ENGLISH-PALI DICTIONARY

AGGAMAHĀPAṆḌITA
A.P. BUDDHADATTA MAHĀTHERA
OF AGGĀRĀMA, AMBALANGODA

BHARATIYA KALA PRAKASHAN
DELHI (INDIA)

First Published : 1954 Cylon
Revised Edition : 2006

Published by **C.P. Gautam**
BHARATIYA KALA PRAKASHAN
3421-A, IInd Floor Narang Colony, Tri Nagar,
Delhi-110035. Phone : 27393083, 32967505 (O), 32492129 (R)

ISBN : 81-8090-114-9

Laser Type Setting by
A-ONE GRAPHICS
JD-18C, IInd Floor, Pitampura, Delhi-110088

Printed By :
BDH Printer at Salasar Imaging Systems
Delhi

FOREWORD

The publication of an English-Pali Dictionary is a notable event in the life of the Pali Text Society; and when our friend of long standing offered this work to us we gladly accepted the privilege of publishing it in the conviction that, although the compiler had had to face a task entailing a number of peculiar difficulties, he was extremely well qualified to do so, having devoted his life to a close and deep study of Pali. It is now thirty years since the Pali Text Society issued its *Pali-English Dictionary ;* this has been twice reprinted in order to meet a constantly growing demand for the aids and means to study Pali and its sacred literature. The time is already ripe to add an English-Pali Dictionary to the Society's long list of publications, and indeed the need for one has been felt for some years. For, although the Venerable Widurupola Piyatissa Thera's *English-Pali Dictionary* has much to commend it, its usefulness is reduced for the English-speaking world by the Pali words being given in Sinhalese script. A publication issued by the Pali Text Society must, on the other hand, follow one of the original 'objects' of the Society: that publications be in roman script.

That this present *English-Pali Dictionary* has been compiled by the Venerable A. P. Buddhadatta Mahāthera, Agga-mahāpaṇḍita, will guarantee the scholarly way in which it has been handled. For he is a grammarian and well known as the author of several Pali grammars written both in Sinhalese and in English; and moreover he has edited *Sammoha-vinodanī*, *Saddhammapajjotika* (3 vols.), *Buddhadatta's Manuals* (2 vols.) for the Pali Text Society, as well as other Pali works published in the Society's Journals.

A Dictionary of the entire English language, each word with a Pali equivalent, would perhaps be impossible; and it would certainly not have been desirable since any such compilation would attain inordinate length, whereas what is more needed is the presentation of as much useful and well chosen material as possible in one volume of a manageable size. It would be impossible, for Pali could not be expected to produce words, for example for plants and birds of a non-Asian habitat. So there are no entries for such things as ' dandelion ', ' buttercup ', ' honey-suckle ' or ' blackbird ', so familiar to English people. ' Tern ' does appear, although not as a bird but as a set of three, a triplet. ' Hawk ', ' kite ' and ' owl ' are however included as well as other birds known also in Asia. Nor have these escaped the notice of the compilers of the Pali Canon and Commentaries, where they are not infrequently referred to. Pali equivalents were therefore already at hand.

But if Pali cannot coin all words, the Venerable Buddhadatta has been indefatigable in coining a great many, particularly perhaps for current English anatomical, medical and botanical terms, for other scientific words and for modern inventions, such as ' emplane ' (verb), 'telephone' and 'telegram', and for which Pali proves very well adapted. This is not altogether surprising for, although it has long been a static language, it yet covers a wide range of thought, enriched by hundreds of narrative stories on a variety of topics and by a multitude of similes drawn from everyday life and things.

Another class of omissions that had to be made concerns certain, but not all, words that are narrowly ' ecclesiastical ' in usage or ' classical ' in reference, such as ' Chasuble ' and ' Doric ' (architecture), and which fall outside the scope of Pali thought.

On the other hand words are included that would not normally find a place in a purely occidental Dictionary. We may give as examples ' Tooth-relic ' and ' false view ', words which, in their technical sense, are not of the common stock of European thought, but they have a decided technical meaning in Buddhist literature. As it is hoped that one of the main uses of this Dictionary will be to provide a further instrument for the study of Pali literature and language, words such as these clearly could not have been omitted ; they are part of the very fabric out of which this literature and language are built.

All first attempts must in time be superseded, as the Venerable Buddhadatta has intimated in his Preface. But that time will not come immediately. For even although everyone may not agree with all the Pali equivalents given, whether they have been freshly coined or composed from words already in Pali usage, I yet believe that the great majority of these equivalents will be found to be precise and apt. I also believe that this *English-Pali Dictionary*, which I hope will meet with every success, is, both on account of its own intrinsic value, and because it is breaking new ground, an important and welcome contribution to the field of Pali studies.

I. B. HORNER.

London, 1955.

ABBREVIATIONS

a. and adj.	..	Adjective
abl.	..	Ablative
abs.	..	Absolutive
adv.	..	Adverb
caus.	..	Causative
conj.	..	Conjunction
cpds.	..	Compounds
f.	..	Feminine
ind.	..	Indeclinable
intj.	..	Interjection
m.	..	Masculine
n.	..	Noun
nt.	..	Neuter
pass.	..	Passive
pl.	..	Plural
p.p.	..	Past Participle
pr.p.	..	Present Participle
pt.p.	..	Potential Participle
v.i.	..	Verb Intransitive
v.t.	..	Verb Transitive
3.	..	Of the three genders

PREFACE

In the preface to my *Concise Pali-English Dictionary*, which was published in 1949, mention was made of the fact that I was preparing an *English-Pali Dictionary*. I compiled a concise *English-Pali Dictionary* during the second World War. While its printing was delayed through more than one obstacle, there appeared an *English-Pali Dictionary* by the Venerable W. Piyatissa Nāyakathera, in the latter half of 1949. In this work the Pali words are given in Sinhalese script ; the gender of the nouns is not defined by designations, but they are given with their different case-endings of the nominative, like *rahado*, *kantā*, *pallalaŋ* and so on. The adjectives also are given sometimes with the masculine case-endings, but occasionally wi h the neuter case-endings. For instance, **Lacteal,** *a.* ඛීරනිස්සිතං, ඛීරමයං[1]. **Lacunal,** *a.* සවිච්ඡෙදො, සච්ඡිද්දො[2] ' appear on page 365 there. An adjective in Pali takes all forms of gender according to the gender of the qualified substantive. To cite adjectives in that manner would naturally lead to confusion in the student's mind. They should have been given without any case-endings.

Although there are many short-comings in his work the Venerable Elder is to be congratulated of embarking on such a bold venture in spite of his poor health.

Under these circumstances the necessity of a well-arranged *English-Pali Dictionary* in full Roman script was still there. Therefore my friends urged me to re-write my work on an enlarged scale, which I agreed to do. Thus this work has become an *English-Pali Dictionary* of considerable size. To cover the whole English language is an enormous task, and to find out Pali words for numerous modern concepts is extremely difficult if not impossible. I had to coin many words for new things, and sometimes I had to give more

1. Khīranissitaŋ, khīramayan. 2. Savicchedo, sacchiddo.

than one Pali word for some English verbs which do not exist in the ancient languages like Pali. As this is only a first attempt it will not be surprising if anyone finds short-comings here too.

In compiling this work I benefited from the preliminary advice and help offered by O. H. de A. Wijesekara, M.A., PH.D., Professor of Sanskrit, University of Ceylon. In the course of my work I had to request Miss I. B. Horner, M.A., the secretary to the Pali Text Society of London, and the well-known translator of the Vinaya texts, to help me in the task. She gladly consented to read the proofs and correct where it was necessary. I received much help from her in defining the exact meaning of some English words and in deciding which words are now not in use though they still appear in some English dictionaries. So I removed many archaic words some of which are often found in the work of the Venerable Piyatissa. I am sorry to say that I could not carry out all of her instructions as I could not sometimes get her corrections in time owing to my being away in Burma for long periods.

I am greatly indebted to the Pali Text Society for undertaking the publication of this work. The Society now has to its credit not only a *Pali-English Dictionary* but also an *English-Pali Dictionary* of medium size. It is left to future scholars to compile an exhaustive *English-Pali Dictionary.*

The printing of this volume has been done by Messrs. Colombo Apothecaries' Co., Ltd., with much care, for which my thanks are due to them.

A. P. BUDDHADATTA.

12th December, 1954.

Aggārāma,
Ambalangoda
Ceylon.

INTRODUCTION

It should be noted that Pali verbs cited here are given in the Third Person singular of the Present Indicative. Their respective Past Participles appear after such verbs. In giving the Past Participles it was found necessary in some instances to give them in compound form with the addition of certain nouns; this need arose when there was no single Pali word exactly parallel to the English verb. For example, the English verb *Forge* is translated here as *kūṭavidhānan karoti*, and its P.P. is given as *katakūṭavidhāna*. Actually this latter is a compound noun, only its first member is a P.P., but, as explained above, it was found convenient to place these too in the category of the Past Participles.

There is some difference in defining Transitive and Intransitive verbs in the two languages. For instance, *Forget* is given as a *v.t.* in English dictionaries, but the Pali verb of the same meaning is reckoned as an Intransitive. It is to be noted that the definition of verbs given here is according to English dictionaries and not after the Pali grammars. This variance exists only in very few instances.

In the *Pali-English Dictionary* of the P.T.S. stems of some Pali nouns, such as *satthar*, *pitar*, and *brahman*, are given with consonantal endings. I did not follow this method as none of the Pali Grammarians has accepted it. They have given them as *sutthu*, *pitu*, and *brahma*, respectively.

The secondary derivatives ending in *-tā*, such as *dakkhatā*, *dhammikatā*, have their neuter forms ending in *-tta* or *ttana*, but for the sake of brevity only one form, either ending in *-tā* or *-tta* is given in one place.

The masculine nouns ending in *-ī* have their feminine stems ending in *-inī*; e.g. *hatthī*, *hatthinī*. Many masculine nouns ending in *-a*, such as *kāka*, *miga*, *nāga*, have their feminine stems ending in *-ī*, and seldom in *-inī* ; e.g.

Masculine	*Feminine*
kāka	kākī
miga	migī
nāga	nāgī, nāginī

Some other masculine nouns having the same ending have their feminine forms ending in *-ā* or *-ānī*, or in both ; e.g.

Masculine	*Feminine*
khattiya	khattiyā, khattiyānī
mātula	mātulānī

The adjectives ending in *-vantu* and *-mantu* form their feminine stems by adding an *ī*, and sometimes dropping the *n* of the suffix ; e.g.

guṇavantu>guṇavantī, guṇavatī
satimantu>satimantī, satimatī

There are two forms of the Present Participle : one ending in *-nta* and the other in *-māna*. Those ending in *-nta*, form their feminine stems by adding an *ī*, and those ending in *māna* by adding an *ā* ; e.g.

gacchanta>gacchantī
pacamāna>pacamānā

Their neuter stems are similar to those of the masculine.

Some Primary Derivatives such as *dāyaka* form their feminine stems by substituting an *i* before the last syllable and an *ā* at the end ; e.g.

dāyaka>dāyikā
pācaka>pācikā
ārocaka>ārocikā

Occasionally I have given some phrases both in English and Pali in order to make clear the meanings of some adverbs and indeclinables and to show how and where to use them.

A. P. BUDDHADATTA.

ENGLISH-PALI DICTIONARY

A, An, use the adj. *eka* for the indefinite, and the *pron. ta* for the definite article, both declined according to the gender, etc. of the substantives connected with them, e.g. *Eko puriso,* a man. *Ekā gāvī,* a cow. *So coro,* the thief. *Sā nārī,* the woman. Very often the definite article is not required in Pali; simply *rājā* stands for 'the king'.

Aback, *adv.* 1. pacchato; paṭimukhaŋ; 2. sahasā.

Abandon, *v.t.* cajati; jahāti; pajahati; vijahati; vajjeti. *p.p.* catta; jahita; pajahita; vijahita; vajjita.

Abandonment, *n.* cajana; pahāna; vijahana; vajjana, *nt.*

Abase, *v.t.* avajānāti; avamaññati. *p.p.* avaññāta; avamānita *or* avamata.

Abasement, *n.* avaññā, *f.* avamāna, *nt.* paribhava, *m.*

Abash, *v.t.* lajjāpeti. *p.p.* °pita.

Abate, *v.t.* hāpeti; passambheti. *p.p.* hāpita; °bhita. *v.i.* hāyati; passambhati. *p.p.* hīna; passaddha.

Abbacy, *n.* vihārādhipacca, *nt.*

Abbey, *n.* mahāvihāra; padhānassama, *m.*

Abbot, *n.* vihārādhipati; assamasāmī, *m.*

Abbreviate, *v.t.* saṅkhipati; samāseti. *p.p.* saṅkhitta; samāsita. °**ion,** *n.* saṅkhepa; saṅgaha, *m.* samasana, *nt.*

Abdicate, *v.t.* dhuraŋ nikkhipati; rajjā apagacchati. *p.p.* nikkhittadhura; apagatarajja. °**ion,** *n.* dhuranikkhepa; rājattāpagama, *m.*

Abdomen, *n.* udara; jaṭhara, *nt.* kucchi, *m.f.*

Abdominal, *a.* udarābaddha.

Abduct, *v.t.* avaharati; pasayha harati. *p.p.* avahaṭa. °**ion,** *n.* avahāra, *m.* sahasāharaṇa, *nt.*

Aberrant, *a.* uppathagāmī.

Aberration, *n.* uppathagamana, *nt.* aññāya, *m.*

Abet, *v.t.* duccarite upatthambheti; aparādhaŋ nigūhati. *p.p.* °bhita; °hitāparādha.

Abeyance, *n.* tāvakālika-passaddhi, *f.* sannisīdana, *nt.*

Abhor, *v.t.* jigucchati; harāyati. *p.p.* °chita; °yita.

Abhorrence, *n.* jigucchā; harāyanā, *f.* °**ent,** *a.* jigucchājanaka; jigucchaka.

Abide, *v.t. i.* vasati; viharati; anuvattati. *p.p.* vusita; vuttha; °tita. — **by his promise,** attano paṭiññāya tiṭṭhati.

Abiding, *a.* ciraṭṭhāyī ; thira.

Ability, *n.* sāmatthiya, *nt.* bhabbatā ; kallatā, *f.*

Abject, *a.* dīna ; hīna ; nīca ; adhama. °**ion,** *n.* dīnatta ; hīnatta ; nīcatta, *nt.*

Abjuration, *n.* sapatha, *m.*

Abjure, *v.t.* sapati ; sapathaŋ karoti. *p.p.* sapita ; katasapatha.

Ablative, *n.* apādāna, *nt.* pañcamī vibhatti, *f.*

Ablaze, *a.* āditta ; pajjalita ; sajotibhūta.

Able, *a.* 1. samattha ; bhabba ; 2. dakkha ; paṭibala ; 3. paṭu ; nipuṇa. °**bodied,** *a.* balavantu.

Ablution, *n.* 1. pakkhālana ; dhovana ; sodhana ; 2. suddhajala, *nt.*

Abnegate, *v.t.* paccakkhāti ; paṭikkhipati. *p.p.* °khāta ; °khitta. °**ion,** *n.* 1. paccakkhāna, *nt.* 2. pahitattatā, *f.*

Abnormal, *a.* pakativiruddha ; niyāmapaṭipakkha.

Abode, *n.* nivāsa ; nilaya ; upassaya, *m.* nivesana ; niketana, *nt.* — **of monks,** vihāra ; saṅghārāma, *m.* — **of heretics,** titthiyārāma, *m.*

Abolish, *v.t.* ucchindati ; vināseti ; niddhamati ; vyantīkaroti. *p.p.* ucchinna ; vināsita ; niddhanta ; °kata.

Abolition, *n.* samuccheda ; samugghāta, *m.* niddhamana ; samūhanana, *nt.*

Abominable, *a.* jegucchа ; paṭikkūla.

Abominate, *v.t.* jigucchati. *p.p.* °chita. °**ion,** *n.* jigucchā ; aṭṭīyanā ; harāyanā, *f.*

Aboriginal, *a.* ādikappika ; ādikālika.

Aborigines, *n.* ādikālikā, *m. pl.*

Abortion, *n.* 1. gabbhapātana ; 2. nipphalīkaraṇa, *nt.*

Abortive, *a.* gabbhapātaka ; vañjhabhāvapāpaka.

Abound, *v.i.* bahulībhavati. *p.p.* °bhūta. °**ing** (with), aḍḍha ; sampanna ; bahula.

About, *prep. adv.* parito. — **a week,** sattāhamattaŋ, *adv.* — **to die,** maraṇāsanna, *a.* **It is about noon,** idāni majjhaṇhakappo. **Speaks about him,** taŋ sandhāya bhāsati.

Above, *adv.* upari ; uddhaŋ, *prep.* — **calculation,** saṅkhyātiga ; pamāṇātikkantа, *a.* °**said,** yathāvutta, *a.*

Abrasion, *n.* ghaŋsana ; ghaŋsitaṭṭhāna, *nt.*

Abreast, *adv.* samasamaŋ, anūnānadhikaŋ ; urena uram āhacca.

Abridge, *v.t.* saṅkhipati ; saŋharati. *p.p.* saṅkhitta ; saŋhaṭa. °**ment,** *n.* saṅkhepa; saṅgaha, *m.* saŋharaṇa, *nt.*

Abroad, *adv.* 1. vitthatākārena ; 2. bahi ; 3. videse.

Abrogate, *v.t.* samūhanati ; samudācāraŋ nivatteti. *p.p.* samūhata. °**ion,** *n.* samūhanana, appavattikaraṇa, *nt.*

Abrupt, *a.* 1. sāhasika ; taṅkhaṇika ; 2. papātasahita. °**ion,**

n. khaṇḍaso bhijjana, *nt.* °**ly,** *adv.* sahasā; khaṇena. °**ness,** *n.* accāyikatta, *nt.*

Abscission, *n.* balavachindana, *nt.*

Abscond, *v.i.* aviditaŋ palāyati. °**er,** *n.* palāyaka; nilīyaka, *m.*

Absence, *n.* 1. anupaṭṭhiti, *f.* vippavāsa; 2. abhāva, *m.* avijjamānatta, *nt.* — **of mind,** sativippavāsa, *m.* **In one's —,** parammukhā, *adv.*

Absent, *a.* 1. anupaṭṭhita; 2. avijjamāna. — **from one's home,** vippavuttha, *a.*

Absentee, *n.* anupaṭṭhitaka; pavāsī, *m.*

Absolute, *a.* 1. paripuṇṇa; 2. kevala; ekaŋsika; 3. asīmita; abādhita; 4. nicca; dhuva; asaṅkhata, *noun:* paramattha, *m.* °**ly,** *adv.* paripuṇṇaŋ; aparādhīnaŋ; ekaŋsena; sabbaso.

Absolution, *n.* pāpamocana; dosanirākaraṇa; santidāna, *nt.*

Absolutism, *n.* serīpālana, *nt.*

Absolve, *v.t.* pāpā *or* aparādhāmoceti. *p.p.* pāpamocita.

Absonant, *a.* 1. viruddha; 2. kharassara.

Absorb, *v.t.* pariyādiyati; antogataŋ karoti. *p.p.* pariyādinna.

Absorbed (in), *a.* āsatta; nirata; vyāvaṭa; parāyaṇa.

Absorbent, *a.* pariyādiyaka.

Absorption, *n.* 1. pariyādiyana; 2. sussana, *nt.* 3. niratabhāva, *m.*

Abstain, *v.i.* viramati; uparamati. *p.p.* virata; uparata.

Abstemious, *a.* mattaññū; mitabhoji. °**ly,** *adv.* mattaññutāya.

Abstention, *n.* virati, *f.* viramana, *nt.*

Abstergent, *a.* sodhaka; saŋsodhaka.

Abstinence, *n.* viramaṇa, *nt.* veramaṇī, *f.* — **from food,** anasana, *nt.* upavāsa, *m.*

Abstinent, *a.* virata; uparata.

Abstract, *v.t.* 1. samuddharati; 2. saṅkhipati. *p.p.* samuddhaṭa; saṅkhitta. *noun:* saṅkhepa; sāraŋsa, *m.* adj. kevala; amissa. °**ion,** *n.* uddharaṇa; avaharaṇa; puthakkaraṇa, *nt.*

Abstruse, *a.* gūḷha; duradhigama; apākaṭattha. °**ness,** *n.* gambhīratta; duradhigamatta, *nt.*

Absurd, *a.* nindita; ñāyaviruddha; ayogga. °**ity,** *n.* ñāyavirodha, *m.* ayutti, asaṅgati, *f.*

Abundance, *n.* bāhulla; vepulla; ussannatta, *nt.*

Abundant, *a.* bahula; vipula; pahūta; ussanna. °**ly,** *adv.* bahuso; pāyena; yebhuyyena.

Abuse, *v.t.* akkosati; paribhavati; nindati. *p.p.* akkuṭṭha; paribhūta; nindita. *noun:* akkosa; paribhava, *m.* garahā; nindā, *f.*

Abusive, *a.* gārayha; nindājanaka; kucchita.

Abut, *v.i.* āhacca tiṭṭhati. *p.p.* °ṭhita.

Abutment, *n.* upakārikā, *f.* uddāpa; upatthambhaka, *m.*

Abysmal, *a.* atalampassa ; agādha.

Abyss, *n.* pātāla ; narakāvāṭa, *m.*

Academic, *a.* vijjāvisayaka. °**al**, *a.* vijjaṭṭhānavisayaka. °**ian**, *n.* vijjālayaniyutta.

Academy, *m.* 1. vijjālaya, *m.* 2. paṇḍitasabhā, *f.*

Accede, *v.i.* 1. anujānāti ; anumaññati. *p.p.* anuññāta ; anumata ; 2. sambandhībhavati. *p.p.* °bhūta.

Accelerate, *v.t.* turitayati. *v.i.* appamādī *or* sīghakārī bhavati. °**ing**, *a.* turitayamāna. °**ion**, *n.* 1. sīghattapāpaṇa, *nt.* 2. sīghatā ; turitatā, *f.* vega, *m.* °**ive**, *a.* sīghattapāpaka. °**or**, *n.* vegajanaka, *m.*

Accent, *v.t.* vegaŋ janetvā katheti ; uccassaralakkhaṇaŋ ṭhapeti, *noun:* uccassara ; tāra, *m.*

Accept, *v.t.* paṭigaṇhāti ; sampaṭicchati ; sādiyati. *p.p.* paṭiggahita ; °chita ; sādita. °**able**, *a.* ādeyya ; tuṭṭhijanaka ; sampaṭicchiya. °**ance**, *n.* paṭiggahana ; sampaṭicchana ; sādiyana, *nt.*

Acceptation, *n.* sammatattha ; visesattha, *m.*

Acceptor, *n.* paṭiggāhaka, 3.

Access, *n.* pavesa ; otāra, *m.* °**ible**, *a.* upagamanīya ; pattabba ; sukhopasaṅkamiya.

Accession, *n.* 1. sampatti, *f.* 2. rajjappatti, *f.* 3. atirekavatthu, *nt.*

Accessory, *n.* upakaraṇa ; parikkhāra, *nt.* adj. upakārabhūta.

Accident, *n.* sahasāpatti, *f.* anapekkhitantarāya, *m.* °**al**, *a.* anapekkhita ; sahasāpatta. °**ally**, *adv.* asambhāvitaŋ ; kākatālīyena.

Acclaim, *v.t.* unnadati ; ukkuṭṭhiŋ karoti. *p.p.* unnadita, *noun:* ukkuṭṭhi ; ugghosanā, *f.*

Acclamation, *n.* jayaghosa ; ugghosa, *m.*

Acclimation, **Acclimatization**, *n.* desaguṇaparicaya, *m.*

Acclivity, *n.* pabbatanitamba, *m.*

Accommodate, *v.t.* 1. sandhāneti ; 2. vāseti ; nivāsaŋ deti. *p.p.* °nita ; vāsita ; dinnanivāsa. °**ion**, *n.* 1. sandhāna ; 2. nivāsadāna, *nt.* sakkāra, *m.*

Accompaniment, *n.* anugamana ; sahacaraṇa, *nt.*

Accompany, *v.t.* parivāreti ; anugacchati. *p.p.* parivuta ; anugata. °**ied with**, sahita ; sameta ; yutta, *a.* °**ied by an army**, sasena, *a.* °**ing**, *a.* saddhiñcara.

Accomplice, *n.* pāpasahāya ; pāpamitta, *m.*

Accomplish, *v.t.* sādheti ; sampādeti ; niṭṭhāpeti. *p.p.* sādhita ; °dita ; °pita. °**ed**, nipuṇa ; vosita. °**ed in learning**, vyatta ; bahussuta. °**ing**, *a.* sādhaka ; nipphādaka ; paripūraka. °**ment**, *n.* saŋsiddhi ; nipphatti ; pariniṭṭhā, *f.* niṭṭhāna ; nipphajjana, *nt.* °**ment in learning**, veyyattiya, *nt.* °**ment of morals**, sīlasampatti, *f.*

Accord, *v.i.* 1. sameti ; ekībhavati. *v.t.* anuppadāti. *p.p.* samita ; ekībhūta ; °padinna. *noun:* samacittatā ; ekamatikatā, *f.* °**ance,** *n.* avirodha, *m.* sāmaggi, *f.* °**ant,** *a.* anulomika ; aviruddha ; anukūla.

According, *adv.* yathānurūpaŋ ; anukūlaŋ. — **to one's convenience,** yathāsukhaŋ, *adv.* — **to one's desire,** yathāruciŋ ; yathākāmaŋ, *adv.* — **to one's strength,** yathābalaŋ ; yathāsattiŋ, *adv.* — **to seniority,** yathāvuddhaŋ, *adv.* °**ly,** *adv.* yathānurūpaŋ ; tadanusārena.

Accost, *v.t.* āmanteti. *p.p.* °tita. *noun:* ālapana ; sambodhana, *nt.*

Accouchement, *n.* vijāyana, *nt.* pasūti, *f.*

Account, *n.* 1. gaṇanā ; saṅkalanā, *f.* 2. pavatti, *f.* vuttanta, *m.* *v.t.i.* gaṇeti ; saṅkaleti ; sallakkheti. *p.p.* gaṇita ; °lita ; °khita. — **for,** kāraṇaŋ *or* hetuŋ dasseti. *p.p.* dassitakāraṇa. **On — of,** ārabbha ; sandhāya ; hetunā. **Taken into —,** sallakkhita, *a.* °**able,** *a.* anuvijjanāraha ; bhāradhāraka. °**ant,** *n.* gaṇaka ; āyakammika, *m.*

Accoutre, *v.t.* pasādheti; sajjeti; sannāheti. *p.p.* °dhita ; sajjita ; sannaddha. °**ment,** *n.* kappana ; sannāha, *m.*

Accredit, *v.t.* 1. vissasati ; 2. bhāram karoti. *p.p.* vissattha ; katabhāra. °**ed,** *a.* paññatta ; sabbasammata ; vissāsāraha.

Accrete, *v.i.* ekībhāvena vaḍḍhati. *p.p.* °ḍhita. °**ion,** *n.* upacaya, *m.*

Accrue, *v.i.* upacayati ; vaḍḍhati. *p.p.* upacita ; vaḍḍhita.

Accumulate, *v.t.i.* sañcināti ; upacināti ; rāsīkaroti. *p.p.* sañcita ; rāsīkata. °**ion,** *n.* sañcaya ; puñja, *m.* rāsīkaraṇa ; āyūhana, *nt.* °**or,** *n.* āyūhaka ; saŋhāraka, *m.*

Accuracy, *n.* tathatā, *f.* tacchabhāva, *m.*

Accurate, *a.* avitatha ; yathābhūta ; yathātatha, °**ly,** *adv.* tattato ; yathābhūtaŋ.

Accurse, *v.t.* abhisapati. *p.p.* abhisatta.

Accusation, *n.* codanā, *f.* apavāda, *m.* dosāropaṇa, *nt.* **False —,** abbhakkhāna, abbhācikkhaṇa, *nt.*

Accusative, *n.* dutiyā vibhatti, *f.* kammakāraka, *nt.*

Accuse, *v.t.* upavadati ; codeti. *p.p.* upavutta ; codita. — **falsely,** abbhācikkhati. °**er,** *n.* codaka, *m.*

Accustom, *v.t.* paricayati ; sikkhati. *p.p.* paricita ; sikkhita.

Acephalous, *a.* 1. sirosuñña ; 2. adhipatirahita.

Acerbity, *n.* 1. ambilatta ; 2. kakkasatta, *nt.*

Ache, *v.i.* rujati. *n.* rujā ; vedanā ; pīḷā, *f.*

Achieve, *v.t.* 1. nipphādeti ; sampādeti ; 2. adhigacchati. *p.p.* °dita ; adhigata. °**ment,** *n.* nipphatti ; saŋsiddhi ; samiddhi, *f.* adhigama, *m.*

Acid, *n. a.* ambila. °**ify,** *v.t.* ambilīkaroti. *v.i.* ambilībhavati. *p.p.* °kata ; °bhūta. °**ity,** *n.* ambilatta, *nt.*

Acknowledge, *v.t.* sampaṭicchati ; paṭijānāti. *p.p.* °chita ; paṭiññāta. °**ment,** *n.* sampaṭicchana ; paṭijānana, *nt.*

Acme, *n.* paramakoṭi, *f.* uparimaparicchedа, *m.*

Acne, *n.* vadanapiḷakā, *f.*

Acolyte, *n.* antevāsī, *m.*

Acoustic, *a.* savaṇavisayaka.

Acquaint, *v.t.* 1. ñāpeti ; nivedeti ; 2. parijānāti ; paricayati. *p.p.* ñāpita ; nivedita ; pariññāta ; paricita. °**ance,** *n.* sañjānana, *nt.* paricaya, *m.* °**ed with,** santhuta ; pariciṇṇa ; vissattha.

Acquiesce, *v.i.* anujānāti ; anumaññati. *p.p.* anuññāta ; anumata. °**nce,** *n.* anuññā ; anumati, *f.* aṅgīkāra , *m.*

Acquire, *v.t.* paṭilabhati ; adhigacchati. *p.p.* paṭiladdha ; adhigata. °**ment,** *m.* paṭilābha ; adhigama, *m.*

Acquisition, *n.* paṭilābha, *m.* anuppatti, *f.* — **of wealth,** dhanasañcaya, *m.*

Acquit, *v.t.* apavādā moceti ; niddosaŋ *or* niravajjaŋ karoti. *p.p.* °mocita ; °kata. °**tal,** *n.* 1. niravajjakaraṇa, *nt.* dosamutti, *f.* 2. iṇamutti, *f.* °**tance,** *n.* 1. iṇamokkha, *m.* iṇasodhana ; 2. iṇamocanapaṇṇa, *nt.*

Acre, *n.* karīsamattaṭṭhāna, *nt.* bhūmāṇavisesa, *m.*

Acrid, *a.* kaṭuka.

Acrimonious, *a.* kakkhaḷa ; pharusa ; niṭṭhura.

Acrimony, *n.* niṭṭhuratta ; pharusatta, *nt.*

Acrobat, *n.* 1. laṅghaka ; rajjukīḷaka, *m.* 2. sīghaparivattī, *m.*

Acropolis, *n.* uccanagara, *nt.*

Across, *adv. prep.* tiriyaŋ ; tiro.

Act, *v.i.* ācarati ; anuyuñjati ; vidahati. *p.p.* ācarita ; anuyutta ; vihita. *noun:* kamma ; kicca, *nt.* kiriyā, *f.*

Acting, *a.* aññassatthāya niyutta. *n.* aṅgahāra ; abhinaya, *m.* — **considerately,** nisammakārī, *a.* — **continuously,** sātaccakārī, *a.* — **for the good,** atthacara ; hitesī, *a.*

Action, *n.* kamma ; kicca, *nt.* payoga, *m.* —**for the good,** atthacariyā, *f.* **Bad** —, duccarita, *nt.* **Good** —, sucarita, *nt.* **Pure** —, sucikamma, *nt.* **One's own** —, sakamma, *nt.* **Wrong** —, duppaṭipatti, *f.* °**able,** *a.* anuyuñjanāraha.

Active, *a.* uyyutta ; ussukka ; analasa. °**ly,** *adv.* analasaŋ ; saussāhaŋ.

Activity, *n.* ussāha ; uyyoga ; ātappa ; viriyārambha, *m.*

Actor, *n.* 1. naṭa ; nattaka ; raṅgakāra, *m.* 2. kiccakārī, *m.*

Actress, *n.* nāṭikā ; nattakī, *f.*

Actual, *a.* yathābhūta ; vijjamāna. °**ity,** *n.* taccha ; tatta ; sacca, *nt.* °**ize,** *v.t.* tathaŋ karoti; tathato vitthāreti. °**ly,** *adv.*

yathātathaŋ; yathābhūtaŋ; paccakkhaŋ.

Acumen, *n.* 1. nipuṇatā; 2. tikhiṇatā, *f.*

Acuminate, *v.t.* tikhiṇīkaroti; tibbayati. *p.p.* °ṇīkata; °yita.

Acute, *a.* tiṇha; tikhiṇa; tibba. **°ness**, *n.* tiṇhatta; tibbatta, *nt.*

Adage, *n.* upamākathā, *f.* viññupadesa, *m.*

Adam, *n.* ādimapurisa, *m.*

Adamant, *n.* 1. vajira; 2. atithaddhavatthu, *nt.* **°ine**, *a.* abhejja; vajirasadisa.

Adapt, *v.t.* yoggaŋ *or* anurūpaŋ karoti. *p.p.* anurūpīkata. **°able**, *a.* anurūpa; kammañña. **°ability**, *n.* anukūlatā; kammaññatā, *f.* **°ation**, *n.* anukūlakaraṇa, *nt.*

Add, *v.t.i.* piṇḍeti; saṅkaleti; samāharati. *p.p.* piṇḍita; °lita; samāhaṭa.

Addendum, *n.* parisiṭṭhasaṅgaha, *m.*

Adder, *n.* gonasa, *m.*

Addict, *v.t.* āsajjati; allīyati. *p.p.* āsatta; allīna. **°ed (to)**, *a.* soṇḍa, āsatta. **°edness**, *n.* soṇḍatta; lolatta, *nt.*

Addition, *n.* saṅkalana; piṇḍana, *nt.* samāhāra, *m.* **°al**, *a.* atireka; adhika. **°al duty**, uttarikaraṇīya, *nt.*

Addle, *v.t.* ākulīkaroti, *v.i.* pūtibhavati. adj. pūtibhūta.

Address, *v.t.* 1. ālapati; āmanteti; 2. vāsaṭṭhānanāmādiŋ likhati. *p.p.* ālapita; °tita. **— in return**, paṭisāveti; paccālapati; paṭilikhati.

Address, *n.* 1. desanā, *f.* 2. thutipaṇṇa, *nt.* 3. vāsaṭṭhānanāma, *nt.* 4. kosalla, *nt.*

Addressee, *n.* lekhanalābhī, *m.*

Adduce, *v.t.* niddisati; udāharati. *p.p.* niddiṭṭha; udāhaṭa. **°ible**, *a.* niddisitabba; udāharaṇīya.

Adept, *n. a.* nipuṇa; kusala; katupāsana; pāragata, 3.

Adequate, *a.* 1. pahoṇaka; 2. paṭibala; bhabba; samattha.

Adhere, *v.i.* laggati; sajjati; abhinivisati. *p.p.* laggita; saṭṭha; abhiniviṭṭha. **°nce**, *n.* laggana, *nt.* āsatti, *f.* saṅga, *m.* **°nt**, *a. n.* 1. saŋlagga; saŋsatta; 2. nissitaka. **— of another faith**, aññaladdhika, *a.*

Adhesive, *a.* lagganasīla.

Adieu, *intj.* sotthy'atthu.

Adjacent, *a.* anantara; sannikaṭṭha.

Adjective, *n.* guṇavacana; visesaṇapada, *nt.*

Adjoin, *v.t.* saŋyojeti; ghaṭeti. *p.p.* °jita; ghaṭita. **°ing**, *a.* upantika; samīpatara; saŋghaṭita.

Adjourn, *v.t.* tāvakālikaŋ nivatteti. *p.p.* °nivattita. **°ment**, *n.* kālikavirāma, *m.*

Adjudge, *v.t.* tīreti; viniccheti; niṇṇeti. *p.p.* tīrita; °chita; niṇṇīta. **°ment**, *n.* vinicchaya, *m.* tīraṇa, *nt.*

Adjudicate, *v.t.* (aṭṭaŋ) vinicchināti. *p.p.* vinicchita. **°ion**, *n.* aṭṭavinicchaya, *m.* **°tor**, *n.* vinicchayāmacca, *m.*

Adjunct, *a.* anubaddha; saŋyutta, *n.* anubandha, *m.* visesaṇa, *nt.* °**ion,** *n.* ghaṭana ; saṅghaṭana, *nt.* °**ive,** *a.* ghaṭitabba ; saŋyojetabba.

Adjure, *v.t.* 1. sasapathaŋ codeti; 2. bāḷhaŋ yācati. *p.p.* °codita ; °yācita.

Adjust, *v.t.* saṇṭhapeti. *p.p.* saṇṭhapita. °**ment,** *n.* saṇṭhapana ; samādhāna, *nt.*

Adjutant, *n.* bhaṭapati-sahakārī, *m.*

Admeasure, *v.t.* bhāgaso miṇāti. *p.p.* °mita. °**ment,** *n.* bhāgaso miṇana, *nt.*

Administer, *v.t.* pasāsati ; vicāreti. *p.p.* pasāsita ; vicārita.

Administration, *n.* 1. pālanā, *f.* sāsana ; vicāraṇa, *nt.* 2. bhesajjaniyamana, *nt.*

Administrator, *n.* 1. kiccādhikārī ; pālaka ; 2. paradhanavicāraka, *m.*

Admirable, *a.* abbhuta ; pasaŋsiya.

Admiral, *n.* nāvikasenāpati, *m.*

Admiration, *n.* vimhaya, *m.* bahumāna, *nt.*

Admire, *v.t.* bahumāneti ; pasaŋsati. *p.p.* bahumata ; pasattha *or* pasaŋsita. °**er,** *n.* pasaŋsaka ; bahumānī, *m.*

Admissible, *a.* pavesanīya ; sampaṭicchiya.

Admission, *n* pavesana ; antokaraṇa, *nt.*

Admissive, *a.* pavesetabba.

Admit, *v.t.* paveseti ; sampaṭicchati. *p.p.* °sita ; °chita.

°**tance,** *n.* pavesa, *m.* antokaraṇa, *nt.* °**tedly,** *adv.* sāṅgīkāraŋ ; sapaṭiññaŋ.

Admix, *v.t.* sammisseti. *p.p.* °sita. °**ture,** *n.* sammissana, *nt.*

Admonish, *v.t.* ovadati ; anusāsati. *p.p.* ovadita ; anusiṭṭha.

Admonition, *n.* ovāda, *m.* anusiṭṭhi ; anusāsanā, *f.*

Ado, *n.* āyāsa ; parissama, *m.*

Adolescence, *n.* vayappatti, *f.* yobbañña, *nt.*

Adolescent, *a.* vayappatta ; yobbanappatta.

Adopt, *v.t.* 1. (a son), puttīyati ; 2. (a conduct, etc.), paṭipajjati ; anucarati. *p.p.* paṭipanna ; anucarita. °**ed,** *a.* 1. puttīkata. °**ion,** *n.* 1. puttīkaraṇa ; 2. paṭipajjana ; anucaraṇa, *nt.*

Adorable, *a.* mahanīya ; vandiya ; pūjiya.

Adoration, *n.* namassana ; vandanā ; apaciti, *f.* paṇāma ; paṇipāta, *m.*

Adore, *v.t.* paṇamati ; namassati ; vandati : pūjeti. *p.p.* °mita ; °sita ; vandita ; pūjita. °**er,** *n.* vandaka ; pūjaka ; sāvaka, *m.*

Adorn, *v.t.* maṇḍeti ; bhūseti ; pasādheti ; alaṅkaroti. *p.p.* maṇḍita ; bhūsita ; pasādhita ; alaṅkata. °**ment,** *n.* maṇḍana ; pasādhana ; alaṅkaraṇa, *nt.*

Adrift, *adv.* plavamānaŋ ; nirālambaŋ. adj. nirālamba.

Adroit, *a.* cheka ; dakkha ; catura ; nipuṇa ; kusala. °**ness,** *n.* nepuñña ; kosalla ; pāṭava, *nt.* chekatā ; dakkhatā, *f.*

Adry, *a.* sukkha ; pipāsita.

Adulate, *v.t.* ullapati ; unnāmeti. *p.p.* °pita ; °mita. °**ion,** *n.* ukkācanā ; ullapanā, *f.*

Adult, *n. a.* vayappatta ; vayaṭṭha.

Adulterate, *v.t.* dūseti ; misseti. *p.p.* dūsita ; missita. °**ion,** *n.* dūsana ; missīkaraṇa, *nt.*

Adulterer, *n.* paradārika ; kāmamicchācārī, *m.*

Adulteress, *n.* aticārinī ; micchācārinī, *f.*

Adultery, *n.* kāmamicchācāra, *m.* aticariyā, *f.* (**— of a male),** paradārakamma, *nt.* (**— of a female),** parapurisasevanā, *f.*

Adumbrate, *v.t.* lesamattaŋ dasseti. *p.p.* °sita. °**ion,** *n.* lesamattadassaṇa, *nt.*

Advance, *v.i.* abhikkamati ; vaḍḍhati. *p.p.* abhikkanta ; vuddha, *v.t.* abhimukhaŋ neti ; vaḍḍheti. *p.p.* °nīta, vaḍḍhita. *noun:* 1. abhikkamana, *nt.* 2. abhivuddhi, *f.* 3. agghavaḍḍhi, *f.* 4. saccakāra, *m.* °**ment,** *n.* saŋvaḍḍhana, *nt.*

Advantage, *n.:* 1. sundarāvatthā ; 2. padhānatā, *f.* 3. payojana, *nt.* attha ; hita, *m.* °**ous,** *a.* hitakara ; sātthaka ; saphala. °**ously,** *adv.* sātthakaŋ ; saphalākārena.

Advent, *n.* āgamana ; pāpuṇana, *nt.*

Adventitious, *a.* asambhāvitasampatta.

Adventure, *v.t.* vīrakammaŋ karoti. *noun:* vīracariyā, *f.* abbhutakamma, *nt.* °**some,** *a.* vīratāsaŋyutta.

Adventurous, *a.* pagabbha ; nibbhaya.

Adverb, *n.* kriyāvisesaṇa, *nt.* °**ial,** *a.* kriyāvisesaka.

Adversary, *n.* paccāmitta ; sapatta ; virodhī ; yugaggāhī, *m.*

Adverse, *a.* viruddha ; vipakkha ; paccanika ; paṭiloma. °**ly,** *adv.* paṭilomaŋ ; viruddhākārena. °**ity,** *n.* vipatti ; āpadā, *f.*

Advertise, *v.t.* nivedeti ; pakāseti ; pākaṭīkaroti. *p.p.* nivedita ; pakāsita ; °kata. °**ment,** *n.* pakāsana ; pākaṭīkaraṇa, *nt.* °**er,** *n.* pakāsaka ; nivedaka, *m.*

Advice, *n.* ovāda ; upadesa, *m.* anusāsanā, *f.*

Advisable, *a.* sammannitabba ; thomanīya.

Advise, *v.t.* ovadati ; anusāsati. *p.p.* ovadita ; anusiṭṭha. °**dly,** *adv.* anuviccakārena. °**er,** *n.* upadesaka ; anusāsaka, *m.* °**ory,** *a.* upadesadāyaka.

Advocacy, *n.* nītyupadesadāna, *nt.*

Advocate, *n.* paratthaṅkathī, *m.* *v.t.* paratthaŋ vadati.

Adze, *n.* tacchanī ; vāsi, *f.*

Aegis, *n.* parittāṇa, *nt.*

Aeon, *n.* kappayuga, *m.*

Aerate, *v.t.* vāyunā misseti. *p.p.* vāyumissita.

Aerial, *a.* 1. vāyumaya ; 2. ākāsagata.

Aeriform, *a.* vātagatika ; acirappavattī.

Aerodrome, *n.* vyomayānaṅgaṇa, *nt.*

Aerogram, *n.* vyomasāsana, *nt.*

Aerolite, *n.* ukkāpāta, *m.*

Aerometor, *n.* vāyumāṇaka, *m.*

Aeronaut, *n.* gagananāvika, *m.*

Aeroplane, *n.* vyomayāna; gaganayāna, *nt.*

Aesthetic, °al, *a.* 1. manorama; 2. sundaratājānanaka. **°ally,** *adv.* rammākārena. **°tics,** *n. pl.* sobhanattavicāraṇā, *f.*

Afar, *adv.* dūrato ; ārā.

Affable, *a.* susīla ; piyaŋvada ; piyasīla.

Affair, *n.* kicca, *nt.* siddhi, *f.*

Affect, *v.t.* 1. ācarati ; 2. abhibhavati. (*the mind*), kampeti ; 3. (*to pretend*), micchā dasseti ; 4. vikatiŋ neti. *p.p.* ācarita ; °bhūta ; kampita ; °sita; vikatinīta. **°ation,** *n.* 1. ayathādassanā, *f.* 2. dappa, *m.*

Affected, *a.* 1. abhūtenāropita; 2. vikatippatta ; 3. gabbita. **°ly,** *adv.* abhūtena ; patirūpena.

Affecting, *a.* hadayaṅgama. **°ly,** *adv.* hadayaṅgamākārena.

Affection, *n.* sineha ; anurāga, *m.* pema, *nt.* **°ate,** *a.* sasneha ; sapema ; anuratta. **°ately,** *adv.* sānurāgaŋ ; sapemaŋ.

Affiance, *n.* paṭiññādāna, *nt.* vivāhapaṭiññā, *f.* *v.t.* vivāhapaṭiññaŋ deti. **°er,** *n.* paṭiññādāyaka, *m.*

Affidavit, *n.* sapathapaṇṇa, *nt.*

Affiliate, *v.t.* 1. saŋyojeti ; 2. puttīkaroti. *p.p.* °jita ; puttīkata. **°ion,** *n.* aṅgīkaraṇa ; saŋyojana, *nt.*

Affined, *a.* ñātibhūta.

Affinity, *n.* 1. ñātisambandha, *m.* bandhutā, *f.* 2. samānatta, *nt.*

Affirm, *v.t.* thirīkaroti ; daḷhīkaroti. *p.p.* thirīkata. **°ation,** *n.* 1. daḷhīkaraṇa ; 2. paṭijānana, *nt.*

Affirmative, *a.* atthyattha ; nicchayakara. **°ly,** *adv.* nicchayākārena ; ekaŋsena.

Affirmatory, *a.* nicchetabba ; daḷhīkaraṇīya.

Affix, *v.t.* sambandheti ; saṅghaṭeti. *p.p.* sambaddha. °ṭita. *noun :* anubandha ; paccaya, *m.*

Afflict, *v.t.* pīḷeti ; santāpeti ; vyathati. *p.p.* pīḷita. °pita ; vyathita.

Afflicted (with), aṭṭita ; abbhāhata ; pareta. — **with pain,** vedanaṭṭa, *a.* — **with grief,** sokapareta, *a.* — **with misery,** dukkhotiṇṇa, *a.*

Affliction, *n.* paritāpa ; kheda, *m.* pīḷā, *f.*

Afflictive, *a.* dukkhāvaha ; pīḷākara.

Affluence, *n.* samiddhi ; mahābhogatā, *f.*

Affluent, *a.* samiddha ; aḍḍha ; mahaddhana. *noun :* sākhānadī, *f.*

Afflux, *n.* samosaraṇa ; pasavana ; sandana, *nt.*

Afford, *v.t.* 1. sampādeti ; 2. sakkoti ; pahoti. *p.p.* sampādita.

Afforest, *v.t.* araññataŋ neti. *p.p.* °nīta

Affranchise, *v.t.* dāsavyā *or* paṭiññāto moceti. *p.p.* °mocita.

Affray, *n.* kalaha ; viggaha, *m.* bhaṇḍana, *nt.*

Affright, *v.t.* tāseti ; bhāyāpeti. *p.p.* tāsita ; °pita.

Affront, *n.* anādara ; agārava ; avamāna, *m.* avaññā, *f.* *v.t.* akkosati ; paribhāsati ; avamaññati. *p.p.* akkuṭṭha ; °sita. avamānita *or* avamata.

Affusion, *n.* āsiñcana ; osiñcana, *nt.*

Afield, *adv.* 1. aṅgaṇe ; 2. dūre.

Afire, *a.* ḍayhamāna.

Aflame, *a.* āditta.

Afloat, *adv.* 1. plavamānaŋ ; 2. pacāritākārena.

Afoot, *adv.* 1. padasā ; 2. sappayogaŋ.

Afore, *adv.* 1. abhimukhe ; purato ; 2. purā ; pure ; paṭhamaŋ. °**named,** °**said,** *a.* pubbevutta ; yathāvutta. °**thought,** *a.* pubbacintita. °**time,** *adv.* purā ; puretaraŋ.

Afraid, *a.* bhīta ; tasita ; bhayaṭṭa ; utrasta.

Afresh, *adv.* abhinavaŋ ; puna.

After, *adv.* pacchā ; anantaraŋ ; tato paraŋ ; anu° — **a long time,** cirena, *adv.* — **that,** atha, *adv.*

After, *a.* pacchima. °**birth,** *n.* gabbhamaŋsa, *nt.* °**crop,** *n.* dutiyasassa, *nt.* °**noon,** *n.* aparaṇha, *m.* pacchābhatta, *nt.* °**pains,** *n.* pasavavedanā, *f.* °**thought,** *n.* anuvitakka, *m.*

Afterwards, *adv.* pacchā ; aparabhāge.

Again, *adv.* puna. — **and again,** punappunaŋ, *adv.*

Against, *prep.* paṭilomaŋ ; paṭimukhaŋ ; paṭi (used as a prefix). — **the order,** uppaṭipāṭiyā. — **the sun,** paṭisuriyaŋ. — **the wind,** paṭivātaŋ. *adv.*

Agamous, *a.* napuŋsaka ; bhāvarūparahita.

Agape, *adv.* vivaṭamukhena. adj. vivaṭamukha.

Age, *n.* 1. āyu ; vaya, *nt.* 2. samaya ; kāla ; yuga, *m.* — **limit,** paramāyu, *nt.* **Come of —,** vayappatta, *a.* **Of the same —,** samavayaṭṭha, *a.* **Old —,** jarā, *f.* mahallakatta, *nt.*

Age, *v.i.* jīrati. *p.p.* jiṇṇa. °**ed,** vuddha ; mahallaka. *a.*

Agenda, *n.* kiccapaṭipāṭi, *f.*

Agency, *n.* niyojitadhura, *nt.* (office :) niyojitakiccālaya, *m.*

Agent, *n.* niyojita ; anuyutta, *m.* (In gram :) kattukāraka, *nt.* kattu, *m.*

Agglomerate, *v.t.* piṇḍīkaroti ; sañcināti. *p.p.* °kata ; sañcita. °**ion,** *n.* piṇḍīkaraṇa, *nt.* sañcaya, *m.*

Agglutinate, *v.t.* samāseti ; smapiṇḍeti. *p.p.* samasita. °ḍita. °**ion,** *n.* samāsana ; sampiṇḍana, *nt.*

Aggrandize, *v.t.* pavaḍḍheti; samukkaŋseti. *p.p.* °ḍhita; °sita. °**ment,** *n.* samukkaŋsa, *m.* samunnati, *f.*

Aggravate, *v.t.* bhāriyaŋ *or* garutaraŋ karoti; uddīpeti. *p.p.* garukata; uddīpita. °**ion,** bhārīkaraṇa; uddīpana, *nt.*

Aggregate, *v.t.* sañcināti; rāsīkaroti. *p.p.* sañcita; rāsīkata. *v.i.* sañcīyati; rāsībhavati. *p.p.* sañcita; rāsibhūta. *noun:* sañcaya; samāgama; samūha, *m.* °**ion,** *n.* sañcinana; rāsīkaraṇa, *nt.* rāsi, *m.*

Aggress, *v.i.* kalaham ārabhati. *p.p.* āraddhakalaha. °**ion,** *n.* kalahārambha; atyācāra, *m.* °**ive,** *a.* kalahakārī, °**or,** *n.* paṭhamakkamaka; dhaŋsaka, *m.*

Aggrieve, *v.t.* dukkhāpeti; sokam uppādeti. *p.p.* °pita; uppāditasoka.

Aghast, *a.* bhayākula; cakita.

Agile, *a.* nipuṇa; dakkha; sīgha; turita. °**lity,** *n.* kosalla; nepuñña; sīghatta, *nt.*

Agitate, *v.t.* 1. khobheti; kampeti; āloleti; phandāpeti. *p.p.* khobhita; kampita. °lita; °pita; 2. (*mentally*), ubbejeti; saŋvejeti. *v.i.* 1. calati; kampati; saṅkhubhati; 2. (*mentally*), ubbijjati; saŋvegam āpajjati. *p.p.* ubbigga; saŋvegāpanna. °**ion,** *n.* iñjana; phandana, *nt.* khobha; saṅkopa, *m.* *Mental* —, ubbega; saŋvega, *m.*

Agitator, *n.* saṅkhobhaka; ālolaka, *m.*

Aglow, *a.* sajotibhūta.

Agnate, *a.* pitupakkhika.

Agnostic, *n.* anissaravādī; lokāyatika, *m.* °**ism,** *n.* anissaravāda, *m.*

Ago, *adv.* purā; pubbe, *with abl.* **Not long** —, nātipure.

Agog, *adv.* accāsāpubbakaŋ.

Agonistic, *a.* 1. kīḷāpaṭibaddha; 2. yugaggāhī.

Agonize, *v.t.* vyathati; santāpeti; ābādheti. *p.p.* vyathita; °pita; ābādhita. *v.i.* aṭṭīyati; santapati.

Agony, *n.* vedanā; rujā, *f.* vyādhi, *m.* **Mental** —, santāpa; upāyāsa, *m.*

Agree, *v.i.* saŋsandati; sameti, *with inst.*; *v.t.* samanujānāti. *p.p.* °dita; samita; samanuññāta. — **upon,** sādiyati; sammannati.

Agreeable, *a.* iṭṭha; kanta; manāpa; manuñña; manohara; ramaṇīya. °**ness,** *n.* ramaṇīyatā; manuññatā, *f.* °**ly,** *adv.* yathāruciŋ; yathāsukhaŋ; avirodhena.

Agreement, *n.* sammuti; anumati; paṭiññā, *f.* saṅgara, *m.*

Agı cultural, *a.* kasikammavisayaka.

Agriculture, *n.* kasikamma, *nt.* °**ist,** *m.* kassaka; ropaka, *m.*

Aground, *adv.* uttīraŋ.

Ah, *intj.* hā; aho; ahaha.

Ahead, *adv.* purato; agge; abhimukhe.

Aid, *v.t.* upakaroti; upatthambheti. *p.p.* upakata; °bhita. *noun:* upakāra; upatthambha, *m.* °**less,** *a.* anātha; asaraṇa; asahāya.

Aide-de-camp, *n.* senāpatisahakārī, *m.*

Ail, *v.t.* pīḷeti; dukkhāpeti. *p.p.* pīḷita; °pita. *v.i.* dukkham vindati *or* anubhavati. °**ment,** *n.* roga; vyādhi; ābādha, *m.* °**ing,** *a.* rujākara; rujamāna; vedanaṭṭa.

Aim, *v.t.* ākaṅkhati; abhipattheti. *p.p.* °khita; °thita. *v.i.* pahāraŋ deti; lakkhaŋ vijjhati. *p.p.* dinnapahāra; viddhalakkha.

Aim, *n.* 1. patthanā; abhilāsā, *f.* ārammaṇa, *nt.* 2. lakkha; vejjha; saravya, *nt.* °**less,** *a.* anabhilakkhita; niṭṭhārahita. °**lessly,** *adv.* anavaṭṭhitaŋ; anabhilakkhitaŋ.

Aiming at (to say something), āhacca; upanīya; sandhāya, *abs.*

Air, *n.* 1. vāta; vāyu; māluta; anila; pavana; samīraṇa, *m.* 2. vesa; ākāsa, *m.* °**course,** vāyupavesamagga, *m.* °**cushion,** vāyupūritanisīdana, *nt.* °**less,** *a.* nivāta; vāyurahita. °**man,** vyomanāvika, *m.* °**ship,** vyomayāna, *nt.* °**tight,** *a.* vātanivāraka.

Air, *v.t.* 1. vātaŋ gāhāpeti; vātena soseti; 2. vesaŋ dasseti. *p.p.* °pitavāta; °sosita; dassitavesa.

Airy, *a.* 1. vāyusahita; 2. vāyusadisa; 3. līlāyutta; salīla.

Aisle, *n.* ālinda, *m.*

Ajar, *adv.* thokaŋ-vivaṭa.

Akin, *a.* sagotta; sajātika.

Alabaster, *n.* setasilā, *f.* khīrapāsāṇa, *m.*

Alack, *intj.* aho; alakkhikaŋ.

Alacrity, *n.* sīghatā; paṭutā, *f.*

Alarm, *v.t.* uttāseti; antarāyaŋ ñāpeti. *p.p.* uttāsita; ñāpitantarāya. *noun:* 1. antarāyañāpana, *nt.* 2. bhīti, *f.* uttāsa, *m.* **Cry of** —, virāva, *m.* — **bell,** *n.* pabodhaka-ghaṇṭā, *f.* °**ing,** *a.* bhayaṅkara; bhayajanaka. °**ist,** *n.* bhāyanasīla; bhītibahula, *m.*

Alas, *intj.* aho dukkhaŋ!

Albeit, *adv.* tathā pi; api ca.

Album, *n.* tucchapotthaka, *m.*

Alchemic, *a.* rasavijjāyatta.

Alchemist, *n.* rasavejja, *m.*

Alchemy, *n.* rasavijjā, *f.*

Alcohol, *n.* majjasāra, *m.* °**ic,** *a.* majjaguṇayutta. °**ize,** *v.t.* majjabhāvaŋ pāpeti; majjena misseti.

Alcoran, *n.* Mahammadīyadhammagantha, *m.*

Alderman, *n.* nigamasāmī, *m.*

Ale, *n.* yavasurā, *f.* °**house,** pānamandira, *nt.*

Alert, *a.* appamatta; atandita. °**ness,** appamāda; ātappa, *m.* dakkhiya; kosalla, *nt.*

Algebra, *n.* bījagaṇita, *nt.*

Alias, *adv.* atha vā; aññathā. *n.* nāmantara, *nt.*

Alien, *a.* bāhira ; videsīya ; paravisayaka. *n.* videsī ; paradesika, *m.*

Alienable, *a.* pārivaṭṭika ; parāyatta-karaṇāraha.

Alienate, *v.t.* 1. parādhīnaŋ karoti; 2. vicchindati ; vighaṭeti. *p.p.* °kata ; vicchinna ; vighaṭita. °**ion,** 1. sāmiparivattana, *nt.* 2. cittavibbhama, *m.*

Alignment, *n.* ujuttāpādana ; ekapantiyā ṭhapana, *nt.*

Alight, *v.i.* otarati ; oruhati ; paccorohati. *p.p.* otiṇṇa ; orūḷha ; paccorūḷha.

Alight, *a.* obhāsita ; sappabha ; pajjalita.

Alike, *a.* samāna ; sadisa ; tulya ; sannibha ; sarikkha.

Aliment, *n.* āhāra, *m.* anna, *nt.* °**ary,** *a.* posaka ; ojādāyaka.

Alimony, *n.* 1. posaṇa, *nt.* 2. bhariyāya laddhabbadhana, *nt.*

Alive, *a.* 1. sajīva ; sacetana ; jīvamāna ; 2. sauyyoga.

Alkali, *n.* khārosadha, *nt.* °**line,** *a.* khārika ; ūsara ; loṇika.

All, *a.* sabba ; sakala ; akhila ; nikhila ; asesa ; nissesa. — **conquering,** *a.* sabbābhibhū. — **embracing,** *a.* sabbavyāpaka. °**knowing,** *a.* sabbaññū; sabbavidū. — **pervading,** *a.* sabbavyāpī. — **pleasing,** *a.* samantabhaddaka. °**seeing,** *a.n.* sabbadassī ; samantacakkhu. — **along,** *adv.* nirantaraŋ ; ādito yāva antā. — **around,** *adv.* samantā ; parito. — **at once,** ekappahārena, *adv.* — **but one,** ekenūnā sabbe.

Allay, *v.t.* upasameti ; passambheti ; nibbāpeti. *p.p,* °mita ; °bhita ; °pita. *v.i.* upasammati ; passambhati ; nibbāti. *p.p.* upasanta ; passaddha ; nibbuta. °**ment,** *n.* upasama, *m.* passaddhi, *f.*

Allegation, *n.* codanā, *f.* pakāsana, *nt.*

Allege, *v.t.* codeti ; pakāseti. *p.p.* codita ; °sita.

Allegiance, *n.* rājabhatti ; rajjapakkhapātitā, *f.*

Allegorical, *a.* rūpakamaya ; upamārūpaka. °**ly,** *adv.* rūpakavasena.

Allegory, *n.* rūpakakathā ; upamākathā, *f.*

Alleviate, *v.t.* tanukaroti ; sameti ; upasameti. *p.p.* °kata ; samita. °**ion,** *n.* upasamana ; tanukaraṇa, *nt.*

Alliance, *n.* sambandha ; saŋyoga, *m.* sandhāna, *nt.*

Allied, *a.* sambaddha ; saŋyutta ; sandhibhūta.

Alligation, *n.* saŋyojana ; sandhikaraṇa, *nt.*

Alligator, *n.* kumbhīla ; suŋsumāra, *m.*

Alliteration, *n.* anuppāsa, *m.* samānakkharatā, *f.*

Allocate, *v.t.* onojeti ; koṭṭhāse niyameti. *p.p.* onojita ; niyamitakoṭṭhāsa. °**ion,** *n.* onojana ; bhāganiyamana, *nt.*

Allot, *v.t.* saŋvibhajati ; bhāgaso deti. *p.p.* saŋvibhatta ; bhāgaso-dinna. °**ment**, *n.* 1. vibhatta-koṭṭhāsa, *m.* 2. puthakkaraṇa, *nt.*

Allow, *v.t.* anujāṇāti ; anumaññati ; aṅgīkaroti. *p.p.* anuññāta ; anumata ; °kata. °**able**, *a.* anuññātabba; aṅgīkaraṇīya. °**ance**, *n.* anuññā ; anumati, *f.* (—granted to someone), vetana ; posāvanika, *nt.*

Alloy, *v.t.* misseti ; dūseti. *p.p.* missita ; dūsita. *n.* 1. missitaloha, *m.* 2. missana ; dūsana, *nt.*

Allude, *v.i.* aniyamena vadati ; sandhāya *or* upādaya bhāsati. *p.p.* °vutta ; °bhāsita.

Allure, *v.t.* palobheti ; sammoheti. *p.p.* °bhita ; °hita. °**ment**, *n.* palobhana ; sammohana, *nt.* °**ing**, *a.* palobhaka.

Allusion, *n.* upanītavācā, *f.* āsajjavacana, *nt.*

Alluvial, *a.* kalalamaya.

Ally, *v.t.* sambandhati ; saŋyojeti ; sandhāti. *p.p.* sambaddha ; saŋyutta ; sandhita. *n.* sahāya ; mitta ; ekapakkhika, *m.* **Allied army**, mittasenā, *f.*

Almanac, *n.* nakkhattapañcaṅga, *m.* dinadassana, *nt.*

Almighty, *a. n.* nikhilabaladhara.

Almoner, *n.* dānasaŋvibhajaka, *m.*

Almonry, *n.* dānasālā, *f.*

Almost, *adv.* pāyo ; bhīyoso. — **the whole**, kevalakappaŋ, *adv.* — **dead**, *a.* matapāya.

Alms, *n.* bhikkhā, *f.* piṇḍapāta, *m.* dāna, *nt.* — **bowl**, patta, *m.* — **collector**, piṇḍapātika ; bhikkhaka, *m.* — **collection**, bhikkhācāra, *m.* uñchācariyā, *f.* °**giver**, piṇḍadāyī, *m.* °**giving**, bhikkhādāna, *nt.* °**hall**, bhattagga, *nt.* dānasālā, *f.* **Distributor of** —, dānaveyyāvaṭika, *m.*

Aloe, *n.* agaru ; agalu, *m.*

Aloft, *adv.* upari ; uddhaŋ.

Alone, *adv.* kevalaŋ. adj. ekaka ; adutiya ; asahāya.

Along, *adv.* ādito yāv'antā. **Goes** —, anuyāti. — **shore**, anutīraŋ, *adv.* — **side**, passato, *ind.* — **with**, saha ; saddhiŋ, *ind.*

Aloof, *adv.* ārā ; ārakā ; dūrato. °**ness**, *n.* āratta ; dūratta, *nt.*

Aloud, *adv.* uccassarena.

Alphabet, *n.* vaṇṇamālā, *f.* °**ical**, *a.* vaṇṇamālānugata.

Already, *adv.* pageva.

Also, *adv. conj.* apica ; puna ca ; aparañ ca.

Altar, *n.* pūjāsana, *nt.* yāgavedikā, *f.*

Alter, *v.t.* viparivatteti ; vipariṇāmeti. *p.p.* °tita ; °mita. *v.i.* viparivattati. *p.p.* °vatta. °**ative**, *a.* viparivattaka ; vipariṇamanta. °**ation**, *n.* vipariṇāmana ; aññathākaraṇa, *nt.*

Altercate, *v.i.* vivadati. *p.p.* vivadita. °**ion**, *n.* vivāda, *m.* bhaṇḍana, *nt.*

Alternate, *v.t.* vārena karoti. *v.i.* vikappena pāpuṇāti. *p.p.* °kata ; °patta. adj. ekantarika ; vikappāgata ; vārānugata. °**ly,** *adv.* vārena vāraŋ ; aññamaññaŋ. °**ion,** *n.* aññamaññaparivattana, *nt.* pariyāya, *m.*

Alternative, *n.* vikappa ; itaravidhi, *m.* adj. vikappayutta ; itarītara. °**ly,** *adv.* vikappavasena.

Although, *conj.* yadi pi ; sace pi ; api.

Altitude, *n.* ubbedha, *m.*

Altogether, *adv.* sabbaso ; sabbathā ; sabbasaṅgahavasena.

Altruism, *n.* parahitakāmitā, *f.*

Altruist, *n.* paratthakārī, *m.* °**ic,** *a.* parahitakara.

Aluminium, *n.* lahu-setaloha, *nt.*

Always, *adv.* satataŋ ; niccaŋ ; santataŋ ; anavarataŋ.

Amain, *adv.* ativegena.

Amalgamate, *v.t.* misseti ; saŋyojeti. *p.p.* missita ; °jita. adj. missībhūta. °**ion,** *n.* missīkaraṇa ; saŋyojana, *nt.*

Amass, *v.t.* sañcināti , rāsīkaroti. *p.p.* sañcita ; rāsīkata. °**ment,** *n.* sañcaya ; puñja, *m.* rāsīkaraṇa, *nt.*

Amateur, *a.* kalābhirata ; vinodakāmī.

Amative, *a.* pemayutta ; sānurāga. °**ness,** *n.* pemayuttatā ; sānurāgatā, *f.*

Amatory, *a.* pemabahula ; siṅgārappiya ; pemānubaddha.

Amaze, *v.t.* vimheti. *p.p.* vimhita. °**ment,** *n.* vimhaya, *m.* acchariya, *nt.* °**ing,** *a.* vimhayāvaha ; acchariyajanaka.

Amazon, *n.* yuddhakāminī, *f.*

Ambassador, *m.* rājadūta, *m.* °**ship,** *n.* dūtakicca, *nt.*

Amber, *n.* tiṇamaṇi ; vaŋsavaṇṇa, *m.*

Ambiguity, *n.* ubhayatthatā ; silesakathā, *f.*

Ambiguous, *a.* sandiddha ; apākaṭattha ; silesattha. °**ly,** *adv.* sasandehaŋ ; sāsaṅkaŋ.

Ambition, *n.* īhā ; yasākaṅkhā ; unnatikāmatā, *f.*

Ambitious, *a.* unnatikāmī ; īhāyutta. °**ly,** *adv.* īhāya ; unnatikāmatāya.

Amble, *v.i.* saṇikaŋ gacchati. *p.p.* °gata.

Ambrosia, *n.* sudhā, *f.* amata ; pīyūsa, *nt.* °**al,** *a.* amatasadisa.

Ambulance, *n.* gilānaratha, *m.*

Ambulate, *v.i.* parikkamati ; anupariyāti. °**tory,** *a.* jaṅgama.

Ambuscade, *v.i.* nilīyati ; nilīyitvā tiṭṭhati. *p.p.* nilīna. *v.t.* nilīyāpeti. *p.p.* °pita. *noun* . 1. nilīnaṭṭhāna, *nt.* nilīnasenā, *f.*

Ambush, *v.t.* nilīyāpeti. *p.p.* °pita. *v.i.* nilīyati. *p.p.* nilīna. *n.* 1. nilīyana ; 2. nilīyāpana, *nt.*

Ameliorate, *v.t.i.* unnāmeti ; saŋvaḍḍheti. *p.p.* °mita ; °ḍhita. °**ion,** *n.* unnāmanā ; saŋvaḍḍhanā, *f.*

Amen, *intj.* sādhu ; evam atthu !

Amenability, *n.* suvacatā ; assavatā, *f.*

Amenable, *a.* suvaca ; assava ; anuvattaka.

Amend, *v.t.* paṭisaṅkharoti ; saŋsodheti. *p.p.* °khata ; °dhita. *v.i.* duccaritaŋ pajahati. °**able,** *a.* saṅkharaṇāraha ; saŋsodhetabba. °**ment,** *n.* paṭisaṅkharaṇa ; saŋsodhana, *nt.*

Amenity, *n.* manuññatā ; rammatā, *f.* *pl.* manoharaguṇā, *m.*

Amerce, *v.t.* daṇḍaŋ paṇeti. °**ment,** *n.* daṇḍādāna, *nt.*

Amethyst, *n.* ambaṅkuramaṇi, *m.*

Amiable, *a.* pemanīya ; suhada ; pāsādika. °**ness,** *n.* pemanīyatā ; pāsādikatā, *f.*

Amicable, *a.* suhada ; samaggārāma. °**ness,** *n.* mettā ; sāmaggi, *f.* sohajja, *nt.* °**bly,** *adv.* suhadatāya ; mittabhāvena.

Amid, Amidst, *prep.* majjhe ; antare (with genitive).

Amiss, *adv.* ayathā. adj. anucita ; uppaṭipāṭika.

Amity, *n.* mettā ; metti, *f.* sohajja ; sakhya, *nt.*

Ammunition, *n.* yuddhopakaraṇa, *nt.*

Amnesty, *n.* dosavimocana ; aparādhakhamana, *nt.*

Among, Amongst, *prep.* see **Amid.**

Amorous, *a.* anurāgī ; kāmuka ; rasika. °**ly,** *adv.* sānurāgaŋ ; savibbhamaŋ. °**ness,** *n.* anurāga, *m.*

Amount, *n.* pamāṇa, *m.* saṅkhyā ; mattā, *f.* *v.i.* — **(to),** upeti ; saṅkhaŋ gacchati. *p.p.* upeta ; °gata.

Amphibian, *n.* *a.* thala-jalacārī, *m.* °**bious,** *a.* thalajalagocara.

Amphibology, *n.* dveḷhakavācā, *f.* silesavākya, *nt.*

Amphitheatre, *n.* aṇḍākararaṅgamaṇḍala, *nt.*

Ample, *a.* 1. visāla ; vipula ; vitthiṇṇa ; 2. pahūta ; pacura ; sambahula. °**ness** ,*n* vipulatta, *nt.*

Amplification, *n.* visālīkaraṇa, *nt.* vitthāra, *m.*

Amplify, *v.t.* bahulīkaroti ; abhivaḍḍheti ; bhāveti. *p.p.* °kata ; °ḍhita ; bhāvita. *v.i.* abhivaḍḍhati. *p.p.* abhivuddha. °**ier,** *n.* saŋvaddhaka, *m.*

Amplitude, *n.* mahatta ; vepulla ; bāhulla, *nt.*

Amputate, *v.t.* vikalaṅgaŋ *or* aṅgacchedaŋ karoti. *p.p.* kataṅgaccheda. °**ion,** *n.* aṅgaccheda, *m.*

Amuck, *adv.* ummattākārena.

Amulet, *n.* kavaca ; antarāyanivāraka, *m.* *nt.*

Amuse, *v.t.* rameti ; vinodayati. *p.p.* ramāpita ; vinodita. °**ment,** abhirati ; kīḷā, *f.* abhiramana, *nt.* — **oneself,** ramati ; dibbati ; nandati. *p.p.* rata ; nandita. °**ing,** *a.* ramma ; manuñña ; tuṭṭhijanaka.

Anachronic, *a.* kālānanurūpa. °**nism,** *n.* kālavirodha, *m.*

Anaconda, *n.* ajagara, *m.*

Anaemia, *n.* rudhirakkhaya, *m.*

Anaesthetize, *v.t.* visaññīkaroti. *p.p.* °kata. °**tic,** *a.* visaññākara.

Anagram, *n.* vacanavipallāsa; akkharavipallāsa, *m.* °**atize,** *v.t.* vacanavipallāsaŋ *or* akkharavipallāsaŋ karoti. *p.p.* katavacana°.

Analects, *n.* subhāsitamālā, *f.*

Analogical, *a.* tulya; sadisa; samāna; sarikkha.

Analogize, *v.t.i.* samāneti; upamāto dasseti. *p.p.* samānita, °dassita.

Analogous, *a.* see **Analogical.**

Analogy, *n.* 1. tulyatā; sarūpatā, *f.* samānatta; sadisatta, *nt.* 2. upamā, *f.* opamma, *nt.*

Analyse, *v.t.* vibhajati; paricchindati; vavatthapeti. *p.p.* vibhatta; °chinna; °pita.

Analysis, *n.* vibhajana, *nt.* vyavaccheda; viccheda, *m.*

Analyst, *n.* vicchedaka, *m.*

Analytic, *a.* vicchedāyatta; pabhedagata. *n. pl.* pabhedavijjā, *f.* — **insight,** paṭisambhidā, *f.*

Anarchic, *a.* nītiviruddha.

Anarchist, *n.* rajjavirodhī; rājapaccatthika, *m.*

Anarchy, *n.* arājakatta, *nt.* rājaviraha, *m.* °**ism,** rājavirodhitā, *f.*

Anathema, *n.* abhisāpa, *m.*

Anathematize, *v.t.* abhisapati. *p.p.* °sapita.

Anatomical, *a.* vyavacchedavisayaka.

Anatomize, *v.t.* (sarīraŋ) vicchindati. *p.p.* vicchinna.

Anatomy, *n.* sarīravicchedavijjā, *f.* °**ist,** *n.* dehavicchedaka, *m.*

Ancestor, *n.* papitāmaha; ādipurisa; pubbapurisa, *m.* °**tral,** *a.* ādipurisāyatta; paramparāgata.

Ancestry, *n.* paramparā; kulapaveṇī, *f.* gotta, *nt.*

Anchor, *n.* nāvābandha; nāvaṅkusa, *m.* *v.t.* nāvaŋ bandhati; niccalaŋ karoti. *p.p.* baddhanāva; niccalīkata. °**age,** *n.* 1. nāvābandhana; 2. bandhanaṭṭhāna, *nt.* 3. nāvāsuṅka, *m.*

Anchoret, Anchorite, *n.* tāpasa; isi, *m.*

Ancient, *a. n.* purāṇa; purātana; porāṇaka; porāṇika; sanantanika. °**ness,** purāṇatta, *nt.* °**ly,** *adv.* purā; bhūtapubbaŋ.

Ancillary, *a.* upakāraka; upatthambhaka.

And, *conj.* ca; api; api ca. — **then,** tato; atha. — **yet,** atha ca pana.

Androgynous, *a.* ubhayaliṅgika; ubhatobyañjanaka.

Androgyny, *n.* ubhayaliṅgī, *m.*

Anecdote, *n.* upākhyāna, *nt.* saṅkhittapavatti, *f.*

Anemometer, *n.* vāyuvegamāṇaka, *nt.*

Anent, *prep.* adhikicca; uddissa; sandhāya, *ind.*

Anew, *adv.* abhinavaŋ; puna pi.

Angel, *n.* devadūta, *m.* °**ic**, °**ical**, *a.* dibba ; amānusika ; devadūtāyatta.

Anger, *n.* kopa ; kodha ; rosa ; paṭigha, *m.* kujjhana, *nt.*

Angle, *v.t.* balisena hanati. *p.p.* balisahata. *n.* 1. balisa, *nt.* 2. koṇa ; aŋsa, *m.* °**er**, *n.* bālisika, *m.*

Anglicize, *v.t.* Eṅglaṇḍiyaŋ karoti. *p.p.* °kata.

Anglo-Saxon, *n.* Eṅglaṇḍiya-Sakasūnu, *m.*

Angrily, *adv.* kopena ; rosena ; sakopaŋ.

Angry, *a.* kuddha ; kupita ; ruṭṭha ; sakopa ; dosākula.

Anguish, *n.* tibbavedanā, *f.* pariḷāha ; atitāpa, *m.* **Free from —**, niddaratha ; nippariḷāha, *a.*

Angular, *a.* sakoṇaka.

Animal, *n.* satta ; pāṇī ; dehī ; jīvī, *m.* — **kingdom**, jīvaloka, *m.* °**cule**, *n.* sukhumapāṇī, *m.*

Animalism, *n.* indriyāsattatā, *f.*

Animalize, *v.t.* sajīvaŋ karoti. *p.p.* °kata.

Animate, *v.t.* 1. sajīvaŋ karoti ; 2. uttejeti ; ussukkāpeti. *p.p.* sajīvakata ; °jita ; °pita. adj. sajīva ; sacetana. °**ion**, *n.* uttejanā, *f.*

Animism, *n.* attaváda, *m.*

Animist, *n.* attavādī, *m.* °**ic**, *a.* attavādāyatta.

Animosity, *n.* vera, *nt.* viddesa, *m.*

Animus, *n.* vyāpāda, *m.*

Ankle, *n.* gopphaka, *m.*

Anklet, *n.* nūpura, *nt.*

Anna, *n.* rūpiyassa soḷasamabhāga, *m.*

Annalist, *n.* itihāsalekhaka, *m.*

Annals, *n.* vassikavuttanta ; itihāsa, *m.*

Annex, *v.t.* saŋyojeti ; sambandhati. *p.p.* °jita ; sambaddha. °**ation**, *n.* sambandhana ; saŋyojana ; ghaṭana, *nt.*

Annihilate, *v.t.* ucchindati ; nirodheti ; vyantīkaroti. *p.p.* ucchinna ; niruddha ; °kata. °**ion**, *n.* uccheda ; nirodha, *m.* visaṅkharaṇa, *nt.* °**tor**, ucchedaka, *m.*

Anniversary, *n.* vassikussava, *m.* adj. saŋvaccharika.

Annotate, *v.t.i.* vyākhyāti ; vaṇṇeti. *p.p.* vyākhyāta ; vaṇṇita. °**ion**, *n.* vyākhyāna, *nt.* atthavaṇṇanā, *f.* °**tor**, *n.* vyākhyātu ; ṭīkākāra, *m.*

Announce, *v.t.* anusāveti ; pakāseti ; nivedeti. *p.p.* °vita ; °sita ; nivedita. °**ment**, *n.* anusāvana ; nivedana ; ārocana ; pakāsana, *nt.* °**er**, *n.* anusāvaka ; ārocaka ; nivedaka, *m.*

Annoy, *v.t.* viheṭheti ; kopeti ; upaddaveti. *p.p.* °ṭhita ; kopita ; upadduta. °**ance**, *n.* vihesā ; viheṭhanā ; pakopanā, *f.* °**ing**, *a.* viheṭhaka ; pīḷākara.

Annual, *a.* anuvassika. *n.* anuvassikasaṅgaha, *m.* °**ly**, *adv.* anuvassaŋ ; anusaradaŋ.

Annuity, *n.* vassikavetana, *nt.*

Annul, *v.t.* lopeti ; samucchindati. *p.p.* lutta ; °chinna.

Annular, *a.* vaṭṭula ; valayākāra.

Annunciate, *v.t.* (ādito) pakāseti *or* viññāpeti. *p.p.* °sita ; °pita. °**ion**, *n.* pakāsanā ; pageva ñāpanā, *f.* °**tor**, *n.* pakāsaka ; nivedaka, *m.*

Anodyne, *n. a.* rujāpahāraka ; vedanānāsaka.

Anoint, *v.t.* ālepeti ; vilimpeti ; abbhañjati ; añjeti. *p.p.* °pita ; °jita ; añjita. — **as a king**, rajje abhisiñcati. *p.p.* °abhisitta. °**ment**, *n.* abbhaṅga, *m.* vilepana, *nt.*

Anomalous, *a.* niyāmaviruddha ; uppaṭipāṭika. °**ly**, *adv.* vidhivirodhena.

Anomaly, *n.* vyabhicāra ; vidhivirodha, *m.*

Anon, *adv.* muhuŋ ; tāvad eva ; sapadi. **Ever and** —, muhuŋ muhuŋ, *adv.*

Anonym, *n.* ninnāmika, *m.* °**ous**, *a.* aññātanāma ; apākaṭanāma. °**ously**, *adv.* nāmanidassanaŋ vinā.

Another, *a.* apara ; itara ; añña ; para. — **country**, desantara, *nt.* — **day**, aññadā, *adv.* **One after** —, anupaṭipāṭiyā, *adv.*

Answer, *v.t.i.* vissajjeti ; paṭivacanaŋ deti. *p.p.* vissajjita ; dinnapaṭivacana. *n.* paṭivacana ; paccuttara ; vissajjana, *nt.* °**able**, *a.* paṭivacanīya ; vissajjitabba.

Ant, *n.* pipīlikā ; kipillikā, *f.* °**hill**, *n.* vammika, *m.*

Antagonism, *n.* virodha, *m.* vipakkhatā, *f.*

Antagonist, *n.* virodhī ; vipakkhaka ; paṭipakkhī, *m.*

Antarctic, *a.* dakkhiṇantagata.

Antecedence, *n.* pubbaṅgamatā, *f.* °**dent**, *a.* puregāmī ; pubbaṅgama, *n.* purevuṭṭapada, *nt.*

Antechamber, *n.* antogabbha, *m.*

Antedate, *v.t.* niyamadinato pubbadinaŋ yojeti. *n.* kālaniyamato pubbadina, *nt.*

Antelope, *n.* eṇimiga ; kuruṅga, *m.*

Anterior, *a.* pubbatara.

Anthem, *n.* devatthutigīta, *nt.*

Anthology, *n.* sāravākyasaṅgaha, *m.*

Anthrax, *n.* antogaṇḍa, *m.*

Anthropoid, *a.n.* māṇavasadisa ; mahāvānara, *m.*

Anthropology, *n.* māṇavavijjā, *f*

Anthropomorphous, *a.* manussākāra.

Antibilious, *a.* pittūpasamaka.

Anti-aircraft, *n.* vyomayānanāsaka, *m.*

Antic, *a. n.* hāsuppādaka ; parihāsaka, *m.*

Antichristian, *a.* Kiṭṭhasamayaviruddha.

Anticipant, *n. a.* abhikaṅkhī ; apekkhaka.

Anticipate, *v.t.* apekkhati ; abhikaṅkhati. *p.p.* °khita. °**ion**, *n.* 1. apekkhā, *f.* 2. pubbābhoga, *m.*

Antidote, *n.* visanāsakosadha, *nt.* °**tal**, *a.* visanāsaka.

Antimony, *n.* kapotañjana *nt.*

Antinomy, *n.* vidhivirodha, *m.*
Antipathetic, *a.* pakativiruddha ; viruddhasabhāva.
Antipathy, *n.* pakativirodha, *m.* sahajavirodhitā, *f.*
Antipode, *n.* paṭipakkhika ; paṭiviruddha, 3. *pl.* pātālavāsino; paṭipakkhadesā, *m.*
Antipole, *n.* paṭiviruddha-akkha, *m.*
Antiquarian, *a.* purāṇavatthuvisayaka. *n.* purātattaññū, *m.*
Antiquary, *n.* purātattagavesaka, *m.*
Antiquate, *v.t.* appacāraŋ *or* atītakālikaŋ karoti. *p.p.* appacārīkata. °**ed,** *a.* parijiṇṇa.
Antique, *a.* purāṇa ; atītāyatta. *n.* purāṇavatthu, *nt.*
Antiquity, *n.* 1. atītakāla, *m.* 2. purāṇatta, *nt.*
Antiseptic, *a. n.* pūtināsaka.
Antisocial, *a.* samājaviruddha.
Antitheist, *n.* anissaravādī, *m.*
Antithesis, *n.* viruddhatthatā ; paṭipakkhatā, *f.*
Antithetic, *a.* aññamaññaviruddha.
Antitype, *n.* paṭhamanidassana, *nt.*
Antler, *n.* sākhāyutta-siṅga ; migasiṅga, *nt.* °**ed,** *a.* visāṇī ; migasiṅgayutta.
Anus, *n.* guda, *nt.* vaccamagga, *m.*
Anvil, *n.* adhikaraṇī, *f.*
Anxiety, *n.* ubbega ; manovilekha, *m.*
Anxious, *a.* sāpekkha ; cintāpara ; ussuka. °**ly,** *adv.* saussāhaŋ ; sāpekkhaŋ.
Any, *a.* kiŋ *with* ci *and* ya. See the following compounds.
Anybody, *n.* yo ko ci.
Anyhow, *adv. conj.* yathā kathañci pi.
Anything, *n.* yaŋ kiñci.
Anyway, Anywise, *adv.* yena kena ci ākārena.
Anywhere, *adv.* yattha kattha ci.
Aorist, *n.* Ajjatanī Vibhatti ; atītakriyā, *f.*
Apace, *adv.* turitaŋ ; tuvaṭaŋ.
Apart, *adv.* visuŋ ; puthu ; ekamantaŋ.
Apartment, *n.* ovaraka.
Apathetic, *a.* upekkhaka ; udāsīna. °**ally,** *adv.* udāsīnākārena ; nirīhaŋ.
Apathy, *n.* upekkhā ; udasīnatā, *f.*
Ape, *n.* vānara ; kapi ; sākhāmiga ; makkaṭa, *m. v.t.* anukaroti ; vilambeti. *p.p.* anukata ; vilambita.
Apepsy, *n.* mandagahaṇitā, *f.*
Aperient, Aperitive, *a. n.* virecaka ; virecana, *nt.*
Aperture, *n.* vivara ; randha ; kuhara, *nt.*
Apetalous, *a.* dalarahita.
Apex, *n.* agga ; sikhara, *nt.* koṭi, *f.* matthaka, *m.*
Aphasia, *n.* kathetum asakyatā, *f.* vācānāsa, *m.*
Aphorism, *n.* sutta ; manta, *nt.* kārikā, *f.*
Aphrodisiac, *a.* kāmuddīpaka.
Apiary, *n.* madhukarāgāra, *nt.*
Apiculture, *n.* madhukarapālana, *nt.*

Apiece, *adv.* khaṇḍaso; bhāgaso; aṅgavasena.

Apish, *a.* jaḷa; vānarasama. **°ly,** *adv.* vānarasamaŋ. **°ness,** *n.* eḷamūgatta; kapisadisatta, *nt.*

Apocope, *n.* antakkharalopa, *m.*

Apocryphal, *a.* ayathābhūta; saṅkitabba.

Apod, *n.* apadasatta, *m.*

Apodictic, *a.* visada; pākaṭa; suvitthārita.

Apollo, *n.* suriyadeva, *m.*

Apologetic, *n. a.* khamāyācaka; accayadesaka. **°ally,** *adv.* accayadesanāya.

Apologist, *n.* sakamatapatiṭṭhāpaka, *m.*

Apologize, *v.i.* khamāpeti; attadosam āvikaroti. *p.p.* °pita. āvikatattadosa.

Apologue, *n.* upadesakathā, *f.*

Apology, *n.* khamāyācanā, *f.* accayapaṭiggahaṇa, *nt.*

Apoplectic, *a.* mucchājanaka.

Apoplexy, *n.* mucchā, *f.* satippavāsa, *m.*

Apostasy, *n.* sadhammacāga, *m.*

Apostate, *n.* sadhammacāgī, *m.*

Apostatize, *v.i.* dhammaŋ paccakkhāti; samayaŋ cajati. *p.p.* paccakkhātadhamma; cattasamaya.

Apostle, *n.* paṭhamadhammadūta; paṭhamārambhaka, *m.*

Apostolate, *n.* dhammadūtādhipacca, *nt.*

Apostrophe, *n.* lopasaññā, *f.*

Apothecary, *n.* bhesajjasampādaka, *m.*

Apotheosis, *n.* devattāropaṇa, *nt.*

Apotheosize, *v.t.* devattam āropeti. *p.p.* āropitadevatta.

Appal, *v.t.* bhāyāpeti; tāseti. *p.p.* °pita; tāsita. **°ling,** *a.* bhayajanaka; bhayānaka.

Apparatus, *n.* upakaraṇa, *nt*

Apparel, *n.* vatthābharaṇa, *nt.* *v.t.* nivāseti; paridahati. *p.p.* nivāsita *or* nivattha, °dahita.

Apparent, *a.* dissamāna; pākaṭa; visada. **°ly,** *adv.* dissamānākārena.

Apparition, *n.* 1. bhūtadassana, *nt.* 2. amanussa, *m.*

Appeal, *v.t.i.* uttarādhikaraṇaŋ yācati; accantaŋ yācati. *noun:* uttarivinicchayāyācanā, *f.*

Appear, *v.i.* āvibhavati; pātubhavati; sandissati. *p.p.* °bhūta; sandiṭṭha. **°ance,** *n.* 1. pātubhāva; uppāda; udaya, *m.* 2. ākāra, *m.* dassana, *nt.*

Appease, *v.t.* upasameti; sannisīdāpeti. *p.p.* °mita; °pita. **°ment,** *n.* upasamana; sannisīdāpana, *nt.*

Appellant, *n.* uttarivincchayākaṅkhī, *m.*

Appellation, *n.* nāma; abhidhāna, *nt.* saññā; samaññā; paññatti, *f.*

Append, *v.t.* anubandheti; olambeti; anughaṭeti. *p.p.* anubaddha; °bita; °ṭita. **°age,** anubandha, *m.* **°ant,** *a.* anughaṭita; upanibaddha.

Appendix, *n.* avasiṭṭhasaṅgaha; upagantha, *m.*

Appendicitis, *n.* antaganṭhikābādha, *m.*

Appertain, *v.i.* sambajjhati. *p.p.* sambaddha.

Appetence, *n.* īhā; taṇhā, *f.* °**tent,** *a.* īhāyutta.

Appetite, *n.* 1. icchā; abhilāsā, *f.* 2. khudā; jighacchā, *f.*

Appetize, *v.t.* jighacchaŋ janeti.

Applaud, *v.t.i.* 1. pasaŋsati; thometi; abhitthavati; 2. appoṭheti. *p.p.* pasattha; thomita; abhitthuta; °ṭhita.

Applause, *n.* thomanā; abhitthuti; kittanā, *f.* sādhukāra, *m.*

Apple, *n.* sītāphala, *nt.*

Appliance, *n.* 1. appaṇā, *f.* 2. upakaraṇa, *nt.*

Applicable, *a.* anucchavika; kammañña; payojiya. °**ly,** *adv.* yathānurūpaŋ.

Applicant, *n.* āyācaka; ākaṅkhī; apekkhaka, *m.* °**cation,** *n.* 1. āyācanā, *f.* yācanapaṇṇa, *nt.* 2. samappaṇā; abhiniropanā, *f.*

Apply, *v.t.i.* 1. appeti; 2. āyācati; upaṭṭhāti; (**some medicine to**), añjati; ālepeti. *p.p.* appita; āyācita; upaṭṭhita; añjita; ālitta. — **oneself to,** niyojeti; upayojeti.

Appoint, *v.t.* 1. niyameti; niyojeti; adhikaroti; 2. sammannati. *p.p.* °mita; °jita; adhikata; sammata. °**ment,** *n.* 1. adhikāra, *m.* ṭhānantara; pada, *nt.* 2. niyama; saṅketa, *m.*

Apportion, *v.t.* onojeti; vibhajati; vikappeti. *p.p.* onojita; vibhatta; °pita.

Apposite, *a.* ucita; anurūpa; saṅgata. °**ly,** *adv.* yathocitaŋ; yathārahaŋ.

Apposition, *n.* 1. samānādhikaraṇa; 2. muddāpatiṭṭhāpana, *nt.*

Appraisal, *n.* agghaniyamana, *nt.*

Appraise, *v.t.* agghāpeti; mūlaŋ niyameṭi. *p.p.* °pita; niyamitamūla. °**ment,** *n.* agghāpana, *nt.* °**er,** *n.* agghakāra; agghāpaka, *m.*

Appreciate, *v.t.i.* 1. anumodati; agghaŋ *or* guṇaŋ jānati; 2. agghaŋ vaḍḍheti. *p.p.* °dita; ñātaggha; ñātaguṇa; vaḍḍhitaggha. °**ion,** *n.* 1. anumodanā; guṇāpaciti, *f.* 2. agghavaḍḍhi, *f.*

Apprehend, *v.t.* 1. rodheti; gaṇhāti; 2. avabujjhati; 3. āsaṅkati; parisaṅkati. *p.p.* rodhita *or* ruddha; avabuddha; °kita.

Apprehension, *n.* 1. rodhana; gahaṇa, *nt.* 2. avabodha, *m.* 3. parisaṅkā, *f.* °**sive,** *a.* sāsaṅka; sappaṭibhaya. °**sively,** *adv.* sāsaṅkaŋ; sabhayaŋ.

Apprentice, *n.* sekkha; sippantevāsi, *m.* °**ship,** *n.* sissatta; antevāsikatta, *nt.*

Apprise, *v.t.* nivedeti; āroceti. *p.p.* nivedita; °cita.

Approach, *v.t.i.* upagacchati; upasaṅkamati; pāpuṇāti; upatiṭṭhati. *p.p.* upagata; upasaṅkanta; patta; upaṭṭhita.

noun: 1. upagamana; pāpuṇana, *nt.* patti, *f.* 2. āgamanamagga, *m.* °**able,** *a.* upagamanīya. °**ing,** *a.* upakaṭṭha; āgāmī.

Approbate, *v.t.* sampaṭicchati; anumaññati. *p.p.* °chita; anumata. °**ion,** *n.* sampaṭicchana, *nt.* anumati, *f.*

Appropriate, *a.* ucita; anurūpa; kappiya. °**ly,** *adv.* ucitākārena; yathānurūpaŋ.

Appropriate, *v.t.* 1. āyattaŋ karoti; 2. visesakiccāya ṭhapeti. °**ion,** āyattakaraṇa, *nt.* pariggaha, *m.*

Approval, *n.* anuññā; anumati; sampaṭicchanā, *f.*

Approve, *v.t.i.* 1. anujānāti; anumaññati; pasaŋsati; 2. tathataŋ dīpeti. *p.p.* anuññāta; anumata; pasattha; dīpitatathatta.

Approximate, *a.* accāsanna; samīpatara. *v.t.* upaneti; samīpaŋ neti. *v.i.* upagacchati; upatiṭṭhati. *p.p.* upanīta; upagata; upaṭṭhita. °**ly,** *adv.* āsannataraŋ; upanayanena. °**ion,** *n.* samīpānayana, *nt.*

Appurtenance, *n.* parikkhāra; upakaraṇa, *nt.* °**nant,** *a.* parikkhārabhūta.

April, *n.* Cittamāsa, *m.*

Apron, *n.* kaṭipaṭicchādana; malaggāhakavattha, *nt.*

Apt, *a.* 1. ucita; yogga; 2. paviṇa; kusala; dakkha. °**ly,** *adv.* pāṭavena; kosallena. °**ness,** pāṭava; kosalla, *nt.*

Aptitude, *n.* 1. kosalla; pāṭava; cāturiya, *nt.* 2. ucitatta; anurūpatta, *nt.*

Aqua, *n.* āpa; paya; jala; vāri, *nt.* °**rium,** *n.* mīnāgāra, *nt.*

Aquarius, *n.* kumbharāsi, *m.*

Aquatic, *a.* jalaja; vārigocara.

Aqueduct, *n.* panālikā; jalanetti; udakamātikā, *f.*

Aqueous, *a.* 1. jalabahula; 2. jalajāta.

Aquiline, *a.* garuḷākāra.

Arab, *n.* Arābidesīya, *m.* °**ian,** *a.* Arābijātika.

Arable, *a.* kasiyogga; kasanāraha.

Arbiter, *n.* niṇṇetu; vinicchayadāyaka; tīretu, *m.*

Arbitral, *a.* majjhaṭṭhatīraṇāyatta.

Arbitrary, *a.* attanomatika; sericārī. °**ily,** *adv.* attanomatiyā; yathākāmaŋ.

Arbitrate, *v.t.i.* tīreti; niccheti; niṇṇeti. *p.p.* tīrita; nicchita; niṇṇīta. °**ion,** majjhattavinicchaya, *m.* °**tor,** see **Arbiter.**

Arboreal, *a.* rukkhajīvī.

Arboriculture, *n.* rukkharopaṇa, *nt.*

Arbour, *n.* nikuñja; latāmaṇḍapa, *m.*

Arc, *n.* addhavaṭṭula; candavaṅka, *m.*

Arcade, *n.* toraṇacchannamagga; channapatha, *m.*

Arcadian, *a.* jānapadika.

Arch, *n.* toraṇa; addhamaṇḍala, *nt.* adj. 1. uttama; seṭṭha;

padhāna ; 2. keḷisīla. *v.t.* addhamaṇḍalaŋ yojeti. *v.i.* addhavaṭṭulo bhavati. *p.p.* yojitaddha° ; °lībhūta. °**angel,** *n.* seṭṭhadevadūta, *m.* °**bishop,** *n.* devapūjakādhipati, *m.* °**duke,** *n.* seṭṭhādipāda ; padhānakumāra, *m.*

Archaeology, *n.* purāvatthuvijjā, *f.* °**ist,** *n.* purātattavedī, *m.*

Archaic, *a.* addhagata ; kālātīta. °**ism,** *n.* atītānugamana, *nt.*

Archer, *n.* issāsa ; dhanuddhara. °**ry,** *n.* dhanusippa ; issattha, *nt.*

Archetype, *n.* mūlapaṭibimba, *nt.*

Archipelago, *n.* 1. dīparāsi ; 2. bahudīpakasamudda, *m.*

Architect, *n.* nimmāṇasippī, *m.* °**ure,** *n.* nimmāṇasippa, *nt.*

Archives, *n.* 1. itihāsalekhanāgara, *nt.* 2. itihāsalipi, *f.* purāvuttanta, *nt.* °**vist,** *n.* purāvuttantapālaka, *m.*

Arctic, *a.* uttarantāyatta ; Merupadesīya. — **circle,** *n.* Meruparivaṭṭa, *nt.*

Ardency, *n.* ātāpa ; ussāha, *m.*

Ardent, *a.* 1. uttatta ; 2. ātāpī ; pahitatta ; ussuka. °**ly,** *adv.* saussāhaŋ ; sānurāgaŋ.

Ardour, *n.* 1. adhikatāpa, *m.* 2. ātappa ; ussāha ; vāyāma, *m.*

Arduous, *a.* 1. durāroha ; 2. dukkara ; dussādhiya.

Area, *n.* 1. bhūmippadesa, *m.* aṅgaṇa, *nt.* 2. āyāmavitthāra, *m.*

Areca, *n.* pūga ; kamuka, *m.* °**nut,** *n.* pūgaphala, *nt.*

Arena, *n.* mallabhūmi, *f.* raṅgamaṇḍala, *nt.*

Argent, *a.* rajatavaṇṇa. °**ine,** *a.* rajatopama.

Argil, *n.* kumbhakāramattikā, *f.*

Argue, *v.t.i.* vivadati ; pamāṇayati ; yuttiŋ katheti. *p.p.* °dita ; pamāṇita ; kathitayuttika. °**ment,** *n.* vivāda, *m.* yuttikathā, *f.* °**er,** *n.* vādī ; yuttikathī, *m.*

Argumentation, *n.* vivadana ; takkavitakkana, *nt.* °**tive,** *a.* takkika ; vādappiya.

Arid, *a.* sukkha ; nissāra.

Aries, *n.* mesarāsi, *m.*

Aright, *adv.* sammā ; yathātathaŋ.

Arise, *v.i.* udeti ; uppajjati ; ubbhavati ; uṭṭhāti ; uggacchati ; pabhavati. *p.p.* udita ; uppanna ; ubbhūta ; uṭṭhita ; uggata ; pabhūta. °**ing,** *n.* jāti ; uppatti ; nibbatti, *f.* udaya ; uggama, *m.* uṭṭhāna, *nt.* adj. jāyamāna ; uppajjanaka. °**ing together,** sahabhū, *a.* °**ing from a cause,** hetuppabhava, *a.*

Aristocracy, *n.* 1. issarajanatā, *f.* 2. adhipatīhi pālana, *nt.*

Aristocrat, *n.* issarajana, *m.*

Arithmetic, *n.* aṅkavijjā, *f.* gaṇita, *nt.* °**al,** *a.* aṅkavijjānugata. °**ian,** *n.* gaṇitaññū ; gaṇaka, *m.*

Ark, *n.* 1. mañjūsā ; peḷā, *f.* 2. taraṇī ; nāvā, *f.*

Arm, *n.* bāhu ; bhuja, *m.* bāhā, *f.* °**ful,** *a.* pasatamatta. °**pit,** *n.* upakaccha, *nt.*

Arm, *v.i.* sannayhati. *p.p.* sannaddha. *v.t.* sannāhayati ; sannaddhaŋ karoti. *p.p.* °yita. *noun: pl.* āyudha ; sattha, *nt.*

Armada, *n.* yuddhanāvāsamūha, *m.*

Armadillo, *n.* kapālagodhā, *f.*

Armament, *n.* 1. sannaddhasenā, *f.* 2. yuddhopakaraṇasamūha, *m.*

Armchair, *n.* āsandi, *f.*

Armistice, *n.* kālika-yuddhavirati, *f.*

Armlet, *n.* keyūra ; bāhumūlavibhūsana, *nt.*

Armour, *n.* sannāha ; kavaca, *m.* vamma, *nt.* *v.t.* sannāheti. *p.p.* sannaddha. °**er,** *n.* 1. āyudhasampādaka ; 2. āyudhādhikārī, *m.*

Armoury, *n.* āyudhāgāra, *nt.*

Army, *n.* yuddhasenā ; camū ; vāhinī, *f.* yuddhabala, *nt.* **Array of an —,** aṇīkagga, *nt.* **— of chariots,** rathasenā, *f.* **— of elephants,** hatthisenā, *f.*

Aroma, *n.* sugandha ; surabhi, *m.* °**tic,** *a.* sugandhī ; surabhiyutta. °**tics,** sugahajātayo, *pl. m.*

Around, *adv.* abhito ; parito ; samantato ; samantā.

Arouse, *v.t.* pabodheti ; uttejeti ; ussukkāpeti. *p.p.* °dhita ; °jita ; °pita. °**ing,** *n.* pabodhana ; uttejana, *nt.*

Arrack, *n.* tālasurā ; nāḷikerī, *f.*

Arraign, *v.t.* codeti ; vinicchayaŋ ṇeti. *p.p.* codita ; °nīta. °**ment,** *n.* codanā, vinicchayapāpanā, *f.*

Arrange, *v.t.i.* saŋvidahati ; paṭipādeti ; paṭiyādeti ; racayati. *p.p.* °hita ; °dita ; racita. °**ment,** *n.* saŋvidhāna ; paṭiyādana, *nt.* vinyāsa, *m.* **Well arranged,** susaŋvihita ; sannihita ; suyutta, *a.*

Arrant, *a.* duṭṭha ; vañcaka ; saṭha. °**ly,** *adv.* duṭṭhākārena ; saṭhena.

Array, *v.t.* 1. byūhayati ; 2. bhūseti ; vibhūseti ; maṇḍeti. *p.p.* byūhita ; bhūsita ; maṇḍita. *noun:* 1. racaṇā, *f.* byūha ; vyūha, *m.* 2. maṇḍana ; pasādhana, *nt.* alaṅkāra, *m.*

Arrear, *n.* (*pl.*) avasiṭṭha-iṇa, *nt.* °**age,** *n.* asodhita-iṇa, *nt.*

Arrest, *v.t.* 1. rundhati ; sannirumbheti ; 2. vikkhambheti. *p.p.* ruddha ; °bhita. *noun:* 1. rundhana ; rodhana ; gahaṇa ; 2. vikkhambhana, *nt.*

Arrival, *n.* āgamana ; upagamana ; pāpuṇana, *nt.* patti ; anuppatti, *f.*

Arrive, *v.i.* pappoti ; pāpuṇāti ; upagacchati ; avasarati. *p.p.* patta ; upagata ; avasaṭa.

Arrogance, *n.* dappa ; abhimāna ; ahaṅkāra, *m.*

Arrogant, *a.* unnala ; dappita ; gabbita ; abhimānī. °**ly,** *adv.* sadappaŋ ; sābhimānaŋ.

Arrogate, *v.t.* aññāyena sakāyattaŋ karoti. °**ion,** *n.* ayuttiyā gahaṇa, *nt.*

Arrow, *n.* usu ; sara ; bāṇa, *m.* asana ; tejana, *nt.* °**headed,** *a.* saratuṇḍākāra.

Arsenal, *n.* yuddhāyudhāgāra, *nt.*

Arsenic, *n.* visapāsāṇa, *nt.* adj. visapāsāṇayutta.

Arson, *n.* gehadāhana, *nt.*

Art, *n.* 1. sippa, *nt.* kalā, *f.* 2. kosalla ; nepuñña, *nt.* 3. (painting), cittakamma, *nt.* °**ful,** *a.* saṭha ; kapaṭa ; māyāvī. °**fulness,** *n.* 1. māyāvitā, *f.* 2. cāturiya, pāṭava, *nt.*

Artery, *n.* dhamanī ; kaṇḍarā, *f.* °**ial,** *a.* dhamanīsambandha.

Article, *n.* 1. nibandha, *m.* visesalipi, *f.* 2. bhaṇḍa ; upakaraṇa ; vatthu, *nt.* **Definite —,** niyamanipāta, *m.* **Indefinite —,** aniyamanipāta, *m.* **— of trade,** paṇiya, *nt.*

Articulate, *v.t.i.* udīreti ; uccāreti, *p.p.* °rita. adj. vyatta ; paripphuṭa. °**ion,** *n.* vyattuccāraṇa, *nt.*

Artifice, *n.* 1. upāya, *m.* sippakosalla, *nt.* 2. sāṭheyya, *nt.* °**er,** *n.* sippī ; nimmāpaka, *m.*

Artificial, *a.* kittima ; sippinimmita ; apākatika. °**ly,** *adv.* kittimākārena.

Artillery, *n.* nāḷīyantasenā, *f.*

Artisan, *n.* sippī ; kalāvedī, *m.*

Artist, *n.* sippī ; cittakāra, *m.* °**ic,** *a.* sippānugata ; kalānukūla ; kosalladīpaka.

Artless, *a.* 1. adakkha ; anipuṇa ; 2. asaṭha ; amāyāvī.

Aryan, *n.* *a.* ariya ; ariyāyatta ; ariyavaŋsika.

As, *adv. conj.* iva ; viya ; yathā. **— before,** yathā pure. **— far as,** yāva . . . tāva ; yāvatā . . . tāvatā. **— follows,** taŋ yathā ; seyyathīdaŋ. **— if,** viya. **— soon as,** tāvad eva. **— well as,** tath'eva.

Asafetida, Asafoetida, hiṅgu, *nt.*

Asbestos, *n.* adayhatantu, *nt.*

Ascend, *v.t.i.* āruhati ; abhiruhati ; ārohati. *v.i.* uggacchati. *p.p.* ārūḷha ; uggata.

Ascendancy, °**ency,** *n.* adhipālana ; adhirohaṇa, *nt.*

Ascendant, °**ent,** *a.* āruhamāna ; uggacchanta. *n.* ārohī ; pabalī, *m.*

Ascension, *n.* uggamana ; āruhaṇa, *nt.* **— to the heaven,** saggārohaṇa, *nt.*

Ascent, *n.* 1. uggamana ; 2. unnataṭṭhāna, *nt.*

Ascertain, *v.t.* vavatthapeti ; nirūpeti ; niccheti. *p.p.* °pita ; nicchita. °**ment,** *n.* sanniṭṭhāna ; avadhāraṇa ; niddhāraṇa, *nt.* nicchaya, *m.*

Ascetic, *a.* *n.* tāpasa ; muni ; yati ; isi ; samaṇa, *m.* °**ism,** *n.* tapacaraṇa, *nt.* samaṇadhamma, *m.* **— practice,** tapa ; tapokamma, *nt.* **Naked —,** acelaka ; digambara, *m.*

Ascribe, *v.t.* ajjhāropeti ; upakkhipati. *p.p.* °pita ; upakkhitta.

Ascription, *n.* ajjhāropaṇa ; upanayana, *nt.*

Asexual, *a.* aliṅgika.

Ash, *n.* 1. (tree), bhasmavaṇṇataru, *m.* 2. chārikā, *f.* bhasma, *nt.* **Hot —,** kukkuḷa, *m.*

Ashame, *v.t.* lajjāpeti. *p.p.* °pita. *v.i.* lajjati. *p.p.* lajjita.

Ashen, *a.* dhūsara; bhasmavaṇṇa.

Ashore, *adv.* tīre; taṭe; kūle, (*Loc.*).

Ashy, *a.* 1. dhūsara; 2. basmacchanna.

Asian, Asiatic, *a.* Āsiāmahādīpāyatta.

Aside, *adv.* ekamantaŋ; ekapasse.

Ask, *v.t.* 1. pucchati; 2. yācati. *p.p.* puṭṭha; yācita. — **in return,** paṭipucchati.

Askance, *adv.* 1. tiro; tiriyaŋ; kuṭilaŋ; 2. sāsaṅkaŋ.

Askew, Aslant, *adv.* anujuŋ; vaṅkākārena; vimukhākārena.

Asleep, *a.* sutta; niddopagata, *adv.* antoniddāya.

Aslope, *a.* poṇa; ninna, *adv.* pabbhārākārena.

Asparagus, *n.* satāvarī; satamūlī, *f.*

Aspect, *n.* 1. vesa; vilāsa; ākāra, *m.* 2. avaṭṭhiti, *f.*

Asperity, *n.* kakkhaḷatta; lūkhatta; kharatta, *nt.*

Asphalt, *n.* asmalepa, *m.*

Aspirant, *n. a.* ākaṅkhī; patthetu, *m.*

Aspirate, *v.t.* saghosam uccāreti. *p.p.* °rita. *n.* ghosakkhara, *nt.* adj. saghosa.

Aspiration, *n.* 1. assāsa, *m.* 2. ākaṅkhā; abhilāsā; patthanā, *f.* abhinīhāra, *m.*

Aspire, *v.i.* pattheti; abhilasati; ākaṅkhati. *p.p.* °thita; °sita; °khita.

Asquint, *a.* valira; kekara, *adv.* kekarākārena.

Ass, *n.* gadrabha, *m.*

Assail, *v.t.* āhanati; paharati; paripāteti. *p.p.* āhata; pahaṭa; °tita. °**ant,** *n.* āhanaka; paripātetu; omaddaka, *m.*

Assassin, *n.* ghātaka; māretu; pāṇahara, *m.* °**ation,** *n.* māraṇa; ghātana; hanana, *nt.*

Assassinate, *v.t.* māreti; ghāteti; hanati. *p.p.* mārita; ghātita; hata.

Assault, *v.t.* paharati; pahāraŋ deti. *p.p.* pahaṭa; dinnapahāra. *n.* pahāradāna; paharaṇa, *nt.*

Assay, *v.t.* loham upaparikkhati. *n.* lohaparikkhā, *f.* °**er,** *n.* lohaparikkhaka, *m.*

Assemblage, *n.* samūha; samudāya; saṅgha; gaṇa, *m.*

Assemble, *v.t.* sannipāteti. *v.i.* sannipatati; samosarati; samāgacchati. *p.p.* °pātita; °patita; samosaṭa; samāgata.

Assembly, *n.* parisā; sabhā; samiti, *f.* samāgama; sannipāta, *m.*

Assent, *v.i.* anujānāti; paṭissuṇāti. *p.p.* anuññāta; paṭissuta. *n.* anumati; anuññā, *f.* paṭissava, *m.*

Assert, *v.t.* daḷhīkaroti; sādhakehi dasseti. *p.p.* °kata; dassitasādhaka. °**ion,** *n.* daḷhīkaraṇa; pamāṇīkaraṇa, *nt.*

Assess, *v.t.* agghaŋ *or* karaŋ nirūpeti; baliŋ niddhāreti. *p.p.* nirūpitakara; niddhāritabali.

°**ment**, *n.* karaniyamana ; agghanirūpaṇa, *nt.* °**or**, *n.* agghanirūpaka, *m.*

Assets, *n.* iṇamocaka-vibhava, *m.*

Asseverate, *v.t.* sanicchayaŋ pakāseti, *p.p.* °sita. °**ion**, sanicchaya-pakāsana, *nt.*

Assiduity, *n.* uyyāma ; uyyoga, *m.* tapparatā, *f.*

Assiduous, *a.* uyyutta ; tappara ; parāyaṇa. °**ly**, *adv.* saussāhaŋ. °**ness**, *n.* tapparāyaṇatā, *f.*

Assign, *v.t.* niyyādeti ; niyameti, *p.p.* °dita ; °mita. °**ment**, *n.* 1. niyyātana ; niyamana ; 2. niyyātanapaṇṇa, *nt.* °**ation**, *n.* 1. onojaṇa, *nt.* 2. pubbaniyama ; niyamitavelādi, *m.* °**ee**, *n.* niyojita ; nīyādetabba ; 3. °**or**, *n.* nīyādaka, *m.*

Assimilate, *v.t.* 1. samāneti ; sadisīkaroti ; 2. paripāceti ; pariṇāmeti, *v.i.* samataŋ yāti, *p.p.* samānita ; °kata ; °cita ; °mita ; °yāta. °**ion**, *n.* 1. samatāpādana ; sadisatta ; tulyatta ; samānatta, *nt.* 2. pariṇāma, *m.*

Assist, *v.t.* anuggaṇhāti ; upatthambheti ; upakaroti, *p.p.* anuggahita ; °bhita ; upakata. °**ance**, *n.* anuggaha ; upakāra, *m.* sahāyatā, *f.*

Assistant, *n.* sahāya ; upatthambhaka, *m.* Upa *in cpds.*, e.g. *upācariya*, assistant teacher.

Assizes, *n.* adhikaraṇavāra, *m.* °**er**, *n.* aggha-māṇanirūpaka, *m.*

Associable, *a.* sevitabba ; bhajitabba.

Associate, *v.t.i.* sevati ; bhajati ; nisevati ; payirupāsati ; saŋvasati. *p.p.* sevita ; bhajita ; °sita ; saŋvuttha. *noun*: sahāya ; sahacara ; anucara ; payirupāsaka, *m.*

Association, *n.* 1. sevana ; bhajana ; payirupāsana, *nt.* saŋsagga ; santhava, *m.* 2. sabhā ; samiti, *f.* saṅgama ; saŋsada, *m.* °**al**, *a.* samājāyatta.

Assonance, *n.* samānassaratā, *f.* °**nant**, *a.* samānasarayutta.

Assort, *v.t.* pantivasena puthakkaroti. *v.i.* āsevati. *p.p.* °kata, āsevita. °**ment**, *n.* uccinana, *nt.* vinyāsa, *m.*

Assuage, *v.t.* upasameti ; sannisīdāpeti. *p.p.* °mita ; °pita. °**ment**, *n.* upasamana, *nt.*

Assuasive, *a.* upasamaka ; santidāyaka.

Assume, *v.t.i.* 1. ādāti ; 2. vesaŋ gaṇhāti ; 3. gabbito hoti ; 4. saccaŋ viya parikappeti. *p.p.* ādinna ; gahitāvesa ; °pita. °**ing**, *a.* gabbita ; sadappa.

Assumption, *n.* 1. ādāna ; 2. vesagahaṇa ; 3. parikappana ; 4. āyattakaraṇa, *nt.*

Assurance, *n.* 1. saccāpana, *nt.* 2. sanicchayakathā, *f.* 3. saccakārapaṇṇa, *nt.*

Assure, *v.t.* 1. surakkhitaŋ karoti ; 2. niccheti ; saŋsayam apaneti. *p.p.* °kata ; nicchita ; apanītasaŋsaya. °**dly**, *adv.* ekantaŋ ; niyataŋ ; nissaŋsayaŋ. °**dness**, *n.* surakkhitatta ; sanicchayatta, *nt.*

Assurgent, *a.* uggacchamāna.

Assyriology, *n.* Asurapurāvijjā, *f.*

Asterisk, *n.* tārālañchana, *nt.*

Asterism, *n.* nakkhatta, *nt.* tārāsamūha, *m.*

Astern, *adv.* nāvāya pacchābhāge.

Asteroid, *a.* tārakākāra.

Asthma, *n.* sāsaroga, *m.* °**tic**, *n.* 1. sāsarogī, *m.* adj. sāsarogāyatta.

Astir, *a.* saṅkhubhita.

Astonish, *v.t.* vimhayāpeti ; kutūhalaŋ janeti. *p.p.* °pita ; janitakutūhala. °**ment**, *n.* vimhaya, *m.* acchariya ; abbhuta, *nt.* °**ing**, *a.* vimhayakara ; acchariyāvaha.

Astound, *v.t.* vimoheti ; ākulīkaroti. *p.p.* vimohita ; °kata.

Astral, *a.* dibba ; sukhuma ; tārakāyatta.

Astray, *adv.* uppathaŋ. adj. uppathagāmī ; maggamūḷha.

Astrict, *v.t.* rundhati ; daḷhaŋ bandhati. *p.p.* ruddha ; daḷhabaddha.

Astride, *adv.* pāde viyūhitvā.

Astringe, *v.t.* saṅkoceti. *p.p.* °cita.

Astringent, *a.* kaṭuka ; kasāva ; santhambhaka.

Astrologer, *n.* muhuttika ; jotisatthaññū, *m.* °**logy**, *n.* horāsattha, *nt.* nakkhattavijjā, *f.* °**gical**, *a.* jotisatthāyatta.

Astronomer, *n.* jotisatthavidū, *m.* °**my**, *n.* jotisattha, *nt.* °**mical**, *a.* jotisatthāyatta. °**mically**, *adv.* jotisatthānusārena.

Astute, *a.* catura ; nipuṇa, °**ly**, *adv.* caturākārena.

Asunder, *adv.* puthu ; visuŋ.

Asylum, *n.* leṇaṭṭhāna, *nt.* assama, *m.*

Asymmetry, *n.* asobhanatā, *f.*

At, *prep.* In many cases it is expressed by the locative, and sometimes by the instrumental or accusative. **At last**, ante ; pariyosāne. **At ease**, yathāsukhaŋ, *adv.* **At first**, ādito ; paṭhamaŋ, *adv.* **At once**, ekappahārena. **At that moment**, tāvade ; taṅkhaṇe. **At that time**, tadā, *adv.*

Ataxy, *n.* sarīrakriyāsaṅkhobha ; kriyāviraha, *m.*

Atheism, *n.* anissaravāda, *m.* adevadiṭṭhi, *f.* °**ist**, *n.* adevadiṭṭhī ; anissaravādī, *m.*

Athirst, *a.* pipāsita ; sataṇha.

Athlete, *n.* malla ; kīḷaka, *m.*

Athletic, *a.* balavantu ; thāmasampanna. *n.* mallayodha, *m.*

Athwart, *adv.* vilomaŋ ; paṭilomaŋ ; tiriyaŋ.

Atlantic, *a.* Atalapabbatāyatta.

Atlas, *n.* bhūmicitta, *nt.*

Atmosphere, *n.* vāyumaṇḍala, *nt.* °**ical**, *a.* vāyumaṇḍalāyatta.

Atom, *n.* paramāṇu, *m.* °**ic**, *a.* paramāṇuvisayaka.

Atomism, *n.* paramāṇuvāda, *m.*

Atomize, *v.t.* paramāṇubhāvaŋ pāpeti. *p.p.* °pāpita.

Atomy, *n.* 1. kisadeha, *m.* 2. aṭṭhikaṅkala, *m.* 3. aṇuppamāṇajīvī, *m.*

Atone, *v.t.i.* paṭikaroti ; paṭikammaŋ *or* daṇḍakammaŋ karoti. *p.p.* paṭikata ; katapaṭikamma. °**ment,** *n.* paṭikamma, *nt.*

Atonic, *a.* aghosa. *n.* aghosakkhara, *nt.*

Atop, *adv.* matthake.

Atrocious, *a.* ghora ; dāruṇa. °**ly,** *adv.* ghorākārena.

Atrocity, *n.* ghoratta ; dāruṇatta, *nt.*

Atrophy, *n.* mandaposaṇa, *nt.*

Attach, *v.t.* 1. laggeti ; sambandhati ; 2. rañjeti. *v.i.* 1. āsajjati ; laggati ; 2. sārajjati. *p.p.* laggita ; sambaddha ; rañjita ; āsatta ; lagga ; sāratta. °**ment,** *n.* 1. āsajjana ; laggana ; rajjana, *nt.* rāga ; anurāga ; saṅga, *m.* rati ; nandi ; nikanti, *f.*

Attack, *v.t.* paharati ; āhanati ; paripāteti. *p.p.* pahaṭa ; āhata ; °tita. *noun* : paharaṇa ; āhanana ; paripātana, *nt.* °**ed by a disease,** rogāpahata ; rogapīḷita, *a.*

Attain, *v.i.* labhati ; paṭilabhati ; adhigacchati ; abhisameti. *p.p.* laddha ; adhigata ; °mita. *v.t.* upeti ; pāpuṇāti. *p.p.* upeta ; patta. °**able,** *a.* laddhabba ; pattabba ; abhisametabba. °**ment,** *n.* paṭilābha ; adhigama ; abhisamaya, *m.*

Attar, *n.* sogandhikasāra, *m.*

Attemper, *v.t.* santataŋ neti ; kammaññaŋ karoti. *p.p.* °nīta ; kammaññakata.

Attempt, *v.t.* ussahati ; vāyamati ; upakkamati. *p.p.* ussahita ; °mita. *n.* ussāha ; vāyāma, *m.* viriya, *nt.*

Attend, *v.t.* 1. upatiṭṭhati ; anuyāti ; parivāreti ; 2. upaṭṭhāti ; upāsati ; sevati. *p.p.* upaṭṭhita ; anuyāta ; °rita ; upaṭṭhita ; upāsita ; sevita. *v.i.* 1. samāgacchati ; 2. manasikaroti. *p.p.* samāgata ; °kata. °**ance,** *n.* 1. upaṭṭhāna ; upāsana, *nt.* sevā, *f.* 2. sampattaparisā, *f.* 3. parivāra, *m.* 4. āvajjanā ; sussūsā, *f.* manasikāra, *m.*

Attendant, *n. a.* sevaka ; upaṭṭhāka ; paricāraka ; veyyāvaccakara, *m.* **Female —,** sevikā ; paricārikā, *f.* **— on a patient,** gilānupaṭṭhāka, *m.*

Attention, *n.* avadhāna ; apekkhana ; odahana, *nt.* abhinivesa, *m.* **— to one subject,** ekaggatā, *f.*

Attentive, *a.* sāvadhāna ; samāhita ; sussūsaka. °**ly,** *adv.* sāvadhānaŋ.

Attenuate, *v.t.* tanuŋ *or* sallahukaŋ karoti ; balaŋ hāpeti. *p.p.* tanukata ; hāpitabala. *v.i.* khīyati ; hāyati ; tanubhavati. *p.p.* khīṇa ; hīna ; tanubhūta. °**ion,** *n.* tanukaraṇa ; hāyana ; khīyana, *nt.*

Attest, *v.t.i.* sakkhiŋ karoti ; sakkhī bhavati ; samatthayati. *p.p.* sakkhikata ; °bhūta ; samatthita. °**ation,** *n.* pamāṇīkaraṇa ; samatthana, *nt.*

Attic, *n.* kūṭāgāra, *nt.*

Attire, *v.t.* acchādeti ; paridahati ; nivāseti. *p.p.* °dita ; °hita ; nivāsita *or* nivattha. *n.* vatthābharaṇa, *nt.*

Attitude, *n.* ākāra ; vilāsa, *m.* saṇṭhiti, *f.*

Attorney, *n.* paṭinidhi ; parakiccasādhaka, *m.* — **General,** *n.* padhānanītivedī, *m.*

Attract, *v.t.* 1. ākassati ; ākaḍḍhati ; 2. palobheti. *p.p.* °sita ; °ḍhita ; °bhita. °**ion,** *n.* ākassana ; palobhana, *nt.* °**ive,** *a.* ākassaka ; palobhaka ; manohara ; hadayaṅgama. °**iveness,** *n.* manoharatta ; manuññatta, *nt.*

Attribute, *v.t.* āropeti ; niropeti. *p.p.* āropita. *n.* guṇavisesa, *m.* visesaṇa, *nt.* °**able,** *a.* ajjhāropanīya. °**tive,** *a.* visesaka ; guṇavācaka.

Attrition, *n.* 1. ghaŋsana, *nt.* 2. anutāpa, *m.*

Attune, *v.t.* tulyassarataŋ pāpeti. *p.p.* °pāpita.

Atwain, *adv.* dvidhā.

Auburn, *a.* tambavaṇṇa.

Auction, *n.* anusāvita-vikkaya, *m.* °**eer,** *n.* anusāvitavikkayī, *m.*

Audacious, *a.* sappagabbha. °**ly,** *adv.* pāgabbhiyena.

Audacity, *n.* pāgabbhiya, *nt.* nillajjatā, *f.*

Audible, *a.* sotagocara ; savaṇakkhama. °**bly,** *adv.* savaṇīyākārena.

Audience, *n.* 1. savaṇa ; nisāmana, *nt.* 2. sāvakagaṇa, *m.* nisāmaka-parisā, *f.*

Audit, *v.t.* gaṇanam upaparikkhati. *n.* saṅkhyāparikkhā, *f.* °**or,** *n.* gaṇaka ; saṅkhyāparikkhaka, *m.*

Audition, *n.* savaṇa, *nt.* sotappasāda, *m.*

Auditive, Auditory, *a.* savaṇānubaddha. — **sensation,** sotindriya, *nt.* — **cognition,** sotaviññāṇa, *nt.*

Auger, *n.* vedhanī, *f.*

Aught, *n.* kiñci ; yaŋ kiñci.

Augment, *v.t.* brūheti ; vaḍḍheti. *p.p.* brūhita ; vaḍḍhita. *v.i.* abhivaḍḍhati. *p.p.* abhivuddha. °**ation,** *n.* vaḍḍhi ; vuddhi, *f.* vaḍḍhana, brūhana, *nt.* °**ative,** *a.* abhivaḍḍhaka.

Augur, *n.* nimittapāṭhaka, *m.* *v.t.* subhāsubham apekkhati. °**al,** *a.* nimittāyatta ; anāgatadassaka. °**y,** *n.* nimittapaṭhana, *nt.*

August, *a.* mahanīyatara ; mahāmahima. *n.* Sāvaṇamāsa, *m.* °**ness,** mahāmahimatā, *f.*

Aunt, *n.* (father's sister :) pitucchā, *f.* (mother's sister :) mātucchā, *f.* (maternal uncle's wife :) mātulānī, *f.* (paternal uncle's wife :) cūlamātā, *f.*

Aura, *n.* tejomaṇḍala, *nt.*

Aural, *a.* sotavisayaka.

Aurelian, *a.* suvaṇṇavaṇṇa.

Aureole, *n.* sīsappabhāmaṇḍala, *nt.* ketumālā, *f.*

Auricular, *a.* sotavisayaka ; rāhaseyyaka. °**ly,** *adv.* kaṇṇajappanena.

Aurora, *n.* 1. akkhāsannāloka, *m.* 2. aruṇa ; aruṇobhāsa, *m.*

Auspicate, *v.t.* ārabhati ; patiṭṭhāpeti. *p.p.* āraddha ; °pita.

Auspice, *n.* pubbanimitta ; subhanimitta, *nt. pl.* maṅgalādhipacca, *nt.*

Auspicious, *a.* subha ; maṅgala ; kalyāṇa ; bhaddaka. **°ness,** *n.* subhatta ; maṅgalatta, *nt.* — **moment,** *n.* sukhaṇa ; sumuhutta, *m.*

Austere, *a.* kaṭhina ; pharusa ; ugga ; tibba. **°ly,** *adv.* pharusākārena. **°ness,** *n.* pharusatta ; kharatta ; tibbatta, *nt.*

Austral, *a.* dakkhiṇāyatta.

Authentic, *a.* saddheyya ; pamāṇika ; yathātatha. **°ally,** *adv.* yathābhūtaŋ ; yathātathaŋ. **°ity,** *n.* tathatā ; saddheyyatā, *f.*

Authenticate, *v.t.* pamāṇīkaroti ; saccattaŋ dīpeti. *p.p.* °kata ; °dīpita.

Author, *n.* 1. ganthakāra, *m.* 2. sampādaka ; uppādaka, *m.* **°ess,** *n.* ganthasampādikā, *f.* **°ship,** *n.* sampādakatta. *n.*

Authoritative, *a.* mahesakkha ; āṇāsampanna. **°rity,** *n.* issariya ; ādhipacca ; pabhutta, *nt.* **°ly,** *adv.* mahesakkhatāya.

Authorize, *v.t.* adhikāraŋ deti ; niyojeti ; sammannati. *p.p.* dinnādhikāra ; niyojita ; sammata.

Autobiography, *n.* sayaŋlikhita-cariyā, *f.*

Autocar, *n.* sayaṅgāmī-ratha, *m.*

Autocracy, *n.* serīpālana, *nt.*

Autocrat, *n.* serīpālaka, *m.* **°ic, °ical,** *a.* serīpālanāyatta.

Autograph, *v.t.* sakahatthena likhati. *p.p.* °likhita. *n.* sakahatthalipi, *f.*

Automatic, *a.* sayaŋvattī. **°ally,** *adv.* sakabalena ; attanā va.

Automatism, *n.* sayañcalana, *nt.*

Automobile, *n.* sayaṅgāmīratha, *m.*

Autonomy, *n.* sayaŋpālana ; sakāyattapālana, *nt.* **°mous,** *a.* sakamatānuga.

Autumn, *n.* saradasamaya, *m.* **°al,** *a.* sāradika.

Auxiliary, *a. n.* sahāyabhūta ; upakāraka ; sahakārī, upakārī, *m.*

Avail, *v.t.* upakaroti ; anuggaṇhāti. *v.i.* atthāya *or* hitāya bhavati. *p.p.* upakata ; anuggahita ; °bhūta. *noun* : attha ; hita, *m.* abhivuddhi, *f.* **Of no —,** nipphala ; niratthaka, *a.* **°able,** *a.* sulabha ; laddhabba ; payojanāvaha.

Avalanche, *n.* himasikharapatana, *nt.*

Avarice, *n.* lobha, *m.* macchariya ; kadariya, *nt.*

Avaricious, *a.* luddha ; kadariya ; maccharī. **°ness,** *n.* luddhatta ; macchariya, *nt.*

Avaunt, *intj.* apehi ; apagaccha ; apakkama.

Avenge, *v.t.* veraŋ niyyāteti. *p.p.* niyyātitavera. **°ful,** *a.* verasādhanābhilāsī.

Avenue, *n.* 1. pavesapatha, *m.* 2. ubhato tarupanti ; taruräjiyatta-vīthi, *f.*

Aver, *v.t.* sanicchayaŋ vadati. *p.p.* °vutta. °**ment,** *n.* thirapakāsana, *nt.*

Average, *a.* majjhimappamāṇika, *n.* 1. vattamānasabhāva, *m.* 2. majjhimappamāṇa, *nt.* *v.t.* 1. pamāṇaŋ dasseti ; 2. majjhe pavatteti. *p.p.* dassitapamāṇa ; °tita.

Averse, *a.* paṭikūla ; parammukha ; viratta. — **to, from pain,** dukkhapaṭikūla. °**sion,** *n.* virāga ; anālaya, *m.* nibbidā ; parammukhatā ; vimukhatā, *f.*

Avert, *v.t.* vāreti ; nivāreti ; nivatteti ; vinivaṭṭeti. *p.p.* vārita ; °tita ; °ṭita.

Avian, *a.* sakuṇāyatta.

Aviary, *n.* pakkhipañjara, *m.*

Aviate, *v.i.* nabhasā gacchati. *p.p.* °gata. °**ion,** *n.* nabhogamana, *nt.* °**tor,** *n.* nabhogāmī, *m.*

Avid, *a.* giddha ; luddha ; lola. °**ity,** *n.* giddhatā ; lolatā, *f.*

Avocation, *n.* jīvikāvutti, *f.* vyāpāra, *m.*

Avoid, *v.t.* vajjeti ; parivajjeti ; cajati ; jahati ; pajahati. *p.p.* vajjita ; catta ; jahita. °**able,** *a.* vajjanīya. °**ance,** *n.* vajjana ; jahana ; pajahana ; pahāna ; cajana, *nt.* cāga, *m.*

Avouch, *v.t.i.* sutthiraŋ pakāseti. *p.p.* °sita. °**ment,** *n.* ekaŋsikavācā, *f.*

Avow, *v.t.* aṅgīkaroti ; sampaṭicchati. *p.p.* °kata ; °chita. °**al,** *n.* pakāsana, *nt.* °**edly,** *adv.* supākaṭaŋ ; sāṅgīkāraŋ.

Avulsion, *n.* 1. vidāraṇa, *nt.* 2. bhūmināsa, *m.*

Await, *v.t.* āgameti ; patimāneti ; apekkhati. *p.p.* °mānita ; °khita.

Awake, *v.t.* pabodheti ; vuṭṭhāpeti. *v.i.* pabujjhati ; jāgarati. *p.p.* °dhita ; °pita ; pabuddha. adj. jāgara ; ussuka.

Awaken, see **Awake.** °**er,** *n.* pabodhaka, *m.* °**ing,** *n.* pabodhana ; pabujjhana, *nt.* — **state,** jāgariya, *nt.*

Award, *v.t.* niyameti ; nītiyā dadāti. *p.p.* °mita ; °dinna. *n.* vinicchaya, *m.* nītiyā niyamita, *nt.*

Aware, *a.* jānanta.

Away, *adv.* ārā ; dūre. — **from,** ārakā.

Awe, *n.* gāravayutta-bhaya, *nt.* *v.t.* sagāravabhayaŋ janeti. — **inspiring,** °**some,** *a.* bhayajanaka.

Aweary, *a.* vihesappatta.

Awful, *a.* bhayānaka ; bhayaṅkara ; bherava ; bībhacca. °**ly,** *adv.* bheravākārena. °**ness,** *n.* bhayānakatta, *nt.*

Awhile, *adv.* khaṇamattaŋ ; thokakālaŋ.

Awkward, *a.* 1. asamattha ; adakkha ; 2. virūpa ; dubbaṇṇa. °**ly,** *adv.* adakkhākārena. °**ness,** *n.* 1. apaṭutā ; 2. asobhanatā, *f.*

Awl, *n.* ārā ; sūcivedhanī, *f.*

Awn, *n.* dhaññasūka, *m.*

Awning, *n.* vitāna, *nt.* uttaracchada, *m.*

Axe, *n.* pharasu, *m.* kuṭhārī, *f.* °**head,** *n.* kuṭhārītala, *nt.* °**helve,** *n.* kuṭhārīdaṇḍa, *m.*

Axiom, *n.* siddhanta, *m.* °**atic,** *a.* sayaŋsiddha.

Axis, *n.* akkha, *m.* akkharekhā, *f.*

Axle, *n.* rathakkha, *m.*

Ay, *intj.* āma ; evaŋ.

Ayah, *n.* dhātī, *f.*

Aye, *adv.* satataŋ ; niccaŋ ; sadā.

Azure, *a.* nabhovaṇṇa, *n.* nabhomaṇḍala, *nt.*

B

Babble, *v.i.* vippalapati ; jappati. *p.p.* °pita. °**ing,** *n.* vippalāpa, *m.* pajappana, *nt.* °**er,** *n.* vācāla ; palāpī, *m.*

Babe, Baby, *n.* susu ; bālaka ; potaka ; chāpa, *m.* °**hood,** *n.* bālya, *nt.*

Babel, *n.* 1. aṭṭālavisesa ; 2. kalakala ; saṅkiṇṇanāda, *m.*

Baboon, *n.* mahāvānara, *m.*

Babyish, *a.* manda ; bāla ; dārakasadisa.

Babylon, *n.* Bāveriraṭṭha, *nt.*

Bacchanalia, *n.* majjapānussava, *m.* °**an,** *n.* majjapānussavagata, *m.*

Bacchus, *n.* majjadevatā, *f.*

Bachelor, *n.* 1. kulaputta ; avivāhita ; 2. upādhilābhī, *m.*

Bacillus, *n.* rogabīja, *nt.*

Back, *n.* piṭṭhi, *f.* adj. pacchima ; pacchā. **Behind one's —,** anabhimukhe ; parokkhe. **Lying on one's —,** uttānaseyyaka, *a.* °**bone,** piṭṭhikaṇṭaka, *nt.* °**door,** pacchimadvāra, *nt.* °**ground,** pacchābhūmi, *f.* **— room,** bāhiragabbha, *m.* **— side,** piṭṭhipassa, *m.*

Back, *v.t.* 1. upatthambheti ; 2. piṭṭhim āruhati. *p.p.* °bhita ; °āruḷha. °**ing,** *n.* upatthambhana, *nt.*

Back, *adv.* pati, ni *or* parā *prefixed to verbs give this adverbial meaning,* e.g. **Comes —,** paccāgacchati. **Gives —,** paṭidadāti. **Goes —,** nivattati ; paṭinivattati. **Turns —,** parāvattati.

Backbiter, *n.* parapiṭṭhimaŋsika, *m.* °**ting,** *n.* pesuññakathā ; piṭṭhimaŋsikatā, *f.*

Backslide, *v.i.* olīyati. *p.p.* olīna.

Backward, *a.* dandha ; manda ; hāyanasīla. °**ness,** *n.* dandhatā ; asamatthatā, *f.*

Backwards, *adv.* pacchāmukhaŋ ; paṭilomaŋ.

Bacon, *n.* loṇadhūpita-sūkaramaŋsa, *nt.*

Bacteria, *n. pl.* rogajanakā ; sukhumapāṇino, *m.*

Bad, *a.* 1. duṭṭha ; pāpī ; nindita ; garahita ; asundara ; 2- asuddha ; sadosa. **— coin,** kūṭakahāpaṇa, *nt.* **— debt,** asodhiya-iṇa, *nt.* **— food,** dubbhojana, *nt.* **— friend,** pāpamitta, *m.* **— man,** dujjana ; kāpurisa, *m.* **— smell,** duggandha, *m.*

Badge, *n.* ciṇha ; lañchana, *nt.*

Badly, *adv.* 1. duṭṭhu ; asundaraŋ ; 2. ativiya.

Badness, *n.* duṭṭhatā ; asundaratā, *f.*

Baffle, *v.t.* bādheti ; khaṇḍeti ; nivāreti. *p.p.* bādhita ; khaṇḍita ; nivārita.

Bag, *n.* pasibbaka, *m.* thavikā ; puṭoli, *f.* *v.t.* thavikāya pakkhipati *or* nidahati ; puṭīkaroti. *v.i.* pūrati. *p.p.* °khitta ; °nihita ; puṭīkata ; puṇṇa. °**gy,** *a.* lambamāna.

Bagatelle, *n.* khuddakavatthu ; appakadhana, *nt.*

Baggage, *n.* pātheyya, *nt.*

Bah, *intj.* dhī.

Bail, *n.* 1. paṭibhoga, *m.* *v.t.* 1. saccakāraŋ deti ; 2. pāṭibhogī bhavati ; 3. nāvāto jalam apaneti. *p.p.* dinnasaccakāra ; °bhūta ; apanītajala. °**sman,** *n.* pāṭibhogī, *m.*

Bailiff, *n.* bhaṇḍādhikārī ; āyakammika, *m.*

Bait, *v.t.* 1. āmisena palobheti ; 2. āmisaŋ deti ; 3. pīḷeti ; hiŋsati. *p.p.* °bhita ; dinnāmisa ; pīḷita ; hiŋsita. *n.* āmisa, *nt.* nivāpa, *m.* °**ing,** *n.* 1. pātheyyāhāra, *m.* 2. āmisapalobhana, *nt.*

Baize, *n.* thūla-kambala, *nt.*

Bake, *v.t.* pacati ; randheti. *p.p.* pakka ; randhita. °**house,** pūpāgāra, *nt.* °**er,** *n.* pūpaka ; pūvakāra, *m.* °**ry,** *n.* pūvasālā, *f.*

Baking-pan, *n.* pūvathāli, *f.*

Baksheesh, *n.* pāritosika, *nt.*

Balance, *n.* 1. tulā, *f.* 2. tulārāsi, *m.* 3. samabhāratā ; apakkhapātitā, *f.* 4. avasiṭṭha-bhāga, *m.* — **of mind,** avikkhepa, *m.* **Beam of a —,** tulādaṇḍa, *m.* °**sheet,** *n.* āyavayalekhana, *nt.*

Balance, *v.t.* 1. tuleti ; dhāreti ; pamāṇeti ; 2. tulyataŋ *or* samataŋ neti. *p.p.* tulita ; dhārita ; °ṇita ; °nīta.

Balcony, *n.* upariālinda ; sīhapañjara, *m.*

Bald, *a.* 1. khallāṭa ; muṇḍa ; 2. anāvaṭa ; 3. analaṅkata. °**ly,** *adv.* vivaṭākārena. °**ness,** *n.* 1. muṇḍatta ; 2. anāvaṭatta, *nt.*

Balderdash, *n.* asaṅgatavācā, *f.*

Baldric, *n.* asibandhanī, *f.*

Bale, *n.* vipatti ; vedanā, *f.* °**ful,** *a.* pīḷākara ; tāpakara.

Bale, *n.* bhaṇḍikā, *f.* *v.t.* ussiñcati. *p.p.* ussiñcita *or* ussitta.

Ball, *n.* guḷa ; goḷaka, *nt.* ghaṭikā, *f.* (— for sporting :) kanduka ; bheṇḍuka, *m.* kīḷāgoḷaka, *nt.* (dance :) dvayaŋ-dvayanacca, *nt.* *v.t.* piṇḍeti ; vaṭṭulaŋ karoti. *v.i.* piṇḍībhavati. *p.p.* piṇḍita ; vaṭṭulīkata ; °bhūta.

Ballad, *n.* gītikā, *f.*

Ballast, *n.* pūrakabhāra, *m.* *v.t.* ūnabhāraŋ pūreti.

Ballerina, *f.* nāṭakitthī, *f.*

Ballet, *n.* naccavisesa, *m.*

Balloon, *n.* nabhogāmīgoḷa, *nt.* °**ist,** *n.* nabhogoḷagāmī, *m.*

Ballot, *n.* chandasalākā, *f.* chandapaṇṇa, *nt.* *v.i.* raho chandaŋ deti. — **box,** *n.* chandapeḷā, *f.*

Balm, *n.* 1. niyyāsa, *m.* 2. vilepana, *nt.* *v.t.* ālepeti ; vilepeti. *p.p.* °pita. °**y,** *a.* santidāyaka ; surabhigandhika.

Balsam, *n.* sugandhālepa, *m.* abbhañjana, *nt.*

Baluster, *n.* khuddakatthambha ; vedikāvayava, *m.*

Balustrade, *n.* laghu-thambhapanti ; vedikāvati, *f.*

Bamboo, *n.* veṇu ; veḷu ; vaŋsa, *m.* — **grove,** veḷuvana, *nt.* **Split** —, bidala, *nt.* **Worker in** —, vilīvakāra, *m.*

Bamboozle, *v.t.* vañceti ; palambheti. *p.p.* vañcita ; °bhita.

Ban, *n.* 1. abhisāpa ; 2. nisedha ; paṭisedha, *m.* *v.t.* 1. abhisapati ; 2. nisedheti ; paṭisedheti. *p.p.* abhisatta ; °dhita.

Banal, *a.* lāmaka.

Banana, *n.* moca ; kadalitaru, *m.* rambhā, *f.* (fruit :) kadaliphala, *nt.*

Band, *n.* (of something :) paṭṭikā, *f.* (of persons :) samūha ; gumba, *m.* seṇī, *f.* (of musicians :) vādakagaṇa, *m.* — **master,** padhānavādaka, *m.*

Band, *v.t.* 1. veṭheti ; paṭṭena bandhati ; 2. saṅgameti ; samūheti. *v.i.* saṅgacchati ; ekībhavati. *p.p.* veṭhita ; paṭṭabaddha ; °mita ; °hita ; saṅgata ; ekībhūta °**age,** *n* bandhana, *nt.* paṭṭikā, *f.* vaṇapaṭicchādaka, *m.* *v.t.* veṭheti. *p.p.* veṭhita.

Bandeau, *n.* siroveṭhana, *nt.*

Bandit, *n.* gāmaghātaka ; panthadūbhī, *m.*

Bandy-legged, *a.* vaṅkajāṇuka.

Bane, *n.* 1. visa, *nt.* 2. vināsahetu, *m.* anatthakāraṇa, *nt.* °**ful,** *a.* ahitakara ; vināsadāyaka.

Bang, *v.t.* tāḷeti ; abhihanati ; vādeti. *v.i.* unnadati. *p.p.* tāḷita ; abhihata ; vādita ; °dita. *n.* unnāda ; nigghosa, *m.* abhihanana, *nt.*

Bangle, *n.* valaya, *m.* kaṅkana, *nt.* karabhūsā, *f.* — **for arm,** keyūra, *nt.* — **for feet,** nūpura, *m.*

Banian, *n.* adhokañcuka, *m.*

Banish, *v.t.* pabbājeti ; paṇāmeti ; apanudati. *p.p.* °jita ; °mita ; °dita. °**ment,** *n.* paṇāmana ; pabbājana, *nt.*

Bank, *n.* 1. tīra ; kūla ; taṭa, *nt.* 2. dhanāgāra. — **bill,** *n.* dhanāgārapaṭiññā, *f.* — **credit,** *n.* dhanāgārikavaḍḍhi, *f.* — **note,** *n.* dhanapaṇṇa, *nt.* °**er,** *n.* dhanāgārapati, *m.* **Along the** —, anutīraŋ, *adv.* **Further** —, pāra ; pārimatīra, *nt.* **Near** —, ora ; orimatīra, *nt.*

Bank, *v.t.* 1. kūlaŋ bandhati ; taṭena āvarati. *p.p.* baddhakūla ; °āvaṭa ; 2. dhanāgāre nikkhipati. *p.p.* °nikkhitta.

Bankrupt, *a.* *n.* khīṇadhana ; hatavibhava. *v.t.* iṇasodhanāsamatthataŋ pāpeti. °**cy,** *n.* hatavibhavatā ; naṭṭhadhanatā, *f.*

Bankstock, *n.* dhanāgāre nihitadhana, *nt.*

Banner, *n.* dhaja ; ketu, *m.*

Banns, *n. pl.* vivāhe pubbanāmakittana, *nt.*

Banquet, *n.* parivesanā, *f.* paṇītabhojanadāna, *nt.* *v.t.* bhojanena saṅgaṇhāti. *p.p.* °saṅgahita. *v.i.* yāvadatthaŋ bhuñjati. °**ing hall,** āpānamaṇḍala, *nt.*

Banter, *n.* muduparihāsa, *m.* *v.t.* parihasanto katheti.

Banyan, *n.* nigrodha ; vaṭarukkha, *m.*

Baptism, *n.* jalasekasuddhi, *f.*

Baptize, *v.t.* jalasekasuddhiŋ deti ; jale osīdāpeti. *p.p.* dinnajalasekasuddhī.

Bar, *n.* 1. daṇḍākāravatthu, *nt.* 2. paligha ; dvārarodha, *m.* 3. bādhā, *f.* bādhaka, *m.* *v.t.* rundhati ; bādheti. *p.p.* ruddha ; bādhita.

Barb, *n.* sūlagga, *nt.* saratuṇḍa, *m.* *v.t.* sūlayuttaŋ karoti. °**ed**, *a.* sūlayutta.

Barbarian, *n.* milakkha ; kirāta ; asiṭṭhajana, *m.*

Barbarism, *n.* asabbhatā, *f.*

Barbarous, *a.* asabbha ; niṭṭhura. °**ly**, *adv.* niṭṭhuraŋ ; niddayaŋ.

Barbarity, *n.* niṭṭhuratta, *nt.*

Barber, *n.* nahāpita ; kappaka, *m.* °**'s outfit**, khurabhaṇḍa, *nt.* °**shop**, *n.* nahāpitasālā, *f.*

Bard, *n.* vetālika ; vandibhaṭṭa, *m.*

Bare, *a.* 1. anāvaṭa ; apaṭicchanna ; nagga ; 2. kevala ; °matta *in cpds.* — **faced**, *a.* 1. anāvaṭamukha ; 2. nillajja. °**footed**, *a.* anupāhana. °**ly**, *adv.* 1. kasiraŋ ; kicchena ; 2. vivaṭākārena. °**ness**, *n.* naggatā ; vivaṭatā, *f.*

Bare, *v.t.* vivarati ; nibbāhati. *p.p.* vivaṭa ; °hita.

Bargain, *n.* kayavikkayapaṭiññā ; paṇopaṇaviyā, *f.* *v.i.* paṇopaṇaviyaŋ *or* dabbavinimayaŋ karoti.

Barge, *n.* 1. keḷināvā, *f.* 2. bhaṇḍavāhinī, *f.*

Bark, *n.* 1. taca, *m.* 2. potavisesa, *m.* 3. (of a dog :) bhussana ; bhuṅkaraṇa, *nt.* **Outer** —, papaṭikā, *f.* — **garment**, vākacīra ; vakkala ; tirīṭaka, *nt.*

Bark, *v.t.* tacaŋ apaneti. *p.p.* apanīta-taca. *v.i.* bhussati ; bhuṅkaroti. *p.p.* bhussita ; bhuṅkata.

Barley, *n.* yava, *m.*

Barm, *n.* majjapheṇa, *nt.* °**y**, *a.* pheṇākiṇṇa.

Barn, *n.* kusūla ; dhaññakoṭṭhaka, *m.*

Barology, *n.* bhāravijjā, *f.*

Barometer, *n.* vāyutulā, *f.* vāyumāṇaka, *nt.*

Baron, *n.* abhijāta ; kulīna, *m.* °**ess**, *n.* abhijātā ; kulīnā, *f.*

Baronet, *v.t.* seṭṭhipadaŋ pāpeti. *p.p.* pāpitaseṭṭhipada ; khuddakaseṭṭhī, *m.*

Barrack, *n.* bhaṭanivāsa, *m.* senāgāra, *nt.*

Barrage, *n.* setubandha, *m.* āli, *f.*

Barred, *a.* 1. rundhita ; 2. palighaṅkita.

Barrel, *n.* dīgha-vaṭṭula-bhājana, *nt.* — **of a gun**, nāḷī, *f.*

Barren, *a.* 1. vañjha ; viphala ; nipphala ; 2. ujjaṅgala. °**ness**, *n.* vañjhatta, *nt.* — **woman**, vañjhā, *f.*

Barricade, *v.t.* āvarati ; rundhati. *p.p.* āvaṭa ; ruddha *or* rundhita. *n.* avarodha, *m.* āvaraṇa, *nt.*

Barrier, *n.* sambādhaka, *m.* *v.t.* sambādheti; āvarati. *p.p.* °dhita; āvarita *or* āvaṭa.

Barring, *prep.* vinā; hitvā; ṭhapetvā.

Barrister, *n.* adhinītivedī, *m.*

Barrow, *n.* 1. sakaṭikā, *f.* 2. unnatabhūmi, *f.*

Barter, *v.t.* vinimeti; nimināti; bhaṇḍāni parivatteti. *p.p.* °mita; °nita, *n.* bhaṇḍavinimaya, *m.*

Base, *n.* patiṭṭhāna, *nt.* pada; ādhāra, mūlabhāga, *m.* adj. adhama; nīca; nihīna. — **born,** *a.* avajāta. °**less,** *a.* amūlaka; nirādhāra; patiṭṭhārahita. °**ly,** *adv.* nīcākārena. °**ment,** *n.* heṭṭhātala, *nt.* °**ness,** *n.* adhamatā; nikiṭṭhatā, *f.*

Base, *v.t.* patiṭṭhāpeti. *p.p.* °pita.

Bash, *v.t.* daḷhaŋ paharati. *p.p.* °pahaṭa.

Bashful, *a.* hirimana; salajja. °**ly,** *adv.* lajjitākārena. °**ness,** *n.* lajjā; hiri; vinītatā, *f.*

Basil (plant), tulasī; sulasā, *f.*

Basin, *n.* 1. thālī, *f.* 2. jalāsaya, *m.* 3. (of a river :) gaṅgādhāra, *m.*

Basis, *n.* pādaka; ādhāra; nissaya, *m.* patiṭṭhā, *f.*

Bask, *v.i.* ātapaŋ nisevati. *p.p.* nisevitātapa.

Basket, *n.* piṭaka, *m.* *v.t.* piṭake pakkhipati. *p.p.* °pakkhitta. °**maker,** *n.* naḷakāra, *m.* **Hand —,** pacchi, *f.*

Bas-relief, *n.* silāpattharullekhana, *nt.*

Bassia (tree), madhuka, *m.*

Bastard, *n.* avajāta; jāraja, *m.* °**ize,** *v.t.* avajātataŋ pakāseti. *p.p.* °sitāvajātatta. °**y,** *n.* avajātatta, *nt.*

Baste, *v.t.* 1. potheti; tāḷeti; 2. vasāya makkheti. *p.p.* pothita; tāḷita; °khita.

Bastion, *n.* uddāpa, *m.* upakārikā, *f.*

Bat, *n.* 1. jatukā; ajinapattā, *f.* (Small —) vagguli, *f.* 2. kandukapaharaṇa, *nt.* *v.i.* kandukaŋ paharati. °**sman,** *n.* kandukapahāraka, *m.*

Batch, *n.* rāsi; samūha, *m.*

Bate, *v.t.* hāpeti; upasameti; ūnaŋ karoti. *p.p.* hāpita; °mita; ūnīkata.

Bath, *n.* nahāna; sināna, *nt.* — **attendant,** nahāpaka, *m.* — **chair,** cakkayuttapīṭha, *nt.* — **powder,** nahānacuṇṇa, *nt.* °**room,** nahānakoṭṭhaka, *m.*

Bathe, *v.t.* nahāpeti, *v.i.* nahāyati. *p.p.* °pita; nahāta. °**ing,** *n.* nahāna, *nt.* °**ing cloth,** jalasāṭikā, *f.*

Bathos, *n.* adhopatana, *nt.*

Bating, *prep.* vinā; ṭhapetvā; muñcitvā.

Baton, *n.* gadā, *f.* muggara, *m.*

Batta, *n.* gamanaparibbaya, *m.*

Battalion, *n.* senādala, *nt.*

Batten, *v.i.* adhikaŋ bhuñjati. *v.t.* paṭṭikāhi daḷhīkaroti. *p.p.* °bhutta; °kata.

Batter, *v.t.* viddhaŋseti; khaṇḍākhaṇḍaŋ karoti. *p.p.* °sita; °kata.

Battery, *n.* 1. viddhaŋsana, *nt.* 2. nāḷīyantaṭṭhāna ; 3. vijjuppādakopakaraṇa, *nt.*

Battle, *n.* yuddha ; raṇa, *nt.* saṅgāma ; āhava, *m.* āyodhana ; samara, *nt.* *v.i.* yujjhati. — **array**, *n.* senāvyūha, *m.* °**axe**, yuddhakuṭhārī, *f.* °**field**, yuddhabhūmi, *f.* °**ment**, sacchiddapākāra, *m.*

Bauble, *n.* vibhūsanapatirūpaka, *m.* kiñcikkha, *nt.*

Bawd, *n.* gaṇikāpālaka, *m.* °**y**, *a.* asabbha ; kāmuka.

Bawl, *v.i.* ugghoseti ; aṭṭassaraŋ karoti, *p.p.* °sita ; kataṭṭassara. °**er**, *n.* ugghosaka, *m.* °**ing**, *n.* kandana, *nt.*

Bay, *n.* 1. mahātittha, *nt.* 2. ubhato sambādhaṭṭhāna, *nt.* *v.t.* bhussitvā anubandhati. *p.p.* °anubaddha.

Bayonet, *n.* mahāchūrikā, *f.* nettiŋsa, *m.*

Bay-salt, *n.* sāmuddikalavaṇa, *nt.*

Bazaar, *n.* āpaṇa, *m.* paṇyasālā, *f.*

Be, *v.i.* bhavati ; hoti ; atthi. *p.p.* bhūta.

Beach, *n.* velā, *f.* samuddatīra, *nt.* *v.t.* tīraŋ pāpeti. *p.p.* tīrapāpita.

Beacon, *n.* maggadesakapadīpa, *m.*

Bead, *n.* guḷikā, *f.* akkha, *m.* **String of — s**, akkhamālā ; japamālā, *f.* *v.t.* guḷikā āvuṇāti ; akkhe sampādeti. *p.p.* āvutaguḷika ; sampāditakkha.

Beadle, *n.* daṇḍadharadūta, *m.*

Beak, *n.* mukhatuṇḍa ; tuṇḍaka, *nt.*

Beaker, *n.* pānabhājana, *nt.*

Beam, *n.* tulādhāra, *m.* — **of a balance**, tulādaṇḍa, *m.* — **of a carriage**, dhura, *nt.* — **of ray**, kara ; kiraṇa ; mayūkha, *m.* °**less**, *a.* nippabha. °**y**, *a.* ujjala ; pabhassarra.

Bean, *n.* māsa, *nt.*

Bear, *n.* accha ; issa ; bhallūka, *m.* °**ish**, *a* avinīta.

Bear, *v.t.* 1. vahati ; dhāreti ; 2. janeti ; 3. bharati ; pariharati. *v.i.* sahati. *p.p.* vahita ; dhārita ; janita ; bhata ; parihaṭa ; sahita. °**able**, *a.* sayha. — **down**, nipāteti. — **enmity**, upanandhati. — **fruit**, phalati. — **in mind**, manasikaroti ; dhāreti. — **with**, upekkhati.

Beard, *n.* massu, *nt.* — **dressing**, massukamma, *nt.* °**less**, *a.* nimmassuka.

Bearer, *n.* vāhī ; dhārī ; dhāraka ; gāhī, *m.*

Bearing, *n.* 1. ācaraṇa, *nt.* saṇṭhiti, *f.* 2. dhāraṇa ; ubbahana, *nt.* adj. sandhāraka ; sahamāna.

Beast, *n.* pasu ; tiracchāna, *m.* °**liness**, *n.* pasutulyatta, *nt.* °**ly**, *a.* pasutulya. — **of burden**, dhorayha ; vāhakapasu, *m.* — **of prey**, vāḷa ; vāḷamiga, *m.*

Beat, *v.t.* 1. paharati ; potheti ; tāḷeti ; āhanati ; ākoṭeti ; 2. (to defeat :) parājeti ; abhibhavati. *p.p.* pahaṭa ; pothita ;

tāḷita; āhata; ākoṭita; parājita; abhibhūta. *v.i.* phandati; kampati; calati. *p.p.* °dita; °pita; calita. — **down,** nihanati; nipāteti. — **off,** palāpeti. — **out,** ākoṭetvā sampādeti. — **up,** sahasā paharati.

Beaten, *a.* pahaṭa; parājita; maddita; abhibhūta.

Beatific, *a.* paramasukhada. **°ation,** *n.* paramasukhatā; devattapatti, *f.*

Beatify, *v.t.* sukhaŋ pāpeti; devattapattiŋ pakāseti.

Beating, *n.* paharaṇa; pothana; tāḷana, *nt.* — **of a drum, etc.,** vādana; āhanana, *nt.*

Beatitude, *n.* paramasukha, *nt.*

Beauteous, Beautiful, *a.* sobhana; rucira; cāru; dassanīya; pāsādika; surūpa; ramma; manuñña.

Beautify, *v.t.* sobheti; maṇḍeti; bhūseti; alaṅkaroti. *p.p.* sobhita; °ḍita; bhūsita; °kata.

Beauty, *n.* sobhā; surūpatā; pokkharatā, *f.* sobhagga, *nt.* **Personal —,** rūpasiri; vaṇṇapokkharatā, *f.* — **spot,** tilaka, *m.*

Beaver, *n.* jalamuṅgusa, *m.*

Becalm, *v.t.* upasameti; nibbāpeti. *p.p.* °mita; °pita.

Because, *adv. conj.* yasmā . . . tasmā; yato . . . tato. Often expressed by the suffix *-ttā*; the word annexed to it is preceeded by Genitive, e.g. *Tassa gatattā,* because he has gone. — **of this,** iminā kāraṇena.

Beck, *n.* kāyaviññatti; hatthādisaññā, *f.* **°on,** *v.t.i.* kāyena viññāpeti. *p.p.* °pita.

Becloud, *v.t.* tirokaroti; paṭicchādeti. *p.p.* °kata; °dita.

Become, *v.i.* 1. hoti; bhavati; sampajjati; 2. jāyati; uppajjati. *p.p.* bhūta; sampanna; jāta; uppanna. *v.t.* vaṭṭati; kappati. **°able,** sakkoti; pahoti; visahati. — **absent,** vippavasati. — **adequate,** sambhunāti. — **afflicted,** aṭṭīyati. — **agitated,** saṅkhubhati; (mentally:) khijjati. — **alarmed,** uttasati. — **allayed,** passambhati. — **angry,** kujjhati; kuppati. — **annoyed,** vihaññati. — **appeased,** upasammati. — **attached,** sajjati; piyāyati. — **aware,** abhijānāti. — **bashful,** lajjati; hirīyati. — **bewildered,** sammuyhati; pamuyhati. — **bound,** bajjhati. — **bright,** vippasīdati. — **clean,** parisujjhati. — **clear,** pasīdati, sujjhati. — **concentrated,** samādhiyati. — **contented,** santussati. — **corrupted,** padussati. — **dejected,** visīdati. — **disgusted with,** jigucchati. — **dirty,** kilissati, — **disheartened,** nibbijjati. *p.p.* nibbinna. — **dissatisfied,** ukkaṇṭhati. — **dissolved,** vilīyati. *p.p.* vilīna. — **doubtful,** kaṅkhati; vicikicchati. — **dried,** sukkhati; sussati. *p.p.* sukkha. — **dull,** muyhati. — **exhausted,** kilamati. — **excited,** paritassati. — **extinguished,**

vijjhāyati ; nibbāti ; nirujjhati. — fatigued, vihaññati ; kilamati. — fond of, piyāyati. — free, pamuccati. *p.p.* pamutta. — full, paripūrati. *p.p.* paripuṇṇa — heated, santappati. *p.p.* santatta.—indefferent, upekkhati. — impure, kilissati. — infatuated, sammucchati. — late, cirāyati. — neutral, samupekkhati. — pleased, santussati. — quiet, sannisīdati. *p.p.* sannisinna. — released, vimuccati. — remorseful, anutappati. — selfish, maccharāyati. — sluggish, olīyati. *p.p.* olīna. — soiled, malinībhavati. — steadfast, pabbatāyati. — vexed, vyāpajjati. *p.p.* vyāpanna. — weary, āgilāyati.

Becoming, *a.* ucita ; anurūpa. *n.* pātubhāva, *m.* bhavana, *nt.* °**ly,** *adv.* yathocitaŋ ; yathārahaŋ.

Bed, *n.* 1. seyyā, *f.* sayana, *nt.* 2. ādhāra, *m.* patiṭṭhā, *f.* 3. bhūmitala ; tala, *nt.* °**ding,** *n.* sayanopakaraṇa, *nt.* °**room,** *n.* sayanighara, *nt.* °**sheet,** *n.* santhara, *m.* attharaṇa, *nt.* °**stead,** *n.* mañca, *m.* **Frame of a —,** aṭani, *f.*

Bedaub, *v.t.* (paṅkādīhi) ālimpeti. *p.p.* °pita *or* ālitta.

Bedeck, *v.t.* alaṅkaroti ; maṇḍeti ; bhūseti. *p.p.* °kata ; maṇḍita ; bhūsita.

Bedevil, *v.t.* niṭṭhuraŋ pīḷeti *or* hiŋsati. *p.p.* °pīḷita ; hiŋsita. °**ment,** *n.* bhūtagāha, *m.* amanussapīḷā, *f.*

Bedew, *v.t.* tusārena chādeti. *p.p.* tusāracchanna.

Bedim, *v.t.* timirayati ; malinīkaroti. *p.p.* °yita ; °kata.

Bedlam, *n.* ummattakāgāra, *nt.* °**ite,** *n.* ummattaka, *m.*

Bedrabbled, *a.* udakacikkhallamalina.

Bee, *n.* madhukara ; madhupa ; ali ; chappada, *m.* °**bread,** *n.* reṇu ; parāga, *m.* °**hive,** *n.* madhupaṭala, *nt.*

Beef, *n.* gomaŋsa, *nt.*

Beer, *n.* yavasurā, *f.*

Beeswax, *n.* madhusitthaka, *nt.*

Beetle, *n.* 1. sapattapāṇaka, *m.* 2. kaṭṭhahattha, *m.* *v.t.* kaṭṭhahatthena paharati. *p.p.* °pahaṭa.

Befall, *v.i.* āpatati ; anupatati ; sijjhati. *p.p.* °tita ; siddha.

Befit, *v.i.* yujjati ; kappati ; vaṭṭati. °**ting,** *a.* yutta ; anucchavika ; anurūpa.

Befog, *v.t.* tirokaroti. *p.p.* °kata.

Befool, *v.t.* moheti ; vilambeti. *p.p.* mohita ; °bita.

Before, *adv.* purato ; abhimukhe, *prep.* purā ; pure, *conj.* yāva . . . tāva, e.g. **Finish your work before he comes,** yāva so n'āgacchati tāva tava kammaŋ niṭṭhāpehi. **As —,** yathā pure. °**hand,** *adv.* pageva ; puretaraŋ ; paṭigacc'eva. — **long,** aciraŋ, *adv.* — **mentioned,** yathāvutta ; pure vutta, *a.*

Befoul, *v.t.* dūseti ; malinīkaroti. *p.p.* dūsita ; °kata.

Befriend, *v.t.* anuggaṇhāti ; upatthambheti. *v.i.* mettāyati. *p.p.* °gahita ; °bhita ; °yita.

Beg, *v.t.* yācati ; āyācati. *v.i.* bhikkhati. *p.p.* yācita. **°ging,** *n.* yācana ; bhikkhana, *nt.*

Beget, *v.t.* janeti ; uppādeti. *p.p.* janita ; °dita. **°ter,** *n.* janaka ; uppādaka, *m.*

Beggar, *n.* kapaṇa ; yācaka ; bhikkhaka, *m.* *v.t.* niddhanaŋ *or* nippabhaŋ karoti. *p.p.* niddhanīkata. **°ly,** *a.* akiñcana ; duggata ; hīnapuñña. **°y,** *n.* atidaḷiddatā, *f.*

Begin, *v.t.* ārabhati ; paṭṭhapeti. *v.i.* pabhavati. *p.p.* āraddha ; °pita ; pabhavita. **°ner,** *n.* ādikammika ; navaka ; ārambhaka, *m.* **°ning,** *n.* 1. ārambha ; 2. ādi ; pabhava, *m.* **°ning from,** pabhuti ; paṭṭhāya (*with abl.*) *ind.*

Begird, *v.t.* parikkhipati ; paḷiveṭheti. *p.p.* °khitta ; °ṭhita.

Begone, *intj.* apehi ; apayāhi ; apakkama.

Begrime, *v.t.* atimalinayati. *p.p.* °yita.

Begrudge, *v.t.* usūyati ; issaŋ bandhati ; na sahati. *p.p.* °yita ; issābaddha ; asahita.

Beguile, *v.t.* 1. moheti ; vañceti ; 2. palobheti ; 3. (time :) khepeti ; atikkāmeti. *p.p.* mohita ; vañcita ; °bhita ; khepita ; °mita. **°ment,** *n.* 1. vañcana ; palobhana, *nt.* 2. kālakkhepa, *m.*

Behalf, *n.* attha ; hita, *m.* **On behalf of,** atthāya ; hetu ; kāraṇā (*with gen.*).

Behave, *v.i.* ācarati ; samācarati ; irīyati ; paṭipajjati. *p.p.* paṭipanna.

Behaviour, *n.* ācāra, *m.* ācaraṇa, vattana, *nt.* cariyā ; paṭipatti, *f.* **Good —,** sadācāra, *m.* **Wrong —,** micchācāra, *m.* duppaṭipatti, *f.*

Behead, *v.t.* sīsaŋ chindati. *p.p.* chinnasīsa. **°ing,** *n.* sīsaccheda, *m.*

Behest, *n.* āṇā, *f.* niyoga, *m.*

Behind, *adv. prep.* pacchato ; piṭṭhito ; anvad eva ; piṭṭhipasse. **°hand,** *a.* olīnavuttika ; hānabhāgiya.

Behold, *v.t.* passati ; oloketi ; udikkhati. *p.p.* diṭṭha ; olokita ; °khita. **°er,** *n.* dassāvī ; passitu ; oloketu, *m.* **°ing,** *n.* udikkhana ; olokana, *nt.*

Beholden, *a.* laddhūpakāra.

Behove, *v.i.* (?) vaṭṭati ; yujjati ; arahati, *with infinitive.*

Being, *n.* satta ; pāṇī ; dehī ; jīvī ; jantu, *m.* *pr. p. of* **be :** santa. **— late,** cirāyitvā, *abs.* **— thus,** itthambhūta, *a.*

Belabour, *v.t.* potheti. *v.i.* vāyamati. *p.p.* pothita ; °mita.

Belate, *v.i.* cirāyati. **°ed,** cirāyita ; pamatta.

Belay, *v.t.* daḷhaŋ veṭheti. *p.p.* °veṭhita.

Belch, *v.i.* uggirati ; udrekayati. *v.t.* asabbhaŋ bhaṇati. *n.* uggāra ; unnāda, *m.*

Beldame, *n.* mahallikā, *f.*

Beleaguer, *v.t.* orundhati ; uparundhati. *p.p.* oruddha ; uparuddha.

Belfry, *n.* ghaṇṭātthambha, *m.*

Belie, *v.t.* visaŋvādeti ; musābhaṇati. *p.p.* °dita.

Belief, *n.* 1. bhatti ; diṭṭhi ; laddhi, *f.* 2. vissāsa, *m.* saddahana, *nt.* **Right —**, sammādiṭṭhi, *f.* **Wrong —**, dulladdhi ; micchādiṭṭhi, *f.*

Believe, *v.t.* saddahati ; vissasati. *p.p.* saddahita ; vissaṭṭha. °**er**, saddahāna ; saddahitu, *m.* °**ing**, *a.* bhattimantu ; pasanna ; saddahanta. °**ing in**, diṭṭhika ; laddhika, *in cpds.*

Belike, *adv.* siyā.

Belittle, *v.t.* 1. avamāneti ; omaññati ; 2. lahukaŋ karoti. *p.p.* °mānita ; omata ; lahukakata.

Bell, *n.* ghaṇṭā ; gaṇḍikā, *f.* *v.t.* ghaṇṭaŋ olambeti. **Small —**, kiṅkiṇī, *f.*

Belladonna, *n.* nididdhikā, *f.*

Belle, *n.* rūpasundarī ; janapadakalyāṇī, *f.*

Bellicose, *a.* raṇakāmī ; kalahakāmī, *m.* °**ity**, *n.* kalahappiyatā, *f.*

Belligerent, *a.* yujjhamāna. *n.* yodha ; yuddhabhaṭa, *m.*

Bellow, *v.i.* dhamati ; nadati ; aṭṭassaraŋ karoti. *p.p.* dhamita, nadita ; kataṭṭasara. *n.* gajjanā, *f.* nāda, *m.* dhamana, *nt.*

Bellows, *n.* bhastā ; gaggarī, *f.*

Bellshaped, *a.* ghaṇṭākāra.

Belly, *n.* udara, *nt.* gabbha, *m.* kucchi, *m.* *f.* °**ache**, *n.* udarasūla, *nt.* kucchirujā, *f.* °**ful**, *adv.* udarāvadehakaŋ ; kucchipūraŋ. °**god**, *n.* udarambharī, *m.* **— of a lute**, vīṇāpokkhara, *m.*

Belock, *v.t.* kuñcikāya pidahati. *p.p.* °pidahita.

Belong, *v.i.* āyattībhavati. °**ed**, *a.* āyatta. °**ing to**, adhīna ; āyatta, *with gen.* °**ing to many**, bāhujañña, *a.* °**ing to others**, parādhīna, *a.*

Belongings, *n. pl.* pariggaha, *m.* sandhana, *nt.*

Beloved, *a.* piya ; kanta ; manāpa.

Below, *adv. prep.* adho ; heṭṭhā.

Belt, *n.* mekhalā ; rasanā, *f.* kāyabandhana, *nt.* *v.t.* bandhati ; veṭheti. *p.p.* baddha ; veṭhita.

Belvedere, *n.* uparivedikā, *f.*

Bemire, *v.t.* kaddamena limpeti. *p.p.* kaddamalimpita.

Bemoan, *v.t.* socati ; paridevati. *p.p.* socita ; °vita.

Bemuse, *v.t.* vimoheti. *p.p.* °hita.

Bench, *n.* 1. dīghāsana ; 2. vinicchayāsana, *nt.* *v.t.* vinicchayāsanaŋ pāpeti.

Bend, *v.t.* nāmeti ; ābhujati ; sammiñjeti. *v.i.* namati. *p.p.* nāmita ; ābhujita ; °jita ; nata *or* namita. **— down**, *v.t.* ninnāmeti. *v.i.* onamati. **— upwards**, *v.t.* unnāmeti. *v.i.* unnamati. °**ing**, *n.* nati ; onati, *f.* namana, *nt.*

Bend, *n.* nataṭṭhāna ; kuṭilatta, *nt.* vaṅkatā, *f.*

Beneath, *adv. prep.* heṭṭhā ; adho.

Benedick, *n.* adhunā vivāhita, *m.*

Benediction, *n.* 1. subhāsaŋsā, vuddhipatthanā, *f.* 2. thuti ; pasaŋsā, *f.* °**tory**, *a.* subhāvaha ; subhāsaŋsaka.

Benefaction, *n.* upakāra ; upatthambha ; hita, *m.* °**tor**, *n.* hitesī ; upakārī ; atthañcara, *m.* °**tress**, *n.* hitesinī ; upakārinī, *f.*

Beneficence, *n.* hitesitā, *f.* paropakāra, *m.* °**ent**, *a.* cāgasīlī ; paratthacārī. °**ently**, *adv.* sānukampaŋ ; cāgasīlitāya.

Beneficial, *a.* atthāvaha ; hitāvaha ; sappāya ; sappayojana. °**ly**, *adv.* sātthakaŋ ; sappayojanaŋ.

Benefit, *n.* 1. upakāra ; anuggaha ; attha ; hita, *m.* 2. phala ; payojana, *nt.* *v.t.* upakaroti ; anuggaṇhāti. *p.p.* upakaṭa ; anuggahita.

Benevolence, *n.* anuddayā ; anukampā ; mettā ; metti, *f.* °**lent**, *a.* dayālū ; anukampaka ; mettacitta.

Bengal, *n.* Vaṅgadesa, *m.* — **madder**, *n.* mañjiṭṭhā, *f.*

Benighted, *a.* 1. tamonaddha ; 2. mandapañña.

Benign, Benignant, *a.* sadaya ; sānukampī ; karuṇāpara. °**ly**, *adv.* sadayaŋ. °**ity**, *n.* dayā ; anukampā, *f.* kāruñña, *nt.*

Benison, *n.* dhaññavāda, *m.*

Benjamin, *n.* tacagandhavisesa, *m.*

Bent, *n.* 1. nati ; 2. poṇatā, *f.* — **of mind**, adhimutti, *f.* abhinivesa, *m.* — **on**, ninna ; paṇihita ; adhimutta. *a.* — **thereon**, tappoṇa; tappabbhāra, *a.* — **over**, avakujja, *a.*

Benumb, *v.t.* thambhīkaroti. *p.p.* °kata.

Bequeath, *v.t.* accayena deti. *p.p.* °dinna.

Bequest, *n.* accaye-dāna, *nt.*

Bereave, *v.t.* viyojeti ; vinākaroti. *p.p.* viyojita ; vinākata. °**ment**, *n.* viyoga ; viraha, *m.*

Bereft, *a.* virahita ; viyutta ; parihīna.

Berry, *n.* khuddakaphala, *nt.*

Berth, *n.* 1. sayanāgāra, *nt.* 2. nāvānivattiṭṭhāna, *nt.* *v.t.* yuttaṭṭhāne nāvaŋ nivatteti.

Beryl, *n.* veḷuriya, *nt.*

Beseech, *v.t.* upanibandhati ; abhiyācati. *p.p.* upanibaddha ; °cita. °**ing**, *a.* abhiyācaka.

Beseem, *v.i.* arahati ; vaṭṭati ; yujjati. °**ing**, *a.* ucita ; anurūpa. °**ingly**, *adv.* ucitākārena.

Beset, *v.t.* 1. sambādheti ; upapīḷeti ; 2. khacati ; antarantare nikkhipati. *p.p.* °dhita ; °ḷita ; khacita ; °nikkhitta. — **with**, avakkanta ; abhibhūta ; otiṇṇa. °**ment**, *n.* orundhana, *nt.*

Beside, *prep.* passe ; antike ; samīpe.

Besides, *adv.* atha ca ; api ca ; athāparaŋ.

Besiege, *v.t.* rundhati ; rodheti. *p.p.* ruddha ; rodhita. *n.* avarodha, *m.* uparundhana, *nt.* °**er,** *n.* avarodhaka, *m.*

Besmear, *v.t.* makkheti ; vilepeti ; anulimpeti. *p.p.* °khita ; °pita.

Besmirch, *v.t.* malinīkaroti. *p.p.* °kata.

Besom, *n.* sammajjanī ; sammuñjanī, *f.* *v.t.* sammajjati. *p.p.* sammaṭṭha.

Besot, *v.t.* moheti ; pamoheti. *p.p.* mohita. °**ted,** *a.* madamatta ; vimohita.

Bespangle, *v.t.* bhāsuravatthūhi vibhūseti. *p.p.* °sita.

Bespatter, *v.t.* 1. osiñcati ; nisiñcati ; 2. pharusena *or* lālappena kileseti. *p.p.* ositta ; °sita.

Bespeak, *v.t.* sūceti ; pākaṭīkaroti. *p.p.* sūcita ; °kata.

Besprinkle, Bespeckle, *v.t.* siñcati ; āsiñcati. *p.p.* sitta ; āsitta.

Best, *a.* vara ; pavara ; seṭṭha ; uttama ; parama. *adv.* yathāsattiŋ ; yathābalaŋ.

Bestial, *a.* pasutulya ; gamma. °**ity,** *n.* pasutulyatā, *f.* °**ize,** *v.t.* pasutulyaŋ karoti. °**ly,** *adv.* gammākārena.

Bestiary, *n.* pasuvijjā, *f.*

Bestir, *v.t.* and *refl.* ussukkāpeti ; paggaṇhāti ; padahati. *p.p.* °pita ; paggahita ; °hita.

Bestow, *v.t.* deti ; dadāti ; pariccajati ; vissajjeti. *p.p.* dinna ; pariccatta ; vissajjita. °**er,** dāyaka ; dātu, cāgī, *m.* °**al,** *n.* dāna ; vitaraṇa, *nt.* cāga ; pariccāga, *m.*

Bestrew, *v.t.* ākirati ; vikirati. *p.p.* ākiṇṇa ; vikiṇṇa.

Bestride, *v.t.* piṭṭhim āruhati ; pādantare katvā tiṭṭhati. *p.p.* °ārūḷha ; °ṭhita.

Bestud, *v.t.* khacayati. *p.p.* khacita.

Bet, *v.t.* paṇeti ; abbhutaŋ karoti. *p.p.* paṇayita ; katabbhuta. *n.* paṇa ; abbhuta, *m.*

Betake, *v.i.* niyuñjati ; pāpuṇāti. *p.p.* niyutta ; patta.

Betel (creeper), *n.* nāgalatā ; tāmbūlī, *f.* — **leaf,** *n.* tambūla, *nt.* — **server,** *n.* tambūlapeḷā, *f.* °**nut,** *n.* pūgaphala, *nt.*

Bethink, *v.i.* jhāyati ; cinteti ; upaṭṭhāti ; sarati. *p.p.* jhāyita ; cintita ; upaṭṭhita ; sarita.

Betide, *v.i.* see **Befall.**

Betimes, *adv.* 1. yathākāle ; ucitavelāyaŋ ; 2. pageva.

Betoken, see **Bespeak.**

Betray, *v.t.* 1. sattu hatthe appeti ; 2. rahassam āvīkaroti ; 3. dubbhati. *p.p.* °appita ; āvīkatarahassa ; dubbhita. °**al,** *n.* dubbhana ; amittahattapāpana, *nt.* °**er,** *n.* mittaddu ; vissāsaghātī, *m.*

Betroth, *v.t.* vāreyyaŋ karoti. *p.p.* katavāreyya. °**al,** *n.* vāreyya, *nt.* vivāhapaṭiññā, *f.*

Better, *a.* varatara ; sundaratara, *adv.* suṭṭhu ; sādhukaŋ ; suṭṭhutaraŋ. *noun* : seyyo ; varaŋ. *v.t.* sundarattaŋ pāpeti ; abhivaḍḍheti. *p.p.* °pāpita ; °vaḍḍhita. °**ment,** *n.* 1. unnati, *f.* 2. saŋsodhana, *nt.*

Better, Bettor, *n.* kandukatāḷaka, *m.*

Between, *adv. prep.* antarā; antare; majjhe; antarena.

Beverage, *n.* pāna; pānaka; peyya, *nt.*

Bevy, *n.* gaṇa, pūga, nikara, *m.*

Bewail, *v.i.* vilapati; socati; anusocati.

Beware, *v.i.* sāvadhāno *or* appamatto bhavati. *p.p.* sāvadhānabhūta.

Bewilder, *v.t.* moheti; pamoheti; muccheti; sambhameti. *p.p.* mohita; mucchita; °mita. °**ment,** *n.* sammoha; sammosa; sativippavāsa, *m.* °**ed,** *a.* mūḷha; sammūḷha; vimohita.

Bewitch, *v.t.* vasīkaroti; sammoheti. *p.p.* °kata; °hita. °**ment,** *n.* vasīkaraṇa; mohana, *nt.* °**ing,** *a.* vasavattaka; mohanaka.

Beyond, *adv. prep.* dūre; pāre; pāraŋ; atikkamma; aticca; ati *in cpds.*, e.g. atimattaŋ = *beyond measure.*

Bezoar, *n.* gorocanā, *f.*

Biangular, *a.* dvikoṇaka.

Biannual, *a.* dvivassika.

Bias, *n.* pakkhapātitā; poṇatā, *f.* *v.t.* agatiŋ gacchati; pakkhapātī hoti. *p.p.* agatigata.

Biaxial, *a.* dviakkhaka.

Bibber, *n.* majjapāyī, *m.*

Bible, *n.* Kiṭṭhava-dhammapotthaka, *m.*

Bibliography, *n.* ganthavaŋsa, *m.* ganthasūci, *f.*

Bibliolatry, *n.* ganthapūjā, *f.*

Bibliophile, *n.* ganthappiya, *m.*

Bibulous, *a.* 1. surāsoṇḍa; 2. pariyādiyaka.

Bicentenary, *n.* dvisatavassikussava, *m.* adj. dvisatavassika.

Bicephalous, *a.* dvisīsaka.

Bicker, *v.t.* kalahaŋ karoti; bhaṇḍeti. *p.p.* katakalaha; bhaṇḍita. °**ing,** *n.* kalaha, *m.* bhaṇḍana, *nt.*

Bicycle, *n.* cakkayuga, *nt.*

Bid, *v.t.* 1. ādisati; āṇāpeti; 2. pakkosati; nimanteti; 3. aggharŋ niyameti. *p.p.* ādiṭṭha; āṇāpita; °sita; °tita; niyamitaggha. °**dable,** *a.* vidheyya. °**der,** *n.* agghaniyāmaka, *m.* °**ding,** *n.* 1. āṇāpana; 2. agghaniyamana, *nt.*

Bide, *v.i.* āgameti. *v.t.* sahati; dhāreti. *p.p.* sahita; dhārita.

Bidental, *a.* dvirada; dvidanta.

Biennial, *a.* dvivassika. *n.* dvivassajīvī, *m.*

Bier, *n.* vilāta, *nt.* chavādhāra, *m.*

Bifold, *a.* diguṇa; duvidha.

Biformed, *a.* yugalakāya; dvivesa.

Bifurcate, *v.t.* aggaŋ dvidhā bhindati. adj. viṭapībhūta; dvisikhara.

Big, *a.* mahanta; visāla; uru. °**ness,** *n.* mahatta; visālatta; vipulatta, *nt.*

Bigamist, *n.* 1. dvibhariya, *m.* 2. dvipatikā, *f.*

Bigamy, *n.* 1. dvipatitā; 2. dvibhariyatā, *f.*

Bigot, *n.* kumbhīlagāhī; duppaṭinissaggī, *m.* °**ed,** kumbhīlagāhayutta, *a.* °**ry,** *n.* ādhānagāhitā; duppaṭinissaggitā, *f.*

Bilateral, *a.* dvipassika.
Bile, *n.* pitta, *nt.*
Bilingual, *a.* dvibhāsika. °**guist**, *n.* dvibhāsāvādī, *m.*
Bilious, *a.* pittādhika.
Bilk, *v.t.* vañceti. *p.p.* vañcita.
Bill, *n.* 1. (beak :) cañcuka ; mukhatuṇḍa, *nt.* 2. (note :) nivedanapaṇṇa, *nt.* 3. (account :) saṅkhyādīpaka, *nt.* 4. (of law :) nītipaṇṇa, *nt.* *v.i.* cumbati ; āliṅgati, *v.t.* nivedeti. *p.p.* °bita ; °gita ; °dita.
Billet, *v.t.* senāsanaŋ niyameti ; nivāsaŋ deti, *n.* nivāsasalākā, *f.*
Billhook, *n.* dātta ; asita, *nt.*
Billion, *n.* koṭilakkha, *nt* — **billion**, *n.* koṭippakoṭi, *f.*
Billow, *n.* kallola, *m.*
Billy-goat, *n.* puŋaja, *m.*
Bimetallic, *a.* dvilohika.
Bimonthly, *a.* dvimāsika.
Bin, *n.* koṭṭhaka ; piṭaka, *m.*
Binary, *a.* diguṇa ; dupaṭṭa.
Bind, *v.t.* bandhati ; vinandhati ; saŋyojeti. *p.p.* baddha ; vinaddha ; saŋyutta. °**er**, *n.* ābandhaka ; sanyojetu, *m.* °**ing**, *n.* bandhana ; vinandhana ; ābandhana, *nt.* °**ing**, *a.* ābandhaka ; saŋyojaka.
Binocular, *a.* nettadvayopayogī. *n.* dvinettadūradassaka, *nt.*
Biography, *n.* jīvanacarita, *nt.* °**pher**, *n.* caritalekhaka, *m.*
Biology, *n.* jīvavijjā, *f.* °**ical**, *a.* jīvavijjāyatta. °**ist**, *n.* jīvavijjāvidū, *m.*
Bioplasm, *n.* jīvamūlapakati, *f.*
Bipartition, *n.* dvidhā vibhajana, *nt.*
Biped, *n. a.* dvipada ; dipada. °**al**, *a.* dvipādaka.
Biplane, *n.* dvibhūmakavyomayāna, *nt.*
Bipolar, *a.* ubhayantayutta ; dviakkhaka.
Birch, *n.* bhujapatta, *m.* *v.t.* daṇḍena tāḷeti. *p.p.* °ḷita.
Bird, *n.* pakkhī ; sakuṇa ; dija ; vihaga ; khaga ; vihaṅgama, *m.* — **catcher**, *n.* sākuṇika, *m.* °**fancier**, *n.* pakkhivāṇija, *m.* — **lime**, pakkhilepa, *m.*
Birth, *n.* uppatti ; nibbatti ; jāti ; sañjāti, *f.* pabhava ; ubbhava, *m.* jāyana ; janana, *nt.* **Of low** —, hīnajacca ; nīcakulīna, *a.* **Of noble** —, abhijāta ; uccākulīna, *a.* °**day**, *n.* jātadivasa, *m.* — **place**, *n.* jātibhūmi, *f.* uppattiṭṭhāna, *nt.* °**right**, *n.* dāyāda ; jaccādhikāra, *m.* — **story**, *n.* jātakakathā, *f.*
Biscuit, *n.* piṭṭhapūpa, *m.*
Bisect, *v.t.* samasamaŋ dvidhā vibhajati. *p.p.* °vibhatta. °**ion**, *n.* dvidhāvibhajana, *nt.*
Bisexual, *a.* dviliṅgika ; ubhatovyañjanaka.
Bishop, *n.* dhammādhikārī, *m.* °**ric**, *n.* dhammādhikāra, *m.*
Bison, *n.* vanūsabha, *m.*
Bit, *n.* 1. khaṇḍa, *nt.* khaṇḍikā, *f.* 2. (— of a horse :) mukkhādhāna, *nt.* khalīna, *m.* (— of food :) ālopa, *m.*
Bitch, *n.* 1. sunakhī ; 2. sigālī ; 3. kokī, *f.*
Bite, *v.t.* ḍasati ; khādati. *p.p.* daṭṭha ; khādita. *n.* ḍasana ; daṭṭhaṭṭhāna, *nt.* °**er**, *n.* ḍasaka ; vañcaka, *m.*

Biting, *a.* tiṇha ; tikhiṇa ; rujākara. °**ly,** *adv.* tiṇhākārena.

Bitter, *a.* 1. titta ; 2. tibba ; tippa ; kaṭuka, *n.* tittarasa, *m.* °**gourd,** *n.* kāravella, *m.* °**ly,** *adv.* tibbākārena. °**ness,** *n.* 1. tittabhāva, *m.* 2. tibbatā ; kaṭukatā, *f.* °**ish,** *a.* īsaŋtittaka.

Bitumen, *n.* asmaja, *nt.* asmalepa, *m.* bhūmilasa, *m.* °**ous,** *a.* asmalasayutta.

Bivalve, *a.* dvipidhānaka.

Biweekly, *a.* addhamāsika ; dvisattāhika.

Bizarre, *a.* virūpākāra ; asaṅgata.

Black, *a.* 1. kaṇha ; kāḷa ; asita ; mecaka ; sāma ; 2. andhakāra ; apākaṭa ; 3. duṭṭha ; pāpaka. *noun* : kāḷavaṇṇa, *m.* *v.t.* kaṇhayati ; kāḷavaṇṇena lepeti. — **ant,** *n.* kāḷakipillikā, *f.* — **art,** *n.* bhūtavijjā, *f.* °**board,** *n.* akkharaphalaka, *m.* °**guard,** *n.* adhama ; khala, *m.* °**lead,** *n.* kāḷatipu, *nt.* °**eyed,** *a.* kaṇhanetta. — **leg,** *n.* vañcaka, *m.* — **sheep,** *n.* saṭha ; parisadūsaka, *m.* °**smith,** *n.* kammāra, *m.*

Blacken, *v.t.* kalaṅketi ; dūseti. *p.p.* °kita ; dūsita.

Blackish, *a.* īsaŋkaṇha.

Bladder, *n.* vatthi, *f.* muttāsaya, *m.*

Blade, *n.* (of grass) patta ; dala, *nt.* (of a weapon) dhārā, *f.* phala, *nt.* e.g. *asidhārā,* blade of a sword, *satthaphala,* blade of a knife.

Blame, *v.t.* upavadati ; codeti ; nindati. *p.p.* upavutta ; codita ; nindita. — **in return,** paṭicodeti. *noun* : codanā, *f.* apavāda ; upavāda, *m.* °**able,** *a.* sāvajja ; codanāraha ; upavajja. °**ful,** *a.* sadosa ; sopārambha. °**less,** *a.* anavajja ; anupavajja ; niddosa. °**lessness,** *n.* anavajjatā, *f.* °**worthy,** *a.* upavaditabba ; codetabba.

Blanch, *v.t.* 1. dhavalīkaroti ; 2. thusam apaneti. *p.p.* °kata ; apanīta-thusa.

Bland, *a.* mudu ; komala. — **in speech,** piyaŋvada. °**ness,** *n.* maddava ; komalatta, *nt.*

Blandish, *v.t.* upalāleti. *p.p.* °lita. °**ment,** *n.* upalālanā, *f.*

Blank, *a.* ritta ; tuccha ; lipirahita. *n.* rittapaṇṇa ; alikhitaṭṭhāna, *nt.* °**ness,** *n.* rittatā ; tucchatā, *f.*

Blanket, *n.* kambala ; pāpuraṇa, *nt.* *v.t.* kambalena acchādeti *or* pārupati. *p.p.* °dita ; °pāruta. — **dealer,** *n.* kambalika, *m.*

Blankly, *adv.* ujukam eva ; vinā vitthārakathanā.

Blare, *v.t.* uccaŋ nadati. *p.p.* °nadita. *n.* unnāda, *m.*

Blaspheme, *v.t.* (ariye) upavadati. °**ous,** *a.* ariyūpavādaka. °**my,** *n.* ariyūpavāda, *m.*

Blast, *n.* 1. vāyuvega, *m.* 2. (of horns) dhamana, *nt.* 3. (explosion) vidhamana ; viddhaŋsana, *nt.* *v.t.* viddhaŋseti ; vināseti. *p.p.* viddhasta ; °sita.

Blatant, *a.* mukhara ; gajjanasīla. °**ly,** *adv.* saghosaŋ ; mukharākārena.

Blaze, *n.* ditti ; pabhā ; ābhā ; juti, *f.* ujjalana, *nt.* *v.i.* jalati ; ujjalati ; dippati. *p.p.* jalita ; ditta. °**ing,** *a.* jalamāna ; dippamāna ; ujjala ; pabhassara.

Blazon, *v.t.* 1. lakkhaṇehi aṅketi ; 2. vibhūseti ; 3. pakāseti ; uttānīkaroti. *p.p.* °aṅkita ; °sita ; °kata.

Bleach, *v.t.* dhavalīkaroti ; dhovati. *p.p.* °kata ; dhota.

Bleak, *a.* 1. atisītala ; 2. anāvaṭa ; 3. nirānanda.

Blear, *a.* 1. nippabha ; 2. bappayutta. °**eyed,** *a.* assupuṇṇanetta. *v.t.* nippabhaŋ karoti. *p.p.* °kata.

Bleat, *v.i.* meṇḍaravaŋ ravati. *n.* meṇḍarava, *m.*

Bleed, *v.t.* rudhiraŋ moceti. *v.i.* lohitaŋ paggharati *or* savati. *p.p.* mocitarudhira ; paggharitalohita. °**ing,** *n.* rattapasavana, *nt.*

Blemish, *v.t.* dūseti ; kalaṅketi ; malinīkaroti. *n.* kalaṅka ; kalusa ; dosa, *m.*

Blench, *v.i.* saṅkucati ; apasarati. *p.p.* °cita ; apasaṭa.

Blend, *n.* sammissana, *nt.* *v.t.* misseti ; sammisseti. *p.p.* missita. °**ing,** *n.* missīkaraṇa, *nt.*

Bless, *v.t.* subham āsiŋsati ; sotthiŋ pattheti. *p.p.* āsiṭṭhasubha ; patthitasotthī. °**ing,** *n.* āsī ; subhāsaŋsā, *f.* sotthāna, *nt.*

Blessed, Blest, *a.* dhañña ; subhaga ; bhagavantu. °**ness,** *n.* subhagatā, *f.*

Blether, *v.i.* samphaŋ palapati ; jappati. *p.p.* °pita.

Blight, *n.* sassaroga, *m.* setaṭṭhikā, *f.* *v.t.* vināseti ; viphalīkaroti. *p.p.* °sita ; °kata.

Blind, *a.* andha ; acakkhuka. *n.* āvaraṇa, tirokaraṇa, *nt.* — **from the birth,** jaccandha, *m.* °**ness,** *n.* andhatā, *f.* — **of one eye,** kāṇa, *m.* **Mentally —,** andhabhūta ; aññāṇa, *a.* °**worm,** *n.* gaṇḍuppāda, *m.* mahīlatā, *f.*

Blind, *v.t.* andhīkaroti. *p.p.* °kata, °**fold,** *v.t.* akkhīni chādeti *or* bandhati. °**folded,** *a.* āvutanetta ; pihitanayana. °**ly,** *adv.* avicārena ; asamekkha.

Blink, *v.i.t.* nimisati ; nimīleti. *p.p.* nimisita ; nimīlita. *n.* nimesa, *m.* nimīlana, *nt.*

Bliss, *n.* paramasukha, *nt.* paramānanda, *m.* °**ful,** *a.* paramasukhada ; santikara. °**fulness,** *n.* sukhasamaṅgitā, *f.*

Blister, *n.* phoṭa ; phoṭaka, *m.* piḷakā, *f.* *v.t.* phoṭam uppādeti. *p.p.* uppāditaphoṭa.

Blithe, *a.* pamudita ; pahaṭṭha. °**ly,** *adv.* sānandaŋ ; sahāsaŋ. °**some,** *a.* sānanda ; haṭṭhatuṭṭha.

Blizzard, *n.* vaddalikā, *f.* himapāta, *m.*

Bloat, *v.t.* uddhumātaŋ karoti. *v.i.* uddhumāyati. *p.p.* °māyita *or* uddhumāta. °**ing,** *n.* uddhumāyana, *nt.*

Block, *n.* 1. kaṭṭhakhaṇḍa ; silākhaṇḍa, *m.* 2. (building :)

gharacaturassa, *nt.* 3. (for beheading :) dhammagaṇḍikā, *f.* 4. (pully :) ubbāhanayanta, *nt.* 5. (obstruction :) avarodha, *m.* °**head,** *n.* jaḷa ; eḷamūga, *m.* °**ish,** *a.* mandapañña ; aviññū. — **of land,** bhūmibhāga, *m.* **Butcher's —,** sūnā, *f.*

Block, *v.t.* uparodheti ; sannirumbheti ; bādheti. *p.p.* °dhita ; °bhita ; bādhita. °**ade,** *v.t.* avarodheti ; bādheti. *p.p.* °dhita. *n.* avarodha, *m.* bādhā, *f.*

Blond, Blonde, *a. n.* tambakesa ; sundaravaṇṇa.

Blood, *n.* 1. rudhira ; lohita ; soṇita, ratta, *nt.* 2. gotta, *nt.* vaŋsa, *m.* paramparā, *f.* **Of noble —,** kulīna ; abhijāta, *a.* **Of royal —,** rājavaŋsika, *a.* °**less,** *a.* khīṇalohita. °**letting,** *n.* rudhiramocana, *nt.* °**red,** *a.* lohitavaṇṇa. °**relation,** *n.* sālohita, *m.* °**shed,** *n.* rudhirasāvaṇa, *nt.* pāṇaghāta, *m.* °**shot,** *a.* lohitapuṇṇa ; rattavaṇṇa. °**stained,** *a.* rudhiramakkhita. °**sucker,** *n.* lohitapāyī, *m.* °**thirsty,** *a.* rattapipāsī. °**vessel,** *n.* rattavāhinī, *f.* rudhiranāḷa, *m.*

Bloody, *a.* 1. lohitamakkhita ; 2. ludda ; lohitapāṇī ; dāruṇa. °**iness,** *n.* kurūratta, *nt.* — **flux,** *n.* rattātisāra, *m.*

Bloom, *n.* 1. kusuma ; puppha, *nt.* 2. navatta ; navayobbana, *nt.* 3. (flourishing condition :) samiddhisamaya, *m.* *v.i.* pupphati ; vikasati. *p.p.* °phita ; °sita. °**ing,** *a.* vikasamāna. °**y,** *a.* 1. kusumita ; pupphākiṇṇa ; 2. samiddha.

Blossom, *n.* puppha ; kusuma, *nt.* *v.i.* pupphati ; vikasati. **In —,** phulla ; phullita ; kusumita, *a.*

Blot, *n.* 1. kalaṅka ; kalusa ; kāḷaka, *m.* 2. lopa, *m.* 3. apakitti, *f.* *v.t.* 1. kalaṅketi ; dūseti ; 2. — **out,** lopeti ; 3. kajjalaŋ soseti. *p.p.* °kita ; dūsita ; sositakajjala. °**ting paper,** *n.* kajjalasosaka, *nt.* °**ter,** *n.* 1. dūsaka, *m.* 2. kajjalasosaka, *nt.*

Blotch, *n.* phoṭa ; gaṇḍa, *m.* °**ed,** *a.* phoṭayutta.

Blow, *n.* 1. pahāra ; abhighāta, *m.* (of wind :) vāyana, *nt.* 2. vyasana, *nt.* vipatti ; āpadā, *f.* *v.i.* vāti ; vāyati, *v.t.* 1. samīreti ; kampeti ; 2. (a pipe, etc.) dhamati. *p.p.* vāyita ; °rita ; °pita ; dhanta. °**ing,** *n.* vāyana ; dhamana, *nt.* — **off,** niddhamati. — **on,** abhidhamati. °**out,** nibbāpeti. — **towards,** upavāyati. — **up** (with explosion :) viddhaŋseti ; (with wind :) uddhumāpeti ; vātena pūreti.

Blown, *p.p.* vikaca ; vikasita ; — **off,** niddhanta.

Blub, *v.i.* assuŋ moceti. *p.p.* mocitassuka.

Blubber, *n.* 1. timiṅgalavasā, *f.* 2. rodana, *nt.* adj. uddhumātoṭṭha.

Bludgeon, *n.* gadā, *f.* laguḷa, *m.*

Blue, *a.* *n.* nīla; nīlavaṇṇa. °**black,** *a.* atinīla. — **blood,** *n.* uccākulīna, *m.* °**book,** *n.* mantimaṇḍalapavatti, *f.* — **jay,** *n.* kikī, *f.* °**water-lily,** *n.* indīvara; nīluppala, *nt.*

Bluebeard, *n.* bahupajāpatika, *m.*

Bluff, *a.* asaṇha; avinīta. *n.* 1. dappa; gabba, *m.* 2. sappapātabhūmi, *f.* 3. akkosa, *m.* *v.t.* (paṭimallam) abhibhavati. *p.p.* abhibhūta (paṭimalla).

Bluish, *a.* īsaŋnīlaka.

Blunder, *n.* khalita, *nt.* pamādadosa, *m.* *v.i.* khalati; pakkhalati. *v.t.* asammā pāleti *or* vatteti. *p.p.* khalita; °pālita; °vattita. °**er,** *n.* pamādī; khalanasīla. °**ing,** *a.* pamādabahula; khalamāna. °**ingly,** *adv.* asamekkha; avīmaŋsitvā; pamādena.

Blunt, *a.* 1. kuṇṭha; atikhiṇa; 2. manda; dandha. *v.t.* kuṇṭheti. *p.p.* kuṇṭhita. °**ly,** *adv.* 1. mandaŋ; 2. abahumānena. °**ness,** *n.* 1. kuṇṭhatā; atikhiṇatā; 2. mandabuddhitā, *f.*

Blur, *n.* kalaṅka, *m.* mala, *nt.* *v.t.* dūseti; malinayati. *p.p.* dūsita; °yita.

Blurt, *v.t.* sahasā *or* ananuvicca vadati. *p.p.* °vutta.

Blush, *n.* 1. lajjā; hiri, *f.* 2. kapolarāga, *m.* *v.i.* 1. lajjati; hirīyati.; 2. aruṇībhavati. *p.p.* lajjita: °bhūta. *v.t.* rattavaṇṇaŋ karoti. *p.p.* katarattavaṇṇa. °**ing,** *a.* kapolarāgajanaka. °**ingly,** *adv.* salajjaŋ.

Bluster, *v.i.* gajjati; thanati. *v.t.* uccāsaddena katheti. *p.p.* gajjita; thanita; °kathita. *noun:* unnāda; ugghosa; kalakala, *m.* °**er,** *n.* unnādī, *m.* °**ingly,** *adv.* mahāsaddena; sagajjitaŋ.

Boa (constrictor), ajagara, *m.*

Boar, *n.* vanasūkara; varāha, *m.* °**ish,** *a.* asabbha; avinīta.

Board, *n.* 1. (of wood:) phalaka; padara, *m.* *nt.* phalakādhāra, *m.* 2. (food:) bhojana, *nt.* āhāra, *m.* 3. (of management:) pālakasabhā, *f.* adhikārīgaṇa, *m.* 4. (of a ship:) nāvātala; nāvāpiṭṭha, *nt.* 5. (of paper:) potthakapadara, *nt.* °**er,** *n.* paragehanivāsī, *m.* °**ing house,** sissanivāsa; āvasathāgāra, *m.*

Board, *v.t.* 1. phalakehi chādeti; padarāni attharati. 2. nāvam āruhati. *v.i.* paragehe nivasati. *p.p.* °chādita; atthatapadara; ārūḷhanāva; °nivuttha.

Boast, *n.* katthanā; vikatthanā; attukkaŋsanā, *f.* *v.i.* katthati; vikatthati; ukkaŋseti. °**ful,** *a.* vikatthanasīla. °**fully,** *adv.* sappagabbhaŋ. °**er,** *n.* vikatthī, *m.*

Boat, *n.* (large), nāvā; taraṇī; tarī, *f.* (small), doṇi, *f.* pota, *m.* upavahana, *nt.* *v.i.t.* potena tarati; pote ṭhapeti. °**man,** *n.* potavāha; nāvika, *m.* °**swain,** *n.* kaṇṇadhāra, *m.*

Bob, *n.* khañjana, *nt.* *v.i.* 1. khañjati; 2. uppatanto naccati. *v.t.* rassaŋ katvā chindati. °**tail,** *a.* chinnapuccha. *n.* khañjarīṭa, *m.*

Bobbery, *n.* bhaṇḍana, *nt.* kalaha, *m.*

Bobbin, *n.* tantukhīla, *m.*

Bode, *v.t.* subhāsubhaŋ katheti. *v.i.* subhāsubhaŋ sūceti. *p.p.* kathitasubhāsubha ; sūcita° ; °**ful,** *a.* pubbanimittasahita.

Bodice, *n.* saṅkaccikā, *f.*

Bodily, *a.* sārīrika ; kāyika. *adv.* sayam eva ; sākallena. — **contact,** kāyasaŋsagga, *m.* — **form,** sarīrasaṇṭhāna, *nt.* — **pain,** kāyikadukkha, *nt.* — **relic,** sarīradhātu, *f.*

Body, *n.* 1. kāya ; deha ; vapu ; attabhāva, *m.* sarīra ; gatta ; kalebara, *nt.* tanu, *f.* 2. samūha ; gaṇa, *m.* parisā, *f.* **Attached to the** —, kāyūpaga ; kāyagata. **Connected with the** —, sārīrika ; kāyapaṭibaddha. **Lustre of the** —, sarīrappabhā, *f.* **One's own** —, sadeha, *m.* **Purity of** —, kāyasoceyya, *nt.* **Relating to** —, kāyika, *a.*

Bodyguard, *n.* aṇīkaṭṭha ; aṅgarakkhaka, *m.*

Bog, *n.* anūpa, *m.* cikkhalla, *nt.* °**gy,** *a.* paṅkabahula.

Boggle, *v.i.* pakkhalati ; āsaṅkati. *p.p.* °lita ; °kita.

Bogie, *n.* mahāratha, *m.*

Bogle, *n.* 1. pisāca ; 2. patirūpaka, *m.*

Bogus, *a.* kuttika ; vañcaka, *m.* — **monk,** samaṇakuttika, *m.*

Boil, *n.* gaṇḍa ; phoṭa, *m.* piḷakā, *f.*

Boil, *v.t.* pacati ; randheti. *p.p.* pacita *or* pakka ; randhita. *v.i.* paccati ; kuthati. °**ing,** *n.* randhana ; pacana, *nt.* pāka, *m.* °**er,** *n.* 1. pācaka ; randhaka, *m.* 2. piṭhara, *m.*

Boisterous, *a.* unnādī ; uddāma ; gajjanaka. — **laugh,** aṭṭahāsa, *m.* °**ly,** *adv.* saghosaŋ.

Bold, *a.* 1. sūra ; nibbhaya ; 2. pagabbha ; sadappa ; avinīta ; 3. vibhūta ; atipākaṭa. °**ly,** *adv.* sappagabbhaŋ. °**ness,** *n.* 1. sūratta ; 2. pāgabbhiya ; 3. vibhūtatta, *nt.*

Bole, *n.* daṇḍa, *m.* nāḷa, *nt.*

Bolster, *n.* upadhāna ; apassena, *nt.* bhisi, *f.* *v.t.* upadhānaŋ ṭhapeti. *p.p.* ṭhapitūpadhāna.

Bolt, *n.* 1. aggaḷa, *nt.* ghaṭikā ; laṅghī, *f.* 2. (lightning :) asani, *f.* *v.t.* 1. sahasā palāyati ; 2. asaṅkhāditvā gilati ; 3. ghaṭikaŋ deti ; laṅghiyā pidahati. *p.p.* °yita ; °gilita ; dinnaghaṭika ; °pihita. °**ing,** *n.* sahasā-palāyana, *nt.*

Bolter, *n.* piṭṭhacālanī, *f.*

Bolus, *n.* mahāguḷikā, *f.*

Bomb, *n.* kittimāsani, *f.* *v.t.* kittimāsaniyā paharati. *p.p.* °pahaṭa.

Bombard, *v.t.* 1. kittimāsaniyā vināseti ; 2. nirantaram akkosati. *p.p.* °vināsita ; °akkuṭṭha. °**ment,** *n.* kittimāsaniyā vināsana, *nt.*

Bombast, *n.* atisayutti, *f.* ativākya, *nt.* °**ic,** *a.* atthasāravirahita ; vikatthanasīla.

Bona fide, *a.* avyāja ; akuṭila. *adv.* yathābhūtaŋ.

Bonanza, *n.* samiddhi, *f.* bhāgya, *nt.*

Bond, *n.* 1. bandhana, *nt.* ābandha, *m.* 2. pāsa, *m.* 3. paṭiññāpaṇṇa, *nt.* *v.t.* bandhati. *p.p.* baddha. °**man,** °**sman,** dāsa, *m.* °**maid,** dāsī, *f.* °**servant,** dāsa; bhataka, *m.* °**service,** dāsatta, *nt.*

Bondage, *n.* paravasatta; dāsatta, *nt.* baddhatā, *f.*

Bone, *n.* aṭṭhi; kaṇṭaka, *nt.* *v.t.* aṭṭhīni apaneti. *p.p.* apanītaṭṭhika. °**less,** *a.* anaṭṭhika. °**setter,** *n.* aṭṭhisandhānaka, *m.*

Bonfire, *n.* jayasūcakaggi, *m.*

Bonnet, *n.* vanitāsīsāvaraṇa, *nt.*

Bonny, *a.* sundara; surūpa.

Bonus, *n.* atirekavetana, *nt.*

Bony, *a.* aṭṭhibahula.

Bonze, *n.* mahāyānikabhikkhu, *m.*

Boo, *v.t.* ohīleti; upakkosati. *p.p.* ohīlita; upakkuṭṭha.

Booby, *n.* jaḷa; eḷamūga, *m.*

Boodle, *n.* 1. samudāya, *m.* 2. lañca-dhana, *nt.*

Boohoo, *v.i.* mahāsaddena paridevati.

Book, *n.* potthaka; gantha, *m.* *nt.* °**binder,** *n.* potthakasibbaka, *m.* °**binding,** *n.* potthakasibbana, *nt.* °**case,** potthakādhāra, *m.* °**keeping,** *n.* vāṇijjagaṇanaṅkana, *nt.* °**ing,** *n.* āyavayalikhana, *nt.* °**let,** *n.* khuddakapotthaka, *m.* °**mark,** *n.* potthakasaṅketa, *nt.* °**man,** *n.* bahussuta, *m.* °**seller,** *n.* potthakavāṇija, *m.* °**worm,** *n.* 1. potthakakīṭa, *m.* 2. niccapaṭhanāsatta, *m.*

Book, *v.t.* pageva nāmam aṅketi *or* okāsaŋ niccheti.

Bookstall, *n.* potthakāpaṇa, *m.*

Boom, *n.* gambhīra-nāda, *m.* 2. uḷumpa, *m.* 3. sahasā laddhapasiddhi, *f.* *v.i.* 1. gambhīraŋ nadati; 2. sahasā uggacchati. *p.p.* °uggata.

Boon, *n.* vara; anuggaha, *m.* pasādadāna, *nt.* adj. pamudita; cāgasīlī.

Boor, *n.* jānapadika; gāmika, *m.* °**ish,** *a.* gamma; asiṭṭha. °**ishly,** *adv.* gammākārena. °**ishness,** *n.* gammatta, *nt.*

Boost, *v.t.* ukkhipati; unnāmeti. *p.p.* ukkhitta; °mita.

Boot, *n.* 1. pādāvaraṇa, *nt.* pādukā, *f.* 2. hita; payojana, *nt.* °**lace,** *n.* pādukābandhana, *nt.* °**less,** *a.* niratthaka; nipphala. °**legger,** *n.* rahassena majjavikkayī, *m.*

Booth, *n.* maṇḍapa, *m.*

Booty, *n.* vilutta-dhana, *nt.*

Booze, *v.i.* adhikaŋ pivati. *n.* adhika-pāna, *nt.* pānussava, *m.* °**zy,** *a.* surāsoṇḍa.

Borax, *n.* rasasodhaka; biḷālaloṇa, *nt.*

Border, *n.* pariyanta, *nt.* sīmā, *f.* — **of a garment,** dasā, *f.* — **of a land,** desasīmā, *f.* — **land,** *n.* sīmāsannaraṭṭha, *nt.*

Border, *v.t.* paricchindati; sapariyantaŋ karoti. *p.p.* paricchinna; °kata. °**ing,** *a.* panta; pariyantaṭṭhita.

Bore, *n.* randha ; vivara ; chidda, *nt.* *v.t.* 1. vitudati ; 2. kaṇṇakaṭukaŋ vadati. *p.p.* vitunna ; vuttakaṇṇakaṭuka. °**er,** *n.* vedhaka ; vitudaka, *m.*

Boreal, *a.* uttaradisāyatta.

Boreas, *n.* uttaravāta, *m.*

Born, *p.p. of bear.* jāta ; sañjāta ; uppanna. — **after,** anujāta, *a.* — **before,** purejāta, *a.* — **from moisture,** saŋsedaja, *a.* — **in the hell,** nerayika ; āpāyika, *a.* — **on the hills,** pabbateyya, *a.* — **on the land,** thalaja, *a.* — **together,** sahaja ; sahajāta. *a.* — **well,** sujāta, *a.*

Borne, *p.p. of bear.* dhārita ; vahita.

Borough, *n.* nigama, *m.* kuḍḍanagara, *nt.*

Borrow, *v.t.* 1. iṇaŋ gaṇhāti ; 2. anukaroti. *p.p.* gahita-iṇa ; anukata. °**ed,** *a.* yācitaka. °**er,** *n.* iṇagāhī ; iṇāyika, *m.*

Borstal, *n.* bālāparādhakārīnivāsa, *m.*

Bosh, *n.* micchāpalāpa, *m.* *v.t.* upahāsaŋ pāpeti.

Bosky, *a.* gumbacchanna.

Bosom, *n.* 1. ura ; hadaya, *nt.* 2. thana ; payodhara, *m.* °**friend,** vallabhamitta, *m.*

Boss, *n.* 1. nābhi, *f.* 2. adhikārī ; ajjhakkhaka, *m.*

Botany, *n.* ubbhidavijjā, *f.* °**ist,** *n.* bhūtagāmaññū ; ubbhidavedī, *m.* °**ical,** *a.* ubbhidāyatta.

Botch, *v.t.* asakkaccaŋ saṅkharoti. °**er,** *n.* anipuṇa ; asakkaccakārī, *m.*

Both, *pron.* ubha ; ubhaya. — **ways,** *adv.* ubhayathā. **In — places,** ubhayattha. **On — sides,** ubhato ; ubhayato.

Bother, *v.t.* hiŋsati ; pīḷeti ; bādheti. *p.p.* hiŋsita ; pīḷita ; bādhita. *n.* pīḷā ; hiŋsā, *f.* bādhana, *nt.* °**some,** *a.* khedāvaha ; pīḷājanaka.

Bottle, *n.* nāḷikā, *f.* **Glass —,** kācatumba, *m.* — **of oil,** telanāli, *f.*

Bo-tree, *n.* bodhirukkha ; duminda, *m.*

Bottom, *n.* 1. adhotala, *nt.* 2. pāda, *nt.* patiṭṭhā, *f.* adj. heṭṭhima. °**less,** *a.* agādha ; atalampassa ; atigambhīra.

Bottom, *v.t.* 1. mūlādhāraŋ patiṭṭhāpeti ; 2. adhotalaŋ pāpuṇāti. *p.p.* °pitamūlā ° ; °patta.

Bough, *n.* sākhā, *f.*

Boulder, *n.* vaṭṭapāsāṇa, *m.*

Boulevard, *n.* tarupantiyuttā mahāracchā, *f.*

Bounce, *v.i.* laṅghati. *v.t.* sahasā ajjhottharati. *p.p.* laṅghita ; °ajjhotthaṭa. *n.* 1. mahānāda ; 2. dāruṇappahāra, *m.* 3. vikatthana, *nt.* *adv.* sahasā ; sasaddaŋ. °**er,** *n.* 1. vikatthī, *m.* 2. pākaṭa-musā, *f.*

Bound, *v.t.* paricchindati ; avadhāreti ; sīmaŋ ṭhapeti. *v.i.* uppatati. *p.p.* paricchinna ; °rita ; ṭhapitasīma ; uppatita. *noun:* 1. avadhi ; pariccheda, *m.* sīmā, *f.* pamāṇa, *nt.* 2. uppatana ; laṅghana, *nt.*

Bound, *a.* gantukāma ; gāmī. *p.p. of bind,* baddha ; ābaddha.

Boundary, *n.* sīmā ; mariyādā, *f.* odhi ; avadhi ; pariccheda, *m.*

Bounden, *a.* āvassaka ; anatikkamiya.

Boundless, *a.* amita ; ananta ; aparimita ; appamāṇa. °**ly,** *adv.* anantaŋ ; aparimitaŋ. °**ness,** *n.* anantatā ; appamāṇatā, *f.*

Bounteous, Bountiful, *a.* cāgasīla ; dānasoṇḍa ; bahuppada. °**ly,** *adv.* cāgasīlatāya ; vigatamalatāya. °**ness,** *n.* vadaññutā ; muttacāgatā, *f.*

Bounty, *n.* 1. cāgasīlatā ; payatapāṇitā, *f.* 2. cāga ; pariccāga, *m.*

Bouquet, *n.* kusumatthabaka, mālāguṇa, *m.*

Bout, *n.* kammantavāra ; ussāha, *m.*

Bovine, *a.* gavya ; gavāyatta.

Bow, *n.* 1. dhanu, *nt.* cāpa ; issāsa, *m.* 2. addhamaṇḍala, *nt.* 3. (— of a boat :) nāvābhimukha, *nt.* (— of a lute :) koṇa, *m.* —**man,** dhanuddhara, *m.* °**string,** *n.* jiyā, *f.* dhanuguṇa, *m.*

Bow, *v.i.t.* namassati ; vandati ; paṇamati ; abhivādeti. *p.p.* °sita ; vandita ; paṇamita ; °dita. *n.* paṇāma ; namakkāra, *m.* vandanā ; namassanā ; abhivādanā, *f.*

Bowel, *n.* anta, *nt.*

Bower, *n.* nikuñja ; latāmaṇḍapa, *m.*

Bowl, *n.* 1. patta, *m.* pāti, *f.* 2. goḷaka, *nt.* kanduka, *m.* 3. goḷakakīḷā, *f.* *v.t.* goḷakehi kīḷati. °**er,** *n.* guḷakīḷaka.

Bow-legged, *a.* vaṅkapāda.

Bowling-green, *n.* kandukakīḷābhūmi, *f.*

Bow-wow, *n.* bhuṅkāra, *m.*

Box, *n.* 1. peḷā ; mañjūsā, *f.* 2. muṭṭhippahāra ; pāṇighāta, *m.* °**er,** *n.* muṭṭhimalla, *m.* °**ing,** *n.* mallayuddha, *nt.*

Box, *v.t.* 1. peḷāya pakkhipati ; 2. peḷāyo sampādeti. 3. sambādhe vāseti. *v.i.* muṭṭhinā paharati ; mallayuddhaŋ karoti. *p.p.* °khitta ; °vāsita ; °pahaṭa ; katamallayuddha.

Boy, *n.* bālaka ; dāraka ; kumāra ; susu, *m.* °**hood,** *n.* bālya ; komāra, *nt.* °**ish,** *a.* bālayogga.

Boycott, *v.t.* sahayogaŋ vajjeti. *p.p.* vajjitasahayoga. *noun* : sahayogavajjana, *nt.*

Brace, *n.* 1. sambandhaka, *m.* 2. yuga ; yugala ; yamaka, *nt.* *v.t.* daḷhaŋ bandhati. *p.p.* daḷhabaddha. °**ing,** *a.* santhambhaka.

Bracelet, *n.* valaya ; kaṅkaṇa ; kaṭaka, *nt.* karabhūsā, *f.*

Bracket, *n.* 1. nāgadantaka, *nt.* 2. addhacanda-rekhā, *f.* *v.t.* addhacandarekhāhi viseseti. *p.p.* °sita.

Brackish, *a.* īsaŋloṇika.

Brag, *v.i.* attānaŋ silāghati ; vikatthati. *p.p.* vikatthita. °**gart,** *n.* vikatthī, *m.*

Brahma, (the Creator :) Lokesa ; Pitāmaha, *m.*

Brahman, Brahmin, *n.* vippa ; dvija ; brāhmaṇa, *m.* °**ical,** *a.* brāhmaṇāyatta.

Braid, *n.* veṇī, *f.* dhammilla, *m.* *v.t.* gantheti ; veṇīkaroti. *p.p.* ganthita ; veṇīkata.

Brain, *n.* 1. lasī, *f.* matthaluṅga, *m.* 2. mati ; buddhi, *f.* °**less,** *a.* matihīna ; mandabuddhika. °**pan,** *n.* sīsakapāla, *m.* °**sick,** *a.* bhantacitta ; sativikala.

Brake, *n.* 1. gumbagahaṇa ; kaṇṭakagahaṇa, *nt.* 2. yānanivattaka, *nt.*

Bramble, *n.* kaṇṭakagumba, *m.*

Bran, *n.* thusa ; dhaññataca, *m.*

Branch, *n.* 1. sākhā, *f.* viṭapa, *m.* 2. (of an institution, etc.) ekadesa ; koṭṭhāsa, *m.* sākhā, *f.* °**ing road,** *n.* dvidhāpatha, *m.* °**y,** *a.* bahusâkha; sākhāsampanna.

Branch, *v.i.* sākhāhi vaḍḍhati. *v.t.* vibhajati ; bhājeti. *p.p.* °ḍhita ; vibhatta ; bhājita.

Brand, *n.* 1. lakkhaṇaṅkana ; vāṇijaciṇha, *nt.* 2. alāta ; ummukka, *nt.* *v.t.* tattalohena aṅketi ; lakkhaṇāhataŋ karoti. — **new,** *a.* abhinavatara.

Brandish, *v.t.* uggirati ; āvijjhati ; paribbhameti. *p.p.* āviddha ; °mita.

Brandy, *n.* vāruṇī, *f.* surāsāra, *m.*

Brangle, *n.* kalaha, *m.* *v.i.* kalahaŋ karoti. *p.p.* katakalaha.

Brass, *n.* rīri, *f.* ārakūṭa, *m.* — **netting,** lohajāla, *nt.* — **plate,** rīripaṭṭa, *nt.* — **wire,** lohasalākā ; loharajju, *f.* °**y,** *a.* 1. ārakūṭasama ; 2. nillajja.

Brat, *n.* pillaka ; dāraka, *m.*

Bravado, *n.* nibbhayatta, *nt.* sāṭopavutti, *f.*

Brave, *a.* *n.* sūra ; vīra ; nibbhaya. *v.t.* vikkamati ; nibbhayo hoti. *p.p.* vikkanta ; nibbhayabhūta. °**ly,** *adv.* savikkamaŋ ; sūrākārena. °**ry,** *n.* dhīratta ; vīratta, *nt.* vikkama ; parakkama, *m.*

Bravo, *intj.* sādhu, sādhu. *n.* paratthaŋ manussaghātī, *m.*

Brawl, *n.* kalaha ; viggaha, *m.* *v.i.* vivadati ; bhaṇḍeti. °**er,** *n.* kalahakārī, *m.*

Brawny, *a.* balavantu ; daḷhakāya.

Bray, *v.i.* gadrabharavaŋ ravati. *v.t.* koṭṭeti ; cuṇṇeti. *p.p.* koṭṭita ; cuṇṇita. *n.* gadrabharava, *m.*

Braze, *v.t.* 1. lohena chādeti ; 2. thambhīkaroti. *p.p.* lohachādita ; °kata.

Brazen, *a.* 1. tambamaya ; 2. atithaddha ; 3. nillajja ; niṭṭhura. *v.t.* atithaddho, nillajjo *or* sappagabbho hoti.

Brazier, *n.* 1. lohaṅgārakaṭāha, *m.* 2. lohakāra ; kammāra, *m.*

Breach, *n.* 1. chiddha ; randha ; vivara, *nt.* 2. (of law, etc.) bhaṅga ; bheda, *m.* atikkamana ; laṅghana, *nt.* *v.t.* vinivijjhati ; chiddaŋ karoti. *p.p.* vinividdha ; katachidda. — **of morality,** sīlabheda, *m.* — **of promise,** paṭiññābhaṅga, *m.*

Bread, *n.* 1. godhumapūpa, *m.* 2. āhāra, *m.* bhojana, *nt.* °**fruit,** labuja, *m.* °**winner,** kulaposaka, *m.*

Breadth, *n.* vitthāra, *m.* puthulatta, *nt.*

Break, *v.t.* 1. chindati ; bhañjati ; bhindati ; 2. (law, etc.) ullaṅgheti ; atikkamati. 3. (to stop) nivatteti ; bādheti. *p.p.* chinna ;

bhagga ; bhinna ; °ghita ; atikkanta ; °tita ; bādhita. *v.i.* bhijjati. *p.p.* bhinna. °**able,** *a.* bhijjanadhamma. — **away,** sahasā apagacchati. °**down,** *v.i.* osīdati. *n.* adhopatana ; osīdana, *nt.* — **forth,** sahasā pātukaroti. — **in,** sahasā pavisati. — **into,** dameti ; vineti. — **into pieces,** khaṇḍeti ; cuṇṇeti. — **loose,** pamoceti. — **off,** viyojeti, vicchindati. — **one's word,** visaŋvādeti. — **out,** uggacchati. — **open,** ugghāṭeti. — **upon,** āhanati. — **with,** vivadati.

Breakage, *n.* bhañjana ; padālana ; vidāraṇa, *nt.*

Breaker, *n.* bhettu ; bhañjaka ; phālaka ; vidāraka, *m.*

Breakfast, *n.* pātarāsa, *m. v.i.* pātarāsaŋ bhuñjati. *v.t.* pātarāsaŋ paṭiyādeti. *p.p.* bhuttapā° ; °ditapāta°.

Breaking, *n.* bhindana ; khaṇḍana ; bhijjana, *nt.* bheda ; cheda, *m.* adj. bhañjaka ; vidāraka ; bhedakara. — **of alliance,** mithubheda, *m.*

Breakneck, *a.* atibhayānaka ; jīvitāpahāraka.

Breakwater, *n.* setubandha, *m.* titthāvaraṇa, *nt.*

Breast, *n.* 1. ura, *m. nt.* 2. (of a woman :) thana ; kuca ; payodhara, *m. v.t.* abhimukhīhoti ; uraŋ dadāti. *p.p.* °mukhībhūta ; dinnaura. °**plate,** *n.* uracchada, *m.*

Breath, *n.* sasana, *nt.* assāsapassāsa, *m.*

Breathe, *v.i.* sasati ; aṇati. — **in,** assasati. — **out,** passasati. °**ing,** *n.* pāṇana ; āṇāpāṇa, *nt.* °**ing in,** assāsa, *m.* āṇa, *nt.* °**ing out,** passāsa, *m.* apāṇa, *nt.*

Breathless, *a.* 1. jīvarahita ; 2. nivattitāṇāpāṇa. °**ly,** *adv.* atisīghaŋ.

Breech, *n.* nitamba ; kaṭippadesa, *m.* °**es,** *n.* kaṭivasana, *nt.*

Breed, *v.t.* 1. janeti ; uppādeti ; nibbatteti; 2. poseti; vaḍḍheti. *p.p.* janita ; °dita ; °tita ; posita ; vaḍḍhita. *v.i.* jāyati ; uppajjati. *p.p.* jāta ; uppanna. °**er,** *n.* janaka ; uppādaka ; posaka, *m.* °**ing,** *n.* 1. posaṇa ; pālana ; saŋvaḍḍhana, *nt.* 2. vinayana ; sikkhana, *nt.*

Breed, *n.* pajā ; paramparā, *f.* apacca, *nt.*

Breeze, *n.* mandānila ; mandamāruta, *m.* °**y,** *a.* mandānilayutta. °**less,** *a.* nivāta.

Brethren, *m. pl.* bhātaro ; sahadhammikā.

Brevity, *n.* saṅkhepa ; samāsa, *m.*

Brew, *v.t.* majjaŋ sampādeti. °**er,** *n.* majjasampādaka, *m.* °**ery,** *n.* majjasampādanaṭṭhāna, *nt.* °**age,** *n.* majja, *nt.* surā, *f.*

Bribe, *v.t.* lañcaŋ deti. *p.p.* dinnalañca. *n.* lañca, *m.* °**er,** lañcadāyaka, *m.* °**ee,** lañcakhādaka, *m.* °**ry,** lañcadāna, *nt.*

Brick, *n.* giñjakā ; cayaniṭṭhakā, *f.* °**house,** giñjakāvasatha, *m.* °**layer,** iṭṭhakavaḍḍhakī, *m.* °**maker,** *n.* giñjakāsampādaka, *m.* °**bat,** *n.* iṭṭhakākhaṇḍa, *m.*

Bridal, *a.* vivāhāyatta.

Bride, *n.* navavadhū ; vivāhābhimukhā, *f.* °**groom,** *n.* āvāhaka ; pāṇiggāhaka, *m.* °**smaid,** *n.* navavadhūvayassā, *f.* °**sman,** *n.* āvāhakasakhā, *m.*

Bridge, *n.* setu, *m.* saṅkamaṇa, *nt. v.t.* setuŋ bandhati ; setunā sambandheti. *p.p.* setubaddha ; setusambaddha. — **of the nose,** nāsāpaṇāḷi, *f.*

Bridle, *n.* mukhādhāna ; khalīna, *nt. v.t.* 1. khalīnaŋ yojeti ; 2. saŋyameti ; niggaṇhāti. *p.p.* yojitakhalīna ; saŋyamita ; niggahita.

Brief, *n.* saṅkhepa ; saṅgaha ; sāraŋsa, *m.* adj. appaka ; thoka ; khaṇika ; saṅkhitta. °**ly,** *adv.* saṅkhepena ; samāsato. °**ness,** *n.* saṅkhittatā ; laghutā ; ittaratā, *f.*

Brigade, *n.* senāvibhāga, *m.* vāhinī, *f.* °**ier,** *n.* camūpati, *m.*

Brigand, *n.* cora ; gāmaghātaka, *m.* °**age,** *n.* gāmaghāta, *m.* panthadūhana, *nt.* °**ism,** *n.* corakamma, *nt.*

Bright, *a.* ujjala ; samujjala ; bhāsura ; sappabha ; pabhassara. — **half of the month,** juṇha ; sukkapakkha, *m.* °**ness,** *n.* juti ; ditti ; pabhā ; ābhā, *f.*

Brighten, *v.t.* obhāseti ; pabhāseti ; joteti ; dippeti. *v.i.* jalati ; ujjalati ; pabhāsati ; dippati ; virājati. *p.p.* °sita ; jotita ; dippita ; jalita ; ujjalita ; °sita ; ditta ; virājita.

Brilliance, *n.* kanti ; sobhā ; juti ; ditti ; pabhā, *f.* °**ant,** *a.* jutimantu ; jutindhara ; pabhassara ; virocamāna. *n.* dhotavajira, *nt.*

Brim, *n.* mukhavaṭṭi ; titti, *f. v.t.* āmukhavaṭṭiŋ pūreti. *v.i.* samatittikaŋ pūrati. *p.p.* °pūrita ; °puṇṇa. °**ful,** *a.* paripuṇṇa ; samatittika.

Brimstone, *n.* gandhaka, *nt.*

Brine, *n.* 1. khāra ; loṇajala, *nt.* 2. samudda, *m.* 3. assu, *nt. v.t.* khāre pakkhipati. *p.p.* °pakkhitta.

Bring, *v.t.* āharati ; āneti ; upaneti ; pāpeti. *p.p.* āhaṭa ; ānīṭa ; upanīta ; pāpita. — **about,** sādheti ; sampādeti. — **back,** paccāharati. — **down,** opāteti ; parihāpeti. — **forth,** janeti ; uppādeti. — **forward,** abhinīharati. — **near,** upanāmeti. — **into,** paṭipādeti ; nipphādeti. — **out,** pakāseti ; pākaṭīkaroti. — **to ruin,** vināseti. — **to an end,** pariyosāpeti. — **together,** samāgameti ; rāsīkaroti. — **under,** dameti ; abhibhavati. — **up,** poseti ; paṭijaggati. — **up to,** upaneti.

Bringer, *n.* ānetu ; upanetu ; āharitu, *m.*

Bringing, *n.* āharaṇa ; ānayana, *nt.* — **up,** paṭijaggana ; posaṇa, *nt.*

Brinjal, *n.* vātiṅgana, *m.*

Brink, *n.* 1. tīra ; taṭa ; kūla, *nt.* 2. pariyanta, *m.*

Brisk, *a.* turita ; avilambita. °**ly,** *adv.* khippaŋ ; turitaŋ ; tuvaṭaŋ ; āsu ; lahuŋ. °**ness,** *n.* sīghatta ; turitatta, *nt.*

Bristle, *v.i.* haŋsati. *p.p.* haṭṭha. *n.* kharaloma, *nt.*

Britain, *n.* āṅgaladesa, *m.*

British, *a.* āṅgalika.

Brittle, *a.* bhaṅgura ; pabhaṅgu. °**ness,** *n.* bhaṅguratta, *nt.*

Broach, *n.* 1. salla ; vedhana, *nt.* 2. thūpikā, *f.* *v.t.* nibbijjhati ; chiddaŋ karoti. *p.p.* nibbiddha ; katachidda.

Broad, *a.* vitthata ; vitthiṇṇa ; puthula. °**ness,** *n.* puthulatta ; vepulla, *nt.* vitthāra, *m.* °**ly,** *adv.* bahuso ; vitthatākārena. °**wise,** *adv.* tiriyaŋ.

Broadcast, *v.t.* pakāseti ; pacāreti. *p.p.* °sita ; °rita.

Broadseal, *n.* rājamuddā, *f.*

Brocade, *n.* pupphavikatikā, *f.* *v.t.* pupphavikatikaŋ sampādeti.

Broidery, *n.* suttavikatikā, *f.*

Broil, *n.* 1. kalaha ; viggaha, *m.* 2. bhajjitamaŋsa, *nt.* *v.t.* bhajjati ; randheti. *p.p.* bhajjita ; randhita. *v.i.* paccati. *p.p.* pakka.

Broken, *a.* (*p.p.* of break), bhagga ; bhinna ; obhagga ; asampuṇṇa. — **bit,** khaṇḍikā, *f.* — **down,** vilugga ; onata. — **up,** palugga ; pabhagga, *a.*

Broker, *n.* kayavikkayika ; vohārika, *m.*

Bronchitis, *n.* sāsanāḷikābādha, *m.*

Bronze, *n.* kaŋsa, *m.* — **vessel,** *n.* kaŋsathāla, *m.* *v.t.* kaŋsavaṇṇaŋ karoti. *p.p.* katakaŋsa°.

Brooch, *n.* urabhūsā, *f.*

Brood, *v.i.* 1. usmāpeti ; 2. parivitakketi ; upanijjhāyati. *p.p.* usmāpita ; °kita ; °yita. *n.* pajā ; santati, *f.*

Brook, *n.* kunnadī, *f.* kandara, *m.* *v.t.* sahati ; khamati. *p.p.* sahita ; khanta.

Broom, *n.* sammajjanī ; sammuñjanī, *f.* °**stick,** *n.* sammajjanīdaṇḍa, *m.*

Broth, *n.* sūpa, *m.*

Brothel, *n.* gaṇikānivāsa, *m.*

Brother, *n.* 1. bhātu ; bhātika ; anuja ; sodariya, *m.* 2. samānasaŋvāsaka, *m.* °**hood,** *n.* nikāya ; sahadhammikagaṇa, *m.* °**in law,** *n.* sāla, *m.* °**less,** *a.* abhātuka. °**like,** *a.* bhātusadisa. °**ly,** *a.* bhātupemayutta.

Brought (*p.p.* of Bring). — **for trial,** abhinīta, *a.* — **near,** upanīta ; upakaṭṭha *a.* — **into contact,** phassita, *a.* — **together,** samāhaṭa, *a.* — **up,** posita ; bhata ; saŋvaḍḍhita, *a.* — **up to,** upanāmita, *a.*

Brow, *n.* 1. bhamu ; bhamukā, *f.* 2. mukhavaṭṭi, *f.*

Browbeat, *v.t.* bhākuṭiŋ karoti. °**ing,** *n.* bhākuṭīkaraṇa, *nt.*

Brown, *a.* piṅgala ; tambavaṇṇa. *v.t.* tambavaṇṇaŋ karoti. *v.i.* tambavaṇṇī bhavati. *p.p.* °ṇṇakata ; °bhūta. °**ish,** *a.* īsaŋpiṅgala. °**ness,** *n.* piṅgalatta, *nt.*

Browse, *n.* navapallava ; saddala, *m.* *v.t.* pallave khādati. *p.p.* khāditapallava.

Bruin, *n.* bhallūka ; issa, *m.*

Bruise, *n.* ghaŋsitaṭṭhāna, *nt.* *v.t.* 1. potheti. 2. cuṇṇeti. *p.p.* pothita ; cuṇṇita.

Bruit, *n.* pavatti ; vāttā, *f.* *v.t.* pākaṭīkaroti. *p.p.* °kata.

Brumous, *a.* mahikāyutta.

Brunt, *n.* pahāravega, *m.*

Brush, *n.* koccha ; vālaṇḍupaka, *m.* *v.t.* kocchena parimajjati. *p.p.* °parimaṭṭha. — **aside,** — **away,** atikkāmeti ; na sallakkheti. °**wood,** *n.* kubbanaka, *nt.* °**y,** *a.* 1. gumbāvuta ; 2. bahulomaka.

Brusque, *a.* dandha ; avinīta. °**ly,** *adv.* avinītākārena.

Brutal, Brutish, *a.* pasutulya ; caṇḍa ; avinīta. °**ity,** *n.* niṭṭhuratā, *f.* °**ly,** *adv.* niddayaŋ ; niṭṭhuraŋ. °**ize,** *v.t.* pasutulyaŋ karoti. *p.p.* °kata.

Brute, *n.* pasu ; tiracchāna, *m.* adj. asabbha ; sammūḷha.

Bubble, *n.* 1. bubbula, *nt.* 2. asāravatthu, *nt.* *v.i.* bubbulāyati. *v.t.* bubbulāni uppādeti. *p.p.* °yita ; °ditabubbula.

Bubonic plague, *n.* ahivātakaroga, *m.*

Buccaneer, *n.* sāmuddikacora, *m.*

Buck, *n.* 1. miga ; hariṇa, *m.* 2. amarākumina, *nt.* *v.i.* uppatati. — **up,** turito bhavati. *p.p.* uppatita ; turitabhūta.

Bucket, *n.* udañcana, *nt.*

Buckish, *a.* maṇḍanajātika.

Buckle, *n.* kuḍuba ; gaṇḍaka. *v.t.* kuḍubena sambandheti. *p.p.* sambaddha.

Buckler, *n.* kheṭaka, *nt.*

Bucolic, *a.* jānapadika.

Bud, *n.* makula ; koraka, *m.* **Fresh** —, khāraka, *m.* *v.i.* aṅkurāyati ; makule janeti. *p.p.* aṅkurita ; janitamakula.

Buddha, *n.* Buddha ; Bhagavantu ; Dasabala ; Sugata ; Muninda ; Sabbaññū ; Sakyasīha ; Sakyamuni, *m.* °**hood,** *n.* Buddhatta, *nt.*

Buddhism, *n.* Buddhasamaya, *m.* Buddhabhatti, *f.*

Buddhist, *n. a.* Buddhabhattika ; Sogata. — **canon,** tipiṭaka, *nt.* — **monk,** bhikkhu ; Buddhasāvaka, *m.*

Budge, *v.i.* apasarati ; apeti. *p.p.* apasaṭa ; apeta.

Budget, *n.* 1. pasibbaka, *m.* 2. āyavayasaṅkhyā, *f.*

Buff, *n.* mahisacamma, *nt.* *v.t.* cammena parimajjati. *p.p.* °parimaṭṭha.

Buffalo, *n.* mahisa, *m.*

Buffer, *n.* paṭighātanivāraka, *m.*

Buffet, *n.* pāṇippahāra ; muṭṭhighāta, *m.* *v.t.* muṭṭhinā paharati ; hatthehi yujjhati. *p.p.* °pahaṭa ; °yujjhita.

Buffoon, *n.* hāsaka ; vidūsaka, *m.* *v.i.* hāsam uppādeti. *v.t.* upahāsaŋ pāpeti. *p.p.* uppāditahāsa ; °pāpita. °**ery,** *n.* parihāsa, dava, *m.*

Bug, *n.* maṅkuṇa, *m.* °**gy,** *a.* maṅkuṇabahula.

Bugbear, *n.* micchābhayakāraṇa, *nt.*

Bugle, *n.* dhamanavaŋsa, *m.* *v.t.* dhameti. *p.p.* dhanta.

Build, *v.t.* māpeti ; nimmiṇāti ; navakammaŋ karoti. *p.p.* māpita ; nimmita ; katanavakamma. °**er**, *n.* navakammika ; māpetu ; kāraka (in cpds.), *m.* °**ing**, *n.* nimmāṇa ; ghara, *nt.* °**ing material**, dabbasambhāra, *m.*

Bulb, *n.* 1. kanda ; ālu, *m.* 2. goḷaka, *m. v.i.* goḷībhavati. *p.p.* goḷībhūta. °**ous**, *a.* goḷākāra ; kandākāra.

Bulbul, *n* 1. gāyakasakuṇa ; 2. gāyaka, *m.*

Bulge, *v.i.* bahi lambati. *p.p.* °bita.

Bulk, *n.* 1. parimāṇa ; pamāṇa, *nt.* 2. nāvābhāra, *m.* 3. khandha, *m.* °**y**, *a.* thūla ; vaṭhara ; mahākāya.

Bull, *n.* balivadda ; goṇa ; usabha, *m.* °**like**, *a.* āsabha.

Bullet, *n.* tipuguḷikā, *f.*

Bulletin, *n.* saṅkhitta-nivedana ; visesanivedana, *nt.*

Bullheaded, *a.* anassava ; avidheyya.

Bullion, *n.* hirañña, *nt.*

Bullock, *n.* uddhaṭabīja-usabha, *m.*

Bully, *n.* sūramānī, *m. v.t.* hiŋsati ; pīḷeti. *p.p.* hiŋsita ; pīḷita.

Bulrush, *n.* vetasa, *m.*

Bulwark, *n.* uddāpa, *m.*

Bum, *n.* nitamba, *m.*

Bumble-bee, *n.* mahāmadhukara, *m.*

Bump, *n.* 1. paṭighāta, *m.* saŋghaṭṭana, *nt.* 2. unnatasīsappadesa, *m.* 3. vāyugaṇḍa, *m.* *v.i.* paṭihaññati. *p.p.* paṭihata. *v.t.* ghaṭṭeti ; paṭihanati. *p.p.* ghaṭṭita ; paṭihata.

Bumper, *n.* puṇṇacasaka, *m.*

Bumpkin, *n.* dandha-jānapadika, *m.*

Bumptious, *a.* attukkaŋsaka.

Bumpy, *a.* visama.

Bun, *n.* addhagoḷapūpa, *m.*

Bunch, *n.* thabaka ; gocchaka, *m.* mañjarī ; vallarī, *f. v.t.* gocchake karoti ; ekato bandhati. *p.p.* katagocchaka ; ekatobaddha.

Bundle, *n.* bhaṇḍikā, *f.* kalāpa, *m. v.t.* bhaṇḍikā bandhati ; kalāpe karoti. *p.p.* bhaṇḍikābaddha ; kalāpakata. — **off**, khippaŋ peseti.

Bung, *n.* rodhanī, *f. v.t.* rodhaniyā pidahati. *p.p.* °pihita.

Bungalow, *n.* hammiya, *nt.*

Bungle, *v.i.* khalati ; pamajjati ; ākulīkaroti. *p.p.* khalita ; pamatta ; °kata. °**er**, *n.* adakkha ; akovida.

Bunion, *n.* pādaphoṭa, *m.*

Bunny, *n.* sasaka, *m.*

Bunting, *n.* 1. patākā, *f.* 2. dhajapaṭa, *m.*

Buoy, *v.i.* plavati. *n.* plava ; uḷumpa, *m.* °**ancy**, *n.* lahutā ; anosīdanatā, *f.*

Buoyant, adj. 1. plavanasīla ; anosīdaka ; 2. sallahukacitta. °**ly**, *adv.* lahukākārena ; plavanākārena.

Burden, *n.* 1. bhāra, *m.* 2. dhura, *nt. v.t.* bhāram āropeti. *p.p.* āropitabhāra. °**ed**, *a.* vyathita ; bhārakkanta. °**some**, *a.* bhāriya ; dukkhama ; pīḷākara.

Bureau, *n.* 1. lekhanādhāra, *m.* 2. kiccālaya, *m.* 3. kārakamaṇḍala, *nt.* °**cracy,** *n.* pālakamaṇḍala, *nt.* °**cratic,** *a.* pālakamaṇḍalāyatta.

Burgeon, *v.i.* aṅkurāyati. *p.p.* aṅkurita.

Burgh, *n.* nagara, *nt.* °**er,** *n.* nagaravāsī ; nāgarika, *m.*

Burgler, *n.* sandhibhedaka ; cora, *m.* °**y,** *n.* sandhiccheda, *m.* coriya ; theyya, *nt.*

Burgomaster, *n.* nigamasāmī ; nagarādhipa, *m.*

Burial, *n.* bhūminidahana, *nt.*

Burke, *v.t.* nigūhati ; pākaṭattaŋ vāreti. *p.p.* nigūhita ; vāritapākaṭatta.

Burlesque, *n.* hāsatthāya anukaraṇa, *nt.* adj. hāsuppādaka. *v.t.* anukaronto hāseti.

Burly, *a.* thūlakāya.

Burmese, *n. a.* Marammika ; Brahmadesika.

Burn, *n.* daḍḍhaṭṭhāna, *nt.* *v.t.* jhāpeti ; dahati. *p.p.* jhāpita ; daḍḍha. *v.i.* ḍayhati ; jhāyati ; pajjalati. *p.p.* daḍḍha ; jhāma ; pajjalita. °**er,** *n.* 1. jhāpaka ; ḍāhaka, *m.* 2. dīpavaṭṭi, *f.* vaṭṭidhāraka, *m.*

Burning, *a.* dāhakara ; accuṇha. *n.* dahana ; jalana, *nt.* — **glass,** *n.* suriyakanta - phalika, *m.* — **ground,** *n.* āḷāhanaṭṭhāna, *nt.*

Burnish, *v.t.* (parimajjanena) jutimantaŋ karoti. *v.i.* ābhāya vaḍḍhati. *p.p.* °ḍhita.

Burrow, *n.* bhūmibila, *nt.* *v.t.* bilaŋ khaṇati. *v.i.* bile vasati. *p.p.* khatabila ; °vuttha.

Bursar, *n.* vijjālaya-bhaṇḍāgārika, *m.* °**y,** *n.* vijjālaya-kosa ; vihārakoṭṭhāgāra, *m.*

Burst, *n.* bhijjana ; padālana ; vidāraṇa, *nt.* *v.i.* phalati ; bhijjati. *v.t.* phāleti ; vidāreti ; bhindati. *p.p.* phalita ; bhinna ; phālita ; vidārita ; °ita. — **forth,** ubbhijjati.

Bury, *v.t.* nikhaṇati ; bhūmiyaŋ nidahati. *p.p.* nikhāta ; bhūminihita. °**ing,** *n.* nikhaṇana ; bhūminidahana, *nt.*

Bus, *n.* mahāratha, *m.*

Bush, *n.* gumba ; pagumba, *m.* °**y,** *a.* gumbāvuta.

Bushel, *n.* aṭṭhadoṇaka, *m.*

Busily, *adv.* atanditaŋ ; analasaŋ.

Business, *n.* kammanta, *nt.* vyāpāra, *m.* jīvikāvutti, *f.* °**like,** *a.* sammāvihita.

Buskin, *n.* jaṅghapādukā, *f.*

Buss, *v.t.* cumbati. *p.p.* cumbita.

Bust, *n.* 1. uddhakāya, *m.* 2. uddhakāyapaṭimā, *f.*

Bustle, *n.* kalakala, *m.* *v.t.* ussukkāpeti. *v.i.* sasambhamo hoti. *p.p.* °pita ; °bhamībhūta.

Busy, *a.* niccappayutta ; bahukicca ; vyāvaṭa. *v.t.* vyāvaṭaŋ karoti ; kicce niyojeti. *p.p.* kiccaniyutta. °**ness,** *n.* bahukiccatā ; anokāsatā, *f.*

But, *conj.* tathā pi ; kin tu. *adv.* eva ; kevalaŋ. *prep.* vinā. **All but one,** ekaŋ vinā sabbe. **I do but jest,** ahaŋ kevalaŋ parihasāmi.

Butcher, *n.* māgavika ; pasughātaka, *m.* *v.t.* hanati, ghāteti. *p.p.* hata ; ghātita. **°'s block,** sūnā, *f.* **°'s knife,** govikattana, *nt.* **°ly,** *adv.* vadhakasadisa. **°y,** *n.* 1. pasughātana, māgavikatta ; 2. niṭṭhura-ghātana, *nt.*

Butler, *n.* gehabhaṇḍarakkhaka, *m.*

Butt, *n.* 1. kuṇṭhitakoṇa, *m.* 2. lakkha ; saravya, *nt.* 3. upahāsa ; parihāsa, *m.* *v.t.* 1. siṅgehi *or* sīsena āhanati ; 2. koṭiyā koṭiŋ ghaṭṭeti. *p.p.* °āhata ; °ṭita.

Butter, *n.* nonīta, *nt.* *v.t.* nonītena yojeti. *p.p.* nonītayojita. **°milk,** *n.* takka, *nt.* **Clarified —,** sappi, *nt.*

Butterfly, *n.* cittapaṭaṅga, *m.*

Buttock, *n.* ānisada, *m.* piṇḍikamaŋsa, *nt.*

Button, kañcukagaṇṭhi, *m.* **°hole,** gaṇṭhipāsa, *m.* *v.t.* gaṇṭhiŋ pāse paveseti *or* āvuṇāti. *p.p.* °sitapāsa ; °āvutapāsa.

Buttress, *n.* upakārikā, *f.*

Buxom, *a.* thūla ; surūpa ; sobhana ; pasanna.

Buy, *v.t.* kiṇāti. *p.p.* kīta. **°er,** *n.* ketu ; kayika, *m.*

Buzz, *n.* jhaṅkāra ; kalarava, *m.* *v.i.* jhanati ; ghumughumāyati ; kūjati. *p.p.* jhanita ; °yita ; kūjita.

By, *prep.* generally expressed by the Instrumental. *adv.* samīpe ; nikaṭe ; passe *with genitive.* **— and by,** kamena ; anupubbena, *adv.* **— the by,** aparañ ca. **— day,** divā, *adv.* **— dint of,** vāhasā, *ind.* **— means of,** nissāya ; paṭicca ; hetunā. **Day by day,** patidinaŋ, *adv.* **One by one,** ekekaso, *adv.*

Bygone, *a.* atīta ; atikkanta.

By-lane, *n.* upavīthi, *f.*

By-law, *n.* upanīti, *f.*

By-name, *n.* upādhi, *m.*

Bypath, *n.* upapatha, *m.*

Byre, *n.* goṭṭha, *nt.*

Bystander, *n.* samīpaṭṭhāyī, *m.*

Byword, *n.* janavāda, *m.* ābhāṇaka, *nt.*

Bywork, *n.* appadhānakicca, *nt.*

C

Cab, *n.* ekassaratha, *m.* *v.i.* ekassarathena yāti.

Cabal, *n.* kumantana ; gūḷhamantana, *nt.* *v.i.* kumanteti. *p.p.* °tita. **°ler,** *n.* kumantaka, *m.*

Cabbage, *n.* goḷapattikā, *f.*

Cabbala, Cabala, *n.* gūḷhavijjā, *f.*

Cabin, *n.* kuṭi, *f.* nāvovaraka, *m.* *v.t.* sambādhe vāseti. **°boy,** *n.* nāvikasevaka, *m.*

Cabinet, *n.* 1. sacivasabhā, *f.* 2. khuddakagabbha, *m.* 3. peḷāyutta-lekhanādhāra, *m.*

Cable, *n.* 1. nāvābandhaka-rajju, *f.* 2. antodaka-vijjutantu, *f.* *v.t.* 1. vijjutantuyo yojeti ; 2. vijjusāsanaŋ peseti. *p.p.* yojitavi° ; pesitavijju°. **°gram,** *n.* antodakasāsana, *nt.*

Caboodle, *n.* sakalasamūha, *m.*

Cache, *n.* gutta-paṭisāmanaṭṭhāna, *nt.*

Cachet, *n.* visiṭṭhalañchana, *nt.*

Cachinnate, *v.i.* uccaŋ hasati. °**ion,** *n.* aṭṭahāsa, *m.*

Cackle, *n.* kukkuṭīruta, *nt.* nipphalavācā, *f. v.i.* kukkuṭī viya ravati ; palapati. *p.p.* °ravita ; palapita.

Cacodemon, *n.* 1. pisāca; 2. asappurisa, *m.*

Cacography, *n.* dullikhita, *nt.*

Cacology, *n.* anucitasaddappayoga, *m.*

Cacophony, *n.* kaṭukassaratā, *f.*

Cactus, *n.* apattaka-sakaṇṭakagaccha, *m.*

Cad, *n.* gammajana, *m.*

Cadaverous, *a.* chavatulya.

Cadence, *n.* 1. parihāni, *f.* 2. sarasaṅkāmana, *nt.*

Cadet, *n.* 1. kaṇiṭṭha ; 2. ādhunikabhaṭa ; yuddhasikkhaka, *m.*

Cadge, *v.i.* (bhikkhāya) carati.

Cadger, *n.* kacchapuṭa-vāṇija, *m.*

Cadre, *n.* mūlaracanā, *f.*

Caducity, *n.* bhaṅguratta, *nt.* °**cous,** *a.* bhaṅgura.

Caesura, *n.* virāma, *m.*

Cafe, *n.* peyyamandira, *nt.*

Cage, *n.* pañjara, *m. v.t.* pañjare khipati. *p.p.* °khitta.

Cairn, *n.* citi, *f.* thūpa, *m.*

Caitiff, *n. a.* jamma ; kātara.

Cajole, *v.t.* lāleti ; upalāleti. *p.p.* °lita. °**er,** upalālaka, *m.* °**ry,** *n.* upalālanā, *f.*

Cake, *n.* pūpa ; pūva, *m.* piṭṭhakhajjaka, *nt.*

Calabash, *n.* alābu ; lābu ; tumbī, *f.*

Calamitous, *a.* anatthāvaha ; vipattikara.

Calamity, *n.* āpadā ; vipatti, *f.* vyasana, *nt.* upaddava, *m.*

Calcareous, *a.* sudhāmissaka.

Calcify, *v.t.* sudhābhāvaŋ pāpeti. *p.p.* °pita.

Calcine, *v.t.* bhasmīkaroti ; cuṇṇattaŋ pāpeti. *p.p.* °kata ; °pāpita.

Calcium, *n.* cuṇṇadhātu ; sudhā, *f.*

Calculable, *a.* saṅkheyya.

Calculate, *v.t.* 1. gaṇeti ; saṅkaleti ; 2. pamāṇeti ; nirūpeti. *p.p.* gaṇita ; °lita ; °ṇita ; °pita. °**ion,** *n.* gaṇanā ; saṅkhyā ; nirūpanā, *f.* °**or,** *n.* gaṇaka, *m.*

Calculous, *a.* asmarīsahita.

Calculus, *n.* asmarī ; muttakicchā, *f.*

Caldron, see **Cauldron.**

Calefacient, Calefactive, *a.* usumajanaka.

Calefactory, *n.* jantāghara, *nt.*

Calendar, *n.* 1. dinadassana ; pañcaṅga, *nt.* 2. nāmāvalī, *f. v.t.* nāmāni aṅketi. *p.p.* nāmaṅkita.

Calf, *n.* vaccha ; potaka, *m.* (of the leg :) jaṅghā, *f.*

Caliban, *n.* manussatiracchāna, *m.*

Calico, *n.* kappāsika, *nt.* setapaṭa, *m.* °**printing,** *n.* paṭacittakamma, *nt.*

Caliph, *n.* Mahammadikanetu, *m.*

Calix, *n.* pupphakaṇṇikā, *f.*

Call, *n.* 1. avhāna ; āmantaṇa ; 2. āṇāpana, *nt.* 3. nimantaṇa, *nt.* 4. samīpāgamaṇa, *nt.*

Call, *v.t.* 1. avhāti ; āmanteti ; pakkosati ; 2. voharati ; ākhyāti ; 3. āṇāpeti. *p.p.* avhāta ; °tita ; °sita ; voharita ; ākhyāta. *v.i.* uccāsaddaŋ karoti. — **back**, paccavheti. — **forth**, abhineti. — **names**, paribhavati. — **on**, — **upon**, sammukhībhavati. — **out**, abhiyogaŋ karoti. °**over**, nāmāni uccāreti *or* vāceti. — **to account**, anuyuñjati. — **to mind**, manasikaroti. — **to witness**, apadisati ; sakkhiŋ karoti. °**ed**, *a.* vutta ; abhihita.

Calligraphy, *n.* sundaralipi, *f.*

Calling, *n.* 1. avhāna ; pakkosana, *nt.* 2. vyāpāra ; jīvanopāya, *m.*

Callosity, *n.* kathinattacatā, *f.*

Callous, *a.* 1. kaṭhina ; kakkasa ; 2. niddaya ; niṭṭhura. °**ness**, *n.* kaṭhinatta ; kakkhalatta ; niddayatta, *nt.*

Callow, *a.* 1. ajātapatta ; 2. akovida ; aparicita.

Calm, *n.* santi, *f.* upasama ; viveka ; avikkhepa, *m.* adj. upasanta ; akkhobha ; nissadda. °**ly**, *adv.* niccalaŋ ; santatāya. °**ness**, *n.* passaddhi ; santi, *f.*

Calm, *v.t.* upasameti ; passambheti. *v.i.* sammati ; passambhati. *p.p.* upasamita ; °bhita ; santa ; passaddha.

Caloric, *n.* kāyika-usuma, *m.* uṇhatta, *nt.*

Calorific, *a.* usumajanaka ; tāpajanaka. °**ation**, *n.* usumajanana, *nt.*

Calorimeter, *n.* usumamāṇaka, *nt.*

Calumniate, *v.t.* abbhakkhāti ; abbhācikkhati. *p.p.* °khāta ; °khita. °**ion**, *n.* abbhakkhāna, *nt.* °**or**, *n.* abbhakkhāyī, *m.*

Calumnious, *a.* abbhācikkhaka. °**ly**, *adv.* micchācodanāya ; sāpavādaŋ.

Calumny, *n.* micchopavāda, *m.* abbhakkhāna, *nt.*

Calyx, see **Calix**,

Cambist, *n.* mūlavinimayakārī, *m.*

Cambric, *a. n.* dukūla ; mudusetavattha, *nt.*

Camel, *n.* oṭṭha, *m.* °**eer**, *n.* oṭṭhārohaka, *m.*

Cameleon, *n.* kakaṇṭaka, *m.*

Camera, *n.* 1. puggalikagabbha, *m.* 2. chāyārūpayanta, *nt.*

Camlet, *n.* uṇṇāvattha, *nt.*

Camp, *n.* khandhāvāra, *m.* *v.t.* senaŋ niveseti. *p.p.* niviṭṭhasena.

Campaign, *n.* 1. yuddhabhūmi, *f.* 2. yuddhāvatthā, *f.*

Camphor, *n.* kappūra ; ghanasāra, *m.* *nt.* °**ate**, *v.t.* kappūrena yojeti. *p.p.* °yojita.

Can, *v.i.* sakkoti ; sakkuṇāti. *v.t.* bhājane nidahati. *p.p.* bhājananihita. *noun* : lahubhājana ; tutthāvaraṇa, *nt.*

Canal, *n.* jalamātikā ; jalanetti, *f.* *v.t.* jalamagge sampādeti ; mātikaŋ khaṇati.

Canard, *n.* micchāpavāda, *m.*

Cancel, *v.t.* lopeti ; nisedheti. *p.p.* lutta ; nisedhita.

Cancer, *n.* 1. kakkaṭaka ; kulīra, *m.* 2. maŋsabbuda, *m.*

Candescent, *a.* atitatta; accuṇha.

Candid, *a.* avyāja ; avaṅka ; akapaṭa ; asaṭha. °**ly**, *adv.* asaṭhena ; nivyājaŋ. °**ness**, *n.* avyājatā, amāyāvitā, *f.* ajjava, *nt.*

Candidate, *n.* apekkhaka; atthika; patthetu, *m.* °**ure**, *n.* āyācanā; apekkhā, *f.*

Candle, *n.* sitthavaṭṭikā; sitthadīpikā, *f.* °**stick**, *n.* sitthadīpādhāra, *m.*

Candour, *n.* ajjava; asāṭheyya, *nt.*

Candy, *n.* khaṇḍasakkharā, *f.* *v.i.* khaṇḍikā sampādeti. *v.t.* sakkharāya āvarati. *p.p.* sakkharāvuta.

Cane, *n.* vetta, *nt.* vettalatā, *f.* *v.t.* vettehi tāḷeti. *p.p.* °ḷita. °**chair**, *n.* bhaddapīṭha, *nt.* — **mill**, *n.* ucchuyanta, *nt.*

Canicide, *n.* 1. sunakhamāraṇa, *nt.* 2. sunakhaghātaka, *m.*

Canine, *a.* sunakhāyatta ; kukkurīya. — **tooth**, *n.* dāṭhā, *f.*

Caniyar (tree), *n.* kaṇikāra ; dumuppala, *m.*

Canker, *n.* 1. nāsaka-kimi, *m.* 2. dūsana, *nt.* 3. kimiroga, *m.* *v.t.* dūseti ; vināseti. *p.p.* °sita. °**ous**, *a.* dūsaka ; nāsaka.

Cannibal, *n.* *a.* manussamaŋsakhādī ; porisādaka. °**ism**, *n.* sajātimaŋsakhādana, *nt.* °**istic**, *a.* sajātimaŋsakhādaka.

Cannon, *n.* nāḷīyanta, *nt.*—**ball**, nāḷīyanta-guḷikā, *f.* °**eer**, *n.* nāḷīyantapālaka, *m.*

Cannonade, *n.* ayoguḷavissajjana, *nt.* *v.t.* ayoguḷe vissajjeti ; nāḷīyantapahāraŋ deti. *p.p.* vissaṭṭhāyoguḷa ; dinnanāḷīyantappahāra.

Cannot (can + not), na sakkoti ; na sakkuṇāti ; na sakkā.

Canny, *a.* 1. dakkha ; catura ; 2. mitavaya.

Canoe, *n.* doṇi, *f.*

Canon, *n.* 1. dhammaganthāvali, *f.* 2. vinayapiṭaka, *nt.* niyamāvali, *f.* 3. dhammādhikārī, *m.* °**ical**, *a.* dhammānukūla ; vinayānugata. °**ically**, *adv.* yathādhammaŋ ; yathāvinayaŋ. °**ize**, *v.t.* 1. piṭakantogataŋ karoti ; 2. suddhapuggalesu gaṇeti. *p.p.* °gaṇita.

Canoodle, *v.i.* āliṅgati. *p.p.* °gita.

Canopy, *n.* vitāna ; ulloca, *nt.* *v.t.* vitānaŋ bandhati. *p.p.* baddhavitāna.

Canorous, *a.* madhurassara.

Cant, *n.* 1. padesikavohāra, *m.* 2. kohañña, *nt.* 3. visamapassa, *m.* *v.t.* 1. visamaŋ ṭhapeti ; 2. samullapati. *p.p.* °ṭhapita ; °pita.

Cantankerous, *a.* kalahakāmī. °**ness**, *n.* kalahappiyatā, *f.*

Canteen, *n.* 1. majjasālā, *f.* 2. bhaṭānam āpaṇa, *m.*

Canter, *v.i.* uppatanto gacchati. *n.* mandagati, *f.*

Canto, *n.* pariccheda ; vagga, *m.*

Canton, *n.* bhūmikhaṇḍa ; upapadesa, *m.* *v.t.* padesavasena vibhajati. °**ment,** *n.* khandhāvāra ; senāvāsabhūmi, *f.*

Canvas, *n.* makacivattha, *nt.*

Canvass, *v.t.* 1. pakkhaŋ gāheti ; chandalābhāya vāyamati ; 2. sukhumam upaparikkhati. *p.p.* gāhitapakkha ; °khita. °**er,** *n.* pakkhagāhāpaka ; chandāyācaka, *m.*

Cap, *n.* 1. sirotāṇa, *nt.* nāḷipaṭṭa, *m.* 2. pidhāna, *nt.* *v.t.* 1. sirotāṇaŋ dhāreti ; 2. upādhiŋ deti ; 3. pidahati. *p.p.* dhāritasirotāṇa ; dinnopādhika ; pihita.

Capable, *a.* samattha ; bhabba ; khama. °**ility,** *n.* bhabbatā ; samatthatā, *f.*

Capacious, *a.* visāla ; puthula ; vitthiṇṇa. °**ness,** visālatta, *nt.*

Capacitate, *v.t.* bhabbaŋ karoti ; anucchivikataŋ pāpeti. *p.p.* °pāpita.

Capacity, *n.* 1. dhāraṇasatti, *f.* sāmatthiya, *nt.* 2. thāma, *m.* 3. nītibala, *nt.*

Caparison, *n.* assakappanā, *f.* assatthara, *m.* *v.t.* kappeti ; vibhūseti. *p.p.* kappita ; vibhūsita.

Cape, *n.* 1. antarīpa, *m.* 2. uttarakāyāvaraṇa, *nt.*

Caper, *n.* laṅghana ; naccana, *nt.* *v.i.* laṅghati ; uppatati. *p.p.* °ghita ; °tita. °**er,** *n.* laṅghaka, *m.*

Capillament, *n.* kesara ; kiñjakkha, *nt.*

Capillary, *a.* kesasama. *n.* sukhuma-sirā, *f.*

Capital, *n.* 1. thambhasīsa ; 2. mūladhana, *nt.* 3. agganagara, *nt.* rājadhāni, *f.* 4. vākyamūlakkhara, *nt.* adj. mukhya ; padhāna ; seṭṭha ; pamukha. °**ly,** *adv.* mukhyavasena. — **punishment,** *n.* maraṇavadha, *m.*

Capitalism, *n.* dhanabala, *nt.*

Capitalist, *m.* mahaddhanī, *m.* °**ic,** *a.* dhanabalāyatta.

Capitation, *n.* puggalika-kara, *m.*

Capitulate, *v.* mithupaṭiññāya sattuvasaŋ gacchati. °**ion,** *n.* paṭiññāpubbaka-vasaṅgamana; paṭiññāpaṇṇa, *nt.*

Caprice, *n.* cāpalya, *nt.* icchācāra, *m.*

Capricious, *a.* lolacitta ; icchāvasagata. °**ly,** *adv.* lolākārena ; cāpallena.

Capricorn, *n.* makararāsi, *m.*

Caprine, *a.* ajasama.

Capsize, *v.i.* viparivattati ; adhomukhī bhavati. *v.t.* viparivatteti ; adhomukhīkaroti. *p.p.* °vatta ; °bhūta ; °vattita ; °kata.

Capsule, *n.* bījakosa, *m.* °**ar,** *a.* puṭākāra.

Captain, *n.* 1. senānī ; daṇḍanāyaka, *m.* 2. nāyaka ; netu ; purogāmī, *m.* 3. (of a ship), niyāmaka ; potanāyaka ; nāvāpati, *m.* *v.t.* purogāmī hoti. °**cy,** *n.* nāyakatta ; padhānatta, *nt.* nāvāpatidhura, *nt.*

Caption, *n.* 1. sahasā rundhana, *nt.* 2. lipimātikā, *f.* sīsapāṭha, *m.*

Captious, *a.* randhagavesī; ayathābhūta. °**ness,** *n.* randhagavesitā, *f.*

Captivate, *v.t.* palobheti; vasīkaroti; moheti. *p.p.* °bhita; °kata; mohita. °**ing,** *a.* palobhaka; manohara; hadayaṅgama. °**ion,** *n.* palobhana; vasīkaraṇa, *nt.*

Captive, *n.* 1. bandhanagata; kārābaddha; 2. vasībhūta. adj. dhajāhaṭa; karamarānīta. °**ity,** *n.* baddhavāsa; vasībhāva, *m.* dāsatta, *nt.*

Captor, *n.* bandhaka; rundhaka; vasavattaka, *m.*

Capture, *n.* rodhana; gahaṇa; bandhana, *nt. v.t.* rodheti; bandhati; adhigaṇhāti. *p.p.* rodhita; baddha; °gahita.

Car, *n.* ratha, *m.* sandana, *nt.*

Carafe, *n.* kāca-udakasarāva, *m.*

Carapace, *n.* kapālaṭṭhi, *nt.* kapāla, *m.*

Caravan, *n.* 1. vāṇijasattha, *m.* 2. mahāyāna, *nt.* — **leader,** satthavāha; satthanāyaka, *m.* °**sary,** °**serai,** °**sera,** *n.* pathikasālā, *f.* satthikanivāsa, *m.*

Caraway, *n.* mahājīraka, *nt.*

Carbine, *n.* rassa-agginālī, *f.*

Carbon, *n.* aṅgāradhātu, *f.* °**aceous,** *a.* aṅgāradhātuyutta. °**ic,** *a.* aṅgāraja. °**ate,** *v.t.* aṅgāradhātukaŋ karoti. °**ize,** *v.t.* aṅgārattaŋ pāpeti. *p.p.* °pāpita.

Carbuncle, *n.* 1. lohitaṅka; rattamaṇi, *m.* 2. visagaṇḍa, *m.*

Carcass, Carcase, *n.* chava; kuṇapa, *m.* matasarīra, *nt.*

Card, *n.* 1. ghanapaṭṭikā, *f.* 2. aŋsullekhanī, *f. v.t.* ullikhati; vijaṭeti. *p.p.* °khita; vijaṭita.

Cardamom, *n.* eḷā; bahulā, *f.*

Cardiac, *a.* hadayāyatta.

Cardinal, *n.* Kiṭṭhadhammādhikārī, *m.* adj. padhāna; mukhya; pamukha. — **number,** suddhasaṅkhyā, *f.* — **points,** catasso disā, *f. pl.*

Care, *n.* 1. gopana; rakkhana; pariharaṇa, *nt.* 2. sati, *f.* appamāda, *m. v.i.* avekkhati; manasikaroti; sallakkheti. *p.p.* °khita; °kata; °khita. °**laden,** °**worn,** *a.* khinna; vihesappatta. °**taker,** *n.* paripālaka, *m.* **I do not —,** ahaŋ na gaṇemi. **In his —,** tassa bhāre. **Take —,** appamatto hohi.

Career, *n.* 1. carita, *nt.* cariyā, *f.* 2. gati; pakati; pavatti, *f. v.i.* sīghaŋ dhāvati.

Careful, *a.* appamatta; sāvadhāna; satimantu. °**ly,** *adv.* sādhukaŋ; sakkaccaŋ. °**ness,** *n.* appamāda, *m.* sāvadhānatta, *nt.*

Careless, *a.* pamatta; anavadhāna. °**ly,** *adv.* anādaraŋ; asakkacca. °**ness,** *n.* anādariya, *nt.* pamāda, *m.* asakkaccakāritā, *f.*

Caress, *n.* āliṅgana; parissajana, *nt. v.t.* parāmasati; āliṅgati; apalāleti. *p.p.* parāmaṭṭha; āliṅgita; °lita.

Cargo, *n.* potabhāra, *m.* nāvāropitabhaṇḍa, *nt.*

Caricature, *n.* vikaṭacittakamma, *nt.* *v.t.* vikaṭacittam ālikhati. °**ist,** *n.* vikaṭacittasippī, *m.*

Carious, *a.* jiṇṇa; khīyamāna.

Carking, *a.* vihesājanaka.

Carline, *n.* mahallikā, *f.*

Carminative, *a.* vātanāsaka.

Carmine, *n.* lākhārasa, *m.* adj. lākhāratta.

Carnage, *n.* mahāvadha, *m.* manussaghātana, *nt.*

Carnal, *a.* sāmisa; kāmanissita; visayāyatta. — **desire,** *n.* kāmāsā; visayāsatti, *f.* °**ity,** *n.* kāmukatā, *f.* °**ly,** *adv.* kāmavasena. — **pleasure,** *n.* kāmasukha, *nt.* — **union,** *n.* methuna, *nt.* kāmasambhoga, *m.* ratikīḷā, *f.*

Carnation, *n.* 1. maŋsavaṇṇa, *m.* 2. lohitapupphajāti, *f.*

Carnification, *n.* maŋsavaḍḍhana, *nt.*

Carnival, *n.* samājussava; kīḷāchaṇa, *m.*

Carnivore, *n.* maŋsakhādī, *m.*

Carnivorous, *a.* maŋsabhakkha; maŋsādaka.

Carol, *n.* bhattigīta; ānandagīta, *nt.* *v.i.* bhattigītaŋ gāyati.

Carouse, *n.* āpānussava, *m.* *v.i.* adhikaŋ pivati; pānussavaŋ pavatteti. *p.p.* °pīta; pavattitapānussava. °**al,** *n.* pānussava, *m.*

Carp, *v.t.* dosaŋ gavesati; apavadati. *p.p.* apavutta.

Carpenter, *n.* vaḍḍhakī; thapati, *m.* °**bee,** *n.* bhamara, *m.* °'**s line,** kāḷasutta, *nt.* — **shed,** vaḍḍhakīsālā, *f.* °**ry,** *n.* vaḍḍhakīkamma, *nt.*

Carpet, *n.* kojava, *m.* bhummattharaṇa, *nt.* *v.t.* kojavehi chādeti *or* santharati. *p.p.* °chādita; santhata.

Carpus, *n.* maṇibandha, *m.*

Carriage, *n.* yāna, vayha, *nt.* ratha, *m.* °**able,** *a.* yānagamanīya. — **pole,** *n.* kubbara, *m.*

Carrier, *n.* hāraka; vāhaka; vāhī; hattu, *m.*

Carrion, *n.* kuṇapa, *m.* pūtimaŋsa, *nt.* — **eater,** *n.* kuṇapādaka, *m.*

Carry, *v.t.* harati; vahati; neti. *p.p.* haṭa; vahita; nīta. — **away,** — **off,** apaharati; apaneti. — **on,** pavatteti. — **out,** — **through,** sādheti; niṭṭhāpeti. — **over,** atiharati. — **tale,** kaṇṇe jappati; pesuññaŋ vadati.

Carrying, *n.* haraṇa; vahana, *nt.* — **away,** nīharaṇa, *nt.* — **pole,** vyābhaṅgī, *f.* kāja, *m.* — **out,** pavattāpana, *nt.*

Cart, *n.* sakaṭa, *m.* *v.t.* sakaṭena neti. *p.p.* °nīta. °**er,** *n.* sākaṭika, *m.* °**load,** *n.* sakaṭabhāra, *m.* — **rut,** *n.* cakkamagga, *m.* °**wright,** sakaṭamāpaka; rathakāra, *m.*

Cartage, *n.* sakaṭavāhamūla, *nt.*

Cartoon, *n.* vikaṭacitta, *nt.*

Carve, *v.t.* ullikhati; cundakammaŋ karoti. *p.p.* °khita; katacundakamma. °**ing,** *n.* cundakamma. *nt.* °**er,** *n.* 1. cundakāra; bhamakāra, *m.* 2. likhanasattha, *nt.*

Cascade, *n.* nijjhara, *m.*

Case, *n*. 1. (condition :) avatthā, *f*. siddhi ; dasā, *f*. 2. (covering :) kosa, *m*. sipāṭikā ; thavikā, *f*. 3. (in grammar :) vibhatti, *f*. 4. (litigation :) adhikaraṇa, *nt*. 5. (cause :) hetu, *m*. kāraṇa, *nt*. **In case**, sace ; yadi, *ind*. **In this case**, asmiŋ visaye. **In both cases**, ubhayathā pi. **If such be the case**, yajjevaŋ. **This being the case**, evaŋ sante.

Case, *v.t*. āvarati ; onandhati ; antokaroti. *p.p*. āvaṭa ; onaddha ; antokata.

Casement, *n*. gavakkha, *m*. vātapāna, *nt*.

Cash, *n*. mūla ; jātarūpa, *nt*. *v.t*. 1. mūlaŋ deti *or* gaṇhāti ; 2. jātarūpataŋ pāpeti. *p.p*. dinnamūla ; gahitamūla ; °pita.

Cashew, *n*. kacchuphala, *nt*.

Cashier, *n*. mūlapaṭiggāhaka ; dhanādhikārī, *m*. *v.t*. ṭhānantarā *or* adhikārato cāveti. *p.p*. °cāvita.

Cashmere, *n*. Kasmīrajavattha, *nt*.

Casino, *n*. mahājanaraṅgamaṇḍala, *nt*.

Cask, *n*. dārubhājana, *nt*.

Casket, *n*. karaṇḍa ; samugga ; caṅgoṭaka, *m*.

Cassava, *n*. āluvagaccha, *m*.

Cassia Fistula, *n*. rājarukkha, *m*.

Cast, *v.t*. 1. khipati ; pakkhipati ; 2. jahati ; cajati ; 3. vilīnalohena nimmiṇāti. *p.p*. khitta ; jahita ; catta ; °lohanimmita. — **aside**, paṭikkhipati ; paccakkhāti. °**away**, chaḍḍeti. — **forth**, ussajati ; vamati. — **glances**, diṭṭhiŋ pāteti. — **lots**, salākaŋ pāteti. °**ing**, *n*. khipana, *nt*. khepa, *m*. °**ing off**, nikkhepa, *m*. — **off**, apakaḍḍhati. — **out**, nikkaḍḍhati.

Cast, *n*. 1. khepa, *m*. khipana ; chaḍḍana ; pātana, *nt*. 2. paṭimā, *f*. paṭibimba, *nt*. 3. saṇṭhāna, *nt*. rūpākāra, *m*.

Castaway, *n*. *a*. bahikata ; chaḍḍitaka.

Caste, *n*. kula, *nt*. vaṇṇa, *m*. **Of the same** —, samānakulika. **Of the low** —, hīnajacca. °**less**, *a*. kulahīna.

Castigate, *v.t*. niggaṇhāti. *p.p*. niggahita. °**ion**, *n*. niggaha, *m*. niggaṇhaṇa, *nt*.

Casting vote, *n*. niṇṇaya-chanda, *m*.

Castle, *n*. duggāvāsa ; pākāragutta-pāsāda, *m*.

Castor oil, *n*. eraṇḍatela, *nt*. — **plant**, *n*. eraṇḍagaccha, *m*.

Castrate, *v.t*. bījāni uddharati ; pumbhāvam apaneti. *p.p*. uddhaṭabīja ; apanītapumbhāva.

Casual, *a*. atakkita ; āgantuka ; ninnimitta. °**ly**, *adv*. anapekkhaŋ ; avitakkitaŋ. °**ty**, *n*. āpadā, *f*. antarāya, *m*. *pl*. yuddhe patitānaŋ nāmāvali, *f*.

Casuist, *n*. dhammādhammavicāraka, *m*. °**ry**, *n*. manobhāvavicāraṇā, *f*.

Cat, *n*. biḷāla ; majjāra ; babbu, *m*. **Female** —, majjārī, *f*. °**ling**, *n*. biḷālapotaka, *m*.

Cataclasm, *n*. udrīyana, *nt*.

Cataclysm, *m*. mahāuplava ; āposaŋvaṭṭa, *m*.

Catacomb, *n*. guhāsusāna, *nt*.

Catafalque, *n*. chavakūṭāgāra ; chavādhāna, *nt*.

Catalepsy, *n*. apamāra, *m*. visaññitā, *f*. °**tic**, *n*. *a*. apasmārarogī.

Catalogue, *n*. dabbanāmāvali, *f*. *v.t*. nāmāvaliŋ sampādeti.

Catamaran, *n*. uḷumpa, *m*. paccarī, *f*.

Catameniya, *n*. thīraja, *m*.

Catapult, *n*. gophaṇa ; sakkharāvijjhaka, *nt*.

Cataract, *n*. 1. mahānijjhara, *m*. 2. akkhikāca, *m*.

Catarrh, *n*. pināsa, *m*. °**al**, *a*. pināsayutta.

Catastrophe, *n*. 1. mahāvipatti, *f*. 2. bhūgoḷikavikāra, *m*.

Catch, *v.t*. gaṇhāti ; bandhati ; rundhati. *p.p*. gahita ; baddha ; ruddha. °**able**, *a*. gahaṇūpaga. °**er**, gāhī ; bandhaka ; rodhaka, *m*. °**ing**, *n*. gahaṇa ; rodhana, *nt*. — **cold**, abhissandena rogī bhavati.

Catch, *n*. 1. gahaṇa ; bandhana ; rundhana, *nt*. 2. nivattaka ; ābandhaka ; rodhaka, *nt*. 3. (gain :) laddhalābha, *m*. 4. vañcana, *nt*. °**ment**, *n*. gaṅgādhāra, *m*.

Catchy, *a*. manohara ; sukhagayha.

Catechism, *n*. pucchāvissajjanā, *f*. kathopakathana, *nt*.

Catechize, *v.t*. pañhavissajjanena uggaṇhāpeti. *p.p*. °pita. °**er**, *n*. pañhavissajjaka, *m*.

Catechu, *n*. khadirasāra, *m*.

Categorical, *a*. 1. suvyatta ; 2. sajātyantogata. °**ly**, *adv*. supākaṭaŋ ; niyataŋ.

Category, *n*. samānavagga, *m*. vibhāga, *m*.

Catena, *n*. mālā ; āvali, *f*. °**ate**, *v.t*. āvuṇāti ; uddānīkaroti. *p.p*. āvuta ; uddanīkata. °**tion**, *n*. āvuṇana, *nt*.

Cater, *v.i*. 1. bhojanaŋ sampādeti ; 2. vinodaŋ dāpeti. *p.p*. sampāditabhojana ; dinnavinoda. °**er**, *n*. vinodadāyī, *m*. °**cousin**, *n*. dūraññāti, *m*.

Caterpillar, *n*. kosakimi ; lomasapāṇaka, *m*.

Catharsis, *n*. virecana, *nt*.

Cathartic, *a*. virecaka. *n*. virecanosadha, *nt*.

Cathedral, *n*. desappamukhadevamandira, *nt*.

Catholic, *a*. sabbasādhāraṇa. *n*. Romaka-bhattika. °**ity**, *n*. sabbasādhāraṇatta, *nt*.

Catholicon, *n*. sabbarogaharosadha, *nt*.

Cat's-eye, *n*. veḷuriya, *nt*.

Cat's paw, *n*. 1. biḷālanakhapañjara, *m*. 2. parassupakaraṇabhūta, *m*.

Cattle, *n*. go. — **fold**, *n*. gokula ; goṭṭha, *nt*. vaja, *m*. — **owner**, *n*. gomika, *m*. — **urine**, *n*. pūtimutta ; gomutta, *nt*. — **keeping**, *n*. gorakkhā, *f*. pasupālana, *nt*. °**plague**, *n*. gonāsakavyādhi, *m*.

Caudal, *a*. naṅguṭṭhākāra.

Caudle, *n*. bhesajjayāgu, *f*.

Cauldron, *n*. lohakaṭāha, *m*.

Cauliflower, *n.* goḷakapuppha, *nt.*

Causal, *a.* hetusambhūta; paccayāyatta. °**ly**, *adv.* hetuso; ṭhānaso. °**ity**, *n.* sahetukatā, *f.*

Causation, *n.* 1. hetuvāda, *m.* 2. janakatta; phaluppādana, *nt.*

Causative, *a.* hetubhūta; samuppādaka; (in gram:) hetvatthaka. — **verb**, hetvatthakriyā, *f.*

Cause, *n.* kāraṇa; nidāna; ṭhāna, *nt.* hetu; paccaya, *m.* *v.t.* 1. janeti; uppādeti; 2. kārāpeti; ussukkāpeti. *p.p.* janita; °dita; kārita; °pita. °**less**, *a.* ahetuka; heturahita; appatiṭṭha. °**lessly**, *adv.* ahetukaŋ; appatiṭṭhaŋ.

Causeway, *n.* ussāpita-magga, *m.* padikavedikā, *f.*

Causing, *a.* samuṭṭhāpaka. — **attachment**, ratikara; madanīya, *a.* — **disunion**, bhedakara, *a.* — **injury**, veyyābādhika, *a.* — **remorse**, upatāpaka, *a.*

Caustic, *n.* dāhaka. adj. dāhakara; tikhiṇa. °**ity**, *n.* jhāpakatta, *nt.*

Cauterize, *v.t.* dāhakena jhāpeti. °**ation**, *n.* khārapakkhipana, *nt.*

Caution, *n.* appamāda, *m.* sāvadhānatā, *f.* *v.t.* satim uppādeti; antarāyaŋ nivedeti. *p.p.* uppāditasati; niveditantarāya. — **money**, *n.* pāṭibhogamūla, *nt.*

Cautious, *a.* sāvadhāna; appamatta; satimantu. °**ly**, *adv.* sāvadhānaŋ. °**ness**, *n.* appamāditā; nisammakāritā, *f.*

Cavalcade, Cavalry, *n.* assārohakasenā, *f.* hayāṇīka, *nt.*

Cavalier, *n.* assārohakarakkhī, *m.*

Cave, *n.* guhā, *f.* leṇa, *nt.* *v.t.* guhaŋ khaṇati.

Cavern, *n.* darī, *f.* girigabbhara, *nt.* °**ous**, *a.* guhābahula.

Cavil, *n.* micchābhiyoga, *m.* *v.i.* micchābhiyogaŋ karoti.

Cavity, *n.* kuhara; kūpaka; bila; randha; chidda, *nt.*

Caw, *v.i.* kākarutaŋ ravati. *p.p.* ravitakākaruta.

Cayman, *n.* mahākumbhīla, *m.*

Cease, *n.* nivattana, *nt.* nivutti, *f.* *v.i.* 1. viramati; uparamati; 2. vigacchati; nivattati. *v.t.* nivatteti. *p.p.* virata; uparata; vigata; nivatta; nivattita. °**ing**, *n.* nivattana; vigamana; nirujjhana, *nt.* nirodha, *m.* °**less**, *a.* nirantara; avicchinna. °**lessly**, *adv.* niccaŋ; nirantaraŋ; satataŋ. °**lessness**, *n.* avicchinnatā, *f.*

Cecity, *n.* andhatā, *f.*

Cedar, *n.* khadira, *m.*

Cede, *v.t.* cajati; pajahati. *v.i.* apagacchati; okāsaŋ deti. *p.p.* catta; pajahita; apagata; dinnokāsa.

Ceiling, *n.* dāruvitāna, *nt.*

Celebrate, *v.t.* 1. pakāseti; pākaṭīkaroti; 2. abhitthavati; thometi; 3. ussavaŋ pavatteti. *p.p.* °sita; °kata; abhitthuta; thomita; pavattitussava. °**ed**, *a.* pasiddha; vissuta; vikhyāta; abhiññāta. °**ion**, *n.* 1. ussava; chaṇa, *m.* 2. abhitthavana, *nt.*

Celebrity, *n.* kitti, *f.* guṇaghosa; yasa *m.*

Celerity, *n.* vega; java, *m.*

Celestial, *a.* dibba; devāyatta. — **abode,** devaloka, *m.* — **city,** devanagara, *nt.* — **nymph,** devaccharā, *f.* — **river,** suranadī, *f.* — **tree,** devadduma; kapparukkha, *m.*

Celibacy, *n.* brahmacariyā, *f.* avivāhakatta, *nt.* °**bate,** *n. a.* brahmacārī; avivāhī, *m.*

Cell, *n.* 1. kuṭi, *f.* khuddakagabbha, *m.* 2. sukhumagoḷaka, *nt.*

Cellar, *n.* bhūmigabbha, *m. v.t.* bhūmigabbhe nidahati. *p.p.* °nidahita.

Cellular, *a.* sukhumagoḷapuṇṇa.

Cement, *n.* sudhālepa, *m. v.t.* sudhālepena sambandheti. *p.p.* °sambaddha.

Cemetery, *n.* susāna, *nt.*

Cenobite, *n.* samaṇa; gaṇavāsī, *m.*

Cenotaph, *n.* thūpa; cetiya, *nt.*

Cense, *v.t.* dhūpeti; dhūpena vāseti. *p.p.* dhūpita; dhūpavāsita.

Censer, *n.* dhūpakaṭāha, *m.*

Censor, *n.* upaparikkhaka; vivecaka, *m.* °**ship,** *n.* vivecakadhura, *nt.*

Censorious, *a.* dosagavesaka. °**ly,** *adv.* randhagavesanapubbakaŋ. °**ness,** *n.* chiddagavesitā, *f.*

Censure, *n.* codanā, *f.* upavāda; upārambha, *m. v.t.* upavadati; codeti; niggaṇhāti. *p.p.* upavutta; codita; niggahita. °**able,** *a.* upavajja; codetabba; gārayha. °**er,** *n.* codaka; upavādaka, *m.*

Census, *n.* janasaṅkhyālekhana, *nt.*

Cent, *n.* sataka, *nt.* (of money:) satamabhāga, *m.* **Ten per —,** dasa satamabhāgā, *m. pl.*

Centenary, *a.* satavassika. *n.* satavassikussava, *m.* °**rian,** *n.* satāyuka, *m.*

Centennial, *a.* satavassapūraka. *n.* satavassapūraṇa, *nt.* °**ly,** *adv.* satavassavārena.

Centesimal, *a.* satabhāgayutta.

Centigrade, *a.* sataŋsakayutta.

Centipede, *n.* 1. satapadī, *m.* 2. kaṇṇajalūkā, *f.*

Cento, *n.* pajjasaṅgaha, *m.*

Central, *a.* 1. majjhima; majjhavattī; 2. padhāna. °**ity,** *n.* majjhavattitā, *f.* °**ism,** *n.* majjhavattana, *nt.*

Centralize, *v.t.* vemajjhaŋ pāpeti. *p.p.* °pāpita. °**ation,** *n.* vemajjhapāpaṇa, *nt.*

Centre, Center, *n.* 1. majjha; vemajjha, *m.* 2. mūlaṭṭhāna, *nt. v.t.* samāharati; ekajjhaŋ karoti. *v.i.* samosarati. *p.p.* samāhaṭa; °kata; samosaṭa.

Centrifugal, *a.* majjhato apagantukāma.

Centripetal, *a.* majjhaŋ pattukāma.

Centuple, *n.* sataguṇita, *nt. v.t.* satena guṇeti. *p.p.* °guṇita.

Centuplicate, *v.t.* sataguṇaŋ karoti. *p.p.* sataguṇīkata.

Century, *n.* satavacchara, *nt.*

Cephalic, *a.* sīsāyatta.

Ceramic, *a.* kumbhakammāyatta. °**s,** *n.* kumbhakārasippa, *nt.*

Cereal, *n.* dhañña; sassa, *nt.* adj. dhaññāyatta.

Cerebral, *a.* matthaluṅgāyatta. — **letter,** *n.* muddhajakkhara, *nt.*

Cerebration, *n.* matthaluṅgavutti; acetanikakriyā, *f.*

Cerebrum, *n.* matthaluṅga, *m.*

Cerement, Cerecloth, *n.* sitthakavattha; chavaveṭhana, *nt.*

Ceremony, *n.* 1. ussava; chaṇa; 2. pūjāvidhi, *m.* °**ial,** *a.* pūjāvidhivisayaka. °**ious,** *a.* pūjāvidhiyutta; pūjāvidhiāsatta.

Ceroplastic, *a.* sitthakasippāyatta, *n. pl.* sitthakasippa, *nt.*

Certain, *a.* 1. niyata; nicchita; nissaŋsaya; 2. aññatara; ekacca. °**ly,** *adv.* addhā; have; dhuvaŋ; kāmaŋ; niyataŋ; ekantaŋ. °**ty,** *n.* nicchaya; asandeha, *m.* niyatatta, *nt.*

Certificate, *n.* pamāṇapaṇṇa; sāmatthiyadīpaka, *nt.* *v.t.* pamāṇapaṇṇaŋ deti. °**ion,** *n.* pamāṇīkaraṇa, *nt.*

Certify, *v.t.* saddahāpeti; pamāṇīkaroti; sāmatthiyaŋ dīpeti. *p.p.* °pita; °kata; dīpitasāmatthiya. °**ier,** *n.* pamāṇapaṇṇadāyaka; saddahāpaka, *m.*

Certitude, *n.* nicchitatta, *nt.* ekantabhāva, *m.*

Cerumen, *n.* kaṇṇamala, *nt.*

Cervical, *a.* gīvāyatta.

Cervine, *a.* sāraṅgasadisa.

Cess, *n.* kara; bali, *m.*

Cessation, *n.* nirodha; upasama; abhāva, *m.*

Cession, *n.* vissajjana; pariccajana, *nt.*

Cesspit, *n.* vaccakūpa, *m.*

Cesspool, *n.* candanikā, *f.* oligalla, *m.*

Cetacean, *n.* khīrapāyī, *m.* °**eous,** *a.* khīrapāyīgaṇāyatta.

Chafe, *v.t.* nighaŋseti; ghaṭṭeti; 2. kopeti; roseti. *p.p.* °sita; ghaṭṭita; kopita; rosita. *v.i.* 1. kuppati; kujjhati; 2. saṅkhubhati; 3. santapati. *p.p.* kupita; kuddha; °bhita; santatta. *noun*: 1. kopa; rosa, *m.* 2. saṅkhobha, *m.* 3. ghaṭṭana, *nt.*

Chaff, *n.* thusa; palāpa, *m.* *v.t.* 1. thusam apaneti; 2. palālaŋ khaṇḍeti. *p.p.* apanītathusa; khaṇḍitapalāla. °**less,** *a.* nitthusa. °**y,** *a.* bhusapuṇṇa; nipphala.

Chaffer, *v.i.* paṇopaṇaviyaŋ karoti. *n.* paṇopaṇaviyā, *f.* °**er,** *n.* kayavikkayika; vohārika, *m.*

Chagrin, *n.* āsābhaṅga; ubbega; santāpa, *m.* *v.t.* ubbejeti; santāpeti. *p.p.* °jita; °pita.

Chain, *n.* 1. saṅkhalikā, *f.* dāma; sandāna, *nt.* 2. (series:) santati; paveṇi; paramparā, *f.* — **for a dog,** gaddula, *nt.* *v.t.* nigaḷeti; sandāneti. *p.p.* °ḷita; °nita. °**less,** *a.* uddāma; niddāma.

Chair, *n.* pīṭha; āsana, *nt.* °**man,** *n.* sabhāpati, *m.* °**manship,** *n.* sabhāpatitta, *nt.*

Chair, *v.t.* dhure ṭhapeti ; pīṭhe nisīdāpeti. *p.p.* °ṭhapita ; °pita.

Chaise, *n.* sandana ; ratha, *m.*

Chalcography, *n.* tambālekhasippa, *nt.*

Chalice, *n.* casaka, *m.*

Chalk, *n.* sitopala, *nt. v.t.* sitopalena likhati. *p.p.* °likhita. **Red —,** gerukā, *f.*

Challenge, *n.* abhiyoga, *m. v.t.* kalahāya *or* vivādāya avheti ; abhiyogaŋ karoti. *p.p.* °avhita ; katābhiyoga. °**able,** *a.* abhiyogāraha. °**er,** abhiyogī ; paṭipuggala, *m.*

Chamber, *n.* gabbha ; ovaraka, *m.* **Inner —,** antogabbha, *m.* **Upper —,** uparigabbha, *m.* °**lain,** *n.* sirisayanapālaka ; rājagharapālaka, *m.* °**maid,** *n.* sayanapālikā, *f.* °**pot,** *n.* passāvabhājana, *nt.*

Chameleon, *n.* kakaṇṭaka, *m.*

Chamois, *n.* vātamiga, *m.*

Champ, *v.i.* sasaddaŋ cabbati ; romanthati. *p.p.* °bita ; °thita.

Champac, *n.* campaka-rukkha, *m.*

Champaign, *n.* vivaṭaṅgaṇa, *nt.*

Champion, *n.* vīra ; sūrayodha ; asadisa, *m. v.t.* paratthāya yujjhati. °**less,** *a.* appaṭipuggala. °**ship,** *n.* asadisavīratta, *nt.*

Chance, *n.* 1. avasara ; okāsa, *m.* avatthā, *f.* 2. niyati, *f.* bhāgadheyya, *nt. v.i.* anapekkhitaŋ sijjhati. *p.p.* °siddha. — **comer,** *n.* yadicchāyāgāmī, *m.* °**ful,** *a.* siddhibahula.

Chancellery, *n.* 1. akkhadassadhura, *nt.* 2. akkhadassakiccālaya, *m.*

Chancellor, *n.* akkhadassāmacca, *m.* °**ship,** *n.* adhikaraṇāmaccadhura, *nt.*

Chancery, *n.* uttarādhikaraṇasālā, *f.*

Chancre, *n.* upadaŋsavaṇa, *m.*

Chandelier, *n.* agghikā, *f.* dīpādhāra, *m.*

Chandler, *n.* sitthavaṭṭivāṇija, *m.*

Change, *n.* vikāra ; vipariṇāma ; aññathābhāva, *m.* ruppana ; viparivattana, *nt. v.i.* vipariṇamati ; ruppati. *v.t.* viparivatteti ; vinimeti. *p.p.* vipariṇata ; °vattita ; vinimita. °**able,** *a.* ruppanaka ; aniccasabhāva. °**ful,** *a.* viparivattamāna ; anicca. °**less,** *a.* thāvara ; avikāra. °**ling,** *n.* vinimita-dāraka, *m.*

Channel, *n.* 1. jalamātikā ; paṇālikā, *f.* vārimagga, *m.* 2. samuddasandhi, *f. v.t.* mātikaŋ khaṇati. *p.p.* khatamātika.

Chant, *n.* gīta, *nt.* gītikā, *f. v.i.* gāyati ; paṭhati. *p.p.* gāyita ; paṭhita. °**er,** *n.* 1. gāyaka, *m.* 2. dhamanavaŋsa, *m.* °**ress,** *n.* gāyikā, *f.*

Chaos, *n.* missībhāva, *m.* saṅkiṇṇatā, *f.*

Chaotic, *a.* saṅkiṇṇa ; vyākula. °**ally,** *adv.* vyākulākārena.

Chap, *n.* 1. hanukā, *f.* 2. māṇavaka ; yuva, *m.* 3. khaṇḍaphulla, *nt. v.i.* thokaŋ bhijjati. *p.p.* °bhinna.

Chapel, *n.* 1. puggalikadevaṭṭhāna, *nt.* 2. devamandire dhammasālā, *f.*

Chap-fallen, *a.* pattakkhandha; adhomukha.

Chapiter, *n.* thambhasīsa, *nt.*

Chaplain, *n.* 1. puggalika-devaṭṭhānādhikārī; 2. purohita, *m.*

Chaplet, *n.* sekhara, *m.* āvelā, *f.*

Chapman, *n.* kacchapuṭavāṇija, *m.*

Chapter, *n.* 1. pariccheda; ajjhāya; vagga, *m.* 2. (of monks :) gaṇa; kārakasaṅgha, *m.* — **house,** sīmāghara; uposathāgāra, *nt.*

Char, *v.t.* aṅgārīkaroti; īsakaŋ dahati. *p.p.* °kata; °daḍḍha.

Character, *n.* 1. sabhāva, *m.* pakati, *f.* sīla, *nt.* 2. akkhara; vaṇṇa, *nt.* 3. visesalakkhaṇa, *nt.* 4. abhiññātapuggala, *m.* °**istic,** *n.* pakati, *f.* liṅga; lakkhaṇa, *nt.* adj. sabhāvadīpaka; pakatiyāgata. °**istically,** *adv.* yathāsabhāvaŋ. °**less,** *a.* apākaṭa; avisiṭṭha.

Characterize, *v.t.* viseseti; vyañjayati. *p.p.* °sita; °jita.

Chare, Chore, *v.i.* gehasodhanādikammaŋ karoti.

Charge, *n.* 1. gahaṇappamāṇa, *nt.* 2. dhura, *nt.* bhāra, *m.* 3. samappaṇa; 4. gutti; rakkhā, *f.* 5. codanā; dosāropaṇā, *f.* 6. āṇā, *f.* 7. paṭihaṇana, *nt.*

Charge, *v.t.* 1. pūreti; āropeti; 2. niyojeti; bhāraŋ karoti; 3. codeti; abhiyuñjati. *v.i.* paṭihanati. *p.p.* pūrita; °pita; °jita; katabhāra; codita; abhiyutta; paṭihata. °**er,** *n.* 1. codaka, *m.* 2. yuddhassa, *m.*

Chariot, *n.* sandana; assaratha, *m.* — **body,** *n.* rathapañjara, *m.* — **pole,** *n.* rathadhura, *nt.* — **rug,** *n.* rathatthara, *nt.*

Charioteer, *n.* rathācariya; sūta; sārathi, *m.*

Charitable, *a.* cāgasīlī; vadaññū. °**ness,** *n.* vadaññutā; cāgasīlitā, *f.*

Charity, *n.* 1. dāna; vitaraṇa, *nt.* pariccāga, *m.* 2. dayā; anukampā, *f.*

Charlatan, *n.* 1. vikatthī; māyāvī, *m.* 2. kūṭavejja, *m.* °**ism,** *n.* vikatthanā; kūṭatikicchā, *f.*

Charm, *n.* 1. manta; vasīkaraṇa, *nt.* 2. kavaca, *m.* 3. (fascination :) manuññatā; manoharatā, *f.* kalyāṇa, *nt.* *v.t.* vasīkaroti; moheti. *p.p.* vasīkata; mohita. °**er,** *n.* palobhaka, *m.* °**ing,** *a.* cāru; manuñña; rammа; manāpa; hadayaṅgama. °**less,** *a.* nissirīka; amanāpa.

Charnel, *a.* chavāyatta. — **grove,** *n.* āmakasusāna, *nt.* °**house,** *n.* susānaghara, *nt.*

Chart, *n.* samuddālekha, *nt.* *v.t.* samuddalakkhaṇaŋ nirūpeti. *p.p.* nirūpita°

Charter, *n.* adhikārapaṇṇa, *nt.* *v.t.* adhikāraŋ deti; adhikārapaṇṇena appeti. *p.p.* dinnādhikāra; °appita.

Chary, *a.* samekkhakārī; mitabbaya. °**iness,** *n.* mitabbayatā, *f.*

Chase, *n.* 1. anubandhana; palāpana, *nt.* 2. (hunting :) migava, *m.* *v.t.* 1. anubhandhati; 2. palāpeti; 3. maggati. *p.p.* anubaddha; °pita; maggita. °**er,** *n.* anubandhaka, *m.*

Chasm, *n.* darī, *f.* bhūvivara, *nt.*

Chassis, *n.* vāhanapañjara, *m.*

Chaste, *a.* suddha ; nimmala ; anavajja ; niddosa. °**ity,** *n.* anavajjatā, *f.* anatikkamana, *nt.* — **of a husband,** sadārasantosa, *m.* — **of a wife,** patibbata, *nt.*

Chasten, *v.t.* dameti ; sodheti. *p.p.* damita ; sodhita.

Chastise, *v.t.* daṇḍeti ; tajjeti ; santajjeti ; niggaṇhāti. *p.p.* °ḍita ; °jita ; niggahita. °**er,** *n.* santajjaka ; niggahetu, *m.* °**ment,** *n.* niggaṇhana ; santajjana, *nt.*

Chat, *n.* sallāpa, *m.* niratthakakathā, *f.* *v.i.* sallapati ; sambhāsati. *p.p.* °pita ; °sita.

Chattel, *n.* jaṅgamadhana, *nt.*

Chatter, *v.i.* 1. kūjati ; 2. palapati ; pajappati. *p.p.* kūjita ; °pita. *noun* : palāpa, *m.* kūjana, *nt.* °**er,** *n.* pajappaka ; vikatthaka, *m.*

Chatty, *n.* cāṭi, *f.* mattikābhājana, *nt.*

Chauffer, *n.* pārihāriya-uddhana, *nt.*

Chauffeur, *n.* sārathī ; rathapājaka, *m.*

Cheap, *a.* appaggha ; °**ly,** *adv.* appamūlena. °**ness,** *n.* appagghatā, *f.*

Cheapen, *v.t.* agghaŋ osādeti. *p.p.* osāditaggha.

Cheat, *n.* saṭha ; vañcaka ; nekatika, *m.* *v.t.* vañceti ; palambheti. *p.p.* vañcita ; °bhita. °**ing,** *n.* nikati ; vañcanā, *f.* sāṭheyya, *nt.*

Check, *n.* 1. nivattana ; nivāraṇa ; sannirumbhana, *nt.* 2. samānana, *nt.* *v.t.* 1. nivāreti ; nivatteti ; nirumbheti. 2. samāneti ; upaparikkhati. *p.p.* °rita ; °tita ; °bhita ; °nita ; °khita. °**er,** *n.* 1. paṭisedhaka ; 2. ūnādhikatta-pariyesaka, *m.*

Checkmate, *v.t.* parājeti. *p.p.* °jita.

Cheek, *n.* kapola ; kaṭa, *m.*

Cheeky, *a.* dubbinīta ; mukhara.

Cheer, *n.* 1. hāsa ; tosa, *m.* 2. sādhukāra ; jayaghosa, *m.* *v.t.* hāseti ; toseti ; pamodeti. *p.p.* hāsita ; °dita. *v.i.* tussati ; nandati ; pamodati. *p.p.* tuṭṭha ; °dita. °**ful,** *a.* sumana ; haṭṭhacitta ; sānanda. °**fulness,** *n.* attamanatā ; santuṭṭhi, *f.* °**less,** *a.* dummana ; asantuṭṭha. °**lessness,** *n.* dummanatā ; asantuṭṭhi, *f.* °**ily,** *adv.* tuṭṭhākārena ; sānandaŋ. °**y,** *a.* attamana ; pamudita.

Cheese, *n.* loṇika-nonīta, *nt.* °**monger,** *n.* loṇikanonītavikkayī, *m.* °**paring,** *a.* kadariya ; luddha.

Cheetah, *n.* ajina-dīpi, *m.*

Chemical, *a.* rasāyanika. — **compound,** rasāyana, *nt.*

Chemist, *n.* rasāyanavidū, *m.* °**ry,** rasāyanavijjā, *f.*

Cheque, *n.* dhanapaṇṇa, *nt.*

Chequer, *n.* sāriphalaka, *m.* *v.t.* caturassa-maṇḍalāni karoti ; nānāvaṇṇena citteti. *p.p.* katacatu° ; °tita.

Cherish, *v.t.* 1. mamāyati ; 2. niveseti ; saŋvaḍḍheti. *p.p.* °yita ; °sita ; °ḍhita. °**er,** posaka ; gopaka, *m.* — **hatred,** veraŋ bandhati; upanandhati. — **love,** mettāyati.

Cheroot, *n.* dhūmavaṭṭikā, *f.*

Cherub, *n.* devadūta, *m.* °**ic,** *a.* dibba.

Chess, *n.* aṭṭhāpadakīḷā ; caturaṅgakīḷā, *f.* °**board,** sāriphalaka, *m.*

Chest, *n.* 1. peḷā, *f.* 2. ura, *m.*

Chestnut, *n.* tambavaṇṇaphala, *nt.* tambaphala-rukkha, *m.*

Chevalier, *n.* vīra-assārohaka, *m.*

Chevy, *n.* migava, *m.* *v.t.* anubandhati. *p.p.* anubaddha.

Chew, *v.t.* cabbati ; saṅkhādati. *p.p.* °bita ; °dita. — **the cud,** romanthati. *p.p.* °thita.

Chicanery, *n.* vyājavacana, *nt.*

Chick, *n.* sakuṇapotaka, *m.* °**peas,** canaka, *m.*

Chicken, *n.* kukkuṭacchāpa, *m.* °**hearted,** *a.* bhīruka ; mandadhitika. °**pox,** *n.* khuddakamasūrikā, *f.*

Chide, *v.t.* tajjeti ; paribhāsati. *p.p.* tajjita ; °sita.

Chief, *a.* padhāna ; jeṭṭha ; mukhya. *n.* issara ; īsa ; adhipati ; nāyaka ; netu, *m.* °**ly,** *adv.* padhānavasena ; visesato. — **minister,** mahāmatta, *m.* — **object,** paramattha, *m.* °**tain,** *n.* gaṇādhipa, *m.*

Chignon, *n.* dhammilla, *m.*

Child, *n.* bālaka ; dāraka ; kumāraka, *m.* °**bed,** *n.* pasūtisamaya, *m.* °**birth,** *n.* pasūti, *f.* °**hood,** *n.* bālya, *nt.* °**ish,** *a.* bālocita. °**less,** *a.* vañjha ; aputtaka. °**like,** *a.* bālasadisa ; niddosa.

Children, *m. pl.* dārakā.

Chill, *n.* sīta, *nt.* sītaroga, *m.* *v.t.* sītalīkaroti ; viriyaŋ hāpeti. *p.p.* °kata ; hāpitaviriya. °**y,** *a.* sītala. *adv.* mandussāhena.

Chilli, *n.* marica, *nt.*

Chime, *n.* samavādana ; anukūlavādita, *nt.*

Chimera, *n.* atathaparikappana ; abbhutavatthu, *nt.* °**ical,** *a.* cintāmaya.

Chimney, *n.* dhūmaniggama, *m.* dhūmanāḷikā, *f.*

Chimpanzee, *n.* manussavānara, *m.*

Chin, *n.* cubuka, *nt.*

China, *n.* Cīnaraṭṭha, *nt.* — **rose,** bandhujīvaka, *m.* °**ware,** setamattikābhaṇḍa, *nt.*

Chine, *n.* piṭṭhikaṇṭaka, *nt.*

Chinese, *a.* Cīnadesīya. *n.* Cīnajātika, *m.*

Chink, *n.* vivara, *nt.* *v.i.* kiṇikiṇāyati. *v.t.* chiddāni karoti. *p.p.* °yita ; katachidda.

Chip, *n.* sakalikā, *f.* *v.t.* 1. tacchati ; 2. khaṇḍeti ; sakalīkaroti. *p.p.* tacchita ; °ḍita ; °kata. — **axe,** *n.* vāsi ; tacchanī, *f.* °**per,** *n.* tacchaka, *m.*

Chippy, *a.* nirassāda ; kopabahula.

Chirp, *v.i.* 1. kūjati ; 2. sallapati. *p.p.* kūjita ; °pita. °**y**, *a.* pītiyutta.

Chirr, Chirrup, *v.i.* dīghaŋ kūjati ; salabho viya nadati.

Chisel, *n.* nikhādana, *nt.* *v.t.* nikhādanena chindati. *p.p.* °chinna.

Chit, *n.* 1. pattikā, *f.* 2. aṅkura, *m.* 3. kisā itthī, *f.* °**chat**, *n.* sallahuka-kathā ; jappanā, *f.*

Chivalrous, *a.* sūra ; vīra ; vikkamayutta.

Chivalry, *n.* vikkama; parakkama, *m.* vīratta, *nt.*

Chloroform, *n.* visaññīkarabhesajja, *nt.* *v.t.* visaññīkaroti. *p.p.* °kata.

Chock, *n.* nivattaka-dārukhaṇḍa, *nt.* *v.t.* dārukhaṇḍena nivatteti. *p.p.* °tita.

Choice, *n.* 1. uccinana, *nt.* 2. ruci ; abhilāsā, *f.* adj. visiṭṭha ; ukkaṭṭha. — **of a husband**, sayaŋvara, *m.*

Choir, *n.* gāyakagaṇa, *m.* *v.i.* gaṇasajjhāyaŋ karoti.

Choke, *v.t.* kaṇṭham uppīḷeti ; sāsam avarodheti. *v.i.* sāso avarujjhati. *p.p.* uppīḷitakaṇṭha ; avaruddhasāsa.

Choler, *n.* 1. pitta, *nt.* 2. kopa, *m.*

Cholera, *n.* visūcikā, *f.*

Choleric, *a.* kodhana.

Choose, *v.t.* uccināti ; roceti. *p.p.* uccinita ; rocita. °**er**, *n.* uccinaka ; rocetu, *m.*

Chop, *n.* sakalikā, *f.* *v.t.* tacchati ; sakalīkaroti. *p.p.* tacchita ; °kata. °**ping**, *n.* tacchana, *nt.* °**per**, *n.* 1. govikatta, *nt.* 2. tacchaka, *m.* °**house**, *n.* lahubhojaṇāgāra, *nt.*

Choppy, *a.* kampanasīla ; athira.

Choral, *a.* gāyakagaṇāyatta.

Chord, *n.* tantu, *m.* tanta, *nt.* *v.t.* tantāni yojeti. °**al**, *a.* tantusambandha.

Chorion, *n.* gabbhāsaya ; jalābu, *m.*

Chorister, *n.* gaṇagāyaka, *m.*

Chorography, *n.* padesa-cittālekha, *m.*

Chorus, *n.* 1. anugāyana, *nt.* 2. anugāyakagaṇa, *m.*

Chouse, *n.* vañcanā, *f.* *v.t.* vañceti. *p.p.* vañcita.

Chowrie, *n.* cāmara, *nt.* vāḷavījanī, *f.*

Chrestomathy, *n.* uddhaṭapāṭhasaṅgaha, *m.*

Christ, *n.* Kiṭṭha-devaputta, *m.* °**ian**, *n.* Kiṭṭhabhattika, *m.* °**mas**, *n.* Kiṭṭhajamma, *nt.*

Christen, *v.t.* 1. udakam ogāheti ; 2. nāmaŋ ṭhapeti. *p.p.* ogāhitodaka ; ṭhapitanāma. °**dom**, *n.* Kiṭṭhabhattikadesa, *m.*

Christianity, *n.* Kiṭṭhabhatti, *f.* Kiṭṭhasamaya, *m.*

Chromatic, *a.* vaṇṇasampanna.

Chronic, *a.* cirappavatta ; anusāyika ; nidhānagata.

Chronicle, *n.* purāvuttakathā, *f.* *v.t.* itihāsaŋ likhati. °**er**, *n.* itihāsalekhaka, *m.*

Chronology, *n.* kālanicchayavijjā, *f.* °**ical,** *a.* kālānugata. °**ist,** *n.* kālaniṇṇayakārī, *m.*

Chronometer, *n.* kālamāṇkayanta, *nt.* °**try,** *n.* kālamāṇa, *nt.* °**trical,** *a.* kālamāṇāyatta.

Chrysoberyl, *n.* mandapītamaṇi, *m.*

Chrysolite, *n.* tiṇamaṇi, *m.*

Chubby, *a.* pīṇa ; pīvara.

Chuck, *n.* kukkuṭavhāna, *nt.* *v.t.i.* agāravam ācarati ; cubukam āhanati.

Chuckle, *n.* 1. kukkuṭīrava, *m.* 2. mandahāsa, *m.* *v.i.* mandaŋ hasati ; 2. kukkuṭī viya ravati. °**headed,** *a.* mandabuddhika.

Chum, *n.* piyamitta ; sahavāsī, *m.*

Chump, *n.* jaḷa ; eḷamūga, *m.*

Chunnam, *n.* sudhācuṇṇa, *nt.*

Church, *n.* devāyatana, *nt.*

Churl, *n.* nihīna ; gamma, *m.* °**ish,** *a.* nīca ; adhama.

Churn, *v.t.* mathati ; abhimanthati ; āviñjati. *p.p.* mathita ; °thita ; āviddha. °**ing,** *n.* mathana, *nt.* °**ing stick,** *n.* mantha, *m.*

Chute, *n.* adhomukhā parikhā *or* panāḷikā, *f.*

Chyme, *n.* jiṇṇāhāra, *m.*

Cicatrice, Cicatrix, *n.* vaṇacinha, *nt.*

Cicatrize, *v.t.* vaṇaŋ rūheti *or* pūrāpeti. *p.p.* rūḷhavaṇa.

Cider, *n.* phala-majjavisesa, *m.*

Cigar, Cigarette, *n.* dhūmavaṭṭikā, *f.*

Cilia, *n.* pakhuma, *nt.*

Cilice, *n.* kesakambala, *nt.*

Cimmerian, *a.* bahalandhakāra.

Cincture, *n.* rasanā ; mekhalā, *f.*

Cinder, *n.* aṅgāra, *m.*

Cinema, *n.* calacittāgāra, *nt.* °**tograph,** *n.* calacittayanta, *nt.* °**tography,** *n.* calacittavijjā, *f.*

Cinerary, *a.* bhasmāyatta.

Cinnabar, *n.* hiṅgula, *nt.*

Cinnamon, *n.* tacagandhī, *m.*

Cinque, *n.* pañcaka, *nt.*

Cipher, *n.* 1. saṅkhyāṅka, *nt.* 2. bindu, *m.* *v.t.* aṅketi ; aṅkāni likhati. *p.p.* aṅkita ; likhitaṅka.

Circa, *n.* vassagaṇanā, *f.*

Circle, *n.* cakka ; parivaṭṭa ; maṇḍala. *v.t.* paribbhameti. *v.i.* paribbhamati ; anuparivattati. *p.p.* °mita ; °tita. — **of rebirths,** saŋsāravaṭṭa, *nt.*

Circlet, *n.* 1. sīsābharaṇa ; 2. khuddaka-maṇḍala, *nt.*

Circuit, *n.* 1. paridhi, *f.* nemimaṇḍala, *nt.* 2. pariyaṭana ; padesāṭana, *nt.* °**ous,** *a.* vaṅkagatika ; anujuka.

Circular, *a.* maṇḍalākāra. *noun* : nivedanapaṇṇa, *nt.* — **road,** parihārapatha, *m.* °**ity,** *n.* vaṭṭulatā, *f.* °**ly,** *adv.* vaṭṭulākārena.

Circulate, *v.t.* pacāreti ; nivedeti. *v.i.* vaṭṭe paribbhamati. *p.p.* °rita ; °dita ; °paribbhanta. °**ion,** *n.* paribbhamaṇa, *nt.* °**ive,** *a.* paribbhamaka. °**tor,** *n.* pacāraka ; bhamāpaka, *m.* °**tory,** *a.* paribbhamaṇāyatta.

Circum, *prep.* parito ; samantā. °**navigate,** *v.t.* parito nāvāya carati.

Circumambulate, *v.i.* padakkhiṇaŋ karoti ; anupariyāti. *p.p.* katapadakkhiṇa ; °yāta. °**ion,** padakkhiṇā, *f.* paritogamaṇa, *nt.*

Circumcise, *v.t.* cammaggaŋ chindati. *p.p.* cinna-cammagga. °**ion,** *nt.* cammaggachedana, *nt.*

Circumference, *n.* paridhi, *f.* parivesa ; āvaṭṭa, *m.*

Circumfluent, *a.* sabbato sandamāna. °**ence,** *n.* sabbato abhissandana, *nt.*

Circumfluous, *a.* jalamajjhagata ; samantodaka.

Circumfuse, *v.t.* parivyāpeti. *p.p.* °pita. °**ion,** *n.* samantā vyāpana, *nt.*

Circumgyrate, *v.i.* parito bhamati. *p.p.* °bhanta.

Circumjacent, *a.* samantā patiṭṭhita.

Circumlocution, *n.* vācābāhulla, *nt.* vaṅkutti, *f.*

Circumscribe, *v.t.* pamāṇeti ; paricchindati. *p.p.* °ṇita ; paricchinna. °**er,** *m.* paricchindaka, *m.*

Circumscription, *n.* paricchindana ; sīmāṭhapana, *nt.*

Circumspect, *a.* samantadassī ; samekkhakārī. °**ion,** *n.* vīmaŋsā ; upaparikkhā, *f.* °**ly,** *adv.* sāvadhānaŋ ; nisamma.

Circumstance, *n.* 1. avatthā ; dasā ; siddhi, *f.* 2. vuttanta, *m.* **According to —,** yathāsambhavaŋ, *adv.* **In bad —s,** dukkhita, *a.* **In good —s,** sukhita, *a.* **Under any —s,** yena kenaci ākārena.

Circumstantial, *a.* āvatthika ; āgantuka. °**ly,** *adv.* āvatthikavasena.

Circumvallate, *v.t.* pākārena parikkhipati. *p.p.* pākāraparikkhitta. °**ion,** *n.* pākāraparikkhipana, *nt.*

Circumvent, *v.t.* vañceti ; palambheti. *p.p.* °cita ; °bhita.

Circumvolution, *n.* samantā paribbhamaṇa, *nt.*

Circus, *n.* kīḷāmaṇḍala, *nt.* abbhuta-kīḷā, *f.*

Cistern, *n.* jalāsaya, *m.*

Citadel, *n.* dugganagara, *nt.*

Cite, *v.t.* 1. āṇāpeti ; 2. uddharitvā paṭhati ; udāharati. *p.p.* °pita ; °paṭhita ; udāhaṭa. °**able,** *a.* udāharaṇīya. °**ation,** *n.* nidassana ; paṭhana, *nt.*

Citizen, *n.* nāgarika ; puravāsī, *m.*

Citron, *n.* dantasaṭha, *m.*

City, *n.* pura ; nagara, *nt.* purī ; nagarī, *f.* **— belle,** *n.* nagarasobhinī, *f.* **— gate,** *n.* nagaradvāra ; gopura, *nt.* **— wall,** *n.* pākāra, *m.*

Civet, *n.* gandha-majjāra, *m.*

Civic, *a.* porī ; nāgarika.

Civil, *a.* 1. mahājanika ; 2. susīla ; piyaŋvada. °**ian,** *n.* ayujjhakajana, *m.* °**ity,** *n.* sosīlya, *nt.* sadācāra, *m.* °**ly,** *adv.* yathāpaññattaŋ ; sabbhākārena.

Civilization, *n.* siṭṭhācāratā ; sabbhatā, *f.*

Civilize, *v.t.* sadācāre vineti; siṭṭhataŋ pāpeti. *p.p.* °vinīta; °pāpita.

Clack, *v.i.* kharasaddaŋ pavatteti; pajappati. *p.p.* °pita.

Clad, *p.p.* nivattha.

Claim, *v.t.* dahati; sakīyattaŋ ñāpeti. *p.p.* dahita; ñāpitasakīyatta. *n.* 1. āyācanā; 2. sakattapaṭipādanā, *f.* °**ant,** *n.* abhiyācaka, *m.*

Clairaudience, *n.* dibbasota, *m.*

Clairvoyance, *n.* dibbacakkhu, *nt.* °**nt,** *n.* dibbacakkhuka, *m.*

Clamant, *a.* ugghosaka; mukhara.

Clamber, *v.i.* āyāsena āruhati. *p.p.* °ārūḷha.

Clammy, *a.* allīyanasabhāvaka.

Clamour, *n.* ugghosa; mahārava; ninnāda, *m.* *v.i.* ugghoseti; unnadati. *p.p.* °sita; °dita. °**ous,** *a.* ugghosaka; unnādī. °**ously,** *adv.* mahāravena; sanigghosaŋ.

Clamp, *n.* sambandhaka; daḷhīkara, *m.* *v.t.* khīlena sambandheti. *p.p.* khīlasambaddha.

Clan, *n.* gotta; kula, *nt.* vaŋsa, *m.* °**sman,** *n.* kulaputta, *m.*

Clandestine, *a.* gūḷha; rāhaseyyaka; paṭicchanna. °**ly,** *adv.* gūḷhākārena.

Clang, *n.* jhaṅkāra, *m.* *v.i.* saṇati; jhanati. *p.p.* °ṇita. °**ourous,** *a.* jhaṅkārayutta.

Clank, *n.* kiṅkiṇisadda, *m.* *v.i.* kiṇikiṇāyati.

Clap, *v.t.* saṅghaṭṭeti; tāḷeti. *v.i.* (hands:) appoṭheti; (wings:) vidhunāti. *p.p.* °ṭita; tāḷita; °ṭhita; °nita. *n.* saṅghaṭṭana; tāḷana; appoṭhana, *nt* °**per,** *n.* vādaka; saṅghaṭṭaka, *m.*

Clapperclaw, *v.t.* 1. vilikhati; 2. niranukampaŋ nindati. *p.p.* °khita; °dita.

Claptrap, *n.* pasaŋsatthikakathā, *f.*

Clarification, *n.* nimmalīkaraṇa; visodhana, *nt.*

Clarify, *v.t.* sodheti; visodheti; vimalīkároti. *p.p.* °dhita; °kata. *v.i.* visujjhati; nimmalībhavati. *p.p.* visuddha; °bhūta.

Clarity, *n.* nimmalatta, *nt.* visuddhi; suddhi, *f.*

Clash, *n.* ghaṭṭana, *nt.* virodha; viggaha, *m.* *v.t.* ghaṭṭeti; āhanati. *v.i.* virujjhati; vivadati. *p.p.* ghaṭṭita; āhata; viruddha; vivadita. °**ing,** *a.* paṭihaññamāna; ghaṭṭiyamāna.

Clasp, *n.* 1. āliṅgana; parissajana, *nt.* 2. sambandhaka, *m.* *v.t.* 1. āliṅgati; parissajati; 2. sambandheti; veṭheti. *p.p.* °gita; parissaṭṭha; °dhita; veṭhita. —**hands,** pāṇiŋ gaṇhāti.

Class, *n.* seṇi; panti, *f.* vagga; sissagaṇa, *m.* *v.t.* vaggavasena vibhajati. *p.p.* °vibhatta. °**fellow,** °**mate,** *n.* sahasikkhaka, *m.*

Classic, *n.* mahāpaññānaŋ ganthāvali, *f.* °**al,** *a.* seṭṭhaganthāyatta.

Classify, *v.t.* pantivasena bhājeti. *p.p.* °bhājita. °**ication,** *n.* vibhatti, *f.* vibhaṅga, *m.*

Clatter, *n.* kala-kalanāda, *m.* *v.i.* unnadati ; kaṭakaṭāyati.

Clause, *n.* 1. khaṇḍa-vākya, *nt.* 2. nītikhaṇḍa, *nt.*

Claustral, *a.* ārāmapaṭibaddha.

Clavate, Claviform, *a.* muggarākāra.

Clavicle, *n.* gīvaṭṭhi, *nt.*

Claw, *n.* pasunakha ; nakhapañjara, *m.* *v.t.* nakhehi vilikhati. *p.p.* °khita. — **of a crab,** aḷa, *m. nt.*

Clay, *n.* mattikā, *f.* **Made of —,** mattikāmaya, *a.* — **vessel,** āmattika, *nt.* °**ish,** *a.* mattikābahula.

Clean, *a.* suddha ; vimala ; amala ; nimmala ; accha ; pasanna. *v.t.* sodheti ; visodheti ; puṇāti ; pariyodapeti. *p.p.* °dhita ; pūta ; °pita. *adv.* paripuṇṇaŋ ; aparisesaŋ. °**handed,** niddosa, *a.* °**liness,** *n.* sucitā ; nimmalatā, *f.* °**ly,** *adv.* parisuddhākārena. adj. amalinasabhāva. — **slate,** sabbadosamuttatā, *f.* — **sweep,** puṇṇa-nidāsatta, *nt.*

Cleanse, *v.t.* see **Clean,** *v.t.* °**ing,** *n.* visodhana ; vodapana ; puṇana, *nt.* adj. vodapaka ; parisodhaka.

Clear, *a.* 1. pasanna ; anāvila ; nimmala ; 2. visada ; pākaṭa ; nijjaṭa ; 3. amissa ; 4. asambādha. *v.t.* 1. see **Clean,** *v.t.* 2. visadīkaroti ; nijjaṭīkaroti ; 3. apaneti. *p.p.* °kata ; apanīta. *v.i.* 1. sujjhati ; 2. apagacchati. *p.p.* suddha ; apagata. — **a debt,** iṇaŋ sodheti. — **a doubt,** kaṅkhaŋ vinodeti. — **from the husk,** tacam apaneti ; nitthusam karoti. °**ly,** *adv.* suvisuddhaŋ ; nijjaṭaŋ. °**ness,** *n.* suddhatā ; nimmalatā ; pākaṭatā, *f.* — **oneself,** attānam anavajjaŋ karoti. — **one's throat,** ukkāsati. °**ance,** *n.* 1. sodhana ; 2. apagamana ; 3. nibbāhana, *nt.* °**ing,** *n.* 1. sodhana ; 2. visadīkaraṇa ; 3. sodhita-bhūkhaṇḍa, *m.*

Cleat, *n.* khīlaka, *nt.*

Cleavage, *n.* dārī, *f.* vivara, *nt.*

Cleave, *v.t.* phāleti ; vidāreti. *p.p.* °lita ; °rita. *v.i.* āsajjati ; laggati. *p.p.* āsatta ; lagga. °**ing,** *n.* 1. vidāraṇa ; phālana ; 2. sajjana, *nt.* saṅga, *m.*

Cleaver, *n.* maŋsakantaka, *m.*

Cleft, *n.* vivara ; phullaṭṭhāna, *nt.*

Cleg, *n.* piṅgalamakkhikā, *f.*

Clemency, *n.* dayā ; anukampā ; karuṇā, *f.*

Clement, *a.* dayālu ; kāruṇika. °**ly,** *adv.* sadayaŋ ; sakaruṇaŋ.

Clench, *v.t.* santhambheti. *p.p.* °bhita. — **the first,** muṭṭhiŋ saṅkoceti.

Clergy, *n.* samaṇagaṇa, *m.* °**man,** *n.* samaṇa ; sāmayikācariya, *m.*

Clerical, *a.* 1. sāmaṇaka ; pabbajitāyatta ; 2. lekhakāyatta. — **error,** lipidosa, *m.*

Clerk, *n.* lekhaka ; lipikāra, *m.*

Clever, *a.* dakkha ; cheka ; kusala ; catura ; kovida ; paṭu ; nipuṇa. °**ly,** *adv.* dakkhākārena.

°**ness**, *n*. pāṭava ; kosalla ; cāturiya ; nepuñña, *nt*. (in learning :) veyyattiya, *nt*.

Client, *n*. 1. nissitaka ; anuyutta ; 2. abhiyojaka, *m*.

Cliff, *n*. pabbatasikhara ; papātataṭa, *m*.

Climate, *n*. 1. utuguṇa ; desaguṇa, *m*. 2. padesa, *m*. °**ic**, *a*. desaguṇāyatta. °**ically**, *adv*. desaguṇavasena. °**ology**, *n*. utuguṇavijjā, *f*.

Climax, *n*. pariyanta, *m*. antimāvatthā, *f*. *v.i*. pariyantaŋ pappoti. *p.p*. °patta.

Climb, *v.t*. āruhati ; abhiruhati ; ārohati. *p.p*. ārūḷha ; abhirūḷha. °**er**, *n*. 1. ārohaka, *m*. 2. latā, *f*. °**ing**, *n*. āruhana, *nt*.

Clinch, see **Clench**.

Cling, *v.i*. āsajjati ; allīyati ; laggati ; nivisati. *p.p*. āsatta ; allīna ; lagga ; niviṭṭha. °**ing**, *n*. sajjana ; laggana, *nt*. adj. visatta ; pagiddha.

Clinic, *n*. bāḷhagilāna, *m*. °**al**, *a*. gilānasayanāyatta.

Clink, *n*. 1. kārāghara, *nt*. 2. kiṇikiṇisadda, *m*. *v.i* kiṇikiṇāyati. *p.p*. °yita.

Clip, *v.t*. agge chindati. *p.p*. aggacchinna. *n*. aggachindana, *nt*. °**per**, *n*. chindaka, *m*. kattarikā, *f*. °**ping**, *n*. 1. chinnavatthu, *nt*. 2. ch ndana; kappana, *nt*.

Clitoria, *n*. aparājitā ; girikaṇṇī, *f*.

Cloak, *n*. pāpuraṇa, *nt*. kañcuka; pāvāra, *m*. — **seller**, pāvārika, *m*. *v.i*. pārupati ; paridahati. *p.p*. pāruta ; °hita.

Clock, *n*. yāmanāḷī, *f*. ghaṭikāyanta ; horālocana, *nt*. — **tower**, ghaṭikāthambha, *m*.

Clod, *n*. leḍḍu ; mattikākhaṇḍa, *m*. *v.t*. leḍḍunā paharati. *p.p*. °pahaṭa.

Clog, *n*. 1. bādhaka ; bandhana, *nt*. 2. pāsa ; nigaḷa, *m*. 3. kaṭṭhapādukā, *f*. *v.t*. bādhati ; rundhati ; paṭibāhati. *p.p*. bādhita ; ruddha ; paṭibāhita. °**gy**, *a*. lagganasīla.

Cloister, *n*. assama ; tāpasārāma ; vihāra, *m*. *v.t*. assame vāseti. *p.p*. °vāsita.

Close, *n*. 1. osāna ; pariyanta, *m*. 2. niṭṭhāna, *nt*. nipphatti, *f*. 3. pidahana, *nt*. 4. āvaritaṭṭhāna, *nt*. adj. 1. āsanna ; samīpa ; 2. pihita ; saŋvuta ; āvaṭa ; 3. sambādha ; 4. ekābaddha ; 5. vivitta ; 6. daḷha ; 7. vissattha ; 8. ekagga. — **behind**, anupadaŋ, *adv*. — **by**, samīpe. — **connection**, upanibandha, *m*. °**ly**, *adv*. nirantaraŋ ; daḷhaŋ ; āsannataraŋ. °**ness**, 1. samīpatta ; 2. āvaṭatta ; 3. sambādhatta ; 4. nivātatta ; 5. daḷhatta, *nt*.

Close, *v.t*. 1. pidahati ; thaketi ; āvarati ; (eyes :) nimīleti ; 2. niṭṭhāpeti ; samāpeti ; osāpeti ; 3. chādeti ; onayhati. *p.p*. pihita ; thakita ; āvaṭa ; °lita ; °pita ; °dita *or* channa ; onaddha. *v.i*. saṅgacchati ; samāgacchati ; 2. niṭṭhāti ; 3. pithīyati. *p.p*. saṅgata ; niṭṭhita ;

pihita. — **fisted**, amuttacāga; maccharī, *a.* — **fistedness**, *n.* amuttacāgatā. — **upon**, niṭṭhāpeti; paripūreti. — **with**, ekamatikataŋ yāti.

Closet, *n.* kuṭikā, *f.* koṭṭhaka, *nt.* *v.t.* mantanāya antokuṭiŋ paveseti. **Bathing** —, nahānakoṭṭhaka, *nt.*

Closure, *n.* 1. pidahana; thakana, *nt.* 2. niṭṭhāpana, *nt.*

Clot, *n.* ghanapiṇḍa, *m.* guḷikā, *f.* *v.i.* piṇḍībhavati; ghanīyati. *p.p.* °bhūta.

Cloth, *n.* vattha; ceḷa; dussa, *nt.* coḷa; paṭa; sāṭaka, *m.* — **of fibre**, khoma, *nt.* — **of cotton**, kappāsika, *nt.* °**less**, *a.* acelaka; nagga. **New** —, ahatavattha, *nt.* **Old** —, nantaka, *nt.* **Silk** —, koseyya, *nt.* **Woolen** —, kambala, *nt.*

Clothe, *v.t.* nivāseti; acchādeti; paridahati. *p.p.* nivattha; °dita; °hita. *n.* acchādana, *nt.* °**ing**, *n.* paridahana, *nt.*

Clothes, *n. pl.* nivāsana-pārupaṇa, *nt.*

Cloud, *n.* valāhaka; ambuda; jaladhara; jalada; meghapaṭala, *m.* — **of dust**, rajakkhandha, *m.* — **of smoke**, dhūmarāsi, *m.* °**ed**, *a.* meghacchanna. °**less**, *a.* vigatavalāhaka.

Cloud, *v.t.* āvarati; paṭicchādeti; andhīkaroti. *p.p.* āvaṭa; °dita; °kata. °**y**, *a.* valāhakayutta. °**y day**, duddina, *nt.* °**iness**, *n.* apākaṭatā; meghacchannatā, *f.*

Clough, *n.* kandara, *m.*

Clout, *n.* kappaṭa, *m.* nantaka, *nt.*

Clove, *n.* lavaṅga, *nt.*

Cloven, *a.* dvidhā-bhinna. — **footed**, *a.* sakhura.

Clown, *n.* 1. hāsaka; 2. jānapadika, *m.* *v.i.* hāsakavesaŋ gaṇhāti. °**ish**, *a.* gamma; pothujjanika.

Club, *n.* 1. muggara, *m.* gadā, *f.* 2. samāja, *m.* samiti, *f.* *v.t.* muggarena paharati. *v.i.* samāgacchati. *p.p.* °pahaṭa; °gata. °**foot**, *a.* thullapāda. °**house** samājāgāra, *nt.*

Cluck, *n.* kukkuṭīruta, *nt.* *v.i.* kukkuṭīrutaŋ pavatteti.

Clue, *n.* 1. sutta, *nt.* 2. upaparikkhāhetu, *m.*

Clump, *n.* gumba; kalāpa, *m.* — **of grass**, thambha, *m.* °**y**, *a.* gumbasahita.

Clumsy, *a.* asobhana; akovida. °**ness**, *n.* asobhanatta; adakkhatta, *nt.*

Cluster, *n.* gocchaka; thabaka; *m.* ghaṭā; mañjarī; vallarī, *f.* *v.i.* ekattha samosarati. *v.t.* ekajjhaŋ neti; sampiṇḍeti. *p.p* °saṭa; °nīta; °dita.

Clutch, *n.* daḷhagahaṇa, *nt.* *v.t.* upādāti; daḷhaŋ gaṇhāti. *p.p.* upādinna; daḷhagahita.

Clutter, *n.* kalakala, *m.* *v.i.* kalakalāyati; ākulīkaroti. *p.p.* °kata.

Clyster, *n.* vatthi, *f.* *v.t.* vatthiyā sodheti; vatthikammaŋ karoti. *p.p.* °dhita; katavatthikamma.

Coach, *n.* ratha ; sandana, *m.* *v.i.* rathena yāti. *v.t.* rathena neti. *p.p.* °yāta ; °nīta. °**man,** *n.* rathācariya ; sūta, *m.* °**box,** sūtāsana, *nt.*

Co-act, *v.t.* ekato karoti. °**ive,** *a.* sahakārī. °**ively,** *adv.* sahakaraṇena.

Coadjutor, *n.* sahakārī ; upatthambhaka, *m.*

Coadunate, *a.* sahayogī.

Coagulate, *v.i.* ghanībhavati. *v.t.* ghanīkaroti. *p.p.* °bhūta ; °kata. °**ion,** *n.* ghanīkaraṇa, *nt.*.

Coal, *n.* khaṇijaṅgāra, *m.* *v.t.* aṅgāraŋ pakkhipati. *p.p.* pakkhittaṅgāra. °**black,** *a.* aṅgāravaṇṇa. °**field,** *n.* aṅgārāyatana, *nt.* °**ing station,** aṅgāragahaṇaṭṭhāna, *nt.* °**mine,** aṅgārākara, *m.* °**pan,** aṅgārakapalla, *nt.* °**tar,** aṅgārasilesa, *m.*

Coalesce, *v.i.* saṅgacchati ; missībhavati. *p.p.* saṅgata ; °bhūta. °**nce,** *n.* ekībhāva ; saṅgama, *m.* sammilana, *nt.*

Coalition, *n.* sāmaggi ; saṅgati, *f.*

Coarse, *a.* 1. thūla ; lūkha ; kakkasa ; 2. asabbha ; gamma. — **cloth,** thūlasāṭaka, *m.* — **food,** lūkhāhāra, *m.* °**ness,** lūkhatta ; oḷārikatta ; thūlatta, *nt.*

Coarsen, *v.t.* pharusattaŋ neti. *p.p.* °nīta.

Coast, *n.* velā, *f.* tīra ; taṭa, *nt.* *v.i.* anutīre sañcarati. °**line,** *n.* tīrarekhā, *f.* °**er,** *n.* anutīragāmī nāvā, *f.*

Coat, *n.* 1. kañcuka, *m.* 2. bāhirālepa, *m.* bāhirapaṭala, *nt.* *v.t.* ālepeti ; lepena paṭicchādeti. *p.p.* °pita ; °dita. °**ing,** *n.* lepa ; ālepa, *m.* paṭala ; āveṭhana, *nt.* — **of mail,** kavaca ; sannāha, *m.*

Coax, *v.t.* upalāleti. *p.p.* °lita. °**er,** *n.* upalālaka, *m.* °**ing,** upalālana, *nt.* °**ingly,** *adv.* upalālanena.

Cobble, *n.* vaṭṭula-pāsāṇa, *m.* *v.t.* 1. vaṭṭulapāsāṇe attharati ; 2. aggaladānena paṭisaṅkharoti. *p.p.* °khata.

Cobbler, *n.* pādukā-saṅkhāraka, *m.*

Cobra, *n.* phaṇī ; nāga, *m.*

Cobweb, *n.* makkaṭakajāla, *nt.* adj. pabhaṅgura.

Cock, *n.* kukkuṭa ; tambacūḷa, *m.* — **of a gun,** nāḷīyantapaṭihanaka, *m.* — **of a pipe,** nāḷamukha, *nt.* °**'s comb,** kaku, *m.* cūḷā, *f.* °**'s crow,** kukkuṭarava, *m.* °**fighting,** *n.* kukkuṭayuddha, *nt.*

Cock, *v.t.* ukkhipati ; (a gun :) ghaṭṭeti; (hay :) puñjetī. *v.i.* unnamati. *p.p.* ukkhitta ; °ṭita ; puñjita ; unnata.

Cockade, *n.* sīsābharaṇavisesa, *m.*

Cockatoo, *n.* mahāsuka, *m.*

Cockboat, *n.* upavahana, *nt.*

Cockchafer, *n.* telapāyikā, *f.*

Cockle, *n.* jalasambukā, *f.* *v.i.* saṅkucati ; valiŋ gaṇhāti. *p.p.* °cita ; valiggahita.

Cock-loft, *n.* candikāsālā, *f.*

Cockpit, *n.* kukkuṭayuddhabhūmi, *f.*

Cockroach, *n.* telapāyikā, *f.*

Cock-sure, *a.* nissaṅka ; ekantabhāvī.

Cocky, *a.* sappagabbha ; avinīta.

Coconut, nāḷikera, *nt.* — **tree,** nāḷikerataru, *m.* — **shell,** nāḷikerakapāla, *m.*

Cocoon, *n.* kimikosa, *m.* *v.i.* kosena onayhati. *p.p.* kosonaddha.

Coction, *n.* 1. kasāya ; 2. pāka, *m.*

Cod, *n.* 1. macchavisesa, *m.* 2. bījakosa, *m.*

Coddle, *v.t.* lāleti ; sapemaŋ poseti. *p.p.* lālita ; °posita. *n.* mamāyaka, *m.*

Code, *n.* saŋhitā, *f.* nītikkhandha ; sikkhāsamūha, *m.*

Codex, *n.* likhita-gantha, *m.*

Codicil, *n.* upalekhana, *nt.*

Codify, *v.t.* nītikkhandhe antokaroti. *p.p.* °kata. °**ication,** *n.* ganthagatakaraṇa, *nt.*

Co-education, *n.* pumitthimissajjhāpana, *nt.*

Coefficient, *n.* 1. samānaniyojita ; sahakārī, *m.* 2. guṇīkāraka, *m.* °**ly,** *adv.* sahakārībhāvena.

Coeliac, *a.* udarāyatta.

Coenobite, *n.* samaṇa, *m.*

Coequal, *a.* sahadhammika ; samānapadaṭṭha. °**ity,** *n.* tulyatta *nt.* samatā, *f.* °**ly,** *adv.* samānākārena.

Coerce, *v.t.* balena kāreti. *p.p.* °kārita. °**ion,** *n.* balakkāra, *m.* °**ive,** *a.* bakkārāyatta.

Coessential, *a.* tulyaguṇa ; samagatika.

Coeternal, *a.* sassatasama.

Coeval, *a.* *n.* samavayaṭṭha.

Coexist, *v.i.* samakāle vattati *or* jīvati. °**ence,** *n.* samakālavattana, *nt.* sahapavatti. *f.* °**ent,** *a.* samakālika ; ekakālavattī.

Coextensive, *a.* samaṭṭhānavyāpī ; samakālavyāpī.

Coffee, *n.* 1. kāphībīja, *nt.* 2. kāphīpāna, *nt.*

Coffer, *n.* dhanapeḷā.

Coffin, *n.* chavadoṇi, *f.* *v.t.* chavadoṇiyaŋ nidahati. *p.p.* °nihita.

Cog, *n.* nemidanta, *nt.* *v.t.* dantasahitaŋ karoti.

Cogency, *n.* sāmatthiya, *nt.*

Cogent, *a.* 1. pabala ; akampiya ; 2. suviññāpaya.

Cogitate, *v.i.* vitakketi ; nijjhāyati. *p.p.* °kita ; °yita. °**able,** *a.* boddhabba. °**ion,** *n.* vitakkana ; nijjhāyana, *nt.* °**ive,** *a.* vitakketabba.

Cognate, *a.* samānajātika ; ekavaggika. *n.* bandhu ; sālohita, *m.* °**ion,** *n.* bandhutta ; ñātitta, *nt.* sambandha, *m.*

Cognition, *n.* parijānanā ; sañcetanā, *f.* — **of smell,** ghāṇaviññāṇa, *nt.* — **of sound,** sotaviññāṇa, *nt.* — **of taste,** jivhāviññāṇa, *nt.* — **of touch,** kāyaviññāṇa, *nt.* — **of vision,** cakkhuviññāṇa, *nt.* °**tive,** *a.* vijānanaka.

Cognize, *v.t.* vijānāti ; abhijānāti. *p.p.* viññāta ; abhiññāta. °**able,** *a.* viññeyya. °**ance,** 1. viññāṇa ; vijānana, *nt.* 2. viessalañchana, *nt.* °**ant,** *a.* vijānanaka ; bujjhanaka.

Cognomen, *n*. 1. kulanāma ; gotta, *nt*. 2. upahāsanāma, *nt*.

Cohabit, *v.i.* saŋvasati ; sahavasati. *p.p.* °vusita ; sahavuttha. **°ation**, *n*. sahavāsa ; saŋvāsa, *m*.

Coheir, *n*. samapariggaha ; samānadāyādī, *m*.

Cohere, *v.i.* saŋyujjati ; ābandhīyati. *p.p.* saŋyutta ; ābaddha. **°nce**, *n*. sambandha ; avirodha, *m*. **°nt**, *a*. anukūla ; aviruddha ; ābaddha ; saṅgata. **°ntly**, *adv*. anukūlatāya ; saṅgatākārena.

Cohesion, *n*. ābandhana, *nt*. āsatti, *f*. **°sive**, *a*. ābandhaka ; ālaggaka. **°sively**, *adv*. saṅlagganākārena.

Coiffeur, *n*. kesamaṇḍetu, *m*.

Coil, *n*. 1. āvaṭṭa ; kuṇḍala, *nt*. 2. rajjupāsa, *m*. 3. aṇḍūpaka, *nt*. — **of a serpent**, bhoga, *m*. *v.i.* kuṇḍalīyati ; āvaṭṭīyati. *v.t.* āvaṭṭīkaroti. *p.p.* °kata.

Coin, *n*. jātarūpa ; kahāpaṇa, *nt*. muddā, *f*. *v.t.* muḍḍaṅketi, *p.p.* °kita. **°age**, *n*. 1. mūlamuddaṅkana, *nt*. 2. parikappa, *m*. nimmāṇa, *nt*.

Coincide, *v.i.* ekībhavati ; ghaṭīyati ; samakāle *or* ekaṭṭhāne ; pavattati. *p.p.* ekībhūta ; °pavatta. **°nce**, *n*. 1. samakālapavattana, *nt*. 2. ekamatikatā, *f*. **°nt**, *a*. samakālika ; anukūla. **°ntly**, *adv*. apubbaŋ acarimaŋ ; samakālaŋ.

Coiner, *n*. vyājamūla-muddāpaka, *m*.

Co-inhere, *v.i.* samadāyādī hoti.

Co-inheritance, *n*. samadāyajja, *nt*.

Coinstantaneous, *a*. ekakkhaṇika.

Coir, *n*. nāḷikeratantu, *nt*. — **matting**, *n*. rajjukilañja, *m*.

Coition, *n*. methuna, *nt*. dvayaŋdvayasnvāsa, *m*.

Colander, *n*. 1. cuṇṇacālikā, *f*. 2. khīraparissāvana, *nt*. *v.t.* parissāveti. *p.p.* °vita.

Cold, *n*. 1. sīta, *nt*. 2. semhapaṭissava, *m*. adj. sītala ; sisira. **°blooded**, *a*. kopahetuvirahita. **°hearted**, *a*. niddaya. **°ly**, *adv*. anādaraŋ ; nirussāhaŋ. **°ness**, *n*. 1. sītalatta, *nt*. 2. virattatā, *f*. — **season**, hemanta, *m*. — **welcome**, udāsīnapaṭiggahaṇa, *nt*.

Colic, *n*. udarasūla, *nt*. **°ky**, *a*. udarasūlāvaha.

Collaborate, *v.i.* ekato kammaŋ karoti. **°ion**, *n*. ekato karaṇa ; samānakicca, *nt*. **°or**, *n*. sahāyaka ; ekato kiccakārī, *m*.

Collapse, *v.i.* saŋsīdati ; paripatati. *p.p.* saŋsīna ; °tita. *n*. laya ; vilaya, *m*. paripatana ; osīdana, *nt*.

Collar, *n*. gīveyyaka, *nt*. kaṇṭhabhūsā, *f*. **°bone**, *n*. akkhaka, *nt*.

Collate, *v.t.* samāneti ; saŋsandeti. *p.p.* °nita ; °dita. **°ion**, *n*. saŋsandana, *nt*.

Collateral, *a*. anugāmika ; anupavattamāna. **°ly**, *adv*. anugāmikatāya.

Colleague, *n*. samānadhurīna ; ekakiccaniyutta, 3.

Collect, *v.t.* ocināti; ācināti; samāharati; rāsīkaroti. *p.p.* ocita; samāhaṭa; °kata. *v.i.* samosarati; upacīyati. *p.p.* samosaṭa; upacita. **°ion,** *n.* rāsi; samavāya; sañcaya; samuccaya; nicaya, *m.* **°ion of alms,** piṇḍapāta, *m.* — **of taxes,** balisaŋharaṇa, *nt.*

Collective, *a.* gaṇībhūta; ekībhūta; (in grammar:) samūhavācaka. — **compound,** dvandasamāsa, *m.* **°ly,** *adv.* rāsivasena.

Collector, *n.* saŋhāraka, *m.* — **of customs,** suṅkika, *m.* — **of income,** āyakammika, *m.* — **of revenue,** karagāhaka, *m.* **°ship,** *n.* karaggāhakadhura, *nt.*

College, *n.* 1. vijjālaya, *m.* 2. paṇḍitagaṇa, *m.* ācariyasaŋhati, *f.* **°ian,** *n.* vijjālayika, *m.* **°iate,** *a.* vijjālayāyatta.

Collide, *v.i.* paṭihaññati; ghaṭṭīyati. *p.p.* paṭihata; ghaṭṭita.

Collier, *n.* aṅgārākarika, *m.*

Colligate, *v.t.* sambandheti; saŋyojeti. *p.p.* sambaddha; °jita. **°ion,** *n.* saŋyoga, *m.* sandhāna, *nt.*

Collision, *n.* saṅghaṭṭana, *nt.* paṭighāta, *m.*

Collocate, *v.t.* niveseti; patiṭṭhāpeti; samodahati. *p.p.* °sita; °pita; °hita. **°ion,** *n.* saŋvesana; samodahana; patiṭṭhāpana, *nt.*

Collocution, *n.* sambhāsana, *nt.* saṅkathā, *f.* **°or,** *n.* sambhāsaka, *m.*

Collogue, *v.i.* rahasi manteti. *p.p.* °tita.

Collop, *n.* maŋsapesi, *f.*

Colloquial, *a.* mahājanakathāyatta.

Colloquy, *n.* mahājanālāpa, *m.*

Collude, *v.i.* kumanteti. *p.p.* °tita.

Collusion, *n.* kumantaṇa, *nt.*

Collyrium, *n.* nettañjana, *nt.*

Colon, *n,* 1. mahā-anta, *nt.* 2. vākyaccheda-(:) lakkhaṇa, *nt.*

Colonel, *n.* gumbapati, *m.*

Colonist, *n.* janapadavāsī, *m.*

Colonize, *v.t.* 1. janapadaŋ patiṭṭhāpeti; 2. janapade vāseti. **°ation,** *n.* janapadapatiṭṭhāpana, *nt.*

Colonnade, *n.* thambhapanti, *f.*

Colony, *n.* 1. videsīya-janapada, *m.* 2. nikāya; samūha, *m.* **°ial,** *a.* janapadāyatta.

Colophon, *n.* ganthakattu-sandassana, *nt.*

Colorific, *a.* vaṇṇuppādaka.

Colorimeter, *n.* vaṇṇamāṇaka, *nt.*

Colossal, *a.* atimahanta.

Colossus, *n.* mahāpaṭimā, *f.* mahāsarīra, *m.*

Colour, *n.* vaṇṇa; raṅga, *m.* vaṇṇadhātu, *f.* *pl.* dhaja, *m.* *v.t.* rañjeti. *p.p.* rañjita; ratta. *v.i.* lajjati; vivaṇṇībhavati. *p.p.* lajjita; °bhūta. **°able,** *a.* vyājayutta. **°blind,** *a.* vaṇṇavivecanākkhama. **°ing,** *n.* 1. rañjitākāra, *m.* 2. vaṇṇālepa, *m.* **°ist,** *n.* rañjaka; raṅgājīva, *m.* **°less,** *a.* vaṇṇahīna. **Change** —, vivaṇṇī bhavati. **Fast** —, ciraṭṭhāyī-vaṇṇa, *m.* **One's true** —, sabhāva, *m.* pakati, *f.* **To give** —, ucitattam āropeti.

Colt, *n.* 1. kisora, *m.* 2. akovida-purisa, *m.* °**ish,** *a.* dandha; capala.

Colubrine, *a.* sappasadisa.

Column, *n.* 1. thambha; yūpa, *m.* 2. (of an army:) senādala, *nt.* — **of smoke,** dhūmakkhan-dha, *m.* — **of printing,** muddaṅkana-vibhāga, *m.* °**ar,** *a.* thambhākāra.

Coma, *n.* balavaniddā, *f.*

Co-mate, *n.* sahavāsī, *m.*

Comb, *n.* 1. kesullekhanī, *f.* vijaṭaka, *m.* 2. cūḷā; sikhā, *f.* *v.t.* ullikhati; vijaṭeti. *p.p.* °khita; °ṭita. °**ing,** *n.* vijaṭana; ullikhana, *nt.*

Combat, *n.* yuddha, *nt.* saṅgāma, *m.* *v.t.* 1. yujjhati; 2. khaṇḍeti; nirākaroti. *p.p.* °jhita; °ḍita; °kata. **Hand to hand** —, bhujayuddha; bāhābāhavī, *nt.* °**ant,** *n.* yodha; malla, *m.* °**ive,** *a.* kalahappiya; raṇakāmī.

Combine, *v.t.* saŋyojeti; samodhāneti; piṇḍeti. *p.p.* °jita; °nita; piṇḍita. *v.i.* saŋyujjati; piṇḍībhavati. *p.p.* saŋyutta; °bhūta. °**ation,** *n.* sandhi; ghaṭanā, *f.* saŋyoga; samavāya, *m.*

Combustible, *a.* sahasā jalanasīla; dahanasīla.

Combustion, *n.* dahana, *nt.* mahāaggiḍāha, *m.*

Come, *v.i.* āgacchati; āyāti; eti; upeti; pāpuṇāti. *p.p.* āgata; āyāta; upeta; patta. — **about,** sijjhati; sambhavati. — **again,** puneti; paṭieti. — **at,** pāpuṇāti; labhati. — **away,** samuṭṭhāti; udeti. — **by,** paṭilabhati. — **back,** paccāgacchati; paṭinivattati. — **down,** 1. paccorohati; 2. nihīyati; hāyati. — **down upon,** pakkhandati; ajjhottharati. — **forth,** niggacchati; 2. udeti; uppajjati. — **in,** pavisati. — **into trouble,** āpadam āpatati. — **near,** — **nigh,** upasaṅkamati; upagacchati. — **of age,** vayappatta, *a.* — **off,** 1. niggacchati; 2. sijjhati. — **on,** abhivaḍḍhati; abhiyāti. — **out,** udeti; pākaṭībhavati. — **out from,** viniggacchati. — **out of water,** uttarati. — **out with,** pakāseti. — **over,** atikkamati; adhivattati. — **round,** pakatim āpajjati. — **short of,** nappahoti. — **to,** upeti; pappoti. — **to blows,** kalahaŋ karoti. — **to one's self,** satiŋ paṭilabhati. — **to the surface,** ummujjati. — **to nothing,** viphalībhavati. — **to pass,** sijjhati. — **to terms,** sandhīyati. — **together,** samosarati. — **to an end,** osānam āpajjati. — **to ruin,** nihīyati. — **to the final release,** parinibbāti. — **up,** uggacchati. — **up to,** upagacchati. — **up with,** adhigaṇhāti. — **upon,** āpatati.

Come-at-able, *a.* upagamanīya ; laddhabba.

Comedy, *n.* hāsadāyaka-nāṭaka, *nt.* °**ian,** *n.* 1. naṭa ; hāsaka, *m.* 2. nāṭakasampādaka, *m.*

Comely, *a.* surūpa ; sundara ; sobhana ; dassanīya. °**iness,** *n.* surūpatā ; sobhanatā, *f.*

Comer, *n.* āgantu ; āgāmī, *m.*

Comet, *n.* dhūmaketu, *m.* °**ic,** *a.* dhūmaketvāyatta.

Comfit, *n.* madhurakhajjaka, *nt.*

Comfort, *n,* sukha ; sāta, *nt.* phāsu, *m.* *v.t.* sukheti ; samassāseti. *p.p.* sukhita ; samassattha. °**able,** *a.* sukhada ; phāsukara. °**ably,** *adv.* sukhena ; yathāphāsukaŋ. °**less,** *a.* aphāsuka ; anassāsa. °**er,** *n.* assāsaka ; sukhada, *m.*

Comic, Comical, *a.* hāsajanaka. °**ly,** *adv.* vikaṭākārena.

Coming, *n.* āgamana ; pāpuṇana, *nt.* adj. āgāmī.

Comity, *n.* mittabhāva ; sadācāra, *m.*

Comma, *n.* appatara-virāma, *m.*

Command, *n.* āṇā ; āṇatti, *f.* vidhāna, *nt.* niyoga, *m.* *v.t.* āṇāpeti ; niyameti. *p.p.* °pita *or* āṇatta ; °mita. °**ant,** *n.* āṇāpaka ; vidhāyaka, *m.* °**ing,** *a.* āṇāsampanna ; mahesakkha. °**ment,** *n.* āṇā, *f.* niyama, *m.* sikkhāpada, *nt.*

Commander, *n.* vidhāyaka ; āṇādāyī, *m.* — **of an army,** senānī ; camūpati, *m.* °**ship,** *n.* senānīdhura, *nt.*

Commemorate, *v.t.* 1. anussarati ; 2. anussaraṇussavaŋ pavatteti. *p.p.* °rita ; pavattitānussara°. °**ion,** *n.* anussaraṇussava, *m.* °**ive,** *a.* anussarāpaka.

Commence, *v.i.* ārabhati ; paṭṭhapeti. *p.p.* āraddha ; °pita. °**ment,** *n.* ārambha ; mūlārambha, *m.* ārabhana, *nt.*

Commend, *v.t.* 1. samappeti ; bhāraŋ karoti ; 2. pasaŋsati ; abhitthavati ; vaṇṇeti. *p.p.* °pita ; katabhāra ; °sita *or* pasattha ; abhitthuta ; vaṇṇita. °**able,** *a.* pasaŋsiya ; thomanīya. °**ably,** *adv.* thomanīyākārena. °**ation,** *n.* 1. samappaṇā, *f.* 2. pasaŋsā ; thuti, *f.* °**atory,** *a.* 1. pasaŋsāvaha ; 2. anupālanāyatta.

Commensal, *a. n.* 1. sahabhottu, *m.* 2. paraputtha ; parūpajīvī. °**ism,** *n.* sahabhojitā ; parūpajīvitā, *f.*

Commensurable, *a.* 1. samappamāṇika ; 2. samabhāgayutta. °**ness,** *n.* samamāṇayuttatā, *f.*

Commensurate, *a.* samamāṇayutta ; anūnādhika ; tulyappamāṇa.

Comment, *v.t.* vyākhyāti ; vitthāreti ; vaṇṇeti. *p.p.* vyākhyāta ; °rita ; °ṇita. °**ary,** *n.* aṭṭhakathā ; vyākhyā ; atthavaṇṇanā, *f.* °**ator,** *n.* vyākhyākāra ; aṭṭhakathācariya, *m.*

Commerce, *n.* vaṇijjā, *f.* vohāra ; kayavikkaya, *m.* *v.i.* vaṇijjaŋ karoti. °**ial,** *a.* vaṇijjāyatta. °**ially,** *adv.* vaṇijjānurūpena.

Commination, *n.* apāyabhayatajjana, *nt.* °**tory,** *a.* tajjanāyatta.

Commingle, *v.i.* missībhavati. *v.t.* sammisseti. *p.p.* missībhūta ; °sita.

Comminute, *v.t.* 1. kaṇaso karoti ; 2. vibhājeti. *p.p.* °kata ; °jita.

Commiserate, *v.t. i.* sahasocati ; anukampati. *p.p.* °cita ; °pita. °**ion,** *n.* sahasocanā ; anukampā, *f.*

Commissary, *n.* 1. anuyuttaka ; niyojita ; 2. bhaṭāhārasampādaka, *m.*

Commission, *n.* 1. kārakasabhā, *f.* niyojitamaṇḍala, *nt.* 2. ācaraṇa, *nt.* 3. samappaṇa, *nt.* 4. niyoga ; 5. adhikāra, *m.* 6. āṇattipaṇṇa, *nt.* 7. lābhabhāga, *m.* °**agent** lābhabhāgena vikketu, *m.* °**er,** *n.* adhikārī ; niyojita, *m.*

Commission, *v.t.* niyojeti ; adhikaroti ; adhikārapaṇṇaŋ deti. *p.p.* °jita ; adhikata ; dinnādhikārapaṇṇa. °**ed with,** adhikata ; payutta, *a.*

Commissure, *n.* sandhiṭṭhāna, *nt.*

Commit, *v.t.* 1. niyyādeti ; appeti ; 2. ācarati ; āpajjati ; pasavati ; 3. niyojeti. *p.p.* °dita ; appita ; ācarita ; āpanna ; °vita. — **adultery,** aticarati ; micchācarati. — **a crime,** aparajjhati. — **a sin,** vippaṭipajjati. — **to memory,** dhāreti ; manasi nidahati.

Commitment, Committal, *n.* 1. ācaraṇa ; anuṭṭhāna, *nt.* 2. kārāpakkhipana, *nt.*

Committee, *n.* sampādakasabhā, *f.* kārakamaṇḍala, *nt.*

Commix, *v.t.* sammisseti. *v.i.* missībhavati. *p.p.* °sita ; °bhūta. °**ture,** *n.* sammissaṇa, *nt.* saŋyoga, *m.*

Commodious, *a.* 1. asambādha ; vitthiṇṇa ; 2. sopakaraṇa ; 3. patirūpa ; anurūpa.

Commodity, *n.* paṇiyabhaṇḍa, *nt.*

Common, *a.* 1. sādhāraṇa ; saṅghika ; 2. bahula ; avisiṭṭha. *n.* sādhāraṇuyyāna, *nt.* — **law** desācāra, *m.* alikhita-nīti, *f.* °**ly,** *adv.* bahuso ; sāmaññena. °**place,** *a.* avisiṭṭha ; appaggha. — **sense,** pakatinicchaya, *m.* — **sin,** lokavajja, *nt.*

Commonalty, *n.* mahājana, *m.* janatā, *f.*

Commoner, *n.* raṭṭhavāsī ; gahapati, *m.*

Commons, *n. pl.* mahājana, *m.* **House of** —, mahājanikamantisabhā, *f.*

Commonwealth, *n.* janasammatarajja, *nt.*

Commotion, *n.* saṅkhobha ; viplava ; pakopa, *m.*

Communal, *a.* padesavisayaka. °**ism,** *n.* janasammutivāda, *m.* °**ize,** *v.t.* mahājanāyattaŋ karoti.

Commune, *v.i.* sākacchati ; sambhāsati. *p.p.* °sita.

Communicable, *a.* nivedetabba ; viññāpetabba.

Communicate, *v.t.* ācikkhati ; nivedeti ; viññāpeti. *p.p.* °khita ; °dita ; °pita. *v.i.* sambandhaŋ pavatteti ; sahabhāgī hoti.

°ion, *n.* 1. nivedana, *nt.* 2. aññamaññasambandha, *m.* **°ive,** *a.* nivedetukāma ; sambhāsanappiya ; sāsanapesaka. **°or,** *n.* nivedaka ; sāsanapesaka ; sambandhaka, *m.*

Communion, *n.* 1. sahayogitā ; ekamatikatā, *f.* 2. ekamatikagaṇa, *m.* **°ist,** *n.* ekanikāyika, *m.*

Communique, *n.* rājakiccanivedana, *nt.*

Communism, *n.* samasambhogavāda, *m.* **°nist,** *n.* samasambhogavādī, *m.* **°nistic,** *a.* samasambhogāyatta.

Communitarian, *n.* samasambhogika, *m.*

Community, *n.* 1. samasambhoga ; 2. sāvakasaṅgha ; nikāya, *m.*

Communize, *v.t.* samasambhogattaŋ pāpeti. *p.p.* °pita.

Commute, *v.t.* vinimeti ; parivatteti. *p.p.* °mita ; °tita. **°able,** *a.* vinimetabba ; parivattiya. **°ation,** *n.* vinimaya, *m.* parivattana, *nt.* **°ative,** *a.* vinimayāyatta.

Comose, *a.* lomasa.

Compact, *n.* paṭissava, *m.* paṭiññā, *f.* adj. saŋhata ; saṅgata ; ghana. *v.t.* sandahati ; sampiṇḍeti ; ghanīkaroti. *p.p.* °hita ; ḍita ; °kata. **°ly,** *adv.* saŋhatākārena. **°ness,** *n.* saŋhatatta, *nt.*

Compaginate, *v.t.* daḷhaŋ sambandheti. *p.p.* daḷhasambaddha.

Companion, *n.* sahacara ; anucara ; sahāya, *m.* *v.t.* anugacchati ; sevati. *p.p.* anugata ; sevita.

Bad —, pāpamitta, *m.*
Good —, kalyāṇamitta, *m.*
°ship, *n.* sahāyatā ; sahacāritā, *f.* mittabhāva, *m.*

Company, *n.* 1. parisā ; sabhā ; samiti, *f.* 2. sahacariyā ; saṅgati, *f.* sahavāsa, *m.* *v.t.* sevati ; bhajati. *p.p.* sevita ; bhajita.

Comparable, *a.* tulanāraha ; upameyya.

Comparative, *a.* saŋsandaka ; tulanavisayaka. *In gram.* adhikatthadīpaka. **°ly,** *adv.* diṭṭhasaŋsandanena.

Compare, *v.t.* samāneti ; saŋsandeti ; upameti. *p.p.* °nita ; °dita ; °mita. **°ison,** *n.* saŋsandana ; upamāna, opamma, *nt.* upamā, *f.*

Compart, *v.t.* bhāgaso vibhajati. *p.p.* °vibhatta. **°ment,** *n.* vibhattabhāga ; rathovaraka, *m.*

Compass, *v.t.* parivāreti ; parikkhipati ; anupariyāti. *p.p.* °rita ; parikkhitta ; °yāta. *n.* 1. maṇḍala, *nt.* paridhi, *f.* 2. mālimayanta, *nt.* pl. maṇḍalamāṇaka, *m.*

Compassion, *n.* dayā ; anukampā ; karuṇā, *f.* kāruñña, *nt.* **°ate,** *a.* kāruṇika ; anukampaka ; dayālu. **°ately,** *adv.* sadayaŋ ; sakaruṇaŋ.

Compatible, *a.* anukūla ; aviruddha ; sahavattī. **°bility,** *n.* anukūlatā ; aviruddhatā, *f.*

Compatriot, *n.* sadesika ; sakaraṭṭhika, 3.

Compeer, *n.* samānapadaṭṭha, *m.*

Compel, *v.t.* pasayha *or* anicchāya kāreti ; uyyojeti. *p.p.* °kārita ; °jita.

Compendious, *a.* saṅkhitta ; sāraŋsabhūta. °**ly,** *adv.* saṅkhepena. °**ness,** *n.* saṅkhittatā, *f.*

Compendium, *n.* sārasaṅgaha, *m.*

Compensate, *v.t.* nitthāreti ; paṭikammaŋ karoti ; hāniŋ pūreti. *p.p.* °rita ; °kata ; pūritahānī. °**ion,** *n.* paṭikamma ; hānipūraṇa, *nt.* °**tory,** *a.* hānipūraka.

Compete, *v.i.* sampayojeti ; vijigiŋsati ; yugaggāhī hoti. *p.p.* °jita ; °sita ; °hībhūta. °**ncy,** °**nce,** *n.* sāmatthiya ; pāguñña, *nt.*

Competent, *a.* paṭibala ; bhabba ; samattha.

Competition, *n.* yugaggāha, *m.* ahamahamikā, *f.*

Competitive, *a.* vijigiŋsaka.

Competitor, *n.* paṭipuggala ; yugaggāhī, *m.*

Compile, *v.t.* saṅgaṇhāti ; saṅkaleti. *p.p.* saṅgahita ; saṅkalita. °**ation,** *n.* saṅkalana ; samāharaṇa ; saṅghaṇhana, *nt.* °**er,** *n.* saṅgāhaka ; ganthakāra, *m.*

Complacence, °**cy,** *n.* pasāda, *m.* pīti ; anukūlatā, *f.* °**nt,** *a.* pasanna ; santuṭṭha ; anukūla. °**ntly,** *adv.* sānandaŋ ; sappasādaŋ.

Complain, *v.i.* 1. codeti ; ujjhāyati ; 2. vilapati. *p.p.* codita ; °yita. °**ant,** *n.* codaka ; ujjhāyaka ; dukkhanivedaka, *m.*

Complaint, *n.* 1. codanā ; dosāropaṇā ; 2. dukkhanivedanā, *f.*

Complaisance, *n.* anurodha, *m.* anukūlatta ; sagāravatta, *nt.*

Complaisant, *a.* aviruddha ; anukūla ; sagārava. °**ly,** *adv.* sagāravaŋ ; anukūlena.

Complement, *n.* 1. ūnapūraṇa, *nt.* 2. paripuṇṇatā, *f.* *v.t.* paripūreti. *p.p.* paripūrita. °**ary,** °**al,** *a.* ūnapūraka ; paripūraka.

Complete, *v.t.* 1. paripūreti ; 2. osāpeti ; niṭṭhāpeti. *p.p.* °rita ; °pita. adj. 1. sampuṇṇa ; paripuṇṇa ; anūna ; 2. niṭṭhita ; saŋsiddha. °**ly,** *adv.* anūnaŋ ; asesaŋ ; nissesaŋ. °**ness,** *n.* anūnatta ; puṇṇatta, *nt.* °**ion,** *n.* 1. pūraṇa, *nt.* pāripūri, *f.* 2. samāpana ; osāpana ; niṭṭhāna, *nt.* °**ing,** *a.* paripūraka ; niṭṭhāpaka.

Complex, *a.* saṅkiṇṇa ; nānāvibhāgayutta. *n.* saṅkiṇṇarāsi, *m.* °**ity,** *n.* saṅkiṇṇatā, *f.*

Complexion, *n.* chavivaṇṇa ; mukhavaṇṇa, *m.*

Compliable, *a.* anuvattanīya.

Compliance, *n.* anuvattana ; aṅgīkaraṇa, *nt.*

Compliant, *a.* anuvattī ; vidheya ; assava ; suvaca.

Complicacy, *n.* saṅkiṇṇatta, *nt.*

Complicate, *v.t.* ākulīkaroti ; sammisseti. *p.p.* °kata ; °sita. adj. ākula ; vyākula ; missita. °**ion,** *n.* ākulīkaraṇa, *nt.*

Complice, *n.* pāpasahāya, *m.* °**ity,** *n.* aparādhasahāyatta, *nt.*

Compliment, *n.* abhinandanavācā ; sammodanā, *f.* *v.t.* ānandaŋ pakāseti ; tuṭṭhiŋ nivedeti.

p.p. pakāsitānanda ; niveditatuṭṭhī. °**ary,** *a.* abhinandanapubbaka.

Comply, *v.i.* anuvattati ; anujānāti. *p.p.* °tita ; anuññāta.

Component, *a.* antogata ; sambaddha. — **part,** aṅga ; antogata-koṭṭhāsa, *m.* — **thing,** saṅkhāra ; saṅkhata, *m.*

Comport, *v.i.* ācarati ; vattati. °**ment,** *n,* ācāra, *m.* pavatti, *f.*

Compose, *v.t.* 1. racayati ; gantheti ; nibandhati ; 2. ghaṭayati ; yojeti ; 3. upasameti. *p.p.* racita ; °thita ; nibaddha ; ghaṭita ; yojita ; °mita. °**ed,** *a.* samāhita. °**edly,** *adv.* samāhitākārena. °**er,** racaka ; nibandhaka, *m.* °**ition,** *m.* racanā, *f.* nibandha ; gantha, *m.* °**ure,** *n.* upasama ; asambhama ; samādhi, *m.*

Compositor, *n.* vaṇṇayojaka, *m.*

Compost, *n.* bhūmisāramissaṇa, *nt.*

Compote, *n.* phāṇitena rakkhitaphala, *nt.*

Compound, *v.t.* saŋyojeti ; misseti ; samāseti. *p.p.* °jita ; °sita. adj. saŋsaṭṭha ; sampayutta. *noun.* 1. saŋyoga ; samāsa, *m.* 2. aṅgaṇa ; ājira, *nt.* °**er,** *n.* missetu ; saŋyojaka, *m.* — **word,** samāsapada, *nt.*

Comprehend, *v.t.* bujjhati ; paṭivijjhati ; parijānāti ; adhigacchati. *p.p.* buddha ; paṭividdha ; pariññāta ; adhigata. °**nsible,** *a.* viññeyya ; adhigamanīya. °**nsion,** *n.* avabodha ; adhigama ; paṭivedha, *m.* pariññā, *f.*

Comprehensive, *a.* 1. vyāpaka ; 2. vitthiṇṇa. °**ly,** *adv.* 1. saṅkhepena ; samāsato ; 2. vyāpakattena. °**ness,** *n.* 1. vyāpakatta ; 2. saṅkhittatta, *nt.*

Compress, *v.t.* sampīḷeti ; saṅghāteti. *p.p.* °ḷita ; °tita. °**ible,** *a.* saṅkocanīya. °**ion,** *n.* sampīḷana ; saṅkocana, *nt.* °**ive,** *a.* saṅkocakara.

Comprise, *v.t.* antokaroti ; sampaveseti. °**able,** *a.* antokaraṇasamattha.

Compromise, *n.* mithupaṭiññā, *f.* sādhāraṇa-niyama, *m.* *v.i.* 1. mithupaṭiññaŋ deti ; 2. kukkuccāyati. *p.p.* °yita.

Comprovincial, *a.* samānapadesika.

Compulsion, *n.* balakkāra, *m.* anicchāya kārāpana, *n* . °**sive,** *a.* anivāriya. °**sory,** *a.* āvassaka ; anivāriya ; avassa-karaṇīya.

Compunction, *n.* anutāpa, *m.*

Compurgation, *n.* dosamocana ; niddosikaraṇa, *nt.*

Compute, *v.t.* gaṇet ; pamāṇeti. *p.p.* gaṇita, °ṇita. °**ation,** *n.* saṅkhyāna ; pamāṇakaraṇa, *nt.*

Comrade, see **Companion.**

Con, *v.t.* uggaṇhāti ; vācuggataŋ karoti. *p.p.* uggahita ; °kata.

Conation, *n.* cittādhiṭṭhāna, *nt.*

Concatenate, *v.t.* āvuṇāti. *p.p.* āvuta. °**ion,** *n.* āvuṇanā, *nt.*

Concave, *a.* puṭākāra. °**ity,** *n.* kuhara, *nt.*

Conceal, *v.t.* nigūhati ; āvarati ; paṭicchādeti. *p.p.* nigūḷha ; āvaṭa ; paṭicchanna. °**ment,** *n.*

nigūhana ; apanidahana ; tiro-karaṇa, *nt.*

Concede, *v.t.* 1. sampaṭicchati ; 2. anujānāti ; 3. appeti. *p.p.* °chita ; anuññāta ; appita.

Conceit, *n.* ahaṅkāra ; micchāsaṅkappa ; māna, *m. v.t.* micchā saṅkappeti. *p.p.* °pita. °**ed,** *a.* dappita ; uddhata. °**edly,** *adv.* uddhatākārena.

Conceivable, *a.* cintāvisayaka ; bodhanīya. °**ness,** *n.* bodhanīyatta, *nt.* °**ly,** *adv.* bodhanīyākārena.

Conceive, *v.t.* 1. anubujjhati ; 2. gabbhaŋ dhāreti. *v.i.* paṭisandhiŋ gaṇhāti. *p.p.* anubuddha ; dhāritagabbha ; gahitapaṭisandhika.

Concentrate, *v.t.* samādahati ; samannāharati. *p.p.* samāhita ; °āhaṭa. °**ed,** *a.* ekagga ; avikkhitta. °**ion,** ekaggatā, *f.* avikkhepa ; samādhi, *m.* — **of mind,** cetosamatha, *m.* °**ive,** *a.* ekattapāpaka.

Concentre, *v.t.* samodahati ; ekaṭṭhānaŋ pāpeti. *p.p.* °hita ; °pāpita. °**ic,** *a.* ekagga ; ekaṭṭhānagāmī.

Concept, *n.* saṅkappa, *m.* mati, *f.* °**ion,** *n.* 1. saṅkappa ; avabodha, *m.* 2. gabbhāvakkanti, *f.* paṭisandhigahaṇa, *nt.* °**ive,** *a.* bujjhanāraha. °**ual,** *a.* saṅkappāyatta ; avabodhāyatta.

Conceptualism, *n.* viññāṇavāda, *m.*

Concern, *n.* sambandha, *m.* apekkhā, *f. v.t.* sambandhī bhavati ; ussukko hoti. *p.p.* °bhūta ; jātussukka. **This does not — me,** idaŋ mamāyatta-kiccaŋ na hoti. **I am concerned about this,** imasmiŋ kāraṇe 'haŋ dukkhito *or* saṅkito homi. **I do not — myself,** ahaŋ majjhaṭṭho homi.

Concerning, *prep.* sandhāya ; paṭicca ; ārabbha ; uddissa.

Concernment, *n.* kicca, *nt.* vyāpāra, *m.*

Concert, *n.* 1. saṅgīta ; 2. sammantana, *nt.* sahakāritā, *f. v.t.* sammanteti ; saŋvidahati. *p.p.* °tita ; saŋvihita.

Concession, *n.* 1. sampaṭicchana ; 2. sampadāna ; varadāna, *nt.*

Conch, *n.* saṅkha ; kambu, *m.*

Conchiferous, *a.* sakalikāsahita.

Conchology, *n.* saṅkhavijjā, *f.* °**ist,** *n.* saṅkhavijjādhārī, *m.*

Conciliate, *v.t.* anuneti ; ārādheti ; sandahati. *p.p.* anunīta ; °dhita ; °hita *or* sandhita. °**ion,** *n.* sandahana, *nt.* °**tor,** *n.* sandhātu ; ārādhaka, *m.* °**tory,** *a.* sandhānakara.

Concise, *a.* saṅkhitta ; samāsita. °**ly,** *adv.* saṅkhittena ; saṅkhepena. °**ness,** *n.* saṅkhittatā, *f.*

Concision, *n.* 1. cammaggachedana, *nt.* 2. saṅkhepatta, *nt.*

Conclamation, *n.* kalakala ; mahāghosa, *m.*

Conclave, *n.* rahosammilanaṭṭhāna, *nt.*

Conclude, *v.t.* 1. samāpeti ; niṭṭhāpeti ; pariyosāpeti ; 2. niccheti ; upadhāreti. *p.p.* °pita ; °chita ; °rita. °**ing,** *a.* niṭṭhāpaka ; osāpaka.

Conclusion, *n.* 1. niṭṭhāna ; nigamana ; pariyosāna, *nt.* 2. sanniṭṭhāna, *nt.* nicchaya, *m.* °**sive,** *a.* nicchayāvaha ; saŋsayacchedaka. °**sively,** *adv.* nicchayena ; nissaŋsayaŋ.

Concoct, *v.t.* missetvā pacati. *p.p.* °pakka. °**ion,** *n.* missitapāka, *m.* kasāya, *nt.*

Concolorous, *a.* anukūlavaṇṇa.

Concomitance, *n.* sampayoga ; samavāya, *m.*

Concomitant, *a.* sahavattī ; sahagata ; sampayutta. °**ly,** *adv.* sahitaŋ ; ekato.

Concord, *n.* sāmaggi ; ekamatitā, *f.* avirodha, *m.* anusandhāna, *nt.* °**ance,** samānatta ; sadisatta, *nt.* °**ant,** *a.* aviruddha ; samagatika.

Concourse, *n.* mahāsannipāta ; mahāsamāgama ; pavāha, *m.*

Concrete, *a.* saŋhata ; piṇḍībhūta. *n.* ghanacaya, *m.* *v.t.* ghanīkaroti ; ābandhati. *v.i.* ghanībhavati. *p.p.* °kata ; ābaddha ; °bhūta. °**ion,** *n.* ekaghanīkaraṇa, *nt.*

Concubine, *n.* upabhariyā ; antepuritthī, *f.* °**age,** *n.* 1. orodhavutti, *f.* 2. avivāhitadampativāsa, *m.* °**ary,** *a. n.* orodhajāta.

Concupiscence, *n.* ratilolatā ; kāmukatā, *f.* °**scent,** *a.* kāmuka ; kāmātura.

Concur, *v.i.* saṅgacchati ; ekībhavati. *p.p.* saṅgata ; ekībhūta. °**rence,** *n.* sammuti ; ekamatitā, *f.* °**rent,** *a.* sahayogika ; samakālika ; ekamatika. °**rently,** *adv.* samakālaŋ ; ekamatitāya.

Concuss, *v.t.* bāḷhaŋ kampeti ; santajjeti. *p.p.* °pita ; °jita. °**ion,** *n.* atikampana ; balavaghaṭṭana, *nt.*

Condemn, *v.t.* dosam āropeti ; sāvajjaŋ karoti ; daṇḍaŋ paṇeti. *p.p.* āropitadosa ; °kata ; paṇitadaṇḍa. °**able,** *a.* sāvajja ; daṇḍanāraha. °**ation,** *n.* 1. daṇḍana, *nt.* vadhaniyama, *m.* 2. garahā ; nindā, *f.* °**atory,** *a.* sāvajjatāpakāsaka.

Condense, *v.t.* ghanīkaroti ; saṅkhipati. *p.p.* °kata ; saṅkhitta. °**able,** *a.* ghanīkaraṇīya. °**ation,** *n.* ghanīkaraṇa, *nt.* °**er,** *n.* ghanīkara, *m.*

Condescend, *v.i.* nihatamānībhavati. °**ing,** *a.* nihatamāna.

Condescension, *n.* samānattatā ; nihatamānatā, *f.*

Condign, *a.* bhabba ; samattha. °**ly,** *adv.* bhabbākārena.

Condiment, *n.* vyañjana ; āsittaka, *nt.*

Condition, *n.* 1. avatthā ; dasā ; vutti, *f.* sabhāva ; ākāra, *m.* 2. niyama, *m.* mithupaṭiññā, *f.* *v.t.* paṭijānāti ; niyameti. *p.p.* paṭiññāta ; °mita. °**al,** *a.* niyamayutta ; paṭiññānugata ; avatthānugata. °**al mood,** sattamīvibhatti, *f.* °**ally,** *adv.* saniyamaŋ ; paṭiññānurūpaŋ. °**ed,** *a.* 1. nipphanna ; sappaccaya ; 2. sammāvihita.

Condolatory, *a.* anusocaka.

Condole, *v.i.* anukampati ; samadukkhī bhavati. °**nce,** *n.* anukampā ; sama-dukkhatā, *f.*

Condone, *v.t.* khamati ; titikkhati. *p.p.* khanta. °**ation,** khamā ; titikkhā, *f.*

Conduce, *v.i.* āvahati ; upaneti. °**ive,** *a.* āvaha ; saŋvattanika ; pāpaka. °**iveness,** *n.* āvahanatā ; pāpakatā, *f.*

Conduct, *n.* 1. ācaraṇa, *nt.* cariyā ; paṭipatti, *f.* ācāra, *m.* 2. nayana ; āvahana, *nt. v.t.* 1. ācarati ; paṭipajjati ; 2. pāpeti ; 3. vidahati ; nibbāhati. *p.p.* ācarita ; paṭipanna; pāpita ; vihita ; °hita. **Good —,** sucarita, *nt.* samācāra, *m.* **Proper—,** sammāvattanā, *f.* **Right —,** sammākammanta, *nt.* **Wrong—,** duccarita, *nt.* °**ible,** *a.* pāpanīya. °**ion,** *n.* pāpana ; nayana, *nt.* °**ive** *a.* āvaha; sampāpaka. °**tor,** *n.* netu ; pāpaka ; pālaka, *m.*

Conduit, *n.* paṇālī ; jalanetti, *f.* vārimagga, *m.*

Cone, *n.* sikhā, *f.* thūpākāravatthu, *nt.* °**ical,** *a.* thūpākāra.

Confabulate, *v.i.* sallapati ; sambhāsati. °**ion,** *n.* sallāpa, *m.* sambhāsana, *nt.*

Confection, *n.* khajjakamissana, *nt. v.t.* khajjakaŋ sampādeti. °**ary,** *n.* khajjakasampādaka, *m.* adj. khajjakāyatta. °**er,** *n.* khajjakasampādaka, *m.* °**ery,** *n.* khajjakasampādana, *nt.*

Confederate, *v.t.* sandhīkaroti. *p.p.* °kata. °**ion,** *n.* 1. sandhikaraṇa, *nt.* paṭiññābandha, *m.* 2. samohitagaṇa, *m.*

Confer, *v.t.* sampadāti ; paṭipādeti. *p.p.* sampadinna ; °dita. *v.i.* sākacchati ; sambhāsati. °**rable,** *a.* 1. sākacchitabba ; 2. dātabba.

Conference, *n.* sākacchā, *f.* sammantaṇa ; sammelana, *nt.*

Confess, *v.t.* sakavajjam āvīkaroti ; āpattiŋ deseti. *p.p.* āvīkatavajja ; desitāpattika. °**edly,** *adv.* nissaŋsayaŋ. °**ion,** *n.* āpattidesanā ; vajjapakāsanā, *f.*

Confidant, *n.* vissāsī ; vallabha, *m.*

Confide, *v.t.* vissasati ; saddahati. *p.p.* vissattha ; °hita °**nce,** *n.* vissāsa, *m.* saddahana, *nt.* °**nt,** *a.* jātavissāsa ; nikkaṅkha. °**ntial,** *a.* vissasanīya ; rāhaseyyaka ; gutta. °**ntly,** *adv.* nirāsaṅkaŋ ; nissaŋsayaŋ.

Configure, *v.t.* sasaṇṭhānaŋ karoti. °**ation,** *n.* ākārālikhana, *nt.*

Confine, *n.* sīmā, *f.* avadhi, *m. v.t.* sīmeti ; avarodheti. *p.p.* sīmita ; avaruddha. °**ment,** *n.* avarodhana, *nt.* (of bowels :) malāvarodha, *m.* (of a woman :) pasūtikāla, *m.* °**ed to bed,** mañcaparāyaṇa, *a.* °**ed woman,** pasūtikā, *f.*

Confirm, *v.t.* daḷhayati ; santhambheti. *p.p.* °yita ; °bhita. °**ation,** *n.* daḷhīkaraṇa, *nt.* °**ative,** *a.* santhambhaka ; sādhaka.

Confiscate, *v.t.* rājāyattaŋ karoti ; sabbassaŋ harati. *p.p.* °yattīkata ; haṭasabbassa. °**ion,** *n.* rajjāyattīkaraṇa, *nt.*

Conflagration, *n.* mahā-aggiḍāha ; dāvaggi, *m.*

Conflict, *n.* virodha, viggaha, *m.* saṅghaṭṭana, *nt.* *v.i.* vivadati; virujjhati; saṅghaṭṭīyati. *p.p.* °dita; viruddha; °ṭita. °**ing,** *a.* viruddha; paṭiloma; vivādāpanna.

Confluence, *n.* saṅgama; samavāya, *m.* — **of rivers,** nadīsaṅgama, *m.*

Confluent, *a.* ekato sandamāna.

Conflux, *n.* ekato-sandana, *nt.*

Conform, *v.i.* anuvattati; anulometi. *v.t.* samāneti; tulyaŋ karoti. *p.p.* °nita; tulyakata. °**able,** *a.* anurūpa; ghaṭanakkhama. °**ance,** °**ity,** *n.* samarūpatā; anukūlatā, *f.* °**ation,** *n.* racitākāra, *m.*

Confound, *v.t.* 1. vikkhipati; ākulīkaroti; 2. sambhameti; sammoheti. *p.p.* vikkhitta; °kata; °mita. °hita. °**ed,** *a.* saṅkula; saṅkiṇṇa. °**edly,** *adv.* atisayena; kucchitākārena. °**ing,** *a.* sandehakara; saŋsayāvaha.

Confront, *v.t.* abhimukhī bhavāti; abbhuyyāti; purato tiṭṭhati. *p.p.* °bhūta; °yāta; °ṭhita. °**ing road,** paṭimagga; paṭipatha, *m.*

Confuse, *v.t.* vikkhipati; vyākulīkaroti. *p.p.* vikkhitta; °kata. °**ed,** *a.* bhanta; sammūḷha; vyākula. °**ing,** *a.* vikkhepaka; sammohaka. °**ion,** *n.* vikkhepa; vibbhama; sammoha, *m.*

Confute, *v.t.* nirākaroti; niddosataŋ dīpeti. *p.p.* °kata; dīpitaniddosatta. °**ation,** *n.* nirākaraṇa; paccakkhāna, *nt.*

Congeal, *v.t.* saŋhanati; ghanīkaroti. *v.i.* ghanībhavati. *p.p.* saŋhata; °kata; °bhūta.

Congelation, *n.* saŋhati, *f.* piṇḍībhāva, *m.*

Congener, *n.* *a.* samajātika. °**ous,** *a.* sajātika. °**ic,** *a.* samajātyāyatta.

Congenial, *a.* 1. anukūla; samānākāra; 2. hitakara; sukhāvaha. °**ity,** *n.* samasīlatā; anukūlatā; anurūpatā, *f.* °**ly,** *adv.* anukūlatāya.

Congenital, *a.* samānuppattika; sahajāta. °**ly,** *adv.* sahajātavasena.

Congeries, *n.* nicaya; rāsi; samūha, *m.*

Congest, *v.t.* rāsīkaroti; sampiṇḍeti. *v.i.* rāsībhavati. *p.p.* °kata; °ḍita; °bhūta. °**ion,** *n.* sañcaya, *m.* °**ed,** *a.* samphuṭa; janākiṇṇa.

Conglobate, *v.t.* goḷīkaroti. *p.p.* °kata. *v.i.* goḷībhavati. *p.p.* °bhūta. adj. goḷākāra.

Conglomerate, *v.t.* piṇḍīkaroti. *v.i.* piṇḍībhavati. *p.p.* °kata; °bhūta. adj. piṇḍākāra. °**ion,** *n.* piṇḍīkaraṇa, *nt.*

Conglutinate, *v.t.* alliyāpeti. *v.i.* allīyati. *p.p.* °pita; allīna. °**ion,** *n.* allīyana, *nt.*

Congratulate, *v.t.* abhinandati; pītiŋ nivedeti. *p.p.* °dita; niveditapītī. °**ion,** *n.* abhinandana; pītinivedana, *nt.* dhaññavāda, *m.* °**tory,** *a.* abhinandanasūcaka.

Congregate, *v.t.* see **Collect.** *v.i.* see **Assemble.** °**ion,** *n.* 1. sannipāta, *m.* 2. sabhā, *f.* sammilana, *nt.* °**ional,** *a.* sammilanāyatta.

Congress, *n.* niyojitasabhā, *f.* mahāsamaya, *m.* °**ional,** *a.* mahāsamayāyatta.

Congruence, *n.* sāmaggi ; anukūlatā, *f.* avirodha, *m.*

Congruent, Congruous, *a.* aviruddha ; anukūla ; saṅgata. °**ly,** *adv.* yathocitaŋ ; yathāyogaŋ.

Conjecture, *v.t.* vitakketi ; anumāneti. *p.p.* °kita ; °nita. *n.* vitakka, *m.* ūhanā, *f.* °**able,** *a.* vitakketabba ; anumeyya.

Conjectural, *a.* anumānika ; vitakkamūlaka.

Conjoin, *v.t.* saŋyojeti ; sandhāneti ; ghaṭeti. *p.p.* °jita ; °nita ; ghaṭita. *v.i.* ghaṭīyati ; sandhīyati. *p.p.* ghaṭita ; sandhita.

Conjoint, *a.* ekābaddha ; saṅgata. °**ly,** *adv.* yuganaddhaŋ ; ekābaddhavasena.

Conjugal, *a.* vivāhavisayaka.

Conjugate, *v.t.* ākhyātarūpāni vibhajati. adj. ekābaddha. °**ion,** *n.* 1. vibhajana ; 2. saŋyojana, *nt.* °**ional,** *a.* vibhajanāyatta.

Conjunct, *a.* sambaddha ; sampayutta ; sahagata. °**ion,** *n.* samāyoga ; saṅgama, saŋsagga, *m.* sandhi, *f.* °**ive,** *a.* saŋyojaka. °**ly,** *adv.* samasamaŋ ; ekato. °**ure,** *n.* 1. saŋyoga, *m.* 2. avatthā, *f.* avasara, *m.*

Conjure, *v.t.* saccāpeti. *v.i.* 1. sapathaŋ karoti ; 2. mantāni jappati. *p.p.* °pita ; katasapatha ; jappitamanta. °**ation,** *n.* 1. saccāpana ; sapathakaraṇa, *nt.* 2. mantajappana, *nt.* °**er,** *n.* māyākāra ; indajālika, *m.*

Connate, *a.* sahajāta.

Connatural, *a.* pākatika ; ajjhattika.

Connect, *v.t.* sambandhati ; sampayojeti ; ghaṭeti. *p.p.* sambaddha ; °jita ; ghaṭita. *v.i.* ābandhīyati ; upayujjati. *p.p.* ābaddha ; upayutta. °**ed,** *a.* sampayutta ; sannissita ; sahagata. °**ion,** *n.* sahayoga ; sampayoga, *m.* sandhi ; samaṅgitā, *f.* ābandhana ; sampiṇḍana, *nt.* °**ive,** *a.* sambandhaka ; saŋyojaka.

Connive, *v.i.* paravajjam upekkhati *or* anujānāti. °**ance,** *n.* paravajjupekkhā, *f.*

Connivent, *a.* anupubbapabbhāra.

Connoisseur, *n.* visesaññū ; guṇadosavicāraka, *m.*

Connote, *v.t.* vyañjayati ; lakkheti. *p.p.* °jita ; lakkhita. °**ation,** *n.* upalakkhaṇā, *f.* °**ative,** *a.* guṇavācaka.

Connubial, *a.* vivāhāyatta.

Conquer, *v.t.* jeti ; jināti ; abhibhavati. *p.p.* jita ; abhibhūta. °**able,** *a.* jetabba. °**or,** *n.* jetu ; arindama ; abhibhū, *m.*

Conquest, *n.* jaya ; vijaya, *m.*

Consanguine, °**guineous,** sālohita ; bandhubhūta. °**nity,** *n.* sālohitatta.

Conscience, *n.* manoviññāṇa, *nt.* vivekabuddhi, *f.*

Conscientious, *a.* amāyāvī ; ujugatika ; kukkuccaka. °**ly,** *adv.* avyājaŋ ; ujutāya. °**ness,** *n.* ajjava, *nt.* amāyāvitā, *f.*

Conscious, *a.* sasaññī ; sacetana ; saviññāṇaka. °**ly,** *adv.* sañcicca ; sacetanaŋ. °**ness,** *n.* viññāṇa, *nt.* cetanā, *f.*

Consecrate, *v.t.* 1. dikkhati ; 2. sammannati ; 3. abhisiñcati ;

4. nimmalīkaroti. *p.p.* dikkhita; sammata; abhisitta; °kata; °**ion,** *n.* abhiseka, *m.* nimmalīkaraṇa, *nt.*

Consectary, *n.* upasiddhanta, *m.*

Consecution, *n.* anukkama; anvaya, *m.* anupubbatā; paramparā, *f.*

Consecutive, *a.* anukkamāgata; ānupubbika. °**ly,** *adv.* anukkamena; yathākkamaŋ. °**ness,** *n.* sānukkamatā, *f.*

Consensual, *a.* paṭiññāya pavattamāna.

Consensus, *n.* ekamatitā, *f.*

Consent, *n.* anuññā; anumati; ekamatitā, *f.* *v.i.* anujānāti; anumaññati. *p.p.* anuññāta; anumata. **Against one's —,** anicchāya; balena. °**ient,** *a.* ekamatika; anukūlacitta.

Consentaneous, *a.* anukūla; ekamatika; ekakkhaṇika. °**ly,** *adv.* ekamatikatāya.

Consequence, *n.* 1. phala, *nt.* vipāka, *m.* 2. garutta, *nt.* mahima, *m.* **As a — of your efforts,** tava ussāhassa phalavasena. **In — of this,** iminā hetunā. **It is of no —,** taŋ na sallakkhaṇīyaŋ. **Of no —,** niratthaka, *a.*

Consequent, *a.* anusaṅgika. °**ial,** *a.* phalavasenāgata. °**ly,** *adv.* phalavasena; tena hetunā.

Conservation, *n.* saŋrakkhana; ciraŋ-pavattāpana, *nt.* °**tive,** *a.* cirappavattaka; saṅkharaṇaviruddha. °**tor,** *n.* saŋrakkhaka; cirānupālaka, *m.* °**tory,** *n.* anupālakaṭṭhāna, *nt.*

Conserve, *v.t.* saŋrakkhati; ciraŋ pavatteti. *p.p.* °khita; °tita.

Consider, *v.i.* anucinteti; vicāreti; vīmaŋsati; parituleti; samekkhati; upadhāreti. *p.p.* °tita; °rita; °sita; °lita; °khita; °rita. °**able,** *a.* sallakkhetabba; anappaka. °**ably,** *adv.* bhiyyo; bhusaŋ; amandaŋ. °**ate,** *a.* vīmaŋsaka; appamatta; samekkhakārī. °**ately,** *adv.* sadayaŋ; sāpekkhaŋ. °**ation,** *n.* ābhoga; manasikāra, *m.* upanijjhāna; paccavekkhana, *nt.* ālocanā; vīmaŋsā, *f.*

Considering, *prep.* nissāya; sallakkhetvā. °**ly,** *adv.* vicāraṇapubbakaŋ.

Consign, *v.t.* appeti; pāpeti; peseti. *p.p.* °pita; pesita. °**ation,** samappaṇa; nītyanugata-mūladāna, *nt.* °**ee,** *n.* bhaṇḍasampaṭicchaka, *m.* °**ment,** *n.* samappita-bhaṇḍasamūha, *m.* samappaṇa, *nt.* °**er,** °**or,** *n.* samappaka; bhaṇḍapesaka, *m.*

Consilient, *a.* ekamatika; anukūla. °**ence,** *n.* ekamatitā, *f.*

Consist, *v.i.* sahavattati; samannāgato hoti. °**ence,** °**ency,** *n.* 1. ghanatā; 2. thiratā; 3. avirodhitā; 4. yuttatā, *f.* °**ent,** *a.* 1. anurūpa; aviruddha; 2. thira; acapala; 3. ghana. °**ently,** *adv.* avirodhena. °**ing of,** patimaṇḍita; samannāgata.

Consistory, *n.* sāmayikādhikaraṇa, *nt.*

Consociate, *v.t.* saṅgacchati; saŋsevati. *n.* sahacara; sahāya, *m.* adj. saŋyutta. °**ion,** *n.* saṅgama, *m.* sevana, *nt.* sahakāritā, *f.*

Console, *v.t.* assāseti ; sokaŋ vinodeti. *p.p.* assattha ; vinoditasoka. °**able,** *a.* assāsetabba. °**ation,** *n.* assāsana ; sokavinodana, *nt.* °**atory,** °**ing,** *a.* assāsakara ; sokāpahāraka.

Consoler, *n.* assāsetu ; sokahārī, *m.*

Consolidate, *v.t.* saŋhanati ; ghanīkaroti. *p.p.* saŋhata ; ghanīkata. *v.i.* ghanībhavati. *p.p.* °bhūta. °**ion,** *n.* saŋhati, *f.* ghanīkaraṇa, *nt.* °**tor,** *n.* sambandhaka, *m.* °**tory,** *a.* sambandhanāyatta.

Consonance, *n.* samānassaratā ; sarānukūlatā, *f.*

Consonant, *a.* aviruddha ; anukūla. *n.* vyañjanakkhara, *nt.* °**ly,** *adv.* 1. anukulatāya ; 2. samasaratāya.

Consort, *n.* (wife :) dutiyikā ; sahacārinī ; bhariyā, *f.* (husband :) sahacārī ; pati ; sāmika ; bhattu, *m.* *v.i.* sahavasati ; saŋvasati. *p.p.* °vuttha.

Conspectus, *n.* sāranidassana, *nt.*

Conspicuous, *a.* supākaṭa ; ativisada. °**ly,** *adv.* vyattākārena. °**ness,** *n.* visadatta ; pākaṭatta ; visiṭṭhatta, *nt.*

Conspire, *v.t.* 1. kumanteti ; 2. saṅgacchati. *p.p.* °tita ; saṅgata. °**acy,** *n.* kumantana, *nt.* °**ator,** *n.* kumantaka ; dubbhaka ; mittaddu, *m.*

Constable, *n.* rājapurisa, *m.*

Constancy, *n.* thiratā, niccalatā, *f.*

Constant, *a.* acala ; thira ; nicca ; nirantara ; nibaddha. °**ly,** *adv.* satataŋ ; niccaŋ ; nirantaraŋ ; abhiṇhaŋ ; nibaddhaŋ.

Constellation, *n.* nakkhatta, *nt.* tārāsamūha, *m.*

Consternate, *v.t.* vikkhipati ; bhāyāpeti. *p.p.* vikkhitta ; °pita. °**ion,** *n.* vikkhepa ; santāsa, *m.* chambhitatta, *nt.*

Constipate, *v.t.* ābandhati. *p.p.* ābaddha. °**ion,** *n.* malabandha ; malatthambha, *m.*

Constituency, *n.* chandadāyakajanatā, *f.*

Constituent, *a.* aṅgabhūta.

Constitute, *v.t.* 1. patiṭṭhāpeti ; nimmiṇāti ; vidahati ; 2. racayati. *p.p.* °pita ; nimmita ; vihita ; racita. °**ion,** *n.* 1. patiṭṭhāpana, *nt.* nimmāṇa, *nt.* 2. racanā, *f.* 3. avatthā ; dasā ; vutti ; 4. vavatthā ; nīti, *f.* vidhi ; niyama, *m.* 5. pakati, *f.* sabhāva, *m.* °**ional,** *a.* nītyanugata ; vavatthānubaddha. °**ionally,** *adv.* niyamānurūpaŋ.

Constitutive, *a.* 1. patiṭṭhāpaka ; māpaka ; 2. sārabhūta.

Constrain, 1. pasayha kāreti ; 2. balena orundhati. *p.p.* °kārita ; °oruddha.

Constraint, *n.* balakkāra, *m.* avarodhana, *nt.*

Constrict, *v.t.* saṅkoceti ; sampīḷeti. *p.p.* °cita ; °ḷita. °**ion,** saṅkocana, *nt.* °**ive** *a.* saṅkocakara. °**or,** *n.* saṅkocetu ; sampīḷaka, *m.*

Construct, *v.t.* māpeti ; yojeti ; ghaṭeti. *p.p.* māpita ; yojita ; °ṭita. °**ion,** *n.* nimmāṇa ; māpana, *nt.* °**ional,** *a.* nimmāṇāyatta. °**ive,** *a.* 1. nimmāṇakara ; māpanāyatta ; 2. pariyāyavutta. °**ively,** *adv.* sasādhanaŋ. °**iveness,** *n.*

nimmāṇasatti, *f.* °**or**, *n.* māpaka ; nimmātu ; vidhāyaka, *m.*

Construe, *v.t.* attha-padāni vaṇṇeti. *p.p.* vaṇṇitatthapada.

Construpation, *n.* kaññādūsana, *nt.*

Consubstantial, *a.* samadabbamaya.

Consubstantiate, *v.t.* ekavatthumhi yojeti. *p.p.* °yojita.

Consuetude, *n.* cāritta, *nt.* °**inary,** *a.* cārittānugata.

Consul, *n.* rajjaniyojita, *m.* °**ate,** *n.* rajjaniyojitāvāsa, *m.*

Consult, *v.t.* 1. sākacchati ; manteti ; 2. sādhakāni pariyesati. *p.p.* °chita ; mantita ; pariyesitasādhaka. °**ation,** *n.* mantaṇa, *nt.* sākacchā, *f.* °**able,** *a.* sākacchitabba ; mantaṇīya. °**ant,** *n.* sākacchaka ; mantaka, *m.*

Consume, *v.t.* khepeti ; vināseti ; pariyādiyati. *p.p.* °pita ; °sita ; pariyādinna. °**able,** *a.* khepanīya. °**dly,** *adv.* atisayena ; nissesaŋ. °**er,** *n.* khepaka ; sosaka, nāsaka, *m.* °**ing,** *a.* khepaka.

Consummate, *v.t.* samāpeti ; niṭṭhāpeti. *p.p.* °pita. adj. paripuṇṇa ; aṇūna ; ukkaṭṭha. °**ion,** *n.* samāpana ; niṭṭhāpana, *nt.*

Consumption, *n.* 1. kāsaroga, *m.* 2. khaya, *m.* pariyādāna, *nt.* °**tive,** *a.* khayagāmī. *n.* kāsarogī, *m.*

Contact, *n.* phassa ; samphassa ; abhighāta, *m.* phusanā, *f.* phoṭṭhabba, *nt.*

Contagion, *n.* rogasaṅkamaṇa, *nt.*

Contagious, *a.* saṅkamanīya. °**ness,** *n.* saṅkamanasabhāva, *m.*

Contain, *v.t.* dhāreti ; antokaroti. *p.p.* dhārita ; °kata. °**able,** *a.* dhāranīya ; antokātabba. °**er,** *n.* dhāraka ; puṭa, *m.* bhājana, *nt.*

Contaminate, *v.t.* dūseti ; misseti. *p.p.* dūsita ; missita. °**ion,** *n.* dūsana ; missaṇa, *nt.*

Contemn, *v.t.* avamaññati ; avajānāti ; paribhavati. *p.p.* avamata ; avaññāta ; °bhūta. °**er,** *n.* paribhavitu ; avamānetu, *m.*

Contemplate, *v.i.* jhāyati ; takketi ; paccavekkhati. *p.p.* °yita ; takkita ; °khita. °**ion,** *n.* jhāyana ; jhāna ; paccavekkhana, *nt.* °**ive,** *a.* jhāyaka ; cintāparāyaṇa. °**tor,** *n.* jhāyī ; vipassaka ; vicāraka, *m.*

Contemporaneous, *a.* samakālika. °**ly,** *adv.* samakālam eva. °**ness,** *n.* samakālikatta, *nt.*

Contemporary, *a. n.* samakālavattī ; samavayaṭṭha.

Contemporize, *v.t.* samakālikaŋ karoti. *p.p.* °kata.

Contempt, *n.* avaññā ; hīlanā ; vambhanā, *f.* avamāna ; anādara ; paribhava, *m.* — **of others,** paravambhanā, *f.* °**ible,** *a.* jeguccha ; kucchita ; gārayha. °**ibly,** *adv.* gārayhākārena.

Contemptuous, *a.* vambhanasīla ; hīlaka. °**ly,** *adv.* vambhanākārena. °**ness,** *n.* vambhanatā, *f.*

Contend, *v.t.* vivadati ; virujjhati. *p.p.* °dita ; viruddha. °**ing,** *a.* vivādāpanna.

Content, *n.* 1. antogata-vatthu, *nt.* 2. titti ; santuṭṭhi, *f.* adj. santuṭṭha ; santappita. *v.t.* toseti ;

tappeti ; santappeti. *p.p.* tosita ; °pita. °**ment,** *n.* santuṭṭhi ; titti ; abhirati, *f.*

Contention, *n.* vivāda ; virodha ; kalaha, *m.*

Contentious, *a.* vivādasīlī ; kalahappiya. °**ly,** *adv.* kalahakāritāya. °**ness,** vivādappiyatā, *f.*

Conterminal, *a.* sannihita ; samānamariyādaka.

Conterminous, *a.* samānasīmāyutta ; koṭiyākoṭipaṭipādaka.

Contest, *n.* vivāda ; yugaggāha. *v.t.* vivadati ; yugaŋ gaṇhāti ; sampayojeti. *p.p.* °dita ; yugaggahita ; °jita, °**able,** *a.* vivādabhājana. °**ant,** *n.* vivādī ; yugaggāhī ; paccāmitta, *m.* °**ed,** *a.* vivādāpnna ; vivādavisayabhūta. °**ation,** *n.* vivadana, *nt.*

Context, *n.* padanvaya ; padasambandha, *m.* °**ure,** *n.* 1. padavinyāsa ; 2. vāyitākāra, *m.*

Contiguity, *n.* samīpatā, *f.*

Contiguous, *a.* ekābaddha ; anantaraṭṭha. °**ly,** *adv.* samīpaṭṭhatāya.

Continence, *n.* indriyadamana, *nt.* cittasaŋvara, *m.* °**nent,** *a.* jitindriya ; santacitta.

Continent, *n.* mahādīpa, *m.* °**al,** *a.* mahādīpika. *n.* mahādīpavāsī, *m.*

Contingency, *n.* anapekkhitasiddhi, *f.*

Contingent, *a. n.* avinicchita ; aniyamita. °**ly,** *adv.* aniyatākārena.

Continue, *v.t.* anuppavatteti; anuppabandheti. *p.p.* °tita ; °dhita. *v.i.* pavattati ; vattati. *p.p.* pavatta. °**able,** *a.* pavattanāraha. °**al,** °**ous,** *a.* avicchinna ; nibaddha; nirantara. °**ance,** °**ation,** °**ity,** *n.* aviccheda ; anuppabandha, *m.* santati ; pavatti, *f.* °**ator,** *n.* pavattaka ; pavattāpaka, *m.*

Continuum, *n.* avicchinnapavaha, *m.*

Contort, *v.t.* ākuñceti ; vyāvaṭṭeti. *p.p.* °cita ; °ṭita. °**ion,** *n.* ākuñcana ; ākuñcitatta, *nt.*

Contour, *n.* bāhirasaṇṭhāna, *nt.* bhājakalekhā, *f.* *v.t.* rekhāhi aṅketi. *p.p.* rekhaṅkita.

Contra, *prep.* paṭi.

Contraband, *n.* guttabhaṇḍaharaṇa. adj. theyyena nīyamāna. °**ist,** *n.* guttabhaṇḍahārī, *m.*

Contraceptive, *a.* gabbhanāsaka.

Contract, *n.* paṭiññātakammanta, *m.* *v.t.* saṅkoceti ; saŋharati ; saṅkhipati. *p.p.* °cita ; saŋhaṭa ; saṅkhitta. *v.i.* 1. mithupaṭiññaŋ karoti ; 2. saṅkucati. *p.p.* kata° ; °cita. —**a debt,** iṇaŋ gaṇhāti. —**a disease,** rogī bhavati. —**a friendship,** mittasanthavaŋ karoti. °**ion,** *n.* saṅkoca, *m.* saŋharaṇa ; saṅkhipana, *nt.* °**or,** *m.* 1. saṅkocaka ; 2. paṭiññāsādhaka, *m.*

Contradict, *v.t.* paṭikkhipati ; paccakkhāti ; virujjhati. *p.p.* °khitta ; °khāta ; viruddha. °**ion,** *n.* 1. paccakkhāna, *nt.* paṭisedha ; virodha, *m.* 2. vesamma, *nt.* vipakkhatā, *f.* °**ory,** *a.* vipakkha ; visabhāga ; paṭiloma ; (— itself :) pubbāparaviruddha. °**orily,** *adv.* paṭilomākārena. °**oriness,** *n.* viruddhatā ; visamatā, *f.*

Contradictious, *a.* vipakkhapakatika.

Contradistinction, *n.* paṭiviruddhatā, *f.* visabhāgalakkhaṇa, *nt.*

Contradistinguish, *v.t.* visabhāgattena viseseti. *p.p.* °sita.

Contraposition, *n.* virodha, *m.* vesamma, *nt.*

Contraption, *n.* tāvakālika-upāya, *m.*

Contrary, *a.* vipakkha ; paṭipakkha. *n.* virodha, *m.* **On the —,** tappaṭipakkhato, *ind.* **°iety,** *n.* vipakkhatā, *f.* **°ious,** *a.* viruddha. **°iwise,** *adv.* viruddhākārena ; paṭilomato.

Contrast, *n.* visesa ; bheda, *m.* vesamma, *nt.* *v.t.* antaraŋ *or* vesammaŋ dasseti. *v.i.* vibhijjati. *p.p.* dassitantara ; vibhinna.

Contravene, *v.t.* ullaṅgheti ; atikkamati ; nisedheti. *p.p.* °ghita ; atikkanta ; °dhita. **°ntion,** *n.* ullaṅghana, *nt.* vītikkama ; nisedha, *m.*

Contribute, *v.t.* chandakaŋ deti ; upatthambheti. *p.p.* dinnachandaka ; °bhita. **°ion,** *n.* sakabhāgadāna, *nt.* **°ive, °ory,** *a.* upatthambhaka ; saŋvaḍḍhaka. **°or,** *n.* bhāgadāyaka ; upakāraka, *m.*

Contrite, *a.* vippaṭisārī ; anutāpahata.

Contrition, *n.* kukkucca, *nt.* pacchātāpa ; vippaṭisāra, *m.*

Contrive, *v.t.* payojeti ; parikappeti. *p.p.* °jita ; °pita. **°ance,** *n.* payoga ; upāya ; upakkama, *m.* upāyacintā, *f.* **°er,** *n.* upāyacintaka, *m.*

Control, *v.t.* dameti ; saŋyameti ; pāleti. *p.p.* damita ; °mita ; pālita. *n.* dama ; saŋyama, *m.* vasavattana, *nt.* **Difficult to —,** duddamaya ; dunniggayha. *a.* **°able,** *a.* dametabba ; vineyya. **°ler,** *n.* pālaka ; vasavattaka, *m.* **°ler of revenues,** rāsivaḍḍhakāmacca, *m.*

Controversy, *n.* vivāda, *m.* **°ial,** *a.* vivādavisayaka. **°ialist,** *n.* vādakāmī ; vivādī, *m.*

Controvert, *v.t.* vivadati ; nirākaroti ; mataŋ khaṇḍeti. *p.p.* °dita ; °kata ; khaṇḍitamata. **°ible,** *a.* khaṇḍanīya.

Contumacious, *a.* avidheyya ; anassava ; dubbaca. **°ness,** *n.* dovacassatā ; anassavatā, *f.*

Contumacy, *n.* dovacassa ; anassavatta, *nt.*

Contumelious, *a.* avamaññanasīla ; uddhata.

Contumely, *n.* avamāna, *m.* avaññā, *f.* paribhava, *n.*

Contuse, *v.t.* antokhataŋ karoti. *p.p.* antokhata. **°ion,** *n.* tacavidāraṇarahita-paharaṇa, *nt.*

Conundrum, *n.* paheḷikā, *f.* gūḷhapañha, *m.*

Convalesce, *v.i.* gelaññā vuṭṭhāti ; ārogyaŋ labhati. *p.p.* °vuṭṭhita ; laddhārogya. **°nce,** *n.* rogūpasama, *m.* **°nt,** *a.* aciravuṭṭhitagelañña.

Convection, *n.* tejoharaṇa, *nt.*

Convene, *v.t.* 1. sammileti ; sannipāteti ; 2. adhikaraṇaŋ āṇāpeti. *v.i.* sannipatati. *p.p.* °lita ; °tita ; °pita ; °tita.

Convenience, *n.* anucchavikatā, *f.* phāsuvihāra, *m.*

Convenient, *a.* sukhakara; phāsuka; anucchavika. °**ly,** *adv.* yathāphāsukaŋ; yathākāmaŋ.

Convent, *n.* assama; paribbājikārāma, *m.*

Convention, *n.* 1. sammuti; 2. sabhā; niyojitaparisā, *f.*

Converge, *v.i.* saṅgacchati; ekattha samosarati. *p.p.* saṅgata; °samosaṭa. °**rice,** *n.* samosaraṇa, *nt.* samavāya, *m.* °**nt,** °**ing,** *a.* samosaramāna.

Conversance, °**cy,** *n.* paricaya, *m.* katahatthatā, *f.* pāṭava; nepuñña, *nt.* °**sant,** *a.* nipuṇa; paṭu; kovida.

Converse, *v.i.* sallapati; sambhāsati. *p.p.* °pita; °sita. *n.* desanā; sākacchā, *f.* °**ation,** *n.* sallāpa, *m.* sambhāsana, *nt.* °**ational,** *a.* sākacchāyatta.

Converse, *a.* paṭiviruddha; viparita. °**sion,** *n.* 1. viparivattana, *nt.* 2. parasamayagahaṇa, *nt.* °**ly,** *adv.* vipariyāyena; viruddhākārena.

Convert, *v.t.* parivatteti; aññathā karoti. *v.i.* viparivattati. *p.p.* °tita; °kata; °**ibility,** *n.* viparivattanīyatā, *f.* °**ible,** *a.* viparivattiya.

Convex, *a.* kummapiṭṭākāra.

Convey, *v.t.* harati; neti; pāpeti. *p.p.* haṭa; nīta; pāpita. °**ance,** *n.* 1. yāna; vāhana, *nt.* 2. haraṇa; nayana; pāpaṇa; niyyātana, *nt.* °**ancer,** *n.* samappaṇalekhanādhikārī, *m.*

Convict, *v.t.* vadhaŋ pāpeti; vajje patiṭṭhāpeti. *p.p.* °pāpita; °pita. *n.* aparādhī; vadhāraha; daṇḍanāraha. °**ion,** *n.* 1. daṇḍaniyamana, *nt.* 2. sakapaṭibhāṇa, *nt.*

Convince, *v.t.* saddahāpeti; bodheti. *p.p.* °pita; bodhita. °**ed,** *a.* jātanicchaya; chinnasaŋsaya. °**ing,** *a.* viññāpaka; avabodhaka. °**ingly,** *adv.* vissāsajanakattena.

Convivial, *a.* ussavākārayutta.

Convocation, *n.* 1. sākacchāsabhā; saṅgīti, *f.* 2. sannipātana, *nt.* °**al,** *a.* sākacchāsabhāyatta.

Convoke, *v.t.* sannipāteti; samavheti. *p.p.* °tita; °hita.

Convolute, *a.* āvalībhūta. *n.* āvalī, *f.* °**ion,** *n.* āvalīkaraṇa, *nt.*

Convolve, *v.t.* āvaṭṭeti; paḷiveṭheti. *p.p.* āvaṭṭita; °ṭhita.

Convoy, *n.* 1. ārakkhaṇa, *nt.* 2. rakkhitanāvāsamūha, *m. v.t.* rakkhanattham anugacchati. *p.p.* °anugata.

Convulse, *v.t.* khobheti; kampeti; cāleti. *p.p.* °bhita; °pita; cālita. °**ion,** *n.* saṅkhobha, *m.* kampā, *f.* calana, *nt.* °**ive,** *a.* kampājanaka.

Coo, *v.i.* kūjati. *p.p.* kūjita. °**ing,** *n.* kūjana, *nt.* adj. kūjamāna.

Cook, *n.* sūda; rasaka; sūpika. *v.t.* pacati; randheti. *p.p.* pakka *or* pacita; randhita. °**ery,** *n.* sūpasattha, *nt.* pākavijjā, *f.* °**ing,** *n.* pacana, *nt.* pāka, *m.* adj. pacanta.

Cool, *n.* sīta, *nt.* adj. 1. sītala; sītibhūta; 2. upasanta; avikkhitta. *v.t.* sītalīkaroti; nibbāpeti.

v.i. sītalībhavati ; nibbāti ; upasammati. *p.p.* °kata ; °pita ; °bhūta ; nibbuta ; upasanta. °**er,** *n.* sītalīkarabhājana, *nt.* °**headed,** *a.* akkhobha ; acala. °**ing,** *a.* sītikara ; tāpahara ; nibbāpaka. °**ness,** *n.* sītalatta, *nt.*

Coolie, *n.* bhataka, *m.*

Coon, *n.* saṭha, *m.*

Coop, *v.t.* pañjare pakkhipati. *p.p.* °khitta.

Cooper, *n.* kosakāraka, *m.* *v.t.* bhaṇḍāvaraṇāni sampādeti. °**age,** *n.* āvaraṇasampādana, *nt.*

Co-operate, *v.i.* sahayogī *or* sahakārī bhavati. *p.p.* °bhūta. °**ion,** *n.* sahayoga, *m.* gaṇabandhana, *nt.* °**ive,** *a.* sahayogika. °**tor,** *n.* sahayogī ; seṇibaddha, *m.*

Co-ordinate, *v.t.* samabalataŋ neti ; yathākkamaŋ yojeti. *p.p.* °nīta ; °yojita. adj. ekākāra ; samabala ; samappamāṇa. °**ion,** *n.* samattapāpaṇa, *nt.*

Copartner, *n.* samabhāgī ; samakoṭṭhāsī ; sahabhāgī, *m.* °**ship,** *n.* sahabhāgitā ; samānabhāgatā, *f.*

Cope, *n.* dīghakañcuka, *m.* *v.i.* (with :) abhibhavati ; abhimaddati. *p.p.* °bhūta ; °dita.

Copious, *a.* bahula ; pacura ; pahūta ; vipula. °**ly,** *adv.* yebhuyyena ; bahuso ; bahulākārena. °**ness,** *m.* bāhulla ; pahūtatta, *nt.*

Copper, *n.* tamba ; tambaloha, *nt.* °**coin,** lohamāsaka, *m.* °**plate,** tambapaṭṭa, *nt.* °**smith,** lohakāra, *m.* °**ware,** lohabhaṇḍa, *nt.*

Coppery, *a.* tambavaṇṇa ; tambamissa.

Copra, *n.* sukkha-nāḷikeramiñjā, *f.*

Copula, *n.* sandhāna, *nt.*

Copulate, *v.i.* saŋvasati ; methunam abhiyuñjati. *p.p.* saŋvuttha ; methunābhiyutta. °**ion,** *n.* methuna, *nt.* saŋvāsa, *m.* dvayandvayasamāpatti *f.* °**ive,** *a.* 1. methunāyatta ; 2. sambandhakara.

Copy, *n.* 1. lipiputtikā ; paṭilekhā, *f.* 2. anukaraṇa ; paṭirūpaka, *nt.* *v.t.* paṭilikhati ; puttikaŋ karoti. *p.p.* °khita ; puttikākata. °**ist,** *n.* lipikāra ; anukārī, *m.* °**right,** *n.* muddāpaṇādhikāra, *m.*

Coquet, *v.t.* hāvaŋ *or* vilāsaŋ dasseti ; vilasati. *p.p.* dassitahāva ; vilasita. °**ry,** *n.* hāva, *m.* līlā ; vilāsitā, *f.* kutta, *nt.* °**tee,** *n.* vilāsinī, *f.* °**tish,** *a.* hāvayutta. °**tishly,** *adv.* vilāsitāya.

Coral, *n.* pavāḷa, *nt.* °**tree,** koviḷāra ; pāricchattaka, *m.* °**line,** *a.* pavāḷaratta. °**loid,** *a.* pavāḷasadisa.

Corbel, *n.* bhittiniggati, *f.* *v.t.* bhittiniggamanāni māpeti.

Corbie, *n.* kākola ; vanakāka, *m.*

Cord, *n.* tantu ; guṇa, *m.* tanta, *nt.* — **of a lute,** vīṇātanti, *f.* *v.t.* bandhati. *p.p.* baddha. °**age,** *n.* bandhaka-rajjusamūha, *m.* °**ed,** *a.* rajjubaddha.

Cordate, *a.* hadayasaṇṭhāna.

Cordial, *a.* 1. vallabha ; sambhatta ; daḷhasohajja ; 2. rucikara ; jaṭharadīpaka. *n.* dīpakabhesajja, *nt.* °**ity,** *n.* sohajja ; sakhya ;

susīlatta, *nt.* °**ly,** *adv.* suhadatāya; vallabhattena.

Cordon, *n.* 1. rakkhakāvali, *f.* 2. rājadattiya-pāmaṅga, *nt.*

Core, *n.* miñjā, *f.* antobhāga, *m.* *v.t.* miñjaṃ apaneti. *p.p.* apanītamiñja.

Corelative, *a.* aññoññasambandha.

Co-religionist, *n.* samānabhattika; sahadhammika, *m.*

Co-respondent, *n.* ekābhiyogabhāgī, *m.*

Corf, *n.* mahāpiṭaka, *nt.*

Coriander, *n.* dhaniya, *nt.*

Cork, *n.* nāḷikāpidhāna, *nt.* °**screw,** *n.* thakanakākaḍḍhanī, *f.* °**y,** *a.* niratthaka; appaggha.

Cormorant, *n.* udakakāka, *m.*

Corn, *n.* 1. dhañña, *nt.* 2. sassa, *nt.* 3. cammaphoṭa, *m.* *v.t.* saŋrakkhati. *p.p.* °khita. °**flour,** *n.* dhaññapiṭṭha, *nt.* °**measure,** nāḷi, *f.* **Growing —,** kiṭṭha, *nt.*

Cornea, *n.* akkhisukkamaṇḍala, *nt.*

Corneous, *a.* siṅgasadisa; siṅgayutta.

Corner, *n.* koṇa, *m.* kaṇṇa, *nt.* *v.t.* 1. koṇaŋ māpeti; 2. paṇiyāni pāleti. **— of the eye,** apāṅga, *m.* °**stone,** koṇasilā, *f.*

Cornet, *n.* kāhala, *m.*

Cornice, *n.* bhittisīsālaṅkāra, *m.*

Cornuted, *a.* siṅgayutta.

Corny, *a.* dhaññabahula.

Corollary, *n.* upasiddhanta, *m.*

Corona, *n.* raŋsimaṇḍala, *nt.* raŋsimālā, *f.*

Coronal, *n.* sīsābharaṇa, *nt.* sekhara; makuṭa, *nt.* adj. muddhāyatta.

Coronation, *n.* kirīṭapilandhana; makuṭabandhana; chattamaṅgala, *nt.* rajjābhiseka, *m.*

Coroner, *n.* akālamata-vīmaŋsaka, *m.*

Coronet, *n.* khuddakakirīṭa, *nt.*

Coronoid, *a.* kākatuṇḍasadisa.

Corporal, *a.* sārīrika; sarīrāyatta. *n.* upagumbādhikārī, *m.* °**ity,** *n.* kāyikatta; rūpatta, *nt.*

Corporate, *a.* saŋsaṭṭha. °**ion,** *n.* seṇī, *f.* pūga; gaṇabandha, *m.* °**ly,** *adv.* gaṇabaddhavasena. °**ive,** *a.* pūgāyatta. °**tor,** *n.* seṇika, *m.*

Corporeal, *a.* sasarīra; dehasita; kāyasamaṅgī. °**ity,** *n.* dehasamaṅgitā, *f.* °**ly,** *adv.* sarīren'eva.

Corps, *n.* senādala, *nt.*

Corpse, *n.* chava, *m.* matakalebara, *nt.*

Corpulent, *a.* pīvara; thullasarīra. °**ency,** *n.* thūlatta; pīvaratta, *nt.*

Corpus, *n.* nītikkhandha, *m.*

Corpuscle, *n.* kaṇa; lava; lesa, *m.*

Corral, *n.* vaja, *m.* pasurodhanaṭṭhāna, *nt.*

Correct, *a.* niddosa; avitatha; anavajja. *v.t.* 1. sodheti; dosaṃ apaneti; 2. ovadati; tajjeti. *p.p.* sodhita; apanītadosa; °dita; tajjita. °**ion,** *n.* 1. niddosīkaraṇa; sodhana, *nt.* 2. anusāsana, *nt.* °**ive,** *a.* saŋsodhaka; paṭikara; suppathagamaka. °**ly,** *adv.* avitathaŋ; yathātathaŋ. °**ness,** *n.* anavajjatā; akalaṅkatā; tathatā, *f.* °**or,** *n.* saŋsodhaka; yathāmaggapaṭipādaka, *m.*

Correlate, *n.* aññamaññasambandhī, *m.* *v.i.* sambandhībhavati. °**ion,** *n.* aññoññasambandha, *m.* °**ive,** *a.* itarītarasambandhaka.

Correspond, *v.i.* 1. saŋsandīyati ; ghaṭīyati ; 2. sandesavinimayaŋ karoti. *p.p.* °dita ; ghaṭita ; katasandesavinimaya. °**ence,** *n.* 1. anukūlatā ; sadisatā, *f.* 2. sandesavinimaya, *m.* °**ent,** *n.* sandesapesaka, *m.* adj. saŋsandiyamāna. °**ing,** *a.* ghaṭīyamāna.

Corridor, *n.* antarāpatha ; uparichanna-magga, *m.*

Corrigendum, *n.* pamādadosa, *m.* sodhyaṭṭhāna, *nt.*

Corrigible, *a.* damanakkhama ; vineyya.

Corrival, *n.* paṭiyogī, *m.*

Corroborate, *v.t.* daḷhayati ; samattheti. *p.p.* daḷhita ; °thita, °**ive,** °**tory,** *a.* daḷhattakara.

Corrode, *v.t.* anukkamena vināseti. *p.p.* °sita.

Corrosion, *n.* anupubbavilayana, *nt.* °**sive,** *a.* nāsaka ; vilīyāpaka.

Corrugate, *v.i.* valiŋ gaṇhāti. *v.t.* valiŋ gaṇhāpeti ; valiyo uṭṭhāpeti. *p.p.* valiggahita ; °pita ; uṭṭhāpitavali. °**tor,** *n.* bhamusaṅkocaka, *m.*

Corrupt, *v.t.* dūseti ; kalusayati. *p.p.* dūsita ; kalusita. *v.i.* dussati ; kilissati ; pūtibhavati. *p.p.* duṭṭha ; kiliṭṭha ; pūtibhūta. adj. vyāpanna ; malina. °**er,** *n.* dūsaka ; lañcadāyī, *m.* °**ible,** *a.* dūsanakkhama. °**ion,** *n.* dūsana ; kalusīkaraṇa ; kilissana, *nt.* pūtibhāva, *m.* °**ive,** *a.* dūsanakara. °**ly,** *adv.* duṭṭhākārena. °**ness,** *n.* duṭṭhatta ; dūsitatta, *nt.*

Corset, *n.* saṅkaccikā, *f.*

Corslet, *n.* uracchada, *m.*

Cortege, *n.* parivāra, *m.* anugāmikaparisā, *f.*

Cortex, *n.* taca, *m.* bāhiramatthaluṅga, *nt.*

Cortical, *a.* tacāyatta.

Coruscate, *v.t.* vipphāreti. *p.p.* °rita. °**ion,** *n.* vipphuraṇa, *nt.*

Corvine, *a.* kākasadisa ; kākāyatta.

Coryza, *n.* pināsa, *m.*

Co-signatory, *n.* *a.* saha hatthalanchanadāyī, 3.

Cosily, *adv.* yathāphāsukaŋ.

Cosmetic, *n.* aṅgarāga, *m.* gandhavilepana, *nt.* °**al,** *a.* aṅgarāgāyatta.

Cosmogony, *n.* lokanimmāṇavijjā, *f.*

Cosmography, *n.* lokavaṇṇanā, *f.*

Cosmopolitan, *a.* sabbasādhāraṇa ; sabbalokavyāpī.

Cosmopolite, *n.* *a.* jātyantarabhedarahita ; sabbalokika.

Cosmorama, *n.* akhiladesa-dassaka.

Cosmos, *n.* lokadhātu, *f.*

Cosset, *v.t.* lāleti. *p.p.* lālita.

Cost, *n.* 1. aggha ; 2. vaya ; paribbaya, *m.* *v.i.* agghati. °**less,** *a.* appaggha. °**ly,** *a.* mahaggha. °**liness,** *n.* mahagghatā, *f.*

Costume, *n.* 1. acchādanavidhi ; vesa, *m.* 2. acchādanavisesa, *m.*

Cosy, *a.* sukhāvaha.

Cot, *n*. 1. dārakadolā, *f*. 2. dolāmañca, *m*. 3. kuṭi, *f*. °**tage**, *n*. kuṭi ; paṇṇasālā, *f*.

Cote, *n*. vaja, *m*. pasukuṭi, *f*.

Co-temporary, *a*. samavayaṭṭha; samakālika.

Co-tenant, *n*. sahavāsī, *m*.

Coterie, *n*. seṇī, *f*.

Cotton, *n*. picu ; tūla, *nt*. kappāsa, *m*. — **cloth**, kappāsika, *nt*. — **mattress**, tūlikā, *f*. °**plant**, kappāsī, *f*.

Couch, *n*. pallaṅka ; mañcaka, *m*. *v.i*. seti. *v.t*. sayāpeti ; sanniveseti. *p.p*. sayita ; °pita ; °sita. °**ant**, *a*. sannisinna.

Cough, *n*. ukkāsana, *nt*. *v.i*. ukkāsati. *p.p*. °sita.

Council, *n*. vidhāyakasabhā, *f*. **District** —, padesasabhā, *f*. **Legislative** —, nītidāyakasabhā, *f*. **Municipal** —, nāgarasabhā, *f*. **Privy** —, sacivasabhā, *f*. **State** —, rājamantisabhā, *f*. — **Chamber**, mantaṇasabhā (-sālā), *f*.

Councillor, *n*. mantī ; amacca, *m*.

Counsel, *n*. 1. mantaṇā ; vicāraṇā, *f*. 2. upadesa, *m*. 3. upadesaka, *m*. *v.t*. upadisati ; anusāsati. *p.p*. upadiṭṭha ; anusiṭṭha. °**lor**, *n*. upadesaka ; nītividū, *m*.

Count, *n*. gaṇanā ; saṅkhyā, *f*. *v.t*. gaṇeti ; saṅkaleti. *v.i*. gaṇīyati. *p.p*. gaṇita ; °lita. °**less**, *a*. asaṅkheyya ; gaṇanātīta.

Count, seṭṭhī, *m*. °**ess**, seṭṭhijāyā, *f*.

Countenance, *n*. 1. vadana ; ānana, *nt*. 2. mukhavaṇṇa, *m*. *v.t*. anuggaṇhāti ; upatthambheti. *p.p*. anuggahita ; °bhita.

Counter, *n*. 1. gaṇanāphalaka, *m*. 2. gaṇaka, *m*. adj. viruddha ; paṭiloma, *adv*. paṭilomaŋ ; paṭiviruddhaŋ. °**charge**, paṭicodanā, *f*. °**current**, paṭisota, *m*. — **evidence**, viruddha-sakkhī, *m*. — **fire**, paṭaggi, *m*. — **message**, paṭisāsana, *nt*. — **plea**, paccuttara, *nt*.

Counteract, *v.t*. nisedheti ; nivāreti ; bādheti. *p.p*. °dhita ; °rita ; bādhita. °**ion**, *n*. paṭikriyā, *f*. nivāraṇa, *nt*. nisedha, *m*.

Counter-attraction, *n*. paccākaḍḍhana, *nt*.

Counterbalance, *n*. samabhāra, *m*. *v.t*. samabhārīkaroti. *p.p*. °kata.

Counterblast, *n*. adhika-virodha, *m*.

Counterbuff, *n*. paṭighāta, *m*.

Counterchange, *v.t*. vinimeti. *p.p*. °mita.

Countercheck, *n*. paṭirodha, *m*.

Counter-claim, *n*. paccabhiyoga, *m*. viruddhāyācanā, *f*.

Counterfeit, *n.a*. kittima ; patirūpaka ; kūṭa. *v.t*. 1. kittimaŋ karoti ; vañceti ; 2. micchā dasseti. *p.p*. vañcita ; °dassita. °**er**, *n*. nekatika ; vañcaka ; patāraka, *m*.

Counterfoil, *n*. paṭipotthaka ; itarakoṭṭhāsa, *m*.

Countermand, *v.t*. paṭiavhāti ; paccādisati. *p.p*. °hāta ; paccādiṭṭha.

Countermarch, *n*. paṭidisāgamana. *v.i*. paṭidisaŋ abhiyāti. *p.p*. °yāta.

Countermark, *n.* atireka-lañchana, *nt.*

Counterpane, *n.* paccattharaṇa ; pārupaṇa, *nt.*

Counterpart, *n.* 1. paṭimā, *f.* paṭibimba, *nt.* 2: samānalipi, *f.*

Counterplot, *n.* paṭikumantaṇa, *nt.* viruddhopāya, *m.* *v.t.* viruddhopāyaŋ yojeti.

Counterpoise, *v.t.* samabhāraŋ karoti. *p.p.* °kata.

Countersign, *n.* abhiññāṇa, *nt.* abhiññāṇavācā, *f.* *v.t.* puna hatthalañchanaŋ ṭhapeti.

Countervail, *v.t.* tulyabhāraŋ károti. *p.p.* °kata.

Counterwork, *n.* viruddhakicca, *nt.* *v.t.* bādheti ; nisedheti. *p.p.* °dhita.

Countrified, *a.* gāmika ; jānapadika.

Country, *n.* raṭṭha ; vijita, *nt.* desa, *m.* —**folk,** jānapadika, *m.* °**man,** *n.* raṭṭhavāsī ; saraṭṭhika ; sadesika, *m.* °**side,** paccanta, *m.*

County, *n.* desamaṇḍala, *nt.* — **council,** maṇḍalikasabhā, *f.*

Coup, *n.* anapekkhita *or* sahasāgata-parivattana, *nt.*

Couple, *n.* yuga ; yugala ; yamaka ; dvanda ; mithuna, *nt.* *v.t.* saŋyojeti ; samāgameti. *v.i.* saŋvasati ; methunam abhiyuñjati. *p.p.* °jita ; °mita ; saŋvuttha ; °abhiyutta. °**ing,** *n.* sandhāna, *nt.* saŋvāsa ; methunābhiyoga, *m.*

Couplet, *n.* gāthāpadadvaya, *nt.*

Coupon, *n.* salākā, *f.*

Courage, *n.* viriya, *nt.* dhiti ; abhīrutā, *f.* parakkama, *m.* °**ous,** *a.* sūra ; vīra ; dhitimantu ; viriyavantu. °**ously,** *adv.* savikkamaŋ. °**ousness,** *n.* sūratta ; vīratta, *nt.*

Courier, *n.* dūta ; sandesahara, *m.*

Course, *n.* 1. gati, *f.* anvaya ; 2. patha, *m.* 3. kama ; vidhi, *m.* 4. ācāra, *m.* *v.t.* anubandhati ; anudhāvati. *v.i.* dhāvati. *p.p.* anubaddha ; °vita. — **of action,** kriyāvidhi, *m.* paṭipatti, *f.* — **of study,** sikkhāmagga, *m.* **A woman in —,** utunī; rajassalā, *f.* **In — of time,** gacchante kāle. **In the — of,** antare ; majjhe. **Of —,** nūnaŋ ; niyataŋ ; have ; khalu, *ind.* **Proper —,** sammāpaṭipatti, *f.* supatha, *m.* **Wrong —,** kupatha, *m.* micchāpaṭipadā, *f.*

Courser, *n.* javanassa, *m.*

Court, *n.* aṅgaṇa ; ājira, *nt.* **King's —,** rājamandira, *nt.* rājasabhā, *f.* —**favour,** rājappasāda, *m.* — **musician,** vetālika, *m.* — **of justice,** adhikaraṇamaṇḍala, *nt.* °**yard,** aṅgaṇa, *nt.*

Court, *v.t.* anurañjeti ; ārādheti. *p.p.* °jita ; °dhita. °**ship,** *n.* pemabandhana, *nt.*

Courteous, *a.* vinīta ; piyaŋvada. °**ly,** *adv.* savinayaŋ ; sānunayaŋ. °**ness,** *n.* vinītatta, *nt.*

Courtesan, °**zan,** *n.* gaṇikā ; vaṇṇadāsī ; abhisārikā, *f.*

Courtesy, *n.* sosīlya ; vinītatta, *nt.* gārava, *m.* **By —,** anuggahena.

Courtier, *n.* rājavallabha ; rājapārisajja, *m.*

Courtly, *a.* 1. vinīta ; poriya ; sabbha ; 2. cāṭukara. °**iness,** *n.* uttamappakati, *f.*

Court-martial, *n.* yuddhādhikaraṇa, *nt.*

Cousin, *n.* (maternal aunt's son) : mātucchāputta, *m.* (paternal aunt's son) : pitucchāputta, *m.* (maternal uncle's son) : mātulaputta, *m.* (paternal uncle's son) : cūlapituputta, *m.* In case of their daughters add *dhītu* instead of *putta.*

Cove, *n.* 1. khuddakaloṇī, *f.* 2. channapatha, *m. v.t.* anto nāmeti ; addhamaṇḍalākāraŋ karoti.

Covenant, *n.* paṭissava, *m.* paṭiññāpaṇṇa, *nt. v.t.* saṅgaraŋ *or* paṭissavaŋ karoti. *p.p.* katasaṅgara ; katapaṭissava, *m.* °**ee,** *n.* paṭiññālābhī, *m.* °**or,** *n.* paṭiññādāyī, *m.*

Coventry, *n.* sahayogavajjana, *nt.*

Cover, *n.* āvaraṇa ; chādana ; attharaṇa, *nt.* chada ; santhara, *m. v.t.* chādeti ; āvarati ; saŋvarati ; pacchādeti. *p.p.* channa ; āvaṭa ; saŋvaṭa ; pacchanna. — **over,** pariyonahati ; avattharati. °**ing,** *n.* pidhāna ; āvaraṇa, *nt.* °**ing over,** oguṇṭhana ; pariyonahana, *nt.* °**let,** *n.* khuddakattharaṇa, *nt.*

Covert, *n.* nilīyanaṭṭhāna, *nt.* adj. gutta ; paṭicchanna. °**ure,** *n.* 1. pidhāna ; āvaraṇa, *nt.* 2. ārakkhā, *f.*

Covet, *v.t.* anugijjhati ; abhijjhāyati. *p.p.* anugiddha. °**ous,** *a.* lolupa ; giddha ; luddha. °**ously** *adv.* luddhākārena. °**ousness,** *n.* giddhi ; lolatā ; abhijjhā, *f.* gedha, *m.*

Covey, *n.* potakagaṇa, *m.*

Covin, *n.* kumantaṇa, *nt.* °**ous,** *a.* vañcaka.

Cow, *n.* gāvī ; dhenu, *f. v.t.* santajjeti. *p.p.* °jita. °**dung,** gomaya, *nt.* °**herd,** gopāla, *m.* °**keeping,** gorakkhā, *f.* °**pen,** °**shed,** goṭṭha ; gokula, *nt.* vaja, *m.*

Coward, *n. a.* adhīra ; bhīruka ; °**ice,** *n.* bhīrukatā ; kātaratā, *f.* °**ly,** *a.* bhāyanasīla.

Cowboy, *n.* gopa-dāraka, *m.*

Co-wife, *n.* sapattī ; samānapatikā, *f.*

Cowl, *n.* sīsāvaraṇa, *nt.*

Cowrie, *n.* sippikā, *f.* varāṭaka, *m.* kākaṇikā, *f.*

Coxcomb, *n.* vikatthaka ; uddhatākāra, *m.* °**ry,** *n.* vikatthana, *nt.* ahaṅkāra, *m.* uddhacca, *nt.*

Coy, *a.* salajja ; hirimana ; mitavacana. °**ly,** *adv.* salajjaŋ. °**ness,** *n.* lajjā, *f.*

Cozen, *v.t.* vañceti ; patāreti. *p.p.* vañcita ; °rita. °**age,** *n.* vañcanā, *f.*

Crab, *n.* kuḷīra ; kakkaṭa, *m.*

Crabbed, *a.* kakkasa ; pharusa. °**ly,** *adv.* niṭṭhuraŋ. °**ness,** *n.* kakkasatta, *nt.*

Crack, *v.t.* bhindati ; khaṇḍeti. *p.p.* bhinna ; °ḍita. *v.i.* 1. bhijjati ; phalati ; 2. unnadati. *p.p.* bhinna ; phalita. *n.* 1. vivara ; phulla, *nt.* 2. mahārava, *m.* — **a joke,** parihasati.

Cracker, *n.* unnādaka, *m.*

Crackle, *v.i.* paṭapaṭāyati. *n.* paṭapaṭāyana, *nt.*

Cracksman, *n.* sandhicchedakacora, *m.*

Cracky *a.* 1. vivarapuṇṇa ; 2. kadariya.

Cradle, *n.* dārakadolā, *f. v.t.* dolāyaŋ sayāpeti. *p.p.* °pita.

Craft, *n.* 1. sāṭheyya ; 2. pāṭava, nepuñña, *nt.* 3. sippa, *nt.* kalā, *f.* 4. taraṇī, *f.* °**sman,** *n.* sippī, *m.* °**y,** *a.* saṭha ; vañcanika. °**iness,** *n.* sāṭheyya, *nt.* °**ily,** *adv.* saṭhena.

Crag, *n.* visama-kūṭa *or* taṭa, *nt.* °**gy,** *a.* visamakūṭayutta.

Cram, *v.t.* atimattaŋ pūreti. *v.i.* atimattam ajjhoharati. *p.p.* °pūrita ; °haṭa. °**mer,** *n.* atimattabhojī, *m.*

Cramp, *v.t.* saṅkoceti ; sambādheti. *p.p.* °cita ; °dhita. adj. saṅkucita ; dubbiññeyya. *n.* saṅkoca ; sambandhaka, *m.*

Crane, *n.* 1. baka, *m.* 2. bhārubbāhaka-yanta, *nt. v.t.* 1. yantena ussāpeti ; 2. gīvaŋ pasāreti. *p.p.* °pita ; pasāritagīva. **Brown** —, balākā, *f.*

Cranial, *a.* sīsakapālāyatta.

Cranium, *n.* sīsakaṭāha, *m.*

Crank, *a.* dubbala ; cañcala. *n.* capala, *m.* °**y,** *a.* 1. athiravuttī ; cañcala ; 2. bavhāvaṭṭa.

Crankle, *v.i.* ito tato namati. ubhato āvaṭṭati. *p.p.* °nata ; °ṭita.

Cranny, *n.* randha ; vivara, *nt.*

Crapulence, *n.* madaccayaroga, *m.* °**lent,** °**lous,** *a.* madaccayābhibhūta.

Crash, *n.* 1. bhijjana, *nt.* 2. mahārava, *m. v.t.* cuṇṇeti ; khaṇḍeti. *v.i.* bhijjati ; khaṇḍīyati. *p.p.* cuṇṇita ; °ḍita ; bhinna ; khaṇḍita.

Crass, *a.* thūla ; oḷārika ; ghana. °**ness,** *m.* thūlatta ; ghanatta, *nt.* °**itude,** *n.* oḷārikatta, *nt.*

Cratch, *n.* pasu-ghāsadoṇi, *f.*

Crater, *n.* narakāvāṭa, *m.*

Cravat, *n.* gīvāveṭhana, *nt.*

Crave, *v.t.* kāmeti ; gijjhati ; abhijjhāyati. *v.i.* abhiyācati. *p.p.* kāmita ; giddha ; °cita.

Craven, *a.* dīna ; kātara.

Craving, *n.* taṇhā ; nikanti ; abhijjhā, *f.* **Free from** —, nibbanatha ; nittaṇha. **Snare of** —, bhavanetti, *f.* taṇhāpāsa, *m.*

Crawl, *v.i.* saŋsappati. *p.p.* °pita. °**ing,** *n.* saŋsappanā, *f.*

Crayon, *n.* sitthavaṭṭikā ; sudhātūlikā, *f.*

Craze, *n.* cittavibbhama, *m. v.t.* 1. ummādeti ; cittaŋ vikkhipati ; 2. phullāni uppādeti. *p.p.* °dita ; vikkhittacitta ; uppāditaphulla.

Crazy, *a.* 1. dubbala ; khittacitta ; capala ; 2. dugghaṭita. °**ily,** *adv.* ummattākārena.

Creak, *n.* kiri-kirisadda, *m. v.i.* kirikirāyati.

Cream, *n.* 1. dadhimaṇḍa ; matthu, *nt.* 2. sāra ; sāraŋsa, *m. v.t.* 1. dadhisāram apaneti ; 2. sāraŋsaŋ gaṇhāti. *p.p.* apanīta-sāra ; gahitasāraŋsa. °**coloured,** *a.* setapīta. °**y,** *a.* matthuvaṇṇa.

Creamer, *n.* matthubhājana, *nt.* °**ry,** *n.* nonītasālā, *f.*

Create, *v.t.* māpeti ; nimmiṇāti ; pātukaroti. *p.p.* māpita ; nimmita ; °kata. °**ion,** *n.* māpana ; nimmaṇā, *nt.* °**ive,** *a.* uppādaka ; māpaka.

Creator, *m.* nimmātu ; vidhātu ; Issara, *m.* °**ship,** *n.* māpakatta ; Brahmatta, *nt.*

Creature, *n.* satta ; pāṇī ; dehī ; jīvī, *m.*

Creche, *n.* sādhāraṇa-dārakāgāra, *nt.*

Credence, *n.* vissāsa, *m.*

Credential, *n.* saddheyyapaṇṇa, *nt.* pl. pamāṇapaṇṇa, *nt.*

Credible, *a.* saddheyya ; paccayika. °**bility,** *n.* vissasitabbatā ; saddheyyatā, *f.*

Credit, *n.* 1. vissāsa, *m.* 2. pasaŋsā ; thuti, *f.* 3. iṇadāna, *nt. v.t.* vissasati ; saddahati. *p.p.* vissattha ; °hita. °**able,** *a.* pasaŋsiya ; saddheyya. °**ably,** *adv.* pasatthākārena. °**or,** *n.* iṇasāmī, *m.*

Credulous, *a.* saddhahanasīla ; avisaṅkī.

Creed, *n.* diṭṭhi ; laddhi, *f.*

Creek, *n.* samuddasākhā ; sākhānadī, *f.*

Creel, *n.* macchapacchi, *f.*

Creep, *v.i.* saŋsappati ; sanikaŋ pavisati. *p.p.* °pita ; °paviṭṭha. °**ing,** *n.* sappana, *nt.* °**ing animal,** uraga ; dīghajātika, *m.*

Creeper, *n.* 1. saŋsappaka, *m.* 2. latā ; valli, *f.*

Creepy, *a.* lomahaŋsajanaka.

Creese, *n.* chūrikā, *f.*

Cremate, *v.t.* jhāpeti ; dahati. *p.p.* jhāpita ; dahita. °**ion,** *n.* jhāpana ; ādahana, *nt.*

Crematorium, Crematory, *n.* ālāhanaṭṭhāna, *nt.* chavadahanasālā, *f.*

Crenate, *a.* passe dantayutta.

Crenellate, *v.t.* vijjhanatthāya chiddasahitaŋ karoti.

Crepitate, *v.i.* ciccitāyati.

Crepuscular, *a.* aruṇālokāyatta.

Crescent, *n.* navacanda, *m.* — **shaped,** *a.* navacandākāra.

Cress, *n.* sākajāti, *f.*

Cresset, *n.* dīpagghikā, *f.*

Crest, *n.* 1. sikhā ; cūḷā, *f.* sikhara, *nt.* 2. sekhara, *nt.* avataŋsa, *m.* *v.t.* sikharayuttaŋ karoti. °**ed,** 1. sikhī ; cūḷī ; 2. sekharī ; kirīṭī. °**fallen,** *a.* maṅkubhūta ; pattakkhandha. — **gem,** — **jewel,** *n.* cūḷāmaṇi ; siromaṇi, *m.*

Cretaceous, *a.* sudhāsadisa.

Crevice, *n.* randha ; vivara ; chiddha, *nt.*

Crew, *n.* nāvikagaṇa, *m.*

Crib, *n.* 1. kuṭikā ; dārakakuṭi, *f.* 2. kumiṇa, *nt. v.t.* 1. sambādhe ṭhapeti ; theyyena anulipiŋ gaṇhāti.

Cribriform, *a.* khuddaka-chiddayutta.

Cricket, *n.* 1. cīrikā ; 2. kandukakīḷā, *f.* *v.i.* kandukena kīḷati. — **ball,** *n.* kanduka ; bheṇḍuka, *m.* °**er,** *n.* kandukakīḷaka, *m.*

Crier, *n.* ugghosaka, *m.*

Crime, *n.* aparādha, *m.* kibbisa, *nt.* °**less,** *a.* niraparādha.

Criminal, *a.* aparādhāyatta ; daṇḍanāraha, *n.* aparādhī ; āgucārī, *m.* — **law,** daṇḍanīti, *f.* °**ly,**

adv. sāhasikena. °**ity,** *n.* sāparādhitā, *f.*

Criminate, *v.t.* vadhayoggaŋ karoti ; dosam āropeti. *p.p.* °kata ; āropitadosa. °**ion,** *n.* aparādhacodanā, *f.* dosāropaṇa, *nt.* °**ive,** °**tory,** *a.* aparādhadīpaka ; vajjadassaka.

Criminology, *n.* aparādhaparikkhā, *f.*

Crimp, *v.t.* valiŋ gaṇhāpeti ; saṅkoceti. *p.p.* valiggahita ; °cita.

Crimson, *a.* lohitavaṇṇa, *v.t.* rattavaṇṇena rañjeti. *p.p.* °rañjita.

Cringe, *n.* nipaccakāra ; atimattagārava, *m. v.i.* dāso viya paṇāmati ; nīcavuttī hoti.

Crinite, *a.* lomasa ; lomabahula.

Crinkle, *n.* vyāvaṭṭa ; veṭhana, *nt. v.t.* veṭheti ; vyāvaṭṭeti. *p.p.* veṭhita ; °ṭita.

Crinoline, *n.* vālakambala, *nt.*

Cripple, *n.* paṅgula ; pīṭhasappī, *m. v.t.* aṅgavikalaŋ karoti. *p.p.* vikalaṅgīkata. *v.i.* khañjati. °**hood,** *n.* aṅgavikalatta, *nt.*

Crisis, *n.* sandehasamaya, *m.* antimāvatthā, *f.*

Crisp, *a.* 1. bhaṅgura ; 2. kuṇḍalāvaṭṭa. *v.t.* kuṇḍalayuttaŋ karoti. *v.i.* kuṇḍalī bhavati. °**ate,** *a.* kuñcitagga.

Cristate, *a.* sikhāyutta ; cūḷī.

Criterion, *n.* nicchayalakkhaṇa ; pamāṇadīpaka, *nt.*

Critic, *n.* vivecaka ; guṇadosanirūpaka, *m.* °**al,** *a.* 1. vicāraṇayutta ; dosagavesī ; 2. bhāriya ; saŋsayāvaha. °**ally,** *adv.* sukhumaŋ ; savicāraṇaŋ.

Criticise, *v.t.* viveceti ; guṇadosaŋ vicāreti. *p.p.* °cita ; vicāritaguṇadosa. °**ism,** *n.* vivecana ; guṇadosanirūpana, *nt.*

Critique, *n.* tattanirūpakalipi, *f.*

Croak, *n.* maṇḍūkarava, *m. v.t.* vilapati. *v.i.* asubhaŋ sūceti. °**er,** *n.* asubhasūcaka, *m.*

Croceate, *a.* kuṅkumavaṇṇa.

Crochet, *n.* ganthita-vatthu, *nt. v.t.* gantheti. *p.p.* °thita.

Crock, *n.* 1. mattikābhājana, *nt.* 2. dandhapurisa, *m.* 3. dubbalassa, *m. v.t.* dubbalīkaroti. *p.p.* °kata. °**ery,** *n.* āmattika, *nt.*

Crocodile, *n.* kumbhīla ; suŋsumāra, *m.*

Croft, *n.* khuddaka-khetta, *nt.*

Crone, *n.* mahallikā, *f.*

Crony, *n.* daḷhamitta, *m.*

Crook, *n.* 1. aṅkusa, *m.* ākaḍḍhanī, *f.* 2. saṭha ; dhutta, *m. v.t.* vañceti. *v.i.* onamati. *p.p.* vañcita ; onata. °**ed,** *a.* vaṅka ; kuṭila ; kuñcita. °**edness,** *n.* vaṅkatta, *nt.*

Crop, *n.* 1. sassa ; 2. kasājaṭa, *nt.* 3. kesakappana, *nt. v. t.*1. luṇāti ; chindati ; agge kappeti *or* chindati ; 2. vapati. 3. phalam uppādeti. *p.p.* luta ; chinna ; °kappita ; vapita ; °ditaphala. — **out,** sahasā pākaṭībhavati *or* āvibhavati. °**sick,** *n.* atibhojanātura. °**per,** *n.* 1. lāyaka ; 2. suphaladāyī, *m.*

Crore, *n.* koṭi, *f.* lakkhasata, *nt.*

Cross, *n.* 1. kākapadalakkhaṇa, *nt.* 2. siṅghāṭaka, *nt.* adj. 1. tiriyaŋ-ṭhita ; 2. paṭiviruddha ; 3. dummana. °**action,** paṭicodanā, *f.* °**bar,** tulāsaṅghāṭa, *m.* °**beam,** tirosaṅghāṭa, *m.* °**bearer,** siṅghāṭakadhārī, *m.* °**breeding,** *n.* (pasūnaŋ) jātisaṅkalana, *nt.* °**examine,** *v.t.* virodhaŋ pucchati. °**eyed,** *a.* kekara. °**road,** caccara, *nt.* maggasandhi. *f.* °**wind,** paṭilomavāta, *m.* °**wise,** *adv.* tiriyaŋ.

Cross, *v.t.* tarati ; atikkamati ; tiriyaŋ gacchati ; paṭidisaŋ gacchati. *p.p.* tiṇṇa ; atikkanta ; tiriyaṅgata. °**ing,** *n.* 1. tiriyaŋ taraṇa, *nt.* 2. sammissaṇa, *nt.* °**ly,** *adv.* viruddhākārena. °**ness,** *n.* asantuṭṭhatā, *f.*

Cross-question, *n.* paṭipucchā, *f.* *v.t.* anupucchati. *p.p.* anupuṭṭha.

Croton, *n.* jayapāla, *m.*

Crouch, *v.i.* saṅkucitvā nisīdati. *p.p.* °nisinna.

Croup, *n.* 1. assa-nitamba ; 2. kumāra-galaroga, *m.*

Crow, *n.* 1. kāka, *m.* 2. kukkuṭarava, *m.* *v.i.* ravati ; nadati. *p.p.* ruta ; nadita.

Crowd, *n.* samūha ; samavāya ; gaṇa, *m.* *v.i.* sannipatati. *v.t.* sambādheti. *p.p.* °tita ; °dhita. °**ed,** *a.* janākiṇṇa ; sambādha.

Crown, *n.* 1. makuṭa, kirīṭa ; sekhara, *nt.* moḷi, *m.* *f.* 2. rajja, *nt.* 3. sikhā ; cūḷā, *f.* sikhara ; agga, *nt.* 4. (— of the head:) muddhā, matthaka, *m.* 5. (— of cash:) kahāpaṇa, *nt.* *v.t.* 1. abhisiñcati ; kirīṭam āropeti ; 2. samāpeti ; niṭṭhāpeti. *p.p.* abhisitta ; āropitakirīṭa ; °pita. °**ed,** *a.* muddhābhisitta. °**land,** rajjāyattabhūmi, *f.* — **post,** majjhimatthambha, *m.* — **prince,** yuvarāja, *m.* — **with success,** saŋsiddhim āpādeti.

Crucible, mūsā, *f.*

Crucify, *v.t.* siṅghāṭake uttāseti. *p.p.* °sita. °**ixion,** uttāsana, *nt.*

Crude, *a.* apariṇata ; aniṭṭhita ; asakkaccakata. °**ly,** *adv.* asakkaccaŋ. °**ness,** *n.* apariṇatatta ; asampuṇṇatta, *nt.*

Cruel, *a.* kurūra ; niddaya ; niṭṭhura ; kakkhaḷa. °**ly,** *adv.* niddayaŋ ; niṭṭhuraŋ. °**ty,** °**ness,** *n.* kurūratta ; niddayatta, *nt.* vihiŋsā, *f.*

Cruise, *v.i.* nāvāya ito tato sañcarati. °**er,** *n.* sañcāraka-yuddhanāvā, *f.*

Crumb, *n.* sakalikā, *f.* khuddakakhaṇḍa, *m.* *v.t.* sakalikāhi āvarati. *p.p.* °āvaṭa.

Crumble, *v.i.* palujjati ; cuṇṇībhavati. *v.t.* cuṇṇeti. *p.p.* palugga ; °bhūta ; cuṇṇita.

Crummy, *a.* 1. pīvara ; 2. abhirūpa.

Crump, *a.* khujja. *v.t.* daḷhaŋ ghaṭṭeti *or* khipati. *p.p.* daḷhakhitta.

Crumple, *v.t.* saṅkoceti ; valiŋ gaṇhāpeti. *v.i.* saṅkucati. *p.p.* °cita ; gaṇhāpitavali ; °cita.

Crunch, *v.t.* 1. dantehi khaṇḍeti ; 2. pādehi sakkharā omaddati. *p.p.* °ḍita ; °dita. *n.* kharasadda, *m.*

Crupper, 1. assa-nitamba, *m.* 2. pucchabanda, *m.*

Crusade, *n.* suddhadesīyayuddha, *nt.*

Crush, *n.* sammaddana, *nt.* *v.t.* 1. sammaddati ; sampīḷeti ; pamaddati ; 2. vicuṇṇeti ; 3. abhimanthati. *p.p.* °dita ; °ḷita ; °ṇita ; abhimathita. °**ing**, *n.* nimmathana, *nt.* °**ing**, *a.* nimmathaka.

Crust, *n.* bāhirataca ; kaṭhinabhāga, *m.* *v.t.* tacena āvarati. *v.i.* kaṭhinībhavati. *p.p.* °āvaṭa; °bhūta. °**y**, *a.* kaṭhina ; thaddhāvaraṇa.

Crustacea, *n.* kosamaccha, *m.* °**ceous**, *a.* kosayutta ; kaṭhinattaca.

Crutch, *n.* kacchayaṭṭhi ; khañjādhāra, *m.*

Crux, *n.* gaṇṭhiṭṭhāna, *nt.*

Cry, *n.* 1. rodana ; kandana ; paridevana, *nt.* 2. rava ; nāda, *m.* *v.i.* rodati ; kandati ; paridevati. *p.p.* °ḍita ; °vita. — **of an animal**, vassita, *nt.* — **of distress**, virāva, vissara, *m.* — **for**, anurodati. — **out**, ugghoseti. — **up**, pasaŋsati. °**ing**, *n.* rodana, *nt.* °**ing**, *a.* rodanta ; rodamāna.

Crypt, *n.* bhūmiguhā, *f.* °**ic**, *a.* gūḷha ; dubbiññeyya.

Cryptography, *n.* guttalipividhi, *m.*

Crystal, *n.* 1. phaḷika, *nt.* 2. sakkharā, *f.* — **of salt**, loṇasakkharā, *f.* **Made of** —, phaḷikamaya, *a.* °**line**, *a.* phalikasadisa. °**lize**, *v.t.* 1. thāvaraŋ karoti ; 2. sakkharābhāvaŋ pāpeti. *p.p.* thāvarīkata ; °pāpita.

Cub, *n.* potaka ; chāpa, *m.*

Cube, *n.* caturassa-ghaṭikā, *f.* °**age**, *n.* ghanaphala, *nt.* °**ical**, *a.* ghaṭikākāra. °**root**, *n.* ghanamūla, *nt.*

Cubicle, *n.* khuddaka-sayanighara, *nt.*

Cubit, *n.* ratana ; hattha ; kukku, *m.* °**al**, *a.* hatthāyatta.

Cuboid, *a.* ghaṭikākāra.

Cuckoo, *n.* kokila ; pika, *m.* **Indian** —, kuṇāla ; karavīka, *m.*

Cucumber, *n.* kakkārī, *f.* elāḷuka, *nt.*

Cucurbit, *n.* alābu ; lābu, *m.*

Cud, *n.* romantha, *m.*

Cuddle, *n.* āliṅgana ; upagūhana, *nt.* *v.t.* āliṅgati ; upagūhati ; palissajati. *p.p.* °gita ; upagūḷha; °jita *or* °saṭṭha.

Cuddy, *n.* gadrabha, *m.*

Cudgel, *n.* muggara ; laguḷa, *m.* *v.t.* muggarena paharati. *p.p.* °pahaṭa.

Cue, *n.* 1. iṅgita ; saññāṇa, *nt.* 2. dhammillaveṇī *f.*

Cuff, *n.* muṭṭhippahāra ; pāṇippahāra, *m.* *v.t.* pāṇinā paharati. *p.p.* °pahaṭa.

Cuirass, *n.* 1. khandha-sannāha, *m.* 2. antosaṅkaccikā, *f.*

Cuisine, *n.* 1. pacanākāra, *m.* 2. pākaṭṭhāna, *nt.*

Cuisse, *n.* ūruttāṇa, *nt.*

Culinary, *a.* pākavisayaka ; mahānasika.

Cull, *v.t.* 1. ocināti ; 2. uccināti. *p.p.* ocita ; uccinita.

Cully, *n.* sukhavañcanīya ; mandapañña, *m.*

Culminant, *a.* muddhanaṭṭha.

Culminate, *v.i.* antaŋ, pāraŋ *or* koṭiŋ pāpuṇāti. *p.p.* antappatta; pārappatta ; koṭippatta. °**ion**, antappatti ; uccatarāvatthā, *f.*

Culpable, *a.* sāparādha ; daṇḍāraha. °**ness**, sāvajjatā, *f.* °**ly**, *adv.* gārayhatāya ; sāvajjatāya.

Culprit, see **Criminal.**

Cult, see **Creed.**

Cultivate, *v.t.* 1. kasati ; 2. ropeti ; 3. bhāveti ; vaḍḍheti. *p.p.* kaṭṭha *or* kasita ; ropita ; °vita ; °ḍhita. °**ion**, *n.* 1. kasi, *f.* kasikamma, *nt.* 2. bhāvanā ; vaḍḍhanā, *f.* °**tor**, *m.* 1. kassaka ; ropaka, *m.* 2. bhāvaka ; vaḍḍhaka, *m.*

Culture, *n.* 1. kasi, *f.* 2. sabbhatā, *f.* sadācāra, *m.* *v.t.* bhāveti ; vaḍḍheti. *p.p.* bhāvita ; °ḍhita. °**al**, *a.* sadācāravisayaka. °**ed**, *a.* 1. kasita ; ropita ; 2. sabbha.

Culvert, *n.* chādita-jalaniggama, *m.*

Cumber, *n.* bādhaka, *m.* *v.t.* 1. bādheti ; 2. kasirena vahati. *p.p.* bādhita ; °vahita. °**some**, *a.* kasira ; bhāriya ; dukkhāvaha.

Cumbrance, *n.* atibhāra, *m.* kiccha, *nt.*

Cummin, *n.* jīraka, *nt.*

Cumulate, *a.* sañcita ; rāsīkata. *v.t.* sañcināti ; rāsīkaroti. *p.p.* sañcita ; °kata. *v.i.* sañcīyati. *p.p.* sañcita. °**ive**, *a.* abhivaḍḍhamāna.

Cumulus, *n.* puñja ; rāsi, *m.* valāhakarāsi, *m.*

Cuneate, Cuneiform, khīlākāra ; sūlākāra.

Cunning, *n.* 1. sāṭheyya ; 2. pāṭava, *nt.* upāya, *m.* adj. 1. saṭha ; vañcanasīla ; 2. upāyakusala. °**ly**, *adv.* upāyena ; cāturiyena ; saṭhatāya.

Cup, *n.* casaka ; saraka, *m.* °**board**, *n.* casakādhāna, *nt.*

Cupid *n.* anaṅga ; madana ; manobhū, *m.* °**ity**, *n.* kāmukatā, *f.*

Cupola, *n.* vaṭṭula-pāsādasīsa ; addhavaṅkachadana, *nt.*

Cupric, *a.* tambamissa.

Cur, *n.* 1. sunakhādhama ; 2. adhamapurisa, *m.* °**rish**, *a.* sunakhūpama ; nīcagatika.

Curate, *n.* upayājaka ; upapūjaka, *m.*

Curative, *a.* rogahara ; vyādhināsaka.

Curator, *n.* adhikārī ; pālaka, (as in uyyāna°), *m.*

Curb, *n.* mukhādhāna, *nt.* *v.t.* saŋyameti ; niggaṇhāti ; avarodheti. *p.p.* saŋyata ; niggahita ; avaruddha.

Curcuma, *n.* haḷiddī, *f.*

Curd, *n.* dadhi, *nt.*

Curdle, *v.t.* ghanīkaroti. *v.i.* ghanībhavati. *p.p.* °kata ; °bhūta.

Cure, *n.* tikicchā, *f.* bhesajja, *nt.* *v.t.* 1. tikicchati ; rogam upasameti ; 2. saŋrakkhati. *p.p.* °chita ; upasamitaroga ; °khita, °**able**, *a.* tekiccha. °**ability**, *n.* satekicchatā, *f.* °**less**, *a.* atekiccha.

Curfew, *n.* dīpanibbāpanavelā, *f.* — **bell**, dīpanibbāpaka-ghaṇṭā, *f.*

Curiosity, *n.* 1. kutūhala, *nt.* vimhaya, *m.* 2. abbhutavatthu, *nt.*

Curious, *a.* 1. abbhutākāra ; adiṭṭhapubba ; 2. ñātukāma ; kotūhalika. °**ly**, *adv.* sābbhutaŋ.

Curl, *n.* kuṇḍala ; alaka, *nt.* *v.t.* kuñceti ; kuṇḍalīkaroti. *p.p.* kuñcita ; °kata. °**y,** *a.* kuṇḍalāvatta ; vellita.

Curlew, *n.* koñcā ; kuntanī, *f.*

Currant, *n.* abīja-sukkha-muddikā, *f.*

Currency, *n.* 1. pacārita-mūla, *nt.* 2. pavattanakāla, *m.*

Current, *a.* 1. pavattamāna ; 2. patthaṭa ; 3. sādhāraṇa ; lokavissuta. *n.* 1. sota ; ogha ; pavāha, *m.* 2. gati ; pavatti, *f.* vega, *m.*

Curriculum, *n.* ajjhayana-paddhati ; °vavatthā, *f.*

Currier, *n.* cammakāra, *m.*

Curry, *n.* sūpa, *m.* vyañjana, *nt.* °**stuff,** kaṭukabhaṇḍa, *nt.* **Suitable for —,** sūpeyya, *a.*

Curry, *v.t.* assaŋ majjati. *p.p.* majjitassa. — **comb,** assamajjanī, *f.*

Curse, *v.t.* abhisapati. *p.p.* abhisatta. *n.* sāpa, *m.* abhisapana, *nt.* — **in return,** paṭisapati. °**ed,** *a.* jeguccha ; vajjanīya.

Cursory, *a.* turita ; asamekkhita. °**ily,** *adv.* asamekkhitākārena ; turitaŋ.

Curt, *a.* atirassa ; atisaṅkhitta. °**ly,** *adv.* atisaṅkhepena. °**ness,** *n.* saṅkhittatā, *f.*

Curtail, *v.t.* laghuŋ karoti ; saṅkhipati ; avacchindati. *p.p.* laghukata ; saṅkhitta ; avacchinna.

Curtain, *n.* javanikā ; tirokaraṇī, *f.* *v.t.* javanikāya parikkhipati ; tirokaroti. *p.p.* javanikāparikkhitta ; tirokata.

Curtsy, Curtsey, *n.* nipaccakāra, *m.*

Curvature, *n.* jimhatā, *f.*

Curve, *n.* addhāvaṭṭa ; addhamaṇḍala. *v.t.* ākuñceti ; nāmeti. *p.p.* °cita ; nāmita.

Curvilinear, *a.* vaṅkarekhāyutta.

Cushion, *n.* bhisi, *f.* upadhāna, *nt.* *v.t.* bhisiyā āvarati. *p.p.* °āvaṭa.

Cushy, *a.* sukhada.

Cuspidore, *n.* khelamallaka, *m.*

Cuss, *n.* sāpa, *m.*

Custard, *n.* āsecanaka, *nt.*

Custody, *n.* ārakkhā ; gutti, *f.* pālana, *nt.* °**ian,** *n.* pālaka ; ārakkhaka, *m.*

Custom, *n.* 1. cāritta ; vatta, *nt.* ācāra, *m.* 2. bali ; rājakara, *m.* °**ary,** *a.* cārittāyatta ; niccappavatta. °**arily,** *adv.* yathāsabhāvena ; niccappavattiyā. °**er,** *n.* kayika, *m.* °**house,** suṅkaṭṭhāna, *nt.*

Cut, *n.* cheda, *m.* chindana ; chinnaṭṭhāna, *nt.* *v.t.* chindati ; kantati ; lunāti. *p.p.* chinna ; kantita ; lūna, *v.i.* pacchijjati. *p.p.* pacchinna. — **all around,** saṅkantati. — **into,** anukanteti. — **into pieces,** avalikhati. — **off,** vicchindati ; upacchindati. — **open,** vikanteti. — **out,** ukkanteti. — **short,** pacchindati. °**ter,** *n.* chettu ; ukkantaka, *m.* — **throat,** *n.* kaṇṭhacchedaka, *m.* °**ting,** chedana, *nt.* °**ting off,** viccheda, *n.*

Cutaneous, *a.* cammāyatta.

Cute, *a.* cheka. °**ly,** *adv.* chekākārena.

Cuticle, *n.* bāhiracamma, *nt.*

Cutlass, *n.* rassa-asi, *m.*

Cutler, *n.* satthavāṇija ; satthakāra, *m.* °**y**, satthasamūha, *m.*

Cycle, *n.* cakka, *nt.* āvaṭṭa, *m.* maṇḍala, *nt. v.i.* 1. āvaṭṭati ; 2. cakkayugena yāti. *p.p.* āvaṭṭita ; °yāta. °**lic**, *a.* punappunaŋ parivattamāna. °**list**, *n.* cakkārohī, *m.*

Cyclone, *n.* vātāvaṭṭa, *m.*

Cyclopaedia, *n.* vissakosa, *m.*

Cygnet, *n.* haŋsapotaka, *m.*

Cylinder, *n.* dīghavaṭṭikā, *f.* °**ical**, *a.* vaṭṭikākāra.

Cymbal, *n.* sammatāḷa, *m.*

Cynic, *n.* sabbattha-dosadassī ; sabbavivecaka ; sabba-jegucchī, *m.* °**al**, *a.* sabbavivecanasīla. °**ally**, *adv.* sabbajigucchāya. °**ism**, *n.* sabbajigucchā, *f.*

Cynosure, *n.* dhuvatārakā, *f.*

Cypher, see **Cipher**.

Cypress, *n.* devadāru, *m.*

Cyst, *n.* vatthi, *f.* āsaya (as in pittāsaya), *m.* °**ic**, *a.* vatthivisayaka.

Cystine, *n.* asmarī, *m.*

D

Dab, *v.t.* sanikaŋ phusati. *p.p.* °phuṭṭha. *n.* 1. mudupahāra, *m.* muduphusana, *nt.* 2. tanumacchavisesa, *m.*

Dabble, *v.t.* (siñcanena) temeti. *v.i.* 1. temīyati ; 2. udake kīḷati. *p.p.* temita ; °kīḷita. °**ing**, *n.* 1. jalakīḷā, *f.* 2. paṇḍitamāna, *m.* °**er**, *n.* 1. jalakīḷaka ; 2. paṇḍitamānī, *m.*

Dabster, *n.* nipuṇa ; visārada, *m.*

Dacoit, *n.* gāmaghātaka, *m.*

Dactyl, *n.* bha-gaṇa, ⏑ – – °**ology**, *n.* hatthamuddā, *f.* °**onomy**, *n.* aṅguligaṇita, *nt.*

Dad, Daddy, *n.* tāta, *m.*

Daedal, *a.* 1. catura ; dakkha ; 2. saṅkiṇṇa ; nānākāra.

Daff, *v.t.* apanidahati .*p.p.* apanihita.

Daft, *a.* muddha ; mūḷha.

Dagger, *n.* chūrikā ; asiputtī, *f.*

Daggle, *v.t.* malena dūseti ; paṅkena lepeti. *p.p.* maladūsita ; paṅkalitta.

Daily, *adv.* patidinaŋ ; devasikaŋ. *a.* devasika.

Dainty, *a.* 1. madhura ; sādurasa ; 2. mudu ; komala. *n.* paṇītabhojana, *nt.* — **bits**, uttaribhaṅga, *m.*

Dairy, *n.* duhanaṭṭhāna ; gorasāgāra, *nt.* °**maid**, gopakaññā, *f.* °**man**, gorasa-sampādaka, *m.*

Dais, *n.* savitāna-vedikā, *f.*

Dale, *n.* upaccakā ; ninnabhūmi, *f.*

Dally, *v.t.* lāleti. *v.i.* vilasati ; ramati. *p.p.* lālita ; °sita ; rata. — **away**, kālaŋ khepeti. °**iance**, *n.* 1. lāsana ; ramana ; kīḷana, *nt.* abhirati, *f.* 2. kālakkhepa, *m.*

Daltonism, *n.* vaṇṇa-andhatā, *f.*

Dam, *n.* āḷi ; pāḷi, *f. v.t.* āḷiŋ bandhati ; jalaŋ santhambheti. *p.p.* ālibaddha ; °bhitajala.

Damage, *n.* 1. hāni, *f.* nāsa, *m.* 2. hānippamāṇa, *m. v.t.* hāpeti ; nāseti ; khepeti. *p.p.* hāpita ; nāsita ; °pita. *v.i.* dussati. *p.p.* duṭṭha.

Damask, *n.* cittadukūla, *nt.* adj. puppharattavaṇṇa.

Dame, *n.* gahapatānī ; ayyā, *f.* *voc.* bhoti ; ayye.

Damn, *v.t.* 1. daṇḍanaŋ pāpeti ; 2. nirayena abhisapati. *p.p.* pāpitadaṇḍana ; °abhisatta. °**able,** *a.* vajjha ; daṇḍanīya. °**ation,** *n.* nirayavadhapāpana, *nt.*

Damp, *a.* adda ; alla ; tinta. *v.t.* 1. temeti ; 2. visādeti ; āsābhaṅgaŋ pāpeti. *p.p.* temita ; °dita ; °pāpita. °**ness,** addatta, *nt.* °**ish,** *a.* īsaŋtinta.

Dampen, *v.t.* kiledayati ; temeti. *p.p.* °yita ; temita.

Damper, *n.* 1. uppīḷaka ; 2. addakārī, *m.*

Damsel, *n.* kaññā ; kumārī ; yuvatī, *f.*

Dance, *n.* nacca ; naṭṭa ; nattanā ; lāsana, *nt.* *v.i.* naccati. *v.t.* naccāpeti. *p.p.* naccita ; °pita. °**er,** *n.* naṭa ; naccaka ; raṅgakāra, *m.* °**ing,** *n.* naccana, *nt.* °**ing girl,** nāṭikā, *f.*

Dander, *n.* kopa ; rosa, *m.*

Dandle, *v.t.* aṅke lāleti. *p.p.* °lālita.

Dandy, *a.* *n.* maṇḍanappiya ; vilāsī, *m.* °**ify,** *v.t.* pasādheti ; vibhūseti °**ism,** vilāsitā, *f.*

Danger, *n.* antarāya ; upaddava ; paripantha, *m.* vipatti ; īti, *f.* °**ous,** *a.* saupaddava ; antarāyāvaha ; pāripanthika. °**ously,** *adv.* bhayānakākārena. °**ousness,** saupaddavatā, *f.* **Free from —,** anupaddava ; khema ; anītika.

Dangle, *v.i.* olambati. *p.p.* °bita.

Dank, *a.* aṭitinta.

Dap, *v.t.* phandāpeti. *p.p.* °pita.

Dapper, *a.* suvesa ; līlāyutta.

Dapple, *n.* kammāsavaṇṇa, *m.* *v.t.* nānāvaṇṇaŋ karoti. *v.i.* kammāsī bhavati. *p.p.* °kata ; bhūta.

Darbies, *n.* hatthasaṅkhalikā, *f.*

Dare, *v.t.* 1. sakkoti ; visahati ; yugaŋ gaṇhāti. *p.p.* gahitayuga. °**ing,** *n.* vīrabhāva, *m.* dhiti, *f.* °**ing,** *a.* vīra ; nibbhaya. °**ingly,** *adv.* nibbhayākārena.

Dark, *a.* 1. tamonaddha ; timirāvuta ; 2. kaṇha ; kāḷa ; asita. *n.* tama ; andhakāra, *m.* timisa, *nt.* °**brown,** *a.* kaṇhapīta, °**ish,** *a.* īsaŋ-kaṇha. °**ness,** *n.* tama ; andhakāra, *m.* °**spot,** kāḷaka, *nt.* °**yellow,** *a.* maṅguravaṇṇa.

Darken, *v.t.* 1. timirāyati ; tamasā āvarati ; 2. kalusayati. *p.p.* °yita ; °āvuta ; °yita.

Darkle, *v.i.* nilīyitvā sayati.

Darkling, *adv.* andhakāre. **adj.** kaṇhavaṇṇa ; nirānanda.

Darling, *n.* atippiya ; vallabha ; 3. adj. piyatama.

Darn, *v.t.* aggaḷaŋ deti. *p.p.* dinnaggaḷa.

Darnel, *n.* sassadūsaka, *nt.*

Dart, *n.* salla ; saṅku, *m.* *v.t.* sallena vitudati. *v.i.* javena dhāvati. *p.p.* sallavitunna.

Dash, *n.* 1. abhighāta, *m.* saṅghaṭṭana, *nt.* 2. ūmisadda, *m.* *v.t.* āhanati ; paṭihanati ; sahasā khipati. *p.p.* āhata ; paṭihata ; °khitta. *v.i.* 1. pakkhandati ; sahasā pavisati ; 2. āhaññati.

p.p. pakkhanta ; °paviṭṭha ; āhata. — **to pieces,** khaṇḍākhaṇḍikaŋ karoti. — **off,** sahasā sampādeti.

Dashing, *a.* tejassī ; pagabbha ; sappabha.

Dastard, *n.* kātara ; bhīruka, *m.* °**ly,** *adv.* kātaratāya.

Data, *n.* paṭiggahita-sacca, *nt.*

Date, *n.* kālaniyama, *m. v.t.* kālaniyamaŋ likhati. °**less,** *a.* kālaniyamarahita. °**palm,** khajjūrī, *f.* °**ing from,** pabhutika, *a.* paṭṭhāya (with abl.) *ind.*

Dative, *n.* sampadānakāraka, *nt.* catutthī vibhatti, *f.*

Datum, *n.* upaññāsa, *m.* ñātasacca, *nt.*

Datura, *n.* mātula-rukkha, *m.*

Daub, *n.* ālepa, *m. v.t.* lepeti ; makkheti. *p.p.* litta ; makkhita. °**er,** *n.* lālapaka, *m.*

Daughter, *n.* dhītu ; duhitu ; tanayā ; atrajā, *f.* °**in-law,** *n.* suṇisā, *f.*

Daunt, *v.t.* santajjeti ; nirussāhayati. *p.p.* °jita ; °hita. °**less,** *a.* abhīruka ; nissaṅka ; ātāpī. °**lessly,** *adv.* abhītaŋ ; nissaṅkaŋ.

Daw, *n.* vanakāka, *m.*

Dawdle, *v.i.* kālaŋ khepeti. °**er,** *n.* alasa ; kālakaṇṇī, *m.*

Dawn, *n.* 1. aruṇa ; pabhāta, *m.* dinamukha, *nt.* 2. aruṇodaya, *m.* aruṇuggamana, *nt. v.i.* udeti ; āvibhavati ; uggacchati. *p.p.* udita ; °bhūta ; uggata. °**ing,** *n.* udaya, *m.*

Day, *n.* divasa ; vāsara, *m.* aha ; dina, *nt.* — **after tomorrow,** parasuve, *ind.* — **and night,** ahoratta, *nt.* — **before yesterday,** parahīyo, *ind.* °**break,** vibhāta, *m.* — **by day,** patidinaŋ ; devasikaŋ, *adv.* °**light,** *n.* divāloka, *m.* °**long,** *a.* sabbadivasāyatta, *adv.* sabbadivasaŋ. °**time,** divasabhāga, *m.* **By —,** divā, *ind.* **Next —,** punadivasa, *m.* **On another —,** aññadā, *adv.*

Day-dream, *n.* nipphalacintā, *f.* °**er,** nipphalacintī, *m.*

Daze, *n.* sammoha ; vibbhama, *m. v.t.* sammoheti ; vibbhameti. *p.p.* °hita ; °mita *or* vibbhanta.

Dazzle, *n.* 1. cakkhumosana, *nt.* 2. adhikappabhā, *f. v.t.* cakkhuŋ moseti. *v.i.* atibhāti ; ativirocati. *p.p.* mositacakkhu ; °cita. °**ing,** cakkhumosaka ; dudikkha.

Dead, *a. n.* mata ; cuta ; peta ; kālakata 3. *adv.* atīva ; accantaŋ. adj. accanta. — **body,** matakalebara, *nt.* °**born,** matappasūta, *a.* — **calm,** accantaniccalatā, *f.* — **certainty,** ekantanicchaya, *m.* — **colouring,** paṭhama-vaṇṇālepa, *m.* — **language,** vohārāpagata-bhāsā, *f.* — **letter,** anappitasāsana, *nt.* — **level,** akhaṇḍa-samatala, *nt.* °**lock,** accantabādhā, *f.* °**ly,** *a.* māraka ; pāṇahara. °**stand,** thiravirodha, *m.* °**wall,** acchidda-bhitti, *f.* — **weight,** avayha-bhāra, *m.*

Deaden, *v.t.* visaññaŋ *or* dubbalaŋ karoti ; moheti. *p.p.* dubbalīkata ; mohita.

Deaf, *a. n.* 1. badhira ; 2. anohitasota, *m.* °**en,** *v.t.* badhirīkaroti. *p.p.* °kata. °**ness,** badhiratta, *nt.* — **mute,** mūgabadhira, *m.*

Deal, *n.* bhāga ; koṭṭhāsa, *m. v.i.* paṇeti ; kayavikkayaŋ karoti. *v.t.* vibhajati ; vissajjeti. *p.p.* vibhatta ; vissaṭṭha. — **with,** ācarati. **A good** —, bhusaŋ ; accantaŋ, *adv.* **A good** — **of,** pacura ; bahula, *a.*

Dealer, *n.* vāṇija ; vohārika, *m.* — **in cloth,** vatthika, *m.* — **in carpets,** pāvārika, *m.* — **in liquor,** soṇḍika, *m.* — **in oil,** telika, *m.* — **in rice,** taṇḍulika, *m.* — **in swine,** sūkarika, *m.* — **in wood,** kaṭṭhika, *m.*

Dealing, *n.* ācaraṇa, *nt.*

Dean, *n.* 1. mahādevāyatanapati ; 2. vijjāyatanapati, *m.*

Dear, *a.* 1. piya ; manāpa ; 2. bavhagghanaka. — **as life,** pāṇasama, *a.* — **madam,** ayye ; bhoti, *voc.* — **Sir,** bhavaŋ ; mahāsaya, *voc.* **Most** —, piyatama, *a.* °**ly,** *adv.* 1. ādarena ; 2. bahumūlena. °**ness,** *n.* 1. piyatta, *nt.* 2. mahagghatta, *nt.*

Dearth, *n.* dullabhatta ; dubbhikkha, *nt.*

Death, *n.* maraṇa ; nidhana, *nt.* cuti ; kālakiriyā, *f.* jīvitakkhaya ; dehanikkhepa, *m.* *Personified:* maccu ; māra ; namuci. *m.* °**agony,** maraṇavedanā, *f.* °**bed,** maraṇamañca, *m.* °**blow,** maraṇīyappahāra, *m.* °**less,** *a.* amara. °**lessness,** amatapada, *nt.* °**rate,** maraṇasaṅkhyā, *f.* °**rites,** petakicca, *nt.* °'**s door,** māramukha, *nt.* °'**sman,** vadhaka, *m.* °**warrant,** vadhāṇā, *f.* **Messenger of** —, yamadūta ; devadūta, *m.* **Power of** —, maccuvasa, *m.* **Sphere of** —, maccudheyya, *nt.* **Subject to** —, maraṇadhamma, *a.*

Debar, *v.t.* nisedheti ; paṭisedheti. *p.p.* °dhita.

Debase, *v.t.* dūseti ; misseti. *p.p.* dūsita ; missita. °**ment,** dūsana ; missana, *nt.*

Debate, *n.* vivāda, *m. v.i.* vivadati ; kāraṇaŋ dasseti. *p.p.* vivadita. °**able,** *a.* vivādāraha. °**er,** vivādī, *m.* °**ful,** *a.* vādatthī.

Debauch, *n.* kāmāvesa, *m. v.t.* vippaṭipajjati ; kāmāsāya dūseti. *p.p.* vippaṭipanna ; °dūsita. °**er,** *n.* kāmāsatta ; durācāra ; itthidhutta, *m.* °**ery,** *n.* visayarati ; durācāratā, *f.* itthidūsana, *nt.* °**ee,** *n.* itthidhutta, *m.*

Debenture, *n.* paṭiññāpaṇṇa, *nt.*

Debilitate, *v.t.* dubbalīkaroti ; balaŋ hāpeti. *p.p.* °kata ; hāpitabala.

Debit, *n.* dātabbamūla, *nt. v.t.* iṇabhāgaŋ likhati. *p.p.* likhitaiṇabhāga.

Debonair, *a.* pasādajanaka.

Debouch, *v.i.* araññato niggacchati. *p.p.* °niggata.

Debris, *n.* vikiṇṇa-jiṇṇāvasesa, *m.*

Debt, *n.* iṇa, *nt.* **Discharging of** —, iṇasodhana, *nt.* **Free from** —, aṇana, *a.* **Freedom**

from —, āṇanya, *nt.* °**or**, *n.* iṇāyika ; iṇaṭṭha, *m.*

Debut, *n.* ādikamma, *nt.* paṭhamapaññāyanā, *f.* °**ant**, *n.* ādikammika, *m.*

Decade, *n.* dasaka ; dasavassa, *nt.*

Decadence, *n.* khaya ; vaya, *m.* parihāni, *f.* jīraṇa, *nt.* °**ent**, *a.* khayagāmī ; parihāyamāna.

Decagon, *n.* dasakoṇaka ; dasaŋsika, *m. nt.*

Decalcify, *v.t.* cuṇṇadhātum apaneti. *p.p.* apanīta°.

Decalogue, *n.* dasapaññatti, *f.*

Decamp, *v.t.* khandhāvārā apagacchati *or* palāyati. *p.p.* °apagata ; °palāta. °**ment**, *n.* khandhāvārapariccāga, *m.*

Decant, *v.t.* sanikaŋ vāheti *or* āsiñcati. *p.p.* °vāhita ; āsitta. °**er**, *n.* bhiṅkāra, *m.* kuṇḍikā, *f.*

Decapitate, *v.t.* sīsaŋ chindati. *p.p.* sīsacchinna. °**ion**, *n.* sīsaccheda, *m.*

Decapod, *n.* dasapadī, *m.*

Decay, *n.* jīraṇa, *nt.* jarā, *f.* palujjana, *nt. v.i.* jīrati ; jīyati ; hīyati ; khīyati ; palujjati. *p.p.* jiṇṇa ; hīna ; khīṇa ; paluṭṭha.

Decease, *v.i.* marati ; kālaŋkaroti. *p.p.* mata ; kālakata. *noun:* see **Death.**

Deceit, *n.* kerāṭiya ; sāṭheyya, *nt.* nikati ; vañcanā, *f.* °**ful**, *a.* nekatika ; kerāṭika ; vañcaka.

Deceive, *v.t.* vañceti ; vimoheti. *p.p.* vañcita ; °hita. °**er**, *n.* vañcaka ; pamohaka ; kuhaka, *m.* °**ing**, *a.* vañcanaka.

December, *n.* Māgasiramāsa, *m.*

Decency, *n.* 1. sabbhatā ; vinītatā ; 2. ucitatā, *f.*

Decen(n)ary, *n.* dasavassa, *nt.* adj. dasavassika.

Decennial, *a.* dasavassakālika. °**ly**, *adv.* dasavassavārena.

Decent, *a.* 1. sabbha ; vinīta ; ācārasampanna ; 2. ucita. °**ly**, *adv.* vinītākārena ; ucitākārena.

Decentralize, *v.t.* padhānaṭṭhānattam apaneti.

Deception, *n.* nikati ; vancanā, *f.* mohana, *nt.*

Deceptive, *a.* vañcanika ; nekatika ; kerāṭika. °**ly**, *adv.* nikatiyā. °**ness**, *n.* vañcakatta, *nt.*

Decide, *v.t.* tīreti ; niccheti ; niṇṇeti. *p.p.* tīrita ; nicchita ; niṇṇita. °**dly**, *adv.* nicchayena ; nūnaŋ ; ekantaŋ.

Deciduous, *a.* pariṇatakāle patanasīla.

Decimal, *a.* dasabhāgika. °**ize**, *v.t.* dasabhāgataŋ pāpeti. °**ly**, *adv.* dasabhāgavasena.

Decimate, *v.t.* dasasu ekekaŋ māreti ; dasamabhāgaŋ vināseti. °**ion**, *n.* dasamabhāganāsana, *nt.*

Decipher, *v.t.* gūḷhakkharāni visadīkaroti ; purālipīnaŋ atthaŋ pakāseti. °**ment**, *n.* purālipivisadīkaraṇa, *nt.*

Decision, *n.* nicchaya, *m.* tīraṇa ; sanniṭṭhāna, *nt.*

Decisive, *a.* nicchayakara ; vavatthāpaka. °**ly**, *adv.* niyataŋ ; ekaŋsena ; sanicchayaŋ. °**ness**, *n.* avadhāraṇa, *nt.* vavatthāpakatta, *nt.*

Decivilize, *v.t.* sabbhataŋ hāpeti. *p.p.* hāpitasabbhatta.

Deck, *n.* nāvāya uparitala, *nt.* *v.t.* maṇḍeti ; bhūseti ; alaṅkaroti. *p.p.* °ḍita ; °sita ; °kata. °**chair,** āsandi, *f.*

Declaim, *v.i.* uccāsaddena vadati ; vācuggataŋ karoti. *p.p.* °vutta ; °kata. °**ation,** *n.* paṭiyattadesanā ; vegayuttakathā, *f.*

Declare, *v.t.* pakāseti ; nivedeti ; sāveti ; ugghoseti. *p.p.* °sita ; °dita ; sāvita ; °sita. °**ant,** *n.* pakāsaka ; nivedaka, *m.* °**ation,** *n.* nivedana ; sāvaṇa, *nt.* pakāsanā ; anusāvanā, *f.* °**ation on oath,** saccakiriyā, *f.* °**ative,** *a.* pakāsaka ; nivedaka. °**atory,** *a.* sūcaka ; vācaka. °**edly,** *adv.* sanicchayaŋ.

Declension, *n.* 1. parihāni, *f.* 2. vibhattiyojanā, *f.*

Decline, *v.i.* 1. hāyati ; khīyati ; parābhavati ; 2. onamati. *p.p.* hīna ; khīṇa ; °bhūta ; onata. *v.t.* 1. paṭisedheti ; paṭikkhipati ; 2. onāmeti ; (in gram.) padarūpāni vibhajati. *p.p.* °dhita ; °khitta ; onāmita ; vibhattapadarūpa. *noun*: onati ; parihāni, *f.* khaya ; vaya ; parābhava, *m.* °**able,** *a.* 1. paṭikkhepāraha ; 2. vibhajanāraha. °**ate,** *a.* onata. °**ation,** *n.* onamana ; adhogamana, *nt.*

Declinometer, *n.* onatattamāṇaka, *nt.*

Declivity, *n.* poṇabhūmi, *f.* nitamba, *m.*

Declivous, Declivtious, *a.* poṇa ; anupubbaninna.

Decoct, *v.t.* kuthati ; pacati. *p.p.* kuthita ; pakka. °**ion,** *n.* kasāya, *nt.*

Decohere, *v.t.* puthakkaroti. *p.p.* puthakkata.

Decollate, *v.t.* sīsaŋ chindati. *p.p.* sīsacchinna. °**ion,** *n.* sīsaccheda, *m.*

Decolourize, *v.t.* vaṇṇaŋ nāseti. *p.p.* nāsitavaṇṇa. °**ration,** *n.* vivaṇṇakaraṇa, *nt.*

Decompose, *v.t.* viyojeti ; vinibbhujati ; puthakkaroti. *v.i.* vilīyati ; pūtibhavati. *p.p.* °jita ; vinibhutta ; °kata ; vilīna ; °bhūta. °**ition,** *n.* 1. viyojana, *nt.* 2. pūtibhāva, *m.*

Decomposite, *a.* *n.* punasamāsita.

Decompound, *a.* *n.* punamissīkata.

Deconsecrate, *v.t.* visuddhattam apaneti. *p.p.* apanīta°.

Decontrol, *v.t.* pālanam apaneti. *p.p.* apanīta°.

Decorate, *v.t.* maṇḍeti ; bhūseti ; vibhūseti ; alaṅkaroti. *p.p.* °ḍita ; °sita ; °kata. °**ion,** *n.* maṇḍana, *nt.* alaṅkāra, *m.* °**ive,** *a.* maṇḍanakara. °**tor,** *n.* vibhūsaka ; maṇḍetu, *m.*

Decorous, see **Decent.**

Decorum, *n.* soracca, *nt.* vinaya ; sadācāra, *m.*

Decoy, *n.* 1. palobhana, *nt.* gahanūpāya, *m.* 2. aghammiga, *m.* *v.t.* palobheti ; vimoheti. *p.p.* °bhita ; °hita.

Decrease, *n.* parihāni, *f.* hāyana, *nt.* apacaya, *m.* *v.i.* parihāyati ; mandībhavati. *p.p.* parihīna ; °bhūta.

Decree, *n.* 1. āṇā ; paññatti, *f.* 2. aṭṭavinicchaya, *m.* *v.t.* ādisati ; āṇāpeti ; paññāpeti. *p.p.* ādiṭṭha ; āṇatta ; paññatta.

Decrement, *n.* apacaya ; khaya, *m.* hānippamāṇa. *nt.*

Decrepit, *a.* jiṇṇa ; jajjarita ; ativuddha. °**ude,** *n.* jiṇṇāvatthā ; atimahallakatā, *f.*

Decrescent, *a.* hāyamāna ; khayadhamma.

Decrown, *v.t.* rajjapadā apaneti. *p.p.* °apanīta.

Decry, *v.t.* upavadati ; apavadati ; nindati. *p.p.* upavutta ; nindita.

Decumbent, *a.* nipanna ; sayamāna.

Decuple, *a.* dasaguṇita. *v.t.* dasena guṇeti. *p.p.* °guṇita.

Decussate, *v.t.* siṅghāṭakaŋ aṅketi. *p.p.* aṅkita°.

Dedicate, *v.t.* samappeti ; upahāraŋ karoti. *p.p.* °pita ; katūpahāra. °**ion,** *n.* samappaṇā, *f.* °**tory,** *a.* samappaṇāyatta.

Deduce, *v.t.* anumāneti ; upalakkheti. *p.p.* °nita ; °khita. °**ible,** *a.* anumeya ; upalakkhitabba.

Deduct, *v.t.* uddharati ; vikalaŋ *or* ūnaŋ karoti. *p.p.* uddhaṭa ; vikalīkata ; ūnīkata. °**ion,** *n.* 1. uddharaṇa ; 2. anumāna, *nt.* anumiti, *f.* °**ive,** *a.* uddhāraka ; ūnakara.

Deed, *n.* 1. kamma ; kicca, *nt.* kiriyā, *f.* 2. appaṇāpaṇṇa, *nt.*

Deem, *v.t.* maññati ; gaṇeti. *p.p.* maññita ; gaṇita.

Deep, *a.* 1. gambhīra ; agādha ; anuttāna ; 2. gūḷha ; sukhuma ; 3. ninna ; nīca. *n.* samudda, *m.* °**darkness,** *n.* ghanandhakāra ; andhantama, *m.* °**love,** daḷhapema, *nt.* °**ly,** gāḷhaŋ ; accantaŋ. °**ness,** gambhīratā ; gāḷhatā, *f.* °**rooted,** baddhamūla, *a.* °**sigh,** dīghanissāsa, *m.* **Knee —,** jaṇṇumatta, *a.*

Deepen, *v.t.* gambhīraŋ *or* gāḷhaŋ karoti. *p.p.* °kata.

Deer, *n.* miga ; hariṇa ; sāraṅga, *m.* °**hunter,** migaluddaka, *m.* °**park,** migadāya, *m.*

Deface, *v.t.* 1. virūpeti ; kalusayati ; 2. apamajjati ; lopeti. *p. p.* °pita ; °sita ; apamaṭṭha ; lutta. °**ment,** *n.* 1. virūpakaraṇa ; 2. apamajjana, *nt.*

De facto, *adv.* saccato ; thetato.

Defalcate, *v.t.* nikatiyā apaharati. *p.p.* °apahaṭa. °**ion,** nikatiyāpaharaṇa, *nt.* °**tor,** nikatiyā apahārī, *m.*

Defame, *v.t.* vivaṇṇeti ; guṇaŋ makkheti. *p.p.* °ṇita ; °khitaguṇa. °**ation,** *n.* apavāda, *m.* abbhakkhāna, *nt.* °**atory,** *a.* guṇanāsaka ; akittikara ; yasohāyaka. °**er,** *n.* makkhī ; avaṇṇavādī, *m.*

Default, *n.* 1. ūnatta, *nt.* 2. sammukhānāgamana, *nt.* 3. vītikkama ; paṭiññābhaṅga, *m.* *v.i.* 1. paṭiññaŋ bhañjati; 2. adhikaraṇaŋ na pāpuṇāti. *v.t.* paṭiññābhaṅge daṇḍaŋ paṇeti. *p.p.* bhaṭṭha-paṭiñña. °**er,** *n.* paṭiññābhañjaka, *m.*

Defeasance, *n.* nibbalīkaraṇa ; nipphalīkaraṇa, *nt.*

Defeasible, *a.* nirākaraṇīya ; vipphalīkaraṇīya.

Defeat, *n.* parājaya ; parābhava, *m.* *v.t.* parājeti ; abhimaddati ; pebhañjati ; jeti. *p.p.* °jita ; °dita ; pabhaṭṭha ; jita.

Defeature, *v.t.* aññavesaŋ gaṇhāpeti ; asañjāniyaŋ karoti. *p.p.* gāhitaññavesa ; °kata.

Defecate, *v.t.* hadati ; ūhadati ; malam apaharati. *p.p.* apahaṭamala. **°ion,** *n.* malāpaharaṇa ; ūhadana, *nt.*

Defect, *n.* ūnatta ; vikalatta ; vajja, *nt.* **°ive,** *a.* ūna ; vikala ; sadosa ; vikalaṅga.

Defection, *n.* pakkhāpagamana ; pakkhavijahana, *nt.*

Defence, *n.* 1. gutti ; ārakkhā, *f.* 2. codanāpaharaṇa *nt.* **°less,** *a.* agutta ; arakkhita ; nirāvudha. **°lessness,** *n.* anārakkhatā, *f.*

Defend, *v.t.* rakkhati ; gopeti. *v.i.* niravajjataŋ pakāseti ; codanam apaharati. *p.p.* °khita ; gopita *or* gutta ; apahaṭacodana. **°ant,** cuditaka, *m.* **°er,** *n.* rakkhaka ; pālaka, *m.*

Defensible, *a.* sukharakkhiya ; paṭivacanīya. **°sive,** *n.* gopakavatthu ; rakkhāvidhāna, *nt.* adj. guttidāyaka ; ārakkhāvaha.

Defer, *v.t.* papañceti ; vilambeti ; kālam ākaḍḍhati. *v.i.* pamajjati ; cirāyati. *p.p.* °cita ; °bita ; pamatta ; cirāyita. — **to,** vasībhavati. **°ence,** *n.* anuvattana, *nt.* vasībhāva, *m.* **°ent,** *a.* sagārava ; vasībhūta ; paramatānuvattaka. **°entially,** *adv.* sagāravaŋ ; sānunayaŋ.

Defiance, *n.* kalahāya avhāna ; paṭippharaṇa, *nt.*

Defiant, *a.* paṭāṇika ; anoṇata ; paccanika.

Deficiency, *n.* ūnatta ; vekalla ; asampuṇṇatta, *nt.* **°ent,** *a.* ūna ; vikala ; aparipuṇṇa.

Deficit, *n.* ūnabhāga, *m.* ūnamūlasaṅkhyā, *f.*

Defile, *n.* kandarapatha ; duggamagga, *m.* *v.t.* padūseti ; malinīkaroti. *v.i.* paṭipāṭiyā gacchati. *p.p.* °sita ; °kata ; °gata. **°er,** *n.* dūsaka, *m.* **°ment,** *n.* 1. dussana ; kilissana ; 2. rajjana, *nt.*

Define, *v.t.* upalakkheti ; viseseti ; paricchindati ; niccheti. *p.p.* °khita ; °sita ; paricchinna ; °chita. **°er,** *n.* nirūpaka ; paricchindaka *m.*

Definite, *a.* nicchita ; niyamita ; paricchinna. **°ly,** *adv.* ekantena ; saniyamaŋ. **°ion,** *n.* upalakkhaṇa ; paricchindana, *nt.* nicchaya, *m.* vavatthā, *f.* **°ive,** *a.* niyāmaka ; paricchindaka ; asandiddha.

Deflagrate, *v.t.* khippaŋ dahati. *v.i.* sīghaŋ jalati. *p.p.* °daḍḍha ; °jalita. **°ion,** *n.* sīghadāha ; mahādāha, *m.*

Deflate, *v.t.* vāyupūriŋ hāpeti. **°ion,** *n.* opātana, *nt.*

Deflect, *v.t.* passato nāmeti. *v.i.* vyāvaṭṭati ; uppathena yāti. *p.p.* °nāmita ; °ṭita ; °yāta. **°ion,** *n.* uppathagamana ; vyāvaṭṭana, *nt.*

Defloration, *n.* 1. kusumavigama, *m.* 2. kaññādūsana, *nt.*

Deflower, *v.t.* 1. kusumahāniŋ karoti ; 2. kaññaŋ dūseti. *p.p.* °kata ; dūsitakañña.

Defluent, *n. a.* adhosandamāna ; yathāninnappavatta.

Deforest, *v.t.* vivanaŋ karoti. *p.p.* °kata.

Deform, *v.t.* virūpeti ; dubbaṇṇīkaroti. *p.p.* °pita ; °kata. °**ed,** *a.* virūpa ; vikalaṅga ; duddasika. °**ation,** *n.* virūpakaraṇa, *nt.* °**ity,** *n.* vevaṇṇiya ; virūpatta, *nt.*

Defraud, *v.t.* vañceti ; patāreti. *p.p.* vañcita ; °rita.

Defray, *v.t.* paribbayaŋ *or* vayamūlaŋ deti. *p.p.* dinnaparibbaya.

Deft, *a.* dakkha ; kusala ; nipuṇa ; catura.

Defunct, *a.* mata ; gatāyuka ; appavattamāna.

Defy, *v.t.* 1. abhiyuñjati ; yugaggāhāya avhāti ; 2. bādheti ; paṭānī hoti. *p.p.* °yutta ; °avhāta ; bādhita ; °bhūta. °**iance,** *n.* abhiyoga ; yugaggāha, *m.* °**iant,** *n.* paṭipuggala ; yugaggāhī, *m.*

Degenerate, *a. n.* hāyamagatika ; khīṇapuñña ; paribhaṭṭha. *v.i.* parihāyati. *p.p.* parihīna. °**ion,** *n.* parihāni, *f.* parābhava, *m.* °**ness,** *n.* parihīnatta, *nt.* guṇahāni, *f.* °**racy,** *n.* kulācārahāni, *f.*

Deglutition, *n.* gilana ; ajjhoharaṇa, *nt.*

Degrade, *v.t.* adhikārā cāveti ; nīcaṭṭhānaŋ pāpeti. *v.i.* uccaṭṭhānā patati. *p.p.* °cāvita ; °pāpita ; °patita. °**ation,** *n.* adhikārabhañjana ; ṭhānācāvana, *nt.* °**ing,** *a.* ayasakara ; nīcattapāpaka.

Degree, *n.* 1. dasā ; ṭhiti ; avatthā, *f.* 2. upādhi, *m.* 3. bhāga ; koṭṭhāsa, *m.* cakkaŋsaka, *nt.* 4. kulatanti, *f.* **By degrees,** anukkamena ; thoka-thokaŋ, *adv.* **In the highest —,** accantaŋ ; atisayena, *adv.*

Dehort, *v.t.* akaraṇāya ovadati. °**ation,** *n.* akaraṇāyovāda, *m.* °**ative,** *a.* nivāraka ; anusāsaka.

Dehumanize, *v.t.* manujagatiŋ nāseti. *p.p.* nāsita°.

Dehydrate, *v.t.* nirudakaŋ karoti. *p.p.* nirudakīkata.

Dehypnotize, *v.t.* visaññaniddā apaneti. *p.p.* °apanīta.

Deicide, *n.* devanāsana, *nt.*

Deictic, *a.* abhidhāyaka ; vācaka.

Deiform, *a.* devasadisa.

Deify, *v.t.* devattam pāpeti *or* āropeti. *p.p.* °pita. °**ication,** *n.* devattāropana, *nt.*

Deign, *v.t.* arahatīti sallakkheti ; anukampati. *p.p.* °khita ; °pita.

Deism, *n.* devabhatti, *f.* issaravāda, *m.*

Deist, *n.* Brahmavādī, *m.*

Deity, *n.* 1. deva, *m.* devatā, *f.* Paramissara, *m.* 2. devatta, *nt.*

Deject, *v.t.* visādeti ; ukkaṇṭhāpeti. *p.p.* °dita ; °pita. *v.i.* visīdati ; ukkaṇṭhati. *p.p.* visinna ; °ṭhita. °**ed,** *a.* khinna ; visādāpanna ; nibbinna ; maṅkubhūta ; adhomukha ; saŋvigga. °**edly,** *adv.* ukkaṇṭhitākārena ; savisādaŋ. °**ion,** *n.* visāda ; kheda, *m.* ukkaṇṭhā, *f.*

Dejecta, *n.* asuci ; karīsa ; mala, *nt.* °**tory**, *a.* virecaka ; malasodhaka.

Delate, *v.t.* codeti ; dosam āropeti. *p.p.* codita ; āropitadosa. °**ion**, codanā ; dosāropaṇā, *f.*

Delay, *v.t.* papañceti ; vilambeti ; kālaŋ khepeti. *p.p.* °cita ; °bita ; °pitakāla. *v.i.* cirāyati ; pamajjati. *p.p.* °yita ; pamatta. *noun* : pamāda, *m.* cirāyana ; vilambana ; dīghasuttiya, *nt.*

Delectable, *a.* pītijanaka ; manohara ; manuñña ; ramanīya. °**bility**, *n.* rammatta, *nt.*

Delectation, *n.* ānanda ; pamoda, *m.* vitti ; tuṭṭhi, *f.*

Delectus, *n.* uddhaṭa-pāṭhasaṅgaha, *m.*

Delegacy, *n.* 1. niyojitatta, *nt.* 2. niyojita-sabhā, *f.*

Delegate, *n.* niyojita ; paṭinidhi, *m.* *v.t.* niyojeti ; paṭinidhiŋ karoti. *p.p.* °jita ; °kata. °**ion**, *n.* 1. niyojana ; 2. paṭinidhimaṇḍala, *nt.*

Delete, *v.t.* lopeti ; apamajjati. *p.p.* lutta ; apamaṭṭha. °**ion**, *n.* lopa, *m.* apamajjana, *nt.*

Deleterious, *a.* hiŋsākara ; asagguṇa.

Deliberate, *a.* 1. sacetanika ; 2. samekkhakata; nisammakata; asāhasa ; suvicārita ; vīmaŋsita. *v.i.* tuleti ; vicāreti ; vīmaŋsati. *p.p.* lulita ; °rita ; °sita. °**ion**, *n.* vicāraṇā ; vīmaŋsā ; upaparikkhā, *f.* °**ive**, *a.* vicārasīlī ; samekkhakārī. °**ly**, *adv.* anuvicca ; sañcicca ; vicārapubbakaŋ. °**ness**, *n.* samekkhakāritā, *f.* appamāda, *m.*

Delicacy, *n.* 1. paṇītabhojana ; madhuranna, *nt.* 2. madhuratta ; lāvañña, *nt.* 3. maddava, *nt.* 4. dubbalatta, *nt.* 5. sadācāra, *m.*

Delicate, *a.* 1. mudu ; komala ; sukumāra ; sukhumāla ; 2. madhura ; paṇīta ; ojavantu ; 3. vinīta ; 4. visiṭṭha ; ukkaṭṭha ; 5. rogātura ; dubbala ; 6. tanu ; sukhuma. °**ly**, *adv.* sukhumaŋ ; mudutāya. °**ness**, *n.* mudutā ; sukhumālatā ; paṇītatā, *f.*

Delicious, *a.* atimadhura ; atipaṇīta ; sādurasa ; asecanaka. °**ly**, *adv.* sumadhuraŋ ; paṇītākārena. °**ness**, madhuratta, *nt.*

Delict, *n.* vītikkama ; nītibhaṅga, *m.* dukkata, *nt.*

Delight, *n.* pīti ; tuṭṭhi ; santuṭṭhi ; modanā, *f.* ānanda ; pamoda ; āmoda, *m.* pāmojja ; somanassa, *nt.* *v.i.* tussati ; ramati ; nandati ; modati. *v.t.* toseti ; modeti ; rameti ; pīṇeti. *p.p.* tuṭṭha ; rata ; nandita ; modita ; tosita ; modita ; ramita ; pīṇita. — **in company**, saṅganikārāmatā, *f.* °**ful**, °**some**, *a.* iṭṭha ; kanta ; manāpa ; manorama ; pītijanaka. °**fully**, *adv.* sānandaŋ. °**ing in**, ramamāna, *a.*

Delimit, *v.t.* paricchindati ; samariyādaŋ karoti. *p.p.* °chinna ; °dīkata. °**ation**, *n.* sīmāṭhapana ; paricchindana, *nt.*

Delineate, *v.t.* 1. sarūpam ālikhati ; 2. vitthāreti. *p.p.* ālikhitasarūpa ; °rita. °**ion**, *n.* sarūpālikhana, *nt.*

Delinquency, *n.* kiccākaraṇa; kattabbāpaharaṇa, *nt.*

Delinquent, *a. n.* sakiccāpahārī; paṭiññābhañjaka.

Deliquesce, *v.i.* vilīyati. *p.p.* vilīna, °**nce,** vilīyana, *nt.* °**nt,** *a.* vilīyanasabhāva.

Delirious, *a.* bhantacitta; sativikala.

Delirium, *n.* mucchā; visaññatā, *f.*

Delitescent, *a.* anusayita.

Deliver, *v.t.* 1. moceti; pamoceti; 2. hatthaŋ pāpeti; 3. deseti; udāharati; 4. (an arrow, etc.) vissajjeti; khipati; 5. (a child:) janeti; pasavati. *p.p.* mocita; °pita; desita; udāhaṭa; vissaṭṭha; kitta; janita; pasūta. °**ance,** *n.* mutti; vimutti, *f.* mokkha; pamokkha, *m.* °**er,** *n.* 1. mocaka; pamuñcaka; 2. tāyaka; 3. desaka; 4. appetu, *m.* — **up,** parivajjeti; pariccajati.

Delivery, *n.* 1. vissajjana; 2. sampappaṇa, *nt.* 3. desanā, *f.* 4. nivedana; viññāpana, *nt.* — **of a child,** gabbhavuṭṭhāna, *nt.* pasūti, *f.*

Dell, *n.* khuddaka-ninnabhūmi, *f.* kuñja; nikuñja, *m. nt.*

Delta, *n.* nadīmukha-dīpa, *m.*

Delude, *v.t.* vañceti; moheti; palobheti. *p.p.* vañcita; mohita; °bhita.

Deluge, *n.* mahogha; āposaŋvaṭṭa, *m.* kappanāsakavuṭṭhi, *f.* *v.t.* ottharati; jalena chādeti. *p.p.* otthaṭa; jalacchanna.

Delusion, *n.* sammoha; vibbhama, *m.* pamuyhana, *nt.*

Delusive, Delusory, *a.* pamohaka; bhantikara. °**ness,** *n.* vañcanikatā, *f.*

Delve, *v.t.* 1. khaṇati; 2. kāraṇaŋ pariyesati. *p.p.* khata °sita.

Demagnetize, *v.t.* ayokantabhāvam apaneti. *p.p.* apanīta°.

Demagogue, *n.* 1. janaāyaka; 2. pakkhagāhīdesaka, *m.*

Demand, *n.* āyācanā, *f.* yuttikathana, *nt.* *v.t.* āyattabhāvaŋ katheti; sakāyattaŋ yācati. *p.p.* kathitāyattabhāva; °yācita. °**ant,** *n.* āyācaka; patthetu, *m.*

Demarcate, *v.t.* sīmeti; paricchindati; mariyādaŋ ṭhapeti. *p.p.* sīmita; paricchinna; ṭhapitamariyāda. °**ion,** *n.* mariyādāṭhapana; sīmāniyamana, *nt.*

Dematerialize, *v.t.* dabbattam apaneti. *v.i.* addabbaŋ bhavati. *p.p.* apanītadabbatta; °bhūta.

Demean, *v.i.* ācarati. *v.t.* attānaŋ onāmeti. *p.p.* onāmitatta. °**our,** *n.* ācāra, *m.* ācaraṇa, *nt.* vutti, *f.*

Dement, Dementate, *v.t.* ummādayati; cittaŋ vikkhipati. *p.p.* °yita; vikkhittacitta. °**tia,** *n.* ummāda; cittakkhepa, *m.*

Demerit, *n.* 1. akusala; pāpa, *nt.* 2. aguṇa; dosa, *m.*

Demi, *prep.* addha; upaddha.

Demi-god, *n.* vimānapeta; siddha; devattapāpita, *m.*

Demi-lune, *n.* 1. addhacanda, *m.* 2. pākāragutti, *f.*

Demi-man, *n.* kinnara, *m.*

Demi-monde, *n.* gaṇikā, *f.*

Demi-rep, *n.* kulaṭā, *f.*

Demise, *n.* 1. maraṇa, *nt.* kālakiriyā, *f.* accaya, *m.* 2. dāyādappaṇā, *f.* *v.t.* dāyādīkaroti. *p.p.* °kata.

Demission, *n.* adhikāravijahana, *nt.*

Demit, *v.i.* adhikāraŋ *or* ṭhānantaraŋ vijahati. *p.p.* vijahitādhikāra.

Demiurge, *n.* lokamāpaka, *m.*

Demobilize, *v.t.* (senaŋ, nāvaŋ, etc.) viyojeti ; puthakkaroti. *p.p.* °jita ; °kata. °**ation**, *n.* viyojana ; puthakkaraṇa, *nt.*

Democracy, *n.* janasammatapālana ; pajāpabhutta, *nt.*

Democrat, *n.* pajāpabhuttavādī, *m.* °**ic**, *a.* janasammatavādāyatta.

Demography, *n.* cuti-uppattyādidīpaka-lipi, *f.*

Demolish, *v.t.* viddhaŋseti ; vināseti ; vidhameti ; adhopāteti. *p.p.* °sita ; °mita ; °pātita. °**er**, *n.* viddhaŋsaka ; nāsaka, *m.*

Demolition, *n.* vināsana ; ummūlana ; ucchindana, *nt.*

Demon, *n.* 1. amanussa ; bhūta ; yakkha ; pisāca, *m.* 2. niṭṭhura ; kakkhaḷa, *m.* °**iac**, *a.* 1. pisācasadisa ; 2. bhūtāviṭṭha. °**ical**, *a.* yakkhasadisa, *f.* °**ism**, *n.* bhūtabhatti, *f.* °**ize**, *v.t.* yakkhāviṭṭhaŋ *or* bhūtasadisaŋ karoti. °**olatry**, *n.* bhūtapūjā, *f.* °**ology**, *n.* bhūtavijjā, *f.*

Demonstrable, *a.* sandassitabha ; nidassanīya.

Demonstrate, *v.t.* niddisati ; nidasseti ; sandasseti. *p.p.* niddiṭṭha ; °sita. °**ion**, *n.* nidassana ; sādhana ; nirūpana, *nt.* °**ive**, *a.* nidassaka ; nirūpaka. °**tor**, *n.* sandassetu, *m.*

Demoralize, *v.t.* sadācārā cāveti ; caritaŋ dūseti ; guṇadhammaŋ hāpeti. *p.p.* °cāvita ; dūsita-carita ; hāpita°. °**ation**, *n.* ācārabhaṅga, *m.* caritadūsana, *nt.* guṇahāni, *f.*

Demos, *n.* 1. pajā ; janatā, *f.* 2. janasammatavāda, *m.*

Demotic, *a.* gamma ; mahājanika.

Demulcent, *a.* samanakara ; sītidāyaka.

Demur, *v.i.* 1. saṅkati ; 2. bādheti. *p.p.* saṅkita ; bādhita. *n.* virodha, *m.* °**rable**, *a.* virodhāraha.

Demure, *a.* santa ; vinīta ; upasanta ; samāhita. °**ness**, *n.* santatta, *nt.* upasama, *m.*

Demurrage, *n.* hānipūrakamūla, *nt.*

Den, *n.* bila, *nt.* guhā, *f.*

Denationalize, *v.t.* jātikalakkhaṇaŋ hāpeti. *p.p.* hāpitajā°.

Denaturalize, *v.t.* sabhāvalakkhaṇaŋ nāseti. *p.p.* nāsitasabh°.

Denature, *v.t.* see the above.

Dendriform, *a.* rukkhasaṇṭhāna.

Dendrology, *n.* rukkhavijjā, *f.*

Denegation, *n.* paccakkhāna, *nt.* paṭikkhepa ; nisedha, *m.*

Dengue, *n.* sandhirujākara-jara, *m.*

Deniable, *a.* nirākaraṇīya ; paṭikkhipitabba.

Denial, *n.* paṭikkhepa, *m.* paccakkhāna, *nt.*

Denigrate, *v.t.* kaṇhayati ; kalaṅketi. *p.p.* °yita ; °kita.

Denizen, *n.* nivāsī ; serijana, *m.*

Denominate, *v.t.* abhidhāti ; nāmaŋ karoti. *p.p.* abhihita ; katanāma. °**ion,** *n.* nāmakaraṇa ; abhidhāna ; nāmadheyya, *nt.* samaññā, *f.* °**ive,** *a.* abhidhāyaka. (In gram.) nāmadhātuka. °**tor,** *n.* 1. nāmadāyaka ; 2. vibhajaka, *m.*

Denote, *v.t.* vyañjayati ; sūceti ; upalakkheti ; viseseti. *p.p.* vyañjita ; sūcita ; °khita ; °sita. °**ation,** *n.* niddesa, *m.* upalakkhaṇa ; sūcana, *nt.* °**ative,** *a.* abhidhāyaka ; vācaka. °**ing,** *a.* sūcaka ; nidassaka.

Denouement, *n.* kumantaṇāvīkaraṇa, *nt.*

Denounce, *v.t.* dosam āvīkaroti ; pākaṭavasena tajjeti. *p.p.* āvīkatadosa ; °jita. °**ment,** *n.* dosāvīkaraṇa, *nt.* °**er,** *n.* codaka ; dosāropaka, *m.*

Dense, *a.* ghana ; sanda ; bahala ; avirala. °**ity,** *n.* bahalatta ; sandatta ; ghanatta, *nt.*

Dent, *n.* pahāra-lañchana, *nt.* *v.t.* lakkhaṇaŋ chindati. *p.p.* chinnalakkhaṇa.

Dental, *a.* dantaja ; dantāyatta.

Dentate, *a.* dantayutta.

Denticle, *n.* khuddaka-danta, *m.*

Dentifrice, *n.* dantadhāvana ; dantabhesajja, *nt.*

Dentist, *n.* dantavejja, *m.* °**ry,** *n.* dantatikicchā, *f.*

Dentition, *n.* 1. dantakantana ; dantasamakaraṇa, *nt.* 2. dantuppāda, *m.* 3. dantavinyāsa, *m.*

Denture, *n.* dantāvali, *f.* kittimadanta, *m.*

Denude, *v.t.* naggaŋ *or* acelakaŋ karoti. *p.p.* naggīkata.

Denunciation, *n.* codanā, *f.* dosāvīkaraṇa, *nt.*

Deny, *v.t.* paṭikkhipati ; paccakkhāti ; no ti vadati. *p.p.* paṭikkhitta ; °khāta ; °vutta.

Deobstruct, *v.t.* bādhakam apaneti. *p.p.* apanītabādhaka.

Deodand, *n.* devadaṇḍa, *m.* puññatthāya rājāyattīkata-dhana, *nt.*

Deodar, *n.* devadāru, *m.*

Deodorize, *v.t.* gandhaŋ nāseti. *p.p.* nāsitagandha. °**ation,** *n.* gandhanāsana ; rogabījanāsana, *nt.*

Depart, *v.i.* apagacchati ; pakkamati ; nissarati ; apakkamati ; apeti. *p.p.* apagata ; pakkanta ; nissaṭa ; apakkanta ; apeta. *v.t.* cajati ; jahāti ; apaneti. *p.p.* catta ; jahita ; apanīta. °**ed from,** mata, kālakata, *a.* °**ure,** *n.* niggamana ; apagamana, *nt.* apakkama, *m.*

Department, *n.* 1. viccheda ; vibhāga, *m.* 2. kāriyaŋsa, *m.* kāriyamaṇḍala, *nt.*

Depasture, *v.i.* gocaraŋ gaṇhāti. *p.p.* gahitagocara.

Depauperize, *v.t.* sadhanaī-karoti. *p.p.* °kata.

Depend, *v.i.* nissayati ; avalambati ; avassayati. *p.p.* nissita ; °bita ; avassita. °**able,** *a.* avassayitabba. °**ing on,** nissāya ; upādāya ; paṭicca, *ind.* —**on,** upajīvati ; anujīvati.

Dependant, °**ent,** *a.* nissita ; parādhīna ; parāyatta. *n.* upajīvī ; anujīvī, *m.* —°**origination,** paṭiccasamuppāda, *m.*

Dependence, *n.* 1. nissaya ; avalambana, *nt.* 2. paravasatā, *f.* °**cy,** *n.* parādhīnadesa, *m.*

Depict, *v.t.* 1. ālikhati ; 2. vaṇṇeti. *p.p.* ālikhita ; vaṇṇita. °**ion,** *n.* ālikhana, *nt.*

Depilate, *v.t.* lome nāseti. *p.p.* nāsitaloma. °**ion,** *n.* lomanāsana, *nt.* °**tory,** *a.* lomanāsaka.

Deplete, *v.t.* riñcati ; suññaŋ karoti. *p.p.* ritta. °**ed,** *a.* suñña ; tuccha. °**ion,** *n.* riñcana, *nt.*

Deplore, *v.t.* anusocati ; anutthunāti. *p.p.* °cita ; anutthuta. °**able,** *a.* anusocanīya. °**ably,** *adv.* socanīyākārena.

Deplume, *v.t.* sakuṇapatte luñcati. *p.p.* luñcitapatta.

Depolarize, *v.t.* ujubhāvam apaneti ; kampeti. *p.p.* apanītaujubhāva ; kampita.

Deponent, *n.* sasapatha-sakkhika, *m.*

Depopulate, *v.t.* vijanīkaroti ; nibbāseti. *p.p.* °kata ; nibbāsita. °**ion,** *n.* janasuññakaraṇa, *nt.*

Deport, *v.t.* apaharati ; vippavāseti ; desantaraŋ peseti. *v.i.* ācarati ; vattati. *p.p.* apahaṭa ; °sita ; °pesita. °**ation,** *n.* pabbājanā ; vivāsanā, *f.* °**ment,** *n.* ācaraṇa, *nt.* ākappa ; iriyāpatha, *m.*

Depose, *v.t.* 1. ṭhānantarā cāveti ; 2. sakkhiŋ katheti. *p.p.* °cāvita ; kathikasakkhī.

Deposit, *n.* 1. āsaya, *m.* nikkhepaṭṭhāna, *nt.* 2. nidahana, *nt.* 3. nihita-dhana, *nt.* 4. adhonicita-mala, *nt.* *v.t.* nidahati ; nikkhipati. *p.p.* nihita *or* nidahita ; nikkhitta. °**ary,** *n.* nihitadhanarakkhaka, *m.* °**or,** *n.* nidahaka ; nikkhipaka, *m.* °**ory,** *n.* nihitaṭṭhāna ; nidhāna, *nt.*

Depot, *n.* bhaṇḍāgāra ; senāgāra, *nt.*

Deprave, *v.t.* dūseti ; kileseti. *p.p.* °sita. °**ed,** *a.* duṭṭha ; durācāra. °**edness,** °**ity,** *n.* bhaṭṭhācāratā, *f.* kilesa, *m.*

Deprecate, *v.t.* 1. apasādeti ; avamāneti ; 2. (aggham) osādeti. *p.p.* °dita ; °nita ; osāditaggha. °**ion,** *n.* 1. apasādana ; 2. agghosīdana, *nt.*

Depreciate, *v.t.* agghaŋ hāpeti. *p.p.* hāpitaggha. °**ion,** *n.* agghosādanā, *f.*

Depredation, *n.* vilumpana, *nt.* °**tor,** *n.* vilumpaka, *m.*

Depress, *v.t.* onāmeti ; omaddati ; visādaŋ pāpeti. *p.p.* °mita ; °dita ; °pita. °**ed,** *a.* visādāpanna ; khinnacitta ; maṅkubhūta. °**ion,** *n.* omaddana ; adhopatana, *nt.* visāda ; kheda, *m.*

Deprive, *v.t.* viyojeti ; voropeti ; vinākaroti. *p.p.* °jita ; °pita ;

°kata. **°ation,** *n.* viyojana; vinākaraṇa, *nt.* hāni; jāni, *f.*

Depth, *n.* 1. gambhīratta; agādhatta; 2. bahalatta, *nt.* 3. agādhajala, *nt.* 4. abbhantara, *nt.*

Depurate, *v.t.* sodheti; puṇāti; nimmalīkaroti. *p.p.* sodhita; pūta; °kata.

Depute, *v.t.* niyojeti; dūtakicce yojeti. *p.p.* °jita. **°ation,** *n.* 1. niyojana, *nt.* 2. niyojita-maṇḍala, *nt.*

Deputy, *n.* niyuttapurisa; upādhikārī, *m.*

Deracinate, *v.t.* ummūleti. *p.p.* °lita.

Derail, *v.i.* ayopathā apagacchati. *v.t.* ayopathā apagameti. *p.p.* °apagata; °mita. **°ment,** *n.* ayopathāpagamana, *nt.*

Derange, *v.t.* vikkhipati; khobheti; ākulīkaroti. *p.p.* vikkhitta; khobhita; °kata. **°ed,** *a.* vipallattha; anavaṭṭhita. **°ed of mind,** khittacitta; ummattaka, *a.* **°ment,** *n.* vikkhepa, *m.* anavaṭṭhiti, *f.*

Derelict, *a. n.* pariccatta; vivajjita; assāmika. **°ion,** *n.* 1. vivajjana, *nt.* 2. kiccākaraṇa; pamajjana, *nt.*

Deride, *v.t.* parihasati; uppaṇḍeti. *p.p.* °sita; °ḍita.

Derision, *n.* upahāsa; parihāsa, *m.* uppaṇḍanā, *f.*

Derisive, Derisory, *a.* 1. upahāsakara; 2. agaṇetabba; upahasitabba.

Derive, *v.t.* nikkaḍḍhati; ādāti. *v.i.* pabhavati; ubbhavati. *p.p.* °ḍhita; ādinna; °vita. **°ation,** *n.* 1. nikkaḍḍhana, *nt.* pabhava, *m.* 2. nibbacana, *nt.* nirutti, *f.* **°ative,** *a. n.* tabbhava; vyuppanna.

Derm, *n.* taca, *m.* **°atologist,** *m.* cammarogatikicchaka, *m.*

Derogate, *v.i.* hāyati; ūnībhavati; parihāyati. *p.p.* hīna; °bhūta; parihīna. **°ion,** *n.* parihāni, *f.* parābhava, *m.* **°tory,** *a.* parihānikara; nindākara.

Derrick, *n.* bhārubbāhakayanta, *nt.*

Dervish, *n.* Mahammadīya-tāpasa, *m.*

Descant, *v.i.* deseti; vyākhyāti. *p.p.* desita; °āta.

Descend, *v.i.* 1. otarati; oruhati; okkamati; 2. paramparāya āgacchati. *p.p.* otiṇṇa; orūḷha; okkanta; °agāta. **°ant,** *n.* apacca, *nt.* vaŋsaja; kulaja, *m.* pl. puttanattuparamparā, *f.* **°ed,** *a.* sambhūta; jāta.

Descension, *n.* oruhana; adhopatana, *nt.*

Descent, *n.* 1. otaraṇa; oruhana, *nt.* adhogati, *f.* 2. santati; paveṇi, *f.* vaŋsa; gotta, *nt.* ubbhava; pabhava, *m.* **Of noble —,** udicca; uccākulīna, *a.*

Describe, *v.t.* vaṇṇeti; vitthāreti; vyākhyāti. *p.p.* °ṇita; °rita; °āta. **°able,** *a.* vaṇṇanīya.

Description, *n.* vaṇṇanā, *f.* vivaraṇa; vyākhyāna, *nt.* vitthāra, *m.* **°tive,** *a.* vitthāraka; vaṇṇanāvisayaka.

Descry, *v.t.* dūrato passati; raho vīmaŋsati. *p.p.* °diṭṭha; °sita.

Desecrate, *v.t.* suddhataŋ dūseti *or* nāseti. *p.p.* dūsitasuddhatta.

Desert, *n.* 1. kantāra ; jaṅgaladesa, *m.* 2. vipāka, *m.* adj. vijana ; asāra ; nipphala.

Desert, *v.t.* pajahati ; jahāti. *v.i.* hitvā palāyati. *p.p.* °hita ; °palāta. °**ed,** *a.* nibbhoga. °**ed village,** suññagāma, *m.* °**er,** *n.* palāyaka, *m.* °**ion,** *n.* °jahana ; cajana, *nt.*

Deserve, *v.i.* arahati ; vaṭṭati. °**ed,** *a.* yogga ; ucita. °**edly,** *adv.* yathocitaŋ. °**ing,** *a.* araha ; bhabba ; anucchavika.

Desiccate, *v.t.* soseti. *p.p.* sosita. °**ion,** *n.* sosana, *nt.*

Desiderate, *v.t.* apekkhati ; icchati ; pattheti. *p.p.* °khita ; icchita ; °thita. °**ive,** *a.* icchāpakāsaka.

Desideratum, *n.* icchitavatthu, *nt.*

Design, *n.* 1. parikappanā, *f.* upāya ; 2. ālekha, *m.* *v.t.* 1. parikappeti ; 2. ālikhati ; lekhāhi aṅketi. *p.p.* °pita ; °khita ; °aṅkita. °**er,** *n.* 1. cintaka ; parikappaka ; 2. ālekhasampādaka, *m.* °**ing,** *a.* upāyadakkha ; vañcanika.

Designate, *v.t.* upalakkheti ; vavatthapeti ; viseseti. *p.p.* °khita ; °pita ; °sita. adj. adhikārāya uccinita. °**ion,** *n.* 1. abhidhāna ; visesalakkhaṇa ; 2. adhikārapāpaṇa, *nt.*

Desilverize, *v.t.* rajatam puthakkaroti. *p.p.* puthakkata°.

Desipience, *n.* accantamūḷhatā ; jaḷatā, *f.*

Desire, *n.* icchā ; āsā ; abhilāsā ; ākaṅkhā ; ruci, *f.* manoratha, *m.* *v.t.* icchati ; kāmeti ; ākaṅkhati ; abhikaṅkhati ; apekkhati ; pattheti. *p.p.* icchita ; kāmita ; °khita ; °thita. °**able,** *a.* icchitabba ; pāṭikaṅkha. — **for gain,** lābhakamyatā, *f.* — **for proficiency,** sādhukamyatā, *f.* °**less,** *a.* nirālaya ; nirāsa ; nittaṇha, — **much,** gijjhati. — **to do,** kattukamyatā, *f.* — **to drink,** pivāsati. — **to eat,** bubhukkhati. — **to have,** jigiŋsati. — **to hear,** sussūsati.

Desirous, *a.* atthika ; jigiŋsasaka ; patthetu ; apekkhaka. — **to do,** kattukāma. — **to go,** gantukāma. — **to eat,** bhottukāma.

Desist, *v.i.* viramati ; nivattati. *p.p.* virata ; nivatta.

Desk, *n.* lekhanaphalaka, *nt.*

Desolate, *a.* vijana ; vivitta ; suñña. *v.t.* vivittaŋ *or* vijanaŋ karoti ; vināseti. *p.p.* vijanīkata ; °sita. °**er,** *n.* chaḍḍaka ; anāthakārī, *m.* °**ion,** *n.* chaḍḍana ; anāthakaraṇa ; pariccajana, *nt.*

Despair, *n.* visāda ; kheda ; āsābhaṅga, *m.* *v.i.* visīdati ; nirāso hoti. °**ing,** *a.* āsābhaṅgakara ; visādāvaha. °**ingly,** *adv.* savisādaŋ.

Despatch, *v.t.* peseti ; pahiṇāti. *p.p.* pesita ; pahita. *n.* 1. pesana ; 2. sāsana ; 3. sīghatta, *nt.* 4. attaghāta, *m.*

Desperate, *a.* jīvitanirapekkha ; aticaṇḍa ; atibhayānaka. °**ness,**

n. jīvitanirapekkhā ; atisāhasikatā, *f.* °**ly,** *adv.* ummattākārena ; aticaṇḍatāya.

Despicable, *a.* nindiya ; kucchita ; gārayha. °**ly,** *adv.* gārayhākārena.

Despise, *v.t.* avajānāti ; vambheti ; jigucchati. *p.p.* avaññāta ; vambhita ; °chita. °**er,** paravambhī, *m.* °**ingly,** *adv.* sāvaññaŋ ; sāvamānaŋ.

Despite, *n.* 1. virodha, *m.* jigucchā, *f.* 2. accusūyā, *f.* *prep.* aganetvā, asallakkhetvā. °**ful,** *a.* atiViruddha ; atiusūyaka. °**fully,** *adv.* saveraŋ ; sāvamānaŋ. °**fulness,** *n.* usūyā, *f.* macchariya, *nt.*

Despoil, *v.t.* vilumpati ; acchindati. *p.p.* vilutta ; acchinna. °**er,** *n.* vilumpaka, *m.* °**ment,** *n.* vilumpana, *nt.*

Despond, *v.i.* visīdati ; khijjati ; khedam āpajjati. *p.p.* visinna ; khinna ; khedāpanna. °**ency,** *n.* visāda ; kheda ; ubbega, *m.* °**ent,** *n.* visādappatta ; khedappatta. °**ently,** °**ingly,** *adv.* sakhedaŋ ; savisādaŋ.

Despot, *n.* yathākāmapālaka ; serirāja, *m.* °**ism,** *n.* serīpālana ; pajāpīḷana, *nt.*

Desquamate, *v.t.* bahittacam apaneti. *p.p.* apanita°.

Dessert, *n.* khajjaka-phalāhāra, *m.*

Destine, *v.t.* gatiŋ niyameti. *p.p.* niyamitagatika. °**ation,** *n.* 1. nirūpitaṭṭhāna ; adhippetaṭṭhāna, *nt.* 2. gatiniyāma, *m.*

Destiny, *n.* niyati, *f.* vidhi, *m.* bhāgadheyya, *nt.*

Destitute, *a.* 1. dīna ; anātha ; asaraṇa ; 2. parihīna ; vivajjita ; virahita. °**ion,** *n.* 1. dīnatta, *nt.* anāthabhāva, *m.* 2. parihāni, *f.* abhāva ; viraha ; viyoga, *m.*

Destroy, *v.t.* vināseti ; vidhameti ; viddhaŋseti ; vighāteti ; ucchindati. *p.p.* °sita ; °mita ; °sita ; °tita ; ucchinna. °**er,** *n.* nāsaka ; vidhamaka ; upacchindaka, *m.*

Destructible, *a.* bhaṅgura ; bhijjanasabhāva.

Destruction, *n.* nāsa ; vināsa ; ghāta ; upaghāta, *m.* viddhaŋsana ; vidhamana, *nt.*

Destructive, *a.* nāsakara ; pabhañjaka ; vidhamaka. °**ly,** *adv.* nāsakākārena. °**ness,** *n.* nāsakatta, *nt.*

Destructor, *n.* saṅkārajhāpaka, *m.*

Desuetude, *n.* abhāvitattapāpana, *nt.* payogābhāva, *m.*

Desulphurize, *v.t.* gandhakarahitaŋ karoti.

Desultory, *a.* anavaṭṭhita ; athira ; cañcala.

Detach, *v.t.* viyojeti ; puthakkaroti ; vicchindati. *p.p.* °jita ; °kata ; vicchinna. °**ed,** *a.* asaŋsaṭṭha ; visaŋyutta ; vippayutta. °**ment,** *n.* 1. visaŋyoga ; viyoga ; viccheda ; 2. senādala, *nt.*

Detail, *v.t.* vitthāreti ; papañceti ; vaṇṇeti. *p.p.* °rita ; °cita ; °ṇita. *n.* vitthāra ; visesavibhāga, *m.* **In —,** vitthārena.

Detain, *v.t.* avarodheti; nivatteti; bādheti. *p.p.* °dhita; °tita; bādhita. °**er,** *n.* avarodhaka, *nt.*

Detect, *v.t.* vajjaŋ gavesati; apākaṭaŋ pakāseti. *p.p.* gavesitavajja. °**ion,** *n.* vajjagavesana, *nt.* °**ive,** *n. a.* vajjagavesaka; carapurisa, *m.*

Detention, *n.* nivattāpana; bādhana; avarodhana, *nt.*

Deter, *v.t.* nivāreti; nisedheti. *p.p.* °rita; °dhita. °**ment,** *n.* balena nivāraṇa, *nt.*

Detergent, *n.* sodhaka-bhesajja, *nt.*

Deteriorate, *v.t.* dūseti; parihāpeti. *v.i.* parihāyati; dussati. *p.p.* dūsita; °pita; parihīna; duṭṭha. °**ion,** *n.* dussana, *nt.* parihāni, *f.*

Determine, *v.t.* niccheti; adhiṭṭhāti; vavatthapeti. *p.p.* °chita; °ṭhita; °pita. °**ant,** *a.* nicchayakara. °**ate,** *a.* sīmita; paricchinna; parimita. °**ately,** *adv.* sanicchayaŋ. °**ation,** *n.* adhiṭṭhāna, *nt.* nicchaya, *m.* °**ative,** *a.* niddhāraka; nicchayakara. °**ed,** *a.* thiracitta; daḷhādhiṭṭhāna. °**edly,** *adv.* daḷhanicchayena.

Determinism, *n.* niyativāda, *m.*

Detersive, *a. n.* malasodhaka, *nt.*

Detest, see **Abhor.** °**able,** *a.* gārayha; dessiya. °**ation,** *n.* jigucchā, *f.* °**er,** *n.* dessī; viddesī, *m.* °**ful,** *a.* jegucchа; amanāpa.

Dethrone, *v.t.* rājattā apaneti. sīhāsanā cāveti. *p.p.* °apanīta; °vita. °**ment,** rājattāpanayana, *nt.*

Detonate, *v.i.* mahāsaddena vipphurati. *p.p.* °rita. °**ion,** *n.* vipphuraṇa, *nt.*

Detour, *n.* vaṅkagamana; ṭhānāpagamana, *nt.*

Detract, *v.t.* apakaḍḍhati; hāpeti; ūnayati. *p.p.* °ḍhita; hāpita. °**ion,** *n.* apakaḍḍhana; hāpana, *nt.* °**ive,** *a.* hāpaka; hānikara.

Detrain, *v.t.* rathā oruhati. *p.p.* °urūḷha.

Detriment, *n.* hāni, *f.* anattha; alābha, *m.* °**al,** *a.* hānikara; ahitāvaha.

Detrited, *a.* puthakkata.

Detrition, *n.* ghaŋsanena khayagamana, *nt.*

Deuce, *n.* pāpimantu; Māra, *m.*

Deuced, *a.* 1. mahanta; adhikatara; 2. atiduṭṭha.

Deuteronomy, *n.* dutiyavivāha, *m.*

Devastate, *v.t.* viddhaŋseti; vināseti; ucchindati. *p.p.* °sita *or* viddhasta; °sita; ucchinna. °**ion,** *n.* ucchindana; viddhaŋsana, *nt.*

Develop, *v.t.* vaḍḍheti; bhāveti; brūheti; paripāceti; bahulīkaroti. *p.p.* °ḍhita; °vita; °hita; °cita; °kata. *v.i.* abhivaḍḍhati; samijjhati. *p.p.* abhivuddha; samiddha °**ment,** *n.* abhivuddhi; bhāvanā; brūhanā, *f.* bahulīkāra, *m.*

Deviate, *v.i.* apakkamati; uppatham okkamati; vītikkamati. *p.p.* apakkanta; °okkanta; °mita. *v.t.* apaneti; uppathaŋ pāpeti. *p.p.* apanīta; °pāpita. °**ion,** *n.* uppathagamana; apakkamana, *nt.* vītikkama, *m.*

Device, *n.* 1. upāya ; payoga, *m.* parikappanā, *f.* 2. visesalakkhaṇa, *nt.*

Devil, *n.* 1. amanussa ; yakkha, *m.* bhūta, *nt.* 2. Māra ; 3. dujjana ; niṭṭhura, *m.* — **dancing,** *n.* bhūtatikicchā, *f.* °**ish,** *a.* yakkhasadisa ; atidāruṇa. °**ishly,** *adv.* atiduṭṭhākārena. °**ism,** *n.* 1. yakkhapūjā, *f.* 2. dāruṇakamma, *nt.* °**ry,** *n.* 1. dāruṇakamma, *nt.* 2. bhūtanamassanā, *f.*

Devious, *a.* 1. vaṅka ; kuṭila ; 2. dūravattī. °**ly,** *adv.* savaṅkaŋ. — **way,** ummagga ; kupatha, *m.*

Devise, *n.* 1. upāya ; ākāra, *m.* 2. dāyādapaṇṇa *nt.* *v.t.* 1. parikappeti ; payojeti ; 2. dāyādaŋ deti. *p.p.* °pita ; °jita ; dinnadāyāda. °**er,** *n.* 1. parikappaka ; payojaka ; 2. dāyādadāyī, *m.*

Devitalize, *v.t.* nijjīvaŋ karoti. *p.p.* °kata.

Devoid, *a.* ritta ; tuccha ; suñña ; vippayutta.

Devolute, *v.t.* adhikāraŋ parivatteti. °**ion,** *n.* 1. adhikārasaṅkāmaṇa, *nt.* 2. santatiparihāni, *f.*

Devolve, *v.t.* saṅkāmeti ; paramparāya pāpeti. *v.i.* paramparāya saṅkamati. *p.p.* °mita ; °pāpita ; °saṅkanta.

Devote, *v.t.* 1. niyyāteti ; 2. saddahati ; bhattim uppādeti ; 3. pūjeti. *p.p.* °tita ; °hita ; uppāditabhattī ; pūjita. °**ed,** *a.* saddha , pasanna , abhiniviṭṭha ; tapparāyaṇa ; bhattiyutta. °**edly,** *adv.* saddhāya ; tapparatāya ; bhattiyā. °**edness,** °**ion,** *n.* saddhā ; bhatti ; tapparatā, *f.* pasāda, *m.* °**ional,** *a.* bhattipara ; saddhānugata.

Devotee, *n.* bhattimantu ; saddha ; upāsaka ; sāvaka, *m.*

Devour, *v.t.* 1. gilati ; ajjhoharati ; 2. khādati ; bhakkhati ; 3. vināseti ; viddhaŋseti ; 4. lolatāya suṇāti *or* paṭhati. *p.p.* gilita ; ajjhohaṭa ; khādita ; °khita ; °sita ; °suta ; °paṭhita. °**er,** *n.* bhakkhaka. °**ing,** *n.* gilana ; bhakkhana, *nt.*

Devout, *a.* bhattimantu ; dhammika. °**ly,** *adv.* bhattiyā ; avyājaŋ. °**ness,** *n.* bhattiyuttatā ; dhammikatā, *f.* — **wife,** patibbatā, *f.*

Dew, *n.* tuhiṇa, *nt.* ussāva, *m.* °**lap,** *n.* galakambala, *nt.*

Dexter, *a.* dakkhiṇa. °**ity,** *n.* dakkhatā, *f.* pāṭava ; kosalla ; nepuñña, *nt.*

Dexterous, *a.* dakkha ; nipuṇa ; paṭu ; cheka. °**ly,** *adv.* nipuṇākārena ; chekatāya.

Dextral, *a.* dakkhiṇāyatta.

Dhobie, *n.* rajaka ; dhovaka, *m.*

Diabetes, *n.* madhumeha, *m.* °**tic,** *a.* 1. madhumehī, *m.* madhumehāyatta.

Diablerie, *n.* 1. bhūtavijjā , *f.* 2. niṭṭhurakamma, *nt.*

Diabolic, °**cal,** *a.* 1. pisācopama ; 2. ghora ; dāruṇa ; atikakkhaḷa. °**ally,** *adv.* sudāruṇaŋ ; ghorākārena.

Diabolism, *n.* 1. bhūtapūjā ; bhūtabhatti, *f.* 2. dāruṇakamma, *nt.*

Diacritical, *a.* visesakara ; visesatta-ñāpaka.

Diadem, *n.* 1. uṇhīsa, *nt.* siromaṇi ; sekhara, *m.* āvelā, *f.* 2. rājapada, *nt.*

Diagnose, *v.t.* rogaŋ niṇṇeti *or* tīreti. *p.p.* niṇṇitaroga.

Diagnosis, *n.* rogaviññāṇa ; roganirūpana, *nt.*

Diagnostic, *n.* rogalakkhaṇa, *nt.* adj. roganicchayakara.

Diagonal, *a. n.* koṇagatarekhā, *f.*

Diagram, *n.* lekhācitta, *nt.*

Dial, *n.* ghaṭikāmaṇḍala ; māṇadassaka ; ghaṭīyantamukha, *nt.*

Dialect, *n.* padesabhāsā, *f.* °**al**, *a.* padesabhāsāyatta.

Dialectic(s), *n.* takkasattha, *nt.* hetuvijjā, *f.* °**al**, *a.* hetuvijjāyatta ; takkānugata ; ñāyānugata. °**ian**, *n.* takkika, *m.*

Dialogic, *a.* pucchā-vissajjanāyatta. °**gist**, *n.* pucchā-vissajjana-ganthakāra, *m.*

Dialogue, *n.* kathopakathana, *nt.* saŋvāda, *m.*

Diameter, *n.* vikkhambha, *m.* cakkamajjharekhā, *f.* °**trical**, *a.* 1. vikkhambhāyatta; 2. ujuvipaccanika ; paṭiviruddha. °**trically**, *adv.* ujukam eva ; vipaccanikākārena.

Diamond, *n.* vajira, *nt. v.t.* vajirehi khacati *or* bhūseti. *p.p.* vajirakhacita.

Diana, *n.* vyādhadevī, *f.*

Diaper, *n.* vicitta-dukūla, *nt.*

Diaphanous, *a.* vinivijjhadassaka.

Diaphoretic, *a.* sedamocanaka.

Diaphragm, *n.* sasanopakārapesī, *f.*

Diarchy, *n.* dvidhāpālitarajja, *nt.*

Diarist, *n.* dinapotthakasāmī, *m.* °**ic**, *a.* dinapotthakāyatta.

Diarize, *v.t.* dinapotthake āropeti. *p.p.* °pita.

Diarrhoea, *n.* atisāra, *m.* **Bloody —**, rattātisāra, *m.*

Diary, *n.* devasika-potthaka, patidina-lekhana, *nt.*

Diastole, *n.* hadayaphandana, *nt.*

Diathesis, *n.* sārīrika-poṇatā ; roganinnatā, *f.*

Diatomic, *a.* dviaṇuka.

Diatribe, *n.* kaṭuka-paribhāsanā, *f.*

Dibasic, *a.* dvitalayutta.

Dibble, *n.* khuddaka-khaṇittī, *f.*

Dice, *n.* (*pl.* of **Die**), akkha ; pāsaka, *m. v.i.* akkhehi dibbati. °**box**, *n.* akkhanāḷi, *f.*

Dicephalous, *a.* dvisīsaka.

Dichotomy, *n.* dvidhāvibhajana, *nt.*

Dichroic, *a.* dvivaṇṇadassaka.

Dicky, Dickey, *n.* 1. gadrabha. *m.* 2. rathācariyāsana, *nt.* adj. cañcala.

Dictate, *v.t.* 1. ādisati ; āṇāpeti ; 2. likhanāya paṭhati. *p.p.* ādiṭṭha ; āṇatta ; °paṭhita. °**ion**, *n.* 1. āṇāpana ; niyojana ; 2. anuvācana, *nt.* °**tor**, *n.* āṇāpaka ; ekādhipa, *m.*

Diction, *n.* vācāvilāsa ; uccāraṇavilāsa, *m.*

Dictionary, *n.* saddakosa ; akārādikosa, *m.*

Dictum, *n.* 1. siddhanta, *m.* subhāsita, *nt.* 2. uccāraṇa, *nt.*

Didactic, *a.* upadesagabbhaka ; anusāsanakara.

Diddle, *v.t.* vañceti ; patāreti. *p.p.* vañcita ; °rita.

Die, *v.i.* marati; cavati; kālaṅkaroti. *p.p.* mata; cuta; °kata.

Diet, *n.* 1. bhojana, *nt.* āhāra; ghāsa, *m.* 2. pālakasabhā, *f.* *v.t.* mitaŋ *or* sappāyaŋ bhuñjati. *p.p.* °bhutta. °**ary**, *n.* *a.* niyamitāhāra, *m.* °**etic**, *a.* bhojanāyatta.

Differ, *v.i.* pabhedaŋ gacchati; bhinnamatiko hoti. *p.p.* pabhedagata. °**ence**, 1. *n.* nānatta; vematta; antara, *nt.* visesa, *m.* 2. nānāmatitta, *nt.*

Different, *a.* vividha; nānākāra; asamāna; visabhāga; nānāvidha. °**ia**, *n.* visesa-lakkhaṇa, *nt.* °**ial**, *a.* visekaka; vyavacchedaka; nānattakara. °**iate**, *v.t.* viseseti; vyavacchindati; niddhāreti. *p.p.* °sita; °chinna; °rita; °**ly**, *adv.* visuŋ visuŋ; nānākārena; vividhā.

Difficult, *a.* dukkara; dussādhiya; kiccha; duravabodha. — **to bear**, asayha, *a.* — **to endure**, dukkhama, *a.* — **to follow**, durannaya, *a.* — **to give**, duddada, *a.* — **to see**, duddasa, *a.* °**ly**, *adv.* kicchena; kasirena. °**ty**, *n.* āyāsa, *m.* dukkaratta, *nt.*

Diffidence, *n.* 1. kaṅkhā; vimati, *f.* 2. atilajjā, *f.*

Diffident, *a.* āsaṅkī; avisārada; lajjamāna. °**ly**, *adv.* avisāradatāya.

Diffluent, *a.* sandamāna; vilīyamāna.

Diffract, *v.t.* ālokaŋ bhājeti *or* nānāvaṇṇattaŋ pāpeti.

Diffuse, *v.t.* vyāpeti. *v.i.* pattharati; pharati. *p.p.* vyāpita; patthaṭa; phuṭa. °**ly**, *adv.* savipphāraŋ. °**ion**, *n.* vipphāra, *m.* pharaṇa; vyāpana, *nt.* °**ive**, *a.* vyāpaka; vipphāraka. °**iveness**, vyāpakatta, *nt.*

Dig, *v.t.* khaṇati. *p.p.* khata. °**ger**, *n.* khaṇanta, *m.* °**ging**, *n.* khaṇana, *nt.* — **into**, nikhaṇati. — **up**, abhikkhaṇati.

Digamy, *n.* dvibhariyatā, *f.*

Digest, *v.t.* jīreti; pariṇāmeti; paripāceti. *v.i.* pariṇamati; paccati. *p.p.* jiṇṇa; °mita; °cita; pariṇata; pakka. °**ion**, *n.* jīraṇa, *nt.* pariṇāma; paripāka, *m.*

Digestive, *a.* paripācaka; gahaṇivaḍḍhaka. *n.* pācakosadha, *nt.* — **faculty**, *n.* gahaṇī, *f.* udaraggi, *m.* pācakindriya, *nt.*

Digit, *n.* 1. aṅgulimattā, *f.* 2. aŋsaka, *m.* kalā, *f.*

Digitate, *a.* visuŋbhūtaṅgulika.

Dignify, *v.t.* ukkaŋseti; uccaṭṭhānaŋ pāpeti. *p.p.* °sita; °pāpita. °**ied**, *a.* mahita; sammānita; mahesakkha.

Dignitary, *n.* mahādhikārī; seṭṭhapadaṭṭha, *m.*

Dignity, *n.* 1. pabhāva; patāpa; mahima; teja, *m.* mahesakkhatā, *f.*

Digress, *v.i.* uppathaŋ yāti; adhippetatthā bahi katheti. °**ion**, *n.* 1. uppathagamana, *nt.* 2. asambandhakathā, *f.* °**ive**, *a.* mātikāto bahigāmī.

Dike, Dyke, *n.* 1. āḷi; pāḷi, *f.* setubandha, *m.* 2. parikhā, *f.* *v.t.* āḷiŋ bandhati. *p.p.* āḷibaddha.

Dilapidate, *v.i.* jīrati; jajjarati; vināsaŋ yāti. *v.t.* vināsamukhaŋ pāpeti. *p.p.* jiṇṇa ; jajjarita ; °yāta ; °pāpita. °**ion**, *n.* avasīdana ; vināsagamana, *nt.* jarappatti, *f.*

Dilate, *v.t.* vyāpeti ; vitthāreti ; vitanoti. *v.i.* pattharati. *p.p.* vyāpita ; °rita ; vitata ; patthaṭa. °**ion**, *n.* vyāpana ; pattharaṇa, *nt.* °**tory**, *a.* vilambaka ; dīghasuttika. °**toriness**, *n.* vilambana ; dīghasuttiya, *nt.*

Dilemma, *n.* dvejjhakathā, *f.* ubhatokoṭika-pañha, *m.*

Dilettante, *n.* kalāsipparata, *m.*

Diligence, *n.* uyyāma ; paggaha, *m.* analasatta ; atanditatta, *nt.*

Diligent, *a.* atandita ; analasa ; āraddhaviriya. °**ly**, *adv.* analasatāya.

Dilly-dally, *v.i.* kālakkhepaŋ karoti ; ito tato bhamati.

Dilute, *v.t.* jalena misseti. *p.p.* jalamissita. adj. vilīna ; āposahita.

Diluvial, *a.* jaloghāyatta.

Diluvium, *n.* āposaŋvaṭṭanicita, *nt.*

Dim, *a.* mandappabha ; avisada. *v.t.* mandappabhaŋ karoti ; malinayati. *v.i.* mandāloko *or* avisado hoti. °**ly**, *adv.* avisadākārena. °**ness**, *n.* avisadatta, *nt.*

Dimension, *n.* āroha-pariṇāha, *m.* parimāṇa, *nt.*

Diminish, *v.t.* khepeti ; hāpeti ; mandīkaroti. *p.p.* khepita ; hāpita ; °kata. *v.i.* khīyati ; hāyati ; mandībhavati. *p.p.* khīṇa ; hīna ; °bhūta.

Diminution, *n.* 1. khaya, apacaya, *m.* mandībhavana, *nt.* 2. khīṇappamāṇa, *nt.*

Diminutive, *a.* khuddaka ; appaka. °**ness**, *n.* khuddakatta, *nt.*

Dimple, *n.* kapolabhaṅga ; kapolāvaṭṭa, *m.*

Din, *n.* ninãda ; kalakala, *m.* *v.t.* mahānādaŋ pavatteti.

Dine, *v.i.* (sāyaṇhe) bhuñjati. *v.t.* bhojeti. *p.p.* bhutta ; bhojita. °**ing-room**, bhojanāgāra, *nt.* °**er**, *n.* bhojī, *m.*

Ding-dong, *n.* (parivattamāna-) ghaṇṭānāda, *m.*

Dingle, *n.* nikuñja, *m.*

Dingy, *a.* malinavaṇṇa.

Dinky, *a.* sundaradassana.

Dinner, *n.* divābhojana; sāyaṇhabhojana, *nt.*

Dinosaur, *n.* ādikappikagodhā, *f.*

Dint, *n.* 1. pahāra ; abhighāta, *m.* 2. sāmatthiya, *nt.*

Diocese, *n.* nāyaka-pūjakāyattapadesa, *m.*

Dip, *v.t.* ogāheti ; paveseti. *v.i.* nimujjati ; ogāhati. *p.p.* °hita ; °sita ; nimugga ; ogāḷha. *n.* ogāhana ; nimujjana, *nt.* °**per**, *n.* 1. nimujjāpaka, *m.* 2. dabbivisesa, *m.*

Dipthong, *n.* saŋyutta-saradvaya, *nt.*

Diploma, *n.* adhikārapaṇṇa, *nt.*

Diplomacy, *n.* 1. dūteyya ; niyojitabala ; 2. kerāṭiya, *nt.*

Diplomat, °**matist**, *n.* dūteyyanipuṇa ; rājanītikusala, *m.* °**ical**, *a.* dūteyyavisayaka.

Diplopia, *n.* diṭṭhiroga, *m.*

Dipsomania, *n.* majjalolatā, *f.*

Dire, *a.* ghora ; dāruṇa ; bherava. °**ful**, *a.* bhayānaka.

Direct, *a.* 1. uju ; avaṅka ; akuṭila ; 2. paṭipāṭiyāgata ; 3. supākaṭa ; suvisada. *v.t.* vidahati ; upadisati ; kāreti. *p.p.* vidahita; upadiṭṭha ; kārita. °**ly,** *adv.* ujukaŋ. °**ive,** *a.* nidassaka ; niyojaka. — **wrongly,** micchāpaṇidahati.

Direction, *n.* 1. niyoga ; niyama, *m.* vidhāna, *nt.* āṇā, *f.* 2. disā, *f.* **Intermediate** — , anudisā, *f.*

Director, *n.* vidhāyaka ; ajjhakkhaka, *m.* °**ate,** *n.* adhikārīsabhā, *f.* °**ry,** *n.* nāmādisūci, *f.*

Dirge, *n.* sokagīta, *nt.*

Dirk, *n.* chūrikā, *f.*

Dirt, *n.* mala ; kalusa, *nt.* uklāpa ; kilesa. °**ily,** *adv.* malinākārena ; kiliṭṭhatāya. °**y,** *a.* kiliṭṭha ; malina ; asuddha.

Disability, *n.* akkhamatā ; asamatthatā ; asakyatā, *f.*

Disable, *v.t.* avasādeti ; dubbalīkaroti. *p.p.*° dita ; °kata.

Disabuse, *v.t.* moham apaneti ; vibbhamaŋ nirākaroti. *p.p.* apanītamoha ; nirākatavib°.

Disaccord, *n.* virodha, *m.* asāmggi, *f.* *v.i.* virujjhati ; vematiko hoti *p.p.* viruddha.

Disadvantage, *n.* ādīnava ; anattha, *m.* ahita, *nt.* °**ous,** *a.* anatthāvaha ; ahitakara.

Disaffect, *v.i.* virajjati. *p.p.* viratta. °**ed,** *a.* duṭṭhacitta. °**ion,** *n.* vipakkhatā ; appiyatā, *f.*

Disaffirm, *v.t.* pubbanicchayaŋ vipallāseti. *p.p.* °sita.

Disafforest, *v.t.* nibbanaŋ karoti. *p.p.* °kata.

Disaggregate, *v.t.* puthakkaroti ; viyojeti. *p.p.* °kata ; °jita.

Disagree, *v.i.* virujjhati ; vilometi. *p.p.* viruddha. °**able,** *a.* appiya ; akanta ; amanāpa. °**able to ear,** kaṇṇakaṭuka. °**ment,** *n.* virodha, *m.* asaŋsandanā, *f.*

Disallow, *v.t.* nānujānāti ; nisedheti ; pacchakkhāti. *p.p.* nānuññāta ; °dhita ; °khāta.

Disannul, *v.t.* nirākaroti ; lopeti; paccādisati. *p.p.* °kata ; lutta ; paccādiṭṭha.

Disappear, *v.i.* antaradhāyati ; vigacchati ; adassanaŋ yāti. *p.p.* antarahita ; vigata ; °yāta. °**ance,** *n.* antaradhāna ; vigamana ; *nt.* abhāva ; atthagama ; vilaya, *m.*

Disappoint, *v.t.* visādaŋ *or* āsābhaṅgaŋ pāpeti. *p.p.* °pāpita. °**ed,** *a.* bhaṭṭhāsa; visādappatta. °**ing,** *a.* āsābhaṅgakara. °**ment,** *n.* āsābhaṅga; visāda ; kheda, *m.*

Disapprobation, *n.* ananujānanā; asampaṭicchanā, *f.*

Disapprove, *v.t.* nānujānati ; garahati. *p.p.* nānuññāta ; °hita. °**al,** *n.* ananuññā ; anabhimati, *f.* garahana, *nt.*

Disarm, *v.t.* nirāyudhaŋ karoti. *p.p.* °kata. °**ament,** *n.* āyudhanikkhepa ; yuddhapariccāga, *m.*

Disarrange, *v.t.* vyākulīkaroti ; vikkhobheti. *p.p.* °kata ; °bhita. °**ment,** *n.* vyākulatta, *nt.*

Disarray, *v.t.* ayathā ṭhapeti ; kamaŋ virodheti. *p.p.* °ṭhapita ; virodhitakkama.

Disassociate, *v.t.* viyojeti ; puthakkaroti. *p.p.* °jita ; °kata.

Disaster, *n.* vipatti ; āpadā, *f.* upaddava, *m.* vyasana, *nt.*

Disastrous, *a.* vipattikara ; āpadāvaha. °**ly,** *adv.* vipattikaratāya.

Disavow, *v.t.* paccakkhāti ; paṭikkhipati. *p.p.* °khāta ; °khitta. °**al,** *n.* paccakkhāna, *nt.*

Disband, *v.t.* visileseti ; senaŋ viyojeti. *p.p.* °sita ; viyojitasena.

Disbar, *v.t.* nītiññavuttito apaneti. *p.p.* °apanīta.

Disbelief, *n.* assaddhiya; asaddahana, *nt.*

Disbelieve, *v.i.* na saddahati ; na vissasati. *v.t.* asaddahāpeti. *p.p.* asaddahita ; avissattha. °pita. °**er,** *n.* asaddahitu, *m.*

Disbranch, *v.t.* sākhā apaneti. *p.p.* apanītasākha.

Disburden, *v.t.* bhāram oropeti *or* nikkhipati. *p.p.* oropitabhāra ; nikkhitta°.

Disburse, *v.t.* vissajjeti ; vayaŋ karoti. *p.p.* °jita ; vayakata. °**ment,** *n.* vayakaraṇa ; vissajjana, *nt.*

Disc, see **Disk.**

Discard, *v.t.* apanudati ; nissajati ; odhunāti. *p.p.* °dita ; nissaṭa ; odhūta.

Discern, *v.t.* paricchindati ; viveceti. *v.i.* parijānāti. *p.p.* paricchinna ; °cita ; pariññāta. °**ible,** *a.* diṭṭhigocara ; abhiññeyya. °**ing,** *a.* abhijānanaka ; sukhumabuddhika. °**ment,** *n.* abhijānana ; sallakkhaṇa ; dūradassana, *nt.* pariññā, *f.*

Discerption, *n.* vidāraṇa, *nt.* visilesa, *m.*

Discharge, *v.t.* 1. bhāram apaneti ; 2. adhikārā cāveti ; 3. (bandhanā) moceti ; 4. (a missile) vissajjeti ; 5. (an arrow) vijjhati. *v.i.* nikkhipati ; nicchāreti ; vamati. *p.p.* apanītabhāra ; °cāvita ; °cita ; vissaṭṭha ; viddha ; nikkhitta ; °rita ; vamita *or* vanta. — **a debt,** iṇaŋ sodheti. — **a duty,** vattaŋ karoti. — **from an accusation,** codanā moceti. — **urine,** omutteti.

Discharge, *n.* 1. (matter emitted:) nissanda, *m.* mala, *nt.* vissaṭṭhi, *f.* 2. (act of discharging:) mocana ; nikkhipana, *nt.* 3. (release from:) mutti ; vimutti, *f.* mokkha, *m.*

Disciple, *n.* sāvaka ; sissa ; antevāsika, *m.*

Discipline, *n.* vinaya ; dama ; niggaha, *m.* sikkhā, *f.* *v.t.* vineti ; sikkheti ; dameti. *p.p.* vinīta ; sikkhita ; damita *or* danta. °**ary,** *a.* vinayadāyaka ; sikkhāyatta.

Disclaim, *v.t.* paccakkhāti ; pariggahaŋ paṭikkhipati. *p.p.* °khāta ; paṭikkhitta°. °**er,** *n.* paṭikkhipana ; pariggahapaccakkhāna, *nt.*

Disclose, *v.t.* vivarati ; pakāseti ; pākaṭīkaroti. *p.p.* vivaṭa ; °sita ; °kata. °**ure,** *n.* vivaraṇa ; pākaṭīkaraṇa, *nt.*

Discoid, *a.* maṇḍalākāra.

Discolour, *v.t.* vivaṇṇataŋ pāpeti ; vaṇṇaŋ hāpeti. *p.p.* °pāpita ; hāpitavaṇṇa. °**ation,** *n.* dubbaṇṇakaraṇa, *nt.*

Discomfit, *v.t.* parājeti. *p.p.* °jita. °**ure,** *n.* parājaya ; āsābhaṅga, *m.*

Discomfort, *n.* pīḷā, *f.* aphāsu, *m.* *v.t.* viheṭheti ; uppīḷeti. *p.p.* °ṭhita ; °ḷita.

Discommend, *v.t.* nindati ; garahati. *p.p.* °dita ; °hita.

Discommode, *v.t.* āyāseti ; viheseti. *p.p.* °sita.

Discompose, *v.t.* vikkhipati ; asamāhitaŋ karoti. *p.p.* vikkhitta ; °kata. °**edly,** *adv.* vikkhittākārena. °**ure,** *n.* vikkhepa, *m.* ākulatta, *nt.*

Disconcert, *v.t.* vyākulīkaroti. *p.p.* °kata.

Disconnect, *v.t.* viyojeti ; visaŋyojeti. *p.p.* °jita. °**ed,** *a.* asambandha ; asaṅgata. °**ion,** *n.* viyojana ; visuŋkaraṇa, *nt.*

Disconsolate, *a.* vimana ; khinnacitta ; ukkaṇṭhita. °**ly,** *adv.* ukkhaṇṭhitākārena.

Discontent, *a.* anabhirata ; asantuṭṭha. *n.* anabhirati ; asantuṭṭhi, *f.* *v.t.* anabhiratiŋ janeti. °**edly,** *adv.* anabhiratiyā. °**ment,** *n.* atitti, *f.*

Discontinue, *v.t.* upacchindati ; nivatteti. *p.p.* upacchinna ; °tita. °**ance,** *n.* viccheda, *m.* °**ous,** *a.* vicchinna. °**ously,** *adv.* vicchinnākārena.

Discord, *n.* bheda ; virodha, *m.* asāmaggi, *f.* °**ant,** *a.* visama ; viruddha ; paṭiloma. °**antly,** *adv.* paṭilomākārena.

Discord, *v.i.* virujjhati. *p.p.* viruddha. °**ant,** *a.* visama ; paṭiloma.

Discount, *n.* uddhaṭabhāga, *m.* *v.t.* lābhato bhāgam uddharati.

Discountenance, *v.t.* nānumodati ; nirussāheti. *p.p.* °dita ; °hita.

Discourage, *v.t.* visādeti ; ussāhaŋ hāpeti. *p.p.* °dita ; hāpitussāha. °**ing,** *a.* ussāhabhañjaka. °**ingly,** *adv.* visādajanakākārena. °**ment,** *n.* ussāhabhaṅga, *m.* osīdana, *nt.*

Discourse, *n.* desanā, *f.* suttanta, *nt.* *v.t.* deseti ; pavadati. *v.i.* sambhāsati. *p.p.* desita ; pavutta ; °sita.

Discourteous, *a.* avinīta ; dubbinīta ; ācārahīna.

Discourtesy, *n.* avinītatā, *f.* agārava, *m.*

Discover, *v.t.* āvīkaroti ; pākaṭattaŋ neti. *p.p.* °āvīkata ; °nīta. °**er,** *n.* āvīkattu, *m.* °**ry,** *n.* āvīkaraṇa, *nt.*

Discredit, *v.t.* na saddahati ; na vissasati. *p.p.* asaddahita ; avissattha. *n.* apakitti, *f.* avissāsa, *m.* akittikaravatthu, *nt.* °**able,** *a.* avissasanīya ; ayasakara.

Discreet, *a.* vicārapubbaka , samekkhakārī. °**ly,** *adv.* vicārapubbakaŋ.

Discrepant, *a.* vibhinna , vividhākāra. °**nce,** °**ncy,** *n.* vibhinnatā, *f.* nānatta, *nt.*

Discrete, *a.* viyutta ; vibhinna. °**ness,** *n.* vibhinnatā, *f.*

Discretion, *n.* viññutā, *f.* sakapaṭibhāṇa, *nt.*

Discriminate, *v.t.* viveceti ; upalakkheti ; viseseti ; niccheti. *p.p.* °cita ; °khita ; °sita ; °chita. °**ion,** *n.* vivecana, *nt.* vinicchaya ; niṇṇaya, *m.* °**ive,** °**ing,** *a.* vivecaka ; paricchindaka. °**ly,** *adv.* sañcicca ; savivecanaŋ.

Discrown, *v.t.* rājapadā apaneti. *p.p.* apanītarājapada.

Discursive, *a.* 1. athira ; anavaṭṭhita ; 2. anumānita ; takkita.

Discus, *n.* cakkāyudha, *nt.*

Discuss, *v.t.* manteti ; sākacchati ; āloceti ; vicāreti. *p.p.* mantita ; °chita ; °cita ; °rita. °**ion,** *n.* mantaṇā ; sākacchā ; vicāraṇā, *f.*

Disdain, *n.* avaññā ; hīḷanā, *f.* *v.t.* avamāneti ; hīḷeti. *p.p.* avamata ; hīḷita. °**ful,** *a.* sāvañña ; sāvalepa. °**fully,** *adv.* sāvamānaŋ.

Disease, *n.* roga ; vyādhi ; ābādha ; ātaṅka, *m.* gelañña, *nt.* *v.t.* rogena vyathati *or* pīḷeti. *p.p.* °vyathita ; °pīḷita. °**ed,** *a.* rogātura ; gilāna.

Disembark, *v.i.* nāvāya otarati. *v.t.* nāvāto otāreti. *p.p.* °otiṇṇa ; °otārita. °**ation,** *n.* orohana ; oropana, *nt.*

Disembarrass, *v.t.* saŋsayato *or* jaṭāto moceti. *p.p.* °cita.

Disembellish, *v.t.* vibhūsā-rahitaŋ karoti. *p.p.* °kata.

Disembody, *v.t.* 1. sarīrato viyojeti ; 2. yuddhasevāto moceti. *p.p.* °jita ; °mocita.

Disembogue, *v.t.* nadīmukhato jalaŋ nikkhāmeti. *p.p.* °mitajala.

Disembosom, *v.i.* hadayagataŋ pakāseti. *p.p.* °sitahada°.

Disembowel, *v.t.* antāni apaneti. *v.i.* antaŋ ṭhānato apagacchati. *p.p.* apanītanta ; apagatanta.

Disembroil, *v.t.* vijaṭāto moceti. *p.p.* °mocita.

Disenchant, *v.t.* vasaṅgamanato moceti. *p.p.* °mocita. °**ment,** *n.* vasībhāvāpaharaṇa, *nt.*

Disencumber, *v.t.* bhārato *or* bādhakato moceti. *p.p.* °mocita.

Disengage, *v.t.* viyojeti. *v.i.* muccati ; mokkhati. *p.p.* °jita ; mutta. °**ment,** *n.* viyojana ; muccana, *nt.*

Disenroll, *v.t.* nāmāvalito apaneti. *p.p.* °nīta.

Disentangle, *v.t.* viniveṭheti ; vijaṭeti. *p.p.* °ṭhita ; vijaṭita. °**ed,** nijjaṭa ; niggumba. °**ment,** *n.* vijaṭana, *nt.*

Disestablish, *v.t.* vavatthitam *or* saṇṭhapitaŋ apaneti.

Disfame, *n.* ayasa, *m.* akitti, *f.*

Disfavour, *v.t.* na anuggaṇhāti nānujāneti. *p.p.* ananuggahita ananuññāta.

Disfeature, *v.t.* virūpeti. *p.p.* °pita.

Disfigure, *v.t.* vikalīkaroti ; virūpeti. *p.p.* °kata ; °pita °**ation,** *n.* virūpakaraṇa ; vevaṇṇiya, *nt.*

Disforest, *v.t.* nibbanaŋ karoti. *p.p.* nibbanīkata.

Disfranchise, *v.t.* chandabalaŋ nāseti. *p.p.* nāsita°.

Disfurnish, *v.t.* upakaraṇāni apaneti. *p.p.* apanītūpakaraṇa.

Disgorge, *v.i.* vamati ; uggirati. *p.p.* vamita *or* vanta ; °rita.

Disgrace, *n.* ayasa, *m.* akitti, *f.* parābhava, *m.* *v.t.* paribhavati ; ayasaŋ pāpeti. *p.p.* paribhūta ; °pāpita. °**ful,** *a.* ayasakara ; avamānajanaka. °**fully,** *adv.* sāvamānaŋ.

Disgruntle, *v.i.* kupito *or* dummukho hoti. °**ed,** *a.* asantuṭṭha.

Disguise, *n.* vesaparivattana, *nt.* *v.t.* vesantaraŋ gaṇhāti ; pakatiŋ parivatteti. *p.p.* gahitavesantara ; parivattitapakatika.

Disgust, *n.* aṭṭīyanā ; harāyanā ; jigucchā, *f.* ubbega ; saŋvega, *m.* *v.i.* virajjati ; ubbijjati. *p.p.* viratta ; ubbigga. °**ful,** °**ing,** *a.* jeguccha ; paṭikkūla.

Dish, *n.* thāla, *m.* thālaka, *nt.* thālī, *f.* *v.t.* thāliyaŋ pakkhipati. *p.p.* °khitta. °**ful,** *a.* pātipūra.

Dishabille, *n.* avibhūsita ; omuttavatthābharaṇa, *m.*

Dishabituate, *v.t.* anabbhāsaŋ karoti. *p.p.* °kata.

Dishallucination, *n.* vipallāsāpanayana, *nt.*

Disharmonize, *v.t.* sāmaggiŋ nāseti ; visamattaŋ neti. *p.p.* nāsita° ; °nīta.

Disharmony, *n.* 1. asāmaggi, *f.* 2. vesamma, *nt.* °**ious,** *a.* 1. visama ; visabhāga ; nānāmatika ; 2. asamassara.

Dishearten, see **Discourage.**

Dishevel, *v.t.* (kese) vikirati ; vippakirati. *p.p.* vikiṇṇa ; vippakiṇṇa.

Dishome, *v.t.* gehā nikkaḍḍhati ; vippavāseti. *p.p.* °ḍhita ; °sita.

Dishonest, *a.* saṭha ; kapaṭa ; vañcaka ; vaṅka. °**ly,** *adv.* savyājaŋ ; nikatiyā ; sāṭheyyena. °**y,** *n.* sāṭheyya, *nt.* nikati, *f.*

Dishonour, *n.* agārava ; ayasa, *m.* akitti, *f.* *v.t.* agarukaroti ; anādarayati. *p.p.* °kata ; °rita. °**able,** *a.* ayasakara ; akittijanaka. °**ably,** *adv.* nindiyākārena.

Dishorn, *v.t.* siṅgāni apaneti. *p.p.* apanītasiṅga.

Dishouse, *v.t.* nijjanaŋ karoti. *p.p.* °janīkata.

Disillusion, *n.* sammohāpanayana, *nt.* *v.t.* sammohaŋ apaneti. *p.p.* apanītasammoha.

Disincline, *v.t.* virajjeti ; aruciŋ uppādeti. *p.p.* °jita ; uppaditāruci. °**ation,** *n.* anicchā ; aruci, *f.*

Disincorporate, *v.t.* samitiŋ *or* pūgaŋ visaŋyojeti. *p.p.* °jitapūga.

Disinfect, *v.t.* rogabījāni apaneti *or* nāseti. *p.p.* apanīta *or* nāsita-rogabīja. °**ant,** *a.* rogabījanāsaka. °**ion,** *n.* visabījanāsana, *nt.*

Disingenuous, *a.* kuṭilajjhāsaya.

Disinherit, *v.t.* adāyādiŋ karoti ; dāyādā apaneti. *p.p.* °kata ; °nīta.

Disintegrate, *v.t.* visileseti ; viyojeti ; vinibbhujati. *p.p.* °sita ; °jita ; vinibbhutta. °**ion,** *n.* viyojana ; puthakkaraṇa, *nt.*

Disinter, *v.t.* nikhaṇitam uddharati. *p.p.* uddhaṭa°.

Disinterest, *n.* upekkhā ; udāsīnatā, *f.* *v.t.* udāsīnaŋ karoti. *refl.* udāsīno hoti ; upekkhati. *p.p.* °kata ; udāsīnabhūta ; upekkhita. °**ed,** *a.* 1. majjhaṭṭha ; apakkhapātī ; 2. muttāsa ; attānapekkha. °**edness,** *n.* 1. nissaṅga ; virāga, *m.* apakkhapātitā, *f.*

Disjoin, *v.t.* viyojeti ; visandhīkaroti. *p.p.* °jita ; °kata. *v.i.* visaŋyujjati. *p.p.* °yutta.

Disjoint, *v.t.* sambandham apaneti ; visaŋyojeti. *p.p.* apanīta° ; °jita.

Disjunct, *a.* visaŋsaṭṭha ; vippayutta. **°ion,** *n.* visaŋsaṭṭhatā ; asambaddhatā, *f.* **°ive,** *a.* viyojaka. *n.* vicchedakapada, *nt.*

Disk, *n.* maṇḍala ; bimba, *nt.*

Dislike, *n.* arati ; aruci ; jigucchā; appiyatā, *f.* *v.t.* jigucchati ; virajjati ; na icchati. *p.p.* °chita; viratta ; na icchita.

Disload, *v.t.* bhāraŋ apaharati *or* otāreti. *p.p.* apahaṭa *or* otāritabhāra.

Dislocate, *v.t.* ṭhānā cāveti ; apasāreti. *p.p.* °cāvita ; °rita. **°ion,** *n.* apasandhikaraṇa ; ṭhānā cāvana, *nt.*

Dislodge, *v.t.* āvāsato apaneti ; nikkaḍḍhati. *p.p.* °nīta ; °ḍhita. **°ment,** *n.* aññaṭṭhānapāpaṇa, *nt.*

Disloyal, *a.* bhattihīna ; dubbhaka. **°ty,** *n.* bhattihīnatā ; dūbhitā, *f.*

Dismal, *a.* 1. udāsīna ; nirussāha ; 2. nirānanda ; dukkhita ; paribhūta. **°ly,** *adv.* savisādaŋ. **°ness,** *n.* maṅkubhāva, *m.* udāsīnatta, *nt.*

Dismantle, *v.t.* 1. āvaraṇam apaneti ; 2. attāṇaŋ karoti. *p.p.* apanītāvaraṇa ; attāṇīkata.

Dismay, *n.* domanassa, *nt.* *v.t.* santāseti ; vyākulīkaroti. *p.p.* °sita ; °kata.

Dismember, *v.t.* aṅgāni vicchindati *or* puthakkaroti. *p.p.* vicchinnaṅga ; puthakkataṅga. **°ment,** *n.* aṅgaviyojana, *nt.*

Dismiss, *v.t.* 1. paṇāmeti ; 2. nissajati ; 3. (senaŋ) visileseti ; 4. (aññattha) pahiṇāti. *p.p.* °mita ; nissaṭṭha ; °sita ; °pahita. **°al, °ion,** *n.* paṇāmana ; nissajjana ; vissajjana, *nt.*

Dismount, *v.i.* (assapiṭṭhito, etc.) otarati ; oruhati. *v.t.* otāreti. *p.p.* otiṇṇa ; orūḷha ; otārita.

Disobedience, *n.* dubbacatā ; anassavatā, *f.* āṇātikkama, *m.* **°ent,** *a.* anassava ; dubbaca.

Disobey, *v.i.* āṇam ullaṅgheti *or* atikkamati ; na sussūsati ; ovādaŋ nānuvattati. *p.p.* ullaṅghitāṇa ; atikkantāṇa ; nānuvattitovāda.

Disoblige, *v.t.* sākacchituŋ na icchati ; āyāseti. *p.p.* °anicchita ; °sita. **°ing,** *a.* ananukūla. **°ingly,** *adv.* ananukūlatāya.

Disorder, *n.* 1. ākulatā ; vyākulatā ; uppaṭipāṭi, *f.* saṅkhobha, *m.* 2. roga ; ābādha, *m.* *v.t.* ākulīkaroti ; vyathati. *p.p.* °kata ; vyathita. **°ly,** *a.* ākula ; saṅkula ; anavaṭṭhita. **°liness,** *n.* uppaṭipāṭi ; vyākulatā, *f.*

Disorganise, °ze *v.t.* vyākulīkaroti ; saŋvidhānaŋ bhañjati. *p.p* °kata ; bhaṭṭhasaŋvidhāna. **°ation,** *n.* vyākulīkaraṇa ; saṅkhobhana, *nt.*

Disown, *v.t.* paccakkhāti ; paṭikkhipati. *p.p.* °khāta ; paṭikkhitta.

Disparage, *v.t.* apasādeti ;

avamaññati; paribhavati. *p.p.* °dita; avamata; paribhūta. °**ment,** *n.* nindā; avaññā; apasādanā, *f.* °**ingly,** *adv.* avaññāvasena.

Disparate, *a. n.* visadisa; vilakkhaṇa.

Disparity, *n.* vesamma; vilakkhaṇatta, *nt.*

Dispart, *v.t.* viyojeti; visuŋkaroti; vibhajati. *v.i.* saṅgamā apagacchati. *p.p.* °jita; °kata; vibhatta; °apagata.

Dispassion, *n.* virāga, *m.* nirāsā, *f.* °**ate,** *a.* viratta; upekkhaka. °**ately,** *adv.* virattākārena.

Dispatch, *n.* 1. pesana; pahiṇana; 2. sāsana, *nt. v.t.* 1. peseti; pahiṇāti. *p.p.* pesita; pahita; 2. khippaŋ niṭṭhāpeti; 3. maraṇīyappahāraŋ deti. *p.p.* °pita; dinna°.

Dispel, *v.t.* nudati; panudati; vinodeti. *p.p.* °dita. °**ler,** *n.* panudaka. °**ling,** *n.* apanudana, *nt.*

Dispensary, *n.* osadhālaya, *m.* bhesajjāgāra, *nt.*

Dispense, *v.t.* 1. bhesajjaŋ payojeti; 2. vissajjeti; vibhajati. *p.p.* payojita°; vissaṭṭha; vibhatta. — **with,** 1. visesavaraŋ deti; 2. āṇaŋ paṭisedheti; 3. taŋ vinā kiccaŋ karoti. *p.p.* dinnavisesavara; paṭisedhitāṇa. °**able,** *a.* 1. vebhaṅgiya; 2. anavassaka; 3. vinā-sādhiya. °**ation,** *n.* 1. vissajjana; vibhajana; 2. saŋvidahana, *nt.* 3. niyati, *f.* °**er,** *n.* 1. bhesajjayojaka; 2. saŋvidahitu, *m.*

Dispeople, *v.t.* nijjanaŋ karoti. *p.p.* °nīkata.

Disperse, *v.t.* vikirati; vikkhipati; dūrīkaroti. *p.p.* vikiṇṇa; vikkhitta; °kata. °**ion,** *n.* vikiraṇa; vikkhipana, *nt.*

Dispirit, *v.t.* ubbejeti; visādeti. *p.p.* °jita; °dita. °**edly,** *adv.* olīnākārena.

Displace, *v.t.* osakketi; ṭhānā cāveti; aññassa ṭhānaŋ gaṇhāti. *p.p.* °kita; °cāvita; gahitaññaṭhāna. °**ment,** *n.* ṭhānācāvana; osakkāpana, *nt.*

Displant, *v.t.* ummūleti. *p.p.* °lita.

Display, *n.* sandassana; pākaṭīkaraṇa, *nt. v.t.* sandasseti; dassanāya pasāreti. *p.p.* °sita; °rita.

Displease, *v.t.* kopeti; roseti; anattamanaŋ karoti. *p.p.* kopita; rosita; °kata. °**ed,** *a.* appasanna; vimana; dummana. °**ing,** *a.* appiya; amanāpa. °**ure,** *n.* asantosa; appasāda, *n.* asantuṭṭhi, *f.*

Disport, *n.* kīḷā, *f. v.i.* sayam eva kīḷati; ramati.

Dispose, *v.t.* vidahati; niyameti. *v.i.* poṇo *or* ninno bhavati. *p.p.* vihita; °mita; poṇībhūta; ninnabhūta. — **of,** 1. appeti; 2. vissajjeti. *p.p.* appita; vissaṭṭha. °**al,** *n.* 1. racanā; paṭipāṭi, *f.* vinyāsa, *m.* 2. vitaraṇa, *nt.* 3. samappaṇa, *nt.* °**er,** *n.* vidhāyaka; vissajjaka, *m.* °**ed to go,** gantukāma, *a.* °**ed to quarrel,** kalahappiya, *a.* **Well disposed,** susīla, *a.*

Disposition, *n*. 1. ajjhāsaya, *m*. adhimutti ; pakati, *f*. 2. racanā, *f*. vinyāsa ; ṭhapitākāra, *m*. **Good —**, sabbhāva, *m*. sosīlya, *nt*.

Dispossess, *v.t*. 1. assāmikaŋ *or* anāyattaŋ karoti ; 2. bhūtagāhato moceti. *p.p*. anāyattīkata ; °mocita. °**ion**, *n*. anāyattabhāva, *m*. assāmikaraṇa, *nt*.

Dispraise, *v.t*. vivaṇṇeti ; nindati ; garahati. *p.p*. °ṇita ; nindita ; °hita. *n*. nindā; garahā, *f*. apavāda, *m*.

Disproof, *n*. nirākaraṇa ; matakhaṇḍana, *nt*.

Disproportion, *n*. vesamma ; asamānatta, *nt*. °**ate**, *a*. visamappamāṇayutta ; ananurūpa.

Disprove, *v.t*. nirākaroti ; mataŋ khaṇḍeti. *p.p*. °kata ; khaṇḍitamata.

Dispute, *n*. vivāda ; kalaha, *m*. bhaṇḍana, *nt*. *v.t*. vivadati ; kalahaŋ karoti. *p.p*. °dita ; katakalaha. °**able**, *a*. vivādāraha ; sasandeha. °**ant**, *n*. vivādī ; viggāhī, *m*. °**ation**. *n*. vivadana, *nt*. **Desirous of —**, vādakāma ; vādatthī, *m*. **Ground for —**, vādapatha, *m*. **Upset in a —**, vādakkhitta, *a*.

Disqualify, *v.t*. anadhikāraŋ *or* akammaññaŋ karoti. °**ication**, *n* akkhamatā ; ananucchavikatā ; anadhikāratā, *f*.

Disquiet, *a*. ubbigga ; kampita. *v.t*. ubbejeti ; khobheti. *p.p*. °jita ; khobhita. °**ude**, °**ness**, vikkhepa ; saṅkhobha, *m*. °**ing**, *a*. vikkhepakara.

Disquisition, *n*. vīmaŋsā ; upaparikkhā, *f*.

Disregard, *n*. anādariya, *nt*. nirapekkhā ; avaññā, *f*. *v.t*. avagaṇeti ; avamāneti ; upekkhati. *p.p*. °ṇita ; °khita. °**ful**, *a*. 1. anādara ; 2. nirapekkha.

Disrelish, *n*. aruci ; jigucchā, *f*. *v.t*. nakkhamati ; jigucchati. *p.p*. akkhanta ; °chita.

Disremember, *v.t*. nassarati ; vissarati ; pamussati. *p.p*. °rita ; pamuṭṭha.

Disrepair, *n*. appaṭisaṅkharaṇa, *nt*.

Disrepute, *n*. ayasa, *m*. akitti, *f*. °**able**, *a*. ayasāvaha ; akittikara.

Disrespect, *n*. agārava ; anādara ; avamāna, *n*. avaññā, *f*. *v.t*. avamāneti ; avajānāti. *p.p*. °nita ; avaññāta. °**ful**, *a*. agārava ; sāvañña; sāvamāna. °**fully**, *adv*. sāvamānaŋ ; agāravena.

Disrobe, *v.t*. omuñcati ; vatthāni apaneti. *v.i*. uppabbajati. *p.p*. omutta ; apanītavattha ; °jita.

Disroot, *v.t*. ummūleti. *p.p*. °lita.

Disrupt, *v.t*. pabhañjati ; vidāreti. *p.p*. pabhaṭṭha ; °rita. °**ion**, *n*. pabhañjana ; vidāraṇa, *nt*. °**ive**, *a*. pabhañjaka ; vidāraka.

Dissatisfy, *v.t*. na pīṇeti ; atittaŋ karoti. *v.i*. ukkaṇṭhati. *p.p*. apīṇita ; atittikata ; °ṭhita. °**faction**, *n*. atitti ; asantuṭṭhi ; ukkaṇṭhanā, *f*.

Dissect, *v.t*. (upaparikkhāya) vicchindati *or* vibhindati. *p.p*. vicchinna ; vibhinna. °**ion**, *n*. viccheda, *m*. °**or**, *n*. vicchedaka, *m*.

Disseize, *v.t.* assāmikaŋ karoti. *p.p.* assāmikata.

Dissemble, *v.t.* 1. yathāsabhāvaŋ paṭicchādeti; 2. ajānanto viya carati; 3. kuhako hoti. *p.p.* paṭicchāditayathāsabhāva; kuhakabhūta.

Disseminate, *v.t.* pacāreti; vyāpeti; vitanoti. *p.p.* °rita; °pita; vitata. °**ion,** *n.* pacāraṇa; vyāpana, *nt.* °**or,** *n.* pacāraka; vyāpetu, *m.*

Dissension, *n.* bheda; virodha; vivāda, *m.*

Dissent, *n.* bhinnamatitā, *f.* matabheda; vivāda, *m.* *v.i.* na saŋsandati; matabhedaŋ yāti. *p.p.* asaŋsandita; °yāta. °**er,** °**ient,** *n.* bhinnamatika. °**ing,** *a.* asaŋsandamāna.

Dissert, *v.i.* deseti; vaṇṇeti. *p.p.* desita; °ṇita. °**ion,** vivaraṇa; vyākhyāna, *nt.*

Disserve, *v.t.* apakaroti. *p.p.* apakata. °**ice,** *n.* anupakāra, *m.*

Dissever, *v.t.* viyojeti; visileseti. *v.i.* viyujjati. *p.p.* °jita; °sita; viyutta.

Dissidence, *n.* vematikatā; bhinnamatitā, *f.* °**ent,** *a.* bhinnamatika.

Dissimilar, *a.* asamāna; visadisa; visabhāga. °**ity,** vesamma; visadisatta, *nt.*

Dissimilate, *v.t.* asamānaŋ *or* visadisaŋ karoti. *p.p.* asamānakata.

Dissimilitude, *n.* asamānatta; visadisatta, *nt.*

Dissimulate, *v.t.* yathāsabhāvaŋ-chādeti; kohaññaŋ dasseti. *p.p.* chāditaya°; dassita°. °**ion,** *n.* sabhāvachādana; kohañña, *nt.*

Dissipate, *v.t.* 1. apaneti; apanudati; 2. vikirati. *p.p.* apanīta; °dita; vikiṇṇa. °**ed,** *a.* durācāra; kāmāsatta. °**ion,** *n.* 1. vikiraṇa, *nt.* 2. duccarita, *nt.*

Dissociable, *a.* asaṅgamāraha.

Dissocialize, *v.t.* asaṅgamārahaŋ karoti.

Dissociate, *v.t.* viyojeti; visileseti. *p.p.* °jita; °sita.

Dissoluble, *a.* visilesanīya; vilayanāraha.

Dissolute, *a.* 1. anavaṭṭhita; 2. durācāra; kāmuka. °**ness,** durācāra, *m.* duccarita, *nt.*

Dissolution, *n.* vilaya; nāsa; bhaṅga; nirodha, *m.*

Dissolve, *v.t.* 1. vilīyāpeti; 2. vicchindati. *v.i.* 1. vilīyati; 2. ucchijjati. *p.p.* °pita; vicchinna; vilīna; ucchinna. °**nt,** *n.* visilesaka; viyojaka, *m. nt.*

Dissonant, *a.* visamassara. °**ly,** *adv.* vissaratāya. °**nce,** *n.* visamasaratā, *f.*

Dissuade, *v.t.* viramāpeti; nivāreti; nisedheti. *p.p.* °pita; °rita; °dhita. °**er,** *n.* nivāraka; viramāpaka, *m.*

Dissuasion, *n.* viramāpana; nivāraṇa, *nt.* °**sive,** *a.* viramāpaka; nivāraka.

Dissymmetry, *n.* asaṅgati; ananukūlatta, *nt.* °**ical,** *a.* asaṅgata; aghaṭiyamāna.

Distaff, *n.* tasara, *m.*

Distance, *n.* dūra ; antara, *nt.* *v.t.* dūre karoti. *p.p.* °kata.

Distant, *a.* dūraṭṭha ; anāsanna.

Distaste, *n.* aruci ; arati, *f.* °**ful,** *a.* 1. arucikara ; amadhura ; 2. appiya ; akanta ; amanāpa.

Distemper, *v.t.* 1. vikkhipati ; vikatiŋ pāpeti ; 2. vaṇṇālepaŋ karoti. *p.p.* vikkhitta ; °pāpita ; katàvaṇṇālepa, *noun*: 1. sārīrikavikāra ; ubbega, *m.* 2. vaṇṇālepa, *m.*

Distend, *v.i.* uddhumāyati. *p.p.* °yita. *v.t.* vātena pūrāpeti. *p.p.* °pita.

Distension, *n.* uddhumāyana, *nt.*

Distich, *n.* upaḍḍhagāthā, *f.*

Distil, *v.t.* parissāveti. *v.i.* parissavati ; sandati. *p.p.* °vita ; parissavita ; sandita. °**ler,** *n.* parissāvaka ; majjasampādaka, *m.* °**lery,** *n.* majjasampādanaṭṭhāna, *nt.*

Distinct, *a.* visiṭṭha ; vibhūta ; nānākāra. °**ion,** *n.* visesa ; pabheda, *m.* visiṭṭhatta, *nt.* °**ive,** *a.* upalakkhaka ; visesaka. °**ively,** *adv.* visesato ; pākaṭākārena. °**ly** *adv.* vibhūtaŋ ; supākaṭaŋ. °**ness,** *n.* visiṭṭhatta ; nānatta ; bhinnatta, *nt.*

Distinguish, *v.t.* viseseti ; upalakkheti. *p.p.* °sita ; °khita. °**able,** *a.* upalakkhaṇīya ; vibhūta ; supākaṭa. °**ed,** *a.* vikhyāta ; patīta ; vissuta ; abhiññāta ; paññāta. °**ing,** *a.* visesakara ; paricchindaka.

Distort, *v.t.* 1. saṅkoceti ; 2. virūpeti. *p.p.* °cita ; °pita. °**ion,** *n.* saṅkoca ; vikāra ; vipallāsa, *m.*

Distract, *v.t.* vikkhipati ; sambhameti. *p.p.* vikkhitta ; °mita. °**ed,** *a.* asamāhita ; aññavihita. °**ion,** *n.* sambhama ; vikkhepa, *m.* anavaṭṭhiti, *f.* °**ive,** *a.* cittakkhobhaka ; vikkhipaka.

Distrain, *v.i.* iṇasādhanatthaŋ iṇāyikāyattaŋ gaṇhāti.

Distrait, *a.* aññavihita ; anohitasota.

Distraught, *a.* atikampita ; saŋkhubhita.

Distress, *n.* vipatti ; āpadā, *f.* vyasana, *nt.* upaddava ; vighāta, *m.* °**ed,** *a.* dukkhita ; aṭṭita ; pīḷita; vyathita ; upadduta. °**ful,** *a.* pīḷākara ; dukkhāvaha ; vipattidāyaka.

Distress, *v.t.* vyathati ; upaddaveti ; pīḷeti. *p.p.* °thita ; upadduta ; pīlita. °**ing,** *a.* dukkhāvaha.

Distribute, *v.t.* vitarati ; vissajjeti ; onojeti. *p.p.* vitarita ; vissaṭṭha ; onojita. °**able,** *a.* onjetabba ; vissajjanīya ; vebhaṅgiya. °**or,** *n.* onojaka ; vissajjaka ; bhājaka, *m.* °**ion,** *n.* onojana ; vibhajana ; vitaraṇa, *nt.* °**ive,** *a.* saŋvibhajaka ; pabhedavācaka.

District, *n.* padesa, *m.* — **court,** disādhikaraṇa, *nt.* — **judge,** disādhikaraṇika, *m.*

Distrust, *v.t.* āsaṅkati ; parisaṅkati ; na saddahati. *p.p.* °kita ; asaddahita. *n.* avissāsa, *m.* āsaṅkā, *f.* °**ful,** *a.* apaccayika ; sāsaṅka. °**fully,** *adv.* sāsaṅkaŋ.

Disturb, *v.t.* vikkhipati ; khobheti ; āloḷeti. *p.p.* vikkhitta ;

khobhita ; °lita. °**ance**, *n.* vikkhepa ; khobha ; ālola, *m.* kampā, *f.* calana, *nt.* °**ing**, *a.* khobhakara ; vikkhipaka.

Disunion, *n.* asāmaggi, *f.* viyoga, *m.*

Disunite, *v.t.* bhedeti ; viyojeti ; *v.i.* viyujjati. *p.p.* bhedita ; °jita ; viyutta. °**ed**, *a.* asamagga ; bhedappatta.

Disuse, *n.* anāsevana, *nt.* abbohāra, *m.* *v.t.* vohārā *or* āsevanā apaneti. *p.p.* °apanīta.

Ditch, *n.* digghikā ; parikhā, *f.*

Ditto, *a.* yathāvutta ; pubbe vutta, *n.* tad eva ; sadisam eva.

Ditty-bag, *n.* macchikassa *or* nāvikassa pacchi, *f.*

Diuresis, *n.* bahumuttaroga, *m.*

Diuretic, *a.* muttavaḍḍhaka.

Diurnal, *a.* 1. ekāhika ; 2. devasika. °**ly**, *adv.* anudinaŋ ; devasikaŋ.

Divagate, *v.t.* apakkamati. *p.p.* apakkanta. °**ion**, *n.* apakkamana, *nt.*

Divan, *n.* 1. mantisabhā ; 2. dīghāsana, *nt.* 3. dhūmavaṭṭikāgāra, *nt.*

Divaricate, *v.i.* dvidhā bhijjati *or* gacchati. *p.p.* °bhinna ; °gata. °**ion**, *n.* dvidhāgamana, *nt.*

Dive, *n.* ogāhana ; nimujjana, *nt.* *v.i.* ogāhati ; nimujjati. *p.p.* ogāḷha ; nimugga. °**er**, *n.* 1. ogāhī ; nimujjaka, *m.* 2. jalacarapakkhī, *m.*

Diverge, *v.i.* 1. apasarati ; apagacchati ; 2. ekaṭṭhānato nānādisāsu gacchati. *p.p.* apasaṭa ; apagata ; nānādisāgata. °**nce**, *n.* apasaraṇa, *nt.* °**nt**, *a.* apasaramāna.

Divers, *a.* °**se**, vividha ; nānāvidha ; nānākāra ; anekavidha. °**ely**, *adv.* vividhā ; nānākārena. °**ity**, *n.* nānatta ; vividhatta, *nt.*

Diversify, *v.t.* vividhaŋ *or* vicittaŋ karoti. *p.p.* vividhākata ; vicittakata. °**ied**, *a.* vicitta ; nānāvaṇṇa.

Diversion, *n.* 1. parivattana, *nt.* 2. vinoda, *m.* anurañjana, *nt.*

Divert, *v.t.* 1. rañjeti ; rameti ; toseti ; 2. aññathā karoti. *p.p.* rañjita ; ramita ; tosita ; °kata. °**ing**, *a.* manorañjaka.

Divest, see **Deprive**. °**ment**, *n.* acchindana, *nt.*

Divide, *v.t.* vibhajati ; bhājeti. *v.i.* vibhijjati ; pabhedaŋ gacchati. *p.p.* vibhatta ; bhājita ; vibhinna ; pabhedagata. °**er**, *n.* bhājaka, *m.*

Dividend, *n.* 1. paṭiviŋsa ; koṭṭhāsa, *m.* 2. bhājiyasaṅkhyā, *f.*

Dividual, *a.* bhājiya.

Divination, *n.* anāgatādisana, *nt.*

Divine, *a.* dibba ; devāyatta. *v.t.* dibbañāṇena katheti *or* pakāseti. *p.p.* °kathita ; °sita. °**eye**, dibbacakkhu, *nt.* — **mansion**, vimāna ; vyamha, *nt.* °**er**, *n.* nimittapāṭhaka, *m.* °**ity**, *n.* devatta, *nt.* — **power**, *n.* devānubhāva, *m.* deviddhi, *f.*

Divisible, *a.* vibhājiya. °**bility**, *n.* bhājanīyatta, vibhajanakkhamatta, *nt.*

Division, *n.* 1. vibhajana, *nt,* vibhāga ; vibhaṅga ; viccheda.

m. 2. koṭṭhāsa ; vagga ; padesa, *m.* °**al,** *a.* koṭṭhāsāyatta ; padesika.

Divisor, *n.* bhājaka, *m.* bhājakasaṅkhyā, *f.*

Divorce, *v.t.* vivāhaŋ nirākaroti *or* lopeti. *p.p.* nirākatavivāha, *n.* vivāhanirākaraṇa, *nt.* °**ment,** *n.* vivāhavisilesa, *m.*

Divulge, *v.t.* (rahassaŋ) pakāseti *or* pākaṭīkaroti. *p.p.* pakāsitarahassa, °kata.

Dizzy, *a.* mucchākara ; bhamuppādaka. °**iness,** *n.* mucchā, *f.* muṭṭhasacca, *nt.* satippavāsa, *m.*

Do, *v.t.* karoti ; vidahati ; sādheti. *p.p.* kata ; vihita ; sādhita. °**all,** sabbatthaka, *a.* °**away with,** alaŋ, *ind.* °**er,** *n.* kārī ; kattu ; sādhetu, *m.* °**ing,** *a.* karonta. °**ing,** *n.* karaṇa ; kicca, *nt.* kriyā, *f.* — **not, (don't),** mā (with imperative or aorist).

Docile, *a.* subbaca ; vineyya ; vidheya ; damma ; sakhila. °**ity,** *n.* vidheyyatā ; subbacatā ; sovacassatā, *f.*

Dock, *n.* 1. nāvānivāsa, *m.* 2. kārāgabbha, *m.* 3. vāladhikantana, *nt.* 4. kesakappanā, *f.* *v.t.* 1. pucchaŋ chindati ; 2. kese kappeti ; 3. nāvaŋ niveseti. *p.p.* chinnapuccha ; kappitakesa ; nivesitanāva. °**er,** nāvātaḷāke kammakarī, *m.*

Docket, *n.* mātikāsūci ; saṅkhittalipi, *f.* *v.t.* adhikaraṇavinicchayaŋ potthake likhati.

Doctor, *n.* 1. bahussuta ; paṇḍita ; 2. vejja ; tikicchaka, *m.* *v.t.* tikicchati. °**ship,** *n.* ācariyapada, *nt.*

Doctrine, *n.* dhamma, *m.* diṭṭhi, *f.* vāda, *m.* **False —,** micchādiṭṭhi, *f.* **True —,** sammādiṭṭhi, *f.* °**al,** *a.* dhammāyatta.

Document, *n.* lekhana, *nt.* lipi, *f.* *v.t.* lekhanena sādheti ; lekhanāni sampādeti. *p.p.* °sādhita ; °ditalekhana. °**ary,** *a.* lekhanāyatta.

Dodder, *v.i.* (dubbalatāya) kampati. *p.p.* °pita.

Dodecagon, *n.* dvādasakoṇaka.

Dodge, *n.* nikati, *f.* sāṭheyya ; ketava, *nt.* *v.t.* (pahārādiŋ) vañceti *or* apaharati. *v.i.* ṭhānā apasarati ; ito cito bhamati. *p.p.* vañcita ; apahaṭa ; °apasaṭa. °bhanta. °**er,** *n.* nekatika ; saṭha, *m.*

Doe, *n.* migī ; hariṇī, *f.*

Doff, *v.t.* omuñcati ; apaneti. *p.p.* omutta ; apanīta.

Dog, *n.* sunakha ; suvāna ; sārameya; kukkura ; sā, *m.* *v.t.* anubandhati ; padā padaŋ yati. *p.p.* °baddha ; °yāta. — **eater,** sapaca ; sapāka, *m.* °**gish,** *a.* sunakhasadisa. — **trough,** suvānadoṇi, *f.* **Mad —,** atisuna ; alakka, *m.*

Dogged, *a.* adamma ; daḷhagāhayutta.

Dogma, *n.* diṭṭhi, *f.* matavisesa ; siddhanta, *m.* °**tic,** *a.* 1. diṭṭhivisayaka ; 2. daḷhadiṭṭhika. °**tically,** *adv.* daḷhagāhena. °**tism,** *n.* diṭṭhigāha ; kumbhīlagāha, *m.* °**tist,** *n.* sakamatadesaka, *m.*

Dogmatize, *v.i.* sakamataŋ deseti *or* patiṭṭhāpeti. *p.p.* desitasakamata.

Doit, *n.* atiappaggha-vatthu ; atikhuddaka-jātarūpa, *nt.*

Dole, *n.* 1. soka ; parideva, *m.* 2. paṭiviŋsa ; koṭṭhāsa, *m.* *v.t.* thoka-thokaŋ deti *or* vibhajati. *p.p.* °dinna ; °vibhatta. °**ful,** *a.* sokātura ; dukkhita. °**fully,** *adv.* sasokaŋ. °**fulness,** *n.* kheda ; visāda, *m.*

Doll, *n.* dhītalikā ; puttalikā, *f.* °**ish,** *a.* mandapañña. °**ishly,** *adv.* mūḷhākārena.

Dollop, *n.* puñja ; piṇḍa ; ālopa, *m.*

Dolmen, *n.* atipurāṇa-susānathūpa, *m.*

Dolorous, *a.* sokātura; dummana.

Dolphin, *n.* macchakinnarī, *f.*

Dolt, *n.* dandha ; jaḷa ; mūḷha, *m.* °**ish,** *a.* mandapañña.

Domain, *n.* 1. sakavisaya, *m.* āṇāvattiṭṭhāna ; 2. ādhipacca ; sāpateyya, *nt.*

Dome, *n.* addhagoḷa-sikhara, *nt.*

Domestic, *n.* gehasevaka, *m.* adj. 1. gehanissita ; gharāvāsāyatta ; 2. sadesāyatta.

Domesticate, *v.t.* 1. vineti; dameti ; 2. (gehe) niveseti. *p.p.* vinīta ; damita ; °sita. °**ion,** *n.* 1. vinayana ; 2. nivesāpana, *nt.*

Domesticity, *n.* 1. gharāvāsa, *m.* 2. gehāsattatā ; sakagharaŋ viya maññanā, *f.*

Domicile, *n.* nivesana ; vāsaṭṭhāna, *nt.* *v.i.* niccavāsam upeti. *p.p.* °upeta. °**iate,** *v.t.* niccavāsappattaŋ karoti.

Dominant, *a.* pabala ; padhāna ; ukkaṭṭha. °**nce,** *n.* pabalatta ; padhānatta, *nt.*

Dominate, *v.t.* vase vatteti ; issariyaŋ *or* ādhipaccaŋ pavatteti. *p.p.* °tita ; pavattita-issariya. °**ion,** *n.* ādhipacca ; issariya, *nt.*

Domineer, *v.i.* abhibhavati ; attano matiyā pāleti. *p.p.* °bhūta ; °lita. °**ing,** *a.* vasavattaka ; attanomatika. °**ingly,** *adv.* attanomatiyā ; seribhāvena.

Dominion, *n.* 1. ādhipacca ; pabhutta, *nt.* 2. adhīnadesa, *m.*

Don, *n.* mahābhāgya, *m.* *v.t.* paridahāpeti ; nivāseti. *p.p.* °pita ; °sita *or* nivattha.

Donate, *v.t.* dadāti ; vitarati ; pariccajati. *p.p.* dinna ; °rita ; pariccatta. °**ion,** *n.* dāna, *nt.* pariccāga, *m.* °**ive,** *a.* paricāgāyatta. *n.* tuṭṭhidāya, *m.*

Done (*p.p.* of **Do**), kata. —**away,** apakata, *a.* — **before,** katapubba, *a.* **Badly** —, dukkata, *a.* **Well** —, sukata, *a.*

Donee, *n.* paṭiggāhaka ; dānalābhī, *m.*

Donkey, *n.* gadrabha ; khara, *m.*

Donor, *n.* dāyaka ; dātu ; cāgī, *m.*

Do-nothing, *n.* alasa ; kusīta, *m.*

Doodle, *n.* jaḷa ; mūḷha, *m.* *v.t.* lāleti. *p.p.* lālita.

Doom, *n.* 1. vadha, *m.* daṇḍana, *nt.* 2. niyati, *f.* *v.t.* vadhaŋ pāpeti ; daṇḍaŋ paṇeti. *p.p.* °pita ; paṇītadaṇḍa. °**sday,** *n.* lokavinicchaya-dina, *nt.*

Door, *n*. 1. dvāra, *nt*. 2. pavesa, *m*. °**frame**, dvārabāhā, *f*. °**keeper**, dvārapāla, *m*. °**mat**, pādapuñchanī, *f*. °**post**, esikātthambha, *m*. °**sill**, °**step**, ummāra, *m*.

Dope, *v.t*. madeti ; mattaŋ karoti. *p.p*. madita *or* matta. *n*. majjajāti, *f*.

Dormancy, *n*. akammaññatā, *f*.

Dormant, *a*. anusayita ; kriyāvirahita.

Dormitory, *n*. sayanighara ; sayanāgāra, *nt*.

Dormouse, *n*. rukkhamūsikā, *f*.

Dorsal, *a*. paṭṭhinissita.

Dose, *n*. pātabba-pamāṇa, *nt*. bhesajja-mattā, *f*. *v.t*. misseti. *p.p*. missita. °**age**, *n*. pātabbabhāga *or* pamāṇa, *m*.

Dossier, *n*. lipi-bhaṇḍikā, *f*.

Dot, *n*. binduciṇha, *nt*. *v.t*. bindūhi aṅketi. *p.p*. °kita.

Dotage, *n*. 1. adhikasineha; 2. atisammosa, *m*.

Dotard, *n*. jarājiṇṇa ; jarātura.

Dote, *v.i*. 1. pamuyhati; 2. atimamāyati. *p.p*. pamūḷha ; °yita. °**ing**, *a*. pemātura. °**ingly**, *adv*. 1. atimuddhatāya ; 2. atisinehena.

Dotty, *a*. kalaṅkita.

Double, *n*. duka ; dvitta, *nt*. adj. 1. diguṇa ; 2. dvippakāra ; duvidha. *v.t*. 1. diguṇīkaroti ; 2. nāmeti. *p.p*. °kata ; nāmita. *v.i*. diguṇīhoti. *p.p*. °bhūta. °**dealer**, saṭha ; vañcaka, *m*. °**edged**, *a*. ubhatodhāra. — **entry**, *n*. dvidhā likhana, *nt*. °**meaning**, *a*. ubhayattha ; sasandeha. — **minded**, *a*. calacitta.

Doubling, *n*. diguṇakaraṇa, *nt*.

Doubly, *adv*. dvidhā ; diguṇaŋ.

Doubt, *n*. kaṅkhā ; saṅkā ; vimati, *f*. sandeha, *m*. *v.i*. saṅkati ; kaṅkhati ; vicikicchati. *p.p*. °kita ; °khita ; °chita. *v.t*. na saddahati. *p.p*. asaddahita. °**ful**, *a*. sasandeha ; āsaṅkī ; kaṅkhī. °**fully**, *adv*. sāsaṅkaŋ. °**less**, *a*. nirāsaṅka ; nikkaṅkha ; asandiddha ; akathaṅkathī. °**lessly**, *adv*. nirāsaṅkaŋ ; nissandehaŋ.

Douce, *a*. amatta ; satimantu.

Dough, *n*. maddita-piṭṭha, *nt*.

Doughty, *a*. vīra ; pabala.

Dour, *a*. avidheya ; thaddhapakatika.

Dove, *n*. kapota ; pārāpata, *m*. °**cot**, *n*. kapotapālikā, *f*. viṭaṅka, *m*. °**like**, *a*. suvinīta.

Dowager, *n*. (laddhadāyādā) vidhavā, *f*.

Dowdy, *n*. dubbasanā ; virūpinī, *f*. adj. asobhana.

Dowel, *n*. khīlaka, *nt*.

Dower, *n*. 1. vidhavāya bhāga, *m*. 2. bhariyāyatta-dhana, *nt*. 3. buddhippabhāva, *m*.

Down, *n*. 1. sukhuma-pakkhipatta, *nt*. 2. aṅgaṇaṭṭhāna, *nt*. *adv*. heṭṭhā ; adho. *v.t*. opāteti ; onāmeti. *p.p*. opātita ; onāmita. °**cast**, *a*. adhomukha ; pattakkhandha. °**castness**, maṅkubhāva, *m*. dummukhatta, *nt*. °**fall**, *n*. parābhava, *m*. parihāni, *f*. °**hearted**, *a*. dīnamana ; khinnacitta. °**pour**, *n*. dhārānipāta, *m*. °**right**, *a*. akuṭila ;

avaṅka, *adv.* ujuŋ ; akuṭilaŋ. °**stairs,** adhotale ; heṭṭhāpāsāde (loc.). °**trodden,** *a.* omaddita. °**ward,** *a.* adhogāmī ; hāyamāna. °**wards,** *adv.* adhomukhaŋ.

Downy, *a.* mudulomayutta ; mudutiṇayutta.

Dowry, *n.* itthidhana, *nt.*

Doxology, *n.* devatthutigīta, *nt.*

Doze, *n.* pacalāyanā, *f.* *v.i.* pacalāyati.

Dozen, *n.* dvādasaka, *nt.*

Drab, *n.* 1. gaṇikā, *f.* 2. mandappabhā, *f.* *v.i.* gaṇikāya samāgacchati. *p.p.* °gata.

Drabble, *v.i.* udakaŋ kampento gacchati ; malino bhavati. *v.t.* malinīkaroti. *p.p.* malinībhūta ; °kata.

Drachm, *n.* dhaññamāsa, *m.*

Draconic, *a.* daḷha ; pīḷākara.

Draft, *n.* 1. niyamita-purisagaṇa, *m.* 2. mūluddhārapaṇṇa, *nt.* 3. paṭhamaracanā, *f.* *v.t.* 1. ālikhati ; saṇṭhānaŋ dasseti ; 2. gaṇam uccināti. *p.p.* °khita ; dassitasaṇṭhāna ; uccinitagaṇa. °**sman,** *n.* ālekhaka, *m.*

Drag, *n.* mahā-assaratha, *m.* *v.t.* ākaḍḍhati ; ākassati. *p.p.* °ḍhita ; °sita. *v.i.* āyāsena gacchati. — **about,** parikassati. — **along,** samparikaḍḍhati. °**ging,** *n.* ākaḍḍhana, *nt.* — **in,** (anavassaŋ) āharati. — **near,** upakaḍḍhati. — **out,** nikkaḍḍhati. °**net,** mahājāla, *nt.*

Draggle, *v.t.* paṅkena makkheti. *v.i.* paṅkena makkhīyati. *p.p.* °makkhita.

Dragoman, *n.* bhāsāparivattaka, *m.*

Dragon, *n.* sapakkha-nāga ; vyāla, *m.*

Dragoon, *n.* assārohī-bhaṭa, *m.* *v.t.* balena kāreti.

Drain, *n.* niddhamana, *nt.* jalaniggama, *m.* *v.t.* apavāheti ; jalaŋ nissāreti. *p.p.* °hita ; nissāritajala. °**age,** *n.* jalāpavāhana, *nt.* °**er,** *n.* jalāpavāhī, *m.*

Drake, *n.* kādamba ; kalahaŋsa, *m.*

Dram, *n.* aṭṭhamāsakapamāṇa, *nt.*

Drama, *n.* nāṭaka ; nāṭya, *nt.* °**tic,** *a.* 1. nāṭakāyatta ; 2. vimhayāvaha. °**tically,** *adv.* nāṭakarūpena. °**tist,** *n.* nāṭyasampādaka, *m.* °**tize,** *v.t.* nāṭakattaŋ parivatteti ; nāṭyaŋ likhati. *p.p.* °tita ; likhitanāṭya.

Dramaturgy, *n.* nāṭyakalā, *f.*

Drape, *v.t.* 1. vatthehi chādeti ; 2. nivāseti ; 3. vatthe pasāreti. *p.p.* °chādita ; nivattha ; °ritavattha. °**er,** *n.* dussavāṇija, *m.* °**ry,** *n.* 1. dussavaṇijjā ; 2. vatthajāti, *f.* °**ry shop,** paggāhikasālā, *f.*

Drastic, *a.* 1. atidaḷha ; anatikkamanīya ; 2. ativirecaka. °**ally,** *adv.* atidaḷhatāya.

Draught, *n.* 1. bhāravahana, *nt.* 2. (udaka-) gaṇḍūsa, *m.* 3. ālekhacitta, *nt.* 4. jālagata-maccharāsi, *m.* 5. nimujjanappamāṇa, *nt.* 6. mūladānapaṇṇa, *nt.* 7. (dragging :) ākaḍḍhana, *nt.* 8. vātapāna-vāyuvega, *m.* °**board,** sāriphalaka, *m.* °**horse,**

vāhakassa, *m.* °**sman,** ālekhya-sampādaka, *m.*

Draw, *n.* 1. ākaḍḍhana, *nt.* 2. salākapātana, *nt. v.t.* ākaḍḍhati. *v.i.* apagacchati. *p.p.* °ḍhita ; apagata. — °**ashore,** thalaŋ pāpeti. — **aside,** apakassati. — **away,** apaneti ; apal aḍḍhati. — **back,** osakkati; paṭilīyati. — **breath,** assasati. — **a line,** rekhaŋ aṅketi. — **the curtain,** tirokaraṇiŋ pāteti; tirokaroti. — **lots,** salākaŋ gaṇhāti. — **money,** mūlam apaneti. — **near,** upasaṅkamati. — **off,** abbūhati. — **out,** nikkaḍḍhati. — **together,** saŋharati. — **up,** ubbāhati.

Drawback, *n.* apasakkana, *nt.* parihāni, *f.*

Drawbridge, *n.* jaṅgamasetu, *m.*

Drawer, *n.* 1. ākaḍḍhaka, *m.* 2. kaḍḍhanīya-samugga, *m.* — **for lots,** bhaddaghaṭa, *m.*

Drawing, *n.* 1. ākaḍḍhana, *nt.* 2. ālekhacitta, *nt.* — **back,** *n.* paṭilīyana ; avakaḍḍhana, *nt.* — **master,** ālekhācariya, *m.* — **near,** upasaṅkamana, *nt.* °**room,** paṭikkamana, *nt.* āsanasālā, *f.*

Drawl, *v.i.* āyatassarena vadati. *p.p.* °vutta.

Draw-well, *n.* ghaṭīyantayuttakūpa, *m.*

Dread, *n.* uttāsa, *m.* bhaya, *nt.* bhīti, *f. v.i.* bhāyati ; uttasati. *p.p.* bhīta ; uttasita. °**ful,** *a.* bhayānaka; bherava ; bībhaccha ; bhiŋsanaka ; bhayajanaka. °**fully,** *adv.* bheravākārena. °**less,** *a.* nibbhaya. °**naught,** *n.* 1. yuddhanāvā, *f.* 2. vārikañcuka, *m.*

Dream, *n.* supina, *nt. v.i.* 1. supinaŋ passati ; 2. upanijjhāyati. — **away,** mudhākālaŋ khepeti. °**er,** *n.* supinadassī; upanijjhāyī, *m.* — **land,** *n.* cintānimuggatā, *f.* — **teller,** supinapāṭhaka, *m.* °**y,** *a.* supinopama ; asāra.

Dreary, *a.* timirayutta ; nirānanda ; suñña ; nijjana.

Dredge, *n.* uddhāraka-yanta, *nt. v.t.* (jalato paṅkādiŋ) uddharati. *p.p.* uddhaṭa.

Dree, *v.t.* sahati ; khamati. *p.p.* sahita ; khanta.

Dreg, *n.* mala, *nt.* kasambu, *m.*

Drench, *n.* 1. osadhakoṭṭhāsa, *m.* 2. adhikatemana, *nt. v.t.* 1. adhikaŋ pivati ; 2. bhusaŋ temeti. *p.p.* °pīta ; °temita. °**er,** *n.* mahāmegha, *m.*

Dress, *n.* acchādana ; vatthābharaṇa, *nt. v.t.* 1. acchādeti ; pasādheti ; 2. paṭiyādeti ; saṅkharoti. *p.p.* °dita ; °dhita ; °dita ; saṅkhata. *v.i.* paridahati. *p.p.* °hita. °**ed with,** āmukka *or* āmutta ; nivattha. °**er,** *n.* 1. kappaka ; 2. saṅkhāraka ; 3. mahānasaphalaka, *m.* °**ing,** *n.* 1. vesavidhāna, *nt.* 2. vaṇaveṭhana, *nt.* 3. tajjana, *nt.* 4. vatthakhali, *f.* 5. bhūmisāra, *m.* °**room,** pasādhanāgāra, *nt.*

Dressy, *a.* maṇḍanappiya.

Dribble, *n.* pasavana, *nt. v.i.* pasavati ; binduvasena galati *or* sandati. *p.p.* °vita ; °galita ; °sandita.

Driblet, *n.* kaṇa ; lava ; lesa, *m.*

Drift, *n.* 1. plavana ; pavahana, *nt.* 2. adhippāya ; neyyattha, *m.* *v.i.* uplavati ; vuyhati. *v.t.* plāveti ; pavāheti. *p.p.* plavita ; vūḷha ; plāvita ; pavāhita. — **wood,** vūḷhadāru, *nt.*

Drill, *n.* 1. ārā, *f.* 2. dīgha-paŋsupuñja, *m.* 3. yuddhasikkhā, *f.* yuddhābhyāsa, *m.* *v.t.* 1. ārāya vijjhati ; 2. yuddhasippaŋ sikkhati. *p.p* °viddha ; sikkhita°.

Drink, *n.* pāna ; peyya, *nt.* *v.t.* pivati ; pāti. *p.p.* pīta. °**able,** *a.* pātabba ; peyya. °**er,** *n.* pāyī ; pānarata, *m.* °**ing,** *n.* pivana, *nt.*

Drinking, *a.* pivanta. — **cup,** casaka, *m.* pānīyathālaka, *nt.* — **festival,** surāchaṇa ; pānussava, *m.* — **hall,** āpāna ; pānamandira, *nt.* — **vessel,** āpānīyakaŋsa, *m.*

Drip, *v.i.* binduso paggharati. *p.p.* °rita. *v.t.* binduso pāteti. *p.p.* °tita. *noun* : chadanagga, *nt.* °**ping,** *a.* paggharanta ; sodaka ; saphusitaka. *n.* 1. paggharaṇa ; galana, *nt.* 2. maŋsarasa, *m.*

Drive, *n.* 1. rathagamana, *nt.* 2. yānabhūmi, *f.* *v.t.* pājeti ; sāreti. *v.i.* rathena yāti. *p.p.* pājita ; sārita ; °yāta. — **away,** nikkaḍḍhati ; apanudati. °**ing,** *n.* pājana ; sāraṇa, *nt.* — **out,** nissāreti ; nikkhāmeti.

Drivel, *n.* 1. bālajappanā, *f.* 2. lālā, *f.* khela, *m.* *v.i.* 1. pajappati ; lālappati ; 2. lālaŋ sandeti ; 2. jaḷo bhavati. °**ler,** *n.* 1. pajappaka, *m.* 2. khelāsaka ; eḷamūga, *m.*

Driver, *n.* pājaka ; sārathi ; sūta ; rathācariya, *m.* °'**s stick,** patoda, *m.* patodalaṭṭhi, *f.*

Drizzle, *n.* sīkara, *nt.* *v.i.* mandaŋ vassati. °**ing,** *n.* sīkaravassa, *nt.*

Droit, *n.* pariggaha ; upādhi, *m.*

Droll, *n.* *a.* parihāsakara ; hāsajanaka. *v.i.* parihāseti ; vikaṭaŋ dasseti. *p.p.* °sita ; dassitavikaṭa. °**ery,** *n.* parihāsana, *nt.*

Drone, *n.* 1. nāyakachappada, *m.* 2. alasa ; nirīha ; tandibahula. *v.i.* huṅkaroti ; jhanati. °**ish,** *a.* kusīta ; nibbiriya.

Droop, *v.i.* onamati ; osīdati ; sithilībhavati. *v.t.* onāmeti. *p.p.* onata ; osīna ; °bhūta ; onāmita. °**ing,** *a.* kilanta ; milāyamāna.

Drop, *n.* 1. bindu ; phusita, *nt.* theva, *m.* 2. pāta. *m.* patana, *nt.* *v.i.* patati. *v.t.* pāteti ; okkhipati. *p.p.* patita ; pātita ; okkhitta. °**ping,** *n.* galana ; sandana, *nt.* °**pings,** *pl.* pasumala, *nt.*

Dropsy, *n.* 1. jalodara, *nt.* 2. sopha, *m.*

Dross, *n.* maṇḍa ; mala, *nt.* asuddhabhāga, *m.*

Drought, *n.* nidāgha, *m.* dubbuṭṭhi, *f.*

Drove, *n.* 1. pasugaṇa ; 2. macchagumba, *m.* 3. phaṇahattha, *m.* cuṇṇadabbikā, *f.* °**er,** *n.* pasugaṇapājaka, *m.*

Drown, *v.t.* 1. nimujjāpeti ; 2. abhibhavati. *v.i.* nimujjitvā marati *p.p.* °pita ; abhibhūta ; °mata.

Drowse, *n.* tandi, *f.* middha, *nt.* *v.i.* pacalāyati ; niddāyati. °**sy,** *a.* middhī ; tandita ; niddālu.

°**iness**, *n.* niddālutā ; pacalāyanā, *f.*

Drub, *v.t.* lagulena tāleti. *p.p.* °tālita. °**bing**, *n.* tālana ; paharana, *nt.*

Drudge, *n.* dāsa ; dukkarakārī, *m.* *v.i.* parissamati ; dukkaraŋ karoti. *p.p.* parissanta ; katadukkara. °**ry**, *n.* dāsavutti, *f.* niccaparissama, *m.*

Drug, *n.* osadha ; bhesajja, *nt.* *v.t.* 1. visena misseti ; 2. osadhaŋ yojeti ; 3. osadhena visaññīkaroti. *p.p.* °sita ; yojitosadha ; °ññīkata. °**gist**, osadhavāṇija, *m.*

Drum, *n.* 1. bheri ; dundubhi, *f.* 2. bherisadisavatthu, *nt.* *v.i.* bheriŋ vādeti *or* āhanati. *p.p.* vādita° ; āhata°. °**mer**, *n.* bherivādaka, *m.* °**stick**, bheridaṇḍa, *m.*

Drunk, *a.* surāmatta. °**ard**, *n.* surāsoṇḍa ; surādhutta, *m.* °**en**, *a.* madamatta. °**enness**, *n.* surāsoṇḍatā, *f.*

Dry, *a.* 1. sukkha ; asāra ; nirasa ; 2. majjarahita. *v.t.* soseti ; visoseti ; sukkhāpeti. *v.i.* sussati. *p.p.* sosita ; °pita ; sukkha. °**ing**, *n.* sosana ; sussana, *nt.* — **meat**, vallūra, *nt.* °**ness**, *n.* 1. sukkhatta ; nissāratta, *nt.* 2. majjarahitatta, *nt.*

Dryad, *n.* vanadevatā, *f.*

Dual, *n.* duka ; dvika ; yugala ; dvanda, *nt.* adj. duvidha ; dvikayutta. °**ism**, *n.* dvittavāda, *m.* °**ity**, *n.* dvittatā, *f.*

Dub, *v.t.* navādhikāraŋ *or* upādhiŋ deti. *p.p.* dinna-navādhikāra.

Dubiety, *n.* saŋsaya ; sandeha ; anicchaya, *m.*

Dubious, *a.* 1. saŋsayāpanna ; 2. saṅkanīya. °**ly**, *adv.* sāsaṅkaŋ.

Dubitation, *n.* kaṅkhā ; saṅkā ; vimati, *f.* °**tive**, *a.* āsaṅkanīya ; saŋsayajanaka.

Duck, *n.* 1. kādamba, *m.* 2. nimujjana, *nt.* *v.i.* nimujjati ; osīdati. *p.p.* nimugga ; osīna. °**ing**, *n.* ogāhana, *nt.*

Duct, *n.* paṇālī, *f.* nāḷa, *m.*

Ductile, *a.* 1. kammañña ; vidheya ; 2. subbaca ; veneyya. °**ity**, *n.* 1. kammaññatā ; 2. vineyyatta ; subbacatta, *nt.*

Dude, *n.* suvesappiya.

Dudgeon, *n.* appasāda, *m.*

Due, *a.* yogga ; anurūpa ; ucita, *n.* 1. labhitabba, *nt.* pattakoṭṭhāsa ; 2. pariggaha, *m.* 3. suṅka ; kara, *m.* 4. iṇa, *nt.* *adv.* nissāya ; hetunā. **The debt is due**, iṇaŋ sodhetabbaŋ. **Your failure is due to your carelessness**, tava pamādo yeva asāmatthiyā kāraṇaŋ.

Duel, *n.* dvandayuddha, *nt.* *v.i.* dvandayuddhaŋ karoti. °**list**, *n.* dvandayodha, *m.*

Duff, *v.t.* patirūpakena vañceti. *p.p.* °cita. °**er**, *n.* vyājavāṇija ; kūṭavāṇija, *m.*

Dug, *n.* thana ; thanagga, *nt.*

Duke, *n.* ādipāda, *m.* °**dom**, *n.* 1. ādipādāyatta-padesa ; 2. ādipādadhura, *nt.*

Dulcet, *a.* sotarasāyana.

Dulcify, *v.t.* 1. madhurayati ; 2. muduŋ karoti. *p.p.* °yita ; mudukata.

Dull, *a.* 1. momuha ; mandapañña ; 2. nippabha ; nitteja ; 3. kuṇṭha ; 4. alasa ; kusīta ; 5. thūla ; 6. nirānanda. *v.t.* 1. moheti ; 2. kuṇṭheti ; 3. malinīkaroti. *v.i.* 1. muyhati ; 2. kuṇṭhati ; 3. malinībhavati. *p.p.* mohita ; °ṭhita ; °kata ; mūḷha ; kuṇṭhita ; °bhūta. °**ness,** *n.* 1. jaḷatā ; 2. malinatā ; 3. atikhiṇatā, *f.* °**sighted,** *a.* mandadiṭṭhika. °**witted,** *a.* mandabuddhika.

Duly, *adv.* yathārahaŋ ; yathocitaŋ ; yathākālaŋ.

Dumb, *a.* mūga. °**ly,** *adv.* tuṇhī. °**ness,** *n.* mūgatta, *nt.* °**show,** *n.* vācārahita-nacca, *nt.*

Dumbfound, *v.t.* vimoheti ; sambhameti. *p.p.* °hita ; °mita.

Dummy, *n.* 1. potthalikā, *f.* 2. jaḷa, *m.* 3. vyājabhaṇḍikā, *f.*

Dump, *n.* 1. thūlavāmana, *m.* 2. agghosādana, *nt.* 3. sahasā pātana, *nt.* *v.t.* 1. kacavaraŋ nidahati ; 2. thāmasā khipati. *p.p.* nihitakacavara ; °khitta.

Dumps, *n. pl.* ubbega ; kheda, *m.*

Dumpy, *a. n.* pīvaravāmana.

Dun, *n.* sanibandha-iṇasodhaka, *m.* adj. kāḷapiṅgala. *v.t.* iṇamocanāya āyācati.

Dunce, *n.* dandha ; mandamati, *m.*

Dunderhead, *n.* mandabuddhika ; atimūḷha, *m.*

Dune, *n.* vālukānicaya, *m.*

Dung, *n.* mala ; vacca ; karīsa, *nt.* ukkāra, *m.* *v.t.* gomayādiŋ bhūmiyaŋ yojeti. °**hill,** *n.* ukkāranicaya, *m.*

Dungeon, *n.* sabbatopihita-bandhanāgāra, *m.*

Duodecimal, *a.* dvādasabhāgayutta.

Duologue, *n.* ubhayabhāsanayutta-nacca, *nt.*

Dupe, see **Cheat.**

Duplex, *a.* diguṇa.

Duplicate, *n.* paṭilekhā ; puttikā ; anulipi, *f.* adj. diguṇa ; duvidha. *v.t.* 1. diguṇīkaroti ; 2. anulipiŋ likhati. °**ion,** *n.* dvittakaraṇa, *nt.*

Duplicity, *n.* 1. dvejjhabhāva, *m.* 2. vañcanā ; māyā, *f.*

Durable, *a.* ciraṭṭhāyī ; thira ; dhuva. °**bility,** *n.* thāvariya ; thiratta, *nt.*

Durance, *n.* rundhana ; bandhana, *nt.*

Duration, *n.* ciraṭṭhiti, *f.* aviccheda, *m.* saṇṭhiti, *f.*

Durbar, *n.* rājasabhā, *f.*

During, *prep.* vattamāne. *Expressed by the Loc. Abs.* e.g. Brahmadatte rajjaŋ kārente (= during the reign of Brahmadatta).

Dusk, *n.* sañjhā, *f.* padosa, *m.* °**y,** *a.* 1. mandāloka ; 2. īsaŋkaṇha.

Dust, *n.* dhūli, *f.* raja ; reṇu, *m.* *v.t.* 1. rajam ākirati ; 2. dhūlim apaneti ; pappoṭheti ; vidhunāti. *p.p.* rajākiṇṇa ; apanītadhūli ; °ṭhita ; °nita *or* vidhūta. °**bin,** *n.* saṅkārakūṭa, *m.* paŋsukūla, *nt.* °**ed,** *a.* virajīkata. °**er,** *n.* 1. rajoharaṇa, *nt.* 2. rajohārī, *m.* °**y,** *a.* 1. saraja ; rajokiṇṇa ; 2. nirasa.

Duteous, Dutiful, *a.* vattasampanna ; vidheyya ; yuttigaruka.

Duty, *n.* 1. veyyāvacca; karaṇīya; kattabba, *nt.* 2. kara; suṅka, *m.* **— free,** *a.* suṅkamutta. °**iable,** *a.* karaggāhāraha. **— of a king,** rājadhamma, *m.* **One's own —,** sakicca, *nt.*

Dux, *n.* jeṭṭhantevāsī, *m.*

Dwarf, *n.* vāmana; lakuṇṭaka, *m.* *v.t.* vāmanaŋ *or* kuṇṭhaŋ karoti. *p.p.* vāmanīkata. °**ish,** *a.* vāmanasabhāva; rassajātika.

Dwell, *v.i.* vasati; nivasati; viharati. *p.p.* vuttha; nivuttha; **— abroad,** pavasati; pavāsaŋ yāti. *p.p.* pavuttha; °yāta. °**er,** *n.* nivāsī; nevāsika, *m.* °**ing,** *n.* nivāsa; āvāsa; upassaya, *m.* geha; ghara; vāsaṭṭhāna, *nt.*

Dwindle, *v.i.* mandībhavati; parihāyati. *p.p.* °bhūta; parihīna.

Dyad, *n.* duka; yamaka, *nt.*

Dye, *n.* rajana, *nt.* raṅga; rāga, *m.* *v.t.* rañjeti; vaṇṇamaṭṭhaŋ karoti. *p.p.* rañjita; °kata. °**er,** *n.* rañjaka; rajaka, *m.*

Dying, *a.* mīyamāna; maramāna; maranta.

Dyke, see **Dike.**

Dynamic, *a.* vegayutta. *pl.* vegavijjā, *f.*

Dynamite, *n.* sahasā vidāraka, *m.* *v.t.* vidārakaŋ yojeti.

Dynamo, *n.* vijjuveguppādaka (-yanta), *nt.*

Dynast, *n.* pālaka; vaŋsaṭṭhāpaka. °**y,** *n.* rājaparamparā, *f.* rājavaŋsa, *m.*

Dysentery, *n.* atisāra, *m.* pakkhandikā, *f.*

Dyspepsia, *n.* ajiṇṇaroga, *m.* alasaka, *nt.*

Dyspeptic, *a.* ajiṇṇarogātura.

Dyspnoea, *n.* sāsatthambha, *m.*

Dysuria, *n.* muttakicchābādha, *m.*

E

Each, *a.* ekeka; pacceka; itarītara. **— day,** patidinaŋ, *adv.* **— his own,** yathāsakaŋ, *adv.* **— other,** aññamaññaŋ, *adv.*

Eager, *a.* 1. lola; āsatta; 2. ussuka; tibbāsa. °**ly,** *adv.* sahaŋ; sāpekkhaŋ. °**ness,** *n.* 1. ākaṅkhā, *f.* lolatta, *nt.* 2. ussāha, *m.*

Eagle, *n.* mahāsena; garuḷa, *m.* °**eyed,** *a.* sukhumadiṭṭhī.

Ear, *n.* 1. sota, *nt.* kaṇṇa, *m.* 2. (of corn, etc.) kaṇṇa, *nt.* kaṇṇikā; mañjarī, *f.* *v.t.* saŋlakkheti; visuŋ ṭhapeti. *p.p.* °khita; °ṭhapita. °**ache,** kaṇṇasūla, *nt.* °**drop,** *n.* kuṇḍala, *nt.* °**drum,** *n.* kaṇṇodara, *nt.* °**lap,** *n.* kaṇṇasakkhalikā, *f.* °**lobe,** *n.* kaṇṇavalli, *f.* °**mark,** *n.* visesa lakkhaṇa, *nt.* *v.t.* visesena lakkheti. °**pick,** *n.* kaṇṇasūci, *f.* °**ring,** *n.* kuṇḍalābharaṇa, *nt.* kaṇṇabhūsā, *f.* °**shot,** *n.* sotapatha, *m.* °**wax,** *n.* kaṇṇamala, *nt.* °**witness,** *n.* sutasakkhika, *m.*

Early, *a.* ādima; paṭhamatara. *adv.* pageva; kālass'eva. **— morning,** paccūsa, *m.* °**iness,** *n.* pubbataratta, *nt.* °**ier than,** purimataraŋ, *adv.*

Earn, *v.t.* sambharati; ajjati. *p.p.* sambhata; ajjita. °**ing,** *n.* ajjitadhana, *nt*

Earnest, *a.* appamatta ; ātāpī ; saussāha. *n.* 1. saccakāra, *m.* 2. yathatthatā ; avitathatā, *f.* °**ly**, *adv.* ussāhena. °**ness**, *n.* tapparatā, *f.* ātappa ; appamāda, *m.*

Earth, *n.* bhūmi ; paṭhavī ; medinī ; avani ; vasundharā, *f.* *v.t.* paṭhaviyaŋ nidahati. *v.i.* paṭhavigabbhe vasati. *p.p.* °hita ; °vuttha. °**born**, *a.* bhummaja ; thalaja. °**en**, *a.* mattikāmaya. °**enware**, mattikabhājana ; āmattika, *nt.* °**ling**, *n.* lokiyajana, *nt.* °**ly**, *a.* lokiya. °**quake**, paṭhavikampā, *f.* °**worm**, gaṇḍuppāda, *m.* mahīlatā, *f.* °**y**, *a.* paŋsusadisa.

Ear-wig, *n.* kaṇṇajalūkā, *f.* *v.t.* kaṇṇajappanena vasīkaroti. *p.p.* °kata.

Ease, *n.* phāsu, *m.* sukha ; sāta, *nt.* *v.t.* sukheti ; sameti. *v.i.* (malādiŋ) nicchāreti *or* nikkhāmeti. *p.p.* sukhita ; samita ; °rita ; °mita. °**ful**, *a.* sukhāvaha °**fully**, *adv.* sukhena. °**fulness**, *n.* sukhitatta, *nt.* °**ment**, *n.* 1. upasamana, *nt.* 2. atirekāgāra ; bhaṇḍāgāra, *nt.*

East, *n.* 1. pubbadisā ; pācī ; puratthimā, *f.* 2. pācīnadesa, *m.* adj. puratthima. °**erly**, *a.* pācīnābhimukha. °**ern**, *a.* 1. puratthima ; 2. pācīnadesīya. °**ward**, *a.* puratthābhimukha.

Easter, *n.* matakuṭṭhānadivasa, *m.*

Easy, *a.* 1. sukara ; phāsuka ; 2. subodha. — **to do**, sukara, *a.* — **to obtain**, sulabha, *a.* — **to see**, sudassa, *a.* °**chair**, āsandi, *f.* °**ily**, *adv.* sukhena. °**ily supported**, subhara, *a.* °**iness**, *n.* sukaratā, *f.* phāsubhāva, *m.*

Eat, *v.t.* khādati ; bhuñjati ; asati ; bhakkhati ; anubhavati ; ghasati. *p.p.* khādita ; bhutta ; asita ; °khita ; anubhutta ; ghasta. °**able**, *a.* bhojja ; bhakkhiya. °**er**, *n.* bhuñjaka ; adaka ; bhottu, *m.* °**er of flesh**, maŋsabhojī, *m.* °**er of grass**, tiṇabhakkha, *m.* °**er of carcases**, kuṇapādaka, *m.* °**ing**, *n.* khādana ; bhuñjana ; asana ; bhakkhana, *nt.*

Eaves, *n.* nimbakosa, *m.* chadanagga, *nt.* °**drop**, *v.i.* upassutiŋ tiṭṭhati. °**dropper**, *n.* upassutika ; rahassagavesaka, *m.*

Ebb, *n.* 1. jalogamana ; 2. hāyana, *nt.* *v.i.* hāyati ; khīyati. *p.p.* hīna ; khīṇa.

Ebony, *n.* kāḷasāra, *m.* adj. kāḷasāramaya.

Ebriety, *n.* madamattatā, *f.*

Ebrious, *a.* pānasoṇḍa.

Ebullient, *a.* 1. phenuddehaka ; 2. ativegayutta.

Ebullition, *n.* 1. pheṇuddehana, *nt.* 2. adhikavega, *m.*

Eccentric, *a.* niyamaviruddha ; lokācāra-paṭipakkha. °**ity**, *n.* ācāravirodha, *m.* visamatta, *nt.*

Ecclesia, *n.* dhammikasabhā, *f.*

Ecclesiast, *n.* desaka, *m.* °**ic**, *n.* pabbajita, *m.* °**ical**, *a.* pabbajitāyatta.

Ecclesiology, *n.* devāyatanavijjā, *f.*

Echo, *n.* paṭighosa ; paṭirava, *m.* *v.i.* anunadati ; paṭiravati. *v.t.* paṭirāveti *p.p.* °dita ; °vita ; °rāvita.

Eclat, *n.* ukkuṭṭhi, *f.* jayaghosa, *m.*

Eclectic, *a.* *n.* nānāmatuddhāraka, *m.* °**ism,** *n.* satthantaruddharaṇa, *nt.*

Eclipse, *n.* gāha, *m.* gahaṇa, *nt.* *v.t.* tirokaroti ; āvarati. *p.p.* tirokata ; āvaṭa. *v.i.* āvarīyati. — **of the moon,** candaggāha, *m.* — **of the sun,** suriyaggāha, *m.*

Ecliptic, *a.* gāhāyatta.

Economic, *a.* mitabbayāyatta. *n.* *pl.* dhanapālanavijjā, *f.* atthasattha, *nt.* °**al,** *a.* dhanapālanāyatta. °**ally,** *adv.* mitabbayena.

Economist, *n.* atthasatthaññū ; mitabbayī, *m.*

Economize, *v.t.* mitabbayaŋ karoti. *p.p.* katamitabbaya.

Economy, *n.* 1. atthasattha, *nt.* 2. vayaparimiti ; sallahukavutti, *f.*

Ecstasy, *n.* pamoda ; pahāsa, *m.* ubbegapīti, *f.*

Ecstatic, *a.* ubbegapītiyutta.

Ecumenic, *a.* sabbasādhāraṇa.

Eczema, *n.* pāmā, *f.*

Edacious, *a.* giddha ; mahābhakkha. °**ly,** *adv.* sagedhaŋ.

Edacity, *n.* loluppa, *nt.* giddhi, *f.* gedha, *m.*

Eddy, *n.* āvaṭṭa ; bhama ; salilabbhama, *m.*

Edema, *n.* sopha, *m.*

Edentate, *a.* *n.* dantarahita.

Edge, *n.* mukhavaṭṭi, *f.* pariyanta, *m.* (of a weapon :) dhārā, *f.* (of a garment :) dasā, *f.* *v.t.* tejeti ; tikhiṇayati ; nisāṇeti. *p.p.* tejita ; tikhiṇita ; nisita. °**ed,** *a.* nisita ; tikhiṇa. °**less,** *a.* kuṇṭha ; atikhiṇa.

Edible, *a.* bhojja ; bhojanāraha.

Edict, *n.* rājasāsana, *nt.*

Edifice, *n.* mahāmandira, *nt.*

Edify, *v.t.* abhivaḍḍheti ; ñāṇaguṇehi vaḍḍheti. *p.p.* °vaḍḍhita. °**ication,** *n.* guṇavuddhi, *f.* buddhivaḍḍhana, *nt.* °**ied,** *a.* ñāṇavuddha ; guṇavuddha. °**ing,** *a.* guṇavaḍḍhaka.

Edit, *v.t.* abhisaṅkharoti ; (lekhaṇāni) sodheti. *p.p.* °khata ; sodhita-lekhana. °**ion,** *n.* saŋsodhana ; abhisaṅkharaṇa, *nt.* °**or,** *n.* ganthasodhaka ; pavattisaṅkhāraka, *m.* °**orial,** *n.* sampādakavākya, *nt.* °**orship,** *n.* sodhakadhura ; saṅkhārakapada, *nt.*

Educate, *v.t.* sikkhāpeti ; uggaṇhāpeti. *p.p.* °pita. °**ion,** *n.* sikkhāpana ; ajjhāpana, *nt.* °**ional,** *a.* ajjhāpanāyatta. °**ive,** *a.* uggahadāyaka. °**tor,** *n.* sikkhetu ; ajjhāpaka, *m.*

Educe, *v.t.* nīharati ; nikkaḍḍhati. *p.p.* nīhaṭa ; °ḍhita.

Edulcorate, *v.t.* ambilattam apaneti. *p.p.* apanīta°.

Eel, *n.* amarā, *f.*

Eerie, °**y,** *a.* atibhīruka.

Efface, *v.t.* lopeti ; apamajjati. *p.p.* lutta ; apamaṭṭha. °**ment,** *n.* lopa, *m.* apamajjana, *nt.*

Effect, *n.* 1. phala, *nt.* vipāka; nissanda, *m.* 2. attha, *m.* payojana, *nt.* 3. nipphatti, *f.* *v.t.* sādheti; sampādeti; nipphādeti. *p.p.* °dhita; °dita. **Of no —,** nipphala; niratthaka. **To take —,** phalituŋ; vipaccituŋ. **To what —,** kimatthāya. **°ive,** *a.* sādhaka; nipphādaka. **°ual,** *a.* phaluppādaka; kiccasādhaka. **°ually,** *adv.* saphalaŋ; amoghaŋ.

Effectuate, *v.t.* sādheti; sampādeti. *p.p.* sādhita; °dita.

Effeminate, *a.* dubbala; sukumāra; itthigatika; porissahīna. **°ly,** *adv.* itthigatikatāya.

Efferent, *a.* apavāhaka.

Effervesce, *v.i.* bubbulāyati. *p.p.* °yita. **°nce,** *n.* bubbuluppādana, *nt.*

Effete, *a.* jiṇṇa; dubbala.

Efficacy, *n.* sāmatthiya, *nt.* pabhāva, *m.* **°ious,** *a.* pabala; samattha; pahoṇaka; phaladāyaka.

Efficient, *a.* kiccasādhaka; kammakkhama. **°ncy,** *n.* nepuñña; kosalla, *nt.* kammakkhamatā, *f.*

Effigy, *n.* paṭimā, *f.* paṭibimba; paṭirūpa, *nt.*

Effloresce, *v.i.* 1. pupphati; 2. vikasati; 3. cuṇṇattaŋ yāti. *p.p.* pupphita; °sita; °yāta. **°nce,** *n.* 1. pupphana; vikasana, *nt.* 2. sukhumattagamana, *nt.*

Effluence, *n.* 1. pasavana; niggamana; 2. (āloka-) vipphuraṇa, *nt.* **°ent,** *a.* sandamāna. *n.* upagaṅgā; mātikā, *f.*

Effluvium, *n.* ghāyana, *nt.* (duggandha-) vāta, *m.*

Efflux, *n.* pavāha; pasava, *m.* sandana, *nt.*

Effort, *n.* ussāha; vāyāma; uyyāma; uyyoga, *m.* viriya, *nt.* **°less,** *a.* nibbiriya; nirīha. **Right —,** sammāvāyāma, *m.* **Wrong —,** micchāvāyāma, *m.*

Effrontery, *n.* pāgabbhiya, *nt.* nillajjatā, *f.*

Effulgence, *n.* juti; ābhā; pabhā; ditti, *f.* obhāsa; mayūkha; kiraṇa, *m.* **°gent,** *a.* jutimantu; bhāsura; pabhassara.

Effuse, *v.t.* sandeti; vāheti; osiñcati. *p.p.* °dita; vāhita; ositta. **°ion,** *n.* nisecana; paggharāpana, *nt.* **°ive,** *a.* avabodhaka; vitthāraka.

Egg, *n.* aṇḍa; bīja, *nt.* *v.t.* ussāheti; uttejeti. *p.p.* °hita; °jita. **°plant,** vātiṅgaṇa, *m.* **°shaped,** *a.* aṇḍākāra.

Ego, *n.* atta; jīva, *m.* **°ism,** *n.* attadiṭṭhi, *f.* attakāmatā, *f.*

Egotism, *n.* ahaṅkāra, *m.* mamatta; mamāyitatta, *nt.*

Egotist, *n.* attābhimānī; mamāyanayutta, *m.* **°ic,** *a.* ahaṅkārayutta; attatthagavesī. **°ically,** *adv.* attakāmatāya.

Egregious, *a.* pamāṇātikkanta; adhikatara. **°ly,** *adv.* accantaŋ; balavataraŋ. **°ness,** *n.* atisaya, *m.* balavataratta, *nt.*

Egress, *n.* niggama, *m.* nikkhamana; nissaraṇa, *nt.* *v.i.* nikkhamati; nissarati. *p.p.* nikkhanta; nissaṭa.

Eh, *ind.* kiŋ? kim etaŋ?

Eidolon, bhūta; pisāca, *m.*

Eight, *a.* *n.* aṭṭha; 3. **°een,** aṭṭhārara; 3. **°fold,** *a.* aṭṭhavidha;

aṭṭhaguṇa. °**th**, *a.* aṭṭhama. — **hundred**, aṭṭhasata, *nt.* **Group of** —, aṭṭhaka, *nt.* **In — ways**, aṭṭhadhā, *adv.*

Eighty, *a.* asīti, *f.* °**four**, caturāsīti, *f.* °**ieth**, *a.* asītima. °**two**, dvāsīti, *f.* °**nine**, ekūnanavuti, *f.*

Eirenicon, *n.* sāmopāya, *m.* sāmayojanā, *f.*

Either, *adv. conj.* vā; atha vā. *adj.* ubhaya. *pron.* dvīsu eko.

Ejeculate, *v.t.* udāneti ; sahasā uccāreti. *p.p.* °nita ; °rita. °**ion**, *n.* sahasā udīraṇa, *nt.*

Eject, *n.* parikappa, *m. v.t.* nīharati ; nikkaḍḍhati ; paṇāmeti ; apanudati. *p.p.* nīhaṭa ; °ḍhita ; °mita : °dita. °**ion**, *n.* nīharaṇa ; apanudana, *nt.* °**ive**, *a.* nīharaka ; apakaḍḍhaka.

Eke, *v.t.* 1. abhivaḍḍheti ; 2. jīvikaŋ sampādeti. *p.p.* °ḍhita ; °pitajīvika.

Elaborate, *a.* vicitta ; suṭṭhuniṭṭhāpita. *v.t.* āyāsena sādheti *or* niṭṭhāpeti. °**ly**, *adv.* mahussāhena ; bavhāyāsena. °**ion**, *n.* vicittakaraṇa; āyāsa-sādhita, *nt.*

Elan, *n.* sahasā-pavisana, *nt.*

Elapse, *v.i.* acceti ; atikkamati. *n.* accaya, *m.* **By the** —, accayena, *adv.* °**ed**, *a.* atikkanta.

Elastic, *a.* pakatyavijahaka. °**ity**, *n.* 1. pakatyavijahana; 2. namanīyatta, *nt.*

Elate, *v.t.* unnāmeti ; pamodeti ; dappitaŋ karoti. *p.p.* °mita ; °dita. adj. 1. pamudita ; pahaṭṭha ; 2. gabbita ; dappita. °**ion**, *n.* 1. pamoda ; pahāsa, *m.* 2. dappa ; abhimāna, *m.*

Elbow, *n.* kappara, *m. v.t.* kapparena apaneti. *p.p.* °nīta. °**grease**, *n.* 1. balavamajjana, *nt.* 2. bāḷhakammakaraṇa, *nt.* °**room**, pahoṇakokāsa, *m.*

Elder, *a.* jeṭṭha ; vuddha ; vuddhatara. *n.* thera, *m.* — **brother**, jeṭṭhabhātu, *m.* °**ly**, *a.* vayovuddha. — **sister**, jeṭṭhabhaginī, *f.*

Eldest, *a.* vuddhatama ; jeṭṭhatama.

Eldritch, *a.* virūpa ; bībhaccha.

Elect, *a.* uccinita ; sammata. *v.t.* uccināti ; vareti. *p.p.* °nita ; varita. °**ion**, *n.* uccinana ; varaṇa, *nt.* °**or**, *n.* uccinitu, *m.* °**orate**, *n.* uccinakagaṇa ; uccinanāyatta-padesa, *m.* °**ress**, *n.* uccinanakā, *f.*

Electric, *n.* vijjubala, *nt.* adj. vijjumaya. °**ity**, *n.* vijjubala, *nt.* vijjutā, *f.*

Electrify, *v.t.* vijjusaŋyuttaŋ karoti. °**ication**, *n.* vijjugoga, *m.*

Electrocution, *n.* vijjuyogena māraṇa, *nt.*

Electrology, *n.* vijjuvijjā, *f.*

Electron, *n.* vijju-aṇu, *m.*

Electroplate, *v.t.* vijjubalena (suvaṇṇādiŋ) lepeti. *p.p.* °litta.

Electrum, *n.* suvaṇṇa-rajatamissaṇa, *nt.*

Electuary, *n.* leyyosadha, *nt.*

Elegance, *n.* lāvañña, *nt.* sobhā ; sulalitatā, *f.* °**nt**, *a.* cāru ; sundara ; surūpa ; lāvaññayutta. °**ntly**, *adv.* sulalitaŋ.

Elegiac, *a. n.* 1. karuṇāpuṇṇa ; 2. sokākula.

Elegy, *n.* sokagīta, *nt.* °**ist**, *n.* sokagītaracaka, *m.* °**ise**, *v.t.* sokagītaŋ racayati.

Element, *n.* dhātu, *f.* mahābhūta, *nt.* — **of cohesion**, āpodhātu, *f.* — **of extension**, paṭhavīdhātu, *f.* — **of heat**, tejodhātu, *f.* — **of motion**, vāyodhātu, *f.* — **of space**, ākāsadhātu, *f.*

Elementary, *a.* mūlika ; amissa. °**ily**, *adv.* mūlikavasena.

Elenchus, *n.* matipaccakkhāna, *nt.*

Elenctic, *a.* paṭipucchāyatta.

Elephant, *n.* hatthī ; mātaṅga ; kuñjara ; gaja ; vāraṇa ; karī ; dantī ; ibha, *m.* °**driver**, hatthāroha, *m.* °**keeper**, hatthigopaka, *m.* °**rug**, hatthatthara, *m.* °**stable**, hatthisālā, *f.* °**tamer**, hatthācariya ; hatthidamaka, *m.* °**training**, hatthisippa, *nt.* °**trappings**, hatthābharaṇa, *nt.* hatthikappanā, *f.* — **to be trained**, hatthidamma, *m.* **Female** —, hatthinī ; kareṇu, *f.* **Young** —, kalabha ; gajapotaka, *m.*

Elephantiasis, *n.* sīpada, *nt.* — **of the scrotum**, vātaṇḍa, *nt.*

Elevate, *v.t.* 1. unnāmeti ; ussāpeti ; 2. pahaŋseti. *p.p.* °mita ; °pita ; °sita. °**ion**, *n.* unnati, *f.* udaya, *m.* seṭṭhattapāpaṇa, *nt.*

Eleven, *a. n.* ekādasa ; 3. °**th**, *a.* ekādasama.

Elf, *n.* pisāca ; vetāla, *m.*

Elicit, *v.t.* nikkhāmeti ; āvīkāreti. *p.p.* °mita ; °kārita.

Elide, *v.t.* lopeti ; paccuddharati. *p.p.* lutta ; °ddhaṭa.

Eligible, *a.* ādeya ; gāhiya ; kammakkhama ; uccinitabba.

Eliminate, *v.t* nāseti ; lopeti ; apaneti. *p.p.* nāsita ; lutta ; apanīta. °**ion**, *n.* nāsana ; paccuddharaṇa.

Elision, *n.* (akkhara-) lopa, *m.*

Elite, *n.* sundaratara-bhāga, *m.*

Elixir, *n.* rasāyana ; amatapāna, *nt.*

Elk, *n.* gokaṇṇa, *m.*

Ellipse, *n.* aṇḍākāra-maṇḍala, *nt.*

Ellipsis, *n.* luttapada ; peyyāla, *nt.*

Elliptic, *a.* 1. aṇḍākāra ; 2. saṅkhitta. °**al**, *a.* ajjhāharitabba ; peyyālayutta.

Elocution, *n.* vacanapaṭutā ; cittakathikatā, *f.* °**ary**, *a.* cittakathāyatta. °**ist**, *n.* cittakathī ; vyattakathika, *m.*

Eloge, *n.* mataguṇakathana, *nt.*

Elongate, *v.t.* vitanoti ; āyataŋ karoti. *p.p.* vitata ; āyatīkata. °**ed**, āyata ; dīgha. °**ion**, *n.* āyatakaraṇa ; añchana, *nt.*

Elope, *v.i.* raho palāyati. *p.p.* °yita. °**ment**, rahopalāyana, *nt.*

Eloquent, *a.* vāgīsa ; kathāpaṭu. °**ly**, *adv.* vāgīsatāya. °**nce**, *n.* cittakathikatta, *nt.*

Else, *adv.* api ca ; itarathā. adj. apara ; itara ; añña. °**where**, *adv.* aññattha. **What** —, kim aññaŋ ?

Elucidate, *v.t.* vyākhyāti ; vyākaroti. *p.p.* °khyāta ; °kata. °**ion**, *n.* vissajjana ; vivaraṇa, *nt.* °**tor**, *n.* vissajjaka ; vyākhyātu, *m.* °**ive**, *a.* pakāsaka ; visadattakara.

Elude, *v.t.* raho apasarati. *p.p.* °apasaṭa.

Elusion, *n.* raho niggamana, *nt.*

Elusory, Elusive, *a.* apakkamanasīla ; pamohaka ; vañcaka. °**siveness,** *n.* apagamana ; pamohana ; sāṭheyya, *nt.*

Elysium, *n.* sagga ; devaloka, *m.*

Emaciate, *v.i.* hāyati ; khīyati ; kisībhavati. *p.p.* hīna ; khīṇa ; °bhūta. *v.t.* khepeti ; hāpeti ; kisaŋ karoti. *p.p.* khepita ; hāpita ; kisīkata. °**ion,** *n.* khīyana ; kisatta, *nt.*

Emanate, *v.i.* niccharati ; pabhavati. *p.p.* °rita ; pabhūta. °**ion,** *n.* pabhava, *m.* niccharaṇa, *nt.*

Emancipate, *v.t.* (bandhanā *or* dāsattā) moceti ; vimoceti ; uddharati. *p.p.* mocita ; uddhaṭa. °**ion,** *n.* mutti ; vimutti, *f.* mokkha, *m.* °**tor,** *n.* vimocaka ; muttidāyaka, *m.*

Emasculate, *v.t.* 1. aṇḍāni uddharati ; bījam uppāṭeti ; pumbhāvaŋ nāseti ; 2. dabbalīkaroti. *p.p.* uddhaṭaṇḍa ; uppāṭitabīja ; nāsitapumbhāva ; °kata. °**ion,** *n.* bījuddharaṇa, *nt.*

Embalm, *v.t.* osadhehi lepeti ; matadehaŋ surakkhitaŋ karoti. *p.p.* osadhalitta. °**ment,** *n.* osadhālepa, *m.* chavasaṅkharaṇa, *nt.*

Embank, *v.t.* āḷiŋ *or* setuŋ bandhati. *p.p.* āḷibaddha ; setubaddha. °**ment,** *n.* āḷibandhana, *nt.*

Embargo, *n.* videsīya-nāvāsañcāra-nivāraṇa, *nt.* *v.t.* videsīyanāvāsañcāraŋ nivāreti *or* nisedheti. *p.p.* nivārita-nāvāsañcāra.

Embark, *v.i.* nāvam abhiruhati *or* āruhati. *p.p.* ārūḷhanāva. *v.t.* nāvāyaŋ bhaṇḍam āropeti. °**ation,** *n.* 1. nāvāruhaṇa ; 2. nāvāropaṇa, *nt.*

Embarrass, *v.t.* ubbāḷhayati ; sambādheti ; vikkhepeti ; sambhameti. *p.p.* ubbāḷha ; °dhita ; °pita ; sambhanta. °**ing,** *a.* bādhaka ; paripanthakara. °**ment,** *n.* sambādha ; sambhama, *m.*

Embassy, *n.* 1. rājadūteyya, *nt.* 2. dūtamaṇḍala, *nt.* 3. dūtanivāsa, *m.*

Embattle, *v.t.* senāvyūhaŋ racayati ; yuddhāya sajjeti. *p.p.* racita° ; °jita.

Embed, *v.t.* khacati ; antopaveseti. *p.p.* khacita ; °sita.

Embellish, *v.t.* bhūseti ; sobheti ; pasādheti ; maṇḍeti. *p.p.* °sita ; sobhita ; °dhita ; °ḍita. °**ment,** *n.* bhūsana ; maṇḍana, *nt.*

Ember, *n.* jalitaṅgāra, *m.*

Embezzle, *v.t.* theyyena attano santakaŋ karoti. °**ment,** theyyāvahāra, *m.*

Embitter, *v.t.* tittaŋ *or* āyāsajanakaŋ karoti ; vajjaŋ daḷhayati. °**ment,** *n.* arucikaraṇa, *nt.* āyāsa, *m.*

Emblazon, *v.t.* vaŋsaciṇhāni aṅketi. *p.p.* aṅkitavaŋsaciṇha.

Emblem, *n.* 1. lañchana ; ciṇha, *nt.* 2. patākā, *f.* °**atical,** *a.* visesadīpaka.

Emblic myrobalan, *n.* āmalakī, *f.*

Embody, *v.t.* dehavantaŋ karoti. *p.p.* °kata. °**iment,** *n.* sarīritā, *f.* dehanimmāṇa, *nt.*

Embolden, *v.t.* ussāheti ; nibbhayaŋ karoti. *p.p.* °hita ; °kata.

Embolism, *n.* rudhirarundhana, *nt.*

Embonpoint, *n.* (itthīnaŋ) thullatā ; pīvaratā, *f.*

Emborder, *v.t.* dasāyuttaŋ karoti. *p.p.* °kata.

Embosom, *v.t.* āliṅgati ; upagūhati ; aṅke nidahati. *p.p.* āliṅgita ; °hita ; °nihita.

Emboss, *v.t.* rūpāni ukkirati *or* uṭṭhāpeti. *p.p.* ukkiritarūpa ; uṭṭhāpitarūpa.

Embowel, *v.t.* antāni nīharati ; *p.p.* nīhaṭanta.

Embower, *v.t.* kuñjayuttaŋ karoti. *p.p.* °kata.

Embrace, *n.* āliṅgana ; parissajana, *nt. v.t.* āliṅgati ; parissajati ; upagūhati. *p.p.* °gita ; parissaṭṭha ; upagūḷha.

Embranchment, *n.* sākhāvasena vibhajana, *nt.*

Embrangle, *v.t.* jaṭeti ; ākulīkaroti. *p.p.* jaṭita ; °kata.

Embrasure, *n.* pākāracchidda, *nt.*

Embrocate, *v.t.* (uṇhodakena) tāpeti *or* sedeti. *p.p.* tāpita ; sedita. °**ion**, *n.* tāpana ; sedana, *nt.*

Embroider, *v.t.* sūcikammena alaṅkaroti. *p.p.* °kata. °**ry**, *nt.* sūcikammālaṅkāra, *m.*

Embroil, *v.t.* saṅkhobheti ; āloleti. *p.p.* °bhita ; ālolita. °**ment**, saṅkhobha, *m.* kalahe niyojana, *nt.*

Embrown, *v.t.* piṅgalaŋ karoti.

Embryo, *n.* 1. kalalarūpa, *nt.* gabbhagata, *m.* 2. paṭhamārambha, *m.* °**logy**, *n.* gabbhaseyyakavijjā, *f.*

Emend, *v.t.* dose apaneti. *p.p.* apanītadosa. °**ation**, *n.* saŋsodhana ; paṭisaṅkharaṇa, *nt.* °**ator**, *n.* saŋsodhaka ; saṅkhāraka, *m.*

Emerald, *n.* 1. marakata (maṇi), *m.* 2. marakatavaṇṇa, *m.*

Emerge, *v.i.* ummujjati ; pātubhavati. *p.p.* °jita ; °bhūta. °**nce**, *n.* ummujjana, *nt.* °**ncy**, *n.* accāyika, *nt.* āpadā, *f.*

Emeritus, *a.* sagārava-vissāma, *m.*

Emersion, 1. *n.* ummujjana ; uggamana, *nt.* 2. pātubhāva, *m.*

Emery, *n.* lohamajjakasilā, *f.*

Emetic, *n. a.* vamathukara ; vamāpaka, *nt.*

Emigrant, *n.* sadesacāgī, *m.*

Emigrate, *v.i.* desantaravāsaŋ yāti. °**ion**, *n.* sadesapariccāga, *m.*

Eminence, *n.* pamukhatā ; uḷāratā, *f.* seṭṭhabhāva, *m.*

Eminent, *a.* seṭṭha ; visiṭṭha ; ukkaṭṭha ; pamukha. °**ly**, *adv.* visiṭṭhākārena.

Emissary, *n.* dūta ; sandesahara, *m.*

Emission, *n.* virecana; muñcana, nicchāraṇa, *nt.* vissaṭṭhi, *f.*

Emit, *v.t.* pamuñcati ; nicchāreti. *p.p.* pamutta ; °rita. — **a smell**, vāti. °**smoke**, padhūpāyati. °**ting**, *a.* vissajjaka ; muñcaka.

Emmet, see **Ant**.

Emolument, *n.* āya ; lābha ; udaya, *m.*

Emotion, *n.* cittavega ; cittabhāva, *m.* °**al**, *a.* cittavegāyatta ; bhāvavisayaka.

Emotive, *a.* cittakkhobhaka ; cittavegajanaka.

Emperor, *n.* adhirāja, *m.*

Emphasis, *n.* avadhāraṇa ; uccakathana, *nt.*

Emphasize, *v.t.* daḷhayati ; avadhāreti ; gambhīram uccāreti. *p.p.* °yita ; °rita.

Emphatic, *a.* daḷha ; nicchita ; avadhāraṇīya. °**ally,** *adv.* sāvadhāraṇaŋ.

Empire, *n.* adhirajja, *nt.*

Empiric, *a.* paricayāyatta, *n.* vejjapatirūpaka, *m.* °**al,** *a.* satthaviruddha. °**ally,** *adv.* satthavirodhena. °**ism,** *n.* kuvejjakamma, *nt.*

Emplacement, *n.* patiṭṭhāpana, *nt.*

Emplane, *v.i.* vyomayānam āruhati. *p.p.* °ārūḷha.

Employ, *v.t.* 1. niyojeti ; adhikaroti ; 2. anuyuñjati. *p.p.* °jita ; °kata ; anuyutta. °**ee,** *n.* niyutta, *m.* °**er,** *n.* niyojaka, *m.* °**ment,** *n.* anuyuñjana, *nt.* vyāpāra, *m.* jīvikāvutti, *f.*

Empoison, *v.t.* 1. visayuttaŋ karoti ; 2. tuṭṭhiŋ nāseti. *p.p.* °kata ; nāsitatuṭṭhi.

Emporium, *n.* vāṇijasamosaraṇa; puṭabhedana, *nt.*

Empower, *v.t.* adhikārabalaŋ deti. *p.p.* dinnādhikārabala.

Empress, *n.* adhirājinī, *f.*

Empressment, *n.* sohajjadassana, *nt.*

Empty, *a.* suñña ; tuccha ; ritta. *v.t.* riñcati ; suññaŋ karoti. *p.p.* ritta ; suññakata. °**handed,** *a.* tucchahattha. °**headed,** *a.* mandapañña. °**iness,** *n.* suññatā, *f.* tucchatta ; rittatta, *nt.*

Empurple, *v.t.* lohitavaṇṇaŋ karoti. *p.p.* katalohitavaṇṇa.

Empyrean, *n.* uddhantama-devaloka, *m.* adj. taddevalokāyatta.

Emulate, *v.t.* unnatim icchati. °**ion,** *n.* unnatikāmatā, *f.* °**ive,** *a.* unnatipāpaka *or* unnatikāma. °**tor,** *n.* unnatikāmī, *m.*

Emulsion, *n.* telodakamissana, *nt.* khīravaṇṇa-saŋyoga, *m.*

Enable, *v.t.* samatthaŋ *or* sakyaŋ karoti. *p.p.* samatthakata.

Enact, *v.t.* paññāpeti ; ādisati ; sammannati. *p.p.* °pita ; ādiṭṭha ; sammata. °**ment,** *n.* paññatti ; sikkhā ; vavatthā, *f.*

Enamel, *n.* bāhiramaṭṭha, *nt.* *v.t.* bāhiramaṭṭhena lepeti. *p.p.* °ṭhalepita.

Enamour, *v.t.* anurañjeti. *p.p.* °rañjita *or* anuratta. °**ed,** *a.* āsattacitta ; paṭibaddhacitta.

Encage, *v.t.* pañjare pakkhipati. *p.p.* °khitta.

Encamp, *v.t.* senaŋ niveseti ; khandhāvāraŋ bandhati. *p.p.* nivesitasena ; baddha°. °**ment,** *n.* senāsannivesa, *m.*

Encase, *v.t.* kose pakkhipati ; pariyonahati. *p.p.* °khitta ; °naddha. °**ment,** *n.* pariyonahana ; kosenāvaraṇa, *nt.*

Encash, *v.t.* jātarūpataŋ parivatteti. *p.p.* °tita.

Enceinte, *n.* vatiparikkhepa, *m.* adj. sañjātagabbhā.

Encephalic, *a.* matthaluṅgāyatta.

Encephalon, *n.* matthaluṅga, *m.*

Enchafe, *v.t.* ghaŋsetvā usmīkaroti. *p.p.* °kata.

Enchain, *v.t.* nigaḷehi bandhati. *p.p.* nigaḷabaddha. °**ment,** *n.* nigaḷabandhana, *nt.*

Enchant, *v.t.* moheti ; vasīkaroti. *p.p.* mohita ; vasīkata. °**er,** *n.* vasavattaka ; mohaka, *m.* °**ing,** *a.* pamohaka; manohara. °**ment,** *n.* mohana ; vasīkaraṇa, *nt.* °**ress,** *n.* vasavattikā ; yoginī, *f.*

Enchase, *v.t.* khacati. *p.p.* khacita.

Enchiridion, *n.* hatthasāragantha, *m.*

Encircle, *v.t.* parikkhipati ; parivāreti. *p.p.* °khitta ; parivuta *or* °vārita.

Enclasp, *v.t.* āliṅgati ; upagūhati. *p.p.* °gita ; °gūhita.

Enclitic, *a.n.* padapūraka; visesattha-rahita.

Enclose, *v.t.* āvarati ; pidahati ; antokaroti. *p.p.* āvaṭa ; pihita ; °kata. °**ure,** *n.* parikkhepa, *m.* koṭṭhaka, *nt.*

Encloud, *v.t.* meghehi chādeti. *p.p.* meghacchanna.

Encomiast, *n.* vandibhaṭṭa ; thutipāṭhaka, *m.*

Encomium, *n.* silāghā ; vandī, *f.*

Encompass, *v.t.* 1. samantato āvarati ; 2. anupariyāti. *p.p.* °āvaṭa ; °yāta. °**ment,** *n.* anuparigamana ; samantāvaraṇa, *nt.*

Encore, *ind.* puna pi ; bhīyo pi.

Encounter, *n.* 1. saṅgama ; sammukhībhāva, *m.* 2. saṅgāma, *m.* *v.t.* samāgacchati ; sammukhī hoti ; paṭippharati. *p.p.* samāgata ; °bhūta ; °rita.

Encourage, *v.t.* ussāheti ; uttejeti ; upatthambheti. *p.p.* °hita ; °jita ; °bhita. °**ment,** *n.* uttejana, *nt.* upatthambha, *m.* °**ing,** *a.* ussāhajanaka.

Encroach, *v.i.* parimaddati ; adhammena pariggaṇhāti. *p.p.* °dita ; °gahita. °**ment,** *n.* nikatiyā pariggaha, *m.*

Encrust, *v.t.* paṭalena chādeti. *p.p.* paṭalacchanna. °**ed,** *a.* ghanībhūta.

Encumber, *v.t.* uparodheti ; sambādheti. *p.p.* °dhita. °**brance,** *n.* 1. uparodha, *m.* bādhā, *f.* 2. bhāra, *m.*

Encyclical, *a.* 1. vaṭṭula ; 2. bahusādhāraṇa.

Encyclopaedia, *n.* nikhilakosa, *m.* °**dic,** *a.* sabbavidū ; sabbasatthavisārada.

End, *n.* 1. anta ; pariyanta, *m.* koṭi, *f.* 2. osāna ; pariyosāna ; niṭṭhāna, *nt.* 3. nāsa ; viccheda, *m.* nivutti, *f.* 4. adhippetattha, *m.* *v.t.* 1. osāpeti ; niṭṭhāpeti. 2. nivatteti. *p.p.* °pita ; nivattita. *v.i.* niṭṭhāti ; osānaŋ yāti. *p.p.* niṭṭhita ; °yāta. °**ing,** *n.* antakiriyā, *f.* niṭṭhāna, *nt.* °**less,** *a.* ananta ; aparimita. °**most,** *a.* sabbantima.

Endanger, *v.t.* antarāyaŋ pāpeti. *p.p.* °pāpita.

Endear, *v.t.* piyāyati. *p.p.* °yita. °**ment,** *n.* piyāyanā, *f.*

Endeavour, *v.i.* vāyamati ; ussahati ; parisakkati. *p.p.* °mita ; °hita ; °kita. *n.* vāyāma ; ussāha, *m.* payatana, *nt.* īhā, *f.*

Endemic, *a.* desa-jātivisayaka.

Endermic, *a.* tacavisayaka.

Endogamy, *n.* samajātikavivāha, *m.*

Endorse, *v.t.* piṭṭhiyaŋ likhati; paṭilikhati; daḷhayati. *p.p.* °likhita; °yita. °**ment,** *n.* paṭilikhana, *nt.*

Endow, *v.t.* dāyādaŋ deti; sanāthīkaroti; samaṅgīkaroti. *p.p.* dinnadāyāda; °kata. °**ed with,** yutta; sahagata; samupeta; samannāgata; sameta; sampanna, *a.* °**ment,** 1. dāyāda, *m.* 2. vuttisamappaṇa, *nt.*

Endue, *v.t.* pasādheti; samaṅgīkaroti. *p.p.* °dhita; °kata.

Endure, *v.t.* sahati; adhivāseti; titikkhati. *p.p.* sahita; °sita; °khita. °**able,** *a.* khamanīya; sayha. °**ance,** *n.* khamā; titikkhā; adhivāsanā, *f.* °**er,** *n.* sahitu; adhivāsaka, *m.* °**ing,** *a.* 1. sahamāna; 2. ciraṭṭhitika.

Enema, *n.* 1. vatthikamma; 2. vatthiyanta, *nt.*

Enemy, *n.* 1. ari; ripu; verī; sattu; disa; paccatthika; paccāmitta; amitta, *m.* 2. sattusenā, *f.*

Energetic, *a.* daḷhaparakkama; dhitimantu; ātāpī. °**ally,** *adv.* daḷhaviriyena.

Energize, *v.t.* pabalaŋ karoti. *p.p.* pabalīkata.

Energumen, *n.* 1. bhūtāviṭṭha; 2. daḷhagāhī, *m.*

Energy, *n.* viriya, *nt.* ussāha; uyyāma, *m.* satti, *f.* thāma, *m.*

Enervate, *v.t.* dubbalīkaroti. adj. dubbala; sattihīna. °**ion,** *n.* dubbalīkaraṇa, *nt.* balahāni, *f.* viriyakkhaya, *m.*

Enfeeble, *v.t.* sithilīkaroti; abalīkaroti. *p.p.* °kata.

Enfetter, *v.t.* saṅkhalikāhi bandhati. *p.p.* °kābaddha.

Enfold, *v.t.* oguṇṭheti; paliveṭheti. *p.p.* °ṭhita.

Enforce, *v.t.* 1. balena kāreti; 2. upatthambheti. *p.p.* °kārita, °bhita. °**ment,** *n.* **1.** pasayhavidhāna; 2. senābalaposaṇa, *nt.*

Enframe, *v.t.* kosakavāṭe pakkhipati. *p.p.* °pakkhitta.

Enfranchise, *v.t.* seripālanaŋ *or* uccinanādhikāraŋ deti. °**ment,** *n.* bhujissakaraṇa; uccinanādhikāradāna, *nt.*

Engage, *v.t.* payojeti; niyojeti. *v.i.* 1. anuyuñjati; 2. paṭiññaŋ deti. *p.p.* °jita; anuyutta; dinnapaṭiñña. °**ment,** *n.* 1. anuyuñjana, *nt.* 2. vivāhapaṭiññā, *f.* °**ing,** *a.* manohara; hadayaṅgama. °**ingly,** *adv.* manoharākārena.

Engender, *v.t.* uppādeti; nibbatteti; janeti. *p.p.* °dita; °tita; °janita.

Engine, *n.* yanta, *nt.* °**driver,** yantadhāvaka, *m.* °**er,** *n.* yantasippī, *m.* *v.i.* vidhānaŋ karoti; māpeti. *p.p.* katavidhāna.

Engird, Engirdle, *v.t.* parikkhipati; parito bandhati. *p.p.* °khitta; °baddha.

England, *n.* Āṅgaladesa, *m.*

English, *a.* Āṅgaladesīya. *n.* Āṅgalabhāsā, *f.*

Engorge, *v.t.* sagedhaŋ gilati. *p.p.* °gilita.

Engraft, *v.t.* ghaṭeti; ropeti. *p.p.* ghaṭita; ropita.

Engrain, *v.t.* bāḷhaŋ rañjeti. *p.p.* °rañjita, see *Ingrain.*

Engrave, *v.t.* rūpāni ukkirati; cundakammaŋ karoti. *p.p.* ukkiritarūpa; katacundakamma. °**ing,** *n.* ukkiraṇasippa; cundakamma, *nt.*

Engross, *v.t.* 1. vipulaŋ karoti; 2. sabbam ādāti; 3. vibhūtaŋ likhati. *p.p.* vipulīkata; °ādinna; °khita. °**er,** *n.* 1. sabbādayī; 2. sundaralekhaka, *m.* °**ment,** *n.* nissesagahaṇa, *nt.*

Engulf, *v.t.* osīdāpeti; nimujjāpeti. *p.p.* °pita. °**ment,** *n.* osīdāpana, *nt.*

Enhance, *v.t.* abhivaḍḍheti. *p.p.* °ḍhita. °**ment,** *n.* abhivaḍḍhana, *nt.*

Enhearten, see **Encourage.**

Enigma, *n.* gūḷhapañha, *m.* paheḷikā, *f.* °**tical,** *a.* gūḷhattha.

Enjoin, *v.t.* niyameti; āṇāpeti. *p.p.* °mita; °pita *or* āṇatta.

Enjoy, *v.t.* 1. abhiramati; nandati; 2. assādeti. upabhuñjati. *p.p.* abhirata; °dita. upabhutta; °**able,** *a.* upabhojiya; ramaṇīya; assādetabba. °**er,** *n.* upabhuñjaka; anubhavitu; assādetu, *m.* °**ment,** *n.* abhirati; assādanā, *f.* abhiramaṇa; anubhavana, *nt.*

Enkindle, *v.t.* ujjāleti; pajjāleti. *p.p.* °lita.

Enlace, *v.t.* paḷiveṭheti. *p.p.* °ṭhita.

Enlarge, *v.t.* vitthāreti; visālīkaroti. *p.p.* °rita; °kata. *v.i.* abhivaḍḍhati. *p.p.* °vuddha. °**ment,** *n.* abhivaḍḍhana; visālīkaraṇa, *nt.*

Enlighten, *v.t.* bodheti; dīpeti; sammādiṭṭhiŋ gaṇhāpeti. *p.p.* bodhita; dīpita; °pita. °**ed One,** Buddha; sabbaññū, *m.* °**ment,** *n.* sambodhi, *f.* saccāvabodha, *m.* °**ing,** *a.* bodhakara; mohanāsaka.

Enlink, *v.t.* saŋyojeti; ghaṭeti. *p.p.* °jita; ghaṭita.

Enlist, *v.t.* nāmāvaliŋ āropeti. *p.p.* °pita. °**ment,** *n.* nāmāvaliāropaṇa, *nt.*

Enliven, *v.t.* ussāheti; uttejeti; pahāseti. *p.p.* °hita; °jita; °sita *or* pahaṭṭha.

Enmesh, *v.t.* jālena bandhati. *p.p.* jālabaddha.

Enmity, *n.* vera, *nt.* upanāha; viddesa, *m.*

Ennoble, *v.t.* unnāmeti; seṭṭhattaŋ pāpeti. *p.p.* °mita; °pāpita. °**ment,** *n.* uccapadappatti, *f.*

Ennui, *n.* anabhirati; appossukkatā, *f.*

Enormity, *n.* 1. mahatta; 2. ghoratta; 3. dāruṇakamma, *nt.*

Enormous, *a.* 1. atimahanta; ativisāla; 2. atidāruṇa. °**ly,** *adv.* ativiya; accantaŋ. °**ness,** *n.* atimahantatta; atidāruṇatta, *nt.*

Enough, *a.* pahoṇaka. *adv.* alaŋ. *n.* pahoṇakamatta, *nt.*

Enounce, *v.t.* uccāreti; udīreti. *p.p.* °rita.

Enquire, *v.t.* āpucchati. *p.p.* °chita. °**ry,** *n.* āpucchā; upaparikkhā, *f.*

Enrage, *v.t.* kopeti; roseti. *p.p.* kopita; rosita *or* ruṭṭha.

Enrapture, *v.t.* paramānandaŋ pāpeti. *p.p.* °pāpita *or* patta.

Enravish, *v.t.* atīva hāseti. *p.p.* °hāsita *or* haṭṭha.

Enrich, *v.t.* aḍḍhaŋ *or* sadhanaŋ karoti. *p.p.* sadhanīkata.

Enrobe, *v.t.* cīvaraŋ pārupāti. *p.p.* pārutacīvara.

Enroll, Enrol, *v.t.* nāmāni aṅketi. *p.p.* aṅkitanāma. °**ment,** *n.* nāmaṅkana, *nt.*

Enroot, *v.t.* sammā ropeti. °**ed,** *a.* baddhamūla.

En route, *adv.* antarāmagge.

Ensanguine, *v.t.* lohitena makkheti. *p.p.* °khita.

Ensconce, *v.t.* nigūheti. *p.p.* nigūhita *or* nigūḷha.

Ensemble, *n.* sabbasamodhāna, *nt.*

Ensheath, *v.t.* kose pakkhipati. *p.p.* °khitta.

Enshrine, *v.t.* nidahati. *p.p.* nidahita *or* nihita.

Enshroud, *v.t.* paṭicchādeti ; āvarati. *p.p.* °dita *or* paṭicchanna ; āvaṭa.

Ensign, *n.* 1. dhaja, *m.* patākā, *f.* 2. visesalakkhaṇa, *nt.* 3. dhajaggāhī, *m.*

Enslave, *v.t.* dāsattaŋ neti. *p.p.* °nīta. °**ment,** *n.* dāsattapāpaṇa, *nt.*

Ensnare, *v.t.* pāsena bandhati. *p.p.* pāsabaddha.

Ensoul, *v.t.* jīvayuttaŋ karoti. *p.p.* °kata.

Ensue, *v.i.* phalavasena uppajjati ; anvāgacchati. *p.p.* °uppanna ; anvāgata. °**ing,** *a.* āgāmī.

Ensure, *v.t.* niccheti ; daḷhīkaroti ; saŋsayam apaneti. *p.p.* nicchita ; °kata ; apanītasaŋsaya.

Enswathe, *v.t.* uparūpari veṭheti. *p.p.* °veṭhita.

Entail, *v.t.* paramparāyattaŋ karoti. *n.* paramparayattatā, *f.*

Entangle, *v.t.* paḷiguṇṭheti ; jaṭeti ; vyākulīkaroti. *p.p.* °ṭhita ; jaṭita ; °kata. °**ed,** *a.* ākula ; saṅkiṇṇa. °**ment,** *n.* jaṭā ; vyākulatā, *f.*

Enter, *v.i.* pavisati ; ogāhati. *p.p.* paviṭṭha ; ogāḷha. *v.t.* 1. paveseti ; anto neti ; 2. nāmaŋ likhati. *p.p.* °sita ; antonīta ; likhitanāma.

Enteric, *a.* antāyatta ; sannipātika. — **fever,** *n.* sannipātajara, *m.*

Enterology, *n.* antavijjā, *f.*

Enteropathy, *n.* antarogā, *m.*

Enterprise, *n.* vyāpāra ; vāyāma, *m.* °**ing,** *a.* uṭṭhānasīla ; saussāha ; dhitimantu.

Entertain, *v.t.* 1. sakkaroti ; sammāneti ; 2. rameti ; 3. paṇidahati. *p.p.* sakkata ; °nita ; ramita ; °hita. °**er,** *n.* sakkāraka ; vinodetu, *m.* °**ing,** *a.* saṅgahakara ; atithipūjaka. °**ment,** *n.* 1. sakkāra, *m.* agghiya ; ātitheyya, *nt.* 2. ramāpana, *nt.* 3. ussava, *m.*

Enthral, *v.t.* vasīkaroti. *p.p.* °kata.

Enthrone, *v.t.* rajje *or* sīhāsane patiṭṭhāpeti. *p.p.* °pita. °**ment,** *n.* rajje patiṭṭhāpana, *nt.*

Enthusiasm, *n.* mahussāha ; saddhātisaya, *m.*

Enthusiast, *n.* mahussāhī, *m.* °**ic,** *a.* uyyutta ; saddhābahula. °**ically,** *adv.* accantānurāgena.

Entice, *v.t.* palobheti ; ussukkāpeti. *p.p.* °bhita ; °pita. °**ing,** *a.* palobhaka. °**ment,** *n.* palobhana ; mohana, *nt.*

Entire, *a.* sakala ; kevala ; asesa ; nissesa ; akhila ; nikhita ; anūna ; niravasesa. °**ly,** *adv.* asesaŋ ; nissesaŋ. °**ty,** *n.* asesatta ; sampuṇṇatta, *nt.*

Entitle, *v.t.* 1. nāmaŋ karoti ; 2. adhikāraŋ deti ; 3. niyameti. *p.p.* katanāma ; dinnādhikāra ; °mita.

Entity, *n.* 1. satta, *m.* 2. vijjamānatā ; pavatti, *f.*

Entomb, *v.t.* thūpe nidahati *or* nikhaṇati. *p.p.* °hita ; °nikhāta.

Entomology, *n.* kīṭakavijjā, *f.*

Entrails, *n.* antāni. *nt. pl.*

Entrain, *v.i.* dhūmarathaŋ pavisati ; *v.t.* dhūmaratham āropeti. *p.p.* °paviṭṭha ; °āropita.

Entrammel, *v.t.* bādheti ; ākulīkaroti. *p.p.* bādhita ; °kata.

Entrance, *n.* 1. dvāra ; mukha, *nt.* pavesa, *m.* 2. pavisana, *nt.*

Entrance, *v.t.* moheti ; muccheti. *p.p.* mohita ; mucchita. °**ment,** *n.* mohana, *nt.*

Entrant, *n.* pavesī ; adhikāragāhī, *m.*

Entrap, *v.t.* see **Ensnare.**

Entreat, *v.t.* upanibandhati ; abhiyācati. *p.p.* °baddha ; °cita. °**ing,** *a.* abhiyācanaka. °**y,** *n.* abhiyācanā ; upanibandhanā, *f.*

Entrée, *n.* pavesādhikāra, *m.*

Entrench, *v.t.* parikhāhi parikkhipati. *p.p.* °khitta. °**ment,** *n.* parikhāyojana, *nt.*

Entrepôt, *n.* vāṇijabhaṇḍāgāra, *nt.*

Entrust, *v.t.* samappeti ; bhāraŋ karoti. *p.p.* °pita ; katabhāra.

Entry, *n.* 1. pavesa, *m.* 2. potthake likhāpana, *nt.*

Entwine, *v.t.* gantheti ; saŋsibbeti. *p.p.* ganthita ; °bita.

Entwist, *v.t.* āveṭheti. *p.p.* °ṭhita.

Enucleate, *v.t.* visadīkaroti. *p.p.* °kata ; °**ion,** *n.* visadīkaraṇa, *nt.*

Enumerate, *v.t.* gaṇeti ; saṅkaleti. *p.p.* gaṇita ; °lita. °**ion,** *n.* saṅkhyā ; gaṇanā ; parikittanā, *f.*

Enunciate, *v.t.* uccāreti ; udāharati ; pakāseti. *p.p* °rita ; udāhaṭa ; °sita. °**ion,** *n.* udīraṇa ; parikittana, *nt.* °**ive,** *a.* parikittaka.

Envelop, *v.t.* paliveṭheti ; pariyonahati. *p.p.* °ṭhita ; pariyonaddha. °**ing,** *a.* paṭicchādaka. °**ment,** *n.* paṭicchādana, *nt.*

Envelope, *n.* paṭala ; āvaraṇa, *nt.* kosa, *m.* — **for a letter,** sāsanāvaraṇa, *nt.*

Envenom, *v.t.* visayuttaŋ karoti ; visena misseti. *p.p.* °kata ; visamissita.

Enviable, *a.* usūyuppādaka.

Envious, *a.* issāsahagata ; issukī ; usūyaka.

Environ, *v.t.* parikkhipati. *p.p.* °khitta. °**ment,** *n.* parikkhepa ; parisara, *m.*

Environs, *n.* sāmanta-padesa, *m.* samīpaṭṭhāna, *nt.*

Envisage, *v.t.* 1. abhimukhī bhavati ; 2. sahajabuddhiyā jānāti. *p.p.* °bhūta ; °ñāta.

Envoy, *n.* 1. rājadūta ; rajjaniyojita, *m.* 2. gantha-parisamāpana-vākya, *nt.*
Envy, *n.* issā ; usūyā ; akkhanti, *f.* *v.t.* usūyati. *p.p.* °yita.
Enwind, *v.t.* kuṇḍalākārena veṭheti. *p.p.* °ṭhita.
Enwomb, *v.t.* gabbhaŋ gaṇhāpeti. *p.p.* gāhitagabbha.
Enwrap, *v.t.* oguṇṭheti. *p.p.* °ṭhita.
Enwreathe, *v.t.* mālāhi āvarati *or* pilandheti. *p.p.* °āvaṭa ; °dhita.
Epaulet, *n.* (yodhānaŋ) aŋsabhūsā, *f.*
Ephemeral, *a.* 1. ekāhika ; 2. katipayadivasappavattaka.
Ephemeris, *n.* *p.* gahasañcāradīpaka, *m.*
Epic, *n.* mahākabba ; vīracarita, *nt.* yuddkakathā, *f.* °**al,** *a.* vīracaritāyatta.
Epicure, *n.* paṇītabhojī, *m.* °**an,** *n.a.* bhogāsatta ; udarambharī, *m.* °**ism,** *n.* 1. odarikatta, *nt.* 2. visayāsatti, *f.*
Epideictic, *a.* padassanāyābhimata.
Epidemic, *n.a.* saṅkantikaroga, *m.* °**al,** *a.* saṅkamanaka ; sabbavyāpī.
Epidemiology, *n.* saṅkantikarogavijjā, *f.*
Epidermic, *a.* bahittacāyatta, *nt.*
Epigastrium, *n.* bāhirodara, *nt.* udarūparibhāga, *m.*
Epiglottis, *n.* upajivhā, *f.*
Epigram, *n.* sāratthadīpakagāthāvali, *f.*
Epigraph, *n.* silālipi ; paṭimādilipi, *f.* °**ics,** purālipivijjā, *f.* °**ist,** *n.* purālipividū, *m.*
Epilepsy, *n.* apamāra ; apasmāra, *m.*
Epileptic, *n.* *a.* apamārarogī, *m.*
Epilogue, *n.* nigamanakathā, *f.*
Episcopacy, *n.* dhammādhikārīsabhā, *f.* °**pal,** *a.* dhammādhikārāyatta.
Episode, *n.* upakathā, *f.* upākhyāna, *nt.* °**ical,** *a.* pāsaṅgika ; antarāgata.
Epistle, *n.* sandesa, *m.*
Epistolary, *a.* sandesāyatta.
Epistoler, *n.* 1. sandesapāṭhaka, *m.* 2. sandesapesaka, *m.*
Epitaph, *n.* thūpalipi, *f.*
Epithalamium, *n.* vivāhagīta, *nt.*
Epithet, *n.* vevacana ; visesana, *nt.*
Epitome, *n.* samāhāra ; sārasaṅgaha, *m.* °**ize,** *v.t.* saṅkhipati ; samāseti. *p.p.* saṅkhitta ; °sita. °**ist,** *n.* saṅgahetu, *m.*
Epoch, *n.* yuga ; kālantara, °**al,** *a.* yugāyatta.
Eponym, *n.* ṭhānassa vā gottassa attano nāmadātā.
Epopee, *n.* vīrakathā-pajja, *nt.*
Equable, *a.* ekākāra ; samāna ; samacitta. °**ility,** *n.* samānatta ; nibbikāratta, *nt.*
Equal, *a.* samāna ; sadisa ; sabhāga ; sama ; tulya. *v.t.* sameti ; tulyataŋ neti. *p.p.* samita ; °nīta. *n.* tulyabala; paṭipuggala, *m.* — **to,** saṅkāsa, sannibha, *a.* — **in mind,** samacitta, *a.* °**ity,** *n.* samānatta ; tulyatta ; sadisatta, *nt.* °**ly,** *ad.* samaŋ ; sadisākārena. °**ize,** *v.t.* samāneti ; sadisaŋ karoti. *p.p.* °nita ; sadisīkata. °**ization,** *n.* samīkaraṇa ; sadisa āpādana, *nt.*

Equanimity, *n.* upekkhā ; majjhattatā, *f.* °**mous**, *a.* upekkhaka ; majjhatta.

Equate, *v.t.* samāneti ; samīkaroti. °**ion**, *n.* samīkaraṇa, *nt.*

Equator, *n.* bhūparidhi ; nirakkharekhā, *f.* °**ial**, *a.* nirakkhadesīya.

Equerry, *n.* assādhikārī, *m.*

Equestrian, *n.* assādhikārī ; assārohī, *m.* adj. hayavisayaka.

Equiangular, *a.* samakoṇaka.

Equidistant, *a.* samantara ; samadūra.

Equilateral, *a.* samaŋsika ; samabhuja.

Equilibrate, *v.t.* samabhāraŋ karoti. *v.i.* samabhārena vattati. *p.p.* °kata ; °tita.

Equilibrist, *n.* rajjugāmīnaṭa, *m.* °**brium**, *n.* samabhāratā, *f.*

Equine, *a.* assasadisa ; assāyatta.

Equinoctical, *a.* samarattindiva.

Equinox, *n.* samarattindivakāla, *m.*

Equip, *v.t.* sajjeti ; sannayhati ; kappeti ; (upakaraṇāni) sampādeti. *p.p.* sajjita ; sannaddha ; kappita ; °dita. °**age**, *n.* parivāra, *m.* °**ment**, *n.* 1. upakaraṇa ; parikkhāra, *nt.* 2. sajjanā ; kappanā, *f.*

Equipoise, *n.* samabhāratā ; antadvayasamatā, *f.* *v.t.* samabhāratāya vatteti. *p.p.* °tita.

Equipollent, *a.* tulyabala.

Equiponderate, *v.t.* samabhārataŋ neti. *p.p.* °nīta.

Equitable, *a.* dhammaṭṭha ; apakkhapātī. °**ness**, *n.* dhammānuvattanā, *f.* °**ly**, *adv.* dhammena ; samena.

Equitation, *n.* assārohaṇa, *nt.*

Equity, *n.* sādhāraṇatta, *nt.* yutti, *f.* ñāya, *m.*

Equivalence, *n.* 1. tulyagghatā ; 2. samabalatā, *f.* °**ent**, *a.* 1. samānattha ; 2. tulyabala. *n.* pariyāyavacana, *nt.*

Equivocal, *a.* yugalattha ; dvandattha ; sasandehattha. °**ity**, *n.* yugalatthatā, *f.*

Equivocate, *v.t.* pariyāyena katheti. °**ion**, *n.* pariyāyakathana, *nt.*

Equivoke, °**que**, *n.* sandiddhakathā ; vaṅkutti, *f.*

Era, *n.* kālapariccheda, *m.* vassaparimāṇa, *nt.*

Eradiate, *v.t.* obhāseti ; pabhāseti. *p.p.* °sita.

Eradicate, *v.t.* ucchindati ; ummūleti ; atthaṅgameti ; nāseti. *p.p.* ucchinna ; °lita ; °gamita ; nāsita. °**ion**, *n.* viddhaŋsana ; antagamana, ucchindana, *nt.*

Erase, *v.t.* apamajjati ; lopeti. *p.p.* apamaṭṭha ; lutta. °**er**, *n.* apamajjaka, *m.*

Erasure, *n.* apamajjanā, *f.*

Ere, *prep. conj.* pubbe ; purā ; puretaraŋ.—**long**, acirena, *adv.* — **now**, ito pubbe, *adv.*

Erebus, *n.* andhakāraniraya, *m.*

Erect, *a.* ujuṭṭhita ; anonata. *v.t.* 1. nimmiṇāti ; māpeti ; 2. ujukaŋ ṭhapeti. *p.p.* nimmita ; māpita ; °pita. °**ion**, *n.* nimmāṇa ; patiṭṭhāpana, *nt.* °**ly**, *adv.* ujukaŋ.

Eremite, *n.* tāpasa ; vanavāsī, *m.*

Erewhile, *adv.* adūrātīte.

Ergo, *adv.* tato ; tasmā.

Eristic, *a.* randhagavesī ; vivādasīlī, *m.*

Erne, *n.* garuḷa, *m.*

Erode, *v.t.* sanikaŋ vināseti. *p.p.* °sita.

Erosion, *n.* bhūmivilayana, *nt.* sanikavināsa, *m.*

Erotic, *a.* kāmuka ; visayalola. — **sentiment**, *n.* siṅgāra, *m.*

Erotomania, *n.* kāmamucchā ; kāmāturatā, *f.*

Err, *v.i.* khalati ; vippaṭipajjati ; uppathaŋ yāti. *p.p.* khalita ; vippaṭipanna ; °yāta. °**ing**, *a.* sāvajja ; uppathagāmī.

Errand, *n.* sandesa, *m.* sāsana, *nt.* dūteyya, *nt.*

Errant, *n.* paribbhamaka ; pariyaṭaka, *m.* °**ry**, *n.* pariyaṭana, *nt.*

Erratic, *a.* pariyaṭanasīla ; aniyatagatika.

Erratum, *n.* asuddhapāṭha (-saṅgaha), *m.*

Erroneous, *a.* sadosa ; ataccha. °**ly**, *adv.* micchā ; sadosaŋ ; atathaŋ.

Error, *n.* dosa ; pamāda, *m.* khalita, *nt.*

Erstwhile, *ad.* 1. purā ; pubbe ; 2. adūrātīte.

Eructation, *n.* 1. uggāra, *m.* 2. bhūdarito aṅgārādi-uggama, *m.*

Erudite, *a.* vyatta ; bahussuta. °**ion**, *n.* bāhusacca ; paṇḍicca ; veyyattiya, *nt.*

Erupt, *v.t.* uggirati ; ubbhijjati ; niggacchati. *p.p.* °rita ; ubbhinna ; niggata. °**ion**, *n.* uggiraṇa ; ubbhijjana ; niggamana, *nt.* °**ive**, *a.* ubbhijjanaka.

Erythema, *n.* kilāsakuṭṭha, *nt.*

Escalade, *n.* nisseṇīhi pākārārohaṇa, *nt.*

Escapade, *n.* bandhanamokkha, *m.*

Escape, *n.* mutti, *f.* nissaraṇa ; parimuccana ; palāyana, *nt.* *v.i.* parimuccati ; palāyati. *p.p.* parimutta ; °yita. °**ment**, *n.* nikkhamaṇa (-dvāra), *nt.*

Escarpment, *n.* papāta ; kaṭaka, *m.*

Eschatology, *n.* punaruppattivāda, *m.*

Escheat, *v.t.* rājasantakaŋ karoti. *p.p.* °kata.

Eschew, see **Avoid**.

Escort, *n.* rakkhakaparisā, *f.* *v.t.* ārakkhāya anugacchati.

Esculent, *a.* bhojanāraha.

Esoteric, *a.* gūḷha ; asabbasādhāraṇa.

Especial, *a.* visiṭṭha ; savisesa ; asādhāraṇa. °**ly**, *adv.* visesena.

Espionage, *n.* caravutti, *f.*

Esplanade, *n.* nagaropavana, *nt.*

Espouse, *v.t.* 1. āvāha-vivāhaŋ karoti ; 2. vāreyyapaṭiññaŋ deti ; 3. anupāleti. *p.p.* kataāvā° ; dinnavāre° ; °lita.

Esprit, *n.* cāturiya ; paṭibhāṇa, *nt.*

Espy, *v.t.* 1. dūrato passati ; 2. randhaŋ gavesati. *p.p.* °diṭṭha ; gavesitarandha.

Esquire, *n.* 1. ayya ; ayyaputta, *m.* 2. sannaddhayodha ; senādhipasevaka, *m.*

Essay, *n.* 1. ussāha ; 2. navārambha ; 3. nibandha, *m.* *v.t.* 1. ārabhati ; 2. ussahati ; 3. thāmam upaparikkhati. *p.p.* āraddha ; °khitathāma. °**ist,** *n.* nibandhakārī, *m.*

Essence, *n.* 1. sāra ; maṇḍa, *m.* ojā, *f.* 2. sāraŋsa ; piṇḍattha, *m.*

Essential, *a.* āvassaka ; sārabhūta. °**ly,** *adv.* sārato ; avassam eva.

Establish, *v.t.* patiṭṭhāpeti ; saṇṭhapeti. *p.p.* °pita. °**ment,** *n.* 1. patiṭṭhāpana, *nt.* 2. āyatana, *nt.* 3. kuṭumbasaṇṭhāpana, *nt.*

Estate, *n.* 1. avatthā ; dasā, *f.* 2. sampatti, *f.* vibhava, *m.* 3. kulatanti, *f.* pettikadhana, *nt.* 4. ārāmavatthu, *nt.* ropitabhūmi, *f.* 5. ṭhānantara, *nt.*

Esteem, *n.* gārava, *m.* bahumāna, *nt.* *v.t.* sammāneti ; sambhāveti. *p.p.* °nita ; °vita.

Estimate, *n.* vayalekhana ; vayanirūpana, *nt.* *v.t.* vayaŋ nirūpeti *or* pamāṇeti. *p.p.* nirūpitavaya. °**ion,** *n.* 1. gārava, *m.* 2. agghanirūpaṇa, *nt.*

Estival, *a.* gimhika.

Estivate, *v.t.* gimhānam atikkāmeti. *p.p.* atikkantagimhāna.

Estrade, *n.* ussāpita-vedikā, *f.*

Estrange, *v.t.* virodheti ; viyojeti. *p.p.* °dhita ; °jita. °**ment,** *n.* viyojana ; bhedana, *nt.*

Estuary, *n.* 1. mahānadīmukha, *nt.* 2. thalantaragata-samudda, *m.*

Etcetera, *n. pl.* ādika ; pabhutika ; iccādi, *m.* ādayo, *pl.*

Etch, *v.t.* muddaṇāya chāyārūpe nipphādeti.

Eternal, *a.* dhuva ; sassata ; anādyanta ; avipariṇāma. °**ly,** *adv.* niccaŋ ; dhuvaŋ ; sassataŋ. °**ism,** *n.* sassata-diṭṭhi, *f.* °**ist,** *n.* sassatavādī, *m.*

Eternity, *n.* sassati ; niccatā, *f.*

Eternize, *v.t.* niccataŋ pāpeti. *p.p.* °pāpita.

Etesian, *n.* pacchimuttaravāta, *m.*

Ether, *n.* ākāsadhātu, *f.* °**ic,** °**eal,** *a.* ākāsadhātvāyatta.

Ethic(s), *a. n.* 1. nītisattha, *nt.* 2. ācāravidhi ; guṇadhamma, *m.* °**al,** *a.* 1. nītivisayaka ; 2. sīlāyatta. °**ally,** *adv.* guṇadhammavasena.

Ethnic, °**al,** *a.* 1. māṇavajātivisayaka ; 2. bhinnadesīya.

Ethnography, *n.* vijjānukūlamāṇavapabheda-dīpana, *nt.*

Ethnology, *n.* māṇavajātivijjā, *f.* °**ic,** *a.* māṇavavijjāyatta. °**ist,** *n.* māṇavavijjāvidū, *m.*

Ethology, *n.* cariyāvisesavijjā, *f.*

Ethos, *n.* cariyāvisesa, *m.*

Etiolate, *v.t.* paṇḍuvaṇṇaŋ *or* uppaṇḍukataŋ pāpeti. *p.p.* °pāpita.

Etiology, *n.* rogaviniccaya, *m.*

Etiquette, *n.* cārittavidhi, *m.* sadācāra-paddhati, *f.*

Etymology, *n.* nirutti ; saddavyuppatti, *f.* °**ical,** *a.* niruttisatthāyatta. °**ist,** *n.* neruttika ; niruttikusala, *m.* °**ize,** *v.t.* niruttiŋ gavesati *or* uggaṇhāti. *p.p.* gavesitanirutti.

Etymon, *n.* mūlika-saddapakati, *f.*

Euclid, *n.* bhūmitivijjā, *f.*

Eugenic, *n.* sundarasantatijanaka-sattha, *nt.*

Eulogy, *n.* pasaŋsā ; thuti ; thomanā, *f.* abhitthavana, *nt.* °**ist,** *n.* thutipāṭhaka, *m.* °**ize,** *v.t.* thometi ; pasaŋsati. *p.p.* thomita ; °sita.

Eunuch, *n.* napuŋsaka, *m.*

Eupeptic, *a.* suddhagahaṇiyutta ; jaṭharaggibahula.

Euphemism, *n.* guttapharusavacana, *nt.* aññālāpa, *m.* °**stic,** *a.* aññālāpī.

Euphony, *n.* sukhuccāraṇa, *nt.* siliṭṭhakkharatā, *f.* °**ic,** *a.* sutimadhura ; siliṭṭhakkhara.

Euphuism, *n.* adhikālaṅkārayutta-lipi, *f.*

Euphuist, *n.* atipaṇḍitatādassāvī, *m.*

Eurasian, *n. a.* Yuropā-Āsiyādesāyatta.

Eureka, *n.* udānavākya, *nt.*

European, *a.n.* Yuropādesāyatta.

Euthanasia, *n.* anāyāsamaraṇa, *nt.*

Evacuate, *v.t.* vireceti ; apaharati ; suññaŋ karoti. *p.p.* °cita ; apahaṭa ; °kata. °**ion,** virecana ; apanayana ; uccāravossajana ; riñcana ; sodhana, *nt.*

Evade, *v.t.* pariharati ; bādheti. *v.i.* upakkamena apasarati. *p.p.* parihaṭa ; bādhita ; °apasaṭa.

Evaluate, *v.t.* agghaŋ nirūpeti. *p.p.* nirūpitaggha.

Evanesce, *v.i.* antaradhāyati ; vinassati. *p.p.* antarahita ; vinaṭṭha. °**nce,** *n.* antaradhāna, *nt.* vināsa, *m.* °**nt,** *a.* khaṇabhaṅgura ; anicca.

Evangel, *n.* dhammalipi, *f.* °**ic,** *a.* dhammalipivisayaka. °**ist,** *n.* dhammalipisampādaka, *m.*

Evanish, *v.i.* antaradhāyati. *p.p.* antarahita.

Evaporate, *v.i.* ussussati ; sukhumarūpataŋ yāti. *v.t.* bappataŋ pāpeti. *p.p.* ussukkha ; °yāta ; °pāpita. °**ion,** *n.* ussussana ; sukhumattagamana, *nt.*

Evasion, *n.* apasaraṇa ; parivajjana, *nt.* °**sive,** *a.* 1. parivajjaka ; vañcanasīla ; kūṭa.

Eve, Evening, *n.* sañjhā, *f.* sāyaṇha ; dinaccaya, *m.* **Good —,** susañjhā, *f.* **In the —** sāyaŋ, *ind.* **Last —,** abhidosa, *m.* **Late in the —,** atisāyaŋ, *ind.*

Even, *a.* sama. *v.t.* sameti ; samaŋ karoti. *p.p.* samita ; samīkata. *adv.* api. **— if, — though,** yadi pi ; yajjapi, *ind.* **— as,** yathā ; yath'eva, *ind.* **— handed,** *a.* apakkhapātī. °**ly,** *adv.* samaŋ. °**ness,** *n.* samatta ; tulyatta, *nt.* **— now,** ajjāpi, *ind.* **— so,** tath'eva ; evam eva, *ind.*

Event, *n.* 1. siddhi, *f.* 2. vuttanta, *m.* 2. pariṇāma, *m.* phala, *nt.* °**ful,** *a.* visiṭṭhasiddhiyutta. °**ual,** *a.* 1. anusaṅgika ; 2. antima. °**ually,** *adv.* ante ; pariyosāne.

Eventuate, *v.i.* sijjhati ; niṭṭhāti ; sampajjati. *p.p.* siddha ; niṭṭhita ; sampanna.

Ever, *adv.* 1. sadā ; niccaŋ ; nirantaraŋ ; satataŋ; 2. yadā ; yadā kadāci; kudācana. **For —,** sadātanāya, *ind.* **— following,** sadānugata, *a.* °**green,** sadānīlapatta, *a.* °**lasting,** sassatika, *a.* **— moving,** sadāgatika, *a.*

°**more**, sadā ; sadātanāya, *ind.* — **recurring**, sadā-sijjhamāna, *a.*

Evert, *v.t.* viparivatteti, *p.p.* °tita.

Every, *a.* sabba ; sakala ; nikhila. °**body**, sabbajana, *m.* °**day**, sabbadā, *adv.* °**one**, sabbajana ; ekeka, *m.* — **other**, ekantarika, *a.* °**thing**, sabba, *nt.* °**where**, sabbattha, *adv.* **In** — **respect**, sabbaso ; sabbākārena, *adv.* **In** — **way**, sabbathā, *adv.* **On** — **side**, sabbato ; samantato, *adv.*

Evict, *v.t.* nītiyā nikkhāmeti *or* nissāreti. *p.p.* °mita ; °rita.

Evidence, *n.* 1. pākaṭatta ; nidassana, *nt.* 2. sakkhi, *m.* *v.t.* pamāṇaŋ *or* sakkhiŋ karoti. *p.p.* pamāṇīkata.

Evident, *a.* pākaṭa ; paccakkha ; yathābhūta. °**ial**, *a.* sasakkhika ; sādhakasahita. °**ly**, *adv.* paccakkhaŋ ; pākaṭaŋ.

Evil, *n.* anattha, adhamma, *m.* vipatti, *f.* vyasana ; pāpa, *nt.* °**conduct**, *n.* durācāra, *m.* °**consequence**, kaliggaha, *m.* °**course**, kupatha, *m.* °**disposition**, duṭṭhatā, *f.* °**doer**, pāpakārī, *m.* °**eye**, diṭṭhavisa, *nt.* °**minded**, pāpāsaya ; dummedha, *a.* — **One**, Antaka ; Māra ; Namuci, *m.* °**speaking**, durālāpa, *a.* °**thought**, pāpasaṅkappa, *m.*

Evince, *v.t.* nidasseti ; pakāseti ; samattheti. *p.p.* °sita ; °thita.

Evirate, *v.t.* bījaŋ *or* aṇḍam uddharati *or* nibbaṭṭeti. *p.p.* uddhaṭabīja ; nibbaṭṭitaṇḍa. °**ion**, *n.* bījuddharaṇa, *nt.*

Eviscerate, *v.t.* antāni bahikaroti *or* nikkhāmeti. *p.p.* bahikatanta.

Evoke, *v.t.* 1. pabodheti ; uttejeti ; 2. avhāti. *p.p.* °dhita ; °jita ; avhāta.

Evolution, *n.* pariṇāma ; kamavikāsa, *m.* °**al**, *a.* pariṇāmavisayaka. °**ist**, *n.* pariṇāmavādī, *m.*

Evolve, *v.i.* (kamena) vikasati ; pariṇamati ; saŋvaṭṭati. *p.p.* °sita ; pariṇata ; °ṭita.

Evulsion, *n.* luñcana, *nt.*

Ewe, *n.* uranī ; eḷikā, *f.*

Ewer, *n.* kuṇḍikā, *f.* kamaṇḍalu, *m.*

Exacerbate, *v.t.* vaḍḍheti ; uddīpeti. *p.p.* °ḍhita ; °pita.

Exact, *a.* yathābhūta ; taccha ; yāthāva. *v.t.* balena ādāti ; pasayha gaṇhāti. *p.p.* °ādinna ; °gahita. °**ion**, *n.* balakkāragahaṇa, *nt.* °**ly**, *adv.* yāthāvato ; yathābhūtaŋ.

Exaggerate, *v.t.* adhikaŋ vaṇṇeti *p.p.* °ṇita. °**ion**, *n.* adhikavaṇṇaṇā, *f.*

Exalt, *v.t.* unnāmeti ; ukkaŋseti. *p.p.* °mita ; °sita. °**ation**, *n.* unnati ; uccapadappatti, *f.* °**ed**, *a.* uttama ; parama ; seṭṭha.

Examine, *v.t.* upaparikkhati ; upadhāreti ; vīmaŋsati. *p.p.* °khita ; °rita ; °sita. °**ation**, upaparikkhā ; vīmaŋsā ; vicāraṇā, *f.* °**er**, *n.* parikkhaka ; vīmaŋsaka *m,*

Example, *n.* udāharaṇa ; nidassana, *nt.*

Exanimate, *a.* nijjīva.

Exasperate, *v.t.* pakopeti ; saṅkhobheti ; roseti. *p.p.* °pita ; °bhita ; rosita *or* ruṭṭha. °**ion,** *n.* pakopana, *nt.*

Excavate, *v.t.* paḷikhaṇati ; abhikhaṇati. *p.p.* °khata. °**ion,** *n.* paḷīkhaṇana, *nt.* °**tor,** *n.* paḷikhaṇaka, *m.*

Exceed, *v.i.* atiriccati ; adhiko bhavati. *v.t.* atikkamati. *p.p.* atiritta ; adhikabhūta ; atikkanta. °**ing,** *a.* adhika ; adhimatta ; accanta. °**ingly,** *adv.* accantaŋ ; atisayena ; atīva ; atimattaŋ.

Excel, *v.t.* abhibhavati ; atiyāti. *v.i.* unnamati ; visissati. *p.p.* abhibhūta ; atiyāta ; unnata ; visiṭṭha. °**lence,** *n.* seṭṭhatā ; visiṭṭhatā, *f.* °**lency,** *n.* mahānubhāvatā ; mahesakkhatā ; seṭṭhatā, *f.*

Excellent, *a.* atiuttama ; atisundara ; pavara ; parama. *In cpds. this meaning is expressed by* nāga, puṅgava, usabha *and* sīha, e.g. purisanāga ; purisasīha. °**ly,** *adv.* suṭṭhutaraŋ ; atisundarākārena.

Except, *prep.* vinā ; vajjetvā ; pahāya. *v.t.* vajjeti ; pajahati. *p.p.* vajjita ; °hita. °**ing,** *adv.* vinā ; rite ; hitvā. °**ion,** *n.* 1. vajjana ; 2. visesakāraṇa, *nt.* °**ional,** *a.* asādhāraṇa ; visiṭṭha.

Excerpt, *n.* uddhaṭapāṭha, *m.* *v.t.* uddharitvā dasseti. *p.p.* °sita. °**ion,** pāṭhuddharaṇa, *nt.*

Excess, *n.* 1. adhikatā ; bahulatā, *f.* atisaya ; atireka, *m.* 2. pamāṇātikkama, *m.* amattaññutā, *f.* — **of rain,** ativuṭṭhi *f.* — **of wind,** vātakopa, *m.*

Excessive, *a.* accanta ; atimatta ; ussanna. °**ly,** *adv.* atisayena ; ativiya ; accantaŋ ; adhikataraŋ.

Exchange, *n.* vinimaya, *m.* parivattana, *nt.* *v.t.* vinimeti ; nimiṇāti. *p.p.* °mita ; °ṇita.— °**able,** *a.* parivattiya.

Exchequer, *n.* rājakosa, *m.* rājabhaṇḍāgāra, *nt.*

Excise, *n.* rājabali ; kara ; suṅka, *m.* *v.t.* karaŋ nirūpeti. *p.p.* nirūpitakara. °**able,** *a.* karadānāraha. °**man,** *n.* karaggāhī, *m.*

Excise, *v.t.* ukkantati ; uppāṭeti. *p.p.* °tita ; °ṭita. °**ion,** *n.* ukkantana ; uppāṭana, *nt.*

Excite, *v.t.* uttejeti ; ussāheti ; saṅkhobheti. *p.p.* °jita ; °hita ; °bhita. °**ed,** *a.* tasita ; vikkhitta. °**able,** *a.* vikopanaka ; ubbegakara. °**ant,** *n.a.* uttejaka ; uddīpaka ; saṅkhobhaka. °**ation,** °**ment,** *n.* vikkhepa ; sambhama, *m.* °**ing,** *a.* saṅkhobhanaka.

Exclaim, *v.t. i.* ugghoseti ; pakāseti. *p.p.* °sita.

Exclamation, *n.* 1. ugghosana ; pakāsana ; 2. āmeṇḍita, *nt.*

Exclamatory, *a.* vimhayasūcaka.

Exclude, *v.t.* nikkhāmeti ; nikkaḍḍhati ; bahikaroti. *p.p.* °mita ; °ḍhita ; °kata.

Exclusion, *n.* nikkaḍḍhana ; vajjana, *nt.*

Exclusive, *a.* nisedhaka ; nivāraka. °**ly,** *adv.* kevalaŋ ; anaññasādhāraṇaŋ. °**ness,** *n.* asādhāraṇatta, *nt.*

Excogitate, *v.t.* anucinteti ; parikappeti. *p.p.* °tita ; °pita. °**ion,** *n.* anucintā ; parikappanā, *f.*

Excommunicate, *v.t.* (gaṇā) nikkaḍḍhati *or* ukkhipati. *p.p.* °ḍhita ; ukkhitta. °**ion,** *n.* nikkaḍḍhana ; paṇāmana, *nt.*

Excoriate, *v.t.* tacaŋ vikopeti. *p.p.* vikopita-taca. °**ion,** *n.* tacavikopana, *nt.*

Excorticate, *v.t.* tacam uppāṭeti. *p.p.* °ṭita-taca. °**ion,** *n.* tacuppāṭana, *nt.*

Excrement, *n.* mala ; karīsa ; mīḷha ; vacca, *nt.*

Excrescence, *n.* 1. cammakhīla, *nt.* 2. nipphalāvayava, *m.*

Excreta, *n.pl.* asuci ; malamuttādi, *m.*

Excrete, *v.t.* nissajati ; ossajati ; vissajjeti. *p.p.* nissaṭṭha ; ossaṭṭha ; vissaṭṭha. °**ion,** *n.* malossajana, *nt.*

Excruciate, *v.t.* abhimanthati ; abhipīḷeti. *p.p.* °mathita ; °ḷita. °**ion,** *n.* abhimanthana, *nt.*°**ing,** *a.* atipīḷaka.

Exculpate, *v.t.* dosā *or* vajjā moceti. *p.p.* dosamocita. °**ion,** *n.* dosamocana, *nt.* °**tory,** *a.* dosamocaka.

Excurrent, *a.* niccharamāna ; bahisandamāna.

Excurse, *v.i.* āhiṇḍati ; pariyaṭati. °**ion,** *n.* āhiṇḍana ; pariyaṭana, *nt.* cārikā ; jaṅghāvihāra, *m.* °**ive,** *a.* bhamanasīla.

Excursus, *n.* upagantha, *m.* ūnapūraṇa, *nt.*

Excuse, *n.* paccāhāra ; khamāhetu, *m.* vajjamocana, *nt.* *v.t.* khamati ; titikkhati ; vajjaŋ paṭiggaṇhāti. *p.p.* khanta ; paṭiggahitavajja. °**able,** *a.* khamitabba.

Exeat, *n.* kālikāvasara, *m.*

Execrable, *a.* jeguccha.

Execrate, *v.t.* jigucchati ; nindati. *v.i.* abhisapati. *p.p.* °chita ; nindita ; abhisatta. °**ion,** *n.* 1. jigucchā, *f.* 2. abhisāpa, *m.*

Execute, *v.t.* 1. karoti ; 2. sādheti ; sampādeti ; nipphādeti ; 3. vadheti ; ghāteti. *p.p.* kata ; sādhita ; °dita ; hata ; ghātita. °**ant,** *n.* sampādaka ; vādaka, *m.* °**ion,** *n.* 1. vidahana ; anuṭṭhāna ; sampādana, *nt.* 2. hanana ; ghātana, *nt.* °**ive,** *a.* kāriyasādhaka ; vidhāyaka.

Executioner, *n.* vadhaka ; ghātaka, *m.* —'**s block,** dhammagaṇḍikā, *f.* —'**s drum,** vajjhabheri, *f.*

Executor, *n.* (matassa) dhanapālaka, *m.* °**ship,** *n.* dhanapālakatta, *nt.*

Exegesis, *n.* vyākhyāna, *nt.* atthavaṇṇanā, *f.*

Exegetical, *a.* atthappakāsaka. °**tist,** *n.* vyākhyākāra, *m.*

Exemplar, *n.* ādisitabba ; nidassanīya ; 3. mūlādesa, *m.* °**y,** *a.* anugantabba ; anukaraṇīya.

Exemplify, *v.t.* udāharati ; nidasseti. *p.p.* udāhaṭa ; nidassita. °**ication,** *n.* nidassanena pākaṭakaraṇa, *nt.*

Exempt, *n. a.* vimutta ; abaddha. *v.t.* vimoceti ; abaddhaŋ karoti. *p.p.* °cita ; °kata. °**ion,** *n.* vimutti, *f.* atirekavara, *m.*

Exequatur, *n.* videsarajjena sampaṭicchana, *nt.*

Exequies, *n.* petakicca, *nt.* matasakkāra, *m.*

Exercise, *n.* paricaya ; payoga, *m.* paṭipajjana ; nisevana, *nt.* *v.t.* ācarati ; paricayati ; parisīleti. *v.i.* paṭipajjati ; vāyamati. *p.p.* ācarita ; °yita ; °lita ; paṭipanna.

Exercitation, *n.* paguṇakaraṇa ; vācuggatakaraṇa, *nt.*

Exert, *v.t.* vāyamati ; parakkamati ; ussahati. *p.p.* °mita ; °hita. °**ion,** *n.* vāyāma ; ussāha ; parakkama ; ātappa, *m.* padahana, *nt.*

Exfoliate, *v.i.* papaṭikā pāteti. *p.p.* pātitapapaṭika.

Exhale, *v.t.* passasati. *v.i.* vāyati. *p.p.* °sita ; vāyita. °**ation,** *n.* passasana ; vāyana, *nt.*

Exhaust, *v.t.* khepeti ; pariyādiyati ; atikilameti. *p.p.* °pita ; pariyādinna ; °mita. °**ible,** *a.* khayagamanīya. °**ion,** *n.* pariyādiyana ; atikilamana, *nt.* °**ive,** *a.* pariyādiyaka; khepaka. °**less,** *a.* akkhaya.

Exhibit, *n.* 1. pamāṇapaṇṇa, *nt.* 2. padassanīya-vatthu, *nt.* *v.t.* padasseti ; āvīkaroti. *p.p.* °sita ; °kata. °**ion,** *n.* padassana ; āvīkaraṇa, *nt.*

Exhilarate, *v.t.* pīṇeti ; toseti ; hāseti. *p.p.* pīṇita ; tosita *or* tuṭṭha ; hāsita *or* haṭṭha. °**ing,** *a.* tosakara. °**ion,** *n.* hāsa ; tosa, *m.* tuṭṭhi, *f.* pāmojja, *nt.*

Exhort, *v.t.* 1. ovadati ; anusāsati ; 2. ussāheti. *p.p.* °dita ; anusiṭṭha ; °hita. °**ation,** *n.* ovāda, *m.* anusāsanā ; anusiṭṭhi, *f.* °**ative,** *a.* anusāsaka ; ovādadāyaka ; pabodhaka.

Exhume, *v.t.* (matadehaŋ) ukkhaṇati ; nikhātam uddharati. *p.p.* ukkhata ; uddhaṭanikhāta.

Exigence, °**cy,** *n.* 1. accāyika ; accāvassaka, *nt.* 2. kālavipatti, *f.* vipattikāla, *m.*

Exigent, *a.* aparihāriya ; āvassaka ; accāyika.

Exiguity, *n.* appatā ; thokatā, *f.*

Exiguous, *a.* appaka ; thoka.

Exile, *n.* vippavāsa, *m.* pabbājana ; nibbāsana, *nt.* *v.t.* pabbājeti ; vippavāseti. *p.p.* °jita ; °sita.

Exility, *n.* tanutta ; sukhumatta, *nt.*

Exist, *v.i.* bhavati ; sambhavati ; pavattati ; saŋvijjati ; atthi. *p.p.* bhūta ; sambhūta ; °tita. °**ence,** *n.* pavattana, *nt.* atthitā ; vijjamānatā, *f.* sambhava, *m.* °**ent,** *a.* pavattamāna ; vijjamāna ; paccuppanna. °**ing for a day,** ekāhika, *a.*

Exit, *n.* niggama, *m.* nikkhamaṇadvāra, *nt.*

Ex-monk, *n.* uppabbajita, *m.*

Exodus, *n.* apagamana ; nikkhamaṇa, *nt.*

Ex-officio, *adv.* ṭhānantarabalena. adj. ṭhānantarena laddhabala.

Exonerate, *v.t.* dosato moceti. *p.p.* °mocita. °**ion,** *n.* niddosīkaraṇa. *nt.*

Exorbitance, *n.* pamāṇātikkama, *m.* °**ant,** *a.* atikkantapamāṇa ; adhikatara ; sīmātikkanta.

Exorcize, *v.t.* bhūtāvesā moceti ; mantehi bhūte apaneti. *p.p.* °mocita ; °apanītabhūta.

Exorcism, *n*. bhūtāpasāraṇa, *nt*. °**cist**, *n*. bhūtavejja, *m*.

Exordium, *n*. mukhabandha, *m*.

Exoteric, *a*. *n*. sugama ; agūḷha.

Exotic, *a*. videsābhata ; parabhāsāyatta.

Expand, *v.t.* vikāseti ; vitthambheti ; vipphāreti. *v.i.* vikasati ; pattharati ; vippharati. *p.p.* °sita ; °bhita ; °rita ; °sita ; patthaṭa ; vipphuṭa.

Expanse, *n*. āyāmavitthāra ; vivittokāsa ; okāsa, *m*. °**ion**, *n*. vikāsa ; vipphāra ; vitthāra, *m*. vikasana, *nt*. °**ive**, *a*. vyāpaka ; vitthata ; vitthiṇṇa.

Ex-parte, *adv*. ekapakkhatthāya. adj. pakkhagāhī.

Expatiate, *v.i.* 1. atipapañceti ; 2. anārammaṇo āhiṇḍati. °**ion**, *n*. 1. atipapañca ; ativitthāra, *m*. 2. paribbhamaṇa, *nt*.

Expatriate, *v.t.* raṭṭhavāsittam apaneti ; raṭṭhā pabbājeti. *p.p.* apanīta° ; °jita. *n*. pabbājita ; pavāsita, *m*.

Expect, *v.t.* ākaṅkhati ; apekkhati ; āgameti ; āsiŋsati. *p.p.* °khita ; āgamita ; āsiṭṭha. °**ance**, °**ancy**, apekkhā ; ākaṅkhā, *f*. °**ant**, *a*. *n*. apekkhī ; ākaṅkhī ; pāṭikaṅkhī. °**ing**, *a*. apekkhanta ; āgamayamāna. °**ation**, *n*. apekkhā ; āsiŋsanā, *f*. °**ative**, *a*. apekkhājanaka.

Expectorate, *v.t.* ukkāsati ; niṭṭhubhati. *p.p.* °sita ; °bhita. °**ion**, *n*. ukkāsana ; niṭṭhubhana, *nt*. °**ive**, °**rant**, *a*. semhuggāraka.

Expedient, *n*. upāya; upakkama, *m*. adj. anurūpa ; ucita ; yogga. °**ly**, *adv*. yathocitaŋ ; yathāyoggaŋ. °**nce**, *n*. ocitya ; yoggatta, *nt*.

Expedite, *v.t.* sīghaŋ sādheti. °**ion**, *n*. 1. sīghatā, *f*. sīghasādhana, *nt*. 2. dūragāmī senā, *f*. °**ious**, *a*. turita. °**iously**, *adv*. sīghaŋ ; turitaŋ.

Expel, *v.t.* nikkaḍḍhati ; paṇāmeti ; nibbāheti. *p.p.* °ḍhita ; °mita ; °hita. °**lant**, *a*. nibbāhita ; nikkaḍḍhita.

Expend, *v.t.* vissajjeti ; vayaŋ karoti. *p.p.* vissaṭṭha ; vayakata. °**iture**, *n*. vaya ; paribbaya, *m*.

Expense, *n*. vaya, *m*. °**ive**, *a*. mahaggha ; mahabbayakara. °**ively**, *adv*. bahuparibbayena.

Experience, *n*. 1. vindana ; anubhavana ; 2. pāṭava ; nepuñña, *nt*. paricaya, *m*. *v.t.* 1. vindati ; anubhavati ; paṭisaŋvedeti ; 2. paricayati ; sikkhati. *p.p.* vindita ; anubhūta ; °dita ; °yita, sikkhita. °**ing**, *a*. anubhavamāna ; paṭisaŋvedī.

Experiential, *a*. paricayāyatta ; anubhavanāyatta.

Experiment, *n*. vīmaŋsā ; uparikkhā, *f*. *v.t.* vīmaŋsati ; uparikkhati. *p.p.* °sita ; °khita. °**al**, *a*. parikkhanamūlaka ; anubhavaladdha. °**alist**, *n*. vīmaŋsaka, *m*.

Expert, *a*. *n*. katahattha ; katupāsana ; pavīṇa ; nipuṇa. °**ly**, *adv*. nipuṇākārena. °**ness**, *n*. nipuṇatta ; kosalla ; nepuñña, *nt*.

Expiate, *v.t.* paṭikaroti ; accayaŋ deseti. *p.p.* paṭikata ; desitaccaya. °**ion,** *n.* paṭikamma, *nt.* accayadesanā, *f.* °**tory,** *a.* pāpanāsaka ; pāpasodhaka.

Expire, *v.i.* marati ; cavati. *p.p.* mata ; cuta. °**ation,** *n.* 1. cuti, *f.* cavana, *nt.* 2. accaya ; saṅkhaya, *m.* °**ing,** *a.* mīyamāna ; cavamāna ; āsannamaraṇa.

Explain, *v.t.* vitthāreti ; vaṇṇeti ; vibhāveti ; kitteti. *p.p.* °rita ; °ṇita ; °vita ; kittita.

Explanation, *n.* visadīkaraṇa ; vivaraṇa, *nt.* vibhāvanā , vaṇṇanā ; atthakathā, *f.* °**tory,** *a.* paridīpaka ; atthappakāsaka.

Expletive, *n.* padapūraṇa, *nt.* adj. padapūraka ; vākyabhūsaka.

Explicate, see Explain. °**tory,** *a.* atthappakāsaka.

Explicit, *a.* pākaṭa ; uttāna. °**ly,** *adv.* visadākārena. °**ness,** *n.* visadatta ; pākaṭatta, *nt.*

Explode, *v.i.* mahāsaddena pabhijjati. *v.t.* pākaṭattam *or* ayasaŋ pāpeti. *p.p.* °pabhinna ; °pāpita.

Exploit, *n.* vikkama, *m.* vīrakriyā, *f.* *v.t.* attatthāya payojeti; saphalākārena yojeti. *p.p.* °jita. °**ation,** *n.* attalābhāya niyojana, *nt.*

Explore, *v.t.* āvaṭaŋ vivarati ; aviditadesaŋ pariyesati. °**ation,** *n.* anāvaraṇa ; parivīmaŋsana, *nt.* °**er,** *n.* anāvaraka ; gavesaka, *m.*

Explosion, *n.* sanāda-bhijjana ; sasadda-phuṭana, *nt.*

Explosive, *a.* vidāraṇakara. *n.* vidāraka-vatthu, *nt.* °**ness,** *n.* vidārakatta, *nt.*

Exponent, *a. n.* desaka ; pakāsaka, *m.*

Export, *n.* 1. videsapesana, *nt.* 2. videsapesīya-bhaṇḍa, *nt.* *v.t.* videsaŋ peseti. *p.p.* °pesita. °**ation,** *n.* videsapesana, *nt.*

Expose, *v.t.* 1. vivarati ; pakāseti ; 2. arakkhitattaŋ pāpeti. *p.p.* vivaṭa ; °sita ; °pāpita ; °**ition,** *n.* parikathā ; saŋvaṇṇanā, *f.* uttānīkaraṇa, *nt.* °**ure,** *n.* 1. anāvaraṇa ; pakāsana ; 2. rakkhāpaharaṇa, *nt.*

Expositor, *n.* atthapakāsaka; vyākhyātu, *m.*

Expostulate, *v.t.* viramaṇāya ovadati. °**ion,** *n.* viramanāyovāda, *m.*

Expound, *v.t.* akkhāti ; deseti ; pakāseti. *p.p.* akkhāta ; desita ; °sita.

Express, *a.* 1. nicchita ; visesita ; ekantika ; 2. sīghagāmī ; 3. anāvaṭa ; pākaṭa. *v.t.* 1. sūceti ; pakāseti ; 2. katheti ; udīreti ; 3. nippīḷeti. *p.p.* sūcita ; °sita ; kathita ; udīrita ; °ḷita. °**ion,** *n.* 1. pakāsana ; kathana, *nt.* 2. nippīḷana, *nt.* 3. iṅgita, *nt.* °**ive,** *a.* vyañjaka ; sūcaka, °**iveness,** *n.* sātthakatta ; vyañjakatta, *nt.* °**ly,** *adv.* ujukam eva ; ekantena.

Expropriate, *v.t.* assāmikaŋ karoti. *p.p.* °kata.

Expulsion, *n.* nissāraṇa ; nikkaḍḍhana, *nt.* °**sive,** *a.* nikkaḍḍhanāraha.

Expunction, *n.* lopa, *m.* apamajjana, *nt.*

Expunge, *v.t.* apamajjati ; lopeti. *p.p.* apamaṭṭha ; lutta.

Expurgate, *v.t.* saŋsodheti. *p.p.* °dhita. °**ion**, *n.* saŋsodhana, *nt.* °**tory**, *a.* dosāpahāraka.

Exquisite, *a.* 1. visiṭṭha ; ukkaṭṭha ; 2. atisukhuma. °**ness**, *n.* visiṭṭhatta, *nt.* °**ly**, *adv.* ativisiṭṭhākārena.

Exsanguinate, *v.t.* rudhiraŋ vāheti. *p.p.* vāhitarudhira.

Exsanguine, *n.* rudhirahīnatā, *f.*

Exsert, *a.* bahinikkhanta.

Ex-service, *a.* rājakiccāpagata.

Exsiccate, *v.t.* soseti. *p.p.* sosita.

Extant, *a.* pavattamāna ; vijjamāna.

Extemporaneous, Extemporary, *a.* avihitapubba ; aparikappita ; taṅkhaṇānurūpa. °**ly**, *adv.* pubbatakkanaŋ vinā.

Extempore, *adv.* pubbavidhānaŋ vinā ; taṅkhaṇānurūpaŋ.

Extemporize, *v.t.* aparikappetvā katheti. *p.p.* °kathita.

Extend, *v.t.* tanoti ; vitthāreti ; vipphāreti. *v.i.* pharati ; pattharati. *p.p.* tata; vitthata *or* vitthārita ; °rita ; phuṭa ; patthaṭa.

Extension, *n.* visālatta, *nt.* āyāma-vitthāra, *m.* pamāṇa, *nt.*

Extensive, *a.* visāla ; vipula ; pacura. °**ly**, *adv.* adhikavasena ; bāhullena ; atimattaŋ. °**ness**, *n.* vipulatta ; visālatta ; patthaṭatta, *nt.*

Extent, *n.* pariṇāha, *m.* parimāṇa, *nt.* vitthāra, *m.*

Extenuate, *v.t.* tanukaroti ; mandīkaroti ; upasameti. *p.p.* °kata ; upasamita. °**ion**, *n.* tanukaraṇa ; upasamana, *nt.*

Exterior, *n.* bahibhāga, *m.* adj. bāhira ; bahiṭṭhita. °**ly**, *adv.* bāhirato. °**ity**, *n.* bāhiratta, *nt.*

Exterminate, see **Eradicate**, °**ion**, *n.* uppāṭana ; ummūlana ; ucchindana, *nt.*

External, *a.* bāhira ; bahiddhā. °**ity**, *n.* bāhiratta, *nt.* °**ly**, *adv.* bāhiravasena ; bahito.

Extinct, *a.* atthagata ; nibbuta ; abhāvappatta. °**ion**, *n.* atthagama ; nirodha, *m.* nibbuti, *f.* °**ion of passions**, āsavakkhaya, *m.*

Extinguish, *v.t.* upasameti ; nirodheti ; nibbāpeti. *p.p.* °mita ; °dhita ; °pita.

Extirpate, *v.t.* samucchindati ; vināseti. *p.p.* samucchinna ; °sita. °**ion**, *n.* samucchindana. *nt.* °**tor**, samucchindaka, *m.*

Extol, *v.t.* pakitteti; abhitthavati ; pasaŋsati. *p.p.* °tita ; abhitthuta ; pasattha. °**ler**, *n.* vaṇṇavādī, *m.*

Extort, *v.t.* pasayha ādāti ; aññāyena gaṇhāti. *p.p.* ādinna ; °gahita. °**er**, *n.* pasayhagāhī ; upapīḷaka, *m.* °**ion**, *n.* pasayhagāha, *m.*

Extra, *a.* atireka ; adhika ; atiritta.

Extract, *n.* 1. rasa ; niyyāsa ; sāra, *m.* 2. saṅkhepa ; uddhaṭabhāga, *m.* *v.t.* nikkhāmeti ; uppīḷetvā gaṇhāti. *p.p.* °mita ; °gahita. °**ion**, *n.* 1. nikkaḍḍhana ; uddharaṇa, *nt.* 2. santati ; paramparā, *f.* °**able**, *a.* ākaḍḍhanīya. °**or**, *n.* ākaḍḍhaka, *m.*

Extradite, *v.t.* karamarānītaŋ paṭidadāti. °**ion**, *n.* paṭiappaṇā, *f.*

Extramundane, *a.* lokuttara.

Extraneous, *a.* bāhira ; bahigata.

Extraordinary, *a.* anaññasādhāraṇa ; ativisiṭṭha. °**ily,** *adv.* abhivisiṭṭhatāya.

Extravagance, *n.* amattaññutā, *f.* sīmātikkamana, *nt.*

Extravagant, *a.* sīmātīta ; amattaññū ; atibbayakārī. °**ly,** *adv.* atibbayena ; adhikacāgena.

Extravagate, *v.i.* sīmaŋ atikkamati. *p.p.* atikkantasīma.

Extravasate, *v.t.i.* bahiddhā vāheti ; nissāveti. *p.p.* °vāhita ; °vita. °**ion,** *n.* nissāvaṇa, *nt.*

Extreme, *n.* agga ; anta, *nt.* paramakoṭi, *f.* adj. 1. accanta ; adhikatama ; parama ; antagata. °**ity,** *n.* pariyanta ; paramāvadhi, *m.* °**ly,** *adv.* accantaŋ ; atisayena.

Extricate, *v.t.* parimoceti ; vijaṭeti. *p.p.* °cita ; °ṭita. °**ion,** *n.* vimocana ; vijaṭana.

Extrinsic, *a.* āgantuka ; bāhira ; anavassa. °**ally,** *adv.* bāhiravasena.

Extrude, *v.t.* nikkaḍḍhati ; palāpeti. *p.p.* °ḍhita ; °pita.

Extrusion, *n.* nikkaḍḍhana ; palāpana, *nt.*

Exuberance, *n.* gaṇḍa ; phoṭa, *m.* uddhumāta, *nt.*

Exuberant, *n.* samiddha ; phīta ; pacura. °**ly,** *adv.* samiddhākārena. °**ance,** *n.* samiddhi ; pacuratā, *f.* °**ate,** *v.i.* samijjhati ; abhivaḍḍhati. *p.p.* samiddha ; abhivuddha.

Exude, *v.i.* sandati ; (sedo) muccati. *p.p.* sandita ; muttaseda. °**ation,** *n.* 1. niccharaṇa, *nt.* 2. niyyāsa, *m.*

Exult, *v.i.* pamodati ; atitussati. *p.p.* pamudita ; atituṭṭha. °**ant,** *a.* pahaṭṭha ; udagga. °**ation,** *n.* pāmojja, *nt.* pamoda, *m.* °**ingly,** *adv.* sānandaŋ.

Eye, *n.* akkhi ; cakkhu ; nayana ; locana ; netta, *nt.* — **of a net,** jālakkhika, *nt.* — **of wisdom,** dhammacakkhu ; ñāṇacakkhu, *nt.* °**ball,** *n.* akkhitārā, *f.* °**brow** *n.* bhamu ; bhamukā, *f.* °**glass,** *n.* upanetta, *nt.* °**lash,** *n.* pamha ; pakhuma, *nt.* °**less,** *a.* andha. °**lid,** *n.* akkhidala, *nt.* °**reach,** °**shot,** diṭṭhipatha, *m.* °**sight,** diṭṭhi, *f.* °**sore,** nettarujā, *f.* °**witness,** paccakkhadassī ; diṭṭhasakkhī, *m.*

F

Fable, *n.* ākhyāna, *nt.* kappitakathā, *f.* *v.t.* 1. ākhyānāni katheti ; 2. atacchaŋ pabandheti. *p.p.* kathitākhyāna.

Fabric, *n.* 1. racanā ; ghaṭanā, *f.* nimmāṇa, *nt.* 2. vattha, *nt.* 3. geha ; mandira, *nt.*

Fabricate, *v.t.* 1. sampādeti ; māpeti ; 2. ayathākaroti ; micchālipiŋ sampādeti. *p.p.* °dita ; māpita ; °kata °dita. °**ion,** *n.* 1. sampādana ; nipphādana, *nt.* 2. micchāracanā, *f.* parikappana, *nt.* °**tor,** *n.* racaka ; nibandhaka ; māpaka, *m.*

Fabulist, *n*. ākhyāsampādaka, *m*.
Fabulous, *a*. kittima ; asaddheyya ; micchākathāyatta.
Façade, *n*. pāsādamukha, *nt*.
Face, *n*. 1. vadana ; ānana ; mukha, *nt*. 2. tala ; piṭṭha ; matthaka, *nt*. *v.t. i*. abhimukhī bhavati. *p.p*. °bhūta. — **to face**, sakkhi ; paccakkhaŋ, *adv*. — **to face with**, sammukha, *a*. — **downward**, avakujja ; adhomukha, *a*. °**ial**, *a*. vadanāyatta. °**ing**, *a*. abhimukha.— **upward**, ummukha, *a*. **Before one's** ~, sammukhe ; purato, *adv*. **Make —s**, mukhavikāraŋ dasseti.
Facet, *n*. aŋsa, *m*. passa, *nt*.
Facetiae, *n*. *pl*. vikaṭavākyāni ; vikaṭarūpāni, *nt*. *pl*
Facetious, *a*. nammālāpī ; hāsuppādaka ; vinodasīlī. °**ly**, *adv*. parihāsapubbaŋ.
Facia, *n*. (pamukhe) nāmaphalaka, *nt*.
Facile, *a*. 1. sukara ; sukhasādhiya ; 2. anukūla ; sakhila ; saṇha. °**ity**, *n*. sukaratta ; susādhiyatta ; sulabhatta, *nt*.
Facilitate, *v.t*. sukarattaŋ neti ; upatthambheti. *p.p*. °nīta ; °bhita.
Facsimile, *n*. paṭilipi ; sadisalipi, *f*.
Fact, *n*. sacca ; taccha avitatha, *n*.
Faction, *n*. pakkha ; janapakkha, *m*. °**al**, *a*. pakkhāyatta.
Factious, *a*. pakkhapātī. °**ly**, *adv*. pakkhapātitāya. **ness**, *n*. pakkhapātitā, *f*.
Factitious, *a*. kittima ; sippanimmita. °**ly**, *adv*. kittimākārena.
Factitive, *a*. hetubhūta ; sādhaka.
Factor, *n*. 1. vāṇijaniyojita, *m*. 2. aṅga ; avayava, *m*. 3. guṇaka ; guṇīkara, *m*.— **of wisdom**, bojjhaṅga, *m*. °**age**, *n*. niyojitasuṅkabhāga, *m*.
Factory, *n*. kammantasālā, *f*.
Factotum, *n*. sabbakiccakārī, *m*.
Factual, *a*. avitatha ; yathātatha. °**ly**, *adv*. yathātathaŋ.
Facula, *n*. suriyakalaṅka, *m*.
Facultative, *a*. indriyāyatta.
Faculty, *n*. 1. sāmatthiya, *nt*. satti, *f*. 2. indriya, *nt*. 3. vijjāyatana-sākhā, *f*. — **of hearing**, sotindriya, *nt*. — **of senses**, pasādarūpa, *nt*. — **of smelling**, ghāṇindriya, *nt*. — **of tasting**, jivhindriya, *nt*. — **of touch**, kāyindriya, *nt*.
Fad, *n*. adhigama-māna, *m*. °**dist**, adhimānī, *m*.
Fade, *v.i*. milāyati. *v.t*. milāyāpeti. *p.p*. milāta ; °pita. °**ing**, *a*. milāyamāna.
Faeces, *n*. mala, *nt*. sarīranissanda, *m*.
Faerie, *n*. vanadevaloka, *m*. adj. vanadevatāyatta.
Fag, *v.i*. ussahati ; yatati. *v.t*. kilameti. *p.p*. °mita.
Faggot, *n*. dāru ; indhana, *nt*. *v.t*. kalāpe bandhati. *p.p*. baddhakalāpa.
Fail, *v.i*. vipajjati ; virajjhati ; viphalībhavati. *p.p*. vipanna ; viraddha ; °bhūta. *v.t*. parihāpeti ; virādheti. *p.p*. °pita ; °dhita. *n*. ananuṭṭhāna ; udāsīnatta, *nt*. **Without** —, avassam eva ; bādhārahitaŋ ; niyataŋ, *adv*. °**ing**, *n*. vajja, khalita, *nt*.

Failure, *n.* asamiddhi ; virajjhanā ; vipatti, *f.* visīdana, *nt.*

Fain, *a.* (kātu-) kāma, *adv.* sānandaŋ.

Faint, *a.* 1. dubbala ; milāta ; 2. mandappabha ; vivaṇṇa, *v.i.* mucchati ; visaññī bhavati. *p.p.* °chita °bhūta. °**hearted**, *a.* adhīra ; kātara ; dīna. °**ing,** *n.* mucchā visaññā, *f.* °**ly** *adv.* mandaŋ ; īsakaŋ ; dubbalatāya. °**ness**, *n.* dubbalatta ; milātatta, *nt*

Fair, *n.* kālika-dabbavinimayaṭṭhāna, *nt.* adj. 1. sobhana ; sundara cāru ; manuñña ; 2. suci ; dhammika ; 3. nimmala ; visada ; 4. pasādajanaka. °**ly,** *adv.* dhammena ; sobhanākārena. °**ness,** *n.* 1. sundaratta ; sobhanatta *nt.* 2. avaṅkatā ; akuṭilatā, *f.* ajjava, *nt.*—**minded,** *a.* samacitta.—**play,** *n.* sādhāraṇavutti, *f.* — **seeming,** *a.* bahisobhana. — **sex,** nārijana, *m.* °**spoken,** *a.* piyaŋvada.

Fairy, *n.* vanadevatā ; vijjādharī, *f.* adj. manokappita.

Faith, *n.* bhatti ; saddhā, *f.* °**ful,** *a.* 1. sasaddha ; pasanna ; bhattimantu ; 2. vissattha ; paccayika ; saccasandha. °**fully,** *adv.* avyājaŋ ; saddhāya. °**fulness,** *n.* 1. saddhāluṭā ; pasannatā, *f.* 2. paccayikatā, *f.* °**less,** *a.* 1. assaddha ; 2. vissāsahīna. °**lessness,** *n.* 1. assaddhiya, *nt.* 2. avissāsa, *m.*

Fake, *n.* 1. rajjuvaṭṭi, *f.* 2. patirūpakavatthu, *nt.* *v.t.* 1. rajjuyā veṭheti ; 2. vañceti. *p.p.* °ṭhita ; °cita.

Fakir, *n.* Mohammadika-samaṇa, *m.*

Falcate, Falciform, *a.* dāttākāra.

Falcon, *n.* sena ; kulala ; sakuṇagghī, *m.* °**er,** *n.* senagopaka, *m.*

Falderal, *n.* appagghavatthu, *nt.*

Fall, *v.i.* 1. patati ; nipatati ; 2. cavati ; 3. parihāyati ; 4. sijjhati ; 5. virujjhati. *p.p.* °**tita** ; cuta ; parihīna ; siddha ; viruddha. *noun*: 1. patana, *nt.* 2. parihāni, *f.*—**among,** antaraŋ pāpuṇāti. — **apart,** palujjati. — **asleep,** niddam okkamati.— **away,** paccosakkati.—**back to,** parāvattati. —**down,** opatati : bhassati.—**into,** okkamati ; āpatati—. **into pieces,** paripaṭati. —**in with,** sammukhībhavati. — **off,** papatati — **on,** āpatati — **out,** 1. sijjhati ; 2. virujjhati ; 3. bahipatati. — **short,** ūno bhavati. — **together,** sampatati.—**under,** antogadhataŋ yāti.—**upon,** anupatati ; avatthāti.

Fallacious, *a.* matibbhamajanaka ; ataccha. °**ly,** *adv.* ayathā ; micchā.

Fallacy, *n.* micchādiṭṭhi, *f.* matibbhama, *m*

Fal-lal, *n.* appagghālaṅkāra, *m.*

Fallen, *a.* patita ; paribhaṭṭha. — **off,** saŋsīna, *a.*

Fallible, *a.* patanasīla ; matibbhamajanaka. °**bility,** *n.* virajjhana, *nt.*

Falling, *n.* patana, *nt.* pāta, *m.* °**against,** abhinipāta, *m.*

Fallow, *n.* kaṭṭhā avapitā bhūmi, *f.* adj. 1. piṅgala; 2. aropita. *v.t.* kasati. *p.p.* kaṭṭha *or* kasita. **ness,** *n.* vañjhatā, *f.* — (of mind), cetokhila, *nt.*

False, *a.* 1. atacoha; vitatha; ayathābhūta; 2. kittima; patirūpaka; 3. saṭha; māyāvī. °**ascetic,** kūṭajaṭila, *m.* — **friend,** pāpamitta; mittapatirūpaka, *m.* °**hood,** asacca; abhūta; alika, *nt.* °**ly** *adv.* abhūtena; micchā. — **suit** kūṭaṭṭa, *nt.* —**witness,** kūṭasakkhi *m.*

Falsetto, *n.* vikatisadda, *m.*

Falsify, *v.t.* 1. micchā *or* ayathā dasseti; vañceti; 2. vitathīkaroti; asaccataŋ dīpeti. *p.p.* °dassita; °cita; °kata; °pita. °**ication,** *n.* kūṭaracanā; micchāghaṭanā; nikati, *f.* °**ier,** *n.* nekatika, *m.*

Falter, *v.i.* pakkhalati; khalanto bhaṇati. *p.p.* °lita. °**ingly,** *adv.* sagaggadaŋ; sakampaŋ. °**ing,** *n.* pakkhalana, *nt.* gaggadavācā, *f.*

Fame, *n.* yasa; siloka, *m.* kitti; pasiddhi, *f.* °**ous,** *a.* vissuta; vikhyāta; abhiññāta; paññāta; pākaṭa; patīta.

Familiar, *a.* paricita; santhuta; vallabha. °**ity,** *n.* vallabhatta, *nt.* santhava; vissāsa; paricaya, *m.* °**ize,** *v.t.* paricayati; suviditaŋ karoti. *p.p.* °yita; °kata. °**ly,** *adv.* vallabhatāya.

Family, *n.* 1. kuṭumba, *nt.* gehajana, *m.* 2. kula, *nt.* vaŋsaparamparā; santati, *f.* 3. samānagaṇa, *m.*

Famine, *n.* chātaka; dubbhikkha, *nt.*

Famish, *v.i.* khudāya milāyati; atichāto hoti. *v.t.* khudāya pīḷeti; nirāhāraŋ karoti. *p.p.* °milāta; °pīḷita; nirāhārīkata. °**ed,** *a.* chinnabhatta; khudābhibhūta.

Famulus, *n.* indajālikānucara, *m.*

Fan, *n.* vījanī, *f.* vidhūpana; tālavaṇṭa, *nt.* *v.t.* vījeti; vidhūpeti. *p.p.* °jita; °pita. °**ning,** *n.* vījana, *nt.*

Fanatic, *n. a.* bhattyummatta; sandiṭṭhiparāmāsī. °**ally,** *adv.* atisaddhāya; bhattyummādena. °**ism,** *n.* idaŋsaccabhinivesa; diṭṭhummāda, *m.*

Fancy, *n.* vikappanā; attanomati, *f.* *v.t.* parikappeti; saṅkappeti. *p.p.* °pita. °**iful,** *a.* 1. saṅkappita; cintāmaya; 2. capala; calacitta. °**ifully,** *adv.* yathākāmaŋ; yathāruciŋ. °**ifulness,** *n.* capalatā; sericāritā, *f.*

Fandangle, *n.* vikaṭābharaṇa, *nt.*

Fane, *n.* devāyatana, *nt.*

Fanfare, *n.* kāhalasamūhanāda, *m.*

Fanfaronade, *n.* vikatthana, *nt.*

Fang, *n.* dāṭhā; āsī, *f.* °**ed,** *a.* daṭhī. °**less,** *a.* galitadāṭha; uddhaṭa-dāṭha.

Fan-light, *n.* dvāropari-kavāṭa, *m.*

Fantast, *n.* parivitakkī, *m.* °**ic,** *a.* asaṅgata; vilakkhaṇa; virūpa. °**ical,** *a.* parivitakkāyatta. °**ically,** *adv.* asaṅgatavasena.

Fantasy, *n.* 1. vilakkhaṇarūpa, *nt.* 2. manokappita-bimba, *m.*

Fantom, *n.* bhūtadassana, *nt.*

Far, *n.* dūra ; dūraṭṭhāna, *nt.* adj. dūra ; dūraṭṭha ; anāsanna. *adv.* adhikaŋ.—**and wide,** putthu, *ind.*—**away,** dūre.—**from,** ārā, *ind.* — **off,** dūraṭṭha, *a.* °**famed,** *a.* mahāyasa. °**fetched,** *a.* dūrasambandha ; dūrānīta. °**reaching,** *a.* dūragāmī. °**seeing** *a,* dūradassī. **As — as,** yāva. *ind.* **Not—from,** avidūra, *a.*

Farce, *n.* upahāsanacca, *nt. v.t.* kaṭukabhaṇḍaŋ yojeti. °**ical,** *a.* hāsajanaka.

Fardel, *n.* bhaṇḍikā, *f.*

Fare, *n.* 1. āhāra, *m.* bhojana, *nt.* 2. vetana, *nt.* 3. sañcāravaya, *m.* niyamitamūla, *nt. v.i.* 1. irīyati ; pavattati ; 2. pariyaṭati ; āhiṇḍati.

Farewell, *n.* sotthi, *f.* subhāsiŋsana, *nt.* bhaddaŋ te !

Farina, *n.* 1. dhaññapiṭṭha, *nt.* 2. parāga, *m.* °**ceous,** *a.* piṭṭhamaya.

Farm, *n.* ārāma, *m.* vatthu, *nt.* °**er,** *n.* khettājīvī ; kassaka, *m.* °**house,** *n.* ārāmakuṭi, *f.* °**ing,** *n.* kasikamma, *nt.* °**yard,** *n.* khalamaṇḍala, *nt.*

Farm, *v.t.* kasaṇāya aññassa bhūmiŋ gaṇhāti. *v.i.* kasati ; kasikammaŋ karoti. *p.p.* kasita *or* kaṭṭha ; katakasikamma.

Farrago, *n.* missitabhaṇḍasamūha, *m.*

Farrier, *n.* 1. assavejja, *m.* 2. assapādughaṭaka, *m.*

Farther, *a.* dūratara. — **shore,** paratīra, *nt.* °**est,** *a.* dūratama.

Farthing, *n.* tambamuddā ; kākaṇikā, *f.*

Fascicle, Fasciculus, *n.* 1. thabaka ; gocchaka, *m.* 2. potthakabhāga, *m.*

Fascinate, *v.t.* moheti ; vasīkaroti ; rameti. *p.p.* mohita ; °kata ; ramita. °**ion,** *n.* mohana ; vasīkaraṇa ; ramāpana, *nt.* °**ing,** *a.* pamohaka ; palobhaka.

Fash, *n.* hiŋsā, *f. v.t.* hiŋsati ; pīḷeti. *p.p.* °sita ; pīḷita.

Fashion, *n.* 1. vilāsa ; 2. lokācāra, *m. v.t.* vidahati ; racayati ; alaṅkaroti. *p.p.* vihita ; racita ; alaṅkata. °**able,** *a.* lokavohārocita ; ācārānurūpa.—**monger,** *n.* siṅgārappiya, *m.*

Fast, *a.* 1. daḷha ; gāḷha ; thira ; acala ; 2. sīgha ; turita ; avilambita, *adv.* 1. daḷhaŋ ; gāḷhaŋ ; thiraŋ ; 2. sīghaŋ ; turitaŋ ; tuvaṭaŋ.—**friend,** daḷhamitta, *m.* °**ness,** 1. thiratta ; daḷhatta, *nt.* 2. sīghatta ; turitatta, *nt.*

Fast, *n.* upavāsa, *m.* anasana, *nt. v.i.* upavasati ; āhāraŋ paṭikkhipati. *p.p.* upavuttha ; paṭikkhittāhāra. °**er,** *n.* upavāsī ; uposathika, *m. adv.* khippataraŋ. °**day,** *n.* uposathadivasa, *m.*

Fasten, *v.t.* bandhati ; ghaṭeti. *p.p.* baddha ; ghaṭita.

Fastidious, *a.* dutappiya, durārādhiya. °**ly,** *adv.* dutappiyākārena. °**ness,** *n.* dutappiyatā, *f.*

Fastness, *n.* balakoṭṭhaka, *m.* dugga, *nt.*

Fat, *n* vasā, *f.* meda, *m.* adj. 1. thūla ; thulla ; pīvara ; pīṇa ; 2. dhanavantu ; 3. lagganasīla. °**ness,** pīvaratta ; thullatta, *nt.*

°**ten**, *v.t.* poseti ; vaḍḍheti, *v.i.* saŋvaḍḍhati ; pīvaro bhavati. *p.p.* posita ; °ḍhita ; saŋvaḍḍha ; pīvarībhūta. °**ty**, *a.* medabahula.

Fatal, *a.* 1. avassabhāvī ; anivāriya ; 2. pāṇahara ; jīvitanāsaka. °**ism**, *n.* niyativāda, *m.* °**ist**, *n.* niyativādī, *m.* °**ity**, *n.* 1. niyatiparāyaṇatā, *f.* kammavipāka, *m.* 2. pāṇahāritā, *f.* jīvitasaŋsaya, *m.* °**ly**, *adv.* 1. jīvitasaŋsayāvahākārena ; 2. niyatiyā.

Fate, *n.* 1. niyati, *f.* vidhi ; kammaniyāma, *m.* 2. vināsa, *m.* 3. bhāgyadevī, *f.* °**ful**, *a.* niyatisiddha ; kammaniyamita. **Ill —**, dubbhāgya, *nt.* **Ill-fated**, *a.* duddasāpanna ; mandabhāgya. **Well-fated**, *a.* subhaga ; dhañña ; mahābhāgya.

Father, *n.* pitu ; janaka ; tāta ; janetu, *m.* °**hood**, pitupada, *nt.* °**in-law**, sasura, *m.* °**less**, *a.* nippitika. °**ly**, *a.* pitusadisa. °**land**, *n.* jātabhūmi, *f.* **— 's elder brother**, mahāpitu, *m.* **— 's younger brother**, cūlapitu, *m.*

Father, *v.t.* pituttaŋ pāpuṇāti. *p.p.* °patta.

Fathom, *n.* vyāma, *m.* *v.t.* ogāhati ; pamāṇeti. *p.p.* ogāḷha ; °ṇita. °**less**, *a.* agādha ; atigambhīra. °**lessly**, *adv.* atigambhīratāya.

Fatidical, *a.* anāgataŋsañāṇī.

Fatigue, *n.* parissama ; kilamatha, *m.* *v.t.* kilameti ; āyāseti. *p.p.* °mita ; °sita. °**less**, *a.* akilanta.

Fatling, *n.* thūla-taruṇapasu, *m.*

Fatten see under **Fat.**

Fatuity, *n.* muṭṭhasaccatā, *f.*

Fatuous, *a.* jaḷa ; muṭṭhassati. °**ness**, *n.* jaḷatā, *f.*

Faugh, *intj.* dhī ; dhiratthu.

Fault, *n.* khalita ; vajja, *nt.* accaya ; dosa ; pamāda, *m.* °**less**, *a.* niravajja ; niddosa ; nimmala ; akalaṅka. **— finder**, randhagavesī, *m.* °**ily**, *adv.* sadosākārena. °**y**, *a.* sadosa ; sāvajja ; sāparādha.

Fauna, *n.* pasugaṇa ; tiracchānaloka, *m.*

Favour, *n.* 1. anuggaha ; pasāda, *m.* anukampā, *f.* 2. anuññā ; anumati, *f.* *v.t.* 1. anuggaṇhāti ; upatthambheti ; varaŋ deti ; 2. anujānāti. *p.p.* anuggahita ; °bhita ; dinnavara ; anuññāta. °**able**, *a.* anukūla ; hitakara. °**ably**, *adv.* sānuggahaŋ ; anukūlatāya. °**ite**, *n.* vallabha ; 3. adj. piyatama. °**itism**, *n.* pakkhapātitā, *f.*

Fawn, *n.* 1. nīcavutti, *f.* 2. migapotaka, *m.* adj. dhūsara. *v.i.* upalāleti. *p.p.* °lita. °**er**, *n.* upalālaka. *m,* °**ing**, *n.* upalālanā, *f.* °**ingly**, *adv.* cāṭukamyatāya.

Fealty, *n.* sāmibhatti, *f.* anurāga, *m.*

Fear, *n.* bhaya, *nt.* santāsa, *m.* bhīti, *f.* *v.i.* bhāyati ; uttasati. *p.p.* bhāyita *or* bhīta ; °sita. °**ful**, *a.* 1. bhayānaka ; bhayāvaha ; bhīma ; bherava ; bhayaṅkara ; bhayajanaka ; 2. *Timid*, bhīruka ; bhayaṭṭa ; uttrasta. °**fully**, *adv.* 1. dāruṇākārena ;

2. sabhayaŋ. °**less,** *a.* nibbhaya ; abhīruka ; nissārajja ; abhīta. °**lessly,** *adv.* nibbhayatāya; nirāsaṅkaŋ. °**some,** *a.* bhayāvaha ; bhītijanaka.

Feasible, *a.* sukara ; susādhiya ; sakya.

Feast, *n.* 1. ussava ; chaṇa, *m.* 2. parivesanā, *f.* maṅgalabhojana, *nt.* *v.t.* bhojanena santappeti. *v i.* yathākāmaŋ bhuñjati. *p.p.* °pita ; °bhutta.

Feat, *n.* vīrakriyā, *f.* vikkama, *m.* adj. sobhana.

Feather, *n.* patta ; piñja, *nt.* (sakuṇa) pakkha, *m.* *v.t.* 1. pakkhipattehi bhūseti; 2. pattāni luñcati; 3. kāyaŋ cāleti. °**brained,** *a.* mandamatika, °**ed,** *a.* pakkhayutta. — **of an arrow,** vāja ; puṅkha, *m.* °**less,** *a.* pakkharahita ; ajātapakkha. °**y,** *a.* bahupiñjaka. °**ing,** *n.* pattasamūha, *m.*

Feature, *n.* ākāra ; liṅga ; saṇṭhāna ; lakkhaṇa, *nt.* pl. mukhasaṇṭhāna ; sarīralakkhaṇa, *nt.* °**less,** *a* visesākāra-rahita.

Febrifuge, *n.* jaranāsī-bhesajja, *nt* °**gal,** *a.* jararoganāsaka.

February, *n.* māgha (-māsa), *m.*

Feculence, *n.* āvilatta; samalatta, *nt.* °**lent,** *a.* āvila ; lulita.

Fecund, *a.* bahuputtaka ; bahuphalada. °**ate,** *v.t.* saphalīkaroti ; phalaŋ janeti. *p.p.* °kata ; janitaphala. °**ation,** °**ity,** *n.* avañjhatā, *f.* saphalīkaraṇa, *nt.*

Federal, *a.* sāmūhika ; saŋhata ; sandhita. °**ize,** *v.t.* samūheti ; gaṇabandhaŋ karoti. *p.p.* °hita; °kata.

Federate, *a.* same as **Federal,** *v.t.* gaṇaŋ bandhati. *p.p.* gaṇabaddha. °**ion,** gaṇabandhana, *nt.*

Fee, *n.* vetana ; nibbisa, *nt.* *v.t.* vetanaŋ deti. *p.p.* dinnavetana. — **for bringing up,** posāvanika, *nt.*

Feeble, *a.n.* dubbala ; appathāma ; sattihīna ; sithila. °**ness,** *n.* dubbalya ; asāmatthiya, *nt.* °**ly,** *adv.* mandaŋ ; sithilaŋ ; dubbalatāya.

Feed, *v.t.* 1. bhojeti ; parivisati ; 2. poseti ; bharati. *p.p.* bhojita ; °vesita ; °sita ; bhata. — **on,** adati ; khādati ; asnāti ; bhuñjati. °**er,** *n.* 1. bhojaka ; posaka, *m.* 2. bhuñjaka, *m.* °**ing,** *n.* 1. parivesanā, *f.* 2. posaṇa, *nt.* —°**ing on,** bhojī, *m.* °**ing on blood,** lohitabhakkha, *a.* °**ing on flesh,** maŋsabhojī, *a.*

Feel, *v.t.* phusati ; vedeti ; anubhavati. *v.i.* maññati. *p.p.* phuṭṭha ; vedita ; anubhūta ; mata. *n.* muta ; phusana, *nt.* °**er,** *n.* phusanāvayava, *m.* — **friendly,** mettāyati. — **hungry,** jighacchati. °**ing,** *n.* 1. vedanā, *f.* anubhavana, *nt.* 2. phusana ; parāmasana, *nt.* 3. dayā ; anukampā, *f.* 4. saññā, *f.* °**ing,** *a.* sacetana ; paṭisaŋvedī. °**ingly,** *adv.* sānukampaŋ. — **pity,** anukampati. — **remorse,** anutappati.

Feign, *v.t.* vyājena dasseti ; kuhayati. *p.p.* °sita ; °yita. °**ed,** *a.* kapaṭa ; vyāja. — **illness,** gilānālayaŋ dasseti.

Feint, *n.* 1. micchāvyapadesa ; 2. vyājapahāra, *m.* *v.i.* kuhako hoti.

Felicific, *a.* sukhāvaha; phāsujanaka.

Felicitate, *v.t.* ānandaŋ pakāseti; abhinandati. *p.p.* pakāsitānanda; °dita. °**ion**, *n.* muditā; abhinandanā; tuṭṭhipavedanā, *f.*

Felicitous, *a.* 1 pītijanaka; 2. atisukhita; atidhañña. °**ly**, *adv.* atidhaññatāya.

Felicity, *n.* 1. accantasukha, *nt.* paramānanda, *m.* mahāpuññatā, *f.* 2. sundaravākya, *nt.*

Feline, *a.* biḷālāyatta.

Fell, *n.* camma; ajina, *nt.* adj. kakkhaḷa; dāruṇa, *v.t.* pāteti; avacchindati; obhañjati; opāteti. *p.p.* pātita; avacchinna; obhaṭṭha.

Felloe, Felly, *n.* 1. cakkanemi, *f.* 2. nemibhāga, *m.*

Fellow, *n.* 1. sahāya; sahacara, *m.* adj. 1. sajātika; 2. samapadaṭṭha. — **countryman**, sadesīya, *m.* — **feeling**, samānasukhadukkhatā, *f.* °**ship**, *n.* sahāyatta; sahadhammikatta; sāmājikatta, *nt.* — **student**, sahasikkhaka, *m.* — **worker**, sahakammakārī. **Bad** —, ceṭaka, duṭṭhapakatika, *m.*

Felon, *n.* sāhasika; mahāparādhī, *m.* °**ious**, *a.* atidāruṇa; atisāhasika. °**y**, *n.* mahāpātaka, *m.*

Felt, *n.* namataka; kambala, *nt.* adj. uṇṇāmaya.

Female, *n.* itthī; nārī; vanitā; aṅganā, *f.* — **animal**, dhenu, *f.* — **organ**, yoni, *f.* itthinimitta, *nt.*

Feme covert, *n.* vivāhitā, *f.*

Feme sole, *n.* 1. avivāhitā; 2. vidhavā, *f.*

Feminine, *a.* itthibhāvayutta. — **gender**, itthiliṅga, *nt.* — **quality**, itthākappa, *m.* °**ity**, *n.* itthibhāva, *m.*

Feminize, *v.t.* itthittaŋ pāpeti. *v.i.* itthittaŋ pāpuṇāti. *p.p.* °pāpita; °patta.

Femoral, *a.* ūrusambanda.

Femur, *n.* ūraṭṭhi, *nt.*

Fen, *n.* anūpa, *m.* jalabahulabhūmi, *f.*

Fence, *n.* vati, *f.* parikkhepa, *m.* *v.t.* vatiyā parikkhipati; ārakkhati. *p.p.* vatiparikkhitta; °khita. *v.i.* 1. khaggasippam upāsati; 2. thenita-bhaṇḍāni vikkiṇāti. °**er**, *n.* khaggasippavidū; asiyodha, *m.* °**ing**, *n.* 1. satthaparicaya, *m.* satthavijjā, *f.* 2. vatibandhana, *nt.* °**less**, *a.* vatirahita; arakkhita; anāvaṭa.

Fend, *v.t.* āvarati; nivāreti. *p.p.* āvaṭa; °rita. °**er**, *n.* nivāraka, *m.* (of a hearth:) aṅgāragutti, *f.* (of a carriage:) rathagutti, *f.*

Fenestrate, *a.* khuddaka-vātāyana-sahita.

Feracious, *a.* bahuphaladāyī.

Feracity, *n.* bahuphalatā, *f.*

Feral, *a.* avinīta; adanta.

Ferine, *a.* vanacara; vāḷa.

Ferment, *n.* madirābīja; kiṇṇa, *nt.* *v.i.* paccati; pheṇam uppādeti. *v.t.* khobheti. *p.p.* pakka; uppāditapheṇa; °bhita. °**ation**, *n.* paccana; antokhobha, *m.*

Fern, *n.* bahupattaka, *m.*

Ferocious, *a.* dāruṇa ; ludda ; sāhasika. °**ly,** *adv.* dāruṇākārena.

Ferocity, *n.* luddatta ; dāruṇatta, *nt.*

Ferreous, *a.* ayomissa.

Ferret, *n.* 1. nakulavisesa, *m.* 2. vatthapaṭṭikā, *f.*

Ferriage, *n.* 1. titthasuṅka, *m.* 2. titthagamana, *nt.*

Ferric, *a.* ayomaya.

Ferriferous, *a.* ayodāyaka.

Ferrous, see **Ferreous.**

Ferry, *n.* (gaṅgā-) tittha, *nt.* °**boat,** titthataraṇī, *f.* °**man,** titthaniyutta, *m.*

Ferry, *v.t.* tāreti ; pāraŋ neti. *v.i.* tarati ; pāraŋ gacchati. *p.p.* tārita ; °nīta ; tiṇṇa ; pāraṅgata *or* pāragata. °**ing across,** tiriyaŋ-taraṇa, *nt.*

Fertile, *a.* sārayutta ; bahuphalada. °**ity,** *n.* ojavantatā ; phaladatā, *f.* °**ize,** *v.t.* ojavantaŋ *or* phaladāyakaŋ karoti. °**ization,** *n.* ojavantakaraṇa, *nt.*

Ferule, *n.* tāḷanī, *f.v.t.* (vettādīhi) tāḷeti. *p.p.* °tāḷita.

Fervency, *n.* 1. mahussāha, *m.* 2. caṇḍikka, *nt.*

Fervent, *a.* uyyogī ; mahussāhī. °**ly,** *adv.* mahussāhena.

Fervidly, see **Fervently.**

Fervour, *n.* adhimattehā, *f.* adhikaviriya, *nt.*

Festal, *a.* chaṇanissita ; ussavayogga.

Fester, *v.i.* sapūyo bhavati. *p.p.* sapūyībhūta. °**ing corpse,** vipubbaka, *nt.*

Festival, *n.* chaṇa ; ussava, *m.*

Festive, *n.* chaṇanissita ; ussavayutta. — **day,** chaṇadivasa, *m.* — **gathering,** samajja, *nt.* °**ity,** *n.* 1. maṅgala, *nt.* ussava, *m.* 2. pamoda, *m.*

Festoon, *n.* mālāguṇa, *m.* *v.t.* mālāguṇe yojeti ; mālāhi bhūseti. *p.p.* °jita ; °bhūsita. °**ed post,** pupphagghiya, *nt.* °**work,** mālākamma, *nt.*

Fetch, *v.t.* (gantvā) āharati *or* āneti. *p.p.* āhaṭa ; ānīta. *n.* dūragāmī-phala, *nt.*

Fête, *n.* mahussava, *m.* *v.t.* sakkaroti ; bhojeti. *p.p.* sakkata ; bhojita.

Fetich, °**sh,** *n.* milakkhānaŋ pujjavatthu, *nt.*

Fetid, *a.* pūtigandhī.

Fetor, *n.* pūtibhāva ; pūtigandha, *m.*

Fetter, *n.* anduka ; nigaḷa, *m.* saṅkhalikā, *f.* *v.t.* rodheti ; nigaḷeti ; bandhati. *p.p.* rodhita ; °ḷita ; baddha.

Fetus, Foetus, *n.* kalalarūpa, *nt.* apariṇata-gabbha, *m.*

Feud, *n.* 1. cirappavattī-kalaha *or* viggaha, *m.* 2. paveṇibhūmi, *f.* °**al,** *a.* paveṇibhūmyāyatta. °**atory,** *n.* parabhūmivāsī, *m.* adj. bhūmisāmikopajīvī, *m.*

Fever, *n.* 1. jararoga, *m.* 2. pariḷāha, *m.* *v.t.* santāpeti ; jarāturaŋ karoti. °**ish,** *a.* tāpajanaka ; jarayutta. °**ishness,** *n.* jarayuttatā, *f.* °**ous,** *a.* jaruppādaka.

Few, *a.n.* appaka ; thoka ; īsaka ; paritta ; manda. — **days,** katipāha, *nt.* °**ness,** *n.* appatta ; mandatta, *nt.*

Fiancé, *n.* vāritaka, *m.* °**cee**, *n.* vāritakaṅganā, *f.*

Fiasco, *n.* virādhana ; ninditapatana, *nt.*

Fiat, *n.* thirāṇā, *f.* thiraniyama, *m.* *v.t.* adhikārabalaŋ deti. *p.p.* dinnādhi°.

Fib, *n.* tucchamusā, *f.* *v.i.* musā bhaṇati.

Fibre, *n.* tantu ; guṇa, *m.* aŋsu, *nt.* °**ous**, *a.* aŋsuyutta.

Fibula, *n.* khuddaka-jaṅghaṭṭhi, *nt.*

Fickle, *a.* capala ; lola ; anavaṭṭhita. °**ness**, *n.* cāpalya, *nt.* anavaṭṭhiti, *f.*

Fictile, *a.* mattikāmaya.

Fiction, *n.* kappitaracanā ; pabandhakathā, *f.* °**ist**, *n.* pabandhakārī, *m.* °**al**, *a.* parikappanāyatta. °**ive**, *a.* manokappita.

Fictitious, *a.* kappanāmaya ; micchāracita ; kūṭa. °**ly**, *adv.* kūṭākārena.

Ficus, *n.* udumbara, *m.*—**Religiosa**, *n.* assatthataru ; bodhirukkha, *m.*

Fiddle, *n.* vīṇā ; sāraṅgī, *f.* *v.t.* vīṇaŋ vādeti. *p.p.* vāditavīṇa. °**er**, *n.* vīṇāvādaka, *m.*

Fidelity, *n.* anurāga, *m.* āsatti, *f.* vallabhatta, *nt.*

Fidget, *n.* anavaṭṭhiti, *f.* sarīravikkhepa, *m.* *v.t.* kāyaŋ vikkhipati. *v.i.* sambhamati. *p.p.* vikkhittakāya ; sambhanta.

Fiducial, *a.* bahusammata ; paṭiggahita.

Fiduciary, *n.* nikkhittavatthugopaka, *m.* adj. gopakattāyatta.

Fie, *intj.* dhī ; dhiratthu.

Fief, *n.* rājadatta-bhūmi, *f.*

Field, *n.* 1. khetta ; kedāra, *nt.* ropiyabhūmi ; 2. aṅgaṇa, *nt.* 3. visayaṭṭhāṇa, *nt.* 4. āyatana, *nt.* 5. patiṭṭhā, *f.* *v.i.* kandukaŋ khipati. —°**marshal**, mahāsenāpati, *m.* — **of vision**, diṭṭhipatha, *m.*—**sports**, aṅgaṇakīḷā, *f.* **Battle**° yuddhabhūmi, *f.* **Loses the** —, parājīyati. **Takes the** —, yuddham ārabhati.

Fiend, *n.* pisāca, *m.* bhūta, *nt.* °**ish**, °**like**, *a.* 1. pisācasadisa ; 2. atikakkhaḷa.

Fierce, *a.* ghora ; caṇḍa ; dāruṇa. °**looking**, *a.* bhīmadassana. °**ly**, *adv.* ghorākārena. °**ness**, *n.* caṇḍatta ; dāruṇatta, *nt.*

Fiery, *a.* 1. accuṇha ; santatta ; 2. aticaṇḍa ; 3. tibba ; ugga.

Fifteen, *a.n.* pañcadasa ; paṇṇarasa. °**th**, *a.* pañcadasama.

Fifth, *a.* pañcama.

Fifty, *n.* paññāsā ; paṇṇāsā ; paññāsati, *f.* °**eight**, aṭṭhapaññāsā, *f.* °**four**, catupaññāsā, *f.* °**six**, chappaññāsā, *f.* °**three**, tepaññāsā, *f.* °**two**, dvipaññāsā, *f.* °**nine**, ekūnasaṭṭhi, *f.*

Fig, *n.* udumbara, *m.*

Fight, *n.* yuddha ; yujjhana ; pahāradāna, *nt.* *v.t.* yodheti ; yujjhati. *v.i.* yugaŋ gaṇhāti. *p.p.* yodhita ; yujjhita ; gahitayuga. — **a battle**, saṅgāmeti. °**ing**, *n.* āyodhana, *nt.* °**er**, *n.* yodha ; sampahāraka, *m.*

Figment, *n.* manokappanā, *f.*

Figure, *n.* 1. paṭibimba ; saṇṭhāna, *nt.* 2. aṅka ; saṅkhyārūpa, *nt.* 3. vākyālaṅkāra, *m.*

4. (body :) deha, *m.* sarīra, *nt.* *v.t.* 1. rūpāni ālikhati ; 2. aṅkāni likhati. °**ative,** *a.* alaṅkārika ; rūpakāyatta. °**ine,** *n.* khuddakapaṭimā, *f.*

Filament, *n.* (muṇāla-) sutta ; kesara, *nt.*

Filatory, Filature, *n.* suttakantana-yanta, *nt.*

Filch, *v.t.* appaso coreti. *p.p.* °corita. °**er,** *n.* thena, *m.*

File, *n.* 1. lohakhādaka, *m.* 2. panti ; āvali ; seṇī, *f.* *v.t.* 1. āvuṇāti ; yathākkamaŋ yojeti ; 2. lohakhādakena samīkaroti. *p.p.* āvuta ; °yojita ; °kata. *v.i.* paṭipāṭiyā gacchati. °**ings,** *n.* lohacuṇṇa, *nt.*

Filial, *a.* gehasita ; janakajanitāyatta. °**ly,** *adv.* gehasita-pemena.

Filiform, *a.* suttākāra.

Filigree, *n.* suvaṇṇa-tantukamma, *nt.*

Fill, *n.* pūraṇa, *nt.* titti, *f.* anūnasampādana, *nt.* *v.t.* pūreti, *v.i.* pūrati. *p.p.* pūrita ; puṇṇa. °**er,** *n.* pūraka, *m.* — **in,** ūnaŋ pūreti. °**ing,** *n.* paripūraṇa, *nt.* °**ing with,** vyāpaka ; pharaṇaka, *a.*

Fillet, *n.* paṭṭabandhana, *nt.* *v.t.* paṭṭena bandhati. *p.p.* paṭṭabaddha.

Fillip, *n.* 1. nakhapiṭṭhippahāra, *m.* 2. uyyojana ; uttejana, *nt.* *v.t.* 1. nakhena ākoṭeti ; 2. uttejeti. *p.p.* °ṭita ; °jita.

Filly, *n.* 1. kisorī, *f.* 2. keḷisīlā yuvatī, *f.*

Film, *n.* tanupaṭala ; chāyārūpapaṭala, *nt.* °**y,** *a.* paṭalāvuta. °**iness,** *n.* paṭalāvutatta, *nt.*

Filter, *n.* parissāvaṇa ; nissandana ; jalasodhana, *nt.* *v.t.* parissāveti. *v.i.* nissandati. *p.p.* °vita ; °dita.

Filth, *n.* asucikalala, *nt.* °**ily,** *adv.* jegucchākārena. °**y,** *a.* saṅkiliṭṭha ; aparisuddha ; jeguccha.

Filtrate, *n.* āsava, *m.* *v.t.* parissāveti. *p.p.* °vita. °**ion,** *n.* parissāvaṇa, *nt.*

Fin, *n.* macchapakkha, *m.* °**footed,** *a* jālapāda. °**less,** *a.* apakkha. °**ny,** *a.* 1. pakkhasahita ; 2. pakkhasadisa.

Final, *a.* *n.* 1. antima ; carima ; pacchima ; osāna ; 2. sunicchita. —**aim,** paramattha, *m.* —**bliss,** *m.* nibbāṇa ; paramasukha, *nt.* —**examination,** *n.* carimopaparikkhā, *f.* °**ity,** *n.* carimakatta. *nt.* °**ly,** *adv.* osānavasena ; ante ; osāne. — **release,** parimutti, *f.* dukkhanirodha, *m.*

Finale, *n.* niṭṭhā, *f.* osāna, *nt.*

Finance, *n.* āya ; dhanāgama, *m.* °**ial,** *a.* āyāyatta ; dhanāyatta. °**ialist,** *n.* āyakammika, *m.* °**ier,** *n.* āyādhikārī, *m.*

Find, *n.* upalābha, *m.* anāvaṭavatthu, *nt.* *v.t.* upalabhati ; adhigacchati. *p.p.* upaladdha ; adhigata. — **delight in,** abhiramati. — **fault with,** dosam āropeti. — **out,** nirāvarati. — **pleasure in,** rajjati ; rañjati. °**ing,** *n.* 1. upaladdhavatthu, *nt.* 2. vinicchaya, *m.*

Fine, *n.* daṇḍakamma, *nt.* *v.t.* daṇḍaŋ paṇeti ; daṇḍeti. *p.p.* daṇḍita. °**ed**, *a.* daṇḍappatta. **Liable to —**, daṇḍāraha, *a.*

Fine, *a.* 1. sukhuma ; 2. sundara ; sobhana ; surūpa ; 3. tanu ; 4. tikhiṇa ; 5. visuddha ; 6. duravabodha. —**art**, *n.* sundarakalā, *f.* °**ly**, *adv.* 1. sukhumaŋ ; 2. sundarākārena. °**ness**, 1. sukhumatta ; 2. sundaratta ; 3. tanutta, *nt.*

Finer, *n.* lohasodhaka, *m.* °**y**, *n.* 1. sobhanatta, *nt.* 2. vibhūsana, *nt.* 3. kammāruddhana, *nt.*

Finesse, *n.* tikhiṇopāya, *m.* *v.t.* tikhiṇopāyaŋ yojeti.

Finger, *n.* aṅguli, *f.* *v.t.* 1. aṅgulīhi phusati ; 2. aṅguliyā ñāpeti ; 3. vādeti ; 4. lañchaŋ gaṇhāti. *p.p.* °phuṭṭha ; °ñāpita ; vādita ; gahitalañcha. °**less**, *a.* aṅgulirahita. °**joint**, aṅgulipabba, *nt.* °**post**, maggadassakatthambha, *m.* °**print**, aṅgulimuddana, *nt.* °**ring**, aṅgulīyaka, *nt.* **Fourth —**, anāmikā, *f.* **Last —**, kaniṭṭhā, *f.* **Middle —**, majjhimā, *f.* **Second —**, tajjanī, *f.*

Finical, *a.* vilāsakāmī. °**ly**, *adv.* vilāsakāmitāya.

Finicking, *a.* vibhūsanagaruka.

Finis, *n.* anta, *m.* osāna, *nt.* parisamatti, *f.*

Finish, *n.* osāna ; niṭṭhāpana, *nt.* *v.t.* niṭṭhāpeti ; osāpeti ; samāpeti. *v.i.* niṭṭhāti. *p.p.* °pita ; niṭṭhita. °**ing**, *n.* niṭṭhāna ; samāpana, *nt.*

Finite, *a.* paricchinna ; parimita ; tīrita. °**ly**, *adv.* 1. samariyādaŋ ; saparicchedaŋ ; 2. niccayena.

Fiord, *n.* bhūmyantarasamudda, *m.*

Fir(-tree), devadāru, *nt.*

Fire, *n.* aggi ; pāvaka ; hutāsana ; jātaveda ; anala ; accimantu, *m.* *v.t.* 1. jhāpeti ; ālimpeti ; 2. nāḷīyantena vijjhati ; 3. ussāheti ; uddīpeti. *v.i.* jalati ; ḍayhati. *p.p.* °pita ; °viddha ; °hita ; °pita ; jalita ; daḍḍha. °**arm**, aggiyanta ; nāḷīyanta, *nt.* °**brand**, alāta, *nt.* °**brigade**, agginibbāpakaseṇā, *f.* °**eater**, indajālika ; mahāmalla, *m.* °**escape**, aggito muccanūpakaraṇa, *nt.* °**fly**, khajjopanaka, *m.* °**irons**, saṇḍāsa, *m.* °**man**, ujjālaka, *m.* °**place**, 1. uddhana ; 2. jantāghara, *nt.* °**proof**, *a.* adayhamāna. °**sacrifice**, aggihoma, *m.* °**side**, uddhanapassa, *m.* °**wood**, dāru ; indhana, *nt.* °**works**, aggimālā, *f.* °**worship**, aggiparicaraṇa, *nt.*

Firm, *n.* vāṇijasamavāya, *m.*

Firm, *a.* thira ; daḷha ; akampiya ; acala. °**ly**, *adv.* thiraŋ ; daḷhaŋ. °**ly devoted**, aveccappasanna, *a.* °**ly rooted**, baddhamūla, *a.* °**ness**, thiratta ; daḷhatta, *nt.*

Firmament, *n.* ākāsa, *m.* nabha, antalikkha, *nt.*

First, *a.* 1. paṭhama ; ādima ; 2. agga ; mukhya ; padhāna. — **born**, *a.* pubbaja ; paṭhamajāta. — **fruit**, aggaphala, *nt.* °**half**, pubbaddha, *m.* °**ling**, *n.* paṭhamaphala, *nt.* ādima-nipphatti, *f.* °**ly**, *adv.* paṭhamataraŋ. — **part of the day**, pubbaṇha, *m.* — **rate**, *a.* aggatama ;

seṭṭhatara. **From the —**, ādito paṭṭhāya.

Firth, Frith, *n.* sākhāsamudda, *m.*

Fisc, *n.* rājakosa, *m.* °**al,** *a.* rājakosāyatta. *n.* rājakosādhikārī, *m.*

Fish, *n.* maccha ; mīna ; jhasa, *m.* *v.t.* macche bandhati. — **egg,** macchaṇḍa, *nt.* °**er,** °**erman,** dhīvara ; kevaṭṭa ; bālisika, *m.* °**hook,** balisa, *nt.* °**ing,** *n.* macchagahaṇa, *nt.* °**ing rod,** *n.* balisayaṭṭhi, *f.* °**monger,** macchika, *m.* °**net,** khipa, *m.* °**trap,** kumina, *nt.* °**y,** *a.* 1. macchabahula ; 2. macchasadisa.

Fissiped, *a. n.* bhinnasapha (-pasu), *m.*

Fissure, *n.* vivara ; phulla, *nt.* *v.t.* vidāreti. *p.p.* °rita.

Fist, *n.* muṭṭhi, *m.* *v.t.* muṭṭhinā paharati. *p.p.* °pahaṭa. °**icuffs,** muṭṭhippahāra, *m.* mallayuddha, *nt.*

Fistula, *n.* nāḷīvaṇa, *nt.* — **in the anus,** bhagandalā, *f.*

Fit, *a.* yogga ; patirūpa ; ucita ; anurūpa ; anucchavika. *v.t.* yojeti; ghaṭeti; sansandeti; samodhāneti. *p.p.* yojita ; °ṭita ; °dita ; °nita. *v.i.* ghaṭīyati ; saŋsandīyati. *noun:* mucchā, *f.* bhama, *m.* āturatta, *nt.* — **for action,** kammañña, *a.* — **for the purpose,** alaŋkammaniya, *a.* — **for riding,** opavayha, *a.* — **for use,** paribhogāraha, *a.* °**ly,** *adv.* yathārahaŋ. °**ness,** yoggatā; bhabbatā; anurūpatā, *f.* — **of anger,** kopāvesa, *m.* — **of fever,** jaravega, *m.*

Fitful, *a.* nānāvatthāyutta. °**ly,** *adv.* kālantarikavasena.

Fitting, *n.* 1. ghaṭana, *nt.* 2. *pl.* upakaraṇa. adj. anurūpa.

Five, *a. n.* pañca. 3. — **days,** pañcāha, *nt.* °**fold,** *a.* pañcavidha. — **hundred,** pañcasata, *nt.* — **moral precepts,** pañcasīla, *nt.* — **thousand,** pañcasahassa, *nt.* — **times,** pañcakkhattuŋ, *adv.* In — **ways,** pañcadhā, *adv.*

Fix, *v.t.* 1. yojeti ; ghaṭeti ; 2. niyameti ; vavatthapeti ; 3. patiṭṭhāpeti. *p.p.* yojita ; ghaṭita ; °mita ; °pita. — **an arrow,** saraŋ sannayhati. °**ation,** *n.* saṅghaṭana, *nt.* °**ative,** *a. n.* daḷhīkara (-vatthu), *nt.* °**ed,** *a* 1. thira ; daḷha ; 2. nicchita ; niyata ; suppatiṭṭhita. °**edness,** °**ity,** *m.* thiratta ; acalatta, *nt.* °**edly,** *adv.* thiraŋ ; acalaŋ. °**ed resolution,** thirādhiṭṭhāna, *nt.* °**ing,** *n.* 1. ghaṭana ; ābandhana ; 2. niyamana, *nt.* °**ture,** *n.* 1. ghaṭitavatthu, *nt.* 2. niyamita-dina, *nt.*

Fizz, Fizzle, *n.* sūsūyana, *nt.* *v.i.* sūsūyati. *p.p.* °yita.

Flabbergast, *v.t.* sammoheti ; vikkhepeti. *p.p.* °hita ; °pita.

Flabby, *a.* sithila ; lambamāna. °**iness,** *n.* sithilatta, *nt.*

Flabellate, *a.* vījanīsadisa.

Flaccid, see **Flabby.**

Flag, *n.* 1. dhaja ; ketu, *m.* patākā, *f.* 2. silāpatthara, *m.* *v.i.* 1. olambati ; 2. paṭilīyati. *v.t.* silāpaṭṭe attharati. *p.p.* °bita ; paṭilīna ; atthata-silāpaṭṭa. — **bearer,** *n.* dhajaggāhī, *m.* — **ship,** dhajanāvā, *f.* — **staff,** dhajayaṭṭhi, *f*

Flagellant, *a. n.* attakilamatha-yutta.

Flagellate, *v.t.* kasādīhi tāḷeti. *p.p.* °ḷita. °**ion,** *n.* tāḷana, *nt.*

Flageolet, *n.* dhamanavaŋsa, *m.*

Flagging, *n.* silāpaṭṭattharaṇa, *nt.* adj. milāyamāna.

Flagitious, *a.* atiduṭṭha; pāpiṭṭha.

Flagon, *n.* casaka, vittha, *nt.*

Flagrant, *a.* 1. mahāsāvajja; atidāruṇa; 2. ativyāpī; supākaṭa. °**ncy,** *n.* atidāruṇatā, *f.*

Flail, *n.* musala, *m.*

Flair, *n.* sahajabuddhi, *f.*

Flake, *n.* 1. kaṇa; lava, *m.* sakalikā, *f.* 2. himakaṇa, *v.i.* sakalībhavati; kaṇaso patati. *p.p.* °bhūta; °tita.

Flambeau, *n.* ukkā; daṇḍadīpikā, *f.*

Flamboyant, *a.* aggijālāsadisa; adhikavaṇṇayutta.

Flame, *n.* acci; sikhā; jālā, *f.* *v.i.* jalati; dippati. *p.p.* jalita; ditta. °**less,** *a.* vītaccika. °**ing,** *a.* jalanta; tapamāna. — **of a lamp,** dīpasikhā, *f.* °**y,** *a.* sikhāyutta.

Flamingo, *n.* rājahaŋsa, *m.*

Flammable, *a.* dahanīya; sukhaḍayha.

Flank, *n.* 1. passa; pakkha, *m.* 2. phāsulikā, *f.* *v.t.* passe tiṭṭhati; passato rakkhati. *p.p.* °ṭhita; °khita.

Flannel, *a. n.* kambala; uṇṇāmaya, *nt.*

Flap, *n.* 1. cālana; vidhunana; 2. tāḷana, *nt.* *v.t.* tāḷeti; vidhunāti; papphoṭeti. *p.p.* tāḷita; vidhūta; °ṭita, *v.i.* kampati. *p.p.* °pita. °**per,** *n.* 1. makkhikāvāraṇa, *nt.* 2, pakkhitāsakaghaṇṭā, *f.* 3. appattavayā kaññā, *f.*

Flapdoodle, *n.* palāpa, *m.* niratthakakathā, *f.*

Flare, *n.* calamāna-jālā, *f.* *v.i.* calasikhāhi jalati. °**ing,** *a.* dippamāna.

Flash, *n.* vipphuraṇa; niccharaṇa, *nt.* acirappabhā, *f.* *v.i.* 1. niccharati; vipphurati; dippati; 2. sahasāvibhavati; 3. khippaŋ paṭibhāti. *p.p.* °rita; vipphuṭa; ditta; °bhūta. *v.t.* sahasāvikaroti. *p.p.* °kata. °**y,** *a.* bahiramanīya; khaṇika; asāra.

Flask, *n.* 1. cammapasibbaka, *m.* 2. kācatumba, *m.* nāḷikā, *f.*

Flat, *n.* 1. tala; pāsādatala; samaṭṭhāna, *nt.* 2. udakāvaṭa-pulinatala, *nt.* 3. aghosakkhara, *nt.* 4. eḷamūga, *m.* adj. 1. sama; 2. asāra; 3. nirassāda; 4. nitteja; 5. suvyatta; paripphuṭa; 6. tiriyaŋ patita. °**ly,** *adv.* 1. samaŋ; 2. suvyattaŋ. °**ness,** *n.* samatā, *f.* — **nosed,** *a.* cipiṭakanāsa. — **roof,** muṇḍacchada, *m.* — **surface,** samatala, *nt.* °**ten,** *v.t.* 1. samīkaroti; 2. oṇāmeti; 3. virasīkaroti. *v.i.* samībhavati. *p.p.* °kata; °mita; °kata; °bhūta.

Flatter, *v.t.* upalāleti; micchā pasaŋsati. *p.p.* °lita; °sita. °**er,** *n.* upalālaka; ullapaka, *m.* °**ingly,** *adv.* cāṭukamyatāya; lālanapubbakaŋ. °**y,** *n.* ullapanā; cāṭukamyatā, *f.*

Flatulent, *a.* udaravātika ; vātabahula. °**ence,** *n.* udaravātābādha, *m.*

Flatus, *n.* udaravāta, *m.*

Flaunt, *n.* ketukamyatā ; attukkaŋsanā, *f.* *v.i.* sadappaŋ carati. *v.t.* attānam ukkaŋseti ; paraŋ vambheti. *p.p.* °sitatta ; °bhita. °**ing,** *a.* ussannamāna.

Flautist, *n.* veṇudhama, *m.*

Flavescent, *a.* mandapīta ; paṇḍuvaṇṇa.

Flavour, *n.* rasa ; assāda, *m.* *v.t.* sarasaŋ karoti. *p.p.* sarasīkata. °**ed with,** vidhūpita, *a.* °**ing,** *n.* rasayojana, *nt.* °**less,** *a.* virasa. °**ous,** *a.* surasa ; paṇīta.

Flaw, *n.* 1. dosa, *m.* randha ; vekalla, *nt.* 2. vātavega, *m.* °**less,** *a.* avikala ; niddosa. °**y,** *a.* sadosa ; vikala.

Flax, *n.* khoma, *nt.* ummā, *f.* °**en,** *a.* khomamaya.

Flay, *v.t.* cammam uppāṭeti ; nittacaŋ karoti. *p.p.* uppāṭitacamma ; nittacīkata. °**er,** *n.* cammuppāṭaka, *m.* °**ing,** *n.* cammuppāṭana ; tacāpaharaṇa, *nt.*

Flea, *n.* adhipātikā, *f.* uppātaka, *m.*

Fleck, *n.* kalaṅka, *m.* *v.t.* kalaṅketi ; kammāsaŋ karoti. *p.p.* °kita ; °kata. °**less,** *a.* akalaṅka.

Flecker, *v.t.* nānāvaṇṇaŋ karoti. *p.p.* °ṇīkata.

Fledge, *v.t.* pakkhe sampādeti ; pakkhehi bhūseti. *p.p.* sampāditapakkha ; °sita. °**ed,** *a.* jātapakkha. °**ling,** sakuṇapotaka, *m.*

Flee, *v.i.* 1. palāyati ; apakkamati ; 2. vajjeti ; pariharati. *p.p.* palāta ; apakkanta ; vajjita ; °rita *or* parihaṭa.

Fleece, *n.* uṇṇā, *f.* meṇḍaloma, *nt.* *v.t.* 1. lomāni chindati ; 2. (vatthādīni) acchindati *or* apaharati. *p.p.* lomacchinna ; acchinna ; apahaṭa. °**cy,** *a.* lomasa.

Fleer, *n.* upahāsa, *m.* *v.i.* upahasati ; parihasati.

Fleet, *n.* yuddhanāvāgaṇa ; nāvāsamūha, *m.* *v.i.* sīghaŋ yāti ; vegena calati ; antaradhāyati. *p.p.* °yāta ; °lita ; antarahita. adj. turitagatika ; sīghagāmī. —**horse,** javanassa, *m.* °**ing,** *a.* aciraṭṭhāyī. °**ingly,** *adv.* turitaŋ ; sīghaŋ. °**ness,** *n.* java, *m.* turitatta, *nt.*

Flesh, *n.* 1. maŋsa ; pisita, *nt.* 2. miñjā, *f.* 3. sattaloka, *m.* 4. kāmataṇhā, *f.* °**ly,** *a.* lokika ; sārīrika ; visayāyatta. °**monger,** *n.* maŋsavikkayī, *m.* °**y,** *a.* maŋsabahula. **Dried —,** vallūra, *nt.*

Flex, *n.* namya-lohatantu, *nt.* *v.t.* nāmeti. *p.p.* nāmita. °**ible,** *a.* namanakkhama. °**ibility,** *n.* namyatta ; anukūlatta, *nt.* °**ile,** *a.* kammañña. °**ion,** *n.* namitatta ; vaṅkatta, *nt.*

Flexuous, *a.* āvalibahula.

Flexure, *n.* nati, *f.* natatta, *nt.* addhacandākāra, *m.*

Flibbertigibbet, *n.* vācāla ; abhijappaka, *m.*

Flick, *n.* mandappahāra, *m.* *v.t.* mandaŋ paharati. *p.p.* °pahaṭa.

Flicker, *n.* kampana ; calana, *nt.* *v.t.* 1. calanto jalati ; 2. pakkhe vidhunāti ; kampati. *p.p.* vidhunitapakkha ; °pita. °**ing**, *a.* cañcala.

Flight, *n.* 1. palāyana, *nt.* 2. (of birds :) uḍḍīyana ; uppatana, *nt.* — **of steps**, sopāṇapanti, *f.*

Flighty, *a.* yathākāmacārī.

Flim-flam, *n.* tucchabhāsana, *nt.*

Flimsy, *a.* tanu ; asāra ; dubbala ; bhaṅgura. °**iness**, *n.* dubbalatta ; baṅguratta, *nt.*

Flinch, *v.i.* apasakkati ; olīyati. *p.p.* °kita ; olīna.

Flinders, *n. pl.* sakalikāni, *nt.*

Fling, *n.* 1. khipana ; vissajjana, *nt.* 2. āsajjavacana, *nt. v.t.* sahasā khipati ; vissajjeti. *v.i.* sahasā dhāvati *or* niccharati. *p.p.* °khitta ; vissaṭṭha ; °rita.

Flint, *n.* jotipāsāṇa ; aggipatthara, *m.* °**hearted**, *a.* thaddhahadaya. °**y**, *a.* 1. jotipāsāṇamaya ; 2. kaṭhinahadaya.

Flip, *n.* mandappahāra, *m. v.t.* ākoṭanena kampeti ; vidhunāti. *p.p.* °piṭa ; °nita.

Flippancy, *n.* vācālatā, *f.* cāpalla, *nt.*

Flippant, *a.* lahuggāhī ; agarukārī. °**ly**, *adv.* lahuggāhitāya.

Flirt, *n.* 1. sahasā-khepa, *m.* 2. (woman) : vilāsavatī ; līlāvatī, *f. v.t.* sahasā khipati, *v.i.* avahasati. *p.p.* °khitta ; °sita. °**ation**, *n.* līlā, *f.* hāva, *m.* °**atious**, *a.* hāva-bhāvappiya. °**ingly**, *adv.* salīlaŋ ; savilāsaŋ.

Flit, *n.* pariyaṭana ; paribbhamaṇa, *nt. v.i.* ito tato bhamati ; ṭhānā ṭhānam uḍḍeti. °**ting**, *n.* paribbhamaṇa ; turituḍḍīyana, *nt.*

Flitter, *v.i.* pakkhe vidhunāti ; paribbhamati. *p.p.* vidhūtapakkha ; °bhanta. — **mouse**, ajinapattā, *f.*

Float, *v.i.* plavati ; vuyhati. *v.t.* plāveti. *p.p.* plavita ; vūḷha ; plāvita. *n.* uḷumpa ; kulla, *m.* °**ing**, *a* plavamāna ; vuyhamāna ; °**age**, 1. udakayānasamūha, *m.* 2. vārito upari dissamāna-bhāga, *m.* °**sam**, *n.* vuyhamānavatthu, *nt.*

Flock, *n.* 1. yūtha ; gaṇa, *m.* 2. lomavaṭṭi, *f. v.i.* yuthavasena sammilati.

Floe, *n.* vuyhamāna-hima, *nt.*

Flog, *v.t.* (kasādīhi) āhanati *or* tāḷeti. *p.p.* °āhata ; tāḷita. °**ging**, *n.* āhanana ; tāḷana, *nt.*

Flood, *n.* 1. ogha ; pavāha, *m.* 2. udakottharaṇa, *nt. v.t.* pavāheti ; udakena osīdāpeti. *v.i.* (udakam) ottharati. *p.p.* °hita ; °pita ; otthaṭa. — **gate**, *n.* jaladvāra, *nt.*

Floor, *n.* 1. bhūtala, *nt.* saṅkhatabhūmi, *f. v.t.* 1. (phalakādīni) santharati ; 2. bhūmiyaŋ pāteti ; 3. (vivāde) parājeti. *p.p.* phalakasanthata ; °tita ; °jita. °**ing**, *n.* talanimmāṇa, *nt.* °**er**, *n.* 1. bhūmipātaka-pahāra, *m.* 2. atikaṭhina-pañha, *m.* °**less**, *a.* talarahita ; appatiṭṭha.

Flop, *n*. 1. kampana, *nt*. 2. kampanasadda, *m*. *v.i*. 1. saddāyanto patati ; 2. dolāyati ; 3. khalanto yāti.

Flora, *n*. bhūtagāma ; rukkhalatādi, *m*. °**al**, *a*. pupphavisayaka; bhūtagāmāyatta.

Florescence, *n*. pupphasamaya, *m*.

Floriate, *v.t*. pupphavikatīhi alaṅkaroti. *p.p*. °kata.

Floriculture, *n*. mālāvaccharopaṇa, *nt*. °**ist**, *n*. mālāropī, *m*.

Florid, *a*. 1. pupphākiṇṇa ; 2. aruṇavaṇṇa ; 3. accalaṅkata. °**ness**, *n*. 1. adhikālaṅkāratā; 2. vācāvibhūsā, *f*.

Floriferous, *a*. bahupupphajanaka.

Floriform, *a*. pupphasaṇṭhāna.

Florilegium, *n*. madhura-pajjasaṅgaha, *m*.

Florist, *n*. mālākāra ; pupphasampādaka, *m*.

Flotilla, *n*. lahunāvāsamūha, *m*.

Flounce, *v.i*. aṅgāni vikkhipati. *p.p*. vikkhittaṅga. *n*. aṅgavikkhepa, *m*. *noun*. dasāvikati, *f*.

Flounder, *v.i*. vipphandati. *p.p*. °dita. *noun*. macchavisesa, *m*.

Flour, *n*. (dhañña-) piṭṭha, *nt*. *v.t*. 1. sañcuṇṇeti ; 2. piṭṭhena ākirati. *p.p*. °ṇita ; piṭṭhākiṇṇa. °**mill**, *n*. dhaññapiŋsaka-yanta, *nt*.

Flourish, *n*. 1. samiddhi, *f*. 2. bāhirālaṅkāra, *m*. 3. dappitavācā, *f*. 4. paribbhamāpana, *nt*. *v.i*. abhivaḍḍhati. *v.t*. 1. maṇḍeti ; sobheti; 2. paribbhameti. *p.p*. abhivuddha ; °ḍita ; °bhita ; °mita. °**ing**, *a*. abhivaḍḍhamāna.

Flout, *n*. hīḷanā ; ohīḷanā, *f*. *v.t*. ohīḷeti. *p.p*. °ḷita.

Flow, *n*. galana ; sandana ; paggharaṇa, *nt*. abhissanda, *m*. *v.i*. 1. galati ; sandati ; abhissavati ; 2. vātena kampati ; 3. sithilībhavati. *p.p*. galita ; sandita ; abhissuta; °pita; °bhūta.—**continually**, anusandati.—**down**, pabhavati. °**forth**, paggharati. °**ing**, *a*. sandamāna. — **out**, vissandati.

Flower, *n*. 1. puppha ; kusuma, *nt*. mālā, *f*. 2. uttamaŋsa, *m*. *v.i*. pupphati; vikasati. *v.t*. pupphehi maṇḍeti. *p.p*. °phita ; °sita ; °ḍita. °**bed**, *n*. mālāvaccha, *m*. °**bud**, *n*. makula, *nt*. °**ed**, *a*. kusumita; pupphayutta.—**garden**, pupphārāma, *m*. °**ing**, *a*. pupphajanaka. °**less**, *a*, apupphaka.—**plant**, mālāgaccha, *m*. °**y**, *a*. 1. pupphākiṇṇa ; 2. vicittavācāyutta.

Flown, *a*. 1. vikasita ; 2. uddhumāta.

Fluctuate, *v.i*. vipphandati. *p.p*. °dita. °**ing**, *a*. phandamāna ; anavaṭṭhita. °**ion**, *n*. vipphandana, *nt*. anavaṭṭhiti, *f*.

Flue, *n*. 1. dhūmanāḷa, *m*. 2. vātāyana, *nt*.

Fluency, *n*. 1. vācāpaṭutā ; 2. asambādhatā, *f*.

Fluent, *a*. 1. sandamāna ; 2. akkhalitavacana ; caturakathī. °**ly**, *adv*. vyattākārena.

Fluff, *n*. muduloma, *nt*. *v.t*. mudulomehi āvarati. *p.p*. °āvaṭa.

Fluid, *n.* vilīnavatthu, *nt.* rasa, *m.* adj. jalamaya ; āpobahula ; vilīna. °**ify**, *v.t.* vilīyāpeti. *p.p.* °pita. °**ity**, *n.* vilīnatta, *nt.*

Fluke, *n.* bhāgyasampatti, *f.*

Flume, *n.* udakappaṇālī, *f.* *v.t.* mātikāya jalaŋ neti.

Flummery, *n.* 1. ghanayāgu, *f.* 2. abhūtappasaŋsā, *f.*

Flummox, *v.t.* vikkhepayati. *p.p.* vikkhepita.

Flump, *v.i.* sasaddaŋ patati. *v.t.* sasaddaŋ pāteti. *p.p.* °patita ; °pātita.

Flunkey, *n.* 1. visesita-sevaka, *m.* 2. cāṭupara, *m.*

Flurry, *n.* sambhama, *m.* vyākulatta, *nt.* *v.t.* bhameti ; khobheti. *p.p.* bhanta ; °bhita.

Flush, *n.* 1. kapolarāga, *m.* rattabhāva ; 2. ubbega, *m.* 3. samiddhi ; phullatā, *f.* adj. abhinava ; samiddha. *v.t.* 1. rattavaṇṇaŋ karoti ; 2. uttejeti ; pahaŋseti. *v.i.* lohitāyati. *p.p.* °ṇīkata ; °jita ; °sita ; °yita.

Fluster, *n.* khobha ; sambhama, *m.* *v.i.* mandaŋ matto hoti. *v.t.* mattaŋ *or* bhantaŋ karoti.

Flute, *n.* dhamanavaŋsa, *m.* *v.t. i.* vaŋsaŋ dhamati. °**player**, vaŋsadhama, *m.*

Flutter, *n.* phandana ; vidhunana, *nt.* *v.i.* pakkhe vidhunāti. *v.t.* phandāpeti. *p.p.* vidhūtapakkha ; °pita. °**ing**, *a.* kampamāna.

Fluvial, *a.* nadīnissita.

Flux, *n.* 1. pavāha, *m.* galana, *nt.* 2. lohitapakkhandikā, *f.* *v.t.* pavāheti. *v.i.* pasavati. *p.p.* °hita ; °vita. °**ion**, *n.* pasavana, *nt.*

Fly, *n.* 1. makkhikā, *f.* 2. uḍḍīyana, *nt.* 3. uḍḍitappamāṇa, *nt.* °**blow**, āsāṭikā, *f.* °**flap**, makkhikāvāraṇa, *nt.* °**leaf**, potthakante alikhitapaṇṇa, *nt.* °**'s egg**, makkhikāṇḍa, *nt.* āsāṭikā, *f.* °**trap**, makkhikā-adūhala, *nt.*

Fly, *v.i.* 1. uḍḍeti ; uppatati ; nabhasā gacchati ; 2. palāyati ; 3. kampati. *p.p.* uḍḍita, °tita ; °gata ; °yita ; °pita. *v.t.* 1. uḍḍīyāpeti ; 2. pariharati ; vajjeti ; 3. vijjhati (of an arrow, etc.) *p.p.* °pita ; parihaṭa ; vissaṭṭha. — **at**, — **upon**, abhipatati ; nipatati. °**er**, *n.* palāyī ; ākāsagāmī, *m.* — **in the face of**, sammukhā virujjhati. — **open**, sahasā vidāreti. °**past**, vītipatati.

Flying, *n.* ḍīyana ; ākāsagamana, *nt.* — **fox**, ajinapattā, *f.* — **squirrel**, pakkhabilāla, *m.* — **upon**, nipātī, *a.*

Foal, *n.* kisora, *m.* *v.t.* kisoram uppādeti. *p.p.* uppāditakisora.

Foam, *n.* pheṇa. *nt.* *v.i.* pheṇam uppādeti *or* uppajjati. *p.p.* uppannapheṇa.

Fob, *n.* ghaṭikākosa, *m.* *v.t.* appagghena vañceti. *p.p.* °cita.

Focus, *n.* majjhaṭṭhāna, *nt.* *v.t.* upasaŋharati ; ekajjhaŋ karoti. *p.p.* °saŋhaṭa, °kata.

Focal, *a.* majjhaṭṭhānāyatta.

Fodder, *n.* ghāsa ; nivāpa ; gocara, *m.* *v.t.* ghāsaŋ deti. *p.p.* dinnaghāsa.

Foe, see **Enemy**.

Foetus, *n*. 1. kalalarūpa, *nt*. 2. apariṇatagabbha, *m*.

Foeticide, *n*. gabbhanāsana; gabbhapātana, *nt*.

Fog, *n*. mahikā, *f*. °**gy**, *a*. 1. mahikāyutta; 2. sasandeha.

Foible, *n*. 1. dubbalaṭṭhāna; 2. guṇavekalla, *nt*. 3. khaggakoṭi, *f*.

Foil, *n*. 1. parājaya, *m*. 2. kuṇṭhita-khagga, *m*. 3. tanulohapaṭṭa, *nt*. 4. sobhājanakavatthu, *nt*. *v.t*. 1. parājeti; 2. viphalayati; 3. kuṇṭheti.

Foist, *v.t*. nikatiyā payojeti *or* paveseti. *p.p*. °jita; °sita.

Fold, *n*. 1. yūtha; gaṇa, *m*. 2. āvali, *f*. 3. sappabhoga, *m*. 4. rajjuvaṭṭi, *f*. 5. namiṭṭhāna, *nt*. 6. vaja, *m*. *v.t*. 1. saŋharati; guṇīkaroti; 2. (of hands, etc.) sammiñjeti; 3. (of cows, etc.) vajaŋ paveseti; rāsīkaroti. *p.p*. saŋhaṭa; °kata; °jita; °sita; rāsīkata.

Foliaceous, *a*. paṇṇasadisa; paṇṇāyatta.

Foliage, *n*. pattasamūha, *m*.

Foliar, *a*. paṇṇāyatta.

Foliate, *a*. pattayutta. *v.t*. 1. āvalīhi vibhūseti; 2. pattāni aṅketi. *p.p*. °sita; aṅkitapatta.

Folio, *n*. kākacapaṭṭa; potthakapatta, *nt*.

Folk, *n*. janatā, *f*. janasamūha, *m*. °**lore**, *n*. janakathā, *f*.

Follicle, *n*. kimikosa; suttakosa, *m*.

Follow, *v.t*. 1. anugacchati; anucarati; 2. (a method), paṭipajjati; 3. (an action), anusikkhati; anukaroti. *v.i*. anusijjhati; anupāpuṇati. *p.p*. anugata; anucarita; paṭipanna; °khita; °kata; anusiddha; anuppatta.—**a business**, kammante abhiyuñjati. °**ed by**, parivuta; purakkhata. °**er**, 1. anugāmī; sāvaka, *m*. 2. parijana; sevaka; anucara; nissitaka, *m*. °**ing**, *a*. 1. anvāyika; anubaddha; 2. vuccamāna. °**ing**, *n*. 1. anugamana, *nt*. 2. parivāra; sāvakagaṇa, *m*. — **on**, upanibandhati. **As follows**, seyyathīdaŋ, *ind*.

Folly, *n*. 1. bālya, *nt*. 2. mūḷhakamma, *nt*.

Foment, *v.t*. 1. uṇhodakena sedeti; 2. vivādāya ussāheti. *p.p*. sedita; °hita. °**ation**, sedana; sedakamma, *nt*.

Fond, *a*. āsatta; anuratta; sānurāga. *In cpds*. — piya; — kāma; — lālasa. °**ly**, *adv*. sānurāgaŋ. °**ness**, anurāga, *m*. piyāyana; mamatta, *nt*. — **of drinking**, pānāsatta, *a*. — **of sport**, kiḷārata, *a*. — **of women**, itthilola, *a*.

Fondle, *v.t*. lāleti; āliṅgati. *p.p*. lālita; °gita. °**ing**, *n*. 1. lālana; āliṅgana, *nt*. 2. pemabhājana, *nt*.

Font, *n*. suddhajalabhājana, *nt*. parittodakādhāra, *m*.

Fontal, *a*. mūlappabhavāyatta.

Food, *n*. āhāra; āmisa, *m*. bhojana; anna, *nt*.—**and drink**, anna-pāna, *nt*. °**less**, *a*. nirāhāra; bhojanavikala.—**supply**, pākavaṭṭa, *nt*. **Hard** —, khajjaka; khādanīya, *nt*. **Liquid** —, peyya, *nt*. **Soft** —, bhojja, *nt*.

Fool, *n*. duppañña ; dummedha ; mandamati. *v.t*. 1. moheti ; vañceti ; 2. uppaṇḍeti ; parihasati. *p.p*. mohita ; °cita ; °ḍita ; °sita. °**ery**, *n*. uppaṇḍanā, *f*. parihāsa, *m*. — **hardiness**, *n*. aññāṇavīsatā, *f*. — **hardy**, *a*. anisammakārī ; anavassa-vīrakriyā. °'**s errand**, alabbhaṇeyya-pariyesana, *nt*.

Foolish, *a*. dandha ; momuha. °**ly**, *adv*. mūḷhākārena. °**ness**, *n*. mūḷhatta ; dandhatta ; bālatta, *nt*.

Foot, *n*. 1. pāda ; pada, *m*. caraṇa, *nt*. 2. mūla, *nt*. patiṭṭhā, *f*. adhotala, *nt*. *v.t*. pādena paharati. *v.i*. pādaŋ ṭhapeti ; pādehi vītikkamati. *p.p*. °pahaṭa ; ṭhapita-pada ; °vītikkanta. °**ball**, *n*. pādakanduka, *m*. °**board**, pādaphalaka, *m*. °**bridge**, padikasetu, *m*. °**fall**, padapāta ; padanikkhepa, *m*. °**guards**, rakkhakapadātigaṇa, *m*. °**hold**, padapatiṭṭhāna ; avaṭṭhāna, *nt*. upatthambha, *m*. °**ing**, *n*. 1. padapatiṭṭhā, *f*. 2. samārambha, *m*. patiṭṭhāpana, *nt*. °**less**, *a*. apada. °**man**, padāti-bhaṭa, *m*. °**mark**, °**print**, padavalañja, *m*. padalañchana, *nt*. °**note**, adholipi, *f*. °**path**, jaṅghamagga ; ekapadika-patha, *m*. °**soldier**, padāti, *m*. °**step**, padanikkhepa, *m*. °**stool**, pādapīṭha, *nt*. °**way**, padikamagga, *m*. — **of a wall**, kuḍḍamūla, *nt*. — **of a mountain**, pabbatapāda, *m*.

For, *prep*. uddissa. *In Pali its meaning is expressed by the Dative or the words :* hetu ; nimittaŋ ; kāraṇā, *and Conj*. yasmā ; tasmā ; tena. °**ever**, sadātanāya. — **long**, cerāya, *ind*. — **once**, sakiŋ, *adv*. — **the most part**, bhīyoso, *ind*. — **the sake of**, atthāya. **Craft for craft**, saṭhassa sāṭheyyaŋ. **Easy for you**, sukaraŋ tayā. — **how many years ?** kati vassāni ? — **want of time**, kālassa ūnatāya. **He started for Colombo**, so Koḷambanagaraŋ pati gato. **He took it for truth**, so taŋ saccan ti gaṇhi. **He waits for money**, so mūlatthāya āgameti.

Forage, *n*. ghāsa, *m*. *v.t*. ghāsaŋ pariyesati ; ghāsaŋ vilumpati. pariyiṭṭhaghāsa ; viluttaghāsa. *v.i*. ghāsatthāya āhiṇḍati. *p.p*. °**er**, *n*. ghāsavilumpaka, *m*.

Forasmuch as, *conj*. yato ; yasmā.

Foray, *n*. aviditappavesa, *m*. *v.i*. (sahasā gantvā) vilumpati.

Forbear, *n*. ādimapurisa, *m*. *v.i*. adhivāseti ; sahati ; titikkhati ; 2. viramati. *v.t*. parivajjeti. *p.p*. °sita ; sahita ; °khita ; virata ; °jita. °**ance**, *n*. khamā ; adhivāsanā ; titikkhā, *f*. °**ing**, *a*. sahanta ; khamamāna.

Forbid, *v.t*. vāreti ; nivāreti ; nisedheti. *p.p*. °rita ; °dhita. °**dance**, *n*. nisedha, *m*. nivāraṇa ; paṭibāhana, *nt*. °**den**, *n*. paṭisedhita ; paṭibāhita. °**ding**, *a*. arucikara ; jigucchājanaka.

Force, *n.* 1. bala, *nt.* vega; thāma, *m.* satti, *f.* 2. patāpa; ānubhāva, *m.* 3. balakkāra, *m.* pasahana, *nt.* 4. yuddhasenā, *f.* *v.t.* 1. balena *or* pasayha kāreti; 2. kaññaŋ dūseti. °**ed,** *a.* accāvassaka; anatikkamiya. °**ful,** *a.* pabala; samattha; tejassī. — **from,** pasayha gaṇhāti. — **in,** pasayha pavisati. — **out,** nikkaḍḍhati.

Forceps, *n.* saṇḍāsa, *m.*

Forcible, *a.* 1. pabala; 2. daḷha; tikhiṇa; 3. sāhasika. °**bly,** *adv.* balakkārena; pasayha.

Ford, *n.* nadītittha, *nt.* *v.t.* padasā tarati. *p.p.* °tiṇṇa. °**able,** *a.* padasā taraṇīya. °**less,** *a.* atittha; tittharahita.

Fore, *a.* ādima, purima; agga; abhimukha. °**arm,** aggahattha, *m.* °**finger,** tajjanī, *f.* °**foot,** pādagga, *nt.* °**front,** abhimukhaṭṭhāna, *nt.* °**ground,** puratobhūmi, *f.* °**leg,** purima-pāda, *m.* °**mast,** aggakūpaka, *m.* °**mentioned,** pubbe vutta; yatthāvutta, *a.* °**noon,** pubbaṇha, *m.* °**part,** purimabhāga, *m.* °**rank,** paṭhama-panti, *f.* °**teeth,** pamukhadanta, *m.*

Forearm, *v.t.* pageva sannayhati. *p.p.* °sannaddha.

Forebode, *v.t.* pageva sūceti *or* pakāseti; pageva maññati. *p.p.* °sūcita; °sita; °ñita. °**ing,** *n.* pageva-sūcana; pubbanimitta, *nt.*

Forecast, *n.* pageva-dassana, *nt.* puretarāvabodha, *m.* *v.t.* pageva niddisati. *p.p.* °niddiṭṭha.

Forecastle, *n.* nāvāpubbabhāga, *m.*

Forechosen, *a.* pageva-nicchita.

Foreclose, *v.t.* pageva pidahati *or* paṭibāhati. *p.p.* °hita.

Forecourt, *n.* pamukhājira, *nt.*

Foredate, *v.t.* pubbataradinaŋ likhati. *p.p.* likhita°.

Foredoom, *v.t.* pageva niyameti *or* daṇḍeti. *p.p.* °mita; °ḍita.

Forefather, *n.* ādipurisa; pitāmaha, *m.*

Forefend, Forfend, *v.t.* pageva ārakkhaŋ yojeti. *p.p.* °yojitārakkha.

Forefront, puratobhāga, *m.*

Forego, *v.t.* 1. purato gacchati; 2. cajati; jahati. *p.p.* °gata; catta; jahita. °**ing,** *a.* heṭṭhāvutta.

Forehead, *n.* nalāṭa; lalāṭa, *nt.*

Foreign, *a.* videsika; paradesīya. °**er,** *n.* videsī; vijātika, *m.*

Forejudge, *v.t.* pageva tīreti *or* niccheti. *p.p.* °tīrita; °chita.

Foreknow, *v.t.* pageva jānāti. *p.p.* °ñāta. °**ledge,** *n.* pagevajānana; anāgatañāṇa, *nt.*

Forelock, *n.* alaka, *m.* lalāṭakesajāri, *f.*

Foreman, *n.* 1. kammantapālaka, *m.* 2. pamāṇapurisajeṭṭhaka, *m.*

Foremost, *a.* mukhya; padhāna; pamukha.

Forensic, *a.* adhikaraṇavisayaka.

Foreordain, *v.t.* pageva adhikāraŋ deti. *p.p.* °dinnādhikāra.

Fore-reach, *v.i.* paṭhamataraŋ pāpuṇāti. *p.p.* °patta.

Forerun, *v.t.* purato dhāvati. °**ner,** *n.* purecara; puregāmī, *m.*

Fore-say, *v.t.* pageva vadati. *p.p.* °vutta.

Foresee, *v.t.* pageva passati. *p.p.* °diṭṭha. °**ing**, *a.* dūradassī.

Foreshadow, *v.t.* pubbanimittaŋ dasseti. *p.p.* dassita°.

Foreshow, *v.t.* pageva dasseti. *p.p.* °dassita.

Foresight, *n.* dūradassitā, *f.*

Forest, *n.* arañña ; vana ; kānana, *nt.* aṭavi, *f.* *v.t.* araññaŋ ropeti *or* patiṭṭhāpeti. *p.p.* ropitārañña. °**er**, *n.* 1. vanavāsī, *m.* 2. aṭavipālaka, *m.* °**ry**, *n.* 1. vanagatadesa, *m.* 2. aṭavipālana, *nt.*

Forestall, *v.t.* pageva saŋvidahati. *p.p.* °saŋvihita.

Foretaste, *n.* pubbūpaladdhi, *f.* *v.t.* puretaraŋ sāyati *or* vindati.

Foretell, *v.t.* anāgataŋ vyākaroti ; bhavitabbaŋ katheti. *p.p.* vyākātānāgata ; kathita°.

Forethought, *n.* pubbavicāraṇā ; paṭhamacintā, *f.*

Foretoken, *n.* pubbanimitta, *nt.* *v.t.* pubbanimittaŋ dasseti. pageva sūceti. *p.p.* dassitapubba° ; °sūcita.

Forewarn, *v.t.* pagev'antarāyaŋ nivedeti ; paṭhamataraŋ ñāpeti. *p.p.* °ditantarāya ; °ñāpita.

Foreword, *n.* pubbikā, *f.* mukhabandha, *m.*

Forfeit, *n.* 1. (sammutibhedāya) daṇḍana, *nt.* 2. daṇḍāya dinnavatthu, *nt.* *v.t.* daṇḍavasena deti. °**ed**, *a.* apahaṭadhana. °**ure**, *n.* daṇḍanena dhanāpaharaṇa, *nt.*

Forgather, *v.i.* saṅgacchati ; sammilati. *p.p.* saṅgata ; sammilita.

Forge, *n.* kammāruddhana, *nt.* *v.t.* 1. lohena nimmiṇāti ; 2. kūṭavidhānaŋ karoti. *v.i.* kasirena abhiyāti. *p.p.* °mita ; katakūṭavidhāna ; °yāta. — **a letter**, kūṭalekhanaŋ sampādeti. °**er**, kūṭavidhānakārī, *m.* °**ry**, *n.* kūṭasaŋvidhāna, *nt.* °**ing**, *n.* kūṭanimmāṇa, *nt.*

Forget, *v.t.* pamussati ; vissarati ; *v.i.* sammuyhati. *p.p.* pamuṭṭha ; °rita ; sammūḷha. °**ful**, *a.* muṭṭhassati ; pamussanasīla. °**fulness**, *n.* muṭṭhasacca, *nt.* satisammosa, *m.*

Forgive, *v.t.* khamati ; titikkhati. *p.p.* khanta ; °khita. °**ing**, *a.* khamanasila. °**ness**, *n.* khamā ; khanti, *f.*

Forgo, *v.t.* viramati ; pajahati ; jahāti. *p.p.* virata ; jahita.

Fork, *n.* bahusūlaka, *m.* (— **of a tree** :) viṭapa ; pasāka, *m.* *v.t.* bahusūlakena khaṇati. *v.i.* viṭapī bhavati ; dvisikhāhi vaḍḍhati. °**ed**, *a.* dvisikha.

Forlorn, *a.* anātha ; asaraṇa ; nirālamba ; chaḍḍita.

Form, *n.* 1. rūpa ; saṇṭhāna, *nt.* ākati, *f.* 2. pakāra ; vidhi, *m.* 3. sissapanti, *f.* 4. ākatipaṇṇa, *nt.* 5. nisīdanaphalaka, *m.* 6. muddaṇakkharaphalaka, *m.* *v.t.* 1. māpeti ; 2. racayati. *v.i.* 1. sijjhati ; 2. jāyati ; 3. rāsībhavati. *p.p.* māpita ; racita ; siddha ; jāta ; °bhūta. °**ation**, *n.* nimmāṇa ; sampādana, *nt.*

°**ative**, *a.* nimmāpaka ; nimmāṇavisayaka. °**less**, *a.* arūpa ; nirākāra. Well °**ed**, *a.* susaṇṭhāna.

Formal, *a.* niyamānusārī ; sārabhūta. °**ist**, *n.* cārittānuyāyī ; yathāniyamakārī, *m.* °**ity**, *n.* ācāraniyama, *m.* yathāvidhivattanā, *f.* °**ize**, *v.t.* vidhiniyamaŋ ṭhapeti ; ācaraṇaŋ niyameti. °**ly**, *adv.* yathāvidhiŋ ; yathāniyamaŋ.

Former, *a. n.* ādima ; purima ; paṭhamatara. — **connection**, pubbayoga, *m.* — **existence**, purimabhava, *m.* °**ly**, *adv.* pure; puretaraŋ ; atīte. — **wife**, purāṇa-dutiyikā, *f.*

Formic, *a.* kipillikājāta. °**acid**, kipillikāvisa, *nt.* °**ary**, kipillikālaya ; vammika, *m.*

Formidable, *a.* 1. mahabbala ; 2. bhayāvaha. °**ness**, *n.* mahabbalatta, *nt.*

Formula, *n.* sutta, *nt.* niyamāvali, *f.* °**ry**, *a.* suttasaṅgaha, *m.* suttāvali, *f.*

Formulate, *v.t.* vavatthapeti ; suttehi racayati. *p.p.* °pita ; suttaracita. °**ion**, *n.* suttaracanā, *f.* vavatthāpana, *nt.*

Fornicate, *v.t.* kāme aticarati *or* micchā-carati. °**ion**, *n.* kāmamicchācāra, *nt.* °**tor**, kāmamicchācārī, *m.* — **tress**, aticārinī, *f.*

Forsake, *v.t.* pajahati ; vijahati ; pariccajati ; vajjeti ; parivajjeti ; nissajati. *p.p.* °hita ; pariccatta ; °jita ; nissaṭṭha. °**er**, *n.* pajahaka ; vivajjetu, *m.* °**ing**, *n.* vivajjana ; pajahana, *nt.* cāga ; paṭinissagga, *m.* — **the Order**, vibbhamati ; uppabbajati. *p.p.* vibbhanta ; °jita.

Forsooth, *adv.* nūnaŋ ; dhuvaŋ ; ekantaŋ ; khalu ; nāma.

Forswear, *v.i.* micchā sapati. *v.t.* paccakkhāti. *p.p.* °sapita ; °khāta.

Fort, *n.* balakoṭṭhaka ; dugga, *m.* °**alice**, *n.* khuddakadugga, *m.*

Forte, *n.* 1. guṇātisaya, *m.* 2. khaggatala, *nt.*

Forth, *adv.* purato ; agge. *prep.* pabhuti ; paṭṭhāya (with *abl.*) °**coming**, *a.* āgāmī ; upakaṭṭha. °**going**, *a.* bahigāmī ; nikkhamanta. °**right**, *a.* ujugatika ; thiravacana. *adv.* ujukam eva. °**with**, *adv.* āsu ; sapadi ; sajju ; taṅkhaṇaŋ ; tāvad eva.

Fortieth, *a.* cattāḷīsatima.

Fortify, *v.t.* suguttaŋ karoti; balakoṭṭhake patiṭṭhāpeti. *p.p.* °kata ; °pita-bala°. °**ication**, *n.* rakkhāvaraṇa; pākāraparikkhipana, *nt.*

Fortitude, *n.* dhiti, *f.* dhīratta ; porisa, *nt.* vikkama, *m.*

Fortnight, *n.* addhamāsa ; pakkha, *m.* °**ly**, *a.* addhamāsika. *adv.* anvaddhamāsaŋ.

Fortress, see **Fort.**

Fortuitism, *n.* ahetuvāda, *m.*

Fortuitous, *a.* asambhāvitasampatta ; kākatālīya. °**ly**, *adv.* asambhāvitākārena.

Fortuity, *n.* ninnimitta, *nt.* yadicchāsiddhi, *f.*

Fortunate, *a.* dhañña ; subhaga ; lakkhika ; mahābhāgya. °**ly**, *adv.* subhagatāya.

Fortune, *n.* 1. bhāgya ; bhāgadheyya, *nt.* 2. sampatti ; lakkhī ; siri, *f.* 3. subha ; maṅgala ; kalyāṇa, *nt.* °**teller,** *n.* nemittika ; ikkhaṇika, *m.* **Bad —,** dubbhāgya, *nt.* **Good —,** sobhagga, *nt.*

Forty, *n.* cattāḷīsati, *f.* °**nine,** ekūnapaññāsā, *f.* °**one,** ekacattāḷīsati, *f.* °**two,** dvicattāḷīsati, *f.*

Forum, *n.* (Romaka-) santhāgāra, *m.* sammilanaṭṭhāna, *nt.*

Forward, *a.* 1. puregāmī ; pubbaṅgama ; 2. ussuka ; uyyutta ; 3. (bold:) pagabbha. *v.t.* 1. anuggaṇhāti ; 2. (niyamitaṭṭhānaŋ) peseti ; 3. abhivḍḍheti. *p.p.* anuggahita ; °pesita. °ḍhita. *adv.* abhimukhaŋ ; (ito) paṭṭhāya *or* pabhuti. °**ness,** 1. ussāha ; uyyoga, *m.* 2. pāgabbhiya, *nt.*

Fosse, *n.* parikhā, *f.*

Fossick, *v.i.* pariyesati. *p.p.* °sita.

Fossil, *n.* pāsāṇībhūta-vatthu, *nt.* adj. pāsāṇībhūta. °**ize,** *v.t.* pāsāṇattaŋ pāpeti.

Foster, *v.t.* 1. poseti ; saŋvaḍḍheti ; bharati ; 2. (a love, etc.) baṇdhati. *p.p.* posita ; °ḍhita ; bhata ; baddha. °**age,** *n.* posakatta, *nt.* °**brother,** *n.* vemātikabhātu, *m.* °**child,** *n.* positadāraka, *m.* °**father,** *n.* posakapitu, *m.* °**mother,** *n.* upamātu, āpādikā, *f.* °**parents,** posakamātāpitaro, *m. pl.* °**sister,** *n.* vemātikabhaginī, *f.* °**son,** *n.* positaputta, *m.* °**ing,** *n.* paṭijaggana, *nt.*

Foul, *a.* 1. kucchita ; gārayha ; 2. malina ; asuddha ; 3. saṭha ; kūṭa. *v.t.* dūseti ; malinīkaroti. *p.p.* dūsita ; °kata. °**ly,** *adv.* duṭṭhākārena. °**mouthed,** *a.* mukhara ; vācāla. °**ness,** *n.* duṭṭhatta, *nt.* — **play,** *n.* duccarita ; sāṭheyya, *nt.* — **smell,** pūtigandha, *m.* — **weather,** duddina, *nt.*

Found, *v.t.* patiṭṭhāpeti ; ārabhati. *p.p.* °pita ; āraddha. °**ation,** *n.* pādaka, *nt.* mūlapatiṭṭhā, *f.* °**er,** *n.* patiṭṭhāpetu ; ārambhaka, *m.* °**er of a religious order,** titthaṅkara, *m.*

Founder, *v.i.* paripatati. *v.t.* 1. (udakaŋ pūretvā) osīdāpeti ; 2. adhikaŋ viheseti. *p.p.* °tita ; °pita ; °sita.

Foundling, *n.* amātāpitika, *m.*

Foundry, *n.* kammārasālā, *f.*

Fount, *n.* vāripasava ; ubbhida, *m.*

Fountain, *n.* jalavipphāraka, *m.* °**pen,** *n.* nāḷalekhanī, *f.*

Four, *a. n.* catu. °**cornered,** *a.* catukkaṇṇa. °**edged,** *a.* caturaŋsa. °**fold,** *a.* catubbidha ; catugguṇa. °**footed,** *a.* catuppadika. °**hundred,** catusata, *nt.* °**score,** asīti, *f.* °**teen,** *a. n.* catuddasa ; cuddasa. °**teenth,** *a.* catuddasama. °**th,** *a.* catuttha. °**thly,** *adv.* catutthavasena. °**times,** catukkhattuŋ, *adv.*

Fourth, *n.* pāda ; catutthaŋsa, *m.*

Fowl, *n.* 1. sakuṇa ; pakkhī ; 2. kukkuṭa, *m.* *v.i.* sakuṇe ghāteti. °**er,** *n.* sākuṇika, *m.* °**ing,** *n.* sakuṇaghāta, *m.*

Fox, *n.* sigāla ; jambuka ; kotthu, *m.* *v.i.* vañceti. °**brush,** sigālanaṅguṭṭha, *nt.* °**chase,** °**hunt,** sigālavadha, *m.* °**hunter,** sigālavedhī, *m.* °**y,** *a.* kapaṭa ; sigālasadisa.

Fracas, *n.* kalaha, *m.*

Fraction, *n.* bhāga ; aŋsa ; koṭṭhāsa, *m.* kalā, *f.* °**al,** *a.* bhāgayutta ; asampuṇṇa.

Fractious, *a.* kalahasīlī ; kopabahula.

Fracture, *n.* 1. bhaṅga, *m.* 2. bhaggaṭṭhāna, *nt.* *v.t.* bhañjati. *v.i.* bhijjati. *p.p.* bhagga ; bhinna.

Fragile, *a.* bhaṅgura ; bhijjanadhamma. °**ity,** *n.* bhaṅguratta, *nt.*

Fragment, *n.* khuddakakhaṇḍa, *m.* sakalikā, *f.* °**ary,** *a.* sakalībhūta.

Fragrance, *n.* sugandha ; surabhi, *m.* °**ant,** *a.* sugandhī ; iṭṭhagandhī.

Frail, *a.* 1. dubbala ; bhaṅgura ; 2. sithilaviriya. °**ty,** *n.* dubbalya; bhaṅguratta, *nt.*

Frame, *n.* 1. racanā, *f.* saŋvidhāna, *nt.* 2. ādhāra ; kosa, *m.* 3. dhārakapañjara, *m.* *v.t.* 1. vidahati; racayati; 2. ādhārake nidahati. *p.p.* vihita ; racita ; °nihita.

Franchise, *n.* chandadānabala, *nt.*

Francolin, *n.* tittira, *m.*(?)

Frank, *a.* akuṭila ; asaṭha ; ujugatika. °**ly,** *adv.* akuṭilaŋ ; ajjavena. °**ness,** *n.* ajjava ; avaṅkatta, *nt.*

Frank, *n.* hatthamuddā, *f.* *v.t.* phāsugamanaŋ vidahati. *p.p.* vihitaphāsu°.

Frankincense, *n.* dhūpeyyagandha, *m.*

Frantic, *a.* atikopāviṭṭha ; ummatta ; khittacitta. °**ally,** *adv.* ummattarūpena. °**ness,** *n.* cittavikkhepa, *m.*

Frap, *v.t.* daḷhaŋ bandhati. *p.p.* daḷhabaddha.

Fraternal, *a.* bhātusadisa ; sahadhammika. °**ly,** *adv.* sahadhammikatāya. °**nity,** *n.* nikāya ; gaṇa ; saṅgha, *m.* °**nize,** *v.t.* sahadhammikataŋ pāpeti.

Fratricide, *n.* (person :) bhātughātaka, *m.* (act :) bhātughātana, *nt.*

Fraud, *n.* nikati, *f.* kerāṭiya ; sāṭheyya, *nt.* °**ulence,** *n.* ketava ; kerāṭiya, *nt.* °**ulent,** *a.* nekatika ; kuhaka. °**ulently,** *adv.* nikatiyā ; saṭhena.

Fraught, *a.* pūrita ; bharita. — **with,** sampayutta ; samākiṇṇa.

Fray, *n.* bhaṇḍana, *nt.* viggaha, *m.* *v.i.* (dasā) khīyati *or* jirati. *p.p.* khīṇadasa.

Frazzle, *n.* kilantabhāva, *m.*

Freak, *n.* 1. capalatā ; sericāritā, *f.* °**ish,** *a.* 1. capala ; lola ; 2. pakativiruddha.

Freckle, *n.* tilaka, *m.* *v.t.* tilakayuttaŋ karoti. *v.i.* tilakayutto hoti. °**ed,** *a.* tilakāhata.

Free, *a.* 1. abaddha ; mutta ; sādhīna ; 2. vigata ; rahita ; apalibuddha ; 3. asambādha ; 4. aparādhīna ; 5. cāgasīlī ;

6. sabbasādhāraṇa ; 7. nimmūlaka. *v.t.* pamoceti.— **boarding house,** puññanivāsa, *m.* °**booter,** panthadūsaka, *m.* °**born** *a.* bhujissa. °**dom,** 1. vimutti, *f.* pamokkha, *m.* 2. aparādhīnatā, *f.* 3. abhāva, viraha, *m.* —**from debt,** anaṇa, *a.* — **from doubt,** nikkaṅkha, *a.* — **from dust,** viraja, *a.* — **from pride,** nimmāna ; appagabbha, *a.* — **hearted,** agativirahita, *a.* °**holder,** bhūmisāmī, *m.* °**ly,** *adv.* yathākāmaŋ ; yathicchitaŋ. — **of charges,** nimmūlena, *adv.* °**thinker,** *n.* abaddhamatika ; adevavādī, *m.* °**will,** *n.* sakamati ; seritā, *f.*

Freeze, *v.i.* ghanībhavati. *v.t.* ghanīkaroti. *p.p.* °bhūta ; °kata.

Freight, *n.* nāvābhāra, *m.* nāvāgata-bhaṇḍajāta, *nt. v.t.* nāvāya āropeti. *p.p.* °pita. °**age,** *n.* 1. bhaṇḍaharaṇapaṭiññā, *f.* 2. nāvāya dātabbamūla. *nt.* °**er,** *n.* bhaṇḍapesaka, *m.*

Frenzy, *n.* kālika-ummāda ; cittavikkhepa, *m.* °**ied,** *a.* bhantacitta ; ummatta.

Frequence, °**cy,** *n.* sātatikatta, *nt.* abhiṇhasiddhi, *f.* bahulatta, *nt.*

Frequent, *a.* abhikkhaṇika ; satata ; nirantara. *v.t.* āsevati ; nisevati ; samudācarati. *p.p.* °vita ; °āciṇṇa. °**ation,** *n.* niccupagamana, *nt.* °**er,** *n.* niccupasevī, *m.* °**ing,** *a.* abhiṇhaŋsijjhamāna ; nisevaka ; upasevaka. °**ly,** *adv.* satataŋ ; bhusaŋ ; nirantaraŋ.

Fresco, *n.* bhitticittakamma, *nt. v.t.* bhittiŋ citteti. *p.p.* cittitabhittī.

Fresh, *a.* 1. nava ; abhinava ; ahata ; nūtana ; 2. sarasa ; harita ; amilāta.— **butter,** nonīta, *nt.* °**ly,** *adv.* abhinavaŋ. °**ness,** 1. navatā ; amilātatā, *f.* 2. aloṇatā, *f.* °**man,** ādhunika, *m.* — **water,** sādujala, *nt.*

Freshen, *v.t.* navataŋ pāpeti. *p.p.* °pāpita.

Fret, *v.t.* 1. nānāsaṇṭhānehi citteti ; 2. ḍasanena *or* ghaŋsanena khepeti ; 3. vyathati ; santāpeti. *v.i.* ujjhāyati. *p.p.* °cittita ; °pita ; °thita ; °pita ; °yita. *noun:* 1. ujjhāyana, *nt.* 2. (of sea :) saṅkhobha, *m.* 3. (of mind :) ubbega ; manotāpa, *m.* °**ful,** *a.* dummana ; ubbigga ; ukkaṇṭhita. °**fully,** *adv.* ubbegena ; sasaŋvegaŋ.

Friable, *a.* sukhabhañjiya.

Friar, *n.* tāpasa ; muni ; yogī, *m.* °**y,** *n.* tāpasārāma, *m.*

Fribble, *n.a.* mandamatika ; jaḷa. °**er,** *n.* vikatthī ; mandamati, *m.*

Friction, *n.* 1. saṅghaṭṭana ; nighaŋsana, *nt.* 2. virodha, *m.*

Friday, *n.* sukkavāra, *m.*

Friend, *n.* mitta ; sakha ; sahāya ; suhada, *m.* samma, *is used in the Vocative only.* °**less,** *a.* asahāya. °**liness,** *n.* anunaya ; avirodha, *m.* hitakāmatā, *f.* °**ship,** *n.* sohajja ; sakhya, *nt.* metti, *f.* **Bad —,** pāpamitta, *m.* **False —,** mittapatirūpaka, *m.* **Intimate —,** sambhatta, *m.* **True —,** kalyāṇamitta, *m.*

Friendly, *a.* hitakāma ; anukūla ; vissattha. —**talk**, samullāpa, *m.* —**treatment**, paṭisanthāra, *m.*

Frigate, *n.* pabala-yuddhanāvā, *f.*

Fright, *n.* bhaya, *nt.* tāsa ; santasā, *m.* bhīti, *f.* °**ful**, *a.* ghora ; bhīma ; bhayānaka. °**fully**, *adv.* ghorākārena.

Frighten, *v.t.* bhāyāpeti ; uttāseti ; santajjeti. *p.p.* °pita ; °sita ; °jita. °**ed**, *a.* bhīta ; tasita ; utrasta. °**ing**, *n.* bhāyāpana ; santajjana, *nt.* °**ing**, *a.* bhayāvaha.

Frigid, *a.* 1. atisītala ; himayutta ; 2. nirussāha ; nissineha. °**ity**, *n.* 1. atisītalatta, *nt.* 2. virāga ; sinehābhāva, *m.* — **zone**, *n.* sisirapabba, *m.*

Frill, *n.* ābhujitadasā, *f.* *v.t.* ābhujita-dasaŋ yojeti.

Fringe, *n.* dasā ; vaṭṭi, *f.* *v.t.* dasāyuttaŋ karoti. °**ed**, *a.* dasāyutta.

Frippery, *n.* niratthakālaṅkāra, *m.*

Friseur, *n.* kesakappaka ; kesapasādhaka, *m.*

Frisk, *n.* sauppatana-kīḷana, *nt.* *v.t.* uppatanto kīḷati. °**y**, *a.* 1. sānanda ; sallahuka ; 2. turita ; sīgha. °**iness**, *n.* kīḷāparatā, *f.*

Fritter, *n.* bhajjita (-phalādi-) khaṇḍa, *m.* *v.t.* 1. sakalīkaroti. *p.p.* °kata ; 2. (-away), kālaŋ vināseti.

Frivol, *v.i.* kālakkhepī hoti. *v.t.* niratthakaŋ khepeti. *p.p.* °bhūta ; °pita. °**ity**, *n.* nissāratā ; agarukāritā, *f.* °**ous**, *a.* nissāra ; niratthaka ; capala. °**ously**, *adv.* nipphalākārena.

Fro, *adv.* **To and fro**, ito tato.

Frock, *n.* 1. uttarīya ; cīvara, *nt.* 2. lomakañcuka, *m.* *v.t.* 1. cīvarena acchādeti ; 2. pūjakadhuraŋ appeti. *p.p.* °dita ; appita°.

Frog, *n.* 1. maṇḍūka ; bheka, *m.* 2. khaggapāsa, *m.*

Frolic, *v.i.* dibbati ; ramati ; kīḷati. *n.* abhiramaṇa, *nt.* keḷi, *f.* adj. pamudita ; haṭṭha-tuṭṭha. °**some**, *a.* keḷisīla ; kīḷāpasuta. °**somely**, *adv.* kīḷāpasutākārena.

From, *prep.* To be expressed by the Abl. —**afar**, dūrato ; ārakā, *ind.* — **above**, uparito, *ind.* — **behind**, pacchato, *ind.* —**hence**, ito, *ind.* —**the beginning**, ādito *or* mūlato paṭṭhāya. — **this day forth**, ajjatagge, *ind.* — **without**, bāhirato, *ind.* — **within**, abbhantarato, *ind.*

Frond, *n.* bahupattaka-kaḷīra, *m.* °**ous**, *a.* pattabahula.

Front, *n.* 1. pamukha, *nt.* 2. lalāṭa, *nt.* 3. abhimukhabhāga, *m.* adj. abhimukha ; purato-bhūta. *v.t.* abhimukhe tiṭṭhati. °**age**, *n.* purimabhāga, *m.* °**al**, *a.* lalāṭasambandha. °**al of an elephant**, gajakumbha, *m.* °**let**, *n.* lalāṭapaṭṭa, *nt.* —**of an army**, senāmukha, *nt.* **In the** —, purato ; agge, *adv.*

Frontier, *n.* rajjasīmā, *f.* paccantadesa, *m.*

Frontispiece, *n.* 1. padhānagharapamukha ; 2. cittita-pamukha, *nt.*

Frontless, *a.* 1. nillajja; ahirika; 2. pamukharahita.

Frost, *n.* tuhina, *nt.* mahikā, *f.* °**bitten,** *a.* tuhinopahata. °**y,** *a.* tuhinayutta; atisīta.

Froth, *n.* pheṇa, *nt.* *v.t.* pheṇam uppādeti, *v.i.* pheṇaŋ vamati. *p.p.* uppāditapheṇa; vamita°. °**y,** *a.* 1. pheṇayutta; pheṇila. °**iness,** pheṇilatta, *nt.*

Froward, *a.* dubbineya; dubbaca. °**ness,** *n.* dovacassatā, *f.*

Frown, *n.* bhūbhaṅga, *m.* *v.i.* bhākutiŋ karoti. *v.t.* appasādaŋ pakāseti. *p.p.* °ṭīkata; pakāsitappasāda. °**ing,** *a.* bhākuṭika.

Frowzy, *a.* duggandha; malina.

Fructiferous, *a.* phaluppādaka.

Fructify, *v.i.* saphalīkaroti. *v.t.* phalam uppādeti. *p.p.* °kata; °dita°. °**ication,** *n.* saphalīkaraṇa, *nt.*

Fructose, *n.* phalasakkharā, *f.*

Fructuous, *a.* phalabharita; avañjha.

Frugal, *a.* mitabbaya; sallahukavuttī. °**ity,** *n.* mitabbayatā, *f.* °**ly,** *adv.* mitabbayena.

Frugivorous, *a.* phalabhakkha.

Fruit, *n.* 1. phala, *nt.* 2. vipāka, *m.* kammaphala, *nt.* 3. payojana, *nt.* lābha, *m.* 4. pajā, *f.* apacca, *nt.* *v.i.* phalaŋ dhāreti. °**age,** *n.* phalabhāra, *m.* °**arian,** *n.* phalakhādī, *m.* °**bearing,** *a.* phaluppādaka. °**er,** *n.* phalārāmaropaka, *m.* °**erer,** *n.* phalavikkayī, *m.* °**ery,** *n.* 1. phalasamūha, *m.* 2. phalāgāra, *nt.* °**ful,** *a.* 1. saphala; avañjha; 2. uppādaka; janaka. °**fully,** *adv.* saphalākārena. °**fulness,** *n.* saphalatta, *nt.* °**less,** *a.* 1. aphala; 2. niratthaka; mogha; vañjha. °**lessly,** *adv.* nipphalākārena. °**lessness,** *n.* nipphalatta, *nt.* — **season,** phalasamaya, *m.*

Fruition, *n.* 1. vipākadāna; phalānubhavana, *nt.* 2. patthitalābha, *m.*

Fruity, *a.* phalāyatta; phalarasayutta.

Frustrate, *v.t.* viphalīkaroti; vyāhanati. *p.p.* °kata; vyāhata. °**ion,** *n.* viphalīkaraṇa; vyāhanana, *nt.*

Fry, *v.t.* bhajjati. *p.p.* bhaṭṭha *or* bhajjita. °**ed flour,** sattu; mantha, *m.* °**ed grain,** lāja, *m.* °**ing,** *n.* bhajjana, *nt.* °**ing pan,** tatta-kapāla, *m.*

Fubsy, *a.* thulla-sarīra.

Fuddle, *n.* mattabhāva, *m.* *v.i.* majjati; muyhati. *v.t.* madayati; moheti. *p.p.* matta; mūḷha; °yita; mohita.

Fudge, *n.* tucchavatthu, *nt.* asaṅgatakathā, *f.* *v.t.* micchā pabandheti *or* ghaṭeti. *p.p.* °dhita; °ghaṭita.

Fuel, *n.* indhana; upādāna, *nt.* *v.t.* indhanaŋ sampādeti; aggimhi (dārūni) khipati. *p.p.* °ditindhana. °**less,** *a.* nirindhana; anedha. — **of life,** upadhi, *m.*

Fuggy, *a.* dhūlisahita; saraja.

Fugacious, *a.* khaṇabhaṅgura; aticañcala. °**ness,** *n.* khaṇabhaṅguratta, *nt.*

Fugitive, *n.* palāyī, *m.* adj. capala; cañcala.

Fugleman, *n.* pubbaṅgama; purato-ṭhita, *m.*

Fulfil, *v.t.* sādheti ; nipphādeti ; sampādeti. *p.p.* sādhita ; °dita. °**ing**, *a.* paripūraka. °**ler**, *n.* sampādaka ; paripūraka, *m.* °**ment**, *n.* samijjhana, *nt.* pāripūri ; nipphatti, *f.*

Fulgency, *n.* juti ; ditti ; pabhā ; ābhā, *f.*

Fulgent, *a.* ujjala ; bhāsura ; jalamāna.

Fuliginous, *a.* kajjalāvuta.

Full, *a.* 1. puṇṇa; sampuṇṇa; 2. sakala. — **aged**, *a.* paripuṇṇavaya, — **blown**, *a.* samphulla ; vikasita. — **eyed**, *a.* visālakkha. °**grown**, *a.* pavaddha ; vayappatta. °**ly**, *adv.* sabbaso ; nissesaŋ. — **moon**, puṇṇacanda, *m.* — **moonday**, puṇṇamī, *f.* °**ness**, puṇṇatta ; bāhulla, *nt.* pāripūri, *f.* — **of**, bharita ; ākiṇṇa ; saṅkiṇṇa. — **of flowers**, supupphita, *a.* — **of mirth**, haṭṭhapahaṭṭha, *a.* — **to the brim**, samatittika ; kākapeyya, *a.*

Fulminate, *v.i.* gajjati, nadati. *v.t.* tajjeti. *p.p.* gajjita ; nadita ; °jita. °**ion**, *n.* gajjana ; tajjana, *nt.*

Fulmine, *v.t.* asaniŋ peseti. *v.i.* thanati. *p.p.* pesitāsani ; thanita.

Fulsome, *a.* 1. kucchita ; jegucchа ; gārayha; 2. vyājakathā, *f.* °**ness**, *n.* gārayhatā, *f.*

Fulvous, *a.* piṅga ; rattapīta.

Fumble, *v.i.* adakkhākārena parāmasati. *p.p.* °parāmaṭṭha. °**er**, *n.* anipuṇa-vāyāma, *m.*

Fume, *n.* dhūpa, *m.* *v.i.* dhūpāyati ; dhūmāyati. *v.t.* gandhena vāseti. *p.p.* °yita ; gandhavāsita.

Fumigate, *v.t.* dhūpeti ; dhūpena vāseti. *p.p.* °pita ; °vāsita. °**ion**, *n.* sandhūpana ; gandhavāsana, *nt.* °**tor**, *n.* sandhūpaka, *m.*

Fun, *n.* dava ; parihāsa, *m.* keḷi, *f.*

Funambulist, *n.* rajjunaṭaka, *m.*

Function, *n.* 1. kicca, *nt.* kiriyāvidhi, *m.* anuṭṭhāna, *nt.* 2. niyamitādhikāra, *m.* 3. indriyabala, *nt.* *v.i.* (sakakiccaŋ) sādheti *cr* sampādeti. *p.p.* °sādhita ; °dita. °**al**, *a.* niyamāyatta. °**ary**, *n.* kiccasampādaka, *m.*

Functionate, see **Function**, *v.i.*

Fund, *n.* nihitadhana; mūladhana, *nt.* *v.t.* mūladhanaŋ sampādeti. *p.p.* °ditamūladhana.

Fundament, *n.* 1. mūlādhāra, *m.* 2. piṇḍikamaŋsa, *nt.*

Fundamental, *a.* mūlika ; padhāna ; sārabhūta. *n.* mūlatatta ; padhānakāraṇa, *nt.* °**ly**, *adv.* mūlikavasena. °**ity**, *n.* mūlikatta ; padhānatta, *nt.* °**ist**, *n.* purāṇadhammarakkhaka, *m.*

Funeral, *n.* petakicca ; matakicca, *nt.* adj. matakiccāyatta. °**pile**, °**pyre**, citaka, *m.*

Funerary, *a.* petakiccāyatta.

Funereal, *a.* matakiccasadisa ; sokasūcaka ; nirānanda.

Fungible, *a.* parivaṭṭanakkhama.

Fungicide, *n.* ahicchattanāsī, *m.*

Fungous, *a.* ahicchattasadisa ; aciraṭṭhāyī.

Fungus, *n.* ahicchattaka, *nt.*

Funicular, *a.* rajjubalāyatta.

Funk, *n.* mahabbhaya, *nt.* *v.i.* paṭilīyati. *v.t.* bhāyāpeti. *p.p.* paṭilīna ; °pita. °**y**, *a.* atibhīta ; uttrasta.

Funnel, *n.* dhūmanetta, *nt.* dhūmaniggama, *m.*

Funny, *a.* hāsajanaka; upahasanīya.

Fur, *n.* 1. loma, *nt.* uṇṇā, *f.* 2. jivhāmala; 3. bhājanamala, *nt.* *v.t.* lomehi āvarati. *p.p.* lomāvuta, °**rier,** *n.* lomavāṇija, *m.* °**ry,** *a.* lomabahula; lomasa.

Furbish, *v.t.* parimajjati; malam apaneti. *p.p.* °jita; apanītamala. °**er,** *n.* malāpahārī, *m.*

Furcate, *a.* dvi-sūlaka. *v.i.* dvisūlībhavati. °**ion,** *n.* dvisūlatta, *nt.*

Furious, *a.* aticaṇḍa; kopāviṭṭha; madamatta. °**ly,** *adv.* aticaṇḍākārena. °**ness,** *n.* dāruṇatta; caṇḍatta, *nt.*

Furl, *v.t.* saṅkoceti; saŋveṭheti; saŋharati. *v.i.* saṅkucati. *p.p.* °cita; °ṭhita; saŋhaṭa; saṅkucita.

Furlong, *n.* gāvutassa soḷasamabhāga, *m.*

Furlough, *n.* bhaṭavirāmapaṭiññā, *f.* *v.t.* bhaṭavirāmapaṭiññaŋ deti.

Furnace, *n.* uddhana, *nt.* āvāpa, *m.* kammāruddhana, *nt.*

Furnish, *v.t.* (upakaraṇāni) sampādeti. *p.p.* sampāditopakaraṇa. °**ed,** *a.* sopakaraṇa; saparikkhāra. °**ed with,** upeta; samupeta, *a.* °**ing,** *n.* upakaraṇasampādana, *nt.*

Furniture, *n.* dārubhaṇḍa; gehopakaraṇa, *nt.*

Furore, *n.* balava-īhā, *f.* accantābhinivesa, *m.*

Furrow, *n.* halapaddhati; sītā, *f.* naṅgalamagga, *m.* *v.t.* 1. kasati; 2. vinivijjhati. *p.p.* kaṭṭha *or* kasita; vinividdha.

Further, *a.* dūratara; adhikatara; *adv.* 1. uttariŋ; 2. api ca; atha ca; puna c'aparaŋ. *v.t.* saŋvaḍḍheti; anuggaṇhāti. *p.p.* °ḍhita; °hita. °**ance,** *n.* saŋvaḍḍhana, *nt.* anuggaha, *m.* °**er,** *n.* pavaḍḍhaka; upakāraka, *m.* °**more,** *adv.* aparañ ca; kiñca bhīyo. °**most,** *a.* dūratama.

Furthest, *a.* dūratama. *adv.* dūratamaŋ; atidūraŋ.

Furtive, *a.* thenita; avahaṭa. °**ly,** *adv.* theyyena; rahassena.

Furuncle, *n.* gaṇḍa; phoṭa, *m.*

Fury, *n.* caṇḍikka, *nt.* kopavega, *m.*

Fuse, *n.* tejovāhaka, *m.* *v.i.* vilīyati; missībhavati. *v.t.* 1. vilīyāpeti; sammisseti; 2. tejovāhakaŋ yojeti. *p.p.* °pita; °sita; yojita-tejovāhaka. °**ible,** *a.* 1. vilīyanasīla; 2. tejopharaka. °**ion,** *n.* 1. vilīyana; 2. saŋyujjana; 3. tejovahana, *nt.*

Fusiform, *a.* dhūmavaṭṭikākāra.

Fusillade, *n.* agginālihi asesaviddhaŋsana, *nt.* *v.t.* aggināḷihi vijjhati.

Fuss, *n.* mahākalakala, *m.* *v.t.* kalakalaŋ uppādeti. *v.i.* saṅkhubhati. *p.p.* °ditakalakala; °bhita. °**y,** *a.* kalakalayutta; saṅkhubhita. °**ily,** *adv.* sasambhamaŋ; sakhobhaŋ. °**iness,** *n.* khubhitatta, *nt.*

Fustigate, *v.t.* muggarena paharati. *p.p.* °pahaṭa. °**ion,** *n.* muggara-paharaṇa, *nt.*

Fusty, *a.* 1. sakaṇṇika; pūtigandha; 2. purāṇabhūta.

Futile, *a.* niratthaka; mogha; asāra; tuccha. °**ity,** *n.* niratthakatta, *nt.*

Future, *n.* 1. anāgatakāla, *m.* āyati, *f.* 2. paraloka; samparāya, *m.* adj. anāgata; āgāmī; āyatika. °**less,** *a.* anāgatāpekkhārahita. °**ist,** anāgatavādagāhī, *m.* °**ity,** *n.* 1. anāgatakāla, *m.* 2. paralokagati, *f.*

Fuzzy, *a.* 1. kuñcitakesa; 2. āvila; avibhūta.

G

Gab, *n.* vippalāpa, *m.*

Gabble, *n.* palāpa, *m.* niratthakakathā, *f.* *v.i.* pajappati; samphaŋ katheti. *p.p.* °pita; kathitasampha. °**er,** *n.* pajappī; palāpī, *m.*

Gable, *n.* kūṭāgāra; gehasikhara, *nt.*

Gaby, *n.* jaḷa; dandha, *m.*

Gad, *n.* 1. patoda, *m.* 2. saratuṇḍa; sūlagga, *nt.* *v.i.* ito tato āhiṇḍati. °**ling,** *n.* sahacara, *m.*

Gad-fly, *n.* piṅgalamakkhikā, *f.*

Gaffer, *n.* mahallaka-jānapadika, *m.*

Gag, *n.* mukharodhakavatthu, *nt.* *v.t.* 1. mukham āvarati; 2. mukhādhānaŋ yojeti; 3. vañceti. *p.p.* āvaṭamukha; yojita°; °cita.

Gage, *n.* nyāsa; upanidhi, *m.* *v.t.* upanidahati; paṭiññaŋ deti. *p.p.* upanihita; dinnapaṭiñña.

Gaggle, *v.i.* kalakalāyati.

Gaiety, *n.* āmoda; pamoda, *m.* pāmojja, *nt.*

Gain, *n.* lābha; āya; phalodaya, *m.* *v.i.* labhati; adhigacchati. *v.t.* ārādheti; vasam āneti. *p.p.* laddha; adhigata; °dhita; °ānīta. °**er,** *n.* labhī, *m.* °**ful,** *a.* saphala; sātthaka; phalada. —**ground,** abhivaḍḍhati; samijjhati. — **upon,** samīpaŋ yāti. **One's own** —, salābha, *m.*

Gainsay, *v.t.* paccakkhāti; paccādisati. *p.p.* °khāta; paccādiṭṭha. °**er,** *n.* viruddhavādī; paṭikkhipaka, *m.*

Gait, *n.* gati; gamanalīlā, *f.*

Gaiter, *n.* jaṅghāvaraṇa, *nt.*

Gala, *n.* ussava; chaṇa, *m.* — **day,** *n.* chaṇadivasa, *m.*

Galaxy, *n.* 1. ākāsagaṅgā, *f.* cakkavāḷa, *nt.* 2. mahesakkha-parisā, *f.*

Gale, *n.* pabalavāta; caṇḍānila, *m.*

Gall, *n.* 1. pitta, *nt.* 2. domanassa, *nt.* *v.t.* 1. cammaŋ vikopeti; 2. pariḷāhaŋ janeti. *p.p.* vikopita°; janita°; °**ing,** *a.* kaṭuka; mammacchedaka.

Gallant, *a.* 1. sūra; vīra; abhīta; 2. cārudassana; 3. susīla. °**ly,** *adv.* savikkamaŋ. °**ry,** *n.* 1. sūratta; vīratta, *nt.* 2. mahesakkhatā, *f.* 3. itthilolatā, *f.*

Gall-bladder, *n.* pittāsaya, *m.*

Gallery, *n.* 1. samussiṭṭhāna, *nt.* 2. channālinda, *m.* 3. cittāgāra, *nt.*

Galley, *n.* 1. purāṇa-nāvāvisesa, *m.* 2. yojitakkharadhāraka, *m.* 3. nāvāya mahānasa, *m.*

Gallic, *a.* Pransadesāyatta.

Gallivant, *v.i.* pariyāhiṇḍati.

Gallon, *n.* doṇamatta-māṇa, *m.*

Gallop, *n.* plavana; uppatana, *nt.* *v.i.* plavanto dhāvati.

Gallows, *n.* vadhaṭṭhāna; māraka-yanta, *nt.*

Galore, *n.* bāhulla, *nt.* *adv.* bāhullena.

Galumph, *v.i.* vijaye naccati.

Galvanism, *n.* rasāyanikavijjubala, *nt.*

Galvanize, *v.t.* rasāyanikavijjuyā loham ālepeti.

Gamble, *n.* jūtakīḷā, *f.* *v.i.* jūtaŋ kīḷati; akkhehi dibbati. °**er,** *n.* jūtakāra; akkhadhutta, *m.* °**ing,** *n.* jūtakīḷana, *nt.*

Gamboge, *n.* Kamboja-pītaniyyāsa, *m.*

Gambol, *n.* lāsana, *nt.* līlā; kīḷā, *f.* *v.i.* dibbati; kīḷati.

Game, *n.* 1. kīḷā; keḷi, *f.* 2. pasu; vadhitabba-pāṇigaṇa, *m.* 3. migava, *m.* *v.i.* kīḷati; dibbati. °**cock,** yuddhakukkuṭa, *m.* °**ful,** *a.* kīḷāpara. °**ing,** *n.* jūta, *nt.* °**ing house,** jūtasālā, *f.* °**keeper,** migarakkhaka, *m.* °**ly,** *adv.* sūrākārena. °**ster,** dhutta; jūtakāra, *m.* °**some,** *a.* kīḷālola; vinodasīlī.

Gammer, *n.* mahallikā, *f.*

Gammon, *n.* 1. nikati; vañcanā, *f.* 2. sūkara-vallūra, *nt.* *v.t.* sokaraŋ lavaṇīkaroti. *p.p.* lavaṇīkatasokara.

Gamp, *n.* mahāchatta, *nt.*

Gamut, *n.* niravasesa-visaya, *m.*

Gamy, *a.* migabahula.

Gander, *n.* cakkavāka, *m.*

Gang, *n.* gaṇa; samūha, *m.* °**er,** *n.* gaṇajeṭṭha, *m.*

Ganges, *n.* Bhāgīrathī; Gaṅgānadī, *f.* °**getic,** *a.* Gaṅgāyatta.

Ganglion, *n.* nahārusaṅghāta, *m.*

Gangrene, *n.* jīvamaŋsa-pūtiroga, *m.* *v.t.* jīvamaŋsaŋ putittaŋ neti.

Gangster, *n.* pūgāyatta; gaṇasahāya, *m.*

Gangway, *n.* antarāpatha; nāvoruhana-patha, *m.*

Gaol, *n.* kārā, *f.* bandhanāgāra, *nt.* *v.t.* kārāgāre khipati. °**er,** *n.* kārāpālaka, *m.*

Gap, *n.* 1. vivara; chidda; 2. antara; antarakāla, *m.*

Gape, *n.* vivaṭamukha, *nt.* vijambhanā, *f.* *v.i.* vijambhati; mukhaŋ vivarati. *p.p.* °bhita; vivaṭamukha. °**er,** *n.* vivaṭamukhī, *m.*

Garage, *n.* rathasālā, *f.*

Garb, *n.* nivāsana-pārupaṇa, *nt.* *v.t.* nivāseti; acchādeti. *p.p.* nivattha; °dita.

Garbage, *n.* 1. chaḍḍiyavatthu, *nt.* 2. nindiyalipi, *f.*

Garble, *v.t.* 1. uccināti; 2. ayathā dasseti. *p.p.* uccinita; °sita.

Garden, *n.* uyyāna, *nt.* ārāma, *m.* uyyānaŋ ropeti. *p.p.* ropituyyāna. °**er,** *n.* uyyānapāla, *m.* °**ing,** *n.* uyyānaropaṇa, *nt.* **Flower —,** pupphārāma, *m.* **Fruit —,** phalārāma, *m.* **Pleasure —,** kīḷuyyāna, *nt.*

Gargantuan, *a.* atimahanta; ativisāla.

Gargle, *n.* mukhavikkhālana; kaṇṭhasodhanosadha, *nt.* *v.t.* (osadhena) kaṇṭhaŋ sodheti; mukhaŋ vikkhāleti. *p.p.* sodhitakaṇṭha; °litamukha.

Gargoyle, *n.* vicittasaṇṭhānapaṇālīmukha, *nt.*

Garish, *a.* atibhāsura; accalaṅkata. °**ly,** *adv.* atibhāsuratāya.

Garland, *n.* āvelā; mālā, *f.* mālādāma, *m.* *v.t.* mālaŋ piḷandheti. *p.p.* piḷandhitamāla. — **for the head,** uttaŋsa; sekhara, *m.* — **maker,** mālākāra, *m.*

Garlic, *n.* lasuṇa, *nt.*

Garment, *n.* vasana; acchādana; nivāsana, *nt.* **Under —,** antaravāsaka, *m.* **Upper —,** uttarīya, *nt.*

Garner, *n.* kusūla, *n.* dhaññāgāra, *nt. v.t.* kusūle nidahati. *p.p.* °nihita.

Garnet, *n.* lohitaṅka; rattamaṇi, *m.*

Garnish, *n.* alaṅkāra, *m.* vibhūsana, *nt. v.t.* alaṅkaroti; bhūseti. *p.p.* °kata; °sita.

Garniture, *n.* 1. vibhūsābhaṇḍa; pilandhanopakaraṇa, *nt.* 2. alaṅkaraṇa, *nt.*

Garret, *n.* vehāsakuṭi, *f.* °**eer,** *n.* vehāsakuṭivāsī, *m.*

Garrison, *n.* dugga-rakkhakasenā, *f. v.t.* duggarakkhake payojeti.

Garrulous, *a.* vācāla; mukhara. °**ness, Garrulity,** *n.* mukharatta, *nt.* bahubhāṇitā, *f.*

Garter, *n.* jaṅghābandhana, *nt.*

Garth, *n.* gehaṅgaṇa, *nt.*

Gas, *n.* vāyurūpa-vatthu, *nt.* °**eous,** *a.* vāyurūpaka.

Gasconade, *n.* vikatthana, *nt. v.i.* vikatthati. *p.p.* °thita.

Gash, *n.* dīgha-khata, *nt. v.t.* dīghakhataŋ sādhedi.

Gasolene, *n.* asuddha-bhūmitela, *nt.*

Gasometer, *n.* vāyurūpakāsaya, *m.*

Gasp, *n.* nissasana, *nt. v.i.* kicchena sasati.

Gastric, *n.* āmāsayaṭṭha. —**juice,** jaṭharaggi, *m.*

Gastrology, *n.* sūpasattha, *nt.*

Gastronome, *n.* sūpasatthaññū, *m.* °**my,** *n.* subhojanavijjā, *f.* °**er,** 1. sūpasatthaññū, *m.* 2. udarambharī, *m.*

Gate, *n.* bahidvāra; pākāradvāra, *nt.* °**house,** dvārakoṭṭhaka, *nt.* °**keeper,** dvārapāla, *m.* °**tower,** gopura, *nt.* °**way,** dvāramagga, *m.*

Gather, *v.t.* 1. ācināti; upacināti; samāharati; 2. anumāneti. *v.i.* saṅgacchati; sannipatati; rāsībhavati. *p.p.* ācita; upacita; samāhaṭa; °nita; saṅgata; °tita; rāsibhūta. °**er,** *n.* saŋhāraka; saṅgāhaka, *m.*

Gathering, *n.* 1. ācaya; upacaya, *m.* samāharaṇa, *nt.* 2. sannipāta; samāgama, *m.* sammelana, *nt.*

Gauche, *a.* asobhaṇa; adakkha.

Gaud, *n.* appagghābharaṇa, *nt.*

Gaudy, *n.* mahābhojanasaṅgaha, *m.* adj. nānāvaṇṇa; asippānurūpa.

Gauge, *n.* 1. pamāṇita-māṇa, *nt.* 2. antogatappamāṇa, *nt. v.t.* yathāpamāṇaŋ miṇāti; samapamāṇaŋ neti. *p.p.* °mita; °nīta.

Gaunt, *a.* kisa; tanu; dubbala. °**ness,** *n.* kisatta, *nt.*

Gauntlet, *n.* hatthaparittāṇa, *nt.*

Gauze, *n.* sukhumavattha; jālavattha, *nt.*

Gavial, *n.* Bhāratīya-kumbhīla, *m.*

Gawk, *n.* mandamatika; asobhanagatika, *m.* °**y,** *a.* asobhana; dandha.

Gay, *a.* 1. pahaṭṭha; udagga; 2. sobhana. **Gaily,** *adv.* sahāsaŋ; sānandaŋ; sobhanākārena.

Gaze, *n.* samekkhana ; nirikkhaṇa, *nt.* *v.i.* samekkhati. *p.p.* °khita. °**er**, *n.* samekkhaka, *m.*
Gazelle, *n.* haripa ; sāraṅga, *m.*
Gazette, *n.* pavattipatta, *nt.* *v.t.* pakāseti ; nivedeti. *p.p.* °sita ; °dita.
Gear, *n.* 1. upakaraṇa, *nt.* 2. saṅghaṭṭita-cakkadvaya, *nt.* *v.t.* kappeti ; sannāheti. *p.p.* kappita ; sannaddha.
Gecko, *n.* gharagoḷikā, *f.*
Gee-gee, *n.* haya, *m.*
Gelatin, *n.* (jīva-) silesa, *m.* °**ous**, *a.* lagganasīla ; miñjasadisa.
Gelation, *n.* sītena thambhīkarṇa, *nt.*
Geld, *v.t.* bījam uppāṭeti. *p.p.* uppāṭita-bīja. °**ing**, *n.* bījuddharaṇa, *nt.*
Gelid, *a.* himasadisa.
Gem, *n.* maṇi, *m.* *v.t.* maṇīhi sobheti. *p.p.* maṇisobhita. °**cutter**, maṇikāra, *m.* °**med**, *a.* maṇikhacita. °**my**, *a.* maṇimaya ; ratanālaṅkata.
Geminate, *a.* yugalabaddha. *v.t.* yugalabaddhaŋ *or* diguṇaŋ karoti. *p.p.* diguṇīkata.
Gemini, *n.* yuga ; mithuna ; yamaka, *nt.* **Sign of** —, mithunarāsi, *m.*
Gemmate, *a.* aṅkurayutta. *v.i.* aṅkurāni pātukaroti. *p.p.* pātukataṅkura. °**ion**, *n.* aṅkurapātubhāva, *m.*
Gemmiferous, *a.* 1. ratanuppādaka ; 2. aṅkuruppādaka.
Gender, *n.* liṅga, *nt.* pakati, *f.*
Genealogy, *n.* vaŋsāvalī ; paramparā, *f.* °**ical**, *a.* paramparāvisayaka. °**ist**, *n.* vaŋsāvalīvidū ; anvayaññū, *m.*
General, *n.* senānī ; camūpati ; senānātha, *m.* adj. sādhāraṇa ; avisiṭṭha ; sabbavyāpī. — **fact**, dhammatā, *f.* °**issimo**, *n.* aggasenāpati, *m.* °**ity**, *n.* sāmañña ; sādhāraṇatta, *nt.* °**ness**, *n.* sāmaññatā, *f.* — **opinion**, sammuti, *f.* — **practice**, lokācāra ; lokavohāra, *m.* °**ship**, senāpacca, *nt.*
Generalize, *v.t.* samataŋ neti ; samānanāmaŋ yojeti. *p.p.* °nīta ; °mayutta. °**ation**, *n.* samānattapāpaṇa ; vaggīkaraṇa, *nt.*
Generally, *adv.* sāmaññena ; pāyo ; bahuso.
Generate, *v.t.* janeti ; uppādeti. *p.p.* janita ; °dita. °**ing**, *a.* uppādaka. °**ion**, *n.* 1. janana ; pasavana ; uppādana, *nt.* 2. kulaparivaṭṭa, *nt.* pajā, *f.* °**ive**, *a.* janaka, nibbattaka.
Generator, *n.* uppādetu ; janetu; nibbattaka, *m.*
Generic, °**cal**, *a.* uppattyāgata ; jātivisayaka. — **property**, jātisabhāva, *m.* °**ally**, *adv.* jātisabhāvena.
Generosity, *n.* vadaññutā ; uḷāracittatā ; dānasoṇḍatā, *f.*
Generous, *a.* 1. cāgasīlī ; dānasoṇḍa ; muttahatta ; 2. khamanasīla. °**ly**, *adv.* cāgasīlitāya ; uḷārajjhāsayeṇa. °**ness**, *n.* cāgasīlitā, *f.*
Genesis, *n.* 1. mūluppatti ; 2. lokuppattikathā, *f.*
Genetic, *a.* mūlārambhāyatta. *pl.* pettikaguṇa, *m.*
Genial, *a.* 1. sukhāvaha ; ramaṇīya ; manohara ; 2. pasanna ; kāruṇika ; 3. uppattivisayaka. °**ity**, *n.* pasannatā ; rammatā,

°**ly**, *adv.* sānandaŋ ; pasannākārena.

Genie, *n.* pisāca ; 'amanussa, *m.*

Genital, *a.* jananāyatta. — **organ**, janakindriya, *nt.*

Genitive, *n.* sāmivacana, *nt.* chaṭṭhī vibhatti, *f.*

Genitor, *n.* janetu, *m.*

Genetrix, *n.* janettī, *f.*

Genius, *n.* 1. visiṭṭhabuddhi, *f.* 2. visiṭṭhapañña, *m.* 3. ārakkhadevatā, *f.* 4. visesaciṇha, *nt.*

Genre, *n.* jātivisesa; vaggabheda, *m.*

Gent, see **Gentleman**.

Genteel, *a.* abhijāta ; sabbha ; ācārakusala ; kulīna. °**ness**, *n.* vinītatā ; abhijātatā, *f.*

Gentile, *a.n.* 1. Yādavetarajātika ; 2. micchādiṭṭhika, *m.*

Gentility, *n.* vinītatā ; sabbhatā, *f.*

Gentle, *a.* 1. mudu ; komala ; somma ; sukumāra ; 2. uccākulīna ; abhijāta ; 3. santa ; danta; anukampaka. — **breeze**, mandānila, *m.* °**folk**, kulīnajana, *m.* °**man**, ayya ; ariya ; mahāsaya, *m.* °**ness**, mudutā ; komalatā ; santatā, *f.* °**woman**, ayyā ; kulitthī, *f.*

Gentlemanly, *a.* vinīta ; susīla ; ācārasīlī.

Gently, *adv.* sadayaŋ ; muduŋ ; mandaŋ.

Gentry, *n.* (majjhima-) kulīnajana, *m.*

Genual, *a.* jaṇṇukāyatta.

Genuflect, *v.i.* jaṇṇūhi patati. *p.p.* °patita. °**flexion**, *n.* jaṇṇūhi nipatana, *nt.* jāṇunati, *f.*

Genuine, *a.* 1. amissajātika ; 2. avitatha ; avyāja ; yathābhūta. °**ly**, *adv.* yathātathaŋ ; avyājaŋ. °**ness**, *n.* avitathatā, *f.*

Genus, *n.* visesajāti, *f.* vagga ; gaṇa, *m.*

Geocentric, *a.* paṭhavippadhāna ; paṭhavito gaṇīyamāna.

Geodesy, *n.* paṭhavitalamāṇasattha, *nt.*

Geognosy, *n.* bhūpadesavijjā, *f.*

Geography, *n.* bhūgoḷasattha, *nt.* °**ical**, bhumisatthāyatta. °**ically**, *adv.* bhūgoḷavijjānurūpaŋ.

Geology, *n.* bhūgabbhavijjā, *f.* °**ical**, *a.* bhūgabbhavijjāyatta. °**ist**, *n.* bhūtattaññū, *m.*

Geomancy, *n.* paŋsunimittapaṭhana, *nt.* °**cer**, paŋsunimittapāṭhaka, *m.*

Geometer, *n.* bhūmāṇavidū, *m.*

Geometry, *n.* jyāmiti, *f.* bhūmānasattha; rekhāgaṇita, *nt.* °**ical**, *a.* bhūmitivisayaka. °**ician**, bhūmitisattaññū, *m.* °**ically**, *adv.* bhūmitisatthānusārena. °**ize**, *v.t.* bhūmitiŋ karoti.

Geoponic, *a.* kasivijjāyatta.

Georgic, *n.* kasinissitakabba, *nt.*

Germ, *n.* bīja ; mūlabīja, *nt.* yoni, *f.* *v.i.* see **Germinate**.

Germane, *a.* sālohita ; sasambandha.

Germicide, *a.n.* visabījanāsaka, *nt.*

Germinal, *a.* mūlabījāyatta.

Germinate, *v.i.* ubbhijjati ; virūhati; aṅkurīyati. *p.p.* ubbhinna; virūḷha ; °rita. °**ion**, *n.* aṅkurapātubhāva, *m.* °**ive**, *a.* aṅkurajanaka.

Gerund, *n.* bhāvapada, *nt.* °**ive**, *a.n.* bhāvapadasadisa ; bhāvapadāyatta.
Gestation, *n.* gabbhadhāraṇa, *nt.* garugabbhatā, *f.*
Gestatory, *a.* gabbhanissita.
Gesticulate, *v.t.* aṅgāni vikkhipati. *p.p.* vikkhittaṅga. °**ion**, kāyaviññatti, *f.* °**tor**, *n.* aṅgavikkhepaka, *m.*
Gesture, *n.* kāyavikāra ; aṅgavikkhepa, *m.* iṅgita, *nt. v.i.* kāyena viññāpeti. *p.p.* °pita.
Get, *n.* pajā, *f.* apacca, *nt. v.t.i.* labhati ; adhigacchati. *p.p.* laddha ; adhigata. — **along**, abhiyāti ; abhivaḍḍhati. — **at**, pappoti. — **away**, vigacchati ; apakkamati. — **back**, paccāgacchati ; paṭilabhati. — **behind**, avasīdati. — **clear**, vimuccati. — **down**, oruhati. — **drunk**, majjati. — **forward**, abbhuyyāti. — **free**, muccati. — **in**, pavisati. — **into**, āpajjati ; nigacchati. — **into debt**, iṇaṭṭho bhavati. — **off**, apayāti. — **on**, pavattati ; jīvikaŋ kappeti. — **out**, nikkhamati ; apeti. — **over**, — **rid of**, vinodeti ; vyantīkaroti. — **through**, atikkamati ; acceti ; tarati ; niṭṭhāpeti. — **up**, uṭṭhāti. — **upon**, āruhati. °**ting**, *n.* labhana ; ajjana, *nt.*
Geyser, *n.* uṇhajalubbhida, *m.*
Ghastly, *a.* 1. bhīma ; ghora ; dāruṇa ; 2. uppaṇḍuka ; chavasama ; kilantindriya.
Ghee, *n.* ghata ; sappi, *nt.*
Ghost, *n.* pisāca ; peta ; amanussa, *m.* °**ly**, *a.* pisācākāra.
Ghoul, *n.* vetāla, *m.*
Giant, *a.* mahākāya. *n.* rakkhasa; asura, *m.* °**like**, visāladeha ; mahābala ; asurasadisa. °**ess**, rakkhasī, *f.*
Gibber, *n.* avyatta-jappana, *nt. v.i.* avyattaŋ jappati. °**ish**, *n.* niratthakālāpa, *m.*
Gibbet, *n.* vadhatthambha, *m. v.t.* vadhatthambhe ālaggeti.
Gibbon, *n.* dīghabāhu-vānara, *m.*
Gibe, *n.* upahāsa, *m.* ohīlanā, *v.t.* upahasati ; ohīleti. °**er**, *n.* ohīlaka, *m.* °**ingly**, *adv.* ohīlanākārena.
Giddy, *a.* 1. bhanta ; matta ; 2. lola ; cañcala ; 3. uddhata ; dappita. *v.t.* sambhameti. *v.i.* sambhamati. *p.p.* °bhamita ; sambhanta. °**ily**, *adv.* bhantākārena. °**iness**, *n.* sambhama, *m.* cañcalatta ; anavadhāna, *nt.*
Gift, *n.* pābhata ; upāyana, *nt.* upahāra ; paṇṇākāra ; pariccāga, *m.* °**ed**, *a.* upeta ; yutta ; sampanna. — **in faith**, saddhādeyya, *nt.*
Gigantic, *a.* ativisāla ; atimahanta.
Giggle, *n.* adhamahāsa, *m. v.i.* avinīto viya hasati.
Gild, *v.t.* 1. suvaṇṇena limpeti. 2. virājeti. *p.p.* suvaṇṇalitta ; °jita. °**ing**, *n.* suvaṇṇālepa, *m.*
Gill, *n.* 1. (macchādīnaŋ) āṇāpāṇindriya, *nt.* 2. khuddakanijjhara, *m.* 3. māṇavaka, *m.*
Gilt, *a.* suvaṇṇālitta.
Gimcrack, *a.* asammāpaṇihita.
Gimlet, *n.* ārā ; vijjhanasūci, *f.*
Gin, *n.* 1. pāsa, *m.* jāla, *nt.* 2. dhaññasurā, *f.* 3. bhārubbahanayanta, *nt. v.t.* pāsam oḍḍeti. *p.p.* oḍḍitapāsa.

Ginger, *n*. siṅgivera, *nt*. *v.t*. 1. siṅgiveraŋ pakkhipati; 2. ussukkāpeti. *p.p*. pakkhitta°. °pita. **Dry —**, mahosadha, *nt*. °**beer**, siṅgiverāsava, *m*. °**ly**, *adv*. sanikaŋ; sāvadhānaŋ. adj. sāvadhāna.

Gingili, *n*. tila, *nt*.

Gipsy, Gypsy, *n*. abaddhanivāsa; ahituṇḍika, *m*.

Giraffe, *n*. dīghagīvamiga, *m*.

Gird, *n*. upahāsa, *m*. *v.i*. upahasati. *v.t*. 1. ābandhati; kacchaŋ bandhati; 2. khaggaŋ sannayhati; 3. parikkhipati. *p.p*. °sita; ābaddha; baddhakaccha; sannaddhakhagga; parikkhitta.

Girder, *n*. mahādhava, *m*.

Girdle, *n*. 1. rasanā; mekhalā, *f*. kaṭisutta; kāyabandhana, *nt*. 2. paribhaṇḍa; parikkhepa, *m*. 3. rāsicakka, *nt*. *v.t*. parikkhipati; paḷiveṭheti. *p.p*. °khitta; °ṭhita.

Girl, *n*. daharā; kaññā; kumārī, *f*. °**hood**, kaññābhāva, *m*. °**ish**, *a*. kaññānurūpa.

Girt, *n*. visamavatthu-māṇa, *nt*. *v.t*. visamavatthuŋ miṇāti.

Girth, *n*. varattā; naddhi; nandī, *f*.

Gist, *n*. sāraŋsa; piṇḍattha. *m*.

Give, *v.t*. dadāti; deti; vitarati. *p.p*. dinna; vitarita. — **away**, appeti; paṭipādeti. — **back**, paṭidadāti. — **birth to**, janeti; vijāyati. — **ear**, sussūsati; sotam odahati. °**er**, dāyaka; dāyī; dātu, *m*. °**forth**, pakāseti. °**ground**, paccosakkati. — **in**, anuvattati. — **in charge**, niyyādeti. — **off**, — **up**, pajahati; cajati; nissajati. — **notice**, apaloketi. — **out**, anuppadāti; niveḍeti. — **over**, *v.i*. viramati. *v.t*. niyyādeti. — **rise to**, uppādeti. — **way**, osīdati; viramati; okāsaŋ deti.

Given, *p.p*. dinna. — **over**, padinna. — **up**, catta; ossaṭṭha; vissaṭṭha. *a*. — **well**, sudinna. *a*.

Giving, *n*. dāna; vitaraṇa; anuppadāna, *nt*. pariccāga. *m*. — **birth**, pasavana; vijāyana, *nt*. — **over**, sampadāna, *nt*. °**up**, pajahana; pahāṇa, *nt*. paṭinissagga, *m*.

Gizzard, *n*. (pakkhi-macchānaŋ) dutiyāmāsaya, *m*.

Glabrous, *a*. nikkesa; khallāṭa.

Glacial, *a*. himamaya; himayutta.

Glaciated, *a*. himagaṅgāvuta.

Glacier, *n*. himanadī, *f*. himakkhandha, *m*.

Glacis, *n*. pākārato bahi poṇabhūmi, *f*.

Glad, *a*. mudita; pamudita; haṭṭha; tuṭṭha; sumana; attamana, santuṭṭha. *v.t*. modeti; toseti; pamodeti. *p.p*. °dita; tosita. °**ly**, *adv*. sānandaŋ. °**ness**, *n*. tuṭṭhi; santuṭṭhi, *f*. ānanda; āmoda; pamoda, *m*.

Gladden, *v.t*. toseti; modeti; hāseti; rameti; pahaŋseti. *p.p*. tosita; modita; hāsita; ramita; °sita. °**ing**, *n*. pahaŋsana, *nt*. °**ing**, *a*. pahaŋsaka.

Glade, *n*. vanamagga, *m*. araññaṅgaṇa, *nt*.

Gladiator, *n*. asikīḷaka; khaggasippī, *m*.

Glair, *n*. setasilesa, *m*.

Glamour, *n.* 1. māyā, *f.* vasīkaraṇa ; 2. atisobhanatta, *nt.* *v.t.* moheti ; vasīkaroti. *p.p.* mohita ; °kata.

Glance, *n.* lesamattolokana, *nt.* diṭṭhipāta, *m.* *v.i.* khippam oloketi, *v.t.* phusanākārena paharati. *p.p.* °kita ; °pahaṭa.

Gland, *n.* maŋsaganṭhi ; mudumaŋsapiṇḍa, *m.* °**ular**, *a.* maŋsapiṇḍākāra.

Glare, *n.* 1. atiditti ; adhikapabhā, *f.* 2. kuddhapekkhana, *nt.* *v.i.* 1. pajjalati ; sandippati ; 2. kodhena oloketi. *p.p.* °lita ; sanditta ; °kita. °**ing**, *a.* daddallamāna ; sampajjalita. °**ingly**, *adv.* atiphuṭaŋ ; supākaṭaŋ.

Glass, *n.* 1. kāca, *m.* 2. kācabhājana. adj. kācamaya. *v.t.* kācapatthare yojeti. — **bottle**, kācatumba, *m.* °**like**, °**y**, kācasadisa. °**ware**, kācabhaṇḍa, *nt.*

Glaucoma, *n.* akkhi-kācaroga, *m.*

Glaucous, *a.* samuddavaṇṇa.

Glaze, *n.* ujjalavaṇṇa, *m.* *v.t.* 1. kācena ālimpeti ; 2. vaṇṇujjalaŋ karoti; 3. kāce yojeti *or* ghaṭeti. *p.p.* °ālitta ; °līkata ; yojitakāca.

Glazier, *n.* kācayojaka, *m.*

Glazing, *n.* 1. kācayojana, *nt.* 2. ujjalavaṇṇadhātu, *f.*

Gleam, *n.* mandajuti, *f.* *v.i.* mandam ujjalati *or* vilasati. *p.p.* °lita ; °sita. °**y**, *a.* mandappabha ; calajjutika.

Glean, *v.i.* uñchati ; thokathokam uccināti. *p.p.* °chita ; °nita. °**ings**, *n.* uñchā ; bhikkhā, *f.* piṇḍapāta, *m.* °**er**, *n.* uñchaka, *m.*

Glee, see **Delight**.

Glen, *n.* kuñja, *m.* avitthiṇṇasamatala, *nt.*

Glib, *a.* 1. turitavacana ; 2. asambādha ; 3. picchila. °**ly**, *adv.* 1. mukharatāya ; 2. picchilākārena ; 3. akkhalitaŋ. °**ness**, mukharatta, *nt.*

Glide, *n.* saŋsappana, *nt.* *v.i.* saŋsappati. *p.p.* °pita. °**ing**, *n.* saŋsappamāna. °**ingly**, *adv.* saŋsappanākārena. — **off**, vinivaṭṭati.

Glimmer, *n.* mandappabhā, *f.* *v.i.* mandaŋ jalati. *p.p.* °jalita. °**ing**, *a.* mandajutika.

Glimpse, *n.* khaṇikadassana ; avibhūta-diṭṭhi, *f.* *v.t.* avibhūtaŋ passati, *v.i.* khaṇamattaŋ dissati. *p.p.* °diṭṭha.

Glint, *n.* khaṇikapabhā, *f.* *v.i.* sahasā jotati.

Glissade, *v.i.* himapapāte sappati.

Glisten, *n.* calajuti, *f.* *v.i.* khaṇe khaṇe jotati. °**ing**, *a.* samujjala ; calajjutika.

Glitter, *n.* pabhāsa, *m.* *v.i.* pabhāsati. *p.p.* °sita. °**ing**, *a.* bhāsamāna ; ujjala.

Gloaming, *n.* sañjhāloka, *m.*

Gloat, *v.i.* ativiya tussati ; lobhena oloketi. *p.p.* atituṭṭha ; °kita.

Globe, *n.* 1. goḷa ; maṇḍala, *nt.* 2. bhūgoḷa, *nt.*

Globular, *a.* goḷākāra.

Globule, *n.* goḷaka ; bindu, *m.*

Glomerate, *a.* piṇḍībhūta. *v.t.* piṇḍīkaroti. *p.p.* °kata. °**ion**, *n* piṇḍīkaraṇa, *nt.*

Gloom, *n.* 1. timira ; tama, *nt.* 2. domanassa, *nt.* arati, *f. v.t.* timirenāvarati. *v.i.* ukkaṇṭhati. *p.p.* timirāvuta ; °ṭhita. °**y**, *a.* 1. tamāvuta ; 2. ukkaṇṭhita. °**ily**, *adv.* 1. savisādaŋ ; 2. nippabhaŋ. °**iness**, *n.* 1. nippabhatta, *nt.* 2. visāda ; kheda, *m.*

Glorify, *v.t.* ukkaŋseti ; vaṇṇeti. *p.p.* °sita ; vaṇṇita. °**ication**, *n.* guṇavaṇṇanā ; pakittanā, *f.*

Gloriole, *n.* pabhāmaṇḍala, *nt.*

Glorious, *a.* kittimantu ; yasavantu ; sirindhara ; mahānubhāva ; vikhyāta. °**ly**, *adv.* pasatthākārena; mahānubhāvena.

Glory, *n.* 1. kitti ; vissuti ; siri, *f.* teja ; patāpa ; ānubhāva, *m.* 2. mahesakkhatā, *f.* 3. sirivibhūti, *f.* 4. saggasampatti, *f. v.i.* 1. accantaŋ modati ; 2. attānaŋ thometi *or* ukkaŋseti. *p.p.* °dita ; °mita ; °sita. **Vain —**, ahaṅkāra, *m.*

Gloss, *n.* 1. ṭīkā, *f.* atthavivaraṇa, *nt.* 2. ditti ; juti, *f. v.t.* 1. vyākhāti ; 2. bāhirato sobheti. °**y**, *a.* maṭṭha ; siniddha ; ujjala. °**al**, *a.* 1. jivhāvisayaka ; 2. vācāvisayaka. °**ary**, *n.* gaṇṭhipadavivaraṇa, *nt.* °**ator**, ṭīkākāra, *m.* °**iness**, *n.* maṭṭhatā, *f.*

Glossitis, *n.* jivhādāha, *m.*

Glossographer, *n.* ṭīkākāra ; gaṇṭhipadavivaraka, *m.* °**phy**, *n.* ṭīkākaraṇa, *nt.*

Glossology, *n.* paribhāsā, *f.* °**ist**, *n.* paribhāsāsampādaka, *m.*

Glottal, *a.* kaṇṭhanāḷanissita.

Glottis, *n.* kaṇṭhanāḷa, *m.*

Glove, *n.* karatalacchada, *m. v.t.* karatalaŋ chādeti.

Glow, *n.* 1. ditti; juti, *f.* 2. tāpa ; dāha, *m. v.i.* dippati ; jotati. *p.p.* ditta ; jotita. °**ing**, *a.* dippamāna ; santatta ; paditta. °**ingly**, *adv.* sadāhaŋ ; satāpaŋ. °**worm**, *n.* khajjopanaka, *m.*

Gloze, *n.* upalālanā, *f. v.t.* 1. upalāleti ; 2. vitthāreti. *p.p.* °lita ; °rita. °**ingly**, *adv.* cāṭukamyatāya.

Glucose, *n.* muddikā-sakkharā, *f.*

Glue, *n.* silesa ; picchila, *m. nt. v.t.* sileseti ; laggāpeti. *p.p.* °sita ; °pita.

Glum, *a.* dummukha ; anattamana. °**ly**, *adv.* asantuṭṭhiyā. °**ness**, *n.* domanassa, *nt.*

Glume, *n.* thusa ; dhaññataca, *m.* °**aceous**, *a.* thusayutta.

Glut, *n.* atimattabhojana, *nt. v.t.* ghasati ; atimattaŋ bhuñjati. *p.p.* ghasita ; °bhutta.

Gluten, *n.* niyyāsa, *m.*

Glutinize, Glutinate, *v.t.* niyyāsena alliyāpeti. *p.p.* °pita.

Glutinous, *a.* lagganasīla.

Glutton, *a.* mahagghasa ; odarika, *m.* °**ous**, *a.* mahagghasa ; atilola. °**ously**, *adv.* atilolākārena. °**y**, *n.* mahābhakkhatā, *f.* atibhakkhana, *nt.*

Glycerine, *n.* medasāra, *m.*

Glyconic, *a.* tisūlaka.

Glycosuria, *n.* mutte sakkharābahulatā, *f.*

Glyptic, *a.* kārusippāyatta.

Glyptography, *n.* maṇikārasippa, *nt.*

Gnarl, *n.* kukku ; gaṇṭhi, *m. v.i.* ghuru-ghurāyati. °**ed**, *a.* sakukkuka ; gaṇṭhiyutta.

Gnash, *v.t.* dante ghaŋseti. *p.p.* ghaŋsitadanta. °**ing,** *n.* dantavidaŋsana, *nt.*

Gnat, *n.* vanamakkhikā, *f.*

Gnathic, *a.* hanusambandha.

Gnaw, *v.t.* ḍasati ; dantehi chiṇdati. *p.p.* daṭṭha ; dantacchinna.

Gneiss, *n.* kāḷasilā, *f.*

Gnome, *n.* 1. kārikā, *f.* sutta, *nt.* 2. nidhipālaka-bhūta, *m.* °**ic,** *a.* kārikāyutta. °**ish,** a. pisācasadisa.

Gnomon, *n.* chāyāmāṇakatthambha, *m.*

Gnosis, *n.* paramatthavijjā, *f.*

Gnostic, *a.n.* paramatthavidū, *m.* °**ism,** *n.* paramatthañāṇa, *nt.*

Go, *v.i.* 1. gacchati ; vajati ; yāti ; carati ; 2. pavattati. *p.p.* gata ; yāta ; °tita. — **about,** anupariyāti.—**against,** abhiyāti; virujjhati. — **ahead,** abhigacchati. —**along,** paṭipajjati.— **ashore,** tarati; uttarati. —**away,** apakkamati. — **back,** paṭikkamati. — **between,** sandhīkaroti. — **beyond,** atikkamati; ativatteti. — **by,** anuyāti. — **down,** ogacchati ; atthaṅgacchati. °**er,** gantu ; gāmī, *m.* —**forth,** abhiyāti. —**forth from,** abhinikkhamati. —**in,** pavisati. —**into,** anupavisati. — **off,** apasarati. — **on,** pavattati. —**out,** nikkhamati ; niggacchati. —**over,** 1. upaparikkhati ; 2. laṅgheti ; saṅkamati. — **round,** anupariyāti. — **through,** 1. vindati ; 2. sevati ; paṭipajjati ; 3. osāpeti ; 4. tiriyaŋ gacchati. — **to,** — **up to,** upagacchati. — **to ruin,** parābhavati ; vinassati. — **up,** uggacchati ; udeti. — **with,** sahagacchati — **without,** viramati. — **wrong,** virajjhati.

Goad, *n.* patoda, *m.* pājana, *nt.* *v.t.* codeti; uyyojeti. *p.p.* codita; °jita.

Goal, *n.* abhimataṭṭhāna, *nt.* paramaniṭṭhā, *f.*

Goat, *n.* eḷaka ; aja, *m.* — **herd,** ajapāla, *m.* °**ish,** *a.* ajagandhī. **She —,** ajī ; eḷikā, *f.*

Gobbet, *n.* kabala, *nt.* piṇḍa, *m.*

Gobble, *v.t.* sīghaŋ *or* sasaddaŋ bhuñjati. *v.i.* kaṇṭhasaddaŋ pavatteti. *p.p.* °bhutta ; pavattita°.

Go-between, *n.* gahabandhanayojaka, *m.*

Goblet, *n.* āpānīya-kaŋsa, *m.*

Goblin, *n.* pisāca, *m.*

God, *n.* deva ; sura ; amara ; tidasa, *m.* devatā, *f.* °**dess,** *n.* accharā ; devakaññā, *f.* °**dess of luck,** lakkhī ; sirī, *f.* °**father,** sāmayika-pitu, *m.* °**head,** *n.* devatta, *nt.* devasabhāva, *m.* °**less,** *a.* adevadiṭṭhika. °**lessness,** *n.* adevadiṭṭhi, *f.* °**like,** *a.* dhammika. °**liness,** 1. dhammikatā ; 2. devabhatti, *f.* °**send,** *a.* devadattiya. °**ship,** *n.* devatta, *nt.* **City of the gods,** tidasapura, *nt.* **Lord of the gods,** devarāja ; tidasinda, *m.*

Godown, *n.* bhaṇḍasālā, *f.*

Goggle, *n.* valira ; kekara, *m.* *v.i.* akkhīni bhameti. *p.p.* bhamitakkhī.

Goglet, *n.* kuṇḍikā, *f.*

Going, *n.* gamana, *nt:* gati, *f.* adj. gacchanta. — **about**, sañcāra, *m.* — **across**, taraṇa, *nt.* — **ashore**, uttaraṇa, *nt.* — **back**, paṭinivattana, *nt.* —**forward**, abhikkamana, *nt.* —**out**, nikkhamana, *nt.* —**out to meet**, paccuggamana, *nt.* — **over**, saṅkamana, *nt.* — **over the limits**, sīmātikkamana, *nt.* — **round**, parikkamana, *nt.* — **afar**, dūragāmī, *a.* — **before**, pubbaṅgama, *a.* —**downward**, adhogāmī, *a.* — **on**, pavattamāna, *a.* — **out**, nikkhamanta, *a.* — **round**, āvijjhamāna, *a.* — **to be**, bhāvī, *a.* — **upwards**, uddhaṅgama, *a.*

Goitre, *n.* galagaṇḍaroga, *m.* °**rous**, *a.* galagaṇḍī.

Gold, *n.a.* suvaṇṇa ; kanaka ; kañcana ; hema ; cāmīkara ; jātarūpa. —**bullion**, hirañña, *nt.* — **coin**, nikkha ; nekkha, *nt.* —**coloured**, *a.* hemavaṇṇa; harittaca ; kanakappabha. °**en**, *a.* hemamaya ; sovaṇṇa. °**smith**, herañññika ; suvaṇṇakāra, *m.*

Gone, (*p.p.* of **go**), gata ; pakkanta ; yāta. — **astray**, vibbhanta ; maggamūḷha, *a.* — **away**, apakkanta, *a.* — **beyond**, pāragata ; pārappatta, *a.* °**forth**, abhikkanta, *a.* — **out**, nikkhanta, *a.* — **over**, tiṇṇa ; atikkanta, *a.* — **wrong**, vyāpanna, *a.*

Gong, *n.* kaŋsatāḷa, *m.*

Goniometer, *n.* koṇamāṇaka, *nt.*

Gonorrhoea, *n.* sukkadosa ; setabindumeha, *m.*

Good, *a.* 1. sundara ; bhaddaka ; subha ; kalyāṇa ; sobhana ; 2. dhammika ; susīla ; 3. hitakāma ; 4. adūsita ; 5. anappaka. *noun:* 1. attha ; hita, *m.* 2. maṅgala, *nt.* samiddhi, *f.* 3. payojana, *nt.* 4. puñña ; sucarita, *nt.* *intj.* sādhu ! bhavatu ! — **breeding**, sosīlya; soracca, *nt.* °**bye**, sotthi; subhaŋ bhavatu! — **conditioned**, *a.* niroga ; suṭṭhita. — **evening**, susañjhā, *f.* — **fortune**, bhāgya, *nt.* —**fellow**, sappurisa, *m.* —**for nothing**, akammasīlī ; payojanarahita, *a.* — **humour**, cittappasāda, *m.* — **humoured**, vivaṭacitta, *a.* °**ly**, — **looking**, *a.* surūpa ; piyadassana. — **manners**, sadācāra, *m.* vinītatta, *nt.* — **morning**, suppabhātaŋ ! — **nature**, sabbhāva, *m.* °**ness**, sādhutā ; sundaratā ; dhammikatā, *f.* — **sense**, suvinicchaya, *m.* °**will**, hitakāmatā ; anukūlatā, *f.* — **wishes**, subhāsiŋsanā, *f.* **As good as his word**, yathāvādī tathākārī. **In good time**, yathākāle. **Makes good**, 1. paripūreti ; 2. tathattaŋ pakāseti. **Of good breeding**, kulīna ; abhijāta, *a.* **So good as**, anuggahapubbakaŋ. *adv.* **Stands good**, 1. pahoti ; 2. patiṭṭhāti.

Goods, bhaṇḍajāta, *nt.* vatthusamūha, *m.*

Goody, *n.* 1. duggatamahallikā, *f.* 2. khajjakavisesa, *m.* °**goody**, *a.* anavatthānurūpa ; tucchābhimānī.

Goose, *n.* kalahaŋsa, *m.*

Gorbelly, *n.* thūlodara, *m.*

Gore, *n.* nikkhanta-lohita, *nt.* *v.t.* siṅgena *or* dāṭhāya vijjhati *or* āhanati. *p.p.* °viddha, °āhata.

Gorge, *n.* 1. kaṇṭhanāḷa ; gala, *m.* 2. girigabbhara ; duggamagga, *m.* *v.t.* bhakkhati ; ghasati ; gedhena bhuñjati. *p.p.* °khita ; ghasta ; °bhutta.

Gorgeous, *a.* adhikavaṇṇa ; nānāvaṇṇujjala. °**ly**, *adv.* vaṇṇujjalatāya. °**ness**, *n.* ujjalavaṇṇatta, *nt.*

Gorget, *n.* 1. kaṇṭhatāṇa, *nt.* 2. kaṇṭhabhūsā, *f.* gīveyya, *nt.* 3. vanitāmukhāvaraṇa, *nt.*

Gorilla, *n.* mahāvānara, *m.*

Gormandize, *n.* mahagghasatā, *f.* *v.i.* adhikaŋ bhuñjati. *p.p.* °bhutta. °**er**, *n.* mahagghasa ; amitabhojī, *m.*

Gory, *a.* lohitamakkhita.

Gosling, *n.* haŋsapotaka, *m.*

Gospel, *n.* sādhucarita, *nt.* sāmayikappavatti, *f.*

Gossamer, *n.* makkaṭajāla, *nt.*

Gossip, *n.* 1. jappanā ; janakathā, *f.* 2. (person :) jappaka ; palāpī, *m.* °**y**, *a.* palapanasīla.

Gossoon, *n.* māṇavaka, *m.*

Got (*p.p.* of **Get**), laddha ; — **down**, oruḷha ; otiṇṇa, *a.* — **into**, pariyāpanna, *a.* — **near**, upasaṅkanta, *a.* — **out of**, nikkhanta; uttiṇṇa, *a.* — **up**, uṭṭhita, *a.* — **well**, suladdha, *a.*

Gouge, *n.* paṇāli-nikhādana, *nt.* *v.t.* nikhādanena chindati. *p.p.* °chinna.

Gourd, *n.* tumbī ; alābu ; lābu, *f.* **Bitter** —, tittālābu, *f.*

Gourmand, *a.* *n.* bahubhakkha.

Gourmet, *n.* rasaloḷa ; pānarata, *m.*

Gout, *n.* vātaratta. °**y**, *a.* vātarattika.

Govern, *v.t.* 1. sāsati ; paripāleti ; 2. dameti ; vasam āneti. *v.i.* vidhānaŋ karoti. *p.p.* sāsita ; °lita ; damita ; °ānīta ; katavidhāna. °**able**, *a.* vineyya ; damma. °**ance**, *n.* pālanakkama, *m.* pālana, *nt.* °**ess**, *n.* puggalikācariyānī, *f.* °**ment**, *n.* rajjānusāsana ; desapālana, *nt.* °**or**, *n.* pālaka ; maṇḍalissara, *m.* °**orship**, *n.* ādhipacca ; maṇḍalissaradhura, *nt.* °**or-General**, rājapaṭinidhi, *m.*

Gown, *n.* vanitānivāsana, kaṭivattha, *nt.*

Grab, *n.* ḍasitvā-gahaṇa, *nt.* *v.t.* ḍasitvā *or* pasayha gaṇhāti. *p.p.* °gahita.

Grabble, *v.i.* andho viya parāmasati ; migo viya sappati.

Grace, *n.* 1. līlā ; sobhā, *f.* lāvañña, *nt.* 2. dayā ; karuṇā, *f.* 3. khanti, *f.* 4. ānubhāva, *m.* *v.t.* sobheti ; bhūseti. *p.p.* °bhita ; °sita. °**ful**, *a.* lalita ; sundaravilāsa. °**fully**, *adv.* salīlaŋ ; sasobhaŋ. °**fulness**, 1. kāruñña ; salīlatta, *nt.* °**less**, *a.* 1. nissirīka ; virūpa ; dubbaṇṇa ; 2. nillajja ; durācāra.

Gracious, *a.* sadaya ; sānubhāva ; susīla. °**ly**, *adv.* sānukampaŋ.

Gracula religiosa, *n.* sārikā, *f.*

Gradate, *v.t.* anukkamena yojeti; *v.i.* paṭipāṭim anugacchati. *p.p.* °jita ; °anugata. °**ion**, *n.* anukkama, *m.* paṭipāṭi, *f.* °**ory**, *a.* kamānurūpa ; yathākkama.

Grade, *n.* vagga ; anukkama, *m.* vaggapaṭipāṭi, *f.* *v.t.* vaggīkaroti. *p.p.* °kata.

Gradely, *a.* 1. atisundara ; 2. avitatha.

Gradient, *n.* anupubbapoṇatta, *nt.*

Gradual, *a.* anukkamika; ānupubbika. °**ly**, *adv.* anukkamena; anupubbena.

Graduate, *n.* upādhidhārī, *m.* *v.t.* 1. upādhiŋ deti; 2. māṇarekhāhi aṅketi. *v.i.* upādhiŋ labhati. *p.p.* laddhopādhī; °aṅkita. °**ion**, *n.* 1. vaggīkaraṇa; *nt.* 2. upādhilābha, *m.* 3. māṇarekhaṅkana, *nt.*

Graft, *n.* aṅkura, *nt.* *v.t.* aṅkurāni sampayojeti. *p.p.* °jitaṅkura.

Grain, *n.* 1. dhañña; sassa, *nt.* 2. bīja, *nt.* 3. goḷaka, *nt.* 4. (in weighing:) dhaññamāsa, *m.* — **husk**, thusa, *m.* **Fried** —, puthuka; lāja, *m.*

Gram, *n.* caṇaka, *m.*

Graminaceous, Gramineous, *a.* tiṇasadisa; tiṇabahula.

Graminivorous, *a.* tiṇabhakkha.

Grammar, *n.* vyākaraṇa; saddasattha, *nt.* °**ian**, *n.* veyyākaraṇika; vyākaraṇasampādaka, *m.*

Grammatical, *a.* vyākaraṇāyatta; vyākaraṇānukūla. °**ly**, *adv.* vyākaraṇānurūpena.

Gramme, Gram, *n.* māṇavisesa, *m.*

Gramophone, *n.* saddavāhakayanta, *nt.*

Granary, *n.* dhaññakoṭṭhaka, *m.* koṭṭhāgāra, *nt.*

Grand, *a.* 1. mahanta; visāla; tumula; 2. uttama; mukhya; agga; 3. mahānubhāva. °**child**, paputta; nattu, *m.* °**daughter**, paputtī, *f.* °**eur**, *n.* mahatta; uḷāratta, *nt.* patāpa, *m.* °**father**, ayyaka; pitāmaha, *m.* °**ly**, *adv.* mahānubhāvena. °**mother**, ayyikā, *f.* °**ness**, mahatta; uttamatta, *nt.* °**son**, nattu; paputta, *m.*

Grandee, *n.* mahākulaja, *m.*

Grandiloquent, *n.* gabbitavāca, *m.* °**ence**, *n.* atisayutti, *f.*

Grandiose, *n.* mahattadassaka; attukkaŋsaka, *m.*

Grange, *n.* kassakaghara, *m.*

Graniferous, *a.* dhaññuppādaka.

Granite, *n.* meghapāsāṇa, *m.*

Granivorous, *a.* dhaññakhādaka.

Granny, *n.* ayyikā, *f.*

Grant, *n.* dānapaṭiññā, *f.* varadāna; adhikāradāna, *nt.* *v.t.* anuppadāti; anumaññati. *p.p.* anuppadinna; anumata. °**ee**, *n.* paṭiggāhaka, *m.* °**or**, *n.* anuppadātu, *m.* **Royal** —, rājadāya, *m.*

Granular, *a.* dhaññasadisa.

Granulate, *v.t.* dhaññabījasamaŋ karoti. *v.i.* dhaññabījasamo hoti.

Granule, *n.* dhaññabīja, *nt.*

Grape, *n.* muddikāphala, *nt.* °**ry**, *n.* muddikārāma, *m.* °**vine**, *n.* muddikālatā, *f.*

Graph, *n.* pamāṇālekha, *m.* °**ical**, *a.* suniddiṭṭha; sucittita; yathābhūtajotaka.

Graphite, *n.* abbhaka, *nt.*

Graphology, *n.* akkharehi caritanirūpana, *nt.*

Grapnel, *n.* nāvā-gāhakaṅkusa, *m.*

Grapple, *n.* 1. kakkaṭayanta, *nt.* 2. daḷhagāha, *m.* bāhuyuddha, *nt.* *v.t.* daḷhaŋ gaṇhāti. *v.i.* (-with) yujjhati. *p.p.* °gahita; yujjhita.

Grasp, *n.* daḷhagāha ; parāmāsa, *m.* upādāna, *nt.* *v.t.* 1. upādāti ; 2. āmasati ; 3. sammasati. *p.p.* upādinna ; āmaṭṭha ; °sita *or* sammaṭṭha. °**ing,** *n.* paṭivedha, *m.* bujjhana, *nt.*

Grass, *n.* tiṇa, *nt.* tiṇabhūmi, *f.* °**clump,** tiṇagumba, *m.* — **eating,** *a.* tiṇabhakkha. °**hopper,** *n.* salabha ; paṭaṅga, *m.* °**y,** *a.* tiṇacchanna. °**y land,** saddala, *m.* **Mat of —,** tiṇasanthara, *m.* **Mattress of —,** tiṇabhisi, *f.*

Grate, *n.* ayosalākāvaraṇa, *nt.* *v.t.* kakkasākārena ghaŋseti ; ghaŋsetvā kaṇe pāteti. *p.p.* °sita ; pātitakaṇa. °**ing,** *n.* 1. lohajāla, *nt.* 2. aññoññaghaṭṭana, *nt.* 3. jālakavāṭa, *m.*

Grateful, *a.* 1. kataññū ; katavedī ; 2. ramaṇīya ; sukhāvaha. °**ly,** *adv.* kataññutāya. °**ness,** kataññutā, *f.*

Gratify, *v.t.* 1. toseti ; rameti ; pamodeti ; pasādeti. *p.p.* tosita; ramita ; °dita. °**ication,** *n.* 1. paritosana ; pasādana, *nt.* ārādhanā, *f.* 2. saŋsiddhi, *f.*

Gratis, *adv.* mudhā ; vinā mūlaŋ.

Gratitude, *n.* katavedità, *f.*

Gratuitous, *a.* 1. mudhā dinna ; nimmūlaka ; 2. ahetuka. °**ly,** *adv.* nimmūlena.

Gratuity, see **Gift.**

Gratulate, see **Congratulate.**

Grave, *n.* chavāvāṭa, *m.* susānabhūmi, *f.* *v.t.* see **Engrave.** °**stone,** *n.* thūpatthambha, *m.* °**yard,** susāna, *nt.*

Grave, *a.* garuka ; bhāriya. —**action,** *n.* bhāriyakamma, *nt.* °**ity,** *n.* 1. bhāra ; gārava, *m.* 2. dhīratta, *nt.* 3. ākaḍḍhakasatti, *f.* °**ly,** *adv.* garutāya. °**ness,** *n.* bhāriyatta, *nt.* — **offence,** *n.* thullaccaya ; mahāpātaka, *m.*

Gravel, *n.* 1. sakkharā, *f.* 2. (disease :) asmarī, *f.* muttakicchābādha, *m.* *v.t.* sakkharā attharati. *p.p.* atthatasakkhara. °**ly,** *a.* sakkharābahula.

Gravid, *a.* gabbhinī ; āpannasattā, *f.*

Gravitate, *v.i.* ākaḍḍhīyati. *p.p.* °ḍhita. °**ion,** *n.* ākaḍḍhana, *nt.*

Gravy, *n.* maŋsasāra, *m.*

Gray, *a.* dhūsara. °**beard,** *a.* mahallaka. — **hair,** palita, *nt.* °**ness,** palitatta ; dhūsaratta, *nt.* °**ness of hair,** pālicca, *nt.*

Graze, *n.* īsaŋghaŋsana, *nt.* *v.t.* 1. tiṇaŋ khādati ; 2. īsakaŋ ghaṭṭeti. *p.p.* khāditatiṇa ; °ṭita. °**ing,** *n.* 1. tiṇabhakkhaṇa ; 2. īsaŋghaṭṭana, *nt.* °**ing ground,** gocaraṭṭhāna, *nt.* tiṇabhūmi, *f.*

Grazier, *n.* gavavāṇija, *m.*

Grease, *n.* vasā, *f.* meda, *m.* *v.t.* vasāya lepeti. *p.p.* vasālitta. °**sy,** *a.* vasāyutta ; medabahula.

Great, *a.* *n.* 1. mahanta ; visāla ; tumula ; vipula ; uru ; 2. uttama ; seṭṭha ; parama ; 3. (—in, number :) pacura ; bahula. — **being,** mahāsatta, *m.* — **man,** mahāpurisa, *m.* — **eminence,** accunnatatta, *nt.* °**en,** *v.t.* vaḍḍhāpeti. °**er,** *a.* mahantatara. — **flood,** mahogha, *m.* — **grandfather,** payyaka ; papitāmaha, *m.* — **grandmother,**

payyikā, *f.* — **grandson,** panattu, *m.* — **leader,** vināyaka, *m.* °**ly,** *adv.* ativiya ; bahuso. — **mass,** khandha, *m.* °**ness,** mahatta; uḷāratta; seṭṭhatta, *nt.* — **sage,** — **seer,** mahesi, *m.* — **toe,** pādaṅguṭṭha, *m.*

Greed, *n.* lobha ; gedha, *m.* giddhi, *f.* gijjhana, *nt.* °**ily,** *adv.* giddhākārena ; mahicchatāya. °**iness,** loluppa ; mahicchatta, *nt.* °**less,** *a.* appiccha ; nittaṇha. °**y,** *a.* luddha ; giddha ; lolupa. **Excessive** —, atricchā, *f.*

Greek, *a.* Yonakadesāyatta.

Green, *n.* 1. haritavaṇṇa, *m.* 2. saddalaṭṭhāna, *nt.* adj. 1. (colour:) harita; 2. (fresh:) alla; nava ; amilāta; 3. (inexperienced :) aparicita ; asanthuta. °**ginger,** siṅgivera, *nt.* °**grocer,** paṇṇika, *m.* °**horn,** sukhavañciya, *m.* °**ish,** *a.* īsaŋharita. °**ness,** haritatta; amilātatta, *nt.* °**pea,** mugga, *m.*

Greet, *v.t.* subham āsiŋsati ; sādaraŋ sampaṭicchati, *v.i.* (aññamaññam) abhinandati. *p.p.* āsiṭṭhasubha ; °chita ; °dita. °**ing,** *n.* abhinandana ; subhāsiŋsana, *nt.*

Gregarious, *a.* gaṇabaddha ; samūhacārī. °**ness,** *n.* gaṇabaddhatā, *f.*

Grenade, *n.* hatthakhittaphuṭaka, *nt.* °**ier,** *n.* 1. hatthaphuṭakakkhipa ; 2. aṅgarakkhagaṇa, *m.*

Grey, see **Gray.**

Grid, *n.* lohasalākāvaraṇa, *nt.*

Griddle, *n.* pūvabhajjakathāli, *f.*

Gride, *n.* ghaŋsanasadda, *m.* *v.i.* (sodhetuŋ) ghaŋseti *or* nipiŋseti. *p.p.* °sita.

Grief, *n.* soka ; kheda ; ubbega, *m.* **Dispelling** —, sokanuda, *a.* **Freed from** —, vītasoka, *a.* **Overcome with** —, sokapareta, *a.*

Grievance, *n.* pīḷāhetu, *m.* khedakāraṇa; *nt.*

Grieve, *v.i.* socati ; khijjati ; ubbijjati. *v.t.* santāpeti ; socāpeti. *p.p.* socita ; khinna ; ubbigga ; °pita. °**ingly,** *adv.* sasokaŋ ; sakhedaŋ. °**ous,** *a.* 1. pīḷājanaka ; socanīya ; garuka ; bhāriya. °**ously,** *adv.* bhāriyākārena.

Grill, *n.* bhaṭṭhamaŋsa, *nt.* *v.t.* bhajjati. *p.p.* bhaṭṭha.

Grim, *a.* 1. vikaṭa ; bhīma ; 2. bhīmadassana ; ghorākāra. °**faced,** *a.* caṇḍamukha ; dummukha. °**ly,** *adv.* ghorākārena. °**ness,** *n.* ghoratta ; virūpatta, *nt.*

Grimace, *n.* mukhavikāra, *m.*

Grimalkin, *n.* 1. vuddhabiḷālī ; 2. appiyamahallikā, *f.*

Grime, *n.* nicitamasi, *m.* *v.t.* malinīkaroti. *p.p.* °kata. °**my,** *a.* malina.

Grin, *n.* dantavikasana, *nt.* *v.i.* dante vidaŋseti. *p.p.* °sitadanta. °**ner,** *n.* dantavidaŋsaka, *m.*

Grind, *v.t.* piŋsati ; saṇheti ; cuṇṇeti. *p.p.* °sita ; °hita ; °ṇita. °**er,** *n.* 1. piŋsaka, *m.* 2. saṇhakara-yanta, *nt.* °**ing,** *n.* piŋsana ; saṇhakaraṇa, *nt.* °**stone,** nisada, *m.* saṇhakaraṇī, *f.*

Grip, *n*. daḷhagāha, *m*. *v.t*. daḷhaŋ gaṇhāti. *p.p*. °gahita. °**per**, *n*. daḷhagāhī, *m*.

Gripe, *n*. 1. udarasūla ; 2. uppīḷana, *nt*. *v.t*. 1. hatthena uppīḷeti ; 2. udarasūlaŋ janeti. *p.p*. °ḷita ; janitūdarasūla. °**er**, *n*. uppīḷaka ; gāhaka, *m*.

Grisly, *a*. bhīma ; ghoratara.

Grist, *n*. piŋsita *or* piŋsitabbadhañña, *nt*.

Grit, *n*. 1. sukhumavālikā, *f*. 2. dhiti, *f*. *v.t*. ghaŋsanasaddam uppādeti. *v.i*. ghaŋsanasaddena calati. °**ty**, *a*. vālukābahula.

Grizzled, *a.n*. palitakesa.

Grizzly, *a*. dhūsara. — **bear**, *n*. mahāaccha, *m*.

Groan, *n*. nitthunana, *nt*. aṭṭassara, *m*. *v.i*. nitthunāti ; anutthunāti. °**ing**, *a*. nitthunanta.

Grocer, *n*. kaṭukabhaṇḍādivikkayī, *m*. °**y**, *n*. kaṭukabhaṇḍādi, *m*.

Groggy, *a*. surāmatta ; vedhamāna.

Groin, *n*. 1. ūrumūla, *nt*. ūrusandhi, *m*. 2. bhittisandhi, *m*.

Groom, *n*. 1. paricāraka ; sevaka, *m*. 2. assagopaka, *m*. *v.t*. asse gopeti. *p.p*. gopitassa.

Groove, *n*. dīghasusira ; paviddhakuhara, *nt*. *v.t*. pavijjhati ; vinivijjhati. *p.p*. °viddha.

Grope, *v.i*. andho viya gavesati.

Gross, *n*. 1. padhānaŋsa, *m*. 2. dvādasakānaŋ dvādasaka, *nt*. adj. 1. thūla ; thulla ; oḷārika ; 2. gamma ; nīca ; asabbha ; nindiya ; 3. adhikatara ; 4. niravasesa. — **headed**, *a*. muṭṭhassatī. °**ly**, *adv*. 1. sākallena ; 2. thūlākārena ; 3. accantaŋ. °**ness**, *n*. 1. thūlatta; 2. adhikatta, *nt*. — **weight**, niravasesabhāra, *m*.

Grotesque, *a*. virūpa ; vilakkhaṇa. °**ly**, *adv*. virūpākārena. °**ness**, *n*. vikaṭatā, *f*.

Grotto, *n*. kittimaguhā, *f*.

Ground, *n*. 1. bhūmi ; chamā, *f*. thala, *nt*. 2. ādhāra, *m*. patiṭṭhā, *f*. mūlakāraṇa, *nt*. 3. (in painting :) mūlavaṇṇālepa ; cittādhāra, *m*. — **floor**, heṭṭhimatala, *nt*. °**less**, *a*. amūlaka ; nirālamba ; ahetuka. °**lessly**, *adv*. ahetukaŋ ; amūlakaŋ. °**lessness**, patiṭṭhārahitatta, *nt*. — **work**, pādaka-kamma, *nt*. **Breaks** —, paṭhamārambhaŋ karoti. **Falls to the** —, vinassati ; paripatati. **Gains** —, abhivaḍḍhati ; pattharati. **Gives** —, osakkati. **Loses** —, parihāyati ; osakkati. **Stands one's** —, thiro tiṭṭhati. **Surface of the** —, bhūtala, *nt*.

Ground, *v.t*. paṭhamam ārabhati. *v.i*. thale āhanīyati. *p.p*. paṭhamāraddha ; thalāhata. °**ing**, *n*. 1. bhūmisaṅkharaṇa ; 2. patiṭṭhāpana, *nt*. °**age**, *n*. nāvātitthabali, *m*.

Groundsel, *n*. ummāra, *m*.

Group, *n*. samūha; gaṇa; vagga; nikāya, *m*. *v.t*. samūheti ; gaṇīkaroti ; vaggavasena ṭhapeti. *p.p*. °hita ; °kata ; °ṭhapita. °**ing**, *n*. vaggīkaraṇa; gaṇabandhana, *nt*. **Belonging to a** —, vaggiya, *a*.

Grouse, *v.i*. 1. ghuru-ghurāyati ; 2. ujjhāyati. *p.p*. °yita.

Grout, *v.t.* mukhatuṇḍena khaṇati. *p.p.* °khata.

Grove, *n.* vanasaṇḍa, *m.* tarugahaṇa ; upavana, *nt.*

Grovel, *v.i.* bhūmiyaŋ avattharati ; nipaccakāraŋ dasseti. *p.p.* °avatthata ; dassitani°. °**ler**, *n.* nīcavuttika, *m.*

Grow, *v.i.* vaḍḍhati ; abhivaḍḍhati ; virūhati. *v.t.* 1. vaḍḍheti ; virūheti ; 2. bharati ; poseti. *p.p.* °vuddha ; virūḷha ; °ḍhita ; virūhita ; bhata ; posita. — **again**, paṭivirūhati. °**ing**, *a.* vaḍḍhamāna. °**er**, *n.* vaḍḍhaka ; ropetu, *m.*

Growl, *v.i.* guggurāyati. *n.* guggurāyana, *nt.*

Grown, *p.p.* of **Grow**. — **long**, parūḷha, *a.* — **from a seed**, phalaruha, *a.* — **strong**, balappatta, *a.*

Growth, *n.* vaḍḍhi ; virūḷhi, *f.* vaḍḍhana, *nt.*

Grub, *n.* kosakimi, *m.* *v.t.* paŋsuŋ viyūheti ; mūlāni uddharati. *p.p.* viyuhita° ; uddhaṭamūla. °**by**, *a.* kimisaṅkiṇṇa ; malina.

Grudge, *n.* 1. issā ; usūyā, *f.* 2. viddesa, *m.* *v.i.* usūyati, *v.t.* anicchāya deti. *p.p.* °dinna. °**ingly**, *adv.* samaccheraŋ.

Gruel, *n.* yāgu, *f.* *v.t.* hiŋsati. °**ling**, *a.* āyāsakara.

Gruesome, *a.* 1. jeguccha ; paṭikkūla ; 2. bhayajanaka.

Gruff, *a.* kakkasa ; pharusa.

Grumble, *n.* ujjhāyana ; nitthunana, *nt.* *v.i.* khīyati ; ujjhāyati. °**ing**, *n.* khīyana ; ujjhāyana, *nt.*

Grume, *n.* 1. ghanībhūtalohita, *nt.* 2. siṅghānikā, *f.* °**ous**, *a.* piṇḍībhūta.

Grumpy, °**pish**, *a.* dosabahula ; asantuṭṭha.

Grunt, *n.* sūkararava, *m.* *v.i.* sūkararavaŋ ravati. °**er**, *n.* sūkara, *m.*

Guana, *n.* godhā, *f.*

Guarantee, *n.* pāṭibhoga ; paṭiññābandha, *m.* *v.t.* pāṭibhogo hoti ; saccakāraŋ ṭhapeti. *p.p.* pāṭibhogabhūta ; ṭhapitasa°.

Guard, *n.* 1. ārakkhā ; gutti, *f.* 2. rakkhaka ; pālaka ; gopaka ; anurakkhī ; pāletu, *m.* *v.t.* rakkhati ; gopeti ; pāleti ; tāyati. *p.p.* °khita ; gopita ; pālita ; tāyita. °**ian**, *n.* āpādaka ; ārakkhaka, *m.* °**ian-ship**, pālakadhura. °**ing**, *n.* anurakkhana, *nt.* **Life** —, aṇīkaṭṭha ; aṅgarakkhī, *m.* **Rear** —, pacchimasenā, *f.* **Van** —, pamukhasenā, *f.*

Guerdon, *n.* phala, *nt.* vipāka, *m.* *v.t.* vipākaŋ deti. *p.p.* dinnavipāka.

Guerrilla, *n.* nilīnayuddha, *nt.*

Guess, *n.* anumāna, *nt.* parikappanā, *f.* *v.i. t.* ūhati ; takketi ; anumāneti. *p.p.* ūhita ; °kita ; °nita.

Guest, *n.* atithi ; āgantuka ; abbhāgata, *m.* °**rite**, ātitheyya, *nt.*

Guffaw, *n.* aṭṭahāsa, *m.* *v.i.* uccāsaddena hasati.

Guide, *n.* maggadesaka ; netu, *m.* *v.t.* maggaŋ dasseti ; upadisati ; anusāsati. *p.p.* dassitamagga ; upadiṭṭha ; anusiṭṭha. °**ance**, *n.* magguddisana ; upadesadāna, *nt.* —**post**, maggadassakatthambha, *m.*

Guild, *n.* seṇī ; pūga ; gaṇa, *m.* — **hall**, pūgāvāsa, *m.* seṇighara, *nt.* — **master**, seṇiya ; satthavāha, *m.*

Guile, *n.* māyā, nikati, *f.* sāṭheyya, *nt.* °**ful**, *a.* nekatika ; māyāvī, °**less**, *a.* asaṭha; amāyāvī. °**lessly**, *adv.* asaṭhena.

Guillotine, *n.* 1. sīsacchedakayanta ; 2. antokantakasalla, *nt.* *v.t.* yantena (sīsaŋ) chindati. *p.p.* °chinnasīsa.

Guilt, *n.* aparādha, *m.* pāpakamma, *nt.* °**ily**, *adv.* sāparādhaŋ. °**less**, *a.* niddosa ; niraparādha. °**lessly**, *adv.* anavajjākārena. °**y**, *a.* sāvajja ; katapāpa.

Guise, *n.* vesa ; ākāra, *m.*

Guitar, *n.* vallakī-vīṇā, *f.*

Gulden, *n.* suvaṇṇa-nikkha, *nt.*

Gulf, *n.* 1. samuddavaṅka, *m.* 2. mahāvivara, *nt.* 3. salilabbhama, *m.* *v.t.* ajjhottharati. *p.p.* ajjhotthaṭa.

Gull, *n.* 1. jalakukkuṭa, *m.* 2. nikati, *f.* sāṭheyya, *nt.* *v.t.* vañceti. *p.p.* vañcita. °**ible**, *a.* sukhavañciya.

Gullet, *n.* kaṇṭhanāḷa, *m.*

Gully, *n.* 1. gambhīra-parikhā, *f.* 2. govikattana, *nt.* *v.t.* parikhā khaṇati. *p.p.* khataparikha.

Gulosity, *n.* mahagghasatā; rasagiddhatā, *f.*

Gulp, *n.* 1. gilana, *nt.* 2. mahāālopa, *m.* *v.t.* sahasā bhakkhati ; gilati. *p.p.* °khita ; gilita.

Gum, *n.* 1. dantamaŋsa, *nt.* 2. niyyāsa ; silesa, *m.* °**my**, *a.* picchila ; niyyāsayutta.

Gumption, *n.* visāradatta, *nt.*

Gun, *n.* aggināḷī, *f.* nāḷīyanta, *nt.* °**ner**, *n.* nāḷīyantadhara, *m.* — **powder**, aggināḷīcuṇṇa, *nt.*

Gunny, *n.* 1. sāṇa, *nt.* 2. sāṇapasibbaka, *m.*

Gurgle, *n.* gaggadāyana, *nt.* *v.i.* gaggadāyati. °**ing**, *n.* galagalāyana, *nt.*

Gush, *n.* 1. balavasandana ; vegena nissaraṇa, *nt.* 2. dhārānipāta, *m.* *v.i.* vegena sandati. *p.p.* °sandita.

Gust, *n.* 1. pabalavāyu ; caṇḍānila, *m.* 2. āhāraruci, *f.* °**able**, *a.* rucikara. °**ful**, *a.* sarasa ; madhura. °**ative**, °**atory**, *a.* rucijanaka. °**less**, *a.* virasa. °**y**, *a.* pabala-vāyusahita.

Gusto, *n.* abhiruci, *f.*

Gut, *n.* antavaṭṭi, *f.* *v.t.* 1. antāni nīharati ; 2. sabbassam apaharati. *p.p.* nīhaṭanta ; apahaṭasabbassa.

Guttae, *n.* *pl.* bindupanti, *f.*

Gutter, *n.* jalaniggama, *m.* paṇāḷī, *f.* *v.t.* paṇāḷiŋ vivarati, *v.i.* abhisandati. *p.p.* vivaṭa° ; °dita.

Guttural, *a.n.* kaṇṭhaja. °**ize**, *v.t.* kaṇṭhaṭṭhaŋ karoti.

Guy, *n.* 1. upatthambhakarajju, *f.* 2. visūkavesagāhī, *m.* *v.t.* avahasati ; patirūpakaŋ dasseti.

Guzzle, *v.i.t.* atimattaŋ pibati *or* ghasati. *p.p.* atimattapīta.

Gymkhana, *n.* mallakīḷābhūmi, *f.*

Gymnasium, *n.* vāyāmabhūmi, *f.* keḷimaṇḍala, *nt.*

Gymnast, *n.* mallayodha, *m.* °**ic**, *a.* kāyabalāyatta. °**ics**, *n.* *pl.* mallakīḷā, *f.*

Gymnosophist, *n.* digambara ; nibbasana, *m.*

Gynaeceum, *n.* orodha, *m.* itthāgāra, *nt.*

Gypsy, *n.* abaddhavāsa, ahituṇḍika, *m.*

Gyrate, *a.* valayehi racita ; sappabhogākāra. *v.i.* maṇḍalākārena *or* addhamaṇḍalakārena gacchati. °**ion,** *n.* paribbhamaṇa, *nt.*

Gyve, *n.* saṅkhalikā, *f. v.t.* saṅkhalikāhi bandhati. *p.p.* °likābaddha.

H

Ha, *intj.* hā ; aho ; handa.

Haberdasher, *n.* khuddakabhaṇḍa-vāṇija, *m.*

Habile, *a.* nipuṇa ; paṭu ; cheka.

Habiliment, *n.* paridhāna, *nt. pl.* sabbatthaka-paridhāna, *nt.*

Habilitate, *v.t.* 1. mūladhanaŋ sampādeti ; 2. adhikārayoggaŋ karoti. *p.p.* °ditamūla° ; °kata.

Habit, *n.* 1. pakati, *f.* sabhāva ; ācāra ; paricaya, *m.* 2. nivāsanākāra, *m. v.t.* 1. vāseti ; 2. nivasati. °**ual,** *a.* abhiṇha ; sātatika ; paricita ; abhiciṇṇa. °**ually,** *adv.* satataŋ ; niccaŋ ; pakatiyā ; yathāciṇṇaŋ. °**uate,** *v.t.* sikkheti ; paricayati. *p.p.* °khita ; °yita. °**ude,** *n.* daḷhaparicaya, *m.* pubbavāsanā, *f.*

Habitable, *a.* vāsayogga.

Habitat, *n.* jammabhūmi, *f.*

Habitation, *n.* vāsaṭṭhāna ; nivesana, *nt*

Hack, *n.* 1. khuddakapharasu, *m.* 2. pahāramukha, *nt.* 3. bhatakassa, *m.* 4. ghāsaphalaka, *nt. v.t.i.* 1. vicchindati ; 2. pādena paharati ; 3. assapiṭṭhiyaŋ yāti. *p.p.* vicchinna ; °pahaṭa ; °yāta.

Hackery, *n.* ekabalivaddayāna, *nt.*

Hackle, *n.* 1. sāṇullekhanī, *f.* 2. kaṇṭhakesara, *nt. v.t.* vicchindati. *p.p.* vicchinna.

Hackney, *n.* 1. bahusādhāraṇā, *f.* 2. bhatakassa, *m. v.t.* hīnakamme niyojeti. °**ed,** *a.* jiṇṇa ; ativiheṭhita. — **coach,** upakkītaratha, *m.*

Hades, *n.* adhobhuvana, *nt.* yamaloka ; paraloka, *m.*

Haecceity, *n.* puggalikatta, *nt.* idambhāva, *m.*

Haemal, *a.* rudhirāyatta.

Haematic, *n.* rudhirosadha, *nt.* adj. rudhirasahita.

Haematite, *n.* rattavaṇṇa-ayopāsāṇa, *m.*

Haemoglobin, *n.* lohitarūpakalāpa, *m.*

Haemorrhage, *n.* rattassavaṇa, *nt.*

Haemorrhoids, *n.* arisaroga, *m.*

Haft, *n.* tharu, *m. v.t.* tharuŋ yojeti. *p.p.* yojitatharu.

Hag, *n.* 1. virūpa-mahallikā ; 2. pisācī ; 3. māyākārī, *f.*

Haggard, *a. n.* kisa ; milātānana.

Haggle, *v.i.* 1. paṇopaṇaviyaŋ karoti ; 2. adakkhākārena chindati. *p.p.* katapa° ; °chinna.

Hagiarchy, *n.* munīnaŋ āṇā, *f.*

Hagio-graphy, *n.* municaritalikhana, *nt.* °**pher,** *n.* sādhucaritasampādaka, *m.*

Hail, *n.* 1. karakā, *f.* 2. dūravhāna, *nt.* 3. subhāsiŋsana, *nt. intj.* svāgataŋ ! suvatthi ; sotthi ! (followed by Dative). *v.i.* 1. karakavassaŋ vassati ; 2. vegena patati. *v.t.* 1. vandati ; abhivādeti ; 2. āmanteti ; 3. subham āsiŋsati. *p.p.* vaṭṭhakaraka° ; °patita ; °dita ; °tita ; āsiṭṭhasubha.

Hair, *n.* kesa ; uttamaṅgaruha, *m.* — **on the body,** loma ; tanuruha, *nt.* °**breadth,** lesamatta, *nt.* kesappamāṇa, *m.* °**brush,** *n.* kesamajjanī, *f.* °**dresser,** *n.* kappaka, *m.* °**dressing,** *n.* kesakappanā, *f.* °**less,** *a.* nikkesa. °**pin,** *n.* kesasūci, *f.* °**relic,** *n.* kesadhātu, *f.* °**splitting,** *n.* vālavedhana, *nt.* adj. vālavedhanākāra. °**y,** *a.* lomasa ; kesava. **Beauty of —,** kesakalyāṇa, *nt.* **Braided —, Plaited —,** veṇī, *f.* **Curled —,** kuñcitakesa, *m.* **Lock of —,** sikhaṇḍa, *m.* sikhā, *f.* **Knot of —,** dhammilla, *m.* **Matted —,** jaṭā, *f.* **Tress of —,** kesakalāpa, *m.*

Halberd, *n.* kuṭhārī, *f.* °**ier,** *n.* kuṭhāridhārī, *m.*

Hale, *a.* aroga ; agilāna ; kalla. *v.t.* ākaḍḍhati. °**ness,** nirogitā, *f.*

Half, *a.* *n.* aḍḍha ; upaḍḍha ; addha, *nt.* **— baked,** *a.* 1. mandapakka ; 2. mandamatika. **— bred,** *a.* avinīta. **— brother,** vemātikabhātu, *m.* **— dead,** *a.* matapāya ; matakappa. **— hearted,** *a.* nirussāha ; hīnaviriya. °**moon,** addhacanda, *m.* **— pay,** upaḍḍhavetana, *nt.* **— sister,** vemātika-bhaginī, *f.* **— starved,** *a.* chātajjhatta. **— truth,** saccālika, *nt.* °**way,** *adv.* upaḍḍhamagge ; addhānamajjhe. °**yearly,** *a.* chammāsika ; addhavassika.

Hall, *n.* sālā, *f.* maṇḍapa, *m.*

Hallo, *intj.* he ; bho ; are ; hare. *v.i.* dūrato avheti. *p.p.* °avhāta.

Halloo, *v.i.* sunakhe payojento saddāyati.

Hallow, *n.* nikkilesī, *m.* *v.t.* 1. suddhattaŋ pāpeti ; 2. pūjeti. *p.p.* °pāpita ; pūjita.

Hallucinate, *v.t.* micchāsaṅkappam uppādeti. °**ion,** matibbhama, *m.* °**tory,** *a.* vyāmohaka ; matibbhamajanaka.

Halo, *n.* pabhāmaṇḍala, *nt.* ketumālā, *f.* *v.t.* ketumālāy'alaṅkaroti. *p.p.* °kata.

Halt, *n.* nivattana ; avaṭṭhāna, *nt.* *v.i.* 1. nivattati ; avaṭṭhāti ; 2. khañjati. *p.p.* nivatta ; avaṭṭhita. °**ing,** *a.* khañjamāna. °**ing place,** nivattanaṭṭhāna, *nt.*

Halter, *n.* kaṇṭhapāsa, *m.* *v.t.* kaṇṭhapāsena bandhati; ubbandhati. *p.p.* °baddha.

Halve, *v.t.* dvidhā bhājeti. *p.p.* °bhājita.

Ham, *n.* 1. nigama ; gāma, *m.* 2. satthi, *f.* 3. loṇita-sūkarasatthi, *f.*

Hamlet, *n.* khuddakagāma, *m.*

Hamadryad, *n.* 1. rukkhadevatā, *f.* 2. ghorasappavisesa, *m.*

Hammer, *n.* ayomuṭṭhi, *f.* ayokūṭa, *m.* *v.t.* kūṭena nihanati. *v.i.* paṭiyatati. *p.p.* °nihata. °**ed,** *a.* abhitāḷita. °**ing,** *n.* kūṭābhighāta, *m.*

Hammock, *n.* vatthadolā, *f.*

Hamper, *n.* mahāpiṭaka, *m.* *v.t.* bādheti ; rundheti. *p.p.* °dhita.

Hand, *n.* 1. hattha ; bhuja ; kara, *m.* 2. disā, *f.* 3. sahāya-kammakāra, *m.* *v.t.* 1. hatthe appeti ; niyyādeti ; 2. upatthambheti. *p.p.* °appita ; °dita ; °bhita. °**basket,** pacchi, *f.* °**bill,** muddita-pattikā, *f.* °**book,** sārasaṅgaha; saṅkhittapotthaka, *m.* — °**cart,** hatthavaṭṭaka, *m.* °**cuff,** saṅkhalikā, *f.* *v.t.* saṅkhalikāhi bandhati. °**ful,** *a.* *n.* pasatamatta. **— loom,** *n.* hattavāyanayanta, *nt.* °**maid,** paricārikā, *f.* °**mill,** hatthavaṭṭitayanta, *nt.* — **over,** samappeti. °**writing,** hatthalipi, *f.* **At** —, samīpaṭṭha, *a.* **Asks the hand of,** vāreyyaŋ karoti. **Changes hands,** adhīnattaŋ parivatteti. **Claps hands,** appoṭheti. **Gets the upper** —, abhibhavati. **Hand in** —, saddhiŋ; samavāyena. — **down,** paramparānugataŋ karoti. **If on the other** —, sace; yadi, *ind.* **In** —, hatthāgata, *a.* **Lays hands on,** gaṇhāti; paharati. **Lends a** —, upakaroti. **Off** —, akicchena. **On all hands,** sabbathā, *adv.* **On the one** —, ekato, *ind.* **On the other** —, aññato; itarathā, *ind.* **Out of** —, sapadi; taṅkhaṇe, *adv.* **Second-hand,** *a.* paribhutta; valañjita. **Shakes hands,** karadānena paṭiggaṇhāti. **Subject in** —, upaṭṭhitakāraṇa, *nt.* **Sword in** —, khaggahattha, *a.* **With clean hands,** niraparādha, *a.*

Handicap, *n.* bādhā, *f.* avarodha, *m.* *v.t.* bādheti; avarodheti. *p.p.* bādhita; °dhita.

Handicraft, *n.* hatthakamma; sippa, *nt.*

Handiwork, *n.* hatthasampādita, *nt.*

Handkerchief, *n.* hatthapuñchana, *nt.*

Handle, *n.* tharu; muṭṭhi, *m.* jaṭa, *nt.* *v.t.* āmasati; sañcopeti. *p.p.* āmaṭṭha; °pita. — **of a knife,** vāsijaṭa, *nt.*

Handsel, *n.* 1. paṭhama-vikkaya, *m.* 2. vassārambhe tuṭṭhidāya, *m.*

Handsome, *a.* abhirūpa; surūpa; dassanīya. °**ly,** *adv.* cārutāya; sobhanākārena. °**ness,** vaṇṇapokkharatā, *f.*

Handy, *a.* 1. āsanna; samīpa; 2. dakkha; nipuṇa; 3. sukhaneyya. °**ily,** *adv.* paṭutāya; nipuṇākārena. °**iness,** pāṭava; kosalla, *nt.*

Hang, *n.* olambana; olaggana, *nt.* *v.t.* olambeti; olaggeti; ubbandhati. *v.i.* olambati; ubbandhīyati. *p.p.* °bita; °gita; ubbaddha. — **about,** vilambati. °**dog,** *n.a.* adhama; nīcavuttika. °**er,** *n.* 1. ubbandhaka, *m.* 2. ussāpaka-vatthu, *nt.* °**ing,** *n.* 1. ubbandhana; olambana, *nt.* 2. javanikā, *f.* °**man,** vadhaka, *m.* — **on,** — **upon,** upajīvati; nissayati. — **on to,** ālambati. — **out,** abbhokāse olaggeti.

Hank, *n.* rajjuvalaya; tantuvalaya, *m.*

Hanker, *v.i.* pattheti; abhilasati. *p.p.* °thita; °sita. °**ing,** *n.* abhilāsā; patthanā, *f.*

Hanky-panky, *n.* 1. indajāla, *nt.* 2. rahassena vikkaya, *m.*

Hansard, *n.* mantisabhāpavatti, *f.*

Hap, *n.* bhāgya; asambhāvitasampatta, *nt.* *v.t.* yadicchāya pāpuṇāti *or* sijjhati. *p.p.* °patta; °siddha. °**less,** *a.* bhāgyahīna. °**ly,** *adv.* vidhiyogena; ninnimittaŋ.

Haphazard, *adv.* asamekkha; avicāriya. adj. bhāgyāyatta. °**ly,** *adv.* aniyamena; yadicchāya.

Happen, *v.i.* sijjhati; bhavati; āpatati. *p.p.* siddha; bhūta;

āpatita. °**ing**, *n*. siddhi, *f*. āpatana, *nt*.

Happy, *a*. 1. sukhita ; santuṭṭha ; pamudita ; 2. dhañña ; bhāgyavantu. °**ily**, *adv*. sukhena ; vidhiyogena. °**iness**, *n*. 1. somanassa, *nt*. ānanda, *m*. pīti, *f*. 2. sampatti ; samiddhi, *f*. **Bringing happiness**, sukhāvaha, *a*.

Hara-kiri, *n*. (Japandesīnaŋ) attavadhakkama, *m*.

Harangue, *n*. tārassarena kathana, *nt*. sālaṅkārakathā, *f*. *v.i.* sālaṅkāraŋ katheti. °**er**, *n*. cittakathī, *m*.

Harass, *v.t.* bādheti ; viheseti ; ubbejeti. *p.p.* bādhita ; °sita ; °jita. °**ment**, *n*. viheṭhana, *nt*. °**ing**, *a*. viheṭhaka ; bādhaka.

Harbinger, *n*. 1. āgamanasūcana; pubbanimitta, *nt*. 2. purecārī ; sandesahara, *m*. *v.t.* āgamanaŋ sūceti *or* pakāseti. *p.p.* sūcitāgamana.

Harbour, *n*. 1. nāvātittha ; khemaṭṭhāna, *nt*. 2. āsaya, *m*. vāsaṭṭhāna, *nt*. *v.t.* vāseti ; nissayaŋ deti. *p.p.* vāsita ; dinnanissaya. °**less**, *a*. asaraṇa ; anissaya. —**town**, paṭṭana ; doṇamukha, *nt*.

Hard, *a*. 1. thaddha ; kaṭhina ; 2. niddaya ; niṭṭhura ; 3. duravabodha; duviññeyya ; 4. dukkhāvaha; 5. dussādhiya; 6. dukkhama ; dussaha. *adv*. 1. āyāsena; kicchena; 2. saussāhaŋ. —**by**, samīpe; nikaṭe. —**drinker**, pānarata, *m*. —**earned**, kicchāladdha; kasiren'ajjita. —**fisted**, *a*. luddha. —**ground**, patthaṇḍila, *nt*. —**hearted**, *a*. kaṭhinahadaya. °**ly**, *adv*. 1. dullabhākārena ; 2. kicchena ; kasirena. °**ness**, *n*. thaddhatta ; kaṭhinatta, *nt*. °**ship**, *n*. āyāsa, *m*. kiccha ; kasira, *nt*. °**ware**, lohabhaṇḍa, *nt*.

Harden, *v.t.* kaṭhinīkaroti ; daḷhayati. *p.p.* °kata ; °yita.

Hardy, *a*. 1. sūra ; vīra ; nissaṅka ; dhitimantu ; 2. sāhasika. °**ihood**, *n*. nibbhayatta ; sāhasikatta, *nt*. °**ily**, *adv*. dhitiyā ; pāgabbhiyena.

Hare, *n*. sasa ; sasaka, *m*. °**brained**, *a*. anisammakārī. —**in the moon**, sasalañchana, *nt*. °**lip**, *n*. dvidhābhinna-uparoṭṭha, *nt*.

Harem, *n*. itthāgāra ; antepura, *nt*. orodha, *m*.

Hark, *v.i.* suṇāti ; nisāmeti. *p.p.* suta ; °mita. *intj*. suṇātha. —**back**, anussarati.

Harlequin, *n*. vidūsaka ; hāsaka, *m*.

Harlot, *n*. gaṇikā ; vesiyā ; abhisārikā ; rūpūpajīvinī, *f*. °**ry**, gaṇikāvutti, *f*.

Harm, *n*. 1. hiŋsā ; pīḷā, *f*. 2. anattha ; apakāra, *m*. hāni, *f*. *v.t.* hiŋsati ; apakaroti ; upaddaveti. *p.p.* hiŋsita ; apakata ; upadduta. °**ful**, *a*. ahitāvaha ; hiŋsājanaka. °**less**, *a*. 1. ahiŋsaka ; nirupaddava ; 2. niddosa. °**lessness**, *n*. anavajjatā ; ahiŋsakatā, *f*. °**lessly**, *adv*. ahiŋsakākārena.

Harmony, *n*. 1. laya, *m*. tālasāmaggi, *f*. 2. sussaratā, *f*. 3. avirodha, *m*. ekamatikatta, *nt*. °**ic**, °**ious**, *a*. saŋsandamāna ; samassara ; yuganaddha. °**ium**, *n*. peḷāturiya, *nt*. °**ize**, *v.i.* saŋsandati. *v.t.* saŋsandeti ; sameti. *p.p.* °dita ; sameta.

Harness, *n.* kappanā, *f.* sannāha, *m.* assābharaṇa, *nt. v.t.* kappeti ; sannāheti ; yojeti. *p.p.* °pita ; sannaddha ; yojita.

Harp, *n.* vīṇā ; vallakī, *f. v.i.* vīṇaŋ vādeti. °**er,** *n.* veṇika, *m.*

Harpoon, *n.* timivedhanī, *f.*

Harpy, *n.* 1. sapakkhā yakkhinī, *f.* 2. vilumpaka, *m.*

Harridan, *n.* kisamahallikā, *f.*

Harrow, *n.* bahudantaka ; leḍḍubhedaka, *nt. v.t.* 1. accantaŋ pīḷeti ; santāpeti ; 2. bahudantakena samīkaroti. *p.p.* °ḷita ; °pita ; °samīkata. °**ing,** *a.* atipīḷākara ; mammacchedaka.

Harry, *v.t.* vilumpati ; acchindati. *p.p.* vilutta ; acchinna.

Harsh, *a.* kakkasa ; pharusa ; kaṭhina. °**ly,** *adv.* niṭṭhuraŋ ; pharusākārena. °**ness,** *n.* niṭṭhuratta ; pharusatta ; niṭṭhuriya, *nt.* —**word,** *n.* pharusavacana, *nt.*

Hart, *n.* puŋmiga, *m.*

Harum-scarum, *a.n.* asamekkhakārī.

Harvest, *n.* dhaññaphala ; lāyitasassa, *nt. v.t.* sassaŋ lunāti. °**man,** sassalāyaka, *m.* —**time,** sassakāla, *m.*

Hash, *n.* missita-maŋsabhojana, *nt. v.t.* vicchindati. *p.p.* vicchinna.

Hasp, *n.* aggalasūci, *f. v.t.* aggalasūciyā thaketi.

Hassock, *n.* 1. jāṇubhisi, *f.* 2. silāvisesa, *m.*

Haste, *n.* 1. vega ; java, *m.* 2. turitagati, *f. v.i.* vegaŋ janeti ; turitayati. *p.p.* janitavega ; °yita. °**en,** *v.t.* tarayati ; vegīkaroti. *p.p.* °yita ; °kata. °**ily,** *adv.* sahasā ; anisamma. °**iness,** *n.* turitatta, *nt.* asamekkhakāritā, *f.* °**ty,** *a.* sāhasika ; āsukārī.

Hat, *n.* sirotāṇa, *nt.* nāḷipaṭṭa, *m. v.t.* sirotāṇaŋ piḷandhati. *p.p.* °dhita°.

Hatch, *n.* 1. pavesadvāra, *nt.* 2. potakasamūha, *m.* 3. kumantaṇa, *nt. v.t.* 1. janeti; 2. aṇḍāni sedeti ; 3. kumanteti. *v.i.* sedīyati. *p.p.* janita ; seditaṇḍa ; °tita.

Hatchet, *n.* cullakuṭhārī, *f.*

Hate, *n.* vera, *nt.* viddesa, *m. v.t.* 1. upanandhati ; 2. jigucchati. *p.p.* upanaddha ; °chita. °**ful,** *a.* kucchita ; garahita ; dessiya. °**fully,** *adv.* dessiyākārena.

Hatred, *n.* vera, *nt.* virodha ; viddesa, *m.*

Hauberk, *n.* dāmakañcuka, *m.*

Haughty, *a.* sadappa ; dappita ; uddhata. °**ily,** *adv.* sadappaŋ. °**iness,** *n.* uddhacca, *nt.* gabba ; dappa ; ahaṅkāra, *m.*

Haul, *n.* jālagata-maccharāsi, *m. v.t.* thāmasā ākaḍḍhati. *p.p.* °ḍhita.

Haulm, *n.* vaṇṭanāḷa ; daṇḍa, *m.*

Haunch, *n.* jaghana, *nt.* kaṭi ; soṇi, *f.*

Haunt, *n.* āsaya, *m.* niccasevitaṭṭhāna, *nt. v.t.i.* adhivasati ; abhiṇham ācarati. *p.p.* adhivuttha ; °rita.

Have, *v.t.i.* Expressed by roots *bhū* and *as,* with genetive of possessor. **I have two sons,** mama dve puttā santi. **He**

had many sons, tassa bahavo puttā ahesuŋ. **They have seen him,** tehi so diṭṭho (hoti). **He has gone,** so gato (hoti). **I have it done,** ahaŋ taŋ kārāpesiŋ. With infinitives it is to be expressed by *pt. p.* e.g. **I have to go,** mayā gantabbaŋ. **Having,** (adj.) is expressed by the terminations : *vantu, mantu, ika, ī, vī, ssī,* or by the words *upeta, yutta, anvita, samannāgata.* **Having** as auxiliary is expressed by the absolutive endings such as *tvā, tvāna,* e.g. **Having gone,** gantvā. **Having come,** āgamma.

Haven, see **Harbour.**

Haversack, *n.* yodhānaŋ makacipasibbaka, *m.*

Havoc, *n.* vināsa, *m.* viddhaŋsana, *nt.* *v.t.* vināseti ; viddhaŋseti. *p.p.* °sita.

Haw, *n.* vati, *f.*

Haw-haw, *n.* aṭṭahāsa, *m.*

Hawk, *n.* sena ; kulala ; sakuṇagghī, *m.* *v.i.* ukkāsati. *v.t.* 1. āhiṇḍanto vikkiṇāti ; 2. seṇehi sakuṇe gaṇhāpeti. *p.p.* °sita ; °vikkīta ; °pita. °**er,** *n.* 1. seṇaposaka; 2. kacchapuṭa-vāṇija, *m.*

Hay, *n.* palāla, *nt.* *v.t.* palālaŋ nipphādeti. °**maker,** tiṇasukkhāpaka, *m.* °**cock,** °**rick,** °**stack,** palāla-puñja, *m.*

Hazard, *n.* 1. saŋsaya, *m.* anāgatabhaya, *nt.* 2. akkhakīḷā, *f.* *v.t.* abhīto karoti ; antarāyābhimukhī hoti. °**ous,** *a.* sasandeha ; antarāyika ; sappaṭibhaya.

Haze, *n.* 1. mahikā, *f.* 2. cittāvilatā, *f.* *v.t.* 1. malinīkaroti ; 2. vyathati ; tajjeti. *p.p.* °kata ; vyathita ; tajjita.

Hazel, *n.* mañjeṭṭhī, *f.* adj. mañjeṭṭhavaṇṇa.

Hazy, *a.* apākaṭa ; mahikonaddha.

He, *pron.* so (mas. sing, of *ta*). °**goat,** pumeḷaka, *m.*

He, *intj.* he ; bho.

Head, *n.* 1. sīsa ; sira ; uttamaṅga, *nt.* muddha ; matthaka, *m.* 2. adhipati ; nātha ; nāyaka, *m.* 3. mātikā, *f.* upaññāsa, *m.* 4. mūlaṭṭhāna, *nt.* pabhava, *m.* 5. pamukhabhāga, *m.* 6. agga ; sikhara, *nt.* matthaka, *m.* adj. padhāna ; mukhya. *v.i.* pubbaṅgamo hoti. *v.t.* purato *or* matthake ṭhapeti. °**ache,** sīsarujā, *f.* °**band,** siroveṭhana ; lalāṭapaṭṭa, *nt.* °**dress,** sirobhūsana, *nt.* °**ed by,** pamukha ; purakkhata, *a.* °**ing,** *n.* mātikāpāṭha, *m.* °**land,** bhūnāsikā, *f.* °**less,** *a.* chinnasīsa. °**long,** *a.* 1. adhomukha; 2. sāhasika, *adv.* adhomukhaŋ. °**man,** jeṭṭhapurisa, *m.* — **master,** padhānācariya, *m.* °**most,** *a.* pamukhatara. — **of an army,** senāpati, *m.* — **quarters,** padhāna-kiccālaya, *m.* majjhaṭṭhāna, *nt.* °**sman,** sīsacchedaka, *m.* °**stone,** sandhisilā ; koṇasilā, *f.* °**strong,** dubbaca ; anassava. — **wind,** paṭivāta, *m.*

Heady, *a.* caṇḍa ; sāhasika.

Heal, *v.t.* tikicchati. *v.i.* gilānā vuṭṭhāti; arogī hoti. *p.p.* °chita; °ṭhita ; °bhūta. °**er,** *n.* tikicchaka ; rogahārī, *m.* °**ing,** *n.*

tikicchana ; rogāpaharaṇa, *nt.* °**ing art,** vejjakamma, *nt.* tikicchā, *f.*

Health, *n.* ārogya ; anāmaya, *nt.* °**ful,** °**y,** *a.* nirāmaya ; nirātaṅka ; agilāna. °**ily,** *adv.* nirogākārena.

Heap, *n.* rāsi ; puñja ; nicaya ; sañcaya, *m.* *v.t.* cināti ; rāsīkaroti. *p.p.* cita ; °kata. °**ing,** *n.* sañcinana, *nt.*

Hear, *v.t.* suṇāti ; nisāmeti. *p.p.* suta ; °mita. °**er,** *n.* sotu ; sāvaka ; nisāmaka, *m.* °**ing,** *n.* savaṇa, *nt.* suti, *f.* °**say,** anussuti, *f.* **Willing to —,** sotukāma, *a.*

Hearken, *v.i.* sussūsati.

Hearse, *n.* vilāta ; chavakūṭāgāra, *nt.*

Heart, *n.* 1. hadaya, *nt.* 2. (mind :) citta ; mana, *nt.* 3. majjhabhāga ; antosāra, *m.* 4. viriya, *nt.* dhiti, *f.* °**ache,** hadayasantāpa, *m.* °**breaking,** *a.* ubbegajanaka. °**broken,** *a.* khinnacitta ; sokātura. °**ily,** *adv.* 1. asaṭhaŋ ; avyājaŋ ; 2. saussāhaŋ ; sānandaŋ. °**less,** *a.* 1. niddaya ; 2. nitteja ; nirussāha. °**lessness.** 1. niddayatā; 2. hīnaviriyatā, *f.* °**rending,** *a.* hadayavidāraka ; mammacchedaka. °**some,** *a.* samassāsaka. °**thrilling,** *a.* manonandaka. °**whole,** *a.* anuratta ; paṭibaddhacitta. °**y,** *a.* 1. asaṭha ; avyāja ; 2. hadayaṅgama. **Learn by —,** vācuggataŋ karoti. **Out of —,** khinnacitta, *a.* **With all one's —,** sabbatthāmena.

Hearten, *v.t.* ussāheti ; pamodeti. *p.p.* °hita ; °dita.

Hearth, *n.* uddhana, *nt.* cullī, *f.*

Heat, *n.* 1. uṇhatta; ghamma, *nt.* tāpa ; dāha, *m.* 2. suriyātapa, *m.* 3. (Hot season :) nidāgha ; gimhāna, *m.* **— of excitement,** rosavega, *m.* **— of youth,** yobbanamada, *m.*

Heat, *v.t.* tāpeti ; santāpeti. *v.i.* santapati. *p.p.* °pita ; santatta. °**edly,** *adv.* sakopaŋ ; sarosaŋ. °**er,** *n.* santāpaka ; uṇhakara, *m.* °**ing,** *n.* santāpana, *nt.* adj. tāpakara.

Heath, *n.* 1. gumbajāti, *f.* 2. gumbacchannabhūmi, *f.*

Heathen, *a.n.* micchādiṭṭhika. °**ism,** *n.* micchādiṭṭhi, *f.*

Heave, *n.* unnāmana; ukkhipana, *nt.* *v.t.* unnāmeti ; ussāpeti. *v.i.* phandati ; kampati. *p.p.* °mita ; °pita ; °dita ; °pita. °**ing,** *n.* phandana ; kampana, *nt.* °**ing,** *a.* kampamāna.

Heaven, *n.* 1. devaloka ; tidasālaya; sagga, *m.* 2. see **Sky.** °**ly,** *a.* dibba ; saggāyatta. °**ly assembly,** devakāya, *m.* °**ly bliss,** dibbasampatti, *f.* °**wards,** *adv.* saggābhimukhaŋ. **Leading to —,** saggasaŋvattanika, *a.*

Heavy, *a.* 1. garuka ; bhāriya. 2. ugga ; tibba ; bāḷha. 3. mandamatika ; alasa ; 4. ākulacitta. °**ily,** *adv.* garukaŋ ; bhāriyākārena. °**iness,** *n.* bhāriyatta ; garutta, *nt.*

Hebdomad, *n.* sattāha, *nt.* °**al,** *a.* sattāhika. °**ally,** *adv.* anusattāhaŋ.

Hebetate, *v.t.* kuṇṭheti ; dandhayati. *p.p.* °ṭhita ; °yita.

Hecatomb, *n.* sabbasatakayāga, *m.*

Heck, *n.* maccharodhaka, *m.*

Heckle, *n.* sāṇullekhanī, *f.* *v.t.* 1. ullikhati; 2. adhikaŋ paṭipucchati. *p.p.* °khita; °chita.

Hectic (fever), *n.* kāsasūcakajara, *m.*

Hector, *n.* vikatthaka; santajjaka, *m.* *v.t.* santajjeti. *p.p.* °jita.

Hedge, *n.* vati, *f.* parikkhepa, *m.* āvaraṇa, *nt.* *v.t.* vatiŋ bandhati; parikkhipati. *p.p.* vatibaddha; °khitta. °**hog**, *n.* sallaka, *m.* °**sparrow**, kalaviṅka, *m.*

Heed, *n.* apekkhā; sāvadhānatā, *f.* *v.t.* avekkhati, manasikaroti. *p.p.* °khita; °kata. °**ful**, *a.* sāvadhāna; appamatta. °**fully**, *adv.* sāvadhānaŋ; samekkhiya. °**less**, *a.* nirapekkha; anavadhāna; pamatta. °**lessly**, *adv.* pamattākārena. °**lessness**, *n.* pamāda, *m.* anavadhānatā; asamekkhakāritā, *f.*

Heel, *n.* paṇhi, *f.* *v.i.* 1. paṇhīhi sañcarati; 2. anubandhati; 3. ekapassena parivatteti. *p.p.* anubaddha; °tita. °**s over head**, avaŋsira; uddhapāda. *a.* **Takes to his heels**, palāyati.

Heft, *n.* 1. tharu, *m.* 2. uyyoga; ussāha, *m.* *v.t.* ussāpeti; ukkhipati. *p.p.* °pita; ukkhitta.

Hefty, *a.* thūla; balavantu.

Hegemony, *n.* nāyakatta, *nt.* °**ic**, *a.* ekādhipaccāyatta.

He-goat, *n.* chakalaka, *m.*

Heifer, *n.* vacchatarī, *f.*

Heigh, *intj.* (samussāhane nipāto).

Height, *n.* ubbedha; uccaya, *m.* — **of a man**, purisappamāṇa, *nt.*

Heighten, *v.t.* ussāpeti; unnāmeti; uttejeti. *v.i.* abhivaḍḍhati; unnamati. *p.p.* °pita; °mita; °jita; abhivaddha; unnata.

Heinous, *a.* pāpiṭṭha; atiduṭṭha. °**ly**, *adv.* atiduṭṭhatāya. °**ness**, *n.* pāpiṭṭhatā, *f.*

Heir, *n.* dāyādaka, *m.*—**apparent**, *n.* yuvarāja, *m.* °**loom**, paramparāgata-bhaṇḍa, *nt.* °**ess**, dāyādinī, *f.* — **presumptive**, *n.* anumānita-dāyādī, *m.* °**ship**, dāyādikatta, *nt.*

Heliacal, *a.* suriyāyatta.

Helianthus, *n.* suriyakantapuppha, *nt.*

Helical, *a.* saṅkhavaṅkākāra.

Helicopter, *n.* vyomayānavisesa, *m.*

Helio —, suriya, *m.* °**graphy**, *n.* suriyavaṇṇanā, *f.* °**latory**, *n.* suriyavandanā, *f.* °**scope**, *n.* suriyasamikkhaka, *nt.*

Helium, *n.* suriyagatavāyu, *m.*

Helix, *n.* kuṇḍalāvaṭṭa, *m.*

Hell, *n.* niraya; naraka; apāya, *m.* °**fire**, nirayaggi, *m.* °**ish**, *a.* 1. āpāyika; 2. atidāruṇa. **Fear of** —, nirayabhaya, *nt.* **Leading to** —, nirayasaŋvattanika, adj. **Sufferer in** —, nerayika, *m.* **Torturer in** —, nirayapāla, *m.*

Hellenic, *a.* Yavanadesīya.

Hellenism, *n.* Yavanasabbhatā, *f.*

Hello, see **Hallo**.

Helm, *n.* keṇipāta, *m.* °**sman**, kaṇṇadhāra, *m.*

Helmet, *n.* lohasirotāṇa, *nt.*

Help, *n.* upakāra ; upatthambha ; anuggaha, *m.* paṭisaraṇa ; anubala, *nt.* patiṭṭhā, *f.* *v.t.* upakaroti ; upatthambheti ; anuggaṇhāti. *p.p.* °kata ; °bhita ; anuggahita. °**er,** *n.* upakāraka ; sahāyaka, *m.* °**ful,** *a.* upakārī ; upatthambhaka. °**less,** *a.* 1. asahāya ; anātha ; asaraṇa; 2. appaṭikāra. °**lessly,** *adv.* anāthākārena. °**lessness,** *n.* asahāyatta, *nt.* **He could not help laughing,** so hāsaŋ nivāretuŋ nāsakkhi. **I cannot help going,** avassaŋ mayā gantabbaŋ.

Helter-skelter, *adv.* sasambhamaŋ.

Helve, *n.* tharu, *m.*

Hem, *n.* 1. dasā, *f.* anuvāta, *nt.* 2. ukkāsana, *nt.* *v.t.* 1. dasaŋ yojeti ; 2. paḷiveṭheti. *p.p.* yojitadasa ; °ṭhita. *v.i.* ukkāsati. *p.p.* °sita.

Hemeralopia, *n.* 1. divāndhatā ; 2. rattyandhatā, *f.*

Hemicycle, *n.* addhacakka, *nt.*

Hemisphere, *n.* goḷaddha, *nt.*

Hemistich, *n.* gāthāpādaddha, *nt.*

Hemlock, *n.* visagacchavisesa, *m.*

Hemorrhage, *n.* rudhirassavaṇa, *nt.*

Hemp, *n.* sāṇa, *nt.* °**en,** *a.* sāṇamaya. °**en cloth,** bhaṅga, *nt.* °**sack,** sāṇipasibbaka, *m.*

Hen, *n.* 1. kukkuṭī ; 2. pakkhidhenu, *f.* — **hearted,** *a.* bhīruka. — **pecked,** *a.* itthivasagata. — **roost,** *n.* kukkuṭālaya, *m.*

Hence, *adv.* 1. ito ; 2. tato ; tena ; tasmā. °**forth,** °**forward,** ajjatagge ; ito pabhuti, *ind.* **From** —, ito paṭṭhāya, paraŋ, *or* pabhuti.

Henchman, *n.* 1. niccupaṭṭhāka ; 2. pālanasahāya, *m.*

Hepatalgia, *n.* yakanābādha, *m.*

Hepatic, *a.* yakanāyatta.

Heptad, *n.* sattaka, *nt.*

Heptagon, *n.* sattakoṇaka, *nt.*

Heptarchy, *n.* sattarājapālana, *nt.*

Herald, *n.* aggesara ; puretarapakāsaka, *m.* *v.t.* puretaraŋ sūceti. *p.p.* °sūcita. °**ry,** *n.* 1. dūteyya ; 2. vaŋsāvalijānana, *nt.* — **sign,** pubbanimitta, *nt.*

Herb, *n.* sāka ; ḍāka, *m.* osadhī, *f.* °**age,** *n.* harita, *nt.* °**ivorous,** *a.* paṇṇakhādaka ; sākabhakkha.

Herbal, *n.* osadhīsattha, *nt.* adj. sākāyatta. °**ist,** *n.* osadhīsatthaññū, *m.*

Herbarium, *n.* sukkhosadhisālā, *f.*

Herbary, *n.* osadhīropaṇaṭṭhāna, *nt.*

Herborize, *v.t.* osadhī samāharati. *p.p.* samāhaṭosadhī.

Herculean, *a.* atidukkara.

Herd, *n.* yūtha ; gaṇa, *m.* *v.i.* yūthavasena carati.—**of cattle,** gogaṇa, *m.* °**sman,** *n.* gopa ; pasupālaka, *m.*

Here, *adv.* idha ; atra ; ettha. *intj.* bho ! bho ! — **and there,** ito tato tattha tattha. °**about,** avidūre. °**after,** ito paraŋ ; paraloke. °**at,** etth 'antare ; atha. °**by,** anena. °**in,** idha ; ettha. °**of,** ito, iminā hetunā. °**tofore,**

adv. ito pubbe. °**unto,** *adv.* yāvajjatanā. °**upon,** *adv.* ito uddhaŋ, anantaraŋ. °**with,** *adv.* anena saha.

Hereditable, *a.* paramparānugāmī.

Hereditament, *n.* dāyādavatthu, *nt.*

Hereditary, *a.* paramparāgata. — **disease,** vaŋsāgataroga, *m.* — **servant,** kuladāsa, *m.* °**ily,** *adv.* vaŋsānukkamena.

Heredity, *n.* pettikaguṇa, *m.* sahajapakati, *f.*

Heresy, *n.* micchāmati, *f.*

Heretic, *n.* micchādiṭṭhika ; aññatitthiya, *m.* °**al,** *a.* dhammaviruddha. °**ally,** *adv.* dhammavirodhena.

Heritable, *a.* dāyādayogga.

Heritage, *n.* dāyāda, *m.* mātāpettika-dhana, *nt.*

Heritor, *n.* dāyadalābhī, *m.*

Hermaphrodite, *n.* ubhatovyañjanaka, *m.*

Hermeneutic, *n.* anuvāda, *m.* adj. anuvādāyatta. °**tist,** *n.* anuvādaka, *m.*

Hermetic, *a.* rasāyanika ; gūḷhavijjāyatta.

Hermit, *n.* tāpasa ; isi, *m.* °**age,** *n.* assama ; tāpasārāma, *m.* tapovana, *nt.* **Female**—, tapassinī, *f.*

Hernia, *n.* antavuddhi, *f.*

Hero, *n.* sūra ; vīra ; mahāparakkama, *m.* (In dramas :) kathānāyaka, *m.* °**ic,** °**ical,** *a.* vīrāyatta ; vikkamāyatta. °**ically,** *adv.* vīrākārena ; savikkamaŋ. °**ism,** *n.* sūratta, *nt.* vikkama, *m.*

Heroine, *n.* 1. vīravanitā ; 2. kathānāyikā, *f.*

Heron, *n.* sārasa ; lohapiṭṭha, *m.*

Herpes, *n.* vitacchikā, *f.*

Herpetology, *n.* sappavijjā, *f.*

Herself, *pron.* sā yeva ; sā attanā va.

Hesitate, *v.i.* āsaṅkati ; kaṅkhati ; vicikicchati ; vilambati. *p.p.* °kita ; khita ; °chita ; °bita. °**ing,** *a.* āsaṅkamāna ; vilambamāna. °**ingly,** *adv.* sāsaṅkaŋ ; savilambaŋ. °**ion,** *n.* 1. kaṅkhā ; saṅkā ; vimati, *f.* saŋsaya, *m.* 2. vilambana ; pakkhalana, *nt.*

Hesperian, *a.* apācīna.

Hesperus, *n.* osadhī-tārakā, *f.*

Hesternal, *a.* hīyattana.

Hetaera, Hetaira, *n.* gaṇikā ; abhisārikā, *f.*

Hetaerism, *n.* gaṇikāvutti, *f.*

Heterochromous, *a.* nānāvaṇṇa.

Heteroclite, *n.* aniyatarūpikapada, *nt.* adj. niyatavidhiviruddha ; visesarūpika.

Heterodox, *a.* asatthasammata ; uppathagāmī. °**y,** *n.* viruddhadhamma, *m.* micchādassana, *nt.*

Heterogeneity, *n.* bhinnajātikatta, *nt.* °**neous,** *a.* bhinnajātika.° **neously,** *adv.* bhinnajātitāya.

Heterogenesis, *n.* opapātikuppatti, *f.*

Heteromorphic, *a.* nānārūpika.

Heteronomy, *n.* paratantarajja, *nt.*

Heteropathy, *n.* visamatikicchā, *f.*

Hew, *v.t.* chindati ; kantati. *p.p.* chinna ; kantita. °**er,** chettu, *m.*

Hexad, *n*. chakka, *nt*.
Hexagon, *n*. chaḷaŋsika. °**al**, *a*. chaḷaŋsayutta.
Hexameter, *n*. chappadikagāthā, *f*.
Hexapod, *n*. chappada, *m*. adj. chappadika.
He, *intj*. he ; bho ; ambho.
Heyday, *n*. 1. samiddhikāla, *m*. 2. pamoda ; ullāsa, *m*. — **of youth**, navayobbana, *nt*.
Hiatus, *n*. virāma ; padaccheda, *m*. ūnaṭṭhāna, *nt*. (**In gram** :) pubbāpara-saradvaya, *nt*.
Hibernal, *a*. hemantika.
Hibernate, *v.i*. sītakālaŋ khepeti *or* atikkāmeti. °**ion**, *n*. kriyāviraha, *m*.
Hiccup, *n*. hikkā, *f*. *v.i*. hikkāyati. *v.t*. hikkam uppādeti. *p.p*. °yita ; °ditahikka.
Hid, **Hidden**, *p.p*. of **Hide**. tirohita ; paṭicchanna.
Hide, *v.t*. gūheti ; nigūheti ; apanidahati ; nilīyāpeti. *p.p*. gūhita *or* gūḷha ; apanihita ; °pita. *v.i*. nilīyati. *p.p*. nilīna. °**ing**, *n*. nilīyana ; nigūhana, *nt*. — **and seek**, nilīna-pariyesana-kīḷā, *f*.
Hide, *n*. camma ; ajina, *nt*. °**bound**, *a*. ghanattaca ; kaṭhinattaca.
Hideous, *a*. bībhaccha ; ghorarūpa ; virūpa. °**ly**, *adv*. bībhacchākārena. °**ness**, *n*. bhīmatā ; ghoratā, *f*.
Hidrotic, *a*. sedajanaka.
Hierarch, *n*. saṅgharāja, *m*. °**y**, *n*. saṅgharājatta, *nt*.
Hieratic, *a*. 1. samaṇāyatta ; 2. atiporāṇaka.
Hieroglyph, *n*. cittalipi, *f*. cittarūpakkhara, *nt*. °**ic**, *a*. cittalipiāyatta. °**ist**, *n*. cittalipividū, *m*.
Higgle, *v.i*. paṇopaṇaviyaŋ karoti. *p.p*. kata°.
High, *a*. 1. ucca ; unnata ; uttuṅga ; uggata ; 2. mukhya ; padhāna ; agga ; uttama ; 3. adhika ; tibba ; pabala, *adv*. uddhaŋ ; upari. — **and low**, uccāvaca, *a*. — **bed**, uccāsayana, *nt*. — **birth**, kulīnatta ; abhijātatta, *nt*. — **bred**, sadācārasampanna, *a*. — **caste**, *n*. uccakula, *nt*. — **day**, 1. majjhaṇha ; 2. chaṇadivasa, *m*. °**er**, *a*. uccatara. °**fed**, atipuṭṭha ; suposita. — **flown**, dappita, *a*. °**handed**, *a*. uddhata ; sericārī, *m*. °**land**, unnatabhūmi, *f*. °**lander**, pabbatavāsī, *m*. — **mettled**, *a*. adīnamana ; mahussāha. — **minded**, *a*. 1. uḷāracitta ; mahajjhāsaya ; 2. gabbita. °**ness**, *n*. 1. uccatta ; 2. seṭṭhatta, *nt*. — **noon**, ṭhitamajjhantika, *m*. — **pitched**, *a*. uccassara. — **principled**, *a*. sādhucarita ; sundaravata. — — **priest**, nāyakapūjaka, *m*. — **road**, mahāpatha, *m*. — **seas**, mahāsamudda, *m*. — **souled**, *a*. uḷārajjhāsaya. — **spirited**, *a*. alīnacitta. — **toned**, tārassara, *m*. — **treason**, rājadubbhana, *nt*. — **water**, jaluggama ; jaluppāta, *m*. °**wayman**, panthadūhaka, *m*. — **wrought**, *a*. āyāsena sampādita. **Very** —, accuggata ; atyucca, *a*.
Highest, *n*. 1. uccatama ; 2. seṭṭhatama. — **fame**, yasagga, *m*.

— **gain**, 1. uttamattha, *m.* 2. lābhagga, *m.* — **path**, aggamagga, *m.* — **wisdom**, sambodhi, *f.*

Highly, *adv.* adhikaŋ ; accantaŋ ; atīva. — **prized**, *a.* cittīkata ; anaggha.

Hilarious, *a.* sānanda ; pamudita.

Hilarity, *n.* ānanda ; pamoda, *m.* vitti, *f.*

Hill, *n.* giri ; addi, *m.* °**iness**, *n.* pabbatabahulatā, *f.* °**y**, *a.* girisañchanna. °**ock**, khuddaka-giri, *m.*

Hilt, *n.* tharu ; muṭṭhidaṇḍa, *m.* *v.t.* tharuŋ yojeti.

Himself, *pron.* so sayam eva ; so attanā va.

Hind, *n.* migī ; hariṇī, *f.*

Hind, *a.* pacchima ; carima. °**most**, *a.* sabbapacchima. — **part**, pacchimabhāga, *m.*

Hinder, *v.t.* vāreti ; āvarati ; rundhati. *p.p.* vārita ; āvaṭa ; ruddha *or* rundhita. °**drance**, *n.* bādhā, *f.* paḷibodha, *m.* nīvaraṇa, *nt.* °**er**, *n.* nivāraka ; bādhaka, *m.*

Hindu, *a. n.* Indīya. °**ism**, Hindusamaya, *m.* °**stānī**, Indubhāsā, *f.*

Hinge, *n.* dvārāvaṭṭaka, *m.* *v.t.* ghaṭeti ; sambandheti. *v.i.* ghaṭīyati. *p.p.* ghaṭita ; sambaddha.

Hinny, *n.* assatara, *m.*

Hint, *n.* iṅgita, *nt.* saññā, *f.* *v.t.* viññāpeti ; iṅgitena sūceti. *p.p.* °pita ; °sūcita.

Hip, *n.* kaṭi, *f.* jaghana, *nt.* nitamba, *m.*

Hip, *intj.* sādhu sādhu. *v.t.* maṅkukaroti. *p.p.* °kata.

Hipe, *v.t.* paṭimallaŋ nipāteti. *p.p.* nipātita°.

Hippodrome, *n.* rathadhāvanamaṇḍala, *nt.*

Hippogriff, *n.* valāhakassa, *m.*

Hippopotamus, *n.* hatthivarāha ; jalamahisa, *m.*

Hircine, *a.* ajākāra.

Hire, *n.* vetana, *nt.* bhati, *f.* *v.t.* bhatiyā (kammaŋ) kāreti ; bhatiyā gaṇhāti. *p.p.* °kārita ; °gahita. °**ling**, *n.* bhataka ; vetanika, *m.*

Hirsute, *a.* lomabahula ; akappitakesa.

Hispid, *a.* kharalomayutta ; lambakesa.

Hiss, *n.* sūsūyana, *nt.* *v.i.* sūsūyati.

Hist, *intj.* tuṇhī bhavatha.

Histology, *n.* maŋsapesivijjā, *f.*

Historiated, *a.* puggalarūpādiyutta.

Historicity, *n.* (itihāse) tathabhāva, *m.*

Historiographer, *n.* itihāsasampādaka, *m.*

History, *n.* itihāsa ; purāvuttanta, *m.* °**ic**, °**ical**, *a.* itihāsika ; purāvuttagata. °**ically**, *adv.* itihāsānusārena. °**ian**, *n.* itihāsaññū, *m.*

Histrion, *n.* nattaka ; naṭaka, *m.* °**ic**, *a.* 1. naṭakocita ; 2. kuhanāyatta.

Hit, *n.* pahāra ; abhighāta, *m.* saṅghaṭṭana, *nt.* *v.t.* āhanati ; paharati ; ghaṭṭeti. *p.p.* āhata ; pahaṭa ; °ṭita. °**upon**, sahasā pappoti.

Hitch, *n*. bādhā, *f*. antarāya, *m*. *v.t.* 1. saŋyojeti; 2. sasaddaŋ ukkhipati. *v.i.* saŋyujjati; bandhīyati. *p.p.* °jita; °ukkhitta; saŋyutta; baddha.

Hither, *adv*. atra; ettha; idha. °**most**, *a*. āsannatama. °**shore**, ora, *nt*. °**to**, yāvajjatanā, *adv*.

Hive, *n*. madhupaṭala; gaṇavāsa, *m*. *v.t.* madhum saŋharati. *v.i.* gaṇabandhena vasati. *p.p.* saŋhaṭamadhu; °vuttha.

Hives, *n. pl.* antadāha, *m*. cammavipphuraṇa, *nt*.

Hoar, *n.a.* palitakesa; mandadhavala. °**y**, *a*. palitakesa; vayovuddha; paṇḍara.

Hoard, *n*. puñja; nicaya; sannicaya, *m*. *v.t.* sañcināti; rāsīkaroti; nidahati. *p.p.* sañcita; °kata; °hita. °**ed**, *a*. ajjita; nicita.

Hoarse, *a*. kakkasa; pharusa, (of voice.) *m*. °**ly**, *adv*. lūkhassarena. °**ness**, *n*. kakkasatta, *nt*.

Hoax, *n*. vañcanā, *f*. sāṭheyya, *nt*. *v.t.* vañceti; apanidheti. *p.p.* °cita; °nihita.

Hob, *n*. uddhanāvaraṇa, *nt*.

Hobble, *v.i.* khañjati. *p.p.* °jita. *n*. dubbalagamana; khañjana, *nt*.

Hobby, *n*. 1. abhiruci, *f*. atirekavinoda, *m*. 2. dārumayassa, *m*.

Hobgoblin, *n*. 1. duṭṭhapisāca; 2. tiṇapurisa, *m*.

Hobnail, *n*. chattāṇi, *m*.

Hob-nob, *v.i.* ekato pivati; santhavaŋ pavatteti. *p.p.* °pīta; pavattitasanthava.

Hocus, *v.t.* surāya moheti. *p.p.* °mohita.

Hocus-pocus, *n*. 1. indajāla, *nt*. 2. mantapada, *nt*. *v.t.* vañceti.

Hodge-podge, *n*. nānādabbasambhāra, *m*.

Hodiernal, *a*. ajjatana; ajjadivasāyatta.

Hodometer, *n*. rathagamanamāṇaka, *nt*.

Hoe, *n*. kuddāla, *m*. *v.t.* bhūmiŋ kasati *or* vidāreti. *p.p.* kaṭṭhabhūmi; °rita°.

Hog, *n*. sūkara; varāha, *m*. °**gish**, *a*. sūkaropama. °**gishly**, *a*. sūkarākārena. °**pen**, °**sty**, *n*. sūkaravaja, *m*. °**plum**, ambāṭaka, *m*.

Hog, *v.t.* majjhato unnāmeti. *p.p.* °mita.

Hogshead, *n*. mahāsurābheri. *f*.

Hoist, *n*. ussāpana, *nt*. ussāpakaupakaraṇa, *nt*. *v.t.* ussāpeti. *p.p.* °pita. °**ed**, *a*. samussita.

Hoity-toity, *n*. avinītacariyā, *f*. adj. 1. kīḷāpara; 2. dappitā. *intj*. aho!

Hold, *n*. 1. gahaṇa; dhāraṇa, *nt*. 2. ādhāra, *m*. patiṭṭhā, *f*. 3. balakoṭṭhaka, *nt*. 4. gayhaṭṭhāna, *nt*. 5. bhājana, *nt*. 6. nāvodara, *nt*. *v.t.* 1. sandhāreti; 2. gaṇhāti; 3. avarodheti. 4. (to contain:) ādhāti; 5. (to continue:) avicchinnaŋ pavatteti. *p.p.* °rita; gahita; °dhita; ādahita; °tita. *v.i.* 1. saṇṭhāti; patiṭṭhāti; 2. viramati; nivattati. *p.p.* saṇṭhita; virata; nivatta. —**back**, *v.t.* nivāreti. *v.i.* osakkati. — **a consultation**, sammanteti. — **dear**, piyāyati. — **enmity**, upanandhati. — **forth**, pākaṭaŋ katheti. °**in**, niggaṇhāti.

— in contempt, avamaññati. —in esteem, bahumāneti. —it true, saddahati. —a meeting, sannipāteti. —off, apagacchati. — on, pavatteti. — on to, parāmasati. — one's tongue, vācaŋ rakkhati. — one's peace, tuṇhībhavati. — an opinion, mataŋ dhāreti. — out, pasāreti. — a sword, khaggaŋ dhāreti. — to his promise, paṭiññāya tiṭṭhati.

Holder, *n.* 1. dhāraka ; gāhaka, *m.* 2. ādhāraka, *m.*

Holding, *n.* 1. gahaṇa ; dhāraṇa, *nt.* 2. pariggahita-bhūmi, *f.* — **out,** paggahaṇa, *nt.*

Hole, *n.* chidda ; vivara, susira ; randha, *nt.* *v.t.* vinivijjhati ; chiddaŋ karoti. *v.i.* bilaŋ gacchati. *p.p.* vinividdha ; katachidda ; bilagata. — **of the yoke,** yugacchiggala, *nt.* **Full of holes,** vicchiddaka ; chiddāvacchiddaka, *a.*

Holiday, *n.* nikkammadivasa ; uposathadina, *m.*

Hollo, *intj.* he ; bho ; ambho. *v.t.* uccāsaddena pakkosati. *p.p.* °sita.

Hollow, *n.* 1. bila, koṭara, *nt.* 2. āvāṭa ; opāta, *m.* 3. puṭa, *nt.* adj. 1. antosusira ; 2. nissāra ; niratthaka ; 3. tuccha ; suñña ; 4. vitatha. *v.t.* bilaŋ khaṇati; puṭaŋ karoti. *p.p.* khatabila ; puṭīkata. °**hearted,** *a.* vaṅkacitta. °**ness,** *n.* asāratta ; tucchatta, *nt.* — **of the hand,** hatthapuṭa, *m.* °**tree,** kolāpa, *m.*

Holocaust, *n.* 1. sabbassadāna, *nt.* 2. niravasesa-vināsa, *m.*

Holograph, *a.n.* sahatthalikhita, *nt.*

Holt, *n.* vanasaṇḍa, *m.*

Holy, *a. n.* visuddha ; pūjiya. — **land,** suddhabhūmi, *f.* — **person,** arahanta ; anāsava, *m.* — **place,** pujjaṭṭhāna, *nt.* °**iness,** visuddhatta ; nikkilesatta, *nt.* — **orders,** pabbajjā, *f.* °**writ,** dhammalipi, *f.*

Holy-stone, *n.* sodhakasilā, *f.* *v.t.* mudusilāya ghaŋseti. *p.p.* °sita.

Homage, *n.* apaciti, *f.* gārava ; paṇāma ; namakkāra ; paṇipāta, *m.* abhivādanā, *f.* **Paying** —, apacāyī, *a.*

Home, *n.* 1. geha ; agāra, nivesana ; ghara, *nt.* āvāsa ; nilaya, *m.* adj. gehāyatta. °**bred,** *a.* gehaja ; gharasaŋvaddha. °**less,** *a.* anagārika. °**lessness,** *n.* anagāriya, *nt.* °**ly,** *a.* analaṅkata ; avisiṭṭha. °**liness,** *n.* analaṅkatatta, *nt.* — **made,** *a.* gehe sampādita. — **sick,** *a.* gharavirahapīḷita. °**spun,** *a.* ghare kantita. °**stead,** gehavatthu, *nt.* °**ward,** *a.* sagehābhimukha ; saraṭṭhābhimukha. °**y,** *s.* sakagharasadisa.

Homicide, *n.* 1. manussaghātī, *m.* 2. manussaghātana, *nt.* °**al,** *a.* naravadhāyatta.

Homiletic, *n.* desanāvilāsa, *m.* adj. dhammadesanāyatta.

Homily, *n.* suttanta, *m.* dhammadesanā, *f.*

Homoeopathy, *n.* samatikicchā, *f.*

Homogeneity, *n.* samajātikatā, *f.*

Homogeneous, °**neal,** *a.* samānajātika ; sahadhammika. °**ness,** samajātikatta, *nt.*

Homologate, *v.t.* sampaṭicchati. *p.p.* °chita.

Homologize, *v.t.* samānattaŋ pāpeti. *v.i.* samattaŋ yāti. *p.p.* °pāpita ; °yāta.

Homologue, *n.* samānavatthu, *nt.*

Homology, *n.* samānatta ; sarūpatta, *nt.* °**ous,** *a.* samānākāra.

Homonym, *n.* anekatthanāma, *nt.* °**ous,** °**ic,** *a.* anekatthaka (-samānasadda).

Homophony, *n.* sarasāmañña, *nt.*

Hone, *n.* nikasa, *m.* *v.t.* nisāṇayati ; tejeti. *p.p.* °ṇita ; tejita.

Honest, *a.* avaṅka ; asaṭha ; akapaṭa ; amāyāvī. °**ly,** *adv.* ujuŋ ; avyājaŋ ; asaṭhatāya. °**y,** *n.* ajjava ; akuṭilatta, *nt.*

Honey, *n.* madhu, *nt.* — **of flowers,** puppharasa, *m.* °**comb,** madhupaṭala, *nt.* °**moon,** ānandakāla, *m.* —**tongued,** *a.* madhubhāṇī.

Honorarium, *n.* sammānadakkhiṇā, *f.*

Honorary, *n.* 1. sammānavasena laddha ; 2. nimmūlena sādhiyamāna.

Honorific, *n.* sammānavacana, *nt.* adj. gāravāyatta.

Honour, *n.* gārava ; bahūmāna ; sammāna, *m.* apaciti ; pūjanā, *f.* *v.t.* 1. garukaroti ; māneti ; sammāneti ; pūjeti. *p.p.* °kata ; mānita ; pūjita ; 2. gāravopādhiŋ deti. *p.p.* dinnagāravopādhī. °**able,** *a.* pūjanīya ; pujja ; garukātabba; mānanīya. °**ably,** *adv.* pujjākārena ; sagāravaŋ.

Hood, *n.* 1. phaṇa, *nt.* 2. sīsāvaraṇa, *nt.* *v.t.* 1. sīsam āvarati ; 2. aŋsakūṭesu laggeti. *p.p.* āvaṭasīsa ; °laggita.

Hoodlum, *n.* dhuttamāṇava, *m.*

Hoodwink, *v.t.* 1. vañceti ; 2. akkhīni pidahitvā bandhati. *p.p.* °cita ; °baddha.

Hoof, *n.* khura, *nt.* *v.t.* khurena paharati. *v.i.* padasā yāti. *p.p.* °pahaṭa ; °yāta.

Hook, *n.* ākaḍḍhanī, *f.* aṅkusa, *m.* *v.t.* 1. aṅkusaŋ yojeti ; 2. balisena ākaḍḍhati. *p.p.* yojitaṅkusa ; °ḍhita. **Fish —,** balisa, *nt.* °**ed,** *a.* vaṅka ; kuṭila.

Hookah, *n.* Indīya-dhūmaneṭti, *f.*

Hooligan, *n.* panthadūsaka, *m.*

Hoop, *n.* valaya ; āvaṭṭa, *m.* kīḷācakka, *nt.* *v.t.* valaye yojeti ; parikkhipati. *p.p.* yojitavalaya ; °khitta. — **ing cough,** *n.* dahaṛānaŋ ukkāsanaroga, *m.*

Hoot, *n.* dhikkāra, *m.* *v.t.* ayasaŋ pakāseti. *v.i.* huṅkaroti. *p.p.* °sitāyasa ; °kata.

Hop, *n.* laṅghana, *nt.* *v.i.* uppatanto yāti ; laṅghati. *p.p.* °ghita. °**per,** *n.* laṅghaka, *m.*

Hope, *n.* apekkhā ; ākaṅkhā ; abhilāsā ; patthanā, *f.* *v.t.* āsiŋsati ; pattheti ; apekkhati. *p.p.* āsiṭṭha ; °thita ; °khita. °**ful,** *a.* sāpekkha ; ākaṅkhī. °**fully,** *adv.* sāpekkhaŋ. °**less,** *a.* nirapekkha. °**lessly,** *adv.* asādhiyākārena ; apekkhābaṅgena. °**lessness,** *n.* nirapekkhatā ; asādhiyatā, *f.*

Hopper, *n.* 1. (yante) dhaññappavesaka-bhājana, *nt.* 2. pūvavisesa, *n.*

Hopple, *n.* pādasaṅkhalikā, *f.* *v.t.* pāde ekato bandhati.

Hora, *n*. horā ; ghaṭikā, *f*. °**ry**, *a*. horāyatta ; anuhoraŋ pavattanaka.

Horde, *n*. mahāsamūha, *m*. *v.i.* samūhavasena vasati *or* carati. *p.p.* °vuttha.

Horizon, *n*. disāmaṇḍala, *nt*. °**tal**, *a*. disānugata ; tiriyaṅgata. °**tally**, *adv*. tiriyaŋ.

Horn, *n*. 1. siṅga ; visāṇa, *nt*. 2. kāhaḷa, *nt*. *v.t.* 1. siṅgayuttaŋ karoti ; 2. siṅgena āhanati. *p.p.* °āhata. °**blower**, *n*. kāhalavādaka, *m*. °**ed**, *a*. siṅgayutta ; visāṇī. °**er**, *n*. 1. ullekhanīsampādaka ; 2. kāhalika, *m*. °**y**, *a*. kaṭhina ; siṅgabahula.

Hornbill, *n*. cātaka, *m*.

Hornet, *n*. bhamara, *m*.

Horologe, *n*. horālocana, *nt*.

Horology, *n*. horāmāṇavijjā, *f*.

Horoscope, *n*. jātipatta, *nt*. nakkhattayoga, *m*.

Horrent, *a*. lomahaŋsaka.

Horrible, *a*. bhayaṅkara ; bhiŋsanaka. °**ness**, *n*. bhīmatta, *nt*. °**ly**, *adv*. bhīmākārena.

Horrid, *a*. bherava ; bībhacca. °**ness**, *n*. bheravatta, *nt*.

Horrify, *v.t.* uttāseti ; bhāyāpeti. *p.p.* °sita ; °pita. °**ication**, *n*. bhāyāpana, *nt*.

Horripilation, *n*. lomahaŋsa, *m*.

Horror, *n*. mahābhaya, *nt*. santāsa ; uttrāsa, *m*. — **stricken**, *a*. bhayatajjita.

Horse, *n*. haya ; assa ; turaga ; turaṅgama ; ghoṭa, *m*. °**back**, assapiṭṭhi, *f*. — **born in Sindh**, sindhava, *m*. — **boy**, assabandha, *m*. — **coper**, — **dealer**, assavāṇija, *m*. — **fly**, piṅgalamakkhikā, *f*. — **groom**, °**keeper**, assagopaka, *m*. — **laugh**, aṭṭahāsa, *m*. — **leech**, mahājalūkā, *f*. °**man**, assāroha, *m*. °**manship**, assasippa, *nt*. °**power**, assabala, *nt*. — **radish**, siggu, *nt*. °**rug**, assatthara, *m*. °**sacrifice**, assamedha, *m*. °**shoe**, khurāvaraṇa, *nt*. — **trainer**, assadamaka, *m*. — **trappings**, assakappana, *m*. °**whip**, kasā, *f*. **Drawn by a** —, hayavāhī, *a*. **Untamed** —, khaluṅka, *m*.

Hortative, *a*. ovādadāyaka ; samuttejaka. °**tion**, *n*. ovāda; upadesa, *m*.

Horticulture, *n*. uyyānapālanavijjā, *f*. °**ist**, *n*. uyyānaropaṇaññū, *m*.

Hosanna, *n*. sādhukāranāda, *m*.

Hose, *n*. 1. uṇṇāmaya-pādatāṇa, *nt*. 2. jalasiñcakanāḷa, *m*.

Hosier, *n*. pādatāṇavāṇija, *m*. °**y**, *n*. uṇṇāmayabhaṇḍasamūha, *m*.

Hospice, *n*. pathikasālā, *f*.

Hospitable, *a*. atithipūjaka ; sakkārasīlī. °**bly**, *adv*. sabahumānaŋ ; sādaraŋ.

Hospital, *a*. ārogyasālā ; sotthisālā, *f*.

Hospitality, *n*. sakkāra, *m*. ātitheyya, *nt*.

Host, *n*. 1. nimantaka ; bhojāpaka, *m*. 2. mahāsamūha, *m*. 3. senābala, *nt*. °**ess**, *n*. nimantikā ; gahapatānī, *f*.

Hostage, *n*. sarīrapāṭibhogī, *m*.

Hostel, *n*. 1. pathikasālā, *f*. 2. sissanivāsa, *m*.

Hostile, *a.* viruddha ; vipakkha ; paccanika. — **army**, sattusenā, *f.* — **king**, paṭirāja, *m.* °**ity**, *n.* virodha, *m.* vipakkhatā, *f.* — **warrior**, paṭiyodha, *m.*

Hot, *a.* 1. uṇha ; santatta ; 2. kopāviṭṭha ; sāhasika. — **blooded**, *a.* caṇḍapakatika.— **headed**, *a.* kopabahula. °**house**, *n.* usumāgāra, *nt.* °**ly**, *adv.* sakopaŋ ; savirodhaŋ. — **season**, *n.* nidāgha ; gimhāna, *nt.*

Hotchpotch, *n.* missitāhāra, *m.* vividhavatthusamūha, *m.*

Hotel, *n.* bhojanāgāra, *nt.*

Hound, *n.* migava-sunakha, *m.* *v.t.* sunakhehi anubandhati. *p.p.* °anubaddha.

Hour, *n.* horā ; ghaṭikā, *f.* — **glass**, ghaṭikāyanta, *nt.* °**ly**, *a.* anughaṭika. *adv.* anughaṭikaŋ.

House, *n.* geha ; ghara ; gaha ; nivesana ; niketana, *nt.* ālaya ; āvāsa ; nilaya, *m.* bhavana ; mandira ; sadana, vesma, *nt.* *v.t.* nivāseti ; vāsaŋ deti. *v.i.* nivasati. *p.p.* °sita ; dinnavāsa ; nivuttha. °**breaker**, sandhicchedaka (-cora), *m.* °**door**, gharadvāra, *nt.* °**gate**, gopura, *nt.* °**hold**, kuṭumba, *nt.* gehajana, *m.* °**holder**, gahapati ; kuṭumbika. °**hold life**, gharāvāsa, *m.* °**keeper**, gehapālaka, *m.* °**keeping**, gharasaŋvidhāna, *nt.* °**less**, *a.* anāgāra. — **lizzard**, gharagoḷikā, *f.* °**maid**, gehadāsī; paricārikā, *f.* — **warming**, navagharappavesa, *m.* °**wife**, gharasāminī, *f.* — **yard**, gehaṅgaṇa, ājira, *nt.*

Hovel, *n.* bāhirakuṭi, *f.*

Hover, *v.i.* parito uḍḍeti ; nabhe paribbhamati. *p.p.* °uḍḍita ; °paribbhanta. °**ing**, *n.* paribbhamaṇa, *nt.*

How, *adv.* kathaŋ ? kenākārena ? —**acting**, kathaṅkara, *a.* °**beit**, tathā pi, *ind.* °**ever**, kathañci pi ; yathākathañci, *ind.* °**evermuch**, yattaka ; yāvataka, *a.* —**far**, kīvadūre. — **long**, kīvaciraŋ, *ind.* — **many**, kittaka ; kati, *a.* — **many times**, kīvakkhattuŋ, *adv.*—**much**, kittaka ; kīva, *a.* °**soever**, evam pi sati.

Howdah, *n.* hatthipiṭṭhāsana, *nt.*

Howl, *n.* 1. dīgha-bhuṅkāra ; 2. aṭṭassara, *m.* *v.i.* dīghaŋ bhuṅkaroti ; vassati. °**ing**, *n.* ravana ; vassana, *nt.*

Hoy, *intj.* āmantana ; pasupalāpana, *nt.*

Hub, *n.* (cakka-) nābhi, *f.*

Hubble-bubble, *n.* missitanāda ; kalakala, *m.*

Hubbub, *n.* kalahasadda, *m.*

Huckle, *n.* jaghana, *nt.* kaṭi, *f.*

Huckster, *n.* kacchapuṭavāṇija, *m.* *v.i.* paṇopaṇaviyaŋ karoti.

Huddle, *n.* saṅkhobha, *m.* saṅkiṇṇatā, *f.* *v.t.* sammisseti ; ekato khipati. *v.i.* missīyati. *p.p.* °sita ; °khitta ; missita.

Hue, *n.* 1. vaṇṇa, *m.* 2. raṅga, *m.* rajana, *nt.* 3. ugghosana, *nt.*

Huff, *n.* kopāvesa, *m.*

Hug, *n.* āliṅgana ; parissajana, *nt.* *v.t.* āliṅgati ; parissajati. *p.p.* °gita ; parissaṭṭha.

Huge, *a.* atimahanta ; ativisāla ; vipula. °**ly**, *adv.* atimattaŋ ; accantaŋ. °**ness**, visālatta, *nt.*

Hugger-mugger, *n.* gūḷhatta, *nt.* rahobhāva, *m.* adj. gūḷha; gutta. *adv.* raho.

Hulk, *n.* 1. nāvākhandha, *m.* 2. mahākāya, *m.* °**ing**, *a.* atithūla; virūpa.

Hull, *n.* sipāṭikā, *f.* bījakosa, *m.* *v.t.* sipāṭikam *or* tacam apaneti. *p.p.* apanīta-taca.

Hull, *n.* nāvāsaṅkhalikā, *f.*

Hullabaloo, *n.* kalakalasadda, *m.*

Hum, *n.* jhaṅkāra; huṅkāra, *m.* *v.t.* jhaṅkaroti; huṅkaroti. *p.p.* °kata. °**ming**, *a.* 1. huṅkaronta; 2. viriyavantu.

Human, *a.* mānusika; manussāyatta. °**ism**, mānusikatta, *nt.* sadācāra, *m.* °**ist**, *n.* mānusācāra-sikkhaka, *m.* °**ity**, *n.* dayā, *f.* °**ize**, *v.t.* sadācāraŋ sikkhāpeti. — **kind**,manussasantati, *f.* °**ly**, *adv.* mānusagatiyā.

Humane, *a.* kāruṇika. °**ly**, *adv.* sadayaŋ; sānukampaŋ.

Humanitarian, *n.* *a.* janahitakāmī, *m.* °**ism**, *n.* parahitaniratatā, *f.*

Humble, *a.* 1. hīna; dīna; nīcavuttika; 2. vinīta; nirahaṅkāra; 3. duggata. *v.t.* abhibhavati; mānaŋ bhañjati. *p.p.* abhibhūta; bhaṭṭhamāna. — **bee**, *n.* madhukarādhipa, *m.* °**ing**, *n.* mānabhañjana, *nt.* °**ly**, *adv.* savinayaŋ; sagāravaŋ. °**ness**, nīcavuttitā; sagāravatā, *f.* nipaccakāra, *m.*

Humbug, *n.* vañcanā; upalālanā, *f.* *v.t.* vañceti. *p.p.* °cita.

Humdrum, *n.* dandhatta; avisesatta, *nt.* adj. udāsīna.

Humeral, *a.* akkhakāyatta.

Humerus, *n.* bāhaṭṭhi, *nt.*

Humid, *a.* adda; tinta; kilinna. °**ity**, *n.* addatta; kilinnatta, *nt.*

Humiliate, *v.t.* see **Humble.** °**ed**, *a.* avamānita; hatadappa. °**ing**, *a.* dappahara. °**ion**, *n.* avamānana; mānabhañjana, *nt.*

Humility, *n.* sagāravatā; nihatamānatā, *f.*

Hummock, *n.* unnatabhūmi, *f.*

Humoral, *a.* pittādisannissita.

Humorist, *n.* vinodaka, *m.*

Humour, *n.* 1. manovutti; cittapakati, *f.* 2. hāsuppādakatā, *f.* 3. pitta-semhādi, *m.* *v.t.* anulometi; ārādheti. *p.p.* °mita; °dhita. °**ous**, *a.* hāsajanaka; vinodakara. °**ously**, *adv.* savinodaŋ; hassādhippāyena. °**some**, *a.* calacitta; lolamati. **Bad** —, domanassa, *nt.* **Disorder of** —, dhātukopa, *m.* **Good** —, sabbhāva, *m.* susīlatta; somanassa, *nt.*

Hump, *n.* kaku; kakudha, *m.* °**backed**, *a.* khujja; gaṇḍula.

Humpty-dumpty, *n.* thulla-vāmana, *m.*

Hunch, *n.* piṇḍī, *f.* piṇḍa, *m.* *v.t.* nāmeti; vaṅkīkaroti. *p.p.* nāmita; °kata. °**back**, khujja, *a.*

Hundred, *n.* sata, *nt.*—**and fifty**, diyaḍḍhasata, *nt.* — **and ten**, dasuttarasata, *nt.* °**billion**, pakoṭi, *f.* °**fold**, *a.* sataguṇika. — **million**, dasakoṭi, *f.* °**th**, *a.* satama. — **thousand**, satasahassa, *nt.* — **times**, satakkhattuŋ, *adv.*

Hunger, *n.* khudā; jighacchā, *f.* *v.i.* jighacchati; bubhukkhati. *v.t.* nirāhārīkaroti. *p.p.* °chita;

°khita ; °kata. — **and thirst,** khuppipāsā, *f.*

Hungry, *a.* chāta ; khudāpareta. **°ily,** *adv.* chātākārena. **°iness,** *n.* chātatta, *nt.*

Hunks, *n.* maccharī, *m.*

Hunt, *n.* migava, *m.* *v.t.* 1. migavadhaŋ karoti ; 2. anvesati. *p.p.* °kata ; °sita. **°er, °sman,** vyādha ; nesāda ; luddaka, *m.* **°ing,** *n.* 1. migava, *m.* 2. gavesana, *nt.*

Hurdle, *n.* sūcidvāra, *nt.* *v.t.* sūcidvāraŋ yojeti. **°er,** sūcidvārasampādaka, *m.*

Hurl, *n.* khepa, *m.* khipana, *nt.* *v.t.* khipati ; vissajjeti. *p.p.* khitta ; vissaṭṭha. — **down,** avakkhipati. **°ing,** *n.* pātana ; vissajjana ; khipana, *nt.*

Hurly-burly, *n.* kolāhalasadda ; missitanāda, *m.*

Hurrah, °ray, *intj.* jaya ! jaya ! *n.* jayunnāda, *m.* *v.i.* unnadati.

Hurricane, *n.* caṇḍānila ; verambhavāta, *m.*

Hurry, *n.* sambhama ; vega, *m.* adhikāsā, *f.* *v.i.* turitaŋ yāti ; turitayati. *v.t.* sīghaŋ peseti. *p.p.* °yita ; °sita. **°iedly,** *adv.* sīghaŋ ; turitaŋ ; avilambitaŋ.

Hurt, *n.* 1. hiŋsā ; pīḷā, *f.* dukkhāpana, *nt.* 2. hāni, *f.* apakāra, *m.* *v.t.* hiŋsati ; vyathati ; dukkhāpeti. *p.p.* °sita ; vyathita ; °pita. **°ful,** *a.* pīḷākara ; hiŋsaka. **°fully,** *adv.* piḷākaratāya ; hānipubbakaŋ. **°less,** *a.* pīḷārahita.

Hurtle, *n.* ghaṭṭanasadda, *m.* *v.t.* turitaŋ khipati ; saṅghaṭṭeti. *p.p.* °khitta ; °ṭita.

Husband, *n.* pati ; bhattu ; sāmika ; dhava, *m.* *v.t.* 1. mitabbayaŋ karoti ; 2. kasikamme yujjati. *p.p.* katamitabbaya ; °yutta. — **and wife,** jāyāpatī ; jayampatī, dampatī, *m. pl.* **°less,** *a.* vidhavā, *f.* **°'s brother,** devara, *m.* **°'s family,** patikula, *nt.* **°'s sister,** nanandā, *f.* **°man,** kassaka, *m.*

Husbandry, *n.* 1. kasikamma, *nt.* 2. mitabbayatā, *f.*

Hush, *n.* nissaddatā, *f.* *v.t.* upasameti ; nissaddaŋ karoti. *v.i.* upasammati ; tuṇhībhavati. *p.p.* °samita ; nissaddīkata ; upasanta ; °bhūta. *intj.* tuṇhī hohi.

Husk, *n.* taca ; thusa, *m.* *v.t.* nitthusayati ; nittacayati. *p.p.* °yita. **°y,** *a.* 1. tacasahita ; 2. kakkasa. **°ily,** *adv.* kharassarena. **°iness,** *n.* kakkasatā ; kharassaratā, *f.*

Hussy, *n.* 1. dubbinītitthī, *f.* 2. avinītadārikā, *f.*

Hustle, *n.* sammadda, *m.* *v.t.* sammaddati ; ekato rāsibhavati. *p.p.* °dita ; °bhūta.

Hut, *n.* kuṭi ; paṇṇasālā, *f.* *v.t.* kuṭiyaŋ niveseti. *p.p.* °sita.

Hutch, *n.* pañjara ; sasapañjara, *m.*

Huzza, *n.* ukkuṭṭhi, *f.* *intj.* sādhu ! sādhu !

Hyena, Hyaena, *n.* taraccha ; migādana, *m.*

Hybrid, *a.* saṅkarajātika. **°ity,** *n.* sankiṇṇajātikatta, *nt.* **°ize,** *v.t.* missanena sañjaneti. *p.p.* °janita. **°ization,** *n.* missanena uppādana, *nt.*

Hydra, *n.* jalavāḷa, *m.* °**headed**, bahusīsaka, *a.*
Hydrate, *v.t.* jalena misseti. *p.p.* °missita.
Hydraulic, *a.* jalavahanāyatta ; jalabalasampādita.
Hydriad, *n.* jaladevatā, *f.* varuṇa, *m.*
Hydrocele, *n.* aṇḍavuddhi, *f.*
Hydrocephalus, *n.* matthaluṅgasopha, *m.*
Hydrogen, *n.* ujjalanakavāyu ; jalakaravāyu, *m.* °**ate**, *v.t.* jalakaravāyunā misseti. *p.p.* °missita.
Hydrography, *n.* jalāsayamāṇavijjā, *f.* °**pher**, *n.* jalāsayamāṇavidū, *m.*
Hydrology, *n.* jalavijjā, *f.* °**gist**, jalavijjāvidū, *m.*
Hydromel, *n.* jalamissitamadhu, *nt.*
Hydrometer, *n.* jalagaruttamāṇaka, *nt.*
Hydropathy, *n.* jalatikicchā, *f.* °**thic**, *a.* jalatikicchāyatta.
Hydrophobia, *n.* jalabhītikaroga, *m.*
Hydrous, *a.* sajala ; vāriyutta.
Hygiene, *n.* ārogyavijjā, *f.* °**ical**, *a.* ārogyavijjāyatta. °**ics**, *n.* ārogyasattha, *nt.*
Hylic, *a.* mahābhūtika.
Hymn, *n.* devatthutigīta, *nt.* *v.t.* gītena abhitthavati. *p.p.* °abhitthuta. °**ic**, °**al**, *a.* thutigītāyatta. °**ist**, *n.* thutigāyaka, *m.* °**ody**, *n.* 1. thutigāyana, *nt.* 2. thutippabandha, *m.* °**ographer**, thutigīta-sampādaka, *m.* °**ology**, *n.* 1. thutigītavijjā, *f.* 2. thutigītasamūha, *m.*
Hypaethral, *a.* abbhokāsika ; chadanarahita ; uparivivaṭa.
Hyperbole, *n.* atisayutti, *f.* °**ical**, *a.* atisayuttipubbaka.
Hypercritic, *n.* ativivecaka ; sukhumarandhagavesī, *m.* °**al**, *a.* ativivecanāyatta. °**ism**, *n.* ativivecana, *nt.*
Hyperphysical, *a.* lokuttara ; arūpāyatta.
Hypersensitive, *a.* sukhumasaññāyutta ; sukhumavedaka, *m.*
Hypertrophy, *n.* atithūlatta, *nt.*
Hyphen, *n.* sambandhalakkhaṇa, *nt.*
Hypnosis, *n.* mohananiddā, *f.*
Hypnotic, *a.* visaññīkara ; niddājanaka. °**tism**, *n.* vasīkaraṇavijjā, *f.* °**tize**, *v.t.* vasīkaroti ; mohaniddaŋ janeti. *p.p.* °kata ; janitamohanidda.
Hypocrisy, *n.* kohañña ; kerāṭiya, *nt.* kuhanā, *f.*
Hypocrite, *n.* kuhaka ; vañcaka, *m.* °**ical**, *a.* kerāṭika ; vañcanika.
Hypostasis, *n.* rudhirabāhulla *nt.*
Hypothecate, *v.t.* upanidhivasena ṭhapeti. *p.p.* °ṭhapita. °**ion**, *n.* nyāsaṭṭhapana, *nt.*
Hypothesis, *n.* saṅkappitattha ; anumāna, *m.*
Hypothetic, °**al**, *a.* saṅkappanāyatta ; pakappita. °**ally**, *adv.* anumānena.
Hypothesize, *v.t.* anumitiŋ sampādeti. *p.p.* °ditānumitī.
Hysteria, *n.* vātummāda, *m.* mucchā, *f.*
Hysterical, *a.* mucchābahula ; mucchanasīla.

I

I, *pron.* ahaŋ. (nom. sing. of amha.)

Ibex, *n.* pabbateyya-chagalaka, *m.*

Ibidem, *adv.* tatth eva ; tad eva.

Ice, *n.* hima ; tusāra, *nt. v.t.* himena chādeti *or* sītalīkaroti. *p.p.* himacchanna ; °kata. °**berg,** *n.* plavamāna-himapabbata, *m.* — **cold, icy,** *a.* himasītala. — **cream,** himaduddha, *nt.* —**fall,** *n.* himapāta, *m.* — **field,** himakhetta; himatala, *nt.* — **house,** *n.* himarakkhanāgāra, *nt.*

Ichneumon, *n.* nakula ; muṅgusa, *m.*

Ichnography, *n.* bhūmisaṇṭhānalekhā, *f.*

Ichor, *n.* vaṇassavaṇa, *nt.*

Ichthyoid, *a.* macchasadisa.

Ichthyology, *n.* jalacaravijjā, *f.*

Ichthyophagy, *n.* macchabhakkhana, *nt.*

Icicle, *n.* himakaṇa, *m.*

Icily, *adv.* sītalākārena.

Iciness, *n.* himasītalatta, *nt.*

Icon, *n.* devapaṭimā ; pujjapaṭimā, *f.* °**ic,** *a.* paṭimāyatta.

Iconoclast, *n.* paṭimābhindaka ; adhammagaruka, *m.* °**lasm,** *n.* paṭimābhindana, *nt.*

Iconography, *n.* paṭimākaraṇa, *nt.* paṭimāsaṅgaha, *m.*

Iconolatry, *n.* paṭimāvandanā, *f.*

Iconology, *n.* paṭibimbavijjā, *f.*

Icy, *a.* himabahula ; himasadisa.

Idea, *n.* mati, *f.* mata, *nt.* adhippāya ; saṅkappa, *m.*

Ideal, *n.* paramattha, *m.* adj. 1. manokappita ; 2. visiṭṭha ; uttama. °**ism,** *n.* viññattimattavāda, *m.* °**ist,** *n.* viññāṇavādī; manovikappī, *m.* °**ity,** *n.* paṭibhāṇasampadā, *f.* °**ly,** *adv.* visiṭṭhākārena.

Ideate, *v.i.* parikappeti ; cinteti. *p.p.* °pita ; °tita. °**ion,** *n.* vitakkana, *nt.*

Idem, *n. adv.* tad'eva ; tatth'eva.

Identical, *a.* tammaya; abhinna; nibbisesa. °**ly,** *adv.* nibbisesaŋ ; abhinnatāya.

Identify, *v.t.* samāneti ; abhisañjānāti ; abhinivisati. *p.p.* °nita ; abhiniviṭṭha. °**ication,** *n.* 1. abhisañjānana, *nt.* abhinivesa, *m.* 2. samānana, *nt.*

Identity, *n.* ekībhāva ; abheda ; nibbisesa, *m.*

Ideograph, *n.* cittarūpakkhara, *nt.* °**ic,** *a.* cittarūpakkharāyatta.

Ideology, *n.* mānasikavijjā, *f.*

Idiocy, *n.* jaḷatā ; eḷamūgatā, *f.*

Idiom, *n.* bhāsārīti, *f.* racanāvilāsa, *m.* °**atic,** *a.* bhāsārītyanugata.

Idiopathy, *n.* anaññaroguṭṭhitagelañña, *nt.*

Idiosyncrasy, *n.* āveṇikasabhāva, *m.* °**cratic.** *a.* āveṇikasabhāvāyatta.

Idiot, *n.* hīnapañña; buddhihīna; jaḷa, *m.* °**ic,** *a.* appapañña ; mandabuddhika.

Idle, *a.* 1. alasa ; kusīta ; nirussāha. *v.i.* nikkammo *or* alaso hoti. *v.t.* kālaŋ khepeti *or* vināseti. *p.p.* khepitakāla. °**ness,** *n.* ālasiya ; ālasya ; kosajja, *nt.* °**er,** kiccavimukha ; akiñcikara; avyāvaṭa, *m.*

Idly, *adv.* ālasiyena ; nirussāhena.

Idol, *n*. (deva-) paṭimā, *f*. paṭibimba, *m*. °**ator**, *n*. paṭimāpūjaka, *m*. °**atry**, *n*. paṭimāvandanā, *f*. °**ize**, *v.t*. ativiya sammāneti. *p.p*. °nita.

Idolum, *n*. mata, *nt*. (micchā-) mati.

Idyll, *n*. khuddaka-vaṇṇanā-kabba, *nt*.

If, *conj*. ce ; sace ; yadi. **If you are tired we will sit down,** sace tvaŋ kilanto'si mayaŋ nisīdissāma. **If he has found it he will send it,** sace so taŋ alabhissā (so) taŋ pahiṇissati. *Ce* is not placed at the beginning of a sentence.

Igneous, *a*. pāvakāyatta.

Ignescent, *a*. vipphuliṅgavissajjaka.

Ignis fatuus, *n*. anaggikaujjalana, *nt*.

Ignite, *v.t*. 1. aggiŋ nibbatteti *or* jāleti ; 2. atitattaŋ karoti. *p.p*. jālitaggi ; °kata. *v.i*. jalati. *p.p*. jalita. °**ion**, *n*. 1. aggijālana ; 2. atitattakaraṇa, *nt*.

Ignoble, *a*. adhama ; nīca ; nihīna; anariya. °**ness**, *n*. nihīnatta; nīcatta, *nt*. °**ly**, *adv*. kucchitākārena.

Ignominy, *n*. ayasa, *m*. *nt*. akitti, *f*. avaññā, *f*. °**ious**, *a*. ayasakara ; nindāvaha. °**iously**, *adv*. gārayhākārena.

Ignoramus, *a*. andhaputhujjana; paṇḍitamānī, *m*.

Ignorance, *n*. avijjā, *f*. aññāṇa, *nt*. moha, *m*.

Ignorant, *a*. apañña ; aññāṇa ; assutavantu. °**ly**, *adv*. aññāṇapubbakaŋ.

Ignore, *v.t*. na gaṇeti ; na sallakkheti. *p.p*. agaṇita ; asallakkhita.

Iguana, *n*. godhā, *f*.

Iliac, *a*. antābādhanissita.

Ilk, *a*. anañña ; abhinna.

Ill, *n*. 1. pāpa ; akusala ; duccarita, *nt*. 2. āpadā ; vipatti, *f*. anattha, *m*. 3. roga ; vyādhi, *m*. adj. 1. duṭṭha ; gārayha ; kucchita ; 2. asubha ; avamaṅgala ; 3. gilāna; rogaṭṭa, *adv*. asammā ; asādhu. °**advised**, *a*. asamekkhita ; anupadhārita. °**affected**, *a*. ahitakāma. °**arranged**, *a*. duppayutta. °**behaved**, °**natured**, *a*. avinīta ; durācāra. °**conditioned**, *a*. duggata, °**dressed**, *a*. kucelaka.—**fame**, ayasa, *m*. akitti, *f*. °**fated**, *a*. alakkhika. °**favoured**, *a*. virūpa ; dubbhaga. °**fitted**, *a*. ayogga; anucita. °**gotten**, *a*. adhammaladdha. °**grounded**, *a*. athira. °**health**, akallatā, *f*. gelañña, *nt*. —**humour**, *n*. duṭṭhapakati, *f*. — **judged**, *a*. anālocita ; asamekkhita.—**looking**, *a*. kudassana. °**luck**, *n*. dubbhaga, *nt*. alakkhī, *f*. — **nature**, *n*. duṭṭhatta, *nt*. duppakati, *f*. °**ness**, *n*. roga ; ātaṅka ; vyādhi, *m*. gelañña, *nt*. °**omen**, asubhanimitta, *nt*. °**repute**, ayasa, *m*. *nt*. °**thatched**, *a*. ducchanna. °**timed**, *a*. akālapayutta. °**treatment**, vihesā, *f*. — **will**, vyāpāda ; manopadosa, *m*.

Illation, *n*. nigamana, *nt*. anumiti, *f*. °**tive**, *a*. anumeya.

Ill-bred, *a.* dubbinīta.

Ill-breeding, *n.* avinaya, *m.* asiṭṭhaṭṭa, *nt.*

Illegal, *a.* adhammika ; nītiviruddha. °**ity,** *n.* aññāya, *m.* nītivirodha, *m.* °**ly,** *adv.* aññāyena ; adhammena.

Illegible, *a.* duppaṭhiya ; avisadakkhara. °**bly,** *adv.* avāceyyākārena.

Illegitimacy, *n.* nītivirodha, *m.* avajātatta, *nt.* °**mate,** *a.* 1. avajāta ; 2. vidhiviruddha. °**mately,** aññāyena ; nītivirodhena.

Illiberal, *a.* adānasīla ; maccharī. °**ity,** *n.* acāgasīlatā, *f.* °**ly,** *adv.* samaccheraŋ.

Illicit, *a.* nītiviruddha ; apaṭiññāta. °**ly,** *adv.* nītivirodhena ; adhammena.

Illimitable, *a.* ananta ; aparimita ; appameya. °**ly,** *adv.* aparimitākārena.

Illiteracy, *n.* asatthaññutā ; anakkharaññutā, *f.*

Illiterate, *a.* vijjāhīna ; anakkharaññū.

Illogical, *a.* takkaviruddha ; ayuttisiddha. °**ly,** *adv.* takkavirodhena.

Illumine, *v.t.* joteti ; pabhāseti ; obhāseti ; pākaṭīkaroti. *p.p.* jotita ; °sita ; °kata. °**ing,** *a.* jotaka ; paridīpaka ; pabhaṅkara.

Illuminate, *v.t.* dīpeti ; pakāseti ; pabhāseti. *p.p.* dīpita ; °sita. °**ion,** *n.* 1. obhāsana ; jotana, *nt.* 2. dīpamālā, *f.*

Illusion, *n.* micchāvabodha ; saññāvipallāsa, *m.* māyā, *f.* °**sive,** °**sory,** *a.* vipallāsajanaka. °**ist,** *n.* 1. māyākāra, *m.* 2. vipallatthacitta ; viparītagāhī, *m.*

Illustrate, *v.t.* paridīpeti ; uttānīkaroti ; visadīkaroti. *p.p.* °pita ; °kata. °**ion,** *n.* 1. udāharaṇa ; nidassana, *nt.* 2. vivaraṇa ; uttānīkaraṇa, *nt.* °**ive,** *a.* uddīpaka ; jotaka ; nidassaka. °**or,** *n.* 1. nidassaka ; paridīpetu ; vaṇṇetu ; 2. ālekhaka, *m.*

Illustrious, *a.* vikhyāta ; vissuta ; abhiññāta ; paññāta ; supākaṭa. °**ly,** *adv.* visiṭṭhākārena. °**ness,** *n.* vissuti ; vikhyātatā ; visiṭṭhatā, *f.*

Image, *n.* 1. paṭimā, *f.* paṭibimba ; paṭirūpa, *nt.* 2. ākāra, *m.* upaṭṭhiti, *f.* *v.t.* 1. paṭibimbeti ; ākāraŋ sallakkheti ; 2. supākaṭaŋ dīpeti. *p.p.* °bita ; sallakkhitākāra ; °pita. °**house,** paṭimāghara, *nt.* °**worship,** rūpavandanā, *f.*

Imagery, *n.* 1. manokappita, *nt.* 2. paṭimāsamūha, *m.*

Imagine, *v.t.* saṅkappeti ; parikappeti. *v.i.* maññati. *p.p.* °pita ; maññita. °**able,** *a.* cintāvisayaka. °**ably,** *adv.* cintiyākārena. °**ary,** *a.* saṅkappaja ; cintāmaya. °**ation,** *n.* saṅkappa, *m.* maññanā, *f.* °**ative,** *a.* parikappaka ; cintāpara. °**atively,** *adv.* parikappanavasena.

Imbecile, *a.* *n.* dubbala ; mandamatika ; mandapañña. °**ity,** *n.* dubbalya ; buddhivekalla, *nt.*

Imbed, *v.t.* anto paveseti. *p.p.* °sita.

Imbibe, *v.t.* 1. āpibati ; 2. adhigaṇhāti ; manasā dhāreti. *p.p.* āpīta ; adhiggahita ; °dhārita.

Imbricate, *v.t.* chadane iṭṭhakā viya attharati.

Imbroglio, *n.* 1. saṅkiṇṇarāsi, *m.* 2. saṅkhubhitāvatthā, *f.*

Imbrue, *v.t.* kiledeti; (lohitena, etc.) makkheti. *p.p.* °dita, °ita.

Imbrute, *v.t.* pasusamaŋ karoti. *p.p.* °kata.

Imbue, *v.t.* rañjeti; paripphoseti. *p.p.* rañjita; °sita.

Imitate, *v.t.* 1. anukaroti; anuyāti; 2. katam anukaroti. *p.p.* °kata; anuyāta. °**ion**, *n.* 1. anukaraṇa; 2. paṭirūpaka; vyājavatthu, *nt.* 3. diṭṭhānugati, *f.* °**ive** *a.* anukaraṇasīla. °**tor**, *n.* anukārī; anusārī, *m.*

Immaculate, *a.* nimmala; anavajja; akalaṅka. °**ly**, *adv.* nimmalākārena; anavajjatāya. °**ness**, *n.* nimmalatta, *nt.*

Immanent, *a.* abbhantarika; antogata. °**nence**, *n.* antogadhatta; pariyāpannatta, *nt.*

Immaterial, *a.* 1. addabba; arūpa; 2. anavassa; niratthaka. °**ity**, *n.* addabbatā, *f.* °**ism**, arūpavāda, *m.*

Immature, *a.* apariṇata; appatta-kāla. °**ity**, *n.* apariṇatatta, *nt.* °**ly**, *adv.* apariṇate.

Immeasurable, *a.* appameya; aparimita; amita; appamāṇa. °**ably**, *adv.* aparimeyyākārena. °**bility**, °**ness**, *n.* appameyatta, *nt.*

Immediate, *a.* 1. ānantarika; 2. upakaṭṭha; āsanna. °**ly**, *adv.* sapadi; sajju; taṅkhaṇaŋ; tāvad eva. °**ness**, *n.* āsannatta; āsukātabbatta, *nt.*

Immedicable, *a.* atekiccha; asādhiya; appatikāra.

Immemorial, *a.* aviditārambha; sativisayātīta; cirantana.

Immense, *a.* atimahanta; ativisāla; atipatthaṭa. °**ity**, *n.* atimahatta; visālatta, *nt.* °**ly**, *adv.* vipulākārena.

Immerge, *v.t.* ogāheti; nimujjāpeti. *v.i.* nimujjati; ogāhati. *p.p.* °hita; °pita; nimugga; ogāḷha.

Immerse, see **Immerge**. °**ion**, *n.* ogāhana, *nt.*

Immethodical, *a.* ayathākkamika; uppaṭipāṭika. °**ly**, *adv.* uppaṭipāṭiyā; kamavirodhena.

Immigrant, *n.* sadesacāgī; (vāsāya) videsagāmī, *m.*

Immigrate, *v.i.* desantaraŋ saṅkamati. *p.p.* °saṅkanta. °**ion**, *n.* sadesacāga; videsasaṅkamaṇa; *nt.*

Imminent, *a.* 1. upantika; accāsanna; 2. jīvitasaŋsayāvaha. °**ly**, *adv.* accāsannavasena; atisayena. °**nence**, *n.* accāsannatā; bhayānakatā, *f.*

Immiscible, *a.* asaŋyujjamāna.

Immission, *n.* antopesana, *nt.*

Immit, *v.t.* antopeseti; antogameti. *p.p.* °sita; °mita.

Immitigable, *a.* alahukāraṇīya.

Immix, *v.t.* sammisseti. *p.p.* °sita. °**ture**, *n.* sammissaṇa, *nt.*

Immobile, *a.* thira; acala; aniñja; akampa. °**ity**, *n.* thāvariya; niccalatta, *nt.* °**ize**, *v.t.* santhambheti; akampiyaŋ karoti. *p.p.* °bhita; °kata.

Immoderate, *a.* amattaññū; sīmātikkamaka. °**ly**, *adv.* amattaññutāya; atimattaŋ. °**ion**, *n.* sīmātikkama, *m.*

Immodest, *a.* avinīta ; nillajja. °**ly**, *adv.* avinītākārena. °**y**, *n.* pāgabbhiya ; avinītatta, *nt.* nillajjatā, *f.*

Immolate, *v.t.* yāgāya hanati. *p.p.* °hata. °**ion**, *n.* yajana ; yāgakaraṇa, *nt.* °**tor**, *n.* yājaka, *m.*

Immoral, *a.* dussīla ; pāpadhamma ; durācāra ; adhammika. °**ity**, *n.* dussīlya ; duccarita, *nt.* adhamma, *m.* °**ly**, *adv.* adhammena.

Immortal, *a.* ajarāmara ; nicca ; sassata ; dhuva. °**ity**, *n.* avinassaratta : ajarāmaratta, *nt.* °**ize**, *v.t.* ajarāmaraŋ karoti. °**ly**, *adv.* sassatākārena.

Immovable, *a.* acala ; akampiya ; thāvara ; asaŋhārima. °**bility**, *n.* acalatta ; akampiyatta ; thāvariya, *nt.* °**ably**, *adv.* thiraŋ ; nibbikāraŋ.

Immune, *a.* vippamutta ; virahita. °**ity**, *n.* vimutti, *f.* abhāva ; viraha, *m.*

Immure, *v.t.* avarodheti ; parikkhipati. *p.p.* °dhita ; °khitta. °**ment**, *n.* avarodhana, *nt.*

Immutable, *a.* nibbikāra ; avipariṇāma. °**bility**, *n.* avikāratā ; niccatā, *f.*

Imp, *n.* 1. yakkhapotaka ; 2. dubbinīta-dāraka, *m.*

Impact, *n.* paṭighāta, *m.* saṅghaṭṭana, *nt.* *v.t.* daḷhaŋ sandahati. *p.p.* °hita.

Impair, *v.t.* vikalīkaroti ; hāpeti. *v.i.* vikalībhavati ; hāyati. *p.p.* °kata ; hāpita ; °bhūta ; hīna. °**ed**, *a.* vikala ; ūna. °**ment**, *n.* vekalla ; ūnatta, *nt.* hāni, *f.*

Impale, *v.t.* uttāseti ; sūle āropeti. *p.p.* °sita ; sūlāropita. °**ment**, *n.* uttāsana ; sūlāropaṇa, *nt.*

Impalpable, *a.* 1. phusanāvisaya ; atisukhuma ; 2. duravabodha. °**ably**, *adv.* avyattaŋ ; apphuṭaŋ ; dujjānākārena.

Impanel, *v.t.* nāmāvaliyaŋ antokaroti. *p.p.* °kata.

Impardonable, *a.* akkhamitabba ; akkhamāraha.

Imparity, *n.* vesamma ; asamānatta, *nt.*

Impark, *v.t.* upavane paveseti. *p.p.* °sita.

Impart, *v.t.* 1. anuppadāti ; vitarati ; 2. pakāseti ; viññāpeti. *p.p.* anuppadinna ; vitarita ; °sita ; °pita.

Impartial, *a.* majjhaṭṭha ; apakkhapātī. °**ity**, *n.* apakkhapātitā ; upekkhā ; majjhattatā, *f.* °**ly**, *adv.* apakkhapātena.

Impartible, *a.* avebhaṅgiya ; avibhajiya.

Impassable, *a.* duratikkama ; duggama ; sambādha.

Impasse, *n.* 1. alaṅghanīyāvatthā, *f.* 2. sambādhamagga, *m.*

Impassible, *a.* acetana ; akampiyasabhāva.

Impassion, *v.t.* kilese khobheti. *p.p.* khobhitakilesa. °**ed**, *a.* anuratta ; āsattacitta. °**able**, *a.* sukhobhiya. °**ate**, *a.* kilesavegayutta.

Impassive, *a.* akampiya ; nibbikāra ; upasanta. °**ly**, *adv.* nibbikaraŋ ; upasantākārena. °**ity**, *n.* ananurattatā ; upasantatā, *f.*

Impaste, *v.t.* 1. lepaŋ sampādeti ; 2. ālepeti.

Impatient, *a.* asahamāna ; atiussuka. °**ence,** *n.* akkhanti ; asahanatā, *f.* °**ly,** *adv.* akkhantiyā ; atisīghaŋ.
Impeach, *v.t.* codeti ; upavadati ; dosam āropeti. *p.p.* codita ; upavutta ; āropitadosa. °**ment,** *n.* codanā ; dosāropaṇā, *f.*
Impearl, *v.t.* muttāhi alaṅkaroti. *p.p.* °kata.
Impeccable, *a.* niddosa ; pāpabhīruka. °**bly,** *adv.* agārayhākārena.
Impeccancy, *n.* anindiyatta ; agārayhatta, *nt.* °**cant,** *a.* nippāpa ; niddosa.
Impecunious, *a.* niddhana ; daḷidda.
Impede, *v.t.* sannirumbheti ; rundheti. *p.p.* °bhita ; °dhita.
Impediment, *n.* antarāya ; uparodha, *m.* bādhā, *f.*
Impel, *v.t.* niyojeti ; payojeti ; vyāpārayati. *p.p.* °jita ; vyāpārita. °**lent,** *a.* *n.* uyyojaka ; payojaka, *m.*
Impend, *v.i.* uparito lambati ; samāpatati. *p.p.* °bita ; °tita. °**ing,** *a.* upakaṭṭha ; paccāsanna.
Impenetrable, *a.* avinivedhiya ; anibbijjhiya ; duravabodha.
Impenitent, *a.* ananutāpī ; khedarahita. °**ence,** *n.* ananutāpa, *m.* ananusocana, *nt.*
Imperative, *a.* *n.* āṇāpaka ; vidhāyaka ; alaṅghiya ; āṇattivācaka. °**ly,** *adv.* avilaṅghiyākārena ; avassam eva. °**ness,** *n.* avilaṅghiyatta, *nt.*
Imperator, *n.* rājādhirāja, *m.* °**trix,** *n.* adhirājinī, *f.*
Imperceivable, *a.* anindriyagocara ; atisukhuma.
Imperceptible, *a.* atisukhuma ; indriyāgocara. °**bility,** *n.* atisukhumatā ; indriyāgocaratā, *f.*
Impercipient, *a.* anupalabbhanaka ; acetanika.
Imperfect, *a.* asampuṇṇa ; ūna ; vikala. °**ly,** *adv.* ūnākārena ; vikalaŋ. °**ion,** *n.* apuṇṇatā, *f.* vikalatta, *nt.* — **memory,** sativekalla, *nt.*
Imperforate, *a.* acchidda ; asusira.
Imperial, *a.* adhirajjāyatta. °**ism,** *n.* adhirājapālana, *nt.* adhirajjavāda, *m.* °**ist,** adhirajjavādī, *m.*
Imperil, see **Endanger.**
Imperious, *a.* 1. uddhata ; sāvalepa ; 2. āṇādāyaka ; avilaṅghiya. °**ly,** *adv.* avilaṅghiyākārena. °**ness,** uddhacca, *nt.* ahaṅkāra, *m.* avilaṅghiyatta, *nt.*
Imperishable, *a.* avyaya ; akkhaya ; avinassara ; dhuva.
Imperium, *n.* ekādhipacca; adhirājatta, *nt.*
Impermanent, *a.* anicca ; adhuva ; bhaṅgura.
Impermeable, *a.* appavesiya ; avinivijjhiya.
Impermissible, *a.* ananuññātabba ; ananujānitabba.
Impersonal, *a.* akattuka ; apāṭipuggalika.—**verb,** bhāvakriyā, *f.*
Impersonate, *v.t.* 1. sacetanattam āropeti ; 2. aññassa vesaŋ gaṇhāti. *p.p.* āropitasace° ; gahitaññavesa. °**ion,** *n.* 1. aññavesagahaṇa ; sacetanattāropaṇa, *nt.*

Impersonify, *v.t.* sacetanattam āropeti. *p.p.* āropitasacetanatta.

Impertinence, *n.* dovacassa, *nt.* anācāra ; avinaya, *m.*

Impertinent, *a.* 1. dubbaca ; avinīta ; 2. anāyatta ; asambandha. °**ly,** *adv.* dubbinītākārena ; parakiccappavesena.

Imperturbable, *a.* akkhobbha ; nibbikāra.

Impervious, *a.* sambādha ; duppavesa ; anibbedhiya. °**ly,** *adv.* duppavesiyattena.

Impetrate, *v.t.* yācanāya labhati. *p.p.* °laddha. °**ion,** *n.* yācanāya labhana, *nt.*

Impetuous, *a.* aticaṇḍa; vegavantu ; sāhasika. °**ly,** *adv.* ativegena; sāhasikatāya. °**ness,** °**osity,** *n.* āvega, *m.* caṇḍatta ; sāhasikatta, *nt.*

Impetus, *n.* 1. vega ; java, *m.* 2. samussāhana, *nt.*

Impiety, *n.* assaddhiya, *nt.* agārava, *m.*

Impinge, *v.t.i.* saṅghaṭṭeti. *p.p.* °ṭita.

Impious, *a.* assaddha ; bhattihīna

Implacable, *a.* avupasamiya ; ciraṭṭhitika. °**bly,** *adv.* avupasamiyākārena.

Implant, *v.t.* abhiropeti ; patiṭṭhāpeti. *p.p.* °pita.

Implausible, *a.* apaccayika ; avissasanīya.

Impledge, *v.t.* nyāsāya ṭhapeti. *p.p.* °ṭhapita.

Implement, *n.* upakaraṇa ; parikkhāra, *nt.* *v.t.* paripūreti ; sampādeti. *p.p.* °rita ; °dita. °**al,** *a.* upakaraṇabhūta.

Impletion, *n.* pūraṇa ; puṇṇatta, *nt.*

Implicate, *v.t.* sambandheti ; jaṭeti ; saŋsileseti. *p.p.* °dhita ; jaṭita ; °sita. °**ion,** *n.* saŋsagga ; sambandha, *m.*

Implicit, *a.* nissaŋsaya ; avisaṅkiya ; vivādarahita. °**ly,** *adv.* nissaŋsayaŋ ; avivādena.

Implore, *v.t.* abhiyācati. *p.p.* °cita. °**ingly,** *adv.* yācanapubbakaŋ.

Imply, *v.t.* 1. upalakkheti ; sūceti ; 2. bodheti ; viññāpeti. *p.p.* °khita ; sūcita ; bodhita ; °pita. °**iedly,** *adv.* ānusaṅgikākārena.

Impolicy, *n.* aññāya ; nītivirodha, *m.*

Impolite, *a.* asabbha ; gamma ; avinīta. °**ly,** *adv.* avinītākārena. °**ness,** *n.* asabbhatā, *f.* avinaya, *m.*

Impolitic, *a.* 1. ñāyaviruddha ; asamekkhakata ; 2. avivekī ; anītiññū.

Imponderous, °**derable,** *a.* sallahuka ; bhārahīna.

Imporous, *a.* acchiddaka.

Import, *v.t.* 1. desantarā āneti ; 2. sūceti ; bodheti. *p.p.* °ānīta ; sūcita ; bodhita, *n.* 1. videsānīta-bhaṇḍa, *nt.* 2. adhippāya, *m.* °**ation,** *n.* desantarānayana, *nt.* °**able,** *a.* videsā āharitabba. °**er,** *n.* videsā bhaṇḍāharaka, *m.*

Importance, *n.* garutta ; sappayojanatta, *nt.* °**ant,** *a.* mukhya ; padhāna ; garuka. °**antly,** *adv.* garutāya ; mukhyatāya.

Importune, *v.t.* nibandhati ; abhiyācati. *p.p.* nibaddha ; °cita. °**ate,** *a.* nibandhaka; atiyācaka. °**ately,** *adv.* sanibandhaŋ. °**ity,** *n.* nibandhana ; atiyācana, *nt.*

Impose, *v.t.* niveseti ; āropeti ; niyameti ; yuttaṭṭhāne ṭhapeti. *p.p.* °sita ; °pita ; °mita ; °ṭhapita. — **upon,** vañceti. °**ing,** *a.* uḷāra ; mahāteja ; vimhayāvaha.

Imposition, *n.* 1. āropaṇa ; niyamana, *n.t.* 2. kara ; bali, *m.* 3. sāṭheyya, *nt.*

Impossible, *a.* asakya ; asādhiya ; abhabba. °**bility,** *n.* asādhiyatta ; asakyatta ; abhabbatta, *nt.* °**bly,** *adv.* asambhavena.

Impost, *n.* kara ; bali ; suṅka, *m.*

Impostor, *n.* kuhaka ; patirūpaka ; vañcaka ; nekatika, *m.*

Imposture, see **Fraud.**

Impotence, *n.* dubbalya.

Impotent, *a.* 1. dubbala ; asamattha; 2. niratthaka. °**ly,** *adv.* dubbalākārena.

Impound, *v.t.* 1. vaje pakkhipati *or* rundheti; 2. rājāyattīkaroti. *p.p.* °pakkhitta ; °ruddha ; °kata.

Impoverish, *v.t.* 1. niddhanīkaroti ; 2. balam apaharati. *p.p.* °kata ; apahaṭabala. °**ment,** *n.* dāḷiddiya ; niddhanatta, *nt.*

Impracticable, *a.* asādhiya; duppayojiya. °**ably,** *adv.* asādhiyākārena.

Impractical, *a.* dukkara ; asādhiya.

Imprecate, *v.t.* abhisapati. *p.p.* abhisatta. °**ion,** *n.* abhisapana, *nt.* sāpa, *m.* °**tory,** *a.* abhisāpayutta.

Imprecision, *n.* ayathākaraṇa, *nt.*

Impregnable, *a.* duppadhaŋsiya; dujjaya ; anabhibhavanīya.

Impregnate, *v.t.* 1. anto vyāpeti ; 2. gabbhaŋ gaṇhāpeti. *p.p.* °pita. °**ed,** *a.* āpannasattā. °**ion,** *n.* gabbhagaṇhāpana, *nt.*

Impress, *v.t.* 1. muddeti ; lañcheti ; 2. daḷhaŋ patiṭṭhāpeti; 3. citte sannidahati. *p.p.* °dita ; °chita ; °pita ; °sannihita. *n.* ciṇha ; lañchana, *nt.* muddā, *f.* °**ion,** *n.* 1. lañchana, *nt.* 2. hadayagata-bhāva, *m.* °**ive,** *a.* cittārādhaka ; hadayaṅgama. °**iveness,** *n.* hadayaṅgamatta, *nt.* °**ively,** *adv.* manoharākārena.

Impressionable, *a.* 1. manorañjaka ; 2. ciṇhapatiṭṭhāpaka.

Imprest, *n.* saccakāra, *m.*

Imprimis, *adv.* paṭhamataraŋ.

Imprint, *v.t.* 1. muddeti ; lañcheti ; 2. (citte) niveseti. *p.p.* °dita ; °chita ; °sita.

Imprison, *v.t.* avarodheti ; kārāyaŋ pakkhipati. *p.p.* °dhita ; °khitta. °**ment,** *n.* rundhana ; kārāpakkhipana, *nt.*

Improbable, *a.* asambhaviya ; bhavitum-asakya. °**bility,** *n.* asambhava, *m.* anupapatti ; bhavitum-asakyatā, *f.*

Improbity, *n.* vaṅkatā, *f.* sāṭheyya ; anajjava, *nt.*

Impromptu, *adv.* nirussāhena ; anāyāsena.

Improper, *a.* anucita ; ayogga ; ananucchavika; appatirūpa. °**ly,** *adv.* ayathā ; asammā ; ayoniso ;

asādhukaŋ. — **place,** aṭṭhāna; anāyatana, *nt.* — **time,** avelā, *f.* akāla, *m.*

Impropriate, *v.t.* puggalādhīnaŋ *or* puggalāyattaŋ karoti. *p.p.* °kata. °**ion,** *n.* puggalāyattakaraṇa, *nt.*

Impropriety, *n.* anucitatta; ayoggatta, *nt.* ayutti, *f.*

Improve, *v.t.* abhivaḍḍheti; bhāveti; brūheti. *p.p.* °ḍhita; bhāvita; brūhita. °**able,** *n.* abhivaḍḍhetabba; vaḍḍhanīya. °**ment,** *n.* abhivaḍḍhana, *nt.* unnati; samiddhi, *f.* udaya, *m.*

Improvidence, *n.* adūradassitā; asamekkhakāritā, *f.*

Improvident, *a.* adūradassī; adīghadassī. °**ly,** *adv.* asamekkha; avivicca.

Improvisate, *v.t.* taṅkhaṇaŋ racayati. °**tor,** *n.* taṅkhaṇa-racaka, *m.*

Improvise, *v.t.* khaṇapaṭibhāṇena karoti *or* vadati; ṭhānocitaŋ karoti. *p.p.* °kata; °vutta.

Imprudence, *n.* 1. adūradassitā; asamekkhā, *f.* 2. agārava; avinaya, *m.*

Imprudent, *a.* avicakkhaṇa; adūradassī; sahasākārī. °**ly,** *adv.* avicārena; ananuvicca.

Impuberal, *a.* appattavaya; nālaṅkammaniya.

Impuberty, *n.* appattavayatā, *f.*

Impudence, *n.* pāgabbhiya; ahirikatta, *nt.* nillajjatā, *f.*

Impudent, *a.* pagabbha; dubbinīta; ahirika. °**ly,** *adv.* sappagabbhaŋ.

Impugn, *v.t.* santajjeti; paccakkhāti. *p.p.* °jita; °khāta. °**ment,** *n.* virodha; paṭikkhepa, *m.* upakkosana, *nt.*

Impuissant, *a.* dubbala; khīṇabala.

Impulse, *n.* 1. cittavega; chanda, *m.* °**ion,** *n.* samussāhana; vegajanana, *nt.* °**ive,** *a.* samussāhaka. °**ively,** *adv.* sahasā. — **of lust,** kāmavega, *m.*

Impunity, *n.* 1. daṇḍamutti; 2. aparihāni, *f.*

Impure, *a.* 1. asuddha; samala; malina; kiliṭṭha; 2. gārayha; kucchita. °**ity,** °**ness,** *n.* asuddhatta; kiliṭṭhatta; mala; kalusa, *nt.* upakkilesa, *m.* **Free from —,** anaṅgaṇa; viraja; nimmala; nikkilesa.

Impute, *v.t.* aññasmiŋ āropeti. *p.p.* °pita. °**able,** *a.* abhisambandhiya. °**ation,** *n.* ajjhāropaṇa; aññasmim āropaṇa, *nt.*

In, *prep.* anto; majjhe. —**another place,** aññattha, *adv.* — **another way,** aññathā, *adv.* — **between,** antarā, *adv.* —**both sides,** ubhato, *adv.* — **both ways,** ubhayathā, *adv.* — **breadth,** vitthārena. — **front,** purato; abhimukhe, *adv.* — **many ways,** anekadhā, *adv.* — **the absence,** parammukhā, *adv.* — **the presence,** sammukhā; abhimukhe. — **the same manner,** tath'eva, *ind.* — **a short time,** acirena, *adv.* — **six days,** chāhena, *adv.* — **that instant,** sapadi, *adv.* — **what respect,** kenākārena? — **what way,** kathaŋ? *adv.*

Inability, *n.* asāmatthiya; dubbalya, *nt.*

Inabstinence, *n.* avirati, *f.*

Inaccessible, *a.* duppavesa; duggama.

Inaccuracy, *n.* vitathatta ; atacchatta, *nt.*

Inaccurate, *a.* vitatha ; ataccha ; ayathābhūta. °**ly**, *adv.* ayathā.

Inaction, Inactivity, *n.* ananuṭṭhāna ; ālasya ; udāsīnatta, *nt.*

Inactive, *a.* akammasīlī ; olīnavuttika ; anuyyogī.

Inadaptable, *a.* akammañña ; nālaŋkammaniya. °**bility**, *n.* akammaniyatta, *nt.*

Inadequate, *a.* akkhama ; asamattha ; appahoṇaka. °**ly**, *adv.* appahoṇākārena. asāmatthiyena. °**quacy**, *n.* asāmatthiya ; appahoṇakatta, *nt.*

Inadherent, *a.* alagga ; asatta.

Inadhesive, *a.* algganasabhāva.

Inadmissible, *a.* anādeyya ; agayha ; asampaṭicchiya.

Inadvertent, *a.* pamatta ; anavadhāna. °**ly**, *adv.* anavadhānena ; pamādena. °**tence**, *n.* pamāda, *m.* anavadhāna, *nt.*

Inalienable, *a.* aviyojiya ; avinibbhoga ; avibhajiya.

Inalterable, *a.* aparivattiya.

Inane, *a. n.* ritta ; suñña ; niratthaka.

Inanimate, *a.* nijjīva ; aviññāṇaka.

Inanition, *n.* suññatta, *nt.*

Inappeasable, *a.* avupasamiya.

Inappellable, *a.* apunavicāraṇīya ; apunavinicchiya.

Inapplicable, *a.* anupayojiya ; anucita. °**cation**, *n.* anupayoga; anuyyoga ; anabhinivesa, *m.*

Inapposite, *a.* aṭṭhānayutta.

Inappreciable, *a.* atyappaka ; avibhūta ; avyatta. °**ciation**, *n.* 1. avibhūtatta ; apākaṭatta ; 2. asampaṭicchana, *nt.*

Inapprehensible, *a.* duravabodha ; duviññeyya. °**sive**, *a.* nirāsaṅka ; vītabhaya.

Inapproachable, *a.* durupasaṅkama ; durāsada.

Inappropriate, *a.* anucita ; ayogga.

Inapt, *a.* asamattha ; anipuṇa ; abhabba. °**itude**, *n.* asāmatthiya ; anipuṇatta ; abhabbatta, *nt.* °**ly**, *adv.* anipuṇākārena ; asammā.

Inarm, *v.t.* āliṅgati ; parissajati. *p.p.* °gita ; parissaṭṭha.

Inarticulate, *a.* avyatta ; apphuṭa ; avisada. °**ly**, *adv.* avisadākārena.

Inartificial, *a.* akittima ; animmita.

Inartistic, *a.* asippānukūla.

Inasmuch, *adv.* yasmā ; yena ; yato.

Inattention, *n.* anavadhānatā ; assavaṇatā, *f.*

Inattentive, *a.* nirapekkha ; anohitasota ; anavadhāna. °**ness**, *n.* anavadhānatta, *nt.*

Inaudible, *a.* savaṇāgocara ; assutigocara.

Inaugural, *a.* ārambhavisayaka.

Inaugurate, *v.t.* 1. ārabhati ; patiṭṭhāpeti ; 2. adhikāre niveseti. *p.p.* āraddha ; °pita ; °sita. °**ion**, *n.* ārambha, *m.* pavesamaṅgala, *nt.*

Inauspicious, *a.* asubha ; avamaṅgala ; abhaddaka. °**ly**, *adv.* abhaddakaŋ ; asubhākārena.

Inborn, Inbred, *a.* sahaja; nesaggika; sabhāvasiddha.

Inbreathe, *v.t.* assasati. *p.p.* °sita.

Incage, *v.t.* pañjare pakkhipati. *p.p.* °khitta.

Incalculable, *a.* asaṅkheyya; appameyya.

Incandesce, *v.t.* uttāpeti. *p.p.* °pita. °**nce,** *n.* accuṇhatta, *nt.* °**nt,** *a.* uttatta; sajotibhūta.

Incantation, *n.* mantajappana, *nt.*

Incapable, *a.* akkhama; asamattha; abhabba. °**bility,** *n.* akkhamatta; abhabbatta, *nt.* °**bly,** *adv.* asamatthākārena.

Incapacious, *a.* aputhula; sambādha.

Incapacitate, *v.t.* abhabbaŋ karoti; vikalayati. *p.p.* abhabbakata; °yita.

Incapacity, *n.* 1. asāmatthiya; abhabbatta, *nt.* anupayogitā, *f.* 2. buddhihīnatā, *f.*

Incarcerate, *v.t.* kārāyaŋ pakkhipati. *p.p.* °khitta. °**ion,** *n.* rundhana; kārāpakkhipana, *nt.*

Incarnadine, *a.* maŋsavaṇṇa, *v.t.* rattavaṇṇaŋ karoti.

Incarnate, *a.* sarīrībhūta; dissamāna. *v.t.* dissamānavesaŋ gaṇhāti; sasarīro bhavati. *p.p.* gahitavesa; sasarīrībhūta. °**ion,** *n.* 1. punaravatāra; 2. sasarīrapātubhāva, *m.*

Incase, *v.t.* kose pakkhipati; ācchādeti. *p.p.* °khitta; °dita.

Incatinate, *v.t.* āvuṇāti. *p.p.* āvuta. °**ion,** *n.* āvuṇana; uddānakaraṇa, *nt.*

Incautious, *a.* pamatta; anavadhāna.

Incendiary, *a. n.* dahanasīla; gehajhāpaka. °**ism,** *n.* gharajhāpana, *nt.*

Incense, *n.* sugandhadhūpa, *m.* *v.t.* 1. dhūpeti; 2. uttejeti; saṅkhobheti. *p.p.* °pita; °jita; °bhita. °**ation,** *n.* gandhadhūpana, *nt.*

Incensory, *n.* dhūpabhājana, *nt.*

Incentive, *a.* uttejaka; palobhaka. *n.* uyyojana; palobhana; samuttejana, *nt.*

Inception, *n.* 1. paṭhamārambha, *m.* 2. paṭisandhi, *f.*

Inceptive, *a. n.* paṭhamārambhaka; paṭṭhāpaka.

Incertitude, *n.* sandeha; saŋsaya, *m.* vimati; kaṅkhā, *f.*

Incessant, *a.* nirantara; avicchinna; sātatika. °**ly,** *adv.* satataŋ; nirantaraŋ.

Incest, *n.* 1. adhammarāga; 2. vyabhicāra, *m.* °**uous,** *a.* ñātimethunāyatta.

Inch, *n.* aṅgula, *nt.*

Inchoate, *a.* āraddhamatta; acirāraddha. *v.t.* ārabhati. *p.p.* āraddha.

Incidence, *n.* siddhi; sabhāvasiddhi, *f.*

Incident, *n.* pasaṅga, *m.* antarāsiddhi, *f.* adj. sijjhamāna; pāsaṅgika; sabhāvasiddha. °**al,** *a.* āgantuka; anusaṅgika. °**ally,** *adv.* pasaṅgavasena; yadicchāya.

Incinerate, *v.t.* bhasmīkaroti. *p.p.* °kata.

Incipient, *a.* mūlabhūta; paṭhamārambhaka. °**ly,** *adv.* ārambhasamakālam eva.

Incise, *v.t.* kantati; nikantati. *p.p.* °tita. °**ion,** *n.* kattana; nikantana; chindana, *nt.* °**ive,** *a.* nikantaka.

Incite, *v.t.* ussāheti; uttejeti; uyyojeti. *p.p.* °hita; °jita. °**ation,** °**ment,** samussāhana; samuttejana, *nt.*

Incivility, *n.* avinītatta; anādariya, *nt.* asabbhatā, *f.*

Inclasp, *v.t.* parissajati; upagūhati. *p.p.* parissaṭṭha; °gūhita.

Inclemency, *n.* niddayatta; kakkasatta, *nt.* °**ment,** *a.* kakkasa; niddaya; niṭṭhura.

Incline, *n.* pabbhāra, *m.* *n.* poṇaṭṭhāna, *nt.* *v.i.* onamati; poṇībhavati. *p.p.* onata; °bhūta. *v.t.* onāmeti; poṇīkaroti. *p.p.* °mita; °kata. °**ation,** *n.* 1. poṇatta; pabbhāratta, *nt.* 2. abhinivesa, *m.* adhimutti, *f.* — **towards,** adhimuccati. °**ed towards,** tanninna; tappoṇa, *a.*

Include, *v.t.* antokaroti; samodahati. *p.p.* °kata; °hita. °**ed,** *a.* antogata; pariyāpanna. °**ing,** *a.* niravasesa; abhivyāpaka.

Inclusion, *n.* saṅgaṇhana; antokaraṇa, *nt.* °**sive,** *a.* niravasesa; abhivyāpaka. °**sively,** *adv.* niravasesena; sākallena; nissesaŋ.

Incoercible, *a.* duppasaha; durāsada.

Incogitable, *a.* acintāvisayaka.

Incognito, *a.* *n.* aññātanāma; paṭicchannavesa. *adv.* apākaṭavesena; paṭicchannākārena.

Incognizance, *n.* asañjānana, *nt.* anupaladdhi, *f.* °**zable,** *a.* anupalakkhiya; asañjāniya. °**zant,** *n.* anupalakkhaka, *m.*

Incoherent, *a.* asambaddha; vippayutta. °**ence,** *n.* asaṅgati; viyuttatā, *f.*

Incohesion, *n.* anallīyana, *nt.* asaṅgati, *f.*

Incombustible, *a.* aḍayha; adahanakkhama.

Income, *n.* āya; udaya; dhanāgama, *m.* °**tax,** *n.* āyabali, *m.* °**ing,** *a.* āgacchamāna.

Incomer, *n.* antopavisaka; videsāgata, *m.*

Incommensurate, *a.* asamaparimāṇa; aghaṭiyamāna. °**surable,** *a.* 1. asamappamāṇa; 2. atakkānugata.

Incommode, *v.t.* āyāseti; pīḷeti. *p.p.* °sita; pīḷita. °**ious,** *a.* aphāsuka; sambādha; pīḷākara.

Incommunicable, *a.* anivedaniya; avattabba. °**cative,** *a.* anivedaka; avadanasīla.

Incommutable, *a.* aparivattiya; avipariṇāmiya.

Incompact, *a.* asambaddha; asaṅgata.

Incomparable, *a.* asadisa; atula; nirupama; anupameya; appaṭisama. °**bly,** *adv.* anupameyākārena.

Incompassionate, *a.* akāruṇika; niddaya.

Incompatible, *a.* ananurūpa; aññamaññaviruddha.

Incompetence, *n.* akosalla, *nt.* adakkhatā, *f.* °**tent,** *a.* asamattha; anipuṇa; abhabba. °**tently,** *adv.* anipuṇākārena.

Incomplete, *a.* asampuṇṇa; aniṭṭhita; asamāpita; ūna. °**ly,** *adv.* sāvasesaŋ; asampuṇṇaŋ. °**ness,** *n.* aparipuṇṇatta; aniṭṭhitatta; ūnatta, *nt.*

Incomplex, *a.* amissita ; asaṅkiṇṇa.

Incomprehensible, *a.* aviññeyya ; duravabodha ; avediya.

Incomputable, *a.* asaṅkheyya ; gaṇanātīta.

Inconceivable, *a.* acintiya ; dubbiññeyya. °**bility,** *n.* acintiyatta ; dubbiññeyyatta, *nt.*

Inconclusive, *a.* nicchayarahita ; anicchita.

Incondensable, *a.* aghanīkaraṇīya.

Inconformity, *n.* ananucchavikatā, *f.* asādissa, *nt.*

Incongruity, *n.* visadisatta ; aghaṭiyamānatta, *nt.*

Incongruous, *a.* visadisa ; aghaṭiyamāna.

Inconsecutive, *a.* kamaviruddha ; uppaṭipāṭika.

Inconsequent, *a.* ñāyaviruddha. °**ence,** *n.* yuttivirodha, *m.* °**ial,** *a.* asāra ; niratthaka.

Inconsiderable, *a.* agaṇetabba ; asallakkhiya ; appamattaka.

Inconsiderate, *a.* avivekī ; asamekkhakārī. °**ly,** *adv.* asamekkha ; ananuvicca. °**ness,** *n.* avicāraṇā ; anupaparikkhā, *f.*

Inconsistent, *a.* aghaṭiyamāna ; pubbāparaviruddha. °**ence,** *n.* asaṅgati ; pubbāparavirodha, *m.* °**ly,** *adv.* pubbāparavirodhena ; asaṅgatiyā.

Inconsolable, *a.* anassāsiya.

Inconspicuous, *a.* avisada ; avyatta ; apākaṭa.

Inconstant, *a.* capala ; cañcala ; athira. °**ancy,** *n.* athiratta, *nt.* anavaṭṭhiti. °**ly,** *adv.* athirākārena.

Inconsumable, *a.* avināsiya.

Incontestable, *a.* vivādarahita ; apaṭikkosiya.

Incontinent, *a.* taṇhāvasika ; atitta. °**nence,** *n.* ajitindriyatā ; āsābahulatā ; atitti, *f.*

Incontrollable, *a.* avidheya ; adamma ; anassava.

Incontrovertible, *a.* avivaditabba ; appaṭikkosiya.

Inconvenience, *n.* aphāsutā, *f.* āyāsa, *m.* °**nient,** *a.* aphāsuka ; āyāsakara. °**niently,** *adv.* kasirena ; aphāsutāya.

Inconvertible, *a.* avinimeyya ; aparivattiya.

Inconvincible, *a.* asaddahāpiya ; anavabodhiya.

Inco-ordination, *n.* asahayogitā, *f.*

Incorporate, *v.t.* saṃyojeti ; sammisseti. *v.i.* ekībhavati ; missīyati. *p.p.* °jita ; °sita ; ekībhūta ; missita. adj. ekībhūta ; gaṇībhūta.

Incorporeal, *a.* asarīrika ; arūpa. °**ity,** *n.* asarīratta, *nt.*

Incorrect, *a.* 1. sadosa ; 2. ataccha ; ayathābhūta. °**ly,** *adv.* sadosaṃ ; atacchākārena. °**ness,** *n.* sadosatta ; vitathatta, *nt.*

Incorrigible, *a.* avidheya ; avineya ; appaṭikamma. °**bility,** *n.* avineyyatā ; anassavatā, *f.* °**bly,** *adv.* avidheyākārena.

Incorrodible, *a.* amalaggāhaka.

Incorrupt, *a.* adūsita ; nimmala. °**ible,** *a.* 1. adūsiya ; 2. apāpavasa. °**ness,** *n.* aduṭṭhatta ; suddhatta, *nt.*

Incrassate, *a.* thūla ; uddhumāta.

Increase, *n*. vuddhi ; abhivuddhi ; samiddhi ; unnati, *f*. udaya ; upacaya, *m*. *v.i*. vaḍḍhati ; virūhati ; unnamati. *v.t*. vaḍḍheti ; brūheti ; bhāveti. *p.p*. °ḍhita ; virūḷha ; unnata ; °ḍhita ; °hita ; °vita. °**ing**, *a*. vaḍḍhamāna.

Incredible, *a*. asaddheya ; apaccayika ; avissāsiya. °**bility**, *n*. asaddheyyatta ; anādeyatta. °**bly**, *adv*. asaddheyyākārena.

Incredulity, *n*. appaccaya ; avissāsa, *m*. āsaṅkā, *f*. °**lous**, *a*. saṅkābahula ; asaddahanta.

Increment, *n*. vuḍḍhi, *f*. lābha, *m*. vuddhippamāṇa, *nt*.

Increscent, *a*. upacīyamāna.

Incriminate, *v.t*. aparādhena codeti. *p.p*. °dita.

Incrustation, *n*. ghanattaca, *m*. papaṭikā, *f*.

Incubate, *v.i*. aṇḍāni sedeti *or* adhisayati. *p.p*. seditaṇḍa. °**ion**, *n*. aṇḍādhisayana, *nt*.

Incubus, *n*. supina-pisāca, *m*.

Inculcate, *v.t*. sādhukaŋ sikkhāpeti ; manasi nivesāpeti. *p.p*. °pita. °**ion**, *n*. manasi nidahana, *nt*.

Inculpate, *v.t*. codeti ; dosam āropeti. *p.p*. codita ; āropitadosa.

Incumbent, *n*. pālakādhipati ; adhikārī, *m*. adj. padhāna ; āvassaka.

Incunabula, *n*. mūlikāvatthā, *f*.

Incur, *v.t*. nigacchati ; pāpuṇāti. — **debt**, iṇaṭṭho hoti. — **sin**, pāpaŋ pasavati. — a **penalty**, daṇḍāraho hoti.

Incurable, *a*. atekiccha ; appatikāra.

Incurious, *a*. akotūhalika.

Incursion, *n*. pakkhandana ; paradesakkamana, *nt*.

Incurvation, *n*. ānamana, *nt*.

Incuse, *n*. uṭṭhāpita-lañchana, *nt*. *v.t*. lañchanaŋ uṭṭhāpeti.

Indebted, *a*. iṇaṭṭha ; iṇāyika. °**ness** *n*. iṇāyikatta, *nt*.

Indecent, *a*. gamma ; anariya ; asabbha. °**cency**, *n*. asiṭṭhatta ; avinītatta, *nt*. °**ly**, *adv*. gammākārena ; nillajjaŋ.

Indecipherable, *a*. dubbāciya ; avisadakkhara.

Indecision, *n*. sandeha ; avinicchaya, *m*. kaṅkhā ; vimati, *f*.

Indecisive, *a*. sandiddha ; dveḷhakajāta ; anavaṭṭhita. °**ly**, *adv*. sasandehaŋ.

Indeclinable, *n*. avyaya, *nt*. nipāta, *m*. adj. avibhajiya ; avibhattika.

Indecorous, *a*. asobhana ; amanuñña ; anucita.

Indecorum, *n*. anācāra, *m*. anucitatta, *nt*.

Indeed, *adv*. addhā ; nūnaŋ ; jātu ; kāmaŋ ; ve ; have ; ekantena.

Indefatigable, *a*. ajeyya ; daḷhatthāma ; thirādhiṭṭhāna. °**bility**, *n*. alīnaviriyatta, *nt*.

Indefeasible, *a*. anapaharaṇīya.

Indefectible, *a*. 1. niddosa ; 2. avirajjhamāna ; akkhaya.

Indefensible, *a*. durakkhiya ; arakkhiya.

Indefinable, *a*. avyākaraṇīya.

Indefinite, *a.* aniyata; avinicchita; atīrita. °**ly,** *adv.* aniyatākārena.

Indelible, *a.* avināsiya; alopiya. °**bly,** *adv.* alopiyākārena.

Indelicate, *a.* pharusa; avinīta. °**ly,** *adv.* pharusākārena. °**cacy,** *n.* pharusatta; avinītatta, *nt.*

Indemnify, *v.t.* 1. paṭikaroti; hāniŋ pūreti; 2. daṇḍanato rakkhati. *p.p.* °kata; pūritahānī; °khita.

Indemnity, *n.* 1. acodiyatā, *f.* 2. abhayadāna, *nt.* 3. paṭikamma; hānipūraṇa, *nt.*

Indemonstrable, *a.* anidassanīya; sayaŋsiddha.

Indentation, *n.* dantasampādana, *nt.*

Indenture, *n.* paṭiññāpaṇṇa, *nt.*

Independence, *n.* aparavasatā; sādhīnatā, *f.*

Independent, *a.* aparādhīna; serī; anissita. °**ly,** *adv.* sādhīnatāya.

Indescribable, *a.* vaṇṇanāvisayātīta. °**ly,** *adv.* avaṇṇiyākārena.

Indescriptive, *a.* vitthārarahita.

Indesignate, *a.* aparicchinna.

Indestructible, *a.* avināsiya; aviddhaŋsiya.

Indeterminable, *a.* anupalakkhiya; tīraṇāvisaya; vinicchayātīta.

Indeterminate, *a.* aniyata; anicchita. °**ion,** *n.* anicchaya, *m.*

Indevotion, *n.* assaddhiya; amāmakatta, *nt.*

Indevout, *a.* assaddha; bhattihīna.

Index, *n.* sūci; anukkamaṇikā, *f.* uddāna, *nt.*

India, *n.* Jambudīpa; Bhāratadesa, *m.* °**an,** *a.* Bhāratīya.

Indicate, *v.t.* sūceti; nirūpeti; niddisati. *p.p.* °cita; °pita; niddiṭṭha. °**ion,** *n.* 1. upadesa, *m.* sūcana; nirūpana; 2. ciṇha; visesalakkhaṇa, *nt.* °**ive,** *a.* °**tory,** *a.* sūcaka; nirūpaka; nidassaka. °**tor,** *n.* nidassaka, *m.*

Indicative mood, *n.* yathatthappakāsaka-kriyā, *f.*

Indict, *v.t.* codeti; upavadati. *p.p.* codita; upavutta. °**ment,** *n.* codanā, *f.* dosāropaṇa, *nt.*

Indifference, *n.* upekkhā; majjhattatā, *f.*

Indifferent, *a.* nirapekkha; upekkhaka; majjhaṭṭha. °**ly,** *adv.* apakkhapātitāya; majjhattatāya.

Indigene, *n.* dāḷiddiya; dīnatta, *nt.*

Indigenous, *a.* sadesajāta; sakadesīya.

Indigent, *a.* duggata; niddhana. °**ly,** *adv.* dīnākārena.

Indigested, *a.* apariṇata; ajiṇṇa. °**tible,** *a.* dujjara. °**tion,** *n.* ajīraka, *nt.* mandagahaṇitā, *f.* alasaka, *nt.*

Indignant, *a.* kopākula; sarosa; ruṭṭha. °**ly,** *adv.* sakopaŋ.

Indignation, *n.* kodha; kopa, *m.* anattamanatā, *f.*

Indignity, *n.* avamāna; paribhava, *m.* avaññā, *f.*

Indigo, *n.* nīlī, *f.*

Indirect, *a.* pariyāyabhūta; anujugāmī. °**ly,** *adv.* pariyāyena.

Indiscernible, *a.* avibhūta; duviññeyya-visesa; adiṭṭhigocara.

Indiscipline, *n.* asikkhitatta, *nt.* avinaya, *m.*

Indiscreet, *a.* avicakkhaṇa ; avivecaka ; adūradassī. °**ly,** *adv.* asamekkha ; avīmaŋsitvā.

Indiscrete, *a.* abhedagata. °**ion,** *n.* avicāraṇā ; anupaparikkhā, *f.* akosalla, *nt.*

Indiscriminate, *a.* 1. avivecaka ; avicāraka ; 2. nibbisesa ; aparicchinna ; 3. saṅkiṇṇā : saṅkula. °**ion,** *n.* avicāraṇā ; aparicchindanā, *f.* °**ing,** *a.* avisesaka ; aparicchindaka.

Indispensable, *a.* āvassaka ; aparihāriya ; apariccajiya. °**ly,** *adv.* avassena.

Indispose, *v.t.* 1. virameti ; 2. gilānayati ; akallataŋ pāpeti. *p.p.* °mita ; °yita ; °pita. °**ed,** *a.* gilāna ; akallaka. °**ition,** *n.* 1. gelañña, *nt.* akallatā, *f.* 2. arati ; aruci, *f.*

Indisputable, *a.* vivādarahita. °**bly,** *adv.* avivādena ; nissaṅkaŋ.

Indissoluble, *a.* avibhājiya ; avinibbhoga ; thira.

Indistinct, *a.* apākaṭa ; avyatta ; avisada. °**ly,** *adv.* avibhūtaŋ ; apākaṭaŋ. °**ness,** avibhūtatta ; apākaṭatta, *nt.*

Indistinguishable, *a.* anupalakkhiya ; aparicchindiya ; avisesiya.

Indistributable, *a.* avebhaṅgiya.

Indite, *v.t.* racayati ; nibandhati. *p.p.* racita ; nibaddha.

Individual, *n.* puggala, *m.* adj. pacceka ; puggalika. °**ity,** *n.* 1. pāṭekkatā ; puggalikatā, *f.* 2. attabhāva ; sakkāya, *m.* °**ly,** *adv.* paccekaŋ ; pāṭekkaŋ ; paccattaŋ. °**ism,** *n.* attakāmatā, *f.*

Individuate, *v.t.* pāṭipuggalikaŋ karoti. *p.p.* °kata.

Indivisible, *a.* abhājiya ; abhejja.

Indocile, *a.* dubbaca ; dubbineya. °**ity,** *n.* dovacassa, *nt.*

Indolence, *n.* ālasya ; kosajja, *nt.* tandī, *f.*

Indolent, *a.* alasa ; nirussāha. °**ly,** *adv.* alasatāya.

Indomitable, *a.* 1. mahussāha ; anivattiya ; 2. duddamiya ; avineya.

Indoor, *a.* gehabbhantarika.

Indoors, *adv.* antogehe.

Indorsation, *n.* thirīkaraṇa, *nt.* punalikhana, *nt.*

Indubitable, *a.* avisaṅkiya ; nissaŋsaya.

Induce, *v.t.* 1. uyyojeti ; 2. palobheti. *p.p.* °jita ; °bhita. °**ment,** *n.* 1. uyyojana ; 2. palobhana, *nt.*

Induct, *v.t.* 1. antokaroti ; 2. adhikāre niyojeti ; 3. abhijānāpeti. °**ion,** *n.* 1. antokaraṇa ; 2. niyojana, *nt.* 3. anumāna, *m.* °**ive,** *a.* 1. anumeya ; 2. (vijju-) vāhaka. °**tor,** *n.* 1. adhikāre niyojaka, *m.* 2. vijjuvāhaka, *m.*

Indulge, *v.i.* abhiramati ; āsajjati ; nirato hoti. *v.t.* abhirameti ; upalāleti. *p.p.* abhirata ; āsatta ; nirata ; °mita ; °lita. °**nce,** *n.* 1. abhiramaṇa, *nt.* āsatti, *f.* 2. tosana ; lālana, *nt.* 3. anuggaha, *m.* °**nt,** *a.* abhiramamāna ; anukūla. °**ntly,** *adv.* sānuddayaŋ ; sābhiratiŋ.

Indurate, *v.t.* kaṭhinayati ; thambheti. *v.i.* kaṭhinībhavati ; thambhīyati. *p.p.* °yita ; °bhita ; °bhūta.

Industrial, *a.* kammantavisayaka. °**ist**, *n.* kammantapayojaka, *m.* °**ly**, *adv.* kammantānusārena.

Industrious, *a.* kiccāsatta ; saussāha. °**ly**, *adv.* saussāhaŋ.

Industry, *n.* 1. kammanta ; sippa, *nt.* 2. uyyoga, *m.* 3. kammasīlitā, *f.*

Indwell, *v.i.* sadā vasati. *p.p.* sadāvuttha. °**ing**, *a.* antovattī.

Inebriant, *a.* ummādakara. °**riate**, *a.* madamatta. *v.t.* madayati.

Inebriety, *n.* ummāda ; mattabhāva, *m.*

Inedible, *a.* abhojanāraha ; abhakkha.

Inedited, *a.* 1. amuddāpita ; 2. asodhitapāṭha.

Ineffable, *a.* vacanapathātīta.

Ineffaceable, *a.* anapamajjiya ; alopiya. °**bly**, *adv.* alopiyākārena.

Ineffective, °**tual**, *a.* 1. niratthaka ; nipphala ; 2. akkhama ; asamattha. °**ly**, *adv.* nipphalākārena.

Inefficacy, *n.* viphalatta ; asāmatthiya ; dubbalatta, *nt.* °**cious**, *a.* asamattha ; pabhāvarahita.

Inefficient, *a.* akāriyakkhama ; apariyatta. °**ncy**, *n.* asāmatthiya ; appahoṇakatta, *nt.* °**ly**, *adv.* anipuṇākārena.

Inelastic, *a.* anamya ; akammañña.

Inelegant, *a.* asobhana ; amanuñña ; aporiya. °**nce**, *n.* asobhanatta ; apāsādikatta, *nt.*

Ineligible, *a.* ananucchavika ; akammāraha. °**bility**, *n.* ananucchavikatta, *nt.*

Ineloquent, *a.* acittakathika ; akovidadesana.

Inept, *a.* anucita ; akovida ; mandamatika. °**ly**, *adv.* akovidākārena.

Ineptitude, *n.* anucitatta ; akovidatta, *nt.*

Inequality, *n.* vesamma ; asamānatta, *nt.*

Inequilateral, *a.* asamaŋsa ; asamabhuja.

Inequitable, *a.* adhammika ; ñāyaviruddha. °**bly**, *adv.* ñāyavirodhena.

Inequity, *n.* aññāya ; adhamma, *m.*

Ineradicable, *a.* anuppāṭanīya ; anuddhāriya.

Inerrable, *a.* anavajja ; appamatta ; avirajjhiya.

Inert, *a.* kriyāhīna ; niccala ; uyyogarahita. °**ia**, *n.* kriyāhīnapavatti ; akriyavutti, *f.* °**ly**, *adv.* kriyāhīnatāya.

Inescapable, *a.* aparihāriya ; avāriya.

Inessential, *a.* anavassaka ; appadhāna.

Inestimable, *a.* anaggha ; agghātīta. °**bly**, *adv.* anagghatāya ; amūlyabhāvena.

Inevitable, *a.* anivāriya ; avassambhāvī. °**bly**, *adv.* avassaŋ ; niyataŋ ; ekantaŋ.

Inexact, *a.* vitatha ; ayathābhūta. °**itude**, *n.* vitathatta ; micchatta, *nt.*

Inexcusable, *a.* akkhamitabba; akkhamāraha. **°bly,** *adv.* akkhamitabbatāya.

Inexecution, *n.* ananuṭṭhāna; avidahana, *nt.* **°table,** *a.* asādhiya; ananuvidheya.

Inexertion, *n.* anīhatā; anuyyogitā, *f.*

Inexhaustible, *a.* akkheyya; avināsiya. **°bility,** *n.* akkheyyatā, *f.*

Inexorable, *a.* adamma; kaṭhinahadaya. **°bly,** *adv.* thaddhahadayena.

Inexpectant, *a.* anapekkhaka; apekkhārahita.

Inexpedient, *a.* anucita; anaraha; anupapanna. **°ency,** *n.* anocitya, *nt.* anupapatti; ayutti, *f.*

Inexpensive, *a.* appaggha; appavaya.

Inexperience, *n.* akosalla; apāṭava; anipuṇatta, *nt.* **°ed,** *a.* adakkha; anipuṇa; aparicita.

Inexpert, *a.* apaṭu; anipuṇa; avisesaññū.

Inexpiable, *a.* appaṭikamma; anupasamiya.

Inexplicable, *a.* avyākaraṇīya; duravabodha. **°bly,** *adv.* avissajjiyākārena.

Inexplicit, *a.* avyatta; avisada; avyākata.

Inexpressible, *a.* vācāvisayātīta. **°bly,** *adv.* avāciyākārena; vattum asakyatāya.

Inexpugnable, *a.* anabhibhavanīya; abhejja.

Inextensible, *a.* avitthāriya.

Inextinct, *a.* avinaṭṭha.

Inextinguishable, *a.* anibbāpiya; anupasamiya.

Inextricable, *a.* avijaṭanīya; amocanīya.

Infallible, *a.* avirādhiya; ekantabhāvī. **°bility,** *n.* avirādhiyatta, *nt.* **°bly,** *adv.* avirādhiyatāya.

Infamy, *n.* ayasa, *m.* akitti, *f.* **°ous,** *a.* ayasakara; gārayha; akittidhara; duṭṭha.

Infancy, *n.* bālya, *nt.* bālāvatthā, *f.*

Infant, *n.* thanapa, *m.* **°ile,** *a.* thanapayogga; bālakocita. **°icide,** *n.* 1. bālaghātana, *nt.* 2. bālaghātaka, *m.* (of female:) dārakaghātikā, *f.*

Infantry, *n.* patti, *m.* bhaṭasenā, *f.*

Infatuate, *v.t.* moheti; muccheti. *p.p.* mohita; °chita. **°ion,** *n.* mohana, *nt.* **°ed,** *a.* giddha; anuratta. **°ing,** *a.* pamohaka; mucchājanaka.

Infeasible, *a.* asādhiya; asakya.

Infect, *v.t.* saṅkāmeti; rogakkantaṃ karoti. *p.p.* °mita; rogakkanta. **°ion,** *n.* (roga-) saṅkamana, *nt.* **°ious,** *a.* saṅkantika.

Infelicity, *n.* dukkha; dubbhāgya, *nt.* **°tous,** *a.* adhañña; alakkhika.

Infelt, *a.* hadayagata.

Infer, *v.t.* anumāneti; saṅkappeti. *p.p.* anumita; °pita. **°able,** *a.* anumeya. **°ence,** *n.* anumāna, *nt.*

Inferential, *a.* anumānasiddha.

Inferior, *a.* 1. omaka; lāmaka; oraka; nīca; 2. ninna; nīcaṭṭha; 3. amukhya; appadhāna. **°caste,** *n.* hīnakula, *nt.* **— in age,** kaṇiṭṭha, *a.* **— in rank,**

orapadaṭṭha, *a.* °**ity,** *n.* omakatta ; hīnatta, *nt.*

Infernal, *a. n.* āpāyika ; nerayika. °**ly,** *adv.* atidāruṇākārena.

Inferno, *n.* apāya, *m.* atibhayaṅkaraṭṭhāna, *nt.*

Infertile, *a.* asāra ; nissāra ; ujjaṅgala.

Infest, *v.t.* upaddaveti ; ubbāheti. *p.p.* upadduta ; ubbāḷha. °**ed with,** niccasevita ; samākiṇṇa, *a.* °**ation,** *n.* upasagga, *m.*

Infestive, *a.* 1. nippītika ; 2. amaṅgala.

Infidel, *n. a.* micchādiṭṭhika ; assaddha. °**ity,** *n.* micchādiṭṭhi ; dubbhitā, *f.*

Infiltrate, *v.t.* parissāveti, *v.i.* sukhumacchiddehi pavisati. *p.p.* °vita ; °paviṭṭha.

Infinite, *a.* ananta ; aparimita ; appamāṇa. °**ly,** *adv.* anantaŋ ; aparimitaŋ. °**ty,** °**tude,** anantatta ; aparimitatta, *nt.*

Infinitesimal, *a.* atisukhuma.

Infinitive, *n.* tum-paccayanta, *m.*

Infirm, *a.* 1. dubbala ; sattihīna ; 2. athira ; adaḷha ; 3. jiṇṇa ; jarātura. °**ity,** *n.* 1. dubbalya, *nt.* balahāni, *f.* 2. vajja, vikalatta, *nt.* 3. vyādhi, *m.*

Infirmary, *n.* gilānasālā, *f.*

Infix, *v.t.* anto paveseti ; daḷhaŋ ṭhapeti. *p.p.* °sita ; °ṭhapita.

Inflame, *v.t.* 1. santāpeti ; uttāpeti ; 2. uddīpeti ; uttejeti ; 3. kopeti ; roseti. *p.p.* °pita ; °sita, *v.i.* santapati ; ḍayhati ; kuppati. *p.p.* santatta ; daḍḍha ; kupita. °**mable,** *a.* dahanasīla ; jalanasabhāva. °**mation,** *n.* ḍāha ; tāpa, *m.* °**matory,** *a.* dāhajanaka ; tāpakara.

Inflate, *v.t.* vitthambheti ; vātena pūreti. *p.p.* °bhita ; °rita. °**ed,** *a.* uddhumāyita. °**ion,** *n.* vitthambhana ; uddhumāyana, *nt.*

Inflect, *v.t.* 1. nāmeti ; 2. (vibhattivasena) vibhajati. *p.p.* nāmita ; °jita. °**ion,** *n.* vibhattivibhāga, *m.*

Inflexible, *a.* 1. anamya ; 2. kathina ; 3. daḷhanicchaya ; thirādhiṭṭhāna. °**bility,** *n.* anamyatta ; daḷhatta ; thirādhiṭṭhānatta, *nt.* °**bly,** *adv.* sudaḷhaŋ ; suthiraŋ.

Inflexion, *n.* padarūpasādhana, *nt.*

Inflict, *v.t.* daṇḍaŋ paṇeti ; vindāpeti ; dukkhaŋ pāpeti. *p.p.* paṇītadaṇḍa ; °pita. °**ion,** *n.* vadhapāpana, *nt.* °**or,** *n.* vadhaka, *m.* — **punishment,** vadhaŋ paṇeti.

Inflorescence, *n.* mālāvaccharopaṇa, *nt.*

Inflow, *n.* anto pavahana, *nt.*

Influence, *n.* ānubhāva ; pabhāva, *m.* vasavattāpana, *nt. v.t.* vasīkaroti ; uyyojeti. *p.p.* °kata ; °jita.

Influent, *a.* antovāhaka.

Influential, *a.* mahānubhāva ; pabala. °**ly,** *adv.* pabhāvena.

Influenza, *n.* semhakopa, *m.*

Influx, *n.* āsavaṇa ; antosamosaraṇa ; antogamana, *nt.*

Inform, *v.t.* nivedeti ; jānāpeti ; āroceti ; ācikkhati. *p.p.* °dita ; °pita ; °cita ; °khita. °**ant,** *n.* nivedaka ; paṭivedaka. °**ation,**

n. 1. nivedana ; ārocana ; viññāpana, *nt.* 2. vuttanta, *m.* °**ative,** *a.* nivedaka ; viññāpaka. °**er,** *n.* dosārocaka ; vajjagavesaka, *m.*

Informal, *a.* niyamaviruddha ; upacārahīna. °**ity,** *n.* niyamavirodha, *m.* °**ly,** *adv.* vidhivirodhena.

Infra, *adv.* adho ; paraṃ.

Infraction, *n.* ullaṅghana, *nt.* vītikkama, *m.*

Infrangible, *a.* abhejja ; abhaṅgura.

Infrequent, *a.* kālika ; asātatika ; aniyatasiddhika. °**ency,** *n.* kālikatta ; anabhiṇhatta, *nt.*

Infringe, *v.t.* ullaṅgheti ; vītikkamati ; aticarati. *p.p.* °ghita ; vītikkanta ; °rita. °**ment,** *n.* ullaṅghana, *nt.* vītikkama, *m.* aticaraṇa, *nt.*

Infructuous, *a.* appasava ; aphaluppādaka.

Infrugal, *a.* aparimitavaya ; vikiraṇasīla.

Infuriate, *v.t.* see **Enrage.**

Infuse, *v.t.* anto paveseti ; nisiñcati ; pharāpeti. *p.p.* °sita ; °cita ; °pita. °**ible,** *a.* pavesanīya ; pharanīya ; siñcitabba. °**ion,** *n.* pavesana ; nisiñcana ; phuraṇa, *nt.*

Infusoria, *n. pl.* jīrakapāṇī, *m.*

Ingate, *n.* pavesadvāra, *nt.*

Ingathering, *n.* sassalāyana, *nt.* sassa-samāhāra, *m.*

Ingeminate, *v.t.* puna vadati. *p.p.* puna-vutta.

Ingenerate, *v.t.* anto uppādeti. *p.p.* °dita.

Ingenious, *a.* vicakkhaṇa ; upāyaññū ; sukhumabuddhika ; nipuṇa. °**ly,** *adv.* nipuṇākārena. °**ness,** *n.* nepuñña ; cāturiya ; pāṭava ; buddhivepulla, *nt.*

Ingenuity, *n.* kosalla, *nt.*

Ingenuous, *a.* 1. avaṅka ; asaṭha ; 2. uḷāracitta ; mahajjhāsaya. °**ly,** *adv.* ujukaṃ ; asaṭhena. °**ness,** *n.* ajjava ; uḷāratta ; mahajjhāsayatta, *nt.*

Ingest, *v.t.* āmāsaye pakkhipati. *p.p.* °khitta.

Ingle, *n.* uddhanaggi, *m.*

Inglorious, see **Infamous.**

Ingoing, *n.* pavisana. *nt.* adj. pavisamāna.

Ingot, *n.* piṇḍa, *m.*

Ingrained, *a.* sahaja ; daḷhapatiṭṭhita. °**ly,** *adv.* sahajavasena.

Ingrate, *a. n.* akataññū ; akatavedī, 3.

Ingratiate, *v.t.* ārādheti ; pasādeti ; anurañjeti. *p.p.* °dhita ; °dita ; °jita.

Ingratitude, *n.* akataññutā ; akataveditā, *f.*

Ingredient, *n.* upakaraṇa, *nt.* sambhāra, *m.*

Ingress, *n.* 1. pavisana, *nt.* 2. pavesādhikāra, *m.* 3. pavisanadvāva, *nt. v.i.* pavisati. *p.p.* paviṭṭha.

Ingrowing, *a.* antovaḍḍhamāna.

Ingulf, *v.t.* ottharati ; nimujjāpeti. *p.p.* otthaṭa ; °pita.

Ingurgitate, *v.t.* sagedhaṃ gilati. *p.p.* °gilita.

Inhabit, *v.t.* vasati ; nivasati ; ajjhāvasati ; viharati. *p.p.* vuttha ; nivuttha ; °vuttha. °**able,** *a.* vāsāraha ; nivāsayogga.

°**ancy**, *n.* thiravāsa, *m.* °**ant**, *n.* vāsī; nivāsī, *m.* °**ion**, *n.* vāsaggahana, *nt.*

Inhale, *v.t.* assasati. *p.p.* °sita. °**ation**, *n.* assāsa, *m.*

Inharmonic, *a.* aghaṭiyamāna; asaŋsandamāna.

Inharmonious, *a.* asaŋsandamāna; visaŋvādaka. °**ly**, *adv.* asaṅgatākārena.

Inhere, *v.i.* anusayati; anto vattati. *p.p.* °yita; °tita. °**nce**, *n.* anusaya; sahajaguṇa, *m.* °**nt**, *a.* anusāyika; antogata; pariyāpanna. °**ntly**, *adv.* pakatiyā; sabhāvena.

Inherit, *v.t.* dāyādī bhavati; paveṇiyā labhati. *p.p.* °bhūta; °laddha. °**able**, *a.* dāyādāraha. °**ability**, *n.* dāyādārahatta, *nt.* °**ance**, *n.* dāyajja; mātāpettika-dhana, *nt.* °**ed**, *a.* anvayāgata; pettika. °**or**, *n.* dāyādī; dāyajjasāmī, *m.*

Inheritress, *n.* dāyādinī, *f.*

Inhibit, *v.t.* see **Forbid**.

Inhospitable, *a.* asakkārasīlī; atithivimukha. °**tality**, *n.* asakkāra; appaṭisanthāra, *m.*

Inhuman, *a.* amānusika; atikakkhaḷa. °**ity**, *n.* niṭṭhuratta, *nt.* °**ly**, *adv.* atidāruṇaŋ.

Inhume, *v.t.* bhūmiyaŋ nikhaṇati *or* nidahati. *p.p.* °nikhāta; nihita. °**ation**, *n.* bhūminidahana, *nt.*

Inimical, *a.* paccatthika; vipakkha; viruddha. °**ly**, *adv.* veribhāvena; viruddhatāya.

Inimitable, *a.* asādhāraṇa; ananukaraṇīya.

Iniquity, *n.* aññāya; adhamma, *m.* °**tous**, *a.* pāpiṭṭha; adhammika. °**tously**, *adv.* adhammena; aññāyena.

Initial, *a.* ādima; purima; paṭhama. *n.* nāmamūlakkhara, *nt.* °**ly**, *adv.* ādo; ādito.

Initiate, *v.t.* 1. dikkhati; upanayati; 2. ārabhati; paṭṭhapeti. *p.p.* dikkhita; upanīta; āraddha; °pita. °**ion**, *n.* dikkhā; pabbajjā, *f.* upanayana, *nt.* °**ive**, *a. n.* paṭhamārambha, *m.* °**tory**, *a.* ādima; paṭhamārambhaka.

Inject, *v.t.* antopaveseti. *p.p.* °sita. °**ion**, *n.* antopavesana, *nt.*

Injudicial, *a.* anītipariyāpanna; ñāyaparibāhira.

Injudicious, *a.* vicārahīna; avivecaka.

Injunction, *n.* āṇā, *f.* sāsana, *nt.* niyoga; ādesa, *m.*

Injure, *v.t.* hiŋsati; vikopeti; viheṭheti. *p.p.* °sita; °pita; °ṭhita. °**ious**, *a.* pīḷākara; antarāyajanaka. °**iously**, *adv.* hiŋsāpubbakaŋ.

Injury, *n.* 1. vikopana; hiŋsana; viheṭhana, *nt.* 2. apakāra, *m.*

Injustice, *n.* ayutti, *f.* aññāya; adhamma, *m.*

Ink, *n.* lekhana-kasaṭa, *nt.* masi, *m.* *v.t.* masinā aṅketi; masiŋ yojeti. °**bottle**, °**pot**, *n.* masibhājana, *nt.* °**stand**, *n.* kajjalādhāra, *m.* °**y**, *a.* masivaṇṇa; kajjalamakkhita.

Inkling, *n.* 1. lesamattajānana; 2. iṅgita, *nt.*

Inland, *n.* desabbhantara, *nt.* adj. desabbhantarika. °**er**, *n.* desamajjhavāsī, *m*

Inlay, *n.* 1. khacita-vatthu; 2. khacana, *nt.* *v.t.* khacati; anuppaveseti. *p.p.* khacita; °sita.

Inlet, *n.* 1. pavesadvāra; āyamukha, *nt.* 2. samuddavaṅka, *m.*

Inlock, *v.t.* antokatvā pidahati. *p.p.* °pihita.

Inly, *adv.* 1. abbhantaravasena; 2. vallabhattena.

Inlying, *a.* antogata.

Inmate, *n.* nevāsika; sahavāsī; parijana, *m.*

Inmost, *a.* accabbhantarika.

Inn, *n.* 1. pathika-nivāsa, *m.* 2. pānamandira, *nt.* °**keeper**, *n.* nivāsapālaka, *m.*

Innate, *a.* nija; sahaja; nesaggika. °**ly**, *adv.* pakatiyā; sahajatāya.

Innavigable, *a.* anāvāgamanīya.

Inner, *a.* abbhantarika; antovattī. — **city**, *n.* antonagara; antepura, *nt.* — **garment**, antaravāsaka, *m.* °**most**, *a.* abbhantaratama. — **room**, antogabbha, *m.*

Innervate, *v.t.* nahāruyuttaŋ karoti.

Innocent, *a.* 1. niddosa; nirapar̄ādha; anavajja; 2. ahiŋsaka; suddhacitta. °**nce**, *n.* anavajjatta; niddosatta, *nt.* °**ly**, *adv.* niddosākārena.

Innocuous, *a.* ahiŋsaka; anapakāraka. °**ly**, *adv.* ahiŋsakākārena.

Innominate, *a.* ninnāmaka.

Innovate, *v.i.* navattaŋ janeti *or* pāpeti. *p.p.* janitanavatta; °pāpita. °**ion**, *n.* navattapāpaṇa, *nt.* navācāra, *m.*

Innoxious, *a.* ahiŋsaka; nirupaddava.

Innumerable, *a.* asaṅkhya; gaṇanātīta.

Innutrition, *n.* posaṇahāni, *f.* mandaposana, *nt.* °**tious**, *a.* aposaṇaka; ojāhīna.

Inobservance, *n.* apaṭipajjana; asallakkhana, *nt.* °**vant**, *a.* duppaṭipanna.

Inobtrusive, *a.* abādhaka.

Inoculate, *v.t.* rogabījāni saṅkāmeti *or* paveseti. *p.p.* °mitarogabīja. °**ion**, rogabījappavesana, *nt.*

Inodorous, *a.* niggandha.

Inoffensive, *a.* aheṭhaka; apīḷaka. °**ness**, *n.* ahiŋsā; adubbhitā, *f.*

Inoperative, *a.* akāriyasādhaka; akiñcikara.

Inopportune, *a.* appattakāla; asamayocita; aṭṭhānapayutta. °**ly**, *adv.* akāle; aṭṭhāne.

Inordinary, *a.* asādhāraṇa; asāmañña.

Inordinate, *a.* atimatta; pamāṇātikkanta. °**ly**, *adv.* atimattaŋ; accantaŋ. °**ness**, *n.* atimattatā, *f.* pamāṇātikkama, *m.*

Inorganic, *a.* nijjīva; anindriyaddha; aviññāṇaka.

Inorganization, *n.* vicchindana, puthakkarana, *nt.*

Inornate, *a.* analaṅkata.

Inosculate, *v.i.* heṭṭhūpariyavasena sandhīyati *or* samosarati. *p.p.* °sandhita; samosaṭa.

Inquest, *n.* upaparikkhā; vicāraṇā, *f.*

Inquire, *v.t.* vīmaŋsati; upaparikkhati; samanuyuñjati. *p.p.* °sita; °khita; °yutta. °**er,** *n.* vīmaŋsaka; upaparikkhaka, *m.* °**ry,** *n.* vīmaŋsā; upaparikkhā; paripucchā, *f.* °**ing,** *a.* anupucchaka. °**ingly,** *adv.* parikkhāvasena; ñātukāmatāya.

Inquisition, *n.* 1. parikkhā, *f.* 2. vinicchayasabhā, *f.* °**tor,** *n.* vīmaŋsaka; vicāraka, *m.*

Inquisitive, *a.* viññātukāma; paripucchaka. °**ly,** *adv.* kutūhalena; ñātukāmatāya. °**ness,** *n.* kutūhala; ñātukāmatta, *nt.*

Inroad, *n.* paradesakkamana, *nt.*

Inrush, *n.* pasayhapavesa, *m.*

Insalivate, *v.t.* (āhāraŋ) khelena misseti. *p.p.* °missita.

Insalubrious, *a.* rogajanaka; akkhema.

Insalutary, *a.* 1. ārogyabādhaka; 2. ācāradūsaka.

Insane, *a.* ummatta; bhantacitta. °**ly,** *adv.* saummādaŋ. °**ity,** °**ness,** *n.* ummāda; cittavibbhama, *m.*

Insanitary, *a.* roguppādaka; ārogyanāsaka.

Insatiable, *a.* mahiccha; atappiya; dutappiya. °**bly,** *adv.* atappiyākārena.

Insatiate, *a.* atitta; asantuṭṭha.

Inscribe, *v.t.* likhati; lekhanam āropeti. *p.p.* likhita; °pita. °**able,** *a.* lekhanīya; likhanakkhama.

Inscription, *n.* 1. lipi; lekhā, *f.* 2. pāsāṇalekhā, *f.*

Inscrutable, *a.* duravabodha; dubbiññeyya. °**bly,** *adv.* duradhigamākārena.

Insect, *n.* kīṭa, *m.* °**icidal,** *a.* kīṭaghātaka. °**ivorous,** *a.* kīṭabhakkha.

Insecure, *a.* akhema; sāsaṅka; sappaṭibhaya. °**ity,** *n.* akhematta; sabhayatta, *nt.*

Inseminate, *v.t.* (bījāni) vapati. *p.p.* vapita (-bīja).

Insensate, *a.* acetana; anindriyabaddha; naṭṭhapasāda.

Insensible, *a.* 1. hataviññāṇa; hīnindriya; naṭṭhapasāda; 2. indriyāgocara; 3. niddaya; 4. kuṇṭhabuddhika. °**bility,** *n.* mucchā; visaññā, *f.* °**bly,** *adv.* alakkhitākārena; mandamandaŋ.

Insensitive, *a.* acetana; pasādahīna. °**ness,** *n.* acetanatta, *nt.*

Insentient, *a.* nijjīva; aviññāṇaka.

Inseparable, *a.* aviyojiya; avibhājiya. °**ly,** *adv.* niccabaddhatāya.

Insert, *v.t.* odahati; antare paveseti. *p.p.* °hita; °sita. °**ion,** *n.* antare pakkhipana, *nt.*

Inset, *n.* antare-pakkhitta, *nt.* *v.t.* antare pakkhipati.

Inshore, *a.* velāsanna. *adv.* velāsanne.

Inside, *n.* abbhantara, *nt.* *adv.* anto; abbhantare.

Insidious, *a.* 1. dubbhī; vissāsaghātaka; 2. rahogata. °**ly,** *adv.* raho; dubbhākārena.

Insight, *n.* pariññā ; vipassanā, *f.* **Analytic —,** paṭisambhidā, *f.*

Insignia, *n.* abhiññāṇa ; visesaciṇha ; adhikāraciṇha, *nt.*

Insignificant, *a.* oramattaka ; asallakkhiya ; agaru ; °**cance,** *n.* lahutā ; oramattatā ; agaṇetabbatā, *f.*

Insincere, *a.* vaṅka ; asaddheyya ; avissāsiya. °**ity,** *n.* vaṅkatā ; saṭhatā, *f.* kohañña, *nt.* °**ly,** *adv.* vissāsabhaṅgena ; vaṅkatāya.

Insinuate, *v.i.* sanikaŋ pavisati *or* pattharati ; 2. pariyāyena katheti. *v.t.* sanikaŋ paveseti. *p.p.* °paviṭṭha ; patthaṭa ; °thita ; °sita. °**ion,** *n.* 1. sanikappavesa, *m.* 2. pariyāyakathā, *f.*

Insipid, *a.* 1. virasa ; niroja ; nirassāda ; 2. nitteja ; anussuka ; 3. nissāra. °**ity,** *n.* 1. virasatā ; 2. asāratā, *f.* °**ly,** *adv.* virasākārena ; aruciyā.

Insist, *v.i.* nibandhati ; daḷhagāhī hoti. *p.p.* nibaddha ; °bhūta. °**ence,** nibandhana ; daḷhāvalambhana, *nt.*

Insnare, see **Ensnare.**

Insobriety, 1. mattabhāva, *m.* soṇḍiya, *nt.* 2. calacittatā, *f.*

Insociable, *a.* asevanīya ; saŋsaggavimukha.

Insolation, *n.* ātapena pācana ; ātapatāpana, *nt.*

Insolent, *a.* unnala ; uddhata ; gabbita ; dappita. °**nce,** *n.* pāgabbhiya ; uddhacca, *nt.* °**ly,** *adv.* dappitākārena.

Insolidity, *a.* aghanatā ; athaddhatā, *f.*

Insoluble, *a.* 1. avilayanīya ; 2. avissajjiya ; atīriya. °**bility,** avilayatta ; avisajjiyatta, *nt.*

Insolvent, *a.* khīṇavibhava ; iṇasodhanakkhama. °**ncy,** *n.* khīṇadhanatā ; iṇasodhanāsakyatā, *f.*

Insomnia, *n.* niddānāsa, *m.*

Insomuch, *a.* tāvataka.

Insouciant, *a.* pamatta ; anapekkhaka.

Inspan, *v.t.* dhure *or* yuge yojeti. *p.p.* °yojita *or* yutta.

Inspect, *v.t.* parivīmaŋsati ; āloceti ; samekkhati. *p.p.* °sita ; °cita ; °khita. °**ion,** *n.* upaparikkhā ; samekkhā ; ālcoanā, *f.* °**or,** *m.* parikkhaka ; samekkhaka ; vīmaŋsī, *m.*

Inspire, *v.t.* 1. ussāheti ; 2. devānubhāvaŋ labhāpeti. *v.i.* 1. assasati ; 2. devānubhāvaŋ labhati. *p.p.* °hita ; °pita ; °sita ; laddhadevānubhāva. °**ation,** *n.* 1. uyyojana, *nt.* 2. devānubhāvalābha, *m.* °**ator,** *n.* uttejaka ; nittudaka, *m.*

Inspirit, *v.t.* samuttejeti. *p.p.* °jita.

Inspissate, *v.t.* ghanīkaroti. *p.p.* °kata.

Instable, *a.* athāvara ; cañcala. °**bility,** *n.* athāvaratta ; cañcalatta, *nt.*

Install, *v.t.* yathāvidhiŋ patiṭṭhāpeti ; adhikāre niyojeti. °**ation,** *n.* 1. adhikāraniyojana ; patiṭṭhāpana, *nt.* 2. rajjābhiseka, *m.*

Instalment, *n.* koṭṭhāsa ; bhāga, *m.*

Instance, *n.* 1. udāharaṇa ; nidassana, *nt.* 2. avasara ; samaya, *m.*

v.t. niddisati; udāharati. *p.p.* niddiṭṭha; udāhaṭa.

Instant, *n.* khaṇa; muhutta, *m.* °**ly,** *adv.* sajju; sapadi; tāvad eva.

Instantaneous, *a.* taṅkhaṇika; aciraṭṭhitika. °**ly,** *adv.* khaṇena; taṅkhaṇe. °**ness,** *n.* taṅkhaṇikatta, *nt.*

Instate, *v.t.* ṭhānantare patiṭṭhāpeti. *p.p.* °pita.

Instauration, *n.* paṭisaṅkharaṇa, *nt.*

Instead, *adv.* Expressed by *ṭhāne,* etc. — **of my brother,** mayhaŋ bhātu ṭhāne. — **of saying,** bhaṇitabbe.

Instep, *n.* piṭṭhipāda, *m.* pādapiṭṭhi, *f.*

Instigate, *v.t.* ussāheti; uttejeti. *p.p.* °hita; °jita. °**tion,** *n.* uttejana; uyyojana, *nt.* °**tor,** *n.* nittudaka; uttejaka, *m.*

Instil, *v.t.* sanikaŋ paveseti *or* sikkhāpeti. *p.p.* °sita; °pita.

Instinct, *n.* sahajañāṇa, *nt.* pakatibuddhi, *f.* adj. sampayutta. °**ive,** *a.* sahaja; pakatisiddha. °**ively,** *adv.* pakatiyā; sahajabuddhiyā.

Institute, *n.* 1. vijjādharaparisā, *f.* 2. vijjāyatana, *nt.* 3. vidhiniyama, *m.* vavatthā, *f.* *v.t.* 1. ārabhati; patiṭṭhāpeti; 2. vavatthapeti; paññāpeti. *p.p.* āraddha; °pita; °**ion,** *n.* 1. patiṭṭhāpana, *nt.* 2. sammuti; paññatti, *f.* 3. vijjālaya, *m.*

Instruct, *v.t.* 1. anusāsati; sikkhāpeti; 2. bodheti; 3. āṇāpeti. *p.p.* anusiṭṭha; °pita; °dhita; aṇātta. °**ion,** *n.* 1. sikkhāpana; vinayana; anusāsana, *nt.* 2. āṇā, *f.* niyoga, *m.* °**ive,** *a.* upadesadāyaka; sikkhāpaka. °**or,** *n.* upadesaka; anusāsaka; ācariya, *m.* °**ress,** *n.* ācariyānī; upajjhāyā, *f.*

Instrument, *n.* upakaraṇa; upakārakavatthu, *nt.* (In law:) paṭiññāpaṇṇa, *nt.* °**al,** *a.* 1. hetubhūta; upakaraṇabhūta; 2. karaṇavibhatti, *f.* °**ality,** *n.* hetubhāva, *m.* kāraṇatta, *nt.* °**ally,** *adv.* kāraṇato; nimittato.

Instrumentation, *n.* 1. turiyavādanakkama, *m.* 2. sallakamma, *nt.*

Insubjection, *n.* aparavasatā; aparādhīnatā, *f.*

Insubmission, *n.* anassavatā; sādhīnatā, *f.*

Insubordinate, *a.* avasavattī; avidheya. °**ion,** avasavattitā, *f.*

Insubstantial, *a.* addabba; avatthuka; asāra.

Insufferable, *a.* asayha; dukkhama; dussaha. °**bly,** *adv.* asayhākārena.

Insufficient, *a.* appahoṇaka; ūna. °**ncy,** *n.* 1. ūnatta; appahoṇakatta, *nt.* 2. ayoggatta, *nt.* °**ly,** *adv.* appahoṇakatāya.

Insular, *a.* 1. jalapariveṭhita; 2. dīpavisayaka; 3. apatthaṭañāṇa.

Insulate, *v.t.* puthakkaroti; kevalattaŋ pāpeti. *p.p.* °kata; °pāpita. °**ion,** puthakkaraṇa, *nt.*

Insult, *v.t.* nindati; akkosati; avajānāti; avamāneti. *p.p.* nindita; akkuṭṭha; avaññāta; avamata, *n.* nindā; avaññā, *f.*

paribhava, *m.* āsajjana,*nt.* °**ing**, *a.* avamānajanaka. °**ingly**, *adv.* sāvamānaŋ.

Insuperable, *a.* alaṅghiya ; dujjaya ; duratikkama ; anabhibhavanīya. °**bly**, *adv.* duratikkamatāya.

Insupportable, *a.* dussaha ; durubbaha. °**bly**, *adv.* durubbahākārena.

Insuppressible, *a.* dunniggayha ; dunnivāriya.

Insure, *v.t.* khemaŋ karoti. *p.p.* khemīkata. °**ance**, *n.* 1. khemakaraṇa, *nt.* 2. khemadhanasañcaya, *m.*

Insurgent, *a.* rājadubbhaka. °**ence**, *n.* rājaviddesitā, *f.*

Insurmountable, see **Insuperable.**

Insurrection, *n.* rājavirodha ; janasaṅkhobha, *m.* °**al**, *a.* rajjavirodhāyatta. °**ist**, *n.* rajjaviddesī, *m.*

Insusceptible, *a.* avikārasabhāva ; avikārakkhama.

Intact, *a.* anāmaṭṭha ; avikala ; abhinna.

Intaglio, *n.* 1. ukkīta-lañchana, *nt.* 2. ukkītavatthu, *nt.* 3. salañchana-maṇi, *m.*

Intake, *n.* 1. udakamagga ; 2. vātappavesaka-nāḷa, *m.*

Intangible, *a.* aphassagocara. °**bility**, *n.* aphusanīyatā, *f.*

Integer, *n.* akhaṇḍasaṅkhyā, *f.*

Integral, *a.* avikala ; anūna ; abhinna.

Integrate, *a.* asesa ; akhaṇḍa ; paripuṇṇa. *v.t.* paripuṇṇaŋ karoti. *p.p.* °kata. °**rity**, *n.* 1. avekalla ; anūnatta, *nt.* 2. avaṅkatta ; dhammikatta, *nt.*

Integument, *n.* taca ; kosa, *m.* āvaraṇa, *nt.*

Intellect, *n.* paññā ; buddhi ; mati, *f.* ñāṇa ; paṭibhāṇa, *nt.* °**ion**, *n.* bujjhana ; avagamana, *nt.* °**ual**, *a.* 1. buddhimantu ; sappañña ; 2. buddhivisayaka.

Intelligence, *n.* 1. ñāṇasatti, *f.* 2. vuttanta, *m.* 3. sandesa, *m.* °**er**, *n.* sandesahara, *m.*

Intelligent, *a.* matimantu ; medhāvī ; visadañāṇa. °**ly**, *adv.* nipuṇākārena ; buddhicāturiyena.

Intelligible, *a.* sugama ; subodha. °**bly**, *adv.* sugamākārena.

Intemperance, *n.* amattaññutā, *f.* pamāṇātikkama ; asaŋyama, *m.* °**rate**, *a.* sīmātīta ; amattaññū. °**rately**, *adv.* asīmitākārena ; atimattaŋ.

Intend, *v.t.* ceteti ; saṅkappeti. *p.p.* °pita. °**ant**, *n.* avekkhaka ; adhikārī, *m.* °**ed**, *a.* adhippeta ; abhimata. °**edly**, *adv.* parikappetvā. °**ment**, *n.* nītyanugatattha, *m.*

Intense, *a.* atimatta ; adhikatara ; gāḷha ; bāḷha ; tibba. °**ify**, *v.t.* balavataraŋ karoti ; gāḷhayati. °**ity**, *n.* atisayatta ; balavatta ; adhimattatta, *nt.* °**ive**, *a.* atimatta ; atibāḷha. °**ively**, °**ly**, *adv.* accantaŋ ; atimattaŋ.

Intent, *a.* abhiniviṭṭha ; niṭṭhaṅgata ; adhiṭṭhānayutta. °**ion**, *n.* parikappa ; adhippāya, *m.* sañcetanā, *f.* °**ional**, *a.* cetanāyatta ; sañcetanika. °**ionally**, *adv.* sañcicca ; cetetvā. °**ness**, *n.*

ekaniṭṭhā, *f.* adhiṭṭhāna, *nt.* — **on**, vyāvaṭa; adhimutta; parāyaṇa, *a.*

Intently, *adv.* sābhinivesaŋ.

Inter, *v.t.* susāne nidahati. *p.p.* °hita. °**ment**, *n.* bhūnidahana, *nt.*

Interact, *n.* antarānacca, *nt.* *v.i.* itarītarabalaŋ pavatteti. °**ion**, *n.* ubhayavyāpīkamma, *nt.*

Intercalary, *n.* adhimāsadina, *m.*

Intercalate, *v.t.* antare paveseti. *p.p.* °sita.

Intercede, *v.i.* 1. paratthāyakatheti; 2. antare tiṭṭhati. *p.p.* °kathita; °ṭhita.

Intercept, *v.t.* avarodheti; upacchindati. °**ion**, *n.* nivāraṇa; paṭibāhana; rodhana, *nt.* °**or**, *n.* rodhaka; bādhaka, *m.* °**ive**, *a.* nivāraka; avarodhaka.

Intercession, *n.* paratthāya āyācanā; parānukampā, *f.* °**cessor**, *n.* paratthagavesī, *m.*

Interchange, *n.* vinimaya, *m.* bhaṇḍaparivattana, *nt.* *v.t.* vinimeti; (bhaṇḍāni) parivatteti. *p.p.* °mita; °titabhaṇḍa.

Intercommunicate, *v.t.* aññamaññasanthavaŋ karoti. *p.p.* °kata-santhava. °**ion**, *n.* aññamaññanivedana, *nt.*

Intercommunion, *n.* aññamaññasahayogitā, *f.*

Intercourse, *n.* saŋsagga; santhava; saŋvāsa; saṅgama, *m.* Sexual —, methuna, *nt.*

Interdependence, *n.* aññamaññāvalambana, *nt.* °**dent**, *a.* aññamaññāvalambī.

Interdict, *n.* paṭisedha; paṭikkhepa, *m.* bādhana, *nt.* *v.t.* nivāreti; nisedheti; paṭisedheti; paṭibāhati. *p.p.* °rita; °dhita; °hita. °**ion**, *n.* paṭibāhana, *nt.* nisedha; paṭisedha, *m.* °**ory**, *a.* nisedhaka; paṭisedhaka.

Interest, *n.* 1. attha, *m.* payojana, *nt.* 2. apekkhā, *f.* anurāga, *m.* 3. (on money:) vaḍḍhi, *f.* *v.t.* anurañjeti; kutūhalam uppādeti. *p.p.* °jita; uppāditakutūhala. °**ed**, *a.* 1. jātāpekkha; anuratta; 2. nirata; niviṭṭha; āsatta; 3. salābhāpekkha. °**ing**, *a.* manohara; vinodakara.

Interfere, *v.i.* 1. anāyattakiccesu abhiyuñjati; 2. aññamaññaŋ virujjhati. *p.p.* abhiyutta; °viruddha. °**nce**, *n.* 1. parakiccappavesa; 2. aññamaññavirodha. °**ing**, *a.* parakiccabādhaka, *a.*

Interfuse, *v.t.* misseti. *v.i.* aññamaññaŋ missīyati. *p.p.* °missita.

Interim, *n.* antaritakāla, *m.* *adv.* etthantare. adj. antarita.

Interior, *n.* abbhantara; antoraṭṭha, *nt.* adj. abbhantarika; antovattī.

Interjacent, *a.* majjhavattī; antarāvattī.

Interject, *v.t.* antare pakkhipati; majjhe khipati. *p.p.* °khitta. °**ion**, *n.* 1. antokhipana; 2. āmeṇḍita, *nt.*

Interlace, *v.t.* saŋsibbeti; gantheti. *p.p.* °bita; °thita.

Interlard, *v.t.* videsavacanehi misseti. *p.p.* °sita.

Interlay, *v.t.* antare niveseti. *p.p.* °sita.

Interleave, *v.t.* antare paṇṇāni pakkhipati. *p.p.* °khittapaṇṇa.

Interline, *v.t.* pantyantare likhati. *p.p.* °likhita. °**ar,** *a.* pantyantare likhita *or* muddita.

Interlock, *v.t.* aññamaññaŋ sambhandheti. *p.p.* °baddha.

Interlocutor, *n.* saŋvādī; sambhāsaka, *m.* °**tion,** *n.* saŋvāda, *m.* sambhāsana, *nt.* °**y,** *a.* saŋvādanissita.

Interloper, *n.* parakiccapakkhandī, *m.*

Interlude, *n.* 1. raṅgantara, *nt.* 2. antarā-raṅga, *m.*

Intermarriage, *n.* vijātikavivāha, *m.*

Intermarry, *v.t.* visadisāvāhavivāhaŋ karoti.

Intermeddle, *v.i.* anāyattakiccesu sandissati.

Intermediary, *a.* antaraṭṭha; majjhavattī.

Intermediate, *v.i.* majjhe *or* antare vattati *or* ācarati. *p.p.* °vattita. *n.* saŋsandakavatthu, *nt.* adj. majjhavattī. °**ly,** *adv.* majjhe; antarāle. °**tor,** *n.* saŋsandaka, *m.* °**ion,** *n.* saŋsandana; majjhe vattana, *nt.*

Intermedium, *n.* majjhavattīvatthu, *nt.*

Interment, *n.* bhūnidahana, *nt.*

Intermigration, *n.* aññamaññadesacāga, *m.*

Interminable, *a.* ananta; apariyanta. °**bly,** *adv.* anantavasena.

Intermingle, *v.i.* sammissīyati. *v.t.* sammisseti. *p.p.* °sita.

Intermission, *n.* kālikanivattana, *nt.* virāma; vissama, *m.*

Without —, nirantaraŋ; avicchinnaŋ, *adv.*

Intermit, *v.i.* kiñci kālaŋ nivattati. *v.t.* antarā nivatteti. *p.p.* °nivatta; °tita. °**tence,** *n.* kālikanivattana, *nt.* virāma, *m.* °**tent,** *a.* antarānivattī.

Intermix, see **Intermingle.**

Intern, *v.t.* sīmantare vāseti. °**ee,** *n.* antovāsī; nevāsī, *m.* °**al,** *a.* abbhantarika; antoṭhita. °**ally,** *adv.* abbhantarikavasena.

International, *a.* jātyantarika; nānādesīya. °**ity,** *n.* jātyantaratta, *nt.* °**ly,** *adv.* jātyantaravasena.

Internecine, *a.* itarītaranāsaka.

Interpenetrate, *v.t.* anto pavisati; pariyogāhati. *p.p.* paviṭṭha; °gāḷha. °**ion,** pariyogāhaṇa, *nt.*

Interplay, *n.* itarītarasiddhi, *f.*

Interplead, *v.i.* aññamaññaŋ vivadati.

Interpolate, *v.t.* antare paveseti. *p.p.* °sita. °**ion** *n.* pakkhitta-pāṭha, *m.*

Interpose, *v.t.* 1. antarā nivatteti; 2. viruddhakāraṇaŋ āharati. *p.p.* °tita. °**sition,** *n.* 1. antarāhaṭakāraṇa; 2. antarānivattāpana, *nt.*

Interpret, *v.t.* 1. anuvādeti; bhāsantaraŋ parivatteti; 2. atthaŋ pakāseti. *p.p.* °dita; °tita; °sitattha. °**ation,** *n.* 1. bhāsāparivattana; 2. atthakathana, *nt.* °**er,** *n.* bhāsānuvādī; atthavaṇṇaka, *m.*

Interregnum, *n.* arājikakāla, *m.*

Interrelation, *n.* itarītarasambandha, *m.* °**ship**, *n.* itarītarasambandhatā, *f.*

Interrogate, *v.t.* paripucchati; anuyuñjati. *p.p.* °chita; anuyutta. °**ion**, *n.* pucchā, *f.* pañha, *m.* °**ive**, *a.* pucchāsabhāva; paripucchaka. °**ively**, *adv.* pucchāsabhāvena. °**tor**, *n.* pucchaka; anuyuñjaka, *m.*

Interrupt, *v.t.* vicchindati; vippakaroti; bādheti. *p.p.* vicchinna; °kata; bādhita. °**er**, *n.* vicchedī; upaghātī, *m.* °**ion**, *n.* bādhana, *nt.* viccheda; upaghāta, *m.* °**ive**, *a.* vicchedakara; bādhaka.

Intersect, *v.t.* aññamaññaŋ vinivijjhati. *p.p.* °vinividdha. °**ion**, *n.* aññamaññacchedana, *nt.*

Interspace, *n.* antarāla, *nt.* majjhe-okāsa, *m.*

Intersperse, *v.t.* vikirati; ito cito ṭhapeti. *p.p* vikiṇṇa; °ṭhapita.

Interstate, *a.* rajjantaraṭṭhita.

Interstice, *n.* 1. antarikā, *f.* 2. chidda; vivara, *nt.*

Intertwine, *v.t.* gantheti; saŋsibbeti. *v.i.* jaṭīyati. *p.p.* °thita; °bita; jaṭita.

Interval, *n.* antarākāla, *m.* virāmavelā, *f.*

Intervene, *v.i.* majjhe *or* antare vattati. *p.p.* °tita. °**ing**, *a.* antarāvattī.

Intervention, *n.* majjhevattana, *nt.*

Interview, *n.* sākacchā; mantanā, *f.* *v.t.* sākacchati; sammanteti. *p.p.* °chita; °tita. °**er**, *n.* sākacchaka, *m.*

Intervolve, *v.t.* aññamaññaŋ saŋveṭheti. *p.p.* °ṭhita.

Interweave, see **Intertwine**.

Intestate, *a.* accayadānalipirahita.

Intestine, *n.* pakkāsaya, *m.* adj. abbhantarika. °**nal**, *a.* antanissita; pakkāsayāyatta.

Intimate, *a.* vallabha; sambhatta; suparicita; cirasanthuta, *n.* daḷhamitta; sambhatta, *m.* *v.t.* viññāpeti; nivedeti. °**ion**, *n.* viññatti; sūcanā, *f.* iṅgita, *nt.* °**ly**, *adv.* suparicitaŋ; vallabhatāya. °**acy**, *n.* vissāsa santhava, *m.*

Intimidate, *v.t.* tajjeti; tāseti. *p.p.* tajjita; tāsita. °**ion**, *n.* tajjana; paribhāsana, *nt.*

Intimity, *n.* puggalikatta; abbhantaratta, *nt.*

Into, prep. Expressed by the Accusative.

Intolerable, *a.* asayha; dukkhama. °**bly**, *adv.* asayhākārena.

Intolerant, *a.* asahanasīla. °**ance**, *n.* akkhanti, *f.* asahana, *nt.* °**ation**, *n.* anokāsakaraṇa, *nt.*

Intomb, see **Entomb**.

Intonate, **Intone**, *v.t.* gītassarena vadati. *p.p.* °vutta. °**ion**, *n.* gambhīra-bhāsana; sarabhañña, *nt.* °**er**, *n.* sarabhāṇaka, *m.*

Intoxicant, *n.* majja, *nt.* adj. madakara.

Intoxicate, *v.t.* madeti; mattaŋ karoti. °**ed**, *a.* sammatta. °**ing**, *a.* madāvaha. °**ion**, *n.* majjana, *nt.* ummāda, *m.*

Intractable, *a.* adamma ; avineya ; dunniggayha. °**bility,** *n.* adammatā, *f.*

Intransitive, *a. n.* akammagāhī.

Intrench, *v.t.* parikhaŋ yojeti ; parikhāya rakkhati. *p.p.* yojitaparikha ; °rakkhita. °**ment,** *n.* 1. parikhākhaṇana, *nt.* 2. khandhāvāra, *m.*

Intrepid, *a.* nissaṅka ; nibbhaya. °**ity,** *n.* sūratta, *nt.* vikkama, *m.* °**ly,** *adv.* savikkamaŋ.

Intricate, *a.* vyākula ; dubbodha ; gūḷha. °**cacy,** *n.* vyākulatta ; gūḷhatta, *nt.* °**ly,** *adv.* ākulākārena. °**ness,** *n.* ākulatta ; dubbodhatta, *nt.*

Intrigue, *n.* kumantana, *nt.* kūṭopāya, *m. v.i.* kumanteti ; kūṭopāyaŋ yojeti. *p.p.* °tita ; yojitakūṭopāya. °**er** *n.* kumantaka, *m.*

Intrinsic, *a.* sahaja ; antovattī ; yathābhūta. °**ally,** *adv.* tattato ; yāthāvato.

Introduce, *v.t.* 1. paveseti ; 2. sañjānāpeti ; 3. paricayaŋ janeti. *p.p.* °sita ; °pita ; janitaparicaya. °**er,** *n.* pavesaka ; viññāpaka ; ārabhaka, *m.*

Introduction, *n.* 1. pavesana ; āharaṇa ; viññāpana, *nt.* 2. nidānakathā, *f.* °**tory,** *a.* pavesaka ; upacārabhūta.

Intromit, *v.t.* anto paveseti. *p.p.* °sita. °**mission,** *n.* antopavesana, *nt.*

Introspect, *v.i.* sakacittam upaparikkhati. °**ion,** *n.* antodassana, *nt.* vipassanā ; attavīmaŋsā, *f.* °**ive,** *a.* antoupanijjhāyaka ; antoparikkhaka.

Introvert, *v.t.* antovyāvaṭṭeti ; cittābhimukhaŋ peseti. *p.p.* °ṭita ; °sita. °**version,** abbhantarāvaṭṭana, *nt.*

Intrude, *v.t.* aṇavhāto pavisati. *p.p.* anavhātappaviṭṭha. °**er,** *n.* animantitāgāmī, *m.*

Intrusion, *n.* anavhātappavesa, *m.* °**sive,** *a.* parakiccappavesī. °**sively,** *adv.* nimantanaŋ vinā.

Intrust, see **Entrust.**

Intuit, *v.i.t.* adhigamena jānāti. *p.p.* °ñāta. °**ion,** *n.* sahajañāṇa ; antoñāṇa, *nt.* °**ive,** *a.* sahajañāṇayutta. °**ively,** *adv.* pakatiñāṇena.

Intumescent, *a.* sophakara. °**nce,** *n.* sopha, *m.* uddhumāyana, *nt.*

Inunction, *n.* abbhañjana, *nt.*

Inundate, *v.t.* ajjhottharati ; jalena ottharāpeti. *p.p.* ajjhotthaṭa ; °pita. °**ion,** *n.* ajjhottharaṇa, *nt.* udakaplava, *m.*

Inurbane, *a.* anāgarika ; gamma.

Inure, *v.t.* paricayati. *p.p.* paricita. °**ment,** *n.* paricaya, *m.*

Inurn, *v.t.* sarīrabhasmaŋ bhājane pakkhipati.

Inutile, *a.* nippayojana ; niratthaka. °**ity,** *n.* niratthakatta, *nt.*

Invade, *v.t.* 1. pakkhandati ; 2. paravisaym abhimaddati. *p.p.* pakkhanta ; °dita° ; °**er,** *n.* abhimaddaka, *m.*

Invalid, *a.n.* dubbala ; gilāna ; nitteja ; rogī ; ātura, *m. v.t.* gilānaŋ *or* akammaññaŋ karoti. °**ity,** *n.* dubbalya ; akkhamatta, *nt.* °**ate,** *v.t.* lopeti ; moghīkaroti. *p.p.* lutta ; °kata.

Invaluable, *a.* anaggha; accagghanaka.

Invariable, *a.* thira; nibbikāra; aparivattiya. °**ly,** *adv.* ekantena; nibbikārena.

Invasion, *n.* paravisayakkamana, *nt.*

Invective, *n.* vācāsannitudana, *nt.*

Inveigh, *v.t.* paribhāsati; daḷham akkosati. *p.p* °sita; °akkuṭṭha.

Inveigle, *v.t.* palobheti; palambheti. *p.p.* °bhita.

Invent, *v.t.* navaŋ parikappeti *or* nimmiṇāti. *p.p.* °pita; °mita. °**ion,** *n.* 1. navanimmāṇa, *nt.* navaparikappa, *m.* 2. kūṭaracanā, *f.* °**ive,** *a.* navanimmāṇakara. °**or,** *n* navanimmātu, *m.* °**ory,** *n.* bhaṇḍasaṅkhyālekhana, *nt.*

Inveracity, *n.* vitathatta, *nt.*

Inverse, *a.n.* viloma; paṭiloma; paṭiviruddha. °**ion,** *n.* virodha, *m.* vilomatta; viparītatta, *nt.* °**ly,** *adv.* viparītena; paṭilomaŋ.

Invert, *v.t.* viparāvatteti; uddham adho-karoti. *p.p.* °tita; °kata.

Invertebrate, *a.* 1. piṭṭhikaṇṭakarahita; 2. dubbala.

Invest, *v.t.* 1. samaṅgīkaroti; 2. acchādeti; 3. adhikāre niyojeti. *p.p.* °kata; °dita; °jita. °**iture,** *n.* adhikāradāna; upanayana, *nt.* °**ment,** *n.* 1. vaḍḍhiyā yojita-dhana; 2. acchādana, *nt.*

Investigate, *v.t.* pariggaṇhāti; samannesati; upaparikkhati. *p.p.* pariggahita; °sita; °khita. °**ion,** *n.* anuvicāraṇā; upaparikkhā, *f.* °**tor,** *n.* anuvijjaka; samannesaka, *m.*

Inveterate, *a.* baddhamūla; ciraṭṭhita; daḷha; thira. °**racy,** *n.* 1. ciraṭṭhitatta; baddhamūlatta, *nt.* 2. upanāha, *m.* °**ly,** *adv.* baddhamūlatāya.

Invidious, *a.* appasādajanaka; kopajanaka. °**ly,** *adv.* appiyākārena. °**ness,** *n.* appiyatta, *nt.*

Invigilate, *v.i.* appamatto hoti; parivīmaŋsati. °**ion,** *n.* parivīmaŋsana, *nt.*

Invigorate, *v.t.* pīṇeti; balaŋ vaḍḍheti. *p.p.* pīṇita; vaḍḍhitabala. °**ing,** *a.* balavaḍḍhaka. °**ion,** *n.* balavaḍḍhana; thāmajanana, *nt.*

Invincible, *a.* ajeyya; anabhibhavanīya.

Inviolable, *a.* alaṅghiya; avītikkamiya; anatikkamiya. °**bly,** *adv.* anatikkamiyattena. °**bility,** *n.* alaṅghiyatta, *nt.*

Inviolate, *a.* akkhata; adūsita; avilaṅghita. °**ly,** *adv.* adūsitākārena.

Invisible, *a.* adissamāna; adiṭṭhigocara; antarahita. °**bly,** *adv.* 1. adissamānākārena; 2. apaccakkhaŋ. °**ness,** *n.* adissamānatā, *f.*

Invite, *v.t.* nimanteti ajjhesati; ārādheti. *p.p.* °tita; °sita; °dhita. °**ation,** *n.* ārādhanā; ajjhesanā, *f.* °**ing,** *a.* palobhaka; manohara. °**ingly,** *adv.* palobhanākārena.

Invocation, *n.* devatujjhāpanā; devatārādhanā, *f.*

Invoice, *n.* (kīta-) bhaṇḍalekhana, *nt.*

Invoke, *v.t.* avhāti ; ujjhāpeti. *p.p.* avhāta ; °pita.

Involuntary, *a.* akāmaka; anicchaka. °**ily,** *adv.* anicchāya ; akāmakaŋ.

Involute, *a.* 1. saŋsaṭṭha ; 2. antokuñcita. °**ion,** *n.* 1. saŋsaṭṭhatā, *f.* 2. kuñcitatta, *nt.*

Involve, *v.t.* 1. āveṭheti ; oguṇṭheti ; 2. saŋyojeti. *p.p.* °ṭhita ; °jita. °**ment,** *n.* 1. āveṭhana ; 2. dhanahīnatta, *nt.*

Invulnerable, *a.* abhejja ; avinivijjhiya. °**bility,** *n.* abhejjatā, *f.* °**bly,** *adv.* abhejjākārena.

Inward, *a.* antovattī. °**ly,** *adv.* abbhantarato. °**ness,** *n.* abbhantaratta, *nt.*

Inward(s), *adv.* antobhimukhaŋ.

Inweave, *v.t.* gantheti. *p.p.* °thita.

Inwrought, *a.* rūpavicitta ; rūpakhacita.

Ionian, *a.n.* Yonaka.

Iota, *n.* lava ; kaṇa ; aṇu, *m.*

Iran, *n.* Pārasikadesa, *m* °**ian,** *a.* Pārasikadesīya.

Irascible, *a.* kodhana ; kujjhanasīla. °**bility,** *n.* kodhabahulatā, *f.*

Irate, *a.* ruṭṭha ; kuddha.

Ire, *n.* kodha ; rosa ; kopa, *m.* °**ful,** *a.* kuddha ; ruṭṭha.

Iridescent, *a.* indadhanusadisa.

Iridium, *n.* setaloha, *nt.*

Iris, *n* 1. Indadhanudevī, *f.* 2. phalikavisesa, *m.* 3. (of the eye :) nettatārā ; kaṇīnikā, *f.*

Irk, *v.t.* hiŋsati ; viheṭheti. *p.p.* °sita ; °ṭhita. °**some,** *a.* hiŋsaka ; pīḷākara.

Iron, *n.* aya ; kāḷāyasa, *m. nt. v.t.* 1. saṅkhalikāhi bandhati ; 2. vatthāni majjati. *p.p* °baddha ; maṭṭhavattha. adj. ayomaya. °**bar,** *n.* ayoghana ; nārāca, *m.* — **chain,** *n.* ayodāma, *m.* — **foundry,** *n.* ayosodhanaṭṭhāna, *nt.* — **monger,** *n.* ayobhaṇḍika, *m.* °**wood,** nāgarukkha, *m.*

Irony, *n.* vyājatthuti, *f.* āsajjavacana, *nt.* adj. ayosadisa; ayomaya. °**nic,** °**nical,** *a.* vyājatthutiyutta. °**nically,** *adv.* āsajja ; upanīya.

Irradiant, *a.* obhāsamāna. °**nce,** *n.* obhāsa, *m.*

Irradiate, *v.t.* obhāseti ; joteti. *p.p.* °sita ; jotita. °**ion,** *n.* obhāsana ; jotana, *nt.*

Irrational, *a.* yuttirahita ; ñāyaviruddha. °**ity,** *n.* aññāya ; yuttivirodha, *m.* hīnabuddhitā, *f.* °**ly,** *adv.* ñāyavirodhena.

Irreclaimable, *a.* appaṭisaṅkharaṇīya ; appaṭilabhiya.

Irrecognizable, *a.* asañjāniya ; sañjānitum asakya.

Irreconcilable, *a.* asandheya ; avupasamiya ; aghaṭiya.

Irrecoverable, *a.* apunalabbha ; appaṭisaṅkhariya. °**bly,** *adv.* alabbhaneyyākārena.

Irrecusable, *a.* sampaṭicchitabba.

Irredeemable, *a.* apunakeyya ; amociya ; anitthāriya. °**bly,** *adv.* amociyākārena.

Irreducible, *a.* avikalakkhama ; akkhaya ; ahāpiya.

Irrefragable, *a.* niruttara ; akhaṇḍiya.

Irrefrangible, *a.* anatikkamiya; alaṅghiya.

Irrefutable, *a.* aparihāriya; avivādiya.

Irregular, *a.* 1. aniyata; ayathāvidhika; uppaṭipāṭika; 2. visama; 3. uppathagāmī. °**ity**, *n.* 1. uppaṭipāṭi, *f.* kamavirodha; 2. niyamābhāva, *m.* 3. vītikkama, *m.* 4. vesamma, *nt.* °**ly**, *adv.* aniyamena; uppaṭipāṭiyā.

Irrelative, *a.* asambandha; asaṅgata; kevala.

Irrelevance, *a.* asaŋyoga, *m.* aghaṭanā, *f.* °**ant**, *a.* aghaṭiyamāna.

Irreligion, *n.* assaddhā, *f.* samayavirodha, *m.* °**gious**, *a.* assaddha; bhattihīna; samayaviruddha. °**giously**, *adv.* adhammena; āgamavirodhena.

* **Irremediable**, *a.* atekiccha; appaṭikamma. °**bly**, *adv.* atekicchākārena.

Irremissible, *a.* akkhamāraha; amocanīya.

Irremovable, *a.* ahāriya; anapaneyya; thāvara.

Irreparable, *a.* appaṭisaṅkharaṇīya; appaṭikamma °**ness**, *n.* appaṭikammatta, *nt.*

Irreplaceable, *a.* apunarāvattiya; apunasādhiya.

Irrepressible, *a.* dunniggayha; duddamiya.

Irreproachable, *a.* anindiya; agārayha; anavajja.

Irreprovable, *a.* atajjanīya; agārayha.

Irresistible, *a.* anivāriya; dunniggayha; dunnivāriya. °**bility**, *n.* dunnivāriyatta, *nt.* °**bly**, *adv.* anivāriyākārena.

Irresolute, *a.* calacitta; akatanicchaya. °**ly**, *adv.* anicchayena. °**ness**, *n.* athirādhiṭṭhānatta; capalatta, *nt.*

Irrespective (of), *v.* nirapekkha; °**ly**, *adv.* agaṇet vā; asallakkhetvā; nirapekkhaŋ; anapekkhiya.

Irresponsible, *a.* niradhikāra; anāpucchitabba. °**bility**, *n.* niradhikāratā, *f.* °**sive**, *a.* anadhikāra; avihāyaka.

Irretentive, *a.* anivattāpanakkhama. °**tion**, nivattetum asakyatā, *f.*

Irretrievable, *a.* apunalabbha; appaṭisaṅkhariya. °**bly**, *adv.* apunalabbhākārena.

Irreverent, *a.* agarukārī; appatissava; avamaññaka. °**ly**, *adv.* agāravena; sāvaññaŋ; anādarena. °**nce**, *n.* agārava; agarukāra; avamāna; anādara, *m.*

Irreversible, *a.* apunarāvattiya; appaṭivattiya.

Irrevocable, *a.* anaññathākaraṇīya; aparivattiya.

Irrigate, *v.t.* jalaŋ paveseti; udakaŋ neti. *p.p.* pavesitajala; nītodaka. °**ion**, *n.* jalanetti, *f.* udakasampādana, *nt.*

Irritable, *a.* kuppanasīla; dosacarita. °**bility**, *n.* dosabahulatā; kuppanasīlitā, *f.*

Irritate, *v.t.* 1. kopeti; roseti; 2. khobheti. *p.p.* kopita; rosita; °bhita. °**ion**, *n.* 1. kopa; rosa; 2. santāpa; dāha, *m.* °**ive**, °**ing**, *a.* 1. kopajanaka; 2. santāpakara.

Irruption, *n.* akkamana, *nt.* pasayha-pavesa, *m.*

Is, *v.i.* atthi; bhavati; vijjati. — **able**, sakkoti.

Isabel, *a.* pītadhūsara.

Ischiatic, *a.* jaghanāyatta.

Ischuria, *n.* muttakicchābadha, *m.*

Island, Isle, *n.* dīpa; antarīpa, *m.* °**er**, *n.* dīpavāsī, *m.*

Islet, *n.* khuddakadīpa, *m.*

Ism, *n.* mata, *nt.* vāda, *m.*

Iso-chromatic, *a.* samānavaṇṇa.

Iso-chronous, *a.* samakālika.

Iso-gonal, *a.* samakoṇaka.

Isolate, *v.t.* viyojeti; vinibbhujati; puthakkaroti. *p.p.* °jita; vinibhutta; °kata. °**ion**, *n.* viniyoga, *m.* putthakkaraṇa, *nt.*

Iso-metric, *a.* samamāṇaka.

Isosceles, *a.* samadvibhuja.

Issue, *n.* 1. niggama; pasava, *m.* nikkhamana, *nt.* 2. vipāka; nissanda; 3. paramparā; santati, *f.* *v.i.* pasavati; niggacchati. *v.t.* nikkhāmeti; pacāreti; pakāseti. *p.p.* pasūta; niggata; °mita; °rita; °sita. °**less**, *a.* anapacca; aputtaka.

Isthmus, *n.* desasandhi; saŋyojakabhūmi, *f.*

It, *pron.* taŋ. *nt.* *sing.* **It behoves**, vaṭṭati.

Italy, *n.* Itālidesa, *m.* °**ian**, *a.* Itālidesīya.

Itch, *n.* kaṇḍuti; kacchu, *f.* *v.i.* kaṇḍūvati. °**y**, *a.* kaṇḍutisahita.

Item, *n.* amissita-visaya, *m.*

Iterate, *v.t.* punappunaŋ vadati *or* karoti. *p.p.* °vutta; °kata. °**ion**, *n.* punarutti, *f.* punakaraṇa, *nt.* °**ive**, *a.* 1. punāgāmī; 2. abhiṇhavācī.

Itinerant, *a.* pariyaṭaka, āhiṇḍaka. °**ary**, *n.* pavāsavuttanta, *nt.*

Itinerate, *v.i.* pariyaṭati; āhiṇḍati.

Itself, *pron.* tad eva.

Ivory, *n.* hatthidanta, *nt.* adj. 1. dantamaya; 2. khīravaṇṇa.

Ivy, *n.* rukkhādanī; tarurohinī, *f.*

J

Jabber, *v.i.* pajappati; palapati. *pp.* °pita. °**ing**, *n.* pajappana, *nt.*

Jack, *n.* 1. bhārukkhepaka-yanta, *nt.* 2. bhaṭakañcuka, *m.* 3. (tree:) panasa, *m.* °**ass**, 1. gadrabha; 2. mahāmūḷha, *m.* °**tar**, nāvika, *m.*

Jackal, *n.* sigāla; kotthuka; jambuka, *m.*

Jackanapes, *n.* 1. vānara; 2. vānaravuttika; capala, *m.*

Jackdaw, *n.* nagarakāka, *m.*

Jacket, *n.* uttarikañcuka, *m.*

Jaconet, *n.* ghana-kappāsikavattha, *nt.*

Jade, *n.* 1. khaluṅkassa, *m.* 2. muggavaṇṇasilā, *f.* *v.t.* khedeti; āyāseti. *p.p.* khedita; āyāsita. °**ish**, *a.* duṭṭha; pāpika.

Jag, *n.* sikhara, *nt.* *v.t.* dantākārena chindati. *p.p.* °chinna.

Jaggery, *n.* guḷa, *m.* sakkharā, *f.*

Jaguar, *n.* dīpibilāla, *m.*

Jail, *n.* kārā, *f.* bandhanāgāra, *nt.* °**bird**, *n.* kārābaddha. °**er**, °**or**, *n.* kārāpāla, *m.*

Jain, *n. a.* niganṭhabhattika, 3.

Jam, *n.* phalasāra, *m. v.t.* sañcuṇṇeti; sammaddati. *p.p.* °ṇita; °dita.

Jamb, *n.* dvārabāhā, *f.*

Jamboree, *n.* samājussava; mahāsannipāta, *m.*

Jangle, *n.* mahānāda, *m. v.i.* kharasaddaŋ pavatteti, *v.t.* kharasaddena vādeti. *p.p.* pavattitakharasadda; °vādita.

Janitor, *n.* dvārapāla, *m.* °**tress**, *n.* dvārapālikā, *f.*

January, *n.* Phussa (-māsa), *m.*

Janus, *n.* dvimukhadevatā, *f.*

Japan, *n.* Japanraṭṭha, *nt.* °**ese**, *a.* Japandesīya.

Jape, *n.* parihāsa, *m.*

Jar, *n.* 1. maṇika; arañjara, *m.* 2. kharasadda, *m. v.i.* khaṭakhaṭāyati.

Jargon, *n.* vippalāpa; kucchitālāpa, *m.*

Jasmine, *n.* jātisumanā, *f.*

Jasper, *n.* suriyakantapāsāṇa, *m.*

Jaundice, *n.* paṇḍuroga, *m.* kāmalā, *f.*

Jaunt, *n.* jaṅghāvihāra, *m. v.i.* anuvicarati.

Jaunty, *a.* ullāsita; sappagabbha. °**ily**, *adv.* ullāsitākārena; kīḷakalīlāya.

Javelin, *n.* satti; heti, *f.*

Jaw, *n.* hanu; hanukā, *f. v.i.* 1. cabbati; 2. atidīghaŋ katheti. *p.p.* cabbita; °thita.

Jay, *n.* kikī; dindibha, *m.*

Jealous, *a.* issukī; maccharī. °**ly**, *adv.* samaccharaŋ; macchariyena. °**y**, *n.* issā; usūyā, *f.* macchariya, *nt.*

Jeer, *n.* upahāsa, *m.* avaññā, *f. v.i.* avahasati; upahasati. *p.p.* °sita. °**ingly**, *adv.* sopahāsaŋ.

Jehovah, *n.* lokamāpaka, *m.*

Jehu, *n.* pharusa-sārathi, *m.*

Jejune, *a.* 1. virala; appaka; 2. asāra; jaṅgala. °**ness**, *n.* viralatta; appakatta, *nt.*

Jelly, *n.* miñjasadisavatthu, *nt. v.t.* miñjasadisaŋ karoti. °**fish**, *n.* sippikā. *f.*

Jemmy, *n.* (corānaŋ) ayosaṅku, *m.*

Jeopardy, *n.* antarāya; sandeha; saŋsaya, *m.* °**ize**, *v.t.* sappaṭibhayaŋ karoti; saŋsaye pāteti. *p.p.* °kata; °tita.

Jerk, *n.* ugghāta, *m.* sahasā calana, *nt. v.t.* sahasā cāleti; ugghāteti. *v.i.* sahasā calati. *p.p.* °lita; °tita; °lita.

Jessamine, see **Jasmine**.

Jest, *n.* keḷi, *f.* parihāsa; nammālāpa, *m. v.t.* parihasati; keḷiŋ karoti. *p.p.* °sita; katakeḷika. °**er**, *n.* vihāsaka, *m.* °**ing**, *n.* sañjagghana, *nt.*

Jet, *n.* 1. dhārā, *f.* jaladhārā, *f.* 2. kāḷasilā, *f. v.t.* nicchāreti; nikkhāmeti. *v.i.* dhārāvasena niggacchati. *pp.* °rita; °mita; °niggata. °**black**, *a.* aṅgāravaṇṇa; atikaṇha.

Jetsam, *n.* (lahubhāvāya) nāvāto khitta-bhaṇḍa, *nt.*

Jettison, *v.t.* (lahubhāvāya) nāvāto bhaṇḍāni khipati. *p.p.* °khitta-bhaṇḍa.

Jetty, *n.* titthasetu, *m.* nāvārohaṇaṭṭhāna, *nt.*

Jew, *n*. Yādava, *m*. *v.t.* vāñceti. *p.p.* °cita.

Jewel, *n*. 1. ratana; ratanābharaṇa, *nt*. 2. maṇi, *m*. 3. anagghavatthu, *nt*. 4. uttamapuggala, *m*. °**ler**, *n*. 1. maṇikāra; 2. ābharaṇavāṇija, *m*. °**lery**, °**ry**, *n*. ratanābharaṇa, *nt*. °**ly**, *a*. ratanopama.

Jewel, *v.t.* ratanehi alaṅkaroti. *p.p.* ratanālaṅkata.

Jewry, *n*. Yādavanivāsaṭṭhāna, *nt*.

Jib, *n*. pamukha-lakāra, *m*. *v.t.* aññaŋ passam ākaḍḍhati. *v.i.* agantum icchati; paccosakkati. *p.p.* °ḍhita; °chita; °kita.

Jibe, *n*. upahāsa, *m*. *v.t.* upahasati; avahasati. *p.p.* °sita.

Jiff(y), *n*. muhuttamatta, *nt*.

Jig, *n*. turita-nacca, *nt*. *v.i.* turitanaccaŋ pavatteti.

Jiggle, *v.t.* sanikaŋ pājeti *or* kampeti. *p.p.* °jita; °pita.

Jimp, *a*. tanu; sukumāra.

Jingle, *n*. kiṇikiṇināda, *m*. *v.i.* jhana-jhanāyati; kiṇikiṇāyati. *v.t.* kiṇikiṇisaddaŋ pavatteti.

Jinks, *n*. saghosa-kīḷā, *f*.

Jinricksha, *n*. hatthavaṭṭakaratha, *m*.

Job, *n*. kicca, *nt*. vyāpāra, *m*. *v.i.* khuddaka-kiccāni karoti. °**ber**, *n*. lahukiccakārī, *m*.

Jockey, *n*. assadamaka, *m*. *v.t.* vañceti. *p.p.* vañcita.

Jocose, Jocular, *a*. keḷisīla; vinodaka; hāsakara, °**ly**, *adv*. hāsapubbakaŋ. °**ity**, °**ness**, *n*. rasikatta, *nt*. hassadhamma, *m*.

Jocund, *a*. pahaṭṭha; pamudita. °**ity**, *n*. pahāsa, *m*.

Jog, *n*. īsañcālana, *nt*. *v.t.* 1. sanikaŋ cāleti; nittudati, *v.i.* vilambanto gacchati. *p.p.* °lita; °dita.

Joggle, *n*. (silā-dāruādīnaŋ) sambandhakaṭṭhāna, *nt*. *v.t.* 1. saṅghaṭeti; 2. punappunaŋ cāleti. *p.p.* °tita; °lita.

Johnny, *n*. kusītamāṇava, *m*.

Join, *n*. sandhi, *m*. *v.t.* ghaṭeti; saŋyojeti; sandhīkaroti. *v.i.* ghaṭīyati; sandhīyati; ekībhavati. *p.p.* °ṭita; °jita; °kata; saŋhita; ekībhūta, °**er**, *n*. vaḍḍhakī; saṅghaṭaka, *m*. °**ery**, *n*. vaḍḍhakīkamma, *nt*. °**ing**, *n*. ghaṭana; sandhikaraṇa; saŋyojana, *nt*.

Joint, *n*. sandhi, *m*. pabba, *nt*. *v.t.* sandahati; ghaṭeti. *p.p.* sandhita; °ṭita. adj. 1. samagga; saŋyutta; 2. sādhāraṇa, — **heir**, *n*. samabhāgī, *m*. °**ly**, *adv*. sahitaŋ; saha; ekato.

Jointure, *n*. vidhavādhana, *nt*.

Joist, *n*. talasiṅghāṭa, *m*.

Joke, see **Jest**.

Joky, *a*. keḷisīla; hāsappiya.

Jolly, *n*. vinoda, *m*. adj. pahaṭṭha; pamudita; kīḷālola. *adv*. atīva. °**ify**, *v.t.* vinodeti; pahaŋseti. *p.p.* °dita; °sita, *v.i.* pahaŋsati. *p.p.* pahaṭṭha. °**ity**, *n*. vinoda; pamoda, *m*.

Jolt, *n*. ugghāta, *m*. *v.t.* ugghāteti. *v.i.* saṅkhubhati; sahasā kampati. *p.p.* °tita; °bhita; °pita. °**y**, *a*. ugghātayutta.

Jolterhead, *n*. dandhapuggala, *m*.

Jonah, *n.* kālakaṇṇī, *m.*

Jostle. *n.* apasāraṇa, *nt.* janasammadda, *m.* *v.t.* apasāreti; aññamaññaŋ ghaṭṭeti. *v.i.* saṅghaṭṭīyati. *p.p.* °rita; °ṭita.

Jot, *n.* thokamattā, *f.* *v.t.* saṅkhepena likhati. *p.p.* °khita. °**ting**, *n.* saṅkhittalipi, *f.*

Journal, *n.* kālikasaṅgaha, *m.* °**ist**, *n.* pattikāsampādaka, *m.* °**ism**, *n.* pattikāsampādana, *nt.*

Journey, *n.* addhānagamana; desāṭana, *nt.* desacārikā, *f.* *v.i.* sañcarati; pariyaṭati. °**ing**, *a.* maggapaṭipanna.

Jovial, *a.* sadāmudita; keḷisīla. °**ity**, *n.* kīḷāparatā, *f.* °**ly**, *adv.* sānandaŋ; sappamodaŋ.

Joy, *n.* ānanda; pamoda, *m.* pīti; tuṭṭhi, *f.* pāmojja, *nt.* *v.i.* santussati; pamodati. *v.t.* pamodeti; toseti. *p.p.* santuṭṭha; pamudita; °dita; tosita. °**ful**, *a.* sumana; haṭṭhacitta. °**fully**, *adv.* pamuditākārena. °**fulness**, *n.* pamuditatta. °**less**, *a.* vittihīna; dummana. °**lessly**, *adv.* dummanākārena. °**lessness**, *n.* anattamanatā; asantuṭṭhi, *f.*

Joyously, *adv.* pamuditākārena.

Jubilant, *a.* atihaṭṭha; pahaṭṭha. °**ly**, *adv.* pahaṭṭhākārena.

Jubilate, *v.i.* tuṭṭhiŋ pakāseti; pamodati. *p.p.* pakāsitatuṭṭhī; °dita.

Jubilee, *n.* cirasamiddhiussava, *m.*

Judge, *n.* daṇḍanāyaka; vinicchayāmacca; adhikaraṇika, *m.* (— in general:) vivecaka; guṇadosaññū, *m.* *v.t.* vinicchcheti; niṇṇeti; tīreti. *v.i.* viveceti. *p.p.* °chita; °ṇita; tīrita; °cita. °**ment**, adhikaraṇa-vinicchaya, *m.* °**ship**, *n.* daṇḍanāyakadhura, *nt.*

Judicatory, *a.* adhikaraṇāyatta.

Judicature, *n.* anuvijjana, *nt.* aṭṭavinicchaya, *m.*

Judicial, *a.* nītyanugata. °**ly**, *adv.* nītyanukūlattena.

Judiciary, *n.* akkhadassasamūha, *m.* adhikaraṇasabhā, *f.*

Judicious, *a.* dhammānugata; yuttiyutta; vīmaŋsakārī. °**ly**, *adv.* suvicāriya; susamekkhiya.

Jug, *n.* kuṇḍikā, *f.* kamaṇḍalu, *m.*

Juggins, *n.* momuha, *m.*

Juggle, *n.* indajāla, *nt.* *v.i.* indajālaŋ dasseti, *v.t.* moheti; vañceti. *p.p.* mohita; °cita. °**er**, *m.* māyākāra; indajālika, *m.* °**ry**, *n.* māyā, *f.* indajāla, *nt.*

Jugular, *a.* kaṇṭhaja; kaṇṭhāyatta.

Jugulate, *v.t.* nāseti; vāreti; nivāreti; nisedheti. *p.p.* nāsita; °rita; °dhita.

Juice, *n.* yūsa; rasa, *m.* ojā, *f.* °**cy**, *a.* yūsabahula.

Jujube (tree :) badarī, *f.* (fruit :) kola; badara, *m.* *nt.*

July, *n.* Āsāḷhi (- māsa), *m.*

Jumble, *n.* saṅkara; missībhāva; saṅkhobha, *m.* *v.t.* saṅkhobheti; āloleti. *p.p.* °bhita; °lita.

Jumbo, *n.* thūladehī, *m.*

Jump, *n.* laṅghana; uppatana, *nt.* *v.t.* laṅgheti; uppatati. *p.p.* °ghita; °tita. °**er**, *n.* laṅghaka, *m.* — **over**, ullaṅgheti. °**y**, *a.* vyākula; avupasanta.

Junction, *n.* sandhiṭṭhāna, *nt.* saṅgama, *m.*

Juncture, *n.* 1. niyamitavelā, *f.* 2. sandhiṭṭhāna, *nt.*

June, *n.* Jeṭṭhamāsa, *m.*

Jungle, *n.* kubbanaka, *nt.* vanasaṇḍa, *m.* °**cock**, *n.* nijjivha, *m.* °**fire**, *n.* dāvaggi, *m.*

Junior, *a.* kaṇiṭṭha. °**ity**, *n.* kaṇiṭṭhatā ; ūnāyukatā, *f.*

Junk, *n.* 1. Cīnanāvā, *f.* 2. rajjukhaṇḍādi, *m.*

Junket, *n.* madhurakummāsa, *m.*

Juno, *n.* suraguru-devī, *f.*

Junto, *n.* pālaka-pakkha, *m.*

Jupiter, *n.* suraguru, *m.*

Jural, *a.* nītyāyatta.

Juridical, *a.* adhikaraṇāyatta.

Jurisdiction, *n.* 1. āṇānuvattīpadesa, *m.* 2. adhikaraṇatīraṇa, *nt.*

Jurisprudence, *n.* nītisattha, *nt.*

Jurist, *n.* ñāyavedī ; nītivedī, *m.*

Juror, *n.* vinicchayasabhika, *m.*

Jury, *n.* vinicchayasabhā, *f.*

Jussive, *a.* āṇāpakāsaka.

Just, *a.* dhammika ; akuṭila ; yuttigaruka. *adv.* sapadi ; aciraŋ. — **after**, samanantarā, *adv.* — **as**, — **like**, iva ; viya, *ind.* — **born**, *a.* jātamatta. °**ly**, *adv.* yathāñāyaŋ. °**ness**, *n.* dhammikatta ; akuṭilatta, *nt.*

Justice, *n.* 1. yutti ; *f.* ñāya, *m.* 2. vinicchayāmacca, *m.* °**ship**, vohārikadhura, *nt.*

Justiciable, *a.* vinicchitabba ; anuvijjitabba.

Justiciary, *n.* adhikaraṇādhikārī, *m.* adj. adhikaraṇānugata.

Justify, *v.t.* niravajjaŋ karoti ; dosā moceti. *p.p.* °kata ; °mocita. °**iable**, *a.* nirākaraṇīyavajja. °**ication**, *n.* dosanirākaraṇa, *nt.* °**ier**, *n.* dosanivāraka ; vajjasodhaka, *m.*

Jut, *n.* bahiniggata-vatthu, *nt.* *v.i.* bahi lambati. *p.p.* °bita.

Jute, *n.* sāṇa, *nt.*

Juvenescent, *a.* yobbanappatta. °**ence**, *n.* yobbanappatti, *f.*

Juvenile, *a.* taruṇa ; komāra ; daharayogga. *n.* yuva, *m.* °**ity**, *n.* yobbana ; bālya, *nt.* taruṇāvatthā, *f.*

Juxtapose, *v.t.* sannidahati ; samīpe ṭhapeti. *p.p.* sannihita ; °ṭhapita. °**ition**, *n.* sannidahana ; samīpe-ṭhapana, *nt.*

K

Kaffir, *n.* Aparagoyānika, *m.*

Kaleidoscope, *n.* rūpadassakakācanāḷa, *nt.*

Kangaroo, *n.* mahāsasavisesa, *m.*

Kaolin, *n.* setamattikā, *f.*

Keck, *v.i.* uggāra-saddaŋ pavatteti. *p.p.* °titauggārasadda.

Keel, *n.* nāvāpādaka, *nt.* *v.t.* nāvam adhomukhīkaroti. *p.p.* °kata.

Keen, *n.* paridevagīta, *nt.* adj. 1. sunisita ; tikhiṇa ; 2. sukhuma ; ugga, *v.i.* paridevati, *v.t.* sokagītaŋ gāyati. *p.p.* °vita ; gāyita°. °**ly**, *adv.* tibbaŋ ; tikhiṇākārena. °**ness**, *n.* tikhiṇatta, *nt.* °**witted**, *a.* tikkhapañña.

Keep, *n.* 1. balakoṭṭhaka, *m.* 2. posaṇa ; bharaṇa, *nt.* *v.t.* 1.

ṭhapeti ; niveseti ; 2. gopeti ; pāleti; 3. (to observe :) ācarati ; anuṭṭhāti. *v.i.* pavattati. *p.p.* ṭhapita ; °sita ; gopita ; pālita; °rita; °ṭhita ; pavatta. — **away,** paṭibāheti.—**away from,** paṭilīyati. — **back,** 1. vigacchati ; apakkamati ; 2. nigūhati. — **company,** sevati ; bhajati. — **down,** nisedheti ; nivāreti. °**er,** pālaka ; rakkhaka, *m.* — **in,** samodahati ; gūheti. — **in check,** uparundhati. — **in mind,** manasikaroti. °**ing,** *n.* gopana, *nt.* °**ing awake,** jāgaraṇa, *nt.* °**ing up,** pariharaṇa, *nt.* — **off,** *v.t.* nivāreti ; nisedheti. *v.i.* viramati. — **out,** bahikaroti ; nikkhāmeti. — **silence,** tuṇhī bhavati. — **still,** saṅkasāyati. — **to,** anuvattati ; daḷhaŋ pavatteti. — **under,** vase vatteti. — **up,** paṭijaggati; poseti.

Keepsake, *n.* sārāṇīyavatthu, *nt.*

Keg, *n.* khuddaka-dārubhājana, *nt.*

Kelpie, *n.* assamukhī jaladevatā, *f.*

Kemp, *n.* thūlauṇṇā, *f.*

Ken, *n.* dassanapatha, *m.* *v.t.* disvā sañjānāti. *p.p.* °nita.

Kennel, *n.* sunakhakuṭi, *f.*

Kerchief, *n.* 1. siroveṭhana, *nt.* 2. hatthapuñchana, *nt.*

Kernel, *n.* miñjā, *f.* miñja, *nt.*

Kerosene, *n.* bhūmitela, *nt.*

Ketchup, *n.* 1. sūparasa, *m.* 2. gacchavisesa, *m.*

Kettle, *n.* jalukhā ; tāpanakumbhī, *f.* °**drum,** paṭaha, *m.*

Key, *n.* kuñcikā, *f.* tāḷa, *m.* avāpuraṇa, *nt.* °**hole,** kuñcikāvivara ; tāḷacchidda, *nt.* °**stone,** *n.* sandhisilā, *f.*

Khaki, *n.* dhūsaravattha, *nt.*

Khan, *n.* 1. Mohammadīyapālaka ; 2. Cīnādhirāja, *m.*

Kibe, *n.* pādaphoṭa, *m.*

Kick, *n.* pādappahāra, *m.* *v.t.* pādena paharati. *p.p.* °pahaṭa.

Kid, *n.* 1. ajapotaka, *m.* 2. sāṭheyya, *nt.* *v.t.* 1. potakaŋ vijāyati ; 2. vañceti. °**dy,** *a.* akammasīlī ; sukumāra.

Kiddle, *n.* macchavati, *f.*

Kidnap, *v.t.* balakkārena apaharati. *p.p.* °apahaṭa. °**per,** *n.* balenāpahārī, *m.* °**ping,** *n.* pasayhāvahāra, *m.*

Kidney, *n.* vakka, *nt.*

Kill, *v.t.* māreti ; ghāteti ; hanati. *p.p.* mārita ; °tita ; hata. °**er,** vadhaka ; māretu ; ghātetu, *m.* °**ing,** *n.* māraṇa ; hanana ; ghātana, *nt.* vadha, *m.*

Kiln, *n.* āvāpa, *m.* °**dry,** *v.t.* āvāpe sukkhāpeti. *p.p.* °pita.

Kin, *n.* 1. ñātibhāva ; 2. ñātigaṇa, *m.* °**ship,** *n.* samānatta ; ñātitta ; sambandhatta, *nt.*

Kinchin, *n.* bālaka, *m.*

Kind, *n.* jāti ; vikati, *f.* gaṇa ; vagga, *m.* adj. kāruṇika ; anukampaka ; sadaya. °**ly,** *adv.* sadayaŋ. °**ness,** karuṇā ; dayā; anukampā ; anuddayā, *f.*

Kindergarten, *n.* dārakapāṭhasālā, *f.* dārakuyyāna, *nt.*

Kindle, *v.t.* jāleti ; ujjāleti ; sandīpeti. *p.p.* °lita ; °pita, *v.i.* jalati ; dippati. *p.p.* jalita ; ditta. °**ing,** *n.* jālana ; dippana, *nt.* °**er,** *n.* jāletu ; ujjāletu, *m.*

Kindred, *n*. ñātigaṇa, *m*. ñātisālohitā, *m. pl*. adj. samānagatika; samajātika.
Kine (*pl*. of **Cow**), go, *m*.
Kinematograph, *n*. calacittadassana, *nt*.
King, *n*. rāja ; bhūpati ; bhūpāla ; narādhipa ; naradeva ; manujinda ; mahīpati ; narinda ; narapati ; narādhipa, *m*. °**craft**, *n*. rajjapālana, *nt*. rājadhamma, *m*. °**dom**, 1. rajja ; vijita ; 2. rājatta, *nt*. — **coconut**, sannīra, *m*. °**fisher**, maccharaṅka, *m*. °**less**, *a*. arājaka. °**ly**, *a*. rājāraha ; rājasadisa. °**ship**, *n*. rājapada ; rājatta, *nt*. °'**s abode**, rājabhavana ; rājamandira, *nt*. °'**s command**, rājāṇā, *f*. °'**s favourite**, rājavallabha, *m*. °'**s retinue**, rājaparisā, *f*. °'**s seal**, rājamuddā, *f*. °'**s sword-bearer**, asiggāhaka, *m*.
Kinsfolk, *n. pl*. bandhugaṇa, *m*.
Kinsman, *n*. bandhu ; bandhava ; ñāti ; sagotta, *m*. °**swoman**, ñātakitthī, *f*.
Kismet, *n*. bhāgya, *nt*. niyati, *f*.
Kiss, *n*. cumbana, *nt*. *v.t*. cumbati. *p.p*. °bita.
Kit, *n*. 1. pātheyya ; 2. puggalikopakaraṇa, *nt*.
Kitchen, *n*. rasavatī, *f*. mahānasa, *nt*. °**garden**, *n*. sākavatthu, *nt*. °**er**, *n*. dānasālādhikārī, *m*.
Kite, *n*. 1. kulala ; sena, *m*. 2. ākāsapatta, *nt*. *v.i*. uḍḍeti. *v.t*. plāveti.
Kith, *n*. bandhuvagga, *m*. ñātigaṇa, *m*.
Kitten, *n*. majjārapotaka, *m*. *v.t*. biḷālapotake vijāyati.
Kittle, *a*. duppariháriya.
Kittul, *n*. hintālataru, *m*.
Kleptomania, *n*. theyyapakatikatā, *f*.
Knack, *n*. upāyakosalla, *nt*. khippanisantitā, *f*. °**er**, *n*. jiṇṇassajiṇṇagehādiŋ ketā, *m*.
Knag, *n*. kukku ; rukkhagaṇṭhi, *m*.
Knap, *n*. sikharaṭṭhāna, *nt*. *v.t*. pāsāṇe (sakkharāpamāṇena) chindati.
Knapsack, *n*. aŋsatthavikā, *f*.
Knar, see **Knag**. °**ed**, *a*. gaṇḍijāta.
Knave, *n*. kitava ; nekatika, *m*. °**ish**, *a*. dhutta ; kapaṭa ; vañcanika. °**ishly**, *adv*. nikatiyā ; sāṭheyyena. °**ry**, °**ishness**, *n*. nikati ; vañcanā, *f*. sāṭheyya ; ketava, *nt*.
Knead, *v.t*. sanneti ; sammaddati. *p.p*. sannita ; °dita.
Knee, *n*. jāṇu ; jaṇṇu, *m*. *v.t*. jaṇṇunā ghaṭṭeti *or* phusati. *p.p*. °ghaṭṭita ; °phuṭṭha. °**cap**, *n*. jāṇumaṇḍala, *nt*. °**deep**, *a*. jaṇṇumatta. °**joint**, ūrupabba, *nt*. °**piece**, jaṅgheyya, *nt*.
Kneel, *v.i*. jaṇṇūhi nipatati. *p.p*. °tita.
Knell, *n*. amaṅgala-ghaṇṭārava, *m*. asubharava, *m*. *v.i*. avamaṅgalaravaŋ pavatteti ; asubhaŋ sūceti
Knick-knack, *n*. sallahukabhaṇḍa, *nt*.
Knife, *n*. chūrikā, *f*. khuddakasattha, *nt*. *v.t*. satthena āhanati. *p.p*. °āhata. — **blade**, vāsiphala, *nt*.
Knight, *n*. vīruttama ; mahāyodha, *m*.

Knit, *v.t.* gantheti. *p.p.* °thita. °**ting**, *n.* ganthana, *nt.*

Knob, *n.* makula, *nt.* gaṇṭhikā. °**by**, *a.* sagaṇḍa; gaṇṭhibahula.

Knock, *v.t.* ākoṭeti; paṭihanati. *v.i.* paṭihaññati. *p.p.* °ṭita; paṭihata. *n.* abhighāta, *m.* āhanana; ākoṭana, *nt.* °**down**, opāteti. °**er**, *n.* āhanaka; ākoṭaka, *m.* °**out**, paharitvā nikkhāmeti. °**off**, apagacchati. °**under**, vasaŋ yāti.

Knoll, *n.* unnatabhūmi, *f.* *v.t.* ghaṇṭaŋ vādeti; gaṇḍiŋ paharati.

Knot, *n.* 1. gaṇṭhi, *m.* ghaṭikā; gaṇṭhikā, *f.* 2. dubbodhaṭṭhāna, *nt.* *v.t.* gantheti; gaṇṭhiŋ yojeti. *p.p.* °thita; yojitagaṇṭhika. — **of hair**, moḷi, *f.* dhammilla, *m.* °**ty**, *a.* 1. pabbayutta; gaṇṭhibahula; 2. gūḷhattha.

Know, *v.i.* jānāti; vijānāti, *v.t.* sañjānāti; bujjhati. *p.p.* ñāta; viññāta; °nita; buddha. — **clearly**, pajānāti; abhijānāti. °**er**, *n.* ñātu; aññātu, *m.* °**ing**, *a.* jānanta. °**ingly**, *adv.* sañcicca; ñatvā. — **perfectly**, parijānāti; sambujjhati. — **thoroughly**, abhisameti. **Difficult to** —, dujjāna; duviññeyya, *a.*

Knowable, *a.* viññeyya; boddhabba.

Knowledge, *n.* ñāṇa, *nt.* paññā; vijjā; bodhi, *f.* **Boundless** —, anāvaraṇañāṇa, *nt.* **Discriminating** —, paṭisambhidā, *f.* **Eye of** —, ñāṇacakkhu, *nt.* **Limited** —, padesañāṇa, *nt.* **Perfect** —, ñāṇadassana, *nt.* **Right** —, sammappaññā, *f.* **Special** —, abhiññā, *f.* **Supreme** —, sammāsambodhi, *f.*

Known (*p.p.* of **Know**), ñāta; avagata; vidita. — **well**, vikkhyāta; pākaṭa.

Knuckle, *n.* aṅgulipabba, *nt.* *v.i.* 1. vasībhavati; 2. guḷaŋ kīḷati. *v.t.* aṅgulīhi ākoṭeti. *p.p.*°bhūta; °ṭita.

Knurl, *n.* gaṇṭhi; gaṇḍa, *m.*

Kobold, *n.* bhūgabbha-pisāca, *m.*

Koel, *n.* kokila, *m.*

Kohl, *n.* añjana, *nt.*

Koran, *n.* Mohammadīyadhammagantha, *m.*

Kosmos, *n.* lokadhātu, *f.*

Kraal, *n.* 1. hatthikoṭṭhaka, *nt.* 2. vatiparikkhittagāma. *m.*

Kris, *n.* chūrikā, *f.*

Kudos, *n.* kitti, *f.* yasoghosa, *m.*

Kyanize, *v.t.* telena makkhetvā ciraṭṭhāyiŋ karoti.

L

Laager, *n.* sakaṭaparivaṭṭa, *nt.* sakaṭakhandhāvāra, *m.*

Labefaction, *n.* hāni; balahāni, *f.* adhopāta, *m.*

Label, *n.* aṅkapaṇṇa; nāmaṅkana; laggitalañchana, *nt.* *v.t.* nāmaṅkitapaṇṇaŋ yojeti.

Labial, *a.* oṭṭhaja; oṭṭhāyatta.

Labiate, *a.* dvidhā-bhinnagga.

Labile, *a.* athāvara.

Laboratory, *n.* rasāyanāgāra, *nt.*

Laborious, *a.* 1. kiccabahula; 2. āyāsakara. °**ly**, *adv.* kicchena; kasirena. °**ness**, *n.* āyāsakāritā, *f.*

Labour, *n.* 1. āyāsa; parissama, *m.* 2. pasūtikāla, *m.* 3. hatthakamma, *nt.* *v.t.* parissamena sādheti. *v.i.* vāyamati; kammaŋ karoti. *p.p.* °sādhita; °mita; katakamma. °**er,** *n.* kammakara; vetanika; bhataka, *m.* °**ious,** *a.* 1. āyāsakara; dukkara; dusādhiya; 2. āyāsakkhama. — **pains,** *n.* pasavavedanā, *f.*

Labyrinth, *n.* 1. dunniggamaṭṭhāna, *nt.* 2. kaṇṇacchidda, *nt.* 3. vyākulatta, *nt.*

Lac, *n.* 1. lākhā, *f.* jatu, *nt.* 2. satasahassa, *nt.*

Lace, *n.* jālabhūsana, *nt.* *v.t.* jālabhūsanaŋ yojeti.

Lacerate, *v.t.* 1. padāḷeti; vidāreti; 2. vyathati; dukkhāpeti. *p.p.* °ḷita; °rita; °thita; °pita. °**ion,** *n.* vidāraṇa; pīḷana, *nt.*

Lacertian, *a.* godhāsadisa.

Laches, *n.* nītividhāna-ananuṭṭhāna, *nt.*

Lachrymal, *a.* assuvisayaka; assumocaka. °**mation,** assupatana, *nt.* °**matory,** *a.* assumocaka.

Lachrymose, *a.* assumukha.

Lack, *n.* abhāva; viraha, *m.* ūnatā, *f.* *v.i.* ūnāyati; ūno bhavati. *p.p.* ūnabhūta. °**ing,** *a.* ūna; hīna. — **all,** *a.* akiñcana. °**lustre,** *a.* mandappabha; maṅkubhūta.

Lackadaisical, *a.* anussuka; anutthunanta.

Lack-a-day, *intj.* aho; ahaha.

Lackey, *n.* pādamūlika; ceṭaka; cullupaṭṭhāka, *m.*

Laconic, °**al,** *a.* saṅkhitta; mitabhāṇī. °**nism,** *n.* mitabhāṇitā, *f.* kathālāghava, *nt.* °**ally,** *adv.* saṅkhepena.

Lacquer, *n.* lākhārasa, *m.* *v.t.* lākhārasena lepeti; lākhāya āvarati.

Lactation, *n.* thaññapāyana, *nt.* thaññapāyanakāla, *m.*

Lacteal, *a.* sakhīra; khīrāyatta; khīramaya.

Lactiferous, *a.* khīravāhī.

Lactometer, *n.* duddhaghanattamāṇaka, *nt.*

Lactory, *n.* khīraduhanaṭṭhāna, *nt.*

Lactogen, *n.* khīrāhāra, *m.*

Lacuna, *n.* 1. cheda, *m.* suññaṭṭhāna, *nt.* 2. naṭṭhapāṭha, *m.* °**al,** *a.* saccheda.

Lacustrine, *a.* sarasija; taḷākagocara.

Lad, *n.* māṇava; māṇavaka, *m.*

Ladder, *n.* sopāṇa, *m.* nissenī, *f.*

Lade, *v.t.* bhaṇḍam āropeti. *p.p.* āropitabhaṇḍa. °**ing,** *n.* nāvābhāra, *m.* nāvāya bhaṇḍajāta, *nt.*

Ladle, *n.* uluṅka, *m.* °**ful,** *a.* uluṅkamatta.

Lady, *n.* ayyā; sāminī; kulitthī, *f.* °'**s finger,** bhaṇḍākī, *f.* °**killer,** *n.* itthidhutta; thīlālaka, *m.* °**like,** *a.* suvinīta. °**love,** *n.* vāritakitthī, *f.* °**ship,** *n.* kulitthībhāva, *m.*

Lag, *v.i.* vilambati; sajjati. *p.p.* °bita; saṭṭha, °**gard,** *n.* mandagāmī; vilambaka; olīyaka, *m.* °**ging,** *n.* vilambana; olīyana; osakkana, *nt.*

Lagoon, *n.* loṇī, *f.*

Laic, *n*. gahaṭṭha; gihī, *m*. adj. gihībhūta. °**al**, *a*. gahaṭṭhāyatta. °**ize**, *v.t*. gahaṭṭhāyattaŋ karoti

Laid, *p.p*. of **Lay**. ṭhapita. — **bare**, vivaṭa, *a*. — **down**, 1. nikkhitta; ohita; 2. paññatta; 3. nipanna.

Lair, *n*. āsaya ; pasunilaya, *m*.

Laity, *n*. 1. gahaṭṭhajana ; 2. gihībhāva, *m*.

Lake, *n*. taḷāka ; sara ; daha, *m*. **Artificial** —, vāpi, *f*. jālāsaya, *m*. **Natural** —, jātassara, *m*. *nt*. **Small** —, pallala, *nt*.

Lakh, *n*. lakkha ; satasahassa, *nt*.

Lama, *n*. Tibbatīya-yati, *m*. °**ism**, Tibbata samaya, *m*. °**sery**, *n*. Tibbatīyārāma, *m*.

Lamb, *n*. meṇḍapotaka, *m*.

Lame, *a*. khañja ; paṅgula. *v.t*. khañjaŋ karoti. °**ish**, *a*. khañjasabhāva. °**ness**, *n*. khañjatta, *nt*. °**ly**, *adv*. vikalagatiyā; khañjākārena. — **person**, paṅgu, *m*.

Lament, *v.i*. vilapati ; anusocati ; paridevati. *p.p*. °pita ; °cita ; °vita. °**able**, *a*. sociya ; socanīya. °**ation**, *n*. vilāpa ; parideva, *m*. ādevanā, *f*. °**ed**, *a*. 1. kālakata ; 2. socitabba.

Lamina, *n*. kharacchavi, *f*. °**ted**, *a*. papaṭikajāta.

Lamp, *n*. padīpa ; pajjota, *m*. *v.t*. obhāseti ; joteti. *v.i*. obhāsati. *p.p*. °sita ; jotita. °**black**, *n*. dīpamasi, *m*. — **stand**, *n*. dīpādhāra, *m*. — **wick**, *n*. dīpavaṭṭi, *f*.

Lampoon, *n*. nindakalipi, *f*. *v.t*. lekhanena nindati. *p.p*. °dita. °**er**, *n*. nindaka, *m*.

Lanate, *a*. lomasa.

Lance, *n*. satti, *f*. tomara ; kuntāyudha, *nt*. *v.t*. sattiyā āhanati. *p.p*. sattiāhata. °**er**, *n*. sattidhara, *m*. **Short**—, kaṇaya, *m*.

Land, *n*. thala, *nt*. bhūmi, *f*. thalappadesa, *m*. *v.t*. thalaŋ pāpeti. *v.i*. thalam otarati *or* pāpuṇāti. *p.p*. °pāpita ; °otiṇṇa ; °patta. °**force**, thalasenā, *f*. °**holder**, °**lord**, bhūmisāmī, *m*. °**ing**, *n*. thalappatti, *f*. nāvotaraṇa, *nt*. °**lady**, *n*. pathikāgārasāminī, *f*. °**less**, *a*. khettavatthurahita. °**mark**, 1. sīmāciṇha, *nt*. 2. thalābhiññāṇa, *nt*. — **route**, thalapatha, *m*. °**scape**, nayanagocara-bhūkhaṇḍa, *m*. — **surveyor**, rajjugāhaka ; bhūmimāṇaka, *m*. **Barren** —, jaṅgala ; marutthala, *nt*. **Living on the** —, thalagocara, *a*. **Marshy** —, anūpa, *m*. kaccha, *m*. *nt*. **Situated on the** —, thalaṭṭha, *a*.

Landed, *a*. khettavatthuyutta.

Landocracy, *n*. khettapatigaṇa, *m*.

Land-pirate, *n*. panthavilopaka, *m*.

Lane, *n*. upapatha, *m*. upavīthi, *f*.

Language, *n*. bhāsā, vāṇī, *f*. — **of Magadha**, Māgadhī, *f*.

Languid, *a*. kilanta ; parissanta ; osīna. °**ly**, *adv*. dubbalākārena. °**ness**, *n*. tandi, *f*. kilamatha, *m*. ālasya, *nt*.

Languish, *v.i.* avasīdati ; kilamati ; milāyati ; *p.p.* osīna ; kilanta ; milāta. °**ing,** *a.* osīdamāna. °**ingly,** *adv.* ukkaṇṭhitākārena. °**ment,** *n.* kilamana ; osīdana, *nt.* ukkaṇṭhā, *f.*

Languor, *n.* dubbalya ; gelañña ; ālasya, *nt.* °**ous,** *a.* dubbala ; gilāna ; alasa.

Laniary, *a.* dāṭhāsadisa ; chindaka. *n.* 1. dāṭhā, *f.* 2. vadhaṭṭhāna, *nt.*

Laniferous, *a.* uṇṇāsahita.

Lank, *a.* kisa ; tanu. °**iness,** *n.* kisatta, *nt.*

Lanner, *n.* vyagghīnasī, *f.*

Lantern, *n.* āvarita-padīpa, *m.*

Lap, *n.* 1. ucchaṅga ; aṅka, *m.* 2. (of a cloth :) dasanta, *m.* *v.t.* oguṇṭheti ; aṅke ṭhapeti. *p.p.* °ṭhita ; °pita. *v.i.* lihati ; (jivhāya) sāyati.

Lapicide, *n.* pāsāṇavidāraka. *m.*

Lapidary, *n.* maṇikāra, *m.* adj. 1. maṇisippāyatta ; 2. silālekhāraha ; silākammāraha.

Lapidate, *v.t.* 1. pāsāṇehi paharati ; 2. silāpahārehi māreti. *p.p.* °pahaṭa ; °mārita. °**ion,** *n.* silāhi paharaṇa, *nt.*

Lapidify, *v.t.* pāsāṇīkaroti. *p.p.* °kata.

Lapis lazuli, *n.* veḷuriya, *nt.* vaŋsavaṇṇa, *m.*

Lappet, *n.* 1. dasanta, *nt.* vatthakoṇa, *m.* 2. lambamāna-pesi, *f.*

Lapse, *n.* accaya ; atikkama, *m.* 2. khalita, *nt.* pamāda, *m.* *v.i.* 1. acceti ; atikkamati ; 2. khalati ; pamajjati. *p.p.* atikkanta ; khalita ; pamatta.

Lapwing, *n.* dindibha, *m.*

Lar, *n.* gharadevatā, *f.*

Larceny, *n.* coriya ; theyya, *nt.* °**ner,** *n.* cora ; thena, *m.*

Lard, *n.* sūkaravasā, *f.* *v.t.* 1. sūkaramaŋsena *or* vasāya missseti ; 2. gambhīrapade yojeti. *p.p.* °sita ; yojita ; °pada.

Larder, *n.* bhojanopakaraṇāgāra, *nt.*

Large, *v.* mahanta ; visāla ; vipula ; uru. °**ly,** *adv.* bahuso ; bhīyo ; yebhuyyena. °**minded,** *a.* uḷāracitta. °**hearted,** uḷārahadaya. °**ness,** *n.* mahatta ; visālatta, *nt.*

Largesse, *n.* vitaraṇa ; vissajjana ; dāna, *nt.* pariccāga, *m.*

Lariat, *n.* pasubandanarajju, *f.*

Lark, *n.* kokila ; paraputtha, *m.* *v.i.* kīḷati ; modati.

Larrikin, *n.* panthadūsaka, *m.*

Larva, *n.* kīṭapotaka, *m.*

Larynx, *n.* galanāḷa ; kaṇṭhanāḷa, *m.*

Lascar, *n.* Bhāratīya-nāvika, *m.*

Lascivious, *a.* kāmāsatta ; kāmuka. °**ly,** *adv.* kāmukatāya. °**ness,** *n.* rāgabahulatā, *f.*

Lash, *n.* kasā ; varattā, *f.* *v.t.* 1. kasāhi tāḷeti ; rajjuyā bandhati. *p.p.* °tāḷita ; baddha. °**ing,** *n.* kasātāḷana, *nt.*

Lass, *n.* kaññā ; kumārī ; yuvatī, *f.*

Lassitude. *m.* kilamatha, *m.* dubbalya ; gelañña, *nt.*

Lasso, *n.* pāsa, *m.*

Last, *a.* 1. antima ; carima ; pacchima ; 2. atīta ; gata ; 3. adhama. *v.i.* dharati ; pavattati, *adv.* ante ; pariyosāne.

°**ing**, *a.* ciraṭṭhāyī; thirapavattika. °**ing long**, addhaniya, *a.* °**ly**, *adv.* osāne; carimavasena.

Latch, *n.* aggaḷa *nt.* *v.t.* aggaḷena thaketi. *p.p.* °thakita.

Latchet, *n.* pādukāveṭhanī, *f.*

Late, *a.* 1. velātīta; pamatta; 2. nūtana; abhinava; 3. atīta; gata; pubbaka. *adv.* cirāyitvā; velam atikkamma; pamajjitvā. °**st**, *a.* pacchimatara. — **in the day**, atisāyaŋ, *ind.* — **in the night**, vītikkantāya rattiyā. °**ly**, *adv.* nāticiraŋ; samīpātīte. °**ness**, *n.* cirāyitatta, *nt.* kālātikkama, *m.* **Of** —, adūrātīte. **Too** —, aticirāyita, *a.* aticirāyitvā, *adv.*

Latency, *a.* apākaṭatā; paṭicchannatā, *f.*

Latent, *a.* nilīna; gūḷha; apākaṭa.

Later, *a.* pacchima, *adv.* pacchā; aparabhāge.

Lateral, *a.* passāyatta. °**ly**, *adv.* passato; passena.

Latescent, *a.* anusāyika. °**ence**, *n.* anusāyikatta, *nt.*

Latex, *n.* rukkhaniyyāsa, *m.*

Lath, *n.* bidala; tanuphalaka, *nt.* *v.t.* bidale yojeti.

Lathe, *n.* bhama, *m.*

Lather, *n.* pheṇa, *nt.* *v.t.* pheṇayuttaŋ karoti. *v.i.* pheṇena āvarīyati. *p.p.* °āvaṭa.

Latitude, *n.* akkhavaṭṭula, *nt.*

Latrine, *n.* vaccakuṭi, *f.*

Latter, *a.* pacchima; pacchāvutta. °**ly**, *adv.* āsannakāle; nātipubbe.

Lattice, *n.* gavakkha; jālakavāṭa, *m.* °**work**, kaṭṭhajāla, *nt.*

Laud, *n.* thuti; pasaŋsā, thomanā; kittanā, *f.* *v.t.* thometi; pasaŋsati; abhitthavati. *p.p.* °mita; pasattha; abhitthuta. °**able**, *a.* pāsaŋsiya; thomanāraha. °**ation**, *n.* thomana, *nt.* °**atory**, *a.* thutipubbaka.

Laugh, *v.i.* hasati; jagghati. °**able**, *a.* hāsakara; hāsajanaka. — **aloud**, ujjagghati. — **at**, parihasati. °**ing**, *a.* hasamāna; hāsayutta. °**ingly**, *adv.* sahāsaŋ. °**ter**, *n.* hāsa, *m.* hasana; jagghana, *nt.* **Horse** —, aṭṭahāsa, *m.*

Launch, *n.* 1. plāvana, *nt.* 2. ārabhana, *nt.* 3. jalapota, *m.* *v.t.* 1. nāvaŋ plāveti; 2. ārabhati. *p.p.* °vita; āraddha.

Launder, *n.* rajaka; dhovaka, *m.* *v.t.* vatthāni dhovati *or* sodheti. °**er**, *n.* ninnejaka; rajaka, *m.* °**dress**, *n.* rajakī, *f.* °**dry**, *n.* rajakasālā, *f.*

Laureate, *n.* aggakavi, *m.*

Laurel, *n.* maṅgala-pattavisesa; punnāga, *m.* *v.t.* 1. maṅgalapattehi maṇḍeti; 2. rājakavittaŋ pāpeti. *p.p.* °dita; °pāpita. **Win the** —, vikhyātiŋ yāti.

Lava, *n.* vilīna-pāsāṇa, *m.*

Lavatory, *n.* 1. vaccakuṭi, *f.* 2. udakakoṭṭhaka, *m.*

Lave, *v.t.* 1. dhovati; pakkhāleti; 2. ussiñcati. *p.p.* dhota; °lita; ussitta. °**er**, *n.* dhovanabhājana, *nt.* °**ment**, *n.* vatthi, *m.*

Lavender, *n.* gandhasāravisesa, *m.*

Lavish, *a.* aticāgī; adhikavayī. *v.t.* bahubbayaŋ karoti; asīmitaŋ deti. *p.p.* °kata; °dinna. °**er**, *n.* ativyayī, *m.* °**ly**, *adv.* atibbayena; aparimitaŋ. °**ness**, *n.* ativyayitā, *f.* asīmitadāna, *nt.*

Law, *n.* 1. nīti; paññatti; vavatthā, *f.* 2. sikkhā; āṇā, *f.* niyoga, *m.* °**abiding**, nītigaruka, *a.* °**book**, *n.* nītigantha, *m.* °**breaker**, *n.* nītyullaṅghaka, *m.* °**court**, vinicchayasālā, *f.* °**giver**, āṇāpaka; nītidāyī, *m.* °**ful**, *a.* nītyanukūla; kappiya. °**fully**, *adv.* ñāyena; dhammena. °**fulness**, dhammikatta; ñāyānugatatta, *nt.* °**less**, *a.* 1. ñāyaviruddha; adhammika; 2. durācāra; sericārī. °**lessly**, *adv.* aññāyena. °**suit**, aṭṭa; adhikaraṇa, *nt.*

Lawn, *n.* tiṇachanna-aṅgaṇa, *nt.*

Lawyer, *n.* nītivedī, *m.*

Lax, *a.* 1. sithila; komala; mudu; 2. durācāra. °**ity**, *n.* sithilatta, *nt.* °**ly**, *adv.* sithilākārena

Laxative, *n.* virecanosadha, *nt.* adj. virecaka.

Lay, *v.t.* 1. ṭhapeti; niveseti; nikkhipati; 2. attharati; 3. nipāteti; 4. āropeti. *p.p.* ṭhapita; °sita; nikkhitta; atthata; °tita; °pita. — **aside**, oropeti. — **down**, nikkhipati. — **hands on**, parāmasati. — **hold of**, gaṇhāti. — **open**, āvīkaroti; vivarati. — **up**, upanikkhipati. — **out**, pasāreti.

Lay, *n.* gīta, *nt.* adj. agārika; gihībhūta. °**man**, *n.* gahaṭṭha; gihī; agārika, *m.* °**woman**, *n.* gihinī; upāsikā, *f.*

Layer, *n.* 1. uparilepa, *m.* 2. sañcitatala, *nt.* 3. patiṭṭhāṭṭhāna, *nt.* 4. nikkhipaka, *m.*

Layfigure, *n.* 1. kaṭṭhapaṭimā, *f.* 2. parikappitapuggala, *m.* 3. agaṇetabba-purisa, *m.*

Laystall, *n.* asucirāsi, *m.*

Lazar, *n.* kuṭṭharogī, *m.* °**et**, *n.* kuṭṭhārogyasālā, *f.*

Laze, *v.i.* ālasiyena kālaŋ khepeti.

Lazy, *a.* alasa; kusīta; akammasīlī. °**ily**, *adv.* kusītākārena. °**iness**, *n.* ālasya; kosajja, *nt.*

Lea, *n.* tiṇabhūmi, *f.* saddala, *m.*

Lead, *n.* tipu; sīsaka, *nt.* *v.t.* tipunā āvarati. °**en**, *a.* 1. tipumaya; 2. bhāriya.

Lead, *n.* nāyakatta; maggadesakatta, *nt.* *v.t.* neti; pāpeti. *v.i.* nāyako hoti. *p.p.* nīta; pāpita; nāyakabhūta. — **back**, paṭineti. — **a bad life**, dujjīvitaŋ jīvati. °**er**, *n.* netu; adhipati; puregāmī; pubbaṅgama, *m.* °**er of a herd**, yūthapati, *m.* °**ership**, *n.* nāyakatta; netutta, *nt.* — **to**, saŋvattati (*with dat.*).

Leading, *a.* 1. āvaha; sampāpaka; 2. maggadesaka; padhāna. — **astray**, mohanaka, *a.* — **bull**, usabha, *m.* — **to**, sampāpaka; āvaha. *a.*—**to rebirth**, ponobhavika, *a.* — **to ruin**, parihāniya; vayagāmī, *a.*

Leaf, *n.* patta; paṇṇa; dala; palāsa, *nt.* °**age**, *n.* pattabhāra, *m.* — **hut**, paṇṇasālā, *f.* °**less**, *a.* pattarahita; galitapatta. °**let**, *n.* pattikā, *f.* °**y**, *a.* sañchannapatta. **Young** —, pallava, *m.*

League, *n.* 1. gāvuta, *nt.* 2. samiti. *v.i.* sandhīyati; saŋyojīyati. *v.t.* sandhānaŋ karoti. *p.p.* sandhita; saŋyutta; katasandhāna. °**er**, *n.* samitigata, *m*

Leak, *n.* chidda ; randha ; vivara, *nt.* *v.i.* savati ; galati ; sandati. *p.p.* savita ; galita ; °dita. °**age**, *n.* 1. sandana ; paggharana ; chiddaṭṭhāna, *nt.* 2. rahassāvībhāva, *m.* °**y**, *a.* sacchidda.

Leal, *a.* akuṭila ; nītigaruka.

Lean, *a.* kisa ; tanu. *v.i.* apasseti ; poṇo bhavati, *v.t.* nipajjāpeti. *p.p.* apassita ; poṇabhūta ; °pita. °**ing**, *n.* poṇatā, *f.* °**ing**, *a.* apassayamāna. °**ing upon**, olubbha ; ālambiya, *abs.* °**ness**, *n.* 1. kisatta ; tanutta ; 2. poṇatta, *nt.*

Leap, *n.* ullaṅghana, *nt.* upplava, *m.* *v.i.* laṅghati ; plavati, *v.t.* laṅgheti. *p.p.* °ghita ; °vita. °**day**, *n.* adhikadivasa, *m.* — **over**, laṅghitvā atikkāmeti. °**ing**, *a.* pakkhandamāna. °**year**, *n.* adhikavassa, *nt.*

Learn, *v.t.* uggaṇhāti ; sikkhati, *v.i.* jānāti ; avagacchati. *p.p.* uggahita ; °khita ; ñāta ; avagata. — **by heart**, vācuggataŋ karoti. °**ed**, *a.* bahussuta ; sutadhara. °**er**, *n.* sikkhaka ; sekkha ; vijjatthī, *m.* °**ing**, *n.* 1. vijjā, *f.* suta ; sippa, *nt.* 2. uggaha, *m.* sikkhana, *nt.* — **well**, samuggaṇhāti.

Lease, *n.* kālikagāha, *m.* *v.t.* kālikavasena deti. *p.p.* °dinna.

Leash, *n.* gaddula, *m.* varattā, *f.* *v.t.* varattāya bandhati. *p.p.* varattābaddha.

Leasing, *n.* musāvāda, *m.* asaccakathana, *nt.*

Least, *n.* *a.* atyappaka ; aṇumatta ; parittaka. **At** —, antamaso. *ind.* °**ways**, °**wise**, *adv.* antimaparicchedena ; antamaso.

Leather, *n.* camma, *nt.* *v.t.* 1. cammena āvarati ; 2. varattāya tāḷeti. *p.p.* °āvaṭa ; °ḷita. °**bag**, cammapasibbaka, *m.* °**dresser**, *n.* cammasaṅkhāraka, *m.* °**n**, *a.* cammamaya.

Leave, *n.* anuññā ; anumati, *f.* okāsa, *m.* āpucchana, *nt.* *v.t.* 1. jahati ; pajahati ; cajati ; ossajati ; vajjeti ; 2. atirittaŋ karoti ; dāyādavasena ṭhapeti, *v.i.* apagacchati ; viramati. *p.p.* jahita ; catta ; ossaṭṭha ; vajjita ; atirittakata ; °pita ; apagata ; virata. — **household life**, pabbajati ; abhinikkhamati. °**ing**, *a.* pajahanta, °**ing**, *n.* pahāna ; vajjana, *nt.* °**over**, seseti. — **the Order**, uppabbajati.

Leaven, *n.* kiṇṇa, *nt.* *v.t.* kiṇṇaŋ pakkhipati. *p.p.* kiṇṇapakkhitta.

Leavings, *n.* *pl.* ucchiṭṭha ; bhuttāvasesa, *nt.*

Lecher, *n.* aticārī ; kāmamicchācārī, *m.* °**ous**, *a.* itthidhutta ; kāmātura. °**ously**, *a.* kāmāturattena. °**y**, *n.* kāmukatta, *nt.*

Lecture, *n.* desanā ; vijjānugatakathā, *f.* *v.t.* deseti ; uddisati. *p.p.* desita ; uddiṭṭha. °**r**, *n.* desaka ; kathika, *m.* °**rship**, kathikapada, *nt.*

Ledge, *n.* bahiniggatavedī, *f.*

Ledger, *n.* 1. āya-vayapotthaka ; 2. susāna-silāpatthara, *m.*

Lee, *n.* 1. vātāvaraṇa, *nt.* nivātapassa, *nt.*

Leech, *n.* 1. jalūkā ; rattapā, *f.* 2. bhisakka, *m.*

Leek, *n.* pattapalaṇḍu, *m.*

Leer, *n.* apāṅgavilokana, *nt.* *v.t.* akkhikoṭiyā oloketi.

Lees, *n. pl.* kakka ; adhosañcitamala, *nt.*

Left, *n.* vāmapassa, *nt.* adj. vāma; savya, *adv.* vāmena ; vāmato. °**handed**, *a.* paricita-vāmahattha. °**ward**, *a.* vāmapassika. °**wards**, *adv.* vāmābhimukhaŋ.

Left, *p.p.* of Leave, — **behind**, ohīna, *a.* — **over**, atiritta ; avasiṭṭha, *a.* — **unfinished**, vippakata, *a.*

Leg, *n.* pāda, *m.* *v.i.* dhāvati. °**less**, *a.* apādaka.

Legacy, *n.* accaye-dāna ; āveṇikadhana, *nt.*

Legal, *a.* ñāyānugata. °**ity**, *n.* nītyanukūlatta, *nt.* °**ize**, *v.t.* vavatthapeti ; paññāpeti ; sammannati. °**ly**, *adv.* ñāyena ; yathānītiŋ.

Legate, *n.* saṅgharājadūta, *m.* *v.t.* dāyādaŋ deti. *p.p.* dinnadāyāda. °**tion**, *n.* 1. dūteyya, *nt.* 2. dūtasabhā, *f.* 3. dūtāvāsa, *m.* 4. dūtakicca, *nt.*

Legatee, *n.* laddhāveṇika-dhana.

Legend, *n.* paramparāgatakathā, *f.* apadāna ; upākhyāna, *nt.* °**ary**, *a.* purāvuttagata.

Legerdemain, *a.* indajāla, *nt.* hatthavyāja, *m.*

Legging, *n.* jaṅghāveṭhana, *nt.*

Leggy, *a.* dīghajaṅgha.

Legible, *a.* vibhūta *or* visadakkhara. °**bility**, *n.* visadakkharatā, *f.* °**bly**, *adv.* suvyattaŋ; suvāciyākārena.

Legion, *n.* 1. senā ; camū, *f.* 2. samūha ; vyūha, *m.*

Legislate, *v.t.* nītiŋ paññāpeti *or* vavatthapeti. *p.p.* °ññattanītika ; °pitanītika. °**ion**, *n.* nītisampādana, *nt.* °**ive**, *a.* vidhāyaka ; nītidāyaka. °**tor**, *n.* vidhāyī ; nītidāyī, *m.* °**ure**, *n.* vidhāyakasabhā, *f.*

Legist, *n.* nītikovida, *m.*

Legitimate, *a.* 1. orasa ; attaja ; 2. nītyanukūla ; 3. yathātatha ; yathābhūta, *v.t.* orasattaŋ pāpeti ; nītyanugataŋ karoti. *p.p.* °pāpita ; °kata. °**ly**, *adv.* yathāñāyaŋ ; yathātathaŋ. °**ness**, *n.* orasatta ; ñāyānugatatta, *nt.*

Legitimacy, *n.* orasatta, *nt.*

Legitimatize, °**mize**, *v.t.* orasattaŋ *or* ñāyanukūlattaŋ pāpeti. *p.p.* °pāpita.

Legitimism, *n.* rājānuvattana, *nt.*

Legume, Legumen, *n.* phalasipāṭikā, *f.* °**minous**, *a.* sipāṭikāyutta.

Leisure, *n.* vivekakāla ; vissamana-samaya, *m.* °**less**, *a.* vivekarahita. °**ly**, *a.* aturita ; yathāvasara, *adv.* manda-mandaŋ ; yathāvasaraŋ.

Lemma, *n.* mātikāpāṭha ; saṅkhitta-visaya, *m.*

Lemon, *n.* jambīra, *nt.* °**ade**, *n.* jambīrapāna, *nt.*

Lemur, *n.* nisāvānara, *m.*

Lend, *v.t.* iṇāya deti. *p.p.* °dinna. °**er**, *n.* iṇadāyī, *m.* °**ing**, *n.* iṇadāna, *nt.*

Length, *n.* āyāma, *m.* dīghatā, *f.* °**en**, *v.t.* āyataŋ karoti. *p.p.* āyatīkata. °**y**, *a.* āyata ; dīgha. °**ways**, °**wise**, anvāyāmaŋ, *adv.*

Lenient, *a.* muduka ; athaddha ; sadaya. °**ly,** *adv.* apharusaŋ ; sadayaŋ. °**ncy,** *n.* maddava, *nt.* mudutā, *f.*

Lenitive, *a.* *n.* upasamakara ; tāpanāsaka.

Lenity, *n.* dayālutā, *f.* kāruñña, *nt.*

Lens, *n.* kācanetta, *nt.* **Convex —,** majjhunnata-kāca, *m.* **Concave —,** majjhaninna-kāca, *m.*

Lentil, *n.* masūraka, *nt.*

Leo, *n.* 1. sīha, *m.* 2. sīharāsi, *m.* °**nine,** *a.* sīhagatika ; sīhajātika.

Leopard, *n.* dīpi ; saddūla, *m.* °**ess,** *n.* dīpinī, *f.*

Leper, *n.* kuṭṭhī, *m.*

Leprosy, *n.* kuṭṭharoga, *m.*

Leprous, *a.* kuṭṭhātura.

Lese-majesty, *n.* rājadubbhana, *nt.*

Lesion, *n.* hāni, *f.* antarāya, *m.* āhanana, *nt.*

Less, *n.* appatara ; ūnaka, *nt.* adj. ūna ; hīna ; appaka. *adv.* ūnataraŋ ; mandataraŋ. *prep.* hitvā ; vihāya. °**er,** *a.* ūnatara; atikhuddaka.

Lessee, *n.* kālikagāhī, *m.*

Lessen, *v.t.* ūnaŋ *or* mandaŋ karoti. *v.i.* hāyati ; khīyati ; mandībhavati. *p.p.* mandīkata ; hīna ; khīṇa ; mandībhūta.

Lesson, *n.* 1. ajjhāya ; uddesa, *m.* 2. upadesa, *m.* *v.t.* sāsati ; upadisati. *p.p.* sāsita ; upadiṭṭha.

Lessor, *n.* kālikagāhadāyī, *m.*

Lest, *conj.* no ce.

Let, *v.t.* 1. anujānāti ; 2. tāvakālikaŋ deti ; 3. moceti. *p.p.* anuññāta ; °dinna ; mocita. — **down,** nikkhipati ; pajahati. — **in,** paveseti. — **loose,** pamuñcati ; vissajjeti. — **off,** vimoceti. — **go,** sithilīkaroti ; gāhaŋ moceti. — **slip,** nissajati.

Letch, *v.t.* bhasmaŋ dhovati. *n.* abhilāsā *f.*

Lethal, *a.* pāṇahara.

Lethargy, *n.* thīna ; ālasya, *nt.* tandī, *f.* °**ic,** *a.* alasa ; tandita. °**ically,** *adv.* alasatāya. °**ize,** *v.t.* alasayati ; tanditaŋ karoti.

Letter, *n.* 1. akkhara, *nt.* vaṇṇa, *m.* 2. lipi, *f.* sāsana, *nt.* sandesa, *m.* *v.t.* akkharehi aṅketi. *p.p.* °aṅkita. — **in reply,** paṭisāsana, *nt.* °**box,** sāsanamañjūsā, *f.* °**ed,** *a.* satthakovida. °**ing,** *n.* akkharalañchana, *nt.* °**less,** *a.* asatthaññū ; assutavantu.

Lettuce, *n.* khādiya-sākavisesa, *m.*

Levant, *v.i.* (iṇam adatvā) palāyati. °**er,** *n.* palāyī, *m.*

Levator, *n.* 1. ukkhipaka-maŋsapesi, *f.* 2. ukkhipakopakaraṇa, *nt.*

Levee, *n.* 1. rājadassana, *nt.* rājasabhā, *f.* 2. nadījala-vārakāḷi, *f.*

Level, *n.* 1. samabhūmi, *f.* samaṭṭhāna, *nt.* 2. samatta ; tulyatta, *nt.* 3. samattadassakopakaraṇa, *nt.* adj. sama ; avisama, *v.t.* samataŋ neti ; samatalaŋ karoti. °**ler,** *n.* samatāpādaka, *m.* °**ly,** *adv.* samākārena. °**ness,** *n.* samatta, *nt.*

Lever, *n.* uttolana-daṇḍa, *m.* *v.t.* ukkhipati ; cāleti. *p.p.* ukkhitta ; cālita. °**age,** *n.* uttolanakicca, *nt.*

Leviathan, *n*. 1. atimahādehī, *m*. 2. ativisālanāvā, *f*. 3. mahāsamudda-makara, *m*.

Levigate, *v.t.* sukhumacuṇṇattaŋ pāpeti. *p.p.* °pāpita.

Levitate, *v.t.* sallahukaŋ karoti, *v.i.* antalikkhe carati. *p.p.* °kata. °**ion**, *n*. ākāsagamana, *nt*.

Levity, *n*. cittalahutā, *f*. lāghava; cāpalla, *nt*.

Levy, *n*. 1. senāsamāhāra, *m*. 2. kara; bali, *m*. *v.t.* 1. senaŋ sañcināti *or* samāharati; 2. karaŋ gaṇhāti. *p.p.* sañcitasena; samāhaṭa°; gahitakara.

Lewd, *a*. 1. kāmāsatta; durācāra. °**talk**, duṭṭhulla, *nt*. °**ly**, *adv*. asabbhākārena. °**ness**, *n*. kāmukatā; asiṭṭhatā, *f*.

Lexicography, *n*. saddakosaracanā, *f*. °**pher**, *n*. saddakosasampādaka, *m*.

Lexicology, *n*. niruttisattha, *nt*.

Lexicon, *n*. saddakosa, *m*.

Lexigraphy, *n*. ekakkharapadika-lipi, *f*.

Liable, *a*. anuyogāraha; upavajja. °**bility**, *n*. upavajjatā, *f*.

Liaison, *n*. aticāra; micchācāra; durācāra, *m*.

Liar, *n*. musāvādī; abhūtakkhāyi, *m*.

Libation, *n*. 1. dakkhiṇodaka, *nt*. 2. dakkhiṇodakapātana, *nt*.

Libel, *n*. abbhakkhāna, *nt*. nindakalipi, *f*. *v.t.* abbhakkhāti; lipiyā nindati. *p.p.* °khāta; °dita, °**ler**, abbhakkhāyī, *m*. °**lous**, *a*. abbhakkhānapubbaka.

Liberal, *n*. sādhīnapuggala, *m*. adj. 1. dānasoṇḍa; cāgasīlī; muttacāga; 2. uḷāracitta; 3. aparādhīṇa. °**ity**, *n*. cāga, *m*. vadaññutā, *f*. °**ly**, *adv*. aluddhatāya; muttahatthatāya.

Liberate, *v.t.* 1. pamoceti; 2. bhujissaŋ karoti. *p.p.* °cita; katabhujissa. °**ion**, *n*. mutti; vimutti, *f*. mokkha, *m*. pamuñcana, *nt*. °**or**, *n*. vimocaka; muttidāyaka, *m*.

Liberticide, *n*. *a*. vimuttināsaka.

Libertine, *n*. *a*. 1. nidāsamatika; sericārī; 2. durācāra, *m*.

Liberty, *n*. sādhīnatā; abaddhatā; aparādhīnatā, *f*.

Libidinous, *a*. kāmuka; rāgaratta.

Libra, *n*. 1. tulā, *f*. 2. tulārāsi, *m*.

Library, *n*. potthakālaya; ganthasamūha, *m*. °**ian**, *n*. ganthālayādhikārī, *m*.

Librate, *v.i.* dolāyati; tulīyati. *p.p.* °yita; tulita. °**ion**, *n*. dolāyana, *nt*.

Licence, *n*. 1. anuññā; anumati, *f*. 2. adhikārapaṇṇa, *nt*. *v.t.* anujānāti; anuññāpaṇṇaŋ deti. *p.p.* anuññāta; dinnānuññāpaṇṇa.

Licensee, *n*. anuññāpaṇṇadhārī, *m*. °**ser**, *n*. anuññāpaṇṇadāyī, *m*.

Licentious, *a*. 1. anītigaruka; asampadāyagaruka; 2. anācārasīlī. °**ly**, *adv*. velātikkamena; nimmariyādaŋ. °**ness**, *n*. sīmātikkama, *m*. durācāratā, *f*.

Lich, Lych, *n*. chava, *m*. matakalebara, *nt*.

Lichen, *n*. vandākā, *f*.

Licit, *a*. dhammika; ñāyānukūla. °**ly**, *adv*. yathāñāyaŋ.

Lick, *v.t.* lihati. *p.p.* lihita. °**ing**, *n*. lihana, *nt*. — **off**, apalihati.

Lickerish, *a.* rasagiddha ; madhurappiya.

Licorice see **Liquorice.**

Lid, *n.* piḍhāna ; thakana ; tirodhāna, *nt.* °**less**, *a.* apihita ; pidhānarahita.

Lie, *n.* asacca ; alika, *nt.* musā, *f.* musāvāda, *m.* *v.i.* vitthāti ; alikaŋ, abhūtaŋ *or* musā bhaṇati. See **Lying.**

Lie, *v.i.* upavisati ; nipajjati. *p.p.* upaviṭṭha ; nipanna. — **awake**, jāgarati. — **dormant**, anuseti. — **down close to**, upanipajjati. — **in**, pasūti-avatthāyaŋ vattati. — **on**, adhiseti. — **with**, ekato nipajjati. See **Lying.**

Lief, *adv.* sānandaŋ.

Liege, *n.* issara ; adhipati, *m.*

Lien, *n.* upanidhiṭhapanādhikāra, *m.*

Lieu (In), atthāya.

Lieutenant, *n.* upādhikārī ; upasenāpati, *m.*

Life, *n.* 1. jīva, *m.* jīvita, *nt.* 2. jīvanacarita, *nt.* 3. jīvana, *nt.* °**belt**, *n.* ummujjāpaka-āvaṭṭa, *m.* °**blood**, 1. antosāra ; 2. padhānahetu, *m.* °**giving**, *a.* jīvada; balajanaka. °**less**, *a.* nijjīva ; acetana. °**lessly**, *adv.* olīnākārena. °**like**, *a.* jīvamānākāra. °**long**, *a.* yāvajīvika. *adv.* yāvajīvaŋ. °**time**, jīvitakāla, *m.* **Endowed with**—, sajīva, *a.* **Faculty of** —, jīvitindriya, *nt.* **For** —, yāvajīvaŋ, *adv.* **Love of** —, jīvitāsā, *f.* **Means of** —, jīvanopāya, *m.*

Lifer, *n.* yāvajīva-kārābaddha.

Lift, *n.* 1. ukkhipana, *nt.* 2. ukkhepaka-yanta, *nt.* *v.t.* ubbāhati ; ukkhipati ; uccāreti. *p.p.* °hita ; ukkhitta ; °rita. °**ed off**, vivatta, *a.*

Ligament, *n.* 1. bandhana, *nt.* 2. aṭṭhisandhi-bandhana, *nt.*

Ligature, *n.* nahārubandhana, *nt.* *v.t.* paṭṭikāhi veṭheti. *p.p.* °ṭhita.

Light, *a.* 1. sallahuka ; agaru ; 2. sukara ; sukhasādhiya. °**fingered**, *a.* coriyanipuṇa. °**hearted**, *a.* sallahukacitta. °**headed**, *a.* bhantacitta. °**heeled**, *a.* turitagatika. °**ly**, *adv.* lahukaŋ ; akasirena. °**minded**, *a.* athiramatika. °**ness**, *n.* lahutā, *f.* — **red**, *a.* aruṇavaṇṇa. °**wood**, *n.* lahudāru-rukkha, *m.*

Light, *n.* āloka ; obhāsa ; kiraṇa, *m.* ābhā ; pabhā ; juti ; ditti ; raŋsi, *f.* marīci, *m.* *f.* *v.t.* obhāseti ; pabhāseti ; ujjāleti ; padīpeti. *v.i.* 1. obhāsati ; ujjalati ; padippati ; 2. otarati. *p.p.* °sita; °lita ; °pita ; paditta ; otiṇṇa. °**er**, *n.* ujjālaka, *m.* °**ing**, *n.* ujjālana, *nt.* °**house**, padīpāgāra, *nt.* °**less**, *a.* nippabha. — **some**, *a.* 1. jutimantu ; salīla ; sappabha ; 2. pamudita ; pītimana.

Lighten, *v.t.* 1. joteti ; pabhāseti; 2. upasameti ; tanukaroti ; lahukaroti. *v.i.* jotati ; pabhāsati. *p.p.* jotita ; °sita ; °mita ; tanukata.

Lighter, *a.* lahukatara. *noun:* bhaṇḍahārī-pota, *m.* *v.t.* potena bhaṇḍāni harati.

Lightning, *n.* vijju ; vijjutā ; akkhaṇā ; acirappabhā, *f.* °**conductor,** °**rod,** *n.* vijju-nivāraka-lohadaṇḍa, *m.*

Ligneous, *a.* dārumaya ; kaṭṭha-sadisa.

Like, *v.t.* roceti ; ruccati (with dat.), *v.i.* icchati ; abhilasati. *p.p.* rocita ; ruccita ; icchita ; °sita. °**able,** *a.* icchitabba. °**ing,** *n.* ruci ; abhilāsā ; icchā, *f.*

Like, *n.* sama ; paṭipuggala, *m.* adj. samāna ; sadisa ; sannibha ; tulya ; nibha ; sarikkhaka ; saṅkāsa. adv. iva ; viya. — **minded,** *a.* samacitta ; samā-najjhāsaya. °**ness,** *n.* 1. samā-natta ; sadisatta ; tulyatta, *nt.* 2. paṭibimba, *m.* °**wise,** *adv.* tath'eva. — **what**? kīdisaŋ ? *ind.* — **this,** īdisaŋ, *ind.* **Of like class,** samānajātika, *a.* **Of like form,** samānarūpa, *a.* **In like manner,** tath'eva, *ind.* **That like,** tādisa, *a.* **This like,** īdisa, *a.* **What like,** kīdisa, *a.* **Which like,** yādisa, *a.*

Liken, *v.t.* upameti ; samāneti. *p.p.* upamita ; °nita.

Likely, *adv.* sakkā ; pāyena ; api nāma. adj. sambhavanīya ; sakya. °**ihood,** *n.* sakyatta ; sambhavanīyatta, *nt.*

Lilliputian, *a. n.* omakappa-māṇika.

Lilt, *n.* madhuragīta, *nt. v.i.* madhurassarena gāyati.

Lily, *n.* uppala, *nt.* **White —,** kumuda, *nt.*

Limb, *n.* avayava, *m.* aṅga-paccaṅga, *nt.* *v.t.* aṅgāni vicchindati. *p.p.* vicchinnaṅga.

Limbate, *a.* nānāvaṇṇapariyanta-yutta.

Limber, *a.* namya ; sīghagatika.

Limbo, *n.* yamaloka ; antarābha-va, *m.*

Lime, *n.* 1. (fruit :) dantasaṭha, *m.* 2. (chunnam :) sudhācuṇṇa, *nt.* 3. pakkhisilesa, *m. v.t.* 1. silesam ālepeti ; 2. sudhā-cuṇṇaŋ vikirati. *p.p.* ālittasilesa ; vikiṇṇa°. °**kiln,** sudhāvāpa, *m.* °**light,** setāloka, *m.* °**stone,** sudhāsilā, *f.* °**wash,** sudhālepa, *m.*

Limit, *n.* sīmā ; mariyādā, *f.* odhi ; pariccheda, *m. v.t* sīmeti ; paricchindati ; odhiŋ ṭhapeti. *p.p.* sīmita ; paricchinna ; ṭha-pitodhika. °**able,** *a.* pari-meyya. °**ation,** *n.* paricchin-dana ; sīmāṭhapana, *nt.* °**ed,** *a.* odhikata ; samariyāda. °**edly,** *adv.* odhiso. °**less,** *a.* ananta ; apariyanta ; appa-māṇa ; aparimeya ; anodhika.

Limitary, *a.* sīmāyatta ; sīmita.

Limitrophe, *a.* desasīmāyatta.

Limn, *v.t.* cittakammaŋ karoti. °**er,** *n.* cittasippī ; cittakāra, *m.*

Limp, *n.* khañjana, *nt. v.i.* khañ-jati. adj. sithila ; komala. °**ingly,** *adv.* khañjagatiyā.

Limpid, *a.* pasanna ; vimala. °**ly,** *adv.* nimmalākārena. °**ness,** *n.* pasannatta ; nimmalatta, *nt.*

Linchpin, *n.* akkhaggakīla, *m.*

Linden, *n.* jambīrarukkha, *m.*

Line, *n.* 1. panti ; paddhati ; pāḷi ; āvali ; rāji ; seṇī, *f.* 2. anuk-kama, *m.* paṭipāṭi, *f.* 3. rajju, *f.* tantu, *m.* sutta, *nt.* 4. santati ; paramparā, *f.* 5. lekhā ; rekhā, *f.* °**age**, *n.* anvaya, *m.* paramparā; kulappaveṇī, *f.* °**al**, *a.* 1. anvayāgata; pāramparika; 2. lekhāmaya. °**ally**, *adv.* paramparāya; vaŋsānukkamena. — **of conduct**, paṭipadā, *f.* — **of a stanza**, gāthāpāda, *m.* **Carpenter's** —, kāḷasutta, *nt.*

Line, *v.t.* 1. rekhāhi aṅketi; 2. pantivasena ṭhapeti; 3. paṭalehi āvarati. *p.p.* rekhaṅkita; °ṭhapita; °āvaṭa. °**ing**, *n.* antopaṭala, *nt.*

Lineament, *n.* vadanalakkhaṇa; visesasaṇṭhāna, *nt.*

Linear, *a.* lekhāyatta.

Lineation, *n.* rekhāhi ālikhana, *nt.*

Linen, *n.* khomavattha. *nt.* adj. khomamaya.

Linger, *v.i.* vilambati; āsāsati. °**er**, *n.* vilambaka; mandagatika, *m.* °**ing**, *a.* āsāsamāna. °**ing**, *n.* vilambana; kālakkhepana, *nt.* °**ingly**, *adv.* savilambaŋ; mandamandaŋ.

Lingo, *n.* parabhāsā, *f.*

Lingua franca, *n.* missitabhāsā; sādhāraṇabhāsā, *f.*

Lingual, *a.* *n.* muddhaja.

Linguiform, *a.* jivhākāra.

Linguist, *n.* bhāsākovida; nānābhāsaññū, *m.* °**ic**, *a.* bhāsāvisayaka.

Liniment, *n.* vedanānāsakālepa, *m.* abbhañjana, *nt.*

Link, *n.* 1. sandhi; saŋyoga; sambandha, *m.* 2. saŋyojakavatthu, *nt.* *v.t.* ghaṭeti; saŋyojeti. *p.p.* ghaṭita; °jita. °**age**, *n.* ghaṭana; yojana, *nt.* yoga, *m.*

Links, *n.* 1. velāsanna-vālukātala, *nt.* 2. goḷakīlābhūmi, *f.*

Linn, *n.* nijjhara, *m.* nijjharapokkharaṇī, *f.*

Linoleum, *n.* sitthālitta-bhummattharaṇa, *nt.*

Linseed, *n.* ummā; atasī, *f.*

Lintel, *n.* uddhadehalī, *f.* uparummāra, *m.*

Lion, *n.* sīha; miginda; migarāja; kesarī, *m.* °**ess**, *n.* sīhī, *f.* °**like**, *a.* sīhasama. — **of man**, narasīha, *m.* °'**s play**, sīhavikkīḷita, *nt.* °'**s roar**, sīhanāda, *m.*

Lip, *n.* oṭṭha; dasanacchada, *m.* dantāvaraṇa, *nt.* *v.t.* oṭṭhehi phusati. *p.p.* oṭṭhaphuṭṭha. °**less**, *a.* oṭṭharahita. °**service**, *n.* vācāmattānuggaha, *m.* °**wisdom**, *n.* bhaṇḍāgārika-pariyatti, *f.*

Lipper, *n.* ūmiyuttatā; asantatā, *f.*

Liquate, *v.t.* vilīyāpeti; vilīyāpetvā sodheti. *p.p.* °pita; °dhita. °**ion**, *n.* vilīyāpana, *nt.*

Liquefy, *v.i.* vilīyati. *v.t.* vilīyāpeti. *p.p.* vilīna; °pita. °**faction**, *n.* vilīyāpana, *nt.* °**factive**, *a.* vilīyanakkhama. °**ier**, *n.* vilīyāpaka, *m.*

Liquescent, *a.* vilīyanasabhāva.

Liqueur, *n.* madhurasurā, *f.*

Liquid, *n.* vilīnavatthu, *nt.* adj. āpogata; vilīna. °**ity**, *n.* davatta; vilīnatta, *nt.*

Liquidate, *v.t.* nittharati; iṇaŋ sodheti. *p.p.* °rita; sodhitaiṇa. °**ion**, *n.* nittharaṇa; iṇasodhana; viyojana, *nt.* °**tor**, *n.* iṇasodhaka; nitthāraka; viyojaka, *m.*

Liquor, *n.* majja; meraya, *nt.* °**ish**, *a.* majjapāyī; majjāsatta.

Distilled —, surā, *f.* **Fermented** —, meraya, *nt.* — **shop,** pānāgāra, *nt.*

Liquorice, *n.* madhulaṭṭhikā; yaṭṭhimadhukā, *f.* **Wild** —, guñjā, *f.* jiñjuka, *m.*

Lira; *n.* Itālidesīya-rūpiya, *nt.*

Lisp, *v.i.* avyattaŋ vadati. *p.p.* °vutta, °**ing,** *n.* gaggadavācā, *f.* avyattavacana, *nt.* °**ingly,** *adv.* avyattasaddena.

Lissom, *a.* namya; kammañña.

List, *n.* 1. sūci; nāmāvali; anukkamaṇikā, *f.* 2. vatthadasā, *f.* *v.t.* 1. nāmāni paṇṇe āropeti; 2. vatthakhaṇḍāni sibbati; *v.i.* 1. pakkhapātī hoti; 2. sotam odahati. *p.p.* āropitanāma; sibbita °da; °pātībhūta; ohitasota; °**less,** *a.* anavaṭṭhita; nirapekkha. °**lessly,** *adv.* anavadhānena; nirapekkhatāya.

Listen, *v.i.* nisāmeti; sussūsati; sotam odahati. *p.p.* °mita; ohitasota. °**er,** nisāmetu; sussūsaka, *m.* °**ing,** *n.* nisāmana, *nt.*

Literal, *a.* saddānugata. °**ism,** *n.* saddānugamana, *nt.* °**ist,** *n.* saddānuyāyī, *m.* °**ly,** *adv.* mūlatthānusārena.

Literalize, *v.t.* padānusārena vyākhyāti. *p.p.* °khyāta.

Literary, *a.* sāhiccavisayaka; ganthasambandha. — **man,** ganthakāra, *m.*

Literate, *a.* 1. akkharaññū; 2. sutavantu. °**tor,** *n.* ādhunikācariya; vyākaraṇaññū, *m.*

Literati, *n.* bahussuta; sutadhara, *m.* °**m,** *adv.* padaso; vyañjanaso.

Literature, *n.* sāhicca, *nt.* ganthasamūha, *m.*

Lithe, *a.* sithila; namya; bhaṅgura.

Lithic, *a.* pāsāṇāyatta; silāvisayaka.

Lithograph, *n.* silāmuddā, *f.* *v.t.* silāpatthare muddāpeti. *p.p.* °pita. °**er,** *n.* silāmuddā-sādhaka, *m.*

Lithology, *n.* pāsāṇavijjā, *f.*

Lithontriptic, *n.* *a.* asmarībhedaka.

Lithotomy, *n.* asmarīchedana, *nt.* °**ic,** *a.* asmarīchedanāyatta. °**ist,** *n.* asmarichedī, *m.*

Lithotrity, *n.* asmarīcuṇṇīkaraṇa, *nt.*

Litigate, *v.i.* aṭṭaŋ karoti; adhikaraṇaŋ yāti. °**ion,** *n.* aṭṭakaraṇa, *nt.* °**gant,** *n.* aṭṭakāra; vivādatthī, *m.*

Litigious, *a.* aṭṭakaraṇasīla; vādappiya.

Litter, *n.* 1. sivikā, *f.* vayha, *nt.* 2. tiṇasanthara, *m.* 3. potakagaṇa, *m.* *v.t.* 1. tiṇam attharati; 2. potake vijāyati; 3. vikirati. *p.p.* tiṇatthata; vijātapotaka; vikiṇṇa.

Little, *a.* appa; thoka; appamatta; lesamatta; aṇumatta; parittaka, *n.* lava; lesa; kaṇa, *m.* thoka; kiñci, *nt.* *adv.* thokaŋ; īsakaŋ; kiñcimattaŋ. — **by little,** thokathokaŋ, *adv.* — **finger,** kaṇiṭṭhaṅguli, *f.* °**less,** *a.* kiñcidūnaka. °**ness,** *n.* khuddakatta; appakatta, *nt.*

Littoral, *a.* velāsanna, *n.* velāsannabhūmi, *f.*

Livable, *a.* 1. vāsāraha; 2. sahavāsocita.

Live, *a.* jīvamāna ; sajīva. *v.i.* 1. jīvati ; dharati ; 2. vasati ; viharati ; 3. *p.p.* vuttha. — **abroad**, vippavasati. — **by**, yāpeti. — **fence**, sajīvarukkhavati, *f.* °**lihood**, *n.* jīvana, *nt.* jīvikā, *f.* jīvanopāya, *m.* °**liness**, *n.* pasannatā ; pahaṭṭhatā ; ussukatā, *f.* °**ly**, *a.* sānanda ; saussāha, *adv.* sānandaŋ ; saussāhaŋ. — **on**, upajīvati. — **together**, saŋvasati. — **under probation**, parivasati.

Liven, *v.t.* pamodeti ; ussukkāpeti. *p.p.* °dita ; °pita.

Liver, *n.* yakana, *nt.* °**ish**, *a.* pittātura.

Livery, *n.* 1. visesitacchādana, *nt.* 2. paribbaya, *m.* °**man**, visiṭṭha-vesadhārī, *m.*

Livid, *a.* tipuvaṇṇa.

Living, *a.* jīvamāna; dharamāna, *n.* 1. jīvana, *nt.* jīvikā, *f.* ājīva, *m.* 2. vāsa, *m.* viharaṇa, *nt.* — **alone**, ekacara ; adutiya, *a.* — **being**, jivī ; pāṇī ; dehī ; satta ; pāṇabhūta, *m.* — **comfortably**, sukhajīvī, *m.* — **in**, adhivuttha, *a.* — **on**, upajīvī, *a.* — **together**, 1. sahajīvī ; sahavāsī, *m.* 2. sahavāsa, *m.*

Lixiviate, *v.t.* udakena (dhovitvā) viyojeti. *p.p.* °jita.

Lizard, *n.* goḷikā, *f.*

Llama, *n.* vāmanoṭṭha, *m.*

Lo, *intj.* passa ; passatha bho !

Load, *n.* 1. bhāra ; haraṇīyabhāra, *m.* *v.t.* 2. bhāram āropeti ; 3. (a gun :) dāhakacuṇṇena pūreti. *p.p.* āropitabhāra ; °pūrita. °**ed**, *a.* 1. pūrita ; 2. bhārāropita. — **carrier**, bhārahārī, *m.* °**ing**, *n.* bhārāropaṇa, *nt.* °**stone**, ayokantapāsāṇa ; lohacumbaka, *m.*

Loaf, *n.* 1. pūvagoḷa, *nt.* 2. piṇḍa, *m.* — **sugar**, piṇḍasakkharā, *f.* *v.i.* kālaŋ khepeti *or* nāseti. *p.p.* khepitakāla. °**er**, *n.* akammasīlī ; kālakaṇṇī, *m.*

Loam, *n.* mudumattikā, *f.*

Loan, *n.* iṇadāna ; kālikagahaṇa, *nt.* *v.t.* iṇaŋ deti ; tāvakālikaŋ deti. *p.p.* dinnaiṇa. °**able**, *a.* kālikavasena dātabba. °**ee**, *n.* iṇāyika ; iṇagāhī, *m.* °**er**, *n.* uttamaṇṇa ; iṇadāyī, *m.*

Loath, *a.* harāyanta ; anicchanta. °**some**, *a.* jigucchitabba. °**someness**, *n.* paṭikkūlatta, *nt.*

Loathe, *v.t.* jigucchati ; harāyati, *v.i.* aṭṭīyati. *p.p.* °chita ; °yita ; aṭṭita. °**ful**, *a.* kucchita. °**ing**, *n.* jigucchā ; aṭṭīyanā ; harāyanā, *f.*

Lob, *v.t.* sanikaŋ khipati, *v.i.* sanikaŋ yāti *or* dhāvati. *p.p.* °khitta, *n.* mandagatika, *m.* — **worm**, mahāpulavaka, *m.*

Lobby, *n.* 1. upasālā ; upaṭṭhānasālā, *f.* 2. abbhantaramagga, *m.*

Lobe, *n.* sakkhalikā, *f.* — **footed**, *a.* jālapāda.

Lobster, *n.* mahākosamaccha, *m.*

Local, *a.* desīya ; padesika. °**ity**, *n.* samīpa-padesa, *m.* °**ize**, *v.t.* padesānugataŋ karoti ; ekattha samodahati. *p.p.* °kata ; °hita. °**ism**, *n.* 1. padesavohāra ; 2. padesānurāga, *m.* °**ly**, *adv.* padesavasena.

Locate, *v.t.* patiṭṭhāpeti ; niveseti. *p.p.* °pita ; °sita. °**ion**, *n.* patiṭṭhāpana ; ṭhapana.

Locative, *a.* patiṭṭhāpaka. *n.* ādhāra-vibhatti, *f.*

Loch, *n.* mahāsara, *m. nt.*

Lock, *n.* 1. kesavaṭṭi, *f.* 2. tāḷayanta, *nt.* 3. jalatthambhana, *nt.* 4. āliṅgana ; upagūhana, *nt.* *v.t.* 1. tāḷena pidahati ; 2. gāḷhaṃ āliṅgati. *p.p.* °pihita ; °gita. **°gate,** mātikādvāra, *nt.* **°jaw,** hanutthambha, *m.* **°up,** tāvakālika-rundhana, *nt.*

Locket, *n.* kavacabhūsā, *f.*

Locomote, *v.i.* ṭhānā ṭhānaŋ saṅkamati. **°ion,** *n.* gamanāgamana, *nt.* calanasatti, *f.* **°ive,** *n.* sayaṅgāmīraṭha, *m.* adj. jaṅgama ; caraṇasīla. **°tory,** *a.* jaṅgama.

Locus, *n.* 1. patiṭṭhitaṭṭhāna, *nt.* 2. gamanapatha, *m.*

Locust, *n.* salabha ; paṭaṅga, *m.*

Locution, *n.* vācāvilāsa, *m.*

Locutory, *n.* assamavāsīnaŋ sambhāsanasālā, *f.*

Lode, *n.* 1. maṇi-lohādi-āyatana, *nt.* 2. anāvaṭaparikhā, *f.* **°star,** *n.* dhuvatārakā, *f.*

Lodge, *n.* kuṭi ; uyyāna-kuṭi, *f.* *v.i.* vasati ; nivasati. *v.t.* vāseti ; niveseti ; patiṭṭhāpeti. *p.p.* vuttha ; nivuttha ; °sita ; °pita. **°ing,** *n.* senāsana ; vāsāgāra, *nt.* **°er,** *n.* nivāsagāhī, *m.* **°ment,** *n.* 1. kālikārakkhā, *f.* 2. nihitadhana, *nt.*

Loft, *n.* 1. kapotapālikā, *f.* 2. uparivedikā, *f.*

Lofty, *a.* 1. uttuṅga ; uḷāra ; 2. sadappa ; uddhata. **°ily,** *adv.* 1. unnatākārena ; 2. sadappaŋ ; sābhimānaŋ. **°iness,** *n.* 1. mahatta; uḷāratta, *nt.* 2. pāgabbhiya, *nt.* abhimāna, *m.*

Log, *n.* dārukhaṇḍa ; kaliṅgara, *m.* *v.t.* dārukhaṇḍe chindati. *p.p.* chinnadā°. **°ger,** *n.* dārukammika, *m.*

Loggerhead, *n.* jaḷabuddhī ; momuha, *m.*

Logic, *n.* takkasattha, *nt.* ñāya, *m.* **°al,** *a.* takkānugata. **°ally,** *adv.* yathāñāyaŋ ; takkānurūpaŋ. **°alness,** *n.* takkānugatatta, *nt.*

Logician, *n.* takkika, *m.*

Logie, *n.* ābharaṇapatirūpaka, *nt.*

Logistics, *n.* senāsannivesopāya, *m.*

Logogram, *n.* laghulekhane padalakkhaṇa, *nt.*

Logographer, *n.* laghulekhaka, *m.*

Logomachy, *n.* vācāvivāda, *m.* vacīyuddha, *nt.*

Loin, *n.* jaghana, *nt.* nitamba, *m.* kaṭi, *f.* **°cloth,** *n.* kaṭivattha, *nt.*

Loiter, *v.i.* vilambati ; kālaŋ khepeti. *p.p.* khepitakāla. **°er,** *n.* vilambaka ; osāsaka, *m.* **°ing,** *n.* vilambana ; osāsana, *nt.* **°ingly,** *adv.* dīghasuttiyena.

Loll, *v.i.* 1. jivhaŋ nicchāreti ; 2. ālasiyena upavisati ; 3. bahi lambati. *p.p.* °ritajivha ; °upaviṭṭha ; °bita.

Lollipop, *n.* modakapūpa, *m.*

Lollop, *v.i.* savilambitaŋ yāti.

Lone, Lonely, *a.* kevala ; asahāya ; ekākī ; pavivitta. **°liness,** *n.* paviveka, *m.* ekākitā, *f.* paṭisallāna, *nt.* — **some,** *a.* vivitta ; anākiṇṇa.

Long, *a.* 1. dīgha ; āyata ; 2. dūra, *adv.* 1. ciraŋ ; 2. dīghaŋ ; 3. dūraŋ ; dīghena addhunā. — **absent,** *a.* cirappavāsī. — **after,** aticirena ; kālantarena, *adv.* — **ago,** atīte ;

purā, *adv.* — **lasting,** *a.* ciraṭṭhitika. °**lived,** *a.* addhagata. — **living,** *a.* cirajīvī. — **pepper,** *n.* pipphalī, *f.* — **since,** cirapaṭikā, *ind.* — **time,** addha; cirakāla, *m.* **As — as,** yāva — tāva, *ind.* **Ere —,** acirena, *adv.* **How —,** kīva ciraŋ, *ind.* **Not very —,** nāticiraŋ, *adv.* **Very —,** suciraŋ, *adv.* atidīgha, *a.*

Long (for), *v.i.* pattheti; apekkhati; icchati; paṭikaṅkhati. *p.p.* °thita; °khita; °chita. °**ing,** *n.* ākaṅkhā; icchā; apekkhā; patthanā, *f.* °**ing,** *a.* icchanta; apekkhamāṅa. °**ing for,** pāṭikaṅkhī; apekkhī; patthenta, *a.* °**ing to go,** gantukāma, *a.* °**ing to hear,** sotukāma, *a.* (So on with all infinitives). °**ingly,** *adv.* sataṇhaŋ; sāpekkhaŋ.

Longanimity, *n.* titikkhā; khamā, *f.* °**mous,** *a.* khantimantu.

Longeval, *a.* dīghāyuka.

Longevity, *n.* cirajīvana, *nt.*

Long-headed, *a.* dīghadassī. °**ness,** dīghadassitā, *f.*

Longimanous, *a.* dīghabāhuka.

Longish, *a.* dīghākāra.

Longitude, *n.* paṭhavīmāṇakadīgharekhā, *f.* °**inal,** *a.* dīghatāyatta; dīgharekhāyatta.

Long-run, *n.* carimaphala, *nt.*

Long-sighted, *a.* dūravatthudassī.

Long-suffering, *a.* ciradukkhita; sahanasīla.

Long-tounged, *a.* mukhara; vācāla.

Longways, Longwise, *adv.* dīghaso.

Long-winded, *a.* cirajaṭita; vihesājanaka.

Looby, *n.* duppañña, *m.*

Look, *n.* 1. olokana; avekkhaṇa, *nt.* 2. vesa; ākāra, *m.* *v.i.* (at) passati; oloketi; avekkhati. *p.p.* diṭṭha; °kita; °khita. — **about,** viloketi. — **after,** vicāreti; (a person:) paṭijaggati; anurakkhati. — **beautiful,** sobhati. — **down,** avaloketi. — **down upon,** avamāneti. °**er,** passitu; avekkhaka, *m.* — **for,** gavesati; samekkhati. — **here,** iṅgha; passa. — **into,** upaparikkhati. — **on,** udikkhati; āloketi. — **out for,** upadhāreti. — **over,** anuviloketi.

Looking, *a.* olokenta; dassī. *n.* olokana, *nt.* — **forward,** ālokaka. *a.* — **after,** paricaraṇā, paṭijagganā, *f.* — **away,** parammukha, *a.* — **glass,** ādāsa, *m.* dappaṇa, *nt.* — **up,** ummukha; ullokaka, *a.*

Loom, *n.* vema, *m.* *v.i.* dūre tiṭṭhati; avibhūtaŋ dissati. *p.p.* °ṭhita; °diṭṭha.

Loon, *n.* nikkamma, *m.* °**y,** *a.* *n.* ummatta, *m.*

Loop, *n.* valaya; pāsa, *m.* *v.t.* pāsena āvuṇāti. *p.p.* °āvuta. °**hole,** niggamadvāra, *nt.*

Loose, *n.* mutti, *f.* adj. 1. sithila; vigalita; 2. aniyata; 3. durācāra; gārayha. *v.t.* sithilīkaroti viyojeti; moceti. *p.p.* °kata; °jita; mocita. *v.i.* sithilībhavati; saŋsīdati. *p.p.* °bhūta; saŋsīna. °**ly,** *adv.* adaḷhaŋ; sithilaŋ. °**ness,** *n.* sithilatta, *nt.*

Loosen, *v.t.* sithilayati; pamoceti. *p.p.* °yita; pamutta. °**ing,** *n.* sithilīkaraṇa, *nt.*

Loot, *n*. viluttadhana, *nt*. *v.t.* vilumpati. *p.p.* vilutta.

Lop, *v.t.* luṇāti; chindati. *p.p.* lūṇa; chinna. *n*. sākhaggachindana, *nt*.

Lop, *v.i.* lambati; olambati. *p.p.* °bita. °**eared**, *a*. lambakaṇṇa. °**sided**, *a*. 1. passato-poṇa; 2. asamapassa.

Loquacious, *a*. mukhara; vācābahula. °**ness**, mukharatta; vācālatta, *nt*.

Lord, *n*. adhipa; adhipati; inda; issara; īsa; nātha; nāyaka; sāmī, *m*. *v.i.* issariyaŋ pavatteti. *v.t.* īsattaŋ pāpeti. *p.p.* pavattitaissariya; °pāpita. °**ly**, *a*. gabbita; abhimānayutta. °**less**, *a*. assāmika; arājaka. °**like**, *a*. 1. tejassī; 2. uddhata. °**liness**, *n*. ādhipacca; issariya, *nt*. °**ling**, *n*. cūlādhipati, *m*. — **of demons**, bhūtapati, *m*. — **of men**, narāsabha, *m*. — **of the world**, lokanātha, *m*. °**ship**, pabhutta; sāmitta, *nt*. — **Chancellor**, akkhadassāmacca, *m*.

Lore, *n*. 1. dhamma, *m*. 2. vijjā, *f*. 3. paṇḍicca; veyyattiya, *nt*.

Loricate, *a*. vammita.

Loris, *n*. pampaka, *m*.

Lorn, *a*. anātha; asaraṇa.

Lorry, *n*. mahābhaṇḍahārīratha, *m*.

Lory, *n*. sukavisesa, *m*.

Lose, *v.t.* virajjhati, *v.i.* vinassati; avajīyati; dhaŋsati. *p.p.* viraddha; vinaṭṭha; avajīna.; dhaŋsita. °**er**, *n*. kaliggāhī; parājita, *m*.

Loss, *n*. hāni; jāni: parihāni, *f*. alābha; nāsa; saṅkhaya, *m*. 2. kaliggaha; parābhava, *m*. — **of memory**, satippavāsa, *m*. — **of wealth**, dhanajāni, *f*.

Lot, *n*. 1. kusapāta, *m*. salākā, *f*. 2. bhāgya; bhāgadheyya, *nt*. niyati, *f*. *v.i.* salākam ākaḍḍhati *or* gaṇhāti.

Lotion, *n*. dhovanosadha, *nt*.

Lottery, *n*. salākagāha; kusapāta, *m*.

Lotus, *n*. paduma; kamala; saroruha; satapatta; aravinda; pokkhara; tāmarasa; ambuja, *nt*. — **bulb**, bhisa, *nt*. — **leaf**, paduminīpatta, *nt*. — **plant**, paduminī, *f*. — **pond**, ambujinī, *f*. padumasara, *nt*. — **root**, muḷāla, *nt*. **Red** —, kokanada, *nt*. **White** —, puṇḍarīka, *nt*.

Loud, *a*. mahāsadda; saghosa. °**ly**, *adv*. saghosaŋ. °**ness**, *n*. uccāsaddatā, *f*. — **noise**, *n*. mahānāda, *m*.

Lough, *n*. mahāsara, *m*. *nt*.

Lounge, *v.i.* ālasyena kālaŋ khepeti. °**er**, *n*. nikkammasīlī, *m*.

Lour, Lower, *n*. 1. bhākuṭī; 2. meghacchannatā, *f*. *v.i.* bhākuṭiŋ *or* bhūkuṭiŋ karoti. °**y**, *a*. meghacchanna.

Louse, *n*. ūkā, *f*. — **egg**, *n*. likkhā, *f*.

Lout, *n*. virūpī; asiṭṭha, *m*. *v.i.* namassati; vandati. *p.p.* °sita; °dita. °**ish**, *a*. dandha; andhabāla.

Lovable, *a*. pemanīya.

Love, *n*. 1. pema, *nt*. sıneha; sneha; anurāga, *m*. 2. mettā, *f. v.t.* 1. piyāyati ; pemaŋ bandhati; 2. mettāyati. *p.p.* °yita; baddhapema. °**begotten,** avajāta, *a.* — **broker,** itthidhutta, *m.* °**child,** jāraja, *m.* °**er,** 1. anurāgī ; 2. vāritaka. *m.* — **god,** anaṅga ; madana, *m.* °**ing,** *a.* sasneha. °**ingly,** *adv.* sasnehaŋ ; sādaraŋ. °**less,** *a.* nissineha. °**liness,** pāsādikatā ; abhirūpatā, *f.* lāvañña, *nt.* °**ly,** *a.* manuñña ; dassanīya ; pāsādika ; abhirūpa. °**sick,** *a.* kāmātura. °**song,** *n.* siṅgāragīta, *nt.*

Low, *n.* gorava, *m. v.i.* goravaŋ nadati, °**ing,** *n.* goravana, *nt.*

Low, *a.* 1. ninna ; adhogata ; 2. hīna ; dīna ; nīca ; adhama ; lāmaka ; gamma ; anariya. °**born,** hīnajātika, adj. °**caste,** *n.* hīnajāti, *f.* adj. hīnajacca. — **country,** ninnaraṭṭha, *nt.* °**er,** *a.* ninnatara ; nīcatara. °**land,** ninnabhūmi, *f.* °**ly,** *a.* 1. nikiṭṭha ; 2. vinīta, *adv.* adhamākārena. °**lying,** *a.* adhovattī ; ninnagata. °**liness,** *n.* nīcavuttitā ; anabhimānatā, *f.* °**ness,** *n.* nīcatta ; ninnatta, *nt.* °**spirited,** *a.* nibbinna ; maṅkubhūta ; udāsīna.

Lower, *v.t.* 1. opāteti ; adhokaroti ; 2. ūnaŋ *or* lahukaŋ karoti *v.i.* ūno bhavati. *p.p.* °tita ; adhokata ; ūnīkata ; ūnabhūta.

Loyal, *a.* assava ; anukūla ; daḷhabhattika ; nītigaruka. — **love,** abhirati, *f.* °**ly,** *adv.* bhattipubbakaŋ. — **husband,** sadārasantuṭṭha, *m.* °**ist,** rājapakkhika, *m.* °**ty,** *n.* sāmibhatti, *f.* anukūlatta, *nt.* — **wife,** patibbatā, *f.*

Lozenge, *n.* dīghacaturassa (pūvādi), *nt.*

Lubber, *n.* thulladehī ; dandhapuggala, *m.* °**ly,** *a.* adakkha, *adv.* dandhākārena.

Lubric, °**ate,** *v.t.* abbhañjati ; siniddhaŋ karoti. *p.p.* °jita ; °kata. °**ation,** siniddhakaraṇa ; abbhañjana, *nt.* °**ant,** *a.* saṇhatāpādaka. °**ity,** *n.* 1. siniddhatta ; 2. kāmukatta, *nt.*

Lucent, *a.* bhāsura ; ujjala.

Lucid, *a.* sappabha ; pasanna ; visada ; accha ; nimmala. °**ity,** °**ness,** *n.* 1. ditti ; kanti ; pabhā ; 2. vimalatā ; pasannatā, *f.* 3. veyyattiya, *nt.* °**ly,** *adv.* vyattaŋ ; visadākārena.

Lucifer, *n.* 1. osadhītārakā, *f.* 2. Sukkagaha, *m.* — **match,** aggisalākā, *f.* °**ous,** *a.* pakāsada ; dittikara.

Luck, *n.* lakkhī ; sirī, *f.* bhāgya, *nt.* °**ily,** *adv.* vidhiyogena. °**iness,** *n.* sobhagga, *nt.* dhaññatā, *f.* °**less,** *a.* alakkhika ; dubbhaga. °**lessly,** *adv.* dubbhagatāya. °**y,** *a.* bhaddaka ; maṅgala ; subha ; dhañña ; kalyāṇa. **Bad** —, alakkhī, *f.* **Good** —, subhagatā, *f.*

Lucre, *n.* lābha ; āya ; dhanāgama, *m.* °**ative,** *a.* lābhuppādaka.

Lucubrate, *v.i.* attanā adhigataŋ pakāseti. °**ion,** *n.* attādhigama-pakāsana, *nt.* visiṭṭharacanā, *f.*

Luculent, *a.* ativisada ; sugama ; subodha.

Ludicrous, *a.* hāsajanaka ; upahasanīya. °**ly**, *adv.* hasanīyākārena.

Lug, *v.t.* vāyāmena ākaddhati. *p.p.* °ḍhita.

Luggage, *n.* gamanopakaraṇa ; pātheyya, *nt.*

Lugubrious, *a.* sasoka ; dummana. °**ly**, *adv.* dummanatāya ; sasokaŋ. °**ness**, *n.* sokāturatā, *f.*

Lukewarm, *a.* 1. nāccuṇha ; 2. hīnaviriya ; anussuka. °**ly**, *adv.* mandussāhena. °**ness**, *n.* 1. udāsīnatta ; 2. manduṇhatta, *nt.*

Lull, *v.t.* upasameti ; lāleti. *v.i.* upasammati. *p.p.* °mita ; lālita ; upasanta. *n.* santi ; nivutti, *f.* upasama, *m.* °**er**, *n.* upasametu ; lālaka, *m.* °**ing**, *n.* lālana, *nt.*

Lullaby, *n.* dārakalālanagīta, *nt.*

Lumbago, *n.* kaṭirujā, *f.*

Lumber, *n.* niratthaka-bhaṇḍa, *nt.* *v.t.* nissārabhaṇḍehi pūreti. *v.i.* mandaŋ calati. *p.p.* °pūrita; °calita. °**man**, *n.* kaṭṭhacchedaka, *m.*

Luminary, *n.* 1. bhānumantu, *m.* ujjalavatthu, *nt.* 2. mahāpañña ; mahāvīra, *m.*

Luminous, *a.* mahājutika ; bhāsura ; tejassī. °**ly**, *adv.* bhāsurākārena.

Luminosity, *n.* mahājutikatā, *f.*

Lump, *n.* 1. piṇḍa, *m.* piṇḍī, *f.* 2. gaṇḍa ; 3. dandhapuggala, *m.* *v.t.* piṇḍeti ; puñjīkaroti. *v.i.* 1. piṇḍībhavati ; vilambanto gacchati. *p.p.* °ḍita ; °kata ; bhūta. °**er**, *n.* nāvābhaṇḍoropaka, *m.* °**ish**, *a.* thūla ; dandha. °**y**, *a.* gaṇḍabahula ; gaṇṭhibahula. **In the** rāsivasena.

Lunacy, *n.* ummāda ; cittavibbhama, *m.*

Lunar, *a.* candāyatta ; candayutta. — **day**, tithi, *f.* — **eclipse**, candaggāha, *m.* — **month**, candamāsa, *m.* — **race**, Candavaŋsa, *m.* °**ian**, candavāsī, *m.*

Lunate, *a.* addhacandākāra.

Lunatic, *a.* *n.* ummatta, *m.* — **asylum**, ummattāgāra, *nt.*

Lunch, Luncheon, *n.* majjhaṇhabhojana, *nt.* lahukāhāra, *m.*

Lunch, *v.i.* divābhojanaŋ bhuñjati. *v.t.* divābhojanaŋ sampādeti. *p.p.* bhutta° ; °ditadivā°.

Lung, *n.* papphāsa, *nt.*

Lunge, *n.* sahasābhitudana, *nt.*

Luniform, *a.* candākāra.

Lunisolar, *a.* candasuriyāyatta.

Lupine, *a.* vakasadisa.

Lupus, *n.* 1. vaka ; koka, *m.* 2. kuṭṭhavisesa, *m.*

Lurch, *n.* 1. āpadāya mittapariccāga, *m.* 2. sahasā-onamana, *nt.* *v.i.* 1. vyasanagatamhā apagacchati ; 2. sahasā onamati. *p.p.* °apagata ; °onata. °**er**, *n.* appagghavatthu-cora, *m.*

Lure, *n.* palobhana ; palobhakavatthu, *nt.* *v.t.* palobheti. *p.p.* °bhita.

Lurid, *a.* 1. bhayaṅkara ; 2. īsaŋpītaka.

Lurk, *n.* nilīyana ; nilīnaṭṭhāna, *nt.* *v.i.* nilīyati ; paṭicchanno tiṭṭhati. *p.p.* nilīna.

Luscious, *a.* sumadhura ; tittikara. °**ly**, *adv.* madhurākārena. °**ness**, *n.* madhuratta ; saojatta, *nt.*

Lush, *a.* ojavantu. *n.* majja, *nt.* *v.i.* majjaŋ pivati. °**y**, *a.* surāmatta.

Lust, *n.* 1. kāmāsā, *f.* rāga, *m.* 2. lobha, *m.* taṇhā ; lālasā, *f.* *v.i.* abhilasati ; kāmeti ; gijjhati. *p.p.* °sita ; kāmita; giddha. °**ful**, *a.* kāmātura; rāgaratta. °**fully**, *adv.* sarāgaŋ ; avassutacittena.

Lustral *a.* pāpasuddhikara.

Lustrate, *v.t.* yāgena sodheti. *p.p.* °dhita. °**ion**, *n.* pāpasodhana, *nt.*

Lustre, *n.* pabhā ; ābhā ; ditti, *f.* obhāsa, *m.* °**less**, *a.* nippabha. °**rous**, *a.* sappabha ; pabhassara ; bhāsura. °**rously**, *adv.* sappabhaŋ ; bhāsurākārena.

Lusty, *a.* sattimantu ; kāyabalī. °**iness**, *n.* mahabbalatā, *f.* °**ily**, *adv.* gāḷhaŋ ; daḷhaŋ ; balavataraŋ.

Lutanist, *n.* veṇika, *m.*

Lute, *n.* 1. vīṇā, *f.* 2. chiddapidahaka-mattikā, *f.* *v.t.* mattikāya chiddaŋ pidahati. *p.p.* °pihitachidda.

Luteous, *a.* rattapītaka.

Luxate, *v.t.* visandhīkaroti ; sandhiŋ bhañjati. *p.p.* °kata ; bhaṭṭhasandhika. °**ion**, *n.* apasandhikaraṇa, *nt.*

Luxury, *n.* 1. sukhopabhoga, *m.* kāmasampatti, *f.* 2. sammiddhi, *f.* 3. paṇītāhāra, *m.* °**iant**, *a.* 1. atisamiddha ; 2. ativibhūsita. °**iantly**, *adv.* samiddhākārena. °**iance**, *n.* samiddhi, *f.* bāhulla, *nt.* °**iate**, *v.i.* abhiramati ; sampattim anubhavati. °**ious**, *a.* atisukhita ; visayāsatta. °**iously**, *adv.* atisamiddhākārena. °**iousness**, *n.* sukhopabhogitā ; vilāsitā, *f.*

Lye, *n.* khārodaka, *nt.*

Lying, *n.* musāvāda, *m.* abhūtakkhāna, *nt.* adj. abhūtavādī ; vañcanika. **Lying** (from *v.i.*), *a.* nipanna. — **in**, *n.* gabbhinīavatthā, *f.* — **in-home**, sūtighara, *nt*

Lyke-wake, *n.* matasarīragopana, *nt.*

Lymph, *a.* vasā, *f.* meda, *m.* °**atic**, *a.* medabahula.

Lyncean, *a.* sukhumadiṭṭhiaka.

Lynch, *v.t.* avinicchitvā daṇḍaŋ paṇeti. *p.p.* °paṇīta-daṇḍa.

Lynx, *a.* vanamajjāra, *m.*

Lyra, *n.* tulārāsi, *m.*

Lyre, *n.* mahāvīṇā, *f.*

Lyric, *a.* vīṇāgeyya, *n.* vīṇāgīta, *nt.* °**al**, *a.* vīṇāgītāyatta.

Lyrist, *n.* veṇika ; vīṇāvādī, *m.*

Lysis, *n.* anupubbūpasama, *m.*

Lysol, *n.* roganivārakosadha, *nt.*

M

Ma, *n.* ammā, *f.*

Ma'am, *n.* ayyā ; bhavantī, *f.*

Macabre, *a.* bherava ; bhiŋsanaka.

Macadam, *a.* khaṇḍapāsāṇayojita. °**ize**, *v.t.* pāsāṇayogena daḷhayati. — **road**, khaṇḍapāsāṇayojita-magga, *m.*

Macaroni, *n.* Itālidesīyapiṭṭhatantu, *nt.*

Macaw, *n.* 1. suvavisesa ; 2. tālavisesa, *m.*

Mace, *n.* 1. (spice :) jātikosa, *m.* 2. (weapon :) kulisa ; gadāyudha ; kunta, *nt.* °**bearer**, kuntadhārī ; gadādhara, *m.*

Macerate, *v.t.* temetvā sithilīkaroti. *v.i.* anasanena kisībhavati. *p.p.* °kata ; °bhūta.

Machinate, *v.t.* kūṭopāyaŋ yojeti. *p.p.* yojitakū°. °**ion**, *n.* kūṭopāyayojana ; kumantana, *nt.* °**tor**, *n.* kumantaka ; upāyayojaka, *m.*

Machine, *n.* yanta, *nt.* *v.t.* yantaŋ sampādeti ; yantakammaŋ karoti. °**ry**, *n.* yantasamūha, *m.* °**ist**, *n.* yantasippī, *m.*

Mackintosh, *n.* udakavārakavatthavisesa, *m.*

Macron, *n.* dīghasaralakkhaṇa, *nt.*

Macrocosm, *n.* lokadhātu, *f.*

Macrology, *n.* ativitthāra, *m.*

Macropod, *a.* dīghapāda. *n.* kakkaṭaka, *m.*

Macula, *n.* kalaṅka ; suriyakalaṅka ; kāḷaka, *m.*

Mad, *a.* 1. ummatta ; khittacitta ; 2. atikuddha ; atibhanta. — **dog**, alakka, *m.* °**ly**, *adv.* ummattākārena. °**ness**, *n.* ummāda ; cittavibbhama, *m.*

Madam, *n.* ayyā ; bhavantī, *f.* *Voc. sing.* bhotī, *f.*

Madden, *v.t.* ummādeti. *v.i.* ummatto hoti. *p.p.* °dita ; ummattabhūta.

Madder, *n.* mañjiṭṭhā, *f.*

Made, *p.p.* (of **Make**), kata; sādhita ; sampādita ; māpita. — **of iron**, ayomaya, *a.* — **known**, pakāsita, *a.*

Madeira, *n.* seta-muddikāsava, *m.*

Madonna, *n.* Kiṭṭhamātupaṭimā, *f.*

Madrigal, *n.* khuddakasiṅgāragīta, *nt.*

Maestro, *n.* saṅgītācariya, *m.*

Magazine, *n.* 1. kālikavisayasaṅgaha, *m.* 2. (of arms :) āyudhāgāra, *nt.* 3. vividhapaṇiyasālā, *f.*

Mage, *n.* 1. māyākāra ; 2. vijjādhara, *m.*

Maggot, *n.* 1. āsāṭikā, *f.* 2. vipallattha-cintā, *f.* °**y**, *a.* 1. āsāṭikākiṇṇa ; 2. vikāramatiyutta.

Magic, *n.* māyā, *f.* indajāla, *nt.* °**al**, *a.* indajālāyatta. °**ally**, *adv.* māyābalena. °**ian**, *n.* māyākāra ; indajālika, *m.*

Magisterial, *a.* adhikaraṇanissita ; nītibalayutta.

Magistral, *a.* sāmikāyatta ; pālakāyatta.

Magistrate, *n.* anuvijjaka ; daṇḍanātha, *m.*

Magna Charta, *n.* mahāpaṭiññāpaṇṇa, *nt.*

Magnanimous, *a.* uḷāracitta ; mahajjhāsaya. °**ly**, *adv.* uḷāracittena. °**mity**, *n.* mahajjhāsayatā, *f.*

Magnate, *n.* aggañña ; mukhyapadaṭṭha, *m.*

Magnesium, *n.* suḍayhaloha, *m.*

Magnet, *n.* ayokanta ; lohacumbaka, *m* °**ic**, *a.* ākaḍḍhakabalayutta. °**ism**, *n.* ayokantaguṇa, *m.* ākaḍḍhakabala, *nt.* °**ize**, *v.t.* ākaḍḍhakabalaŋ yojeti.

Magneto, *n.* vijjuppādakayanta, *nt.*

Magnific, Magnificent, *a.* sobhamāna ; sirimantu ; mahappabha. °**ly**, *adv.* atisobhanākārena. °**cence**, *n.* 1. mahima ; patāpa, *m.* 2. sobhā ; vibhūti, *f.*

Magnify, *v.t.* 1. visālīkaroti ; vaḍḍheti ; 2. atisayena vaṇṇeti. *p.p.* °kata ; °ḍhita ; °ṇita. °**ier**, *n.* vaḍḍhaka ; mahattapāpaka, *m.* °**ing**, *a.* brūhaka ; mahattāpādaka. °**ication**, *n.* visālīkaraṇa, *nt.*

Magniloquent, *a.* vikatthaka. °**ence**, *n.* vikatthana, *nt.*

Magnitude, *n.* 1. pamāṇa, *nt.* 2. uḷāratta ; visālatta, *nt.*

Magpie, *n.* seta-kāḷasakuṇa, *m.*

Mahout, *n.* hatthāroha, *m.*

Maid, *n.* 1. ceṭikā ; paricārikā ; *f.* 2. kaññā, *f.* — **of honour**, rājinī-paricārikā, *f.*

Maiden, *n.* kumārī; yuvatī; taruṇī, *f.* °**hood**, *n.* komāriya, *nt.* °**like**, °**ly**, *a.* komala ; kaññāsadisa.

Mail, *n.* 1. (armour :) kavaca ; sannāha, *m.* vamma, *nt.* 2. (letters :) sandesasamūha, *m.* *v.t.* 1. sannayhati ; 2. sandesaŋ peseti. — **coat**, *n.* vārabāṇa, *nt.*

Maim, *v.t.* aṅgavikalaŋ karoti. *p.p.* °līkata. *n.* aṅgavekalla, *nt.* °**ed**, *a.* vikalaṅga.

Main, *a.* mukhya ; padhāna ; mūlabhūta. — **land**, mahādesa, *m.* °**ly**, *adv.* mukhyavasena ; bahuso. — **sail**, mahālakāra, *m.* °**stay**, mukhyopatthambha, *m.*

Main, *n.* 1. mahaṇṇava, *m.* 2. padhānaṅga, *nt.* mukhyakoṭṭhāsa, *m.* 3. (force :) sakalasatti, *f.* **With might and —**, sakalasattiyā.

Maina, *n.* sālikā, *f.*

Maintain, *v.t.* anupāleti ; poseti ; pavatteti. *p.p.* °lita ; posita ; °tita. °**er**, *n.* posaka ; pavattaka, *m.* °**able**, a. paṭijagganiya.

Maintenance, *n.* 1. bharaṇa ; posaṇa ; paṭijagana, *nt.* 2. jīvikā ; jīvanavutti, *f.* 3. ghāsacchādana, *nt.*

Maize, *n.* dhaññavisesa, *m.*

Majesty, *n.* mahima ; patāpa ; ānubhāva, *m.* °**ic**, a. mahānubhāva ; mahāteja ; mahesakkha. °**ically**, *adv.* mahānubhāvena ; mahimena ; tejasā.

Major, *n.* senādalapati, *m.* adj. 1. padhāna ; mukhya; 2. adhikasaṅkhyaka. °**ship**, *n.* dalapatidhura, *nt.* °**ity**, *n.* 1. bahutarabhāga, *m.* adhikatarasaṅkhyā, *f.* 2. vayappatti, *f.*

Make, *v.t.* 1. karoti ; vidahati ; 2. sampādeti ; sādheti ; 3. (to compel :) kāreti (this is often expressed by the causative form). *p.p.* kata ; vihita ; °dita ; kārita. *noun :* katākāra, *m.* nimmāṇa, *nt.* — **angry**, kopeti ; roseti. — **ashamed**, lajjāpeti. — **clear**, uttānīkaroti. — **for**, upagacchati. — **good**, paṭikaroti ; tathataŋ dīpeti. — **happy**, sukheti ; pīṇeti. — **haste**, abhittharati. — **known**, pavedeti. — **manifest**, upadasseti. — **off**, palāyati. — **out**, 1. nirūpeti ; 2. aṅketi ; 3. sañjānāti. — **over**, appeti ; bhāraŋ karoti. — **stiff,** santhambheti. — **up,** 1. sādheti; nipphādeti ; 2. samāharati ; 3. (a querrel) upasameti ; 4. (one's mind :) niccheti ; adhiṭṭhāti. — **war,** yujjhati. *v.i.* — **against,** virujjhati. — **believe,** vyāja, *m.* nikati, *f.* — **bold,** nibbhayo bhavati. — **light of,** avamaññati. —**peace,** sandhātu, *m.* °**shift,** *n.* tāvakālika-upāya, *m.* — **sure,** vissattho bhavati. — **up,** vesa, *m.* °**er,** *n.* kāraka ; māpaka; sampādaka, *m.* °**ing,** *n.* karaṇa ; sādhana ; nimmāṇa, *nt.*

Make, *n.* katākāra, *m.* nimmāṇa, *nt.*

Maladjustment, *n.* dugghaṭana ; asammāyojana, *nt.*

Maladministration, *n.* dussāsana ; duṭṭhapālana, *nt.*

Maladroit, *a.* adakkha ; anipuṇa; asobhana. °**ly,** *adv.* asobhanākārena.

Malady, *n.* vyādhi ; roga, *m.*

Malaise, *n.* sarīrāphasu, *m.*

Malapropism, *n.* ayathāvācāpayoga, *m.*

Malapropos, *adv.* aṭṭhāne, *a. n.* aṭṭhānayojita.

Malar, *n.* cubukaṭṭhi, *nt.*

Malaria, *n.* visavāta, *m.* °**al fever,** visavātajara, *m.*

Malcontent, *a. n.* 1. atitta ; asantuṭṭha ; 2. rājavipakkha.

Male, *a. n.* puma ; purisa, *m.* — **organ,** pulliṅga ; aṅgajāta, *nt.*

Malediction, *n.* sāpa ; akkosa, *m.* °**tory,** *a.* abhisāpakara.

Malefactor, *n.* dussīla ; durācāra, *m.*

Malefic, *a.* hānikāra ; anatthāvaha. °**ent,** *a.* apakāraka ; aparādhika. °**ence,** *n.* apakāra ; aparādha, *m.*

Malevolent, *a.* anatthakāma ; duṭṭhamana ; dubbhaka. °**ence,** *n.* vyāpāda, *m.* dubbhana, *nt.* °**ly,** *adv.* duṭṭhacittena.

Malfeasance, *n.* dukkata ; ayathācaraṇa, *nt.*

Malformation, *n.* 1. dugghaṭanā ; 2. virūpatā, *f.*

Malice, *n.* palāsa, *m.* ahitakāmatā, *f.* °**cious,** *a.* palāsī. °**ciously,** *adv.* pisuṇatāya ; sapalāsaŋ.

Malign, *v.t.* apavadati; abbhakkhāti. *p.p.* apavutta ; °khāta. adj. ahitakara. °**ancy,** *n.* aniṭṭhatā ; appiyatā, *f.* °**ant,** *a.* 1. ghora ; dāruṇa ; 2. durāsaya ; pāpacitta ; 3. asubha ; aniṭṭha. °**antly,** *adv.* duṭṭhākārena ; duṭṭhacittena. °**ity,** *n.* upanāha, *m.*

Malinger, *v.i.* gilānālayaŋ dasseti. °**er,** *n.* vyājarogī, *m.*

Malism, *n.* lokāsubhadiṭṭhi, *f.*

Mall, *a.* sacchadana-caṅkama, *m.*

Mallard, *n.* vanahaŋsa, *m.*

Malleable, *n.* athaddha ; mudubhūta; kammakkhama. °**bility,** *n.* kammakkhamatā, *f*

Malleate, *v.t.* dārumuṭṭhiyā tāḷeti. *p.p.* °tāḷita.

Mallet, *n.* dāruhatthaka, *m.*

Malnutrition, *n.* mandaposaṇa ; dupposaṇa, *nt.*

Malodorous, *a.* pūtigandhika.

Malpractice, *n.* duṭṭhācāra; ayathācāra, *m.*

Malt, *n.* 1. aṅkurita-yava, *m.* 2. surākiṇṇa, *nt.* — **drink,** *n.* yavasurā, *f.* °**ster,** yavasurā-sampādaka, *m.*

Maltreat, *v.t.* hiŋsati; pīḷeti. *p.p.* hiŋsita; pīḷita. °**ment,** *n.* appiyācāra; apakāra; anādara, *m.*

Malversation, *n.* vissāsabhaṅga, *m.* aññāyacaraṇa, *nt.*

Mamilla, *n.* thanagga; cūcuka, *nt.*

Mamma, *n.* ammā; ambā; jananī; mātu, *f.*

Mammal, *n.* khīrapāyī, *m.* °**ian,** *n.* khīrapāyī-tiracchāna, *m.*

Mammon, *n.* 1. dhanesa; Kuvera, *m.* 2. dhanasampatti, *f.* °**ism,** *n.* dhanaparāyaṇatā, *f.* °**ist,** *n.* kāmabhogī; visayāsatta, *m.*

Mammoth, *a.* mahākāya; atimahanta. *n.* porāṇaka-mahāhatthi-visesa, *m.*

Mammotty, *n.* kuddāla, *m.*

Man, *n.* manussa; nara; manuja; macca, *m.* — **eater,** porisāda, *m.* °**fully,** *adv.* purisathāmena; purisavikkameṇa. °**hood,** manussatta; porisa, *nt.* °**kind,** manussajāti; pajā; janatā, *f.* °**ly,** *a.* dhīra; vīra. °**liness,** porissa, *nt.* purisavikkama, *m.* °**like,** *a.* purisocita. — **of-war,** yuddhanāvā, *f.* — **slaughter,** manussaghātana, *nt.*

Manacle, *n.* hatthasaṅkhalikā, *f.* *v.t.* saṅkhalikāya bandhati. *p.p.* °baddha.

Manage, *v.t.* vidahati; vicāreti; pāleti. *v.i.* ācarati; upāyaŋ yojeti. *p.p.* vihita; °rita; pālita; yojitopāya. °**able,** *a.* vineya; vidheya; damma. °**ment,** *n.* paripālana; saŋvidhāna, *nt.* °**er,** *n.* payojaka; paripālaka, *m.*

Manciple, *n.* (vijjālayādisu) bhojanopakaraṇa-sampādaka, *m.*

Mandamus, *n.* seṭṭhādhikaraṇato adharādhikaraṇaŋ pesitāṇā, *f.*

Mandarin, *n.* (Cīna-) mantī, *m.* — **orange,** *n.* erāvata; mahānāraṅga, *m.*

Mandate, *n.* āṇā, *f.* niyoga, *m.* °**tory,** *a.* āṇāpaka.

Mandible, *n.* adhohanu, *m.*

Mandrake, *n.* visagacchavisesa, *m.*

Mandrill, *n.* caṇḍavānaravisesa, *m.*

Manducate, *v.t.* cabbati. *p.p.* cabbita. °**ion,** *n.* cabbana, *nt.*

Mane, *n.* pasukesara, *nt.* °**ed,** *a.* kesarayutta. °**less,** *a.* gīvā-kesararahita.

Manege, *n.* assasippa, *nt.*

Manes, *n. pl.* ñātipetā, *m.*

Manganese, *n.* kāḷaloha, *m.*

Mange, *n.* pasukuṭṭha, *nt.*

Manger, *n.* godoṇi, *f.* ghāsabhājana, *nt.*

Mangle, *v.t.* vicchindati. *p.p.* vicchinna. *n.* vatthamaṭṭhakaraṇī, *f.* °**ed,** *a.* ākoṭita; majjita.

Mango, *n.* amba, *nt.* — **tree,** ambarukkha, *m.* °**grove,** ambavana, *nt.* ambasaṇḍa, *m.*

Mangonel, *n.* silākhipakayanta, *nt.*

Mangosteen, *n.* madhutimbarū, *m.*

Mania, *n.* cittavibbhama, *m.* °**c,** °**cal,** *a.* vikkhittacitta.

Manifest, *v.t.* āvīkaroti. *v.i.* pātubhavati ; āvibhavati ; sandissati. *p.p.* āvīkata ; pātubhūta ; āvibhūta ; sandiṭṭha. adj. visada ; vibhūta ; pākaṭa. °**ation,** *n.* pātubhāva, *m.* āvīkaraṇa ; visadīkaraṇa, *nt.* °**ly,** *adv.* supākaṭaŋ. °**ness,** *n.* pākaṭatta ; visadatta, *nt.* °**ative,** *a.* pakāsaka ; vyañjaka.

Manifesto, *n.* nivedanapaṇṇa.

Manifold, *a. n.* vividha ; bahuvidha ; nānākāra ; aneka ; anekavidha. *v.t.* bahuttaŋ pāpeti. °**ly,** *adv.* nānākārena. °**ness,** *n.* vividhatā, *f.*

Manikin, *n.* 1. manussavamana, *m.* 2. māṇavadehanirūpakacitta, *nt.*

Manioc, *n.* dīghāluvavisesa, *m.* (Sinhalese : *maññokkā*).

Manipulate, *v.t.* hatthehi sampādeti. *p.p.* °dita. °**ion,** *n.* 1. hatthakamma ; 2. kammakosalla, *nt.*

Mannequin, *n.* 1. acchādanapadassaka, *m.* 2. °rūpa, *nt.*

Manner, *n.* ākāra ; pakāra ; kama ; vidhi, *m.* °**less,** *a.* avinīta ; asiṭṭha. °**ly,** *a.* vinīta ; sabbha ; subbata. **In like —,** tath'eva ; ten'ākārena, *adv.* **In that —,** tathā, *adv.* **In this —,** itthaŋ ; evaŋ, *adv.*

Manners, *n.* cāritta, *nt.* sadācāra, *m.* **Bad —,** anācāra, *m.* **Good —,** sosīlya, *nt.* sadācāra, *m.*

Manor, *n.* rājadāya-bhūmi, *f.* **— house,** *n.* kulīna-mandira, *nt.*

Mansion, *n.* mandira, *nt.* pāsāda, *m.*

Mansuetude, *n.* subbacatta ; assavatta, *nt.*

Mantle, *n.* pāvāra, *m.* uttaracchādana ; upasambyāna, *nt.* *v.t.* pārupati ; acchādeti. *v.i.* āvarīyati. *p.p.* pāruta ; °dita ; āvaṭa.

Manual, *n.* saṅkhittagantha ; sārasaṅgaha, *m.* adj. hatthasādhiya ; bāhābala-karaṇīya. **— art,** hatthakamma, *nt.* **— labour,** bāhābala, *nt.*

Manufactory, *n.* kammantasālā, *f.*

Manufacture, *n.* nimmāṇa ; sampādana, *nt.* *v.t.* sampādeti ; māpeti. *p.p.* °dita ; māpita. °**er,** *n.* sampādaka ; sippī, *m.*

Manumission, *n.* bhujissakaraṇa ; dāsavyamocana, *nt.*

Manure, *n.* bhūtagāmaposaka, *m.* *v.t.* bhūmisāraŋ yojeti. *p.p.* °jita.

Manuscript, *n.* hatthalekhana, *nt.* hatthalipi, *f.*

Many, *a.* bahu ; bahula ; sambahula ; pahūta ; aneka. *n.* janatā, *f.* janasamūha, *m.* **— folk,** bahujana, *m.* **— footed,** *a.* bahuppada. **— sided,** *a.* anekākāra. **— times,** bahukkhattuŋ ; anekavāraŋ, *adv.* **How —,** kittaka, *a.* **In — ways,** bahudhā, *adv.* **So —,** tāvabahuka, *a.*

Map, *n.* bhūmicitta, *nt.* *v.t.* bhūmicittam ālikhati, **— out,** paṭiyādeti ; paṭipāṭiŋ *or* karaṇākāraŋ dasseti. *p.p.* ālikhita — ; dassitapaṭipāṭi.

Maple, *n.* sakkharārukkha, *m.*

Mar, *v.t.* bādheti ; paṭisedheti. *p.p.* °dhita.

Marasmus, *n.* sarīrakkhaya; khayaroga, *m.*

Maraud, *v.t.* vilumpati. *v.i.* vilumpanāya vicarati. *p.p.* vilutta; °**rita.** °**er**, *n.* vilumpaka; panthadūhaka, *m.* °**ing**, *n.* panthadūhana, *nt.*

Marble, *n.* 1. kīḷāgoḷaka, *nt.* 2. khīrapāsāṇa, *m.* kammāsasilā, *f.* *v.t.* kammāsavaṇṇaŋ yojeti.

Marc, *n.* phalakasaṭa, *m.*

March, *n.* Phagguṇa, *m.*

March, *n.* 1. bhaṭasaṅkamaṇa, *nt.* 2. desasīmā, *f.* *v.i.* payāti; samānagatiyā gacchati. — **against**, abbhuyyāti.

Marconigram, *n.* vijjuvegasāsana, *nt.*

Mare, *n.* vaḷavā; assā, *f.*

Maremma, *n.* (roguppādaka-) anūpa-desa, *m.*

Margarine, *n.* kittima-nonīta, *nt.*

Margin, *n.* pariyanta, *m.* *v.t.* 1. sapariyantaŋ karoti; 2. pariyante likhati. °**al**, *a.* pariyantavattī; pariyante likhita. °**ate**, *a.* sapariyanta.

Margosa, *n.* nimbataru; pucimanda, *m.*

Marine, *n.* 1. nāvāsamūha, *m.* 2. nāvābhaṭa, *m.* adj. sāmuddika. °**er**, *n.* nāvika, *m.*

Marionette, *n.* cala-dhītalikā, *f.* suttasañcālikā, *f.*

Marital, *a.* 1. pativisayaka; 2. vivāhavisayaka.

Maritime, *a.* samuddāsanna.

Marjoram, *n.* sugandha-paṇṇavisesa, *m.*

Mark, *n.* lakkhaṇa; lañchana; saṅketa; abhiññāṇa, *nt.* *v.t.* aṅketi; lañcheti. *p.p.* °kita; °chita. °**edly**, *adv.* paripphuṭaŋ; suvyattaŋ. °**er**, *n.* saṅketakārī, *m.* °**ing**, *n.* aṅkana; saṅketakamma, *nt.* °**ing nut**, bhallātakī, *f.* — **on the forehead**, tilaka; cittaka, *nt.* — **out**, paricchindati.

Market, *n.* āpaṇa, *m.* *v.i.* paṇeti; vohāraŋ karoti. °**able**, *a.* kayavikkayāraha. — **place**, paṇyavīthikā, *f.* — **town**, nigama, *m.*

Marksman, *n.* lakkhavedhī, *m.*

Marl, *n.* sudhāmissita-mattikā, *f.* *v.t.* sudhāmattikaŋ yojeti.

Marmalade, *n.* madhurambilaphalasāra, *m.*

Marmelo, *n.* mālūra; beluva; billa, *m.*

Marmoreal, *a.* khīrapāsāṇasadisa.

Maroon, *a.* ghanāruṇa. *n.* palāta-dāsa, *m.* *v.t.* dīpake chaḍḍeti *or* rodheti. *p.p.* °ḍita; °ruddha.

Marplot, *n.* parakiccadūsaka, *m.*

Marquee, *n.* paṭamaṇḍapa, *m.*

Marriage, *n.* pāṇiggaha, *m.* gharabandhana, *nt.* °**able**, *a.* vivāhayogga. (— woman:) alaŋpateyyā, *f.*

Marrow, *n.* miñjā, *f.* (of bones:) aṭṭhimiñjā, *f.* °**less**, *a.* miñjarahita. °**y**, *a.* miñjapuṇṇa.

Marry, *v.t.* pāṇiggahaŋ karoti. (To take a wife:) vivāheti; (To take for husband:) āvāheti. *v.i.* gharabandhanaŋ pāpuṇāti. *p.p.* katapāṇiggaha; °hita; pattagharabandhana.

Mars, *n.* Kujagaha, *m.*

Marsh, *n.* palipa, *m.*

Marshy, *a* anūpa; saḷilappāya. — **date palm,** hintāla, *m.* — **land,** kaccha, *nt. m.*

Marshal, *n.* bhaṭavidhāyaka, *m. v.t.* anukkamena *or* yathākkamaŋ yojeti. *p.p.* °yojita, *v.i.* yathopacāraŋ neti. *p.p.* °nīta.

Marsupial, *a.* pasibbakākāra; potapasibbakayutta.

Mart, *n.* paṇyavīthikā, *f.*

Martial, *a.* yuddhavisayaka; saṅgāmāyatta. — **law,** *n.* yuddhāṇā, *f.* yuddhāyattapālana, *nt.*

Martinet, *n.* daḷhānusāsaka, *m.*

Martyr, *n.* (dhammatthaŋ) pariccatta-jīvita, 3. °**dom,** *n.* sadatthe jīvitapariccāga, *m.* °**ize,** *v.t.* sadatthe jivitaŋ pariccajati.

Marvel, *n.* vimhaya, *m.* abbhuta; acchariya, *nt. v.i.* vimhayam āpajjati. °**lous,** *a.* vimhayāvaha; acchariyajanaka. °**lously,** *adv.* abbhutākārena. °**lousness,** *n.* abbhutatta; vimhayāvahatta, *nt.*

Mascot, *n.* subhanimitta; maṅgalavatthu, *nt.*

Masculine, *a. n.* pulliṅgika; purisindriyayutta. — **gender,** pulliṅga, *nt.* °**ity,** *n.* purisatta, *nt.* pumbhāva, *m.*

Mash, *n.* yāgusadisapāna, *nt. v.t.* 1. piṭṭhādiŋ uṇhodake maddati; 2. siṅgāram uppādeti. *p.p.* maddita; °ditasiṅgāra.

Mask, *n.* vyājamuka; mukhāvaraṇa, *nt. v.t.* vyājamukhaŋ yojeti; vesaŋ parivatteti. *p.p.* yojita —; parivattitavesa.

Mason, *n.* iṭṭhakavaḍḍhakī; sudhājīvī, *m.* °**ry,** *n.* iṭṭhakaracanā, *f.* sudhākamma, *nt.*

Masquerade, *n.* vesaparivattana; kapaṭavesa-gahaṇa, *nt. v.i.* 1. vikaṭavesaŋ gaṇhāti; 2. paṭicchanno carati.

Mass, *n.* 1. rāsi; puñja; nicaya; nikara; khandha, *m.* 2. piṇḍa, *m.* goḷaka, *nt. v.t.* sañcināti; rāsīkaroti; samāharati. *p.p.* sañcita; °kata; °haṭa.

Massacre, *n.* manussaghātana, *nt. v.t.* samūhavasena māreti. *p.p.* °rita.

Massage, *n.* aṅgasambāhana; parimaddana, *nt. v.t.* sambāhati; aṅgāni parimaddati. *p.p.* °hita; °ditaṅga.

Masseur, *n.* sambāhaka, *m.*

Massive, *a.* atimahanta; atibhāriya. °**ness,** *n.* atimahatta, *nt.* atibhāratā, *f.*

Massy, *a.* thūla; bhāriya. °**iness,** *n.* thūlatta; bhāriyatta, *nt.*

Mast, *n.* kūpaka, *m.*

Master, *n.* 1. sāmī; nātha; adhipati; issara; adhīsa; nāyaka; 2. adhikārī; ajjhakkhaka; 3. ajjhāpaka; ācariya; garu; satthu; 4. paṇḍita; pāragata, *m. v.t.* 1. abhibhavati; 2. pāraŋ gacchati; 3. parisahati; 4. (some learning:) pariyāpuṇāti. *p.p.* abhibhūta; pāragata; °hita; pariyāputa. °**ly,** *a.* atinipuṇa. °**hood,** °**ship,** *n.* ādhipacca; issariya, *nt.* °**piece,** *n.* pasatthatamākati, *f.* pasatthanimmāṇa, *nt.* °**ful,** *a.* sericārī; sādhīna. °**fully,** *adv.* sādhīnatāya. °**y,** *n.* 1. pavīṇatta; pāragatatta, *nt.* 2. vasībhāva, *m.*

Masticate, *v.t.* cabbati; saṅkhādati. *p.p.* °bita; °dita. °**ion,** *n.* saṅkhādana, *nt.*

Mastiff, *n.* mahāsunakhavisesa, *m.*

Mastitis, *n.* thanadāha, *m.*

Mastoid, *a.* thanākāra.

Mat, *n.* kilañja; kaṭasāra, *m. v.t.* 1. gantheti; 2. kilañjehi chādeti. *p.p.* °thita; °chādita. *v.i.* thūlākārena vaḍḍhati.

Matted-hair, *n.* kesajaṭā, *f.*

Match, *n.* 1. paṭipuggala; tulyabala, *m.* 2. āvāha-vivāhasaŋsandana, *nt.* 3. aggisalākā, *f.* °**less,** *a.* atula; nirupama; asadisa; appaṭipuggala. °**lessly,** *adv.* anupamatāya. °**lessness,** *n.* nirupamatta; atulyatta, *nt.* °**maker,** *n.* vivāhasaŋsandaka, *m.*

Match, *v.t.* tuleti; samāneti; saŋsandeti, *v.i.* 1. yugaggāhī hoti; 2. pariṇayena sambandhīyati. *p.p.* tulita; °nita; °dita; °sambaddha.

Mate, *n.* 1. kammantasahāya, *m.* 2. upādhikārī, *m.* 3. jāyāpatīnam eko; (male:) pati, *m.* female:) jāyā, *f. v.i.* saŋvasati; santhavaŋ karoti. *v.t.* saŋvāseti; gharabandhanena bandhati. *p.p.* saŋvuttha; katasanthava; °sita; °baddha.

Mater, *n.* ammā; mātu, *f.* °**nity,** *n.* mātubhāva, *m.* mātiṭṭhāna, *nt.*

Material, *n.* dabba, *nt.* dabbasambhāra, *m.* adj. bhūtika; rūpamaya; 2. sārabhūta; 3. garuka; mukhya. — **composition,** rūpīvatthu, *nt.* — **food,** kabaliṅkārāhāra, *m.* — **form,** rūpa, *nt.* °**ism,** lokāyatavāda, *m.* °**ist,** lokāyatika, *m.* °**ize,** *v.t.* dabbabhāvaŋ *or* yathātathattaŋ pāpeti. *v.i.* pātubhavati; sijjhati. *p.p.* °pāpita; pātubhūta; siddha. °**ly,** *adv.* vatthuto; paramatthato. — **world,** saṅkhāraloka, *m.* **Writing —,** lekhanopakaraṇa, *nt.*

Materia medica, *n.* osadhīyavatthu; osadhījāta, *nt.*

Materiel, *n.* sāmūhika-upakaraṇajāta, *nt.* apuggalika-vatthusamūha, *m.*

Maternal, *a.* mattika; mātusantaka. — **uncle,** mātula, *m.*

Mathematical, *a.* gaṇitavisayaka. °**cian,** *n.* gaṇaka; gaṇitaññū, *m.* °**ly,** *adv.* gaṇitānusārena.

Mathematics, *n. pl.* gaṇitasattha, *nt.*

Matin, *n.* udayagīta, *nt.* adj. pubbaṇhika.

Matinee, *n.* aparaṇhika-naccagīta, *nt.*

Matriarchy, *n.* mātupadhānatta, *nt.*

Matricide, *n.* 1. mātughāta, *m.* 2. (person:) mātughātī; mattigha, *m.*

Matriculate, *v.t.* mahāvijjālayaŋ paveseti. *v.i.* mahāvijjālayaŋ pavisati. *p.p.* °sita; °paviṭṭha, °**ion,** *n.* nikhilavijjālayappavesana, *nt.*

Matrimony, *n.* gharabandhana, *nt.* °**ial,** *a.* gharabandhanāyatta. °**ially,** *adv.* pāṇiggahavasena.

Matrix, *n.* 1. gabbhāsaya, *m.* 2. muddākkharasampādaka, *nt.*

Matron, *n.* 1. gahapatānī; 2. nāyakasevikā, *f.* °**age,** °**ship,** nāyakasevikādhura, *nt.*

Mattamore, *n.* bhūmyantaragabbha, *m.*

Matter, *n.* 1. vatthu ; dabba ; bhūtarūpa, *nt.* 2. hetu, *m.* kāraṇa, *nt.* 3. (pus :) pubba ; pūya, *m.* 4. padattha, *m.* 5. visayakāraṇa, *nt.* — **of fact**, sacca, *nt.* yathābhūtattha, *m.* **It does not matter**, tena kiccaŋ natthi. **What does it matter to you ?** kiŋ tena tava payojanaŋ ?

Mattery, *a.* pūyasahagata.

Matting, *n.* 1. kalāla, *m.* bhummattharaṇa, *nt.* 2. kilañjopakaraṇa, *nt.*

Mattock, *n.* ṭaṅka, *m.* khaṇitti, *f.*

Mattoid, *n.* paṇḍitamānībāla, *m.*

Mattress, *n.* bhisi, *f.* santhara, *m.*

Maturate, *v.i.* pariṇamati ; paripaccati. *p.p.* pariṇata ; paripakka. °**ion**, *n.* 1. paripāka ; 2. pūyasañcaya, *m.* °**ive**, *a.* paripācaka.

Mature, *a.* 1. pariṇata ; paripakka ; 2. sampanna ; paripuṇṇa. *v.t.* pariṇāmeti ; paripāceti. *v.i.* pariṇamati. *p.p.* °mita ; °cita ; pariṇata. °**ity**, *n.* pariṇatatta ; pakkatta, *nt.*

Matutinal, Matutine, *a.* pātosijjhamānaka.

Maudlin, *n.* saŋvegādhika ; assupaggharaka, *m.*

Maul, *n.* mahādārukūṭa, *m.* *v.t.* 1. kūṭena tāḷeti ; 2. dosavicārena vināseti. *p.p.* °tāḷita ; °sita.

Maunder, *v.i.* 1. animittam āhiṇḍati ; 2. avyattaŋ jappati. *p.p.* °ḍita ; °pita.

Mausoleum, *n.* visiṭṭha-susānāgāra, *nt.*

Mauve, *n.* *a.* nīlalohitavaṇṇa.

Maw, *n.* jaṭhara, *nt.* — **worm**, udariyapāṇaka, *m.*

Mawkish, *a.* 1. virasa ; 2. jigucchājanaka.

Maxilla, *n.* uparimahanu, *m.* °**ry**, *a.* hanunissita.

Maxim, *n.* siddhanta, *m.* sutta, *nt.* °**ist**, *n.* 1. niyāmarucika, *m.*

Maximum, *n.* 1. uparimakoṭi ; 2. paramasaṅkhyā, *f.* °**ize**, *v.t.* uparimakoṭiŋ pāpeti. *p.p.* °pāpita.

May, *aux. v.* This is expressed by the Potential : **May be**, siyā ; bhaveyya. **May the deity protect us**, devatā amhe rakkhatu.

May, *n.* Vesākha, *m.*

Mayor, *n.* nagarādhipa, *m.* °**alty**, *n.* 1. nagarādhipacca, *nt.* 2. nagarādhipa-samaya, *m.* °**ess**, *n.* nagarādhipatinī, *f.*

Mazarine, *n.* *a.* ghana-nīlavaṇṇa, *m.*

Maze, *n.* 1. duggamagga, *m.* gahanaṭṭhāna, *nt.* 2. vaṅkatta; visamatta, *nt.* 3. saŋsaya ; sandeha, *m.* *v.t.* vyākulīkaroti ; moheti. *p.p.* °kata ; mohita. °**y**, *a.* dunniggama ; atijimha.

Mead, *n.* madhupāna, *nt.*

Meadow, *n.* tiṇabhūmi, *f.* saddala, *m.*

Meagre, *a.* 1. ittara ; appaka ; thoka ; 2. kisa ; tanu. °**ly**, *adv.* appavasena. °**ness**, *n.* appatta ; kisatta, *nt.*

Meal, *n.* 1. dhaññapiṭṭha ; 2. bhojana, *nt.* āhāra, *m.* °**time**, bhattavelā, *f.* **Morning** — , pātarāsa, *m.* *v.i.* bhattaŋ bhuñjati. *p.p.* bhuttabhatta.

Mean, *a.* 1. dīna ; kātara ; nihīna; 2. majjhima. °**ly,** *adv.* nīcākārena. °**ness,** *n.* hīnatta ; dīnatta, *nt.* °**time,** °**while,** tadantare, *adv.*

Mean, *v.t.* adhippeti; parikappeti; cinteti. *v.i.* maññati; sūceti. *p.p.* °peta ; °pita ; °tita ; mata ; sūcita.

Meander, *n.* vaṅkagati, *f.* *v.i.* kuṭilaŋ *or* jimhaŋ gaccati *or* savati. *p.p.* °gata. °**ing,** *a.* saŋsappamāna.

Meaning, *n.* 1. saddattha ; adhippāya, *m.* 2. iṅgita, *nt.* adj. sandīpaka ; sūcaka. °**less,** *a.* attharahita. °**ly,** *adv.* sundarādhippāyena.

Means, *n.* 1. upakkama; upāya; payoga, *m.* 2. upakaraṇa, *nt.* 3. vibhava, *m.* **Beyond one's —,** āyam atikkamma. **By all—,** sabbākārena. **By any —,** kathañci pi ; yena kenaci upāyena. **By no —,** na kathañci pi. **Failure of—,** payogavipatti, *f.* **Having moderate—,** appavibhava, *a.*

Measles, *n.* lahumasūrikā, *f.*

Measure, *n.* 1. māṇa, pamāṇa, *nt.* 2. (plan:) upāya; payoga, *m.* 3. (metre:) chandovutta, *nt.* 4. (a rod for—) māṇadaṇḍa, *m.* *v.t.* miṇāti ; tuleti ; pamāṇeti. *p.p.* mita; tulita; °ṇita. °**able,** *a.* pameyya ; tulanāraha. °**er,** *n.* parimāṇakara, *m.* °**less,** *a.* amita; aparimita; appameyya. °**ing four inches,** caturaṅgula, *a.* °**ment,** *n.* māṇa; tulana, *nt.* **According to—,** pamāṇayutta, *a.* **False —,** māṇakūṭa, *nt.* **Grain —,** tumba, *m.*

Meat, *n.* 1. maŋsa ; āmisa, *nt.* 2. bhojana ; anna, *nt.* °**seller,** maŋsika, *m.*

Mechanic, *n.* yantika ; yantasippī, *m.* °**al,** *a.* yantavisayaka; yantasippānugata. °**ally,** *adv.* yantasippānusārena.

Mechanics, *n.* yantasippa, *nt.* °**nist,** *n.* yantasippī, *m.* °**nism,** *n.* yantaracanā, *f.*

Medal, *n.* kittimuddā, *f.* °**list,** *n.* kittimuddālābhī, *m.* °**lion,** *n.* mahākittimuddā, *f.*

Meddle, *v.i.* parakiccesu pavisati. *p.p.* °paviṭṭha. °**some,** *a.* anāyattakiccakārī.

Mediaeval, *a.* majjhakālīna.

Medial, *a.* majjhima ; majjhavattī.

Mediate, *a.* majjhavattī ; antarāvattī. *v.i.* majjhe vattati. *v.t.* (aññamaññaŋ) sandahati. *p.p.* °tita ; °hita. °**ion,** *n.* antaravattitā, *f.* sandhāna, *nt.* °**tor,** *n.* sandhānakārī ; sandhātu, *m.* °**tory,** *a.* sandhānakara. °**trix,** *n.* sandhānakārinī; majjhavattinī, *f.*

Medicable, *a.* satekiccha ; sappatikāra.

Medical, *a.* osadhīya ; tikicchāvisayaka. °ly, *adv.* vejjasatthānusārena. — **practice,** vejjakamma, *nt.* °**science,** vejjasattha, *nt.* āyubbeda, *m.* — **treatment,** tikicchā, *f.* osadhappayoga, *m.*

Medicament, *n.* osadha ; bhesajja, *nt.*

Medicaster, *n.* kuvejja, *m.*

Medicate, *v.t.* bhesajjaŋ deti. *p.p.* dinnabhesajja. °**ion,** *n.* bhesajjakaraṇa, *nt.*

Medicine, *n.* osadha ; bhesajja, *nt.* agada, *m.* °**al,** *a.* osadhīya ; rogahara. °**al herb,** osadhī, *f.* — **man,** māyākāra, *m.*

Medico, *n.* vejja ; tikicchaka, *m.*

Mediocre, *a.* majjhavattī ; sāmañña. °**crity,** *n.* sāmaññatta; majjhavattitta, *nt.*

Meditate, *v.i.* jhāyati ; upanijjhāyati ; sammasati. *p.p.* °yita ; °sita. °**ion,** *n.* jhāyana; jhāna, *nt.* °**ive,** *a.* cintaka; parikappaka; nijjhāyaka.

Mediterranean, *a.* bhūmajjhaṭṭha.

Medium, *n.* upakārakavatthu, *nt.* saŋsandakapuggala, *m.*

Medley, *n.* 1. pakiṇṇakavatthu ; 2. sammissatta, *nt.*

Medulla, *n.* aṭṭhimiñjā, *f.*

Meed, *n.* pāritosika, *nt.*

Meek, *a.* subbaca ; vinīta ; anuddhata. °**ly,** *adv.* savinayaŋ. °**ness,** *n.* soracca ; subbacatta, *nt.*

Meet, *a.* ucita ; anurūpa ; anucchavika. *v.t.* samāgacchati ; abhimukhībhavati. *p.p.* samāgata ; abhimukhībhūta. °**ing,** *n.* 1. samosaraṇa ; melana ; 2. samiti ; sabhā, *f.* sannipāta, *m.* °**ly,** *adv.* ucitākārena. °**ness,** *n.* ocitya ; anurūpatta, *nt.* — **together,** samosarati ; sannipatati. — **with,** sammukhī hoti.

Megacephalic, *a.* mahāsīsa.

Megalith, *n.* thūpa-mahāsilā, *f.*

Megalomania, *n.* ahaṅkārādhikatā, *f.*

Megaphone, *n.* saddavaḍḍhakakāhala, *m.*

Megrim, *n.* sīsapassarujā, *f.*

Melancholy, *n. a.* domanassa, *nt.* visāda ; kheda, *m. a.* dummana ; visādappatta. °**lia,** *n.* khedummāda, *m.* aṭṭhānabhaya, *nt.* °**lic,** *a.* olīnavuttika; dummanapakatika.

Melange, *n.* missībhāva, *m.* pakiṇṇaka, *nt.*

Melanism, *n.* gattakāḷavaṇṇatā, *f.*

Melee, *n.* 1. saṅkula-yuddha, *nt.* 2. balava-vivāda, *m.*

Meliorate, see **Improve.** °**ion,** *n.* abhivaḍḍhana ; samiddhipāpana, *nt.*

Meliorism, *n.* lokābhivuddhisādhaka-mata, *nt.*

Melliferous, *a.* madhuppādaka.

Mellifluous, *a.* madhusadisa ; atimadhura.

Mellow, *a.* 1. supariṇata ; 2. mudu ; komala. *v.t.* paripāceti ; muduttaŋ pāpeti. *v.i.* paripākaŋ gacchati. *p.p.* °cita ; °pāpita ; °gata. °**ness,** *n.* mudutta ; pakkatta, *nt.*

Melodious, *a.* sotarasāyana. °**ly,** *adv.* madhurassarena. °**ness,** *n.* sotarasāyanatta ; mādhuriya, *nt.*

Melodrama, *n.* abbhutarasikanāṭaka, *nt.*

Melody, madhura-saṅgīta, *nt.* gīta-vādita-laya ; madhurassara, *m.* °**ist,** *n.* gīta-sampādaka, *m.* °**ize,** *v.t.* layānugaŋ karoti.

Melon, *n.* tipusa ; Kāliṅgaphala, *nt.*

Melt, *v.i.* vilīyati. *v.t.* vilīyāpeti. *p.p.* vilīna ; °pita. **°ing,** *n.* vilīyana, *nt.* **°ing pot,** mūsā, *f.*

Member, *n.* 1. avayava, *m.* aṅga, *nt.* 2. (of an assembly :) sāmājika, *m.* 3. (of a council :) pārisajja, *m.* **°ship,** *n.* sāmājikatta, *nt.*

Membrane, *n.* (maŋsa-) paṭala, *nt.* āvarakattaca, *m.*

Memento, *n.* satuppādaka, *m.* anussaraṇavatthu, *nt.*

Memoir, *n.* 1. caritalekhā, *f.* 2. vuttanta, *m.* 3. visayanibandha, *m.*

Memorabilia, *n. pl.* saritabbavatthūni, *nt.*

Memorandum, *n.* sāraka-paṇṇa, *nt.* khuddakalipi, *f.*

Memorial, *n.* 1. anussārakavatthu, *nt.* 2. nivedanapaṇṇa, *nt.* adj. satuppādaka ; sarāpaka. **°ist,** *n.* āyācaka, *m.* **°ize,** *v.t.* 1. lekhanena āyācati ; 2. (ussavādinā) anussarati.

Memory, *n.* sati, *f.* anussaraṇa, *nt.* **°able,** *a.* saritabba ; saranīya ; sāranīya, **°ize,** *v.t.* vācuggataŋ karoti ; manasi dhāreti. *p.p.* °kata ; °dhārita. **Loss of —,** satisammosa, *m.* **Right —,** sammāsati, *f.*

Menace, *n.* santajjana, *nt.* *v.t.* santajjeti ; bhāyāpeti. *p.p.* °jita ; °pita. **°ingly,** *adv.* tajjanākārena.

Menage, *n.* gharasaŋvidhāna ; gharāvāsakicca, *nt.*

Menagerie, *n.* baddha-vālamigasamūha ; pasu-pakkhinivāsa, *m.*

Mend, *n.* paṭisaṅkhataṭṭhāna, *nt.* vuddhigāminī avatthā, *f.* *v.t.* paṭisaṅkharoti. *v.i.* vuddhiŋ *or* unnatiŋ yāti *p p.* °khata; °yāta. **°er,** *n.* paṭijaggaka, *m.* **°ing,** *n.* paṭijaggana, *nt.*

Mendacious, *a.* asaccavādī, *m.* **°city,** *n.* musāvāditā, *f.*

Mendicant, *n.* bhikkhaka ; yācaka, *m.* (Religious :) samaṇa ; muni ; yati, *m.* **°cancy,** *n.* bhikkhubhāva, *m.* **°city,** *n.* bhikkhācāra, *m.*

Menial, *n.* bhacca ; ceṭaka ; kiṅkara, *m.* adj. adhama ; nīca. **— duties,** kāyaveyyāvacca, *nt.*

Meniscus, *n.* addhacandalakkhaṇa, *nt.*

Mensal, *a.* māsika.

Menses, *n.* thīraja ; utu, *m.*

Menstrual, *a.* patimāsika. **— time,** utukāla, *m.* **°uous,** *a.* pupphavatī ; utunī, *f.*

Menstruate, *v.i.* utunī hoti. **— °ion,** *n.* utussavana, *nt.*

Mensurable, *a.* 1. layabaddha ; 2. pameyya. **°ration,** *n.* miti, *f.* māṇa, *nt.*

Mental, *a.* mānasika ; manomaya ; cetasika. **— action,** manokamma, *nt.* **— activity,** saṅkhāra, *m.* **— property,** cetasika, *nt.* **°ity,** *n.* cittuppāda, *m.* **°ly,** *adv.* cittena ; cittavasena.

Mentation, *n.* cintana, *nt.* cetanā, *f.*

Mention, *n.* āvedana ; kathana, *nt.* *v.t.* patisāreti ; niddisati. *p.p.* °rita ; niddiṭṭha. **°able,** *a.* ārocetabba ; vattabba.

Mentor, *n.* sadupadesaka ; satuppādaka, *m.*

Menu, *n.* bhojanasūci, *f.*

Mephitis, *n.* duggandhavāta, *m.*

Mercantile, *a.* vāṇijjavisayaka.

Mercenary, *n.* vetaṇika-bhaṭa ; adj. dhanaluddha ; lābhāpekkha ; vetanika, *m.*

Mercer, *n.* dukūlavāṇija, *m.* °**y,** *n.* dukūlāpaṇa, *m.*

Merchandise, *n.* paṇiya ; vikkāyika-bhaṇḍa, *nt.*

Merchant, *n.* vāṇija ; vohārika ; paṇyājīvī, *m.* — **man,** — **vessel,** vāṇijanāvā, *f.* — **prince,** mahādhana-vāṇija, *m.*

Merciful, *a.* sānukampa ; kāruṇika ; dayālū. °**ly,** *adv.* sadayaŋ. °**ness,** *n.* kāruṇikatta, *nt.*

Merciless, *a.* niddaya ; akāruṇika. °**ly,** *adv.* niddayākārena. °**ness,** *n.* niddayatta, *nt.*

Mercury, *n.* 1. pārada, *m.* 2. (planet :) Budha, *m.* °**ial,** °**ic,** °**rous,** *a.* 1. pāradayutta ; 2. pasannacitta ; pītikara ; 3. capala ; cañcala.

Mercy, *n.* dayā ; karuṇā ; anukampā, *f.*

Mere, *n.* taḷāka, *m.* adj. kevala ; suddha. °**ly,** *adv.* kevalaŋ.

Meretricious, *a.* 1. vesiyāraha ; 2. bahivibhūsita. °**ly,** *adv.* bahimaṭṭhatāya.

Merge, *v.t.* nimujjāpeti ; ogāheti. *v.i.* nimujjati ; ogāhati. *p.p.* °pita ; °hita ; nimugga ; ogāḷha. °**nce,** *n.* nimujjana, *nt.* °**er,** *n.* antogamana, *nt.*

Meridian, *n.* 1. majjhaṇha, *m.* 2. nabhomajjharekhā, *f.* adj. majjhaṇhika.

Meridional, *a.* kha-majjhāyatta, *n.* bhūmajjhavāsī, *m.*

Merit, *n.* 1. puñña ; kusala ; 2. phala, *nt.* vipāka, *m.* 3. guṇavisesa, *m.* *v.t.* arahati. °**ed,** *a.* ucita ; yogga ; araha. **Desirous of** —, puññatthika, *a.* **Share of** —, patti, *f.* puññabhāga, *m.* **Transference of** —, pattidāna, *nt.*

Meritorious, *a.* 1. kusaluppādaka ; 2. pasaŋsiya. °**ly,** *adv.* pasaŋsiyākārena. °**ness,** *n.* pasaŋsiyatta, *nt.*

Merlin, *n.* senavisesa, *m.*

Mermaid, *n.* udakakinnarī ; macchanārī, *f.*

Merman, *n.* jalakinnara ; naramaccha, *m.*

Merry, *a.* sāṇanda ; pamudita ; sumana ; haṭṭha. °**ily,** *adv.* sānandaŋ. °**iment,** *n.* ullāsa ; pamoda ; ussava, *m.* — **andrew,** vikaṭakavi, *m.* — **making,** *n.* pītussava, *m.* **Make** —, ullasati ; santussati. *p.p.* °sita ; santuṭṭha.

Mesdames, see **Madame.**

Meseems, *v.i.* mayhaŋ upaṭṭhāti ; maññe.

Mesentery, *n.* antaguṇa, *nt.*

Mesh, *n.* 1. (of a net :) jālakkhika, *nt.* 2. pāsa, *m.* *v.t.* jālena bandhati *or* bādheti. *p.p.* jālabaddha. °**y,** *a.* jālākāra.

Mesmerism, *n.* mohanavijjā, *f.* vasīkaraṇa, *nt.* °**ist,** *n.* vijjāya pamohaka, *m.* °**ize,** *v.t.* mohanena vasīkaroti. *p.p.* °kata.

Mess, *n.* 1. gaṇabhojana ; missitabhojana, *nt.* 2. saṅkulatta, *nt.* *v.i.* gaṇena bhuñjati. *v.t.* misseti ; saṅkulīkaroti. *p.p.* °bhutta ; °sita ; °kata. °**mate,** sahabhojī, *m.*

Message, *n.* sandesa, *m.* sāsana, *nt.*

Messenger, *n.* dūta ; sandesahara ; pessa, *m.*

Messiah, *n.* lokasivaṅkara, *m.*

Messuage, *n.* sauyyānageha, *nt.*

Metabolism, *n.* rūpajanakasatti, *f.*

Metal, *n.* loha, *m. nt.* °**lic,** *a.* lohāyatta. °**list,** *n.* lohavisesaññū, *m.* °**lography,** *n.* lohavijjā, *f.* °**loid,** *a.* lohasadisa. °**lurgy,** *n.* lohasodhana, *nt.* — **worker,** lohakāra, *m.* **Made of** —, lohamaya, *a.*

Metallize, *v.t.* lohattaŋ pāpeti ; lohena sambandheti. *p.p.* °pita ; °sambaddha.

Metamorphose, *v.t.* rūpantaraŋ *or* vikatiŋ pāpeti. *p.p.* °pita. °**sis,** *n.* rūpantaraparivattana, *nt.*

Metaphor, *n.* 1. diṭṭhanta, *m.* nidassana, *nt.* 2. rūpakopamā, *f.* °**ical,** *a.* upamāvisayaka. °**ically,** *adv.* upacārena ; upamāvasena.

Metaphrase, *n.* bhāsānuvāda, *m.* *v.t.* 1. bhāsantaraŋ parivatteti ; 2. vacanāni parivatteti. *p.p.* °tita.

Metaphysics, *n. pl.* ajjhattavijjā, *f.* paramattha-dhamma, *m.* °**cal,** *a.* ajjhattika ; arūpāyatta. °**cally,** *adv.* paramatthavasena. °**cian,** *n.* paramatthavidū.

Metastasis, *n.* rogassa aññaṭṭhānasaṅkāmana, *nt.*

Metathesis, *n.* 1. vaṇṇavipallāsa ; 2. dhātuvipallāsa, *m.*

Mete, *n.* 1. sīmā, *f.* 2. sīmāpāsāṇa, *m.* *v.t.* 1. miṇāti ; 2. (daṇḍaŋ, etc.) āropeti. *p.p.* mita ; āropita°

Metempsychosis, *n.* punaruppatti, *f.* punabbhava, *m.*

Meteor, *n.* ukkāpāta ; uppāta, *m.* °**ic,** *a.* uppātavisayaka ; ukkāsambhava. °**ite,** patitaukkā, *f.* °**ology,** *n.* antalikkhavijjā, *f.* °**oid,** nabhogāmīvatthu, *nt.*

Meter, *n.* 1. metu, *m.* 2. māṇakayanta, *nt.*

Methinks, *v.* (impersonal), maññe ; evam me hoti.

Method, *n.* ākāra ; pakāra ; naya ; vidhi ; kama, *m.* °**ical,** *a.* kamānugata ; niyamānukūla ; vavatthita. °**ically,** *adv.* yathākkamaŋ ; yathāvidhiŋ. °**ist,** *n.* niyamānugāmī, *m.* °**ize,** *v.t.* vavatthapeti ; yathākkamaŋ ṭhapeti. *p.p.* °pita ; °ṭhapita.

Meticulous, *a.* accāsaṅkī ; kukkuccaka.

Metier, *n.* jīvikāvutti, *f.*

Metre, *n.* 1. chandovutta, *nt.* 2. (dvihatthādhika-) dīghamāṇa, *nt.* °**ician,** *n.* chandovidū, *m.* °**ist,** *m.* pajjabandhaka, *m.*

Metric, *a.* 1. chandāyatta ; 2. dasaŋsikamāṇāyatta. °**al,** *a.* 1. chandobaddha ; 2. māṇāyatta. °**al composition,** pajjabandha, *m.* °**ally,** *adv.* chandovuttavasena. °**ics,** *n.* chandosattha, *nt.*

Metronymic, *a.* mattikanāmalābhī.

Metropolis, *n.* agganagara, *nt.* rājadhānī, *f.*

Mettle, *n.* 1. teja ; viriya, *nt.* ussāha, *m.* 2. pakati, *f.* °**some,** *a.* tejassī ; mahussāha.

Mew, *n.* 1. pakkhipañjara ; 2. biḷāla-rava, *m.* *v.t.* pañjare khipati ; rodheti. *v.i.* biḷālaravaŋ nadati. *p.p.* °khitta ; rodhita.

Mews, *n.* assasālā, *f.*

Miasma, *n.* pūtivāta ; visavāta, *m.*

Mica, *n.* abbhakavisesa, *m.*

Mickle, *a.* bahula ; pacura, *n.* mahatī saṅkhyā, *f.*

Microbe, *n.* sukhumapāṇī ; khuddajantu, *m.*

Microcosm, *n.* 1. jīvattabhāva, *m.* 2. vissapatibimba, *nt.*

Microphone, *n.* saddavipphāraka (-yanta), *nt.*

Microscope, *n.* sukhumadassaka, *m.* °**ic**, *a.* atisukhuma.

Micturition, *n.* abhikkhaṇaŋ passāvakaraṇāsā, *f.*

Mid, *a.* majjhima. °**day**, *n.* majjhaṇha, *m.* °**heaven**, nabhomajjha, *nt.* °**land**, majjhadesa, *m.* °**night**, nisītha, *m.* aḍḍharatta, *nt.* °**summer**, majjhagimhāna, *m.* °**way**, *n.* addhapatha, *m.* *adv.* antarena ; majjhe.

Midwife, sūtikā, *f.* °**ry**, sūtikamma, *nt.*

Midden, *n.* saṅkārakūṭa, *m.*

Middle, *n.* vemajjha, *m.* adj. majjhima ; majjhavattī. °**aged**, *a.* majjhimavayaṭṭha. °**ing**, *a.* sādhāraṇa ; majjhimappamāṇa.

Midge, *n.* makasa ; ḍaŋsa, *m.*

Midget, *n.* ativāmanapurisa, *m.*

Midriff, *n.* udaramajjhavattinī pesī, *f.*

Midst, *adv.* *prep.* majjhe ; antare.

Mien, *n.* ākāra ; vesa, *m.*

Might, *n.* satti, *f.* thāma, *m.* bala, *nt.*

Mighty, *a.* 1. pabala ; uruvikkama ; 2. atimahanta. °**ily**, *adv.* 1. vikkamena ; 2. atīva ; atimattaŋ. °**iness**, *n.* pabalatta ; sāmatthiya, *nt.*

Mignon, *a.* sukumāra.

Migrate, *v.i.* niggacchati ; desantaravāsāya gacchati. *p.p.* °gata. °**ory**, *a.* desantarasaṅkāmī.

Milch, *a.* khīradāyinī, *f.* — **cow**, duddhavatī, *f.*

Mild, *a.* 1. mudu ; komala ; 2. sadaya ; kāruṇika. °**ly**, *adv.* mudukākārena. °**ness**, maddava ; sukumāratta, *nt.*

Mildew, *n.* seṭaṭṭhikā, *f.* setakaṇṇikā, *f.* *v.i.* kaṇṇakitaŋ hoti.

Mile, *n.* addhakosa, *m.* °**age**, *n.* dūrappamāṇa, *nt.* kosasaṅkhyā, *f.* °**stone**, *n.* kosathūṇā, *f.*

Militant, *a.* yuddhakāmī ; vivādakāmī. °**ly**, *adv.* vivādakāmitāya. °**ncy**, *n.* yuddhakāmitā, *f.*

Military, *n.* yuddhasenā, *f.* adj. yuddhāyatta; saṅgāmika. °**ism**, *n.* yuddhanīti, *f.* saṅgāmādhipacca, *nt.* °**ist**, *n.* 1. yuddhasikkhaka ; 2. yuddhakāmī. *m.* — **caste**, khattiyajāti, *f.* — **man**, yuddhabhaṭa; saṅgāmāvacara, *m.* — **science**, yuddhasippa, *nt.*

Militate, *v.i.* virujjhati; paṭippharati. *p.p.* viruddha ; paṭipphuṭa.

Militia, *n.* sacchandāgatasenā, *f.*

Milk, *n.* paya ; khīra ; duddha, *nt.* *v.t.* duhati. *p.p.* duddha. °**ing**, *n.* duhana ; dohana, *nt.* °**maid**, gopī, *f.* °**man**, dohaka, *m.* — °**pail**, khīrupadhāna, *nt.* — °**porridge**, khīrapāyāsa, *m.*

°sop, adhīrajana, *m.* — tooth, khīradanta, *m.* — white, *a.* khīravaṇṇa.

Milky, *a.* 1. khīropama; khīravaṇṇa; 2. khīrayutta. °**iness**, *n.* khīrayuttatā, *f.* — **way**, suranadī; ākāsagaṅgā, *f.*

Mill, *n.* cakkayanta, *nt.* *v.t.* piŋsati; cuṇṇeti. *p.p.* °sita; °ṇita. °**er**, *n.* 1. cakkayantapālaka; piŋsaka, *m.*

Millenary, °**nial**, *a.* sahassavassika.

Millennium, *n.* vassasahassa, *nt.*

Millesimal, *n.* sahassatamabhāga, *m.* adj. sahassabhāgika.

Millet, *n.* kaṅgu, *m.*

Milliard, *n.* satakoṭi, *f.*

Milliner, *n.* nāripiḷandhanasampādaka, *m.* °**y**, *n.* nāriparicchada, *m.*

Million, *n.* dasalakkha, *nt.*

Millionaire, *n.* lakkhapati; mahaddhanī; seṭṭhī, *m.*

Milt, *n.* macchapihaka, *m.* macchaṇḍakosa, *m.*

Mimic, *n.* anukārī; vidūsaka, *m.* *v.t.* upahāsāya anukaroti. °**ry**, *n.* anukaraṇopahāsa, *m.*

Miminy-piminy, *a.* adhikasucigaruka; vicittarucika.

Mimosa, *n.* nidhikumbhīgaccha, *m.*

Minacious, *a.* santajjaka. °**ly**, *adv.* tajjanākārena. °**city**, *n.* santajjana, *nt.*

Minar, *n.* dīpatthambha; aṭṭāla, *m.* °**et**, *n.* khuddakaṭṭa, *m.* pāsādasiṅga, *nt.*

Minatory, *a.* santajjaka.

Mince, *n.* cuṇṇita-maŋsa, *nt.* *v.t.* sukhumaŋ likhati; sañcuṇṇeti. *p.p.* °khita; °ṇita.

Mind, *n.* 1. citta; mana; mānasa, *nt.* 2. saṅkappa, *m.* *v.t.* 1. cinteti; manasikaroti; 2. avekkhati. *p.p.* °tita; °kata; °khita. — **cognition**, manoviññāṇa, *nt.* °**ful**, *a.* satimantu; sāvadhāna; sampajāna. °**fully**, *adv.* sāvadhānaŋ. °**fulness**, *n.* appamāda, *m.* satisampajañña, *nt.* °**less**, *a.* anavadhāna; pamatta. — **made**, manomaya, *a.*

Mine, *n.* ākara, *m.* āyatana; uppattiṭṭhāna, *nt.* *v.t.* khaṇati; antobhūmiŋ khaṇati. *p.p.* khata. °**er**, *n.* ākarika, *m.*

Mine, *a.* madīya. *pron.* *poss.* mama; mayhaŋ; me.

Mineral, *n.* khaṇija-dhātu, *f.* adj. ākaraja; bhūdhātumaya. °**ogist**, *n.* khaṇijatattaññū, *m.* °**ology**, *n.* khaṇijavijjā, *f.* — **salt**, sindhava, *m.*

Minerva, *n.* Sarassatī Devī, *f.*

Mingle, *v.t.* misseti; saŋyojeti. *v.i.* missībhavati. *p.p.* missita; °jita; °bhūta.

Miniate, *v.t.* rattahiṅgulena lepeti. *p.p.* °litta.

Miniature, *n.* khuddaka-cittakamma, *nt.* khuddaka-paṭimā, *f.* adj. atikhuddaka, *v.t.* khuddakasaṇṭhānaŋ dasseti *or* sampādeti.

Minify, *v.t.* pamāṇaŋ parihāpeti. *p.p.* °pitapamāṇa.

Minikin, *n.* hīnaparimāṇapāṇī, *m.*

Minimal, *a.* atikhuddaka; atyappaka.

Minimize, *v.t.* pamāṇaŋ hāpeti; appakaŋ karoti. *p.p.* hāpitapamāṇa; appīkata.

Minimum, *n.* appatamasaṅkhyā, *f.* heṭṭhimaparicchedа, *m.* heṭṭhimapamāṇa, *nt.*

Minion, *n.* 1. piyatamapuggala; iṭṭha-pāṇī; 2. dinasevaka, *m.* 3. muddākkharavisesa, *m.*

Minister, *n.* saciva; rājāmacca, *m.* *v.t.* sevati; upaṭṭhāti. *p.p.* sevita; upaṭṭhita. °**ial,** *a.* 1. amaccāyatta; 2. nītyāyatta; 3. devasevāyatta.

Ministration, *n.* upaṭṭhāna, *nt.* pāricariyā; sevā, *f.*

Ministry, *n.* 1. amaccapada, *nt.* 2. devasevā, *f.* 3. amaccamaṇḍala, *nt.* 4. devasevakadhura, *nt.*

Minor, *a.* 1. kaṇiṭṭha; kaṇiya; 2. appadhāna; amukhya. *n.* appattavaya; ūnavayaṭṭha; 3. °**ity,** *n.* 1. bālya, *nt.* bālāvatthā, *f.* 2. ūnasaṅkhyā, *f.* appatarabhāga, *m.*

Minster, *n.* mahādevālaya, *m.*

Minstrel, *n.* vetālika; thutipāṭhaka; gāyaka, *m.* °**sy,** *n.* 1. vandigīta, *nt.* 2. vandibhaṭṭasamūha, *m.* 3. gāyanasippa, *nt.*

Mint, *n.* mūlaṅkanaṭṭhāna, *nt.* *v.t.* mūlaŋ muddāpeti. °**age,** *n.* rūpiyamuddaṅkana, *nt.*

Minus, *n.* hāpana-ciṇha, *nt.* adj. ūna; ūnaka. — **one,** ekūna, *a.*

Minute, *n.* muhutta; khaṇa, *m.* adj. aṇumatta; atikhuddaka; sukhuma. °**ly,** *adv.* 1. aṇuso; sukhumākārena; 2. anukkhaṇaŋ. °**ness,** *n.* sokhumma; sukhumatta, *nt.*

Minute, *v.t.* 1. yathābhūtavelaŋ gavesati; 2. siddhiŋ likhati.

Minutia, *n.* yathātathavaṇṇanā, *f.*

Minx, *n.* dubbinītā yuvatī, *f.*

Miracle, *n.* pāṭihāriya; vikubbana, *nt.*

Miraculous, *a.* abbhuta; vimhayāvaha; iddhivisayaka. °**ly,** *adv.* abbhutākārena.

Mirage, *n.* marīci; migataṇhikā, *f.*

Mire, *n.* paṅka; kaddama, *m.* kalala; cikkhalla, *nt.* *v.t.* paṅkena dūseti. *p.p.* °sita.

Mirror, *n.* ādāsa; dappaṇa, *m.* *v.t.* 1. ādāse yojeti; 2. ādāsena viya dasseti; parāvatteti.

Mirth, *n.* hāsa; āmoda; ānanda, *m.* °**ful,** *a.* haṭṭha; pamudita. °**fully,** *adv.* sānandaŋ. °**fulness,** *n.* pahaṭṭhatā, *f.* °**less,** *a.* anattamana; ukkaṇṭhita.

Miry, a. kalalapuṇṇa; paṅkayutta.

Misadventure, *n.* vipatti, *f.*

Misadvise, *v.t.* micchā upadisati. *p.p.* °upadiṭṭha.

Misalliance, *n.* ayathāsambandha, *m.*

Misanthrope, °**pist,** *n.* mahājanapaccatthika, *m.*

Misapply, *v.t.* ayathā yojeti. *p.p.* °yojita. °**ication,** *n.* ayathāyojana, *nt.*

Misapprehend, *v.t.* ayathā *or* aññathā avagacchati. *p.p.* °avagata. °**hension,** ayathāvabodha, *m.* °**hensive,** *a.* ayathābujjhaka.

Misappropriate, *v.t.* aṭṭhāne yojeti; ayathā paṭipajjati. *p.p.* °yojita; °paṭipanna. °**ion,** *n.* ayathā yojana. *nt.*

Misbecome, *v.i.* na yujjati; na vaṭṭati.

Misbegotten, *a.* avajāta.

Misbehave, *v.t.* asammā vattati *or* ācarati. °**ed,** *a.* durācāra. °**iour,** *n.* anācāra; duṭṭhācāra, *m.* asammāvattana, *nt.*

Misbelief, *n.* micchādiṭṭhi, *f.* ayathādassana, *nt.*

Miscalculate, *v.t.* virajjhitvā gaṇeti. *p.p.* °gaṇita. °**ion,** *n.* viraddhagaṇanā, *f.* ayathāvinicchaya, *m.*

Miscall, *v.t.* ayahā voharati. *p.p.* °rita.

Miscarry, *v.i.* 1. viphalībhavati; 2. gabbho patati. *p.p.* °bhūta; patitagabbhā. °**iage,** *n.* 1. viphalībhāva, *m.* 2. gabbhapatana, *nt.*

Miscellaneous, *a.* vomissaka; saṅkiṇṇa; nānākāra. °**ly,** *adv.* sammissākārena.

Miscellany, *n.* vividha-nibandhasaṅgaha, *m.*

Mischance, *n.* duddasā, *f.* dubbhāgya, *nt.*

Mischief, *n.* 1. apakāra; anattha, *m.* hiŋsā, *f.* 2. durācāra, *m.* — **maker,** dujjana, *m.*

Mischievous, *a.* anatthakara; duṭṭhapakatika. °**ly,** *adv.* duṭṭhākārena.

Miscible, *a.* missanayogga.

Miscite, *v.t.* ayathā udāharati. *p.p.* °udāhaṭa.

Misconceive, *v.t.* ayathā bujjhati. *p.p.* °buddha.

Misconception, *n.* micchāvabodha, *m.*

Misconduct, *n.* micchācāra; avinaya, *m.* *v.t.* asammā vattati; durācāraŋ carati.

Misconjecture, *n.* micchāvitakka, *m.*

Misconstrue, *v.t.* ayathā sādheti; viparītatthaŋ katheti. *p.p.* °dhita; kathitavipa°. °**truction,** *n.* ayathāsādhana; viparītatthakathana, *nt.*

Miscreant, *n.a.* 1. adhama; nīca; 2. micchādiṭṭhika.

Miscreated, *a.* ayathānimmita.

Misdate, *v.t.* ayathā kālaniyamaŋ likhati.

Misdeed, *n.* dukkata; kukicca; kibbisa; duccarita, *nt.*

Misdeem, *v.t.i.* ayathā cinteti *or* sañjānāti. *p.p.* °tita; °nita.

Misdemeanour, *n.* durācāra; avinaya, *m.*

Misdirect, *v.t.* ayathā neti; kupathaŋ pāpeti. *p.p.* °nīta; °pāpita. °**ion,** *n.* ummagganayana; ayathānusāsana, *nt.*

Misdoer, *n.* pāpakārī; micchāpaṭipanna. °**doing,** *n.* dukkata; kucchitakamma, *nt.*

Miser, *n.* luddha; lolupa; macchari; kadariya, *m.* °**ly,** *a.* adānasīla; maccherābhibhūta.

Misery, *n.* dukkha; vyasana; kiccha; kasira, *nt.* °**able,** *a.* kātara; dīna; duggata; kapaṇa. °**ably,** *adv.* dukkhitākārena.

Misfeasance, *n.* nītiviruddhapayoga, *m.*

Misfit, *n.* ananucchavikatta; asaŋsandiyamānatta, *nt.*

Misfortune, *n.* alakkhī, *f.* vyasana; abhāgya, *nt.* upaddava, *m.*

Misgive, *v.t.* āsaṅkati; parisaṅkati. *p.p.* °kita. °**ing,** *n.* āsaṅkā; vimati, *f.* saŋsaya, *m.*

Misgotten, *a.* adhammaladdha.

Misgovern, *v.t.* asammā pāleti. *p.p.* °lita. °**ment,** *n.* adhammikapālana, *nt.*

Misguide, *v.t.* apathe niyojeti. *p.p.* °jita. °**ed,** *a.* uppathagāmī; ayathānusiṭṭha.

Mishandle, *v.t.* anādarenācarati; pīḷeti. *p.p.* °rita; pīḷita.

Mishap, *n.* vipatti, *f.* abhāgya, *nt.*

Mishear, *v.t.* ayathā *or* avibhūtaŋ suṇāti. *p.p.* °suta.

Mishmash, *n.* saṅkiṇṇa-missaṇa, *nt.*

Misinform, *v.t.* ayathā nivedeti. *p.p.* °dita. °**ation,** *n.* micchānivedana, *nt.*

Misinterpret, *v.t.* ayathā anuvādeti. *p.p.* °dita. °**ation,** *n.* ayathānuvāda, *m.*

Misjudge, *v.t.i.* ayathā tīreti; asammā vicāreti. *p.p.* °rita. °**ment,** *n.* ayathāvinicchaya, *m.*

Mislay, *v.t.* aṭṭhāne ṭhapeti *or* nidahati. *p.p.* °ṭhapita; °nihita.

Mislead, *v.t.* uppathaŋ neti; vimoheti. *p.p.* °nīta; °hita. °**ing,** *a.* pamohaka; kummaggapāpaka.

Mismanage, *v.t.* asammā pāleti *or* pavatteti. *p.p.* °lita; °tita. °**ment,** *n.* ayathāpālana, *nt.*

Misname, *v.t.* aññanāmena voharati *or* ālapati. *p.p.* °rita; °pita.

Misnomer, *n.* ayathānāma; ananucchavikābhidhāna, *nt.*

Misogamy, *n.* vivāhavirodha, *m.* °**ist,** *n.* vivāhavirodhī, *m.*

Misogynist, *n.* itthidessī, *m.* °**gynic,** *a.* vanitāviruddha.

Misology, *n.* hetuvirodha, *m.*

Misplace, *v.t.* aṭṭhāne nikkhipati; micchā paṇidahati. *p.p.* °nikkhitta; °paṇihita. °**ment,** *n.* aṭṭhānanikkhipana; micchāpaṇidahana, *nt.*

Misprint, *v.t.* sadosaŋ muddāpeti, *n.* muddaṅkaṇadosa, *m.*

Misprision, *n.* 1. kumantanagūhana, *nt.* 2. avaññā; ohīlanā, *f.*

Misprize, *v.t.* avagaṇeti; omaññati. *p.p.* avagaṇita; omata.

Mispronounce, *v.t.* asuddham uccāreti. *p.p.* °rita. °**nunciation,** *n.* asuddhuccāraṇa, *nt.*

Misquote, *v.t.* ayathā udāharati. *p.p.* °udāhaṭa. °**tation,** *n.* ayathā-udāharaṇa, *nt.*

Misread, *v.t.* asammā vāceti. *p.p.* °vācita.

Misreckon, *v.t.* ayathā gaṇeti. *p.p.* °gaṇita.

Misrelate, *v.t.* ayathā nivedeti. *p.p.* °dita.

Misreport, *n.* micchānivedana, *nt.* *v.t.* ayathānivedeti. *p.p.* °dita.

Misrepresent, *v.t.* ayathā dasseti; asaccaŋ pakāseti. *p.p.* °sita. °**ation,** *n.* ayathādassana, *nt.* asaccappākāsa, *m.*

Misrule, *n.* adhammikapālana, *nt.*

Miss, *n.* kumārī; yuvatī, *f.*

Miss, *n.* 1. virajjhana; vipajjana, *nt.* 2. abhāva; viraha, *m.* *v.i.* virajjhati; vipajjati; viphalībhavati. *v.t.* 1. virādheti; na vindati. *p.p.* viraddha; vipanna; °bhūta; °dhita; avindita. *v.t.* 2. (to feel the absence of:) abhāvaŋ cinteti; ukkaṇṭhati.

p.p. cintitābhāva ; °ṭhita. °**ing**, *a.* naṭṭha ; galita ; tirohita.

Misshapen, *a.* virūpa ; dussaṇṭhāna.

Missile, *n.* paharaṇa ; khipitabbāyudha, *nt.*

Mission, *n.* 1. dūteyya, *nt.* 2. dūtasamūha, *m.* niyojitasabhā, *f.* °**ary**, *n.* dhammadūta, *m.* adj. dhammadūteyyavisayaka.

Missis, *n.* gahapatānī, *f.*

Missive, *n.* rājakīyasāsana, *nt.*

Mis-spell, *v.t.* sadosaŋ likhati *or* paṭhati. *p.p.* °khita ; °ṭhita.

Mis-spend, *v.t.* ayathā vissajjeti *or* vayaŋ karoti. *p.p.* °vissaṭṭha ; °katavaya.

Mis-state, *v.t.* ayathā nirūpeti *or* katheti. *p.p.* °pita ; °kathita. °**ment**, ayathākathana, *nt.*

Mist, *n.* tuhina, *nt.* dhūmikā, *f.* *v.i.* tuhinena āvarīyati. *p.p.* °āvuta. °**y**, *a.* tuhināvuta.

Mistake, *v.t.* ayathā *or* virajjhitvā aṇhāti. *v.i.* muyhati ; khalati. *p.p.* °gahita ; mūḷha ; khalita. *noun:* khalita, *nt.* pamādadosa ; matibbhama, *m.* °**able**, *a.* virajjhanāraha. °**nly**, *adv.* ayathāvagamena ; vibbhamena.

Mister, *n.* 1. ayya ; sāmī; 2. bhavanta.

Mistime, *v.t.* ayathākāle karoti *or* vadati. *p.p.* °kata ; °vutta.

Mistress, *n.* 1. sāminī ; ayyā ; gharaṇī, *f.* 2. ācariyānī ; 3. vallabhā ; piyā, *f.*

Mistrial, *n.* ayathānuyuñjana, *nt.*

Mistrust, *n.* avissāsa, *m.* āsaṅkā, *f.* *v.t.* āsaṅkati ; parisaṅkati ; na vissasati. *p.p.* °kita; avissattha.

°**ful**, *a.* āsaṅkī. °**fully**, *adv.* sāsaṅkaŋ.

Misunderstand, *v.t.* ayathā bujjhati. *p.p.* °buddha. °**ing**, *n.* viparītāvabodha, *m.* micchāgahaṇa, *nt.*

Misuse, *n.* ayathā-upayoga, *m.* *v.t.* asammā payojeti ; vinipāteti. *p.p.* °jita ; °tita. °**age**, *n.* aṭṭhānopayoga, *m.* vinipātana, *nt.*

Mite, *n.* 1. lava ; kaṇa ; lesa ; 2. appaggha-mūlavisesa, *m.*

Mitigate, *v.t.* upasameti ; lāghavayati. *p.p.* °mita ; °yita. °**ion**, *n.* upasamana ; ūnattapāpaṇa, *nt.* °**ive**, *a.* ūnattapāpaka.

Mitre, *n.* devapūjaka-nāḷipaṭṭa, *m.*

Mix, *v.t.* misseti ; sanneti. *p.p.* missita ; sannita. °**ed**, vokiṇṇa ; saṅkiṇṇa. *a.* °**ed with**, paribhāvita ; saŋsaṭṭha. *a.* °**ture**, *n.* saŋyoga, *m.* sammissaṇa, *nt.*

Mixen, *n.* asucirāsi, *m.*

Mizzle, *v.i.* mandaŋ vassati. *n.* sīkaravuṭṭhi, *f.*

Mnemonic, *a.* satuppādaka. *pl.* sati-uddīpana, *nt.*

Moan, *n.* akkandana, *nt.* vilāpa; aṭṭassara, *m.* *v.* akkandati; vilapati. *p.p.* °dita; °pita. °**ful**, *a.* paridevamāna. °**fully**, *adv.* savilāpaŋ.

Moat, *n.* nagaraparikhā ; digghikā, *f.* *v.t.* parikhaŋ yojeti. °**ed**, *a.* parikhāyutta.

Mob, *n.* 1. janasamūha, *m.* 2. kalahakārī parisā, *f.* *v.t.* kalahaŋ karoti. *v.i.* kalahāya sannipatati. *p.p.* katakalaha ; °tita.

Mobile, *a.* jaṅgama cañcala. °**ity,** *n.* jaṅgamatta ; calana, *nt.* — **principle,** vāyodhātu, *f.* °**ize,** *v.t.* 1. jaṅgamattaŋ pāpeti ; 2. senaŋ sannayhati *or* sajjeti. *p.p.* °pita ; sannaddhasena.

Moccasin, *n.* cammapādukā, *f.*

Mock, *n.* parihāsa, *m.* uppaṇḍanā ; viḷambanā, *f.* adj. kittima. *v.t.* uppaṇḍeti ; parihasati. *p.p.* °ḍita ; °sita. °**er,** *n.* parihasaka, *m.* °**ery,** *n.* parihāsa, *m.* viḷambanā, *f.*

Mode, *n.* 1. ākāra ; pakāra ; vidhi, *m.* 2. ācāra ; vohāra ; sampadāya, *m.*

Model, *n.* 1. ādisiya-rūpa, *nt.* 2. ādisitabba-puggala ; pamāṇabhūta, *m.* *v.t.* paṭirūpāni karoti. *v.i.* saṇṭhānam uppādeti. *p.p.* paṭirūpakata ; uppāditasaṇṭhāna, *nt.* °**led figure,** potthalikā, *f.*

Moderate, *a.* mattāyutta ; parimita ; majjhavattī, *n.* mattaññū ; 3. *v.t.* saŋyameti ; niggaṇhāti. *v.i.* upasammati. *p.p.* °mita ; niggahita ; upasanta. °**ly,** *adv.* mattāyuttaŋ ; mattaññutāya. °**ness,** °**ion,** *n.* mattaññutā, *f.* saŋyama ; sīmānatikkama, *m.*

Modern, *a.* nūtana ; ajjatana ; vattamānika ; ādhunika. °**ism,** *n.* ādhunika-mata, *nt.* °**ity,** °**ness,** *n.* nūtanatta, *nt.* °**ize,** *v.t.* navattaŋ pāpeti.

Modest, *a.* hirimantu ; salajja ; savinaya ; nirahaṅkāra. °**ly,** *adv.* vinītatāya ; nihatamānatāya. °**y,** *n.* vinaya, *m.* nimmānatā ; lajjā ; hiri, *f.*

Modicum, *n.* appamattaka, *nt.*

Modify, *v.t.* 1. saṅkharoti ; pariṇāmeti ; 2. niyameti. *p.p.* saṅkhata ; °mita. °**ication,** *n.* paṭisaṅkharaṇa ; rūpantara-parivattana, *nt.* °**ier,** *n.* saṅkhāraka, *m.* °**icatory,** *a.* parivattanayogga. °**iable,** *a.* paṭisaṅkharaṇāraha.

Modish, *a.* maṇḍanappiya. °**ly,** *adv.* pāsādikavesena.

Modulate, *v.t.* samaŋ pavatteti. *p.p.* °tita. °**ion,** *n.* samaŋpavattāpana, *nt.*

Module, *n.* niyamita-dīghamāṇa, *nt.*

Modus, *n.* ākāra, *m.* — **operandi,** pavattanākāra, *m.*

Mohammedan, *a. n.* Mahammadika.

Mohur, *n.* suvaṇṇanikkhavisesa, *m.*

Moider, *v.t.* vikkhipati. *p.p.* vikkhitta.

Moiety, *n.* upaḍḍha ; samabhāga, *m.*

Moil, *v.i.* 1. vihaññati ; kilamati ; 2. paṅke saṅkamati. *v.t.* paṅkena dūseti. *p.p.* vihata ; kilanta ; °saṅkanta ; °dūsita.

Moist, *a.* temita ; tinta ; alla. °**en,** *v.t.* temeti ; kiledeti. *p.p.* temita ; °dita. °**ure,** *n.* 1. allatta, *nt.* tintabhāva, *m.* 2. vātagata-jala, *nt.*

Molar, *a.* 1. cabbanopakārī ; 2. piŋsanaka. — **tooth,** *n.* piŋsakadanta, *m.*

Molasses, *n. pl.* ucchurasa, *m.* phāṇita, *nt.*

Mole, *n.* 1. tilakālaka, *m.* 2. dīghatuṇḍī, *f.* 3. samuddāḷi, *f.* baddhasetu, *m.* — **eyed,** *a.* khuddakanetta.

Molecule, *n.* aṇu, *m.* °**ar,** *a.* aṇuvisayaka.

Molest, *v.t.* upaddaveti ; paritāpeti. *p.p.* upadduta ; °pita. °**ation,** *n.* pīḷana ; hiŋsana, *nt.*

Mollify, *v.t.* upasameti ; muduŋ karoti. *p.p.* °mita ; mudukata. °**ication,** *n.* upasāmana ; mudukaraṇa, *nt.*

Mollusc, *n.* kosayutta-pāṇī, *m.*

Molly, *n.* nārīsabhāvika-purisa. *m.*

Molten, *a.* uttatta ; vilīna.

Moment, *n.* 1. khaṇa, *m.* muhutta, *nt.* 2. garutta ; mahatta, *nt.* °**ary,** *a.* khaṇika ; athāvara. °**ous,** *a.* garuka; sallakkhaṇīya. **Auspicious —,** sukhaṇa, *m.* **In a —,** khaṇena. *adv.*

Momentum, *n.* vegappamāṇa, *nt.*

Monachal, *a.* tapacariyāyatta.

Monachism, *n.* pabbajjā; tapacariyā,*f.* samaṇadhamma, *m.*

Monad, *n.* abhejjavatthu, *nt.*

Monandry, *n.* ekapatikatā, *f.*

Monarch, *n.* rāja ; adhissara ; bhūpati, *m.* °**ical,** *a.* rājakīya ; rājāyatta. °**y,** *n.* 1. ekādhipacca ; 2. vijita, *nt.*

Monastery, *n.* vihāra ; assama ; yatinivāsa, *m.*

Monastic, *a.* sāmaṇaka; vihārāyatta.

Monday, *n.* Candavāra, *m.*

Monetary, *a.* rūpiyavisayaka.

Monetize, *v.t.* lohamayamūlaŋ upayojeti.

Money, *n.* mūla ; jātarūpa ; rūpiya, *nt.* °**changer,** *n.* rūpiyaparivattaka, *m.* °**lender,** *n.* iṇadāyī, *m.* °**less,** *a.* niddhana.

Monger, *n.* vyāpārika ; vāṇija, *m.*

Mongoose, *n.* nakula ; muṅgusa, *m.*

Mongrel, *a.* saṅkarajāta ; saṅkiṇṇuppattika.

Monism, *n.* advayavāda ; ekattavāda, *m.*

Monition, *n.* pageva nivedana ; paṭhamānusāsana, *nt.*

Monitor, *n.* 1. upadesaka ; 2. jeṭṭhantevāsika, *m.* °**y,** *a.* nivedaka ; upadesadāyaka. *n.* saṅghapituno ovāda, *m.*

Monk, *n.* muni ; samaṇa ; pabbajita ; tapodhana, *m.* °**dom,** *n.* samaṇadhamma, *m.* °**hood,** *n.* samaṇabhāva, *m.* °**ish,** *a.* sāmaṇaka; samaṇāyatta. **Buddhist —,** bhikkhu, *m.*

Monkey, *n.* vānara ; kapi ; makkaṭa ; sākhāmiga, *m.* **Female —,** vānarī ; makkaṭī, *f.*

Monoceros, *n.* khaggavisāṇa; gaṇḍaka, *m.* °**rous,** *a.* ekasiṅgika.

Monochrome, *n. a.* ekavaṇṇikacitta, *nt.* °**atic,** *a.* ekavaṇṇayutta.

Monocle, *n.* ekacakkhupanetta, *nt.*

Monochronic, *a.* ekakālika.

Monocular, *a.* ekanettānucchavika ; ekakkhika.

Monogamy, *n.* ekadārapariggaha, *m.*

Monogram, *n.* ekakkharasaññā, *f.*

Monograph, *n.* ekavisayakanibandha, *m.*

Monolith, *n.* ekapāsāṇamayathambha, *m.* °**ic,** *a.* ekapāsāṇakata.

Monologue, *n.* ekākībhāsana, *nt.* °**gize,** *v.i.* attanā va attānaŋ katheti.

Monomial, *n. a.* ekavacanābhāsana, *nt.*

Mononym, *n.* ekakkharasadda, *m.*

Monoplane, *n.* ekatalagaganayāna, *nt.*

Monopoly, *n.* (vāṇijje) kevalādhikāra, *m.* °**ist,** *n.* kevalādhikārī, *m.* °**ize,** *v.t.* anaññasādhāraṇaŋ karoti.

Monosyllabic, *a.* ekakkharayutta. °**ble,** *n.* ekakkharasadda, *m.*

Monotheism, *n.* ekissaravāda; devanimmāṇavāda, *m.* °**ist,** *n.* ekissaravādī, *m.*

Monotone, Monotony, *n.* ekasadisatta, *nt.* visesābhāva, *m.* °**ic,** *a.* ekasarayutta ; avisiṭṭhākāra.

Monotonous, *a.* abhinnasara ; nibbisesa. °**ly,** *adv.* nibbisesatāya ; samarūpena.

Monsoon, *n.* vassānakāla ; meghasamaya, *m.*

Monster, *n.* rakkhasa ; bhīmadeha ; mahādeha, *m.*

Monstrous, *a.* ghorarūpa ; vikaṭākāra. °**ly,** *adv.* ghorākārena. °**trosity,** *n.* dāruṇatta ; bhayajanakatta, *nt.*

Montane, *a.* pabbateyya.

Month, *n.* māsa, *m.* °**ly,** *a.* māsika. *adv.* paṭimāsaŋ. **Half a —,** addhamāsa ; pakkha, *m.*

Monticule, *n.* khuddaka-pabbata ; vammika, *m.*

Monument, *n.* anussarāpakavatthu, *nt.* susānathūpa, *m.* cetiya, *nt.* °**al,** *a.* 1. anussarāpaka ; 2. (of literary works :) atisambhāvanīya; atyukkaṭṭha. °**alize,** *v.t.* anussaraṇaŋ pavatteti *or* patiṭṭhāpeti. *p.p.* °titānussaraṇa.

Mood, *n.* 1. cittapakati, *f.* manobhāva, *m.* 2. (in gram :) kriyāvibhatti, *f.* °**y,** *a.* udāsīna ; dīnacitta ; dummana. °**iness,** *n.* dummanatta, *nt.*

Moon, *n.* canda ; indu ; sasī ; nisākara ; nisānātha ; sasaṅka ; tārāpati; uḷurāja, *m. v.i.* ālasiyena kālaŋ khepeti. **— beam,** °**light,** *n.* komudī ; candikā, *f.* **— calf,** *n.* eḷamūga ; jaḷa, *m.* °**lit,** *a.* candikāyutta. **— shine,** micchāsaṅkappa, *m.* **— stone,** *n.* 1. pāṭikā, *f.* 2. candakantapāsāṇa, *m.* **Digit of the —,** kalā, *f.* **Full —,** puṇṇacanda, *m.* **New —,** navacanda, *m.* **Orb of the —,** candamaṇḍala, *nt.*

Moony, *a.* 1. candasadisa ; 2. atidandha ; kriyāhīna.

Moor, *n.* tiṇabhūmi ; asārabhūmi, *f. v.t.* rajjuyā (nāvaŋ) bandhati. **— land,** *n.* gumbacchanna-desa, *m.*

Moot, *n.* 1. vādavivāda, *m.* 2. nītisissasabhā, *f. v.t.* uggaṇhanatthaŋ vivadati. *p.p.* °dita.

Mop, *n.* gehasammajjanī, *f. v.t.* gehaŋ (*or* bhaṇḍāni) sammajjati *or* parisodheti. *p.p.* sammaṭṭha ; °dhita.

Mope, *n.* ubbega, *m. v.i.* ubbijjati; khijjati. *p.p.* ubbigga ; khinna. °**ish,** *a.* ubbegayutta. °**ishly,** *adv.* khinnacittena.

Moppet, *n.* pilotika-dhītalikā, *f.*

Moral, *n.* sādhuguṇa ; sadācāra ; dhammopadesa, *m.* adj. dhammika ; ñāyānugata. °**ist,** *n.*

dhammopadesaka; ñāyaññū, *m.* °**ity**, *n.* 1. sīla; sucarita, *nt.* 2. nītisattha, *nt.* °**ize**, *v.t.* ācāraŋ sikkhāpeti; dhammaṭṭhaŋ karoti. °**ly**, *adv.* dhammānurūpaŋ. — **perfection**, moneyya, *nt.* — **practice**, sīla, *nt.* — **transgression**, sīlavipatti, *f.*

Morals, *n. pl.* ācāra, *m.*

Morass, *n.* kacchabhūmi, *f.*

Morbid, *a.* vyādhita; akallaka; dubbala. °**ly**, *adv.* dubbalākārena. °**ness**, *n.* dubbalya, *nt.*

Morbific, *a.* rogāvaha; asappāya.

Mordacity, Mordancy, *n.* mammacchedaka-vacana, *nt.* upārambha, *m.* °**cious**, *a.* garahāpubbaka; sopārambha.

Mordant, *a.* 1. mammacchedaka; 2. malasodhaka. °**ly**, *adv.* kaṭukaŋ; pharusākārena.

More, *a.* adhika; atiritta; bahutara, *adv.* bhīyo; adhikataraŋ. *noun:* atireka; atisaya, *m.* The adj. is often expressed by the suffix *tara*, e.g. *abhirūpatara*, more beautiful. — **and more**, uttaruttariŋ; bhīyoso mattāya. — **over**, uttarim pi; api ca; puna c'aparaŋ. — **than a thousand**, parosahassa, *nt.* **No** —, na ito uddhaŋ. **What** —, kim aññaŋ?

Morgue, *n.* 1. chavasālā, *f.* 2. pāgabbhiya, *nt.*

Moribund, *a.* āsannamaraṇa; matapāya.

Moringa, *n.* siggu, *nt.* sobhañjana, *m.*

Morn, Morning, *n.* pabhāta; paccūsa; pubbaṇha, *m.* — **meal**, pātarāsa, *m.* — **star**, osadhītārakā, *f.* **Good** —, suppabhātaŋ! **In the** —, pāto, *ind.*

Morose, *a.* 1. kakkasa; khara; lūkha; 2. dussīla. °**ly**, *adv.* pharusākārena. °**ness**, *n.* pharusatta, *nt.*

Morphia, *n.* ahipheṇasāra, *m.*

Morphology, *n.* pāṇivisesa-rukkhavisesa-niruttivisesañāṇa, *nt.* °**ist**, *n.* rukkhādivisesaññū, *m.*

Morrow, *n.* punadivasa, *m.* **On the** —, suve, *ind.*

Morse, *n.* saloma-macchavisesa, *m.*

Morsel, *n.* ālopa; kabaḷa, *m.*

Mortal, *n.* macca; manussa, *m.* *a.* 1. maraṇadhamma; nassanasīla; 2. mānusika; 3. pāṇahara; 4. atidāruṇa. °**ity**, *n.* 1. aniccatā; bhaṅguratā, *f.* 2. manussatta, *nt.* 3. maccu, *m.* maraṇa, *nt.* °**ly**, *adv.* pāṇaharākārena.

Mortar, *n.* 1. udukkhala, *m.* 2. sudhālepa, *m.*

Mortgage, *n.* nyāsa; upanidhi, *m.* *v.t.* upanidahati; nyāsaŋ karoti. *p.p.* upanihita; katanyāsa. °**gee**, *n.* nyāsagāhī, *m.* °**ger**, *n.* nyāsadāyī, *m.*

Mortify, *v.t.* 1. ātāpeti; niggaṇhāti; 2. pūtibhāvaŋ neti. *v.t.* 1. pūtibhavati; 2. kāyappasādo nassati. *p.p.* °pita; niggahita; °nīta; pūtibhūta; naṭṭhakāyappasāda. °**ication**, *n.* 1. paritāpana; 2. damana; niggaṇhana; 3. tapacaraṇa, *nt.* 4. aŋsabhaṅga, *m.* °**ing**, *a.* 1. mānabhañjaka; dappahara; 2. santāpaka.

Mortuary, *n.* chavakuṭikā, *f.* adj. petakiccāyatta.

Mosaic, *a.* nānāvaṇṇa-silādi-khacita. — **work,** vividhavaṇṇakhacana, *nt.*

Mosque, *n.* Mahammada-devāyatana.

Mosquito, *n.* makasa; sūcimukha, *m.* °**net,** *n.* makasāvaraṇa; makasajāla, *nt.*

Moss, *n.* nīlikā, *f.* sevāla, *m.* °**y,** *a.* nīlikāyutta; sevālacchanna.

Most, *a.* 1. adhikatama; 2. atiseṭṭha; parama. *n.* bahutamabhāga, *m. adv.* atīva; accantaŋ. °**ly,** *adv.* pāyena; yebhuyyena. — **early,** *adv.* atippage'va; puretaram eva. — **excellent,** *a.* atyuttama; atiseṭṭha. — **high,** *a.* accunnata.

Mot, *n.* caturavacana, *nt.*

Mote, *n.* ratharenu; kaṇa; lava, *m.*

Moth, *n.* 1. vatthakhādaka; 2. paṭaṅga, *m.*

Mother, *n.* ammā; ambā; mātu; janettī; janikā, *f.* °**hood,** *n.* mātubhāva, *m.* — **in-law,** sassu, *f.* °**less,** *a.* nimmātika. —'**s father,** mātāmaha, *m.* —'**s milk,** thañña, *nt.* —'**s mother,** mātāmahī, *f.* —'**s sister,** mātucchā, *f.* —'**s womb,** mātukucchi, *f.*

Mother, *v.t.* 1. mātubhāvaŋ paṭijānāti; 2. mātiṭṭhāne tiṭṭhati; 3. dārake janeti. *p.p.* paṭiññātamātubhāva; °ṭhita; janitadāraka. °**ly,** *a.* mātusadisa. — **land,** *n.* jātabhūmi, *f.* sadesa, *m.* — **language,** *n.* nijabhāsā, *f.* — **tongue,** *n.* sadesabhāsā, *f.*

Motif, *n.* padhānajjhāsaya; nirūpitādhippāya, *m.*

Motile, *a.* jaṅgama. °**ity,** *n.* jaṅgamatta, *nt.*

Motion, *n.* 1. calana; phandana; iñjana, *nt.* 2. vireka, *m.* 3. (sabhāgata-) yojanā, *f. v.t.* viññāpeti; saññaŋ deti. *p.p.* °pita; dinnasañña. °**less,** *a.* niccala; thāvara.

Motive, *n.* nimitta; nidāna; kāraṇa, *nt.* hetu, *m.* adj. 1. cālaka; pavaṭṭaka; 2. hetubhūta. *v.t.* hetuŋ sampādeti. °**ity,** *n.* cālakasatti, *f.* °**less,** *a.* ahetuka; animitta.

Motley, *a.* 1. nānāvaṇṇa; 2. vividha, *n.* 1. anucitasammissaṇa, *nt.* 2. vidūsakamaṇḍana, *nt.*

Motor, *n.* 1. cālaka; pavaṭṭaka, *m.* 2. cālakayanta, *nt.* — **car,** sayaŋvaṭṭaka (-ratha), *m.*

Mottle, *v.t.* sabalavaṇṇaŋ karoti. *p.p.* katasabala°.

Motto, *n.* upadesavākya, *nt.* ādisiyapāṭha, *m.*

Mould, *n.* 1. sithila-paŋsu, *m.* 2. ākati, *f.* saṇṭhāna, *nt. v.t.* saṇṭhānaŋ *or* ākatiŋ nipphādeti. *v.i.* kaṇṇakito bhavati. *p.p.* nipphādita-saṇṭhāna; kaṇṇakita. °**y,** *a.* malaggahita; kaṇṇakita.

Moulder, *n.* ākatisādhaka, *m. v.i.* jīrati; cuṇṇattam āpajjati. *p.p.* jiṇṇa; °āpanna.

Moult, *n.* pakkhapātana, *nt. v.t.* pakkhe pāteti. *v.i.* pakkhāni galanti. *p.p.* pātitapakkha; galitapakkha.

Mound, *n.* 1. lohagoḷa; cūḷāmaṇi, *m.* 2. paŋsukūla, *nt.* silārāsi, *m.* unnataṭṭhāna, *nt.*

Mount, *n.* 1. pabbata, *m.* 2. vāhakapasu, *m.* 3. cittakammādhāra; chāyārūpadhāraka, *m. v.i.* 1. āruhati; 2. unnatiŋ yāti. *v.t.* āroheti; āropeti; patiṭṭhāpeti. *p.p.* ārūḷha; °yāta; °hita; °pita. °**ing,** *n.* ārohaṇa; āropaṇa, *nt.*

Mountain, *n.* pabbata; giri; naga; addi; mahīdhara, *m.* °**eer,** *n.* pabbatavāsī; pabbateyya, 3. °**ous,** *a.* giribahula. — **ridge,** nitamba. — **range,** pabbatāvali, *f.*

Mountebank, *n.* 1. paṇḍitamānī; 2. vañcaka; kūṭatikicchaka, *m.* °**ery,** *n.* 1. vañcanā; 2. kūṭatikicchā, *f.*

Mourn, *v.i.* anusocati; paridevati. *p.p.* °cita; °vita. °**er,** *n.* anusocaka, *m.* °**ful,** *a.* sasoka; sokaṭṭa; sokapareta. °**fully,** *adv.* sasokaŋ. °**ing,** *n.* socana, *nt.* paridēva, *m.*

Mouse, *n.* mūsikā, *f.* ākhu; undura, *m. v.i.* undure gaṇhāti.

Moustache, *n.* dāṭhikā, *f.*

Mouth, *n.* mukha; vadana; pavesadvāra, *nt.* °**ful,** *n.* mukhapūraṇamatta, *nt.* gaṇḍūsa, *m.* °**less,** *a.* pavesadvāravirahita.

Mouth, *v.i.* 1. vikatthati; 2. mukhena phusati *or* khādati. *p.p.* °thita; °phuṭṭha; °dita. °**y,** *a.* vikatthaka.

Move, *n.* 1. saṅkama; 2. upāya; upayoga; 3. apagama, *m. v.t.* 1. cāleti; īreti; pavatteti; 2. dayam uppādeti. *v.i.* calati; iñjati; samīrati. *p.p.* cālita; īrita; °tita; °dita; calita; iñjita; °rita. °**able,** *a.* saŋhārima; cālanīya. *pl.* saŋhāriya-bhaṇḍa, *nt.* — **about,** sañcarati; paribbhamati. — **aside,** apasakkati. — **back,** paṭisakkati; vivaṭṭati. °**er,** *n.* cālaka; payojaka, *m.* °**ing,** *a.* calamāna; jaṅgama; sadaya. °**ing in,** avacara, *a.* °**ment,** *n.* sañcaraṇa; gamana; kampana, *nt.* — **off,** apakkamati. — **on,** abhiyāti; pavattati.

Movingly, *adv.* sānuddayaŋ.

Mow, *v.t.* 1. lāyati; dāyati. *v.i.* mukhavikāraŋ dasseti. *p.p.* lāyita; dāyita; dassitamukhavikāra. *noun.* 1. palālapuñja; palālanicaya, *m.* 2. lāyitadhañña, *nt.* °**er,** *n.* lāyaka, *m.* °**ing,** *n.* lāyana; niddāna, *nt.*

Much, *n.* bahuka, 3. adj. pahūta; anappaka; bhusa; bahula; pacura. *adv.* ativiya; bahuso; bhīyo; yebhuyyena. — **better,** *a.* sādhutara; sundaratara. — **esteemed,** *a.* bahumānita. °**ness,** bahulatta; adhikatta, *nt.* **As — as,** yattaka — tattaka. **How —,** kittaka, *a.* **That —,** tattaka, *a.* **This —,** ettaka, *a.*

Muck, *n.* gomayādi, *m. v.t.* 1. aparisuddhaŋ karoti; 2. laṇḍaŋ pāteti; 3. animittam āhiṇḍati. *p.p.* °kata; °pātita; °ḍita. °**rake,** *n.* kacavarasaṅkaḍḍhanī, *f.* °**worm,** *n.* gūthapāṇaka, *m.*

Mucous, *a.* picchila; lasikāvuta; jallikāsahita; samala.

Mucus, *n.* 1. dehamala, *nt.* lasikā, *f.* 2. rukkhaniyyāsa, *m.* — **of the ear,** kaṇṇamala, *nt.* — **of the nose,** siṅghāṇikā, *f.*

Mud, *n.* paṅka; kalala; kaddama, *m.* °**guard,** *n.* paṅkavāraka, *m.* °**dy,** *a.* sakaddama; kalalayutta. °**diness,** *n.* sapaṅkatta, *nt.* °**slinger,** *n.* usūyaka; dūsaka, *m.*

Muddle, *n.* vikkhepa, *m.* ākulatta; vyākulatta, *nt.* *v.t.* vyākulīkaroti. *v.i.* vikkhitto hoti. *p.p.* °kata; vikkhitta. °**headed,** *a.* vibbhantacitta; mandabuddhika.

Muddy, *a.* vikkhittacitta. *v.t.* vikkhepaŋ janeti. *p.p.* janitavikkhepa.

Muff, *n.* dandhapuggala; akovida, *m.* *v.t.* virādheti. *p.p.* °dhita.

Muffle, *n.* 1. pasu-uttaroṭṭha, *m.* *v.t.* (sīsam) oguṇṭheti *or* āveṭheti. *p.p.* °ṭhita. °**er,** *n.* oguṇṭhakapaṭa, *m.*

Mug, *n.* 1. pānabhājana, *nt.* kuṇḍikā, *f.* 2. jaḷamati, *m.* *v.i.* āyāsena uggaṇhāti. *p.p.* °uggahita.

Mugger, *n.* makara, *m.*

Muggy, *a.* ghammayutta; kilinna.

Mugwump, *n.* (apakkhāyatta-) pabhū, *m.*

Mulberry, *n.* ambilikā, *f.* brahmadāru, *m.*

Mulct, *n.* rājadaṇḍa, *m.* *v.t.* daṇḍaŋ paṇeti; daṇḍeti. *p.p.* daṇḍita.

Mule, *n.* assatara, *m.* °**ish,** *a.* avinīta.

Mull, *n.* 1. sukhumakappāsika, *nt.* 2. vomissita-vatthujāta, *nt.* *v.t.* vomisseti. *p.p.* °sita.

Mullah, *n.* Mahammada-dhammācariya, *m.*

Muller, *n.* nisadapota, *m.*

Mulligrubs, *n.* *pl.* 1. udarasūla, *nt.* 2. dummukhatta, *nt.*

Mullion, *n.* kavāṭasūci, *f.*

Multangular, *a.* bahukoṇaka.

Multeity, *n.* bahuvidhatta, *nt.*

Multifarious, *a.* vividha; bahuvidha; nānārūpa; nānākāra; vividhākāra. °**ly,** *adv.* nānākārena; anekadhā.

Multiform, *a.* anekavidha; nānappakāra. °**ity,** *n.* bahuvidhatta, *nt.*

Multimillionaire, *n.* anekakoṭipati; mahāsāḷa, *m.*

Multipara, *n.* bahuppajā, *f.*

Multiparous, *a.* bahupotaka.

Multipartite, *a.* bahuvibhāga.

Multiped, *a.* bahuppada.

Multiple, *n.* guṇitaka, *nt.* adj. bahuvidha.

Multiply, *v.t.* 1. guṇīkaroti; 2. vaḍḍheti; bahulīkaroti. *p.p.* °kata; °ḍhita; °kata. °**icand,** *n.* guṇetabba, *nt.* °**ication,** *n.* guṇīkaraṇa; bahulīkaraṇa, *nt.* °**cable,** *a.* guṇīkaraṇāraha; vaḍḍhanīya. °**icity,** *n.* bāhulla; anekatta, *nt.* °**ier,** guṇakara; vaḍḍhaka, *m.*

Multitude, *n.* samūha; samudāya; saṅgha; gaṇa, *m.* saŋhati, *f.* (— of animals) yūtha, *m.* °**inous,** *a.* bahusaṅkhyaka; aneka.

Mum, *intj.* tuṇhī! adj. nissadda. *v.i.* nissaddam ācarati.

Mumble, *v.i.* apphuṭaŋ vadati; jappati. *p.p.* °vutta; °pita. °**ing,** *n.* pajappana, *nt.*

Mummer, *n.* mūgābhinayadassaka; potthalikāpayojaka, *m.*

Mummy, *n.* surakkhita-matadeha, *m.* *nt.* °**ification,** *n.* matadeha-saŋrakkhana, *nt.* °**ify,** *v.t.* chavaŋ saŋrakkhati. *p.p.* °khitachava.

Mump, *v.i.* 1. nitthunāti; maṅkubhavati; 2. bhikkhāya carati. *p.p.* °nita; °bhūta.
Mumps, *n.* uḷūkamukharoga; kaṇṇamūlasopha, *m.*
Munch, *v.t.* romanthati. *p.p.* °thita.
Mundane, *a.* ihalokika; diṭṭhadhammika; saŋsārika. °**ness**, *n.* lokikatta, *nt.*
Mungoose, *n.* muṅgusa; nakula, *m.*
Municipal, *a.* nāgarikapālanāyatta, *nt.* °**ity**, *n.* nagarasabhā, *f.* nāgarikapālana, *nt.*
Munificent, *a.* dānasoṇḍa; bahuppada. °**cence**, *n.* uḷāracittatā; muttahatthatā, *f.* °**ly**, *adv.* dānasoṇḍatāya.
Muniment, *n.* pariggahapaṇṇa, *nt.*
Munition, *n.* yuddhopakaraṇa, *nt.*
Mural, *a.* bhittivisayaka. — **painting**, bhitticittakamma, *nt.*
Murder, *n.* manussaghātana, *nt.* *v.t.* māreti; vadheti; hanati. *p.p.* mārita; vadhita; hata. °**er**, *n.* munussaghātī, *m.* °**ous**, *a.* hantukāma; atighora. °**ously**, *adv.* hantukāmatāya.
Mure, *v.t.* agāre rundheti. *p.p.* °dhita.
Murk, *a.* andhakāra; anobhāsa. °**y**, *a.* tamonaddha.
Murmur, *n.* anutthunana, *nt.* mandasadda, *m.* *v.i.* 1. anutthunāti; 2. mandaŋ saddāyati. *p.p.* anutthuta; °yita. °**ous**, *a.* anutthunaka. °**ously**, *adv.* anutthunanākārena.
Murrain, *n.* gosaṅkantikaroga, *m.*
Murrey, *a.* lohitaratta.
Muscle, *n.* maŋsapesī, *f.*
Muscular, *a.* 1. maŋsapesivisayaka; 2. daḷhasarīra. °**ity**, *n.* kāyabalayuttatā, *f.* °**lature**, *n.* maŋsapesi-patiṭṭhitākāra, *m.*
Muse, *n.* kalādevatā, *f.* *v.i.* jhāyati; āvajjeti; manasikaroti. *p.p.* °yita; °jita; °kata. °**ful**, *a.* cintāpara; jhānarata. °**ingly**, *adv.* jhāyanākārena.
Museum, *n.* dullabhavatthusamūha, *m.* kutūhalasālā, *f.*
Mush, *n.* 1. ghanayāgu, *f.* 2. chatta, *nt.*
Mushroom, *n.* ahicchattaka, *nt.* adj. aciraṭṭhāyī.
Music, *n.* gītavādita; tāḷāvacara, *nt.* °**al**, *a.* saṅgītāyatta. °**al instrument**, *n.* turiyabhaṇḍa, *nt.* °**ian**, *n.* turiyavādaka; gandhabba, *m.* **Vocal** —, saṅgīta, *nt.*
Musk, *n.* katthūrikā, *f.* migamada, *m.* °**deer**, gandhamiga, *m.* °**rose**, kareri, *m.*
Musket, *n.* aggināḷikā; guḷikākhipanī, *f.* °**eer**, *n.* aggināḷidhārī, *m.*
Muslin, *n.* sukhuma-kappāsika, *nt.*
Mussal, *n.* daṇḍadīpikā, *f.*
Mussel, *n.* jalasuttī; sambuka, *m.*
Must, *n.* 1. nava-muddikāsava, *m.* 2. kaṇṇakitatta, *nt.* °**y**, *a.* kaṇṇakita. °**iness**, *n.* pūtigandhatā, *f.*
Must, *v.* aux. Expressed by the *pt. p.*, e.g. **Must be**, bhavitabbaŋ.
Mustard, *n.* sāsapa; siddhattha, *m.*

Muster, *n.* sannipātana, *nt.* sannipāta, *m.* *v.t.* sannipāteti. *v.i.* sannipatati; saṅgacchati. *p.p.* °tita; saṅgata.

Mutate, *v.t.* vipariṇāmeti. *p.p.* °mita. °**table,** *a.* vipariṇāmadhamma. °**ion,** *n.* vipariṇāmana; aññathākaraṇa, *nt.*

Mutatis mutandis, *adv.* aññathākaraṇasahitaŋ.

Mute, *n.* 1. mūga, *m.* 2. pakkhimala, *nt.* 3. aghosakkhara, *nt.* adj. mūga; sarahīna. °**ly,** *adv.* nissaddaŋ. °**ness,** *n.* mūgatta; nissaddatta, *nt.*

Mutilate, *v.t.* aṅgacchedaŋ karoti; vikalayati. *p.p.* kataṅgaccheda; °yita. °**ion,** *n.* aṅgacchedana; vikalīkaraṇa, *nt.*

Mutiny, *n.* dāmarikavyāpāra, *m.* *v.i.* rañño dubbhati. °**eer,** *n.* rājadubbhī; rajjadohī, *m.* °**ous,** *a.* dubbhanasīla; avasavattī.

Mutter, *v.i.* jappati; palapati. *p.p.* °pita. °**ing,** *n.* upajappana, *nt.*

Mutton, *n.* eḷakamaŋsa, *nt.*

Mutual, *a.* itaretara; aññamañña; mithu. °**ity,** *n.* itaretaratta, *nt.* aññamaññasambandha, *m.* °**ly,** *adv.* aññamaññaŋ. °**ism,** *n.* sambandhatāvāda, *m.* °**ist,** *n.* sambandhatāvādī, *m.*

Muzz, *v.t.* mattaŋ *or* pamattaŋ karoti. *p.p.* mattakata. °**y,** *a.* 1. matta; 2. tejohīna; udāsīna.

Muzzle, *n.* 1. pasumukhanāsikā, *f.* 2. aggināḷīmukha, *nt.* *v.t.* mukhabandhaŋ yojeti. *p.p.* yojita°.

My, *pron. poss. sing.* mama; mayhaŋ; me. — **dear,** ambho, *ind.*

Mycology, *n.* ahicchattakavijjā, *f.*

Myelitis, *n.* piṭṭhikaṇṭakadāha, *m.*

Myology, *n.* pesīvijjā, *f.*

Myope, *n.* rassadiṭṭhika, *m.*

Myopia, *n.* rassadiṭṭhitā, *f.*

Myosis, *n.* tārāsaṅkucana, *nt.*

Myriad, *n.* nahuta; dasasahassa, *nt.* adj. asaṅkhya; gaṇanātīta.

Myriapod, *a. n.* bahuppadika.

Myrobalan, *n.* tiphala, *nt.* — **belarica,** vibhītakī, *f.* — **emblica,** āmalakī, *f.* **Yellow —,** harītakī, abhayā, *f.*

Myrrh, *n.* sugandha-niyyāsa, *m.*

Mysterious, *a.* 1. gūḷha; paṭicchanna; 2. dubbodha. °**ly,** *adv.* gūḷhākārena. °**ness,** *n.* gūḷhatta, *nt.*

Mystery, *n.* rahassa, *nt.*

Mystic, *n.* yogī; guyhatantavidū, *m.* adj. gūḷha; apākaṭa; dubbodha. °**ally,** *adv.* gūḷhākārena. °**ism,** *n.* gūḷhadhamma, *m.*

Mystify, *v.t.* moheti; vyākulayati. *p.p.* mohita; vyākulita. °**ication,** *n.* sammohana, *nt.*

Myth, *n.* purāvuttakathā, *f.* itihītiha, *nt.* micchāpabandha, *m.* °**ic,** °**ical,** *a.* porāṇika; devakathāyutta. °**ology,** *n.* ākhyāna, *nt.* °**ological,** *a.* devakathāyatta; ākhyānavisayaka. °**ologist,** *n.* purāvuttavidū, *m.*

N

Nab, *v.t.* sahasā gaṇhāti *or* nirundhati. *p.p.* °gahita; °dhita.

Nabob, *n.* Mahammadika-maṇḍalissara, *m.*

Nacarat, *n.* pītarattavaṇṇa, *m.*

Nadir, *n.* adhobhuvana, *nt.*

Nag, *n.* khuddakassa, *m. v.t.* khuŋseti; vambheti. *p.p.* °sita; °bhita. °**ger,** *n.* vambhaka; niggahetu, *m.* °**gish,** *a.* niggaṇhanasīla.

Naiad, *n.* udakadevatā, *f.*

Nail, *n.* 1. (of hand:) nakha, *m.* 2. (of metal:) āṇi, *f.* kīlaka, *m. v.t.* āṇiŋ paveseti; āṇiyā sambandhati. *p.p.* pavesitāṇī; āṇisambaddha.

Naive, *a.* akapaṭa; avyāja; pākatika. °**ly,** *adv.* avyājaŋ. °**ty,** *n.* avyājatta, *nt.*

Naked, *a.* 1. nagga; 2. apaṭicchanna; 3. abhūsita; 4. kevala. °**ly,** *adv.* naggākārena. °**ness,** *n.* naggatta; apaṭicchannatta, *nt.* — **ascetic,** digambara; nigaṇṭha, *m.* — **eye,** pakaticakkhu, *nt.*

Namby-pamby, *a.* 1. ativibhūsita; 2. mandussāha.

Name, *n.* 1. nāma; nāmadheyya; abhidhāna, *nt.* samaññā; ākhyā, *f.* 2. pasiddhi; kitti; patīti, *f. v.t.* 1. nāmaŋ ṭhapeti *or* karoti; 2. apadisati. *p.p.* katanāma; apadiṭṭha. °**ed,** *a.* 1. abhihita; saññita; ākhyāta; 2. nāmaka. °**ing,** *n* nāmakaraṇa; nāmagahaṇa, *nt.* °**less,** *a.* ninnāmaka; apākaṭa. °**ly,** *adv.* yad idaŋ; taŋ yathā; seyyathīdaŋ. °**sake,** *n.* samānanāmaka, 3.

Nanny, *n.* 1. ajī, *f.* 2. dhātī, *f.*

Nap, *n.* 1. mandaniddā, *f.* 2. siniddhaloma, *nt. v.i.* pacalāyati; thokaŋ supati.

Nape, *n.* galavāṭaka, *m.* gīvāpiṭṭhi, *f.*

Napkin, *n.* hatthapuñchana; mukhapuñchana, *nt.*

Nappy, *a.* lomasa.

Narcosis, *n.* madamattatā, *f.*

Narcotic, *n.* niddājanakosadha, *nt.* adj. mohanaka; niddājanaka. °**tism,** *n.* osadhajātaniddā, *f.* °**tize,** *v.t.* osadhena moheti.

Nard, *n.* sugandha-niyyāsavisesa, *m.*

Narrate, *v.t.* vitthāreti; vaṇṇeti; vyākhyāti. °**ion,** *n.* vaṇṇanā, *f.* kittana, *nt.* °**ive,** *n.* kathāmagga, *m.* upākhyāna, *nt.* °**tor,** *n.* kittaka; anussāvaka, *m.*

Narrow, *a.* aputhula; sambādha; anāyata, *v.t.* saṅkhipati; ākuñcati. *p.p.* saṅkhitta; °cita. °**ly,** *adv.* avitthatākārena; appamattakena. — **minded,** *a.* dīnapakatika; aputhulajjhāsaya. °**ness,** *n.* aputhulatta, *nt.*

Nasal, *n.* anunāsikakkhara, *nt.* adj. anunāsika; ghāṇāyatta.

Nascent, *a.* sambhavesī. °**cency,** *n.* sambhavesitā, *f.*

Nasty, *a.* atimalina; accantāsuddha. °**ily,** *adv.* kucchitākārena. °**iness,** malinatta; asuddhatta, *nt.*

Natal, *a.* sahaja; jammāgata.

Nates, *n. pl.* nisadamaŋsa, *nt.*

Nation, *n.* manussajāti; ekasadisa-janatā, *f.*

National, *a.* jātika; desīya. — **custom,** jātikācāra; desācāra, *m.* °**ism,** *n.* desabhatti, *f.* desānurāga, *m.* °**ize,** *v.t.* desāyattaŋ *or* desānugaŋ karoti. °**ity**, *n*. jātivisesa, *m*. desīyatā, *f*. °**ly**, *adv*. jātivasena ; desīyatāya.

Native, *n*. desavāsī ; desubbhūta, 3. adj. 1. desaja ; desīya ; 2. sahaja ; nesaggika. °**ity**, *n*. 1. uppatti, *f*. sambhava, *m*. 2. jammapatta, *nt*. — **country**, uppattidesa, *m*. sakaraṭṭha, *nt*. — **place**, *n*. jātabhūmi, *f*.

Natty, *a*. 1. suvilāsī ; 2. badhirapakatika.

Natural, *a*. nesaggika ; pākatika ; akittima ; sabhāvasiddha. — **condition**, pakati, *f*. °**ist**, *n*. sabhāvadhammavedī, *m*. °**ize**, *v.t*. 1. paricayati ; 2. desīyaŋ karoti. °**ism**, *n*. sabhāvanirūpaṇa, *nt*. — **lake**, jātassara, *m*. *nt*. °**ly**, *adv*. pakatiyā; sabhāvena. °**ness**, *n*. nesaggikatta, *nt*.

Nature, *n*. 1. pakati, *f*. sabhāva, *m*. dhammatā, *f*. 2. lokanimmāṇa, *nt*. °**ed**, *a*. pakatika (in cpds.), e.g. **Good-natured**, sādhupakatika.

Naught, *n*. 1. na kiñci ; suññatā, *f*. 2. bindu, *m*. adj. suñña ; tuccha.

Naughty, *a*. kadācāra ; avinīta.

Nausea, *n*. uggāra, *m*. vamana, *nt*. aruci, *f*. °**eous**, *a*. uggārajanaka ; jigucchāvaha.

Nauseate, *v.t*. aruciŋ uppādeti. *v.i*. jigucchati. *p.p*. uppāditāruci ; °chita.

Nautch, *n*. aṅganānacca, *nt*. °**girl**, nāṭakitthi, *f*.

Nautical, *a*. nāvāyatta ; nāvikavisayaka.

Naval, *a* nāvāvisayaka ; nāvikasenāyatta.

Nave, *n*. 1. nābhi ; piṇḍikā, *f*. 2. devāyatana-majjhabhāga, *m*.

Navel, *n*. 1. sarīranābhi, *f*. 2. majjhaṭṭhāna, *nt*.

Navicular, *a*. nāvākāra.

Navigable, *a*. nāvāgamanīya.

Navigate, *v.t*. 1. nāvāya sañcarati ; 2. nāvaŋ pājeti. *p.p*. °**rita** ; pājitanāva. °**ion**, *n*. 1. nāvāsañcāra, *m*. yātrā, *f*. 2. nāvikavijjā, *f*. °**or**, *n*. nāvika ; samuddagāmī, *m*.

Navy, *n*. 1. nāvāsamūha, *m*. 2. nāvikasenā, *f*.

Nay, *adv*. natthi ; na hi ; no h'idaŋ. *n*. paṭikkhepa, *m*.

Naze, *n*. samuddantaritabhūmi, *f*.

Neap, *n*. sāgaruppāta, *m*. *v.t*. ottharati. *p.p*. otthaṭa. °**tide**, manda-uppāta, *m*.

Neapolitan, *n*. Naples-nagaravāsī, *m*.

Near, *adv*. avidūre ; āsanne. adj. āsanna ; antika ; avidūra ; samīpa ; nikaṭa. *v.t*. upagacchati. *p.p*. upagata. °**er**, *a*. āsannatara. °**est**, *a*. samīpatama ; accāsanna. °**ly**, *adv*. pāyo ; kincid ūnakaŋ. °**ness**, *n*. samīpatta ; āsannatta, *nt*. — **shore**, ora ; orimatīra, *nt*. °**sighted**, *a*. adūradassī.

Neat, *a*. sobhana ; parisuddha ; cāru. — **handed**, *a*. payatapāṇī. °**ly**, *adv*. sobhanākārena ; suṭṭhu. °**ness**, *n*. soceyya ; sobhanatta, *nt*.

Neb, *n*. mukhatuṇḍa, *nt*. cañcu, *m*.

Nebula, *n*. 1. vivaṭṭamānaloka ; tārārāsi, *m*. 2. (of the eye :) setapaṭala, *nt*. °**ous**, *a*. 1. tārāmeghākāra ; 2. apākaṭa ; meghasadisa.

Nebular, *a.* tārāmeghāyatta.

Necessary, *a.* avassakaraṇīya; anivāriya; āvassaka. *n.* parikkhāra; āvassaka-upakaraṇa, *nt.* °**ily,** *adv.* avassam eva; niyataŋ; nūnaŋ.

Necessitate, *v.t.* pasayha niyojeti; āvassakattaŋ pāpeti. *p.p.* °jita; °pita. °**tous,** *a.* niddhana; duggata.

Necessity, *n.* 1. āvassakatta; 2. akiñcanatta; daḷiddatta, *nt.*

Neck, *n.* gīvā, *f.* gala; kaṇṭha, *m.* °**erchief,** *n.* kaṇṭhoguṇṭhanaka, *nt.* °**lace,** *n.* gīveyyaka, *nt.* kaṇṭhabhūsā, *f.* hāra, *m.*

Necrolatry, *n.* petapūjā, *f.* pubbapeta-bali, *m.*

Necrology, *n.* matasaṅkhyālekhana, *nt.* °**ist,** *n.* matanāmalekhaka, *m.*

Necromancy, *n.* bhūtavijjā, *f.* °**cer,** *n.* bhūtavejja; yakkhadāsa, *m.*

Necropolis, *n.* susāna, *nt.*

Necrosis, *n.* kāyaviññāṇāpagama, *m.*

Nectar, *n.* pīyūsa; amata; sudhābhojana, *nt.* °**ean,** °**ous,** *a.* amatopama.

Need, *n.* 1. ākaṅkhā; apekkhā, *f.* attha, *m.* 2. vyasana, *nt.* vipatti, *f.* *v.t.* apekkhati; ākaṅkhati. *v. aux.* **He need not go,** no tena gantabbaŋ. **There needs nothing more,** tato'dhikaŋ na kiñci pi icchitabbaŋ. °**ful,** *a.* 1. ākaṅkhī; apekkhī; 2. āvassaka. °**less,** *a.* 1. niratthaka; 2. nirapekkha. °**lessly,** *adv.* niratthakaŋ. °**lessness,** *n.* niratthakatta, *nt.* °**y,** *a.* 1. atthika; 2. duggata; niddhana.

Needle, *n.* sūci, *f.* °**case,** *n.* sūcighara, *nt.* °**work,** *n.* tuṇṇakamma, *nt.* *v.t.* sibbati.

Needs, *adv.* avassaŋ.

Nefarious, *a.* atiduṭṭha; pāpiṭṭha. °**ly,** *adv.* sāparādhaŋ; duṭṭhākārena.

Negate, *v.t.* nisedheti; paccakkhāti; abhāvaŋ neti. *p.p.* °dhita; °khāta; °nīta. °**ion,** *n.* 1. paccakkhāna, *nt.* nisedha; 2. abhāva, *m.*

Negative, *n.* 1. nisedhatthavācaka, *m.* 2. viparāvattaka, *m.* adj. abhāvavācaka; nisedhapakatika. *v.t.* nisedheti; paṭisedheti. *p.p.* °dhita. °**ly,** *adv.* paṭipakkhena. °**ity,** *n.* abhāvavācakatta, *nt.* nisedhatthatā, *f.* °**tory,** *a.* nisedhaka.

Neglect, *n.* asallakkhaṇa; upekkhana, *nt.* *v.t.* parihāpeti; riñcati; upekkhati; pamajjati. *p.p.* °pita; °cita; °khita; pamatta. °**ful,** *a.* nirapekkha; pamatta; vimukha. °**fully,** *adv.* pamādena; nirapekkhaŋ; asamekkha. °**ing,** *a.* riñcamāna.

Negligent, *a.* pamādī; upekkhī. °**ly,** *adv.* pamādena; savilambaŋ. °**ence,** *n.* pamāda, *m.* asallakkhaṇa, *nt.*

Negligible, *a.* abbohārika; asallakkhetabba.

Negotiate, *v.i.* vinimeti; mithuanumatiŋ pakāseti. *p.p.* °mita; °sita. °**ion,** *n.* vinimaya, *m.* aññamaññānumati, *f.* °**or,** *n.* vinimetu; paṭiññākārī, *m.*

Negro, *n.* kaṇhacchavika. adj. kāḷavaṇṇa.

Neigh, *n.* hesārava, *m.* *v.i.* hesāravaŋ pavatteti.

Neighbour, *n.* paṭivissaka ; samīpavāsī, *m.* adj. samīpaṭṭha. *v.t.* samīpavattiŋ karoti. °**hood,** *n.* samīpaṭṭhāna ; nikaṭa, *nt.* upantika ; sakāsa, *m.* °**ing,** *a.* sāmanta ; āsanna. °**ly,** *a.* vissāsika ; upakāraka ; paṭivissakasadisa. °**liness,** *n.* paṭivissakatta ; vissāsikatta, *nt.*

Neither, *conj. a. adv. pron.* n'eva... na ; n'eko pi. **Neither you nor I know,** n'eva tvaŋ na c' āhaŋ jānāma. **If you do not go, neither will I,** sace tvaŋ na gaccheyyāsi aham pi na gaccheyyaŋ. **I know not, neither can I guess,** ahaŋ n'eva jānāmi, na anumānitum pi sakkomi. **Neither of them knows,** tesu eko pi na jānāti. **Neither of the accusations is true,** codanāsu ekā pi na avitathā.

Nemesis, *n.* vipākadāyinī devī, *f.*

Nenuphar, *n.* uppala, *nt.*

Neolithic, *n.* silāyudhasamaya, *m.*

Neology, *n.* nūtanasaddappayoga, *m.* °**ist,** *n.* nūtanasaddappayojaka, *m.* °**ize,** *v.t.* nūtanasadde payojeti.

Neophyte, *n.* adhunāpabbajita ; adhunā-samayāgata, *m.*

Neoteric, *a.* ādhunika ; adhunāgata ; vattamāna.

Neotropical, *a.* uṇhadesāyatta.

Nepenthes, *n.* sammohakosadha, *nt.*

Nephalism, *n.* majjavirati, *f.*

Nepheloid, *a.* abbhacchanna.

Nephew, *n.* (sister's son :) bhāgineyya, *m.* (brother's son :) bhātuputta, *m.*

Nephralgia, *n.* vakkaroga, *m.*

Nephritic, *a.* vakkarogātura.

Nepotism, *n.* ñātipakkhapātitā : *f.* °**ist,** *n.* ñātipakkhapātī, *m.*

Neptune, *n.* samuddadeva, *m.*

Nervate, *a.* nahāruyutta ; phāsukāyutta.

Nerve, *n.* 1. nahāru, *m.* sirā ; dhamanī, *f.* 2. bala ; viriya, *nt.* *v.t.* balaŋ vaḍḍheti. *p.p.* vaḍḍhitabala. °**less,** *a.* dubbala; akkhama. °**ous,** *a.* 1. hīnabala ; kampanasīla ; 2. nahāruvisayaka. °**ously,** *adv.* 1. sakampaŋ ; 2. saviriyaŋ. °**ousness,** *n.* 1 sirādubbalatta, *nt.* 2. ussāha, *m.*

Nervine, *a.* sirāposanaka ; sattijanaka.

Nervy, *a.* 1. daḷhakāya ; thāmavantu ; 2. pagabbha ; 3. adhīra.

Nescience, *n.* avijjā, *f.* aññāṇa, *nt.*

Nescient, *a.* anabhiñña ; aññāṇī.

Ness, *n.* desatuṇḍa, *nt.*

Nest, *n.* kulāvaka, *nt.* niḍḍa, *m.* vāsaṭṭhāna, *nt.* *v.t.* kulāvakaŋ sampādeti. °**less,** *a.* vikulāvaka. °**ling,** *n.* pakkhipotaka, *m.*

Nestle, *v.i.* niḍḍe sayati, *v.t.* poseti. *p.p.* °sayita ; posita.

Nestor, *n.* sadupadesaka, *m.*

Net, *n.* jāla, *nt.* adj. niravasesa ; suddha. *v. t.* jālena bandhati. *p.p.* jālabaddha. **Netting (of a bed),** mañcavāna, *nt.*

Nether, *a.* adhara ; adhaṭṭha. —**most,** *a.* adhotama. — **region,** — **world,** rasātala ; adhobhuvana, *nt.*

Nettle, *n.* kapikacchu, *m.* *v.t.* 1. kapikacchunā paharati ; 2. paritāpeti; pakopeti. *p.p.* °pahaṭa ; °pita.

Neural, *a.* nahāruvisayaka. °**gia,** *n.* nahārugatavedanā, *f.*

Neurasthenia, *n.* nahārudubbalya, *nt.*

Neuritis, *n.* nahārudāha, *m.*

Neurology, *n.* nahāruviññāṇa, *nt.*

Neurosis, *n.* nahāruvipallāsa, *m.*

Neurotic, *a.* nahārupīḷaka. *n.* nahāruvipallāsayutta, *m.*

Neuter, *n.* 1. napuŋsaka; 2. apakkhagāhaka, *m.* adj. napuŋsakaliṅgika.

Neutral, *a.* apakkhagāhī; majjhaṭṭha; upekkhaka. °**ity,** *n.* majjhattatā; apakkhagāhitā, *f.* °**ize,** *v.t.* dubbalaŋ *or* udāsīnaŋ karoti; balaŋ hāpeti. °**ization,** *n.* balanāsana; dubbalīkaraṇa, *nt.* °**ly,** *adv.* apakkhagāhena; udāsīnatāya.

Never, *adv.* na kudācanaŋ; na kadāci. — **more,** na puna. — °**theless,** *adv.* api ca; tathā pi; evam pi sati.

New, *a.* nava; abhinava; nūtana; navīna. °**born,** jātamatta; sampatijāta, *a.* — **comer,** *n.* āgantuka; ādhunika; navaka, *m.* — **fangled,** *a.* accādhunika; navattakāmī. °**ly,** *adv.* abhinavena. — **moon day,** amāvasī, *f.* — **year,** navavassa, *nt.*

News, *n.* pavatti, *f.* vuttanta; janavāda, *m.* °**boy,** °**man,** *n.* pavattipatta-vikketu, *m.* — **monger,** *n.* pavattihārī, *m.* °**paper,** *n.* pavattipatta, *nt.*

Newt, *n.* jalathalagocarā khuddakagodhā, *f.*

Next, *a.* 1. anantara; accāsanna; 2. āgāmī. *adv.* atha; tad anantaraŋ; anantaraŋ. — **but one,** ekantarika, *a.* — **day,** punadivasa, *m.* — **world,** samparāya; anantarabhava, *m.*

Nexus, *n.* paṭiññābandha, *m.*

Nib, *n.* 1. tuṇḍa; agga, *nt.* 2. lekhanīmukha, *nt.* *v.t.* lekhanīmukhaŋ yojeti.

Nibble, *n.* sanika-chindana, *nt.* *v.t.* thoka-thokaŋ ḍasati *or* chindati. *p.p.* °daṭṭha; °chinna.

Nice, *a.* sundara; sobhana; bhaddaka. °**ly,** *adv.* sammā; ruciraŋ; sobhanākārena. °**ness,** °**ty,** *n.* sundaratta; sobhanatta, *nt.*

Niche, *n.* (paṭimādiṭhapanāya) bhittiguhā, *f.*

Nick, *n.* yuttakāla; pattakāla; yathākāla, *m.* *v.t.* 1. parikham avacchindati; 2. yathākāle paharati. *p.p.* avacchinnaparikha; °pahaṭa. °**nack,** khuddakabhaṇḍajāta, *nt.* °**name,** *n.* vikaṭanāma, *nt.* *v.t.* upahassanāmaŋ deti.

Nickel, *n.* rajatavisesa, *m.* *v.t.* tena lohena limpeti.

Nicotian, *a.* dhūmapaṇṇāyatta.

Nicotine, dhūmapaṇṇasāra, *m.*

Nictate, Nictitate, *v.i.* nimesaummesaŋ pavatteti. *p.p.* pavattita°.

Niddle-noddle, *a.* kampamāna; calamāna. *v.i* sīsaŋ kampeti; pacalāyati.

Nidificate, Nidify, *v.t.* kulāvake karoti. *p.p.* katakulāvaka.

Nid-nod, *v.i.* pacalāyati.

Niece, *n.* (sister's daughter:) bhāgineyyā, *f.* (brother's daughter:) bhātudhītu, *f.*

Niggard, *a. n.* kadariya ; luddha. °**ly**, *a.* maccharī ; lobhādhika. *adv.* appavayena ; luddhākārena. °**liness**, *n.* macchariya, *nt.*

Nigger, *n.* kaṇhadehī, *m.*

Niggle, *v.i.* niratthakakicce kālaŋ khepeti. °**ing**, *a.* appamattaka ; appapayojana.

Nigh, *a.* āsanna ; upakaṭṭha, *adv.* avidūre ; āsanne.

Night, *n.* nisā ; rajanī ; ratti, *f.* — **bird**, *n.* ulūka, *m.* °**blind**, *a.* rattandha. °**fall**, *n.* nisāmukha, *nt.* abhidosa ; padosa, *m.* °**ly**, *a.* nisāyatta. *adv.* anurattiŋ ; paṭinisaŋ. °**mare**, *n.* dussupina, *nt.* °**shade**, nididdhikā, *f.* °**time**, *n.* rattibhāga, *m.* °**stool**, vaccapīṭhikā, *f.* °**watch**, nisārakkhā, *f.* nisārakkhī, *m.*

Nigrescent, *a.* īsaŋkāḷavaṇṇa.

Nigritude, *n.* kaṇhatta, *nt.*

Nihilism, *n.* ucchedavāda ; natthikavāda, *m.*°**ist**, *n.* uccedavādī, *m.* °**ity**, *n.* suññatā ; avijjamānatā, *f.* abhāva, *m.*

Nil, *ind.* na kiñci. *noun.* akiñcanatta, *nt.*

Nimble, *a.* turita ; sīghagatika. °**ness**, *n.* turitatta, *nt.* °**ly**, *adv.* sīghaŋ ; turitaŋ ; āsu ; lahuŋ tuvaṭaŋ.

Nimbus, *n.* ketumālā, *f.* raŋsimaṇḍala, *nt.*

Niminy-piminy, *a.* atvilāsī ; atikomala.

Nincompoop, *n.* jaḷabuddhika, *m.*

Nine, *n. a.* nava. 3. °**fold**, *a.* navaṅgika ; navaguṇika. — **storeyed**, *a.* navabhūmaka. °**teen**, *n.* ekūnavīsati, *f.* °**teenth**, *a.* ekūnavīsatima. °**ty**, *n.* navuti, *f.* °**ty-nine**, ekūnasata, *nt.* °**ty-six**, channavuti, *f.*

Ninny, *n.* dandhapuggala, *m.*

Ninth, *a.* navama.

Nip, *n.* 1. aggacchindana ; ucchindana, *nt.* 2. mammacchedakavacana, *nt v.t.* uppīḷeti; aggaŋ chindati; chinditvā apaneti. *p.p.* °ḷita; aggacchinna; °nīta. °**ping**, *n.* nikantana, *nt.* °**per**, *n.* nakhavilikhaka, *m.*

Nipple, *n.* cūcuka; thanagga, *nt.*

Nit, *n.* likkhā, *f.* ūkaṇḍa, *nt.* °**ty**, *a.* likkhāpuṇṇa.

Nitrate, *n.* yavakhāra, *m. v.t.* yavakhārena misseti. *p.p.* °sita.

Nitric, *a.* jīvantakavāyuppādaka. — **acid**, *n.* jīvantakavisa, *nt.*

Nitrogen, *n.* nigguṇavāyu, *m.*

Nitrous, *a.* jīvantakayutta.

Nix, *n.* 1. na kiñci ; 2 jaladevatā, *f.*

No, *a. adv.* no ; na ; na hi.

Nob, *n.* 1. sīsa, *nt.* 2. uccākulīna ; *m. v.t.* (mallayuddhe) sīsaŋ paharati. *p.p.* pahaṭasīsa.

Nobble, *v.t.* 1. ayathā āyattīkaroti ; 2. ayathā pakkhapātī hoti. *p.p.* °kata ; °tībhūta.

Nobby, *a.* suvesa ; pāsādika.

Nobility, *n.* 1. kulīnatta ; abhijātatta, *nt.* 2. kulīnajanatā, *f.*

Noble, *a. n.* uttama ; abhijāta ; uccākulīna. — **elephant**, gajaratana, *nt.* — **horse**, ājānīya, *m.* °**man**, kulīna, *m.* — **minded**, *a.* uḷārajjhāsaya. °**ness**, *n.* seṭṭhatta ; uttamatta, *nt.* — **person**, purisuttama ; purisājañña ; purisāsabha, *m.* — **practice**, ariyadhamma, *m.* — **truth**, ariyasacca, *nt.*

Nobly, *adv.* pasatthākārena.

Nobody, *n.* na koci.

Nock, *n.* jiyābandhanaṭṭhāna, *nt.* *v.t.* saraŋ āropeti. *p.p.* āropitasara.

Noctambulant, *a.* niddāya āhiṇḍakasabhāva. °**lation**, niddāyāhiṇḍana, *nt.* °**list**, *n.* antoniddāhiṇḍaka, *m.*

Noctiflorous, *a.* rattiŋ-pupphanaka.

Noctilucent, *a.* rattibhāsura.

Noctivagant, *a.* nisācārī.

Nocturnal, *a.* nisācara; nisāgata; rattisiddha.

Nod, *n.* sīsonamana, *nt.* *v.i.* 1. sīsam onamati; 2. pacalāyati, *v.t.* sīsam onāmeti. *p.p.* onāmitasīsa.

Noddle, *v.t.* sīsaŋ okampeti. *p.p.* okampitasīsa.

Noddy, *n.* 1. jalabuddhika, *m.* 2. sāmuddika-pakkhivisesa, *m.*

Node, *n.* 1. pabba, *nt.* gaṇṭhi, *m.* 2. valayadvaya-ghaṭṭitaṭṭhāna, *nt.* 3. vātagaṇḍa, *m.*

Nodose, *a.* gaṇṭhibahula; pabbabahula.

Nodule, *n.* khuddakagaṇṭhi, *m.*

Nodus, *n.* dukkaratta; dubbodhaṭṭhāna, *nt.*

Noetic, *a.* buddhivisayaka.

Nog, *n.* dārusaṅku; aṅkusa, *m.* *v.t.* khīlena santhambheti. *p.p.* °bhita. °**gin**, *n.* dārucasaka, *m.*

Noise, *n.* sadda; rava; nāda; ghosa; nigghosa, *m.* *v.t.* nadati; ravati; ghoseti; ugghoseti; saddāyati. *p.p.* nadita; ravita; °sita; °yita. °**ful**, *a.* saghosa. °**less**, *a.* nissadda. °**lessly**, *adv.* nissaddatāya. °**ily**, *adv.* mahāsaddena. °**iness**, *n.* uccāsaddatā, *f.* °**sy**, *a.* uccāsadda; saghosa.

Noisome, *a.* 1. duggandha; 2. antarāyakara; 3. kucchita.

Noll, *n.* sīsamatthaka, *m.*

Nomad, *n.* *a.* pasukulājīvī; athiranivāsī. °**ic**, *a.* pariyāhiṇḍaka.

Nom de plume, *n.* āropitanāma; *nt.*

Nomenclator, *n.* nāmadāyī, *m.* °**ture**, *n.* 1. nāmavavatthāna, *nt.* 2. paribhāsāvacana, *nt.* 3. nāmāvali, *f.*

Nominal, *a.* 1. nāmasadisa; nāmamattaka; appamattaka; 2. nāmavisayaka. °**ly**, *adv.* nāmamattena; saddavasena. paññattimattavāda, *m.* °**ism**, *n.*

Nominate, *v.t.* 1. nāmaŋ vadati *or* niddisati; 2. adhikārāya uccināti. *p.p.* vuttanāma; niddiṭṭha°; °nita. °**ion**, *n.* nāmayojanā, *f.* °**or**, *n.* nāmayojaka; nāmaniddisaka, *m.*

Nominative, *n.* paṭhamā vibhatti, *f.* kattuvācaka, *nt.*

Nominee, *n.* niddiṭṭhanāma; niyojita, *m.*

Non, *prep.* Often expressed by **a** – prefixed to a noun beginning with a consonant, and **an** – to that which begins with a vowel.

Nonage, *n.* bālya, *nt.* appahoṇakavaya, *m.* appattavayatā, *f.*

Nonagenarian, *a.* *n.* navutivassika.

Nonagon, *a.* *n.* navakoṇaka.

Nonary, *a.* navasaṅkhyaka, *n.* navaka, *nt.*

Nonattachment, *n.* nissaṅga, *m.* alaggana, *nt.* arati, *f.*
Nonattainment, *n.* appatti, *f.* anadhigama, *m.*
Nonattention, *n.* anavadhāna, *nt.*
Nonchalance, *n.* anapekkhatā; udāsīnatā, *f.* °**lant,** *a.* acala; nissaṅka; visārada.
Noncontinuance, *n.* appavatti, *f.* viccheda, *m.*
Nonco-operation, *n.* asahayogitā, *f,*
Nondescript, *a.* duvitthāriya; duvavatthāpiya.
None, *pron.* na koci; na kiñci; n' eko pi. *adv.* natthi kiñci.
Nonendurance, *n.* asahana, *nt.*
Nonentity, *n.* 1. abhāva, *m.* appavatti, *f.* 2. agaṇetabba-vatthu, *nt.*
Nonesuch, Nonsuch *a.* asama; asadisa; appaṭima.
Nonexistent, *a.* asanta, avijjamāna; appavattamāna.
Nonfeasance, *n.* kattabbākaraṇa, *nt.*
Nongrowth, *n.* avirūḷhi, *f.*
Nonhurting, *a.* ahiŋsaka; aviheṭhaka.
Nonkilling, *n.* māghāta, *m.*
Nonobservance, *n.* appaṭipajjana; arakkhaṇa, *nt.*
Nonpareil, *a.* *n.* atulya; asadisa; appaṭipuggala.
Nonplus, *n.* kattabbānicchaya; sambādha, *m.* vyākulatta, *nt.* *v.t.* vyākulīkaroti; kiccaŋ bādheti. *p.p.*°kata; bādhitakicca.
Nonresident, *a.* anevāsika; niccavāsarahita.
Nonreturner, *n.* anāgāmī, *m.*
Nonsense, *n.* vippalāpa, *m.* asambandhakathā, *f.* °**ical,** *a.* attharahita; asambandha. °**ically,** *adv.* attharahitākārena.
Nonsuit, *n.* codanāpaṭikkosana, *nt.* *v.t.* codanaŋ paccākaḍḍhati.
Nontransgression, *n.* avītikkama, *m.*
Nonviolence, *n.* anupaghāta, *m.*
Noodle, *n.* mandamati; duppañña, *m.*
Nook, *n.* koṇa, *m.* viviṭṭaṭṭhāna, *nt.*
Noon, *n.* divā, *ind.* majjhaṇha, *m.* adj. majjhaṇhika. °**tide,** *n.* majjhaṇhakāla, *m.*
Noose, *n.* pāsa, *m.* bandhana, *nt.* *v.t.* pāsena bandhati *or* bādheti. *p.p.* pāsabaddha; °bādhita.
Nor, *conj.* na ca; na vā.
Norm, *n.* niyāma, *m.* sutta; nidassana, *nt.*
Normal, *a.* sābhāvika; niyamānugata; pākatika. °**ity,** *n.* yathākkamatta, *nt.* °**ly,** *adv.* yathāsabhāvena, sāmaññena. °**ize,** *v.t.* pākatikattaŋ pāpeti. — **state,** pakati, *f.* sabhāva, *m.* — **school,** guruvuttivijjālaya, *m.*
North, *n.* uttaradisā; uttarā, *f.* adj. uttarāyatta. *adv.* uttarena. °**east,** *a.* pubbuttara. °**ern,** °**erly,** *a.* udicca; uttaradisika. °**pole,** Sudassana, *m.* °**wards,** *adv.* uttarābhimukhaŋ. °**west,** *a.* pacchimuttara. °**western,** *a.* pacchimuttarīya.
Northener, *n.* uttaradesavāsī, *m.*
Nose, *n.* nāsā; nāsikā, *f.* ghāṇa, *nt.* *v.t.* ghāyati. *p.p.* ghāyita. °**bag,** *n.* (assānaŋ) mukhapasibbaka, *m.* °**string,** kusā, *f.* — **treatment,** natthukamma, *nt.* °**ring,** nāsikābharaṇa, *nt.*
Nosegay, *n.* pupphagocchaka; kusumatthabaka, *m.*

Nosology, *n.* roganidānavijjā, *f.*

Nostalgia, *n.* gharavirahapīḷā; pavāsukkaṇṭhā, *f.*

Nostril, *n.* nāsāpuṭa, *m.* ghānabila, *nt.*

Nostrum, *n.* guttosadha, *nt.*

Nosy, *a.* 1. mahānāsika; 2. duggandhāvaha. *n.* tikhiṇaghānindriya, *m.*

Not, *adv.* na; no; na hi. (Prohibitive:) mā, *ind.* — **done**, akata, adj. — **finding**, *a.* anibbisanta. — **seldom**, abhiṇhaŋ, *adv.*

Notability, *n.* anussaraṇīyatta; visiṭṭhatta, *nt.*

Notable, *a.* saritabba; visiṭṭha; pākaṭa. °**bly**, *adv.* visesato; visesena.

Notalgia, *n.* piṭṭhirujā, *f.*

Notary, *n.* nītilipi-sampādaka, *m.*

Notch, *n.* cheda, *m.* vivara, *nt.*

Note, *n.* 1. aṅkana; abhiññāṇa; 2. saṅkhittavivaraṇa; 3. saṅkhittasāsana, *nt.* 4. dhanapaṇṇa, *nt.* *v.t.* 1. avekkhati; āloceti; 2. paṇṇe āropeti; 3. aṅketi; lañcheti. *p.p.* °khita; °cita; paṇṇāropita; aṅkita; °chita. °**ation**, *n.* aṅkaṇa, *nt.* °**book**, *n.* ciṇhapotthaka, *nt.* °**paper**, sāsanapatta, *nt.* °**worthy**, sallakkhaṇīya, *a.*

Nothing, *n.* na kiñci, *ind.* abhāva, *m.* natthitā, *f.* °**ness**, *n.* suññatta; ākiñcañña, *nt.* *adv.* na kim api.

Notice, *n.* 1. āvedanā; nivedanā, *f.* viññāpana, *nt.* 2. avekkhana; avadhāna; 3. nivedanapaṇṇa, *nt.* *v.t.* sallakkheti; avekkhati. *p.p.* °khita. °**able**, *a.* pākaṭa; sallakkhaṇāraha. **Give** —, nivedeti. **Take** —, manasikaroti.

Notify, *v.t.* ñāpeti; nivedeti; pakāseti. *p.p.* ñāpita; °dita; °sita. °**ication**, *n.* nivedana; viññāpana, *nt.*

Notion, *n.* mati, *f.* saṅkappa, *m.* °**al**, *a.* saṅkappāyatta.

Notoriety, *n.* 1 vikhyāti; 2. akitti, *f.* ayasa, *m.*

Notorious, *a.* 1. pasiddha; pākaṭa; 2. kubuddhika; duṭṭhapakatika. °**ly**, *adv.* supākaṭaŋ; duṭṭhākārena. °**ness**, *n.* pasiddhi; akitti, *f.*

Notwithstanding, *prep.* agaṇetvā; anādiyitvā. *conj.* yadi pi; sace pi. *adv.* evam pi sati.

Nought, *n.* 1. na kiñci pi; 2. suññalakkhaṇa, *nt.* bindu, *m.*

Noumenon, *n.* asaṅkhatārammaṇa, *nt.*

Noun, *n.* nāmapada, *nt.*

Nourish, *v.t.* poseti; bharati; paṭijaggati. *p.p.* posita *or* puṭṭha; bhata; °gita. °**ing**, *a.* ojavantu; puṭṭhikara. °**ment**, *n.* 1. posaṇa; yāpana, *nt.* 2. āhāra, *m.* bhojana, *nt.*

Nous, *n.* mana, *m.* *nt.* buddhi, *f.*

Novel, *n.* navapabandha, *m.* navakathā, *f.* adj. nava; nūtana. °**ette**, *n.* saṅkhitta-pabandha, *m.* °**ist**, *n.* navakathāsampādaka, *m.* °**ty**, *n.* 1. navatā, *f.* 2. abhinavavatthu, *nt.* °**ize**, *v.t.* navapabandhattaŋ pāpeti.

November, *n.* Kattikamāsa, *m.*

Novennial, *a.* navasaŋvaccharika.

Novice, *n.* navaka; sāmaṇera; samaṇuddesa, *m.* °**iate**, *n.* ādhunikatta; sāmaṇeratta, *nt.*

Now, *adv.* adhunā ; idāni ; etarahi. *conj.* atha. °**adays,** imasmiŋ kāle. — **and then,** yadā kadāci. **Just** —, idān'eva. **Till** —, yāvajjatanā, *ind.*

Nowhere, *adv.* na katthaci.

Nowise, *adv.* na kathañci pi.

Noxious, *a.* hiŋsaka ; ahitakara ; sopaddava. °**ly,** *adv.* ahitakaratāya.

Nozzle, *n.* mukharakkhana-khaṇḍa ; ghaṭitakoṭṭhāsa, *m.*

Nuance, *n.* sukhumanānatta, *nt.*

Nubble, *n.* khuddaka-gaṇṭhi, *m.*

Nubile, *a.* vivāhayogga.

Nucleus, *n.* mūlakāraṇa, *nt.* janakasatti, *f.* majjhasāra, *m.*

Nude, *a.* nagga ; acela ; anāvuta. °**ity,** *n.* naggiya, *nt.* °**ly,** *adv.* naggākārena.

Nudge, *v.t.* vitudati ; kapparena saññāpeti. *p.p.* °dita ; °pita. *n.* vitudana, *nt.* sanikappahāra, *m.*

Nugatory, *a.* mogha ; viphala ; appaggha.

Nugget, *n.* asodhita-lohapiṇḍa, *m.*

Nuisance, *n.* pīḷā ; bādhā, *f.* appiyavatthu, *nt.* aniṭṭhakriyā, *f.*

Null, *a.* nitteja ; vigatabala ; nipphala ; mogha. °**ify,** *v.t.* moghīkaroti ; °**ification,** *n.* moghīkaraṇa ; balahāpana, *nt.* °**ity,** *n.* abhāva, *m.* suññatta ; asāmatthiya, *nt.*

Numb, *a.* santhambhita ; naṭṭhapasāda. *v.t.* thambheti ; akammaññaŋ karoti. *p.p.* °bhita ; °kata. °**ness,** *n.* thambhitatta, *nt.*

Number, *n.* 1. saṅkhyā ; gaṇanā, *f.* 2. aṅka, *m.* *v.t.* 1. gaṇeti ; saṅkaleti ; 2. aṅketi. *p.p.* gaṇita, °lita ; aṅkita. °**ing,** *n.* saṅkhyāna, *nt.* °**less,** *a.* asaṅkhya ; gaṇanātīta ; saṅkhyātiga.

Numerable, *a.* saṅkheyya.

Numeral, *n.* saṅkhyā, *f.* adj. saṅkhyāvisayaka. °**ly,** *adv.* yathāsaṅkhyaŋ.

Numerary, *a.* saṅkhyādhīna ; niyatasaṅkhyaka.

Numeration, *n.* saṅkhyāna, *nt.* °**tor,** *n.* 1. gaṇaka, *m.* 2. (gahetabba-) bhāgasaṅkhyā, *f.*

Numerical, *a.* saṅkhyāvācaka. °**ly,** *adv.* gaṇanavasena ; yathāsaṅkhyaŋ.

Numerous, *a.* aneka ; anappaka. °**ly,** *adv.* bahuso ; anekadhā. °**ness,** *n.* anekatta ; bāhulla, *nt.*

Numismatic, *a.* mūlamuddaṅkaṇāyatta ; rūpiyāyatta. °**tology,** *n.* rūpiyavijjā, *f.*

Nummary, *a.* rūpiyāyatta.

Nummet, *n.* divābhojana, *nt.*

Numskull, mūḷhapuggala, *m.*

Nun, *n.* samaṇī ; bhikkhunī, *f.* 3. °**nery,** *n.* bhikkhunīupassaya ; samaṇīnivāsa, *m.* °**ship,** *n.* samaṇībhāva, *m.*

Noncupate, *v.t.* (lekhanaŋ vinā) vācāya pakāseti. *p.p.* °sita.

Nuptial, *n.* pāṇiggaha, *m.* adj. vivāhapaṭibaddha. — **ceremony,** vivāhamaṅgala, *nt.*

Nurse, *n.* 1. dhātī, *f.* gilānupaṭṭhākā ; 2. posikā ; āpādikā, *f.* *v.t.* āpādeti ; poseti ; paṭijaggati. *p.p.* °dita ; posita ; °gita. °**ing,** *n.* posaṇa ; upaṭṭhāna, *nt.* °**ling,** *n.* thanapa, *m.*

Nursery, *n.* posaṇaṭṭhāna, *nt.* °**maid,** *n.* paricārikā dhātī, *f.*

°man, rukkhapotakasaŋrakkhaka, *m*.

Nurture, *n*. 1. posaṇa ; saŋvaḍḍhana ; 2. sikkhāpana, *nt*. *v.t*. 1. poseti; vaḍḍheti; 2. sikkhāpeti. *p.p*. posita ; °ḍhita ; °pita.

Nut, *n*. sakapāla-phala, *nt*. °**cracker,** *n*. kapālabhindaka, *nt*.

Nutate, *v.i*. onamati. *p.p*. onata. °**ion,** *n*. 1. onamana ; kampana ; 2. bhamarikādolāyana, *nt*.

Nutmeg, *n*. jātiphala, *nt*.

Nutrient, *a*. posaṇakara.

Nutriment, *n*. posaṇa, *nt*. āhāra, *m*.

Nutrition, *n*. posaṇakaraṇa, *nt*.

Nutritious, *a*. puṭṭhikara ; ojavantu. °**tive,** *a*. posaṇadāyī.

Nutty, *a*. phalabahula ; phalarasayutta.

Nuzzle, *v.t*. sukhaŋ nipajjati. *p.p*. °nipanna.

Nyctalopia, *n*. rattandhatā, *f*.

Nyctitropic, *a*. rattiyaŋ parivattanasīla.

Nymph, *n*. jaladevatā ; vanadevatā, *f*. °**olepsy,** *n*. alabbhaneyyacintāya laddha-pīti, *f*.

Nymphomania, *n*. balavakāmāsā, *f*. methunummāda, *m*.

O

O, *intj*. 1. he ; bho ; ambho ; 2. (joy and surprise :) aho ; handa ; 3. (sorrow :) hā ; ahaha.

Oaf, *n*. virūpadāraka, *m*. °**ish,** *a*. mandapañña ; dandha.

Oak, *n*. sindūrarukkha, *m*.

Oar, *n*. nāvāpājanī, *f*. keṇipāta, *m*. *v.t*. arittena pājeti. *p.p*. °pājita. °**sman,** *n*. arittadhārī, *m*.

Oasis, *n*. kantāra-khemabhūmi, *f*.

Oat, *n*. dhaññavisesa, *m*.

Oath, *n*. sapatha, *m*. abhisapana, *nt*.

Obdurate, *a*. dubbaca ; anassava ; kaṭhinahadaya. °**racy,** *n*. dubbacatta ; anassavatta, *nt*. °**ly,** *adv*. dubbacākārena.

Obedience, *n*. sovacassa ; subbacatta, *nt*. sussūsā, *f*.

Obedient, *a*. assava ; subbaca ; vidheyya ; vacanakara. °**ly,** *adv*. suvacatāya ; assavākārena.

Obeisance, *n*. paṇāma ; namakkāra, *m*. abhivādanā, *f*.

Obelisk, *n*. sūcisaṇṭhānathambha, *m*. °**lize,** *v.t*. sūcitthambhena aṅketi. *p.p*. °aṅkita.

Obese, *a*. pīṇa ; pīvara ; thūla. °**ness,** *n*. pīṇatta ; thūlatta, *nt*.

Obey, *v.t.i*. anuvattati ; sussūsati. *p.p*. °vattita.

Obfuscate, *v.t*. andhayati ; moheti ; timirāvutaŋ karoti. *p.p*. andhita ; mohita ; °kata. °**ion,** *n*. andhīkaraṇa, *nt*.

Obit, *n*. maraṇānussaraṇussava, *m*.

Obituary, *n*. maraṇanivedana ; matakicca, *nt*.

Object, *n*. 1. vatthu ; gocaravatthu, *nt*. 2. visaya ; gocara, *m*. 3. attha, *m*. phala, *nt*. 4. adhippāya ; manoratha, *m*. 5. (in gram.) kamma, *nt*. upayogattha, *m*. *v.t*. bādheti ; khaṇḍeti. *p.p*. °dhita ; °ḍita. *v.i*. virujjhati. *p.p*. viruddha. °**ion,** *n*. virodha, *m*. °**ionable,** *a*. nisedhetabba ; vajjanīya ; virodhāraha ; sāvajja.

Objectify, *v.t.* visayabhāvaŋ *or* indriyagocarattaŋ pāpeti. *p.p.* °pāpita.

Objective, *a.* 1. kammavācaka; 2. bāhira; 3. padatthanissita. °**ly,** *adv.* bāhirākārena. °**ness,** *n.* bāḥiratta, *nt.*

Objuration, *n.* sapathakaraṇa, *nt.*

Objurgate, *v.t.* nindati; paribhavati; tajjeti. *p.p.* °dita; paribhūta; tajjita. °**ion,** *n.* tajjana; paribhāsana, *nt.* °**tory,** *a.* tajjakasabhāva.

Oblate, *n.* samayānuvattī; saddhapuggala, *m.* adj. koṇa-samatalākāra. °**ion,** *n.* homa; havya; balikamma, *nt.*

Obligation, *n.* yuttibaddhatā, *f.* °**tory,** *a.* āvassaka; aparihāriya.

Oblige, *v.t.* vase vatteti; anuggaṇhāti; niyojeti. *p.p.* °tita; anuggahita; °jita. °**gee,** *n.* anuggahita; paṭiññāgāhī, *m.* °**ing,** *a.* paccupakāraka. °**ingly,** *adv.* kataññutāpubbaṅgamaŋ.

Obligor, *n.* paṭiññādāyī, *m.*

Oblique, *a.* 1. passaninna; 2. anuju; visama; vaṅka. °**ly,** *adv.* visamaŋ; tiro. °**ness,** *n.* visamatta; kuṭilatta, *nt.* °**ity,** *n.* kuṭilatta; visamatta, *nt.*

Obliterate, *v.t.* lopeti; apamajjati. *p.p.* lutta; apamaṭṭha. °**ion,** *n.* lopa, *m.* apamajjana, *nt.*

Oblivion, *n.* vissaraṇa, *nt.* satisammosa, *m.* °**vious,** *a.* pamussanasīla.

Oblong, *a.* āyatacaturassa.

Obloquy, *n.* garahā, *f.* apavāda, *m.*

Obmutescence, *n.* acala-tuṇhībhāva, *m.*

Obnoxious, *a.* kucchita; gārayha; nindiya. °**ly,** *adv.* kucchitākārena. °**ness,** *n.* nindiyatta, *nt.*

Obscene, *a.* gamma; nīca; anariya; asabbha. °**ly,** *adv.* asabbhākārena. °**ness,** *n.* gammatta, *nt.* — **language,** duṭṭhulla, *nt.*

Obscurant, *n.* vivecanavirodhī; avīmaŋsākāmī, *m.* °**ism,** *n.* avivecakatta, *nt.* vīmaŋsāvirodha, *m.*

Obscure, *n.* apākaṭavatthu, *nt.* adj. 1. apākaṭa; anuttāna; 2. malina; nippabha; 3. dubbodha; gūḷhattha, *v.t.* āvarati; chādeti; avisadīkaroti. *p.p.* āvaṭa; chādita *or* channa; °kata. °**ity,** °**ness,** *n.* apākaṭatta; avisadatta; gūḷhatta, *nt.* °**ly,** *adv.* gūḷhaŋ; apākaṭaŋ. °**ation,** *n.* āvaraṇa; malinīkaraṇa, *nt.* — **passage,** ganṭhiṭṭhāna, *nt.*

Obsecration, *n.* balavāyācanā, *f.*

Obsequies, *n.* petakicca, *nt.* °**quial,** *a.* matakiccāyatta.

Obsequious, *a.* atidīna; accantavasānuvattī. °**ness,** *n.* accantānuvattana, *nt.* °**ly,** *adv.* atidīnatāya; cāṭukamyatāya.

Observe, *v.t.* 1. passati; oloketi; 2. rakkhati; ācarati; paṭipajjati; 3. vadati. *p.p.* diṭṭha; °kita; °khita; °rita; paṭipanna; vutta. °**able,** *a.* diṭṭhigocara; paṭipajjitabba. °**ance,** *n.* rakkhaṇa; ācaraṇa, *nt.* paṭipatti, *f.* °**ant,** *n.* nirikkhaka; sāvadhāna; saŋrakkhaka, *m.* °**ation,** *n.* 1. avekkhaṇa, *nt.* 2. vacana; vākya, *nt.* — **a fast,** uposatham upavasati. °**er,** *n.* anupassī; rakkhitu, *m.* °**ingly,** *adv.* appamattākārena; samekkhāya. — silence, monam ācarati.

Observatory, *n.* ākāsavatthuparikkhaṇaṭṭhāna, *nt.*

Obsess, *v.t.* 1. pīḷeti; 2. āvisati. *p.p.* pīḷita; āviṭṭha. °**ion,** *n.* pīḷana; āvisana, *nt.* amanussagāha, *m.*

Obsolescent, *a.* abhāvagāmī; gatabbaya.

Obsolete, *a. n.* gatavohāra; appacāriyamāna. °**ness,** *n.* gatavohāratta, *nt.* appacāra, *m.*

Obstacle, *n.* paripantha; palibodha, *m.* bādhā, *f.* nīvaraṇa, *nt.*

Obstetric, *a.* pasūtivisayaka. *pl.* pasūtivijjā, *f.* °**ian,** *n.* pasūtisādhikā, *f.*

Obstinate, *a.* dubbaca; anassava; dubbinīta. °**ly,** *adv.* dubbacākārena. °**nacy,** *n.* dovacassa; anassavatta, *nt.*

Obstipation, *n.* adhika-malabandha, *m.*

Obstreperous *a.* dunniggayha; ugghosanasīla. °**ly,** *adv.* saghosaŋ; uccāsaddena. °**ness,** *n.* mukharatta; uddāmatta, *nt.*

Obstruct, *v.t.* bādheti; vāreti; rodheti; nivāreti; āvarati. *p.p.* bādhita; vārita; rodhita; āvaṭa. °**ing,** *a.* bādhaka; nivāraka. °**ion,** *n.* bādhana; vāraṇa; rundhana, *nt.* °**ionist,** *n.* bādhākara; antarāyakārī, *m.* °**ive,** *a.* bādhaka; pīḷaka; pāripanthika. °**ively,** *adv.* bādhakākārena. °**iveness,** *n.* bādhakatta, *nt.*

Obtain, *v.t.* labhati; adhigacchati; pappoti. *p.p.* laddha; adhigata; patta. °**able,** *a.* laddhabba; adhigamanīya. °**ment,** *n.* paṭilābha; adhigama, *m.* **Difficult to —,** dullabha, *a.* **Easy to —,** sulabha, *a.*

Obtest, *v.t.* 1. virodhaŋ pakāseti; 2. sakkhiŋ avheti. *p.p.* pakāsitavirodha; avhitasakkhī. °**ation,** *n.* āyācanā, *f.*

Obtrude, *v.i.* balena pavisati, *v.i.* ayācito anusāsati. *p.p.* °paviṭṭha; °anusiṭṭha.

Obtrusion, *n.* anāhūtappavesa, *m.* °**sive,** *a.* balena pavisanasīla. °**sively,** *adv.* āyācanaŋ vinā.

Obtruncate, *v.t.* matthakaŋ chindati. *p.p.* chinnamatthaka.

Obtund, *v.t.* kuṇṭheti; balaŋ hāpeti. *p.p.* °ṭhita; hāpitabala.

Obturate, *v.t.* chiddaŋ pidahati. *p.p.* pihitachidda. °**ion,** *n.* chiddapidahana, *nt.*

Obtuse, *a.* 1. jaḷa; mūḷha; 2. kuṇṭha; atikhiṇa. °**ly,** *adv.* kuṇṭhākārena. °**ness,** *n.* kuṇṭhatta, *nt.*

Obverse, *n.* 1. mukhapassa; abhimukha, *nt.* 2. viruddhapakkha, *m.* adj. itarapassika; paṭilomika.

Obvert, *v.t.* abhimukhīkaroti. *p.p.* °kata.

Obviate, *v.t.* apaneti; apaharati; abhibhavati. *p.p.* apanīta; apahaṭa; abhibhūta. °**ion,** *n.* apaharaṇa, *nt.*

Obvious, *a.* 1. pākaṭa; vyatta; suvisada; 2. sugama. °**ly,** *adv.* supākaṭaŋ; suvisadaŋ. °**ness,** *n.* pākaṭatta; sugamatta, *nt.*

Occasion, *n.* avatthā, *f.* samaya; avasara; vāra, *m.* *v.t.* samuṭṭhāpeti; janeti. *p.p.* °pita; janita. °**al,** *a.* pāsaṅgika; āgantuka;

aniyata. °**ally,** *adv.* antarantarā; kālena kālaŋ. °**ing,** *a.* samuṭṭhāpaka.

Occident, *n.* pacchimadesa, *m.* °**al,** *a.* pacchimadesīya; apācīna. °**alize,** *v.t.* apācīnattaŋ pāpeti. *p.p.* °pita.

Occiput, *n.* sīsapacchābhāga, *m.*

Occlude, *v.t.* paṭicchādeti. *p.p.* °dita. °**lusion,** *n.* pidahana; chādana, *nt.*

Occult, *a.* gūḷha; duviññeyya; rāhassaka. *v.t.* tirokaroti. *v.i.* tirobhavati. *p.p.* °kata; °bhūta. °**ation,** *n.* tirokaraṇa, *nt.* °**ism,** *n.* gūḷhavijjā, *f.* °**ist,** *n.* gūḷhavijjāvidū, *m.*

Occupant, *n.* pariggāhaka; adhivāsī, *m.* °**ncy,** *n.* pariggaha, *m.* adhivāsitā, *f.*

Occupy, *v.t.* 1. pariggaṇhāti; adhivasati; adhigaṇhāti; 2. abhiyuñjati. *p.p.* °gahita; adhivuttha; adhiggahita; abhiyutta. °**pation,** *n.* jīvanopāya; vyāpāra, *m.* °**ied,** *a.* vyāvaṭa; payutta. °**ier,** *n.* sāmī; adhikārī, *m.*

Occur, *v.i.* 1. bhavati; sijjhati; 2. khāyati; paṭibhāti. *p.p.* bhūta; siddha; khāyita. °**rence,** *n.* siddhi, *f.*

Ocean, *n.* samudda; sāgara; sindhu; udadhi; jalanidhi; aṇṇava, *m.* °**ic,** *a.* sāmuddika. °**ography,** *n.* samuddavaṇṇanā, *f.* °**ology,** *n.* samuddavijjā, *f.*

Ocellus, *n.* 1. makkhikālocana; 2. vaṇṇabindu, *nt.*

Ochlocracy, *n.* dāmarikapālana, *nt.*

Ochre, *n.* geruka, *nt.*

Octachord, *a.* aṭṭhatantika.

Octad, *n.* aṭṭhaka, *nt.*

Octagon, *n.* aṭṭhakoṇakavatthu, *nt.* °**al,** *a.* aṭṭhaŋsika.

Octant, *n.* cakkassa aṭṭhamabhāga, *m.*

Octave, *n.* 1. aṭṭhaka, *nt.* 2. saraggāma, *m.* 3. aṭṭhapadikagāthā, *f.*

Octavo, *a.* aṭṭhapattika.

Octennial, *a.* aṭṭhavassika.

Octingentenary, *n.* aṭṭhasatavassikussava, *m.*

October, *n.* Assayuja, *m.*

Octodecimo, *n.* aṭṭhārasapaṇṇaka -(potthaka), *m.*

Octogenerian, *n.* asītivassika, *m.*

Octopod, *n.* aṭṭhapadikapāṇī, *m.*

Octopus, *n.* aṭṭhahaṭṭhakapāṇī, *m.*

Octosyllabic, *a.* *n.* aṭṭhasarayutta.

Octori, *n.* nagarasuṅka, *m.*

Octuple, *a.* aṭṭhaguṇa; aṭṭhavidha.

Ocular, *a.* cakkhuvisayaka; paccakkha. °**ly,** *adv.* paccakkhaŋ.

Oculist, *n.* akkhivejja; nayanatikicchaka, *m.*

Odalisque, *n.* antepuradāsī, *f.*

Odd, *n.* atiritta (-visama-) saṅkhyā, *f.* adj. visama; asaṅgata; vikaṭa. °**ity,** °**ness,** *n.* vesamma; vikaṭatta; asāmaññalakkhaṇa. °**ly,** *adv.* visamākārena.

Odds, *n. pl.* 1. visadisatā, *f.* 2. tulanātireka, *m.*

Ode, *n.* gīta, *nt.* pajjabandha, *m.*

Odious, *a.* kucchita; dessiya; garahita; appiya. °**ly,** *adv.* dessiyākārena; kucchitākārena. °**ness,** *n.* gārayhatta, *nt.*

Odium, *n.* viddesa, *m.* appiyatta, *nt.*

Odontalgia, *n.* dantarujā, *f.*

Odontiasis, *n.* dantakantana, *nt.*

Odontology, *n.* dantavijjā, *f.*

Odorous, *a.* sugandhī ; surabhigandhika. °**ly**, *adv.* sugandhasahitaŋ.

Odour, *n.* gandha, *m.* °**less**, *a.* gandharahita.

Oecumenical, *a.* sabbasādhāraṇa.

Oedima, *m.* sapubba-sopha, *m.* °**tous**, *a.* uddhumāta.

Oesophagus, *n.* galanāḷa, *m.*

Oestrum, *n.* 1. piṅgalamakkhikā, *f.* 2. unnatāsā, *f.*

Of, *prep.* adhikicca ; uddissa. — **course**, ekantaŋ ; dhuvaŋ, *adv.* — **great learning**, bahussuta, *a.* —**late**, acirātīta, *a.* — **old**, purā, *adv.* — **the low caste**, hīnajacca, *a.* **Died of fever**, jararogena mari.

Off, *adv.* dūre ; dūrato. *intj.* apehi. adj. dūravattī ; dūraṭṭha. °**day**, vissamanadivasa, *m.* °**hand**, sukhena, *adv.* °**let**, niggamana, *nt.* °**shoot**, aṅkura, *m.* sākhā, *f.* °**spring**, santati ; pajā, *f.* °**time**, vissamanakāla, *m.*

Offal, *n.* ucciṭṭhabhojana ; chaḍḍanīyavatthu, *nt.*

Offence, *n.* 1. vajja, *nt.* dosa, *m.* 2. aparādha, *m.* 3. āsādana, *nt.* 4. virodha ; 5. kopa ; rosa, *m.* °**less**, *a.* niddosa.

Offend, *v.t.* apasādeti ; āsādeti ; aparajjhati. *v.i.* padussati. *p.p.* °dita ; aparaddha ; paduṭṭha. °**er**, *n.* āsādaka ; pakopaka, *m.*

Offensive, *n.* viruddhakriyā, *f.* virodha, *m.* adj. kopajanaka ; virodhuppādaka ; appiya ; pīḷākara. °**ly**, *adv.* appiyākārena ; viruddhākārena. °**ness**, *n.* pīḷājanakatta ; appiyatta ; sadosatta, *nt.*

Offer, *n.* 1. abhihāra ; upanikkhepa, *m.* paṭiññā, *f.* 2. agghaniyamana, *nt.* *v.t.* appeti ; upanāmeti ; abhiharati. *p.p.* appita ; °mita ; abhihāṭa. °**er**, *n.* abhihāraka ; upanetu, *m.* °**ing**, *n.* pūjā, *f.* upahāra, *m.* yajana; upanayana, *nt.*—**opposition**, paṭivirujjhati. — **violence**, pahāraŋ deti.

Offertory, *n.* (sāmayika-) chandaka-saŋharaṇa, *nt.*

Office, *n.* 1. kicca ; kāriya, *nt.* 2. ṭhānantara ; pada, *nt.* adhikāra, *m.* 3. kiccālaya, *m.* °**bearer**, *n.* ṭhānantarika, *m.* °**er**, *n.* padaṭṭha ; dhurandhara ; adhikārī, *m.* °**cial**, *n.* rājapurisa, *m.* adj. rajjakiccāyatta. °**cially**, *adv.* rajjakiccavasena. °**cialdom**, adhikārīgaṇa, *m.*

Officiate, *v.i.* adhikāre abhiyuñjati ; dhurāyattakiccaŋ sampādeti. *p.p.* °abhiyutta ; sampādita°ca.

Officinal, *a.* vikkeyyosadhāyatta.

Officious, *a.* adhikānuggahasīlī. °**ly**, *adv.* adhikānuggahakāmatāya.

Offing, *n.* samudde dissamānadūraṭṭhāna, *nt.*

Offish, *a.* unnatikāma.

Offscourings, *n. pl.* kacavara ; dhotamala, *nt.*

Offset, *n*. 1. ārambha, *m*. 2. nikkhanta-sākhā, (pabbatādīnaŋ), *f*.

Offshoot, *n*. 1. pāroha, *m*. sākhā, *f*. 2. niggatakoṭṭhāsa, *m*.

Offspring, *n*. 1. pajā, *f*. apacca, *nt*. paramparā, *f*. 2. phala, *nt*.

Oft, **Often**, *adv*. askiŋ ; abhiṇhaŋ ; anekavāraŋ ; anekadā.

Ogle, *v.i*. piyacakkhunā oloketi. *p.p*. °kita.

Ogre, *n*. rakkhasa ; dānava, *m*. °**ss**, *n*. rakkhasī, *f*.

Oh, see **O**.

Oho, *intj*. vimhaye tuṭṭhiyā canipāto.

Oil, *n*. tela, *nt*. sineha, *m*. *v.t*. telena makkheti ; sineheti. *p.p*. °khita ; °hita. °**ing**, *n*. sinehana, abbhañjana, *nt*. °**cake**, telapūva, *m*. °**cloth**, sitthakavattha, *nt*. °**iness** *n*. telagatikatā, *f*. °**man**, *n*. telavāṇija, *m*.—**mill**, *n*. telayanta, *nt*. °**paint**, *n*. telacittakamma, *nt*.

Oily, *a*. 1. satela ; 2. upalālaka.

Ointment, *n*. vilepana ; abbhañjana, *nt*.

Ola, *n*. tālapaṇṇa, *nt*.

Old, *a*. 1. vuddha ; mahallaka ; 2. purāṇa ; jiṇṇa. — **age**, jarā, *f*. vuddhavaya, *m*. °**en**, *a*. purātana ; cirantana. °**er**, *a*. vuddhatara ; jiṇṇatara. °**ish**, *a*. atikkantayobbana.— **maid**, thullakumārī, *f*.— **man**, mahallaka, *m*. °**ness**, *n*. jiṇṇatta ; mahallakatta, *nt*. — **woman**, mahallikā, *f*.

Oleander, *n*. karavīra ; assamāraka, *m*.

Olfaction, *n*. ghāyana, *nt*.

Olfactory, *n*. ghāṇindriya, *nt*. adj. ghāṇāyatta.

Olibanum, *n*. turukkha, *m*.

Olid, *a*. pūtigandhika.

Oligarch, *n*. pālakasabhika, *m*. °**y**, *n*. kuḍḍarajja ; katipayapālana, *nt*.

Oliguria, *n*. mandamuttatā, *f*.

Olio, *n*. missita-bhojana, *nt*.

Olive, *n*. jitarukkha, *m*. °**green**, *a*. haritapītaka.

Ology, (o-logy), vijjā, *f*.

Olympiad, *n*. mahākīḷāsamaya, *m*.

Olympic, *a*. catuvassika-kīḷāyatta.

Ombrology, *n*. meghavijjā, *f*.

Omen, *n*. nimitta ; pubbanimitta, *nt*. Bad —, dunnimitta, *nt*. Good —, subhanimitta, *nt*.

Ominous, *a*. asubhasūcaka ; avamaṅgala. °**ly**, *adv*. avamaṅgalākārena.

Omission, *n*. hāpana ; vajjana, *nt*. pamādadosa, *m*.

Omit, *v.t*. jahāti ; vajjeti ; cajati ; parihāpeti. *p.p*. jahita ; °jita ; catta ; °pita.

Omnibus, mahāratha, *m*. adj. bavhatthasādhaka.

Omnifarious, *a*. sabbākāra.

Omnipotent, *a*. sabbabaladhara. °**ence**, *n*. anantasatti, *f*.

Omnipresent, *a*. sabbavyāpī ; sabbattha-vijjamāna. °**ence**, *n*. sabbavyāpitā, *f*.

Omniscient, *a*. sabbaññū ; sabbavidū. °**ence**, *n*. sabbaññutā.

Omnium gatherum, *n*. sabbapakkhika-sannipāta, *m*.

Omnivorous, *a*. sabbabhakkha.

Omophagic, *a.* āmakamaŋsabhojī.

Omphalos, *n.* nābhi, *f.*

On, *prep. adv.* upari ; matthake. **— account of,** paṭicca ; nissāya ; ārabbha, *ind.* **— all sides,** sabbato ; samantato, *ind.* **°coming,** *n.* upagamana, *nt.* **— his arrival,** tasmiŋ āgate. **°looker,** udikkhaka, *m.* **— the other hand,** aññathā ; itarathā, *adv.* **— the same day,** tadahu, *ind.* **— that account,** tato nidānaŋ ; tannimittaŋ. **°ward,** *a.* abhimukhagāmī. **°wards,** *adv.* agge ; purato ; abhimukhe.

Onager, *n.* vanagadrabha, *m.*

Onanism, *n.* ayathāsukkavissaṭṭhi, *f.*

Once, *adv.* ekadā ; ekavāraŋ ; ekakkhattuŋ ; sakiŋ. **— a week,** sattāhavārena ; anusattāhaŋ, *adv.* **— more,** *adv.* puna pi. **— upon a time,** atīte ; pubbe ; purā. **At —,** sapadi ; taṅkhaṇaŋ, *adv.*

Oncology, *n.* phoṭavijjā, *f.* **°otomy,** *n.* gaṇḍaphālana, *nt.*

One, *a.* eka. *pron.* koci. **— and a half,** diyaḍḍha, *nt.* **— by one,** ekeka, *a.* **— day,** ekadā, *adv.* **°eyed,** ekakkhika, *a.* **—another,** aññamaññaŋ, *adv.* **°ness,** ekatta, *nt.* ekībhāva, *m.* **— pointedness,** ekaggatā, *f.* ekodibhāva, *m.* **°'s own,** nija ; saka ; sakīya, *a.* **°self,** sayaŋ ; sāmaŋ, *ind.* **In — way,** ekadhā, *adv.*

Oneirocritic, *a. n.* supinatthappakāsaka, *m.*

Onerous, *a.* bhāriya ; durubbaha. **°ly,** *adv.* bhāriyākārena. **°ness,** *n.* garutta, *nt.*

Onesided, *a.* ekapassika ; ekadesika.

Onfall, *n.* abhibhavana ; ajjhottharaṇa, *nt.*

Onion, *n.* palaṇḍu, *m.*

Only, *adv.* kevalaŋ ; eva. adj. kevala ; ekākī ; adutiya. **— for,** yāvad'eva. **— once,** sakid'eva.

Onomatopoe, *n.* anukaraṇasadda, *m.* **°tic,** *a.* saddānukaraṇānugata. **°tically,** *adv.* saddānugamanavasena.

Onrush, *n.* ādhāvana ; pakkhandana, *nt.*

Onset, *n.* abhisampāta, *m.* akkamana ; pahāradāna, *nt.*

Onslaught, *n.* abhighāta, *m.* sahasā paharaṇa, *nt.*

Ontology, *n.* sattā-vīmaŋsā, *f.* **°ist,** *n.* sattā-vādī, *m.*

Onus, *n.* kiccabhāra ; adhikāra, *m.*

Onym, *n.* paribhāsā, *f.* **°ous,** *a.* visesanāmayutta.

Onyx, *n.* kabaramaṇi, *m.*

Oof, *n.* rūpiya ; mūla, *nt.* **°y,** *a.* dhanavantu.

Oology, *n.* sakuṇaṇḍavijjā, *f.*

Ooze, *n.* 1. allakaddama, *m.* 2. rajanavisesa, *m.* 3. sanditavatthu, *nt.* *v.t.* paggharati ; passandati. *p.p.* °rita ; °dita. **°zy,** *a.* paggharaṇapakatika. **°iness,** *n.* sandamānatta, *nt.*

Opacity, *n.* anacchatā ; pabhāvinivijjhiyatā, *f.*

Opal, *n.* upalamaṇi, *m.* **°ine,** *a.* upalasadisa.

Opaque, *a.* nippabha ; vinivijjhāpassiya. **°ness,** *n.* anacchatta ; kālusiya, *nt.*

Open, *a.* vivaṭa ; anāvaṭa ; asaŋvuta ; pasārita ; pākaṭa. *v.t.* 1. vivarati ; ugghāṭeti ; 2. āvīkaroti ; pākaṭīkaroti ; 3. (of meaning :) vyākhyāti ; 4. (of eyes :) ummīleti. *v.i.* vikasati ; pupphati. *p.p.* vivaṭa ; °ṭita ; āvīkata ; °kata ; °khyāta ; °lita ; °sita ; pupphita. — **air,** abbhokāsa, *m.* °**armed,** *a.* nivyāja. °**eared,** *a.* ohitasota. °**er,** *n.* vivaritu ; ugghāṭaka, *m.* °**eyed,** *a.* vimhayākula. °**handed,** *a.* payatapāṇī ; vossaggarata, *m.* °**hearted,** *a.* akapaṭa ; akuṭila. °**ing,** *n.* 1. vivaraṇa ; vikasana ; anāvaraṇa, *nt.* 2. vivara ; chidda, *nt.* °**ly,** *adv.* āvī ; pākaṭavasena. °**minded,** *a.* adīnacitta. °**mouthed,** *a.* mukhara ; vācāla. °**ness,** *n.* vivaṭatta ; akuṭilatta, *nt.* — **space,** *n.* aṅgaṇa ; vivaṭaṭṭhāna, *nt.*

Opera, *n.* sasaṅgītanāṭaka, *nt.*

Operate, *v.i.* balaŋ pavatteti ; kiccakārī hoti. *v.t.* sallakammaŋ karoti. *p.p.* pavattitabala ; °bhūta ; katasallakamma. °**ion,** *n.* 1. vyāpāra, *m.* kicca, *nt.* 2. sallakamma, *nt.* °**ive,** *a.* kiccasādhaka ; payojaka. *noun :* sippī ; kammakāra, *m.* °**tor,** *n.* 1. pavattāpaka ; 2. sallavejja ; sallakatta, *m.*

Operose, *a.* kicchasādhiya. °**ly,** *adv.* kicchena ; kasirena. °**ness,** *n.* dukkaratta, *nt.*

Ophiolater, *n.* sappanamassaka ; nāgapūjaka, *m.*

Ophiology, *n.* sappavijjā, *f.*

Ophiophagous, *a.* sappabhakkha.

Ophthalmia, *n.* nettābhisanda ; akkhidāha, *m.* °**mic,** *a.* nettavisayaka ; abhissandayutta. °**mist,** *n.* akkhivejja, *m.*

Ophthalmology, *n.* nayanavijjā, *f.* °**moscope,** *n.* nayanabbhantaranidassaka, *m.* °**motomy,** *n.* nayanasallakamma, *nt.*

Opiate, *a.* niddājanaka ; ahipheṇayutta. *noun :* niddājanakosadha, *nt.* *v.t.* ahipheṇena misseti. *p.p.* °sita.

Opine, *v.t.* ajjhāsayaŋ dhāreti ; mataŋ pakāseti. *p.p.* dharitaj° ; pakāsitamata.

Opinion, *n.* mata, *nt.* mati, *f.* ajjhāsaya ; adhippāya, *m.* °**ative,** °**ated,** *a.* ādhānagāhī ; attanomatika.

Opium, *n.* ahipheṇa, *nt.* *v.t.* ahipheṇena tikicchati.

Oppilate, *v.t.* avarodheti. *p.p.* avaruddha.

Opponency, *n.* virodha, *m.*

Opponent, *n.* paccatthika ; paṭipakkha ; amitta ; verī, *m.* adj. viruddha ; paccanika ; paccatthika.

Opportune, *a.* samayocita ; kālānurūpa ; pattāvasara. °**ly,** *adv.* yathāsamayaŋ ; yathākāle ; yathocitaŋ. °**ism,** *n.* kālocitavutti, *f.* °**ity,** *n.* pattakāla ; avasara ; okāsa ; vāra, *m.*

Oppose, *v.t.* virujjhati. *p.p.* viruddha. °**ed,** *a.* paṭipakkha ; paṭiloma ; viloma ; vipakkha. °**able,** *a.* virujjhitabba ; paṭikkosiya. °**less,** *a.* anivāriya ; bādhārahita.

Opposite, *a.* 1. viruddha ; paṭipakkha ; 2. abhimukha ; paṭimukha; paṭikūla. *n.* vipariyāya, *m.* — **bank,** paratīra, *nt.* °**ly,** *adv.* viparītaŋ; paṭilomaŋ. °**tion,** *n.* virodha, *m.* vipakkhatta, *nt.* — **wind,** paṭivāta, *m.*

Oppress, *v.t.* uppīḷeti; ābādheti; vyathati; heṭheti; omaddati. *p.p.* °ḷita; °dhita; °thita; °dita. °**ion,** *n.* upapīḷana; viheṭhana; bādhana; pajāpīḷana, *nt.* °**ive,** *a.* pīḷaka; bādhaka; viheṭhaka. °**or,** *n.* pajāpīḷaka; visamācāra. °**ively,** *adv.* pajāpīḷanena; vihiŋsāya.

Opprobrious, *a.* sopavāda. °**ly,** *adv.* sopavādaŋ.

Opprobrium, *n.* apakitti; ayasa; apavāda; upavāda, *m.*

Oppugn, *v.t.* vivadati; paṭipucchati. *p.p.* °dita; °chita. °**ation,** *n.* vivadana, *nt.*

Opsimath, *n.* vuddha-sissa, *m.*

Optative, *n.* Sattamī vibhatti, *f.* adj. icchatthaka; icchāpakāsaka.

Optic, *n.* cakkhu; nayana, *nt.* *a.* nayanapaṭibaddha. °**al,** *a.* dassanavisayaka. °**ian,** *n.* 1. upanettavāṇija; 2. diṭṭhisatthaññū, *m.* pl. diṭṭhivijjā, *f.*

Optimism, *n.* sabbasubhavāda, *m.* °**ist,** *n.* sabbasubhavādī, *m.*

Option, *n.* abhiruci; icchā, *f.* abhilāsa, *m.* °**al,** *a.* yathicchaka; vikappasiddha. °**ally,** *adv.* vikappena.

Opulent, *a.* aḍḍha; mahaddhana; mahābhoga. °**nce,** *n.* samiddhi; sampatti, *f.* vibhava, *m.* °**ly,** *adv.* aḍḍhākārena.

Opus, *n.* paccekasaṅgītaracanā, *f.* °**cule,** *n.* khuddakagītaracanā, *f.*

Or, *conj.* vā; atha vā; (In questioning:) uda; udāhu; nu. — **else,** vā pana.

Oracle, *n.* devavākya; anāgatañāṇa, *nt.* °**cular,** *a.* devavākyāyatta.

Oral, *a.* mukhapāṭhābhata. °**ly,** *adv.* paṭhanavasena.

Orange, *n.* jambīra, *m.* °**coloured,** *a.* pītaratta. °**ry,** *n.* jambīravatthu, *nt.*

Orang-outang, °**utan,** *n.* mahāvānaravisesa, *m.*

Orate, *v.t.* deseti. *p.p.* desita. °**ion,** *n.* cittakathā, *f.* sālaṅkāravacana, *nt.* °**tor,** *n.* cittakathī, *m.* °**tory,** *n.* 1. vācāpaṭutta; vāgīsatta, *nt.* 2. puggalikadevāyatana, *nt.*

Orb, *n.* 1. maṇḍala; āvaṭṭa; 2. goḷaka; 3. akkhigoḷa, *nt.* *v.t.* goḷattaŋ pāpeti. *v.i.* goḷībhavati. *p.p.* °pāpita; °bhūta. °**icular,** *a.* vaṭṭula; goḷākāra; cakkākāra.

Orbit, *n.* 1. gahatārāpatha, *m.* 2. akkhikūpa, *m.*

Orchard, *n.* phalārāma, *m.*

Orchestic, *a.* naccāyatta. *pl.* naccakalā, *f.*

Orchestra, *n.* 1. vādakasamūha, *m.* 2. vādittamaṇḍapa, *m.*

Ordain, *v.t.* 1. sammannati; niddisati; 2. pabbājeti. *p.p.* sammata; niddiṭṭha; °jita. °**er,** *n.* paññāpaka; pabbājaka, *m.* °**ment,** *n.* 1. paññāpana; 2. pabbājana; upasampādana, *nt.*

Ordeal, *n.* tattaparikkhā; saccavīmaŋsā, *f.*

Order, *n.* 1. paṭipāṭi, *f.* kama; anukkama; anvaya, *m.* 2. niyoga, *m.* āṇā; āṇatti, *f.* 3. gaṇa;

vagga; nikāya, *m.* *v.t.* āṇāpeti; niyameti; saŋvidahati. *p.p.* °pita; °mita; saŋvihita. °**er,** *n.* āṇāpaka, *m.* °**less,** *a.* ayathākkamaka; bhinnapaṭipāṭika. °**ly,** *a.* vavatthita; kamānugagata; anukkamika. *n.* upaṭṭhambhaka-sevaka, *m.* **Holy —,** ariyasaṅgha, *m.* **In —,** anupubbena; paṭipāṭiyā; yathākkamaŋ. **In — to,** atthāya. **Out of —,** uppaṭipāṭika; bhinnakkama, *a.*

Ordinal, *n.* kamavācakasaṅkhyā, *f.* adj. kamavācī.

Ordinance, *n.* vavatthā; niyamāvali, *f.* niyoga, *m.* °**nant,** *a.* niyāmaka.

Ordinary, *a.* sādhāraṇa; avisiṭṭha; sāmañña. °**ily,** *adv.* sāmaññena; avisesato. °**ness,** *n.* sāmaññatā; avisiṭṭhatā, *f.*

Ordinate, *a.* kamānugata; ānupubbika. °**ion,** *n.* 1. patiṭṭhāpana, *nt.* 2. pabbajjā, *f.*

Ordnance, *n.* yuddhayantasamūha, *m.*

Ordure, *n.* karīsa; mīḷha, *nt.* ukkāra; asuci, *m.*

Ore, *n.* asodhita-khaṇijadhātu, *f.*

Oread, *n.* giridevatā, *f.*

Organ, *n.* 1. mahāturiya, *nt.* 2. avayava, *m.* 3. indriyāyatana, *nt.* 4. (of a society :) kālikasaṅgaha, *m.* °**ic,** *a.* indriyabaddha. °**ism,** *n.* saŋvidahana, *nt.* racanā, *f.* °**ist,** *n.* mahāturiyavādaka, *m.* **— of generation,** aṅgajāta; rahassaṅga, *nt.* **— of smell,** ghāṇāyatana, *nt.* **— of taste,** jivhāyatana, *nt.* **— of touch,** kāyappasāda, *m.*

Organize, *v.t.* saŋvidahati: sammā vavatthapeti. *p.p.* saŋvihita; °pita. °**ation,** *n.* saŋvidahana, *nt.* vinyāsa, *m.* racanā, *f.*

Organology, *n.* avayavavibhāga, *m.*

Organon, *n.* 1. takkanahetu; 2. ñāyagantha, *m.*

Orgasm, *n.* 1. adhikavega, *m.* 2. accantakāmāsā, *f.*

Orgy, *n.* 1. surāchaṇa, *m.* 2. devapūjāvisesa, *m.*

Orient, *n.* 1. pācīnadesa, *m.* 2. pubbadisā, *f.* adj. udenta; uggacchamāna. °**al,** *a.* pācīna; pubbadesīya. *n.* pācīnavāsī, *m.* °**alist,** *n.* pācīnabhāsaññū, *m.*

Orifice, *n.* chidda; vivara, *nt.* **— of the ear,** sotabila; kaṇṇacchidda, *nt.*

Origin, *n.* mūluppatti, *f.* nidāna, *nt.* pabhava; samudaya, *m.* yoni; sañjāti, *f.* °**al,** *a.* ādima; mūlabhūta. *noun :* mūlabhūtavatthu, *nt.* °**ality,** *n.* apubbatā; navakappanā, *f.* sayampaṭibhāṇa. *nt.* °**ally,** *adv.* ādito; mūlato; paṭhamaŋ.

Originate, *v.t.* janeti; uppādeti; nibbatteti; samuṭṭhāpeti. *v.i.* jāyati; pabhavati; uppajjati; samuṭṭhāti, *p.p.* janita; °dita; °tita; °pita; jāta; pabhūta; uppanna; samuṭṭhita. °**ing,** *a.* nibbattaka; uṭṭhāpaka. °**ion,** *n.* uppatti, *f.* ubbhava; samudaya, *m.* samuṭṭhāna, *nt.* °**tor,** *n.* janetu; uppādetu; nibbattetu.

Orinasal, *a.* anunāsika.

Orion, *n.* migasiranakkhatta, *nt.*

Orison, *a.* āyācanā; patthanā, *f.*

Ornament, *n.* ābharaṇa; piḷandhana; pasādhana; vibhūsana, *nt.* alaṅkāra, *m.* *v.t.* bhūseti;

vibhūseti ; maṇḍeti ; pasādheti ; alaṅkaroti. *p.p.* °sita ; °ḍita ; °dhita ; alaṅkata. °**al,** *a.* bhūsanāyatta ; maṇḍanopakāraka. °**ally,** *adv.* maṇḍanavasena. °**ation,** *n.* 1. maṇḍana ; bhūsana ; alaṅkaraṇa ; 2. cittakamma, *nt.*

Ornate, *a.* alaṅkata ; bhūsita.

Ornithology, *n.* pakkhivijjā, *f.* °**ist,** *n.* pakkhivijjāvidū, *m.*

Ornithomancy, *n.* sakuṇarutavijjā, *f.*

Orography, *n.* pabbatavijjā, *f.*

Orology, *n.* giripabhedañāṇa, *nt.*

Orotund, *a.* madhuragambhīra.

Orphan, *n.* *a.* nimmātāpitika. °**age,** *n.* 1. nimmātāpitikatta, *nt.* 2. anāthadārakanivāsa, *m.*

Orpiment, *n.* haritāla, *nt.*

Orrery, *n.* gahagamanadīpakayanta, *nt.*

Orris, *n.* vacā ; golomī, *f.*

Ort, *n.* āhārato chaḍḍanīyavatthu, *nt.*

Orthodox, *a.* dhammaladdhika ; saccānugata. °**y,** *n.* sammādiṭṭhi, *f.*

Orthoepist, *n.* suṭṭhuccāraka, *m.*

Orthogon, *n.* samacaturassa, *nt.* °**al,** *a.* caturaŋsika.

Orthography, *n.* akkharavinyāsa ; akkharasamaya, *m.*

Orthometry, *n.* niddosapajjaracanā, *f.*

Oscillate, *v.i.* dolāyati ; phandati. *p.p.* °yita ; °dita. °**ing,** *a.* dolāyamāna. °**ion,** *n.* dolāyana ; phandana, *nt.*

Oscitant, *a.* vijambhamāna.

Oscitation, *n.* jambhanā, pamattatā, *f.*

Oscular, *a.* mukhāyatta ; vadanāyatta.

Osculate, *v.i.t.* cumbati. *p.p.* cumbita. °**ion,** *n.* cumbana, *nt.* °**tory,** *a.* cumbanāyatta.

Osprey, *n.* ukkuha ; kurara, *m.*

Osseous, *a.* aṭṭhimaya ; aṭṭhibhūta.

Ossicle, *n.* khuddakaṭṭhi, *nt.*

Ossify, *v.t.* aṭṭhisadisaŋ karoti. *p.p.* °kata.

Ossuary, *n.* matakaṭṭhi-agāra, *nt.*

Ostensible, a. vyāja ; ayathābhūta ; kittima. °**bly,** *adv.* vyājena ; ayathā. °**sive,** *a.* ayathādassaka.

Ostentation, *n.* dappa ; ahaṅkāra ; bāhirālaṅkara, *m.*

Ostentatious, *a.* attukkaŋsaka ; dappita. °**ly,** *adv.* sadappaŋ ; sāhaṅkāraŋ.

Osteography, *n.* aṭṭhivaṇṇanā, *f.*

Osteology, *n.* aṭṭhivijjā, *f.*

Ostler, *n.* santhāgāra-assagopaka, *m.*

Ostracize, *v.t.* (raṭṭhā) pabbājeti ; nibbāseti. *p.p.* °jita ; °sita. °**cism,** *n.* nibbāsana, *nt.*

Ostrich, *n.* oṭṭhasakuṇa, *m.*

Other, *a.* itara ; para ; apara. — **gates,** *adv.* aññamaggena. °**ness,** *n.* aparatta, *nt.* °**wise,** *adv.* aññathā ; itarathā. **At — times,** aññadā, *adv.* **The — day,** aparajju, *ind.* **The others,** aññe, apare ; itare, *m. pl.*

Otic, *a.* sotapaṭibaddha.

Otiose, *a.* 1. alasa ; 2. nipphala ; 3. anapekkhita ; 4. kriyāvirahita. °**ly,** *adv.* akammaniyākārena.

Otitis, *n.* kaṇṇapāka, *m.*

Otter, *n.* udda; jalamajjāra, *m.*

Ought, *n.* yaŋ kiñci. *v.i.* arahati; vaṭṭati; yujjati.

Ounce, *n.* 1. cha-dharaṇabhāra, *m.* 2. dīpivisesa, *m.*

Our, *poss. pl.* amhākaŋ.

Ours, *poss. pl. a.* amhāyatta.

Ourself, *pron.* mayam eva; mayaŋ attanā va.

Oust, *v.t.* apanudati; nikkhāmeti; bahikaroti. *p.p.* °dita; °mita; bahikata.

Out, *adv.* bahi; bahiddhā. — **of danger,** antarāyamutta, *a.* — **of food,** nirāhāra, *a.* — **of hope,** gatāsa; nirapekkha, *a.* — **of kindness,** anukampāya, *adv.* — **of office,** bhaṭṭhādhikāra, *a.* — **of one's mind,** vikkhittacitta, *a.* — **of one's reach,** avisaya; apattabba, *a.* — **of order,** uppaṭipāṭika, *a.* — **of pity,** anukampam upādāya. — **of place,** aṭṭhānika; anucita, *a.* — **of print,** apuna-muddita, *a.* — **of sight,** dassanātikkanta, *a.* — **of time,** ayathākālika, *a.* — **of use,** gatavohāra; luttaparibhoga, *a.* — **of the way place,** dūraṭṭhāna, *nt.* — **of work,** nikkamma, *a.* °**ward,** *a.* bāhirābhimukha. °**ward-bound,** *a.* videsagāmī, *a.* °**wardly,** *adv.* bāhirato. °**wards,** *adv.* bahiddhā.

Out, *intj.* apehi; apasara.

Outact, *v.t.* aticarati; atikaroti. *p.p.* °carita; °kata.

Outbalance, *v.t.* atirekataŋ yāti; (pamāṇam) atikkamati. *p.p.* °yāta; atikkanta°.

Outbid, *v.t.* adhikagghaṭhapanena kiṇāti. *p.p.* °kīta.

Outbluster, *v.t.* atirekaŋ gajjati. *p.p.* °jita.

Outbrave, *v.i.* ativiya nibbhayo hoti.

Outbreak, *n.* 1. sahasā uṭṭhāna; ubbhijjana; 2. rogapattharaṇa, *nt. v.i.* 1. pariyuṭṭhāti; 2. sahasā pattharati. *p.p.* pariyuṭṭhita; °patthaṭa.

Outbuilding, *n.* bahighara, *nt.*

Outburst, *n.* sahasā-niggama, *m.* sasaddabhijjana, *nt.*

Outcast, *n.* 1. bahikata; 2. hīnajacca; vasala, *m.*

Outcome, *n.* nissanda; vipāka, *m.* phala, *nt.*

Outcry, *n.* ugghosana, *nt.* tumulanāda, *m.*

Outdare, *v.t.* vikkamena atiseti.

Outdo, *v.t.* acceti; atikkamati; abhibhavati. *p.p.* atikkanta; abhibhūta.

Outdoor, *a.* abbhokāsika.

Outer, *a.* bāhiratara. °**most,** *a.* atibāhira; paribāhira.

Outface, *v.i.* 1. bhākuṭiŋ karoti; 2. antarāyābhimukhaŋ yāti. *p.p.* katabhākuṭī; °yāta.

Outfit, *n.* parivaccha; paricchada, *m.* maggopakaraṇa, *nt. v.t.* parivacchaŋ karoti *or* sajjeti. *p.p.* kataparivaccha.

Outflow, *n.* abhisanda; pasava, *m.*

Outgo, *n.* vaya, *m.* vissajjana, *nt. v.t.* acceti; atikkamati. *p.p.* atikkanta. °**ing,** *n.* vaya; khaya; apacaya, *m.* °**ing,** *a.* bahigāmi.

Outgrow, *v.t.* atikkamma vaḍḍhati. *p.p.* °ḍhita. °**th,** *n.* bāhiravaḍḍhi, *f.*

Outhouse, *n.* upaghara, *nt.*

Outland, *n.* paradesa, *m.* °**ish**, *a.* videsīya. °**er**, *n.* videsī, *m.*

Outlast, *v.i.* cirakālaŋ pavattati. *p.p.* °tita.

Outlaw, *n.* likhita-cora, *m.* *v.t.* sambhogaŋ nivāreti ; nītiyā bahikaroti. *p.p.* °ritasambhoga ; °bahikata. °**ry**, *n.* pabbājanakamma, *nt.*

Outlay, *n.* vaya, *m.* vissajjana, *nt.*

Outleap, *n.* pakkhandana, *nt.*

Outlet, *n.* niggama, *m.* nikkhamaṇadvāra, *nt.*

Outline, *n.* 1. bāhirasaṇṭhāna, *nt.* 2. saṅkhittavaṇṇanā, *f.* *v.t.* 1. saṇṭhānam ālikhati ; 2. saṅkhepato nirūpeti. *p.p.* ālikhita ; °pita.

Outlive, *v.i.* atikkamma *or* dīghatarakālaŋ jīvati.

Outlook, *n.* 1. apekkhā ; paccāsā, *f.* 2. diṭṭhipāta, *m.*

Outlying, *a.* dūraṭṭha ; asaŋsaṭṭha.

Outmarch, *v.i.* agge yāti ; atikkamati. *p.p.* °yāta ; atikkanta.

Outmost, *a.* bāhiratama.

Outnumber, *v.t.* saṅkhyāya atikkamati. *p.p.* atikkantasaṅkhya.

Outpace, *v.t.* hitvā yāti ; atikkamati. *p.p.* °yāta ; atikkanta.

Outpour, *n.* dhārānipāta, *m.* *v.i.* dhārāhi nipatati. *p.p.* °tita.

Output, *n.* nipphādita-pamāṇa, *nt.*

Outquench, *v.t.* nibbāpeti ; upasameti. *p.p.* °pita ; °samita.

Outrage, *n.* 1. dūsana, *nt.* atyācāra ; 2. balakkāra, *m.* *v.t.* 1. dūseti ; kalaṅketi ; 2. pasayha carati. *p.p.* dūsita ; °kita ; °carita. °**ous**, *a.* sāhasika ; atiduṭṭha. °**ously**, *adv.* ghoraŋ ; dāruṇākārena. °**ousness**, *n.* sāhasikatta ; dāruṇatta, *nt.*

Outreach, *v.t.* dūrataraŋ pāpuṇāti *or* pattharati. *p.p.* °patta ; patthaṭa.

Outrider, *n.* pacchārohaka, *m.*

Outright, *adv.* 1. sapadi ; taṅkhaṇaŋ ; 2. sabbathā ; nissesaŋ.

Outrival, *v.i.* visiṭṭhatamo bhavati.

Outroot, see **Eradicate.**

Outrun, *v.t.* atikkamitvā dhāvati.

Outset, *n.* ārambha ; ādi, *m.* paṭṭhapana, *nt.*

Outshine, *v.i.* atirocati. *p.p.* °cita.

Outside, *n.* bāhirabhāga, *m.* adj. bāhira, *adv.* bahiddhā. °**er**, *n.* 1. parajana ; bāhiraka ; 2. aparicita, *m.*

Outskirt, *n.* pariyanta ; paccanta, *m.*

Outspoken, *a.* uttānavacana ; tathavādī ; thiravacana. °**ly**, *adv.* vyattaŋ ; visadaŋ ; uttānaŋ ; ujukaŋ.

Outspread, *v.t.* vitthāreti ; pasāreti ; vitanoti. *p.p.* °rita ; vitata.

Outstanding, *a.* 1. bahiniggata ; sudissamāna ; 2. anipphanna ; 3. asañcita (-iṇa-karādi).

Outstare, *v.t.* bhākuṭikaraṇena lajjāpeti. *p.p.* °pita.

Outstretch, *v.t.* pasāreti ; vitanoti. *p.p.* °rita ; vitata.

Outstrip, *v.t.* atikkamma yāti. *p.p.* °yāta.

Outvie, see **Excel.**

Outwear, *v.t.* ciraŋ nivāseti *or* paridahati. *p.p.* °nivattha ; °hita.

Outweigh, *v.t.* bhārena atiriccati. *p.p.* atirittabhāra.

Outwit, see **Cheat.**

Outwork, *n.* bahiddhārakkhā, *f.*
Outworn, *a.* jiṇṇa; jajjara.
Oval, Ovate, *a.* aṇḍākāra.
Ovary, *n.* aṇḍāṣaya, *m.* °**ious,** *a.* aṇḍuppādaka.
Ovation, *n.* ussavena paṭiggahaṇa, *nt.*
Oven, *n.* āvāpa, *m.* uddhana, *m.*
Over, *adv.* upari; uttariŋ; uddhaŋ. *prep.* ati; abhi; adhi; pati. —**again,** puna pi. —**against,** *adv.* abhimukhaŋ. —**and over,** punappunaŋ. **All** —, 1. sabbattha; 2. paripuṇṇaŋ, *adv.* uparima; upariṭṭha, *a.* **Give** — pajahati; appeti. **Is** —, niṭṭhitaŋ.
Overact, *v.t.* aticarati; pamāṇam atikkamati. *p.p.* °rita; atikkantapamāṇa.
Overalls, *n. pl.* paridhānāvaraṇa, *nt.*
Overawe, *v.t.* bhāyāpeti; abhibhavati. *p.p.* °pita; abhibhūta.
Overbalance, *v.t.* atituleti. *p.p.* °lita.
Overbear, *v.t.* dameti; vasīkaroti. *p.p.* danta; vasīkata. °**ing,** *a.* uddhata; dappita. °**ingly,** *adv.* sadappaŋ; uddhatākāreṇa.
Overbeg, *v.t.* atiyācati. *p.p.* °cita.
Overboard, *adv.* nāvāya bahi.
Overbold, *a.* atinibbhaya; atisāhasika.
Overburden, *v.t.* adhikabhāram āropeti. *p.p.* °pita.
Overcast, *v.t.* paṭicchādeti; āvarati. *p.p.* °dita; āvaṭa. adj. meghacchanna; timirāvuta.
Overcautious, *a.* atisaṅkita.
Overcharge, *v.t.* adhikamūlaŋ niyameti. *p.p.* niyamitādhikamūla. *n.* adhikamūlaniyamana, *nt.*
Overcloud, see **Overcast.**
Overcoat, *n.* bāhira-kañcuka, *m.*
Overcome, *v.t.* ativattati; pasahati; abhibhavati; pamaddati. *p.p.* °tita; °hita; abhibhūta; °dita. adj. aṭṭita; pareta; parājita. °**ing,** *n.* pasahana; abhibhavana, *nt.*
Overcrowd, *v.t.* sambādheti; nirantaraŋ pūreti. *p.p.* °dhita; °pūrita.
Overdo, *v.t.* adhikaŋ viheseti; kilameti. *p.p.* °sita; °mita.
Overdose, *n.* adhika-bhesajjapāna, *nt.*
Overdraw, *v.t.* adhikataramūlaŋ gaṇhāti. *p.p.* gahitādhika°.
Overdress, *v.t.* ujjalavesaŋ dhāreti. *p.p.* dhāritujjalavesa.
Overdue, *a.* niyamitakālātikkanta.
Overeat, *v.t.* atimattaŋ bhuñjati; bhojane amattaññū hoti. *p.p.* °bhutta.
Overestimate, *v.t.* pamāṇādhikaŋ agghāpeti. *p.p.* °pita.
Overfatigue, *n.* adhikaparissama, *m.* *v.t.* atikilameti. *p.p.* °mita.
Overfeed, *v.t.* atimattaŋ bhojeti. *p.p.* °bhojita.
Overflow, *v.t.* ottharati. *v.i.* abhisandati; vissandati. *p.p.* otthaṭa; °dita, *n.* 1. abhisanda; 2. jalogha, *m.* 3. ottharaṇa, *nt.* °**ing,** *a.* 1. abhisandamāna; 2. atibahula.
Overgrow, *v.t.* chādetvā vaḍḍhati. *p.p.* °ḍhita. °**ing,** *a.* sulabha; bahula; ativaḍḍhamāna.
Overhang, *v.t.* upari lambeti. *v.i.* upari lambati. *p.p.* °bita.
Overhasty, *a.* atisāhasika; anisammakārī.

Overhaul, *v.t.* 1. vibhajitvā vīmaŋsati; 2. anubandhitvā pāpuṇāti. *p.p.* °sita; °patta.

Overhead, *adv.* sīsūpari; matthake.

Overhear, *v.t.* anabhilakkhito suṇāti.

Overheat, *v.t.* adhikaŋ tāpeti. *p.p.* °pita.

Overindulgence, *n.* adhikatarāsevana, *nt.*

Overjoy, *n.* pamoda, *m.* *v.t.* pahaŋseti; atipīṇeti. *p.p.* °sita *or* pahaṭṭha; °ṇita.

Overland, *a.* thalagāmī. °**route,** *n.* thalapatha, *m.*

Overlap, *v.t.* vyāpetvā *or* chādetvā tiṭṭhati. *p.p.* °ṭhita.

Overlay, *v.t.* 1. āvarati; paṭicchādeti; 2. adhikabhāram āropeti. *p.p.* āvaṭa; °dita; °pita.

Overleap, *v.t.* ullaṅgheti; uppatitvā yāti. *p.p.* °ghita; °yāta.

Overlie, *v.t.* avattharitvā tiṭṭhati. *p.p.* °ṭhita.

Overload, *v.t.* atibhāram āropeti. *p.p.* āropitātibhāra.

Overlook, *v.t.* 1. na gaṇeti; upekkhati; atikkamitvā passati; 2. anuviloketi. *v.i.* unnato dissati. *p.p.* agaṇita; °khita; °diṭṭha; °kita.

Overlord, *n.* adhissara; pabhū; abhibhū, *m.* °**ship,** *n.* issariyādhipacca, *nt.*

Overmuch, *n.* atibāhulla, *nt.* adj. atimatta. *adv.* accantaŋ; atimattaŋ.

Overnight, *adv.* pubbarattiyaŋ; rattibhāge.

Overpass, *v.t.* atikkamati; vajjeti. *p.p.* atikkanta; vajjita.

Overpay, *v.t.* adhikavetanaŋ deti. *p.p.* dinnādhikavetana.

Overpeople, *v.t.* adhikajanākiṇṇaŋ karoti. *p.p.* °kata.

Overplus, *n.* atirittabhāga; atireka, *m.*

Overpoise, *n.* mahābhāra; adhikabhāra, *m.*

Overpower, *v.t.* abhibhavati; maddati; adhivattati. *p.p.* abhibhūta; maddita; °tita.

Overproduction, *n.* adhikanipphādana, *nt.*

Overrate, *v.t.* adhikagghaŋ niyameti; adhikamūlaŋ niddisati. *p.p.* niyamitādhi°; niddiṭṭhādhika°.

Overreach, *v.t.* 1. atikkamitvā pāpuṇāti; 2. vañceti; 3. uggacchati. *p.p.* °patta; °cita; uggata.

Override, *v.i.* akkamati; atikkamati; abhimaddati. *p.p.* akkanta; atikkanta; °dita.

Overripe, *a.* atiparipakka.

Overrule, *v.t.* ñāyena paṭisedheti. *or* niggaṇhāti; abhibhavati. *v.i.* pasāsati. *p.p.* °dhita; niggahita; abhibhūta; °sita.

Overrun, *v.t.* avattharati; ajjhottharati. *p.p.* avatthaṭa; °thaṭa.

Overscrupulous, *a.* atikukkuccaka.

Oversea, *a.* videsika; pārasāmuddika. °**s,** *adv.* videse; samuddapāre.

Oversee, *v.t.* (kammantaŋ) paripāleti *or* vicāreti. *p.p.* °lita; °rita. °**er,** *n.* pālaka; adhikārī; vicāraka, *m.*

Overset, *v.t.* nikkujjeti; adhomukhīkaroti. *p.p.* °jita; °kata.

Overshadow, *v.t.* chāyāya chādeti *or* tirokaroti. *p.p.* °chādita; °tirokata.
Overshoot, *v.t.* atilakkhaŋ vijjhati. *p.p.* °viddha.
Oversight, *n.* khalita; anavadhāna, *nt.* pamādadosa, *m.*
Oversize, *a.* pamāṇātikkanta.
Oversleep, *v.t.* ativelaŋ supati. *p.p.* °sutta. *n.* dīghasoppa, *nt.*
Overspent, *a.* 1. atikilanta; 2. atikkanta; atikhīṇa.
Overspread, *v.t.* ottharati; vyāpeti; pattharati. *p.p.* otthaṭa; °pita; patthaṭa.
Overstate, *v.t.* adhikaŋ vaṇṇeti. *p.p.* °ṇita.
Overstep, *v.t.* atikkamati; atisarati. *p.p.* atikkanta; atisaṭa.
Overstock, *n.* atisañcaya, *m.* *v.t.* adhikaŋ rāsīkaroti. *p.p.* °kata.
Overstrain, *v.t.* adhikam ussahati. *p.p.* °hita.
Overt, *a.* pākaṭa; vyatta. °**ly,** *adv.* pākaṭākārena. °**ness,** *n.* pākaṭatta, *nt.*
Overtake, *v.t.* anubandhitvā gaṇhāti. *p.p.* °gahita.
Overtax, *v.t.* adhikakaraŋ gaṇhāti. *p.p.* gahitādhikakara.
Overthrow, *v.t.* 1. vināseti; 2. parājeti; 3. ucchindati. *p.p.* °sita; °jita; ucchinna.
Overtime, *n.* (niyamitakālato) adhikakāla, *m.*
Overture, *n.* 1. paṭhamārambha; upaññāsa, *m.* 2. vivecanīyavisaya, *m.*
Overturn, see **Overset.**
Overvalue, *v.t.* adhikagghaŋ ṭhapeti. *p.p.* °ṭhapita.
Overweening, *a.* attukkaŋsaka; adhikamānī.
Overweigh, *v.t.* bhārena atiriccati. *p.p.* °atiritta. °**ght,** *n.* adhikabhāra, *m.*
Overwhelm, *v.t.* 1. abhitudati; 2. osīdāpeti; 3. pariyādiyati. *p.p.* abhituṇṇa; °pita; pariyādinna.
Overwise, *a.* atipaṇḍita; paṇḍitamānī.
Overwork, *n.* adhikakicca, *nt.* atiparissama, *m.* *v.t.* 1. atiparissantaŋ karoti; 2. adhikaŋ kammaŋ karoti.
Overworn, *a.* atikilanta; paribhogajiṇṇa.
Overwrought, *a.* atiparissanta.
Overzeal, *n.* accussukatā, *f.* °**ous,** *a.* adhikussāhī.
Ovicular, *a.* aṇḍanissita.
Oviferous, *a.* aṇḍajanaka.
Oviform, *a.* aṇḍākāra.
Oviparous, *a.* 1. aṇḍajanaka; 2. aṇḍaja.
Ovine, *a.* meṇḍāyatta; meṇḍagatika.
Oviposit, *v.t.* āsāṭikaŋ nikkhipati. *p.p.* nikkhittāsāṭika. °**ion,** *n.* āsāṭikānikkhipana, *nt.*
Ovoid, *a.* aṇḍākāra.
Ovum, *n.* kalalarūpa, *nt.*
Owe, *v.i.* iṇaŋ dhāreti; iṇāyiko hoti. *p.p.* dhāritaiṇa; iṇāyikabhūta. °**ing,** *a.* nittharitabba; dātabba. °**ing to,** nissāya; hetunā.
Owl, *n.* ulūka; vāyasāri, *m.* °**et,** ulūkapotaka, *m.* °**ish,** *a.* ulūkopama; mandabuddhika. °**light,** *n.* padosa; mandāloka, *m.*
Own, *a.* saka; sakīya; nija. *v.t.* āyattaŋ *or* adhīnaŋ karoti; pariggaṇhāti. *v.i.* aṅgīkaroti; paṭi-

jānāti. *p.p.* āyattīkata; aṅgīkata; paṭiññāta. **My —**, mamāyatta. **Your —**, tavāyatta. **Our —**, amhāyatta.

Owner, *n.* sāmī; issara; pati, *m.* °**less**, *a.* assāmika. °**ship**, *n.* sāmitta; pabhutta, *nt.*

Ox, *n.* usabha; goṇa; balivadda, *m.* °**eyed**, *a.* visālakkha.

Oxide, *n.* pāṇadavāyunā missitavatthu, *nt.*

Oxidize, *v.t.* pāṇadavāyunā misseti. *p.p.* °sita.

Oxygen, *n.* pāṇadavāyu, *m.* °**ate**, *v.t.* pāṇadavāyunā tikicchati. *p.p.* °chita.

Oyster, *n.* sambuka, *m.*

Ozone, *n.* ghanībhūtapāṇadavāyu, *m.*

P

Pabulum, *n.* āhāra, *m.*

Pacable, *a.* santikara.

Pacation, *n.* vupasamana, *nt.*

Pace, *n.* 1. padapāta; padavītihāra, *m.* 2. gamana, *nt.* gati, *f.* *v.i.* caṅkamati; samaŋ yāti. *v.t.* padavārehi miṇāti. *p.p.* °mita; °yāta; °mita. °**er**, *n.* aturitagāmī, *m.*

Pacific, *a.* santikara; akkhubhita. °**ation**, *n.* 1. upasama, *m.* santi, *f.* 2. sāmaggikaraṇa, *nt.* °**ism**, *n.* yuddhavirodha, *m.*

Pacify, *v.t.* upasameti; sandhāti. *p.p.* °mita; sandahita. °**ier**, *n.* upasametu, *m.* °**ist**, *n.* yuddapaṭipakkha, *m.* °**ism**, *n.* yuddhavirodha, *m.*

Pack, *n.* 1. bhaṇḍikā, *f.* khandhabhāra, *m.* 2. (of hounds, etc.) gaṇa; yūtha; samūha, *m.* 3. (of cards:) pattikārāsi, *m.* *v.t.* puṭaŋ bandhati; bhaṇḍikaŋ karoti. (— in a box:) sannidahati, *v.i.* 1. samosarati; 2. sahasā apagacchati. *p.p.* puṭabaddha; bhaṇḍikākata; sannihita; °apagata. — **off**, apaneti; sahasā nikkhāmeti. °**horse**, *n.* bhāravāhī-assa, *m.* °**man**, *n.* bhaṇḍavāhī, *m.*

Package, *n.* 1. puṭa, *m.* bhaṇḍikā, *f.* 2. puṭakosa, *m.*

Packet, *n.* khuddaka-bhaṇḍikā, *f.*

Pact, *n.* katikāvatta, *nt.* paṭiññābandha, *m.*

Pad, *n.* 1. upadhāna; cumbaṭaka, *nt.* 2. lekhanapaṇṇanicaya, *m.* 3. panthadūhaka, *m.* *v.i.* padasā yāti. *v.t.* upadhāne sampādeti *or* yojeti; muduvatthunā chādeti. *p.p.* sampāditūpadhāna; °dita. °**ding**, *n.* bhisipūrakadabba, *nt.*

Paddle, *n.* nāvāpājanī, *f.* *v.t.* nāvādiŋ pājeti. *v.i.* jale yāti. *p.p.* pājitanāva; °yāta. °**wheel**, pājaka-cakka, *nt.* °**er**, *n.* nāvāpājaka, *m.*

Paddock, *n.* 1. khuddakakhetta, *nt.* 2. maṇḍūka, *m.*

Paddy, *n.* vīhi, *m.*

Padlock, *n.* tāḷaka; kuñcikāyanta, *nt.*

Padre, *n.* devapūjaka, *m.*

Paean, *n.* thutigīta; jayagīta, *nt.*

Pagan, *n.* *a.* micchādiṭṭhika, *m.* °**ism**, *n.* micchādiṭṭhi, *f.*

Page, *n.* 1. (of a book:) piṭṭha, *nt.* 2. (— boy:) ceṭaka; cullupaṭṭhāka; pādamūlika, *m.*

Pageant, *n*. 1. vilāsadassana, *nt*. vāhanussava, *m*. 2. tucchanidassana, *nt*. °**ry**, *n*. mahānubhāvadassana, *nt*.

Paginal, *a*. (potthaka-) piṭṭhāyatta.

Paginate, *v.t*. piṭṭhāni aṅketi. *p.p*. aṅkitapiṭṭha.

Pagoda, *n*. 1. cetiya, *nt*. thūpa, *m*. 2. soṇṇakahāpaṇavisesa, *m*.

Paideutics, *n*. ajjhāpanavijjā, *f*.

Pail, *n*. thāli-sadisabhājana, *nt*. pāti, *f*. °**ful**, *n*. pātipūra, *m*.

Paillasse, Palliasse, *n*. palālabhisi, *f*.

Pain, *n*. rujā ; vedanā ; pīḷā, *f*. *v.t*. vyathati ; pīḷeti ; upatāpeti ; dukkheti. *p.p*. vyathita ; pīḷita ; °pita ; °khita. **Mental** —, kheda ; ubbega ; manotāpa, *m*. domanassa, *nt*. °**ed**, *a*. dukkhita ; vedanaṭṭa. °**ful**, *a*. rujāvaha ; santāpakara ; dussādhiya. °**fully**, *adv*. kicchena ; kasirena. °**less**, *a*. niruja ; niddukkha. °**lessly**, *adv*. anāyāsena ; nirujaŋ. °**staking**, *a*. uyyogī ; saussāha.

Paint, *n*. vaṇṇaka, *nt*. vaṇṇajāta, *nt*. *v.t*. 1. vaṇṇālepaŋ karoti ; 2. ālikhati ; citteti. *p.p*. katavaṇṇālepa ; ālikhita ; cittita. °**er**, *n*. 1. vaṇṇālepaka ; raṅgājīvī ; 2. cittakāra, *m*. °**er's brush**, tūlikā ; ālekhanī, *f*. °**ing**, *n*. 1. cittakamma ; ālikhana ; 2. cittitavatthu, *nt*. 3. vaṇṇālepa, *m*.

Pair, *n*. yuga ; yugala ; yamaka ; dvanda, *nt*. (— of a male and a female :) mithuna, *nt*. *v.t*. saŋyojeti ; yugaso ṭhapeti. *v.i*. saŋvāsaŋ kappeti. *p.p*. saŋyutta ; °ṭhapita ; kappitasaŋvāsa.

Palace, *n*. pāsāda, *m*. bhavana ; vimāna ; mandira, *nt*. — **garden**, pamadavana, *nt*. — **grounds**, rājantepura, *nt*.

Palaeography, *n*. purālipivijjā, *f*.

Palaeology, *n*. purāvatthuvijjā, *f*.

Palaeontology, *n*. purājīvīvijjā, *f*.

Palaestra, *n*. mallasippālaya, *m*. vāyāmakaraṇaṭṭhāna, *nt*.

Palankeen, Palanquin, *n*. dolā ; sivikā ; pāṭaṅkī, *f*.

Palate, *n*. 1. tālu, *m*. 2. ruci, *f*. assāda, *m*. °**able**, *a*. rucikara ; sādurasa. °**tal**, *a*. tāluja ; tāluvisayaka.

Palatial, *a*. rājāraha. — **building**, mahāmandira, *nt*.

Palatine, *a*. rājādhikārayutta.

Pale, *n*. kaṭṭhasūla, *nt*. saṅku, *m*. adj. vivaṇṇa ; uppaṇḍuka. *v.t*. 1. vaṇṇaŋ hāpeti. ; 2. sūlehi āvarati. *v.i*. vivaṇṇī hoti. *p.p*. hāpitavaṇṇa ; sulāvaṭa ; °bhūta. °**ing**, *n*. saṅkuvati, *f*. °**ness**, *n*. vevaṇṇiya ; uppaṇḍukatta, *nt*. °**ish**, *a*. īsaŋpaṇḍuka.

Palette, *n*. cittakāra-vaṇṇaphalaka, *m*.

Palfrey, *n*. ārohanīyassa, *m*.

Palindrome, *n*. paṭilomayamaka, *nt*.

Palingenesis, *n*. punajīvana, *nt*.

Palinode, *n*. sakamatakhaṇḍakapajja, *nt*.

Palisade, *n*. saṅkupanti, *f*.

Pall, *n*. chavacchādakavattha, *nt*. *v.t*. virasīkaroti. *v.i*. rasahīno bhavati. *p.p*. virasīkata. °**bearer**, *n*. chava-vatthagāhī, *m*.

Palladium, *n*. ārakkhā ; ārakkhadevatā, *f*.

Pallet, *n*. 1. palālabhisi, *f*. 2. kumbhakāra-dāruhattha, *m*.

Palliate, *v.t.* dosalāghavaŋ karoti. °**ion**, *n*. dosalahukaraṇa, *nt*. °**ive**, *n*. samanosadha; sūlanāsana, *nt*. adj. upasamaka; dosahāpaka.

Pallid, see **Pale**, *a*.

Pallor, *n*. vevaṇṇiya; nittejatta, *nt*.

Palm, *n*. 1. karatala; hatthatala, *nt*. 2. (tree:) tāla, *m*. *v.t.* 1. karatalena parimajjati; 2. saṭhena vañceti. *p.p.* karatala-parimaṭṭha; °cita. °**acous**, *a*. tālajātivisayaka. °**ar**, *a*. karatalāyatta. — **leaf**, *n*. tālapaṇṇa, *nt*. — **off**, patāreti; vañceti.

Palma Christi, *n*. eraṇḍa, *m*.

Palmary, *a*. accukkaṭṭha.

Palmate, *a*. karatalākāra.

Palmer, *n*. 1. tālapaṇṇahattha, *m*. 2. paribbājaka; puññatitthasevī, *m*.

Palmistry, *n*. sāmuddikavijjā; hatthalekhāvijjā, *f*.

Palmy, *a*. 1. tālasañchanna; 2. samiddha; puṇṇavibhava. — **days**, samiddhikāla, *m*.

Palmyra, *n*. tālarukkha, *m*.

Palp, *n*. phusanāvayava, *m*. °**able**, *a*. phusanīya; supākaṭa. °**ably**, *adv*. supākaṭaŋ.

Palpate, *v.t.* hatthena phusitvā jānāti. *p.p.* °ñāta.

Palpitate, *v.i.* kampati; phandati; nāḷī vahati. *p.p.* °pita; °dita. °**ion**, *n*. kampana; phandana; nāḷīvahana, *nt*.

Palsy, *n*. aŋsabhaṅga; pakkhaghāta, *m*. *v.t.* aŋsabhaṅgam uppādeti; kriyārahitaŋ karoti. *p.p.* uppāditaŋsabhaṅga.

Palter, *v.i.* nikatiyā carati; ayathā vadati. *p.p.* °rita; °vutta.

Paltry, *a*. 1. adhama; anariya; 2. appaggha; appamattaka.

Paludal, *a*. kacchanissita.

Pamper, *v.t.* atitappeti; adhikaŋ bhuñjati. *p.p.* °pita; °bhutta. °**er**, *n*. atibhojī, *m*. °**ing**, *n*. atibhojana; atilālana, *nt*.

Pamphlet, *n*. khuddakagantha, *m*. °**eer**, *n*. khuddakaganthalekhaka, *m*.

Pamplegia, *n*. sabbaṅgatthambhana, *nt*.

Pan, *n*. kapallaka, *nt*. thālī, *f*. °**cake**, *n*. kapallakapūva, *m*.

Panacea, *n*. sabbaroganāsakosadha, *nt*.

Panache, *n*. sikhā, *f*. sekharapiñja, *nt*.

Pancratic, *a*. mallakīḷāvisārada. °**tium**, *n*. mallayuddha, *nt*.

Pandemic, *a*. opasaggika. *n*. opasaggikaroga, *m*.

Pandemonium, *n*. 1. yakkhanivāsa; 2. anītikapadesa, *m*.

Pander, *n*. pāpasahāya; duṭṭhānusāsaka, *m*. *v.t.* pāpakammesu niyojeti. *v.i.* pāpasaṅkappaŋ sampādeti. °**ess**, *n*. pāpasahāyikā, *f* °**ism**, pāpamittatā, *f* pāpaninnatā, *f*.

Pandiculation, *n*. aṅgappasāraṇa; vijambhana, *nt*.

Pane, *n*. 1. kācaphalaka, *m*. 2. caturassaka, *nt*.

Panegyric, *n*. guṇavaṇṇanā, *f*. adj. thutiyutta; pasaŋsāvisayaka. °**rist**, *n*. thomaka; pasaŋsaka; vandī; thutipāṭhaka, *m*. °**rize**, *v.t.* thomet; pasaŋsati. *p.p.* thomita; pasattha.

Panel, *n.* 1. kavāṭa-phalaka, *m.* 2. tīrakanāmāvali, *f.* *v.t.* 1. assakacchaŋ yojeti; 2. kavāṭaphalakaŋ yojeti. *p.p.* yojita°.

Pang, *n.* balavarujā; vedanā, *f.*

Pangolin, *n.* kapālagodhā, *f.*

Panic, *n.* 1. mahabbhaya; 2. ahetuka-bhaya, *nt.* — **stricken,** mahabbhayabhīta.

Panjandrum, *n.* 1. attukkaŋsakapuggala, *m.* 2. pākaṭapuggalassa vikaṭanāma, *nt.*

Pannage, *n.* sūkaranivāpa, *m.*

Pannier, *n.* satthagāmīnaŋ yamaka-pasibbaka, *m.*

Pannikin, *n.* khuddakasarāvaka, *m.* pānīyathālaka, *nt.*

Panoply, *n.* sabbaṅgasannāha, *m.*

Panorama, *n.* sabbadisādassana, *nt.* °**mic,** *a.* sabbabhāgadassaka.

Panpipe, *n.* dhamana-vaŋsa, *m.*

Pant, *n.* nissasana, *nt.* *v.i.* 1. dīghaŋ nissasati; 2. atigijjhati. °**ing,** *a.* nissasanta.

Pantaloon, *n.* vidūsaka; vihāsaka, *m.*

Pantheist, *n.* issaranimmāṇavādī, *m.* °**ism,** *n.* issaranimmāṇavāda, *m.*

Pantheon, *n.* 1. sakaladevagaṇa, *m.* 2. sakaladevāyatana, *nt.*

Panther, *n.* cittaka-dīpi, *m.*

Pantile, *n.* chadaniṭṭhikāvisesa, *m.*

Pantisocracy, *n.* janasammatapālana, *nt.*

Pantomime, *n.* cāraṇika (-nacca), *nt.*

Pantophagous, *a.* sabbabhakkha.

Pantry, *n.* āhārabhaṇḍāgāra, *nt.*

Pap, *n.* 1. cūcuka; thanagga, *nt.* 2. pāyāsa-sadisāhāra, *m.* mudubhojana, *nt.*

Papa, *n.* tāta, *m.*

Papal, *a.* Romaka-nāyakapūjakāyatta.

Papaw, *n.* vātakumbha, *m.* nāvāphala, *nt.*

Paper, *n.* kākacapaṇṇa, *nt.* *v.t.* kākacapaṇṇehi chādeti. *p.p.* °chādita.

Papilla, *n.* khuddakaphoṭa, *m.*

Papist, *n.* Romakasāmayika, *m.*

Papula, *n.* vadanaphoṭa, *m.* °**lous,** *a.* vadanaphoṭayutta.

Papyraceous, *a.* kākacasadisa.

Par, *n.* samatta; tulyatta, *nt.*

Parable, *n.* upamā; nidassanakathā, *f.* opamma, *nt.*

Parabolic, °**al,** *a.* nidassanabhūta; upamāyatta. °**ally,** *adv.* upamāvasena.

Parachronism, *n.* sadosavassasaṅkhyā, *f.*

Parachute, *n.* gaganotaraṇa-chatta, *nt.*

Parade, *n.* senāvyūha, yuddhaparicaya, *m.* *v.t.* senāvinyāsaŋ dasseti. *v.i.* sadappaŋ carati. *p.p.* dassita°.

Paradigm, *n.* nidassana; udāharaṇa, *nt.* °**atic,** *a.* nidassanabhūta.

Paradise, *n.* Nandanavana, *nt.* devaloka, *m.* °**saic,** *a.* dibba; sovaggika.

Paradox, *n.* sammutiviruddhavāda, *m.* °**ical,** *a.* sammutiviruddha.

Paragon, *n.* ukkaṭṭha-pamāṇa; setthatamavatthu, *nt.* niruttarapuggala, *m.*

Paragraph, *n.* vākyacheda ; vākyakhaṇḍa, *m. v.t.* vākyāni vicchindati. *p.p.* vicchinna-vākya.

Paralipsis, *n.* paṭikkhepālaṅkāra ; ākhepa, *m.*

Parallel, *a. n.* samadūravattī ; sabbathāsama. *v.t.* samadūravattiŋ karoti ; samāneti. *p.p.* °tīkata ; °nita. **°ism,** *n.* samantaratta ; sadisatta, *nt.* **°ogram,** *n.* samantaradīgha-caturassa, *nt.*

Paralogism, *n.* ahetukābhāsa, *m.* atakkānugatakathā, *f.*

Paralyse, *v.t.* santhambheti ; akammaññaŋ karoti. *p.p.* °bhita ; °kata.

Paralysis, *n.* pakkhaghāta ; aŋsabhaṅga, *m.*

Paralytic, *a.* naṭṭhindriya ; pakkhahata.

Paramagnetic, *a.* ayokantākaḍḍhanīya.

Paramount, *a.* sabbaseṭṭha ; atyukkaṭṭha. **°ly,** *adv.* sabbātisayena.

Paramour, *n.* (male :) jāra, *m.* (female :) jārī ; aticārinī, *f.*

Paranoia, *n.* cittabbhama, *m.*

Parapet, *n.* nīcabhitti, *f.* paŋsusilādikata-āvaraṇa, *nt.*

Paraphernalia, *n.* 1. itthidhana, *nt.* 2. upakaraṇa ; parikkhāra, *nt.* Royal —, rājakakudhabhaṇḍa, *nt.*

Paraphrase, *v.t.* vitthāreti ; vyākhyāti. *p.p.* °rita ; vyākhyāta. *n.* atthavaṇṇanā, *f.* vivaraṇa, *nt.* **°stic,** *a.* vyākhyābhūta ; vaṇṇanāvisayaka.

Paraplegia, *n.* adhopakkhaghāta, *m.*

Parasite, *n.* 1. paraputtha ; parabhata ; cāṭupara, *m.* 2. (plant :) rukkhādanī ; vandākā, *f.*

Parasol, *n.* chatta ; ātapatta, *nt.*

Parathesis, *n.* tulyādhikaraṇa ; samānavibhattikatta, *nt.* **°thetic,** *a.* samānavibhattika.

Parboil, *v.t.* addhaŋ pacati. *p.p.* addhapakka.

Parcel, *n.* 1. bhaṇḍikā, *f.* puṭa, *m.* 2. bhāga ; koṭṭhāsa, *m. v.t.* bhāgaso vibhajati. *p.p.* °vibhatta. **°ed,** *a.* puṭabaddha. **— out,** vibhajati ; koṭṭhāse karoti. **°ling,** *n.* bhāgaso-karaṇa, *nt.*

Parcenary, *n.* sahabhāgitā ; bhāgāyattatā, *f.* **°ner,** *n.* sahabhāgī ; koṭṭhāsī, *m.*

Parch, *v.t.* soseti ; bhajjati. *v.i.* sussati ; bhajjīyati. *p.p.* sosita ; bhaṭṭha ; sukkha ; bhajjita. **°ed corn,** lāja, *m.* **°ed flour,** sattu ; mantha, *m.*

Parchment, *n.* cammpaṭṭa ; lipicamma, *nt.*

Pard, *n.* dīpi, *m.*

Pardon, *n.* khamā ; khanti ; titikkhā, *f. v.t.* khamati ; titikkhati. *p.p.* khanta ; °khita. **°able,** *a.* 1. khantabba ; khamāraha ; 2. satekiccha.

Pare, *v.t.* tacchati ; tanukaroti ; (of rind:) tacam apaneti. *p.p.* °chita ; tanukata ; apanītataca.

Paregoric, *a. n.* vedanūpasamaka (– bhesajja), *nt.*

Parent, *n.* 1. mātāpitaro, *pl.* 2. mūlapurisa ; pabhava, *m.* **°age,** *n.* kulaparivaṭṭa, *nt.* **°al,** *a.* 1. mātāpettika ; 2. vacchala. **°hood,** *n.* mātāpitiṭṭhāna, *nt.* **°less,** *a.* nimmātāpitika.

Parenthesis, *n.* 1. nikkhepalakkhaṇa, *nt.* 2. upavākya, *nt.*
Parenthetical, *a.* anusaṅgika. °**ly**, *adv.* pakkhepavasena; anusaṅgavasena.
Parenticide, *n.* 1. mātāpitughāta, *m.* 2. mātāpitughātī, *m.*
Paresis, *n.* addhapakkhaghāta, *m.*
Par excellence, *adv.* accukkaṭṭhatāya.
Parget, *n.* bhittilepa, *m. v.t.* bhittiŋ lepeti.
Pariah, *n.* caṇḍāla; hīnajacca.
Parish, *n.* gocaragāma; vibhattapadesa, *m.* °**ioner**, gocaragāmavāsī, *m.*
Parity, *n.* samānatta; sāmañña, *nt.*
Park, *n.* upavana; uyyāna, *nt.* ārāma, *m. v.t.* 1. uyyānaŋ sampādeti; 2. upavane ṭhapeti. *p.p.* °dituyyāna; °pita.
Parlance, *n.* 1. sallāpa, *m.* sākacchā, *f.* 2. kathanākāra, *m.*
Parley, *n.* sambhāsana, *nt.* sākacchā, *f. v.i.* sākacchati; sammanteti. *p.p.* °chita; °tita.
Parliament, *n.* mantisabhā, *f.* °**ary**, *a.* mantisabhāyatta.
Parlour, *n.* sannipātasālā, *f.* sambhāsanaṭṭhāna, *nt.*
Parlous, *a.* sappaṭibhaya; sopaddava.
Parochial, *a.* sīmitapadesāyatta; padesika.
Parody, *n.* 1. parihāsapajja, *nt.* 2. dubbalānukaraṇa, *nt. v.t.* kucchitākārena anukaroti.
Parole, *n.* apalāyana-paṭiññā, *f.*
Paronomasia, *n.* silesālaṅkāra, *m.*
Parotid, *n.* lālāsaya, *m.* adj. kaṇṇasamīpaṭṭha.
Parotitis, *n.* uḷūkaroga, *m.*
Paroxysm, *n.* 1. rogavega; 2. kopavega, *m.*
Parquet, *n.* nānādārukhacitabhūtala, *nt.*
Parricide, *n.* 1. pitughāta, *m.* 2. pitughātī, *m.*
Parrot, *n.* suka; suva; kīra, *m. v.t.* anubhāsati. *p.p.* °sita.
Parry, *v.t.* pahāraŋ vañceti *or* vāreti. *p.p.* vañcitapahāra. *n.* pariharaṇa, *nt.*
Parse, *v.t.* padavibhāgaŋ karoti. *p.p.* katapadavibhāga. °**ing**, *n.* padavibhajana, *nt.*
Parsimony, *n.* mitavaya, *m.* °**ious**, *a.* mitavyayī; maccharī. °**iously**, *adv.* luddhākārena.
Parsley, *n.* ajamodā, *f.*
Parson, *n.* padesika-devapūjaka, *m.* °**age**, *n.* pūjakāvāsa, *m.*
Part, *n.* 1. aŋsa; bhāga; koṭṭhāsa, *m.* 2. (constituent:) aṅga; avayava. *nt.* 3. (allotted:) pattakoṭṭhāsa, *m.* 4. (turn:) vāra; pariyāya, *m.* 5. (share:) āyattakicca, *nt.* āyattabhāga, *m.* **By parts**, bhāgaso. *ind.* **For my —**, aham pana. **For the most —**, pāyaso, bahuso. *ind.*
Part, *v.t.* bhājeti; viyojeti; puthakkaroti. *v.i.* viyujjati; vigacchati. *p.p.* °jita; puthakkata; viyutta; vigata. °**ing**, *n.* viyoga; viraha; apagama, *m.* °**ly**, *adv.* bhāgaso; addhavasena.
Partake, *v.i.* 1. anubhoti; paribhuñjati; 2. sahabhāgī hoti. *p.p.* anubhūta; paribhutta; °bhūta. °**er**, *n.* sahabhāgī; sahabhojī, *m.*
Parthenogenesis, *n.* saŋvāsarahituppādana, *nt.*

Partial, *a.* 1. pakkhapatita ; asabbavyāpaka ; 2. asampuṇṇa. °**ity,** *n.* pakkhapātitā, *f.* anurāga, *m.* °**ly,** *adv.* ekadesato ; bhāgavasena.

Partible, *a.* vibhajanīya. °**bility,** *n.* vibhajanārahatta, *nt.*

Participate, *v.t.* bhāgaŋ gaṇhāti. *v.i.* pattiko *or* sahabhāgī hoti. *p.p.* gahitabhāga; pattikabhūta, °**ion,** *n.* bhāgagahaṇa ; sahabhāgitā, *f.* saŋvibhāga, *m.* °**pant,** *n.* sahabhāgī ; pattika, *m.*

Participle, *n.* kitakapada, *nt.*

Particle, *n.* 1. lava ; aṇu ; lesa, *m.* 2. (In gram :) avyaya, *nt.*

Parti-coloured, *a.* nānāvaṇṇa ; vicittavaṇṇa.

Particular, *a.* asādhāraṇa; paccеka ; visiṭṭha. *n.* paccekavatthu, *nt.* °**ity,** *n.* paccekatta ; asādhāraṇatta, *nt.* °**ly,** *adv.* visesena ; paccekavasena.

Particularize, *v.t.* viseseti ; visuŋ niddisati. *p.p.* °sita ; °niddiṭṭha. °**ation,** *n.* paricchindana ; visesakaraṇa, *nt.*

Partisan, *n.* 1. pakkhagāhī, *m.* 2. kuṭhārī, *f.* °**ship,** *n.* pakkhagāha, *m.*

Partite, *a.* yāva mūlā vibhatta.

Partition, *n.* vicchedana ; vibhajana, *nt.* *v.t.* vibhajati ; viyojeti. *p.p.* vibhatta ; °jita.

Partitive, *a.* vibhāgadassaka.

Partner, *n.* 1. pattika ; bhāgī ; 2. sahakārī ; sahāya, *m.* °**ship,** *n.* sahabhāgitā ; sahakāritā, *f.*

Partridge, *n.* kapiñjala, *m.*

Parturient, *a.* āsannapasavā, *f.*

Parturition, *n.* pasūti, *f.* vijāyana, *nt.*

Party, *n.* pakkha ; vagga ; gaṇa ; saṅgha, *m.*

Parvanimity, *n.* anuḷārajjhāsayatā, *f.*

Parvenu, *n.* samiddhigabbita.

Pasquinade, *n.* upahāsakabba, *nt.*

Pass, *n.* 1. saṅkama ; sañcāra ; giridugga, *m.* 3. gamanāvasara, *m.* *v.t.* 1. atikkamati ; pāraŋ gacchati ; 2. (time :) khepeti ; vītināmeti ; 3. anumaññati ; aṅgīkaroti. *v.i.* sañcarati. *p.p.* atikkanta ; pāragata ; °pita ; °mita ; anumata ; °kata. °**able,** *a.* gamanakkhama ; taraṇakkhama. — **away,** cavati. — **by,** samīpena yāti ; upekkhati. °**ed,** atīta ; vītivatta. — **for,** maññati ; gaṇeti. °**ing,** *a.* athira ; khaṇika. °**ing,** *n.* atikkamana ; uttaraṇa. °**ing away,** cavana, *nt.* accaya, *m.* — **into,** pavisati. — **off,** apeti. — **on,** pavattati. — **over,** samatikkamati. — **over to,** saṅkamati. — **over the limits,** atidhāvati. — **through,** vinivijjhati.

Passage, *n.* 1. pavesamagga ; saṅkama, *m.* 2. magga ; patha ; 3. gamanāvasara, *m.* 4. pāṭha, *m.* vākya, *nt.*

Passe, *a.* gatayobbana.

Passenger, *n.* sañcāraka ; pariyaṭaka ; gamika ; addhika, *m.*

Passer-by, *n.* samīpena gāmī, *m.*

Passible, *a.* vedanakkhama. °**bility,** *n.* vedanakkhamatā, *f.*

Passim, *adv.* sabbathā ; sabbattha.

Passion, *n.* 1. rāga ; kāma ; āsava ; 2. kopa ; rosa; 3. cittakkhobha, *m.* °**al,** *a.* kilesāyatta. °**less,** *a.* nikkilesa ; anāsava ; vītarāga ; khīṇāsava.

Passionate, *a.* sāraddha ; sarosa ; kāmamucchita ; kodhana. °**ly,** *adv.* sarāgaŋ ; sakopaŋ. °**ness,** *n.* kuppanasīlatā, *f.*

Passive, *a.* 1. udāsīna ; nirīha ; 2. titikkhaka. °**ly,** *adv.* nirīhakatāya. °**ness,** *n.* nirīhatā ; sahanasīlatā, *f.* — **voice,** kammakāraka, *m.* °**ity,** nirīhatā, *f.*

Passport, *n.* gamanānuññāpaṇṇa, *nt.*

Past, *n.* atītakāla, *m.* adj. atīta ; atikkanta. *adv.* parato ; atikkamitvā. **He ran past the house,** so geham atikkamitvā (*or* gehassa parato) dhāvi.

Paste, *n.* sannitavatthu, *nt.* ālepa, *m. v.t.* lepeti ; lepena ābandhati. *p.p.* lepita ; lepābaddha. — **board,** *n.* ghanakākacapaṭṭa, *m.*

Pastil, Pastille, *n.* sugandhasalākā, *f.*

Pastime, *n.* vinodakīḷā, *f.*

Pastor, *n.* devāyatanādhikārī, *m.* °**al,** *a.* devapūjakāyatta.

Pastoral, *n.* janapadakabba, *nt.* adj. pasupālanāyatta ; gocarabhūmyāyatta.

Pastry, *n.* piṭṭhāvuta-maŋsādi, *m.*

Pasture, *n.* 1. gocarabhūmi, *f.* 2. gocara ; ghāsa, *m. v.t.* gocaraŋ gaṇhāpeti ; tiṇaŋ khādāpeti. *v.i.* gocaraŋ gaṇhāti. *p.p.* gaṇhāpitagocara ; gahitagocara. °**age,** *n.* gocarabhūmi, *f.*

Pasty, *a.* sannitapiṭṭhasadisa.

Pat, *n.* 1. vallabha-jīvī, *m.* 2. sanikappahāra, *m.* parāmasana, *nt. v.t.* sādaraŋ paharati ; lāleti ; parāmasati. *p.p.* °pahaṭa ; lālita ; parāmaṭṭha.

Patch, *n.* aggala, *nt.* (vatthādi-) khaṇḍa, *m. v.t.* aggalaŋ deti ; khaṇḍehi saṅkharoti. *p.p.* dinnaggala ; khaṇḍasaṅkhata. °**work,** khaṇḍasaŋyoga, *m.* °**y,** *a.* aggalabahula.

Pate, *n.* sīsa, *nt.* muddhā, *m.*

Patella, *n.* jāṇuphalaka, *m.*

Patent, *n.* asādhāraṇādhikāra, *m.* adj. 1. supākaṭa ; 2. laddhabala. *v.t.* visiṭṭhādhikāraŋ labhati. *p.p.* laddha°kāra. °**ee,** *n.* asādhāraṇādhikāralābhī, *m.* °**ly,** *adv.* supākaṭaŋ.

Pater, see **Father.** °**nal,** *a.* pettika ; pitusantaka. °**nity,** *n.* pitubhāva ; pitudhamma, *m.* °**nal uncle,** cullapitu, *m.*

Path, *n.* magga ; patha ; pantha ; addhā, *m.* añjasa ; ayana, *nt.* **Long** —, addhāna, *nt.* **Right** —, supatha, *m.* **Wrong** —, uppatha ; kummagga, *m.* — **finder,** *n.* maggadesaka, *m.* °**less,** *a.* apatha ; duggama.

Pathetic, °**al,** *a.* khedakara ; anukampājanaka. °**ally,** *adv.* khedajanakatāya.

Pathogenesis, *n.* roganidāna, *nt.*

Pathogeny, *n.* rogapattharaṇākāra, *m.*

Pathognomy, *n.* cittabhāvapākaṭīkaraṇa, *nt.*

Pathology, *n.* rogalakkhaṇavijjā, *f.* °**ist,** *n.* rogalakkhaṇaññū, *m.*

Pathos, *n.* karuṇārasa, *m.*

Patience, *n.* adhivāsanā ; khanti ; dhiti ; khamā, *f.*

Patient, *n*. rogī ; vyādhita, *m*. adj. adhivāsaka ; sahitu, *m*. °**ly**, *adv*. adhivāsanapubbakaŋ ; nibbikāraŋ.

Patina, *n*. antokhacana, *nt*. °**ted**, *a*. antokhacita.

Patio, *n*. antogehaṅgaṇa, *nt*.

Patois, *n*. padesīyabhāsā, *f*.

Patriarch, *n*. 1. kulapati ; kulappadhāna, *m*. 2. padhānadevapūjaka, *m*. °**al**, *a*. kulapativisayaka. °**ate**, *n*. kulapatidhura ; pūjakācariyadhura, *nt*. °**y**, *n*. kulapatipālanakkama, *m*.

Patrician, *n*. kulīnajana, *m*. adj. pālakajanāyatta.

Patricide, *n*. 1. pitughāta, *m*. 2. pitughātī, *m*. °**al**, *a*. pitughātanāyatta.

Patrimony, *n*. pitudāyajja ; pettikadhana, *nt*. °**ial**, pettikadhanāyatta.

Patriot, *n*. sadesānurāgī, *m*. °**ic**, *a*. desabhattika. °**ism**, *n*. desānurāga, *m*.

Patrol, *n*. 1. sañcārakarakkhī, *m*. 2. rakkhāya sañcaraṇa, *nt*. *v.i*. rakkhaṇāya paribbhamati.

Patron, *n*. anuggāhaka ; ārakkhaka, *m*. °**age**, *n*. anuggaha ; paggaha, *m*. °**ize**, *v.t*. anupāleti ; anugganhāti. *p.p*. °lita ; °gahita. °**less**, *a*. nirādhāra ; anātha.

Patronymic, *n*. gottanāma, *nt*.

Pattern, *n*. nidassanarūpa ; paṭirūpa, *nt*. ākati, *f*. *v.t*. ādisiyarūpāni sampādeti ; saṇṭhānāni yojeti.

Patulous, *a*. vitthāriyamāna ; vitthiṇṇa. °**ly**, *adv*. vitthiṇṇākārena. °**ness**, *n*. vitthiṇṇatā, *f*.

Paucity, *n*. appatā ; thokatā, *f*.

Paunch, *n*. udara, *nt*. āmāsaya, *m*. *v.t*. antāni bahikaroti. *p.p*. bahikatanta. °**y**, *a*. mahodara.

Pauper, *n*. vaṇibbaka ; akiñcana, *m*. °**dom**, °**ism**, *n*. akiñcanatta; daḷiddatta, *nt*. °**ize**, *v.t*. akiñcanattaŋ pāpeti. *p.p*. °pita.

Pause, *n*. virāma ; viccheda, *m*. nivatti, *f*. vyavadhāna, *nt*. *v.i*. nivattati ; vissamati. *p.p*. °tita ; vissanta.

Pave, *v.t*. silādīhi attharati. *p.p*. °atthata. °**er**, *n*. attharaka, *m*. °**ment**, *n*. nicitaṭṭhāna, *nt*. vedikā, *f*. atthatamagga, *m*.

Pavilion, *n*. maṇḍapa, *m*.

Pavonian, *a*. mayūrasadisa.

Paw, *n*. nakhapañjara, *m*. *v.t*. nakhapañjarena āhanati. *p.p*. °jarāhata.

Pawky, *a*. kapaṭa ; upāyakusala. °**ily**, *adv*. kapaṭākārena. °**iness**, *n*. kerāṭiya, *nt*.

Pawn, *n*. nyāsa ; upanidhi, *m*. *v.t*. nyasati ; nikkhipati. *p.p*. nyasita ; nikkhitta. — **broker**, *n*. nyāsagāhī ; upanidhivohārika, *m*. °**er**, *n*. nikkhepaka, *m*.

Pay, *n*. vetana, *nt*. bhati, *f*. *v.t*. vetanavasena deti ; nibbisati. *p.p*. °dinna ; nibbiṭṭha. — **a debt**, iṇaŋ sodheti. °**day**, *n*. vetanadivasa, *m*. °**able**, *a*. deyya ; nittharaṇīya. °**bill**, *n*. bhatilekhana, *nt*. °**ee**, *n*. bhatipaṭiggāhī, *m*. °**master**, *n*. vetanādhikārī, *m*. °**ment**, *n*. vetanadāna, *nt*. — **honour**, sakkaroti ; garukaroti. *p.p*. sakkata.

Pea, *n*. kalāya ; māsa, *m*.

Peace, *n*. sāma, *m*. santi ; sāmaggi, *f*. °**able**, °**ful**, *a*. sāmakāmī ;

santa. °**fulness,** *n.* sāmakāmitā; santatā, *f.* °**fully,** *adv.* santākārena; sāmaggiyā. °**maker,** *n.* paṭisandhātu; sāmaggikara. °**making,** *n.* sāmaggikaraṇa, *nt.* —**officer,** *n.* sāmarakkhaka, *m.*

Peacock, *n.* mayūra; mora; sikhaṇḍī; nīlagīva, *m.* *v.i.* 1. uddhato carati; 2. asantaŋ dasseti. °**'s cry,** kekā, *f.* °**'s tail,** bariha; morapiñja, *nt.*

Peahen, *n.* mayūrī, *f.*

Peak, *n.* kūṭa; girisikhara, *nt.* °**ed,** *a.* sikharayutta. °**y,** *a.* niccātura.

Peal, *n.* unnāda; ghaṇṭārava, *m.* *v.i.* nadati; ravati. *v.t.* nādeti; saddāyati. *p.p.* nadita; ravita; nādita; °yita.

Pearl, *n.* muttā, *f.* °**oyster,** *n.* suttikā, *f.* **String of** —, muttāvali, *f.* °**y,** *a.* muttāsadisa. *v.t.* bindūni vikirati. *p.p.* vikiṇṇabinduka.

Peasant, *n.* jānapadika; kassaka, *m.* °**ry,** *n.* kassakagaṇa, *m.*

Pebble, *n.* upala; gulapāsāṇa, *m.* °**bly,** *a.* upalākiṇṇa.

Peccable, *a.* pāpaninna; pāpāsaya.

Peccadillo, *n.* aṇumatta-dosa, *m.*

Peccant, *a.* pāpī; dummatika. °**ncy,** *n.* pāpakāritā, *f.*

Peccavi, *n.* āpattidesanā, *f.* sakadosāvīkaraṇa, *nt.*

Peck, *n.* 1. doṇa-pāda, *m.* 2. nitudana, *nt.* *v.t.* tudati; tuṇḍenāhanati; uñchati. *p.p.* tudita; °āhata; uñchita. °**er,** *n.* vitudaka; kaṭṭhatudaka, *m.* °**ing,** *n.* sakkharākhipana, *nt.* °**ish,** *a.* bubhukkhita.

Pectoral, *n.* vibhūsita-uracchada, *m.* adj. urarogopasamaka.

Peculate, *v.t.* theyyacittena gaṇhāti. *p.p.* °gahita, °**ion,** *n.* nikatiyā gahaṇa, *nt.*

Peculiar, *a.* asādhāraṇa; visiṭṭha; puggalika; paccattika. °**ity,** *n.* asādhāraṇatta; visiṭṭhatta; puggalikatta, *nt.* °**ly,** *adv.* visesena; visesato.

Pecuniary, *a.* mūlanissita; dhanāyatta.

Pedagogue, Pedant, *n.* paṇḍitamānī; attukkhaŋsaka, *m.*

Pedantic, *a.* paṇḍitamānagabbita.

Pedantry, *n.* paṇḍitamāna, *m.*

Pedate, *a.* pādasahita.

Peddle, *v.i.* 1. vāṇijjāya āhiṇḍati; 2. appamattakāya kilamati. °**er,** *n.* kacchapuṭavāṇija, *m.*

Pedestal, *n.* bhūmikā, *f.* mūlādhāra, *m.* patiṭṭhā, *f.*

Pedestrian, *n.* padika; pathika; pattika; addhagū, *m.* °**ism,** *n.* padagamana, *nt.*

Pedicel, Pedicle, *n.* khuddakavaṇṭa, *nt.*

Pedicle, *n.* pādasaṅkhalikā, *f.*

Pedicular, *a.* ūkākiṇṇa.

Pediculation, *n.* ūkākiṇṇatā, *f.*

Pedicure, *n.* pādatikicchā, *f.*

Pedigree, *n.* 1. vaŋsāvali, *f.* 2. anvayalekhā, *f.*

Pedlar, *n.* kacchapuṭavāṇija, *m.* °**y,** *n.* kaccapuṭavaṇijjā, *f.*

Pedometer, *n.* padapāta-māṇakayanta, *nt.*

Peduncle, *n.* vaṇṭa, *nt.* nāḷa; daṇḍa, *m.* °**cular,** *a.* vaṇṭākāra.

Peek, see **Peep.**

Peel, *n.* jalli, *f.* taca, *m.* *v.t.* vitacchati; vipāṭeti; tacam apaneti.

p.p. °chita ; °ṭita ; apanīta-taca °**er**, *n.* tacchaka, *m.* °**ing**, *n.* tacāpaharaṇa, *nt.*

Peep, *v.i.* 1. nilīyitvā *or* paṭicchanno oloketi ; 2. sanikam upagacchati ; 3. kūjati. *p.p.* °kita ; °upagata ; kūjita. *noun :* 1. nilīyitvā olokana ; 2. kūjana, *nt.* 3. paṭhamadassana, *nt.* udaya, *m.*

Peer, *n.* 1. samapadaṭṭha ; 2. mahākulapabhava, *m. v.i.* samataŋ yāti. *v.t.* kulīnattaŋ pāpeti. *p.p.* °yāta ; °pāpita. °**age**, *n.* mahākulikatta, *nt.* °**less**, *a.* asama ; appaṭipuggala ; atulya ; anupama.

Peerish, *a.* kalahappiya ; duṭṭhapakatika. °**ly**, *adv.* duṭṭhākārena. °**ness**, *n.* kodhabahulatā, *f.*

Peg, *n.* nāgadantaka ; dārukīla, *nt. v.t.* 1. nāgadante olambeti ; 2. kīlehi saṅghaṭeti. *p.p.* °bita ; °ṭita.

Pejoration, *n.* avaññā ; ohīlanā, *f.*

Pelagian, Pelagic, *a.* 1. sāmuddika ; samuddāyatta ; 2. samudde pavattāpita.

Pelf, *n.* mūla ; dhana, *nt.*

Pelican, *n.* udakakukkuṭa, *m.*

Pellet, *n.* guḷikā, *f. v.t.* guḷikāhi āhanati. *p.p.* °āhata.

Pellicle, *n.* tanu-taca, *m.*

Pell-mell, *n.* saṅkulatta, *nt.* adj. saṅkinna. *adv.* asamekkha ; ayathākkamaŋ ; saṅkiṇṇatāya.

Pellucid, *a.* nimmala ; vimala ; pasanna. °**ness**, *n.* nimmalatta, *nt.*

Pelt, *n.* 1. khipana ; paharaṇa, *nt.* 2. aparimaddita-camma, *nt. v.t.* abhihanati ; khipati ; (āyudhehi) paharati. *p.p.* abhihata ; khitta ; pahaṭa. °**monger**, *n.* cammavāṇija, *m.*

Pelvis, *n.* vaccamagga, *m.*

Pen, *n.* 1. lekhanī, *f.* 2. vaja, *m. v.t.* 1. vaje orundhati ; 2. likhati ; nibandhaŋ sampādeti. *p.p.* °oruddha ; likhita ; °ditanibandha.

Penal, *a.* daṇḍanāyatta ; daṇḍakammāraha. °**ty**, *n.* daṇḍana, *nt.* niggaha, *m.* °**code**, *n.* daṇḍanīti, *f.* °**ize**, *v.t.* daṇḍārahaŋ karoti.

Penance, *n.* tapa, *m.* tapacaraṇa, *nt.* attakilamatha, *m. v.t.* tapacaraṇe niyojeti. *p.p.* °jita.

Penchant, *n.* poṇatā ; ninnatā ; abhilāsā, *f.*

Pencil, *n.* 1. abbhakalekhanī ; 2. cittakāra-tūlikā, *f. v.t.* vaṭṭikāya likhati. *p.p.* °likhita.

Pendant, °**dent**, *n.* olambakābharaṇa, *nt.* urabhūsā, *f.* kuṇḍalābharaṇa, *nt.* adj. lambamāna ; dolāyamāna.

Pending, *a.* avinicchita ; aniṭṭhita. *prep.* yāva.

Pendulate, *v.i.* 1. dolāyati ; 2. anavaṭṭhito hoti. *p.p.* dolāyita ; anavaṭṭhita.

Penduline, Pendulous, *a.* olambamāna ; dolāyamāna.

Pendulum, *n.* lambaka ; loladaṇḍa, *m.*

Penetralia, *n.* 1. abbhantarimagabbha, *m.* 2. abbhantaracetiya, *nt.*

Penetrate, *v.t.* pariyogāhati ; vinivijjhati ; paṭivijjhati. *p.p* pariyogāḷha ; vinividdha ; paṭividdha. °**ing**, °**ive**, *a.* pariyogāhaka ; vinivijjhaka. °**ion**, *n.* vinivijjhana ; pariyogāhaṇa, *nt.*

Peninsula, *n.* dīpappāyadesa, *m.*

Penis, *n.* purisaliṅga ; mehana, *nt.*

Penitence, *n.* anutāpa ; pacchātāpa, *m.*

Penitent, *a. n.* anutāpī, *m.* °**ial,** *a.* anutāpayutta. °**ly,** *adv.* sānutāpaŋ.

Penitentiary, *n.* 1. tapa niyāmakādhikārī, *m.* 2. paṭisaṅkharaṇāpekkha-nivāsa, *m.*

Penman, *n.* lekhaka ; lipikāra, *m.* °**ship,** *n.* lekhane dakkhatā, *f.*

Penknife, *n.* khuddakasattha, *m.*

Penname, *n.* lipi-rūḷhināma, *nt.*

Pennant, *n.* patākā, *f.*

Penniform, *a.* pakkhipattākāra.

Penniless, *a.* niddhana ; akiñcana.

Pennon, *n.* dīgha-dhaja, *m.*

Penny, *n.* māsaka, *m.* °**wise,** *a.* mandabuddhika ; appamattarakkhaka. °**worth,** *a.* māsakagghanaka.

Pennyroyal, *n.* sugandhasākavisesa, *m.*

Penology, *n.* kārāpālanañāṇa, *nt.* °**ist,** *n.* kārāpālanakovida, *m.*

Pension, *n.* vissāmavetana, *nt.* *v.t.* vissāmavetanaŋ deti. *p.p.* dinnavis°. °**er,** vissāmavetanalābhī, *m.* °**able,** *a.* vissāmavetanāraha.

Pensive, *a.* jhāyaka ; cintāpara. °**ly,** *adv.* jhāyanapubbakaŋ. °**ness,** *n.* cintāparatā, *f.*

Penstock, *n.* niddhamanadvāra, *nt.*

Pent, *a.* oruddha ; rodhita.

Pentachord, *a.* pañcatantika.

Pentad, *n.* pañcaka, *nt.*

Pentagon, *n.* pañcakoṇakavatthu, *nt.* °**al,** *a.* pañcakoṇayutta.

Penultimate, *a.* upantabhūta. *n.* antakkharato purimakkhara, *nt.*

Penumbra, *n.* (candagāhādisu) upacchāyā, *f.*

Penury, *n.* dāḷiddiya ; niddhanatta, *nt.* °**ious,** *a.* 1. daḷidda ; niddhana ; 2. luddha ; kadariya.

Peon, *n.* pesanakara ; paheṇaka, *m.*

People, *n.* janatā ; pajā, *f.* mahājana, *m.* *v.t.* janāvāsaŋ karoti ; manusse nivāseti. *p.p.* janāvāsakata ; nivāsitamanussa.

Pepper, *n.* kolaka ; goḷamarica, *nt.* °**y,** *a.* 1. kaṭuka ; tikhiṇa ; 2. maricabahula.

Pepsin, *n.* udare pācakojā, *f.*

Peptic, *a.* pācakaggidīpaka.

Per, *prep.* 1. vasena ; anu ; 2. anūnaŋ ; paripuṇṇaŋ. — **annum,** vassavasena ; anuvaccharaŋ, *adv.* — **diem,** anudivasaŋ, *adv.*

Peracute, *a.* atitikhiṇa.

Peradventure, *adv.* kadāci ; karahaci.

Perambulate, *v.t.* anupariyāti ; padakkhiṇaŋ karoti. *p.p.* °yāta ; °kata. °**ion,** *n.* pariyāhiṇḍana, *nt.* °**tor,** anupariyāyī, *m.* °**tory.** *a.* paryāhiṇḍaka ; paribbhamaka.

Perceive, *v.t.* vijānāti ; samanupassati ; paccakkhaŋ karoti. *p.p.* viññāta ; °sita ; °kata. °**er,** *n.* boddhu ; ñātu, *m.*

Per cent, *adv.* satabhāgavasena.

Percentage, *n.* 1. sataŋsasaṅkhyā ; 2. paṭisataŋ gaṇanā, *f.*

Percept, *n.* 1. ālambana ; ārammaṇa, *nt.* 2. cittopaladdhi, *f.* °**ion,** *n.* saññā, *f.* vijānana, *nt.* °**ible,** *a.* veditabba ; indriyagocara. °**ive,** *a.* bujjhanasīla ; bujjhanakkhama ; visayagāhaka. °**ibly,** *adv.* paccakkhaŋ.

Perch, *n.* 1. pakkhivāsayaṭṭhi, *f.* 2. ekādasaratanikamāṇa, *nt.* *v.i.* nilīyati ; yaṭṭhiyaŋ nisīdati. *p.p.* nilīna ; °nisinna.

Perchance, *adv.* kadāci ; kismiñci kāle.

Percipient, *n. a.* visayagāhī ; bujjhanakkhama. °**nce,** *n.* visayagāha, *m.* bujjhanakkhamatā, *f.*

Percolate, *v.i.* parisavati ; binduvasena sandati. *v.t.* parissāveti. *p.p* °savita ; °sandita ; °vita. °**ion,** *n.* parisavana, *nt.* °**tor,** *n.* parissāvaka, *m.* parissāvana, *nt.*

Percuss, *v.t.* (aṅguliādīhi) sanikam āhanati. *p.p.* °āhata. °**ion,** *n.* saṅghaṭṭana, *nt.* paṭighāta, *m.*

Perdition, *n.* mahāvipatti ; apāyuppatti, *f.*

Perdu, Perdue, *a.* gūḷha ; paṭicchanna.

Perdurable, *a.* ciraṭṭhāyī. °**bility,** *a.* ciraṭṭhitikatā, *f.*

Peregrinate, *v.i.* āhiṇḍati ; sañcarati. °**ion,** *n.* āhiṇḍana; sañcaraṇa, *nt.*

Peregrine, *a. n.* videsāgata ; videsānīta.

Peremptory, *a.* sunicchita ; avisaṅkiya ; anullaṅghiya. °**ily,** *adv.* sunicchitākārena ; avassaŋ.

Perennial, *a.* sakalasaŋvacchataṭṭhāyī ; nirantara. °**ly,** *adv.* nirantaraŋ ; satataŋ ; niccaŋ. °**ity,** *n.* nirantaratta, *nt.*

Perfect, *a. n.* anūna ; sampuṇṇa ; paripuṇṇa ; avikala. *v.t.* paripūreti ; avikalīkaroti. *p.p.* °rita ; °kata. °**er,** *n.* sampūraka, *m.* °**ion,** *n.* paripūraṇa, *nt.* pāripūri ; saŋsiddhi ; nipphatti; sampuṇṇatā, *f.* °**ive,** *a.* siddhikara ; paripūraka. °**ly,** *adv.* sampuṇṇaŋ ; asesaŋ ; nissesaŋ. °**ness,** *n.* anūnatta ; kevalaparipuṇṇatta, *nt.* °**tense,** parokkhā vibhatti, *f.*

Perfervid, *a.* atigāḷha ; atibāḷha. °**ly,** *adv.* atigāḷhaŋ.

Perfidy, *n.* paṭiññābhaṅga ; vissāsaghāta, *m.* °**ious,** *a.* asaccasandha ; vissāsaghātī. °**iously,** *adv.* dubbhitāya ; vissāsaghātena.

Perforate, *v.t.* vinivijjhati. *p.p.* vinividdha. °**ion,** *n.* vijjhana ; vinivijjhana, *nt.* °**tor,** *n.* vedhanī, *f.*

Perforce, *adv.* balakkārena ; pasayha ; avassatāya.

Perform, *v.t.* sādheti ; karoti ; pavatteti. *v.i.* naccati. *p.p.* sādhita ; kata ; °tita ; naccita. — **a dance,** naccaŋ payojeti *or* pavatteti. °**ance,** *n.* 1. ācaraṇa ; vattana ; sampādana ; 2. naccana, *nt.* °**er,** *n.* 1. sampādaka ; sādhaka ; 2. naṭa ; raṅgakāra, *m.*

Perfume, *n.* sugandha ; surabhi ; vāsa, *m.* *v.t.* parivāseti ; surabhayati. *p.p.* °vāsita ; °yita. °**atory,** *a.* sugandhakara. — **chest,** gandhakaraṇḍaka, *nt.* — **dealer,** °**er,** *n.* gandhika ; gandhājīvī, *m.* °**ing,** *n.* gandhavāsana, *nt.* °**ry,** *n.* 1. gandhāpaṇa ; 2. gandhasambhāra, *m.*

Perfunctory, *a.* asakkaccakārī ; nirussāha ; nirīha. °**ily,** *adv.* anavadhānena ; asakkaccaŋ.

Perhaps, *adv.* app'eva ; kadāci ; kismiñci kāle ; siyā.

Perfuse, *v.t.* siñcati ; upasiñcati ; ajjhottharati. *p.p.* sitta ; upasitta ; ajjhotthaṭa.

Pergola, *n.* latāchannapatha, *m.*

Peri, *n.* vanadevatā, *f.*

Periapt, *n.* ārakkhā-kavaca, *m.*

Pericarditis, *n.* hadayapaṭalaroga, *m.*

Pericarp, *n.* kaṇṇikā, *f.* bījakosa, *m.*

Pericranium, *n.* sīsakapālacamma, *nt.*

Peril, *n.* antarāya ; upaddava, *m.* *v.t.* upaddaveti ; antarāyaŋ pāpeti. *p.p.* upadduta ; °pāpita. °**ous,** *a.* antarāyakara ; sopaddava ; sappaṭibhaya. °**ously,** *adv.* sāsaṅkaŋ ; sāntarāyaŋ ; sopaddavatāya.

Perimeter, *n.* pariṇāha, *m.*

Period, *n.* 1. samaya ; kālantara ; addha, *m.* 2. yuga ; addhāna, *nt.* 3. virāmakāla, *m.* virāmalakkhaṇa, *nt.* °**ic,** °**ical,** *a.* sāmayika ; anukālika. *n.* kālikasaṅgaha, *m.* sāmayika-paṇṇa, *nt.* °**ically,** *adv.* kālena kālaŋ. °**icity,** *n.* sāmayikatā ; kālānugatatā, *f.* — **of fasting,** phaggu ; uposatha, *m.*

Peripatetic, *a.* pariyaṭaka ; paribbājaka ; aniyatavāsa.

Periphery, *n.* paridhi ; bāhirāvaṭṭa, *m.*

Periphrase, °**phrasis,** *n.* vaṅkutti, *f.* vācābāhulla, *nt.* °**rastic,** *a.* vācābahula.

Periphrase, *v.t.* vaṅkuttiyā pakāseti. *p.p.* °sita.

Perish, *v.i.* nassati ; vinassati ; khayaŋ *or* vilayaŋ yāti. *v.t.* vināseti. *p.p.* naṭṭha ; vinaṭṭha ; kayaṅgata ; vināsita. °**able,** *a.* bhaṅgura ; khayadhamma ; nassanasabhāva. °**ableness,** bhaṅguratta, *nt.* °**ingly,** *adv.* asahanīyākārena.

Peristalsis, *n.* antānaŋ bhojanaharaṇasatti, *f.*

Peristyle, *n.* parivāraka-thambhapanti, *f.*

Peritoneum, *n.* kucchipaṭala ; antāvaraṇa, *nt.*

Perjure, *v.t.* micchā sapati ; kūṭasakkhī hoti. *p.p.* °sapita ; °bhūta. °**er,** *n.* micchāsapathakārī ; kūṭasakkhika, *m.* °**ry,** *n.* micchāsapana, *nt.*

Perjurious, *a.* micchāsapathakara. °**ly,** *adv.* micchāsapanena.

Perk, *v.i.* uddhato pakkhandati. °**y,** *a.* abhimānī ; sappagabbha.

Permanence, °**cy,** *n.* niccatta ; thāvaratta ; dhuvatta, *nt.*

Permanent, *a.* nicca ; dhuva ; thāvara ; avikopiya. °**ly,** *adv.* niccavasena ; dhuvattena.

Permeable, *a.* pariyādānakkhama. °**bility,** *n.* pariyādānakkhamatā, *f.*

Permeate, *v.t.* vyāpeti ; pariyādiyati. *p.p.* vyāpita ; pariyādinna. °**ion,** *n.* sabbavyāpana ; pariyādāna, *nt.*

Permission, *n.* anuññā ; anumati, *f.* okāsakamma, *nt.* °**sible,** *a.* anuññātabba ; anuññeyya. °**sive,** *a.* anujānaka ; okāsakara.

Permit, *n.* anuññā, *f.* anumatipaṇṇa, *nt.* *v.t.* anujānāti ; anumaññati ; okāsaŋ karoti. *p.p.* anuññāta ; anumata ; katokāsa.

Permute, *v.t.* 1. viparivatteti ; aññathā karoti ; 2. vinimeti. *p.p.* °tita ; °kata ; °mita. °**ation,** *n.* viparivattana ; aññathākaraṇa, *nt.* vinimaya, *m.* °**able,** *a.* viparivattanāraha; vinimeyya.

Pernicious, *a.* apakāraka; anatthāvaha; nāsakara. °**ly,** *adv.* savināsaŋ; sāpakāraŋ; anatthāvahatāya.

Pernoctation, *n.* sabbarattijāgaraṇa, *nt.*

Perorate, *v.t.* kathaŋ (samodhānetvā) osāpeti. °**ion,** *n.* kathāsamodhāna; kathāpariyosāna, *nt.*

Perpend, *v.t.* vitakketi; saṅkappeti. *p.p.* °kita; °pita.

Perpendicular, *a.* ujulambamāna. °**ly,** *adv.* ujulambākārena.

Perpetrate, *v.t.* duṭṭhakammam ācarati; aparajjhati. *p.p.* ācarita°; aparaddha. °**ion,** *n.* duṭṭhācaraṇa, *nt.* °**tor,** *n.* dukkatakārī; durācārī, *m.*

Perpetual, *a.* avicchinna; satatappavatta; nirantara. °**ly,** *adv.* satataŋ; avicchinnaŋ.

Perpetuate, *v.t.* avicchinnaŋ pavatteti; thirīkaroti. *p.p.* °tita; °kata. °**tuity,** *n.* avicchinnatā; niccapavatti, *f.*

Perplex, *v.t.* sambhameti; moheti. *p.p.* °mita; mohita. °**ing,** *a.* vikkhepaka; sammohaka. °**ity,** *n.* vimati; vicikicchā, *f.* sandeha, *m.* dveḷhaka, *nt.*

Perquisite, *n.* atirekalābha, *m.*

Persecute, *v.t.* vyathati; pīḷeti; vadhaŋ niyameti. *p.p.* vyathita; pīḷita; °mitavadha. °**ion,** *n.* hiŋsana; daṇḍana; vadhaniyamana, *nt.* °**tor,** *n.* vadhaka; hiŋsaka, *m.*

Perseverance, *n.* viriyārambha; paggaha, *m.* sātaccakiriyā; anikkhittadhuratā; appaṭivānitā, *f.*

Persevere, *v.i.* padahati; parakkamati; viriyam ārabhati *or* na ossajati; na olīyati. *p.p.* padahita; parakkanta; āraddhaviriya; anossaṭṭhaviriya. °**ing,** *a.* pahitatta; daḷhaparakkama. °**ingly,** *adv.* sātaccakiriyāya.

Persia, *n.* Pārasikadesa, *m.*

Persiflage, *n.* muduparihāsa, *m.*

Persimmon, *n.* mahākhajjūrīvisesa, *m.*

Persist, *v.i.* nibaddhakārī *or* akhaṇḍakārī hoti. °**ent,** *a.* sātaccakārī; niccappavattaka. °**ently,** *adv.* sanibandhaŋ; daḷhaŋ. °**ence,** *n.* sātaccakiriyā; appamāditā, *f.* °**ive,** *a.* anolīna; akhaṇḍanasīla; avirata.

Person, *n.* 1. puggala; jana, *m.* 2. sarīra, *nt.* 3. (In gram :) purisa, *m.* °**able,** *a.* abhirūpa. °**age,** *n.* seṭṭhapurisa, *m.* °**al,** *a.* puggalika; ajjhattika. °**ality,** *n.* puggalikatta, *nt.* °**ally,** *adv.* sayam eva; attanā va; pāṭipuggalikaŋ. °**nel,** *n.* sabhikagaṇa, *m.* kiccakārīmaṇḍala, *nt.*

Personate, *v.t.* aññassa vesaŋ gaṇhāti. *p.p.* gahitaññavesa. °**ion,** *n.* paravesadhāraṇa, *nt.*

Personify, Personalize, *v.t.* sacetanattam āropeti *p.p.* āropitasacetanatta. °**ication,** *n.* cetanāropaṇa, *nt.*

Perspective, *n.* dūradassana-cittakamma; manodassana, *nt.* adj. dūradassaka. °**ly,** *adv.* dūradassakākārena.

Perspicacious, *a.* dīghadassī. °**city,** *n.* dīghadassitā, *f.*

Perspicuous, *a.* visada; vibhūta; supākaṭa. °**cuity,** *n.* visadatta; pākaṭatta, *nt.* °**ly,** *adv.* visadākārena; supākaṭaŋ.

Perspire, *v.i.* sedo muccati. *v.t.* sedaŋ moceti. *p.p.* muttaseda; sedamocita. °**able,** *a.* sedajanaka; sedamocanopakāraka. °**ation,** *n.* seda, *m.* sedana, *nt.* °**atory,** *a.* sedamocka.

Persuade, *v.t.* anuneti; upalāleti; palobheti. *p.p.* anunīta; °lita; °bhita. °**er,** upalālaka; palobhaka, *m.*

Persuasion, *n.* upalālana; palobhana; āyācana, *nt.*

Persuasive, *a.* upalālaka; palobhaka; niyojaka.

Pert, *a.* 1. sappagabbha; 2. paṭu; dakkha. °**ly,** *adv.* 1. sappagabbhaŋ; 2. paṭutāya. °**ness,** *n.* 1. pāgabbhiya; 2. pāṭava; kosalla, *nt.*

Pertain, see **Belong.**

Pertinacious, *a.* ādhānagāhī; daḷhadiṭṭhika. °**ly.** *adv.* ādhānagāhitāya. °**city,** *n.* daḷhagāha; abhinivesa, *m.*

Pertinent, *a.* anucchavika; ucita; sambaddha; anukūla. °**ly,** *adv.* avirodhena; ucitākārena; anukūlatāya. °**nency,** *n.* anukūlatta; ocitya; yoggatta, *nt.*

Perturb, *v.t.* saṅkhobheti; vyākulayati. *p.p.* °bhita; °lita. °**ation,** *n.* saṅkhobha, *m.* ākulatta, *nt.* °**ed,** *a.* khubhita; vyākula.

Peruke, *n.* kittima-kesakalāpa, *m.*

Peruse, *v.t.* sammā paṭhati; samāhito vāceti. *p.p.* °ṭhita; °cita. °**sal,** *n.* sammāvācana, *nt.*

Pervade, *v.t.* vyāpeti; pharati; pariyādiyati; ajjhottharati. *p.p.* °pita; phuṭa; pariyādinna; °thaṭa. °**ing,** *a.* vyāpaka; pharaṇaka.

Pervasion, *n.* pharaṇa; vyāpana, *nt.* vipphāra, *m.* °**sive,** *a.* abhivyāpaka; anupharaka. °**sively,** *adv.* abhivyāpetvā; pharaṇena.

Perverse, *a.* 1. viparīta; paṭiloma; 2. anassava; dubbaca; duddamma. °**ly,** *adv.* 1. paṭilomaŋ; 2. dubbacatāya. °**ion,** °**ity,** *n.* 1. vipallāsa; vipariyāsa, *m.* 2. dubbacatta, *nt.* 3. micchāpaṭipatti, *f.* °**ive,** *a.* vipallāsakārī; durupayogī.

Pervert, *v.t.* 1. viparivatteti; vipallāseti; 2. micchāpaṭipajjati. *p.p.* °tita; °sita; °paṭipanna.

Pervious, *a.* suppavesiya; pavesadāyī. °**ness,** *n.* suppavesiyatta, *nt.*

Pesky, *a.* pīḷāvaha.

Pessimism, *n.* sabbāsubhavāda, *m.* °**ist,** *n.* sabbāsubhavādī, *m.*

Pest, *n.* 1. māraka-vyādhi, *m.* 2. paḷibodha; papañca, *m.* °**er,** *n.* pīḷaka; bādhaka, *m.* °**house,** *n.* opasaggikarogāyatana, *nt.*

Pester, *v.t.* pīḷeti; bādheti; viheṭheti. *p.p.* °ḷita; °dhita; °ṭhita.

Pestiferous, *a.* opasaggika; saṅkantika; pāṇahara.

Pestilence, *n.* rogavyasana, *nt.* mārakaroga, *m.* °**lent,** *a.* 1. pāṇahara; māraka; 2. hiŋsākara; 3. guṇanāsaka.

Pestle, *n.* musala, *m.* *v.t.* (musalena) koṭṭeti. *p.p.* °ṭita.

Pet, *n.* piyasatta, *m.* piyavatthu, *nt.* adj. pemanīya. *v.t.* lāleti. *p.p.* lālita.

Petal, *n.* (puppha-) dala, *nt.* °**oid**, — **shaped**, *a.* dalākāra. °**ous**, *a.* bahudalayutta.

Petard, *n.* dvārugghāṭakayanta, *nt.*

Peter, *v.i.* niṭṭhāti; osānaŋ pāpuṇāti. *p.p.* niṭṭhita; osānappatta.

Petiole, *n.* pattanāḷa; pattanahāru, *m.*

Petition, *n.* 1. āyācanapaṇṇa, *nt.* abhiyācanā; patthanā, *f.* *v.t.* abhiyācati; abhipattheti. *p.p.* °cita; °thita. °**er**, *n.* abhiyācaka; āyācaka, *m.*

Petrify, *v.t.* pāsāṇīkaroti; santhambheti. *p.p.* °kata; °bhita. °**faction**, *n.* pāsāṇīkaraṇa; santhambhana, *nt.*

Petroglyph, *n.* silāvaḍḍhakīkamma; pāsāṇacittakamma, *nt.*

Petrograph, *n.* silālekhā; silālipi, *f.* °**y**, *n.* pāsāṇasambhava-vijjā, *f.* °**er**, *n.* pāsāṇasambhavavidū, *m.*

Petrol, *n.* sodhita-khaṇijatela. *v.t.* khaṇijatelaŋ yojeti. *p.p.* yojita°.

Petroleum, *n.* bhūmijatela, *nt.*

Petrology, *n.* silāvijjā, *f.*

Petrous, *a.* pāsāṇasadisa.

Petticoat, *n.* itthantaravāsaka. adj. nārīgatika.

Pettifog, *v.t.* appamattake vivadati. °**ger**, *n.* ittara-nītividū, *m.*

Pettish, *a.* kakkasa; kodhana. °**ly**, *adv.* sābhissaṅgaŋ.

Petty, *a.* appaka; lahuka; appamattaka. °**iness**, *n.* appamattakatta, *nt.*

Petulant, *a.* kodhana; upāyāsabahula.

Pew, *n.* (devāyatane) puggalikāsana, *nt.*

Pewit, *n.* dindibha; kikī, *m.*

Pewter *n.* kaŋsaloha, *nt.*

Phalange, Phalanx, *n.* 1. senāmukha; 2. pūgabandhana; vaggabandhana, *nt.*

Phallus, *n.* liṅgasaṇṭhāna; liṅgarūpa, *nt.* °**ic**, *a.* liṅgāyatta.

Phantasm, *n.* 1. bhūtadassana; 2. manonimmāṇa; matapuggala-dassana, *nt.* °**al**, *a.* bhūtadassanāyatta. °**ally**, *adv.* bhūtadassanavasena. °**agoria**, *n.* calarūpadassana, *nt.*

Phantom, *n.* 1. bhūta; pisāca, *m.* 2. manomayarūpa, *nt.* °**atic**, °**ic**, *a.* obhāsanissita; māyāmaya.

Pharisee, *n.* 1. dhammānuvattī; 2. kuhaka; kūṭatāpasa, *m.*

Pharmaceutical, *a.* osadhavidhāna-visayaka. °**tics**, osadhasampādana, *nt.* °**tist**, *n.* osadhasampādaka, *m.*

Pharmacography, *n.* osadhavaṇṇanā, *f.*

Pharmacology, *n.* osadhasampādana-vijjā, *f.* °**ist**, osadhappabhedavidū, *m.*

Pharmacopoeia, *n.* osadhanighaṇḍu, *m.*

Pharmacy, *n.* 1. osadhasampādana, *nt.* 2. bhesajjasālā, *f.* osadhālaya, *m.* °**ist**, osadhavāṇija, *m.*

Pharos, *n.* nāvikadīpāgāra, *nt.* padīpatthambha, *m.*

Pharyngitis, *n.* kaṇṭhaggadāha, *m.*

Pharynx, *n.* sāsanāḷa-kaṇṭhantara, *nt.*

Phase, *n.* 1. candakalā, *f.* 2. dissamānākāra.

Pheasant, *n.* vanakukkuṭa; jīvañjīvaka, *m.*

Phenomenon, *n.* 1. diṭṭhivisaya, *m.* dassana, *nt.* 2. abbhuta, *nt.* °**nal**, *a.* acchariyāvaha.

Phew, *intj.* dhiratthu!

Phial, *n.* kācatumba, *m.*

Philander, *v.i.* sārattākārena carati; pemaŋ bandhati. *p.p.* baddhapema. °**er**, *n.* lahu-pemadassaka; itthivallabha, *m.*

Philanthropy, *n.* parahitakāmitā; lokānukampā; lokatthacariyā, *f.* °**ic**, *a.* parahitakamī; lokānukampī. °**ist**, *n.* parahitākārī; lokatthacārī; parānukampī, *m.*

Philately, *n.* sāsanamuddā-sañcinana, *nt.* °**ist**, *n.* sāsanamuddā-visesavidū; muddāsaŋhāraka, *m.*

Philharmonic, *a.* saṅgītappiya.

Philippic, *n.* mammacchedakavācā, *f.*

Philology, *n.* niruttisattha, *nt.* °**ical**, *a.* neruttika. °**ist**, *n.* bhāsātattaññū, *m.*

Philomath, *n.* vijjāpiya. °**y**, *n.* sutappiyatā, *f.*

Philosophy, *n.* tattañāṇa; ñāyasattha, *nt.* °**pher**, *n.* ajjhattadhammavidū, *m.* °**ical**, *a.* tattañāṇāyatta. °**ically**, *adv.* ñāṇadassanānurūpena; ñāyānusārena. °**ize**, *v.t.* yathāsabhāvaŋ nirūpeti.

Philotechnic, *a.* kalābhirata.

Philtre, Philter, *n.* vasīkaraṇosadha, *nt.*

Phiz, *n.* 1. ānana; vadana, *nt.* 2. mukhavaṇṇa, *m.*

Phlebitis, *n.* dhamanīdāha, *m.*

Phlebotomy, *n.* (arogatāya) rudhirasāvaṇa, *nt.* °**ize**, *v.t.* rudhiraŋ sāveti. *p.p.* sāvitarudhira.

Phlegm, *n.* semha; kapha, *m.* *nt.* °**atic**, *a.* 1. semhādhika; 2. semhajanaka; 3. anussuka, °**agogic**, *a.* semhanāsaka. °**y**, *a.* 1. semhayutta; 2. nirīhaka.

Phoenix, Phenix, *n.* Misarapurāvuttagata-mahāpakkhī, *m.*

Phonate, *v.i.* uccāreti. *p.p.* °rita. °**ion**, *n.* uccāraṇa, *nt.*

Phone, *n.* 1. ekassarasadda, *m.* 2. see **Telephone**.

Phonetic, *a.* saddavisayaka; vācānissita. °**ics**, *n. pl.* saravijjā, *f.* °**ally**, *adv.* saravijjāvasena. °**tist**, *n.* saravijjāvidū, *m.*

Phonic, *a.* saddavisayaka; sarāyatta.

Phonogram, *n.* saddānugatalakkhaṇa, *nt.* °**graph**, *n.* 1. sarānugatalipi, *f.* 2. saddavāhakayanta, *nt.* °**graphy**, *n.* saralekhanakkama, *m.*

Phonology, *n.* saravijjā, *f.* °**ically**, *adv.* saravijjāvasena. °**ist**, *n.* saravijjāvidū, *m.*

Phosphoresce, *v.i.* aggiŋ vinā dippati; andhakāre dippati. °**nt**, *a.* andhakāre dippamāna.

Phosphorus, *n.* pakāsada-rasāyana, *nt.*

Photograph, *n.* chāyārūpa, *nt.* °**er**, *n.* chāyārūpasippī, *m.* °**ic**, *a.* chāyārūpāyatta. °**y**, *n.* chāyārūpasippa, *nt.*

Phrase, *n.* 1. khaṇḍavākya, *nt.* 2. racanāvidhi, *m.* bhāsārīti, *f.* 3. upadesapāṭha, *m. v.t.* 1. pakāseti ; 2. vākyāni racayati. °**ology,** *n.* vākyaracanā, *f.* racanāvidhi, *m.* °**monger,** *n.* sundarapāṭhagavesī, *m.*

Phrenetic, see **Frantic.**

Phrenology, *n.* sīsakapālavijjā, *f.* °**ist,** *n.* kapālalakkhaṇaññū, *m.*

Phthisis, *n.* khayaroga, *m.*

Physic, *n.* 1. tikicchā, *f.* vejjakamma, *nt.* 2. bhesajja, *nt. pl.* 1. rūpadhātuvijjā, *f.* 2. padatthasattha, *nt. v.t.* tikicchati. *p.p.* °chita. °**al,** *a.* 1. sārīrika ; 2. rūpamaya ; 3. osadhīya. °**ally,** *adv.* dehabalena ; dhātuvasena. °**ian,** *n.* vejja ; bhisakka, *m.* °**ist,** *n.* 1. rūpadhammavidū ; 2. padatthasatthaññū.

Physiognomy, *n.* aṅgavijjā, *f.* °**ist,** *n.* aṅgavijjāvidū, *m.*

Physiography, *n.* mahābhūtavaṇṇanā ; bhūvaṇṇanā, *f.*

Physiology, *n.* jīvavijjā ; bhūtagāmavijjā, *f.* °**ist,** *n.* jīvavijjāvedī, *m.*

Physique, *n.* sarīrasaṇṭhāna ; dehalakkhaṇa, *nt.*

Piacular, *a.* paṭikammāyatta ; dosahāpaka.

Pianist, *n.* turiyavisesavādaka, *m.*

Piano, *n.* turiyavisesa, *m.*

Piazza, *n.* 1. bhūmippadesa ; 2. ālinda, *m.*

Pibroch, *n.* saṅgāma-kāhalanāda, *m.*

Pica, *n.* khuddaka-muddākkharavisesa, *m.*

Picaroon, *n.* samuddacora ; vilumpaka, *m. v.i.* vilumpati. *p.p.* vilutta.

Piccaninny, *n.* dāraka ; bālaka, *m.* adj. atikhuddaka.

Pick, *n.* 1. khaṇittī, *f.* 2. dantasodhanī, *f.* 3. uñchana, *nt. v.t.* 1. ocināti ; samāharati ; 2. uccināti ; 3. uñchati ; tuṇḍena gaṇhāti. *p.p.* ocita ; samāhaṭa ; uccinita ; uñchita ; °gahita. °**axe,** *n.* pāsāṇadāraṇī, *f.* — **a bone,** visuŋ karoti. °**ing,** *n.* uddharaṇa ; tudana, *nt.* — **off,** thokathokaŋ bhuñjati. — **one's teeth,** dante sodheti. — **out,** uddharati ; nīharati. °**pocket,** *n.* gaṇṭhibhedakacora, *m.* — **a-back,** *adv.* khandhe āropetvā. — **a pocket,** gaṇṭhiŋ chindati. — **a quarrel,** kalahaṃ ārabhati. **Ear** —, kaṇṇasodhanī, *f.* **Tooth** —, dantasūci, *f.*

Picket, *n.* 1. sūla ; saṅku, *m.* 2. chandagahaṇa, *nt. v.t.* 1. sūlehi āvarati ; 2. rakkhīgumbaŋ ṭhapeti. *p.p.* °āvaṭa ; ṭhapita°.

Pickle, *n.* bilaṅgasūpa, *m. v.t.* bilaṅgena yojeti. *p.p.* bilaṅgayojita.

Picksome, *a.* dutappiya.

Picnic, *n.* 1. vanakīḷā, *f.* 2. kīḷābhojana, *nt.*

Pictorial, *a.* cittakammāyatta ; chāyārūpasahita.

Picture, *n.* 1. cittakamma ; 2. paṭirūpa, *nt.* — **frame,** *n.* cittāvaraṇa, *nt.* cittādhāra, *m.* °**gallery,** *n.* cittāgāra, *nt.* °**maker,** *n.* cittakāra, *m.*

Picture, *v.t.* 1. āloceti ; manasikaroti ; 2. citteti ; ālikhati. *p.p.* °cita ; °kata ; cittita ; °khita.

Picturesque, *a.* vicitta ; dassanīya. °**ness**, *n.* dassanīyatta ; vicittatta, *nt.* °**ly**, *adv.* dassanīyākārena.

Pie, *n.* 1. pakkhivisesa, *m.* 2. piṭṭhāvuta-bhojana, *nt.*

Piebald, Pied, *a.* kammāsa ; sabala ; vividhavaṇṇa.

Piece, *n.* khaṇḍa ; koṭṭhāsa, *m.* sakalikā, *f.* *v.t.* saŋyojeti ; ghaṭeti ; samodhāneti. *p.p.* °jita ; ghaṭita ; °nita. °**meal**, *adv.* khaṇḍaso ; bhāgaso.

Pier, *n.* setubandha, *m.*

Pierce, *v.t.* vinivijjhati. *p.p.* vinividdha. °**ing**, *a.* vedhaka ; tudaka ; 2. tibba ; ugga. °**ing**, *n.* nittudana ; vijjhana, *nt.*

Pierglass, *n.* sabbakāyikādāsa, *m.*

Piety, *n.* dhammikatta, *nt.* saddhā ; bhatti, *f.*

Piffle, *n.* samphappalāpa, *m.* *v.i.* samphaŋ palapati.

Pig, *n.* sūkara ; varāha, *m.* *v.i.* sūkarasadisaŋ vasati. °**gery**, *n.* sūkaravaja, *m.* °**gish**, *a.* sūkaropama ; kucchitavutti. °**headed**, *a.* mandamatika. °**let**, °**ling**, *n.* sūkarapotaka, *m.* °**tail**, *n.* (Cīnadesīyānaŋ) vellita-dhammilla, *m.*

Pigeon, *n.* kapota ; pārāvata, *m.* *v.t.* mañjūsovarake pakkhipati. *p.p.* °khitta. °**hearted**, *a.* adhīra ; kātara. °**hole**, *n.* 1. kapota-bila, *nt.* 2. mañjūsovaraka, *m.* °**ry**, kapotapālikā, *f.*

Pike, *n.* saṅku ; sūla, *m.* °**man**, *n.* sūladhārī, *m.* — **for an elephant**, tutta, *nt.* °**staff**, kuntayaṭṭhi, *m.* *f.*

Pile, *n.* 1. puñja ; rāsi ; nicaya, *m.* 2. sūla ; khīla, *m.* *v.t.* puñjeti ; rāsīkaroti ; cināti. *p.p.* °jita ; °kata ; cita. **Funeral** —, citaka, *nt.*

Piles, *n.* arisa, *nt.*

Pilfer, *v.t.* moseti ; coreti ; avaharati. *p.p.* mosita ; corita ; avahaṭa. °**er**, *n.* mosaka, *m.* °**age**, *n.* mosanā, *f.* coriya, *nt.*

Pilgrim, *n.* puññatitthagāmī, *m.* °**age**, *n.* cetiyacārikā, *f.*

Piliferous, *a.* saloma ; lomāvuta.

Pill, *n.* guḷikā ; vaṭṭikā, *f.*

Pillage, *n.* vilumpana, *nt.* vilopa, *m.* *v.t.* vilumpeti ; acchindati. *p.p.* vilutta ; acchinna. °**er**, *n.* vilumpaka ; acchindaka, *m.*

Pillar, *n.* thambha ; yūpa ; thūṇa, *m.*

Pillion, *n.* pacchāsana, *nt.*

Pillory, *n.* vadhaka-dārubhaṇḍa, *nt.*

Pillow, *n.* bimbohana ; sīsūpadhāna, *nt.* *v.t.* upadhānāni yojeti. *v.i.* bimbohane sīsaŋ ṭhapeti. °**case**, cimilikā ; bimbohanathavikā, *f.*

Pilot, *n.* 1. jalapathadesaka ; 2. kaṇṇadhāra, *m.* *v.t.* nāvāyā maggaŋ dasseti. °**less**, *a.* maggadesakarahita.

Pilule, *n.* khuddakavaṭikā, *f.*

Pimple, *n.* vadanapiḷakā, *f.*

Pin, *n.* sūci ; salākā, *f.* *v.t.* sūciyā āvuṇāti *or* ghaṭeti. *p.p.* sūcyāvuta ; sūcighaṭita. °**prick**, *n.* 1. sūcivijjhana ; 2. appakatudana, *nt.*

Pincers, *n.* saṇḍāsa, *m.*

Pinch, *n*. nakhatudana, *nt*. *v.t*. nakhehi vitudati *or* vilikhati. *p.p.* nakhavitunna ; °khita.

Pine, *n*. devadāru, *m*. *v.i*. milāyati ; osīdati. *p.p.* milāta ; osīna. °**apple**, *n*. bahunettaphala, *nt*. madhuketakī, *m*. — **for**, ākaṅkhati ; ukkaṇṭhati. *p.p.* °khita ; °ṭhita.

Pinfold, *n*. goṭṭha, *nt*. *v.t*. goṭṭhe *or* vaje rundheti. *p.p.* °dhita.

Pingo, *n*. kāja, *m*. — **basket**, sikkā, *f*.

Pinguid, *a*. pīna ; pīvara ; vaṭhara.

Pinion, *n*. 1. pekhuṇa; 2. khuddakacakka, *nt*. *v.t*. 1. pakkhe chindati ; 2. pacchābāhaŋ bandhati. *p.p.* chinnapakkha ; °baddha.

Pink, *a*. pāṭala. *v.t*. satthena vijjhati. *p.p.* satthaviddha. °**y**, *a*. īsaŋpāṭala.

Pinnace, *n*. dvikūpakanāvā, *f*.

Pinnacle, *n*. niyyūha, *m*. pāsādasikhara, *nt*.

Pioneer, *n*. puregāmī ; pubbaṅgama ; netu ; maggadesaka, *m*. *v.t*. purato yāti ; maggaŋ dasseti. *p.p.* °yāta ; dassitamagga.

Pious, *a*. dhammika ; saddha ; bhattimantu. °**ly**, *adv*. saddhāya ; bhattiyā. °**ness**, *n*. dhammikatta, *nt*.

Pip, *n*. 1. phalabīja, *nt*. 2. tilaka, *m*. 3. tārāsaṇṭhāna, *nt*. *v.t*. āhanati. *p.p.* āhata.

Pipe, *n*. 1. nāḷikā ; paṇālī ; āyatikā, *f*. 2. dhamanavaŋsa, *m*. *v.t*. vaŋsaŋ dhamati. °**er**, *n*. vaŋsadhamaka, *m*. °**clay**, *n*. setamattikā, *f*. °**ing**, *n*. vaŋsadhamana, *nt*.

Pipul (tree), assattha (-rukkha), *m*.

Piquant, *a*. 1. tibba ; tikhiṇa ; 2. hadayaṅgama. °**ncy**, *n*. 1. kaṭukatta, *nt*. 2. manoharatta, *nt*. °**ly**, *adv*. 1. tikhiṇākārena ; hadayaṅgamatāya.

Pique, *n*. mandakopa ; appasāda ; asantosa, *m*. *v.t*. kopeti ; roseti. *v.i*. uddāmo hoti. *p.p.* kopita ; rosita ; uddāmabhūta.

Piracy, *n*. nāvāvilumpana, *m*.

Pirate, *n*. 1. sāmuddikacora ; nāvāvilumpaka ; 2. paraganthavilumpaka, *m*. *v.t*. 1. vilumpati ; avaharati ; 2. aññakattukaganthaŋ pakāseti. *p.p.* vilutta ; avahaṭa. °**ical**, *a*. sāhasika ; vilumpaka.

Pirogue, *n*. ekarukkhadoṇi, *f*.

Pirouette, *n*. maṇḍalanacca, *nt*.

Piscatology, *n*. macchappabheda-ñāṇa, *nt*.

Piscatory, *n*. parāyattaṭhāne macchabandhanānumati, *f*.

Pisces, *n*. mīnarāsi, *m*. °**cine**, *a*. macchavisayaka.

Piscivorous, *a*. macchabhakkha.

Pish, *intj*. dhiratthu.

Pisiform, *a*. māsa-saṇṭhāna.

Pismire, *n*. kipillikā, *f*.

Piss, *v.i*. ummihati ; omutteti. *p.p.* °hita ; °tita. *n*. mutta, *nt*.

Pistol, *n*. khuddakagginālikā, *f*. *v.t*. (imāya) vijjhati. *p.p.* °viddha.

Pit, *n*. āvāṭa ; sobbha ; ākara, *m*. *v.t*. 1. āvāṭe pakkhipati ; 2. yujjhanāya payojeti. *p.p.* °pakkhitta ; °jita. — -**a-pat**, *adv*. sahadayaphandanaŋ ; sāsaṅkaŋ. °**fall**, *n*. opāta, *m*. **Small** —, kusobbha, *m*.

Pitch, *n*. 1. yakkhadhūpa, *m*. 2. agga ; sikhara, *nt*. pariyanta, *m*. *v.t*. 1. niveseti ; patiṭṭhāpeti ; 2. khipati ; pāteti ; 3. sajjulasena ālepeti. *v.i*. nipatati ; opatati. *p.p*. °sita ; °pita ; khitta ; pātita ; °ālitta. °tita. **— on**, adhiṭṭhāti ; sanniṭṭhānaŋ yāti.

Pitcher, *n*. kuṇḍikā, *f*. kamaṇḍalu, *m*. **Full —**, puṇṇaghaṭa ; bhaddakumbha, *m*.

Piteous, *a*. dīna ; dukkhita ; dayāraha. °**ly**, *adv*. dukkhitākārena.

Pith, *n*. 1. sāraŋsa ; 2. rukkhasāra, *m*. sāradāru, *nt*. °**less**, *a*. asāra ; nissāra ; pheggumaya. °**y**, *a*. sārayutta.

Pittance, *n*. 1. appapariccāga, *m*. 2. thokavetana, *nt*.

Pituitary, *a*. semhuggāraka.

Pity, *n*. dayā ; karuṇā ; anukampā, *f*. *v.t*. anukampati ; karuṇāyati ; anuddayati. *p.p*. °pita ; °yita. °**iable**, *a*. anukampiya ; dayanīya. °**iful**, *a*. kārunika ; sadaya ; anukampaka. °**iless**, *a*. niddaya ; niṭṭhura. °**ilessly**, *adv*. niddayaŋ ; niranukampaŋ.

Pityriasis, *n*. vitacchikā, *f*.

Pivot, *n*. vivaṭṭana-khīla, *nt*.

Placable, *a*. suvupasamiya ; adhivāsanasīla.

Placard, *n*. nivedanapaṇṇa, *nt*. *v.t*. āvedanapaṇṇea pakāseti. *p.p*. °sita.

Placate, *v.t*. vupasameti ; santataŋ pāpeti. *p.p*. °mita ; °pita.

Place, *n*. ṭhāna, *nt*. padesa ; bhūbhāga, *m*. 2. ṭhānantara, *nt*. adhikāra, *m*. *v.t*. 1. ṭhapeti ; patiṭṭhāpeti ; 2. adhikāre niyojeti. *p.p*. °pita ; °jita *or* niyutta. °**ed**, *a*. nihita ; nikkhitta ; paṇihita. °**ing**, *n*. ṭhapana ; patiṭṭhāpana, *nt*. **— for execution**, āghātana, *nt*. **In one —**, ekattha, *adv*. **In one — or another**, yattha katthaci. **In the first —**, paṭhamaŋ, *adv*. **In the next—**, dutiyaŋ ; anantaraŋ. **Out of —**, aṭṭhāne, *adv*. **Give —**, apakkamati. **Take —**, sijjhati.

Placenta, *n*. gabbhāsaya, *m*.

Placid, *a*. upasanta ; anāvila. °**ly**, *adv*. santākārena. °**ity**, *n*. santatā, *f*. anāvilatta, *nt*.

Plagiarist, *n*. vākya-racanāthenaka, *m*. °**ism**, *n*. vākyaracanācoriya, *nt*. °**ize**, *v.t*. racanādiŋ theneti.

Plagiary, *n*. paravākyathenana, *nt*.

Plagio (in comb.), abbohāragata.

Plague, *n*. 1. uppāta ; upaddava, *m*. 2. saṅkantikaroga ; ahivātakaroga, *m*. *v.t*. pīḷeti ; upaddaveti ; vyathati. *p.p*. pīḷita ; upadduta ; vyathita. °**ing**, *a*. upaddavakara. °**er**, *n*. pīḷaka ; santāpaka, *m*.

Plaguy, *a*. santāpakara. °**ily**, pīḷākaratāya.

Plaid, *n*. vicitta-kambala, *nt*.

Plain, *n*. samatala, *nt*. samabhūmi, *f*. adj. 1. sama ; 2. amissita ; 3. avibhūsita ; 4. visada ; pākaṭa ; 5. akapaṭa ; avyāja ; 6. (of food :) appaṇīta. °**ly**, *adv*. supākaṭaŋ ; avyājaŋ. °**ness**, *n*. 1. samatta ; 2. ajjava ; avyājatta, *nt*.

Plaint, *n*. 1. codanā, *f*. abhiyoga, *m*. 2 vilāpa, *m*. °**iff**, *n*. codaka, *m* °**ive**, *a*. sokāvaha ; dīna. °**ively**, *adv*. sakaruṇaŋ ; dīnākārena.

Plait, *n.* ganthana; veṇīkaraṇa, *nt.* *v.t.* gantheti; veṇīkaroti. *p.p.* °thita; °kata.

Plan, *n.* 1. saṇṭhānālekha; suttapāta, *m.* 2. naya; kama; upāya; upayoga, *m.* *v.t.* 1. saṇṭhānam ālikhati; 2. payojeti; upakkamati. *p.p.* ālikhitasaṇṭhāna; °jita; °mita.

Plane, *n.* 1. tala; samatala, *nt.* 2. (Carpenter's:) kaṭṭhasamakaraṇī, *f.* *v.t.* vitaccheti; samīkaroti. *p.p.* °chita; °kata.

Planet, *n.* gahatārā, *f.* °**ary**, *a.* gahatārāyatta. °**arium**, *n.* gahamaṇḍalākāradassana, *nt.* °**stricken**, *a.* gahapīḷita; vibbhanta.

Plangent, *a.* phandamāna; kampamāna. °**ncy**, *n.* phandamānatta, *nt.*

Plank, *n.* dāruphalaka, *m.* *nt.* *v.t.* phalake attharati; phalakehi chādeti. *p.p.* atthataphalaka; phalakacchanna.

Plant, *n.* 1. osadhī, *f.* gaccha, *m.* 2. yantasamūha, *m.* *v.t.* 1. ropeti; 2. niveseti. *p.p.* ropita; °sita. °**ation**, *n.* 1. ropaṇa, *nt.* 2. ārāma; uyyāna, *nt.* °**er**, *n.* ropaka, *m.*

Plantain, *n.* rambhā; kadalī, *f.* moca, *m.* (Fruit:) kadaliphala, *nt.*

Plantar, *a.* pādatalāyatta.

Plantigrade, *n.* pādatalacārī, *m.*

Plaque, *n.* vicitta-lohaphalaka, *m.*

Plash, *n.* udakasobbha, *m.* *v.i.* udake kīḷati. *v.t.* udakaŋ kampeti. °**y**, *a.* sobbhayutta; salilappāya.

Plasm, *n.* jīvadhātu, *f.*

Plasma, *n.* jīvasāra, *m.*

Plaster, *n.* 1. lepa; cuṇṇālepa, *m.* 2. bhesajjālepa, *m.* *v.t.* 1. ālepeti; sudhāya lepeti; 2. bhesajjālepaŋ yojeti. *p.p.* ālitta; yojita-°pa. °**er**, *n.* sudhālepaka; palagaṇḍa, *m.* °**ing**, *n.* ālepana; sudhākamma, *nt.* °**ed with**, avalitta; parikammakata, *a.*

Plastic, *a.* kammañña; sukhanamya. °**ity**, *n.* muduttа; kammaññatta, *nt.*

Plastron, *n.* cammamaya-urāvaraṇa, *nt.*

Plat, see **Plait**.

Plate, *n.* 1. taṭṭaka; kaŋsa; bhuñjana-patta, *m.* 2. paṭṭa, *nt.* paṭṭikā, *f.* *v.t.* lohena lepeti *or* āvarati. *p.p.* lohalitta; lohāvuta.

Plateau, *n.* adhiccakā, *f.* uccasamatala, *nt.*

Platform, *n.* vedikā, *f.* — **around a pagoda**, cetiyaṅgaṇa, *nt.*

Platitude, *n.* gāmikakathā, *f.* °**inous**, *a.* sāraŋsarahita. °**inously**, *adv.* rasahīnākārena.

Platter, *n.* khuddaka-taṭṭaka; thāla, *m.*

Plaudit, *n.* pasaŋsā, *f.* aṅgīkaraṇa, *nt.*

Plausible, *a.* pasaŋsiya; saccābhāsa; bahiramma. °**bility**, *n.* āpātharammatā, *f.*

Play, *n.* 1. kīḷā; keḷi; khiḍḍā; rati, *f.* vinoda, *m.* 2. raṅga, *m.* nacca, *nt.* *v.i.* 1. kīḷati; ramati; dibbati; 2. naccati. — **at ball**, guḷakīḷā, *f.* °**er**, *n.* kīḷaka, *m.* °**fellow**, °**mate**, *n.* sahakīḷaka, *m.* °**ful**, *a.* kīḷāsatta; kīḷābhirata. °**fully**, *adv.* keḷipubbakaŋ. °**fulness**, *n.* kīḷāratatta; kīḷālola ta, *nt.* °**ground,** *n.* keḷimaṇḍala, *nt.* kīḷābhūmi, *f.* °**thing,** *n.* kīḷābhaṇḍa, *nt.* °**time,** *n.* kīḷāsamaya, *m.* — **a trick,** hassaŋ yojeti. — **upon,** upahasati. °**wright,** *n.* nāṭyaganthasampādaka, *m.*

Plea, *n.* 1. codanāpahāra ; mocanahetu, *m.* 2. patthanā, *f.*

Plead, *v.t.i.* codanaŋ pariharati ; kāraṇākāraṇaŋ dasseti. — **guilty,** 1. sāvajjataŋ paṭijānāti ; 2. savinayaŋ yācati. °**er,** *n.* nītivedī, *m.* °**ing,** *n.* 1. codanāpariharaṇa ; 2. abhiyācana, *nt.*

Pleasance, *n.* 1. pamoda ; vinoda, *m.* 2. kīḷuyyāna ; gehuyyāna, *nt.*

Pleasant, *a.* ramma ; ramaṇīya ; manohara ; manuñña ; cāru ; kanta ; hadayaṅgama. °**ly,** *adv.* rammākārena. — **thing,** laddhaka ; rāmaṇeyyaka, *nt.* — **to hear,** savaṇīya, *a.* — **to touch,** sukhasamphassa, *a.*

Please, *v.t.* toseti ; modeti ; pasādeti ; rañjeti ; ārādheti ; rameti ; pīṇeti. *p.p.* tosita ; modita ; °dita ; °jita ; °dhita ; ramita ; pīṇita. *v.i.* tussati ; nandati ; pasīdati ; ramati ; modati. *p.p.* tiṭṭha ; °dita ; pasanna ; rata ; mudita. °**ed,** *a.* haṭṭha ; pahaṭṭha ; santuṭṭha ; sumana ; patīta. °**ing,** *a.* iṭṭha; kanta; manāpa ; ruccanaka. °**ingly,** *adv.* ruccanākārena.

Pleasure, *n.* āmoda ; pamoda ; ānanda ; santosa, *m.* tuṭṭhi ; vitti ; pīti ; nandi ; rati, *f.* pāmojja, *nt.* °**able,** see **Pleasant.** °**boat,** *n.* keḷināvā, *f.* °**garden,** *n.* kīḷuyyāna, *nt.* °**ground,** *n.* vinodabhūmi, *f.* — **house,** *n.* vilāsamandira, *nt.*

Pleat, *n.* āvali ; vali, *f.* *v.t.* āvaliyo karoti. *p.p.* katāvalī.

Plebeian, *n.* akulīna-jana ; mahājana, *m.* adj. mahājanika.

Plebiscite, *n.* mahājana-matapakāsana, *nt.*

Pledge, *n.* 1. nyāsa ; upanidhi ; saccakāra, *m.* 2. paṭiññā, *f.* *v.t.* 1. saccakāraŋ ṭhapeti ; 2. paṭiññaŋ deti. *p.p.* ṭhapita-saccakāra ; dinnapaṭiñña. °**gee,** *n.* nyāsagāhī, *m.* °**er,** *n.* nyāsadāyī, *m.*

Pleiades, *n.* kattikanakkhatta, *nt.*

Plenary, *a.* anūna ; sampuṇṇa. °**ily,** *adv.* anūnaŋ ; asesaŋ.

Plenipotentiary, *a.* *n.* anūnabaladhāri ; puṇṇabalayutta. °**tence,** *n.* anūnabala, *nt.*

Plenish, *v.t.* sampādeti. *p.p.* °dita.

Plenitude, *n.* puṇṇatta ; sulabhatta, *nt.*

Plenteous, *a.* bahula ; sulabha ; pahūta. °**ly,** *adv.* bahulaŋ ; sulabhatāya ; pahūtākārena.

Plenty, *n.* bāhulla ; pacuratta ; samiddhatta, *nt.* °**iful,** *a.* bahula ; pacura ; sulabha ; pahūta. °**fully,** *adv.* bāhullena ; sulabhattena. °**fulness,** bahulatta ; samiddhatta, *nt.*

Plenum, *n.* sampuṇṇasabhā, *f.*

Pleonasm, *n.* padabahulatta ; punaruttibahulatta, *nt.* °**stic,** *a.* niratthaka-padabahula.

Plethora, *n.* rattapitta ; rudhirabāhulla, *nt.* °**ric,** *a.* rattādhika.

Pleura, *n.* kilomaka, *nt.* °**risy,** *n.* kilomakadāha ; papphāsadāha, *m.*

Plexus, *n.* sirājāla, *nt.*

Pliable, *a.* sunamya; akaṭhina; kammañña. °**bility,** *n.* namyatta; vidheyatta, *nt.*

Pliant, *a.* namya; vidheya; kammañña. °**ncy,** *n.* namyattā; vidheyatta, *nt.*

Plicate, *a.* veṇīkata; puṭībhūta. °**ion,** *n.* saŋhatatta, *nt.*

Pliers, *n. pl.* saṇḍāsavisesa, *m.*

Plight, *n.* 1. paṭiññā; 2. avatthā; gati; pavatti, *f. v.t.* paṭiññaŋ deti. *p.p.* dinnapaṭiñña. °**er,** *n.* paṭiññātu, *m.*

Plinth, *n.* thambhapāda, *m.* bhittimūla, *nt.*

Plod, *v.i.t.* kicchena yāti; sanikaŋ vāyamati; akhaṇḍaŋ pavatteti. *p.p.* °yāta; °mita; °tita. °**ding,** *n.* akhaṇḍavāyāma, *m.*

Plop, *n.* udake patana-sadda, *m. v.i.* sahasā udake patati. *adv.* patanasaddayuttaŋ.

Plot, *n.* 1. bhūbhāga; 2. kūṭopāya, *m.* kumantana, *nt. v.t.* upāyaŋ yojeti; upakkamati. *v.i.* dubbhati; kumanteti. *p.p.* yojitopāya; dubbhita; °tita. °**ter,** *n.* dubbhī; kumantaka, *m.* °**ting,** *n.* dubbhana; padussana; kumantana, *nt.*

Plough, *n.* naṅgala; hala, *nt. v.t.* kasati. *p.p.* kasita *or* kaṭṭha. °**ing,** *n.* kasana; kasikamma, *nt.* °**ing festival,** vappamaṅgala, *nt.* °**man,** *n.* kassaka, *m.* °**share,** *n.* phāla, *m.* **Beam of a —,** naṅgalīsā, *f.*

Plover, *n.* dindibha; soṇṇacūḷa, *m.*

Pluck, *n.* dhiti, *f.* viriya, *nt.* parakkama, *m. v.t.* (off:) luñcati; lunāti; nikkaḍḍhati; (to gather:) ocināti; saŋharati. *p.p.* °cita; lūna; °ḍhita; ocita; saŋhaṭa. °**ing,** *n.* 1. uppāṭana; uddharaṇa; 2. ocinana, *nt.* °**less,** *a.* adhīra; kātara. °**y,** *a.* nibbhaya.

Plug, *n.* thambhanī; rodhanī, *f. v.t.* pidahati; thaketi; rodheti. *p.p.* pihita; thakita; rodhita.

Plum, *n.* kola; badara, *nt.*

Plumage, *n.* pattasamūha, *m.*

Plumassier, *n.* pakkhipattavāṇija, *m.*

Plumb, *n.* lambaka; olambaka, *nt.* adj. lambamāna. *v.t.* lambakaŋ otāreti. *v.i.* olambati. *p.p.* otārita-lambaka; °bita. °**line,** *n.* lambakasutta, *nt.* °**less,** *a.* appameyya.

Plumbago, *n.* abbhaka, *nt.*

Plumbeous, *a.* tipusadisa; tipuālitta.

Plumber, *n.* tipukammakāra; tipusandhānaka, *m.* — **bean,** *a.* tipumaya; tipusadisa.

Plume, *n.* pakkhipatta, *nt. v.t.* pakkhehi alaṅkaroti. *p.p.* °alaṅkata.

Plummet, *n.* lambasīsaka, *nt.*

Plummy, *a.* aḍḍha; samiddha.

Plumose, *a.* pakkhipattākāra.

Plump, *a.* pīna; pīvara; thūla. *v.t.* 1. pīvarīkaroti; 2. sahasā pāteti. *v.i.* thūlo hoti. *p.p.* °kata; °tita; thūlabhūta. °**ness,** *n.* pīvaratta, *nt.* °**y,** *a.* īsaŋpīvara.

Plumper, *n.* ekantamusāvāda, *m.*

Plumy, *a.* piñjamaṇḍita.

Plunder, *n.* vilopa; nillopa, *m.* vilumpana, *nt. v.t.* vilumpati; acchindati; padhaŋseti. *p.p.* vilutta; acchinna; °sita. °**er,** *n.*

vilopaka ; mosaka ; vilumpaka, *m.* °**ing**, *n.* vilumpana, *nt.*

Plunge, *v.t.* osīdāpeti ; udake opilāpeti. *v.i.* osīdati ; nimujjati ; ogāhati. *p.p.* °pita ; osīna ; nimugga ; ogāḷha. °**ing**, *n.* ogāhana ; nimujjana, *nt.*

Pluperfect, *n.* bhūtātīta, *m.*

Plural, *n.* bahuvacana, *nt.* adj. aneka ; bahuvidha. °**ity,** *n.* bahuvidhatta ; anekatta, *nt.* °**ize,** *v.t.* bahuvidhaŋ karoti.

Plus, *n.* saṅkalana-lakkhaṇa, *nt.*

Plutarchy, Plutocracy, *n.* dhanapatipālana ; dhanikādhipacca, *nt.* °**crat,** *n.* dhanabalī, *m.*

Pluto, *n.* Yamarāja, *m.* °**nic,** *a.* Yamarājāyatta. °**nian,** *a.* antobhūmijāta.

Pluvial, *a.* vuṭṭhibahula ; vuṭṭhivisayaka.

Pluvious, *a.* vuṭṭhijāta.

Pluviometer, *n.* vuṭṭhimāṇaka, *nt.*

Ply, *n.* 1. āvali, *f.* 2. ghanatta, *nt.* 3. ajjhāsaya, *m.* *v.t.* ussāhena payojeti ; punappunaŋ vāyamati. *v.i.* nirantaraŋ pavattati. *p.p.* °jita ; °mita ; °tita.

Pneumatic, *a.* vāyupuṇṇa; vāyumaya, *n. pl.* vāyuvijjā, *f.* °**ally,** *adv.* vāyubalena.

Pneumatology, *n.* devattavijjā, *f.*

Pneumogastric, *a.* papphāsa-āmāsayāyatta.

Pneumonia, *n.* papphāsadāha, *m.*

Poach, *v.t.* 1. vitudati ; 2. pasayha pavisati ; 3. aṇḍāni sedeti. ° **er,** *n.* pāṇīthenaka, *m.* *p.p.* vitunna ; °paviṭṭha.

Pock, *n.* masūrikā-piḷakā, *f.*

Pocket, *n.* ovaṭṭikā, *f.* *v.t.* ovaṭṭikāyaŋ nidahati. *p.p.* ni hita. °**able,** *a.* ovaṭṭikāharaṇīya.

Pod, *n.* 1. bījavaṭṭikā, *f.* 2. suttakosa, *m.* *v.i.* bījavaṭṭikā uppādeti. °**ded,** *a.* bījavaṭṭikāyutta ; mañjarīsahita.

Podagra, *n.* vātasopha, *m.*

Podge, *n.* thūla-lakuṇṭaka, *m.*

Poem, *n.* kabba ; pajja, *nt.* pajjabandha, *m.*

Poephagous, *a.* tiṇabhakkha.

Poesy, *n.* 1. pajjabandhana, *nt.* 2. pajjasamūha, *m.*

Poet, *n.* kavi ; pajjasampādaka, *m.* °**ic,** °**ical,** *a.* kabbamaya ; pajjāyatta. °**ics,** *n.* kabbasattha, *nt.* °**ess,** *n.* pajjasampādikā, *f.* — **laureate,** *n.* kavipuṅgava ; mahākavi, *m.* °**ry,** *n.* pajjabandha, *m.* kabba ; kāveyya, *nt.* gāthā, *f.*

Poetaster, Poeticule, *n.* kukavi, *m.*

Poetize, *v.t.* kabbaŋ racayati ; kabbattaŋ pāpeti. *p.p.* racita° ; °pāpita.

Poignant, *a.* tikhiṇa; tibba; ugga. °**ncy,** *n.* tikhiṇatta ; uggatta, *nt.* °**ly,** *adv.* tibbākārena ; uggatāya ; tibbaŋ.

Point, *n.* 1. koṭi, *f.* agga ; sikhara, *nt.* 2. bindulakkhaṇa ; 3. visesalakkhaṇa, *nt.* 4. adhippetattha, *m.* 5. (of land :) bhūnāsikā, *f.* 6. (of directions :) disānudisā, *f.* *v.t.* 1. tejeti ; sikharīkaroti ; 2. ādisati ; nidasseti. *p.p.* tejita ; °kata; ādiṭṭha; °sita. °**edly,** *adv.* tikhiṇaŋ ; phuṭaŋ; vyattaŋ. °**er,** *n.* uddesaka; nidassaka, *m.* °**ing out,** niddisana ; uddisana, *nt.* °**less,** *a.* atikhiṇa ; niratthа,

Point-blank, *adv.* ujukam eva. *a.* ujumagga-yutta ; ekantika.

Pointsman, *n.* (dhūmaratha-) ayosaṅghāṭa-ghaṭaka, *m.*

Poise, *n.* bhārasamatta, *nt.* paṭibhāra, *m.* *v.t.* tuleti ; samabhāraŋ karoti. *p.p.* tulita ; °rīkata.

Poison, *n.* visa, *nt.* *v.t.* visaŋ yojeti *or* pakkhipati ; visena lepeti *or* māreti. *p.p.* visayojita ; visapakkhitta ; visalitta ; °mārita. °**ed,** *a.* visapīta ; visadiddha. °**er,** visayojaka, *m.* °**ous,** *a.* savisa ; visayutta.

Poke, *n.* 1. pasibbaka, *m.* 2. tudana ; āhanana, *nt.* *v.t.* tudati ; āhanati. *p.p.* tunna ; āhata.

Poker, *n.* 1. aṅgāracālaka ; 2. nittudaka, *m.* °**ish,** *a.* hiŋsaka.

Poky, *a.* adhama ; malina ; kucchita.

Polar, *a.* uttara-dhuvāyatta. °**ity,** *n.* dakkhiṇuttaragāmitā, *f.*

Pole, *n.* 1. bhūakkhagga, *nt.* 2. yaṭṭhi, *f.* daṇḍa, *m.* 3. ekādasaratanika-māṇa, *nt.* 4. (of a carriage :) dhura, *nt.* yugadaṇḍa, *m.* *v.t.* daṇḍaŋ yojeti ; daṇḍena apaṇeti. *p.p.* daṇḍayojita; °apanīta. °**axe,** *n.* yuddhakuṭhārī, *f.* °**cat,** *n.* nakulavisesa, *m.* °**star,** *n.* dhuvatārakā, *f.*

Polemic, *n.* vivāda, *m.* adj. vivaditabba ; vivādatthī. *pl.* vādasattha, *nt.* °**al,** *a.* vivādavisayaka ; vivādakusala.

Police, *n.* rakkhakagaṇa, *m.* °**man,** *n.* rājapurisa ; nagararakkhī, *m.* — **magistrate,** daṇḍanātha, *m.*— **officer,** *n.* sāmarakkhī, *m.* — **station,** rakkhinivāsa, *m.* bhaṭāgāra, *nt.*

Policy, *n.* 1. naya ; nītimagga ; 2. upāya ; payoga, *m.* 3. niyamāvali, *f.* 4. pālanapaṭutta, *nt.*

Polish, *n.* 1. maṭṭhatta, *nt.* 2. siṭṭhatā ; sabbhatā, *f.* 3. majjanadabba, *nt.* *v.t.* 1. parimajjati ; vaṇṇamaṭṭhaŋ karoti ; 2. suṭṭhu vineti. *p.p.* parimaṭṭha ; °maṭṭhakata ; °vinīta. °**er,** *n.* vaṇṇamaṭṭhakārī, *m.* °**ing,** *n.* majjana; vaṇṇamaṭṭhakaraṇa, *nt.*

Polite, *a.* vinīta ; susīla ; poriya ; ācārasīlī. °**ly,** *adv.* vinītākārena. °**ness,** *n.* susīlatta; vinītatta, *nt.*

Politic, *n.* nāgarika ; janahitakārī ; vicakkhaṇa ; upāyadakkha. *pl.* desapālanasattha, *nt.* °**al,** *a.* rajjapāḷanāyatta. °**ian,** *n.* desapālanaññū, *m.* °**al science,** *n.* pālanavijjā, *f.*

Polity, *n.* desapālana, *nt.* pālanakkama, *m.*

Poll, *n.* 1. sīsa, *nt.* 2. chandadāyaka-nāmāvali, *f.* 3. chandadānaṭṭhāna, *nt.* 4. suka, *m.* *v.t.* 1. nāmāni likhati; 2. aggāni chindati. *p.p.* likhitanāma ; chinnagga. adj. siṅgarahita.

Pollard, *n.* 1. chinnagga-rukkha ; 2. galitavisāṇa, *m.* *v.t.* aggaŋ chindati. *p.p.* chinnagga.

Pollen, *n.* reṇu ; parāga, *m.* *v.t.* reṇūhi chādeti. *p.p.* reṇuchanna. °**less,** *a.* areṇuka.

Pollicitation, *n.* athirapaṭiññā, *f.*

Pollinate, *v.t.* parāge ākirati. *p.p.* ākiṇṇaparāga.

Poll-tax, *n.* puggala-bali, *m.*

Pollute, *v.t.* dūseti ; kalaṅketi ; kalusayati. *p.p.* dūsita ; °kita ;

°yita. °er, *n.* dūsaka, *m.* °ion, *n.* dūsana; kalusīkaraṇa, *nt.* pūtibhāva, *m.*

Polly, *n.* suvapotaka, *m.*

Polo, *n.* assārohaka-guḷakīḷā, *f.*

Poltroon, *n.* adhīra; kātara, *m.* °**ery,** *n.* dīnatta, *nt.*

Polyandry, *n.* bahupatikatta, *nt.* °**ist,** *n.* bahupatikā itthī, *f.*

Polyarchy, *n.* janasammatarajja, *nt.*

Polycarpous, *a.* bahuphalada.

Polychromatic, *a.* anekavaṇṇa.

Polychrome, *n.* nānāvaṇṇamuddita. °**my,** *n.* anekavaṇṇehi muddaṅkana, *nt.*

Polygamy, *n.* bahubhariyatā, *f.* °**ist,** *n.* bahubhariyaka, *m.* °**mous,** *a.* bahubhariyāhāraka.

Polygenesis, *n.* bahumūlakuppatti, *f.*

Polyglot, *a. n.* nānābhāsika. °**tal,** °**tic,** *a.* nānābhāsāyatta.

Polygon, *n.* bahukoṇaka, *nt.* °**al,** *a.* bahukoṇayutta.

Polyhistor, Polymath, *n.* nānāsatthavidū; mahāpaṇḍita, *m.* °**mathy,** *n.* bāhusacca, *nt.* °**mathic,** *a.* bahussuta.

Polymorphic, *a.* bahurūpaka; nānāsaṇṭhāna.

Polynesia, *n.* bahudīpakapadesa, *m.*

Polypetalous, *a.* bahudalaka.

Polypod, *a. n.* bahuppada.

Polypus, *n.* bahumūlakagaṇḍa, *m.*

Polysyllabic, *a.* bahusarayutta.

Polytechnic, *a.* bahusippaka, *n.* vividhasippadāyakaṭṭhāna, *nt.*

Polytheism, *n.* bahudevavāda, *m.* °**theist,** *n.* bahudevadiṭṭhika, *m.*

Pomade, *n.* sugandha-vilepana, *nt.*

Pomander, *n.* rogavāraka-surabhiguḷikā, *f.*

Pomegranate, *n.* dāḷimaphala, *nt.*

Pomiculture, *n.* phalarukkharopaṇa, *nt.*

Pommel, *n.* gaṇṭhi-bubbulaka, *nt.* *v.t.* tharunā āhanati. *p.p.* °āhata.

Pomology, *n.* phalaropaṇavijjā, *f.*

Pomp, *n.* patāpa, *m.* sobhā; siri, *f.* mahāparihāra, *m.* °**ous,** *a.* mahāteja; sakavibhavadassaka. °**ously,** *adv.* mahāparihārena; uḷārapatāpena. °**ousness,** mahāparihāratta; issariya, *nt.* — **of a king,** rajjasiri, *f.* — **and splendour,** sirivilāsa, *m.*

Pond, *n.* pokkharaṇī, *f.* *v.t.* jalasotaŋ rodheti. *v.i.* pokkharaṇitaŋ pāpuṇāti. *p.p.* rodhitasota; °patta.

Ponder, *v.t.i.* jhāyati; ūhati; anuvitakketi. *p.p.* jhāyita; ūhita; °kita. °**able,** *a.* tulanīya; tulanāraha. °**ation,** *n.* tulana, *nt.* °**ous,** *a.* atibhāriya; dandhagatika. °**ously,** *adv.* atigarukatāya; dandhākārena. °**ousness,** *n.* 1. tulanīyatta; 2. dandhatta, *nt.*

Poniard, *n.* churikāvisesa, *m.*

Pontiff, *n.* mukhyapurohita; nāyaka-devapūjaka, *m.* saṅgharāja, *m.* °**icate,** *n.* nāyakapūjakadhura; saṅgharājatta, *nt.*

Pontoon, *n.* setunāvā; titthanāvā, *f.* *v.t.* titthanāvāhi tarati.

Pony, *a.* ghoṭaka; khuddakassa, *m.*

Pooh, *intj.* dhi; dhiratthu. °**pooh,** *v.t.* dhikkaroti. *p.p.* dhikkata.

Pool, *n.* sobbha, *nt.* pokkharaṇī, *f.* *v.t.* chandakaŋ saŋharati.
Poon, *n.* punnāgataru, *m.*
Poonac, *n.* piññāka, *m.*
Poop, *n.* mandamatika, *m.*
Poor, *a.* 1. daḷidda ; niddhana ; kapaṇa ; akiñcana ; 2. khīṇa ; kisa ; ūna ; 3. asāra ; guṇahīna ; 4. kātara ; 5. anātha.—**asylum**, anāthālaya, *m.* °**ly**, *adv.* dīnākārena. °**ness**, dāḷiddiya, *nt.* — **soil**, nissārabhūmi, *f.* — **spirited**, *a.* adhīra ; nirīha ; kātara.
Pop, *v.i.t.* phuṭanasaddaŋ pavatteti ; sahasā nikkhamati *or* uppatati. *p.p.* °tita ; °nikkhanta ; °tita. °**corn**, lāja, *m.*
Pope, *n.* Romaka-saṅgharāja, *m.* °**dom**, *n.* Romaka-saṅgharājadhura, *nt.*
Popery, *n.* Romaka-samaya, *m.*
Popinjay, *n.* 1. sukarūpa, *nt.* 2. satapatta, *m.* 3. gabbitapuggala, *m.*
Poppy, *n.* ahipheṇa-gaccha, *m.*
Populace, *n.* janatā, *f.* mahājana, *m.*
Popular, *a.* janappiya ; mahājanika. °**ity**, *n* janappiyatta, *nt.* °**ize**, *v.t.* janappiyaŋ *or* atipākaṭaŋ karoti. °**ly**, *adv.* janappiyatāya ; pākaṭatāya.
Populate, *v.t.* janāvāsaŋ karoti. *p.p.* katajanāvāsa. °**ion**, *n.* janāvāsakaraṇa, *nt.*
Populous, *a.* janākiṇṇa ; janasambādha. °**ness**, *n.* bahujanatta, *nt.*
Porcelain, *n.* 1. sukhumasetamattikā, *f.* 2. setamattikābhaṇḍa, *nt.*
Porch, *n.* channa-dvārakoṭṭhaka ; ālinda, *m.*
Porcine, *a.* sūkaropama.
Porcupine, *n.* sallaka, *m.* °**ish**, *a.* sallakasadisa.
Pore, *n.* 1. lomakūpa, *m.* 2. sukhumachidda, *nt.* *v.t.i.* nijjhāyati ; saŋvitakketi. *p.p.* °yita ; °kita. °**ous**, sacchidda ; chiddāvacchidda. °**ousness**, *n.* sacchiddatta, *nt.*
Pork, *n.* sūkaramaŋsa, *nt.* °**er**, *n.* thūlasūkara, *m.* °**ling**, *n.* sūkarapotaka, *m.* °**y**, *a.* 1. sūkaramaŋsasadisa ; 2. saŋvaḍḍhita.
Pornocracy, *n.* gaṇikāpabhutta, *nt.* °**ography**, *n.* gaṇikāvuttivicāraṇā ; asabbhalipi, *f.*
Porosity, *n.* chiddabahulatta, *nt.*
Porpoise, *n.* samuddasūkara, *m.*
Porraceous, *a.* īsaŋharita.
Porridge, *n.* ghanayāgu, *f.*
Porringer, *n.* yāgubhājana, *nt.*
Port, *n.* 1. paṭṭana, *nt.* nāvātittha, *nt.* 2. dvāra ; mukha, *nt.* 3. gamanākāra, *m.* 4. haraṇa, *nt.* *v.t.* dhāreti ; pariharati. *p.p.* dhārita ; °rita *or* parihaṭa. °**able**, *a.* saṅkamanīya ; hāriya. °**age**, *n.* 1. vahana ; haraṇa ; 2. haraṇavetana, *nt.* °**al**, *n.* mahādvāra, *nt.* — **hole**, *n.* nāvāgavakkha, *nt.*
Portative, *a.* vahanasīla ; haraṇopakārī.
Portend, *v.t.* pageva sūceti ; pubbanimittaŋ dasseti. *p.p.* °sūcita ; dassita°.
Portent, *n.* pubbanimitta, *nt.* °**ous**, *a.* pubbanimittasahita ; asubhasūcaka °**ously**, *adv.* pubbanimittavasena.
Porter, *n.* 1. bhārahārī ; 2. dvārapāla, *m.* °**age**, *n.* bhāravahanavetana, *nt.*

Portfolio, *n.* paṇṇakosa, *m.* paṇṇarakkhikā, *f.* lekhanagopaka, *m.*

Portico, *n.* sacchadana-dvārakoṭṭhaka, *m.* ālindamukha, *nt.*

Portion, *n.* bhāga; koṭṭhāsa; paṭiviŋsa, *m. v.t.* bhājeti; vibhajati. *p.p.* bhājita; vibhatta.

Portly, *a.* 1. mahānubhāva; ulāradassana; 2. thūladeha. °**iness**, *n.* gambhīravuttitā; thūlakāyatā, *f.*

Portmanteau, *n.* cammamañjūsā, *f.*

Portrait, *n.* paṭibimba; chāyārūpa, *nt.* °**ist**, *n.* paṭibimbakārī, *m.* °**ure**, *n.* paṭibimbasampādana, *nt.*

Portray, *v.t.* ālikhati; citteti. *p.p.* ālikhita; cittita. °**al**, *n.* cittakamma, *nt.* °**er**, *n.* cittakāra; cittasippī, *m.*

Portress, *n.* dvārapālikā, *f.*

Pose, *n.* līlā, *f.* vilāsa; aṅgavinyāsa, *m. v.t.* 1. purato ṭhapeti; 2. līḷhaŋ gaṇhāpeti; 3. pañhehi sambhamāpeti; 4. niruttaraŋ karoti. *p.p.* °ṭhapita; °pita; niruttarīkata.

Poser, *n.* 1. purato-ṭhāyī; 2. sedamocaka-pañha, *m.*

Posit, *v.t.* nidasseti; patiṭṭhāpeti. *p.p.* °sita; °pita.

Position, *n.* 1. avatthā; dasā; pavatti, *f.* 2. patiṭṭhitaṭṭhāna, *nt.* 3. ṭhānantara; pada, *nt. v.t.* yuttaṭṭhāne patiṭṭhāpeti. *p.p.* °pita.

Positive, *a.* 1. ekanta; niyata; avassaka; 2. paccakkha; 3. sunicchita; yathābhūta. °**ly**, *adv.* 1. niyataŋ; nūnaŋ; avassaŋ; 2. tattato; paramatthato. °**ness**, *n.* asaṅkiyatta, *nt.* daḷhanicchaya, *m.* °**ism**, *n.* yathābhūtañāṇa, *nt.* yathābhūtavāda, *m*

Posology, *n.* osadhamattā-ñāṇa, *nt.*

Posse, *n.* bhaṭadala, *nt.*

Possess, *v.t.* 1. dhāreti; āyattīkaroti; 2. āvisati; adhigaṇhāti. *p.p.* dhārita; °kata; āviṭṭha; adhiggahita. °**ed with**, upeta; samupeta; yutta; upalakkhita; sampanna, *a.* °**ed by a spirit**, bhūtāviṭṭha, *a.* °**ion**, *n.* 1. pariggaha, *m.* adhīnatta, *nt.* 2. āvesa, *m.* adhimuccana, *nt.* 3. vibhava, *m.* vitta, *nt.* °**or**, *n.* sāmī; dhāraka, *m.*

Possessive, *a.* sāmyatthavācaka; adhīnattapakāsaka. — **case**, sambandhavibhatti, *f.*

Possible, *a.* sādhiya; sakkuṇeyya; sakya. °**bility**, *n.* sakyatta; bhabbatta; sādhiyatta, *nt.* °**bly**, *adv.* siyā kadāci.

Post, *n.* 1. thambha, *m.* thūṇā, *f.* 2. pada; ṭhānantara; 3. niyamitaṭṭhāna; 4. sāsanaharaṇa, *nt. v.t.* 1. patiṭṭhāpeti; niyojeti; 2. thambhe bandhati *or* alliyāpeti; 3. sāsanaŋ peseti. *p.p.* °pita; °jita; °baddha; °pita; pesitasāsana. *v.i.* javena dhāvati. *adv.* atisīghaŋ. °**age**, *n.* sāsanaharaṇa-mūla, *nt.* °**age stamp**, sāsana-lañchana, *nt.* °**al**, *a.* sāsanapesanāyatta. — **card**, *n.* sāsanapattikā, *f.* — **horse**, *n.* javassa, *m.* °**man**, *n.* sāsanabhājaka, *m.* °**master**, *n.* sāsanāgārādhipa, *m.* — **office**, sandesāgāra, *nt.*

Postdate, *v.t.* anāgata-dinaniyamaŋ likhati. *p.p.* likhita-anāgata°.

Poster, *n.* mahānivedanapaṇṇa, *nt.*

Posterior, *n.* pacchābhāga, *m.* adj. pacchimakālika. °**rity**, *n.* pacchimajanatā; anāgataparamparā, *f.* °**ly**, *adv.* pacchā.

Postern, *n.* apākaṭa-dvāra, *nt.*

Post-humous, *a.* 1. accaye-jāta; 2. accaye muddāpita. °**ly**, *adv.* maraṇato paraŋ.

Postil, *n.* adholipi, *f.*

Postmark, *n.* sāsanāgāralañchana, *nt.*

Postmeridiem, *adv.* aparaṇhe. °**dian**, *a.* aparaṇhika. *n.* aparaṇha, *m.*

Post-mortem, *n.* maraṇānantaraupaparikkhā, *f.* adj. maraṇānantarika.

Postpone, *v.t.* niyamitakālam avakaḍḍhati. *p.p.* °ḍhita°. °**ment**, *n.* divasākaḍḍhana, *nt.*

Post-script, *n.* pacchālikhita, *nt.*

Postulate, *n.* apaccakkhagahaṇa, *nt.* siddhanta, *m.* *v.t.* siddhantavasena tīreti *or* paṭiggaṇhāti. *p.p.* °tīrita; °gahita. °**ion**, *n.* siddhantavasena gahaṇa, *nt.*

Posture, *n.* aṅgavinyāsa; iriyāpatha, *m.* saṇṭhiti, *f.*

Posy, *n.* 1. pupphatthabaka, *m.* 2. ādisiya-pāṭha, *nt.*

Pot, *n.* 1. (for water :) kumbha; ghaṭa; kalasa, *m.* 2. (for cooking :) cāṭi; ukkhali; khalopī, *f.* *v.t.* kumbhiyaŋ āsiñcati *or* nikkhipati. *p.p.* °āsitta; nikkhitta. °**bellied**, *a.* lambodara. °**herb**, *n.* sākapaṇṇa, *nt.* °**house**, *n.* pānamandira, *nt.* °**sherd**, kapālakhaṇḍa, *m.* °**stand**, cumbaṭaka, *nt.* kumbhādhāra, *m.*

Potable, *a.* pātabba; peyya.

Potamic, *a.* nadīpaṭibaddha. °**mology**, *n.* nadībheda-viññāṇa, *nt.*

Potash, *n.* khāra; yavakhāra, *m.*

Potassium, *n.* yavakhāra-mūladhātu, *f.*

Potato, *n.* goḷāluva, *m.*

Potence, °**cy**, *n.* sāmatthiya, *nt.* balamahima, *m.* iddhi, *f.*

Potent, *a.* pabala; sappabhāva. °**ate**, *n.* pabhū; adhīsa, *m.*

Potential, *a.* 1. sambhavanīya; sakkuneyya; 2. vidhyatthaka. °**ity**, *n.* sakyatā, *f.* °**ly**, *adv.* yathāsambhavaŋ. — **mood**, Sattamī vibhatti, *f.* °**ly**, *adv.* pabalākārena.

Potentiate, *v.t.* balaŋ deti; sakyaŋ karoti. *p.p.* dinnabala; sakyakata.

Pother, *n.* 1. sāsarodhaka-vatthu, *nt.* 2. missitasadda, *m.* *v.t.* pīḷeti; bādheti. *p.p.* pīḷita; bādhita.

Potion, *n.* bhesajjamattā, *f.*

Potpourri, *n.* 1. vāsana-dabba; 2. vividhappasaṅga-nacca, *nt.* 3. nānāracanāsaṅgaha; 4. missitāhāra, *m.*

Pottage, *n.* mudumaŋsabhojana, *nt.*

Potter, *nt.* kumbhakāra, *m.* °'**s wheel**, kulālacakka, *nt.* °**y**, *n.* 1. kulālabhaṇḍa, *nt.* 2. kumbhakārasālā, *f.*

Pottle, *n.* 1. pānaghaṭa, *m.* 2. phalapacchi, *f.*

Potty, *a.* appamattaka; agaṇetabba.

Pouch, *n.* 1. ovaṭṭikā, *f.* 2. upajaṭhara, *nt.* 3. pasibbaka, *m.* *v.t.* ovaṭṭikāya nidahati; pasibbake pakkhipati. *p.p.* °nihita ; °pakkhitta.

Poult, *n.* kukkuṭapotaka, *m.* °**erer,** *n.* kukkuṭavāṇija, *m.* °**ry,** *n.* kukkuṭagaṇa, *m.*

Poultice, *n.* gaṇḍālepa, *m.*

Pounce, *n.* 1. nakhapañjara, *m.* 2. sahasā-ajjhottharaṇa, *nt.* 3. masivāraka-cuṇṇa, *nt.* *v.t.* 1. pakkhandati ; sahasā ajjhottharati ; 2. nakhehi gaṇhāti. *p.p.* pakkhanta ; °ajjhotthaṭa ; °gahita.

Pound, *n.* 1. tulābhāra, *m.* 2. soṇṇanikkha, *nt.* 3. vaja ; koṭṭhaka, *m.* *v.t.* koṭṭeti ; cuṇṇeti. *p.p.* koṭṭita ; °ṇita. °**age,** *n.* 1. bhārānuga-kara ; 2. āyānuga-bali, *m.* °**er,** *n.* 1. koṭṭaka, *m.* 2. musala, *m.*

Pour, *n.* dhārānipāta, *m.* *v.t.* āsiñcati ; osiñcati ; ākirati ; okirati. *p.p.* āsitta ; ositta ; °kirita *or* °kiṇṇa. °**ing,** *n.* secana; siñcana ; osiñcana ; okiraṇa, *nt.*

Pout, *n.* mukhavikāra, *m.* dummukhatta, *nt.* *v.t.* mukhavikāraŋ dasseti. *p.p.* dassita°.

Poverty, *n.* dāḷiddiya ; niddhanatta, *nt.* °**stricken,** *a.* duggata ; dukkhita.

Powder, *n.* cuṇṇa ; piṭṭha, *nt.* *v.t.* cuṇṇeti ; piŋseti. *p.p.* °ṇita ; °sita. °**ed,** *a.* vicuṇṇa; sañcuṇṇa. °**y,** *a.* sacuṇṇa.

Power, *n.* satti, *f.* bala ; sāmatthiya, *nt.* thāma ; pabhāva, *m.* °**ful,** *a.* balavantu; thāmavantu. °**fully,** *adv.* balavākārena. °**fulness,** *n.* thāmavantatā, *f.* °**less,** *a.* abala ; dubbala ; asamattha ; sattihīna. °**lessness,** *n.* abalatta ; dubbalya ; asāmatthiya, *nt.*

Pox, *n.* upadaŋsaroga, *m.*

Practice, *n.* 1. paricaya, *m.* 2. ācaraṇa ; abhiyuñjana; paṭipajjana, *nt.* °**able,** *a.* sādhiya; sukara ; kātuŋsakya. °**ably,** *adv.* sādhiyākārena ; sakyatāya. °**cal,** *a.* ācaraṇīya ; paccakkhakaraṇīya. °**cally,** *adv.* 1. paricayena ; 2. paramatthato ; 3. yathāpaguṇaŋ.

Practise, *v.t.* ācarati ; paṭipajjati ; anuyuñjati ; āsevati ; bhāveti. *p.p.* ācarita ; paṭipanna ; anuyutta ; °vita. °**ing,** *a.* ācaranta ; paṭipajjamāna. **Much °ed,** ajjhāciṇṇa, *a.* **Thoroughly °ed,** suparicita ; vatthukata.

Practitioner, *n.* vejjakammaniyutta, *m.*

Praecognitum, *n.* avassañeyya, *nt.*

Pragmatic, *a.* 1. anubhavamūlaka ; 2. kiccakusala; 3. parakiccappavesī. °**ism,** *n.* 1. anubhavamūlaka-vāda, *m.* 2. cārittānugamana ; nītyanugamana, *nt.* °**cally,** *adv.* anubhūtapubbākārena. °**tize,** *v.t.* saccākārena dasseti.

Praise, *n.* pasaŋsā ; thuti ; thomanā ; kittanā, *f.* abhitthavana, *nt.* *v.t.* pasaŋsati ; thometi ; kitteti; abhitthavati. *p.p.* pasattha; thomita ; °tita ; abhitthuta. °**er,** *n.* pasaŋsaka, *m.* °**ful,** °**worthy,** *a.* pasaŋsiya ; thomanāraha. °**ing,** *a.* vaṇṇavādī ; abhitthavaka.

Prank, *n.* 1. upahāsa, *m.* 2. uppatana, *nt.* *v.t.* sadappaŋ bhūseti.

v.i. vibhūsito hoti. p.p. °bhūsita. °**ish**, a. vinodasīlī ; parihāsappiya.

Prate, n. jappanā, f. palapana, nt. v.i. pajappati ; palapati. p.p. °pita. °**er**, n. jappaka ; palapaka, m.

Prattle, n. bālalapanā ; niratthkakathā, f. v.i, palapati.

Prawn, n. kosamaccha, m.

Praxis, n. 1. sammatacāritta, nt. 2. paricayodāharaṇasamūha, m.

Pray, v.t. āyācati ; pattheti. p.p. °cita ; °thita. °**er**, n. 1. āyācanā ; abhipatthanā, f. 2 āyācaka, m. °**erless**, a. yācanāvimukha.

Preach, v.t. deseti ; pakāseti ; akkhāti. p.p. °sita ; akkhāta. °**er**, n. desetu ; akkhāyī, m. °**ing**, n. desanā, f. pāvacana, nt. **Well °ed**, svākkhāta ; sammadakkhāta.

Pre-admonish, v.t. pageva ovadati. p.p. °dita.

Preamble, n. paṭhamārambha ; mukhabandha, m. patthāvanā, f.

Precarious, a. avinicchita ; sāsaṅka. °**ly**, adv. sāsaṅkaŋ. °**ness**, n. sāsaṅkatta, nt.

Precative, Precatory, a. āyācanatthavācī ; āsiŋsāpubbaka.

Precaution, n. samekkhā, f. pubbopāya, m. °**ary**, a. pubbopāyāyatta ; samekkhāpubbaka.

Precautious, a. samekkhakārī. °**ly**, adv. susamekkhiya.

Precede, v.t. purato yāti ; agge carati. p.p. °yāta ; °carita. °**nce**, n. 1. pubbaṅgamatta ; 2. pamukhatta, nt. purekkhāra, m. °**nt**, n. pubbanidassana, nt. adj. purogāmī. °**ing**, a. pubbaṅgama.

Precedented, a. pubbanidassanayutta.

Precent, v.i. gāyane pubbaṅgamo hoti. °**or**, n. pamukhagāyaka, m.

Precept, n. sikkhāpada, nt. °**or**, n. upajjhāya ; vinayācariya, m. °**orship**, n. upajjhāyadhura, nt. °**ress**, n. upajjhāyā, f.

Precession, n. abhimukhagamana ; ayana, nt.

Precinct, n. 1. āvarita-bhūbhāga ; antogata-padesa, m. 2. sīmā ; mariyādā, f.

Precious, a. mahaggha ; mahāraha. °**ly**, adv. mahagghākārena. °**ness**, n. mahagghatta, nt. — **stone**, maṇi, m.

Precipice, n. papāta, m.

Precipitate, a. sāhasika ; atituritaa; adhomukha. v.t. 1. adhomukhaŋ pāteti ; opāteti ; 2. sahasā kāreti. v.i. adho patati. p.p. °pātita ; °kārita ; °patita. °**tance**, n. sāhasikatta, nt. asamekkhakāritā, f. °**ion**, n. antarāyābhimukhīkaraṇa ; accāyikatta, nt. °**ly**, adv. sahasā ; anisamma ; adhomukhaŋ.

Precipitous, a. 1. atiturita ; 2. papātābhimukha. °**ly**, adv. atituritatāya. °**ness**, n. sāhasikatta, nt. asamekkhā, f.

Precis, n. saṅkhepa, m.

Precise, a. niyata ; paricchinna ; yathābhūta; anūnānadhika. °**ly**, adv. yathābhūtaŋ ; anūnādhikaŋ. °**ness**, n. yathābhūtatta ; anūnādhikatta, nt.

Precisian, n. yathātathakārī ; yathāvidhikārī, m.

Precision, n. yathāvidhitta ; suparicchinnatta, nt.

Preclude, *v.t.* nivāreti ; nisedheti. *p.p.* °rita ; °dhita.

Preclusion, *n.* nivāraṇa ; nivattana ; paṭibāhana, *nt.* nisedha, *m.* °**sive,** *a.* nivāraka ; paṭisedhaka.

Precocious, *a.* akālapakka ; ayathāpariṇata. °**ness,** *n.* ayathāpariṇatatta, *nt.* °**city,** *n.* akālapariṇati, *f.*

Precogitate, *v.t.* puretaraŋ vitakketi. *p.p.* °kita. °**ion,** *n.* puretaracintā, *f.*

Precognition, *n.* puretarāvabodha, *m.*

Preconceive, *v.t.* puretaraŋ bujjhati ; pageva cinteti. *p.p.* °buddha ; °tita. °**ception,** puretaracintā, *f.*

Preconcert, *v.t.* pageva niccheti. *p.p.* °chita.

Preconize, *v.t.* pakāseti ; anusāveti. *p.p.* °sita ; °vita.

Precursor, *n.* 1. aggesara ; purecārī, *m.* 2. pubbanimitta, *nt.* °**y,** *a.* 1. puregāmī ; 2. pubbanimittabhūta.

Predacious, *a.* 1. aññabhakkha ; 2. vilumpaka.

Predatory, *a.* hiŋsaka ; vilumpaka ; upaddavakara.

Predecease, *v.i.* puretaraŋ marati. *p.p.* °mata.

Predecessor, *n.* pubbādhikārī, *m.*

Predestinate, Predestine, *v.t.* puretaraŋ niyameti *or* nirūpeti. *p.p.* °mita ; °pita. °**ion,** *n.* puretaraniyamana, *nt.* °**narian,** *n.* niyativādī, *m.*

Predetermine, *v.t.* puretaraŋ niccheti. *p.p.* °chita. °**ation,** *n.* puretaranicchaya, *m. or* adhiṭṭhāna.

Predicament, *n.* 1. visiṭṭhaguṇādi, *m.* 2. kicchappavatti ; dukkarāvatthā, *f.*

Predicate, *n.* 1. ākhyātapada, *nt.* 2. guṇavisesa, *m.* 3. siddhanta, *m. v.t.* 1. abhidhāti ; niddisati ; 2. thirīkaroti. °**cable,** *a.* abhidheyya. °**ive,** *a.* ākhyātāyatta. °**ion,** *n.* nicchayakaraṇa ; pakāsana, *nt.* °**tory,** *a.* desanāyatta ; desanārata.

Predict, *v.t.* pageva katheti ; puretaram ādisati *or* vyākaroti. *p.p.* °kathita ; °ādiṭṭha ; vyākata. °**ion,** *n.* anāgatakathana, *nt.* °**or,** *n.* anāgatavattu, *m.* °**ive,** *a.* anāgatasūcaka.

Predilection, *n.* 1. pubbavāsanā ; 2. pakkhapātitā, *f.*

Predispose, *v.t.* puretaraŋ poṇīkaroti. *p.p.* °poṇīkata. °**ition,** *n.* tapponatta ; chandānugāmitta, *nt.*

Predominant, *a.* pabala. °**nance,** *n.* pabalatta ; balādhikya, *nt.* °**ly,** *adv.* ādhipaccena.

Predominate, *v.i.* ādhipaccaŋ pavatteti. *p.p.* pavattitādhipacca.

Pre-eminent, *a.* sabbaseṭṭha ; atyuttama. °**nence,** *n.* sabbaseṭṭhatta ; atyuttamatta ; ativisiṭṭhatta, *nt.* °**ly,** *adv.* sabbaseṭṭhākārena.

Pre-emption, *n.* 1. paṭhamatarakaya, *m.* 2. tadatthāyā' vasara, *m.*

Preen, *v.t.* tuṇḍena pakkhe saṅkharoti. *p.p.* °saṅkhatapakkha.

Pre-engage, *v.t.* puretaraŋ paṭijānāti. *p.p.* °paṭiññāta. °**ment,** *n.* puretarapaṭiññā, *f.*

Pre-exist, *v.i.* ādito pavattati. °**ence,** *n.* pubbajāti, *f.* pubbenivāsa, *m.* °**ent,** *a.* ādito pavattamāna.

Preface, *n.* mukhabandha, *m.* bhūmikā, *f.* sabhāvakathana, *nt.* *v.t.* mukhabandhaŋ likhati. *p.p.* likhita°.

Prefatory, *a.* sabhāvañāpaka.

Prefect, *n.* nāyakādhikārī, *m.* °**oral,** *a.* nāyakādhikārīvisayaka. °**ure,** *n.* adhikārīnivāsa; adhikārāyattapadesa, *m.*

Prefer, *v.t.* 1. adhikataraŋ roceti; 2. unnatiŋ pāpeti. *p.p.* °rocita; °pāpita. °**able,** *a.* variya; varatara. °**ence,** *n.* abhiruci, *f.* °**ment,** *n.* unnatipāpana, *nt.*

Preferential, *a.* anuggahapubbaka.

Prefigure, *v.t.* pageva nirūpeti. *p.p.* °pita. °**ation,** *n.* pagevanirūpana, *nt.* °**ative,** *a.* pubbataranirūpaka.

Prefix, *n.* upasagga (-pada), *nt.* *v.t.* purato yojeti. *p.p.* °yojita.

Pregnable, *a.* padhaŋsiya.

Pregnant, *a.* 1. sagabbhā; garugabbhā; 2. bhāriya; garuka; 3. bahussuta. °**nancy,** *n.* gabbhadhāraṇa, *nt.* °**ly,** *adv.* saphalākārena.

Prehensile, *a.* gahaṇakkhama.

Prehension, *n.* 1. gahaṇa, *nt.* 2. manovitakka, *m.*

Prehistoric, *a.* itihāsapubbakālika. °**ry,** *n.* ādikappetihāsa, *m.*

Prejudge, *v.t.* puretaraŋ niccheti. *p.p.* °chita. °**ment,** *n.* puretaranicchaya, *m.*

Prejudice, *n.* pakkhapāta; ayathāgāha, *m.* agati, *f.* *v.t.* agatiŋ yāti; pakkhapātī hoti. *p.p.* °yāta; °bhūta. °**ial,** *a.* anatthakara. °**ially,** *adv.* sāpakāraŋ; agatiyā.

Prelate, see **Bishop.**

Prelect, *v.i.* deseti; pavadati. *p.p.* desita; pavutta. °**ion,** *n.* desanā, *f.* °**or,** *n.* desaka, *m.*

Prelibation, *n.* paṭhamassāda, *m.*

Preliminary, *n.* pubbakicca, *nt.* adj. parikammabhūta; pubbakiccāyatta.

Prelude, *n.* 1. ārambhagīta; 2. upacāra-nacca, *nt.* *v.t.* pubbakiccaŋ karoti.

Premature, *a.* akālapakka; ayathāpariṇata; appattakālika. °**ly,** *adv.* yathākālato pubbe. °**ness,** *n.* akālapariṇāma, *m.*

Premeditate, *v.t.* pageva saṅkappeti; puretaraŋ cinteti. *p.p.* °pita; °tita. °**ion,** *n.* puretaracintā, *f.*

Premier, *n.* padhānāmacca, *m.* adj. pamukha; pāmokkha. °**ship,** *n.* mahāmaccadhura, *nt.*

Premise, *n.* paṭhamavuttakāraṇa, *nt.* *v.t.* sabhāvaŋ pakāseti. *p.p.* °sitasabhāva.

Premises, *n.* *pl.* savatthukaghara, *nt.* vāsabhūmi, *f.*

Premium, *n.* 1. nihitadhana; 2. pāritosikadāna, *nt.*

Premonition, *n.* bhavitabbañāpana, *nt.* °**tive,** °**tory,** pubbanimittabhūta.

Prenotion, *n.* paṭhamataramata, *nt.*

Preoccupy, *v.t.* pageva sasantakaŋ karoti; pageva abhiyuñjati. *p.p.* °kata; °yutta. °**ation**, *n.* pagevābhiyuñjana, *nt.*

Prepare, *v.t.* 1. paṭiyādeti; saŋvidahati; sajjeti; kappeti; 2. saṅkharoti; 3. (a seat, etc.) paññāpeti 4. (a medicine:) yojeti. *v.i.* parivacchaŋ karoti. *p.p.* °dita; saŋvihita; sajjita; °pita; saṅkhata; paññatta; yojita; kataparivaccha. °**ation**, *n.* paṭiyādana; sajjana; parikamma; parivaccha, *nt.* °**atory**, *a.* parikammabhūta. °**er**, *n.* paṭiyādaka, *m.*

Prepay, *v.t.* pageva vetanaŋ deti. *p.p.* °dinnavetana. °**ment**, *n.* puretara-vetana, *nt.*

Prepense, *a.* sañciccakata.

Preponderate, *v.i.*(saṅkhyābalādīhi) atiriccati. *p.p.* °atiritta. °**rance**, *n.* 1. bhārātireka, *m.* 2. ādhipacca; adhikabala, *nt.* °**rant**, *a.* (balādīhi) atiriccamāna.

Preposition, *n.* nipātapada, *nt.* °**tive**, *a.* purato yojetabba. °**al**, *a.* avyayabhūta.

Prepossess, *v.t.* pageva adhigaṇhāti *or* vasaŋ neti. *p.p.* °adhiggahita; °nīta.°**ed**, *a.* jātānurāga. °**ing**, *a.* hadayaṅgama. °**ion**, *n.* poṇatta; anukūlatta, *nt.* pakkhapāta, *m.*

Preposterous, *a.* dhammaviruddha; ananucchavika. °**ly**, *adv.* adhammena. °**ness**, *n.* ayutti, *f.*

Prepotent, *a.* atipabala.

Prepuce, *n.* mehanaggacamma, *nt.*

Prerequisite, *n.* pagevāvassakavatthu, *nt.*

Prerogative, *n.* visesādhikāra, *m.* visesabala, *nt.*

Presage, *n.* pubbanimitta, *nt.* *v.t.* pageva sūceti. *p.p.* °sūcita.

Prescient, *a.* anāgatadassī. °**ence**, *n.* anāgatañāṇa, *nt.* °**ly**, *adv.* anāgatadassitāya.

Prescribe, *v.t.* niyameti; niddisati. *p.p.* °mita; niddiṭṭha.

Prescript, *n.* vidhāna, *nt.* āṇā; nīti; rīti, *f.* °**ion**, *n.* 1. niddesapaṇṇa, *nt.* 2. bhesajjaniyama, *m.* °**ive**, *a.* 1. niddesāyatta; 2. paramparāyāta.

Presence, *n.* 1. vijjamānatta, *nt.* 2. sammukhībhāva, *m.* — **of mind**, satisampajañña, *nt.*

Present, *n.* paṇṇākāra; upahāra, *m.* pābhata; upāyana, *nt.* adj. vattamāna; vijjamāna; paccupaṭṭhita. *v.t.* 1. upahāraŋ deti; 2. abhimukhaŋ neti; 3. sañjānāpeti. *p.p.* dinnopahāra; °nita; °pita. *v.i.* paccupaṭṭhito hoti. °**able**, *a.* 1. cārudassana; 2. sañjānāpetabba; 3. tuṭṭhidāya-yogga. °**ation**, *n.* 1. vitaraṇa, *nt.* pariccāga, *m.* 2. padassana, *nt.* — **existence**, *n.* vattamāna-bhava, *m.* °**ly**, *adv.* adhunā; etarahi; idāni. °**ment**, *n.* 1. pakāsana, *nt.* 2. paṭibimba, *nt.* 3. codanā, *f.* °**ee**, *n.* laddhūpahāra, *m.* °**tense**, *n.* vattamānakāla, *m.*

Presentiment, *n.* pubbopaladdhi, *f.* puretarāvabodha, *m.*

Preserve, *n.* 1. rakkhitāhāra, *m.* 2. migadāya, *m.* abhayabhūmi, *f.* *v.t.* rakkhati; anupāleti; saṅgopeti. *p.p.* rakkhita; °lita; °pita. °**ation,** *n.* saṅgopana; ciraŋ pavattāpana, *nt.* °**ative,** *n. a.* anupālaka; cirappavattaka. °**er,** *n.* saṅgopaka; anupālaka, *m.* °**ing,** *a.* anupālanaka.

Preside, *v.i.* aggāsane nisīdati; ādhipaccaŋ pāpuṇāti. *p.p.* °nisinna; °patta. °**ncy,** *n.* ādhipacca; paripālakatta, *nt.* °**ing,** *a.* sabhāpālaka.

President, *n.* sabhāpati, *m.* °**ial,** *a.* sabhānetuvisayaka. °**ship,** *n.* sabhāpatitta; nāyakatta, *nt.*

Press, *n.* 1. janasammadda; 2. sambādha, *m.* 3. muddāyanta; 4. pīḷakayanta, *nt.* 5. pavattipatta, *nt. v.t.* 1. uppīḷeti; sammaddati; 2. nibandhati; abhiyācati; 3. daḷham āliṅgati; upagūhati. *p.p.* °ḷita; °dita; nibaddha; °cita; °gita; upagūḷha. °**er,** *n.* nibandhaka; uppīḷaka, *m.* °**ing,** *a.* āvassaka; anatikkamiya. °**ure,** *n.* 1. pīḷanavega; 2. sambādha, *m.* nippīḷana, *nt.* 3. kiccabhāra, *m.* 4. nibandhana, *nt.*

Prestidigitator, *m.* indajālika; māyākāra, *m.* °**tion,** *n.* indajāla, *nt.*

Prestige, *n.* cirāgata-garutta, *nt.* cirāgatānubhāva, *m.*

Prestissimo, Presto, *adv.* sīghaŋ; turitaŋ.

Presume, *v.t.* 1. anumāneti; 2. sīmam atikkamati. *v.i.* pāgabbhiyaŋ dasseti. *p.p.* °nita; sīmātikkanta; dassita °ya. °**able,** *a.* anumetabba; ūhanīya. °**ably** *adv.* anumeyākārena. °**edly,** *adv.* anumānena; nayagāhena.

Presumption, *n.* 1. anumānagāha, *m.* 2. pāgabbhiya, *nt.* °**tive,** *a.* anumānasiddha; anumeya. °**tuous,** *a.* sāhasika; pagabbha. °**tuously,** *adv.* sappagabbhaŋ; sadappaŋ.

Presuppose, *v.t.* pageva pakappeti *or* anumāneti. °**ition,** *n.* puretarakappanā, *f.*

Pretend, *v.t.* vyājena dasseti; micchā ñāpeti *or* paṭipajjati. *v.i.* vyājavesaŋ gaṇhāti. *p.p.* °sita; °pita; °paṭipanna; gahita°. °**nce,** *n.* micchācaraṇa; sāṭheyya, *nt.* °**ed,** *a.* vyāja; kapaṭa. °**er,** *n.* ayathāpaṭiñña; micchāpaṭijānanaka. °**edly,** °**ingly,** *adv.* savyājaŋ; kohaññena.

Pretension, *n.* vyājadassana; vyājavesadhāraṇa; micchāpaṭijānana, *nt.*

Pretentious, *a.* attukkaŋsaka; micchāpaṭiññāyutta; sābhimāna. °**ly,** *adv.* micchāpaṭiññāya.

Preter-human, *a.* amānusika; manussabhāvātīta.

Preterit, °**rite,** *n.* Hīyattanī, *f.* adj. atītakālika.

Preterition, *n.* asallakkhaṇa; vajjana; ohāya-gamana, *nt.*

Pretermit, *v.t.* 1. na sāreti; kātuŋ pamussati; 2. parivajjeti. *p.p.* asārita; pamuṭṭha; °jita.

Preternatural, *a.* alokika; sabhāvātīta.

Pretext, *n.* micchāvyapadesa; lesamattagāha, *m. v.t.* lesamattena codeti. *p.p.* °codita.

Pretty, *a.* sobhana; dassanīya; abhirūpa; cārudassana; sundara; manuñña. *adv.* īsakaŋ; thokaŋ. °**ily,** *adv.* sundarākārena.

°**ness**, *n.* sobhanatā ; cārutā, *f.* °**ify**, *v.t.* sobhanaŋ karoti.

Prevail, *v.i.* abhibhavati ; vase vatteti. *p.p.* °abhibhūta ; °tita. °**ing**, *a.* vyāpita ; bahulībhūta. °**ingly**, *adv.* mahānubhāvena ; pabhuttena.

Prevalent, *a.* vyāpita ; bahulībhūta. °**nce**, *n.* bāhulla, *nt.* bahulappavatti, *f.* °**ly**, *adv.* bāhullena ; bhīyo.

Prevaricate, *v.i.* kuṭilaŋ *or* pariyāyena vadati *or* bhāsati. *p.p.* °vutta ; °sita. °**ion**, *n.* vaṅkakathā, *f.* saccapaṭicchādana, *nt.* °**tor**, *n.* saccapaṭicchādī, *m.*

Prevenient, *a.* 1. purogāmī ; purejāta ; 2. paṭibāhaka. °**nce**, *n.* 1. purejātatta ; 2. paṭibāhakatta, *nt.*

Prevent, *v.t.* nivāreti ; nisedheti ; paṭibāhati. *p.p.* °rita ; °dhita ; °hita. °**ion**, *n.* nivāraṇa ; rundhana ; paṭibāhana, *nt.* °**ive**, *a.* nisedhaka ; vibādhaka. °**er**, *n.* nivāretu ; nisedhetu, *m.*

Previous, *a.* pubba ; purima ; puretara. °**ly**, *adv.* puretaraŋ ; purā ; pure. — **birth**, purimabhava, *m.*

Prevision, *n.* puretaradassana ; anāgatañāṇa, *nt.*

Prewarn, *v.t.* pageva ñāpeti. *p.p.* °ñāpita.

Prey, *n.* gocara, *m.* āmisa ; bhakkha, *nt.* *v.t.* (upon), bhakkhati ; adati ; gocaraŋ gaṇhāti. *p.p.* °khita ; adita ; gahitagocara.

Price, *n.* aggha ; mūla, *nt.* *v.t.* aggheti ; agghaŋ niyameti. *p.p.* °ghita ; niyamitaggha. °**less**, *a.* mahaggha ; anaggha. °**lessness**, *n.* anagghatta, *nt.*

Prick, *n.* 1. tudana ; nittudana ; vijjhana, *nt.* 2. tutta, *nt.* patoda, *m.* *v.t.* tudati ; nittudati ; vijjhati ; vyathati. *p.p.* tudita *or* tunna ; viddha ; vyathita. °**er**, *n.* vedhaka ; nittudaka, *m.* vedhanī, *f.*

Prickle, *n.* 1. kaṇṭaka, *m.* sallakasūci, *f.* °**iness**, *n.* kaṇṭakagahanatta, *nt.* °**ly**, *a.* sakaṇṭaka. °**ly-pear**, *n.* sakaṇṭaka-nuhī, *m.* °**ly-night-shade**, *n.* nididdhikā, *f.*

Pride, *n.* mada ; māna ; dappa ; ahaṅkāra, *m.* pāgabbhiya, *nt.* *v.t.* (oneself upon :) vikattheti ; attānaŋ ukkaŋseti. *p.p.* °thita ; °sita. — **of life**, jīvitamada, *m.* — **of youth**, yobbanamada, *m.*

Priest, *n.* 1. samaṇa ; dhammācariya ; 2. devapūjaka; yajaka, *m.* °**ess**, *n.* samaṇī, *f.* °**hood**, *n.* samaṇabhāva, *m.* sāmañña, *nt.* °**ly**, *a.* sāmaṇaka ; samaṇasāruppa. °**liness**, *n.* samaṇākappa, *m.* °**craft**, *n.* samaṇopāya, *m.*

Prig, *n.* 1. ācārānugatatta, *nt.* 2. dappitapuggala ; 3. cora, *m.* *v.t.* coreti ; theneti. *p.p.* corita ; thenita. °**gery**, *n.* ahaṅkāra, *m.* °**gish**, *a.* gabbita ; bahisobhana.

Primacy, *n.* padhānatta, *nt.*

Prima facie, *adv.* āpāthagatavasena ; paṭhamadassanena.

Primal, *a.* 1. purātana; ādikappika ; 2. padhāna.

Primary, *a.* ādima ; mūlika ; paṭhamaka. °**ily**, *adv.* mūḷikavasena ; ādito ; paṭhamaŋ.— **edu-**

cetion, paṭhamakajjhāpana, *nt.* — **school,** mūlika-pāṭhasālā, *f.*

Prime, *n.* 1. uttamaŋsa, *m.* 2. samiddhāvatthā, *f.* 3. ādi ; paṭhamārambha, *m.* adj. paṭhama ; ādima ; padhāna. °**ness,** *n.* visiṭṭhatta ; uttamatta, *nt.* — **minister,** *n.* mahāmacca, *m.* — **of youth,** paṭhamavaya, *m.*

Primer, *n.* paṭhama-pāṭhāvali, *f.*

Primeval, *a.* ādikappika ; sanantana.

Primiparous, *a.* paṭhamavijātā, *f.*

Primitive, *a.* purātana ; pubbakālīna.

Primogenitor, *n.* paṭhamapitu ; mūlapurisa ; ādima, *m.* °**ture,** *n.* paṭhamajātatta ; aggajatta, *nt.*

Primordial, *n.* mūlabhūta ; ādito paṭṭhāya pavattamāna.

Primrose, *n.* mandapīta-pupphavisesa, *m.*

Prince, *n.* rājakumāra, *m.* °**ess,** *n.* rājaputtī ; rājakumārī, *f.* °**ly,** *a.* rājāraha ; rājasadisa.

Principal, *n.* 1. padhānādhikārī ; padhānācariya, *m.* 2. mūladhana, *nt.* adj. padhāna ; mukhya. °**ly,** *adv.* padhānavasena. °**ship,** *n.* padhānācariya-dhura, *nt.*

Principality, *n.* 1. rajjappadesa, *m.* rajjamaṇḍala, *nt.* 2. uparājāyattadesa, *m.*

Principia, *n. pl.* 1. mūlasikkhā ; 2. mūladhātu, *f.*

Principle, *n.* rīti, *f.* vidhi ; niyama, *m.* mūlikasacca, *nt.*

Prink, *v.t.* alaṅkaroti ; pasādheti. *p.p.* °kata ; °dhita.

Print, *n.* 1. muddā, *f.* 2. muddaṅkana, *nt.* 3. cittapaṭa, *m. v.t.* aṅketi ; muddāpeti. *p.p.* aṅkita ; °pita. °**er,** *n.* muddāpaka, *m.* °**ing,** *n.* muddaṅkana, *nt.* °**ing press,** muddāyanta, *nt.* °**ing office,** muddaṅkanālaya, *m.*

Prior, *a.* purima ; puretara. *adv.* puretaraŋ. *n.* vihārādhipati, *m.* °**y,** *n.* vihāra ; ārāma ; assama, *m.* °**ity,** *n.* puretaratta ; purimatta, *nt.*

Prism, *n.* dīgha-tulyaŋsaka, *m.*

Prison, *n.* bandhanāgāra ; andughara, *nt.* kārā ; suruṅgā, *f.* cāraka, *nt.* °**er,** *n.* kārābaddha ; bandhanagata, *m.* — **warder,** *n.* kārāpālaka, *m.*

Pristine, *a.* mūlika ; porāṇaka.

Prithee, *intj.* ahaŋ taŋ yācāmi.

Privacy, *n.* 1. rahassa ; apākaṭatta, *nt.* 2. vivittaṭṭhāna, *nt.*

Private, *a.* 1. puggalika ; ajjhattika ; 2. gutta ; apākaṭa ; 3. vijana ; vivitta. °**ly,** *adv.* 1. raho ; rahassena ; 2. puggalikavasena. °**ness,** *n.* 1. puggalikatta ; 2. rāhasikatta, *nt.* — **apartments,** itthāgāra ; antepura, *nt.* — **parts,** rahassaṅga ; aṅgajāta, *nt.*

Privation, *n.* 1. abhāva ; viraha, *m.* 2. parihāni, *f.* pārijuñña, *nt.*

Privative, *n.* abhāvattha ; nakārattha, *m.* adj. abhāvakara ; nāsakara.

Privilege, *n.* visesādhikāra ; pasāda ; vara, *m. v.t.* visesādhikāraŋ *or* varaŋ deti. *p.p.* dinnavara. °**ed,** *a.* varalābhī.

Privy, *n.* vaccakuṭi, *f.* adj. gūḷha ; rāhaseyyaka. — **cleaner,** vaccasodhaka, *m.* — **council,** rājādhikaraṇa, *nt.* °**ily,** *adv.* raho ;

rahasi; gūḷhākārena. °**ity,** *n.* rahassajānana, *nt.*—**pit,** vaccakūpa, *m.*

Prize, *n.* 1. pāritosika; upāyana, *nt.* 2. karamarānīta, *nt.* 3. kaṭaggāha, *m.* *v.t.* agghaŋ ṭhapeti; 2. bahumaññati. *p.p.* ṭhapitaggha; bahumata. °**giving,** *n.* pāritosikavissajjana, *nt.*

Pro, *prep.* atthāya.

Probable, *a.* sambhavanīya; bhabba; sakya. °**bility,** *n.* sukkuṇeyyatta, *nt.* °**bly,** *adv.* siyā.

Probate, *n.* accayadāna-paṇṇādhikāra, *m.*

Probation, *n.* caritaparikkhaṇa, *nt.* parivāsa, *m.* °**ary,** *a.* parivāsāyatta. °**al,** *a.* parivasamāna. °**er,** *n.* 1. parivāsagāhī; 2. ādhunika, *m.*

Probative, *a.* sasakkhika; sādhanasahita.

Probe, *v.t.* 1. sukhumaŋ nirikkhati; 2. salākāya gavesati. *p.p.* °khita; °sita. °**ing,** *n.* gavesana, *nt.*

Probity, *n.* ajjava; akuṭilatta, *nt.*

Problem, *n.* vicāranīya-visaya; tīranīya-pañha, *m.* °**atical,** *a.* vicāranīya; avinicchita.

Proboscis, *n.* soṇḍā, *f.* soṇḍākāra-avayava, *m.*

Procedure, *n.* vidhāna; anuṭṭhāna, *nt.* anukkama, *m.*

Proceed, *v.i.* abhikkamati; abhiyāti; ārabhati. *p.p.* abhikkanta; abhiyāta; āraddha. — **from,** pabhavati; niggacchati.

Proceeds, *n. pl.* udaya; lābha, *m.*

Process, *n.* pavatti; gati; kiccapaṭipāṭi, *f.* abhikkamana, *nt.* *v.i.* abhikkamati; paṭipāṭiyā gacchati. — **of cognition,** cittavīthi, *f.*

Procession, *n.* ussavayātrā, *f.* paṭipāṭiyā gamana, *nt.*

Proclaim, *v.t.* pakāseti; anusāveti; ugghoseti. *p.p.* °sita; °vita; °sita. °**mation,** *n,* anusāvaṇa; pakāsana, *nt.* °**er.** *n.* anusāvaka; pakāsaka, *m.* °**matory,** *a.* anusāvaṇāyatta.

Proclivity, *n.* poṇatta; ninnatta; sampavaṅkatta, *nt.* °**vious,** *a.* ninna; poṇa.

Procrastinate, *v.i.* vilambati; cirāyati; kālaŋ khepeti; pamajjati. *v.t.* vilambeti. *p.p.* °bita; °yita; khepitakāla; pamatta; °bita. °**ion,** *n.* kālakkhepa, *m.* cirāyana; vilambana; pamajjana; dīghasuttiya, *nt.*

Procreate, *v.t.* janeti; uppādeti. *p.p.* janita; °dita. °**ion,** *n.* janana; pasavana, *nt.* °**ive,** *a.* janaka; uppādaka.

Proctor, *n.* nītividū; paṭivattu, *m.*

Procumbent, *a.* avakujjapatita; adhomukkanipanna.

Procure, *v.t.* 1. sampādeti; adhigacchati; upaṭṭhāpeti; labhati. *p.p.* °dita; adhigata; °pita; laddha. °**er,** *n.* 1. sampādaka; 2. micchācārupatthambhaka, *m.* °**able,** *a.* adhigantabba; labbhaneyya; sādhiya. °**ation,** *n.* 1. sampādana; 2. adhigamana, *nt.* °**ator,** *n.* parakiccasampādaka, *m.*

Procuress, *n.* dhuttitthī; sañcārikā, *f.*

Prod, *n.* vijjhanasūci, *f.* *v.t.* nittudati; vijjhati. *p.p.* nittunna; viddha.

Prodigal, *a.* *n.* atibbayasīlī; dhananāsaka, *m.* °**ize**, *v.t.* adhikavayaŋ karoti. °**ity**, *n.* atibbayakāritā, *f.* °**ly**, *adv.* adhikavayena.

Prodigy, *n.* 1. abbhutapurisa, *m.* acchariyavatthu, *nt.* °**ious**, *a.* atimahanta; abbhutākāra. °**iously**, *adv.* 1. abbhutākārena; 2. atimattaŋ; adhimattaŋ.

Prodrome, *n.* 1. rogapubbanimitta, *nt.* 2. puretara-gantha, *m.*

Produce, *n.* nipphatti, *f.* udaya, *m.* nimmāṇa, *nt.* *v.t.* uppādeti; nipphādeti; samuṭṭhāpeti; nibbatteti. *p.p.* °dita; °tita. °**er**, *n.* nipphādaka; sampādaka; uṭṭhāpetu, *m.* °**ing**, *a.* nibbattaka; sañjanaka; samuṭṭhāpaka. °**ing**, *n.* uppādana; nipphādana, *nt.* °**ible**, *a.* uppādanīya; sampādanakkhama.

Product, *n.* 1. uppannavatthu; sampāditabhaṇḍa, *nt.* 2. vipāka, *m.* phala, *nt.* °**ion**, *n.* abhinipphādana, *nt.* °**ive**, *a.* phaladāyaka; nipphādaka. °**ively**, *adv.* saphalākārena. °**ivity**, *n.* phalāvahatta; saphalatta, *nt.*

Proem, *n.* upaññāsa, *m.* ārambhakathā; bhūmikā, *f.*

Profane, *v.t.* dūseti; asuddhaŋ karoti. *p.p.* dūsita; asuddhakata. adj. anariya; pothujjanika; gamma. °**ation**, °**ity**, *n.* apavittakaraṇa, *nt.* °**ly**, *adv.* adhammikatāya.

Profess, *v.i.t.* 1. paṭijānāti; 2. pakāseti; 3. uggaṇhāpeti; vyapadisati. *p.p.* paṭiññāta; °sita; °pita; upadiṭṭha. °**ed**, *a.* katapaṭiñña. °**edly**, *adv.* paṭiññāpubbakaŋ. °**ion**, *n.* 1. paṭiññā; āpattidesanā, *f.* 2. jīvanopāya, *m.* °**ional**, *a.* ājīvāyatta.

Professor, *n.* paṇḍitācariya; mahajjhāpaka, *m.* °**ship**, *n.* paṇḍitācariyadhura, *nt.*

Proffer, *n.* dātukāmatāpakāsana, *nt.* *v.t.* attano icchāya samappeti; dātukāmataŋ *or* kātukāmataŋ pakāseti. *p.p.* °pita; °sita.

Proficient, *a.* nipuṇa; kusala; pavīṇa; vyatta; dakkha. °**ncy**, *n.* nepuñña; kosalla; pāṭava, *nt.* °**ly**, *adv.* nipuṇatāya; pavīṇatāya.

Profile, *n.* addhadassana; ekapassālekha, *nt.* *v.t.* ekapassikālekham ālikhati. *p.p.* ālikhita°.

Profit, *n.* 1. attha; lābha, *m.* payojana, *nt.* 2. udaya, *m.* vaḍḍhi, *f.* *v.t.* hitam āvahati. *v.i.* atthāya hoti; unnatiŋ yāti; lābham adhigacchati. *p.p.* āvahitahita; °bhūta; °yāta; adhigatalābha. °**able**, *a.* hitāvaha; phaladāyī. °**ableness**, *n.* saphalatta, *nt.* °**ably**, *adv.* saphalākārena. °**eer**, *n.* adhikalābhagāhī, *m.* °**less**, *a.* nipphala; niratthaka.

Profligate, *a.* durācāra; pāparata. °**gacy**, *n.* durācāratā; kāmāsattatā, *f.* °**ly**, *adv.* kāmāsattatāya.

Profound, *a.* 1. duravabodha; atisukhuma; 2. agādha; gambhīra; 3. parama; uttama. *n.*

gambhīratta, *nt.* °**ly**, *adv.* gāḷhaŋ ; bhusaŋ ; accantaŋ. °**ness**, °**fundity**, *n.* gambhīratta ; sukhumatta, *nt.*

Profuse, *a.* 1. cāgādhika ; 2. pahūta ; pacura ; bahula ; vipula. °**ly**, *adv.* bahulaŋ ; bhīyo ; bāhullena. °**ness**, °**ion**, *n.* bāhulla, vepulla ; pacuratta, *nt.* samiddhi, *f.*

Progeny, *n.* santati ; pajā, *f.* kulavaŋsa, *m.* °**itive**, *a.* santatuppādaka. °**itor**, *n.* pajāpati ; pitāmaha ; ādipurisa, *m.* °**itress**, °**itrix**, *n.* paṭhamajanettī ; ādimamātu, *f.* °**iture**, *n.* apaccajanana, *nt.*

Prognathic, *a.* lambahanuka.

Prognosis, *n.* roganimitta, *nt.*

Prognostic, *n.* pubbanimitta, *nt.* °**ation**, *n.* nimittapaṭhana, *nt.* °**ate**, *v.t.* pubbanimittaŋ dasseti; pageva sūceti. °**ative**, °**atory**, *a.* anāgatasūcaka ; pageva nirūpaka. °**ator**, *n.* nimittapāṭhaka ; anāgatasūcaka, *m.*

Programme, *n.* kiccapaṭipāṭi ; kāriya-sūci, *f.* *v.t.* kāriyasūciŋ sampādeti.

Progress, *n.* 1. abhivuddhi, *f.* abbhuṭṭhāna, *nt.* unnati, *f.* 2. abhikkamana, *nt.* *v.i.* abhivaḍḍhati. *v.t.* abhikkamati. *p.p.* abhivuddha ; abhikkanta. °**ion**, *n.* abhigamana ; abhivaḍḍhana, *nt.* °**ive**, *a.* 1. vuddhigāmī ; vaḍḍhamāna ; 2. anukkamika. °**ively**, *adv.* anukkamena.

Prohibit, *v.t.* nivāreti ; nisedheti ; paṭisedheti. *p.p.* °rita ; °dhita. °**er**, °**or**, *n.* nisedhaka ; nivāretu, *m.* °**ive**, *a.* vāraka ; bādhaka. °**ion**, *n.* nisedha ; paṭisedha, *m.* nivāraṇa, *nt.*

Project, *v.t.* 1. upakkamati ; 2. abhikkhipati. *v.i.* bahi niggacchati. *p.p.* °mita ; abhikkhitta ; °niggata. *n.* upāya ; payoga ; saṅkappa, *m.* °**ile**, *n.* paharaṇa ; khipanakāyudha, *nt.* adj. khipanīya. °**ing**, *a.* bahiniggata. °**ion**, *n.* 1. upāya, *m.* 2. bahiniggama, *m.* 3. unnataṭṭhāna, *nt.* °**or**, *n.* upāyayojaka, *m.* °**ure**, *n.* bahiniggama, *m.*

Prolapse, *v.i.* adho bhassati. *p.p.* °bhaṭṭha. °**sus**, *n.* 1. adhopatana ; 2. antabhassana, *nt.*

Prolative, *a.* ākhyātapūraka.

Prolegomenon, *n.* ārambhakathā, *f.* pubbaniddesa, *m.*

Prolepsis, *n.* pubbavuttāpekkhā, *f.*

Proletariat(e), *n.* duggatajanatā, *f.* °**rian**, *n.* duggatajana, *m.*

Prolicide, *n.* apaccaghātana, *nt.*

Prolific, *a.* 1 bahuputtaka ; 2. bahuphalada ; samiddha. °**acy**, °**ness**, *n.* samiddhatta ; bahuphaladatta, *nt.*

Prolix, *a.* ativitthārita ; atipapañcita. °**ity**, *n.* ativitthāra, *m.* °**ly**, *adv.* ativitthārena.

Prologue, *n.* mukhabandha, *m.* ārambhakathā ; paṭhamaviññatti, *f.*

Prolong, *v.t.* vitanoti ; papañceti. *p.p.* vitata ; °cita. °**ation**, *n.* 1. papañcakaraṇa; dīghasuttiya, *nt.* 2. cirappavattikaraṇa, *nt.*

Promenade, *n.* caṅkamana ; anuvicaraṇatthāna, *nt.* *v.i.* anuvicarati ; anusañcarati. *p.p.* °rita.

Prominent, *a.* 1. pamukha ; padhāna; mukhya ; ukkaṭṭha; visiṭṭha; 2. tuṅga ; uggata ; unnata ; 3. supākaṭa. °**ly**, *adv.* visesena ; mukhyavasena. °**nce**, *n.* 1. seṭṭhatta ; mukhyatta, *nt.* 2. unnati ; uttuṅgatā, *f.*

Promiscuous, *a.* saṅkiṇṇa ; saṅkula ; nibbisesa. °**ly**, *adv.* nibbisesena ; missākārena. °**cuity**, *n.* sammissatta ; saṅkiṇṇatta, *nt.*

Promise, *n.* paṭiññā, *f.* paṭissava; saṅgara, *m.* *v.t.* paṭijānāti; paṭissuṇāti. *p.p.* paṭiññāta; paṭissuta. °**see**, *n.* paṭiññālābhī, *m.* °**ser**, °**sor**, *n.* paṭiññādāyī, *m.* °**ing**, *a.* 1. paṭijānamāna ; 2. siddhisūcanaka.

Promissory, *a.* sappaṭiñña. — **note**, iṇapaṇṇa, *nt.*

Promontory, *n.* bhūnāsikā, *f.*

Promote, *v.t.* abhivaḍḍheti ; unnatiŋ pāpeti. *p.p.* °ḍhita ; °pāpita. °**er**, *n.* unnatipāpaka, *m.* °**ion**, *n.* unnatipāpana, *nt.* °**ive**, *a.* abhivaḍḍhaka; unnatipāpaka.

Prompt, *a.* *n.* khippa ; turita ; avilambita ; appamatta. *v.t.* ussāheti ; uttejeti ; pabodheti. °**ing**, *n.* uttejana ; uyyojana, *nt.* °**ness**, °**itude**, *n.* turitatta ; paṭutta, *nt.* ussāha, *m.* (of mind :) paṭibhāṇa, *nt.* °**ly**, *adv.* āsu ; khippaŋ; turitaŋ; tuvaṭaŋ.

Promulgate, *v.t.* pakāseti ; vyāpeti. *p.p.* °sita ; °pita. °**ion**, *n.* pakāsana ; vyāpana, *nt.* °**tor**, *n.* pakāsaka ; vyāpaka, *m.*

Pronate, *v.t.* abhimukhaninnaŋ karoti. °**ion**, *n.* abhimukhapasāraṇa, *nt.* °**tor**, *n.* abhimukhapasāraka-pesi, *f.*

Prone, *a.* poṇa ; nata ; parāyaṇa ; adhomukha. °**ness**, *n.* poṇatta, *nt.* āsattatā ; onatatā, *f.*

Prong, *n.* vijjhana-sūla, *nt.* *v.t.* sūlena vijjhati ; (bahudantakena) paŋsuŋ viyūhati. *p.p.* sūlaviddha ; °hitapaŋsu.

Pronominal, *a.* sabbanāmāyatta.

Pronoun, *n.* sabbanāma, *nt.*

Pronounce, *v.t.i.* 1. nicchayena vadati ; 2. uccāreti ; udāharati. *p.p.* °vutta ; °rita ; udāhaṭa. °**able**, *a.* uccāraṇīya ; udāhariya. °**ment**, *n.* 1. nicchayadāna ; tīraṇa ; 2. udīraṇa, *nt.* °**ed**, *a.* sunicchita ; pakāsita.

Pronunciation, *n.* uccāraṇa; udīraṇa, *nt.*

Proof, *n.* 1. sādhana ; nidassana ; pamāṇa, *nt.* 2. sodhiyapaṇṇa, *nt.* adj. sahanakkhama ; avinivijjhiya. *v.t.* abhejjaŋ *or* avejjhaŋ karoti. *p.p.* avejjhakata. °**less**, *a.* sādhanahīna. °**reader**, *n.* vaṇṇasodhaka, *m.*

Prop, *n.* upatthambha ; ādhāra, *m.* *v.t.* upatthambheti ; ādhāreti. *p.p.* °bhita ; °rita.

Propaedeutic, *n.* paṭhamasikkhāpana, *nt.* vijjārambha, *m.*

Propaganda, *n.* dhammappacāraṇa ; pacārakavidhāna, *nt.* °**ist**, *n.* pacāraniyutta. °**ism**, *n.* pacāraṇavidhi, *m.*

Propagate, *v.t.* 1. vitanoti ; pacāreti ; 2. santatiŋ vaḍḍheti. *p.p.* vitata ; °rita ; vaḍḍhitasantatī. °**ion**, *n.* 1. pacāraṇa ; vyāpana, *nt.* 2. santativaḍḍhana, *nt.* °**tor**, *n.* pacāraka ; vaḍḍhetu, *m.* °**ive**, *a.* pacāraṇāyatta.

Propel, *v.t.* sañcāleti; abhikkamāpeti. *p.p.* °lita; °pita. °**ler,** *n.* sañcālakacakka, *nt.*

Propense, see **Prone.** °**ity,** *n.* poṇatta; parāyaṇatta, *nt.*

Proper, *a.* 1. yogga; ucita; patirūpa; anucchavika; anulomika; yathāraha; 2. nija; saka; attaniya. °**ly,** *adv.* sammā; yathābhūtaŋ; yathārahaŋ. — **course,** sammāpaṭipatti, *f.* — **to eat,** bhojja; khāditabba, *a.*

Property, *n.* 1. dhana; santakavatthu, *nt.* 2. guṇavisesa, *m.* sabhāvalakkhaṇa, *nt.*

Prophecy, *n.* anāgatādisana, *nt.*

Prophesy, *v.t.* anāgatam ādisati. *p.p.* ādiṭṭhānāgata.

Prophet, *n.* anāgatavattu, *m.* °**ess,** *n.* anāgatadassikā, *f.* °**hood,** *n.* anāgatavattubhāva, *m.* °**ic,** *a.* anāgatadesakāyatta; anāgatasūcaka.

Prophylactic, *a. n.* roganivāraka.

Propinquity, *n.* 1. āsannatta; samānatta, *nt.* 2. ñātisambandha, *m.*

Propitiate, *v.t.* ārādheti; pasādeti; paritoseti. *p.p.* °dhita; °dita; °sita. °**tion,** *n.* ārādhanā; pasādanā, *f.* °**tor,** *n.* ārādhaka; pasādetu, *m.* °**tory,** *a.* santikara; vūpasamaka.

Propitious, *a.* 1. pasanna; hitakara; 2. subha; maṅgala; kalyāṇa. °**ly,** *adv.* sadayaŋ; sānuggahaŋ; iṭṭhākārena. °**ness,** *n.* subhatta; anukūlatta, *nt.*

Proponent, *n.* yojanākāra; matadassaka, *m.*

Proportion, *n.* parimāṇa; ārohapariṇāha, *m.* 2. samabhāga, *m.* samappamāṇa, *nt.* °**al,** *a.* samappamāṇa; anurūpa. °**less,** *a.* ocityahīna; asaṅghaṭiyamāna. °**ate,** *a.* saṅghaṭiyamāna. °**ately,** *adv.* anurūpākārena; yathāpamāṇaŋ.

Propose, *v.t.* 1. kattabbaŋ niddisati; mataŋ āvīkaroti; 2. vivāham āpucchati. *p.p.* niddiṭṭhakattabba; āvīkatamata; āpuṭṭhavivāha. °**sal,** *n.* 1. kattabbaniddesa, *m.* yojanā, *f.* 2. vivāhāpucchā, *f.* °**sition,** *n.* 1. kattukamyatāñāpana, *nt.* 2. pakāsana, *nt.* 3. mūladhamma, *m.*

Propound, *v.t.* 1. vicāraṇāya upakkhipati; 2. yojanaŋ āharati. *p.p.* °upakkhitta; āhaṭayojana. °**er,** yojanākārī, *m.*

Proprietary, *a.* adhīnatāvisayaka. *n.* sāmitta, *nt.*

Proprietor, *n.* sāmī; pariggāhī, *m.* °**ship,** *n.* sāmitta; adhīnatta, *nt.*

Propriety, *n.* ucitatta; yoggatta, *nt.* sadācāra, *m.*

Propulsion, *n.* abhikkamāpana; abhinittudana, *nt.* °**sive,** *a.* abhinittudaka.

Prorogue, *v.t.* kālikavasena nivatteti. *p.p.* °tita.

Prosaic, *a.* 1. gajjamaya; 2. kabbarasahīna.

Prosaist, *n.* gajjasampādaka, *m.*

Proscribe, *v.t.* raṭṭhā pabbājeti; ārakkhārahitaŋ karoti. *p.p.* °jita. °**cription,** *n.* pabbājana; rakkhāpanayana, *nt.*

Prose, *n.* gajjabandha, *m.* *v.t.* (pajjaŋ) gajjarūpena likhati; °likhita.

Prosector, *n.* matadehaviccheedaka, *m.*

Prosecute, *v.t.* nirantaraŋ pavatteti. *v.i.* adhikaraṇe codeti; vinicchayaŋ neti. *p.p.* °tita; °dita; °nīta. °**ed,** *a.* codita; daṇḍappatta. °**ion,** *n.* 1. niccānuṭṭhāna; 2. aṭṭakaraṇa, *nt.* °**tor,** *n.* 1. codaka; abhiyuñjaka; 2. niccappavattaka, *m.* °**trix,** *n.* codikā, *f.*

Proselyte, *n.* sadhammacāgī; samayantaragāhī, *m.* °**ism,** *n.* samayantaragahaṇa, *nt.* °**ize,** *v.i.* sakadhammaŋ cajati. *p.p.* cattasakadhamma.

Prosify, *v.t.* gajjaŋ racayati; gajjataŋ pāpeti. *p.p.* gajjaracita; °pita.

Prosody, *n.* chandosattha, *nt.* °**ial,** °**ical,** °**ic,** chandovisayaka. °**ian,** °**ist,** chandovidū, *m.*

Prosopopoeia, *n.* sacetanattāropaṇa, *nt.*

Prospect, *n.* 1. dassanapatha, *m.* 2. anāgatāpekkhā, *f.* °**ive,** *a.* bhavitabba; anāgatāyatta. °**ively,** *adv.* anāgatāpekkhāya. °**us,** *n.* nidassanalipi, *f.* kāriyānukkamadassana, *nt.*

Prospect, *v.t.* khaṇijatthāya (bhūmiŋ) gavesati.

Prosper, *v.i.* samijjhati; sampajjati; abhivaḍḍhati. *v.t.* saŋvaḍḍheti; saphalīkaroti. *p.p.* samiddha; sampanna; abhivuddha; °ḍhita; °kata. °**ity,** *n.* samiddhi; sampatti; abhivuddhi, *f.* abbhudaya, *m.*

Prosperous, *a.* samiddha; sassirīka; phīta; saphala; vaḍḍhamāna. °**ly,** *adv.* samiddhākārena; sobhaggena. °**ness,** *n.* samiddhatta; sāphalya, *nt.*

Prosthesis, *n.* 1. ādyakkharavaḍḍhana; 2. vikalaṅgapūraṇa, *nt.*

Prostitute, *n.* gaṇikā; vesiyā; vaṇṇadāsī, *f.* *v.t.* gārayhakamme niyojeti. *p.p.* °jita. °**ion,** *n.* 1. gaṇikāvutti, *f.* 2. gārayhakamma, *nt.*

Prostrate, *a.* 1. gāravābhinata; 2. abhibhūta; 3. tiriyaŋ nipanna. *v.t.* 1. (oneself:) nipaccakāraŋ karoti; pādamūle patati; 2. abhibhavati; vināseti. *p.p.* katanipaccakāra; °patita; abhibhūta; °sita. °**ion,** *n.* nipaccakāra, *m.* gāravābhinati, *f.*

Protagonist, *n.* (naccādisu) padhānapuggala, *m.*

Protasis, *n.* pubbavākya, *nt.* siddhanta, *m.*

Protean, *a.* bahuvesayutta; vividhasāmatthiyadhara.

Protect, *v.t.* tāyati; rakkhati; gopeti; pāleti. *p.p.* tāyita; °khita; gopita; pālita. °**ion,** *n.* ārakkhā, *f.* tāyana; tāṇa; leṇa; parittāṇa, *nt.* °**ive,** *a.* paṭisaraṇa; tāṇabhūta. °**or,** *n.* pāletu; gopetu; tāyaka; rakkhaka, *m.* °**ress,** *n.* gopikā; rakkhikā, *f.*

Protegé, *n.* saraṇagata, *m.*

Protest, *v.t.i.* paṭikkosati; paṭivirujjhati. *p.p.* °sita; °viruddha. *n.* paṭikkosanā, *f.* paṭivirujjhana, *nt.* viruddhavāda, *m.* °**ation,** *n.* paṭikkosanā; vipaccanikatā, *f.* °**er,** *n.* paṭikkosaka; viruddhavādī. °**ingly,** *adv.* paṭikkosanena.

Protocol, *n.* paṭhamākati, *f.* paṭhamuddesa, *m.*

Protogenetic, *a.* paṭhamavaḍḍhanāyatta.

Protoplasm, *n.* jīvadhātu, *f.*

Prototype, *n.* mūlikapaṭimā, *f.* mūlapaṭibimba, *nt.*

Protract, *v.t.* 1. vilambeti; 2. vitthambheti. *p.p.* °bita; °bhita. °**ion,** *n.* 1. cirāyana; vilambana; dīghasuttiya, *nt.* 2. vitthambhana, *nt.*

Protrude, *v.i.* niggacchati; palambati. *p.p.* niggata; °bita. *v.t.* nikkhamāpeti; palambeti. *p.p.* °pita; °bita. °**nt,** °**ing,** *a.* bahiniggata; palambamāna.

Protrusile, *a.* pasāraṇakkhama.

Protrusion, *n.* bahipasāraṇa, *nt.* bahiniggama, *m.* °**sive,** *a.* pasāraṇīya; pasāraṇakkhama.

Protuberant, *a.* ucchūna; uddhumāta; bahiniggata. °**nce,** *n.* uddhumāyana, *nt.* phoṭa; gaṇḍa, *m.*

Proud, *a.* sadappa; gabbita; mānatthaddha. — **of birth,** jātitthaddha, *a.* — **of wealth,** dhanatthaddha, *a.* °**ly,** *adv.* sadappaŋ; sābhimānaŋ.

Prove, *v.t.* samatthayati; tathattaŋ dīpeti. *v.i.* paññāyati; sandassīyati. *p.p.* °yita; dīpitatathatta; paññāta; sandiṭṭha. °**able,** *a.* samatthanīya; sādhanīya.

Provenance, *n.* ubbhavaṭṭhāna; pabhavaṭṭhāna, *nt.*

Provender, *n.* 1. ghāsa, *m.* pasubhojana, *nt.* 2. sambala, *nt.*

Proverb, *n.* ābhāṇaka, *nt.* °**ial,** *a.* ābhāṇakāyatta. °**ially,** *adv.* ābhāṇakavasena.

Provide, *v.t.* sampādeti; upaṭṭhapeti; paṭiyādeti. *p.p.* °dita; °pita; °dita. °**ed,** *conj.* sace; yadi. °**er,** *n.* sampādaka, *m.*

Providence, *n.* 1. niyati, *f.* pubbakamma, *nt.* 2. dūradassitā, *f.* pubbopāya, *m.*

Provident, *a.* dūradassī; samekkhaka; pubbavīmaŋsī. °**ial,** *a.* vidhiniyamita. °**ially,** *adv.* vidhiniyamena. °**ly,** *adv.* susamekkha; dūradassanena.

Province, *n.* 1. padesa, *m.* 2. niyamitakicca, *nt.* °**cial,** *a.* padesika, *n.* padesavāsī. °**ciality,** *n.* padesikatta, *nt.* °**cialism,** *n.* padesācāra, *m.*

Provision, *n.* 1. saŋvidahana; sampādana, *nt.* 2. sambala; pātheyya; upakaraṇa, *nt.* paribbaya, *m.* 3. niyamāvali, *f.* *pl.* bhojanavatthūni. *v.t.* sampādeti. *p.p.* °dita. °**al,** *a.* sāmayika; tāvakālika. °**ally,** *adv.* tāvakālikaŋ.

Proviso, *n.* paṭiññāpanne visesaniyama, *m.* °**or,** *n.* visesaniyamadhārī, *m.* °**ory,** *a.* visesaniyamayutta.

Provocation, *n.* 1. pakopana; 2. ujjhāpana; 3. uttejana, *nt.* °**tive,** *a.* pakopaka; uddīpaka.

Provoke, *v.t.* 1. kopeti; roseti; 2. ujjhāpeti; 3. uttejeti. *p.p.* °pita; rosita; °pita; °jita.

Provost, *n.* 1. vijjālayādhikārī; 2. saṅghanāyaka, *m.*

Prow, *n.* nāvāsīsa, *nt.* adj. nibbhaya; sūra.

Prowess, *n.* sūratta; vīratta, *n.* vikkama, *m.* porisa, *nt.*

Prowl, *n.* raho-paribbhamaṇa, *nt.* *v.i.* raho paribbhamati *or* pariyaṭati.

Proximate, *a.* samīpa ; āsanna ; upantika. °**ly,** *adv.* āsannatāya.

Proximity, *n.* āsannatta ; antikatta, *nt.*

Proximo, *adv.* āgāmi-māse.

Proxy, *n.* paṭinidhi ; niyojitapuggala, *m.*

Prude, *n.* ativinayadassikā, *f.*

Prudent, *a.* nipaka ; dūradassī ; samekkhakārī. °**nce,** *n.* nepakka ; samekkhā ; dūradassitā, *f.* °**ial,** *a.* vīmaŋsaka ; samekkhāyutta. °**ly,** *adv.* anuvicca ; samekkhāya.

Prudery, *n.* micchāhirottappa, *nt.*

Prune, *n.* 1. sukkha-badara, *nt.* 2. badaravaṇṇa, *m.* *v.t.* aggāni chindati. *p.p.* aggacchinna.

Prunella, *n.* kaṇṭhadāha, *m.*

Prurient, *a.* kāmāsatta. °**nce,** *n.* kāmalolatā, *f.*

Pruritus, *n.* kuṭṭharoga, *m.*

Pry, *n.* 1. sukhuma-nirikkhaṇa, *nt.* 2. anāhūtappavesa, *m.* *v.i.* 1. sukhumaŋ nirikkhati ; 2. parakiccāni gavesati. *p.p.* °khita ; °sita. °**ing,** *n.* parakiccagavesana, *nt.*

Psalm, *n.* bhattigīta ; dhammagīta, *nt.* °**ist,** *n.* dhammagītabandhaka, *m.* °**odist,** *n.* bhattigītagāyaka, *m.*

Pseudograph, *n.* vyājalekhana, *nt.* kūṭalipi, *f.*

Pseudologer, *n.* satatamicchāvādī, *m.*

Pseudonym, *n.* vyājanāma, *nt.* °**ous,** *a.* kūṭanāmadhārī.

Pshaw, *intj.* dhiratthu !

Psilosis, *n.* (kesādi-) luñcana, *nt.*

Psittacine, *a.* sukasadisa.

Psyche, *n.* jīva, *m.* viññāṇa ; citta, *nt.* °**chic,** °**chical,** *a.* mānasāyatta ; ajjhattika.

Psychiater, *n.* manorogatikicchaka, *m.*

Psychology, *n.* cetasikavijjā ; ajjhattavijjā, *f.* °**ical,** *a.* cittavisayaka. °**ist,** *n.* cittadhammavidū, *m.*

Psychopath, *n.* vibbhantacitta, *m.*

Psychosis, *n.* cittavibbhama, *m.*

Pteropus, *n.* tūliya ; pakkhabiḷāla, *m.*

Puberty, *n.* yobbana, *nt.* viññutā ; vayappatti, *f.*

Pubescence, *n.* yobbanappatti, *f.* °**scent,** *a.* pattayobbana ; rajoyutta.

Public, *n.* janatā, *f.* mahājana, *m.* adj. 1. mahājanika ; sabbasādhāraṇa ; 2. pasiddha ; pākaṭa. °**ation,** *n.* (gantha-) pakāsana ; pākaṭīkaraṇa, *nt.* °**ity,** *n.* passiddhi ; vissuti, *f.* pākaṭatta, *nt.* °**ist,** *n.* jananītikovida, *m.* °**ly,** *adv.* supākaṭaŋ ; pasiddhākārena. — **house,** pānāgāra, *nt.* — **road,** mahāpatha, *m.* °**spirited** *a.* paratthanirata.

Publish, *v.t.* pacāreti ; pakāseti ; pākaṭīkaroti. *p.p.* °rita ; °sita ; °kata. °**er,** *n.* pakāsaka ; pacāraka, *m.* °**able,** *a.* pākāṭikattabba.

Pucker, *n.* āvali, *f.* āvalisamūha, *m.* *v.t.* valiŋ gaṇhāpeti ; āvaliyo karoti. *v.i.* valiŋ gaṇhāti. *p.p.* °pita ; āvalīkata ; valiggahita.

Pudding, *n.* madhurabhojja, *nt.* °**head,** *n.* jaḷamati, *m.*

Puddle, *n.* kaddamāvāṭa ; sobbha, *m.* udakacikkhalla, *nt.* *v.t.* āvilaŋ *or* cikkhallaŋ karoti. *p.p.* āvilīkata.

Pudency, *n.* vinītatā, *f.*

Pudendum, *n.* mehana ; vatthaguyha ; rahassaṅga, *nt.* °**virile,** *n.* kāṭa, *m.* °**mulibre,** *n.* koṭacikā, *f.*

Pudge, *n.* thullavāmanaka, *m.* °**gy,** *a.* thullavāmana.

Puerile, *a.* bālocita. °**ity,** *n.* bālocitatta, *nt.* °**ly,** *adv.* bālocitākārena.

Puerperal, *a.* pasūtivisayaka.

Puff, *n.* 1. sahasā-dhamana ; sahasāvāyana, *nt.* 2. sakiŋ mocita-dhūmapuñja, *m.* *v.t.* sahasā dhamati *or* nicchāreti. *v.i.* uddhumāyati. *p.p.* °mita ; °rita; uddhumāta. °**iness,** *n.* uddhumātatta, *nt.* °**y,** *a.* 1. vāyanayutta ; 2. uddhumāta ; atithūla.

Pug, *n.* 1. saṅkhatamattikā, *f.* 2. pasupadalañchana, *nt.* *v.t.* 1. (iṭṭhakādatthāya) mattikaŋ saṅkharoti ; 2. padasaññāya anubandhati. — **faced,** *a.* kapimukha. °**gish,** *a.* cipiṭanāsika. °**mill,** *n.* mattikāpiŋsaka-yanta, *nt.* °**nose,** *n.* cipiṭanāsā, *f.* °**nosed,** *a.* cipiṭanāsika.

Pugilist, *n.* mallayodha, *m.* °**ism,** mallayuddha, *nt.*

Pugnacious, *a.* kalahappiya.

Puisne, *a.* kaṇiṭṭha ; upapadaṭṭha.

Puissant, *a.* pabala ; savikkama. °**nce,** *n.* sūratta, *nt.* vikkama, *m.*

Puke, *n.* vamathu, *m.* chaddikā, *f.* *v.i.* vamati. *v.t.* vamāpeti ; vamanaŋ uppādeti. *p.p.* vanta ; °pita ; °ditavamana.

Pule, *v.i.* nitthunāti ; saṇikaŋ rudati.

Pull, *n.* ākaḍḍhana, *nt.* *v.t.* ākaḍḍhati ; ākassati. *p.p.* °ḍhita ; °sita. — **about,** samparikaḍḍhati. — **along,** samākaḍḍhati. — **down,** nipāteti. — **off,** apakaḍḍhati. — **out,** uddharati ; ubbāhati ; abbūhati ; ūhanati. — **towards,** upakaḍḍhati. — **up,** ummūleti.

Pulley, *n.* ākaḍḍhakacakka ; ghaṭīyanta, *nt.*

Pullulate, *v.i.* aṅkurayati. *p.p.* aṅkurita. °**ion,** *n.* aṅkuruggamana, *nt.*

Pulmonary, Pulmonic, *a.* papphāsanissita.

Pulp, *n.* 1. miñjā, *f.* 2. mudupuñja, *m.* *v.t.* 1. sanneti ; muduvatthutaŋ pāpeti ; 2. miñjam apaneti. *v.i.* miñjasadiso hoti. *p.p.* sannita ; °pita ; apanītamiñja ; °disībhūta.

Pulpit, *n.* dhammāsana ; kathikāsana, *nt.*

Pulse, *n.* 1. rudhiragamana ; hadayaphandana, *nt.* 2. māsajāti, *f.* °**ate,** *v.i.* phandati. °**ation,** *n.* phandana ; nāḷīpatana, *nt.*

Pulverise, °**ze,** *v.t.* cuṇṇeti ; piŋseti. *p.p.* °ṇita ; °sita. °**ation,** *n.* cuṇṇīkaraṇa, *nt.* °**er,** *n.* saṇhakaraṇī, *f.*

Pulverulent, *a.* 1. sukhacuṇṇiya ; 2. papatanakkhama.

Pulvinate, *a.* bhisisamaŋ-uddhumāta.

Pummel, *v.t.* muṭṭhinā punappunaŋ paharati. *p.p.* °pahaṭa.

Pump, *n.* uttolana-yanta, *nt.* *v.t.* uttoleti ; ussiñcati. *p.p.* °lita ; ussitta.

Pumpkin, *n.* kumbhaṇḍa, *m.* **Yellow —**, pītakumbhaṇḍa, *m.*

Pun, *n.* silesatthavacana ; samānasadda-nānattha-vacana, *nt.* *v.i.* (tādisaŋ) vadati.

Punac, *n.* piññāka, *m.*

Punch, *n.* 1. vedhanī, *f.* vinivijjhakayanta, *nt.* 2. abhighāta ; 3. vidūsaka, *m.* *v.t.* 1. abhihanati ; 2. kaṇṭakena vijjhati. *p.p.* abhihata ; °kaviddha.

Puncheon, *n.* 1. upatthambhakakhāṇu, *m.* 2. mahādārubhājana, *nt.*

Punchinello, *n.* 1. thullavāmana ; 2. padhānadārupotthalikā, *f.*

Punctate, *a.* bindvaṅkita.

Punctilio, *n.* sukhumopacāravidhi, *m.* °**us**, *a.* sukhumaparikammānugāmī.

Punctual, *a.* kālaniyamānugata ; niyamānugāmī. °**ity**, *n.* yathākālikatta; niyamānugāmitta, *nt.* °**ly**, *adv.* yathāsamayaŋ.

Punctuate, *v.t.* vicchedalakkhaṇāni yojeti. *p.p.* °ṇayojita. °**ion**, *n.* vicchedalakkhaṇayojanā, *f.*

Punctum, *n.* tilaka ; bindu, *m.*

Puncture, *n.* sūcivedha, *m.* *v.t.* sūciyā vijjhati. *p.p.* sūcividdha.

Pungent, *a.* 1. kaṭuka ; tikhiṇa ; 2. mammacchedaka. °**ncy**, *n.* kaṭukarasatta ; tikhiṇatta.

Punish, *v.t.* daṇḍeti ; niggaṇhāti ; vadhaŋ payojeti. *p.p.* °ḍita ; niggahita ; °jitavadha. °**able**, *a.* daṇḍanīya ; daṇḍāraha. °**ableness**, *n.* daṇḍanīyatta, *nt.* °**ment**, *n.* daṇḍana, *nt.* niggaha, *m.*

Punitive, *a.* daṇḍakammāyatta.

Punk, *n.* 1. gaṇikā, *f.* 2. pūtidāru, *nt.*

Punkah, *n.* olambaka-mahāvījanī, *f.*

Punnet, *n.* phalapacchi, *f.*

Punster, *n.* silesavacanabhāsaka, *m.*

Puny, *a.* 1. khuddaka ; appaka ; 2. dubbala. °**iness**, *n.* appakatta ; dubbalatta, *nt.*

Pup, *n.* kukkura, *m.* *v.t.i.* sunakhapotake vijāyati.

Pupa, *n.* sakosaka-kimi, *m.*

Pupate, *v.i.* kosena āvarīyati. *p.p.* kosāvuta.

Pupil, *n.* 1. sissa ; antevāsika, *m.* 2. (of the eye :) nettatārā ; kaṇīnikā, *f.* °**age**, *n.* sissāvatthā, *f.* °**ary**, *a.* sissavisayaka.

Puppet, *n.* pañcālikā ; potthalikā, *f.* °**show**, potthalikānacca, *nt.*

Puppy, *n.* 1. kukkurapotaka ; 2. dappitamāṇava, *m.* °**ish**, *a.* mandamatika ; dappita.

Purblind, *a.* dubbaladiṭṭhika ; mandabuddhika. *v.t.* ūnadiṭṭhiŋ karoti. °**ness**, *n.* mandadiṭṭhikatta, *nt.*

Purchase, *n.* kaya, *m.* *v.t.* kiṇāti ; mūlena gaṇhāti. *p.p.* kīta ; °gahita. °**able**, *a.* ketabba ; kayāraha. °**er**, *n.* ketu ; kayika, *m.*

Pure, *a.* 1. suddha ; suci ; nimmala ; accha ; pasanna ; pūta ; 2. asaṅkiṇṇa ; amissa ; kevala ; 3. niddosa ; anavajja. °**ly**, *adv.* 1. kevalaŋ ; 2. nimmalākārena. °**ness**, °**ity**, *n.* nimmalatta ; soceyya ; suddhatta ; niddosatta, *nt.* suddhi, *f.*

Purge, *n.* virecakosadha, *nt.* *v.t.* sodheti ; vireceti ; malaŋ vissajjeti. *p.p.* sodhita ; °cita ; vissaṭṭhamala. °**ation,** *n.* sodhana; virecana, *nt.* °**ative,** *n.* virecakosadha, *nt.* adj. virecaka. °**atory,** *n.* pāpasodhaka-niraya, *m.*

Purify, *v.t.* sodheti; visodheti; puṇāti; vodapeti; sampasādeti. *p.p.* °dhita; pūta; °pita; °dita. °**ication,** *n.* saŋsodhana; visodhana; nimmalīkaraṇa; pāvana; vodapana, *nt.* visuddhi; saŋsuddhi, *f.* °**icatory,** *a.* saŋsodhaka. °**ier,** *n.* saŋsodhetu; vodapetu, *m.*

Purist, *n.* suddhikāmī; bhāsāsuddhiniviṭṭha, *m.*

Purity, *n.* 1. suddhatta; nimmalatta; 2. amissatta, *nt.*

Purl, *n.* 1. mandappavāha; 2. pavāhasadda, *m.* *v.i.* sāvaṭṭaŋ sandati. *v.t.* adhomukhīkaroti. *p.p.* °dita; °kata. °**er,** *n.* tiriyaŋpātakapahārā, *m.*

Purlieu, *n.* aṭavipariyanta; araññaparisara, *m.*

Purloin, *v.t.* coreti; theneti. *p.p.* corita; thenita. °**er,** *n.* takkara, mosaka; cora, *m.*

Purple, *n.* nīla-lohita-vaṇṇa, *m.* adj. nīlaratta. *v.t.* nīlarattaŋ karoti. *p.p.* °kata.

Purport, *n.* adhippāya; ajjhāsaya; gamyattha, *m.* *v.t.* ceteti; saṅkappeti. *v.i.* khāyati; paṭibhāti. *p.p.* cetayita; °pita.

Purpose, *n.* āsaya; adhippāya; saṅkappa, *m.* *v.t.* saṅkappeti; cinteti. *p.p.* °pita; °tita. °**ful,** *a.* sādhippāya; katanicchaya. °**less,** *a.* niratthaka. °**lessly,** *adv.* niratthakākārena. °**ly,** *adv.* sañcicca; sanicchayaŋ; saceatnaŋ. **For** the — **of,** atthāya. **For what** —, kimatthāya? **To no** —, niratthakaŋ, *adv.*

Purse, *n.* thavikā, *f.* pasibbaka, *m.* *v.t.* thavikāya pakkhipati. *p.p.* °khitta. °**pride,** *n.* dhanagabba, *m.* °**er,** *n.* nāvāya bhaṇḍāgārika, *m.*

Pursue, *v.t.* 1. anubandhati; 2. anuṭṭhāti; nisevati; ācarati. *p.p.* anuṭṭhita; °vita; °rita. °**ance,** *n.* anugamana; paṭipajjana, *nt.* °**ant,** *a.* anugāmī; paṭipanna. °**er,** *n.* anubandhaka, *m.*

Pursuit, *n.* 1. anubandhana; anvesana; 2. anuṭṭhāna; paṭipajjana; nisevana, *nt.*

Pursuivant, *n.* anucara; sevaka, *m.*

Pursy, *a.* thūladehī.

Purulent, *a.* pūyapuṇṇa; sañjātapūya. °**nce,** *n.* pūyapaggharaṇa, *nt.*

Purvey, *v.t.* sampādeti. *p.p.* °dita; °**ance,** (upakaraṇa) sampādana; bhojanasaŋvidahana, *nt.* °**or,** *n.* bhojanaparikappaka, *m.*

Purview, *n.* 1. padhānavisaya; paramattha, *m.* 2. dassanapatha, *m.*

Pus, *n.* pūya; pubba, *m.*

Push, *n.* khipana; sañcālana; nudana, *nt.* *v.t.* nudati; niṭṭudati; panudati; sañcāleti. *p.p.* °dita; °lita. — **aside,** apasāreti. — **away,** apanudati. °**ing,** *n.* nudana; apasaraṇa, *nt.* °**ing,** *a.* saussāha; dhitimantu. °**cycle,** *n.* cakkayanta, *nt.*

Pusillanimous, *a.* adhīra; kātara. °**mity,** *n.* kātaratta, *nt.*

Puss, Pussy, *n.* biḷāla ; majjāra, *m.*

Pustule, *n.* piḷakā, *f.* phoṭa, *m.* °**late,** *v.i.* piḷakā jāyati. *p.p.* jātapiḷakā. °**lous,** *a.* piḷakābahula.

Put, *n.* ṭhapana ; khipana, *nt.* *v.t.* ṭhapeti ; nikkhipati ; patiṭṭhāpeti. *p.p.* ṭhapita ; °khitta ; °pita.— **aside,** jahāti; pajahati. —**away,** nikkhāmeti ; nissāreti. — **back,** 1. papañceti ; 2. pubbaṭṭhānaŋ pāpeti. — **down,** 1. okkhipati ; otāreti ; 2. abhibhavati ; nihanati. — **forth,** 1. upadisati ; āvīkaroti; 2.upaṭṭhapeti. — **in,** pakkhipati. — **in order,** paṭisāmeti. — **off,** apaneti ; (some attire :) omuñcati. — **on,** (attire :) paridahati ; nivāseti ; paṭimuñcati ; (an armour :) sannayhati ; (a blame :) āropeti. — **out,** pasāreti ; vitanoti ; (a light :) nibbāpeti ; (eyes, etc.) uppāṭeti. — **over,** 1. papañceti; 2. upari ṭhapeti. — **to death,** māreti. — **together,** saŋyojeti ; saṅghaṭeti. — **up,** 1. sañcināti ; 2. nivāsaŋ gaṇhāti ; 3. vikkayāya ṭhapeti. °**ting,** ṭhapana ; nikkhipana, *nt.*

Putative, *a.* anumānita ; pasiddha ; parikappita.

Putid, *a.* duggandha ; pūtika.

Putrefy, *v.i.* pūtibhavati. *v.t.* pūtittaŋ pāpeti. *p.p.* pūtibhūta; °pāpita. °**faction,** *n.* pūtibhāva, *m.* °**factive,** *a.* pūtibhāvajanaka.

Putrescent, *a.* īsaŋpūtika.

Putrid, *a.* pūtika ; pūtigandha. °**ity,** °**ness,** pūtikatta, *nt.* pūtibhāva, *m.*

Puttee, *n.* jaṅghāveṭhana, *nt.*

Putty, *n.* kācaghaṭakālepa, *m.*

Puzzle, *n.* paheḷikā, *f.* sambhama, *m.* *v.t.* vimoheti ; sambhameti. *p.p.* °hita ; °mita. °**ing,** *a.* bhantikara ; vimohaka.

Pyaemia, *n.* lohitadūsana, *nt.*

Pygmy, *a.* *n.* vāmanaka ; lakuṇṭaka, *m.*

Pyjamas, *n.* *pl.* rattivasana, *nt.*

Pylon, *n.* 1. gopura, *nt.* 2. uccatthambha, *m.*

Pyorrhoea, *n.* dantapūyasavana, *nt.*

Pyramid, *n.* Misaradesīyathūpa, *m.* °**al,** *a.* thūpākāra.

Pyre, *n.* citaka, *m.*

Pyretic, *a.* jaruppādaka.

Pyrexia, *n.* jararoga, *m.*

Pyrolatry, agginamassana, *nt.*

Pyrology, *n.* tejoviññāṇa, *nt.* °**ist,** *n.* tejotattavidū, *m.*

Pyromantic, *n.* agginimittapāṭhaka, *m.*

Pyrosis, *n.* antodāha, *m.*

Pyrotechnic, *a.* aggimālāyatta, *n.* aggimālāsampādana, *m.*

Python, *n.* 1. ajagara ; 2. yakkhadāsa ; 3. bhūtāviṭṭhapuggala, *m.*

Pyxis, *n.* karaṇḍaka ; samugga, *m.*

Q

Quack, *n.* 1. haŋsanāda ; 2. kūṭavejja, *m.* *v.t.* 1. haŋso viya nadati ; 2. sasaddaŋ bhāsati ; 3. vikatthati. *p.p.* °sita ; °ṭhita. °**ery,** *n.* 1. kūṭatikicchā, *f.* 2. sāṭheyya, *nt.* °**ish,** *a.* vikatthanasīla.

Quadragenarian, *n.* cattāḷīsavassika, *m.*

Quadrangle, *n.* catukoṇaka; caturassaka, *nt.* °**gular,** *a.* catukkaṇṇa ; caturassa.

Quadrant, *n.* 1. catutthabhāga ; 2. gāthāpāda ; 3. cakkacatutthaŋsa, *m.*

Quadrate, *n.* catukkoṇaka, *nt.* adj. caturaŋsika. *v.t.* caturassaŋ karoti. *p.p.* °kata.

Quadrennial, *a.* catuvassika. °**ly,** *adv.* catuvassikavārena.

Quadrilateral, *a.* catupassika.

Quadruped, *n.* catuppada ; pasu, *m.*

Quadruple, *a. n.* catugguṇika. *v.t.* catugguṇaŋ karoti. *v.i.* catugguṇī hoti. *p.p.* °kata ; °bhūta. °**icate,** *a.* caturūpaka ; catukkabhūta. *n.* catukka, *nt.* *v.t.* catūhi guṇeti. °**icity,** *n.* catugguṇikatā, *f.*

Quaff, *v.t.* yathicchaŋ pivati. *p.p.* °pīta. °**er,** *n.* atipāyī, *m.*

Quag, Quagmire, *n.* sapaṅkasobbha, *m.*

Quail, *n.* vaṭṭakā ; laṭukikā, *f.* lāpa, *m.* *v.i.* olīyati ; osīdati. *p.p.* olīna ; osīna.

Quaint, *a.* apākatika ; vilakkhaṇa ; vikaṭa. °**ly,** *adv.* savikāraŋ; vilakkhaṇaŋ. °**ness,** *n.* vikaṭatta ; vilakkhaṇatta, *nt.*

Quake, *v.i.* kampati ; phandati ; calati. *p.p.* °pita ; °dita ; calita. *n.* kampana ; calana ; phandana, *nt.*

Qualify, *v.t.* 1. viseseti ; paricchindati ; 2. anucchavikaŋ karoti ; yoggattaŋ pāpeti. *p.p.* °sita ; paricchinna ; °kata ; °pita. °**ication,** *n.* 1. guṇavisesa, *m.* 2. yoggatta ; ucitatta, *nt.* °**ied,** *a.* 1. guṇopeta ; 2. alaṅkammaniya ; kammakkhama.

Quality, *n.* 1. guṇa ; sabhāva, *m.* pakati, *f.* lakkhaṇa, *nt.* 2. vagga, *m.* **Bad —,** 1. dugguṇa, *m.* 2. hīnajāti, *f.* **Good —,** 1. sagguṇa, *m.* 2. seṭṭhajāti, *f.*

Qualm, *n.* kālikamucchā, *f.* cittosīdana, *nt.*

Quandary, *n.* 1. dukkarāvatthā ; duddasā, *f.* 2. manovilekha, *m.*

Quantify, *v.t.* pamāṇaŋ nirūpeti. *p.p.* nirūpitapamāṇa.

Quantity, *n.* 1. pamāṇa ; parimāṇa, *nt.*, mattā, *f.* 2. rāsi ; puñja ; sañcaya, *m.* °**ive,** *a.* pameyya.

Quantum, *n.* 1. parimāṇa, *nt.* 2. abhimata-koṭṭhāsa, *m.*

Quarantine, *n.* saŋsagganisedha, *m.* *v.t.* saŋsaggaŋ nisedheti. *p.p.* nisedhitasaŋsagga.

Quarrel, *n.* kalaha ; medhaga, *m.* bhaṇḍana, *nt.* *v.i.* bhaṇḍeti ; vivadati ; kalahaŋ karoti. *p.p.* °ḍita ; °dita ; katakalaha. °**some,** *a.* kalahappiya ; bhaṇḍanakāraka.

Quarry, *n.* 1. pāsāṇākara, *m.* . icchitavatthu, *nt.* *v.t.* pāsāṇe khaṇati. *p.p.* khatapāsāṇa. °**man,** *n.* pāsāṇabhedaka, *m.*

Quartan, *a.* caturāhika.

Quarter, *n.* 1. catutthabhāga, *m.* 2. disā, *f.* 3. padesa, *m.* 4. *pl.* vāsaṭṭhāna, *nt.* nivāsa, *m.* *v.t.* 1. catudhā vibhajati ; 2. nivāseti. *v.i.* vāsaŋ gaṇhāti. *p.p.* °vibhatta; °sita; gahitavāsa. °**ly,** *a.* temāsika. °**age,** *n.* temāsikavetana, *nt.* °**ing,** *n.* catudhā vibhajana, *nt.*

Quartette, *n.* catukka, *nt.*
Quarto, *n.* catupattaka, *nt.*
Quartz, *n.* kācopala, *nt.*
Quash, *v.t.* abalīkaroti ; nirasati ; paccakkhāti. *p.p.* °kata ; °sita ; °khāta.
Quasi, *conj.* tathā hi. adj. expressed by *addha* or *kappa* in cpds., e.g. **Quasi-historical**, *a.* addhetihāsika.
Quatrain, *n.* catuppadika-pajja, *nt.*
Quaver, *n.* lalana, *nt.* *v.i.* kampati; calati ; lalati. *p.p.* °pita ; calita ; lalita. °**ingly**, *adv.* sakampaŋ ; salalitaŋ.
Quay, *n.* nāvotaraṇasetu, *m.*
Quean, *n.* avinītayuvatī, *f.*
Queen, *n.* rājadevī ; rājamahesī ; rājinī, *f.* *v.t.* rājiniŋ karoti. — **consort**, *n.* aggamahesī, *f.* °**ly**, *a.* rājinīsadisa.
Queer, *a.* abbhuta ; apākatika ; vilakkhaṇa. °**ly**, *adv.* abbhutākārena ; vikaṭatāya. °**ness**, *n.* apākatikatta ; vilakkhaṇatta, *nt.*
Quell, *v.t.* abhibhavati ; niggaṇhāti ; upasameti. *p.p.* °bhūta ; niggahita ; °mita.
Quench, *v.t.* apanudati ; (thirst:) upasameti; (fire, etc.) nibbāpeti. *p.p.* °dita ; °mita ; °pita. *v.i.* upasammati ; nibbāti. *p.p.* upasanta ; nibbuta. °**able**, *a.* upasamanakkhama. °**less**, *a.* avupasamiya.
Quern, *n.* piṭṭhapiŋsanī, *f.*
Querulous, *a.* ujjhāyamāna ; dummana.
Query, *n.* pañha, *m.* *v.t.* pucchati ; vīmaŋsati. *p.p.* puṭṭha ; °sita. °**ist**, *n.* pañhapucchaka, *m.*
Quest, *n.* upaparikkhā, *f.* anuvijjana, *nt.* magganā ; gavesanā, *f.* *v.t.* upaparikkhati ; gavesati. *p.p.* °khita ; °sita.
Question, *n.* 1. pañha, *m.* pucchā, *f.* 2. saŋsaya ; sandeha, *m.* 3. vādavisaya, *m.* *v.t.* pucchati ; anuyuñjati. *p.p.* puṭṭha ; anuyutta. °**able**, *a.* saṅkanīya ; pucchitabba. °**er**, *n.* anuvijjaka ; pucchaka, *m.* °**less**, *a.* nissaŋsaya ; aparipucchiya. °**naire**, *n.* pañhāvali, *f.* — **in return**, *v.t.* paṭipucchati. *n.* paṭipucchā, *f.*
Quibble, *n.* silesavacana, *nt.* vyājakathā; lesakathā, *f.* *v.i.* aññen' aññaŋ paṭicarati. °**bler**, *n.* vyājakathika ; amarāvikkhepika, *m.*
Quick, *a.* sīgha ; turita ; savega ; javasampanna. °**ly**, *adv.* sīghaŋ ; khippaŋ ; tuvaṭaŋ ; āsu ; lahuŋ ; sajju. °**en**, *v.t.* turitayati ; vegaŋ janeti ; uttejeti. *p.p.* °yita ; janitavega ; °jita. °**ening**, *a.* vegajanaka. °**eyed**, *a.* sukhumadasssī. — **hedge**, *n.* jīvadaṇḍavati, *f.* °**lime**, sudhācuṇṇa, *nt.* °**ness**, *n.* sīghatta ; turitatta, *nt.* °**sand**, *n.* (nadīādisu) saṅkamamāna-vālukāpuñja. °**silver**, *n.* pārada, *m.* °**witted**, *a.* khippābhiñña ; paṭibhāṇavantu.
Quiddity, *n.* 1. antosāra, *m.* 2. sāṭheyya, *nt.*
Quiddle, *v.i.* mudhā kālaŋ khepeti. *p.p.* °khepitakāla.
Quidnunc, *n.* vuttantagavesaka, *m.*

Quiescence, *n.* niccalatta ; nirīhatta ; santatta, *nt.* °**scent,** *a.* niccala ; nirīha ; upasanta.

Quiet, *a.* appasadda ; anākiṇṇa ; vivitta ; passaddha. *n.* akkhobha ; viveka, *m.* passaddhi ; nissaddatā, *f.* paṭisallāna, *nt.* *v.t.* passambheti ; upasameti. *v.i.* passambhati ; upasammati. *p.p.* °bhita ; °mita ; passaddha ; upasanta. °**ism,** °**ness,** *n.* passaddhi, *f.* upasama, *m.* °**ly,** *adv.* appasaddena ; santākārena.

Quietude, *n.* santi ; samatha, *m.*

Quietus, *n.* 1. bandhanamokkha ; 2. pāṇacāga, *m.*

Quill, *n.* 1. pakkhipatta, *nt.* pattanāḷa, *m.* 2. (of a porcupine :) salala, *nt.* 3. pattalekhanī, *f.* 4. dhamananāḷa, *m.*

Quilt, *n.* tūlikā, *f.* tūlasanthara, *m.* *v.t.* 1. tūlena onandhati ; 2. santhare sampādeti. *p.p.* tūlonaddha ; sampāditasanthara.

Quinary, *a.* pañcaka ; pañcavaggika.

Quinate, *a.* pañcapattaka ; pañcaṅgulika.

Quincentenary, *a.* pañcasatavassika.

Quinine, *n.* jaranāsakosadha, *nt.*

Quinquagenarian, *n.* *a.* paṇṇāsavassika.

Quinquelateral, *a.* pañcapassika.

Quinquennial, *a.* pañcavassika. °**ly,** *adv.* pañcavassavārena.

Quinsy, *n.* kaṇṭhadāha, *m.*

Quintad, *n.* pañcaka, *nt.*

Quintan, *n.* pañcāhavārikajara, *m.*

Quintessence, *n.* antosāra ; yathāsabhāva, *m.*

Quintuple, *a.* *n.* pañcavidha ; pañcavaggika.

Quintuplicate, *a.* pañcaguṇita. *v.t.* pañcahi guṇeti. *p.p.* pañcaguṇita.

Quire, *n.* catuvīsatipattika, *nt.*

Quirk, *n.* upahāsavākya, *nt.*

Quit, *a.* dosamutta ; apeta ; vissaṭṭha ; mocita. *v.t.* 1. cajati ; jahāti ; 2. vimoceti ; vissajjeti. *p.p.* catta ; jahita ; °cita ; vissaṭṭha. °**tance,** *n.* 1. vimutti, *f.* mokkha, *m.* 2. nissajana ; 3. nittharaṇa, *nt.* °**ter,** *v.* pajahaka ; vissajjaka ; vimocaka, *m.*

Quite, *adv.* 1. sabbathā ; sabbaso ; asesaŋ ; nissesaŋ ; 2. accantaŋ ; atīva.

Quiver, *n.* 1 tūnīra ; bāṇadhi, *m.* 2. kampana, *nt.* *v.i.* pariphandati ; pariplavati ; vedhati ; kampati. *p.p.* °dita ; °vita ; °dhita ; °pita.

Quixotic, *a.* vipallatthamatika ; abbhutakāmī ; micchābhimānī. °**tism,** *n.* micchābhimānitā, *f.*

Quiz, *n.* vikaṭadassana ; parihāsakārī, *m.* *v.t.* parihasati ; uppaṇḍeti. *p.p.* °sita ; °ḍita. °**zical,** *a.* kelisīla ; parihāsarata.

Quod, *n.* bandhanāgāra, *nt.* *v.t.* kārāyaŋ rundheti. *p.p.* °dhita.

Quoin, *n.* 1. bhittikoṇa, *m.* 2. koṇasilā, *f.*

Quondam, *a.* bhūtapubba ; kadāci-bhūta.

Quorum, *n.* gaṇapūraṇa, *nt.*

Quota, *n.* niyamitabhāga, *m.*

Quote, *v.t.* 1. udāharati ; nidasseti ; 2. vayappamāṇaŋ dasseti. *p.p.* udāhaṭa ; °sita ; °sitavaya.

°**ation**, *n.* 1. udāharaṇa, *nt.* udāhaṭapāṭha, *m.* 2. vayappamāṇadassana, *nt.*

Quoth, *v.t. past.* 1. avoca ; āha ; 2. avociŋ ; avadiŋ.

Quotidian, *a.* sabbāhika ; devasika.

R

Rabbi, *n.* Yādava-samaṇa, *m.*

Rabbit, *n.* sasa ; sasaka ; pelaka, *m.* °**hutch**, sasakoṭṭhaka, *m.* *v.t.* sase māreti.

Rabble, *n.* 1. adhamajana ; 2. avinītajanasamūha, *m.*

Rabid, *a. n.* 1. ummatta ; atidāruṇa ; 2. alakka ; atisuna, *m.* °**ly**, *adv.* sahummādaŋ ; ummādena.

Rabies, *n.* sunakhummāda, *m.*

Race, *n.* 1. (jayaggāhāya) dhāvana, *nt.* 2. kula ; gotta, *nt.* vaŋsa ; anvaya, *m.* *v.i.* 1. jayaggāhāya dhāvati ; 2. assadhāvane yuñjati. *v.t.* dhāvane niyojeti. *p.p.* °yutta ; °jita. °**course**, *n.* assamaṇḍala, *nt.* dhāvanabhūmi, *f.* °**horse**, *n.* javādhikassa, *m.*

Racer, *n.* dhāvanayugaggāhī, *m.*

Racial, *a.* gottāyatta ; vaŋsāgata. °**ly**, *adv.* kulavasena ; gottavasena.

Rack, *n.* 1. bhājanādhāraka ; 2. ghāsādhāra, *m.* 3. balavavedanā, *f.* 4. añchakayanta, *nt.* 5. vātāhata-megha, *m.* *v.t.* 1. ghāsena pūreti ; ghāsaŋ deti ; 2. ākaḍḍhanto pīḷeti. *p.p.* °rita ; °lita.

Racket, *n.* 1. kala-kala ; saṅkhobha, *m.* 2. guḷapaharaṇī, *f.* *v.i.* ugghosento carati. °**y**, *a.* 1. saṅkhobhakārī ; vinodappiya.

Racy, *a.* 1. vaŋsalakkhaṇayutta ; 2. javasampanna.

Raddle, *n.* gerukamattikā, *f.* *v.t.* gerukena limpeti. *p.p.* gerukalimpita.

Radial, *a.* 1. cakkaŋsakākāra ; 2. raŋsipharaṇākāra. °**ly**, *adv.* cakkaŋsānugamena.

Radiant, *a.* ujjala ; bhāsura ; jutimantu. °**nce**, *n.* juti ; ditti ; pabhā, *f.* obhāsa, *m.* °**ly**, *adv.* sappabhaŋ.

Radiate, *a.* pabhassara ; bhāsura. *v.i.* pabhāsati ; obhāsati ; ujjalati ; dippati. *v.t.* obhāseti ; pabhāseti ; raŋsiyo nicchāreti. *p.p.* °sita ; °lita ; ditta ; °sita. °ritaraŋsī. °**ion**, *n.* obhāsana ; raŋsinicchārana ; ujjalana, *nt.* °**tor**, *n.* tejonicaya-peḷā, *f.*

Radical, *a.* 1. mūlika ; 2. nesaggika ; sabhāvaja. °**ly**, *adv.* sabhāvato ; pakatiyā.

Radio, *n.* ākāsagāmī-saddappacāra, *m.* *v.t.* ākāsagāmī-sandesaŋ peseti.

Radish, *n.* mūlaka ; cuccu, *m.*

Radium, *n.* dāhaka-loha, *nt.*

Radius, *n.* 1. vaṭṭulaŋsa ; addhavikkhambha, *m.* cakkaŋsa, *m.* 2. (of a wheel :) ara ; cakkāra, *m.*

Radix, *n.* mūlasaṅkhyā, *f.*

Raff, *n.* dhuttajana, *m.* °**ish**, *a.* adhama ; nīca.

Raffle, *n.* 1. kusapātena laddhabba, *nt.* 2. kacavara, *m.* *v.t.* kusapātena paveseti. *p.p.* °sita.

Raft, *n.* uḷumpa ; kulla ; tara, *m.* *v.t.* 1. kullaŋ bandhati ; 2. kullena tāreti. *p.p.* baddhakulla ; kullatārita.

Rafter, *n.* chadanatulā ; valabhī, *f.* *v.t.* valabhiyo yojeti. *p.p.* valabhiyojita.

Rag, *n.* 1. kappaṭa, *m.* nantaka, pilotika, *nt.* 2. vatthakhaṇḍa, *m.* *v.t.* akkosati ; paribhāsati. *p.p.* akkuṭṭha ; °sita. °**ged**, *a.* 1. visama ; 2. jajjarībhūta ; 3. kucelaka.

Ragamuffin, *n.* kucelaka ; malinanivasana, *m.*

Rage, *n.* 1. adhikakopa ; rosa ; kopāvesa, *m.* 2. tikhiṇatta ; caṇḍatta, *nt.* *v.i.* 1. kujjhati ; kuppati ; 2. saṅkhubhati. *p.p.* kuddha ; kupita ; °bhita. °**ful**, *a.* kopākula. °**ing**, *a.* vegayutta ; aticaṇḍa ; kopāviṭṭha.

Raid, *n.* desakkamana ; pakkhandana, *nt.* *v.t.* akkamati ; pakkhandati. *p.p.* akkanta ; °dita.

Rail, *n.* lohasaṅku ; vatidaṇḍa ; lohadaṇḍa, *m.* *v.i.* upavadati ; akkosati ; garahati. *v.t.* saṅkūhi *or* salākāhi parikkhipati *or* āvarati. *p.p.* saṅkuparikkhitta ; salākāvaṭa. °**er**, *n.* akkosaka, *m.* °**ing**, *n.* 1. garahana ; 2. saṅkuyojana, *nt.* °**way**, *n.* lohadaṇḍapatha, *m.*

Raillery, *n.* parihāsakeḷi, *f.*

Raiment, *n.* vattha ; vasana ; acchādana, *nt.*

Rain, *n.* vassa, *nt.* vuṭṭhi, *f.* megha ; deva, *m.* *v.i.* vassati. *v.t.* vassāpeti. *p.p.* vuṭṭha ; °pita. °**bow**, *n.* indadhanu, *nt.* — **cloud**, *n.* jalada ; ambuda ; jaladhara ; pajjunna ; vārivaha, *m.* — **down**, ovassati. °**fall**, *n.* vuṭṭhipatana, *nt.* °**gauge**, *n.* vuṭṭhimāṇaka, *nt.* — **god**, *n.* Pajjunna, *m.* °**ing**, *a.* vassanta. °**less**, *a.* avuṭṭhika. — **upon**, abhivassati. *p.p.* abhivuṭṭha. °**y**, *a.* vuṭṭhibahula. °**y season**, vassāna ; pāvusa, *m.*

Raise, *v.t.* ussāpeti ; uṭṭhāpeti ; ukkhipati ; uccāreti. *p.p.* °pita ; ukkhitta ; °rita. °**ing**, *n.* ukkhipana, *nt.* — **water**, ussiñcati. *p.p.* ussitta.

Raisin, *n.* sukkhamuddikā, *f.*

Rake, *n.* 1. bhūmyullekha ; 2. itthidhutta, *m.* *v.t.* bhūmiŋ ullikhati. *v.i.* aticarati. °**ish**, *a.* kāmuka.

Rally, *n.* samosaraṇa ; puna rāsībhavana, *nt.* *v.i.* samosarati ; puna samāgacchati. *v.t.* puna rāsī karoti. *p.p.* samosaṭa ; °samāgata ; °kata.

Ram, *n.* mesa ; meṇḍa ; urabbha, *m.*

Ramble, *n.* pariyāhiṇḍana, *nt.* *v.i.* paribbhamati ; pariyaṭati. *p.p.* paribbhanta. °**er**, *n.* pariyaṭaka ; paribbhamaka, *m.* °**ing**, *a.* āhiṇḍaka.

Ramify, *v.t.* sākhā vitthāreti. *v.i.* sākhā pattharati ; sākhāvasena vibhajīyati. *p.p.* vitthatasākha ; patthaṭasākha ; °vibhatta. °**ication**, *n* 1. aṅgopaṅgavibhāga, *m.* 2. sākhāpattharaṇa, *nt.*

Rammish, *a.* pūtigandha.

Ramp, *v.i.* purimapāde ussāpetvā tiṭṭhati. *v.t.* 1. pakkhandati ; 2. aññāyena lābhaŋ labhituŋ ussahati. *p.p.* °ṭhita ; pakkhanta. *n.* adhikalābhussāha ; adhikakara, *m.*

Rampage, *n.* sāhasikavutti, *f. v.i.* sāhasikaŋ carati ; vilopaŋ karoti. *p.p.* °carita ; katavilopa.

Rampant, *a.* 1. atibahula ; 2. anabhibhavanīya ; 3. pacchimapādehi ṭhita. °**ncy,** *n.* 1. atibahulatta ; 2. uddāmatta, *nt.*

Rampart, *n.* nagarapākāra, *m.*

Ramshackle, *a.* jajjara ; jiṇṇa.

Ranch, *n.* govaḍḍhanaṭṭhāna, *nt.*

Rancid, *a.* pūtigandha-rasika.

Rancorous, *a.* atidubbhaka ; upanāhī. °**ly**, *adv.* upanāhena.

Rancour, *n.* upanāha, *m.* baddhavera, *nt.*

Random, *n. a.* aniyata ; asambhāvita ; yadicchaka. **At —,** aniyamena ; avicāriya ; yadicchāya, *adv.*

Range, *n.* 1. rāji ; panti ; āvali ; pāḷi, *f.* 2. visayaṭṭhāna, *nt.* 3. vegappamāṇa, *nt. v.t.* paṭipāṭiyā yojeti ; pantivasena ṭhapeti. *v.i.* paribbhamati. *p.p.* °yojita ; °ṭhapita ; °bhanta. **— of an arrow,** sarapāta, *m.* **— of sight,** cakkhupatha, *m.*

Ranger, *n.* dāyapāla ; aṭavipālaka, *m.*

Rank, *n.* 1. seṇī, *f.* vagga, *m.* 2. ṭhānantara, *nt.* adj. 1. pacura ; pahūta ; atiphīta ; 2. pūtigandhika ; 3. jeguccha ; 4. dūsita. *v.t.* seṇivasena patiṭṭhāpeti. *v.i.* anukkamena tiṭṭhati. *p.p.* °pita ; °ṭhita. °**ness,** *n.* 1. bāhulla ; adhikatta, *nt.* 2. pūtibhāva, *m.*

Rankle, *v.i.* pūtibhavati. *p.p.* °bhūta.

Ransack, *v.t.* 1. suṭṭhu gavesati ; 2. vilumpati. *p.p.* °sita ; vilutta.

Ransom, *n.* puggalavimuttimūla, *nt. v.t.* agghaŋ datvā vimoceti. *p.p.* °cita.

Rant, *n.* uccāsaddena desanā ; caturakathā, *f. v.i.* mahāsaddena pakāseti. *p.p.* °sita. °**er,** *n.* palapaka, *m.*

Rap, *n.* ākoṭana, *nt. v.t.* 1. ākoṭeti ; 2. khaṭakaŋ deti. *v.i.* kakkasavācaŋ bhāsati. *p.p.* °ṭita ; dinnakhaṭaka.

Rapacious, *a.* vilumpaka ; sabbāvahārī. °**ly,** *adv.* atilobhena ; balakkārena. °**ness,** °**city,** *n.* atiluddhatta ; vilumpakatta, *nt.*

Rape, *n.* 1. balenāvaharaṇa ; 2. kaññādūsana, *nt. v.t.* 1. pasayha avaharati ; 2. itthiŋ dūseti. *p.p.* °avahaṭa ; dūsititthika.

Rapid, *a.* sīgha ; turita ; vegavantu. °**ity,** °**ness,** *n.* sīghatta ; turitatta, *nt.* vega, *m.* °**ly,** *adv.* sīghaŋ ; turitaŋ ; vegena.

Rapids, *n. pl.* sīghasota, *m.* sotapatana, *nt.*

Rapier, *n.* asiputtī ; chūrikā, *f.*

Rapine, see **Plunder.**

Rapport, *n.* sambaddhatā, *f.*

Rapprochement, *n.* punasandhāna, *nt.*

Rapscallion, *n.* kitava ; dhutta ; saṭha, *m.*

Rapt, *p.p. a.* nimugga ; adhimutta ; parāyaṇa ; ninnamānasa. °**ure,** *n.* paramasantosa, *m.* adhikatuṭṭhi, *f.* °**urous,** paramānandayutta ; atituṭṭhidāyaka. °**urously,** *adv.* atisayapītiyā.

Rare, *a.* 1. dullabha ; virala ; 2. apubba ; atulya. °**fication,** tanukaraṇa, *nt.* °**fy,** *v.t.*

viralīkaroti. *v.i.* tanubhavati. *p.p.* °kata; °bhūta. **°ity,** *n.* dullabhavatthu, *nt.* **°ness,** *n.* viralatta; dullabhatta, *nt.* **°ly,** *adv.* dullabhavasena; kālantarena.

Rascal, *n.* dhutta; khala; kitava, *m.* **°ity,** *n.* sāṭheyya; ketava, *nt.* **°ly,** *a.* saṭhākārena.

Rase, Raze, *v.t.* 1. ucchindati; ummūleti; viddhaŋseti; 2. thokaŋ vilikhati. *p.p.* ucchinna; °lita; °sita; °khita.

Rash, *n.* kacchuvisesa, *m.* adj. sāhasika; avicārita. **°ly,** *adv.* sahasā; asamekkha. **°ness,** *n.* sāhasa, *nt.* avicāra, *m.*

Rasp, *n.* lohakhādanī, *f.* *v.t.* khādaniyā ghaŋseti. *p.p.* °sita.

Rat, *n.* undura; ākhu, *m.* mūsikā, *f.* *v.t.* mūsikā māreti. **— snake,** *n.* dhammani; gharasappa, *m.* **— trap,** *n.* mūsikā-adūhala, *nt.*

Ratan, *n.* vetasa; vañjula, *m.*

Rate, *n.* 1. agghappamāṇa, *nt.* 2. niyamitabhāga, *m.* 3. kara; bali, *m.* *v.t.* 1. aggheti; 2. pamāṇaŋ niyameti; 3. paribhāsati. *p.p.* agghita; niyamitapamāṇa; °sita. **°payer,** *n.* suṅkadāyī, *m.* **°er,** *n.* suṅkanirūpaka, *m.*

Rather, *adv.* 1. kiñca; varaŋ; seyyo; 2. kim api; īsakaŋ.

Ratify, *v.t.* daḷhīkaroti; saccāpeti. *p.p.* °kata; °pita. **°ication,** *n.* daḷhīkaraṇa; saccāpana, *nt.* **°ier,** *n.* daḷhīkattu, *m.*

Ratio, *n.* aññamaññappamāṇa, *nt.*

Ratiocinate, *v.t.* takketi; anumeti. *p.p.* °kita; °mita. **°ion,** takkana; ūhana; anumāna, *nt.*

Ration, *n.* niyamitāhārakoṭṭhāsa, *m.* *v.t.* āhārakoṭṭhāsaŋ niyameti.

Rational, *a.* 1. sacetana; saviññāṇaka; 2. ñāyānuga; yuttiyutta. **°ism,** *n.* hetuvāda, *m.* **°ist,** *n.* hetuvādī, *m.* **°ity,** *n.* 1. sacetanatta, *nt.* 2. vicārasatti, *f.* **°ly,** *adv.* yuttipubbakaŋ; ñāyānusārena. **°ize,** *v.t.* hetuvasena vitthāreti.

Ratlin(e), *n.* rajjunisseṇī, *f.*

Rattan, see **Ratan.**

Rattle, *n.* saṭasaṭa-saddakārī, *m.* *v.i.* 1. saṭasaṭāyati; 2. pajappati. **°ing,** *n.* 1. saṭasaṭāyana; pajappana, *nt.* **°brained, °headed,** *a.* lolasabhāva.

Raucous, *a.* kharasaddayutta; bhinnassara. **°ly,** *adv.* bhinnassaratāya; vissaraŋ.

Ravage, *n.* viddhaŋsana, *nt.* vilopa, *m.* *v.t.* viddhaŋseti; vināseti; vilumpati. *p.p.* viddhasta *or* °sita; °pita. **°er,** *n.* viddhaŋsaka, *m.*

Rave, *n.* 1. sakaṭapañjarāvaraṇa, *nt.* 2. vippalāpa, *m.* *v.i.* 1. palapati; pajappati; 2. ummatto hoti. **°ing,** *n.* ummāda; vibbhama, *m.* **°ingly,** *adv.* ummattākārena.

Ravel, *n.* jaṭā, *f.* *v.t.* āveṭheti; vyākulayati; jaṭeti. *p.p.* °ṭhita; °lita; jaṭita. *v.i.* vyākulībhavati. *p.p.* °bhūta. **— out,** *v.t.* viniveṭheti.

Raven, *n.* kākola; vanakāka, *m.* *v.t.* gedhena bhakkhati. *p.p.* °khita. **°ous,** *a.* atichāta; atibhakkha. **°ously,** *adv.* loluppena.

Ravin, *n.* coriya, *nt.* vilopa, *m.*

Ravine, *n.* darī, *f.* kandara, *m.*

Ravish, *v.t.* 1. atipīṇeti; 2. pamoheti; 3. balena harati; 4. itthiŋ dūseti. *p.p.* °ṇita; °hita; °haṭa; °dūsita. °**ing,** *a.* pamohaka; palobhaka. °**ment,** *n.* 1. pamohana; *nt.* 2. pītummāda, *m.* 3. itthidūsana, *nt.*

Raw, *a.* 1. āma; apakka; apariṇata; 2. adda; 3. niccamma; 4. aparicita; 5. amissita; 6. asaṅkhata. — **cemetery,** āmakasusāna, *nt.* — **flesh,** āmakamaŋsa, *nt.* °**ness,** *n.* āmakatta; apakkatta, *nt.*

Ray, *n.* 1. kiraṇa; kara; aŋsu, *m.* raŋsi; ābhā; pabhā, *f.* 2. maṇḍukamaccha, *m.* *v.i.* niccharati. *v.t.* nicchāreti. *p.p.* °rita. °**less,** *a.* nippabha.

Raze, see **Rase.**

Razor, *n.* khura, *m.* *v.t.* khurakammaŋ karoti. *p.p.* katakhurakamma. — **blade,** *n.* khuradhārā, *f.* — **sheath,** khurakosa, *m.* °**strop,** khuracamma, *nt.*

Re, *prep.* uddissa; sandhāya.

Reabsorb, *v.t.* punapariyādiyati. *p.p.* °yādinna. °**tion,** *n.* punapariyādiyana, *nt.*

Reach, *v.t.i.* 1. upagacchati; pāpuṇāti; 2. adhigacchati; paṭilabhati. *p.p.* upagata; patta, adhigata; paṭiladdha. *n.* upagamana, *nt.* patti, *f.* adhigama, *m.* āsannaṭṭhāna, *nt.*

React, *v.t.* 1. puna karoti; 2. aññamaññamhi balaŋ pavatteti. *v.i.* paṭikaroti. *p.p.* °kata; paṭikata. °**ion,** *n.* aññamaññappavatti; paṭikriyā, *f.* °**ive,** *a.* aññamaññamhi balappavattaka. °**ionary,** *a.* paṭigāmī; parihānigāmī.

Read, *v.t.i.* paṭhati; vāceti; sajjhāyati. *p.p.* paṭhita; vācita; °yita. °**able,** *a.* paṭhitabba; vācanāraha. °**er,** *n.* 1. paṭhitu; vācaka, *m.* 2. pāṭhagantha, *m.* °**ing,** *n.* paṭhana; sajjhāyana, *nt.* °**ing room,** paṭhanasālā, *f.*

Readjust, *v.t.* puna pakatiŋ neti; paṭisaṅkharoti. *p.p.* °nīta; paṭisaṅkhata. °**ment,** paṭisaṅkharaṇa, *nt.*

Readmit, *v.t.* puna sampaṭicchati. *p.p.* °chita. °**mission,** *n.* punantokaraṇa, *nt.*

Readopt, *v.t.* puna pariggahaŋ karoti. *p.p.* °katapariggaha.

Readorn, *v.t.* puna alaṅkaroti. *p.p.* °alaṅkata.

Ready, *a.* 1. sajjībhūta; 2. sannaddha; 3. appamatta; nipuṇa; 4. sukara; sulabha. °**ily,** *adv.* 1. sīghaŋ; turitaŋ; 2. saussāhaŋ; 3. anāyāsena. °**iness,** *n.* 1. kammaññatā, *f.* 2. icchā, *f.* 3. ussāha, *m.* 4. sīghatta; dakkhatta, *nt.* — **made,** *a.* sajjitapaṭiyatta. — **wit,** paṭibhāṇa, *nt.*

Real, *a.* 1. avitatha; yathātatha; taccha; 2. akittima. °**ism,** *n.* yathābhūta-nirūpana, *nt.* °**ity,** *n.* tacchatta; vijjamānatta, *nt.* °**istic,** *a.* yāthāvato nirūpita. °**ly,** *adv.* tattato; tathato.

Realize, *v.t.* sacchikaroti; abhisameti; paccakkhaŋ karoti. *p.p.* °kata; °mita; °kata. °**ation,** *n.* sacchikaraṇa, *nt.* abhisamaya, *m.*

Realm, *n.* 1. rajja; raṭṭha, *nt.* 2. bhava; loka, *m.* — **of goblins,** petaloka, *m.* **Formless** —, arūpabhava, *m.*

Realty, *n.* thāvara-sāpateyya, *nt.*
Reanimate, *v.t.* samuttejeti; samussāheti. *p.p.* °jita; °hita.
Reannex, *v.t.* puna sambandheti. *p.p.* °dhita. °**ation**, *n.* punasambandhana, *nt.*
Reap, *v.t.* 1. luṇāti; dāyati; chindati; 2. labhati; adhigacchati. *p.p.* lūṇa; dāyita; chinna; laddha; adhigata. °**er**, *n.* lāyaka, *m.* °**ing**, *n.* lāyana, *nt.*
Reappear, *v.i.* punarāvibhavati; puna paññāyati. *p.p.* °bhūta; °paññāta.
Rear, *n.* pacchābhāga, *m.* *v.t.* 1. bharati; poseti; vaḍḍeti; 2. ukkhipati. *p.p.* bhata; posita; °ḍhita; ukkhitta. °**ing**, *n.* 1. posaṇa; bharaṇa; 2. ukkhipana, *nt.* — **most**, *a.* pacchimatara. — **wards**, *adv.* pacchāmukhaŋ.
Reascend, *v.t.* punāruhati. *p.p.* punārūḷha.
Reason, *n.* 1. kāraṇa; nimitta, *nt.* hetu, *m.* 2. yutti, *f.* ñāya, *m.* 3. vicāraṇasatti, *f.* *v.i.* 1. takketi; vicāreti; yuttiŋ katheti; hetuŋ dasseti. *p.p.* °kita; °rita; °thita; dassitahetuka. °**able**, *a.* 1. ucita; yogga; ñāyānugata; 2. vicārasīlī. °**ableness**, *n.* ocitya, *nt.* yutti, *f.* °**ably**, *adv.* yuttipubbakaŋ; ñāyānurūpena. °**er**, *n.* takkī; vīmaŋsī, *m.* °**ing**, *n.* takkana; ūhana; vicāraṇa, *nt.* °**less**, *a.* ahetuka; akāraṇa.
Reassemble, *v.i.* puna sannipatati. *p.p.* °tita.
Reassert, *v.t.* puna pi pakāseti. *p.p.* °sita.
Reassign, *v.t.* puna nīyādeti. *p.p.* °dita.
Reassume, *v.t.* punārabhati. *v.i.* puna sampaṭicchati. *p.p.* °raddha; °chita.
Reassure, *v.t.* 1. abhayaŋ paṭijānāti; 2. samussāheti; 3. nissaṅkaŋ karoti. *p.p.* paṭiññāta-abhaya; °hita; nissaṅkīkata.
Reave, *v.t.* pasayha gaṇhāti *or* avaharati. *p.p.* °gahita; avahaṭa.
Reavow, *v.i.* puna sampaṭicchati *or* paṭijānāti. *p.p.* °chita; °paṭiññāta.
Rebate, *n.* vyavakalana; apaharaṇa, *nt.* *v.t.* (vegādiŋ) hāpeti; mandīkaroti. *p.p.* hāpita; °kata.
Rebel, *n.* dāmarika; kumantaka; rājadubbhī, *m.* *v.i.* dubbhati; kumanteti. *p.p.* °tita. °**lion**, *n.* janapadasaṅkhobha, *m.* °**lious**, *a.* dāmarika; dubbhaka; dubbaca.
Rebirth, *n.* punaruppatti; abhinibbatti, *f.* punabbhava, *m.* **Craving for** —, bhavataṇhā, *f.* **Wheel of** —, bhavacakka, *nt.*
Reborn, *a.* abhinibbatta; paccājāta.
Rebound, *v.i.* paccāvattati; paṭinivattati; osakkati. *v.t.* osakkāpeti. *p.p.* °tita; °kita; °pita.
Rebuff, *n.* paccāghāta, *m.* *v.t.* 1. paṭihanati; 2. nirākaroti; 3 parājeti. *p.p.* paṭihata; °kata; °jita.
Rebuild, *v.t.* puna nimmiṇāti *or* samuṭṭhāpeti. *p.p.* °mita; °pita.
Rebuke, *n.* akkosa; niggaha, *m.* *v.t.* akkosati; niggaṇhāṭi. *p.p.* akkuṭṭha; niggahita. °**ingly**, *adv.* saniggahaŋ; sopārambhaŋ.

Rebut, *v.t.* paccakkhāti; patikkhipati; nirākaroti. *p.p.* °khāta; paṭikkhitta; °kata. °**ment,** *n.* nirākaraṇa, *nt.* codanāparihāra, *m.*

Recalcitrate, *v.i.* āṇam atikkamati *or* ullaṅgheti. *p.p.* atikkanta-āṇa. °**trant,** *a.* avidheya; anassava; dubbaca. °**tration,** *n.* āṇātikkamana, *nt.*

Recall, *n.* paṭikkosana; paccavhāna, *nt.* *v.t.* paccavheti; abalīkaroti; moghīkaroti; paṭikkosati. *v.i.* (to mind :) anussarati; anucinteti. *p.p.* °vhāta; °sita; °rita; °tita.

Recant, *v.i.t.* sakamataŋ *or* sakasamayaŋ pajahati. *p.p.* °hitasakamata.

Recapitulate, *v.t.* puna sampiṇḍetvā katheti. *p.p.* °thita. °**ion,** *n.* sampiṇḍitakathā, *f.*

Recapture, *v.t.* puna gaṇhāti *or* rodheti. *p.p.* °gahita; rodhita. *n.* punaggāha, *m.*

Recast, *v.t.* puna nimmiṇāti; paṭisaṅkharoti. *p.p.* °mita; °saṅkhata.

Recede, *v.i.* apakkamati; apagacchati; osīdati. *p.p.* apakkanta; apagata; osīna. °**ing,** *n.* apagamana, *nt.*

Receipt, *n.* 1. ādāna, *nt.* paṭilābha, *m.* 2. āya; udaya, *m.* 3. paṭiggaha-paṇṇa, *nt.*

Receive, *v.t.* 1. sampaṭicchati; paṭigganhāti ;2. labhati; paṭilabhati; adhigacchati. *p.p.* °chita; °gahita; laddha; adhigata. °**able,** *a.* laddhabba; paṭiggahetabba. °**ability,** *n.* laddhabbatā, *f.* °**er,** *n.* 1. lābhī; 2. paṭiggahetu, *m.* 3. iṇasodhanādhikārī, *m.*

Recension, *n.* punālocana; punasaŋsodhana, *nt.*

Recent, *a.* nava; nūtana; acirāgata; adhunāgata. °**ncy,** *n.* nūtanatta; ādhunikatta, *nt.* °**ly,** *adv.* adhunā; acirātīte. °**ness,** *n.* ādhunikatta, *nt.*

Receptacle, *n.* upadhāraṇa; bhājana, *nt.* kaṭāha, *m.*

Reception, *n.* 1. paṭiggahaṇa; ādāna, *nt.* 2. sakkāra; paṭisanthāra, *m.* sammānana, *nt.* °**tive,** *a.* paṭiggāhaka. °**tivity,** *n.* paṭiggahaṇakkhamatā; dhāraṇakkhamatā, *f.*

Recess, *n.* 1. koṇa, *m.* vivittaṭṭhāna, *nt.* 2. vissamanakāla, *m.* vissamana, *nt.* 3. osīdana, *nt.* °**ion,** *n.* 1. osīdana; apagamana, *nt.*

Recharge, *v.t.* 1. puna codeti; 2. puna suṅkaŋ niyameti; 3. (aggināḷiŋ) puna pūreti. *p.p.* °dita; °mitasuṅka; °rita.

Recipe, *n.* osadhaniyama, *m.*

Recipient, *n.* ādāyī; gāhī; lābhī, *m.* °**ncy,** *n.* gāhakatta, *nt.*

Reciprocal, *a.* aññamañña; itaretara. °**ly,** *adv.* mithu; añña; maññaŋ.

Reciprocate, *v.t.i.* vinimeti-aññen'aññaŋ parivatteti. *p.p.* °mita; °tita. °**ion,** *n.* vinimaya, *m.* mithuparivattana, *nt.*

Reciprocity, *n.* vinimaya, *m.* aññamaññaparivattana, *nt.*

Recital, *n.* 1. sajjhāyana, *nt.* 2. saṅgāyanā, *f.* 3. itihāsakhaṇḍa, *m.*

Recite, *v.i.t.* paṭhati ; sajjhāyati ; gāyati. *p.p.* °ṭhita ; °yita ; gīta. °**ation,** *n.* paṭhana, *nt.* uddesa ; sajjhāya, *m.* °**er,** *n.* pāṭhaka ; bhāṇaka, *m.*

Reck, *v.i.* pariganeti ; sallakkheti; appamatto hoti. *p.p.* °ṇita ; °khita. °**less,** *a.* pamatta ; anavadhāna. °**lessly,** *adv.* asamekkha ; avicāriya. °**lessness,** *n.* 1. pamāda, *m.* anavadhāna ; 2. sāhasa ; anottappa, *nt.*

Reckon, *v.t.* gaṇeti ; saṅkaleti ; avadhāreti. *v.i.* vitakketi ; anumāneti. *p.p.* gaṇita ; °lita ; °rita ; °kita ; °nita. °**er,** *n.* gaṇetu, *m.* °**ing,** *n.* gaṇanā ; sallakkhanā, *f.*

Reclaim, *v.t.* 1. punarāvatteti ; 2. paṭilabhati ; puna lābhāya ussahati ; 3. pāpato nivāreti. *p.p.* °tita ; paṭiladdha ; °hita ; °rita. °**able,** *a.* paṭikaraṇīya ; suppathapāpiya. °**ant,** *a.* suppathaṭṭha.

Reclamation, *n.* 1. punalābha, *m.* punarāvattana, *nt.* 2. pāpanivutti, *f.*

Recline, *v.i.* apasseti ; saŋvisati ; adhiseti. *p.p.* °sita ; saŋviṭṭha ; adhisayita. °**ing,** *a.* apassayamāna.

Recluse, *n.* samaṇa ; pabbajita ; paribbājaka, *m.* adj. pavivitta. °**ion,** *n.* ekacariyā, *f.* vivittavāsa, *m.* °**ive,** *a.* vivekayutta. °**sory,** *n.* tāpasārāma ; assama, *m.*

Recognition, *n.* sañjānana, *nt.*

Recognize, *v.t.* sañjānāti ; vijānāti ; aṅgīkaroti. *p.p.* °nita ; viññāta ; °kata. °**able,** *a.* sañjānanāraha. °**ance,** *n.* 1. pāṭibhogapaṇṇa, *nt.* 2. paṭibhoga, *m.*

Recoil, *v.i.* paṭikuñcati ; paṭilīyati. *p.p.* °cita ; paṭilīna. °**ment,** *n.* paṭilīyana ; paṭikuñcana, *nt.*

Recollect, *v.t.i.* samanussarati ; satiŋ paccupaṭṭhāpeti. *p.p.* °rita. °ṭhitasati. °**ion,** *n.* anussaraṇa, *nt.* anussati, *f.* °**ing,** *a.* patissata.

Recombine, *v.t.* puna saŋyojeti. *p.p.* °jita.

Recommend, *v.t.* yathābhūtaguṇaŋ katheti *or* ñāpeti. *p.p.* kathita yathābhūtaguṇa. °**ation,** *n.* 1. guṇakittana ; 2. kittanapaṇṇa, *nt.* °**able,** *a.* pāsaŋsiya ; guṇakittanāraha. °**atory,** *a.* kittanapubbaka.

Recommit, *v.t.* puna rundhāpeti *or* jānāpeti. *p.p.* °pita.

Recompense, *n.* hānipūraṇa ; phātikamma, *nt.* *v.t.* phātikammaŋ karoti ; paṭidaṇḍaŋ deti. *p.p.* kataphātikamma ; dinnapaṭidaṇḍa.

Recompose, *v.t.* puna racayati *or* sampādeti. *p.p.* °racita ; °dita.

Reconcile, *v.t.* paṭisandhāneti. *p.p.* °nita. °**able,** *a.* paṭisandahanīya ; susandheyya. °**ment,** °**iation,** *n.* virodhasamana ; saṅghaṭana, *nt.* °**iatory,** *a.* sāmaggisādhaka ; sandhānakara.

Recondite, *a.* dubbodha ; gūḷhattha.

Reconduct, *v.t.* puna neti. *p.p.* °nīta.

Reconnaissance, *n.* paṭhamatarupaparikkhā, *f.*

Reconnoitre, *v.t.* pageva upaparikkhati. *p.p.* °khita.

Reconquer, *v.t.* puna jināti ; paṭijināti. *p.p.* °jita.

Reconsider, *v.t.* puna vitakketi *or* sallakkheti. *p.p.* °kita; °khita. °**ation,** *n.* puna sallakkhaṇa, *nt.*

Reconstruct, *v.t.* puna māpeti *or* karoti. *p.p.* °pita; °kata.

Reconvey, *v.t.* punāharati; puna pāpeti. *p.p.* °haṭa; °pita. °**ance,** *n.* punapāpana, *nt.*

Record, *n.* vuttanta, *m.* pavattilekhā, *f.* *v.t.* abhilikhati; paṇṇe āropeti. *p.p.* °khita; °pita. °**er,** *n.* lekhanāropaka, *m.*

Re-count, *v.t.* ākhyāti; nivedeti. *p.p.* ākhyāta; °dita. °**al,** *n.* ācikkhana; anusāvaṇa, *nt.*

Recoup, *v.t.* 1. hāniŋ pūreti; 2. ūnaŋ karoti. *p.p.* pūritahānika; ūnīkata.

Recourse, *n.* patiṭṭhā, *f.* avalamba; nissaya, *m.* tāṇa; leṇa, *nt.*

Recover, *v.t.* paṭilabhati; paccāharati. *v.i.* gilānā vuṭṭhāti; arogo hoti. *p.p.* paṭiladdha; °haṭa; °ṭhita; arogībhūta. °**y,** *n.* 1. paccāharaṇa, *nt.* 2. rogūpasama, *m.*

Recreant, *a.* *n.* adhīra; kātara; hīnaviriya.

Recreate, *v.t.* 1. puna māpeti; 2. paṭisaṅkharoti. *v.i.* 1. vissamati; balaŋ paṭilabhati; 2. ramati. *p.p.* °pita; °khata; °mita; paṭiladdhabala; rata. °**ion,** *n.* vissamana, *nt.* vinoda, *m.* balāharaṇa, *nt.* °**ive,** *a.* sukhakara; anurañjaka.

Recrement, *n.* kasaṭa, *m.* mala, *nt.* kacavara, *m.*

Recriminate, *v.t.* paṭicodeti; paccabhiyuñjati. *p.p.* °dita; °yutta. °**ion,** *n.* paccabhiyoga, *m.* paṭicodanā, *f.* °**ive,** *a.* paṭicodanāraha.

Recrudesce, *v.i.* puna pabhijjati. *p.p.* °pabhinna. °**nce,** *n.* punapabhijjana, *nt.* °**nt,** *a.* punavaḍḍhanaka.

Recruit, *v.t.* 1. balaŋ vaḍḍheti; 2. navasenā āharati. *v.i.* anubalaŋ labhati. *p.p.* vaḍḍhitabala; āhaṭa °sena; laddhānubala.

Rectangle, *n.* caturassaka, *nt.* °**gular,** *a.* catukoṇayutta.

Rectify, *v.t.* 1. dosam apaharati; saŋsodheti; 2. pākatikaŋ karoti. *p.p.* apahaṭadosa; °dhita; °kata. °**ication,** *n.* dosāpaharaṇa; parisodhana, *nt.*

Rectilinear, *a.* ujurekhāyutta.

Rectitude, *n.* ujutta; ajjava; dhammikatta, *nt.*

Rector, *n.* ajjhakkhaka; vijjālayādhipati, *m.*

Rectum, *n.* pakkāsayanta, *m.*

Recumbent, *a.* nipajjamāna; passena sayamāna. °**nce,** *n.* passena-sayana, *nt.* °**ncy,** *n.* nipajjana, *nt.*

Recuperate, *v.t.* ārogyaŋ paṭilabhati. *v.i.* gilānā vuṭṭhāti. *p.p.* paṭiladdhārogya; °ṭhita. °**ion,** *n.* ārogyapaṭilābha, *m.*

Recur, *v.i.* puna sijjhati. *p.p.* °siddha. °**ence,** *n.* punasiddhi, *f.* °**ing,** °**ent,** *a.* punappuna-sijjhamāna.

Recusant, *a.* *n.* avidheyya; avasavattī.

Red, *a.* *n.* ratta; lohita; rattavaṇṇa.—**ant,** *n.* tambakipillikā, *f.*—**arsenic,** *n.* sindūra, *nt.* —**colour,** *n.* rattavaṇṇa, *m.* —**eyed,** *a.* lohitakkha; tambanetta. — **lead,** *n.* cīnapiṭṭha, *nt.* °**dish,** *a.* piñjara; aruṇavaṇṇa. °**hot,** *a.* uttatta.

Redact, *v.t.* (ganthaŋ) saŋsodheti; saṅkharoti. *p.p.* °dhita; saṅkhata. °**ion,** *n.* saŋsodhana; saṅkharaṇa, *nt.* °**or,** *n.* saŋsodhaka, *m.*

Redden, *v.t.* rattavaṇṇaŋ karoti. *p.p.* °ṇīkata.

Reddle, *n.* gerukamattikā, *f.*

Redeem, *v.t.* 1. dhanaŋ datvā moceti; 2. (a promise:) paṭiññaŋ moceti. *p.p.* °mocita; mocitapaṭiñña. °**er,** *n.* tāyaka; vimocaka; pāpasodhaka, *m.*

Redemption, *n.* 1. parimocana; 2. pāpasodhana; 3. nyāsamocana, *nt.* °**tory,** *a.* muttikara.

Redintegrate, *v.t.* paṭipākatikaŋ karoti. *p.p.* °kata.

Redirect, *v.t.* puna niyojeti. *p.p.* °jita.

Redolent, *a.* uggagandhī; sugandhī. °**nce,** *n.* uggagandhatā, *f.* sugandha, *m.*

Redouble, *v.t.* nirantaraŋ vaḍḍheti; bahulīkaroti; daḷhīkaroti; *p.p.* °ḍhita; °kata, *v.i.* nirantaraŋ vaḍḍhati; bahulībhavati. *p.p.* °bhūta.

Redoubt, *n.* kālika-balakoṭṭhaka, *m.* °**able,** *a.* uruvikkama; mahāpatāpa, °**ed,** *a.* bhīma; duppadhaŋsiya.

Redound, *v.i.* mahato atthāya pavattati; phaladāyī hoti. *p.p.* °tita; °yībhūta.

Redress, see **Recompense.**

Reduce, *v.t.* 1. hāpeti; tanukaroti; 2. (price:) osādeti; 3. abhibhavati; parājeti; 4. pāpeti; 5. (metal:) visuŋ karoti; viyojeti. *p.p.* hāpita; tanukata; °dita; °bhūta; °jita; pāpita; visuŋkata; °jita. °**ible,** *a.* hāpanīya.

Reduction, *n.* 1. hāpana; ūnakaraṇa; 2. pāpana, *nt.* 3. parābhava, *m.*

Redundant, *a.* atiritta; adhika; sātisaya. °**ncy,** *n.* atirittatā, *f.* adhikatta, *nt.* °**ly,** *adv.* sātisayaŋ.

Reduplicate, *v.t.* diguṇīkaroti. *p.p.* °kata. °**ion,** *n.* diguṇīkaraṇa; dvittatāpādana, *nt.*

Re-echo, *v.i.* puna paṭiravati *or* paṭinadati. *p.p.* °nadita.

Reed, *n.* naḷa, *m.* *v.t.* naḷehi acchādeti *or* alaṅkaroti. *p.p.* °dita; °kata. —**hut,** *n.* naḷāgāra, *nt.* **Bundle of —,** naḷakalāpa, *m.* °**y,** *a.* naḷabahula.

Reef, *n.* silāsaṅghāta, *m.* *v.t.* lakāraŋ saŋharati. *p.p.* saŋhaṭalakāra.

Reek, *n.* 1. dhūma; 2. duggandha, *m.* *v.i.* dhūmāyati; duggandhaŋ nicchāreti. *p.p.* °yita; °ritaduggandha.

Reel, *n.* 1. suttāvaṭṭa, *m.* tantuveṭhana, *nt.* 2. bhama, *m.* kampana, *nt.* *v.i.* paribbhamati. *v.t.* bhamāpeti. *p.p.* paribbhanta; °pita. °**ingly,** *adv.* sabbhamaŋ.

Re-embark, *v.i.* puna nāvam abhiruhati; puna vyāvaṭo hoti. *p.p.* °nāvābhirūḷha.

Re-enact, *v.t.* puna paññāpeti. *p.p.* °paññatta.

Re-enforce, *v.t.* balaŋ vaḍḍheti. *p.p.* vaḍḍhitabala.

Re-engage, *v.i.* puna niyujjati; *v.t.* puna niyojeti *or* niyameti. *p.p.* °niyutta; °jita; °mita.

Re-enter, *v.t.* puna pavisati *or* aṅketi. *p.p.* °paviṭṭha; °aṅkita. --**entrance,** *n.* punappavesa, *m.*

Re-establish, *v.t.* puna patiṭṭhāpeti. *p.p.* °pita. °**ment,** *n.* punapatiṭṭhāpana, *nt.*

Re-examine, *v.t.* punānuparikkhati. *p.p.* °khita.

Re-existence, *n.* punabbhava, *m.* punajīvana, *nt.*

Refection, *n.* 1. lahubhojana; 2. balāharaṇa, *nt.* °**tory,** *n.* bhattagga, *nt.* bhojanasālā, *f.*

Refer, *v.t.* 1. niddisati; apadisati; 2. niyyādeti. *p.p.* niddiṭṭha apadiṭṭha; °dita. °**able,** *a.* 1. nidassitabba; 2. niyyādetabba. °**ence,** *n.* apadisana; āvedana, *nt.* — **back,** *v.t.* puna vicāraṇāya paṭipeseti. °**ing to,** upanāyika; uddesika, *a.*

Referee, *n.* tīraṇakārī, *m.* *v.i.* tīreti. *p.p.* tīrita.

Referendary, see **Referee.** *n.*

Refill, *v.t.* punapūreti. *p.p.* °rita.

Refine, *v.t.* visodheti; vimalīkaroti. *v.i.* visujjhati. *p.p.* °dhita; °kata; visuddha. °**ment,** *n.* visodhana; nimmalīkaraṇa, *nt.* °**er,** *n.* saŋsodhaka; visodhaka, *m.* °**ery,** *n.* lohasodhanaṭṭhāna, *nt.*

Refit, *v.t.* puna ghaṭeti. *p.p.* °ṭita.

Reflect, *v.i.* 1. jhāyati; vitakketi; 2. parāvattati. *v.t.* viparāvatteti. *p.p.* °yita; °kita; °vatta; °tita. °**ing,** *a.* 1. jhāyamāna; 2. parāvattamāna. °**ion,** *n.* 1. upanijjhāna; paccavekkaṇa, *nt.* 2. paṭibimba, *m.* °**ive,** *a.* 1. cintāpara; 2. viparāvattaka. °**ively,** *adv.* vicārapubbakaŋ. — **on,** āvajjati. °**or,** *n.* viparāvattaka; paṭibimbadassaka; ādāsa, *m.*

Reflex, *n.* 1. parāvattita-āloka, *m.* °rūpa, *nt.* 2. upanijjhāna, *nt.* °**ion,** *n.* paṭibimba, *m.* °**ible,** *a.* parāvattanakkhama.

Reflexive, *a.* *n.* bhāvarūpaka; kammakattuvācaka.

Refluent, *a.* paṭisandamāna. °**nce,** *n.* paṭisandana, *nt.*

Reflux, *n.* paṭisandana, *nt.*

Reform, *n.* dosāpaharaṇa; paṭisaṅkharaṇa, *nt.* *v.t.* paṭisaṅkharoti; paṭisodheti; dosam apaharati. *p.p.* °khata; °dhita; apahaṭadosa. *v.i.* pāpā *or* dosā viramati. *p.p.* °virata. °**able,** *a.* saŋsodhanāraha; saṅkharaṇakkhama. °**ation,** *n.* paṭisaṅkharaṇa, *nt.* °**ative,** *a.* saŋsodhaka. °**atory,** caritasodhanaṭṭhāna, *nt.* °**er,** *n.* saŋsodhaka; paṭisaṅkhāraka, *m.*

Refract, *v.t.* raŋsiŋ vyāvaṭṭeti. *p.p.* °ṭitaraŋsī. °**ion,** *n.* raŋsivyāvaṭṭana, *nt.*

Refractory, *a.* duddamya; avasavattī; kūṭa; avidheya. °**ily,** *adv.* avidheyyākārena; asādhiyākārena. °**iness,** *n.* avasavattitā, *f.*

Refrain, *v.t.* nivāreti; nivatteti; *v.i.* viramati. *p.p.* °rita; °tita; virata. °**ing,** *n.* vigamana, *nt.*

Refrangible, *a.* namya; vyāvaṭṭanīya. °**bility,** *n.* namyatta, *nt.*

Refresh, *v.t.* kilamathaŋ vinodeti; santappeti; vissamāpeti. *v.i.* vissamati; balaŋ gaṇhāti. *p.p.* vinoditakilamatha; °pita; vissanta; gahitabala. °**ing,** *a.* santappaka. °**ment,** *n.* 1. kilamathavinodana; 2. lahubhojana, *nt.*

Refrigerate, *v.t.* sītalīkaroti. *v.i.* sītalībhavati. *p.p.* °kata; °bhūta. °**rant,** *a.* tāpanāsaka; sītakara. *n.* tāpanibbāpana ; sītalīkaraṇosadha, *nt.* °**ion,** sītikaraṇa, *nt.* °**tory,** *n.* sītalīkaraṇabhājana, *nt.*

Refuge, *n.* saraṇa ; tāṇa ; leṇa, *nt.* patiṭṭhā, *f.* *v.t.* tāṇaŋ *or* leṇaŋ deti ; rakkhati. *p.p.* dinnatāṇa ; °khita. °**gee,** *n.* saraṇāgata ; anātha, *m.* **Take —,** saraṇaŋ gaṇhāti.

Refulgent, *a.* pabhassara ; dippamāna ; bhāsura. °**nce,** *n.* ujjalobhāsa, *m.*

Refund, *n.* paṭidāna, *nt.* *v.t.* (gahitamūlaŋ) paṭidadāti. *p.p.* paṭidinna.

Refuse, *n.* mala ; kasaṭa, *nt* adj. avasiṭṭha ; ucciṭṭha ; asāra. *v.t.* paṭikkhipati ; paṭisedheti ; paccakkhāti. *p.p.* paṭikkhitta ; °dhita ; paccakkhāta. °**sal,** *n.* paccakkhāna, *nt.* paṭikkhepa ; paṭisedha, *m.*

Refute, *v.t.* nirākaroti ; paccādisati. *p.p.* nirākata ; °diṭṭha. °**ation,** *n.* matakhaṇḍana ; nirākaraṇa, *nt.* °**able,** *a.* nirākaraṇīya ; khaṇḍanīya.

Regain, *v.t.* paṭilabhati ; puna adhigacchati. *p.p.* paṭiladdha ; °gata.

Regal, *a.* rājakīya ; rājāyatta. °**ity,** *n.* rājatta, *nt.* °**ly,** *adv.* rājārahākārena.

Regale, *v.t.* bhusaŋ santappeti ; atitoseti.1.*v.i.*paritussati;2.yāvadatthaŋ bhuñjati. *p.p.* °pita ; °sita ; parituṭṭha ; °bhutta. °**ment,** *n.* suṭṭhu santappaṇa, *nt.*

Regalia, *n. pl.* rājakakudhabhaṇḍa ; rājaciṇha, *nt.*

Regard, *n.* sammāna, *m.* avadhāna, *nt.* sambhāvanā, *f.* *v.t.* 1. avekkhati ; sallakkheti ; 2. sammāneti ; sambhāveti ; 3. anuvicinteti. *p.p.* °khita ; °nita ; °vita ; °tita. °**ful,** *a.* sāvadhāna ; sāpekkha. °**fully,** *adv.* sādaraŋ ; sāvadhānaŋ. °**less,** *a.* nirapekkha ; udāsīna. °**lessly,** *adv.* udāsīnatāya. °**lessness,** *n.* upekkhā ; udāsīnatā, *f.*

Regarding, *prep.* sandhāya ; uddissa.

Regency, *n.* rājapaṭinidhitta, *nt.*

Regenerate, *v.t.* punuppādeti ; nūtanattaŋ pāpeti. *v.i.* puna jāyati. *p.p.* °dita ; °pita ; °jāta. °**ion,** *n.* punaruṭṭhāpana, *nt.*

Regenesis, *n.* punabbhava, *m.* punaruppatti, *f.*

Regent, *n.* rājapaṭinidhi, *m.*

Regicide, *n.* 1. rājanāsana, *nt.* 2. rājaghātī, *m.*

Regime, *n.* rajjānusāsana, *nt.* rajjakāla, *m.*

Regimen, *n.* sappāyavidhi, *m.*

Regiment, *n.* senādala ; aṇīka, *nt.* °**al,** *a.* senādalāyatta.

Region, *n.* rajja ; raṭṭha ; vijita, *nt.* desa ; visaya, *m.* °**al,** *a.* padesika.

Register, *n.* lekhānidhāna, *nt.* *v.t.* likhitvā nidahati. *p.p.* °nihita.

Registrar, *n.* lekhanādhikārī, *m.* °**tration,** *n.* likhitvā nidahana, *nt.*

Regnal, *a.* rajjapālanāyatta.

Regnant, *a.* 1. rajjānusasāmāna ; 2. accāvassaka ; atippadhāna.

Regorge, *v.t.* uggirati ; vamati. *p.p.* °rita ; vanta.

Regress, *n*. parāvattana ; paṭinivattana, *nt*. *v.i*. parāvattati ; paccosakkati. *p.p*. °tita ; °kita. °**ion**, *n*. parāvattana ; osakkana, *nt*.

Regret, *n*. anutāpa, *m*. anusocanā, *f*. vippaṭisāra, *m*. *v.t*. anutappati ; anusocati. °**ful**, *a*. sānutāpa ; sasoka. °**fully**, *adv*. sānutāpaŋ. °**table**, *a*. anutapanīya ; socanīya.

Regular, *a*. 1. anukkamika ; niyamānugata ; nibaddha ; 2. ekākāra. °**ity**, *n*. 1. anukkama, *m*. paṭipāṭi, *f*. 2. niyatatta, *nt*. °**ly**, *adv*. 1. niyataŋ ; nibaddhaŋ ; 2. yathāvidhiŋ ; yathākkamaŋ.

Regulate, *v.t*. saŋvidahati ; niyameti ; kamānugataŋ karoti. *p.p*. saŋvihita ; °mita ; °gakata. °**ion**, *n*. saŋvidhāna, *nt*. niyama, *m*. sikkhā ; paññatti, *f*. nīti, *f*. °**ive**, *a*. niyāmaka ; paññāpaka. °**tor**, *n*. vidahaka ; paññāpetu, *m*.

Rehabilitate, *v.t*. puna ṭhānantare ṭhapeti. °**ion**, *n*. pākatikakaraṇa ; punādhikāradāna, *nt*.

Rehearse, *v.t*. saṅgāyati ; sajjhāyati. *p.p*. °yita. °**sal**, *n*. saṅgīti; ekato sajjhāyanā, *f*.

Reign, *n*. 1. rajjapālana ; rajjānusāsana, *nt*. 2. rajjakāla, *m*. *v.i*. rajjam anusāsati *or* pāleti. *p.p*. anusiṭṭharajja. °**ing**, *a*. rajjaŋ kurumāna.

Reimburse, *v.t*. vayakataŋ paṭidadāti. °**ment**, *n*. vayapaṭidāna, *nt*.

Rein, *n*. kusā ; ratharasmi, *f*. *v.t*. saŋyameti ; niggaṇhāti. *p.p*. °mita ; niggahita.

Reincarnation, *n*. punaruppatti, *f*.

Reindeer, *n*. tuhinamiga, *m*.

Reinforce, *v.t*. senābalaŋ vaḍḍheti. *p.p*. vaḍḍhitasenābala. °**ment**, *n*. upatthambhana ; senāvaḍḍhana, *nt*.

Reinsert, *v.t*. puna anto paveseti. *p.p*. °sita.

Reinspection, *n*. punupaparikkhaṇa, *nt*.

Reinstall, *v.t*. puna (adhikāre) patiṭṭhāpeti. *p.p*. °pita.

Reinstate, *v.t*. puna osāreti. *p.p*. °rita. °**ment**, *n*. osāraṇā; punapatiṭṭhāpanā, *f*.

Reiterate, *v.t*. punappunaŋ karoti *or* katheti. *p.p*. °kata ; °kathita. °**ion**, *n*. punarutti, *f*. punakaraṇa, *nt*.

Reject, *v.t*. 1. nudati ; nissāreti ; nissajati ; 2. paṭikkhipati. *p.p*. nudita ; °rita ; nissaṭṭha ; °khitta. °**ion**, *n*. panudana, nissajana, *nt*.

Rejoice, *v.i*. modati ; pamodati ; abhiramati ; nandati ; abhinandati. *v.t*. toseti ; pamodeti ; abhiramāpeti. *p.p*. °dita ; abhirata ; °dita ; tosita ; °dita ; °pita. °**ing**, *n*. ānanda ; āmoda ; pamoda, *m*. abhirati ; modanā, *f*. °**ing**, *a*. modamāna ; ramamāna. °**ing together**, sahanandī, *a*.

Rejoin, *v.t*. paṭisandhāneti ; puna saŋyojeti. *v.i*. paccuttaraŋ deti. *p.p*. °nita ; °jita ; dinnapaccuttara. °**der**, *n*. paccuttara ; paṭivacana, *nt*.

Rejudge, *v.t*. puna tīreti. *p.p*. °rita.

Rejuvenate, *v.t.* yuvattaŋ paṭineti. *p.p.* °nīta. °**ion,** *n.* punayuvattapāpana, *nt.*

Rejuvenescence, *n.* punayobbanappatti, *f.*

Rekindle, *v.t.* puna jāleti *or* dippeti. *p.p.* °jālita ; °pita.

Relapse, *n.* paṭipatana, *nt.* pubbāvatthāpatti, *f.* *v.i.* paṭipatati ; paccāvattati. *p.p.* °tita ; °vattita.

Relate, *v.t.* akkhāti ; ācikkhati ; kitteti ; vaṇṇeti. *v.i.* sambandhībhavati. *p.p.* akkhāta ; °khita ; °tita ; °ṇita ; °bhūta. °**ed,** *a.* ñātibhūta ; sambaddha. °**er,** *n.* akkhātu ; kittetu, *m.* °**ing,** *a.* sambandhī ; sahayogī. °**ion,** *n.* 1. sambandha; saŋsagga; sampayoga, *m.* 2. bandhutta ; sakatta, *nt.* 3. bandhu ; bandhava ; sagotta ; ñāti ; ñātaka, *m.* °**ionship,** *n.* bandhutta ; sambandhatta, *nt.*

Relative, *a* sambandhavācaka ; sāpekkha. *n.* bandhu ; ñāti, *m.* — **compound,** Bahubbīhisamāsa, *m.* °**ly,** *adv.* aññāpekkhāya.

Relax, *v.t.* sithilayati ; dubbalīkaroti. *v.i.* sithilībhavati ; viriyam ossajati. *p.p.* °yita ; °kata ; °bhūta ; ossaṭṭhaviriya. °**ation,** *n.* sithilīkaraṇa ; viriyossajana, *nt.* °**ative,** *a.* sithilakara ; virecaka.

Release, *n.* mutti ; vimutti, *f.* mokkha ; vimokkha, *m.* niyyāna ; pamuccana, *nt.* *v.t.* moceti ; vimoceti ; pari° ; muñcati ; vissajjeti. *p.p.* °cita ; mutta ; vissaṭṭha. — **from debt,** iṇamokkha, *m.* **Well** °**ed,** *a.* sumutta ; vippamutta.

Relegate, *v.t.* vivāseti ; pabbājeti. *p.p.* °sita ; °jita. °**ion,** *n.* nibbāsana ; pabbājana, *nt.*

Relent, *v.i.* anukampati. *p.p.* °pita. °**ingly,** *adv.* sadayaŋ ; sānukampaŋ. °**less,** *a.* niddaya; niranukampa. °**lessly,** *adv.* niddayākārena.

Relevant, *a.* vavatthānurūpa ; anukūla ; opāyika ; saṅgata. °**ly,** *adv.* anukūlatāya ; saṅgatākārena. °**nce,** *n.* anurūpatta ; anukūlatta ; ocitya, *nt.*

Reliable, *a.* saddahitabba ; paccayika ; vissasanīya. °**bility,** *n.* saddheyyatta, *nt.*

Reliance, *n.* saddahana, *nt.* vissāsa, *m.*

Relic, *n.* 1. matakalebara, *nt.* 2. avasiṭṭha-dhātu, *f.* 3. paribhutta-vatthu, *nt.* — **casket,** dhātusamugga, *m.* — **chamber,** dhātugabbha, *m.*

Relict, *n.* vidhavā ; patisuññā, *f.*

Relief, *n.* 1. assāsa ; upasama, *m.* nibbāpana, *nt.* 2. vimokkha, *m.* mutti, *f.* 3. upakāra ; upatthambha, *m.*

Relieve, see **Release.** °**ing Officer,** anātha-sahanadāyī, *m.*

Religion, *n.* samaya, *m.* diṭṭhi, *f.* °**ist,** *n.* samayānuvattī, *m.* °**ize,** *v.t.* samayānugaŋ karoti. °**giose,** *a.* atibhattimantu. °**giosity,** *n.* adhikabhatti, *f.*

Religious, *a.* 1. dhammika ; bhattimantu ; 2. dhammāyatta. — **belief,** *n.* laddhi, *f.* — **life,** brahmacariyā ; sāmayikavutti, *f.* °**ly,** *adv.* yathādhammaŋ; samayānurūpaŋ. — **practice,** sāmayika-paṭipatti, *f.* — **vow,** vata; dhutaṅga, *nt.*

Relinquish, *v.t.* cajati; jahāti; vossajati. *p.p.* catta; jahita; vossaṭṭha. °**ment,** *n.* pajahana, *nt.* vossagga, *m.*

Relish, *n.* 1. sādurasa; 2. assāda; 3. āseka, *m.* upasiñcanaka, *nt.* *v.t.* 1. surasaŋ karoti; 2. assādeti; roceti. *p.p.* surasīkata; °dita; rocita °**able,** *a.* rucikara; surasa.

Relucent, *a.* ujjala; pabhassara.

Reluctant, *a.* akāmaka; anicchamāna. °**ly,** *adv.* akāmaŋ; anicchāya. °**nce,** *n.* anicchā; vimukhatā, *f.*

Rely, *v.i.* vissasati; saddahati. *p.p.* vissattha; °hita. °**ing on,** nissita; avalambī, *a.* °**ing on others,** parapattiya; parapaccayika, *a.*

Remain, *v.i.* 1. ohīyati; nivattati; acchati; 2. avasissati; atiriccati. *p.p.* ohīna; nivatta; avasiṭṭha; atiritta. *pl.* matadeha, *m.* *nt.* °**der,** *n.* sesa; atireka, *m.* °**ing,** *a.* avasiṭṭha; atirekabhūta.

Remand, *n.* puna bandhanappaṇā, *f.* *v.t.* paṭiavheti; kārāpālānaŋ puna appeti. *p.p.* °hita; °pita.

Remark, *n.* bhāsana; kathana; *nt.* utti, *f.* nirūpana, *nt.* *v.t.i.* 1. saŋlakkheti; nirūpeti; 2. vadati; ākhyāti. *p.p.* °khita; °pita; vutta; ākhyāta. °**able,** *a.* visiṭṭha; saŋlakkhaṇīya. °**ably,** *adv.* visiṭṭhākārena.

Remarry, *v.t.* puna vivāheti. *p.p.* °hita.

Remedy, *n.* 1. paṭikāra, *m.* 2. bhesajja; osadha, *nt.* *v.t.* 1. paṭikaroti; 2. tikicchati. *p.p.* paṭikata; °chita. °**iable,** *a.* satekiccha; sappatikāra. °**iless,** *a.* atekiccha; asādhiya. °**ilessly,** *adv.* atekicchākārena.

Remember, *v.t.* sarati; anussarati. *p.p.* °rita. °**brance,** *n.* sati, *f.* anussaraṇa, *nt.*

Remind, *v.t.* sarāpeti. *p.p.* °pita, °**er,** *n.* 1. sārakavatthu, *nt.* 2. sāretu, *m.* °**ing,** *n.* sāraṇā, *f.*

Reminiscence, see **Memory.**

Reminiscent, *a.* saramāna. °**ly,** *adv.* anussatipubbakaŋ.

Remise, *n.* paṭiappaṇā, *f.* nīyātana, *nt.* *v.t.i.* nīyāteti; vasaŋyāti. *p.p.* °tita; °yāta.

Remiss, *a.* pamatta; anohita; nirapekkha. °**ness,** *n.* pamāda, *m.* anavadhāna, *nt.* °**ible,** *a.* khamanāraha. °**ion,** *n.* 1. pāpamocana, *nt.* 2. iṇamutti, *f.* 3. balahāpana, *nt.* °**ly,** *adv.* pamādena; anavadhānena.

Remit, *v.t.i.* 1. peseti; pahiṇāti; 2. sithilīkaroti; 3. (pāpā *or* iṇā) moceti; vissajjeti; 4. dosaŋ khamati. *p.p.* pesita; pahita; °kata; °cita; vissaṭṭha; khamitadosa. °**tal,** *n.* 1. paravasagamana; 2. pariggahanīyātana, *nt.* °**tance,** *n.* pesana; pesitamūla, *nt.* °**tee,** *n.* pesaka; pesetu, *m.* °**tent,** *a.* vārena vāraŋ hāyamāna.

Remnant, *n.* avasiṭṭhabhāga, *m.*

Remodel, *v.t.* navasaṇṭhānena sampādeti. *p.p.* °dita.

Remonstrate, *v.i.t.* viruddhaŋ vadati; virodhaŋ dasseti. *p.p.* °vutta; dassitavirodha. °**trance,**

n. nivāraṇopāya, *m.* virodhadassana, *nt.* °**trant,** *a. n.* virodhadassaka. °**ingly,** *adv.* virodhadassanena.

Remorse, *n.* anutāpa ; upatāpa ; pacchātāpa ; vippaṭisāra, *m.* °**ful,** *a.* vippaṭisārī ; anutāpī. °**less,** *a.* niddaya ; niṭṭhura. °**lessly,** *adv.* niddayākārena. °**lessness,** *n.* niddayatta, *nt.*

Remote, *a.* dūraṭṭha ; pavivitta. °**ness,** *n.* dūravattitā, *f.*

Remount, *v.t.* punāruhati. *p.p.* °rūḷha.

Remove, *n.* 1. apagamana ; 2. visesappamāṇa, *nt. v.t.* apaneti ; apaharati ; pajahati ; dhunāti ; panudati. *p.p.* °nīta ; apahaṭa ; °hita ; dhuta ; °dita. *v.i.* apayāti ; apagacchati. *p.p.* °yāta ; apagata. °**able,** *a.* apasaraṇīya ; jahitabba ; apanetabba. °**al,** *n.* apanudana ; panudana, *nt.* apagama ; apakkama, *m.* °**er,** *n.* apahattu ; apanetu. °**er of darkness,** tamonuda, *m.*

Remunerate, *v.t.* 1. vetanaŋ *or* pāritosikaŋ deti ; 2. paccupakaroti ; 3. yathārahaŋ phalaŋ deti. *p.p.* dinnavetana ; °kata ; °dinnaphala. °**ion,** *n.* phaladāna ; paṭiphala, *nt.* °**ive,** *a.* lābhuppādaka ; phaladāyī. °**ively,** *adv.* phaladāyīvasena.

Renaissance, *n.* punaruddīpana, *nt.*

Renascent, *a.* punarubbhavamāna. °**cence,** *n.* punaruppatti, *f.* punarubbhava, *m.*

Rencounter, *n.* 1. saṅgāma ; 2. asambhāvita-samāgama, *m.*

Rend, *v.t.* phāleti ; dāḷeti ; vidāreti. *p.p.* °lita ; °rita. °**er,** *n.* phālaka ; vidāraka. °**ing,** *n.* vidālana, *nt.*

Render, *v.t.* 1. paṭidadāti ; 2. pāpeti ; 3. anuvādeti *or* bhāsantaraŋ parivatteti. *p.p.* paṭidinna ; pāpita ; °dita ; °tita. *n.* 1. paṭidāna ; 2. karadāna, *nt.* —**help,** upatthambheti. °**ing,** *n.* bhāsānuvāda, *m.* °**ed useless,** viddhasta ; vināsita.

Rendezvous, *n.* saṅketaṭṭhāna ; sannipātaṭṭhāna, *nt.*

Renegade, *n.* dhammabhaṭṭha ; sadhammacāgī, *m. v.i.* sadhammaŋ *or* sapakkhaŋ cajati. *p.p.* cattasadhamma.

Renew, *v.t.* navīkaroti ; pakatiŋ pāpeti. *p.p.* °kata ; °pita. °**al,** *n.* paṭisandahana, *nt.* punārambha, *m.* °**able,** *a.* navattāpādiya. °**er,** *n.* navattāpādaka, *m.*

Renounce, *v.t.* 1. pajahati ; pariccajati ; nissajati ; 2. paccakkhāti ; alan ti vadati. *p.p.* °hita ; pariccatta ; nissaṭṭha ; °khāta ; °vutta. °**ment,** *n.* paccakkhāna, *nt.* paṭinissagga, *m.*

Renovate, see **Renew.**

Renown, *n.* kitti ; vissuti ; pasiddhi, *f.* °**ed,** *a.* vissuta ; vikhyāta ; paññāta ; pākaṭa.

Rent, *n.* 1. kara ; bali, *m.* 2. phuṭana ; vivara ; vidārana, *nt. v.t.* kālikakarena gaṇhāti *or* deti. *p.p.* °gahita ; °dinna. °**al,** *n.* kālikakara. °**able,** *a.* kālikakarena dātabba.

Renumber, *v.t.* puna aṅkāni yojeti. *p.p.* punayojitaṅka.

Renunciation, *n.* paṭinissagga, *m.* abhinikkhamana, *nt.* pabbajjā, *f.* °**tory,** *a.* paṭinissaggāyatta.

Re-occupy, *v.t.* punāyattaŋ karoti. *p.p.* °tīkata.

Reorganize, *v.t.* puna vidahati *or* payojeti. *p.p.* °vihita ; °jita. °**ation,** *n.* punavidhāna, *nt.*

Repair, *n.* 1. paṭisaṅkharaṇa ; paṭijaggana ; 2. hānipūraṇa ; 3. nissitaṭṭhāna, *nt.* *v.t.* paṭisaṅkharoti ; paṭijaggati. *p.p.* °khata ; °gita. *v.i.* yāti ; pāpuṇāti; nissayati. *p.p.* yāta ; patta ; nissita.

Reparable, *a.* paṭisaṅkharaṇīya ; sappatikāra.

Reparation, *n.* hānipūraṇa ; alābhadāna, *nt.*

Repartee, *n.* khippanisantī, *m.* *v.i.* sopahāsaŋ vadati.

Repartition, *n.* punavibhajana, *nt.*

Repast, *n.* bhojana, *nt.* āhāra, *m.* *v.t.* bhojeti. *v.i.* bhuñjati. *p.p.* °jita ; bhutta.

Repatriate, *v.t.* sadesaŋ pāpeti. *v.i* sadesaŋ pāpuṇāti. *p.p.* °pāpita ; °patta.

Repay, *v.t.* 1. paṭidadāti ; nitthāreti ; 2. phalam uppādeti. *p.p.* paṭidinna ; °rita ; °ditaphala. °**able,** *a.* paṭidātabba. °**ment,** *n.* paṭidāna ; phaladāna, *nt.*

Repeal, *n.* lopa, *m.* balāpaharaṇa, *nt.* paccādesa, *m.* *v.t.* lopeti ; paccādisati ; balam apaharati ; moghīkaroti. *p.p.* lutta ; paccādiṭṭha ; apahaṭabala ; °kata. °**er,** *n.* lopaka ; nivāraka.

Repeat, *v.t.* punappuna karoti *or* vadati. *p.p.* °kata ; vutta. °**edly,** *adv.* punappunaŋ ; asakiŋ ; abhikkhaṇaŋ. °**er,** *n.* puṇavādī, *m.*

Repetition, *n.* punarutti, *f.* punakaraṇa, *nt.*

Repel, *v.t.* paṭipalāpeti ; paṭibāhati ; paṭinivāreti. *p.p.* °pita ; °hita ; °rita. °**ling,** *a.* paṭibāhaka. °**lence,** *n.* palāpana ; nivāraṇa, *nt.* °**lent,** *a.* palāpaka ; paṭibāhaka.

Repent, *v.i.* anutapati ; anusocati. *p.p.* °cita. °**ance,** *n.* pacchātāpa ; vippaṭisāra, *m.* °**ant,** *a.* *n.* anutāpī. °**antly,** *adv.* sānutāpaŋ.

Repeople, *v.t.* puna janāvāsaŋ karoti. *p.p.* °kata.

Repercussion, *n.* paṭighāta ; paṭighosa, *m.* parāvattana, *nt.* °**sive,** *a.* parāvattaka.

Repertory, *n.* paṭisāmitaṭṭhāna ; bhaṇḍāgāra, *nt.*

Reperusal, *n.* puna sammāvācana, *nt.*

Repine, *v.i.* khijjati ; nibbijjati ; avasīdati. *p.p.* khinna ; nibbinna ; avasīna.

Replace, *v.t.* paṭiniveseti ; puna yathāṭhāne ṭhapeti. *p.p.* °sita ; °pita. °**ment,** *n.* paṭinidahana ; yathāṭhāne ṭhapana, *nt.*

Replant, *v.t.* puna ropeti. *p.p.* °pita.

Replenish, *v.t.* paṭipūreti. *p.p.* °rita. °**ment,** *n.* paṭipūraṇa ; punasampādana, *nt.*

Replete, *a.* sampuṇṇa ; paripuṇṇa ; aḍḍha ; samiddha. °**ion,** *n.* samiddhatā, *f.*

Replica, *nt.* paṭirūpa, *nt.* samānaputtikā, *f.*

Replicate, *v.t.* 1. dvittaŋ karoti ; 2. paṭirūpaŋ sampādeti ; 3. saŋharati. *p.p.* dvittakata ;

°ditapatirūpa ; saŋhata. °**ion,** *n.* 1. saŋharaṇa ; 2. paccuttaradāna ; 3. puttikākaraṇa, *nt.*

Reply, *n.* paṭivacana; paccuttara; vissajjana, *nt. v.t.* paccuttaraŋ deti ; (pañhaŋ) vissajjeti. *p.p.* dinnapaccuttara ; °jita.

Report, *n.* 1. vuttanta, *m.* 2. anussuti, *f.* 3. āvedana, *nt.* 4. nāda, *m. v.t.* vuttantaŋ likhati, nivedeti *or* viññāpeti ; pavattiŋ katheti. *p.p.* °likhitavuttanta ; kathitapavattī. °**er,** *n.* vuttantanivedaka, *m.*

Repose, *n.* vissama, *m.* nipajjana, *nt.* passaddhi, *f. v.i.* vissamati. *v.t.* 1. passambheti ; 2. vissasati. °**ful,** *a.* vissamanayutta. °**fully,** *adv.* passaddhākārena.

Reposit, *v.t.* nidahati. *p.p.* °hita *r* nihita °**ory,** *n.* 1. ākara, *m.* āyatana, *nt.* 2. nihitaṭṭhāna, *nt.*

Repossess, *v.t.* punāyattaŋ karoti. *p.p.* °tīkata. °**ion,** *n.* punāyattīkaraṇa, *nt.*

Reprehend, *v.t.* santajjeti; dosam āropeti. *p.p.* °jita ; °pitadosa. °**nsible,** *a.* sāvajja ; tajjanīya. °**nsion,** *n.* garahā, *f.* santajjana, *nt.* upārambha, *m.* °**nsive,** *a.* santajjaka ; sopārambha.

Represent, *v.t.* 1. vitthāralakkhaṇaŋ katheti ; paṭinidasseti ; 2. nivedeti ; 3. aññatthāya sandissati ; 4. aññavesena tiṭṭhati. *p.p.* kathitavit° ; °sita ; °dita ; °sandiṭṭha ; °ṭhita. °**ation,** *n.* 1. padassana ; nivedana ; sandissana ; 2. paṭibimba, *nt.* °**ative,** *n.* niyojitapuggala ; āyuttaka, *m.* adj. paṭinidhibhūta.

Repress, *v.t.* rodheti ; abhibhavati ; saŋyameti ; niggaṇhāti. *p.p.* rodhita ; abhibhūta ; °mita ; niggahita. °**ion,** *n.* niggaha ; paṭirodha, *m.* abhibhavana, *nt.* °**ive,** *a.* niggaṇhanaka. °**ively,** *adv.* niggahapubbakaŋ.

Reprieve, *v.t.* daṇḍanakālaŋ *or* vadhakālaŋ atikkamāpeti. *p.p.* °pitavadhakāla.

Reprimand, *n.* nītiyā santajjana, *nt. v.t.* nītiyā santajjeti. *p.p.* °jita.

Reprint, *n.* punamuddāpana, *nt. v.t.* puna muddāpeti. *p.p.* °pita.

Reprisal, *n.* veranīyātana ; karaṇuttarikaraṇa, *nt.*

Reproach, *n.* garahā ; omasanā, *f.* apavāda ; upakkosa, *m. v.t.* garahati ; apavadati ; akkosati. *p.p.* °hita ; upavutta ; akkuṭṭha. °**ful,** *a.* nindiya ; gārayha. °**fully,** *adv.* garahapubbakaŋ ; sopavādaŋ.

Reprobate, *a. n.* dhikkata ; durācāra ; pāpasamācāra. *v.t.* 1. asantuṭṭhiŋ pakāseti ; 2. parivajjeti. °**ion,** *n.* 1. garahaṇa ; 2. parivajjana, *nt.*

Reproduce, *v.t.* 1. abhinibbatteti ; paṭijaneti ; 2. puttikaŋ sampādeti. *p.p.* °tita ; °nita ; °ditaputtika. °**ction,** *n.* paṭijanana ; abhinibbattāpana, *nt.* °**ctive,** *a.* nibbattāpaka.

Reproof, *n.* santajjana ; garahana, *nt.* codanā, *f.*

Reprove, *v.t.* 1. codeti ; 2. niggaṇhāti ; tajjeti. *p.p.* codita ; niggahita ; °jita.

Reptant, *a.* uraga ; saŋsappamāna.

Reptile, *a. n.* uraga; sappa; pannaga; pādūdara. °**lian,** *a.* urogāmī.

Republic, *n.* 1. janasammatarajja; 2. pajāpabhutta, *nt.* °**an,** *n.* pajāpabhuttavādī, *m.* adj. sammutirajjāyatta.

Repudiate, *v.t.* nirākaroti; paccakkhāti. *p.p.* °kata; °khāta. °**ion,** *n.* 1. nirākaraṇa; paccakkhāna, *nt.* 2. vivāhaviyojana, *nt.*

Repugn, *v.i.* virujjhati; appiyākārena carati; vimukhīhoti. *p.p.* viruddha; °bhūta. °**ance,** *n.* virodha; virāga, *m.* vimukhatta, *nt.* °**ant,** *a.* viruddha; viratta; vimukha. °**antly,** *adv.* aruciyā; jigucchāya.

Repulse, *v.t.* paccāvatteti; paṭihanati. *p.p.* °tita; paṭihata. °**ion,** *n.* paccāvattana; paṭihaṇana; nissāraṇa, *nt.* °**ive,** *a.* 1. paccāvattaka; 2. appiya; jeguccha. °**iveness,** *n.* appiyatta; jegucchatta, *nt.*

Repute, *v.t.* sambhāveti; sammāneti. *p.p.* °vita; °nita. °**able,** *a.* 1. mānanīya; pasattha; 2. yasadāyaka; bahumānuppādaka. °**ation,** *n.* kitti, *f.* yasoghosa, *m.* °**ed,** *a.* vissuta; abhiññāta; sambhāvita.

Request, *n.* 1. āyācanā; ajjhesanā; 2. ākaṅkhā; apekkhā, *f.* *v.t.* āyācati; ajjhesati. *p.p.* °cita; °sita. °**ing,** *a.* āyācamāna.

Require, *v.t.* pattheti; apekkhati; ākaṅkhati. *p.p.* °thita; °khita. °**ment,** *n.* 1. apekkhā; icchā, *f.* 2. icchita-vatthu *or* kāraṇa, *nt.*

Requisite, *n.* parikkhāra; upakaraṇa; āvassakavatthu, *nt.* adj. āvassaka. °**ion,** *n.* 1. apekkhā; ākaṅkhā, *f.* 2. upakaraṇasampādanāya āṇā, *f.* *v.t.* 1. upakaraṇasampādanaŋ āṇāpeti; 2. rājakiccāya āṇāpeti. *p.p.* °pita.

Requite, *v.t.* 1. hāniŋ paṭipūreti; 2. phalavasena deti. °**tal,** *n.* 1. paṭidāna; nittharaṇa; vipākadāna, *nt.* 2. paṭikriyā, *f.*

Rescind, *v.t.* balaŋ lopeti *or* hāpeti; abalīkaroti. *p.p.* hāpitabala; °kata °**cission,** *n.* balahāpana, *nt.*

Rescue, *n.* tāṇa; leṇa, *nt.* mutti, *f.* mokkha, *m.* tāyati; rakkhati; vimoceti. *p.p.* tāyita; °khita; °cita. °**er,** *n.* tāyaka; mocaka, *m.*

Research, *n.* anvesanā; gavesanā; magganā; vicāraṇā, *f.* *v.t.* upaparikkhati. *p.p.* °khita. °**er,** *n.* anuvicāraka, *m.*

Resemble, *v.t.* samo *or* sadiso bhavati; sameti. *p.p.* samībhūta; sadisībhūta; samita. °**ance,** *n.* sadisatta; sarikkhatta, *nt.* °**ing,** *a.* sadisa; tulya; sannibha; saṅkāsa.

Resent, *v.t.* appatīto hoti; anattamanataŋ pavedeti. °**ful,** *a.* anattamana; ujjhāyaka. °**ment,** *n.* appiyatta; asahana, *nt.*

Reserve, *n.* 1. nidahana; 2. nidahitavatthu, *nt.* *v.t.* 1. gopeti; saŋrakkhati; 2. visuŋ karoti; 3. nidahati. *p.p.* gopita; °khita; °kata; °hita. °**ation,** *n.* 1. saŋrakkhaṇa; nidahana; 2. avisāradatta; līnatta, *nt.* °**ed,** *a.* 1. visuŋkata; 2. saŋrakkhita; 3. mitabhāṇī; saŋvarayutta. °**edly,** *adv.* mitabhāṇitāya.

Reservoir, *n.* jalāsaya, *m.* vāpī, *f.*

Reset, *v.t.* 1. puna yojeti; 2. thenitabhaṇḍaŋ paṭiggaṇhāti. °**ter**, *n.* thenitabhaṇḍapaṭiggāhī, *m.*

Reside, *v.i.* vasati; āvasati; adhivasati; viharati; vāsaŋ kappeti. *p.p.* vuttha; āvuttha; °rita; kappitavāsa. °**nce**, *n.* nivesana; niketana; vāsaṭṭhāna, *nt.*

Resident, *n. a.* nivāsī; adhivāsī; nevāsika. °**ial**, *a.* nivāsānucchavika; nevāsikāyatta.

Residual, *a. n.* avasiṭṭha; avasesa; sesabhāga, *m.*

Residue, *n.* avasiṭṭhabhāga, *m.* °**duum**, *n.* avasiṭṭha-malādi, *m.*

Resign, *v.t.* adhikāraŋ nissajati; pajahati *or* pariccajati; adhikārā apagacchati. *p.p.* nissaṭṭhādhikāra; °hita; pariccatta; °apagata. *v.i.* vasaŋ yāti; adhivāseti. *p.p.* °yāta; °sita. °**ation**, *n.* 1. adhikāracāga, *m.* 2. vasaṅgamana, *nt.* 3. adhivāsanā, *f.* °**ed**, *a.* 1. adhivāsaka.

Resile, *v.i.* paṭikuñcati. *p.p.* °cita. °**lience**, *n.* paṭikuñcana; pacchato paṭikkamana, *nt.* °**lient**, *a.* paṭikuñcaka.

Resin, *n.* yakkhadhūpa, *m.* *v.t.* yakkhadhūpena ālepeti. *p.p.* ālitta. °**ous**, *a.* yakkhadhūpagatika.

Resipiscence, *n.* dosapaṭiggahaṇa, *nt.* °**scent**, *a.* dosapaṭiggāhī.

Resist, *v.t.* paṭibāhati; bādheti; nivāreti. *p.p.* °hita; bādhita; °rita. °**ance**, *n.* bādhana; vāraṇa, *nt.* virodha, *m.* °**ant**, *a.* paṭibāhaka; bādhaka. °**ibility**, *n.* paṭibāhanīyatta, *nt.* °**ible**, *a.* paṭibāhiya; vāraṇīya. °**less**, *a.* appaṭibāhiya. °**lessly**, *adv.* avāriyākārena.

Resoluble, *a.* bhāgaso karaṇīya.

Resolute, *a.* thirādhiṭṭhāna; daḷhanicchaya. °**ly**, *adv.* daḷhanicchayena. °**ness**, *n.* thirādhiṭṭhānatta, *nt.*

Resolution, *n.* 1. dhiti; adhimutti, *f.* adhimokkha, *m.* sanniṭṭhāna, *nt.* 2. sabhāgatayojanā, *f.*

Resolve, *n.* sanniṭṭhāna, *nt.* nicchaya, *m.* *v.i.* niccheti; adhiṭṭhāti. *v.t.* vilīyāpeti; viyojeti. *p.p.* °chita; °ṭhita; °pita; °jita. °**ed**, *a.* katanicchaya; thirādhiṭṭhāna. °**edly**, *adv.* daḷhanicchayena.

Resolvent, *a. n.* visilesaka (-bhesajja), *nt.*

Resonant, *a.* upakūjita; saṅghuṭṭha.

Resorption, *n.* punapariyādiyana.

Resort, *v.i.* sevati; bhajati; nissayati, *v.t.* puna vaggīkaroti. *p.p.* °kata. *n.* 1. nissaya; upāya, *m.* 2. niccasevitaṭṭhāna, *nt.*

Resound, *v.i.* abhinadati; upakūjati; paṭiravati, *v.t.* nādena pūreti. *p.p.* °dita; °jita; °vita; °pūrita. °**ing with**, saṅghuṭṭha, *a.*

Resource, *n.* 1. upāya; payoga, *m.* 2. *pl.* vibhava; āya, *m.* 3. nicitavatthu, *nt.* °**ful**, *a.* 1. upāyakusala; 2. vibhavasampanna. °**less**, *a.* anupāyakusala; avassayarahita.

Respect, *n*. 1. gārava ; cittīkāra ; nipaccakāra ; bahumāna, *m*. pūjā ; apaciti, *f*. 2. sambandha, *m*. apekkhā, *f*. 3. paṇāma, *m*. abhivādanā, *f*. *v.t.* garukaroti ; māneti ; pūjeti ; apacāyati. *p.p.* °kata ; mānita; pūjita; °cita. °**ability**, *n*. pujjatta ; mānanīyatta, *nt*. °**able**, *a*. garukātabba ; mahanīya ; mānanāraha ; pūjanīya. °**ably**, *adv*. pujjākārena; sabahumānaŋ. °**ed**, *a*. sambhāvita ; bahumata ; sammānita. °**er**, *n*. abhivādaka ; mānetu ; sambhāvetu ; pūjetu, *m*. °**ful**, *a*. sagārava ; sādara ; sappatissa. °**fully**, *adv*. sagāravaŋ ; sabahumānaŋ; sādaraŋ.

Respecting, *adv*. uddissa ; sandhāya ; apekkhiya.

Respective, *a*. yathāsaka ; pacceka. °**ly**, *adv*. yathāsakaŋ ; paccekaŋ.

Respire, *v.i.t.* sasati ; assāsapassāsaŋ karoti. *p.p.* katassāsapassāsa. °**ation**, *n*. sasana, *nt*. assāsapassāsa, *m*. °**atory**, *a*. sasanapaṭibaddha.

Respite, *n*. virāma, *m*. kālikanivattana, *nt*. *v.t.* okāsaŋ deti ; kālam apakaḍḍhati. *p.p.* dinnokāsa ; kālāpakaḍḍhita.

Resplendent, *a*. jutimantu ; jutindhara; samujjala; pabhassara. °**nce**, *n*. pabhassaratā, *f*. samujjalana, *nt*. °**ly**, *adv*. uḷārobhāsena ; abhikkantavaṇṇena.

Respond, *v.i.* 1. paccuttaraŋ deti; 2. paṭissuṇāti ; viditabhāvaŋ ñāpeti. *p.p.* dinna° ra ; paṭissuta. °**ent**, *n*. 1. cuditaka ; 2. paṭivacanadāyī, *m*.

Response, *n*. paṭivacana ; paccuttara, *nt*. °**ibility**, *n*. dhurandharatā ; anuyuñjitabbatā, *f*. °**ible**, *a*. 1. dhuravāhī; 2. anuyuñjitabba; paṭivacanīya. °**ibly**, *adv*. paṭivattabbākārena. °**ive**, *a*. 1. uttaradāyī ; 2. vadaññū ; sānukampī. °**iveness**, *n*. 1. uttaradāyakatta, *nt*. 2. vadaññutā ; anukampitā, *f*.

Rest, *n*. 1. vissama ; viveka, *m*. 2. upasama, *m*. santi, *f*. 3. niddā ; seyyā, *f*. 4. ādhāraka, *nt*. 5. kālakiriyā, *f*. *v.i.* vissamati, *v.t.* vissāmeti ; saŋveseti. *p.p.* vissanta ; °mita ; °sita.—**against**, apassayati. °**ful**, *a*. saviveka ; upasanta. °**house**, *n*. vissāmasālā, *f*. °**ing on**, nissita ; patiṭṭhita. °**ing place**, vissamanaṭṭhāna, *nt*. nilaya, *m*. °**less**, *a*. 1. cañcala ; vyākula ; avupasanta ; 2. uddāma. °**lessly**, *adv*. vyākulākārena. °**lessness**, *n*. ākulatta ; cañcalatta; asantatta, *nt*.

Rest, *n*. 1. atiritta, *nt*. avasesakoṭṭhāsa, *m*. 2. vuttāpara. *v.i.* atiriccati. *p.p.* atiritta.

Restaurant, *n*. lahubhojanāgāra-*nt*.

Restitution, *n*. paṭidāna ; hānipūraṇa, *nt*.

Restive, *a*. avasa ; avidheya ; avupasanta.

Restore, *v.t.* 1. paṭidadāti ; 2. paṭipākatikaŋ karoti. *p.p.* paṭidinna ; °kata. °**able**, *a*. paṭisaṅkharaṇīya. °**ation**, phātikamma ; paṭisaṅkharaṇa, *nt*. °**ative**, *a*. balavaḍḍhaka, *n*. vājīkaraṇosadha, *nt*.

Restrain, *v.t.* avarodheti; sannirumbheti; orundhati; niggaṇhāti; saŋyameti. *p.p.* °dhita; °bhita; oruddha; niggahita; °mita. °**able,** *a.* niggahetabba; paṭibāhiya. °**er,** *n.* niggahetu. saŋyametu, *m.* °**int,** *m.* niggaha; saŋyama; vinaya, *m.* sannirumbhana, *nt.*

Re-strain, *v.t.* atimattaŋ viheseti. *p.p.* °sita.

Restrict, *v.t.* paricchindati; sīmaŋ niyameti; mariyādaŋ ṭhapeti; paṭibāhati. *p.p.* °chinna; °mitasīma; ṭhapitamariyāda; °hita. °**ion,** *n.* paricchindana; sīmāniyamana; paṭibāhana, *nt.* °**ive,** *a.* sīmāniyāmaka; paṭibāhaka.

Result, *n.* vipāka; nissanda; ānisaŋsa, *m.* kammaphala, *nt.* *v.i.* vipaccati; nipphajjati; samudāgacchati. *p.p.* vipakka; nipphanna; °gata. °**ant,** *n.* phala, *nt.* adj. paccayajāta; hetuja. °**less,** *a.* nipphala; niratthaka. °**ing in,** vepakka; phaluppādaka.

Resume, *v.t.* punārabhati; punādāti. *p.p.* °raddha; punādinna. *n.* sārasaṅgaha, *m.*

Resumption, *n.* paccādāna; punārabhana, *nt.* °**tive,** *a.* paccādāyī; punārambhakara.

Resupinate, *a.* avaŋsira; vipallattha.

Resurrect, *v.t.* matam uṭṭhāpeti; punarujjīveti. *p.p.* °pita; °vita. °**ion,** *n.* matakuṭṭhāpana; punarujjīvāpana, *nt.*

Resuscitate, see **Resurrect.**

Ret, *v.t.* temanena muduŋ karoti. *p.p.* °mudukata.

Retail, *n.* appakavikkaya, *m.* *v.t.i.* appamattakaŋ vikkiṇāti. — **merchant,** *n.* khuddakavāṇija; appamattavibhajaka, *m.*

Retain, *v.t.* suṭṭhu niveseti; āyattaŋ katvā ṭhapeti. *p.p.* °sita; °ṭhapita. °**er,** *n.* 1. nikkhipaka, *m.* 2. sevaka; bhacca; kiṅkara, *m.*

Retaliate, *v.t.* 1. paṭikaroti; 2. veraŋ nīyāteti. *p.p.* °kata; nīyātitavera. °**ion,** *n.* paṭikaraṇa; veranīyātana, *nt.* °**ive,** *a.* veranīyātaka; paṭikaraṇasīla.

Retard, see **Obstruct.** °**ation,** paṭibāhana; bādhana, *nt.* °**ative,** *a.* paṭibāhaka. °**ment,** *n.* bādhana; paṭibāhana, *nt.*

Retention, *n.* 1. nivāraṇa; 2. malabādhana, *nt.* muttakicchā, *f.* °**tive,** *a.* 1. pavattāpaka; 2. appamussaka. °**tively,** *adv.* pavattāpakavasena. °**tiveness,** *n.* pavattāpana; appamussana, *nt.*

Reticence, *n.* mitabhāṇitā, *f.* tuṇhībhāva, *m.* °**cent,** *a.* appabhāṇī.

Reticle, *n.* sukhumajālaka, *nt.*

Reticulate, *v.t.* akkhikavasena vibhajati; jālasamaŋ karoti; *p.p.* °vibhatta; °kata. °**ion,** *n.* jālasadisakaraṇa; akkhivasena vibhajana, *nt.*

Retiform, *a.* jālākāra.

Retina, *n.* diṭṭhisirāpaṭala, *nt.* cakkhuppasāda, *m.*

Retinue, *n.* parivāra; parijana, *m.* parisā, *f*

Retire, *v.t.* (adhikārādito) apagacchati; apakkamati. *v.i.* paṭisallīyati. *p.p.* apagata; apakkanta; °līna. °**ment,** *n.* 1. adhikāracāga, *m.* apagamana; 2.

paṭisallīyana, *nt.* °**ing**, *a.* pavivitta; vivekarata. °**ing hall**, paṭikkamanasālā, *f.*

Retort, *n.* paṭivādāropana, *nt.* omasavāda, *m.* *v.t.* paṭivadati; paccāvatteti; omasati. *p.p.* paṭivutta; °tita; omaṭṭha.

Retrace, *v.t.* paṭinivattati; paṭikkamati. *p.p.* °tita; paṭikkanta.

Retract, *v.t.* paṭisaŋharati; paccosakkati. *p.p.* °saŋhaṭa; °kita; °**able**, *a.*paṭisaŋharaṇīya. °**ility**, *n.* saŋharaṇīyatta, *nt.* °**ion**, *n.* paṭisaŋharaṇa, *nt.*

Retreat, *n.* 1. paccosakkana; apagamana; 2. vijanaṭṭhāna, *nt.* *v.i.t.* 1. paccosakkati; paṭinivattati; 2. paṭisallīyati. *p.p.* °kita; °tita; °līna.

Retrench, *v.t.i.* apacināti; vyavacchindati; mandīkaroti. *p.p.* apacita; °chinna; °kata. °**ment**, *n.* 1. apacaya, *m.* 2. mandīkarana, *nt.*

Retribute, *v.i.* pariṇamati; phalati; vipaccati. *p.p.* °ṇata; °lita; vipakka. °**ion**, *n.* paṭidaṇḍa; vipāka, *m.* paṭiphala, *nt.* °**ive**, *a.* vipākadāyaka; paṭiphalajanaka.

Retrieve, see **Recover**.

Retroact, see **React**. °**ion**, *n.* paṭiviruddhakriyā, *f.* °**ive**, *a.* paṭilomavattī.

Retrocede, *v.i.* paccosakkati. *v.t.* (raṭṭhaŋ) paṭinīyādeti. *p.p.* °kita; °dita.

Retrocession, *n.* 1. paṭinīyātana; 2. paccosakkana, *nt.*

Retroflected, *a.* paccāvattita; parāvattita.

Retrograde, *a.* *n.* paṭigāmī; parihāyamāna; osakkamāna. *v.i.* paṭiyāti; paccāvattati; olīyati. °**ation**, *n.* paṭigamana; osakkana; olīyana, *nt.*

Retrogress, *v.i.* paccāvattati; parāvattati; parihāyati. *p.p.* °tita; parihīna. °**ive**, *a.* paccāvattamāna; parihāyamāna. °**ion**, *n.* paccāvattana; parihāyana, *nt.*

Retroject, *v.t.* paccākhipati. *p.p.* °khitta.

Retrospect, *n.* atītāvalokana, *nt.* °**ive**, *a.* atīlālocaka.

Retrovert, *v.t.* paccāvatteti. *p.p.* °tita. °**rsion**, *n.* paccāvattana, *nt.*

Return, *n.* 1. paccāgamana; paṭinivattana, *nt.* 2. paṭinīyātana, *nt.* 3. phala, *nt.* udaya; *m.* *v.i.* paṭinivattati; paccāgacchati. *v.t.* paccāharati; paṭinīyādeti. *p.p.* paṭinivatta; paccāgata; °haṭa; °dita. °**able**, *a.* paccāharaṇīya; paṭinīyādetabba. °**er**, *n.* paccāgāmī, *m.*

Reunion, *n.* paṭisandhāna; punaghaṭana; punasamāgamana, *nt.*

Reunite, *v.t.* paṭisandhāneti; puna ghaṭeti. *p.p.* °nita; °ṭita.

Reveal, *v.t.* vivarati; pakāseti; āvīkaroti; (to the mind:) paṭibhāti. *p.p.* vivaṭa; °sita; °kata. °**er**, *n.* āvīkattu; pakāsetu, *m.*

Revel, *v.i.t.* visayarasam anubhoti; pānussavaŋ pavatteti. *p.p.* anubhūta°sa; °titapānussava. °**ler**, *n.* visayarasabhogī, *m.* °**ry**, *n.* pānussava; surāchaṇa; pītussava, *m.*

Revelation, *n.* āvīkaraṇa; vivaraṇa; pakāsana, *nt.*

Revenge, *n.* veranīyātana, *nt.* *v.t.* veram appeti; paṭihiŋsati. *p.p.* appitavera; °sita. °**ful,** *a.* veranīyātaka. °**fully,** *adv.* veranīyātanavasena. °**less,** *a.* appaṭidubbhanaka.

Revenue, *n.* rājabali; kara, *m.*

Reverberate, *v.i.* paṭinādati. *v.t.* paṭirāveti. *p.p.* °dita; °vita. °**ion,** *n.* paṭirava; paṭighosa, *m.* °**ive,** *a.* paṭiravaka; paṭinādaka. °**tor,** *n.* paccāvattakapadīpa, *m.*

Revere, *v.t.* sammāneti; garukaroti; mahati; pūjeti; bahumāneti. *p.p.* °nita; °kata; mahita; pūjita; bahumata. °**able,** *a.* mānanīya; garukātabba. °**nce,** *n.* gārava; bahumāna, *m.* apaciti, *f.* °**nd,** *a.* pujja; gāravāraha; mānanīya. °**nd Sir,** bhante, *voc.* °**nt,** *a.* sādara; sagārava. °**ntly,** *adv.* sagāravaŋ; sabahumānaŋ.

Reverie, *n.* nijjhāyana, *nt.*

Reverse, *n.* 1. paṭiloma; vipariyāya; 2. pacchābhāga; piṭṭhipassa, *m.* adj. paccanika; paṭipakkha; viparīta. *v.t.* 1. viparivatteti; 2. adhomukhīkaroti. *p.p.* °tita; °kata. °**al,** *n.* paccāvattana, *nt.* vipallāsa, *m.* °**ible,** *a.* viparivattiya; aññathākaraṇīya. °**ion,** *n.* viparivattana, *nt.* vipallāsa, *m.* °**ly,** *adv.* paṭilomato; vipariyāyena.

Revert, *v.i.t.* 1. punarāvattati; 2. punādhikāraŋ labhati. *p.p.* °tita; punaladdhādhikāra. °**ible,** *a.* paccāvattanīya; paṭiladdhabba.

Review, *n.* vivecana; guṇadosavicāraṇa; paccavekkhaṇa, *nt.* *v.t.* viveceti; paccavekkhati. °**er,** *n.* vivecaka; tattadassaka, *m.*

Revile, *v.t.* akkosati; paribhāsati; garahati. *p.p.* °sita; °hita. °**er,** *n.* akkosaka; garahī, *m.* °**ing,** *n.* paribhāsanā, *f.* dhikkāra, *m.* garahā, *f.*

Revise, *v.t.* puna parikkhati *or* saŋsodheti. *p.p.* °khita; °dhita. °**al,** °**ion,** punavicāraṇā; parisodhanā, *f.* °**ional,** *a.* punasodhanāyatta.

Revisit, *v.t.* puna pāpuṇāti. *p.p.* °patta.

Revive, *v.i.* punarujjīvati; atikkamitvā jīvati; pākatiko hoti. *v.t.* punarujjīveti; pākatikaŋ karoti. *p.p.* °vita; pākatikabhūta, °vita; °kakata. °**al,** *n.* 1. punarujjīvana, *nt.* 2. pakatibhāvappatti, *f.*

Revivify, *v.t.* navajīvanaŋ pāpeti; samussāheti. *p.p.* °pāpita; °hita. °**ication,** *n.* navajīvadāna; samussāhana, *nt.*

Revocable, *a.* paccakkhātabba; nisedhetabba. °**cation,** *n.* paccakkhāna; nisedhana; paṭikkhipana, *nt.*

Revoke, *v.t.* nisedheti; paṭisedheti. *p.p.* °dhita.

Revolt, *n.* pajākhobha; rājavirodha; āṇātikkama, *m.* *v.t.* 1. āṇam atikkamati; 2. paṭipakkhaŋ bhajati; dubbhati. *p.p.* atikkantāṇa; bhajita° kha; °bhita. *v.i.* jigucchati; harāyati. *p.p.* °chita; °yita. °**ing,** *a.* bībhaccha; jeguccha.

Revolution, *n.* 1. āvaṭṭana; vivaṭṭana, *nt.* 2. rajjavipallāsa, *m.* °**ary,** *a.* vipallāsakara; parivattanasīla. °**ist,** *n.* vipallāsavādī, *m.* °**ize,** *v.t.* samparivatteti; vipallāseti. *p.p.* °tita; °sita.

Revolve, *v.t.* āvijjhati; bhamāpeti. *v.i.* 1. sambhamati; paribbhamati; āvaṭṭati; 2. parivitakketi. *p.p.* āviddha; °pita; sambhanta; °ṭita; °kita. °**er,** *n.* āvaṭṭaka-aggināḷī, *f.*

Revulsion, *n.* 1. jigucchā; arati, *f.* 2. balavaviraha; 3. cittavikkhepa, *m.* °**sive,** *a.* virāgajanaka.

Reward, *n.* puṇṇapatta; tuṭṭhidāya, *m.* *v.t.* 1. tuṭṭhidāyaŋ *or* pāritosikaŋ deti; 2. saphalīkaroti. *p.p.* dinnatuṭṭhidāya; °kata. °**less,** *a.* viphala.

Rewrite, *v.t.* puna likhati. *p.p.* °khita.

Rex, *n.* vattamāna-rāja, *m.*

Reynard, *n.* sigāla; kotthu, *m.*

Rhabdomancy, *n.* yaṭṭhinā khaṇijagavesana, *nt.*

Rhapsode, *n.* itihāsagāyaka, *m.* °**ize,** *v.t.* itihāsagītaŋ likhati *or* gāyati.

Rhapsody, *n.* itihāsakabba; itihāsa-sarabhañña, *nt.* °**ical,** *a.* itihāsakabbāyatta; vīrakriyāsūcaka.

Rhetoric, *n.* alaṅkārasattha, *nt.* °**al,** *a.* alaṅkārāyatta. °**ian,** *n.* alaṅkārika. — **figure,** silesālaṅkāra, *m.*

Rheumatic, *a.* rattavātika; rattavātāyatta. °**ism,** *n.* pabbavāta; rattavāta, *m.*

Rhinal, *a.* ghāṇāyatta.

Rhinoceros, *n.* khaggavisāṇa; gaṇḍaka, *m.*

Rhododendron, *n.* asokavisesa, *m.*

Rhomb, *n.* visamacaturassa, *nt.* °**ic,** *a.* visamacaturassākāra.

Rhomboid, *n.* dīgha-visama-caturassa, *nt.*

Rhyme, *n.* 1. sandabbha; akkharasamatā; vacanasamatā, *f.* 2. pajjabandha, *m.* °**er,** *n.* sandabbharacaka, *m.*

Rhythm, *n.* laya, *m.* saddasamatta, *nt.* °**ic,** °**ical,** *a.* layānugata. °**ically,** *adv.* layānukūlaŋ.

Rib, *n.* 1. phāsukā; phāsulikā, *f.* 2. vitthambhakadāru, *nt.* tulāsaṅghāṭa, *m.* *v.t.* phāsukā *or* tulā yojeti.

Ribald, *a.* *n.* asabbha; gamma; asabbhavāca. °**ry,** *n.* asabbhavācatā, *f.* asabbhavohāra, *m.*

Ribbon, *n.* dukūlapaṭṭa, *m.*

Rice, *n.* 1. taṇḍula, *m.* 2. (plant :) vīhisassa, *nt.* °**gruel,** yāgu, *f.* — **milk,** *n.* khīrapāyāsa, *m.* — **powder,** *n.* kuṇḍaka, *nt.* **Boiled** —, odana; bhatta, *nt.*

Rich, *a.* *n.* 1. dhanavantu; mahābhoga; 2. mahaggha; mahāraha; 3. samiddha; aḍḍha; 4. bahuphalada; sāravantu; 5. paṇīta; ojavantu; 6. atisobhana; samujjala. *pl.* vibhava, *m.* vitta; dhana, *nt.* °**ly,** *adv.* atisayena; sobhanākārena. °**ness,** *n.* aḍḍhatā; samiddhi; sassirīkatā, *f.*

Rick, *n.* puñja; rāsi; palālapuñja, *m.* *v.t.* puñje karoti. *p.p.* puñjīkata.

Rickets, *n.* aṭṭhidubbalatta, *nt.* °**ty,** *a.* sithilasandhika; sithilaṭṭhika.

Rickshaw, *n.* hatthavaṭṭakayāna, *nt.*

Rid, *v.t.* moceti; vimoceti; apaneti. *p.p.* °çita; °nīta. °**dance,** *n.* mutti; vimutti, *f.* mokkha; pamokkha, *m.* **Get — of,** pajahati; dūrīkaroti.

Riddle, *n.* 1. paheḷikā, *f.* 2. dhaññacālikā, *f.* *v.t.* 1. paheḷikaŋ katheti; 2. cālaniyā sodheti *or* visuŋkaroti. *p.p.* kathita°; °dhita; °kata.

Ride, *n.* āruhitvā gamana, *nt.* *v.t.* āruhati; samāruhati. *v.i.* assapiṭṭhiyā carati. *p.p.* ārūḷha, °rita. **°er,** *n.* ārohaka; assārohī, *m.* **°ing,** *n.* āruhana, *nt.* **°ing on,** ārūḷha; piṭṭhigata; yānagata.

Ridge, *n.* 1. kaṭaka, *m.* pabbatapiṭṭhi, *f.* 2. chadanapiṭṭhi; 3. pabbatāvali, *f.* 4. ālavāla, *m.* *v.t.* paddhatiyo *or* ālavāle sampādeti. **°plate, °pole,** sikharatulā, *f.* **°tile,** *n.* sikhariṭṭhikā, *f.*

Ridicule, *n.* parihāsa; dava, *m.* uppaṇḍanā, *f.* *v.t.* avahasati; uppaṇḍeti. *p.p.* °sita; °ḍita. **°ous,** *a.* upahasanīya; hāsajanaka. **°lously,** *adv.* upahassākāreṇa; hāsajanakatāya.

Rife, *a.* vitthiṇṇa; pahūta; pacura. **°ness,** *n.* bāhulla; pacuratta, *nt.*

Riffraff, *n.* adhamajana, *m.*

Rifle, *n.* khuddaka-nāḷīyanta, *nt.* *v.t.* acchindati; vilumpati. *p.p.* °acchinna; vilutta.

Rift, see **Fissure.**

Rig, *n.* 1. kūṭopāya, *m.* nikati, *f.* 2. nāvārajjuādi, *m.* *v.t.* 1. vañceti; kūṭopāyaŋ yojeti; 2. nāvaŋ upakaraṇehi sajjeti. *p.p.* °cita; yojita; °sajjitanāva. **°ging,** *n.* kūpakarajju, *f.*

Right, *a.* 1. yathābhūta; avitatha; 2. dhammika; 3. dakkhiṇa; 4. uju; 5. niddosa. *n.* 1. yutti, *f.* ñāya; dhamma, *m.* 2. āyattabhāva; pariggaha, *m.* 3. dakkhiṇapassa, *m.* 4. adhikāra, *m.* *adv.* yathocitaŋ; sādhukaŋ. *intj.* bhaddhaŋ; sādhu. *v.t.* ujuŋ *or* niddosaŋ karoti; suppathaŋ pāpeti. *p.p.* °sīkata; °pāpita. **— angle,** *n.* samakoṇa, *m.* **— conduct,** sammākammanta, *m.* **°ful,** *a.* ñāyānugata; nītyanukūla. **°handed,** *a.* paricitadakkhiṇahattha. **°ly,** *adv.* yathātathaŋ; sammā; suṭṭhu. **°ly disposed,** sammāpaṭipanna, *a.* **°ness,** *n.* sammatta; niddosatta, *nt.* **— ward,** *a.* dakkhiṇābhimukha.

Righteous, *a.* dhammika; dhammaṭṭha; anavajja. **°ly,** *adv.* dhammikākārena. **°ness,** *n.* dhammikatta; anavajjatta, *nt.*

Rigid, *a.* 1. daḷha; kaṭhina; 2. kakkasa; pharusa; thaddhahadaya. **°ity,** *n.* anamyatā; thaddhatā; pharusatā, *f.*

Rigmarole, *n.* asaṅgatakathā; attharahita-vācā, *f.*

Rigour, *n.* uggatta; kaṭhinatta; daḷhatta, *nt.* **°ous,** *a.* kaṭhora; ugga; asithila. **°ously,** *adv.* niṭṭhuraŋ; atidaḷhaŋ; gāḷhaŋ.

Rile, *v.t.* pakopeti. *p.p.* °pita.

Rill, *n.* kunnadī; mātikā, *f.*

Rim, *n.* 1. mukhavaṭṭi, *f.* 2. pariyanta, *m.* (of a garment :) dasā, *f.* (of a wheel :) nemi, *f.*

Rime, *n.* tuhina, *nt.* ussāva, *m.* *v.t.* tuhinena chādeti. *p.p.* tuhinacchanna.

Rimose, Rimous, *a.* chiddāvacchidda.

Rind, *n.* taca, *m.* bāhirāvaraṇa, *nt.* *v.t.* tacam apaneti. *p.p.* apanīta-taca.

Rinderpest, *n.* gomāraka-vyādhi, *m.*

Ring, *n.* 1. valaya ; cakka ; maṇḍala, *nt.* 2. (for finger :) aṅgulīyaka, *nt.* aṅgulimuddā, *f.* 3. rava ; nāda, *m.* 4. (of persons :) pūga ; gaṇa, *m.* *v.t.* nādeti ; vādeti. *v.i.* 1. nadati ; saddāyati ; 2. valayākārena āvaṭṭati. *p.p.* °dita ; nadita ; °yita ; °ṭita. — **leader,** *n.* kalahanāyaka, *m.* °**let,** *n.* alakā, *f.* kesakuṇḍali, *f.* — **worm,** *n.* kuṭṭhavisesa, *m.*

Ringent, *a.* vivaṭamukha.

Rinse, *n.* vikkhālana ; ācamana, *nt.* *v.t.* vikkhāleti ; ācameti. *p.p.* °lita ; °mita.

Riot, *n.* janasaṅkhobha, *m.* dāmarikakamma, *nt.* °**er,** *n.* saṅkhobhī ; dāmarika, *m.* °**ous,** *a.* khobhakārī ; viplavakārī. °**ously,** *adv.* viplavakāritāya ; mahānādena. °**ousness,** viplavakāritā, *f.*

Rip, *n.* 1. nibbhogassa ; 2. dhuttapuggala, *m.* 3. vidāritaṭṭhāna, *nt.* 4. jalopāta, *m.* *v.t.* vidāreti ; phāleti. *p.p.* °rita ; °lita.

Riparian, *a.* nadīkūlanissita.

Ripe, *a.* 1. pakka ; pariṇata ; 2. siddha ; sampanna. *v.t.* paripāceti. *v.i.* paripaccati. *p.p.* °cita ; paripakka. °**en,** *v.i.* paccati ; pariṇamati. *v.t.* pāceti ; pariṇāmeti. *p.p.* °cita ; °mita. °**ly,** *adv.* paripakkākārena. °**ness,** *n.* pariṇatatta, *nt.* °**ning,** *a.* paripācaka.

Ripple, *n.* ūmi ; vīci, *f.* khuddakataraṅga, *m.* *v.t.* ūmiyo uṭṭhāpeti. *v.i.* taraṅgāyati. *p.p.* °pitūmika ; °yita.

Rise, *n.* 1. udaya ; samudaya ; uggama ; samuggama ; ubbhava ; samubbhava, *m.* uṭṭhāna ; samuṭṭhāna, *nt.* 2. unnati ; samunnati ; abhivuddhi, *f.* *v.i.t.* udeti ; samudeti ; uṭṭhāti ; samuṭṭhāti ; uggacchati ; ubbhavati ; āruhati ; vaḍḍhati. *p.p.* °dita ; °ṭhita ; uggata ; ubbhūta ; ārūḷha ; °ḍhita. °**ing,** *n.* 1. uggamana, *nt.* 2. mukhapiḷakā, *f.* 3. saṅkhobha, *m.* — **and fall,** udayabbaya, *m.* — **up,** abbhuggacchati ; ajjhāruhati ; (from a seat :) uṭṭhāti ; uṭṭhahati.

Risible, *a.* hāsetukāma. °**bility,** *n.* hāsajanakatā, *f.*

Risk, *n.* antarāya, *m.* hāni, *f.* sandeha, *m.* *v.t.* antarāyābhimukhī hoti *or* karoti. *p.p.* °khībhūta ; °khīkata. °**y,** *a.* sāsaṅka ; sappaṭibhaya.

Rite, *n.* pūjāvidhi ; cārittaniyama, *m.* °**ual,** *n.* pūjāniyama, *m.* adj. pūjānugata ; cārittāyatta. °**ualism,** *n.* pūjāvidhi-anugamana, *nt.* °**ualist,** *n.* pūjānugāmī, *m.*

Rival, *n.* *a.* paṭimalla ; paṭipuggala ; yugaggāhī, *m.* *v.t.* vijigiŋsati ; yugaggāhī hoti ; samataŋ yāti. *p.p.* °sita ; °bhūta ; °yāta. °**ry,** °**ship,** *n.* vijigiŋsā, *f.* yugaggāha, *m.* paṭipuggalatta, *nt.*

Rive, *v.t.* vidāreti ; (vipāṭeti. *v.i.* vidārīyati ; phalati. *p.p.* **(Riven),** °rita ; °ṭita ; phalita.

River, *n.* nadī ; savantī ; gaṅgā ; saritā ; āpagā ; ninnagā, *f.* °**ain,** *a.* gaṅgāsanna ; gaṅgāyatta ; nadītīravāsī. — **bank,** *n.* nadīkūla ; nadītīra, *nt.* — **bed,** *n.* nadītala, *nt.* — **basin,** *n.* gaṅgādhāra, *m.* — **god,** *n.* nadīdevatā, *f.* — **head,** *n.* nadīpabhava, *m.* — **mouth,** *n.* nadīmukha, *nt.*

Rivet, *n.* ayomayabandhana, *nt.* *v.t.* lohakhīlena daḷhaŋ ghaṭeti. *p.p.* °ṭita.

Rivulet, *n.* kunnadī, *f.*

Road, *n.* magga ; pantha ; patha, addhā, *m.* añjasa; ayana; vaṭuma, *nt.* °**side,** *n.* maggapassa, *nt.* **High** —, mahāmagga, *m.*

Roam, *v.i.* pariyaṭati ; pariyāhiṇḍati ; anuvicarati. °**ing,** *n.* āhiṇḍana ; pariyaṭana, *nt.*

Roar, *n.* gajjana, thanita, *nt.* nāda ; unnāda, *m.* *v.i.t.* gajjati ; nadati ; thanayati. *p.p.* °jita ; nadita ; thanita. °**er,** *n.* gajjitu ; naditu, *m.* °**ing,** *n.* gajjanā, *f.* nāda, *m.* °**ing,** *a.* gajjamāna.

Roast, *v.t.* bhajjati. *p.p.* °jita. °**ing,** *n.* bhajjana, *nt.*

Rob, *v.t.* coreti ; theneti ; vilumpati. *p.p.* °rita ; °nita ; °pita. °**ber,** *n.* cora ; mosaka ; thena, *m.* °**bery,** *n.* coriya ; theyya, *nt.* corikā, *f.*

Robe, *n.* pārupaṇa ; cīvara, *nt.* *v.t.* paridahati ; pārupati ; nivāseti. *p.p.* °hita ; pāruta ; nivattha.

Roborant, *a.* balavaḍḍhaka.

Robot, *n.* yantamaya-purisa ; yantasadisapuggala, *m.*

Robust, *a.* niroga ; dehabalī. °**ness,** *n.* ārogya, *nt.*

Rock, *n.* 1. sela ; siluccaya ; pāsāṇa, *m.* 2. kampana, *nt.* *v.t.* dolāpayati ; kampeti. *v.i.* dolāyati ; calati. *p.p.* °yita ; °pita ; calita. —**crystal,** *n.* kācopala, *m.* °**er,** *n.* cālaka ; kampaka, *m.* °**iness,** *n.* pāsāṇabahulatta, *nt.* — **inscription,** *n.* pāsāṇalekhā, *f.*— **pool,** *n.* soṇḍī, *f.*— **salt,** *n.* sindhava, *m.* °**y,** *a.* pāsāṇabahula.

Rocket, *n.* aggibāṇa, *m.*

Rod, *n.* daṇḍa, *m.* yaṭṭhi, *f.*

Rodent, *a.* ḍaŋsaka, *n.* ḍaŋsakapāṇī, *m.*

Rodomontade, *n.* vikatthī, *m.* adj. vikatthanasīla. °**er,** vikatthī, *m.*

Roe, *n.* 1. migī ; harinī, *f.* 2. migavisesa, *m.* 3. macchaṇḍasaṅghāta, *m.* — **buck,** *n.* rohitamiga, *m.*

Rogue, *n.* khala ; dhutta ; saṭha, *m.* °**ry,** *n.* sāṭheyya ; ketava, *nt.* nikati, *f.* °**ish,** *a.* nekatika ; vañcaka.

Roi, *n.* rāja, *m.*

Roil, *v.t.* (telādiŋ) khobhetvā malinīkaroti.

Role, *n.* pāṭekka-kicca ; āyattakamma, *nt.*

Roll, *n.* 1. vaṭṭi ; vaṭṭikā ; 2. nāmāvali, *f.* *v.i.* parivattati ; paribbhamati ; āvaṭṭīyati. *v.t.* parivatteti ; paribbhameti ;

āvaṭṭeti. *p.p.* °tita; °bhanta; °ṭita; °mita. °**able**, *a.* āvaṭṭanīya. — **back**, paṭivatteti. °**er**, *n.* parivaṭṭaka; samīkaraṇayanta, *nt.* — **over**, vinivaṭṭeti.

Rollick, *n.* kīḷā, *f.* vinoda, *m.* *v.i.* sammodati; ramati. *p.p.* °dita; °rata. °**ing**, °**some**, *a.* vinodappiya; kīḷālola.

Romance, *n.* ākhyāyikā; kappitakathā, *f.* °**er**, *n.* 1. ākhyāyikāsampādaka, *m.* 2. musāvādī, *m.*

Romantic, *a.* 1. abbhuta; pakappita; 2. abbhutappiya.

Romp, *n.* 1. potaka-kīḷā, *f.* 2. kīḷāpiyadāraka, *m.* *v.i.* vacchakīḷaŋ kīḷati. °**y**, *a.* keḷipara.

Roof, *n.* chadana, *nt.* *v.t.* chādeti; chadanaŋ māpeti. *p.p.* °dita; māpita-chadana. °**less**, *a.* 1. vivattacchada; nicchadana; 2. anātha.

Rook, *n.* 1. kāka; vāyasa; 2. saṭha; vañcaka, *m.* *v.t.* sāṭheyyena (mūlaŋ) jināti. *p.p.* °jita. °**ery**, *n.* 1. vāyasanivāsa; 2. dīnagharasamūha; 3. lomasamacchāvāsa, *m.*

Room, *n.* 1. gabbha; ovaraka; 2. okāsa, *m.* °**y**, *a.* asambādha; visāla. °**iness**, *n.* asambādhatta; visālatta, *nt.* °**ily**, *adv.* asambādhatāya.

Roost, *n.* vāsayaṭṭhi, *f.* nilīyanaṭṭhāna, *nt.* *v.i.* vāsamupeti; nilīyati. *p.p.* °upeta; nilīna. °**er**, *n.* kukkuṭa, *m.*

Root, *n.* 1. mūla, *nt.* pāda, *m.* 2. hetu, *m.* kāraṇa; nidāna, *nt.* 3. (of a word:) pakatirūpa; dhāturūpa, *nt.* *v.t.* ropeti. *v.i.* mūlehi patiṭṭhāti; mūle vaḍḍheti. *p.p.* ropita; °ṭhita; vaḍḍhitamūla.

Rope, *n.* rajju; naddhi; nandi, *f.* yotta, *nt.* *v.t.* rajjuyā bandhati. — **dancer**, rajjunaṭaka, *m.* — **maker**, rajjukāraka, *m.* — **yarn**, *n.* rajjuvāka, *m.*

Rosary, *n.* japamālā; akkhamālā, *f.*

Rose, *n.* japākusuma, *nt.* sevantī, *f.* — **apple**, *n.* jambuphala, *nt.* °**ate**, *a.* pāṭalavaṇṇa.

Rosy, *a.* pāṭala; setaratta. °**iness**, *n.* pāṭalatta, *nt.* rattabhāva, *m.*

Rosette, japākusumasaṇṭhānavatthu, *nt.*

Roster, *n.* yuddhasenāsu kiccasūci, *f.*

Rostrum, *n.* kathikavedikā, *f.*

Rot, *n.* pūtibhāva, *m.* jīraṇa. *nt.* *v.i.* jīrati; pūtibhavati. *v.t.* jīrāpeti; pūtikaroti. *p.p.* jiṇṇa, °bhūta; °pita; °kata. °**ten**, *a.* pūtika. °**ten egg**, puccaṇḍa, *nt.*

Rotary, *a.* paribbhamaṇaka. — **machine**, muddāyantavisesa, *m.*

Rotate, *v.i.* paribbhamati, *v.t.* paribbhameti. *p.p.* °bhanta; °mita. °**ion**, *n.* paribbhamaṇa, *nt.* °**ive**, °**tory**, *a.* paribbhamanasīla; paribbhamaka.

Rote, *n.* kevala-paricaya, *m.* vācuggatakaraṇa, *nt.*

Rotter, *n.* niratthakapuggala, *m.*

Rotund, *a.* goḷākāra; maṇḍalākāra. °**ity**, *n.* goḷatta.

Rotunda, *n.* maṇḍalākāramandira, *nt.*

Rouge, *n.* kuṅkumacuṇṇa, *nt.* rattālepa, *m.*

Rough, *a.* 1. kakkasa; pharusa; khara; kaṭhina; 2. (in manners:) asiṭṭha; avinīta; 3. saṅkhubhita. *v.t.* kharaŋ *or* visamaŋ karoti. *adv.* pharusākārena; asampuṇṇatāya. — **and ready**, asammāsampādita; tāvakālika, *a.* — **and tumble**, 1. visama; uppaṭipāṭika, *a. n.* kalaha, *m.*—**cast**, kharālepa, *m.* — **diamond**, aporiya-sundarahadaya, *m.* °**ly**, *adv.* 1. pharusākārena; 2. avisesena. °**ness**, *n.* 1. kharattā; lūkhatta; 2. niṭṭhuriya, *nt.* — **neck**, *n.* caṇḍapuggala, *m.* — **rider**, *n.* assadamaka, *m.*

Roughen, *v.t.* kakkasaŋ karoti. *v.i.* kakkasībhavati. *p.p.* °sīkata; °bhūta.

Round, *n.* 1. maṇḍala, *nt.* āvaṭṭa, *m.* 2. vāra, *m.* adj. vaṭṭula; maṇḍalākāra; goḷākāra. *adv.* maṇḍalākārena. *prep.* abhito; parito; samantato. *v.t.* vaṭṭulaŋ *or* goḷākāraŋ karoti. *v.i.* vaṭṭulībhavati. *p.p.* vattulīkata; °bhūta.—**about**, *a.* paritogāmī. *n.* caccarāvaṭṭa, *m.* — **about talk**, pariyāyakathā, *f.* °**ish**, *a.* īsaŋvaṭṭula. °**ly**, *adv.* suparipuṇṇaŋ; ujukam eva. °**ness**, *n.* vaṭṭulatta, *nt.* — **off**, sammā niṭṭhāpeti. — **up**, parito yāti.

Rouse, *n.* 1. pānussava, *m.* 2. uṭṭhiṭṭhana; pabodhana; pabujjhana, *nt. v.t.* uṭṭhāpeti; pabodheti; uttejeti. *v.i.* pabujjhati; uṭṭhāti; vijambhati. *p.p.* °pita; °dhita; °jita; pabuddha; uṭṭhita; °bhita. °**ing**, *a.* pabodhaka; uttejaka.

Rout, *n.* 1. kalahakārīgumba, *m.* 2. viddhaŋsana, *nt.* vināsa, *m.* 3. janasammadda; 4. senābhaṅga, *m. v.t.* bhañjati; viddhaŋseti. *p.p.* bhaṭṭha; °sita.

Route, *n.* gamanamagga; patha, *m. v.t.* gamanamaggaŋ niyameti. **En°**, antarāmagge.

Routine, *n.* kiccapaṭipāṭi; kriyāpaddhati; niyamāvali; dinacariyā, *f.* °**ist**, *n.* kiccapaṭipāṭiyutta-puggala, *m.*

Rove, see **Roam**.

Rover, *n.* 1. pariyāhiṇḍaka; 2. samuddacora, *m.*

Row, *n.* 1. rāji; āvali; pāḷi; panti; seṇī, *f.* 2. kalaha, *m. v.t.* 1. nāvaŋ pājeti; keṇiŋ pāteti; 2. kalahaŋ karoti. *p.p.* pājitanāva; pātitakeṇī; katakaḷaha. °**er**, *n.* 1. nāvika; keṇipātī; 2. kalahakārī, *m.*

Rowdy, *a. n.* kalahakārī; kalahappiya. °**ism**, *n.* kalahakāritā, *f.*

Royal, *a.* rājakīya; rājāyatta; rājāraha. — **bed**, sirisayana, *nt.* — **bed-room**, sirigabbha, *m.* — **chariot**, rājaratha, *m.* — **concubine**, rājorodha, *m.* — **gift**, *n.* rājadāya, *m.* — **harem**, rājantepura, *nt.* °**ism**, rājabhatti; rājapakkhikatā, *f.* °**ist**, *n.* rājabhattika, *m.* °**ly**, *adv.* rājārahatāya. — **pond**, maṅgalapokkharaṇī, *f.* — **power**, rājiddhi, *f.* rājabala, *nt.* rājānubhāva, *m.* — **seal**, rājamuddā.

Royalty, *n.* 1. rājatta, *nt.* 2. rājavaŋsika, *m.* 3. rājakula, *nt.* 4. rājabali, *m.* 5. ganthakattulābhaŋsa, *m.*

Rub, *n.* ghaŋsana; ucchādana, *nt. v.t.* parimaddati; sambāheti; ubbaṭṭeti; (in bathing:) ucchādeti. *p.p.* °dita; °hita; °ṭita; °dita. °**ber**, *n.* 1. ghaŋsaka; parimajjaka, *m.* 2. (substance:) 1. puñchakavatthu, *nt.* 2. niyyāsavisesa, *m. v.t.* niyyāsena āvarati. *p.p.* °āvuta.

Rubbish, *n.* kacavara; kasambu; saṅkāra, *m.* — **heap**, saṅkārakūṭa, *nt.* °**y**, *a.* asāra; tuccha.

Rubble, *n.* khaṇḍita-pāsāṇa; asmakhaṇḍarāsi, *m.*

Rubefy, Rubify, *v.t.* rattavaṇṇaŋ karoti. *p.p.* °ṇīkata. °**faction**, *n.* rattavaṇṇāpādana, *nt.*

Rubicelle, *n.* padumarāgamaṇi, *m.*

Rubicund, *a.* lohitavaṇṇa. °**ity**, *n.* rattavaṇṇatā, *f.*

Rubric, *n.* visesita-mātikāpāṭha, *m.* °**ate**, *v.t.* rattavaṇṇena aṅketi. °**ation**, *n.* rattavaṇṇaṅkana, *nt.*

Ruby, *n.* lohitaṅka; rattamaṇi, *m.* adj. rattavaṇṇī. *v.t.* rattavaṇṇīkaroti. *p.p.* °kata. °**ious**, *a.* lohitaṅkavaṇṇa.

Ruck, *n.* 1. vali, *f.* 2. samudāya; sañcaya, *m.* — **sack**, *n.* piṭṭhipasibbaka, *m.*

Ruckle, *n.* maraṇāsannassa galanāda, *m. v.i.* ghurughurāyati.

Ruction, *n.* kalakala, *m.*

Rudder, *n.* kenipāta, *m.* kaṇṇa, *nt.*

Ruddy, *a.* aruṇavaṇṇa; rattavaṇṇa. *v.t.* rattaŋ karoti. — **goose**, cakkavāka, *m.*

Rude, *a.* 1. avinīta; asabbha; 2. anipuṇa; adakkha. °**ly**, *adv.* 1. avinītākārena; 2. visamākārena. °**ness**, *n.* 1. avinītatta; 2. kakkasatta, *nt.*

Rudiment, *n.* mūlavatthu; mūlikaṅga, *nt.* mūlikasikkhā, *f.* °**al**, °**tary**, *a.* mūlikabhūta.

Rue, *n.* anutāpa; upāyāsa, *m. v.t.* anutappati; anusocati. °**ful**, *a.* sokātura. °**fully**, *adv.* sasokaŋ.

Ruffian, *n.* sāhasika; kakkhaḷa; duṭṭhapakatika, *m.* °**age**, °**ism**, *n.* caṇḍikka; kurūrakamma, *nt.* °**ly**, *a.* caṇḍapakatika.

Ruffle, *n.* 1. saṅkoca, *m.* ākuñcana, *nt.* 2. kuñcitadasā, *f.* 3. saṅkhobha, *m. v.t.* 1. saṅkoceti; ākuñceti; 2. saṅkhobheti; vikopeti. *p.p.* °cita; °bhita; °pita.

Rug, *n.* ghanattharaṇa, *nt.* santhara, *m.*

Rugged, *a.* visama; kakkasa; pāsāṇākiṇṇa. — **land**, jaṅgaladesa, *m.* °**ly**, *adv.* visamākārena. °**ness**, *n.* vesamma; kakkasatta, *nt.*

Ruin, *n.* 1. nāsa; vināsa, *m.* 2. vyasana, *nt.* parihāni. *f. v.t.* vināseti; viddhaŋseti; ucchindati. *p.p.* °sita; ucchinna. °**ation**, *n.* viddhaŋsana, *nt.* °**ous**, *a.* vināsakara; viddhaŋsaka. °**ously**, *adv.* nāsakaratāya.

Ruins, *n. pl.* naṭṭhāvasiṭṭhavatthūni, *nt.*

Rule, *n.* 1. nīti; paññatti, *f.* niyama, *m.* 2. pālana; sāsana, *nt.* 3. pabhutta; ādhipacca, *nt.* 4. lekhādaṇḍa, *m.* *v.t.* 1. sāsati; pāleti; 2. niyameti; āṇāpeti; 3. ujurekhāhi aṅketi. *p.p.* sāsita; pālita; °mita; °pita; °kita. °**er,** *n.* 1. pālaka; sāsitu; 2. ujurekhaka, *m.* °**ing,** *a.* 1. pālayamāna; 2. pavattamāna. °**ing,** *n.* nicchaya; niṇṇaya, *m.*

Rum, *n.* meraya, *nt.*

Rum, Rummy, *a.* 1. vikaṭa; virūpa; 2. bhayānaka.

Rumble, *v.i.* sanikaŋ gajjati. *p.p.* °jita. °**ing,** *n.* mandagajjanā, *f.* thanita, *nt.*

Rumbustious, *a.* ghosanasīla; ugghosaka.

Ruminant, *a. n.* romanthaka, *m.*

Ruminate, *v.t.i.* 1. romanthati; 2. anuvitakketi. *p.p.* °thita; °kita. °**ion,** *n.* 1. romanthana; 2. jhāyana, *nt.* °**tor,** *n.* 1. romanthī; 2. jhāyī, *m.*

Rummage, *n.* suṭṭhuparikkhanā, *f.* *v.t.* suṭṭhu upaparikkhati. *p.p.* °khita.

Rumour, *n.* janappavāda; vuttanta, *m.* pavatti, *f.*

Rump, *n.* nisadamaŋsa, *nt.*

Rumpus, *n.* kalaha, *m.* ugghosana, *nt.*

Run, *n.* 1. dhāvana, javana, *nt.* 2. gati; pavatti, *f.* *v.i.t.* 1. dhāvati; sandhāvati; javati; 2. sandati; savati. — **about,** paridhāvati. — **after,** anudhāvati. — **against,** abhidhāvati. — **away,** palāyati. — **back to,** paṭidhāvati. — **forth,** padhāvati. — **into,** āpajjati. °**ner,** *n.* dhāvaka; javamāna. °**ning,** *n.* dhāvana, *nt.* °**ning up,** ujjavanta, *a.* — **off,** apadhāvati. — **out,** khīyati. — **over,** ottharati. — **round,** anuparidhāvati. — **towards,** ādhāvati. — **up to,** upadhāvati.

Runagate, *n.* vaṇibbaka, *m.*

Rung, *n.* sopāṇaphalaka, *nt.*

Runnel, Runlet, *n.* kunnadī; mātikā, *f.*

Runner, *n.* 1. dhāvaka; sandesahara, *m.* 2. pavattāpaka; 3. daṇḍāropita-valaya, *m.*

Rupee, *n.* rūpiya, *nt.*

Rupture, *n.* 1. bheda, *m.* phulla, *nt.* 2. antavuddhi. *v.t.* bhañjati; vidāḷeti. *v.i.* bhijjati; vidārīyati. *p.p.* °jita; °ḷita; bhaṭṭha; °rita.

Rural, *a.* gāmika; jānapadika. °**ism,** °**ity,** *n.* paccantavohāra, *m.* paccantavāsitā, *f.* °**ist,** *n.* paccantavāsī, *m.* °**ize,** *v.i.* paccantavāsaŋ gaṇhāti; *v.t.* paccantavohāraŋ pāpeti. *p.p.* gahita°; pāpita°.

Ruse, *n.* upāya; kūṭopāya, *m.* adj. nekatika.

Rush, *n.* 1. pakkhandana, *nt.* abhinipāta, *m.* 2. kilañjatiṇa, *nt.* *v.t.i.* pakkhandati; sahasā pavisati. *p.p.* °dita; °paviṭṭha. °**light,** *n.* ukkāloka; mandāloka, *m.* — **of a crowd,** janasammadda, *m.* — **on,** abhinipatati.

Rust, *n.* lohamala, *nt.* *v.i.* malaŋ gaṇhāti. *p.p.* malaggahita. °**eaten,** *a.* malāvuta; malakhādita. °y, *a.* malayutta ; malacchanna. °iness, *n.* malaggahitabhāva, *m.*

Rustic, *n. a.* jānapadika, *m.*

Rusticate, *v.i.* janapade vasati. *v.t.* 1. daṇḍanavasena (vijjālayato) nikkhāmeti ; 2. kharalepaŋ yojeti. *p.p.* °mita ; °yojita.

Rustle, *n.* saṭasaṭāyana, *nt. v.i.* saṭasaṭāyati. *p.p.* °yita.

Rut, *n.* 1. cakkapatha, *m.* 2. madajala, *nt.* migamada, *m. v.t.* cakkacchinnaŋ karoti. *v.i.* rāgaratto hoti. *p.p.* °kata ; rāgaratta. **°ted; °ish,** *a.* madamatta. **°ty,** *a.* cakkacchinna.

Ruth, *n.* dayā ; anukampā, *f.* **°less,** *a.* niddaya. **°lessly,** *adv.* niddayākārena.

Rye, *n.* dhaññavisesa, *m.*

Ryot, *n.* kassaka ; khettājīva, *m.*

S

Sabbath, *n.* uposatha ; vissamanadivasa, *m.* **°tic,** *a.* uposathāyatta. **°tize,** *v.i.* uposatham upavasati. *p.p.* upavutthuposatha.

Sable, *n.* himanakula, *m.* adj. kāḷa ; kaṇha ; mecaka.

Sabot, *n.* kaṭṭhapādukā, *f.*

Sabotage, *n.* hānikarakriyā.

Sabre, *n.* nettiŋsa, *m.*

Sabreur, *n.* khaggadhara-assāroha, *m.*

Sabulous, *a.* vālukābahula.

Sac, *n.* pasibbakākāra-maŋsapesi, *f.* **°ciform,** *a.* pasibbakākāra.

Saccharine, *n.* aṅgārika-sakkharā, *f.* adj. madhura.

Sacerdocy, °dotage, *n.* sāmayikapūjāvidhi, *m.*

Sacerdotal, *a.* samaṇāyatta.

Sack, *n.* 1. pasibbaka, *m.* sāṇapuṭolī, *f.* 2. vilumpana ; acchindana, *nt. v.t.* 1. vilumpati ; gāmaghātaŋ karoti ; 2. pasibbake pakkhipati ; 3. adhikārā cāveti. *p.p.* vilutta ; kata °ta ; °pakkhitta ; °vita. **°age,** *n.* gāmaghāta, *m.* **— cloth,** *n.* sāṇavattha, *nt.* **°ful,** *n.* pasibbakapūraṇappamāṇa, *nt.* **°less,** *a.* ahiŋsaka ; niraparādha.

Sacrament, *n.* sāmayika-pārisuddhi, *f.* parittāṇa, *nt.* **°al,** *a.* parittāṇāyatta.

Sacred, *a.* mahanīya ; pūjanīya ; parisuddha. **°ly,** *adv.* pujjākārena. **°ness,** *n.* mahanīyatta, *nt.* **— place, — spot,** *n.* puññatittha ; pujjaṭṭhāna, *nt.* **— writing,** *n.* dhammalipi, *f.*

Sacrifice, *n.* yāga ; yañña, *m.* āhuti, *f.* juhana, *nt. v.t.* 1. yajati ; havati ; 2. pariccajati. *p.p.* yiṭṭha ; huta ; °ccatta. **°er,** *n.* yajitu ; yājaka, *m.*

Sacrificial, *a.* yāgāyatta. **— grass,** kusa, *m.* barihisa, *nt.* **— ladle,** sujā, *f.* **— pit,** yaññāvāṭa, *m.* **— post,** yūpa, *m.* thūṇā, *f.*

Sacrilege, *n.* pujjaṭṭhānadūsana, *nt.* **°ist,** *n.* suddhaṭṭhānadūsaka, *m.*

Sacrosanct, *a.* anatikkamiya; avajjha; abādhiya. °**ity,** *n.* atisuddhatta, *nt.*

Sad, *a.* 1. dummana; dukkhita; appatīta; sokaṭṭa; 2. socanīya; dukkhāvaha. °**den,** *v.t.* khedeti; sokaṭṭaŋ karoti. *p.p.* °dita; °kata. °**ly,** *adv.* sakhedaŋ; sasokaŋ. °**ness,** *n.* domanassa, *nt.* soka; visāda; ubbega, *m.*

Saddle, *n.* assakacchā, *f.* *v.t.* kacchaŋ yojeti. *p.p.* yojitakaccha.

Safe, *n.* lohapeḷā, *f.* adj. khema; siva; abhaya. — **conduct,** 1. abhayasāsana, *nt.* 2. gamanārakkhā, *f.* — **from every quarter,** akutobhaya, *a.* — **guard,** *n.* gutti; ārakkhā, *f.* *v.t.* paripāleti. °**ly,** *adv.* nirupaddavākārena. °**ty,** *n.* gutti; ārakkhā, *f.* khema, *nt.*

Safflower, *n.* kusumbha, *m.*

Saffron, *n.* kuṅkuma, *nt.* adj. kuṅkumavaṇṇa; aruṇavaṇṇa; *v.t.* kuṅkumavaṇṇena rañjeti. *p.p.* °jita; kuṅkumaratta.

Sag, *v.i.* bhārena onamati *or* olambati. *p.p.* °onata; °bita.

Sagacious, *a.* catura; tikhiṇapaṭibhāṇa; vicakkhaṇa. °**ly,** *adv.* sunipuṇaŋ; sukhumabuddhiyā. °**city,** *n.* cāturiya; buddhisokhumma, *nt.*

Sage, *n. a.* mahāpañña; mahesi, *m.* °**ly,** *adv.* mahāpaññatāya; bāhusaccena. °**ness,** *n.* paṇḍicca; bāhusacca, *nt.*

Sagittarius, *n.* dhanurāsi, *m.*

Sago, *n.* tālapiṭṭhavisesa, *m.*

Sail, *n.* lakāra. *v.i.* udake javati. *v.t.* udakaŋ tarati; nāvāya yāti. *p.p.* °javita; tiṇṇodaka; °yāta. °**er,** *n.* nāvā, *f.* °**or,** *n.* nāvika, *m.* — **downstream,** ojavati. — **upstream,** ujjavati.

Saint, *n.* arahanta; khīṇāsava; visuddhapuggala, *m.* °**hood,** visuddhatta; arahatta, *nt.* °**ly,** *a.* viraja; nikkilesa; vūpasanta.

Sake, *n.* nimitta; kāraṇa, *nt.* hetu, *m.* **For the — of,** atthāya.

Sal, *n.* sāla; assakaṇṇa, *m.* — **grove,** *n.* sālavana, *nt.*

Salaam, *n.* sādarācara, *m.* *v.i.t.* 1. sādarācāraŋ pavatteti; 2. sīsena paṇamati. *p.p.* °titasā°; °mita.

Salacious, *a.* kāmuka; kāmāsatta. °**city,** *n.* kāmukatta, *nt.* °**ly,** *adv.* kāmukatāya.

Salad, *n.* sālava, *m.* āmakasākavyañjana, *nt.*

Salamander, *n.* 1. aggijīvī; 2. tejosahaka; 3. jalagodhāvisesa, *m.*

Salary, *n.* māsikavetana. *v.t.* vetanaŋ deti. *p.p.* dinnavetana.

Sale, *n.* vikkaya, *m.* °**able,** *a.* vikkeyya; vikkiṇeyya. — **price,** vikkeyyamūla, *nt.* °**sman,** *n.* vikketu; vikkayika, *m.*

Salient, *a.* 1. mukhya; padhāna; 2. plavaṅgama; 3. phandamāna; °**ence,** °**ency,** *n.* 1. mukhyatta; 2. phandamānatta, *nt.*

Saliferous, *a.* khārabahula.

Saline, *n.* khārodakubbhida, *m.* adj. khārika; loṇika; ūsara. °**ity,** *n.* khāratta; ūsaratta, *nt.*

Salinometer, *n.* khāramāṇakayanta, *nt.*

Saliva, *n.* lālā; eḷā, *f.* khela, *m.* °**nt**, *a.* lālājanaka.

Salivate, *v.t.* lālaŋ janeti *or* paggharāpeti. *p.p.* janitalāla; °pita. °**ion**, *n.* lālāpaggharāpana, *nt.*

Sallow, *a.* paṇḍuvaṇṇa. °**ness**, *n.* paṇḍuvaṇṇatā, *f.*

Sally, *n.* 1. sahasā pakkhandana, *nt.* 2. nammālāpa, *m.* *v.i.* pakkhandati; sahasā niggacchati. *p.p.* pakkhanta; °niggata.

Saloon, *n.* sālā, *f.* mahāgabbha, *m.*

Salt, *n.* lavaṇa, loṇa, *nt.* *v.t.* loṇaŋ yojeti; loṇena saŋyojeti. adj. loṇika; khārayutta. °**ed fish**, loṇamaccha, *m.* °**ern**, *n.* loṇasampādakaṭṭhāna, *nt.* °**ish**, *a.* īsaŋloṇika. °**less**, *a.* aloṇaka. — **maker**, loṇakāra, *m.* — **pan**, *n.* loṇī, *f.* loṇākara, *m.* °**petre**, *n.* yavakhāraloṇa, *nt.* — **water**, khārodaka, *nt.* °**y**, *a.* loṇayutta.

Saltant, *a.* uppatanaka; laṅghamāna. °**tation**, *n.* naccana; uppatana, *nt.*

Salubrious, *a.* sappāya; sukhadāyaka; arogakara. °**ly**, *adv.* sappāyākārena. °**rity**, *n.* sappāyatā; sukhadāyakatā, *f.*

Salutary, *a.* hitakara; atthāvaha; sukhadāyī.

Salute, *n.* sādarācāra; paṇāma, *m.* *v.t.* garukaroti; sādarācāraŋ pavatteti; sādarena paṭiggaṇhāti. *p.p.* °kata; °titasā°ra; °gahita. °**ation**, *n.* sādarācāra, *m.* garukaraṇa, *nt.* paṇāma, *m.* °**atory**, *a.* ācārasīlī; sammodaka; sagārava.

Salvage, *n.* 1. vināsato uddharaṇa, *nt.* 2. naṭṭhanāvāto uddhaṭabhaṇḍa, *nt.* 3. bhaṇḍarakkhaṇasuṅka, *m.*

Salvation, *n.* 1. mokkha, *m.* mutti, *f.* niyyāna, *nt.* 2. samuddharaṇa; saŋrakkhaṇa, *nt.*

Salve, *n.* vilepana; añjana, *nt.* *v.t.* 1. añjati; 2. vināsato moceti. *p.p.* añjita; °cita.

Salver, *n.* lohataṭṭaka, *nt.*

Salvo, *n.* gāravācāra-thanita, *nt.*

Samaritan, *n.* cāgasīlīpuggala, *m.* adj. Samariyadesīya.

Same, *a.* anañña; nibbisesa; samāna; abhinna. °**ness**, anaññatta; ahinnatta, *nt.*

Sample, *n.* paṭirūpa, *nt.* ākati, *f.* samānavatthu, *nt.* *v.t.* ākatiŋ deti *or* gaṇhāti. *p.p.* dinnākatika; gahitākatika. °**er**, *n.* ākatidassakavatthu, *nt.*

Sanative, Sanatory, *a.* ātaṅkahārī; sappāyabhūta. °**torium**, *n.* sappāyasālā, *f.* sukhavaḍḍhakaṭṭhāna, *nt.*

Sanctify, *v.t.* pavittīkaroti; suddhattaŋ pāpeti. *p.p.* °kata; °pāpita. °**ication**, *n.* visodhana; pāpanāsana, *nt.* °**ing**, *a.* visodhaka.

Sanctimony, *n.* kohañña, *nt.* °**ious**, *a.* kuhakavuttika. °**iously**, *adv.* kohaññena, kuhakatāya.

Sanction, *n.* anumati; anuññā, *f.* *v.t.* anujānāti; anumaññati. *p.p.* anuññāta; anumata.

Sanctitude, Sanctity, *n.* visuddhi, *f.* nimmalatta, *nt.*

Sanctuary, *n.* 1. puññabhūmi, *f.* pujjaṭṭhāna, *nt.* 2. abhayaṭṭhāna, *nt.*

Sanctum, *n.* 1. suddhaṭṭhāna; 2. vivittaṭṭhāna, *nt.*

Sand, *n.* pulina, *nt.* vālikā; vālukā; sikatā; vaṇṇu, *f.* *v.t.* vālikaŋ okirati. *p.p.* valikokiṇṇa. — **bed,** *n.* vālukātala, *nt.* — **dune,** *n.* vātāgatavālukārāsi, *m.* — **flea,** *n.* uppātakapāṇī, *m.* — **glass,** *n.* pulinaghaṭikā, *f.* °**iness,** *n.* sikatābahulatta, *nt.* — **storm,** *n.* pulinavassa, *nt.* °**y,** *a.* pulinabahula; valukāmaya. °**y track,** vaṇṇupatha, *m.* °**y waste,** marukantāra, *m.*

Sandal, *n.* 1. (wood:) candana, *nt.* gandhasāra, *m.* 2. (footware:) upāhana, *m.* *nt.* pādukā, *f.*

Sandwich, *n.* antarita-khādanīya, *nt.* *v.t.* antare pakkhipati. *p.p.* °khitta.

Sane, *a.* 1. pakaticitta; anummatta; 2. nirāmaya. °**ness,** °**ity,** *n.* 1. pakaticittatā, 2. nirāmayatā, f.

Sangfroid, *n.* akampyatā; dhiti, *f.*

Sanguify, *v.t.* rudhirattaŋ pāpeti. *p.p.* °pita. °**ication,** *n.* rudhirattapāpana; rudhirajanana, *nt.*

Sanguine, *a.* 1. lohitavaṇṇa; 2. dhitimantu; 3. sundarattāpekkhī. °**ary,** *a.* lohitapāṇī; niṭṭhuracitta. °**ly,** *adv.* sāpekkhaŋ; sākaṅkhaŋ. °**ous,** *a.* rudhirādhika; rattavaṇṇa. °**ivorous,** *a.* lohitabhakkha.

Sanify, *v.t.* ārogyaŋ vaḍḍheti. *p.p.* °ḍhitārogya.

Sanitary, *a.* ārogyakara. °**ily,** *adv.* rogaharaṇākārena. °**iness,** *n.* ārogyakaratta, *nt.*

Sanitation, *n.* rogāvaraṇa; ārogyarakkhaṇa, *nt.*

Sap, *n.* ojā, *f.* yūsa; rasa; sāra, *m.* *v.t.* 1. yūsam apaharati; 2. viriyaŋ khepeti; 3. ummaggaŋ khaṇati; 4. mūlaŋ khaṇati, *v.i.* sāyāsaŋ uggaṇhāti. *p.p.* apahaṭayūsa; °pitaviriya; khatummagga; khatamūla; °uggahita. °**ful,** *a.* ojavantu. °**less,** *a.* ojārahita. °**ling,** *n.* rukkhapotaka, *m.*

Sapan-wood, *n.* pattaṅgadāru, *nt.*

Sapid, *a.* madhuroja; sādurasa. °**ity,** *n.* madhrojatta, *nt.*

Sapient, *a.* paṇḍitamānī. °**nce,** *n.* paṇḍitamāna, *m.* °**ly,** *adv.* paṇḍitamānitāya.

Sapodilla, *n.* sakkharāphala, *nt.*

Sapphire, *n.* indanīla, *m.* °**ine,** *a.* nīlamaṇisadisa.

Sarcasm, *n.* omasavāda, *m.*

Sarcast, *n.* omasavādī, *m.* °**ic,** *a.* omasavādī; omasaka. °**ically,** *adv.* omasanākārena; sopārambhaŋ.

Sarcology, *n.* maŋsavijjā, *f.*

Sarcoma, *n.* maŋsagaṇṭhi, *m.*

Sarcophagus, *n.* silāmaya-chavādhāna, *nt.*

Sardonic, *a.* niggahasūcaka; sopārambha. °**ally,** *adv.* upahāsapubbakaŋ.

Sarsaparilla, *n.* sāribālatā, *f.*

Sartorial, *a.* tunnakammāyatta.

Sash, *n.* kaṭibandhana; kaṭisutta, *nt.*

Satan, *n.* pāpimantu; Māra, *m.* °**ic,** *a.* pāpiṭṭha; Mārāyatta. °**ism,** *n.* atiluddatta; kakkhalatta, *nt.*

Satchel, *n.* (dārakānaŋ) potthaka-pasibbaka, *m.*

Sate, *v.t.* santappeti. *p.p.* °pita.

Satellite, *n.* 1. upagaha; 2. anucara; anuyāyī, *m.*

Satiate, *v.t.* pīṇeti; santappeti. *p.p.* pīṇita; °pita. adj. santappita; titta; tittippatta. °**ion, Satiety,** *n.* titti, *f.* pīṇitabhāva, *m.* °**ed,** *a.* suhita; dhāta.

Satin, *n.* Cīnapaṭṭa, *nt.* *v.t.* siniddhaŋ karoti. °**y,** *a.* atisiniddha.

Satire, *n.* upārambha-gabbhakapabandha, *m.* °**ical,** *a.* ākkhepapubbaka. °**ist,** ākkhepavādī, *m.* °**ize,** *v.t.* ākkhepayuttaŋ likhati.

Satisfy, *v.t.* 1. santappeti; sampīṇeti; toseti; 2. saŋsayam apaneti. *v.i.* santussati. *p.p.* °pita; °ṇita; tosita; apanītasaŋsaya; santuṭṭha. °**faction,** *n.* 1. tuṭṭhi; titti; abhirati, *f.* assāda, *m.* 2. kaṅkhāvinodana, *nt.* °**factory,** *a.* 1. samattha; pariyatta; tittikara; 2. kaṅkhānuda. °**iable,** *a.* sukhasantappiya. °**ied,** *a.* nicchāta; abhiraddha; santuṭṭha. °**ing,** *a.* 1. santappaka; 2. saŋsayacchedaka. °**ier,** *n.* santappetu, *m.*

Satrap, *n.* maṇḍalissara, *m.* °**y,** *n.* rajjamaṇḍala, *nt.*

Saturate, *v.t.* accantaŋ pūreti *or* sedeti; suṭṭhu temeti. *p.p.* °rita; °mita. °**ion,** *n.* 1. suṭṭhutemana; 2. atipūraṇa, *nt.*

Saturday, *n.* Sanivāra, *m.*

Saturn, *n.* ravisuta, *m.* °**ian,** *a.* ravisutāyatta, *n.* ravisutalokavāsī, *m.*

Saturnine, *a.* dandha; manda; nirīha.

Satyr, *n.* 1. ajarūpadevatā, *f.* 2. kāmukapuggala, *m.* °**iasis,** *n.* kāmamucchā, *f.*

Sauce, *n.* 1. (yūsabahula-) vyañjana, *nt.* 2. avinītatta; pāgabbhiya, *nt.* *v.t.* 1. rasakena yojeti; 2. pāgabbhiyena vattati. °**less,** *a.* yūsavirahita. °**pan,** *n.* rasakathālī, *f.*

Saucer, *n.* rasakādhāra; sarāva, *m.*

Saucy, *a.* avinīta; nillajja. °**ily,** *adv.* avinītākārena. °**iness,** *n.* nillajjatā, *f.*

Saunter, *n.* mantharagamana, *nt.* *v.i.* vilambanto yāti.

Sausage, *n.* maŋsavaṭṭikāvisesa, *m.*

Savage, *n.* 1. vanacārī; asiṭṭhajana, *m.* 2. kakkhalakamma, *nt.* adj. 1. vanacara; asiṭṭhācāra; 2. vāḷa; dāruṇa. °**ly,** *adv.* asiṭṭhākārena; kakkhalatāya. °**ness,** *n.* asiṭṭhatta; dāruṇatta, *nt.* °**ry,** *n.* dāruṇakamma, *nt.*

Savant, *n.* bahussuta; mahāpañña.

Save, *v.t.* pamoceti; ulḷumpati; uttāreti; samuddharati. *p.p.* °cita; °pita; °rita; samuddhaṭa. *v.i.* dhanaŋ samāharati *or* saŋrakkhati. *p.p.* samāhaṭadhana. *prep.* vihāya; vajjetvā; muñcitvā. °**er**, *n.* tāyaka; pamocaka, *m.* °**ing**, *n.* rakkhitadhana, *nt.* °**ing**, *a.* saŋrakkhaka. °**ingly**, *adv.* mitabbayena.

Saviour, *n.* pamocaka; santāraka; mokkhadāyaka, *m.*

Savour, *n.* 1. assāda; sādurasa, *m.* 2. sugandha, *m.* °**iness**, *n.* surasatta; sugandhatta, *nt.* °**less**, *a.* nirasa; niggandha. °**y**, *a.* surasa; rucikara.

Saw, *n.* kakaca, *m.* *v.t.* kakacena chindati. *p.p.* °chinna. °**dust**, *n.* kakacacuṇṇa, *nt.* °**pit**, okantanāvāṭa, *m.* °**yer**, *n.* kantaka; kakacagāhī, *m.* °**teeth**, kakacadanta, *m.*

Say, *v.t.* vadati; bhāsati; katheti; udīreti; brūti. *p.p.* vutta; °sita; °thita; °rita. °**ing**, *n.* bhāsana; kathana; vacana; vākya, *nt.* utti; vācā; kathā, *f.* **Popular** °**ing**, janappavāda, *m.*

Scab, *n.* 1. vaṇakapāla; 2. kacchuvisesa, *m.* 3. adhamajana, *m.* °**by**, *a.* kacchuyutta. °**ies**, *n.* vitacchikā, *f.*

Scabbard, *n.* (khaggādi-) kosa, *m.* kosī, *f.*

Scabrous, *a.* kaṭhinasabhāva.

Scaffold, *n.* vadhavedikā, *f.* āghātana, *nt.* *v.t.* aṭṭakaŋ yojeti. °**ing**, *n.* aṭṭaka, *nt.*

Scald, *n.* uṇhena daḍḍhaṭṭhāna, *nt.* *v.t.* uṇhena dahati; tattavatthunā jhāpeti. *p.p.* uṇhadaḍḍha; °pita. °**ing**, *a.* atitatta. °**head**, *n.* sīsacammaroga, *m.*

Scale, *n.* 1. macchasakalikā, *f.* 2. tulāvaṭṭa, *m.* māṇayanta, *nt.* 3. nisseṇī; adhirohinī, *f.* 4. aṅkita-parimāṇa, *nt.* *v.t.* 1. tuleti; miṇāti; 2. sakalikā apaneti; 3. (nisseṇim) āruhati. *p.p.* tulita; mita; apanīta°; °ārūḷha. °**iness**, *n.* sakalikābahulatta, *nt.*

Scallop, *n.* kapālapiṭṭhika, *m.*

Scallywag, Scalawag, *n.* virūpanīcapuggala, *m.*

Scalp, *n.* 1. sīsamuddhā, *m.* 2. sīsacamma, *nt.* *v.t.* sīsacammaŋ uppāṭeti. *p.p.* °ṭitasīsacamma.

Scamp, *n.* dhutta; saṭha, *m.* *v.t.* asādhukaŋ kammaŋ karoti.

Scamper, *n.* sīghapalāyana, *nt.* *v.i.* bhīto dhāvati.

Scan, *v.t.i.* 1. sukhumaŋ nirikkhati; 2. (in verses:) mattā gaṇeti. *p.p.* °khita; °gaṇitamatta. °**sion**, *n.* mattāgaṇana; patthārakaraṇa, *nt.* °**ning**, *n.* pajjaracanā, *f.* chandovibhāga, *m.*

Scandal, *n.* dūsana, *nt.* kalaṅka; apavāda, *m.* *v.t.* abhūtena abbhācikkhati. *p.p.* °khita. °**monger**, *n.* abhūtabbhakkhāyī, *m.* °**ous**, *a.* 1. akittikara; guṇanāsaka; 2. garahita; jegucchā.

Scandalize, *v.t.* durācārena dummanaŋ karoti; abbhācikkhati. *p.p.* °manīkata; °khita.

Scandent, *a.* (latā viya) āruhanasabhāva.

Scansorial, *a.* (nakhehi) āruhaṇasīla.

Scant, °**ty**, *a.* virala; appaka; dullabha. °**ily**, *adv.* viralākārena. °**iness**, *n.* viralatta, *nt.*

Scantling, *n.* see **Sample.**

Scape, *n.* vaṇṭa, *nt.* °**goat,** *n.* parapāpavāhī (-aja), *m.* °**grace,** *n.* moghapurisa, *m.*

Scapula, *n.* aŋsakūṭa, *m.* °**lar,** *a.* aŋsakūṭāyatta.

Scar, *n.* 1. vanaciṇha ; āhatalañchana, *nt.* 2. pabbatapapāta, *m.* *v.t.* lakkhaṇāhataŋ karoti ; kalaṅkayati. *p.p.* °kata ; °yita.

Scaramouch, *n.* vikatthī ; attasilāghī, *m.*

Scarce, *a.* virala ; dullabha. °**ly,** adj. kicchena ; kasirena. °**ity,** °**ness,** *n.* viralatta ; dullabhatta, *nt.*

Scare, *v.t.* uttāseti ; santāseti. *n.* bhayahetu, *m.* °**crow,** *n.* tiṇapurisa, *m.*

Scarf, *n.* uttarīya, *nt.*

Scarify, *v.t.* lohitaharaṇatthaŋ vijjhati. *p.p.* °viddha.

Scarlet, lohitavaṇṇa.

Scathe, *n.* hāni, *f.* upaddava, *m.* *v.t.* balavahāniŋ pāpeti ; upaddaveti. *p.p.* °pāpita; upadduta °**less,** *a.* akkhata ; anupahata.

Scatter, *v.t.* ākirati ; vikirati ; vippakirati ; viyūheti. *p.p.* ākiṇṇa; vikiṇṇa ; °hita. — **about,** pakirati. °**ing,** *n.* vikiraṇa ; viyūhana, *nt.* °**over,** abbhukkirati.

Scavenge, *v.t.* kacavaraŋ sodheti. °**er,** *n.* kacavarasodhaka ; pupphachaḍḍaka ; pukkusa ; vīthisodhaka, *m.*

Scene, *n.* 1. ṭhāna, *nt.* padesa, *m.* 2. raṅgajavanikā, *f.* 3. naccavibhāga, *m.* 4. diṭṭhipatha, *m.* °**ry,** *n.* desavilāsa, *m.* °**ic,** °**ical,** *a.* 1. raṅganissita ; 2. desadassanassita.

Scenography, *n.* dūradassakacittakamma, *nt.*

Scent, *n.* 1. sugandha ; gandhasāra ; parimala, *m.* *v.t.* 1. parivāseti ; gandhena bhāveti ; 2. ghāyati. *p.p.* °sita ; °vita ; °yita. °**ed powder,** vāsacuṇṇa, *nt.* °**less,** *a.* niggandha. — **organ,** ghāṇindriya, *nt.*

Sceptic, *a.* *n.* kaṅkhī ; natthikadiṭṭhī, *m.* °**ism,** *n.* natthikavāda, *m.*

Sceptre, *n.* rājayaṭṭhi, *f.* jayakunta, *m.* °**less,** *a.* rājayaṭṭhirahita.

Schedule, *n.* 1. niyamāvali, *f.* 2. parisiṭṭha-saṅgaha, *m.* *v.t.* paṇṇe āropeti ; niyamāvaliŋ likhati.

Schema, *n.* 1. saṅkhitta-nirūpana, *nt.* saddālaṅkāra, *m.* °**tic,** *a.* saṅkhittanirūpanāyatta.

Scheme, *n.* 1. upāya ; payoga ; upakkama ; 2. kūṭopāya, *m.* *v.i.* *t.* 1. upakkamati ; parikappeti ; 2. kūṭopāyaŋ yojeti. *p.p.* °mita; °pita ; yojita°. °**er,** *n.* upāyayojaka, *m.* °**ing,** *n.* kumantaṇayojanā, *f.*

Schism, *n.* parisabheda ; saṅghabheda ; matavirodha, *m.* °**atic,** *n.* parisabhedī, *m.* *a.* saṅghabhedakara. °**atically,** *adv.* bhedakaravasena.

Scholar, *n.* 1. sissa ; sekkha, 2. bahussuta ; paṇḍita, *m.* °**ly,** *a.* vibudhocita. °**ship,** *n.* 1. sissabhāva, *m.* 2. paṇḍicca, *nt.*

Scholastic, *a.* vibuddhāyatta ; vijjāvisayaka ; vijjāyatanāyatta. °**ally,** *adv.* vibudhānurūpaŋ ; vijjānurūpaŋ.

Scholiast, *n.* aṭṭhakathācariya ; nyāsakāra, *m.*

Scholium, *n.* adholipi, *f.*

School, *n.* 1. vijjāyatana, *nt.* pāṭhasālā, *f.* 2. (of thought :) sampadāya, *m. v.t.* vineti ; sikkheti. *p.p.* vinīta ; °khita. — **board,** *n.* ajjhāpakasabhā, *f.* — **boy,** *n.* pāṭhasālīyasissa, *m.* —**fellow,** — **mate,** *n.* sahajjhāyaka, *m.* — **master,** *n.* pāṭhasālācariya, *m.*

Schooner, *n.* dvikūpakanāvā, *f.*

Sciatic, *a.* kaṭivisayaka. °**a,** *n.* kaṭivāyu, *m.*

Science, *n.* vijjā, *f.* sattha, *nt.*

Scientific, *a.* 1. vijjānugata ; 2. viññātasattha. °**ally,** *adv.* vijjānukūlatāya.

Scientist, *n.* vijjāvisārada, *m.*

Scilicet, *adv.* seyyathīdaŋ ; kathan ti ce.

Scimitar, *n.* asiputtī, *f.*

Scintilla, *n.* phuliṅga, *nt.* °**late,** *v.i.* phuliṅgāni vissajjeti ; pabhāsati. *p.p.* vissaṭṭhaphuliṅga ; °sita.

Sciolist, *n.* kiñcimattavidū, *m.* °**ism,** *n.* appamattajānana, *nt.*

Scion, *n.* 1. kulaputta ; mahākulāgata, *m.* 2. baddhaṅkura, *m.*

Scissile, *a.* chedanakkhama.

Scission, *n.* chinnaṭṭhāna, *nt.* cheda, *m.*

Scissor, *v.t.* chindati. *p.p.* chinna. **Scissors,** *n. pl.* pipphalaka, *nt.* kattarikā, *f.*

Scoff, *n.* avahāsa ; upahāsa, *m. v.i.* avahasati ; upahasati. *p.p.* °sita. °**er,** *n.* avahāsī, *m.* °**ingly,** *adv.* avahāsapubbakaŋ; sopahāsaŋ.

Scold, *n.* 1. santajjana ; paribhāsana, *nt.* 2. kharavācā nārī, *f. v.t.i.* paribhāsati ; akkosati. *p.p.* °sita ; akkuṭṭha. °**er,** *n.* paribhāsaka, *m.* °**ing,** *n.* garahā ; paribhāsanā, *f.*

Sconce, *n.* 1. sitthadīpādhāra ; 2. khuddaka-balakoṭṭhaka ; 3. sīsamatthaka, *m.*

Scoop, *n.* 1. khaṇittī, *f.* 2. uḷuṅka, *m. v.t.* 1. anto khaṇati ; 2. uluṅkena apaneti. *p.p.* °khata ; °nīta.

Scoot, *v.i.* palāyati. *p.p.* palāta.

Scope, *n.* 1. visaya ; okāsa ; 2. ajjhāsaya ; 3. paramattha, *m.*

Scorch, *n.* cammaḍāha, *m. v.t.* abhitāpeti. *p.p.* °pita. °**ing,** *a.* abhitāpakara.

Score, *n.* 1. gaṇanāciṇha, *nt.* 2. chinnarekhā, *f.* 3. vīsatisaṅkhyā, *f.* 4. nimitta, *nt.* hetu, *m. v.t.* rekhāhi aṅketi. *p.p.* rekhaṅkita.

Scoria, *n.* aggibhūdharika-ayomaṇḍa, *m.*

Scorify, *v.t.* lohamalattaŋ pāpeti. *p.p.* °pita.

Scorn, *v.t.* avajānāti ; avamāneti; hīleti. *p.p.* avaññāta ; avamata ; hīlita. *n.* avamāna, *nt.* anādara ; tirokkāra, *m.* avaññā, *f.* °**er,** *n.*

avamaññaka; hīletu, *m.* °**ful,** *a.* sāvañña, °**fully,** *adv.* sāvaññaŋ.

Scorpio, *n.* vicchikarāsi, *m.* °**ion,** *n.* vicchika, *m.*

Scot, *n.* kara; bali, *m.*

Scotch, *n.* 1. cakkabādhaka; 2. avaccheda, *m.* *v.t.* cakkaŋ bādheti; 2. avacchindati. *p.p.* bādhitacakka; avacchinna.

Scotoma, *n.* akkhidiṭṭhibādhana, *nt.*

Scoundrel, *n.* khala; narādhama, *m.* °**ism,** *n.* ketava, *nt.*

Scour, *v.t.* 1. samparimajjati; ghaŋsitvā sodheti; 2. ativireceti. *v.i.* javena palāyati. *p.p.* °rimaṭṭha; °dhita; °palāta.

Scourge, *n.* 1. kasā, *f.* 2. devadaṇḍa, *m.* *v.t.* 1. kasāhi tāḷeti; 2. accantaŋ pīḷeti. *p.p.* °ḷita; °pīḷita.

Scout, *n.* 1. carapurisa; 2. bālacara, *m.* *v.i.* gūḷhaŋ *or* raho carati. *v.t.* sāvaññaŋ paṭikkhipati. *p.p.* °khitta.

Scow, *n.* titthadoṇi, *f.*

Scowl, *n.* bhūbhaṅga, *m.* bhākuṭīkaraṇa, *nt.* *v.i.* bhākuṭiŋ karoti. *p.p.* bhākuṭīkata.

Scrabble, *v.i.* 1. vilikhati; 2. āyāsena gavesati. *p.p.* °khita; °sita.

Scraggy, *a.* 1. kakkasa; 2. kisa; 3. dīghagīva. °**iness,** *n.* 1. kakkasatta; 2. kisatta; 3. dīghagīvatta, *nt.*

Scramble, *v.t.i.* kicchena āruhati; gaṇhitum ussaheti. *p.p.* °ārūḷha; °hita. °**er,** *n.* kicchenārohī, *m.* °**ing,** *n.* kicchārohaṇa, *nt.* gahaṇussāha, *m.*

Scrannel, *a.* kaṇṇakaṭuka.

Scrap, *n.* 1. chinnakhaṇḍa; bhuttāvasesa, *m.* 2. bhaṇḍana, *nt.*

Scrape, *n.* 1. avalekhana, 2. kiccha; kasira, *nt.* *v.t.* avalikhati; ullikhati. *p.p.* °khita. °**er,** *n.* avalekhaka; piŋsaka, *m.* °**ing,** *n.* nighaŋsana; ullikhana, *nt.*

Scratch, *v.t.* kaṇḍūvati. *n.* kaṇḍuti, *f.* °**er,** *n.* kaṇḍūvaka, *m.* °**ing,** *n.* avisadalekhana, *nt.* °**y,** *a.* vilikhanayutta.

Scrawl, *v.t.* avyattaŋ *or* turitaŋ likhati. *p.p.* °likhita. *n.* avisadalekhana, *nt.*

Scream, *n.* akkandana; viravana, *nt.* *v.i.t.* viravati; akkandati. *p.p.* °dita. °**er,** *n.* virāvakārī, *m.* °**ingly,** *adv.* saviravaŋ. °**y,** *a.* viravamāna.

Screech, *n.* tārassara, *m.* *v.i.t.* uccassarena nadati; vissaraŋ karoti. *p.p.* katavissara.

Screed, *n.* āyāsakara-dīghakathā, *f.* °dīghalipi, *f.*

Screen, *n.* javanikā; tirokaraṇī, *f.* *v.t.* 1. āvarati; tirokaroti; 2. cālaniyā puthakkaroti. *p.p.* āvaṭa; tirokata; °kata. — **wall,** sāṇipākāra, *m.*

Screw, *n.* vyāvaṭṭanī, *f.* valayakhīlaka, *m.* *v.t.* 1. vyāvaṭṭaniyā ābandhati; 2. nippīḷetvā dhanaŋ sañcināti. *p.p.* °ābaddha; °sañcitadhana. — **drawer,** *n.* vyāvaṭṭanīyojaka, *m.* °**pine,** *n.* dhanuketakī, *m.*

Scribble, *n.* avisadalipi, *f.* avyattalekhana, *nt.* *v.t.* avisadaŋ *or* turitaŋ likhati. *p.p.* °khita. °**er,** *n.* avisadalekhaka, *m.*

Scribe, *n.* lekhaka; lipikāra, *m.* *v.t.* likhati. *p.p.* likhita.

Scrimmage, *n.* kalaha, *m.*

Scrimp, *v.t.i.* mitabbayena annapānaŋ sampādeti; maccharāyati. *p.p.* °ditannapāna; °yita.

Scrip, *n.* 1. khuddakathavikā, *f.* 2. mūlapaṭiggahapaṇṇa, *nt.*

Script, *n.* hatthalekhana; mūlalekhana, *nt.* °**orium,** *n.* lekhanāgāra, *nt.*

Scripture, *n.* pāvacana, *nt.* dhammalipi, *f.* °**ral,** *a.* pāvacanāyatta. °**rally,** *adv.* pāvacanāgatavasena.

Scrivener, *n.* 1. nītilipisampādaka; 2. iṇadāyaka, *m.*

Scrofula, *n.* galagaṇḍaroga, *m.* °**lous,** *a.* galagaṇḍātura.

Scroll, *n.* āvaṭṭita-lipi, *f.* *v.t.i.* āvaṭṭeti. *p.p.* °ṭita.

Scrotum, *n.* aṇḍakosa, *m.*

Scrotitis, *n.* aṇḍadāha, *m.*

Scrub, *n.* 1. nighaŋsana; 2. gumbagahana, *nt.* *v.t.* nighaŋseti; pakkhāleti. *p.p.* °sita; °lita. °**ber,** *n.* nighaŋsaka, *m.* °**by,** *a.* gumbacchanna.

Scruff, *n.* khandhaṭṭhi, *nt.*

Scrumptious, *a.* manohara; atimadhura.

Scruple, *n.* kukkucca, *nt.* saŋsaya, *m.* *v.i.* kukkuccāyati; saṅkati. *p.p.* °yita; °kita. °**pulous,** *a.* kukkuccabahula; yutticintaka. °**pulously,** *adv.* atiparikkhāya; yutticintāya. °**pulousness,** *n.* vajjabhayadassavitā, *f.*

Scrutator, *n.* sukhumupaparikkhaka, *m.*

Scrutineer, *n.* vajjaparikkhaka; sukhumanirūpaka, *m.*

Scrutiny, *n.* sukhumaparikkhā, *f.* °**ize,** *v.t.* pariyogāhati; suṭṭhupaparikkhati. *p.p.* °gāḷha; °khita.

Scud, *n.* vātāhata-valāhaka, *m.* *v.i.* tuvaṭaŋ dhāvati.

Scuffle, *n.* vyākula-kalaha, *m.* *v.i.* vyākulaŋ kalahaŋ karoti.

Scull, *n.* khuddakāritta, *nt.* *v.t.* khuddārittena pājeti. *p.p.* °jita. °**er,** *n.* khuddaka-doṇi, *f.* °**ery,** *n.* bhājanadhovanaṭṭhāna, *nt.* °**ion,** *n.* bhājanadhovaka; āḷārikantevāsī, *m.*

Sculptor, *n.* silāvaḍḍhakī; rūpukkiraka, *m.* °**ture,** *n.* paṭimāukkiraṇa; silātacchana, *nt.* *v.t.* (silādīhi) paṭimādayo ukkirati. °**tural,** *a.* ukkiraṇāyatta.

Scum, *n.* pheṇa, *m.* uggatamala, *n.t.* *v.t.* pheṇam apaneti. *p.p.* apanītapheṇa. °**my,** *a.* uggatapheṇayutta.

Scumble, *v.t.* vaṇṇamaṭṭhaŋ karoti. *p.p.* °kata.

Scurf, *n.* cammapapaṭikā, *f.* °**y,** *a.* chavipapaṭikāyutta.

Scurry, *v.i.* lahuŋ dhāvati.

Scurvy, *n.* pūtirattaroga, *m.* adj. nīca; kucchita.

Scut, *n.* rassa-naṅguṭṭha, *nt.*

Scutcheon, *n.* 1. nāmaṅkitapaṭṭa, *m.* 2. tāḷacchiggalāvaraṇa, *nt.*

Scutter, see **Scurry.**

Scutum, *n.* kheṭaka; saraphalaka, *nt.*

Scythe, *n.* asita; dātta; lavitta, *nt.*

Sea, *n.* samudda; sāgara; sindhu; aṇṇava; jalanidhi; udadhi, *m.* °**board,** samuddavelā, *f.* °**born,** *a.* samuddaja. °**breeze,** *n.* samuddāgatavāta, *m.* — **chart,** *n.* samuddagamanākati, *f.* °**coast,** sāgaratīra, *nt.* °**faring,** *a.* samuddagāmī. — **gage,** *n.* nāvāsīdanappamāṇa, *nt.* °**girt,** *a.* sāgaraparikkhitta. °**green,** *a.* sāgaravaṇṇa. °**man,** *n.* nāvika, *m.* °**monster,** *n.* makara, *m.* °**nymph,** aṇṇavadevatā, *f.* °**port,** *n.* nāvāpaṭṭana, *nt.* °**salt,** *n.* sāmuddika-loṇa, *nt.* °**shore,** *n.* samuddatīra, *nt.* °**side,** *n.* sāgarāsannaṭṭhāna, *nt.* °**sickness,** sāmuddika-bhama, *m.* °**ward,** *a.* samuddābhimukha. °**wards,** *adv.* sāgarābhimukhaŋ. °**weed,** *n.* samuddagaccha, *m.* °**worthy,** *a.* yātrāyogga.

Seal, *n.* muddā, *f.* lañchana, *nt.* *v.t.* 1. muddeti; lañcheti; 2. niccheti; niṇṇeti. *p.p.* °dita; °chita; °ṇita. °**ing,** *n.* lañchaṭhapana, *nt.* °**ing wax,** lākhā, *f.* jatu, *nt.*

Seal, *n.* lomasa-maccha, *m.*

Seam, *n.* sibbanīmagga, *m.* *v.t.* sibbanena sandhāti; sibbaniŋ dasseti. *p.p.* °sandhita; dassitasibbana. °**less,** *a.* sibbanīrahita. °**ster,** *n.* tunnavāya, *m.* °**stress,** *n.* tunnavāyikā, *f.*

Seance, *n.* vīmaŋsakasabhā, *f.*

Sear, *a.* sukkha; milāta. *v.t.* soseti; snehaŋ pariyādāti. *p.p.* sosita; pariyādinnasneha.

Search, *n.* esanā; gavesanā; pariyesanā; anvesanā; eṭṭhi; gaveṭṭhi; pariyeṭṭhi, *f.* *v.t.* esati; gavesati; pariyesati; maggati; vicināti. °**er,** *n.* esaka; gavesaka, *m.* °**able,** *a.* gavesiya; pariyesitabba.

Season, *n.* utu; samaya, *m.* *v.t.* saṅkharoti; pariṇāmeti. *v.i.* paricayati; paripākaŋ yāti. *p.p.* saṅkhata; °mita; °yita; °yāta. °**able,** *a.* samayocita; paripācanāraha. °**ably,** *adv.* yathāsamayaŋ; kālānurūpaŋ. °**al,** *a.* samayāyatta. **Out of** —, ayathākālika, *a.* akāle, *adv.* **Wrong** —, akāla, *m.*

Seat, *n.* 1. āsana; nisīdana; 2. ṭhāna; āyatana; niketana, *nt.* *v.t.* 1. (oneself:) nisīdati; upavisati; (someone else:) nisīdāpeti; 2. patiṭṭhāpeti; 3. āsanaŋ paññāpeti. *p.p.* nisinna; upaviṭṭha; °pita; paññattāsana. — **of learning,** vijjāyatana, *nt.* **Lose one's** —, mantidhurā apanīyati.

Sebaceous, *a.* medobahula.

Secant, *n.* chedaka-rekhā, *f.*

Secede, *v.i.* sapakkhato apagacchati. *p.p.* °apagata. °**er,** *n.* pakkhavissajjaka; bhedamatika.

Secession, *n.* sapakkhacāga, *m.*

Seclude, *v.t.* 1. visuŋ vāseti; 2. (oneself:) paṭisallīyati. *p.p.* °vāsita; °līna. °**ed,** *a.* vivitta; vūpakaṭṭha; rahogata; paṭisallīna. °**ed place,** suññāgāra; pantasenāsana, *nt.*

Seclusion, *n.* 1. vinākaraṇa; visuṅkaraṇa; 2. paṭisallāna; sallīyana, *nt.* — **at noon,** divāvihāra, *m.* °**ist,** *n.* vivekakāmī; paṭisallānarata.

Second, *n.* 1. muhutta; accharāsaṅghāta, *m.* 2. sahāya; upatthambhaka, *m.* adj. dutiya. *v.t.* anujānāti; samattheti. *p.p.* anuññāta; °thita. °**ary,** *a.* appadhāna; amukhya. °**arily,** *adv.* amukhyavasena. °**er,** *n.* anumaññaka; daḷhīkattu, *m.* °**hand,** *a.* kataparibhoga. °**ly,** *adv.* dutiyaŋ. **Without a —,** addutiya; appaṭipuggala.

Secret, *n.* rahassa; guyha, *nt.* adj. gūḷha; rāhassaka; paṭicchanna. °**ecy,** *n.* gūḷhatta; rāhassikatta, *nt.* °**ly,** *adv.* raho; gūḷhaŋ. °**ness,** *n.* gūḷhatta; rāhasikatta, *nt.* °**ive,** *a.* rahassākāra; gūḷhasabhāva.

Secretary, *n.* lekhanādhikārī, *m.* — **of state,** mahālekhaka, *m.* °**iate,** mahālekhakālaya, *m.*

Secrete, *v.t.* 1. nikkhāmeti; moceti; 2. nigūhati. *p.p.* °mita; °cita; nigūḷha. °**ion,** *n.* niggatayūsa, *m.* mala, *nt.* °**tory,** *a.* nicchāraka; mocaka.

Sect, *n.* nikāya; gaṇa; pakkha, *m.* °**arian,** *n. a.* nikāyāyatta; pakkhagata; nekāyika. °**arianism,** *n.* nekāyikatta, *nt.* pakkhagāha, *m.* °**ary,** *n.* nikāyāyattapuggala, *m.*

Section, *n.* vagga; khaṇḍa; pabba; pariccheda, *m.* *v.t.* vibhajati; paricchindati. *p.p.* vibhatta; °chinna. °**al,** *a.* koṭṭhāsāyatta. °**ally,** *adv.* paricchedavasena; koṭṭāsavasena.

Sector, *n.* chinnabhāga, *m.*

Secular, *a.* ihalokika; saŋsārika. °**ity,** °**ness,** *n.* lokikatta, *nt.* °**ise,** *v.t.* lokikattaŋ pāpeti. °**ism,** *n.* ihalokaniṭṭhā, *f.* °**ly,** *adv.* lokiyavasena.

Secure, *a.* khema; nibbhaya; nirāsaṅka; nirupaddava. *v.t.* 1. tāyati; rakkhati; 2. daḷhīkaroti. *p.p.* tāyita; °khita; °kata. °**ly,** *adv.* khemena; surakkhitaŋ. °**er,** *n.* abhayadāyī; tāyaka, *m.* °**ity,** *n.* 1. gutti; rakkhā, *f.* tāṇa; leṇa, *nt.* 2. saccakāra, *m.* — **place,** khemaṭṭhāna, *nt.*

Sedan, *n.* sivikā, *f.*

Sedate, *a.* upasanta; nibbikāra. °**ly,** *adv.* nibbikāraŋ. °**ness,** *n.* upasantatā. *f.* °**ive,** *a.* upasamakara. *n.* upasamanosadha, *nt.*

Sedentary, *a. n.* nisajjābahula; udāsīna; akammasīla.

Sediment, *n.* kakka; sañcitamala, *nt.* °**ary,** *a.* malasadisa.

Sedition, *n.* kumantana; dubbhana, *nt.* °**tious,** *a.* dubbhanasīla; °**tiously,** *adv.* dubbhanākārena.

Seduce, *v.t.* vimoheti; palobheti. *p.p.* °hita; °bhita. °**er,** *n.* palobhaka; vimohaka, *m.* °**ction,** *n.* palobhetvā avaharaṇa; vimohana, *nt.* °**ctive,** *a.* palobhaka vimohaka. °**ctively,** *adv.* palobhanena.

Sedulous, *a.* kiççāsatta ; uyyogapara. °**ly,** *adv.* saussāhaŋ. °**ness,** *n.* uyyoga ; kattukamyatā, *f.*

See, *v.t.* passati ; pekkhati ; ikkhati; oloketi. *p.p.* diṭṭha ; °khita ; °kita. °**er,** *n.* passitu ; dassāvī ; dassī, *m.* °**ing,** *a.* passanta; olokenta.

See, *n.* dhammācariyāyattapadesa, *m.*

Seed, *n.* 1. bīja, *nt.* 2. pabhava ; mūlahetu, *m.* 3. (semen :) sukka, *nt.* 4. santati, *f. v.t.* 1. bījam uppāṭeti; 2. bījāni puthakkaroti. *v.i.* bījāni pāteti *or* uppādeti. *p.p.* uppāṭitabīja ; °katabīja ; °ditabīja. °**ling,** *n.* bījaṅkura, *m.* °**less,** *a.* abījaka. °**sman,** *n.* bījavāṇija, *m.* — **time,** *n.* vapanakāla, *m.* — **vessel,** *n.* bījakosa, *m.* °**y,** *a.* bījapuṇṇa.

Seek, *v.t.* 1. gavesati ; pariyesati ; 2. ākaṅkhati ; pattheti. *p.p.* °sita ; °khita ; °thita. °**er,** *n.* gavesī ; ākaṅkhī ; patthetu, *m.* °**ing after,** nibbisanta ; gavesanta, *a.*

Seem, *v.i.* dissati ; khāyati ; paṭibhāti. °**ing,** *a.* kittima ; bāhirato dissamāna. °**ingly,** *adv.* ayathāvato ; bāhirato dissanākārena. °**ly,** *a.* anucchavika ; anurūpa.

Seen, *p.p.* of See, diṭṭha ; — **face to face,** sakkhidiṭṭha, *a.* — **well,** sudiṭṭha, *a.* **Easily —,** sudassa, *a.*

Seer, *n.* anāgatavattu ; anāgatadassī, *m.*

See-saw, *n.* phalakapājanakīḷā, *f. v.i.* phalakena dolāyati.

Seethe, *v.i.* kuthati. *v.t.* sedeti ; kutheti. *p.p.* kuthita ; sedita. °**ing,** *a.* saṅkhubhita ; kuthita.

Segment, *n.* cheda ; chinnakhaṇḍa, *m.*

Segregate, *v.t.* viyojeti ; visuŋkaroti. *p.p.* °jita ; °kata. °**ion,** *n.* visuṅkaraṇa, *nt.* °**ive,** *a.* viyojaka.

Seine, *n.* mahājāla, *nt.*

Seismic, *a.* bhūmicalanāyatta.

Seismography, *n.* bhūmicālavibhāga, *m.*

Seismometer, *n.* bhūmicālasūcakayanta, *nt.*

Seize, *v.t.i.* pasayha gaṇhāti ; āvisati; akkamati. *p.p.* °gahita; āviṭṭha ; akkanta. °**er,** *n.* gāhaka ; gāhī, *m.* °**ure,** *n.* gahaṇa ; akkamana ; āvisana, *nt.*

Sejunction, *n.* viyojana ; puthakkaraṇa, *nt.*

Seldom, *adv.* kadāci ; kālantarena.

Select, *a.* uccinita ; visiṭṭha ; sammata. *v.t.* uccināti ; avadhāreti. *p.p.* °nita ; °rita. °**ion,** *n.* uccinana, *nt.* °**ness,** *n.* mahagghatta ; visiṭṭhatta, *nt.*

Self, *n.* atta, *m.* sayaŋ, *ind.* adj. saka ; nija ; sakīya. — **abnegation,** *n.* nekkhamma, *nt.* —

°applause, *n.* attasilāghā, *f.* °assumed, *a.* attanā āropita. °begotten, °born, sayambhū ; sayañjāta, *a.* °choice, *n.* sayaŋvara, *m.* °collected, *a.* attadanta. °care, *n.* attagutti, *f.* °composed, *a.* bhāvitatta. °command, *n.* attasaŋyama, *m.* °conceit, *n.* ahaṅkāra, *m.* °confidence, *n.* vesārajja, *nt.* °conscious, *a.* saka-sabhāvacintaka. °contained, *a.* attasaññata. °contradictory, *a.* aññamaññavirodhī. °controlled, *a.* saŋyatatta. °denial, *n.* sakatthapariccāga, *m.* °denying, *a.* sakatthacāgī. °destruction, *n.* attaghāta, *m.* °devotion, *n.* paratthacariyā, *f.* °educated, *a.* attanā va uggahita. °esteem, *n.* attasambhāvanā, *f.* °evident, *a.* sayaŋsiddha. °government, *n.* sādhīnapālana, *nt.* °guarded, *a.* attagutta. °help, *n.* attupatthambhna, *nt.* °interest, *n.* sakattha. °love, *n.* sakatthaparāyaṇatā, *f.* °made, *a.* sayaṅkata. °mortification, *n.* attakilamatha, *m.* °mortifying, *a.* attantapa. °possessed, *a.* samāhita; avyaggamana. °praise, *n.* attukkaŋsanā, *f.* °respect, *n.* attābhimāna, *m.* °righteous, *a.* attānavajjatādassī. °same, *a.* anañña ; abhinna. °satisfied, *a.* attasantuṭṭha ; abhimānayutta. °sacrifice, *n.* attapariccāga, *m.* °seeking, *a.* attatthakāmī. °sufficient, *a.* sabbasampuṇṇa ; saka-balayutta. °will, *n.* seritā, *f.* yathākāmācāra, *m.* He himself, so attanā va; so sayam eva. I myself, aham attanā va. They themselves, te attanā va. We ourselves, mayam attanā va.

Selfhood, *n.* puggalabhāva ; attabhāva, *m.*

Selfish, *a.* sakatthapara. °ly, *adv.* sakatthaparatāya. °ness, *n.* sakatthaparatā, *f.*

Selfless, *a.* paratthakāmī. °ness, *n.* paratthakāmitā, *f.*

Sell, *v.t.* vikkiṇāti. *p.p.* vikkīta. °er, *n.* vikketu ; vikkāyika. °ing, *n.* vikkiṇana, *nt.*

Selvage, *n.* dasā ; mukhavaṭṭi, *f.*

Semblance, *n.* samānatta ; sadisatta, *nt.* dissamānākāra, *m.*

Semen, *n.* sukka, *nt.* sambhava, *m.* **Seminal,** *a.* sambhavavisayaka.

Semi, *prep.* addha (in cpds.) ; °annual, *a.* addhavassika ; chammāsika. °circle, *n.* addhāvaṭṭa, addhacakka, *nt.* °circular, *a.* addhavaṭṭula. °colon, *n.* addhavirāmaciṇha, *nt.* °conscious, *a.* addhamucchita. °menstrual, *a.* addhamāsika. °lunar, *a.* addhacandākāra. °vowel, *n.* addhasara ; antaṭṭhakkhara, *nt.* (i.e. y.v.) °weekly, *a.* addhasattāhika.

Seminality, *n.* jananasatti, *f.*

Seminary, *n.* 1. sāmaṇerasikkhālaya, *m.* 2. bījaropaṇaṭṭhāna, *nt.* °niferous, *a.* bījadhārī.

Sempiternal, *a.* sadātana ; sassata.

Senate, *n.* sacivasabhā, *f.* °**tor,** *n.* saciva, *m.*

Send, *v.t.* peseti; pahiṇāti. *p.p.* pesita; pahita. — **after,** anupeseti. — **away,** paṇāmeti; uyyojeti. — **back,** paṭipeseti. °**er,** *n.* pesetu; pesaka, *m.* — **for,** pakkosāpeti. — **forth,** 1. nicchāreti; 2. sāsanaŋ peseti. °**ing,** *n.* pesana, *nt.* °**ing off,** vissajjana, *nt.* °**off,** ossajati; vissajjeti; peseti. — **out,** nicchāreti; nikkhāmeti.

Senescent, *a.* jīyamāna.

Senile, *a.* vayovuddha; jarājiṇṇa. °**ity,** *n.* jarājiṇṇatā, *f.*

Senior, *n.a.* vuḍḍhatara; jeṭṭha. °**ity,** *n.* jeṭṭhatta; vuddhataratta, *nt.* — **monk,** *n.* thera, *m.* — **nun,** *n.* therī, *f.*

Senna, *n.* soṇṇapatta; virecakapaṇṇa, *nt.*

Se'nnight, *n.* sattāha, *nt.*

Sensation, *n.* visayagahaṇa, *nt.* saŋvega, *m.* °**al,** *a.* saŋvegakara; vimhayāvaha. °**ally,** *adv.* saŋvegajanakākārena.

Sense, *n.* 1. (cakkhādi-) indriya, *nt.* 2. padattha, *m.* 3. avabodha; 4. ajjhāsaya; 5. saññā, *f.* 6. sati, *f.* *v.t.* maññati; anumānena jānāti. °**less,** *a.* acetana; aviññāṇaka; visaññī; sammūḷha. °**lessly,** *adv.* visaññitāya; muṭṭhasaccena; mucchitākārena. — **object,** *n.* ālambana; ārammaṇa, *nt.* — **of hearing,** sotindriya, *nt.* — **of sight,** cakkhundriya, *nt.* — **of smell,** ghāṇindriya, *nt.* — **of taste,** jivhindriya, *nt.* — **of touch,** kāyindriya, *nt.* — **organ,** āyatana; pasādarūpa, *nt.* — **perception,** muti, *f.* **According to** —, anvattha, *a.*

Sensible, *a.* 1. indriyagocara; 2. sacetana; 3. anupahatindriya; 4. paṭisaŋvedī; 5. mutimantu; vicakkhaṇa. °**bility,** *n.* 1. jānanasatti; 2. tikhiṇindriyatā, *f.* °**bly,** *adv.* paccakkhato; sappaññākārena. °**ness,** *n.* tikhiṇindriyatā, *f.*

Sensitive, *a.* 1. khippābhiñña; tikhiṇindriya; 2. hirimantu; lajjābahula. °**ly,** *adv.* sukhumasaññāya. °**ness,** *n.* tikkhindriyatā, *f.* — **plant,** namakkārī; nidhikumbhī, *f.*

Sensorium, *n.* matthaluṅga, *nt.*

Sensory, °**sorial,** *a.* visayagahanasamattha; savedana.

Sensual, *a.* 1. indriyabaddha; 2. visayāsatta; 3. (person:) kāmuka; visayarasika. °**ist,** *n.* kāmabhogī; visayarata. °**ity,** °**ness,** *n.* kāmabhogitā, *f.* — **enjoyment,** kāmasevanā; visayarati, *f.* — **pleasure,** kāmarati, *f.*

Sensuous, *a.* indriyagocara; indriyāsatta.

Sentence, *n.* 1. vākya, *nt.* 2. daṇḍaniyama, *m.* *v.t.* daṇḍaŋ paṇeti; vadhāya niyameti. *p.p.* paṇītadaṇḍa; °mitavadha.

Sentient, *a.* sacetanika. °**ence,** *n.* sacetanatta, *nt.*

Sentiment, *n.* 1. saṅkappa; adhippāya, *m.* 2. manobhāva; siṅgārādirasa, *m.* °**al,** *a.* 1. rasabahula; 2. saṅkappamaya. °**ally,** *adv.* manobhāvavasena. °**ality,** °**alism,** *n.* rasaññutā; manobhāvayuttatā, *f.* °**ist,** *n.* nāṭyarasika, *m.*

Sentinel, Sentry, *n.* rakkhīpurisa, *m.*

Separable, *a.* puthakkaraṇīya.

Separate, *a. n.* pacceka; pāṭiyekka; āveṇika; puthubhūta; visumbhūta. *v.t.* viyojeti; puthakkaroti; visuṅkaroti; vinibbhujati. *v.i.* viyujjati; vinābhavati. *p.p.* °jita; °kata; vinibhutta; viyutta; vinābhūta. °**ion,** *n.* visuṅkaraṇa; viyujjana, *nt.* viyoga; vippayoga, *m.* °**ly,** *adv.* visuŋ; puthu; pāṭekkaŋ; paccekaŋ. °**ness,** *n.* pāṭekkatā; paccekatā, *f.* °**ive,** *a.* viyogakara. °**tor,** *n.* viyojaka, *m.* °**ism,** *n.* vinābhavana, *nt.*

Sepoy, *n.* Bhāratīya-yuddhabhaṭa, *m.*

Sepsis, *n.* pūyapaggharaṇa, *nt.*

Septangular, *a.* sattakoṇaka.

September, *n.* Poṭṭhapāda, *m.*

Septenary, *n.* sattaka, *nt.* adj. sattaṅga; sattavaggika.

Septennial, *a.* sattavassika.

Septet, *n.* sattaka, *nt.*

Septic, °**al,** *a.* pūtibhāvagata.

Septuagenarian, *a. n.* sattativassika.

Septuple, *a.* sattaguṇika.

Sepulchre, *n.* susānaghara; chavāgāra, *nt.* *v.t.* chavaŋ thūpe nidahati. *p.p.* thūpanihita-chava. °**al,** *a.* 1. chavāgārāyatta; 2. khedasūcaka.

Sepulture, *n.* bhūnidahana; chavanikkhipana, *nt.*

Sequacious, *a.* dhitihīna; parānuvattī. °**city,** *n.* dhitihīnatā, *f.*

Sequel, *n.* anugāmīphala, *nt.* uttarivipāka, *m.*

Sequence, *n.* anukkama; anvaya, *m.* paramparā, *f.* °**ent,** *a.* anugāmī.

Sequester, *v.* visuŋ vāseti *or* ṭhapeti. *p.p.* °vāsita; °ṭhapita.

Sequestrate, *v.t.* 1. rājasantakaŋ karoti; 2. iṇāyikassa dhanaŋ rundheti. *p.p.* °kata; °rundhitadhana. °**ion,** *n.* dhanarundhana, *nt.* °**tor,** *n.* rundhitadhanapālaka, *m.*

Seraglio, *n.* itthāgāra; antepura, *nt.* orodha, *m.*

Serene, *a.* upasanta; samāhita; passaddha. °**ity,** *n.* passaddhi, *f.* upasama, *m.*

Serf, *n.* kassaka-dāsa, *m.* °**dom,** *n.* kassaka-dāsavya, *nt.*

Serial, *n.* anukkamapaṇṇa, *nt.* adj. kamānugata. °**ly,** *adv.* anukkamena; yathākkamaŋ.

Seriate, *v.t.* anukkamikaŋ *or* kamānugataŋ karoti. *p.p.* °kata.

Seriatim, *adv.* yathānukkamaŋ.

Sericulture, *n.* kosakimiposaṇa, *nt.* °**ist,** *n.* kosakimiposaka, *m.*

Series, *n.* āvali; panti; seṇi; mālā, *f.*

Serious, *a.* 1. bhāriya; garuka; 2. dhīrasabhāva. °**ness,** *n.* garutta; bhāriyatta; dhīratta, *nt.* °**ly,** *adv.* bāḷhaŋ.

Serjeant, Sergeant, *n.* bhaṭasenāya upādhikārī, *m.*

Sermon, *n.* dhammadesanā, *f.* suttanta, *m.* °**ize,** *v.t.* dhammaŋ deseti. *p.p.* desitadhamma.

Serous, *a.* takkavaṇṇa; takkasadisa.

Serpent, *n.* sappa ; ahi ; uraga ; bhujaga ; bhogī ; āsīvisa ; alagadda, *m.* °**charmer,** *n.* ahiguṇṭhika, *m.* °**ine,** *a.* sappopama ; kuṭila ; vaṅka. **Body of a —,** bhoga, *m.* **Fang of a —,** āsī ; sappadāṭhā, *f.* **Slough of a —,** nimmoka, *m.*

Serrate, *a.* kakacasadisa. *v.t.* dante uṭṭhāpeti. *p.p.* °pītadanta.

Serried, *a.* nirantarasaŋhata.

Serum, *n.* vasā, *f.*

Servant, *n.* sevaka ; bhacca ; kiṅkara ; pesanakara ; paricāraka, *m.* — **boy,** *n.* ceṭaka, *m.* — **girl,** *n.* ceṭikā, *f.*

Serve, *v.t.* upāsati ; paricarati ; upaṭṭhāti. *v.i.* sādheti ; pavatteti. *p.p.* upāsita ; °rita ; upaṭṭhita ; sādhita ; °tita. — **out,** bhājeti.—**up food,** 1. bhojanaŋ paṭiyādeti ; 2. parivisati. — **with,** sampādeti.

Service, *n.* 1. sevā ; paricariyā, *f.* upaṭṭhāna ; veyyāvacca, *nt.* 2. kicca ; vatta, *nt.* 3. pūjāvidhi, *m.* °**able,** *a.* kammakkhama ; alaṅkammaniya. **Public —,** rājakicca, *nt.* rājasevā, *f.*

Servile, *a.* parādhīna ; parapessiya ; dāsopama. °**ly,** *adv.* nīcavuttiyā ; adhikagāravena. °**ity,** *n.* atilolatta ; dāsasadisatta, *nt.*

Servitor, *n.* see **Servant,** upaṭṭhāka ; kappiyakāraka, *m.*

Servitude, *n.* parādhīnatta, *nt.*

Sesame, *n.* tila, *nt.* — **paste,** tilakakka, *nt.* — **cake,** tilasaṅguḷikā, *f.*

Session, *n.* sabhāvāra ; adhikaraṇavāra, *m.* °**al,** *a.* sabhāvārāyatta.

Sesspool, *n.* jambālī, *f.* oligalla, *m.*

Set, *n.* 1. samūha, *m.* āvali, *f.* vagga ; gaṇa, *m.* 2. atthagama, *m.* adj. niyata ; thira ; nicchita. *v.t.* 1. nidahati ; niveseti ; ṭhapeti ; 2. payojeti. *v.i.* atthaṅgacchati. *p.p.* nihita ; °sita ; ṭhapita ; °jita ; °gata. — **about,** ārabhati. — **against,** virujjhati. — **apart,** visuŋ karoti *or* ṭhapeti. — **aside,** paṭisāmeti. — **before,** upaṭṭhapeti ; abhiharati. — **down,** nikkhipati. — **forth,** niddisati ; paññāpeti. — **free,** pamoceti. — **in motion,** kampeti ; paribbhameti. — **in order,** saŋsāmeti. — **into agitation,** saŋvejeti. — **on,** payojeti. — **on fire,** ujjāleti. — **out,** nikkhamati ; niggacchati. — **over,** niyojeti ; adhikāraŋ pāpeti. —**up,** 1. payojeti ; 2. ukkujjeti. — **upon,** pakkhandati. °**ting,** *n.* sannivesa, *m.* patiṭṭhāpana, *nt.* °**ting down,** atthagama, *m.*

Set-down, *n.* bādhaka ; balavatajjana, *nt.*

Settee, *n.* dīghāsana, *nt.*

Settle, *n.* dīghaphalakāsana, *nt.* *v.t.* 1. sanniveseti ; 2. saŋvidahati ; 3. sannisīdāpeti ; 4. samathaŋ pāpeti ; 5. vavatthapeti ; 6. thirīkaroti. *v.i.* 1. adhivasati ; 2. sannisīdati ; 3. thirībhavati ; 4. samatham upeti ; 5. gharabandhanam upeti. *p.p.* °sita ; saŋvihita ; °pita ; thirīkata ; adhivuttha ; sannisinna ; thirībhūta ; °upeta. °**er,** *n.* adhivāsī, *m.* °**ment,** *n.* 1. sannivesa, *m.* 2.

vinicchaya, *m.* 3. gharabandhana, *nt.* 4. niviṭṭhaṭṭhāna, *nt.* janapada, *m.*

Seven, *n. a.* satta. °**fold,** *a.* sattaguṇika. °**teen,** *n. a.* sattarasa; sattadasa; 3. °**teenth,** *a.* sattadasama. °**th,** *a.* sattama. — **times,** *adv.* sattakkhattuŋ. — **years old,** sattavassika. **A group of** —, sattaka, *nt.*

Seventy, *n.* sattati, *f.* °**five,** pañcasattati, *f.* °**four,** catusattati, *f.* °**one,** ekasattati, *f.* °**seven,** sattasattati *f.* °**six** chasattati, *f.* °**three,** tesattati, *f.* °**two,** dvisattati; dvāsattati, *f.*

Sever, *v.t.* vicchindati; viyojeti. *p.p.* vicchinna; °jita. °**ance,** *n.* vicchindana, *nt.*

Several, *a.* katipaya. °**ly** *adv.* visuŋ; paccekaŋ. °**ty,** *n.* bhinnatta, *nt.* puthubhāva, *m.*

Severe, *a.* tikhiṇa; tibba; ugga; atimatta; kaṭuka; daḷha. °**ity,** *n.* tibbatta; tikhiṇatta, *nt.* °**ly,** *adv.* atimattaŋ; atitibbaŋ.

Sew, *v.t.* sibbati; tuṇṇakammaŋ karoti. *p.p.* °bita; katatuṇṇa°. °**ing,** *n.* sibbana, *nt.* °**ing machine,** sibbakayanta, *nt.*

Sewer, *n.* paṇālī; malanibbāhinī, *f.* °**age,** *n.* malanibbāhanakamma, *nt.*

Sex, *n.* liṅga; bhāvarūpa, *nt.* **Female** —, itthibhāva, *m.* **Male** —, pumbhāva, *m.*

Sexagenarian, *a. n.* saṭṭhivassika, 3.

Sexangle, *a. n.* chakoṇaka, *m.*

Sexennial, *a.* chabbassika.

Sexology, *n.* kāmasattha, *nt.*

Sextuple, *a.* chakoṭṭhāsika.

Sexual, *a.* liṅgika; methunāyatta. — **intercourse,** methuna, *nt.* (thī-puma-) saŋvāsa, *m.*

Shabby, *a.* lūkha; kucchita; kiliṭṭhavasana. °**ily,** *adv.* kucchitākārena. °**iness,** lūkhavasanatta, *nt.*

Shackle, *n.* nigaḷa; anduka, *m.* *v.t.* andukehi bandhati. *p.p.* andukabaddha.

Shade, *n.* 1. chāyā, *f.* 2. tirokaraṇī, *f.* vitāna, *nt.* 3. lesamattā, *f.* 4. āvaṭaṭṭhāna, *nt.* 5. pacchābhāga, *m.* *v.t.* āvarati; chādeti. *p.p.* āvaṭa; °dita. °**less,** *a.* chāyārahita; anāvaṭa. °**y,** *a.* sacchāya; avivaṭa.

Shadow, *n.* 1. chāyā, *f.* 2. lesamatta, *nt.* *v.t.* 1. chāyāya pattharati; tirokaroti; 2. avisadaŋ nirūpeti. °**y,** *a.* 1. chāyāmaya; chāyābahula; 2. vitatha.

Shaft, *n.* 1. sara; kaṇḍa; usu; bāṇa, *m.* 2. yaṭṭhi, *f.* daṇḍa; tharu; muṭṭhi, *f.*

Shag, *n.* thūlalomakavattha, *nt.* °**gy,** *a.* 1. lomasa; kharalomayutta; 2. atibahula; 3. gumbacchanna.

Shake, *n.* calana; kampana; iñjana; dhunana, *nt.* *v.t.* cāleti; kampeti; dhunāti; īreti; iñjeti. *v.i.* calati; kampati; iñjati; phandati. *p.p.* cālita; °pita; dhuta; īrita; iñjita; calita; °dita. — **about,** mathati; mantheti. — **off,** odhunāti; niddhunāti. °**ing,** *a.* calamāna; kampamāna. °**y,** *a.* lola; capala; cala.

Shall, *v. aux.* Expressed by the Future and Potential forms (such as *-issati, -eyya*). **What**

shall I do, kim ahaŋ karissāmi *or* kareyyaŋ ?

Shallow, *a.* 1. uttāna; agambhīra; 2. appassuta; 3. appamattaka. *v.t.* uttānaŋ karoti. *v.i.* uttānībhavati. *p.p.* uttānīkata; uttānībhūta. °**ly**, *adv.* uttānākārena. °**ness**, *n.* agambhīratta, *nt.* °**hearted**, *a.* athirajjhāsaya.

Sham, *n.* palambhanā; vañcanā, *f.* vyāja, *m.* adj. kūṭa; kittima. *v.t.* palambheti; vañceti. *p.p.* °bhita; °cita. °**fight**, uyyodhikā, *f.*

Shamble, *n.* alalitagati, *f.* *v.i.* asobhanākārena yāti.

Shambles, *n. pl.* āghātana; sūnāghara, *nt.*

Shame, *n.* 1. lajjā; hiri, *f.* 2. avamāna, *m.* apakitti, *f.* *v.t.* lajjāpeti; avamāneti. *v.i.* lajjati. *p.p.* °pita; °nita; lajjita. —**faced**, *a.* lajjanasīla; vinītasabhāva. °**ful**, *a.* lajjitabba; nindanīya; akittikara. °**fully**, *adv.* lajjitabbākārena. °**less**, *a.* nillajja; ahirika. °**lessly**, *adv.* nillajjākārena °**lessness**, *n.* alajjitā; ahirikatā, *f.*

Shampoo, *n.* sambāhana; sedana, *nt.* *v.t.* sambāhati; ubbaṭṭeti. *p.p.* °hita; °ṭita.

Shank, *n.* jaṅghā, *f.*

Shanty, *n.* kuṭi; paṇṇasālā, *f.*

Shape, *n.* saṇṭhāna, *nt.* ākāra, *m.* *v.t.* saṇṭhānaŋ deti; nimmiṇāti. *p.p.* dinnasaṇṭhāna; nimmita. °**less**, *a.* nirākāra; saṇṭhānarahita. °**ly**, *a.* surūpa; susaṇṭhāna.

Shard, *n.* kaṭhalikā, *f.* kapālakhaṇḍa, *m.*

Share, *n.* paṭiviŋsa; koṭṭhāsa; bhāga, *m.* *v.t.* 1. bhājeti; vibhajati; 2. bhāgaŋ labhati. *v.i.* sahabhāgī hoti. *p.p.* °jita; vibhatta; laddhabhāga; °gībhūta. °**holder**, *n.* bhāgasāmī; paṭiviŋsadhārī, *m.* °**er**, *n.* bhāgī; bhāgagāhī; bhājaka, *m.*

Share, *n.* phāla; phālaka, *m.*

Shark, *n.* 1. makara; 2. vañcaka, *m.* *v.i.* sāṭheyyena jīvati.

Sharp, *a.* 1. tikkha; tikhiṇa; tippa; tibba; 2. nisita; tejita; 3. khippanisantika; sukhumabuddhika. *adv.* yathākālaŋ; kālam anatikkamma. °**en**, *v.t.* tejeti; uttejeti; niseti; dhāraŋ ṭhapeti. *p.p.* °jita; nisita; ṭhapitadhāra. °**ener**, *n.* nisāṇakaravatthu, *nt.* °**er**, *n.* vañcaka; saṭha, *m.* °**ly**, *adv.* 1. tiṇhaŋ; tikhiṇaŋ; 2. yathākālam eva. °**ness**, 1. tikhiṇatta; 2. kosalla; pāṭava, *nt.* °**set**, *a.* atijighacchita. °**witted**, *a.* tikhiṇabuddhika.

Shatter, *v.t.* vikirati; vicuṇṇeti; khaṇḍeti. *v.i.* palujjati; vikirīyati. *p.p.* vikiṇṇa; °ṇita; °ḍita; palugga; vikiṇṇa.

Shave, *n.* 1. khurakamma; kesavoropaṇa, *nt.* 2. vañcana; sāṭheyya, *nt.* 3. kicchena mutti, *f.* *v.t.* muṇḍeti; kese ohāreti. *p.p.* °ḍita; °ritakesa. °**er**, nahāpita, *m.* °**ing**, *n.* kesoropaṇa; bhaṇḍukamma, *nt.* °**ling**, *n.* muṇḍaka; muṇḍasīsa, *m.*

Shawl, *n.* pāvuraṇa, *nt.*

She, *pron.* sā, *f.* °**bird**, *n.* sakuṇī, *f.* —**elephant**, *n.* hatthinī, *f.*

Sheaf, *n.* kalāpa, *m.* veṇī ; kaṇṇikā, *f.* *v.t.* veṇīkaroti. *p.p.* veṇīkata.

Shear, *v.t.* (lomādiŋ) luṇāti ; anukantati. *p.p.* lūṇa ; °tita. °**er,** *n.* lomakantaka, *m.* °**ing,** *n.* kantana ; lāyana, *nt.* *pl.* kattarikā, *f.*

Sheath, *n.* kosa, *m.* kosī, *f.*

Sheathe, *v.t.* kose pakkhipati ; paḷiveṭheti. *p.p.* °khitta ; °ṭhita. °**ing,** *n.* kosekhipana, *nt.*

Sheave, *v.t.* veṇīkaroti. *p.p.* °kata.

Shed, *n.* °maṇḍapa, *m.* vivaṭasālā, *f.* *v.t.* moceti ; vāheti ; paggharāpeti. *p.p.* mocita ; vāhita ; °pita. °**der,** *n.* paggharāpaka, *m.* °**ding,** *n.* paggharāpana, *nt.*

Sheen, *n.* kanti ; sobhā ; juti, *f.* bhāsuratta, *nt.* °**y,** *a.* ujjala ; bhāsura.

Sheep, *n.* meṇḍa ; mesa ; urabbha, *m.* — **cot,** °**fold,** *n.* meṇḍavaja, *m.* — **dealer,** *n.* orabbhika, *m.* °**ish,** *a.* nitteja ; lajjaṅasīla. °**ishness,** *n.* momuhatta ; nittejatta, *nt.*

Sheer, *a.* 1. kevala ; amissa ; 2. adhika ; daḷha. *v.i.* vokkamati ; apasarati. *p.p.* vokkanta ; apasaṭa. °**ly,** *adv.* accantaŋ.

Sheet, *n.* 1. paṭṭaka ; 2. attharaṇa, *nt.* *v.t.* attharati ; santharati. *p.p.* atthata ; santhata. —**fish,** sapharī, *m.* —**of metal,** lohapaṭṭa, *nt.* — **of paper,** kāgajapaṇṇa, *nt.* —**of water,** jalatala, *nt.* **Bed —,** mañcattharaṇa, *nt.*

Shelf, *n.* phalakādhāra ; bhittiphalaka, *m.*

Shell, *n.* kaṭāha ; kosa ; ghanattaca, *m.* *v.t.* kaṭāham apaneti ; kosā apaneti ; kapālehi chādeti. *p.p.* apanītakaṭāha ; kosāpanīta ; °chādita. °**fish,** kosamaccha ; kapālamaccha, *m.*

Shellac, *n.* lākhāpaṭṭa, *nt.*

Shelter, *n.* 1. āvaraṇa ; 2. tāṇa ; leṇa ; paṭisaraṇa, *nt.* *v.t.* tāyati ; rakkhati ; āvarati. *p.p.* tāyita ; °khita ; āvaṭa. °**less,** *a.* anāvaraṇa ; asaraṇa.

Shelve, *v.t.* 1. phalakatthare ṭhapeti ; 2. paṭisāmeti. *p.p.* °pita ; °**mita,** *v.i.* īsaŋ poṇāyati.

Shepherd, *n.* meṇḍapāla, *m.* *v.t.* meṇḍe pāleti. *p.p.* pālitameṇḍa. °**ess,** *n.* meṇḍapālī, *f.*

Sherbet, *n.* sītala-pāna, *nt.*

Sheriff, *n.* padesādhikārī, *m.* °**dom,** °**hood,** *n.* padesādhikāritta, *nt.*

Shibboleth, *n.* kulāveṇikavacana, *nt.*

Shield, *n.* 1. kheṭaka ; phalaka ; 2. tāṇa ; leṇa, *nt.* *v.t.* tāyati ; rakkhati. *p.p.* tāyita ; °khita.

Shift, *n.* saṅkamana ; parivattana, *nt.* ṭhānantarappatti, *f.* *v.t.* 1. cāveti ; saṅkāmeti ; upāyaŋ yojeti. *v.i.* ṭhānā cavati ; saṅkamati. *p.p.* cāvita ; °mita ; yojitopāya ; °cuta ; saṅkanta. °**less,** saṅkamanarahita. °**lessly,** *adv.* acalākārena. °**ily,** *adv.* kūṭopāyena. °**y,** *a.* capala ; asaddheyya.

Shikar, *n.* migava, *m.* °**ee,** *n.* vyādha ; migavantevāsī, *m.*

Shilling, *n.* (tannāmaka-) rūpiyavisesa, *m.*

Shilly-shally, *n.* akatanicchayatā, *f.* *v.i.* vicikicchati.

Shimmer, *n.* mandāloka, *m.* *v.i.* mandaŋ jalati.

Shin, *n.* aggajaṅghā, *f.*

Shine, *n.* juti ; ditti, *f.* *v.i.* jotati ; dippati ; pabhāsati ; rājati. *v.t.* joteti ; vaṇṇamaṭṭhaŋ karoti. *p.p.* jotita ; ditta ; °sita ; kata °ṭṭha. °**ing,** *a.* ujjala ; bhāsura ; jutimantu ; virocamāna ; virājamāna. °**y,** *a.* bhāsura ; vaṇṇamaṭṭha.

Shingle, *n.* dārumayachadaniṭṭhakā, *f.* *v.t.* chadanapaṭṭikāhi chādeti. *p.p.* °dita.

Shingles, *n.* vitacchikāroga, *m.*

Ship, *n.* nāvā ; taraṇī ; tarī, *f.* *v.t.* nāvam āropeti. *p.p.* °pita. °**builder,** *n.* nāvānimmāpaka, *m.* °**chandler,** *n.* nāvāya upakaraṇasampādaka, *m.* °**master,** *n.* nāvādhipati, *m.* °**man,** *n.* nāvika, *m.* °**ment,** *n.* nāvāya bhaṇḍajāta, *nt.* °**ping,** *n.* nāvāya pesana ; nāvāropaṇa, *nt.* °**wreck,** *n.* nāvābhaṅga, *m.* °**wrecked,** *a.* bhinnanāva. °**yard,** nāvānimmāpanaṭṭhāna, *nt.*

Shire, *n.* janapadekadesa, *m.*

Shirk, *v.i.* kiccavimukho hoti. *p.p.* °khībhūta. °**er,** *n.* kiccavimuka, *m.*

Shirt, *n.* adhokañcuka, *m.*

Shiver, *n.* 1. kampā, *f.* phandana; vedhana, *nt.* 2. sakalikā, *f.* khaṇḍa, *m.* *v.i.* vedhati ; kampati. *v.t.* sakalī-karoti. *p.p.* °dhita ; °pita ; sakalīkata. °**ingly,** *adv.* kampāsahitaŋ.

Shoal, *n.* 1. agambhīraṭṭhāna ; 2. mahāsamūha ; macchagumba, *m.* 3. jalavālukātala, *nt.* *v.i.* 1. uttānībhavati ; 2. sammilati ; gumbavasena rāsībhavati. *p.p.* °bhūta ; °lita.

Shock, *n.* 1. abhighāta ; 2. saṅkhobha, *m.* vipphandana, *nt.* *v.t.* 1. abhihanati ; saṅghaṭṭeti ; 2. saṅkhobheti ; vikkhipati. *v.i.* saṅkhubhati. *p.p.* abhihata ; °ṭita; °bhita; vikkhitta; °bhita. °**ingly,** *adv.* bībhacchākārena ; vikkhepakatāya.

Shoddy, *a.* lāmaka ; vyāja. *n.* pilotikatantu ; pilotikakhaṇḍa, *m.*

Shoe, *n.* pādatāṇa, *nt.* pādukā, *f.* *v.t.* pādatāṇaŋ *or* khurattāṇaŋ yojeti. *p.p.* yojitakhurattāṇa. °**black,** *n.* pādatāṇamajjaka, *m.* °**maker,** *n.* pādukāsampādaka, *m.*

Shoo, *intj.* apasara. *v.i.* sūsūyati. *v.t.* palāpeti. *p.p.* °yita ; °pita.

Shoot, *v.i.* sahasā niggacchati ; ubbhijjati. *v.t.* vijjhati ; vissajjeti. *p.p.* °niggata ; ubbhinna ; viddha ; vissaṭṭha. *noun.* 1. aṅkura ; kisalaya, *m.* 2. salilāvaṭṭa, *m.* 3. opatanapaṇālikā, *f.* — **ahead,** paṭimalle parājetvā dhāvati. — **down,** vijjhitvā māreti. — **off,** sahasā palāyati. — **home,** yathālakkhaŋ vijjhati. — **up,** sīghaŋ vaḍḍhati. °**er,** *n.* vijjhitu, *m.*

Shooting, *n.* 1. vijjhana, *nt.* 2. migava, *m.* adj. tibba (vedanākara), *m.* — **gallery,** *n.* vijjhanaparicayaṭṭhāna, *nt.* — **range,** *n.* abbhokāse vijjhanaparicaya, *m.* — **star,** *n.* ukkāpāta, *m.*

Shop, *n.* āpaṇa, *m.* paṇyasālā, *f.* *v.t.* āpaṇaŋ yāti. °**keeper,** *n.*

āpaṇika ; paṇyavikkayī, *m.* °**lifter,** *n.* paṇiyacora, *m.* °**ping,** *n.* āpaṇato kiṇana, *nt.*

Shore, *n.* veḷā, *f.* taṭa ; tīra ; kūla, *nt.* *v.t.* thambhādīhi upatthambheti ; ādhārakaŋ yojeti. *p.p.* °bhita ; yojitādhāraka. °**less,** *a.* atīra ; amariyāda.

Short, *a.* (of length :) rassa ; vāmana ; anāyata. (of time :) aciraṭṭhitika ; ittarakālika. (of quantity :) appahoṇaka ; ūna. (of vowel :) laghu. °**coming,** *n.* pamādadosa, *m.* °**cut,** *n.* ujumagga ; adūrapatha, *m.* °**hand,** *n.* laghulekhana, *nt.* — **handed,** *a.* upatthambharahita. — **lived,** *a.* acirajīvī ; aciraṭṭhāyī. °**ly,** *adv.* 1. acirena ; khippaŋ; 2. saṅkhepena ; samāsato. °**ness,** *n.* adīghatta ; rassatta, *nt.* °**sight,** *n.* rassadiṭṭhi ; adūradassitā, *f.* °**sighted,** *a.* rassadiṭṭhika. — **spoken,** *a.* mitabhāṇī. — **tempered,** *a.* kuppanasīla.

Shortage, *n.* ūnatta, *nt.*

Shorten, *v.t.* 1. saṅkhipati ; saṅkoceti ; 2. rassaŋ karoti. *p.p.* saṅkhitta ; °cita ; katarassa.

Shot, *n.* 1. khepa ; pahāra, *m.* vijjhana, *nt.* 2. nāḷīyantaguḷikā, *f.* 3. vijjhaka ; nāḷīyantavedhī, *m.*

Shoulder, *n.* jattu ; aŋsakūṭa, *m.* *v.t.* 1. khandhena vahati ; aŋsakūṭe ṭhapeti ; 2. jattunā paharati. *p.p.* °vahita ; °pita ; °pahaṭa. — **belt,** *n.* aŋsapaṭṭikā, *f.*

Shout, *n.* unnāda ; virava, *m.* *v.i.t.* ugghoseti ; saddāyati ; ravati ; nadati ; unnadati. *p.p.* °sita ; °yita ; ruta ; nadita.

Shove, *n.* ussāraṇā, *f.* āyāsena apanayanā, *f.* *v.t.* ussāreti ; bāhādīhi paharitvā apaneti. *p.p.* °rita ; °nīta.

Shovel, *n.* bhūmidabbī, *f.* *v.t.* bhūdabbiyā pakkhipati. *p.p.* °pakkhitta. °**ler,** *n.* bhūdabbiyā pakkhipaka, *m.*

Show, *n.* 1. sandassana ; āvīkaraṇa; 2. vyājadassana, *nt.* *v.t.* 1. dasseti ; nidasseti ; 2. sūceti ; pakāseti ; āvīkaroti. *p.p.* °sita ; °cita; °sita ; āvīkata. *v.i.* sandissati ; āvībhavati. *p.p.* sandiṭṭha ;° bhūta. °**er,** *n.* dassetu ; nidassaka, *m.* °**ily,** *adv.* dassanīyākārena ; vyājena. °**iness,** *n.* dassanīyatta ; gabbitapadassana, *nt.* °**y,** *a.* dassanīya ; vyājadassanayutta.

Shower, *n.* vuṭṭhi, *f.* mandamegha, *m.* *v.i.* mandaŋ vassati. — °**bath,** *n.* dhārāsināna ; sīkaranahāna, *nt.* °**y,** *a.* meghabahula.

Shred, *n.* sakalikā, *f.* vatthakhaṇḍa, *m.* *v.t.* sakalīkaroti ; khaṇḍaso chindati. *p.p.* °kata; °chinna.

Shrew, *n.* 1. kakkasitthī ; kalahakāriṇī, *f.* 2. mūsikāvisesa, *m.*

Shrewd, *a.* 1. tibba ; tikhiṇa ; 2. catura ; nipuṇa ; sūra. °**ly,** *adv.* 1. chekākārena ; caturatāya ; 2. tibbaŋ. °**ness,** *n.* 1. cāturiya ; nepuñña ; 2. tikhiṇatta, *nt.*

Shriek, *n.* akkandana, *nt.* kaṭukanāda, *m.* *v.i.t.* kaṭukaŋ nadati ; akkandati. *p.p.* °dita.

Shrill, *a.* kaṇṇakaṭuka. *v.i.* kakkasaŋ nadati. °**ness,** *n.* kaṇṇakaṭukatta, *nt.*

Shrimp, *n.* jalavicchika, *m.*

Shrine, *n.* cetiya, pujjaṭṭhāna, *nt.* *v.t.* cetiye nidahati. *p.p.* °hita.

Shrink, *v.i.* saṅkucati ; līyati. *v.t.* saṅkoceti ; saŋharati. *p.p.* °cita ; līna ; °cita ; saŋhaṭa. — **from,** viramati ; apakkamati. °**able,** *a.* saṅkocanāraha. °**age,** *n.* saṅkocana ; paṭilīyana, *nt.*

Shrivel, *v.i.* saṅkuṭati. *v.t.* valiŋ gaṇhāpeti ; saṅkoceti. *p.p.* °ṭita ; °pita ; °cita.

Shroud, *n.* chavapaṭicchādana, *nt.* *v.t.* onandhati ; onahati. *p.p.* onaddha ; onayhita.

Shrub, *n.* gumba; gaccha, *m.* °**bery,** *n.* gumbachannaṭṭhāna, *nt.* °**by,** *a.* gumbayutta.

Shrug, *n.* aŋsasaṅkoca, *m.* *v.i.t.* aŋsakūṭe unnāmeti *or* saṅkoceti. *p.p.* unnāmitaŋsakūṭa.

Shudder, *n.* chambhitatta, *nt.* *v.i.* bhayena kampati *or* phandati. *p.p.* bhayakampita. °**ingly,** *adv.* sacchambhitattaŋ.

Shuffle, *n.* 1. vikkhipana ; missīkaraṇa, *nt.* 2. vañcanā, *f.* *v.t.* vikkhipati ; sammisseti ; opuṇāti. *v.i.* pāde sappanto gacchati. *p.p.* vikkhitta ; °sita ; °ṇita.

Shun, *v.t.* vivajjeti ; parivajjeti ; pajahati. *p.p.* °jita ; °hita.

Shunt, *n.* parāvattana ; aññattha pāpana, *nt.* *v.t.* parāvatteti ; aññattha neti. *p.p.* °tita ; °nīta.

Shut, *v.t.* thaketi ; pidahati ; āvarati. *p.p.* thakita ; pihita ; āvaṭa. — **in,** rodheti. — **out,** nivāreti ; nisedheti. °**ter,** *n.* kavāṭa ; pidhāna, *nt.* °**ting,** *n.* pidahana, *nt.* — **up,** sannirumbheti.

Shuttle, *n.* tasara, *m.*

Shy, *a.* lajjālu ; bhīruka ; hirimana ; janabhīruka. *v.i.* sahasā apakkamati. *v.t.* (paharaṇāya) khipati *or* vissajjeti. *p.p.* °apakkanta ; khitta ; vissaṭṭha. °**ly,** *adv.* salajjaŋ. °**ness,** *n.* hirimanatā ; janabhīrutā, *f.*

Sibilant, *n.* usumakkhara, *nt.*

Sibyl, *n.* devadāsī ; anāgatavādinī, *f.*

Siccative, *a.* *n.* sosanaka.

Sick, *a.* gilāna ; vyādhita ; rogī ; rogātura ; akallaka. °**ish,** *a.* īsaŋ-gilāna. — **leave,** *n.* gilānaviveka, *m.* °**ly,** *a.* rogabahula. °**ness,** roga ; vyādhi ; ātaṅka ; āmaya, *m.* gelañña, *nt.* °**room,** gilānasālā, *f.*

Sicken, *v.t.* 1. gilānaŋ karoti ; 2. jigucchamuppādeti. *v.i.* 1. gilāno hoti ; 2. jigucchati. *p.p.* ° nīkata ; °ditajiguccha ; gilānabhūta ; °chita. °**ing,** *a.* jigucchākara.

Sickle, *n.* asita ; dātta ; lavitta, *nt.* °**man,** *n.* lāyaka, *m.*

Side, *n.* passa ; pakkha ; aŋsa, *m.* *v.i.* pakkhaŋ gaṇhāti ; passe tiṭṭhati. *p.p.* gahitapakkha ; °ṭhita. — **by side,** yuganandhavasena, *adv.* °**long,** *a.* passānugata. °**look,** *n.* apāṅgadiṭṭhi, *f.* °**show,** *n.* amukhyavohāra, *m.* °**splitting,** *a.* atihāsajanaka. °**view,** *n.* ekapassikadassana, *nt.* — **with,** pakkhaŋ gaṇhāti. °**wise,** °**ways,** *adv.* tiriyaŋ. °**wards,** *adv.* passābhimukhaŋ. **At one's —,** passe, *adv.* **On all –s,** samantato, *adv.* °**ing with,** anuvattaka ; pakkhagāhī, *a.*

Sidereal, *a.* nakkhattanissita.

Siderography, *n.* ayoukkiraṇasippa, *nt.*

Sidle, *v.i.* (gāravāya) passena yāti. *p.p.* °yāta.

Siege, *n.* avarodhana; uparodhana; rundhana, *nt.* *v.t.* orundhati; uparundhati; rodheti. *p.p.* oruddha; rodhita.

Siesta, *n.* divāvihāra, *m.* divāseyyā, *f.*

Sieve, *n.* piṭṭhacālanī, *f.* *v.t.* cālaniyā puthakkaroti. *p.p.* °kata.

Sift, *v.t.* 1. opuṇāti; 2. cālaniyā sodheti; 3. sukhumam upaparikkhati. *p.p.* °ṇita; °dhita; °khita. °**ing,** *n.* opuṇana, *nt.* °**er,** *n.* opuṇaka, *m.*

Sigh, *n.* nissāsa, *m.* *v.i.t.* nissasati; nitthunāti. *p.p.* °sita; °nita. °**ingly,** *adv.* sanissāsaŋ.

Sight, *n.* diṭṭhi, *f.* dassana, *nt.* cakkhupatha, *m.* *v.t.* passati; āpāthagataŋ karoti. *p.p.* diṭṭha; °kata. °**less,** *a.* andha, diṭṭhihīna. °**lessness,** *n.* andhatta, *nt.* °**ly,** *a.* dassanīya; cārudassana. °**liness,** *n.* dassanīyatta; abhirūpatta, *nt.* °**seeing,** *n.* nānāṭhānadassana; disāvilokana, *nt.* °**seer,** *n.* sundaraṭṭhānapassī, *m.*

Sigillate, *a.* samuṭṭhāpitarūpa (-bhājana). °**ion,** *n.* bhājanesu rūpasamuṭṭhāpana, *nt.*

Sign, *n.* 1. lakkhaṇa; lañchana; abhiññāṇa, *nt.* 2. iṅgita, *nt.* viññatti, *f.* viññāpana, *nt.* 3. visesadhajа, *m.* *v.i.* 1. hatthalañchaŋ patiṭṭhāpeti. *v.t.* viññāpeti; saññaŋ deti. *p.p.* °pitahattha°; °pita; dinnasañña. °**board,** nāmaphalaka, *nt.* — **language,** *n.* hatthamuddā, *f.* — **on the forehead,** tilaka, *m.* °**post,** *n.* saññātthambha, *m.*

Signal, *n.* saññā, *f.* saṅketa, *m.* adj. visiṭṭha; asādhāraṇa. *v.t.* saññaŋ deti; saṅketaŋ karoti. *p.p.* dinnasañña; katasaṅketa. °**ize,** *v.t.* khyātiŋ gameti; visiṭṭhataŋ pāpeti. °**man,** *n.* saññādāyaka, *m.* °**ly,** *adv.* visiṭṭhākārena.

Signatory, *n.* *a.* hatthalañchanadāyī, *m.*

Signature, *n.* hatthalañchana, *nt.* hatthamuddā, *f.*

Signet, *n.* muddā; muddikā, *f.* °**ring,** *n.* hatthamuddikā, *f.*

Signify, *v.t.* gameti; bodheti; viññāpeti; sūceti. *p.p.* gamita; °dhita; °pita; sūcita. °**icance,** *n.* 1. attha; adhippāya, *m.* 2. mahatta; garutta, *nt.* °**icant,** °**icative,** *a.* 1. viññāpaka; atthayutta; 2. anussaraṇīya.

Signior, Signor, *n.* ayya; sāmī, *m.*

Silent, *a.* nissadda; tuṇhībhūta. °**nce,** *n.* nissaddatā, *f.* tuṇhībhāva, *m.* abhāsana, *nt.* *v.t.* 1. nissaddaŋ karoti; 2. niruttarataŋ pāpeti. *p.p.* nissaddīkata; °pāpita. °**ly,** *adv.* tuṇhībhāvena; nissaddaŋ.

Silhouette, *n.* chāyācitta, *nt.* *v.t.* chāyācittam ālikhati.

Silk, *n.* koseyya; kimijavattha, *nt.* — **cotton tree,** simbalī, *m.* °**en,** *a.* koseyyamaya. — **mercer,** *n.* koseyyavāṇija, *m.* —

worm, *n*. kosakimi, *m*. °**y**, *a*. mudu ; komala ; saṇha.

Sill, *n*. ummāra, *m*. esikā, *f*.

Silly, *a*. momuha ; andhabāla. °**iness**, *n*. mūḷhatta ; mandamatitta, *nt*.

Silt, *n*. vūḷha-paṅkādi, *m*. *v.t.* (paṅkādīhi) rundheti *or* āvarati. *v.i.* rodhīyati. *p.p.* °dhita; °āvaṭa ; rodhita.

Silvan, Sylvan, *a*. āraññaka ; vanacchanna.

Silver, *n*. rajata, *nt*. adj. rajatavaṇṇa; rajatamaya. *v.t.* rajatena āvarati *or* lepeti. *p.p.* rajatāvaṭa ; rajatalitta. — **coin**, rūpiya, *nt*. — **plate**, rajatapaṭṭa, *m*. °**smith**, *n*. rajatakāra, *m*. — **tongued**, *a*. caturakathika. °**y**, *a*. rajatobhāsa.

Simian, *n*. vānara, *m*. adj. vānaragatika.

Similar, *a*. sadisa ; samāna ; tulya ; sannibha ; saṅkāsa ; sarikkha. °**ity**, *n*. sadisatta ; tulyatta ; samānatta, *nt*. °**ly**, *adv*. tath'eva ; evam eva.

Simile, *n*. upamā, *f*. opamma ; rūpaka, *nt*.

Similitude, *n*. samānatta ; samānarūpakatta, *nt*.

Simmer, *v.i.* mandaŋ kuthati ; sanikaŋ paccati. *p.p.* °kuthita ; °pakka.

Simoom, *n*. kantāravāta, *m*.

Simous, *a*. cipiṭanāsika.

Simper, *n*. aññāṇahāsa, *m*. *v.i.* mūḷhākārena hasati.

Simple, *a*. 1. avisiṭṭha ; anacchariya ; 2. amissa ; kevala ; 3. uju ; 4. sugama. °**icity**, *n*. 1. amissatā ; 2. vinītatā ; 3. sugamatā, *f*. °**ification**, *n*. visadīkaraṇa, *nt*. °**ify**, *v.t.* ujuŋ *or* visadaŋ karoti. *p.p.* visadīkata. °**ly**, *adv*. kevalaŋ ; anākulaŋ. °**minded**, *a*. akuṭila ; ujucitta. °**ness**, *n*. avisiṭṭhatta ; analaṅkaṭatta, *nt*. °**ton**, *n*. eḷamūga, *m*.

Simulate, *v.t.* vyājena dasseti ; micchā ñāpeti. *p.p.* °dassita ; °pita. °**ion**, *n*. vyājavesagahaṇa, *nt*.

Simultaneous, *a*. yuganandha ; apubbācarima ; ekakālika. °**ly**, *adv*. apubbaŋ acarimaŋ. °**ness**, *n*. samakālikatta, *nt*.

Sin, *n*. pāpa ; akusala ; apuñña ; agha ; durita ; dukkaṭa, *nt*. *v.i.* pāpaŋ karoti ; duccaritaŋ carati. *p.p.* katapāpa. °**ful**, *a*. pāpī ; pāpakārī ; pāpiṭṭha. °**fulness**, *n*. pāpiyatta ; pāpiṭṭhatta, *nt*. °**less**, *a*. nippāpa ; anagha. °**ner**, *n*. pāpakārī, *m*.

Since, *prep*. pabhuti *with abl*. *conj*. yato ; yasmā. *adv*. tadanantaraŋ ; (tato) paṭṭhāya. — **now**, yāv'ajjatanā. **Ever —**, (tato) sabbadā. **Since I saw you last**, tava mayā antimaŋ diṭṭhakālato paṭṭhāya. **Since he did so**, tena tathā katattā. **How long since is it ?** kīvaciraŋ ito ? **Has since been cut down**, tasmā so chinno.

Sincere, *a*. avyāja ; yathābhūta. °**ity**, °**ness**, *n*. ajjava, avyājatta, *nt*. °**ly**, *adv*. ajjavena ; avyājena.

Sinciput, *n.* sīsapubbaddha, *m.*

Sine, *prep.* vinā. — **qua non,** accāvassaka-kāraṇa, *nt.*

Sinecure, *n.* nikkamma-savetanaṭhānantara, *nt.* °**ist,** *n.* nikkamma-vetanūpajīvī, *m.*

Sinew, *n.* nahāru, *m.* sirā, *f.* °**y,** *a.* thāmavantu.

Sing, *v.i.* gāyati ; (of birds :) kūjati. *p.p.* gāyita ; kūjita. °**er,** *n.* gāyaka, *m.* °**ing,** *n.* gāyana ; gīta, *nt.*

Singe, *v.t.* thokaŋ jhāpeti. *v.i.* thokaŋ ḍayhati. *p.p.* °pita ; °daḍḍha.

Singhalese, Sinhalese, *a.* Sīhaḷadīpika ; Sīhaḷāyatta. — **language,** Sīhaḷabhāsā, *f.*

Single, *a. n.* 1. ekaka ; kevala ; asahāya ; 2. avivāhaka. *v.t.* niddhāreti ; uccināti. *p.p.* °rita ; °nita. — **combat,** dvandayuddha, *nt.* °**handed,** *a.* asahāya. — **hearted,** *a.* advejjhamānasa. — **lined,** *a.* ekapaṭalika. °**ly,** *adv.* ekekaso ; paccekaŋ. °**ness,** *n.* kevalatta ; ekakatta, *nt.*

Singsong, *n.* abhinnassaragīta, *nt.*

Singular, *n.* ekavacana, *nt.* adj. 1. pacceka ; ekībhūta ; 2. ativisiṭṭha ; vimhayāvaha ; anupama ; anaññasādhāraṇa. °**ity,** *n.* asādhāraṇatta ; visiṭṭhatta, *nt.* °**ly,** *adv.* visesato.

Sinister, *a.* 1. asubha ; avamaṅgala ; 2. duṭṭha ; vaṅka ; 3. vāma ; adakkhiṇa.

Sinistrous, *a* durāsaya. °**ly,** *adv.* duṭṭhākārena ; durāsayatāya.

Sink, *n.* pūti-udakāvāṭa, *m. v.i.* 1. nimujjati ; osīdati ; visīdati ; ogacchati ; 2. vilayaŋ yāti. *v.t.* 1. osīdāpeti ; 2. khayaŋ pāpeti. *p.p.* nimugga ; osīna ; visīna ; ogata ; °yāta ; °pita. °**er,** *n.* 1. osīdāpaka ; 2. osīdāpakabhāra, *m.* °**ing,** *n.* 1. osīdāpana ; 2. nimujjana, ogāhana, *nt.* 3. balahāni, *f.*

Sinology, *n.* Cīnabhāsādiñāṇa, *nt.*

Sinuosity, *n.* vaṅkayuttatā, *f.*

Sinuous, *a.* vaṅkagāmī ; kuṭilagatika.

Sinus, *n.* bhagandalā, *f.*

Sip, *n.* thokapibana, *nt. v.t.* thokathokaŋ pivati. *p.p.* °pivita.

Siphon, *n.* unnāmita-nāḷa, *m.*

Sir, *n.* mārisa ; ayya, *m. v.t.* ayyanāmen' ālapati.

Sire, *Voc.* Mahārāja ; Deva ; Ayya. *v.t.* sindhave uppādeti.

Siren, *n.* 1. kinnarī ; jalaṅganā ; 2. unnādinī ; nādanāḷī, *f.*

Siriasis, *n.* 1. adhikātapamucchā, *f.* 2. ātapasināna, *nt.*

Sirius, *n.* ekā mahātārā, *f.*

Sirocco, *n.* uṇhavāta, *m.*

Sirrah, *n. Voc.* are ; hare ; aho sāmī.

Sister, *n.* bhaginī ; anujā, *f.* °**hood,** *n.* 1. bhaginībhāva ; 2. sahadhammika-nārīgaṇa, *m.* °**in-law,** nanandā, *f,* °**ly,** *a.* bhaginīsadisa. °**'s son,** bhāgiṇeyya, *m.* °**'s husband,** sāla, *m.* **Elder** —, jeṭṭhabhaginī, *f.* **Younger** —, kaṇiṭṭhabhaginī, *f.*

Sit, *v.i.* nisīdati ; upavisati ; āsati. *v.t.* nisīdāpeti ; upaveseti. *p.p.* nisinna ; upaviṭṭha ; °pita ; °sita. — **near,** upanisīdati. °**ting,** *n.*

nisajjā, *f.* °**ting room**, pamukhasālā, *f.*

Site, *n.* vatthu ; patiṭṭhāṭhāna, *nt.*

Situate, Situated, *a.* patiṭṭhita ; niviṭṭha. °**tion,** *n.* 1. sannivesa, *m.* patiṭṭhāna, *nt.* 2. avatthā ; dasā, *f.* 3. adhikāra, *m.* pada, *nt.*

Sitz-bath, *n.* nahānabhājana, *nt.*

Six, *a. n.* cha. — **coloured,** *a.* chabbaṇṇa. — **cornered,** *a.* chaḷaŋsika. — **fold,** *a.* chabbidha ; chagguṇa. °**teen,** *a. n.* soḷasa. °**teenth,** *a.* soḷasama. °**th,** *a.* chaṭṭha.

Sixty, *n.* saṭṭhi, *f.* °**five,** pañcasaṭṭhi, *f.* °**four,** catusaṭṭhi, *f.* °**nine,** ekūnasattati, *f.* °**six,** chasaṭṭhi, *f.* °**seven,** sattasaṭṭhi, *f.* °**three,** tesaṭṭhi, *f.* °**two,** dvāsaṭṭhi ; dvisaṭṭhi, *f.*

Sizable, *a.* mahanta ; visāla.

Size, *n.* pamāṇa ; parimāṇa, *nt.* āyāmavitthāra, *m. v.t.* pamāṇayuttaŋ karoti ; vaggīkaroti. *p.p.* °kata.

Size, *n.* vatthakhali, *m. v.t.* khalinā makkheti. *p.p.* khalimakkhita. **Sizy,** *a.* khaliyutta.

Skate, *n.* 1. maṇḍūkamacchavisesa, *m.* 2. himapādukā, *f. v.i.* himapādukāhi visappati.

Skein, *n.* suttaguḷikā, *f.*

Skeleton, *n.* 1. aṭṭhikaṅkala ; aṭṭhisaṅghāṭa, *m.* 2. gehapañjara, *m.* 3. saṅkhittasaṇṭhāna, *nt.* °**ize,** *v.t.* kaṅkalattaŋ pāpeti.

Skep, *n.* 1. veṭṭapiṭaka ; 2. madhukarapañjara, *m.*

Sketch, *n.* 1. saṅkhittanirūpana, *nt.* saṅkhittaracanā, *f. v.t.* saṅkhepena nirūpeti. *p.p.* °pita. °**y,** *a.* saṅkhittanirūpanayutta.

Skew, *a. n.* passonata.

Skewer, *n.* maŋsasūci ; maŋsasalākā, *f.*

Ski, *n.* himapādukāphalaka, *m. v.i.* himapādukāphalakehi yāti.

Skid, *n.* cakkarodhana, *nt. v.i.* khalitvā yāti. *v.t.* cakkaŋ rodheti. *p.p.* °yāta ; rodhitacakka.

Skiff, *n.* lahudoṇikā, *f.*

Skill, *n.* cāturiya, kosalla ; nepuñña, *nt.* °**ful,** *a.* paṭu ; pavīṇa ; nipuṇa ; cheka ; catura. °**fully,** *adv.* cāturiyena ; nepuññena. °**ed,** *a.* katahattha ; katupāsana.

Skim, *v.t.* pheṇam *or* maṇḍam apaneti. *v.i.* vegena parisappati. *p.p.* apanītamaṇḍa ; °pita. °**mer,** *n.* 1. maṇḍuddharaṇakaṭacchu ; 2. udakapakkhivisesa, *m.*

Skimp, *v.t.* ūnappamāṇena annapānādiŋ sampādeti ; maccharāyati. °**ingly,** *adv.* maccharākārena. °**y,** *a.* mitampaca ; maccharī.

Skin, *n.* taca, *m.* camma, *nt. v.t.* cammam uppāṭeti ; niccammaŋ karoti. *v.i.* cammaŋ rūhati. °**ner,** *n.* cammakāra ; cammavāṇija, *m.* — **deep,** *a.* chavimattagambhīra. — **flint,** *n.* thaddhamaccharī, *m.* **Outer —,** chavi, *f.*

Skip, *v.i.* 1. uppatanto kīḷati ; 2. sahasā ṭhānantaraŋ yāti. *n.* ādhāvana-paridhāvana, *nt.* °**per,** *n.* 1. plavaka ; 2. lahunāvādhipa, *m.*

Skip, *n.* 1. ākarotaraṇa-bhājana, *nt.* 2. vijjālayasevaka, *m.*

Skirmish, *n.* antarā-kalaha, *m.* *v.t.* mandasamūhavasena yujjhati. *p.p.* °jhita.

Skirt, *n.* pariyanta, *m.* vaṭṭikā, *f.* (of a clothe:) dasā, *f.* *v.i.t.* pariyantena yāti; pariyante vattati.

Skit, *n.* nindakalipi; ohīlakaracanā, *f.* *v.t.* ohīlakaracanaŋ sampādeti.

Skittish, *a.* 1. capala; avinīta; 2. keḷsīla. °**ly**, *adv.* capalatāya; keḷsīlatāya.

Skive, *v.t.* nipiŋseti; taccheti. *p.p.* °sita; tacchita. °**er**, *n.* cammasodhakasattha, *nt.*

Skulk, *v.i.* nilīyati. *p.p.* nilīna. °**er**, *n.* nilīyaka, *m.*

Skull, *n.* sīsakapāla, *m.*

Sky, *n.* ākāsa; vehāsa; nabha; antaḷikkha; anilapatha; ādiccapatha, *m.* gagana; ambara; kha, *nt.* °**blue**, *a.* mandanīla. °**clad**, *a.* digambara; nagga. °**high**, *a.* atyucca. °**lark**, *n.* bhāradvājapakkhī, *m.* °**light**, *n.* chadanagavakkha, *m.* °**scraper**, *n.* atyucca-pāsāda, *m.* °**wards**, *adv.* nabhābhimukhaŋ.

Slab, *n.* silāpatthara; silāpaṭṭa, *m.* *v.t.* patthare sampādeti.

Slack, *a.* 1. sithila; manda; atikhiṇa; 2. pamatta; anussuka. *n.* dandhagatika, *m.* *v.t.* sithilīkaroti. *p.p.* °kata. °**en**, *v.i.* mandībhavati; sithilībhavati. *v.t.* mandīkaroti. *p.p.* °bhūta; °kata. °**ly**, *adv.* sithilākārena. °**ness**, *n.* sithilatta; mandavegatta, *nt.*

Slake, *v.t.* 1. pipāsam upasameti; 2. jalam āsiñcati. *p.p.* °mitapipāsa; āsittajala.

Slam, *n.* ghaṭṭanasadda, *m.* *v.t.i.* mahāsaddena thaketi *or* ghaṭṭeti. *p.p.* °kita; °ṭita.

Slander, *n.* pesuñña; abbhakkhāna, *nt.* *v.t.* abbhakkhāti; apavadati. *p.p.* °khāta; apavutta. °**er**, *n.* abbhakkhāvī; pisuṇavādī, *m.* °**ous**, *a.* sopavāda; bhedakara. °**ously**, *adv.* sopavādaŋ; abbhakkhānapubbakaŋ.

Slang, *n.* 1. asabbha, *nt.* asiṭṭhavācā; 2. avyattakathā, *f.* °**y**, *a.* avyattapadabahula.

Slant, *n.* opāta, *m.* adj. poṇa; opātayutta. *v.t.* opātayuttaŋ karoti. *v.i.* poṇībhavati. *p.p.* opātakata; °bhūta. °**ing**, *a.* poṇabhūta. °**ingly**, *adv.* poṇākārena.

Slap, *v.t.* pāṇitalena paharati. *p.p.* °pahaṭa. *n.* pāṇippahāra, *m.* — **bang**, *adv.* dāruṇākārena. — **dash**, *adv.* sāhasikatāya; anisamma.

Slash, *n.* 1. dīghapaṭṭikā, *f.* 2. kasāhanana, *nt.* *v.t.* 1. dīghaso chindati; 2. kasāya tāḷeti. *p.p.* °chinna; °tāḷita. °**ing**, *a.* mammacchedaka.

Slat, *n.* dīgha-tanupaṭṭikā, *f.* *v.t.* dīghapaṭṭikāya āhanati. *p.p.* °āhata.

Slate, *n.* silāpaṭṭa, *m.* °**pencil**, *n.* silāpattharalekhanī, *f.* *v.t.* 1. silāpattharehi chādeti; 2. bāḷhaŋ garahati *or* upavadati. *p.p.* °hita; °upavutta. °**er**, *n.* 1. silāpattharavaḍḍhakī; 2. bāḷhagarahī, *m.*

Slattern, *n.* asobhanā *or* dunnivatthā itthī, *f.* °**ly**, *adv.* asobhanākārena.

Slaughter, *n.* hanana ; ghātana ; māraṇa, *nt.* vadha, *m.* *v.t.* māreti ; ghāteti ; hanati. *p.p.* °rita ; °tita ; hata. °**er**, *n.* vadhaka ; ghātaka, *m.* °**house**, *n.* sūnāghara, *nt.* °**ous**, *a.* manussaghātaka. °**ously**, *adv.* atidāruṇatāya.

Slave, *n.* dāsa, *m.* *v.i.* dāsakammaŋ karoti. — **woman**, dāsī, *f.* °**ry**, *n.* dāsatta, *nt.* °**ish**, *a.* dāsopama ; dāsasadisa. °**ishly**, *adv.* dāsākārena.

Slaver, *v.t.* lālā paggharāpeti. *p.p.* °pitalāla.

Slavey, *n.* paricārikā ; ceṭikā, *f.*

Slavocracy, *n.* dāsapatipālanabala, *nt.*

Slay, *v.t.* hanati ; ghāteti ; māreti. *p.p.* hata ; °tita ; °rita. °**er**, *n.* ghātetu ; hantu, *m.*

Sled, **Sledge**, *n.* acakkahimayāna, *nt.* *v.i.* himayānena yāti.

Sledge (-hammer), ayokūṭa ; ayoghana, *m.*

Sleek, *a.* siliṭṭha ; siniddha. *v.t.* maṭṭhaŋ *or* siliṭṭhaŋ karoti. *p.p.* maṭṭhakata. °**ly**, *adv.* saṇhākārena. °**y**, *a.* vañcanasīla ; upajappaka.

Sleep, *n.* niddā ; seyyā, *f.* soppa, *nt.* *v.i.* niddāyati ; sayati ; supati. °**er**, *n.* sayitu, *m.* °**ful**, *a.* niddālu ; niddābahula. °**ing**, *a.* sayāna ; sayamāna. °**iness**, *n.* niddālutā ; middhaparetatā, *f.* °**less**, *a.* vigatanidda ; jāgaranta. °**lessness**, *n.* niddāvigama, *m.* °**y**, *a.* niddālu ; niddhapareta.

Sleet, *n.* jalamissita-himavuṭṭhi, *f.* *v.i.* himamissaŋ vassati.

Sleeve, *n.* kañcukahattha, *m.*

Sleigh, see **Sled.**

Sleight, *n.* 1. nepuñña ; 2. sāṭheyya ; upāyakosalla, *nt.* — **of hand**, indajāladassana, *nt.*

Slender, *a.* tanu ; kisa ; appaka. °**ness**, *n.* tanutta ; kisatta.

Slice, *n.* pesikā, *f.* phāla, *m.* *v.t.* pesīkaroti ; sallikhati. *p.p.* °kata ; °khita. °**er**, *n.* pesīkāraka, *m.*

Slick, *a.* 1. catura ; 2. cāṭukāma ; upajappaka. *adv.* anūnaŋ ; sampuṇṇaŋ.

Slide, *v.i.* visappati ; ṭhānā cavati. *p.p.* °pita ; °cuta. *v.t.* ṭhānā cāveti. *p.p.* °vita, *n.* opātapanāḷikā, *f.* °**ing**, *n.* opatana ; visappana, *nt.*

Slight, *a.* appamattaka. *n.* avaññā, *f.* anādara, *m.* *v.t.* avamaññati. *p.p.* avamata. °**ly**, *adv.* appavasena.

Slim, see **Slender.** °**ness**, *n.* 1. kisatta ; tanutta ; upāyakosalla, *nt.* °**ly**, *adv.* nikatiyā ; upāyena.

Slime, *n.* 1. sevāla, *m.* 2. cikkhalla, *nt.* *v.t.* sevālena onahati. *v.i.* silesitāya gahaṇā muñcati. *p.p.* sevālonaddha ; °mutta.

Slimy, *a.* 1. silesayutta ; agahaṇūpaga ; 2. vañcanaka ; 3. upalālaka. °**ily**, *adv.* kapaṭatāya ; cāṭukamyatāya.

Sling, *n.* sakkharāvijjhakayanta, *nt.* *v.t.* sakkharā vijjhati. *p.p.* °viddha.

Slink, *n.* ayathākāle jātavaccha, *m.* *v.i.* nilīyitvā apakkamati. *v.t.* 1. migīgabbhaŋ pāteti ; 2. kāle aparipuṇṇe pasaveti. *p.p.* °apakkanta ; °pātitami° ; °vita.

Slip, *n.* 1. pakkhalana, *nt.* 2. khalita, *nt.* pamādadosa, *m.* 3. tanupaṭṭikā, *f.* 4. cimilikā, *f.* 5. antaravāsaka, *m.* 6. saṅkhalikā, *f.* *v.i.* 1. khalati ; visappati ; 2. muñcitvā yāti ; alakkhito palāyati ; 3. khalitam āpatati. — **away,** anabhilakkhito apakkamati. °**pery,** *a.* 1. picchila ; khalanasabhāva ; 2. asaddahitabba ; agaṇeyya. °**shod,** *a.* sadosa.

Slipper, *n.* pādukā, *f.* upāhana, *m. nt.*

Slit, *n.* dīghapaṭṭa, *m.* *v.t.* dīghaso chindati *or* phāleti. *p.p.* °chinna ; °lita.

Sliter, *v.i.* pakkhalanto visappati.

Sliver, *n.* dārusakalikā, *f.* *v.t.* sakalīkaroti. *v.i.* sakalībhavati. *p.p.* °kata ; °bhūta.

Slobber, *n.* 1. paggharitalālā ; 2. atimamāyanā, *f.* *v.i.* 1. khelaŋ paggharāpeti ; khelena makkheti ; 2. asammā kiccaŋ karoti. *p.p.* °pitakhela ; °khita ; °katakicca. °**y,** *a.* lālākilinna ; khelapaggharāpaka.

Slog, *v.t.* daḷham abhihanati. *p.p.* °hata. *v.i.* āyāsena kammaŋ karoti. *p.p.* °katakamma. °**ger,** *n.* daḷhābhighātī, *m.*

Sloop, *n.* ekakūpaka-nāvā, *f.*

Slop, *n.* 1. malinajala, *nt.* 2. kacavara, *m.* 3. *pl.* peyyavatthu, *nt.* 4. nāvikanivāsana, *nt.* *v.t.* malinajalena temeti. *p.p.* °temita. °**basin,** *n.* avakkārapāti, *f.* °**seller,** *n.* nivāsanavāṇija, *m.* °**shop,** *n.* nivāsanāpaṇa, *m.* °**py,** *a.* sakaddama. °**piness,** *n.* palipa, *m.*

Slope, *n.* ponatta ; pabbhāratta, *nt.* *v.i.* poṇībhavati. *v.t.* poṇīkaroti. *p.p.* °bhūta ; °kata. °**ping,** *a.* poṇa ; ninna.

Sloth, *n.* ālasya ; kosajja, *nt.* tandī, *f.* °**bear,** *n.* madhubhakkhī-accha, *m.* °**ful,** *a.* alasa ; kusīta ; tandita. °**fully,** *adv.* ālasiyena ; kosajjena. °**fulness,** *n.* ālasiyābhibhūtatā, *f.*

Slouch, *n.* asobhanagati, *f.* *v.i.* onatasīsena gacchati.

Slough, *n.* 1. nimmoka ; jiṇṇataca, *m.* 2. mahāpaṅka, *m.* *v.t.* nimmokam apaneti. *p.p.* apanītanimmoka.

Sloven, *a.* 1. malina ; asobhana ; 2. dandha.

Slow, *a.* dandha ; manda ; manthara ; asīgha. *adv.* mandaŋ ; sanikaŋ. *v.t.* mandīkaroti ; vegaŋ hāpeti. °**ly,** *adv.* mandamandaŋ ; sanikaŋ ; aturitaŋ. °**ness,** asīghatta ; aturitatta, *nt.* °**paced,** *a.* mandagāmī. °**witted,** *a.* mandamatika. °**worm,** *n.* gaṇḍuppāda, *m.*

Slubber, *v.t.* paṅkādīhi dūseti. *v.i.* asakkaccaŋ karoti. *p.p.* °dūsita ; °kata.

Sludge, *n.* ghanakalala, *m.* jambālī, *f.* °**gy,** *a.* sakaddama ; kalalībhūta.

Slug-abed, *n.* ussūrasāyī, *m.*

Sluggard, *n.* alasa ; kusīta ; mandaviriya, *m.*

Sluggish, *a.* olīna ; mandussāha. °**ly,** *adv.* olīnatāya ; kusītākārena. °**ness,** *n.* ālassa ; āḷasiya, *nt.*

Sluice, *n.* vāpijalaniggama, *m.* jaladvāra, *nt.* °**cy,** *a.* sandamānaka.

Slum, *n.* duggatajanāvāsappadesa, *m.* *v.i.* duggatāvāsaŋ passati.

Slumber, *n.* pacalayanā, *f.* *v.i.* pacalāyati; middhī hoti. *p.p.* °yita; °bhūta.

Slummock, *v.t.* giddhākārena gilati. *p.p.* °gilita.

Slump, *n.* sahasā-agghapatana, *nt.* *v.i.* aggho osīdati.

Slur, *n.* apavāda, *m.* abbhācikkhaṇa, *nt.* *v.t.* 1. sammissetvā katheti *or* gāyati; 2. kalaṅketi; dūseti. *p.p.* °thita; °yita; °kita; dūsita.

Slush, *n.* 1. tintakaddama, *m.* 2. vilīyamānahima, *nt.* 3. asabbhagantha, *m.*

Slut, *n.* adhamanārī; kulaṭā, *f.* °**tish**, *a.* kulaṭāsadisa.

Sly, *a.* saṭha; kūṭa; kapaṭa. °**ly**, *adv.* saṭhena. °**ness**, *n.* sāṭheyya, *nt.*

Smack, *n.* 1. rasalesa, *m.* 2. saññāmatta, *nt.* 3. oṭṭhāhanana, *nt.* 4. pāṇippahāra, *m.* 5. sasaddacumbana, *nt.* 6. khuddakanāvā, *f.* *v.i.* 1. rasaleso ñāyati; 2. tālussaraŋ pavatteti; *v.t.* pāṇinā paharati. *adv.* daḷhaŋ; sahasā. °**er**, *n.* 1. sasaddappahāra, *m.* 2. daḷhacumbana, *nt.* 3. mahattaravatthu, *nt.*

Small, *a.* 1. khuddaka; 2. appaka; thoka; 3. omaka. °**er**, *a.* khuddakatara.—**hand**, *n.* khuddakakkharalipi, *f.* — **hours**, pacchimayāma, *m.* °**ish**, *a.* īsaŋkhuddaka. °**minded**, *a.* anuḷārajjhāsaya. °**ness**, *n.* khuddakatta, *nt.* °**pox**, *n.* masūrikā, *f.* — **talk**, *n.* samphappalāpa, *m.*

Smart, *n.* balavavedanā, *f.* *a.* 1. sobhana; suvesa; 2. catura; dakkha; 3. khippābhiñña. *v.i.* tibbavedanaŋ vindati. °**ly**, *adv.* 1. sīghaŋ; 2. sobhanākārena. °**ness**, *n.* 1. paṭutta; 2. sobhanatta, *nt.*

Smarten, *v.t.* samuttejeti. *p.p.* °jita.

Smash, *v.t.* cuṇṇeti; cuṇṇavicuṇṇaŋ karoti. *p.p.* °ṇita; °ṇīkata. *n.* 1. cuṇṇīkaraṇa, *nt.* 2. dhanahāni, *f.* 3. daḷhappahāra, *m.* °**er**, *n.* daḷhappahāradāyī, *m.*

Smatter, *v.i.* lesamattaŋ jānāti. *p.p.* °ñāta. °**er**, *n.* bahussutamānī, *m.* °**ing**, *n.* appassutatta, *nt.* paṇḍitamāna, *m.*

Smear, *n.* lepa-kalaṅka, *m.* *v.t.* ālepeti; abbhañjati; añjeti; makkheti; vilepeti. *p.p.* ālitta; °jita; °khita; vilitta. °**y**, *a.* lepakalaṅkita.

Smell, *n.* gandha, *m.* *v.t.* ghāyati; āghāyati; siṅghati. *p.p.* °yita; °ghita. *v.i.* vāyati; gandhaŋ sūceti. *p.p.* vāyita; sūcitagandha. °**ing**, *n.* ghāyana; siṅghana, *nt.* °**ing**, *a.* gandhayutta; ghāyamāna.

Smelt, *v.t.* (lohaŋ) vilīyāpeti. *p.p.* °pita. °**er**, *n.* vilīyāpaka, *m.* °**ery**, *n.* lohavilīyāpanaṭṭhāna, *nt.*

Smile, *n.* sita, mihita, *nt.* mandahāsa, *m.* *v.i.* mandaŋ hasati; sitaŋ pātukaroti. *p.p.* °sita. °kata. °**ing**, *a.* hasamāna; mihitayutta. °**ingly**, *adv.* mihitapubbakaŋ.

Smirch, *n.* kalaṅka, *m.* *v.t.* kalaṅketi; kalusayati. *p.p.* °kita; °yita.

Smirk, *n.* vyājahāsa, *m.* *v.i.* vyājena hasati. °**y**, *a.* vyājahāsabahula.

Smite, *v.t.* paṭihanati; daḷhaŋ paharati. *p.p.* paṭihata, °pahaṭa. °**er**, *n.* pahāradāyī, *m.*

Smith, *n.* kammāra; lohakāra, *m.* °**ing**, *n.* lohakamma, *nt.* °**y**, *n.* kammārasālā, *f.*

Smock, *n.* bāhirakañcuka, *m.*

Smoke, *n.* dhūma, *m.* *v.i.* dhūmāyati; dhūmapānaŋ karoti. *v.t.* dhūmena sukkhāpeti. *p.p.* °yita; katadhūmapāna; °pita. °**er**, *n.* dhūmapāyī, *m.* °**ing**, *n.* 1. dhūmāyana; 2. dhūmapāna, *nt.* °**ing pipe**, dhūmanetta, *nt.* °**less**, *a.* vidhūmá. °**y**, *a.* dhūmāvuta.

Smooth, *a.* 1. maṭṭa; maṭṭha; siliṭṭha; siniddha; saṇha; 2. acala; akkhobha; 3. nirāyāsa. *v.t.* 1. saṇheti; parimajjati; 2. sameti; upasameti. *p.p.* saṇhita; parimaṭṭha; °mita. °**chinned**, *a.* nimmassuka. °**faced**, *a.* sommānana; bhadramukha. °**ly**, *adv.* saṇhākārena. °**ness**, *n.* 1. maṭṭhatta; saṇhatta, *nt.* 2. akkhobha; upasama, *m.* °**tongued**, *a.* sakhilavāca; piyaŋvada.

Smother, *n.* dhūmapaṭala; dhūlipaṭala, *m.* *v.t.* 1. sāsam avarodheti; sāsarodhanena māreti; 2. aticumbanādīhi viheseti; 3. bhasmanā aggiŋ paṭicchādeti; 4. rahassaŋ rakkhati. *v.i.* kicchena sasati. *p.p.* °dhitasāsa; °mārita; °sita; °ditaggi; °khitarahassa.

Smoulder, *n.* antojhāyana, *nt.* vītaccikaṅgāra, *m.* *v.i.* 1. antojhāyati; padhūpāyati; 2. gūḷhaŋ pavattati. *p.p.* °yita; °tita. °**ing**, *a.* pakkaṭṭhita.

Smudge, *v.t.* masiādīhi dūseti. *v.i.* malinībhavati. *n.* 1. masiciṇha, *nt.* 2. makasavārakadhūma, *m.*

Smug, *a. n.* aṭṭatuṭṭha; yathālābhatuṭṭha, 3. °**ness**, *n.* yathālābhatuṭṭhi, *f.*

Smuggle, *v.t.* suṅkam adatvā bhaṇḍaŋ harati; theyyena harati *or* āharati. °**er**, *n.* theyyabhaṇḍahārī, suṅkaparihārī, *m.* °**ing**, *n.* theyyabhaṇḍaharaṇa, *nt.*

Smut, *n.* 1. masimakkhitaṭṭhāna, *nt.* 2. asabbhakathā, *f.* *v.t.* kalaṅketi; malinayati. *p.p.* °kita; °yita. °**ty**, *a.* 1. kalaṅkita; 2. asabbhayutta.

Smutch, see **Smudge**.

Snail, *n.* manthara; thalasambuka, *m.* *v.t.* manthare rāsīkaroti. — **slow**, *a.* atipapañcaka; atimandagatika.

Snake, see **Serpent**. — **catcher**, *n.* ahiguṇṭhika, *m.* — **fang**, āsī, *f.* °**gourd**, paṭola, *m.* °**y**, *a.* 1. āsivisūpama; 2. kuṭila.

Snap, *n.* 1. bhañjana; 2. sahasā gahaṇa *or* ḍasana; 3. kopena kathana, *nt.* *v.t.* 1. sahasā ḍasati *or* bhañjati; 2. kopena katheti; 3. accharaŋ paharati; 4. acchindivā gaṇhāti. *p.p.* °daṭṭha; °bhaṭṭha; °thita; °pahaṭa; °gahita. °**ping**, *n.* sahasā-gahaṇa, *nt.* accharāsadda, *m.* °**pish**, *a.* kodhana; kaṭukavāca. °**pishly**, *adv.* pharusākārena ; sakopaŋ. **In a —**, muhuttena, *adv.* °**shot**, *n.* sahasā-gahitachāyārūpa, *nt.*

Snare, *n.* pāsa, *m.* vākarā ; migabandhinī, *f. v.t.* pāse yojeti ; pāsena bandhati. *p.p.* pāsayojita ; pāsabaddha.

Snarl, *n.* kakkasasadda, *m.* ghuru-ghurāyana, *nt. v.i.t.* ghurughurāyati ; kakkasasaddaŋ pavatteti. *p.p.* °yita ; °titakak°.

Snatch, *n.* acchindana ; pasayhagahaṇa, *nt. v.t.i.* acchindati ; pasayha gaṇhāti. *p.p.* acchinna ; °gahita. **— off**, avaharati ; theneti. **— out**, uppāṭeti ; ummūleti.

Sneak, *n.* hīnalāmakapuggala, *m. v.i.t.* 1. rahasi vicarati ; 2. kucchitaŋ carati ; 3. pesuññaŋ bhaṇati ; 4. theneti. *p.p.* °rita ; °nita. adj. adhamācāra. °**ingly**, *adv.* gārayhākārena.

Sneck, *n.* aggala, *nt.* dvārabandha, *m. v.t.* aggalena pidahati ; dvāraŋ bandhati. *p.p.* °pihita ; baddhadvāra.

Sneer, *n.* avaññā ; ohīḷanā, *f. v.t.* avahasati ; *v.i.* avaññaŋ dasseti. *p.p.* °sita ; dassitāvañña. °**er**, *n.* ohīḷaka, *m.* °**ingly**, *adv.* sāvamānaŋ ; sopahāsaŋ.

Sneeze, *n.* khipita, *nt. v.i.* khipati. °**ing**, *a.* khipanta. °**y**, *a.* khipitabahula.

Snick, *n.* khuddaka-cheda, *m. v.t.* agambhīraŋ khataŋ sampādeti.

Snicker, *v.i.* pajagghati. *p.p.* °ghita.

Snide, *a.* kūṭa ; kittima.

Sniff, *n.* upasiṅghana, *nt. v.i.* upasiṅghati. °**y**, *a.* gabbita ; ohīḷaka.

Snigger, *n.* saniggaha-hāsa, *m. v.i.* sopahāsaŋ hasati.

Snip, *n.* chinnakhaṇḍa, *m. v.t.* kattarikāya sīghaŋ chindati. *p.p.* °chinna.

Snipe, *n.* vaṭṭaka, *m.*

Snivel, *n.* 1. vyājarodana, *nt.* 2. siṅghānikāpaggharaṇa, *nt. v.i.* siṅghānikaŋ muñcanto rodati.

Snob, *n.* attukkaŋsī ; vyājadappita, *m.* °**bish**, *a.* attukkaŋsaka; nikiṭṭha. °**bishness**, *n.* attamahattakāmitā, *f.*

Snooze, *n.* appaniddā, *f. v.i.* thokaŋ sayati.

Snore, *n.* ghurughurāyanā ; kākacchanā, *f. v.i.* kākacchati ; ghurughurāyati. °**ing**, *a.* kākacchamāna.

Snort, *n.* nāsārāva, *m. v.i.* nāsāya ravati.

Snot, *n.* siṅghāṇikā, *f.* °**ty**, *a.* siṅghāṇikābahula.

Snout, *n.* sanāsika-mukha ; (sūkara-) tuṇḍa, *nt.* soṇḍā, *f.*

Snow, *n.* hima ; tuhina, *nt.* nīhāra, *m. v.i.* himaŋ patati. *p.p.* patitahima. °**ball**, *n.* himaguḷikā, *f.* °**drift**, *n.* himasaŋhati, *f.* °**fall**, *n.* himavuṭṭhi, *f.* °**plough**, *n.* himanaṅgala, *nt.* °**storm**, tuhinavuṭṭhi, *f.* °**white**, himadhavala. °**y**, *a.* 1. himayutta ; 2. himasadisa.

Snub, *n.* 1. ohīḷanā, *f. v.t.* 1. omāneti ; ohīḷeti ; 2. vaḍḍhiŋ nivāreti. *p.p.* °nita ; °ḷita ; °rita. °**nosed**, *a.* cipiṭanāsika.

Snuff, *n.* nāsācuṇṇa, *nt.* *v.t.* 1. nāsācuṇṇam ādāti; 2. dīpavaṭṭiŋ saṅkharati. *p.p.* ādinnanāsācuṇṇa; saṅkhatadīpavaṭṭika. °**box**, *n.* nāsācuṇṇakaraṇḍa, *m.* °**ers**, *n. pl.* dīpavaṭṭisaṅkhāraka, *m.* — **out**, (dīpaŋ) nibbāpeti.

Snuffle, *v.i.* 1. anunāsikasaddaŋ pavatteti; 2. kicchena sasati. °**er**, *n.* mammana, *m.*

Snug, *a.* succhanna; sugutta. °**gery**, *n.* suguttaṭṭhāna, *nt.* °**gle**, *v.i.* samīpe sayati. °**ly**, *adv.* yathāsukhaŋ.

So, *adv. conj.* tathā; tādisaŋ; itthaŋ. — **as**, viya, *ind.* — **and so**, asuka, *a.* — **also**, tath'eva, *ind.*— **big**, tāvamahanta, *a.* — **called**, *a.* saṅkhāta. — **far**, ettāvatā, *adv.* — **long**, tāvatā, *adv.* — **long as**, yāva kīvaŋ, *adv.* — **many**, *a.* tāvataka. — **much so**, apissu, *ind.*

Soak, *v.t.* kiledeti; temeti. *v.i.* kiledīyati. *p.p.* °dita; °mita. °**er**, *n.* 1. mahāvuṭṭhi, *f.* 2. surāsoṇḍa, *m.*

Soap, *n.* nahānīya, *nt.* °**berry tree**, pheṇila, *m.* °**y**, *a.* pheṇabahula.

Soar, *v.i.* uḍḍeti; upari ḍeti. *p.p.* uḍḍita. °**ing**, *n.* uḍḍīyana, *nt.*

Sob, *n.* gaggada, *m.* *v.i.* sagaggadaŋ rodati.

Sober, *a.* 1. santa; dhīra; 2. nimmada; amatta. *v.t.* amattaŋ *or* upasantaŋ karoti. *p.p.* amattakata. °**ly**, *adv.* santākārena. °**ness**, *n.* santatta; nimmadatta, *nt.*

Sobriquet, *n.* parihāsanāma, *nt.*

Sociable, *a.* 1. susīla; 2. saṅgamappiya. °**bility**, *n.* samānattatā, *f.* °**bly**, *adv.* mittākārena.

Social, *a.* samājahita; mahājanika. °**ism**, *n.* samājahitakaraṇa, *nt.* samasambhogatā, *f.* °**ist**, *n.* samasambhogavādī; samājahitakārī, *m.*

Society, *n.* samiti; parisā, *f.* samāgama, *m.* **Fond of** —, saṅgaṇikārata, *a.*

Sociology, *n.* samājadhammavijjā, *f.* °**ist**, *n.* samājadhammavedī, *m.*

Sock, *n.* rassa-pādāvaraṇa, *nt.* *v.t.* 1. khipati; 2. laguḷena paharati. *p.p.* khitta; °pahaṭa.

Socket, *n.* kuhara, *nt.*

Sod, *n.* saddala, *m.* *v.t.* saddala khaṇḍehi attharati *or* āvarati. *p.p.* °atthata; °āvaṭa.

Soda, *n.* sodhakalavaṇa, *nt.*

Sodden, *a.* 1. atitinta; atikilinna; 2. atisayena matta. *v.t.* adhikaŋ temeti. *v.i.* atikiledīyati. *p.p.* °mita; °dita.

Sodomy, *n.* purisamethuna, *nt.*

Soever, *suf.* **Who** —, yo koci. **How** —, yena kenaci ākārena. **What** —, yaŋ kiñci. **Where** —, yattha katthaci.

Sofa, *n.* pallaṅka; mañcaka, *m.*

Soft, *a.* 1. mudu; komala; 2. (in speech:) sakhila; 3. (tender:) sukhumāla; sukumāra; 4. dubbala; 5. mūḷha. °**hearted**, *a.* muducitta. °**ish**, *a.* īsaŋ muduka. °**ly**, *adv.* muduŋ; sanikaŋ; saṇhākārena. °**ness**, *n.* maddava; komalatta, *nt.*

Soften, *v.t.* 1. muduŋ karoti; 2. upasameti. *v.i.* mudubhavati.

p.p. mudukata ; °mita ; °bhūta. °**ing**, *a.* mudubhāvakara ; upasamaka.

Soggy, see **Sodden.**

Soil, *n.* 1. mattikā, *f.* paŋsu, *nt.* 2. bhūmi, *f.* *v.t.* dūseti ; malinīkaroti. *p.p.* dūsita ; °kata.

Sojourn, *n.* kālikavāsa ; aciravāsa, *m.* *v.i.* tāvakālikaŋ vasati. °**ing**, *n.* aciravāsa, *m.* °**er**, *n.* aciranivāsī, *m.*

Solace, *n.* assāsa, *m.* *v.t.* assāseti ; samassāseti. *p.p.* assattha *or* assāsita.

Solar, *a.* suriyāyatta. °**ium**, *a.* ātapasālā, *f.* — **month**, suriyamāsa, *m.*—**race**, *n.* suriyavaŋsa, *m.* — **system**, *n.* suriyāyattagahasamūha, *m.*

Solatium, *n.* hānipūraṇa, *nt.*

Solder, *n.* sandahanaka-loha, *nt.* *v.t.* lohabhaṇḍaŋ sandhāneti. *p.p.* °nitaloha°. °**er**, *n.* lohasandhānakārī, *m.*

Soldier, *n.* yuddhabhaṭa; yodhājīvī; balattha, *m.* °**ly**, *a.* yodhasama. °**ship**, *n.* saṅgāmasūratā, *f.* °**y**, *n.* balasenā, *f.*

Sole, *n.* pādatala, *nt.* *v.t.* pādukātalāni sampādeti *or* yojeti. *p.p.* yojita° tala.

Sole, *a.* kevala ; ekaka ; adutiya. °**ness**, *n.* kevalatta, *nt.* adutiyatā, *f.*

Solecism, *n.* 1. asuddhappayoga; 2. avinītabhāva, *m.* °**cistic**, *a.* ocityahīna.

Solemn, *a.* 1. atisanta ; 2. atigambhīra ; 3. cārittavidhipubbaka. °**ity**, °**ness**, *n.* garutā ; santatā, *f.* carittavidhi, *m.* °**ly**, *adv.* santatāya ; cārittavidhipubbakaŋ.

Solicit, *v.t.* āyācati ; abhiyācati. *p.p.* °cita. °**ant**, *n.* abhiyācaka, *m.* °**ation**, *n.* abhiyācanā, *f.* °**or**, *n.* 1. āyācaka ; 2. nītividū, *m.* °**ous**, *a.* cintāpara ; avupasantacitta. °**ously**, *adv.* cintāparatāya ; sākaṅkhaŋ. °**ude**, *n.* 1. pajjhāyanā ; 2. ukkaṇṭhitatā ; 3. ākaṅkhā, *f.*

Solid, *a.* ghana ; thira ; *n.* ekagghana ; ghanībhūta, *m.* °**arity**, *n.* 1. ekamatikatta, *nt.* 2. samānasambhoga, *m.* °**ify**, *v.t.* ghanattaŋ *or* thirattaŋ pāpeti. *v.i.* ghanībhavati. °**ification**, *n.* ghanīkaraṇa ; thirīkaraṇa, *nt.* °**ity**, °**ness**, *n.* ghanatta ; thiratta, *nt.* °**ly**, *adv.* thiraŋ ; daḷhaŋ. — **measure**, *n.* ghanamāṇa, *nt.*

Solidungular, *a.* abhinnakhura.

Soliloquy, *n.* ekākībhāsana, *nt.* °**qize**, *v.i.* ekākī bhāsati. °**qist**, *n.* ekākī-bhāsaka, *m.*

Soliped, *n.* abhinnakhura-pasu, *m.*

Solitary, *a.* ekākī ; nissaṅga ; adutiya ; vivitta, *m.* *n.* samaṇa ; tāpasa, *m.* °**ily**, *adv.* savivekaŋ ; ekākitāya. °**iness**, *n.* paviveka ; ekākībhāva, *m.*

Solitude, *n.* 1. viveka, *m.* paṭisallāna, *nt.* 2. vivittaṭṭhāna, *nt.*

Solstice, *n.* ayanakāla, *m.* **Summer** —, uttarāyana, *nt.* **Winter** —, dakkhiṇāyana, *nt.*

Soluble, *a.* 1. vilīyanakkhama ; 2. vissajjanāraha.

Solution, *n.* 1. vilīyana ; 2. vilīnavatthu, *nt.* 2. vyākhyāna ; vivaraṇa, *nt.*

Solutive, *a.* 1. vilīyāpanaka ; 2. virecanaka.

Solve, *v.t.* 1. vyākhyāti ; visadīkaroti ; 2. vilīyāpeti. *p.p.* °khyāta ; °kata ; °pita. °**able,** *a.* vivaraṇīya ; vissajjanakkhama. °**ability,** *n.* vilīyanīyatta ; vissajjanasāmatthiya, *nt.*

Solvent, *a. n.* 1. vilīyāpanaka ; 2. iṇasodhanasamattha. °**ncy,** *n.* iṇasodhanasāmatthiya, *nt.*

Somatic, *a.* kāyika ; kāyapaṭibaddha.

Somatology, *n.* kāyikavijjā, *f.*

Sombre, *a.* malinavaṇṇa ; dhūsara ; nippabha. °**ly,** *adv.* nippabhākārena. °**ness,** *n.* nippabhatta, *nt.* °**ously,** *adv.* nirānandaŋ ; nippabhaŋ.

Some, *a. pron.* eka ; ekacca ; ekatiya ; 2. (quantity :) thoka ; kiñci ; appaka. *adv.* pāyo. —**body,** °**one,** koci. °**how,** yathā kathañ ci. °**how or other,** yena kena ci ākārena.—**people,** ekacce. °**thing,** yaŋ kiñci. °**time,** *a.* bhūtapubba. °**times,** *adv.* kadāci ; karahaci. °**what,** *adv.* īsaŋ ; thokaŋ ; manaŋ. —**where,** yattha katthaci.

Somersault, *n.* avaŋsirakkhipana, *nt. v.i.* uddhapādaŋ avaŋsiraŋ laṅgheti. *p.p.* °ghita.

Somnambulate, *v.i.* niddāya āhiṇḍati. °**lism,** *n.* niddāyāhiṇḍana, *nt.* °**list,** *n.* niddayāhiṇḍaka, *m.*

Somni- (niddāvācakaŋ.) °**ferous,** *a.* niddājanaka. °**loquence,** *n.* niddāya jappana, *nt.* °**loquist,** *n.* niddāya jappaka, *m.*

Somnolent, *a.* niddāsīlī ; middhapareta.

Son, *n.* putta ; tanaya ; tanuja ; atraja ; sūnu ; suta, *m.* °**in-law,** *n.* jāmātu, *m.* °**less,** *a.* aputtaka. °**ship,** *n.* puttabhāva, *m.*

Sonant, *n.* ghosakkhara ; dhanitakkhara, *nt.*

Song, *n.* gīta, *nt.* gītikā, *f.* °**ster,** *n.* gāyaka, *m.* °**stress,** *n.* gāyikā, *f.*

Soniferous, *a.* saddavāhaka.

Sonnet, *n.* cuddasapadikapajja, *nt.*

Sonometer, *n.* savaṇa-māṇakayanta, *nt.*

Sonorific, *a.* sadduppādaka ; nādakara.

Sonorous, *a.* ninnādī ; gambhīranādī. °**ly,** *adv.* 1. mahānādena ; 2. sumadhuraŋ. °**ness,** *n.* 1. madhurasaratā ; 2. nādajanakatā, *f.*

Soon, *adv.* sīghaŋ ; khippaŋ ; āsu ; tuvaṭaŋ ; aciraŋ ; avilambitaŋ.

Soot, *n.* masi, *m.* kajjala, *nt. v.t.* masinā lepeti *or* chādetī. *p.p.* masilitta ; °dita. °**y,** *a.* masiyutta.

Sooth, *n.* sacca ; taccha, *nt.* **In —,** tathavasena, *adv.* °**sayer,** *n.* nemittika ; nimittapāṭhaka, *m.*

Soothe, *v.t.* 1. upasameti ; 2. lāleti. *p.p.* °mita ; lālita. °**er,** *n.* lālaka ; upasametu, *m.* °**ing,** *a.* santikara ; nibbāpaka. °**ing,** *n.* upasamana ; lālana, *nt.* °**fast,** *a.* saccasandha.

Sop, *n.* 1. tinta-khādanīya ; 2. lālakavatthu, *nt.* 3. lañca, *m. v.t.* 1. kiledeti ; 2. lañcaŋ deti. *p.p.* °dita ; dinnalañca.

Sophist, *n.* moghatakkī ; vitaṇḍavādī, *m.* °**ical,** *a.* kutakkamohaka. °**icate,** *v.t.* moghatakkena dūseti. °**cation,** micchātakkanena vivadana, *nt.* °**ism,** °**try,** *n.* vitaṇḍavāda, *m.*

Soporific, *a. n.* soppajanaka; niddājanaka.

Sorcerer, *n.* vijjādhara; indajālika, *m.* °**cery,** *n.* māyā, *f.* indajāla, *nt.*

Sordid, *a.* 1. malina; 2. nīca; adhama; nikiṭṭha. °**ly,** *adv.* 1. malinākārena; 2. nīcākārena. °**ness,** *n.* 1. malinatta; 2. nihīnatta, *nt.*

Sore, *n.* vaṇa; aru, *m.* adj. savedana; saruja; dukkhita. *adv.* bāḷhākārena. °**ly,** *adv.* atisayena; tippaŋ; tibbaŋ. °**ness,** *n.* rujā; vedanā, *f.*

Sororal, *a.* bhaginyāyatta.

Sorrel, *n.* paṇṇambilikā, *f.*

Sorrow, *n.* soka; cittasantāpa, *m.* socanā, *f. v.i.* socati; anutapati. *p.p.* socita; °pita. °**ful,** *a.* 1. sasoka; sokī; dummana; dukkhita; sokaṭṭa; 2. socanīya; khedāvaha. °**fully,** *adv.* sasokaŋ. °**less,** *a.* nissoka. °**lessness,** *n.* nissokitā, *f.* °**stricken,** *a.* sokapīḷita; sokātura.

Sorry, *a.* 1. sokaṭṭa; khinna; dukkhita; 2. alakkhika; dīna; lāmaka; 3. dayāraha; socanīya. °**ily,** *adv.* sasokaŋ.

Sort, *n.* vaggabheda, *m.* visesajāti, *f. v.t.* vaggavasena viyojeti; uccināti. *p.p.* °jita; °nita. °**able,** *a.* vaggīkātabba; jātivasena vibhajanīya. °**er,** *n.* vaggīkāraka, *m.*

Sot, *n.* surādhutta, *m. v.i.* surāya majjati. °**tish,** *a.* madamatta; surālola.

Soul, *n.* atta; jīva, *m.* °**less,** *a.* 1. anatta; acetana; 2. nirīha; nibbiriya. °**lessly,** *adv.* nirīhatāya. °**ful,** *a.* dhitimantu; saussāha. °**fully,** *adv.* dhīratāya. °**stirring,** *a.* cittakkhobhakara. —**theory,** *n.* attadiṭṭhi, *f.* **Belonging to the —,** ajjhattika; attaniya.

Sound, *n.* 1. sadda; nāda; rava; ghosa; dhani; ārāva, *m.* 2. avitthata-samuddappadesa, *m.* adj. 1. agilāna; kalla; niroga; 2. avikala; akkhata; 3. niddosa; 4. acchidda; 5. daḷha. *v.i.* nadati; ravati; saddāyati. *v.t.* 1. nādeti; vādeti; 2. suṭṭhu vīmaŋsati; 3. jalagambhīrattaŋ mināti; 4. ajjhāsayaŋ pucchati. *p.p.* nadita; ruta; °yita; °sita; mitajala°; puṭṭhajjhāsaya. *adv.* daḷhaŋ; thiraŋ. °**er,** *n.* 1. unnādī, *m.* 2. saddapaṭiggāhakopakaraṇa, *nt.* 3. vanasūkara, *m.* °**ing,** *n.* 1. jalamāṇa, *m.* 2. velāsannaṭṭhāna, *nt.* °**ing line,** jalamāṇakasutta. *nt.* —**headed,** *a.* satimantu. °**less,** *a.* nissadda. °**ly,** *adv.* sammā; suṭṭhu; daḷhaŋ. °**ness,** *n.* 1. kallatta; nirogatta, *nt.* 2. akkhatatta; 3. daḷhatta, *nt.*

Soup, *n.* pātabba-sūpa, *m.*

Sour, *a.* 1. ambila; 2. kakkasa; appiya. *v.i.* ambilāyati. *v.t.* ambilattaŋ *or* appiyattaŋ pāpeti. *p.p.* °yita; °pāpita. °**ish,** *a.* mandambila. °**ly,** *adv.* appiyākārena. °**ness,** *n.* ambilatta, *nt.* 2. kakkasatta, *nt.*

Source, *n.* pabhava, *m.* ubbhavaṭṭhāna; nidāna; āyatana, *nt.*

South, *n.* dakkhiṇa-disā, *f. a.* dakkhiṇa; apasavya. °**east,** *n.* dakkhiṇapubbā, *f.* °**ern,** *a.* dakkhiṇāyatta. °**erner,** *n.* dākkhiṇadisāvāsī, *m.* — **pole,** *n.* dakkhiṇakkha; assakaṇṇa, *m.* °**wards,** *adv.* dakkhiṇābhimukhaŋ. °**west,** *n.* dakkhiṇapacchimā, *f.* °**wester,** *n.* dakkhiṇapacchimavāta, *m.*

Souvenir, *n.* sārāṇīyavatthu, *nt.*

Sovereign, *a.* 1. sabbabhumma; 2. parama; seṭṭha. *n.* 1. adhirāja; mahārāja, *m.* 2. suvaṇṇa-nikkha, *nt.* °**ty,** *n.* ekarajja; issariyādhipacca, *nt.*

Sow, *n.* varāhī; sūkarī, *f.*

Sow, *v.t.* vapati. *p.p.* vapita. °**er,** *n.* vāpaka, *m.* °**ing,** *n.* vapana, *nt.*

Space, *n.* 1. okāsa, *m.* antara, *nt.* 2. ākāsa, *m. v.t.* antaraŋ ṭhapeti; anāsannaŋ karoti. *p.p.* ṭhapitantara; °kata. — **around,** parikkamana, *nt.* °**ious,** *a.* urunda; mahanta; asambādha. — **of time,** kālantara, *nt.*

Spade, *n.* kuddāla; khaṇittivisesa, *m. v.t.* kuddālena khaṇati. *p.p.* °khata. °**ful,** *n.* khaṇittipūra, *nt.*

Spado, *n.* napuŋsaka, *m.*

Spalpeen, *n.* nīcapuggala, *m.*

Span, *n.* 1. vidatthi, *f.* 2. vitthatappamāṇa, *nt. v.t.* 1. (vidatthiyā) miṇāti; 2. antaraŋ chādetvā tiṭṭhati. *p.p.* °mita; °ṭhita.

Spangle, *n.* ujjala-vibhūsaṇa, *nt. v.t.* ujjalavatthūhi bhūseti. *p.p.* °sita.

Spank, *v.t.* paharitvā assam uyyojeti. *p.p.* °jitassa. °**er,** *n.* 1. assuyyojaka; 2. javanassa, *m.*

Spanner, *n.* 1. vyāvattanī-saṇḍāsa, *m.* 2. setupassa-sambandhaka, *m.*

Spar, *n.* 1. dīgha-vaṭṭa-daṇḍa, *m.* 2. muṭṭhiyuddha, *nt. v.t.* muṭṭhīhi yujjhati. *p.p.* °jhita.

Spare, *a.* 1. atiritta; avasiṭṭha; vinimmutta; 2. kisa; virala. *v.t.* 1. parivajjeti; 2. parimoceti; 3. atirittaŋ karoti. *p.p.* °jita; °cita; °kata. °**ing,** *a.* mitabbaya. °**ingly,** *adv.* pamāṇayuttaŋ; mitabbayena. °**ly,** *adv.* viralavasena. °**ness,** *n.* viralatta, *nt.*

Spark, *n.* vipphuliṅga; phuliṅga, *nt. v.t.* phuliṅgāni vissajjeti. *p.p.* vissaṭṭhaphuliṅga. °**le,** *v.i.* vipphurati. °**ling,** *a.* vipphuranta. °**lingly,** *adv.* vipphuraṇākārena.

Sparrow, *n.* kalaviṅka; caṭaka, *m.*

Sparse, *a.* virala; tanubhūta. °**ly,** *adv.* viralākārena. °**ness,** *n.* viralatta, *nt.*

Spasm, *n.* 1. kāyaphandana, *nt.* 2. cittakkhobha, *m.* °**odic,** *a.* kālika-phandanayutta.

Spate, *n.* mahājalottharaṇa, *nt.*

Spatial, *a.* okāsāyatta.

Spatter, *n.* binduvissajjana, *nt.* pariseka, *m. v.t.* osiñcati; parisiñcati. *p.p.* ositta; parisitta.

Spawn, *n.* macchaṇḍa, *nt. v.i.* aṇḍāni pasavati *or* vijāyati. *p.p.* °vitaṇḍa.

Spay, *v.t.* gabbhāsayam apaneti. *p.p.* apanītagab°.

Speak, *v.i.t.* katheti ; bhāsati ; vadati ; bhaṇati ; sallapati. *p.p.* °thita ; °sita ; vutta ; °ṇita ; °pita. °**able,** *a.* kathanakkhama; kathanīya. °**er,** *n.* kathika ; kathetu ; vattu, *m.* °**ing,** *n.* kathana, *nt.*— **ill of,** apavadati. — **well of,** pasaŋsati. — **together,** sambhāsati.

Spear, *n.* satti ; heti, *f. v.t.* sattiyā āhanati. *p.p.* °āhata. °**man,** *n.* sattidhara, *m.*

Special, *a.* visesa ; asādhāraṇa ; āveṇika. °**ize,** *v.t.* visiṭṭhattaŋ labhati. °**ism,** *n.* visesañāṇa, *nt.* °**ist,** *n.* visesaññū, *m.* °**ity,** *n.* visiṭṭhatta, *nt.* °**ly,** *adv.* visesato. °**ty,** *n.* visesapaṭiññāpaṇṇa, *nt.*

Species, *n.* abhijāti, *f.* vaggabheda ; jātivisesa, *m.*

Specify, *v.t.* viseseti ; vibhajati ; niddhāreti. *p.p.* °sita ; vibhatta; °rita. °**ic,** *a.* visiṭṭha ; paricchinna. °**ically,** *adv.* odhiso ; visesato. °**ication,** *n.* niddhāraṇa ; visesakaraṇa, *nt.*

Specimen, *n.* ākati, *f.* nidassana; paṭirūpa, *nt.*

Specious, *a.* bahimanorama ; saccābhāsa. °**ly,** *adv.* saccābhāsamattena.

Speck, *n.* tilaka; bindu, *m.* °**le,** *v.t.* bindūhi citteti. *p.p.* °tita. *n.* vaṇṇabindu, *m.* °**led,** *a.* kammāsa. °**less,** *a.* akalaṅka.

Spectacle, *n.* visiṭṭha-dassana, *nt. pl.* upanetta, *nt.* °**cular,** *a.* visiṭṭhadassanāyatta.

Spectator, *n.* pekkhaka ; ullokaka, *m.*

Spectre, *n.* pisāca ; bhūta, *m.* °**ral,** *a.* pisācasadisa.

Spectrum, *n.* 1. tiyaŋsakāce dissamāna-chabbaṇṇa, *m.* 2. uggahanimitta, *nt.*

Speculate, *v.i.* vitakketi ; cinteti ; jhāyati ; anumāneti. *p.p.* °kita ; °tita ; °yita ; °nita. °**tion,** *n.* vicāraṇā, *f.* upanijjhāna, *nt.* °**tive,** *a.* vicārasīlī. °**tor,** *n.* vitakkī ; vīmaŋsī ; nijjhāyaka, *m.*

Speech, *n.* kathā ; vācā, *f.* bhāsana ; kathana, *nt.* **Harsh** —, pharusavācā, *f.* **Kind** —, peyyavajja, *nt.* **Right** —, sammāvācā, *f.* °**less,** *a.* 1. tuṇhī ; 2. mūga.

Speed, *n.* vega ; java, *m. v.i.* turitayati ; vegaŋ janeti. *v.t.* sīghataraŋ kāreti. *p.p.* °yita ; janitavega ; °kārita. °**ily,** *adv.* sīghaŋ ; turitaŋ. °**iness,** *n.* sīghatta ; turitatta, *nt.* °**y,** *a.* vegavantu ; javasampanna.

Spell, *n.* 1. manta, *nt.* mohana ; vasīkaraṇa, *nt. v.i.* anvakkharaŋ uccāreti. °**ing,** *n.* akkharaviññāsa, *m.* °**bound,** *a.* mohita ; vasīkata.

Spelter, *n.* tuttha, *nt.*

Spend, *v.t.i.* 1. vayaŋ karoti ; vissajjeti ; 2. (time :) khepeti ; vītināmeti. *p.p.* °kata ; vissaṭṭha ; °pita ; °mita. °**thrift,** *a. n.* dhananāsaka, *m.*

Sperm, *n.* sambhava, *m.* sukka, *nt.* °**atism,** *n.* sukkamocana, *nt.*

Spew, *v.t.* vamati. *p.p.* vamita.

Sphere, *n.* 1. goḷa ; goḷaka ; maṇḍala, *nt.* āvaṭṭa, *m.* 2. āyatana ; visayaṭṭhāna, *nt.* °**ical,** *a.* goḷākāra ; parimaṇḍala. °**ically,** *adv.* goḷākārena. °**ics,** *n.* goḷamāṇakavijjā, *f.* °**oid,** *n.* upagoḷaka, *nt.* °**rule,** *n.* khuddakagoḷa, *nt.*

Sphinx, *n.* 1. nārīmukhasīha ; 2. guttasabhāva, *m.*

Sphygmic, *a.* rattadhāvanāyatta.

Spice, *n.* kaṭukabhaṇḍa, *nt.* *v.t.* kaṭukabhaṇḍaŋ pakkhipati. *p.p.* °khittakaṭuka°. °**ry**, *n.* katukabhaṇḍasamūha, *m.*

Spick, *a.* abhinavatara ; atinūtana.

Spicy, *a.* 1. kaṭukabhaṇḍayojita ; 2. sobhana ; 3. kaṭukākāra. °**ily**, *adv.* dassanīyākārena.

Spider, *n.* lūtikā, *f.* uṇṇanābhi ; makkaṭaka, *m.* °**web**, *n.* lūtikājāla ; makkaṭasutta, *nt.* °**y**, *a.* lūtāsadisa ; atikisa.

Spiflicate, *v.t.* 1. bhusaŋ tāḷeti ; 2. cittaŋ vyākulayati. *p.p.* °ḷita ; vyākulitacitta.

Spike, *n.* 1. khīla ; saṅku ; sūla, *m.* 2. mañjarī ; vallarī, *f.* *v.t.* 1. sūle āropeti ; 2. saṅkūhi āvarati. *p.p.* sūlāropita ; °āvaṭa.

Spile, *n.* 1. nāgadantaka ; 2. mahākhīla, *m.* °**ing**, *n.* khīlavati, *f.*

Spill, *n.* 1. dārupaṭṭikā, *f.* 2. paggharāpana ; avassāvaṇa, *nt.* *v.t.* paggharāpeti ; bahi-pāteti. *v.i.* galati ; paggharati ; bahi patati. *p.p.* °pita ; °tita ; galita ; °rita ; °patita. — **water**, *n.* jalaniggama, *m.*

Spin, *v.t.* 1. (suttaŋ) kantati ; 2. bhamāpeti. *p.p.* °tita ; °pita. °**ner**, *n.* suttakantaka, *m.* °**ning**, *n.* suttakantana, *nt.*

Spinach, *n.* upodikālatā, *f.*

Spindle, *n.* kantanasūci, *f.* *v.i.* kisībhavati. *p.p.* °bhūta. °**legged**, *a.* kisajaṅgha. °**ly**, *a.* kisadīgha.

Spindrift, *n.* vīcipheṇa, *nt.* vīcisīkara, *m.*

Spine, *n.* piṭṭhikaṇṭaka, *m.* °**less**, *a.* piṭṭhikaṇṭakarahita. °**ous**, *a.* sapiṭṭhikaṇṭaka. °**al**, *a.* piṭṭhikaṇṭakāyatta.

Spinster, *n.* 1. vayappatta avivāhikā ; 2. suttakantikā, *f.* °**hood**, *n.* avivāhikatā, *f.*

Spiracle, *n.* khuddajantu-sāsanāḷā, *m.*

Spiral, *n.* vyāvaṭṭa, *m.* *v.t.* vyāvaṭṭeti. *p.p.* °ṭita.

Spire, *n.* 1. sikhara ; siṅga, *nt.* 2. thūpikā ; pāsādakaṇṇikā, *f.* 3. āvaṭṭanī, *f.* *v.i.* sikharākārena uggacchati. *v.t.* sikharaŋ yojeti. *p.p.* °uggata ; yojitasikhara. °**y**, *a.* sikharayutta.

Spirit, *n.* 1. jīva ; atta ; 2. amanussa ; bhūta, *m.* 3. cittasabhāva, *m.* 4. (liquor :) āsava ; 5. sāraŋsa ; 6. uyyoga, *m.* *v.t.i.* 1. bhūtehi viya nīyati ; antaradhāyati ; 2. uttejeti. *p.p.* °nīta ; antarahita ; °jita. °**ed**, *a.* mahussāha. °**edly**, *adv.* saviriyaŋ. °**less**, *n.* nitteja ; hīnaviriya. °**lessly**, *adv.* maṅkubhāvena ; nittejatāya.

Spiritual, *a.* ajjhattika ; mānasika. °**ize**, *v.t.* ajjhattikattaŋ *or* parisuddhattaŋ pāpeti. °**ism**, *n.* bhūtavijjā, *f.* °**ist**, *n.* 1. attavādī ; 2. bhūtavejja, *m.* °**ly**, *adv.* ajjhattikavasena ; paramatthato.

Spirituous, *a.* majjasārabahula.

Spirt, **Spurt**, *n.* bahisandana, *nt.* *v.t.* vegena bahi paggharāpeti. *v.i.* vegena bahi sadanti. *p.p.* °pita ; °dita.

Spit, *n.* 1. maŋsasūla, *nt.* 2. bhūnāsikā, *f.* *v.t.* niṭṭhubhati; 3. nicchāreti; 4. sūlena *or* khaggena vijjhati. *p.p.* °bhita; °rita; sūlaviddha. °**ting,** *n.* niṭṭhubhana, *nt.* °**toon,** *n.* khelamallaka, *m.*

Spite, *n.* viddesa, *m.* *v.t.* dubbhati; veraŋ bandhati; virujjhati. *p.p.* °bhita; baddhavera; viruddha. °**ful,** *a.* viddesī; dubbhī; usūyaka. °**fully,** *adv.* issāya; viddesena. **In — of,** anādariyena, *adv.*

Spitfire, *n.* atikodhana, *m.*

Spittle, *n.* lālā, *f.* khela, *m.*

Splanchnic, *a.* antapaṭibaddha.

Splash, *n.* 1. sittodaka, *nt.* 2. kalaṅka, *m.* *v.t.* udakaŋ *or* kaddamaŋ siñcati *or* khipati. *p.p.* sittodaka; khittakaddama. °**board,** *n.* kaddamāvaraṇaphalaka, *m.* °**y,** *a.* kaddamamakkhita.

Splatter, *v.i.* 1. udakapothanasaddaŋ pavatteti; 2. anavagamanīyākārena katheti. *p.p.* °titasadda; °thita. °**dash,** *n.* mahāghosa, *m.* °**faced,** *a.* vikaṭamukha.

Splay, *a.* anujubhūta; passato nikkhanta; asamakoṇaka. *v.t.* anujukaŋ sampādeti. °**footed,** *a.* khaluṅkapāda.

Spleen, *n.* 1. pihaka, *nt.* kopa, *m.* domanassa, *nt.* °**ful,** °**ish,** *a.* kodhana; dummana.

Splenalgia, *n.* pihakarujā, *f.*

Splendent, *a.* dittiyutta.

Splendid, *a.* 1. tejassī; mahānubhāva; samullasita; bhāsura; 2. seṭṭha; pasattha. °**ly,** *adv.* mahānubhāvena; atisundarākārena.

Splendour, *n.* patāpa; pabhāva, *m.* sirivibhūti, *f.* sirisobhagga, *nt.*

Splenetic, *a.* kodhana; kopabahula.

Splenic, *a.* pihakanissita.

Splice, *n.* saṅghaṭana; sandhikaraṇa, *nt.* *v.t.* saṅghaṭeti; sandhāneti. *p.p.* °ṭita; °nita.

Splint, *n.* dāruhīra, *nt.* °**er,** *n.* sakalikā, *f.* hīra, *nt.* *v.t.* hīra-hīraŋ karoti. *p.p.* hīrīkata. °**ery,** *a.* hīrasadisa.

Split, *n.* phulla; vivara, *nt.* *v.t.* vidāreti; phāleti; vipāṭeti. *v.i.* phalati; bhijjati; vidālīyati. *p.p.* °rita; °lita; °ṭita; °lita; bhinna; vidālita. °**ting,** *n.* vidālana; phālana, *nt.* °**ter,** *n.* vidāraka; phāletu, *m.*

Splodge, *n.* kalaṅka, *m.*

Splutter, *v.i.* 1. avyattaŋ katheti; 2. bindūni pāteti. *p.p.* °thita; °titabindū.

Spoil, *n.* 1. vilutta-dhana; 2. abbhutaladdha, *nt.* *v.t.* 1. padūseti; saṅkileseti; nāseti; 2. vilumpati; pasayha harati. *p.p.* °sita; vilutta; °haṭa. °**er,** *n.* dūsaka; vilumpaka, *m.*

Spoke, *n.* ara; cakkadanta, *m.* *v.t.* are yojeti. *p.p.* yojitāra.

Spoken, *p.p.* of **Speak,** vutta; kathita; akkhāta.

Spokesman, *n.* niyojitakathika, *m.*

Spoliate, *v.t.* vilumpati. *p.p.* vilutta. °**ion,** *n.* 1. vilumpana; 2. sakkhilipidūsana, *nt.* °**tor,** *n.* vilumpaka, *m.*

Sponge, *n.* samuddāhicchatta, *nt.* *v.t.* samuddāhicchattena sodheti *or* ubbaṭṭeti. *p.p.* °dhita; °ṭita. °**er,** *n.* parūpajīvī; parabhata, *m.* °**iness,** *n.* chiddabahulatta, *nt.* °**y,** *a.* chiddāvacchiddaka; pariyādiyaka.

Sponsion, *n.* pāṭibhogitā, *f.*

Sponsor, *n.* pāṭibhoga; ārakkhaka, *m.*

Spontaneous, *a.* yādicchaka; sayañjāta. °**ly,** *adv.* sahasā; yadicchāya; sayam eva. °**ness,** *n.* yādicchakatā; sābhāvikatā, *f.*

Spoof, *n.* sāṭheyya, *nt.* *v.t.* vañceti. °**er,** *n.* saṭha; vañcaka, *m.*

Spook, *n.* pisāca, *m.* °**ish,** *a.* bhūtāviṭṭha.

Spool, *n.* vaṭṭulāvaṭṭa, *m.*

Spoon, *n.* 1. dabbi, *f.* kaṭacchu, *m.* 2. mandamati; adhimattasinehī, *m.* *v.t.* kaṭacchunā gaṇhāti *or* cāleti. *v.i.* adhimattasinehaŋ dasseti. *p.p.* kaṭacchugahita; °lita; dassitātimatta°. °**ful,** *n.* kaṭacchupūra, *nt.* °**fed,** *a.* dabbiposita; sakamatahīna. °**y,** *a.* muduka; pemātura.

Spoor, *n.* migapadavalañja, *m.* *v.t.* (migānaŋ) gatamaggam anuyāti. *p.p.* °yāta.

Sporadic, *a.* tattha tattha jāyamāna; kālena kālaŋ sijjhamāna. °**ally,** *adv.* viralavasena.

Spore, *n.* sukhumabīja, *nt.*

Sport, *n.* 1. keḷi; kīḷā, *f.* 2. migava, *m.* *v.i.* dibbati; ramati; kīḷati. °**ful,** °**ive,** *a.* keḷisīla; khiḍḍāpasuta. °**ively,** °**fully,** *adv.* kīḷāvasena; sopahāsaŋ. °**iveness,** *n.* khiḍḍābhiratatta, *nt.* °**sman,** *n.* kīḷaka; migavakusala, *m.*

Spot, *n.* 1. ṭhāna, *nt.* bhūbhāga; padesa, *m.* 2. tilaka; bindu, *m.* ciṇha, *nt.* 3. kalaṅka, *m.* *v.t.* 1. bindūhi citteti; 2. kalaṅketi; dūseti. *p.p.* °tita; °kita; dūsita. °**less,** *a.* akalaṅka; niddosa. °**ted,** °**ty,** *a.* sabala; kammāsa.

Spouse, *n.* 1. bhattu; pati, *m.* 2. bhariyā; dutiyikā, *f.* (Both together:) dampatī; jāyāpatī; jānipatī; jayampatī, *m. pl.* °**less,** *a.* avivāhika.

Spout, *n.* paṇālī, *f.* *v.t.* sīghaŋ nikkhāmeti *or* nicchāreti. *p.p.* °mita; °rita. °**er,** *n.* turitakathika, *m.*

Sprag, *n.* cakkarodhaka, *m.*

Sprain, *n.* kāyasandhipīḷana *or* vyāvaṭṭana, *nt.* *v.t.* maṇibandhādikaŋ vyāvaṭṭeti. *p.p.* °ṭita.

Sprat, *n.* sālimaccha, *m.*

Sprawl, *v.t.* asammā pasāreti. *v.i.* hatthapāde pasāretvā nipajjati. *p.p.* °rita; °nipanna. *n.* duppasāraṇa, *nt.*

Spray, *n.* 1. sapuppha-sākhābhaṅga, *m.* 2. binduvasena patamāna-vatthu, *nt.* *v.t.* binduvasena khipati. *p.p.* °khitta.

Spread, *n.* patthharaṇa; visaraṇa, *nt.* *v.t.* pasāreti; vitthāreti; vitanoti. *v.i.* pattharati; visarati. *p.p.* °rita; vitata; patthaṭa; visaṭa. °**eagle,** *n.* attasilāghī, *m.* °**ing,** *a.* pattharamāna. —**over,** ottharati. *p.p.* otthaṭa.

Sprig, *n.* pasākhā, *f.*

Sprightly, *a.* saussāha; uyyogī. °**iness,** *n.* uyyoga, *m.* ussukatta, *nt.*

Spring, *n.* 1. (time :) vasanta, *m.* 2. (of water :) ubbhida ; jalapasava, *m.* 3. (an elastic body :) uplavaka ; unnāmaka, *m.* *v.i.* (— **up,**) 1. ubbhijjati ; abbhudeti ; 2. virūhati ; 3. unnamati ; plavati. *v.t.* janeti ; virūheti ; uṭṭhāpeti. *p.p.* ubbhinna ; °dita ; virūḷha ; unnata ; plavita ; janita ; °hita ; °pita. — **forth,** nipphajjati. — **forward,** pakkhandati. — **of life,** navayobbana, *nt.* °**less,** *a.* anupplavaka. °**tide,** *n.* adhika-uppāta, *m.* °**y,** *a.* parāvattanagatika.

Springe, *n.* khuddakapasubāddhana, *nt.*

Sprinkle, *n.* 1. vikiraṇa, *nt.* 2. appavuṭṭhi, *f.* *v.t.* vikirati ; siñcati. *p.p.* vikiṇṇa ; sitta. °**ing,** *n.* vikiraṇa ; secana, *nt.*

Sprint, *v.i.* puṇṇajavena dhāvati. *n.* sīghadhāvana, *nt.*

Sprite, *n.* pisāca ; amanussa, *m.*

Sprout, *n.* aṅkura ; kalīra, *m.* *v.i.* virūhati ; aṅkurīyati. *p.p.* virūḷha ; °rita.

Spruce, *a.* sumaṇḍita ; pasādhita. *v.t.* maṇḍeti ; pasādheti. *p.p.* °ḍita ; °dhita. °**ly,** *adv.* maṇḍitākārena. °**ness,** *n.* sumaṇḍitatta, *nt.*

Spry, *a.* catura ; sūra.

Spud, *n.* khuddaka-khaṇittī, *f.* *v.t.* uddharati. *p.p.* uddhaṭa.

Spume, *n.* pheṇa, *nt.* *v.i.* pheṇam uggacchati. *p.p.* uggatapheṇa. °**y,** *a.* pheṇabahula.

Spunk, *n.* 1. dhiti, *f.* viriya, *nt.* 2. kopa, *m.* °**y,** *a.* dhitimantu.

Spur, *n.* 1. pādukāpatoda, *m.* 2. (of a cock :) pādakaṇṭaka, *m.* *v.t.* patodena vijjhati ; ussāheti ; uttejeti. *p.p.* patodaviddha ; °hita ; °jita.

Spurious, *a.* kūṭa ; kittima. °**ly,** *adv.* kūṭena ; vyājena. °**ness,** *n.* kūṭasabhāva, *m.* kittimatā, *f.*

Spurn, *n.* pāden'apaharaṇa, *nt.* *v.t.* 1. pādena apaharati ; 2. apasādeti. *p.p.* °apahaṭa ; °rita.

Spurt, *n.* sahasā niccharaṇa, *nt.* *v.i.* sahasā vegaŋ janeti. *p.p.* °janitavega.

Sputter, *n.* 1. vegena kathana ; 2. sasadda-niccharana, *nt.* *v.t.* vegena vyākulaŋ katheti. *p.p.* °kathita.

Sputum, *n.* khela, *m.*

Spy, *n.* ocaraka ; payuttaka ; carapurisa, *m.* *v.t.* anabhilakkhito upaparikkhati.

Squab, *a.* *n.* thullavāmana. *adv.* bāḷhapatanena. *n.* 1. pārāpatapotaka, *m.* 2. tūlabhisi, *f.*

Squabble, *n.* bhaṇḍana, *nt.* kalaha, *m.* *v.i.t.* bhaṇḍeti ; kalahaŋ karoti. *p.p.* °ḍita ; katakalaha. °**er,** *n.* kalahakārī, *m.*

Squadron, *n.* 1. yuddhanāvāgaṇa, *m.* 2. bhaṭasamūha ; assārohīgaṇa, *m.*

Squalid, *a.* malina ; kucchita ; adhama. °**ity,** °**ness,** *n.* malinatta ; dīnatta, *nt.*

Squall, *n.* 1. vaddalikā, *f.* 2. viravana, *nt.* *v.i.t.* viravati ; vissaraŋ karoti. *p.p.* °vita ; °kata. °**y,** *a.* vaddalikāsahita. °**er,** *n.* virāvakārī, *m.*

Squander, *v.t.* adhikavayaŋ karoti ; dhanaŋ vināseti. °**er,** *n.* dhananāsaka, *m.* °**ingly,** *adv.* niratthakavayena.

Square, *n.* samacaturassaka-vatthu; caturassaṅgaṇa, *nt.* adj. 1. samacaturaŋsika; 2. avaṅka; 3. samabhūta; 4. anavajja; 5. anucchavika. *v.t.* 1. caturassattaŋ pāpeti; 2. guṇeti; 3. samāneti; 4. iṇaŋ sodheti. *p.p.* °pita; guṇita; °nita; sodhita-iṇa. — **deal**, *n.* sādhāraṇavinimaya, *m.* — **meal**, *n.* yāvadatthabhojana, *nt.* — **measure**, *n.* ghanamāṇa, *m.* °**ly**, *adv.* ujukaŋ. °**root**, *n.* guṇamūla, *nt.*

Squash, *n.* 1. abhimaddana; parimathana, *nt.* 2. lābuvisesa, *m.* *v.t.* parimaddati; abhimanthati. *p.p.* °dita; °mathita.

Squat, *n.* ukkuṭikanisīdana, *nt.* *v.i.* ukkuṭikaŋ nisīdati. °**ter**, *n.* 1. ukkuṭikāsanika; 2. parabhūmibhogī, *m.*

Squeak, *n.* tikhiṇarava, *m.* *v.i.* tikhiṇaŋ ravati *or* nadati. °**er**, *n.* tikhiṇarāvī, *m.*

Squeal, *n.* kaṭukasadda; aṭṭitassara, *m.* *v.i.* aṭṭitasaddaŋ pavatteti. *p.p.* °titaṭṭitasadda. °**er**, *n.* aṭṭitasaddakārī, *m.*

Squeamish, *a.* 1. niccakukkuccaka; 2. dubbala-gahaṇika, °**ly**, *adv.* sakukkuccaŋ. °**ness**, *n.* kukkuccapakatatta; niccasaṅkitatta, *nt.*

Squeeze, *n.* 1. nippīḷana; maddana; 2. daḷhāliṅgana, *nt.* *v.t.* 1. nippīḷeti; maddati; 2. daḷham āliṅgati. *p.p.* °ḷita; °dita; °gita. °**er**, *n.* nippīḷaka, *m.*

Squib, *n.* 1. aggisalākā, *f.* 2. nindakalipi, *f.* *v.t.* omasavādena garahati. *p.p.* °hita.

Squiffy, *a.* īsaŋ-matta.

Squint, *n.* kekaradiṭṭhi, *f.* *a.* valira; kekara. *v.i.* valirākārena passati. °**eyed**, *a.* valirakkhika; visamacakkhula.

Squire, *n.* bhūmisāmī; janapadaseṭṭhī, *m.*

Squirm, *n.* ito c'ito pavaṭṭana, *nt.* *v.i.* ito c'ito parivattati *or* visappati. *p.p.* °tita; °pita.

Squirrel, *n.* kalandaka, *m.*

Squirt, *n.* siṅgaka, *nt.* *v.t.* siṅgakena nicchāreti. *p.p.* °rita.

Stab, *n.* chūriyāhanana, *nt.* *v.t.* chūriyā āhanati. *p.p.* °āhata. °**ber**, *n.* āhanaka, *m.*

Stable, *a.* thira; acala; thāvara; dhuva; ciraṭṭhāyī. °**bility**, *n.* thiratta; dhuvatta; ciraṭṭhitikatta, *nt.* °**bilize**, *v.t.* thirīkaroti. *p.p.* thirīkata. °**bly**, *adv.* thiraŋ; daḷhaŋ.

Stable, *n.* assasālā, *f.* pasunivāsa, *m.* *v.t.* assasālāya pakkhipati. *p.p.* °pakkhitta.

Stack, *n.* (tiṇādīnaŋ) rāsi; puñja; sañcaya, *m.* *v.t.* puñjīkaroti; samāharati. *p.p.* °kata; °haṭa.

Stactometer, *n.* bindumāṇakayanta, *nt.*

Stadium, *n.* samajjamaṇḍala, *nt.* kīḷābhūmi, *f.*

Staff, *n.* 1. yaṭṭhi, *f.* daṇḍa, *m.* kattarayaṭṭhi, *f.* 2. adhikārīgaṇa, *m.*

Stag, *n.* sāraṅga; hariṇa, *m.*

Stage, *n.* 1. raṅgatala; ussāpitaṭṭhāna, *nt.* aṭṭāla, *m.* 2. avatthā; dasā, *f.* 3. naccakalā, *f.* nāṭakagaṇa, *m.* 4. gamanappamāṇa, *nt.* *v.t.* naccaŋ dasseti *or* payojeti. *p.p.* °jitanacca.

Stager, *n.* katahattha; ñāṇavuddha, *m.*

Stagger, *v.i.* dolāyati ; pakkhalati. *v.t.* saŋsayaŋ pāpeti ; pakampeti. *p.p.* °yita ; °lita ; °pita. °**ingly,** *adv.* sapakkhalanaŋ, *m.*

Stagnate, *v.i.* nippasavo hoti ; nappabhavati. *p.p.* °savībhūta ; °vita. °**ion,** *n.* niccalapavattana ; ekattha-vattana, *nt.* °**nant,** *a.* niccala ; asuddha. °**nancy,** *n.* avahanatta ; asuddhatta, *nt.*

Staid, *a.* thirasabhāva. °**ly,** *adv.* thirasabhāvena. °**ness,** *n.* acalatta ; thiratta, *nt.*

Stain, *n.* kalaṅka, *m.* kalusa, *nt.* *v.t.* kalaṅketi ; dūseti ; kalusayati. *p.p.* °kita ; dūsita ; °yita. °**er,** *n.* kalaṅketu ; dūsaka, *m.* °**less,** *a.* akalaṅka ; nimmala ; vimala.

Stair, *n.* sopāṇa, *nt.* ārohanī, *f.* °**case,** *n.* sopāṇapatha, *m.*

Stake, *n.* 1. sūla ; saṅku, *m.* 2. thūṇā, *f.* 3. abbhuta ; paṇa, *m.* *v.t.* 1. paṇeti ; abbhutaŋ karoti ; 2. sūlehi āvarati ; 3. sūle uttāseti. *p.p.* paṇita ; katabbhuta ; °āvaṭa ; °sita.

Stale, *n.* gomutta ; assamutta, *nt.* adj. pārivāsika ; virasa ; navabhāvāpagata. *v.t.* 1. pārivāsikaŋ karoti ; 2. omutteti. *p.p.* °kata ; °tita. °**ness,** *n.* pārivāsikatta, *nt.*

Stalk, *n.* 1. nāḷa ; daṇḍa, *m.* vaṇṭa, *nt.* 2. gabbitagamana, *nt.* 3. pasucoriya, *nt.* *v.i.* uddhatākārena vajati. *v.t.* raho anubandhati ; pasuŋ coreti. *p.p.* °anubaddha ; coritapasuka. °**ing horse,** 1. dīpakassa, *m.* 2. vyājadassana, *nt.*

Stall, *n.* 1. ekapasuvaja, *m.* 2. āpaṇavibhāga ; khuddakāpaṇa, *m.* 3. gāyakāsana, *nt.* *v.t.i.* 1. vaje nikkhipati ; 2. paṅke cakkam osīdati ; 3. dhāvanayantaŋ nivattati. *p.p.* °khitta ; °osīnacakka ; nivatta°. °**age,** *n.* āpaṇasuṅka, *m.* °**fed,** *a.* vaje posita.

Stallion, *n.* anuddhaṭabījassa, *m.*

Stalwart, *a. n.* thāmavantu ; daḷhakāya, *m.* °**ness,** *n.* pabalatta, *nt.*

Stamen, *n.* purisa-kesara, *nt.* puppharēṇu, *m.*

Stammer, *n.* mammanatta, *nt.* *v.i.* mammanāyati. °**er,** *n.* mammana ; khalitavāca, *m.* °**ingly,** *adv.* sagaggadaŋ ; mammanatāya.

Stamp, *n.* 1. muddā ; muddikā, *f.* lañchana, *nt.* 2. padapāta ; padaghāta, *m.* *v.t.* 1. muddeti ; lañcheti ; 2. pādena bhūmim āhanati. *p.p.* °dita ; °chita ; bhūmyāhatapāda.

Stampede, *n.* sasambhamapalāyana, *nt.* *v.i.* sasambhamaŋ palāyati.

Stanch, *v.t.* santhambheti ; sandanaŋ nivatteti. *p.p.* °bhita ; nivattitasandana.

Stanchion, *n.* upatthambhakathūṇā, *f.* *v.t.* upatthambhakaŋ yojeti.

Stand, *n.* 1. ādhāra ; nissaya ; 2. virāma, *m.* 3. avaṭṭhāna, *nt.* santhiti, *f.* *v.t.i.* 1. tiṭṭhati ; avaṭṭhāti ; 2. uṭṭhāti ; 3. vattati ; 4. sahati ; dhāreti ; 5. nivattati. *p.p.* ṭhita ; uṭṭhita ; °tita ; sahita ; °rita ; nivatta. — **aside,** passato tiṭṭhati. — **back,** apakkamati. °**ing,** *a.* pavattamāna ; tiṭṭhamāna. — **by,** upatiṭṭhati. —

fast, — **firmly**, patiṭṭhāti; adhiṭṭhāti; gādhati. — **still**, santiṭṭhāti. — **up**, uttiṭṭhati; uṭṭhāti.

Standard, *n.* dhaja; ketu, *m.* patākā, *f.* adj. pamāṇībhūta; nidassanabhūta. °**bearer**, dhajadhārī, *m.*

Standing, *n.* 1. pavattana; avaṭṭhāna, *nt.* 2. puggalikatatta, *nt.*

Stanza, *n.* gāthā, *f.* pajja, *nt.*

Staple, *n.* 1. aṅkusa, *m.* 2. padhāna-vāṇijabhaṇḍa, *nt.* adj. padhānabhūta; sulabhuṭṭhānaka; mukhya. *v.t.* aṅkusaŋ yojeti. *p.p.* yojitaṅkusa.

Star, *n.* tārā; tārakā, *f.* uḷu, *m.* *v.t.* tārālakkhaṇaŋ yojeti. °**board**, *n.* nāvādakkhiṇapassa, *m.* °**crossed**, *a.* hatalakkhika; dubbhaga. °**gazer**, *n.* nakkhattapāṭhaka, *m.* °**less**, *a*, tārāvirahita. °**light**, *n.* tārāloka, *m.* °**lit**, *a.* tārobhāsita. **Shooting** —, ukkāpāta, *m.*

Starch, *n.* piṭṭhadhātu, *f.* khali, *nt.* *v.t.* khalinā makkheti. *p.p.* khalimakkhita. °**y**, *a.* amuduka; kharasamphassa.

Stare, *n.* thirolokana, *nt.* *v.i.t.* thiram oloketi. *p.p.* °kita. °**er**, *n.* thirolokaka, *m.* °**ingly**, *a.* ativyattaŋ; atiphuṭaŋ.

Stark, *a.* 1. asesa; kevala; 2. asithila; daḷha; thaddha. *adv.* kevalaŋ; accantaŋ.

Start, *n.* 1. ārambha, *m.* 2. phandana, *nt.* *v.i.* 1. ārabhati; 2. sahasā phandati *or* kampati. *p.p.* āraddha, °dita; °pita. °**ing point**, ārabhanaṭṭhāna, *nt.*

Startle, *n.* uttāseti; santāseti; phandāpeti. *p.p.* °sita; ° pita. °**ing**, *a.* phandāpanaka.

Starve, *v.i.* chinnabhatto hoti; khudāya avasīdati. *v.t.* nirāhārena māreti. *p.p.* °avasīna; °mārita. °**ation**, *n.* nirāhāratā; ajaddhumārikā, *f.* °**ing**, *a.* khudāya mīyamāna. °**ling**, *n.* chāta; jighacchita; bubhukkhita.

Stasis, *n.* rudhirāvarodha, *m.*

State, *n.* 1. avatthā; dasā, *f.* 2. sabhāva, *m.* pakati, *f.* 3. rajja; raṭṭha, *nt.* 4. issariya, *nt.* patāpa, *m.* adj. rajjāyatta. *v.t.* ācikkhati; pakāseti; vitthāreti. *p.p.* °khita; °sita; °rita. — **carriage**, rājaratha, *m.* — **elephant**, maṅgalahatthī, *m.* — **horse**, maṅgalassa, *m.* °**ly**, *a.* mahāteja; mahānubhāva. °**liness**, *n.* mahāpatāpatta, *nt.* uḷārasirisobhagga, *nt.* °**ment**, *n.* nivedana; pakāsana, *nt.* °**sman**, rājanītinipuṇa.

Static, °**cal**, *a.* acala; aniñja.

Statics, *n.* *pl.* acalavatthuniyāma, *m.*

Station, *n.* 1. avaṭṭhāna; nivattanaṭṭhāna, *nt.* 2. ṭhānantara, *nt.* adhikāra, *m.* *v.t.* niveseti; patiṭṭhāpeti. *p.p.* °sita; °pita. °**ary**, *a.* acala; thāvara.

Stationer, *n.* lipibhaṇḍavāṇija, *m.* °**y**, *n.* lipibhaṇḍa, *nt.*

Statistics, *n.* *pl.* mahājanikasaṅkhyālekhana, *nt.* °**cally**, *adv.* saṅkhyālekhanānusārena.

Statue, *n.* paṭimā, *f.* paṭibimba, *nt.* °**ary**, *n.* paṭimāsippa; paṭimākaraṇa, *nt.* adj. paṭimāpaṭibaddha. °**sque**, *a.* paṭimāsadisadassana. °**tte**, *n.* khuddakapaṭimā, *f.*

Stature, *n.* ārohapariṇāha, *m.*
Status, *n.* dhana-balādi-pamāṇa, *nt.*
Statute, *n.* vavatthā; paññatti, *f.* niyamitavidhi, *m.* °**able,** °**ory,** *a.* vavatthānugata; nītyanukūla.
Staunch, *a.* daḷhabhattika.
Stave, *n.* 1. dārupaṭṭikā, *f.* 2. gāthāpāda, *nt. v.t.* nivāreti. *p.p.* °rita.
Stay, *n.* 1. kālikavāsa, *m.* 2. nivattana, *nt.* 3. ādhāra; upatthambha, *m.* 4. nivāraṇa, *nt. v.i.* tāvakālikaŋ vasati; nivattati. *v.t.* nivatteti; santhambheti. *p.p.* °vuttha; °tiṭa; °bhita. — **behind,** ohīyati. °**er,** *n.* 1. nivāretu; 2. upatthambhaka, *m.* °**ing,** *n.* viharaṇa, *nt.*
Steadfast, *a.* thira; daḷhādhiṭṭhāna. °**ly,** *adv.* thiravasena. °**ness,** *n.* daḷhatta; thirādhiṭṭhānatta, *nt.*
Steady, *a.* acala; thāvara. *v.t.* thirīkaroti; daḷhayati. °**ily,** *adv.* thirākārena. °**iness,** *n.* thiratta; acalatta; acāpalla, *nt.*
Steak, *n.* maŋsakhaṇḍa, *m.*
Steal, *v.t.* coreti; theneti. °**er,** *n.* takkara; mosaka; cora, *m.* °**ing,** *n.* theyya; coriya, *nt.*
Stealth, *n.* gūḷhatta, *nt.* rahobhāva, *m.* **ily,** *adv.* gūḷhaŋ. °**y,** *a.* gūḷha; paṭicchanna.
Steam, *n.* bappa, *m. v.i.* bappam uppādeti. *v.t.* usmanā sedeti. *p.p.* °ditabappa; °dita. °**bath,** *n.* sedakamma, *nt.* °**boat,** *n.* dhūmayātrā, *f.* °**engine,** *n.* bappayanta, *nt.* °**er,** *n.* dhūmanāvā, *f.*
Steed, *n.* ājaññassa, *m.*
Steel, *n.* ayasāra, *m.* adj. atithaddha. *v.t.* ayasārena chādeti. *p.p.* °dita. °**y,** *a.* atithaddha.
Steep, *n.* papāta, *m.* adj. ukkūla; durāruha; pātālayutta. *v.t.* kiledeti; otāretvā temeti. *p.p.* °dita; °mita.
Steeple, *n.* pāsādasikhara, *nt.*
Steer, *n.* uddhaṭabīja-goṇa, *m. v.t.* nāvaŋ pājeti *or* gantabbamaggaŋ pāpeti. *p.p.* pājitanāva; °pita. °**age,** *n.* nāvācāraṇa, *nt.* °**sman,** *n.* kaṇṇadhāra, *m.*
Stele, *n.* salekha-silāthambha, *m.*
Stellar, *a.* nakkhattapaṭibaddha.
Stellate, *a.* tārakākāra.
Stelliferous, *a.* tārābahula.
Stellular, *a.* tārākārena sampādita.
Stem, *n.* daṇḍa; nāḷa, *m.* vaṇṭa, *nt. v.t.* 1. nivatteti; santhambheti; 2. oghaŋ chindanto tarati. *p.p.* °tita; °bhita; °tarita.
Stench, *n.* pūtigandha, *m.* °**y,** *a.* pūtigandhika.
Stenograph, *n.* saṅkhittakkharalekhana, *nt.* °**er,** *n.* laghulekhaka, *m.* °**y,** *n.* laghulekhanavijjā, *f.*
Stentor, *n.* uccassarayutta, *m.* °**ian,** *a.* gambhīrassara.
Step, *n.* 1. padapāta; padavikkhepa; 2. kama, *m.* paṭipāṭi, *f.* 3. sopāṇaphalaka, *m.* 4. pādalañchana, *nt. v.t.i.* akkamati; padaŋ nikkhipati. *p.p.* akkanta; °khittapada. — **by step,** 1. anupadaŋ; 2. anukkamena, *adv.* — **back,** paṭikkamati. — **forward,** abhikkamati. — **down,** otarati. — **in,** āruhati *or* pavisati.— **out,** turitayati. °**ping,** *n.*

padavikkama; padavītihāra, *m.* °**ping stone,** 1. padapātasilā, *f.* 2. vuddhipadaṭṭhāna, *nt.*

Step, *prep.* °**brother,** vemātikabhātu, *m.* °**father,** dutiyavivāhe pitā, *m.* °**daughter,** dutiyavivāhe dhītā, *f.* °**mother,** dutiyavivāhe mātā, *f.* °**sister,** vemātika-bhaginī, *f.* °**son,** paṭhamavivāhe putto, *m.*

Steppe, *n.* rukkharahita-samabhūmi, *f.*

Stereotype, *n.* ghanīkata-muddākkharaphalaka, *m. v.t.* 1. ekābaddhaŋ karoti; 2. avipariṇāmiyattaŋ pāpeti. *p.p.* °dhakata; °pita.

Sterile, *a.* aphala; vañjha; asāra. °**ity,** *n.* vañjhatā, *f.*

Sterling, *a.* yathābhūta; yathāvatthuka. *n.* soṇṇanikkha, *nt.*

Stern, *n.* nāvāpacchābhāga, *m.* adj. asithila; daḷha; thaddha. °**ly,** *adv.* atidaḷhaŋ. °**ness,** daḷhatta; pharusatta, *nt.*

Sternum, *n.* uraṭṭhi, *nt.*

Sternutation, *n.* 1. khipitaka; 2. natthukamma, *nt.* °**tatory,** *a.* 1. khipitajanaka; 2. natthukammāyatta.

Stertorous, *a.* ghurughurupassāsī.

Stethoscope, *n.* nāḷiviññāṇayanta, *nt. v.t.* hadayaphandanam upaparikkhati.

Stevedore, *n.* nāvābhaṇḍavāhaka, *m.*

Stew, *n.* 1. mandapakka-bhojana, *nt.* 2. manotāpa, *m. v.t.* mandaŋ pacati. *p.p.* °pakka.

Steward, *n.* bhojanādhikārī; bhaṇḍāgārika; āyuttaka, *m.* °**ship,** *n.* āyuttakaṭṭhāna; bhaṇḍāgārikatta, *nt.*

Stick, *n.* kattaradaṇḍa, *m.* kattarayaṭṭhi, *f. v.i.* allīyati; laggati. *v.t.* 1. alliyāpeti; laggeti; 2. nittudati. *p.p.* allīna; lagga; °pita; °gita; °dita. °**ing,** *n.* allīyana, *nt.* abhissaṅga, *m.* °**iness,** *n.* saŋlagganatā, *f.* °**y,** allīyanasabhāva.

Stickle, *v.t.* nibandhati; vivadati. *p.p.* nibaddha; °dita. °**er,** *n.* nibandhaka, *m.*

Stiff, *a.* 1. patthaddha; kaṭhina; anamma; 2. dukkara; 3. ghanībhūta. °**en,** *v.t.* kaṭhinīkaroti. *v.i.* kaṭhinībhavati. *p.p.* °kata; °bhūta. °**ly,** *adv.* daḷhaŋ; sābhimānaŋ. — **necked,** *a.* ādhānagāhī; uddhata. °**ness,** *n.* kaṭhinatta, *nt.*

Stifle, *v.t.* sāsaŋ nirumbheti. *p.p.* °bhitasāsa. °**ing,** *a.* sāsanirumbhaka.

Stigma, *n.* 1. vaṇalañchana, *nt.* 2. apakitti, *f.* °**tize,** *v.t.* kalaṅketi; lañcheti. *p.p.* °kita; °chita.

Stile, *n.* vatidvāra, *nt.*

Still, *n.* parissāvaka-yanta, *nt.* adj. acala; akampa; niccala; nissadda, *v.t.* upasameti; acalaŋ *or* nissaddaŋ karoti. *p.p.* °mita; °kata. *adv.* 1. yāva-tāva; yāvajjatanā; yāv'imaŋ kālaŋ; 2. evaŋ sante pi; tathā pi. °**born,** maritvā-jāta; gabbhamata, *m.* — **more,** bhīyoso mattāya, *adv.* °**ness,** *n.* niccalatta; nissaddatta, *nt.*

Stilt, *n.* pādayaṭṭhi, *f.* °**ed,** *a.* 1. pādayaṭṭhigāmī; 2. gabbita; vikatthaka.

Stimulate, *v.t.* uttejeti; ussāheti; pabodheti. *p.p.* °jita; °hita; °dhita. °**lant,** *a. n.* uttejaka;

uddīpaka, *m. nt.* °**ion**, *n.* uttejana ; samuṭṭhāpana ; anubalappadāna, *nt.* °**ive**, *a.* uttejaka ; paggaṇhanaka.

Stimulus, *n.* 1. uddīpakavatthu; uttejakosadha, *nt.* 2. paggaha, *m.*

Sting, *n.* 1. dāṭhā, *f.* 2. ḍasana, *nt.* *v.t.* 1. ḍasati ; 2. accantaŋ vyathati. *p.p.* daṭṭha; °thita. °**less**, *a.* niddāṭha ; uddhaṭadāṭha.

Stingy, *a.* luddha ; kadariya ; maccharī. °**iness**, *n.* macchariya ; luddhatta, *nt.* °**ily**, *adv.* luddhākārena ; kadariyena.

Stink, *n.* pūtigandha, *m.* *v.t.* pūtigandhaŋ vāyeti. *v.i.* 1. pūti vāyati; 2. ayasaŋ pappoti. *p.p.* vāyitapūti° ; °patta. °**ing**, *a.* pūtigandhāvaha.

Stint, *n.* ūnatta ; ūnappamāṇa, *nt. v.t.* 1. ūnakaŋ deti ; 2. mitaŋ bhuñjati ; 3. viramati. *p.p.* °dinna ; °bhutta; virata. °**ingly**, *adv.* atiluddhākārena. °**less**, *a.* nillobhī ; amaccharī; asīmita.

Stipe, *n.* daṇḍa ; nāḷa, *m.* vaṇṭa, *nt.*

Stipend, *n.* 1. vetana, *nt.* 2. niyamita-aya, *m.* °**iary**, *n.* vetanalābhī, *m.*

Stipulate, *v.i.* paṭiññaŋ ṭhapeti ; saṅgaraŋ karoti ; *v.t.* paṭiññaŋ gaṇhāti. *p.p.* ṭhapitapaṭiñña ; katasaṅgara ; gahitapaṭiñña. °**ion**, *n.* paṭiññā, *f.* saṅgara, *m.*

Stir, *n.* saṅkhobha, *m.* *v.t.* 1. khobheti ; āloleti ; viloleti ; 2. mantheti. *v.i.* saṅkhubhati ; iñjati ; kampati. *p.p.* °bhita ; °lita ; °thita ; iñjita ; °pita. °**ring**, *n.* copana ; kampana ; saṅkhubhana, *nt.* °**ring**, *a.* saṅkhobhaka. °**er**, *n.* khobhakārī, *m.*

Stirrup, *n.* ārohī-pādukā, *f.*

Stitch, *n.* sibbanī, *f.* ārapatha, *m.* *v.t.* sibbati. *p.p.* °bita.

Stithy, *n.* 1. kammārasālā ; 2. adhikaraṇī, *f.*

Stock, *n.* 1. sannidhi ; sañcaya, *m.* 2. mūladhana, *nt.* 3. anvaya ; vaŋsa, *m.* 4. saŋvaḍḍhita-pasugaṇa, *m.* 5. (for feet :) suruṅgā, *f.* 6. khandha ; daṇḍa ; khāṇuka, *m.* *v.t.* sañcināti ; samāharati ; rāsīkaroti. *p.p.* sañcita ; samāhaṭa ; °kata. **Laughing** —, parihāsaṭṭhāna-vatthu, *nt.* °**breeder**, *n.* pasupālaka ; pasuposaka, *m.* °**still**, *a.* khāṇusadisa ; niccala. °**taking**, *n.* bhaṇḍagaṇanolokana, *nt.*

Stockade, saṅkuvati, *f.* *v.t.* saṅkuvatiŋ yojeti.

Stocking, *n.* pādajāla, *nt.*

Stocky, *a.* thulla-vāmanaka.

Stodge, *n.* garukāhāra, *m.* *v.i.* gedhena bhuñjati. *p.p.* °bhutta. °**gy**, *a.* 1. garuka ; dujjara ; 2. ativitthārita.

Stoic, *a. n.* upekkhaka ; mahādhitika. °**ally**, *adv.* upekkhakatāya ; attasaŋyamena.

Stoke, *v.t.* 1. uddhane indhanaŋ khipati ; 2. turitaŋ bhuñjati. *p.p.* °khittindhana ; °bhutta. °**er**, *n.* 1. uddhanaposaka ; 2. turitabhojī, *m.*

Stolid, *a.* momuha ; garukāya ; anussuka. °**ity**, *n.* muṭṭhasacca ; anussukatta ; jaḷatta ; garukāyatta, *nt.* °**ly**, *adv.* mūḷhākārena.

Stomach, *n.* 1. āmāsaya, *m.* udara; jaṭhara, *nt.* 2. abhiruci, *f.* *v.t.* abhiruciyā bhuñjati. °**ic,** *a.* āmāsayāyatta. *n.* rucivaḍḍhakosadha; gahaṇidīpaka, *nt.* °**less,** *a.* mandagahaṇika.

Stone, *n.* 1. silā, *f.* pāsāṇa; asma, *m.* 2. (of fruits:) aṭṭhi; bīja, *nt.* *v.t.* 1. pāsāṇehi paharati; 2. aṭṭhīni apaneti. *p.p.* °pahaṭa; apanītaṭṭhika. — **age,** *n.* pāsāṇāyudha-yuga, *m.* °**blind,** *a.* *n.* jaccandha. — **cutter,** *n.* 1. taṅka; 2. pāsāṇadāraka, *m.* °**deaf,** *a.* *n.* puṇṇabadhira. — **mason,** *n.* silāvaḍḍhakī, *m.* °**still,** *a.* pāsāṇathira. °**ware,** *n.* ghanamattikabhājana, *nt.* **Made of —,** silāmaya, *a.* — **to grind with,** nisadapota, *m.*

Stony, *a.* 1. silābahula; 2. atithaddha. — **hearted,** *a.* niṭṭhura; kaṭhinahadaya. °**iness,** *n.* 1. niṭṭhuratta; pāsāṇabāhulla, *nt.*

Stook, *n.* veṇīkata-sassapuñja, *m.*

Stool, *n.* 1. pādapīṭha, *nt.* 2. uccārossagga, *m.* *v.i.* vaccaŋ karoti; uccāram ossajati. *p.p.* katavacca; ossaṭṭhuccāra.

Stoop, *n.* 1. onamana; 2. vasaṅgamana, *nt.* *v.i.* 1. onamati; 2. vasaŋ yāti. *p.p.* °mita; °yāta.

Stop, *n.* 1. nivattana, *nt.* viccheda; virāma, *m.* 2. virāmalakkhaṇa; 3. rodhana, *nt.* *v.i.* nivattati; 2. viramati; vicchijjati. *v.t.* 1. nivatteti; rundheti; 2. vāreti; nivāreti. *p.p.* nivatta; virata; vicchinna; °tita; °dhita; °rita. — **cock,** *n.* jalanāḷathakanaka, *nt.* °**page,** *n.* rodhana; thambhana; nivattāpana, *nt.* upaccheda, *m.* °**per,** *n.* avarodhaka, *m.* rodhanī, *f.* *v.t.* rodhaniyā pidahati.

Storax, *n.* sugandha-niyyāsavisesa, *m.*

Store, *n.* 1. bhaṇḍanicaya; 2. bhaṇḍasālā, *f.* *v.t.* sañcināti; sannidahati; rāsīkaroti. *p.p.* sañcita; sannihita; °kata. °**age,** *n.* 1. sannidhikaraṇa, *nt.* 2. bhaṇḍāgārāya dātabbamūla, *nt.* °**house,** *n.* sannidhiṭṭhāna; koṭṭhāgāra, *nt.* °**keeper,** *n.* koṭṭhāgārika, *m.*

Storey, *n.* pāsādatala, *nt.* °**ed,** °**ied,** *a.* bhūmiyutta; bhummika. **Three-storeyed,** tibhummika.

Stork, *n.* bakavisesa, *m.*

Storm, *n.* 1. caṇḍavāta; mahāmegha; 2. saṅkhobha, *m.* 3. omaddana, *nt.* *v.i.* saṅkhubhati; vegena vassati; *v.t.* 1. saṅkhobheti; 2. (paravisayaŋ) omaddati. *p.p.* °bhita; °vuṭṭha; °dita. °**y,** *a.* saṅkhubhita; vātavuṭṭhisahita; khobhakara.

Story, *n.* 1. kathāvatthu, *nt.* ākhyāyikā, *f.* 2. tala, *nt.* bhūmi, *f.* See **Storey. Seven-storied,** sattabhūmaka, *a.*

Stout, *a.* thāmavantu; thūladehī; dhitimantu; nibbhaya. °**hearted,** *a.* thiracitta; daḷhanicchaya. °**ly,** *adv.* thiracittena. °**ness,** *n.* pabalatta; thiranicchayatta, *nt.*

Stove, *v.* cullī, *f.* uddhana, *nt.*

Stow, *v.t.* paṭisāmeti; nikkhipati. *p.p.* °mita; nikkhitta. °**age,** *n.* 1. paṭisāmana, *nt.* bhaṇḍāgārika-suṅka, *m.* °**away,** mūlam adatvā nāvā-gāmī, *m.*

Straddle, *v.i.t.* pāde pasāretvā tiṭṭhati *or* nisīdati. *p.p.* °ṭhita; °nisinna.

Straggle, *v.i.* samūhato viyujjati; vikiṇṇākārena yāti; animittam āhiṇḍati. *p.p.* °viyutta; °yāta. °**er,** *n.* sakaparisa-bhaṭṭha; maggamūḷha, *m.* °**ingly,** *adv.* maggamūḷhākārena; samūhaviyogena.

Straight, *a.* uju; ajimha; avaṅka; akuṭila; sarala. *adv.* ujukaŋ; sajju; sapadi. °**en,** *v.t.* ujuŋ karoti. — **away,** sajju; sīgham eva, *ind.* °**forward,** *a.* ujucitta; ajjavayutta.—**line,** *n.* ujurekhā, *f.* °**ly,** *adv.* ujukam eva. °**ness,** *n.* ajjava; akoṭilla, *nt.*

Strain, *n.* 1. āyāsa; parissama, *m.* 2. kriyāsantati, *f.* 3. (musical:) laya, *m.* *v.t.* āyāseti; uppīḷeti; 2. parissāveti; vimalīkaroti. *p.p.* °sita; °ḷita; °vita; °kata. °**er,** *n.* 1. parissāvana, *nt.* 2. sodhanī; cālanī, *f.*

Straits, *n.* 1. duddasā, *f.* kasira; kiccha, *nt.* 2. samuddasandhi, *m.* adj. sambādha; avitthiṇṇa. °**en,** *v.t.* sambādheti; pīḷeti. *p.p.* °dhita; °ḷita. °**ness,** *n.* sambādhatta; dukkaratta, *nt.*

Strand, *n.* kūla; tīra; taṭa, *nt.* *v.t.* kūlaŋ pāpeti; tīre āhanati. *v.i.* ohīyati. *p.p.* °pita; °āhata; ohīna. °**ed,** *a.* kicchāpanna; appaṭisaraṇa.

Strange, *a.* 1. abbhuta; apubba; 2. videsīya; 3. asanthuta; aparicita. — **looking,** *a.* abbhutadassana. °**ly,** *adv.* abbhutākārena. °**ness,** *n.* abbhutatta; aparicitatta, *nt.* °**er,** *n.* āgantuka; atithi; 2. adhunāgata; aparicita, *m.*

Strangle, *v.t.* sāsanirodhena māreti. — **oneself,** ubbandhati; sāsaŋ nirumbhetvā marati. *p.p.* °mārita; ubbaddha; °mata. °**ing,** *n.* ubbandhana; sāsanirumbhana, *nt.*

Strangury, *n.* muttakicchābādha, *m.* °**ious,** *a.* muttakicchābādhī.

Strap, *n.* varattā; naddhi, *f.* yotta, *nt.* *v.t.* varattāya bandhati *or* tāḷeti. *p.p.* °baddha; °ḷita. °**ping,** *n.* varattātāḷana, *nt.* adj. vaḍḍhitadeha.

Stratagem, *n.* kapaṭopāya, *m.*

Strategy, *n.* saṅgāmopāya, *m.* °**ic,** °**ical,** *a.* saṅgāmopāyavisayaka. °**ist,** *n.* saṅgāmopāyadakkha.

Stratum, *n.* bhūmitalatthara, *nt.* °**ticulate,** *a.* talattharayutta. °**tify,** *v.t.* talavasena attharati. *p.p.* °atthata.

Stratus, *n.* meghapaṭala, *m.*

Straw, *n.* palāla; sukkhatiṇa, *nt.* °**y,** *a.* palālamaya; palālasadisa.

Stray, *a.* maggamūḷha; yūthabhaṭṭha. *v.i.* 1. magge muyhati; 2. uppathaŋ yāti. *p.p.* maggamūḷha; °yāta.

Streak, *n.* vaṇṇalekhā, *f.* *v.t.* lekhā yojeti; vaṇṇalekhāhi alaṅkaroti. *p.p.* yojitaleka; °lekhālaṅkata.

Stream, *n.* jalasota ; jalogha, *m.* kunnadī ; jalamātikā, *f.* *v.i.* pasavati ; pabhavati. *p.p.* °vita. °**let,** *n.* khuddakamātikā, *f.*

Streamer, *n.* 1. dīghadhaja, *m.* 2. raŋsikadamba, *m.*

Street, *n.* racchā ; vīthi ; visikhā; rathikā, *f.* °**sweeper,** *n.* vīthisodhaka, *m.* °**walker,** *n.* gaṇikā, *f.*

Strength, *n.* satti, *f.* thāma, *m.* bala ; sāmatthiya, *nt.* °**en,** *v.t.* pabalīkaroti ; daḷhayati. *v.i.* thirībhavati. *p.p.* °kata ; °yita ; °bhūta. °**ener,** *n.* 1. pabalīkāraka, *m.* 2. balajanakosadha, *nt.* °**less,** *a.* sattihīna ; abala ; dubbala.

Strenuous, *a.* āraddhaviriya ; atandita ; ātāpī. °**ly,** *adv.* daḷhaviriyena. °**ness,** *n.* uyyoga ; parakkama, *m.* viriyādhiṭṭhāna, *nt.*

Stress, *n.* 1. āyāsa, *m.* garutta ; bhāriyatta, *nt.* 2. saddagambhīratta, *nt.* *v.t.* daḷhayati ; savisesaŋ udīreti. *p.p.* °yita ; °rita.

Stretch, *n.* pasāraṇa ; pattharaṇa, *nt.* *v.t.* pasāreti ; vitanoti. *v.i.* pasārīyati. *p.p.* °rita ; vitata. °**er,** *n.* 1. pasāretu, *m.* 2. rogīmañca, *m.* —**forth,** paggaṇhāti.

Strew, *v.t.* ākirati ; vikirati ; vippakirati. *p.p.* ākiṇṇa ; vikiṇṇa.

Striate, *a.* sukhumarekhāṅkita.

Stricken, *p.p.* (of Strike), addita ; maddita ; pīḷita ; aṭṭita.

Strict, *a.* 1. daḷha ; asithila ; 2. anullaṅghiya ; anatikkamiya ; niyata. °**ly,** *adv.* sanicchayaŋ ; saniyamaŋ. °**ness,** *n.* daḷhatta ; asithilatta.

Stricture, *n.* 1. tikhiṇa-vivecana, *nt.* 2. sirāsaṅkoca, *m.*

Stride, *v.i.t.* pāde vītiharati ; pādaŋ dūre nikkhipati. *p.p.* vītihaṭapāda ; °khittapāda. *n.* padavītihāra, *m.*

Strident, *a.* kaṭukasaddayutta.

Stridulate, *v.i.* gambhīra-kaṭukasaddaŋ pavatteti.

Strife, *n.* bhaṇḍana, *nt.* kalaha ; viggaha, *m.*

Strike, *v.t.* paharati ; abhihanati ; ghaṭṭeti. *v.i.* āhaññati ; ghaṭṭīyati. *p.p.* pahaṭa ; abhihata ; °ṭita ; āhata ; ghaṭṭita ; 2. mūlādiŋ muddāpeti ; 3. kammantaŋ cajati ; 4. cittaŋ ākaḍḍhati. *p.p.* °pita ; cattakammanta ; °ḍhitacitta. *n.* kammantacāga, *m.* °**er,** *n.* 1. pahāradāyī ; 2. kammantacāgī, *m.* °**ing,** *a.* manohara ; cittākaḍḍhaka. °**ingly,** *adv.* savisesaŋ ; manoharatāya.—**off,** lopeti ; makkheti. — **against,** paṭihanati. — **down,** opāteti ; nighāteti. °**ing,** *n.* paharaṇa ; pothana ; saṅghaṭṭana, *nt.* —**in return,** paṭipaharati. — **out,** (fire), saṅghaṭṭanena janeti. — **through,** vinivijjhati. — **up,** ārabhati.

String, *n.* 1. sutta, *nt.* tanti, *f.* 2. seṇi ; panti ; āvali, *f.* 3. dhanujiyā, *f.* *v.t.* 1. āvuṇāti ; 2. tantūhi bandhati ; 3. jiyaŋ āropeti. *p.p.* āvuta ; tantubaddha ; jiyāropita. — **of contents,** uddāna, *nt.* — **of pearls,** muttāvali, *f.* °**y,** *a.* tantuyutta.

Stringent, *a.* 1. kaṭuka ; tikhiṇa ; 2. avilaṅghiya ; asithila. °**ncy,** *n.* kaṭukatta ; asithilatta ; anullaṅghiyatta, *nt.*

Strip, *n.* cīraka, *nt.* dīghapaṭṭikā, *f.* *v.t.* uddāḷeti ; (of clothes :) acchindati. *p.p.* °ḷita ; acchinna. — **of bark,** vākacīra, *nt.* — **of cloth,** coḷapaṭṭikā, *f.*

Stripe, *n.* 1. paṭṭikā, *f.* 2. visamavaṇṇarekhā, *f.* 3. kasāpahāra, *m.* °**ed,** *a.* lekhācittita.

Stripling, *n.* kumāra ; māṇava, *m.*

Strive, *v.i.* ghaṭati ; vāyamati ; yatati ; īhati ; ussahati. *p.p.* °ṭita ; °mita ; īhita ; °hita. °**ing,** *n.* ghaṭana ; īhana, *nt.* ussāha ; vāyāma, *m.*

Stroke, *n.* 1. pahāra ; āghāta, nigghāta, *m.* 2. rekhā, *f.* 3. parāmasana, *nt.* 4. kenipāta, *m.* 5. khaṇikābādha, *m.* 6. anapekkhita-bhāgya *or* abhāgya, *nt.* *v.t.* parimajjati ; parāmasati. *p.p.* °maṭṭha *or* majjita ; parāmaṭṭha.

Stroll, *n.* mandacārikā, *f.* caṅkamana, *nt.* *v.i.* carati ; āhiṇḍati ; pariyaṭati. °**er,** *n.* pariyaṭaka, *m.*

Strong, *a.* 1. balavantu ; thāmavantu ; pabala ; 2. daḷha ; thira ; 3. tibba ; tikhiṇa ; 4. pahonta ; samattha. °**hold,** *n.* baḷakoṭṭhaka ; dugga, *nt.* °**ly,** *adv.* gāḷhaŋ ; daḷhaŋ ; bāḷhaŋ. — **minded,** *a.* daḷhamānasa.

Strop, *n.* khuracamma, *nt.* khuratejanapaṭṭikā, *f.* *v.t.* paṭṭikāya khuraŋ tejeti. *p.p.* °tejitakhura.

Structure, *n.* 1. nimmāṇa, *nt.* racitākāra, *m.* 2. mandira, *nt.*

Struggle, *n.* daḷhavāyāma ; balavaviggaha, *m.* vipphandana, *nt.* *v.i.* 1. abhiyatati ; daḷhaŋ vāyamati ; 2. vipphandati. *p.p.* °tita ; °mita ; °dita.

Strum, *n.* anipuṇavādana, *nt.* *v.i.* anipuṇākārena vādeti. *p.p.* °vādita.

Struma, *n.* gaṇḍamālaroga, *m.*

Strumpet, *n.* gaṇikā, *f.*

Strut, *v.i.* sābhimānaŋ vicarati.

Strychnia, *n.* tikhiṇavisa-visesa, *m.*

Stub, *n.* khāṇuka, *m.* chinnāvasiṭṭha-mūla, *nt.* *v.t.* mūlāni uddharati. *p.p.* uddhaṭamūla.

Stubble, *n.* chinnāvasiṭṭha-sassa, *nt.*

Stubborn, *a.* avidheyya ; avasa ; duddamma ; mānatthaddha. °**ly,** *adv.* duddammākārena. °**ness,** *n.* duddamyatta ; avidheyyatta, *nt.*

Stucco, *n.* siniddha-sudhālepa, *m.*

Stud, *n.* gaṇṭhi ; kukku, *m.* *v.t.* khacati. *p.p.* khacita.

Student, *n.* sissa ; antevāsī ; vijjatthī, *m.*

Studio, *n.* sippāyatana, *nt.*

Study, *n.* 1. ajjhayana ; uggahaṇa, *nt.* 2. ajjhayana-gabbha, *m.* *v.t.i.* 1. uggaṇhāti ; pariyāpuṇāti ; adhīyati ; anusikkhati ; 2. vīmaŋsati. *p.p.* uggahita ; pariyāputa ; adhīta ; °khita ; °sita. °**ious,** *a.* vijjāsatta ; vīmaŋsāpubbaka. °**iously,** *adv.* vīmaŋsāpubbakaŋ ; upaṭṭhitasatiyā. °**iousness,** *n.* vijjatthikatā ; vīmaŋsakatā, *f.*

Stuff, *n.* 1. dabba ; vatthu ; 2. upakaraṇa, *nt.* 3. kasaṭa ; kacavara, *m.* *v.t.* accantaŋ pūreti. *v.i.* giddho bhuñjati. *p.p.* °rita. °**ing,** *n.* 1. antopūraṇa ; 2. pūrakadabba, *nt.* °**y,** *a.* nivāta ; sambādha.

Stultify, *v.t.* 1. mūḷhattaŋ dasseti; 2. adhikāraŋ nivāreti. *p.p.* °sitamūḷ°; nivāritādhi°.

Stumble, *n.* khalita; pakkhalana, *nt.* pamādadosa, *m.* *v.i.t.* pakkhalati; pamajjati. *p.p.* °lita; pamatta. °**ing,** *a.* pakkhalamāna. °**ing block,** *n.* bādhaka, *nt.* antarāya, *m.*

Stump, *n.* khāṇuka; chinnāvasesa, *m.* *v.t.i.* 1. sasaddaŋ caṅkamati; 2. niruttaraŋ karoti; 3. pacārento āhiṇḍati; 4. sākhādayo chindati. *p.p.* °mita; °kata; chinnasākhādi. °**y,** *a.* thullavāmana.

Stun, *v.t.* badhirīkaroti; mucchāpeti. *p.p.* °kata; °pita. °**ning,** *a.* atisundara; vimhāpanaka. °**ner,** *n.* vesārajjakara, *m.*

Stunt, *n.* 1. vaḍḍhinivattana, *nt.* 2. visiṭṭhakriyā, *f.* *v.t.* vaḍḍhiŋ nirumbheti; vāmanaŋ karoti. *p.p.* °bhitavaḍḍhī; vāmanīkata.

Stupefy, *v.t.* moheti; muccheti. *p.p.* mohita; °chita. °**faction,** *n.* vyāmohana; visaññīkaraṇa, *nt.* °**ing,** *a.* mucchaka; pamohaka.

Stupendous, *a.* 1. ativisāla; 2. vimhayāvaha. °**ly,** *adv.* atimahattena; abbhutākārena.

Stupid, *a.* momuha; mandamatika; dandha; sammūḷha. °**ity,** °**ness,** *n.* dandhatta; mandiya, *nt.* °**ly,** *adv.* dandhākārena.

Stupor, *n.* mucchā; sammucchā; bhantasatitā, *f.*

Stuprate, *v.t.* pasayha (itthiŋ) dūseti. °**ion,** *n.* pasayharamana, *nt.*

Sturdy, *a.* daḷhasarīra; thāmavantu. °**ily,** *adv.* pabalākārena. °**iness,** *n.* thāmasampannatā, *f.*

Stutter, *v.i.* pakkhalanto bhāsati. °**er,** *n.* pakkhalitavāca, *m.* °**ingly,** *adv.* sagaggadaŋ.

Sty, *n.* 1. sūkaravaja, *m.* 2. kucchitaṭṭhāna, *nt.* *v.t.* sūkare vaje khipati.

Stye, *n.* akkhidalapiḷakā, *f.*

Style, *n.* 1. paṇṇalekhanī, *f.* 2. pakāra; ākāra; 3. racanāvilāsa, *m.* *v.t.* abhidhāti; nāmaŋ ṭhapeti; upalakkheti. *p.p.* abhihita; ṭhapitanāma; °khita. °**ish,** *a.* suvesa. °**ishly,** *adv.* sobhanavesena. °**ist,** *a.* lalitaracanāsatta.

Stylograph, *n.* nāḷaḷekhanīvisesa, *m.*

Styptic, *a.* *n.* rudhirasandananivattaka.

Styx, *n.* Vetaranī-nadī, *f.*

Suasion, *n.* palobhana; pakkhagāhana, *nt.* °**sive,** *a.* pakkhagāhāpaka.

Suave, *a.* 1. piyaŋvada; 2. sādurasa; manuñña. °**ly,** *adv.* manuññatāya; saṇhākārena. °**ity,** *n.* 1. piyavāditā; 2. sādurasatā, *f.*

Sub, *pref.* upa; anu; adho.

Subacid, *a.* īsaŋambila.

Subacrid, *a.* īsaŋtittaka.

Subacute, *a.* īsaŋtikhiṇa.

Subaltern, *n.* upasenāpati, *m.*

Subaqueous, *a.* antodakaṭṭha.

Subcommittee, *n.* anukārakasabhā, *f.*

Subcommentary, *n.* ṭīkā, *f.*

Subconsciousness, *n.* bhavaṅga; upaviññāṇa, *nt.*

Subcutaneous, *a.* antocammaṭṭha.

Subdivide, *v.t.* puna vibhajati; upavibhajati. *p.p.* °vibhatta. **°vision,** *n.* upavibhāga, *m.*

Subdue, *v.t.* abhibhavati; pamaddati; dameti; pasahati; abhimanthati. *p.p.* °bhūta; °dita; danta; °hita; °thita. **°able,** *a.* abhibhavanīya; jeyya. **°er,** *n.* abhibhū; pamaddaka; dametu, *m.* **°ing,** *a.* abhimanthaka.

Sub-editor, *n.* upasaṅkhāraka, *m.*

Sub-head, *n.* upamātikā, *f.*

Subjacent, *a.* adhoṭhita.

Subject, *n.* 1. visaya, *m.* 2. pajā; parapālanānugata, *m.* 3. (in gram.) kattu, *m.* 4. vasagamana, *nt.* 5. kathānāyaka, *m.* adj. vasavattī; upajīvī; parādhīna; parāyatta. *v.t.* vasīkaroti; abhibhoti. *p.p.* vasīkata; abhibhūta. **°ion,** *n.* vasībhāva, *m.* parādhīnatta, *nt.* **°ive,** *a.* ajjhattika; mānasika. **°ivity,** *n.* mānasikatta, *nt.*

Subjoin, *v.t.* anughaṭeti; pacchā sambandheti. *p.p.* °ṭita; °dhita.

Subjugate, *v.t.* vasaŋ neti; omaddati; abhibhavati. *p.p.* °nīta; °dita; °bhūta. **°ion,** *n.* vasānayana; abhibhavana, *nt.* **°tor,** *n.* vijetu; dametu; vasavattaka, *m.*

Subjunctive, *a.* aniyamatthavācaka; vikappadīpaka. — **mood,** *n.* Sattamī vibhatti, *f.*

Sub-king, *n.* padesarāja, *m.*

Sublime, *a.* sukhuma; visiṭṭha; ukkaṭṭha. **°ate,** *v.t.* sukhumattaŋ *or* parisuddhattaŋ pāpeti. *p.p.* °pāpita. **°ation,** *n.* sukhumattapāpaṇa; parisodhana, *nt.* **°ly,** *adv.* sukhumatāya; uḷāratāya. **°ity,** *n.* accuḷāratta; atisukhumatta, *nt.*

Subliminal, *a.* bhavaṅgagata; cittānusayita.

Submarine, *a.* antodakavattī. *n.* makarapota, *m.* antodakanāvā, *f.* — **fire,** *n.* vaḷavāmukha, *nt.*

Submerge, *v.t.* ajjhottharati; nimujjāpeti. *v.i.* nimujjati; otthariyati. *p.p.* ajjhotthaṭa; °pita; nimugga. **°nce, °mersion,** *n.* ajjhottharaṇa; nimujjāpana; nimujjana, *nt.*

Submission, *n.* anuvattana; vasaṅgamana, *nt.* **°sive,** *a.* anuvattī; vidheya; vacanakara; assava. **°sively,** *adv.* savinayaŋ; sagāravaŋ **°siveness,** *n.* vasībhāva, *m.* anuvattana; vacanakaratta, *nt.*

Submit, *v.i.* 1. vasaŋ yāti; anuvattati; 2. savinayaŋ vadati. *v.t.* appeti; bhāraŋ karoti. *p.p.* °yāta; °tita; °vutta; °appita; katabhāra.

Subordinate, *a.* amukhya; orapadaṭṭha; appadhāna. *v.t.* anuṭhapeti; vase vatteti; amukhyaŋ karoti. *p.p.* °pita; °tita; °kata. *n.* sahakārī; anuvattaka, *m.* **°ion,** *n.* vasaṅgamana; appadhānatta, *nt.* **°ly,** *adv.* amukhyavasena.

Suborn, *v.t.* kūṭasakkhiŋ otāreti. **°ation,** *n.* kūṭasakkhiotāraṇa, *nt.*

Subpoena, *n.* adhikaraṇavhāna, *nt.* *v.t.* adhikaraṇaŋ avhāti. *p.p.* °avhāta.

Subreption, *n.* nikatiyā gahaṇa, *nt.*

Subscribe, *v.t.* 1. hatthalañchanaŋ yojeti ; 2. niyamitabhāgaŋ deti.' *v.i.* anumaññati. *p.p.* yojitahat° ; dinnaniya° ; anumata. °**er,** *n.* chandakadāyī ; upatthambhaka ; bhāgadāyī, *m.* °**iption,** *n.* 1. nāmalikhana ; 2. chandakadāna ; 3. vassikadeyya, *nt.*

Subscript, *n.* adholipi, *f.*

Subsection, *n.* upavibhāga, *m.*

Subsequent, *a.* anantarāgata ; ānantarika. °**nce,** *n.* vipāka, *m.* anugataphala, *nt.* °**ly,** *adv.* anantaraŋ ; tato paraŋ.

Subserve, *v.t.* upatthambheti ; upakaroti. *p.p.* °bhita ; upakata. °**ient,** *a.* upakāraka ; anukūla. °**ience,** *n.* upatthambha, *m.* anukūlatta, *nt.* °**iently,** *adv.* upatthambhakavasena.

Subside, *v.i.* ogacchati ; sannisīdati. *p.p.* ogata ; sannisinna. °**nce,** *n.* ogamana ; heṭṭhā-osīdana, *nt.* °**iary,** *a. n.* upatthambhaka ; upakāraka. °**ize,** *v.t.* dhanena upatthambheti. *p.p.* °bhita.

Subsidy, *n.* upatthambhaka-dhana, *nt.*

Subsist, *v.i.t.* pavattati ; jīvati ; yāpeti ; jīvikaŋ kappeti. *p.p.* °tita ; kappitajīvita. — **by,** anujīvati ; °**ence,** *n.* jīvana ; pavattana, *nt.* ājīva, *m.* jīvitavutti, *f.* °**ent,** *a.* pavattamāna ; upajīvī. — **on,** upajīvati.

Subsoil, *n.* heṭṭhā-paŋsu, *m.*

Substance, *n.* 1. vatthu ; dabba, *nt.* 2. sāra ; piṇḍattha, *m.* 3. dhana ; vitta, *nt.*

Substantial, *a.* 1. dabbamaya ; 2. tathato-vijjamāna ; 3. sāravantu ; 4. dhanavantu. °**ity,** °**ness,** *n.* dabbatta ; tathatovijjamānatta, *nt.* °**ly,** *adv.* vatthuto ; tattato ; sārato. °**tiate,** *v.t.* tathaŋ *or* paccakkhaŋ kāreti. °**tiation,** *n.* pamāṇīkaraṇa ; tathattadīpana, *nt.*

Substantive, *n.* nāmapada ; visessa, *nt.* adj. sattāvācaka.

Substitute, *n.* niyojita ; paṭinidhi, *m.* *v.t.* aññass'atthāya niyojeti ; (in gram :) ādesaŋ karoti. *p.p.* °jita ; katādesa. °**ion,** *n.* paṭinidahana ; niyojana, *nt.* °**ional,** *a.* paṭinidahanāyatta. °**ive,** *a.* paṭinidheyya.

Substratum, *n.* heṭṭhātala, *nt.* 2. upanissaya, *m.*

Substructure, *n.* vatthucinana, *nt.*

Subsume, *v.t.* antogadhaŋ karoti. *p.p.* °kata. °**sumption,** *n.* antogadhakaraṇa, *nt.*

Subterfuge, *n.* 1. muñcanūpāya, *m.* 2. sāṭheyya, *nt.*

Subterranean, *a.* antobhumma ; bhūmigata.

Subtle, *a.* 1. atisukhuma ; dubbodha ; duggāhiya ; 2. upāyakusala ; kerāṭika ; 3. (of intellect :) kusaggamatika : tikkhapañña. °**ty,** °**ness,** *n.* 1. sukhumatta ; dubbodhatta ; 2. upāyakosalla, *nt.* °**ly,** *adv.* sukhumaŋ ; dubbodhatāya ; nikatiyā.

Subtract, *v.t.* bhāgam uddharati ; ūnaŋ karoti. *p.p.* uddhaṭabhāga ; ūnīkata. °**ion,** *n.* vyavakalana ; bhāguddharaṇa, *nt.* °**ive,** *a.* vyavakalanaka.

Suburb, *n.* upanagara, *nt.* °**an,** *a.* nagarāsanna.

Subvention, see **Subsidy.**

Subvert, *v.t.* viparivatteti ; ummūleti ; vināseti. *p.p.* °tita ; °lita ; °sita. °**version,** *n.* viparivattana, *nt.* °**versive,** *a.* viparivattaka ; ucchindaka.

Subway, *n.* ummagga, *m.*

Succeed, *v.i.* samijjhati ; sampajjati. *v.t.* paṭilabhati ; anupāpuṇāti. *p.p.* samiddha ; sampanna ; paṭiladdha ; anuppatta. °**ing,** *a.* anuyāyī ; āgāmī ; anantarāgāmī.

Success, *n.* samiddhi ; nipphatti ; saŋsiddhi, *f.* sāphalya, *nt.* °**ful,** *a.* samiddha ; saphala. °**fully,** *adv.* samiddhākārena.

Succession, *n.* 1. anukkama, *m.* paṭipāṭi, *f.* 2. paramparā ; santati ; 3. āvali, *f.* °**al,** *a.* anukkamāgata ; yathāpaṭipāṭika. °**sive,** *a.* anukkamika ; pāramparika. °**sively,** *adv.* anukkamena ; anupubbena.

Successor, *n.* anantarāgata ; anukkamappatta, *m.*

Succinct, *a.* saṅkhitta ; laghu. °**ly,** *adv.* saṅkhepena. °**ness,** *n.* saṅkhittatta, *nt.*

Succour, *n.* avassopatthambha, *m.* paṭisaraṇa ; paṭibala, *nt.* *v.t.* yathākāle upatthambeti. *p.p.* °bhita. °**er,** *n.* avassakāle upatthambhaka, *m.* °**less,** *a.* appatiṭṭha ; appaṭisaraṇa.

Succulent, *a.* sarasa ; ojavantu. °**nce,** *n.* ojavantatā, *f.*

Succumb, *v.i.* avasīdati ; vasaŋ yāti. *p.p.* osīna ; vasaŋyāta.

Such, *a.* tathāvidha ; tathārūpa ; tādisa ; etādisa.—**like,** *a.* evaŋvidha. —**likeness,** tathābhāva, *m.* — **and such,** asuka, *a.*

Suck, *v.t.* cūsati ; thaññaŋ viya pibati. °**er,** *n.* cūsaka, *m.* °**ing,** *a.* thanapāyī.

Suckle, *v.t.* pāyeti. *p.p.* pāyita. °**ing,** *n.* thanapa ; khīrapaka, *m.*

Sudation, *n.* sedakamma, *nt.* °**tory,** *a.* sedajanaka.

Sudatorium, *n.* sedanaghara ; jantāghara, *nt.*

Sudden, *a.* sahasāpatta ; taṅkhaṇika. °**ly,** *adv.* sahasā ; taṅkhaṇaŋ. °**ness,** *n.* khaṇikatta ; sahasāgatatta, *nt.*

Sudoriferous, *a.* sedavāhī.

Sudorific, *a.* sedamocaka.

Suds, *n. pl.* pheṇapiṇḍa, *m.*

Sue, *v.t.i.* adhikaraṇe codeti ; aṭṭaŋ karoti ; vinicchayaŋ yāti. *p.p.* °dita ; kataṭṭa ; °yāta.

Suet, *n.* pasumeda, *m.*

Suffer, *v.i.t.* 1. vindati ; vedeti ; paccanubhoti ; 2. adhivāseti ; titikkhati. *p.p.* °dita ; °bhūta ; °sita ; °khita. °**able,** *a.* vedanīya ; sahanīya. °**ance,** *n.* anumati ; khamā, *f.* paramata-sahana, *nt.* °**er,** *n.* vedaka, *m.* °**ing,** *n.* vedanā ; pīḷā ; vyathā, *f.* dukkha. *nt.* °**ingly,** *adv.* savedanaŋ. °**ing from illness,** rogātura, *a.*

Suffice, *v.i.t.* pahoti.

Sufficient, *a.* pahoṇaka ; alambhūta ; °**ncy,** *n.* pahoṇakatta ; sāmatthiya, *nt.* alambhāva. °**ly,** *adv.* pariyattaŋ ; paripuṇṇaŋ ; pahoṇakatāya.

Suffix, *n.* paccaya. *v.t.* padante ghaṭeti. *p.p.* °ṭita.

Suffocate, *v.t.* 1. sāsaŋ rodheti; 2. sāsaŋ nirumbhitvā māreti. *p.p.* rodhitasāsa; °mārita. °**ion**, sāsarodhana, *nt.*

Suffrage, *n.* anumatidāna; chandabala, *nt.*

Suffuse, *v.t.* vyāpeti; vitthambheti; pattharati; pharati. *p.p.* °pita; °bhita; patthaṭa; phuṭa, °**ion**, *n.* pattharaṇa; vyāpana, *nt.*

Sugar, *n.* sukkharā, *f.* *v.t.* sakkharā yojeti. *p.p.* yojitasakkhara. °**candy**, *n.* khaṇḍasakkharā, *f.* °**cane**, *n.* ucchu, *m.* °**mill**, *u.* ucchuyanta, *nt.* °**y**, *a.* sakkharāyutta.

Suggest, *v.t.* samupaṭṭhapeti; sūceti. *p.p.* °pita; sūcita. °**ion**, *n.* parikappanā; matayojanā, *f.* °**ive**, *a.* sūcaka; vyañjaka. °**iveness**, *n.* sūcakatta; vyañjakatta, *nt.*

Suicide, *n.* 1. attavadha; 2. attaghātī, *m.* °**al**, *a.* attanāsaka; attaghātaka.

Suilline, *a.* ṣūkaragaṇika.

Suit, *n.* 1. nivāsanayugala; 2. yuga; yamaka, *nt.* 2. vivāhayojanā, *f.* 3. codanā, *f.* abhiyoga, *m.* *v.i.* kappati; vaṭṭati; yujjati. *v.t.* yoggaŋ karoti; saṅghaṭeti. *p.p.* kappita; yutta; yoggakata; °ṭita. °**able**, *a.* yogga; anurūpa; anucchavika; sāruppa. °**ableness**, *n.* ocitya; yoggatta; sāruppatta, *nt.* °**ably**, *adv.* yathocitaŋ. °**or**, *n.* 1. abhiyuñjaka; 2. vivāhatthī, *m.*

Suite, *n.* 1. parijana; parivāra, *m.* 2. paribhogabhaṇḍarāsi, *m.* 3. ovarakapanti; 4. turiyasāmaggi, *f.*

Sulk, *v.i.* dummukhī hoti. °**iness**, *n.* asantuṭṭhi, *f.* °**y**, *a.* dummana.

Sullen, *a.* khinna; anattamana. °**ly**, *adv.* khinnākārena. °**ness**, *n.* dummukhatta; dummanatta, *nt.*

Sully, *v.t.* kalaṅketi; dūseti. *p.p.* °kita; dūsita.

Sulphur, *n.* gandhaka, *nt.* °**ous**, *a.* gandhakayutta.

Sultry, *a.* gimhādhika; tāpakara. °**iness**, *n.* gimhādhikatta, *nt.*

Sum, *n.* 1. gaṇanā, *f.* saṅkalana, *nt.* 2. samāhāra; 3. piṇḍattha, *m.* 4. sākalla, *nt.* *v.t.* 1. gaṇeti; saṅkaleti; 2. saṅkhipati; samāharati. *p.p.* gaṇita; °lita; saṅkhitta; samāhaṭa. °**mation**, *n.* saṅkalana, *nt.*

Summary, *n.* uddesa; saṅkhittasaṅgaha; saṅkhepa, *m.* °**ily**, *adv.* saṅkhepavasena. °**ize**, *v.t.* saṅkhipati; sāraŋsam uddharati. *p.p.* khitta; uddhaṭasāraŋsa.

Summer, *n.* gimhāna; nidāghasamaya, *m.* *v.i.* gimhānaŋ vītināmeti. °**y**, *a.* gimhika. °**less**, *a.* gimhānarahita.

Summersault, see **Somersault**.

Summit, *n.* kūṭa; sikhara; siṅga, *nt.* matthaka; muddhā, *m.*

Summon, *v.t.* adhikaraṇam avheti; pakkosati; āṇāpeti. *p.p.* avhita; °sita; °pita. *n. pl.* adhikaraṇavhāna; āṇāpana, *nt.*

Summum bonum, *n.* accantasukha; nibbāṇa, *nt.*

Sumpter, *n.* bhāravāhī-assa, *m.*

Sumption, *n.* udāharaṇa, *nt.*

Sumptuary, *a.* paribbayaniyāmaka.

Sumptuous, *a.* bahuparibbaya; tittikara. °**ly,** *adv.* adhikavayena; paṇītākārena.

Sun, *n.* suriya; ādicca; dinakara; ravi; bhānumantu; divākara; sataraŋsi; aŋsumālī; bhānu, *m.* *v.t.* ātape nidahati; *v.i.* ātapaŋ tapati; ātape nisīdati. *p.p.* °nihita; tapitātapa; °nisinna. °**beam,** *n.* ravikiraṇa, *m.* °**burnt,** *a.* ātapatatta. °**day,** *n.* ravivāra, *m.* °**dial,** *n.* suriyaghaṭī, *f.* °**flower,** suriyāvattīpuppha. °**less,** *a.* nirātapa. —**like,** *a.* suriyopama. °**light,** °**shine,** suriyātapa, *m.* °**rise,** *n.* suriyodaya, *m.* °**set,** *n.* suriyatthaṅgamana, *nt.* °**shade,** *n.* chatta; ātapatta, *nt.* °**ny,** *a.* ātapasahita.

Sunder, see **Separate.**

Sundry, *a.* bahuvidha; nānākāra; vividha.

Sup, *v.i.* sāyamāsaŋ bhuñjati. *p.p.* bhuttasā°; °**per,** *n.* rattibhojana, *nt.*

Super, *pref.* ati; adhi; adhika; atisaya. °**able,** *a.* abhibhavanīya; sukhasādhiya. °**abundance,** atibahulatta, *nt.* °**abundant,** *a.* accādhika. °**annuated,** *a.* vayovuddha. °**human,** *a.* manussattātīta; amānusika. °**mundane,** *a.* lokuttara. °**natural,** *a.* alokika; atimānusa. °**structure,** *n.* uparimandira, *nt.*

Superadd, *v.t.* adhikaŋ sambandheti. *p.p.* °dhita. °**ition,** *n.* adhikataraghaṭana, *nt.*

Superb, *a.* atisobhana; atirucira. °**ly,** *adv.* atiruciratāya. °**ness,** *n.* atisobhanatta, *nt.*

Supercargo, *n.* nāvābhaṇḍādhikārī, *m.*

Superciliary, *a.* bhamukopariṭhita.

Supercilious, *a.* atidappita; abhimānī. °**ly,** *adv.* uddhatākārena.

Super-eminence, *n.* atyuttamatta; atiseṭṭhatta, *nt.* °**nent,** *a.* atiseṭṭha; atiuttama.

Super-erogation, *n.* atirekakiccakaraṇa, *nt.* °**tory,** *a.* atirekakiccadāyī.

Super-essential, *a.* accāvassaka.

Superexcellence, *n.* ativisiṭṭhatta, *nt.* °**lent,** *a.* ativisiṭṭha; atiseṭṭha.

Superficial, *a.* 1. uttāna; agambhīra; 2. appamattaka; 3. anipuṇa; 4. bāhira. °**ly,** *adv.* bāhiravasena; agambhīratāya. °**ity,** *n.* uttānatta; appamattakatta, *nt.*

Superfine, *a.* 1. atisukhuma; 2. atisundara; suparisuddha.

Superfluous, *a.* atiritta; accadhika; niratthaka. °**ness,** *n.* adhikatta; niratthakatta, *nt.*

Superimpose, *v.t.* matthake āropeti. *p.p.* °pita.

Superintend, *v.t.* kammantaŋ vicāreti *or* saŋvidahati. *p.p.* vicāritaka°; saŋvihitaka°. °**ence,** *n.* kammantavicāraṇā, *f.* °**ent,** *n.* kammantanāyaka; ajjhakkhaka; avekkhaka, *m.*

Superior, *n.* 1. seṭṭhādhikārī; 2. ārāmādhipati, *m.* adj. uccatarapadaṭṭha; parama; uttama. °**ity,** *n.* seṭṭhataratta; ukkaṭṭhatta, *nt.*

Superlative, *a.* *n.* seṭṭhatama; sabbuttama. °**ly,** *adv.* accantaŋ; atisayena.

Supernal, *a.* devāyatta.

Supernatant, *a.* upari plavamāna.

Superposition, *n.* uparițhapana, *nt.* uparițțhiti, *f.*

Superscribe, *v.t.* upari likhati; silādisu likhati. *p.p.* °khita. °**scription,** *n.* uparilipi, *f.* tale likhita, *nt.*

Supersede, *v.t.* ekam apanetvā aññaŋ niyojeti. °**session,** *n.* aññassa țhāne niyojana, *nt.*

Superstition, *n.* micchāmati, *f.* ayathāsaddahana, *nt.* °**tious,** *a.* micchāmatika. °**tiously,** *adv.* micchāmatānugamanena.

Supervene, *v.i.* anusijjhati; antaraŋ pāpuņāti. *p.p.* anusiddha; antarappatta.

Supervise, *v.t.* paripāleti. *p.p.* °lita, °**ion,** *n.* paripālana; pațiavekkhana, *nt.* °**sor,** *n.* paripāletu, *m.*

Supine, *a.* 1. uttānasaya; 2. nirussāha. *n.* (in gram:) tumantapada, *nt.* °**ly,** *adv.* uttānamukhatāya; ālassena. °**ness,** *n.* 1. uttānamukhatta; 2. nirīhakatta, *nt.*

Supplant, *v.t.* upāyena apaneti; aññassa adhikāraŋ (upāyena) gaņhāti. *p.p.* °nīta; °gahitādhikāra.

Supple, *a.* sunamya; komala.

Supplement, *v.t.* ūnaŋ pūreti; atirekaŋ yojeti. *p.p.* ūnapūrita; yojitātireka. *n.* ūnapūraņa, *nt.* upagantha; parisițțhasangaha, *m.* °**ary,** *a.* ūnapūraka.

Suppliant, *n.* āyācaka; patthetu, *m.* adj. āyācamāna. °**ance,** *n.* abhiyācanā, *f.* °**ly,** *adv.* sagāravaŋ; āyācanapubbakaŋ.

Supplicant, *n.* abhiyācaka, *m.*

Supplicate, *v.t.* sagāravaŋ yācati. *p.p.* °cita. °**ion,** *n.* sagāravāyācanā, *f.* °**tory,** *a.* savinaya; sagārava.

Supply, *v.t.* sampādeti; upațțhapeti. *p.p.* °dita; °pita. *n.* 1. sampādana; 2. sampādita-bhaņḍa, *nt.* °**ing,** *a.* sampādaka.

Support, *n.* upatthambha; nissaya; avassaya; paggaha; ādhāra, *m.* patițțhā, *f.* *v.t.* 1. upatthambheti; sandhāreti; 2. (life:) bharati; poseti; 3. sahati; dhāreti; 4. anumaññati. *p.p.* °bhita; °rita; bhata; posita; sahita; °rita; anumata. °**able,** *a.* upatthambhiya; pațipādanīya. °**er,** *n.* upatthambhaka, *m.* °**less,** *a.* nirādhāra.

Suppose, *v.i.t.* parikappeti; anumāneti. *p.p.* °pita; °nita. °**ition,** *n.* parikappanā, *f.* anumāna, *m.* °**sititious,** *a.* anumānamattaka; parikappamattaka. °**itive,** *a.* anumānavācaka.

Suppress, *v.t.* abhibhoti; nimmathati; nirumbheti. *p.p.* abhibhūta; °thita; °bhita. °**ion,** *n.* niggaha, *m.* nimmathana; nirumbhana, *nt.* °**ive,** *a.* niggaņhaka; nirumbhaka. °**or,** *n.* niggahetu; vikkhambhetu; pațibāhetu, *m.*

Suppurate, *v.i.* pūyaŋ janeti. *p.p.* janitapūya. °**ion,** *n.* pūyajanana, *nt.* °**ive,** *a.* pūyajanaka.

Supreme, *a.* anuttara; sețțhatama; accukkațțha. °**macy,** *n.* atisețțhatā; pāmokkhatā, *f.* ādhipacca, *nt.* °**court,** *n.* sețțhādhikaraņa, *nt.* °**ly,** *adv.* sețțhākārena; visițțhatāya.

Surcease, *n.* nivattana, *nt.* appavatti, *f.* osāna, *nt.* *v.i.* nivattati ; viramati.

Surcharge, *n.* atirekamūlaniyamana, *nt.* *v.t.* 1. accantaŋ pūreti ; 2. atirekamūlaŋ niyameti. *p.p.* °rita ; niyamitātirekamūla.

Surcoat, *n.* sannāhoparikañcuka, *m.*

Surd, *n.* aghosakkhara, *nt.*

Sure, *a.* niyata ; ekanta ; ekaŋsika ; nicchita ; asandiddha ; nissaŋsaya. *adv.* nissaŋsayaŋ. °**ly,** *adv.* addhā ; dhuvaŋ ; nūnaŋ ; ve ; have ; kāmaŋ ; jātu ; ekantaŋ. °**ness,** *n.* nissaŋsayatta ; nicchitatta, *nt.*

Surety, *n.* 1. pāṭibhoga ; 2. pāṭibhogī, *m.* °**ship,** *n.* pāṭibhogitā, *f.*

Surf, *n.* velāvici, *f.* taraṅga, *m.*

Surface, *n.* tala ; piṭṭha, *nt.* matthaka, *m.*

Surfeit, *n.* atimattabhojana ; suhitatta, *nt.* *v.t.* atipūreti. *v.i.* atibhuñjati. *p.p.* °rita ; atibhutta.

Surge, *n.* ullola; kallola, *m.* mahāvīci, *f.* *v.i.* saṅkhubhati ; vīci viya uṭṭhāti. *p.p.* °bhita ; °ṭhita.

Surgeon, *n.* sallakatta ; sallavejja, *m.* °**gery,** *n.* 1. sallakattiya, *nt.* 2. sallakattasālā, *f.*

Surgical, *a.* sallakammāyatta. — **instrument,** *n.* sallāyudha, *nt.*—**operation,** *n.* sallakamma, *nt.*

Surly, *a.* pharusa; kakkhala. °**ily,** *adv.* pharusākārena. °**iness,** *n.* pharusatta, *nt.*

Surmise, *n.* anumāna, *m.* parikappana, *nt.* *v.i.* anumeti ; parikappeti. *p.p.* anumita ; °pita. °**er,** *n.* takkika ; anumetu, *m.*

Surmount, *v.t.* 1. atikkamitvā yāti ; 2. sikharam āruhati ; 3. bādhakam abhimaddati. *p.p.* °yāta ; °ārūḷha ; °ditabādhaka.

Surname, *n.* gottanāma ; kulanāma, *nt.* *v.t.* kulanāmaŋ yojeti.

Surpass, *v.t.* atikkamati; atiseti ; visiṭṭhataŋ yāti. *p.p.* atikkanta; atisita ; °yāta. °**ing,** *a.* visiṭṭhatara. °**ingly,** *adv.* visiṭṭhākārena.

Surplice, *n.* uttarakañcuka, *m.*

Surplus, *n.* atireka ; atirittabhāga, *m.*

Surprise, *n.* vimhaya, *m.* 2. sahasāpakkhandana, *nt.* *v.t.* 1. vimhayāpeti ; sahasā pāpuṇāti. *p.p.* °pita ; °patta. °**ing,** *a.* acchariyāvaha ; vimhayajanaka. °**ingly,** *adv.* vimhayajanakākārena. °**ed,** *a.* vimhita.

Surrender, *n.* 1. paravasagamana ; 2. samappaṇa, *nt.* *v.i.* paravasaŋ yāti ; attādhīnattaŋ cajati. *p.p.* °yāta ; catta°.

Surreptitious, *a.* gūḷha; paṭicchanna ; rahokata. °**ly,** *adv.* gūḷhākārena ; raho.

Surround, *v.t.* parikkhipati ; parivāreti. *p.p.* °khitta ; °rita. °**ing,** *a.* samantāṭhita. °**ings,** *n.* *pl.* parivāra ; parisara, *m.*

Surtax, *n.* átireka-kara, *m.*

Surveillance, *n.* upaparikkhaṇa, *nt.*

Survey, *n.* avekkhaṇa ; parikkhaṇa; parimiṇana, *nt.* saṅkhittappavatti, *f.* *v.t.* 1. avekkhati ;

nirikkhati; anuviloketi; 2. pariminâti; 3. anuvicāreti. *p.p.* °khita; °kita; °mita; °rita. °**or**, *n.* bhūmimāṇaka; rajjugāhaka, *m.*

Survive, *v.t.i.* 1. aticca jīvati; 2. puna jīvati. °**val,** *n.* atikkamma-jīvana; puna-jīvana, *nt.* °**or,** *n.* aticca-jīvī; puna-jīvī; matāvasiṭṭha-puggala, *m.*

Susceptible, *a.* muducitta; onamanasīla. °**bility,** *n.* sunamyatta, *nt.* mudusabhāva, *m.*

Suspect, *a.* saṅkitabba. *n.* saṅkitapuggala, *m. v.t.* āsaṅkati; parisaṅkati; kaṅkhati. *p.p.* °kita; °khita.

Suspend, *v.t.* 1. olambeti; 2. (from office:) adhikārā nirumbheti. *v.i.* olambati; olaggati. *p.p.* °bita; °bhita; olagga. °**nsion,** *n.* 1. olambana; 2. adhikāranirumbhana, *nt.*

Suspense, *n.* 1. avinicchaya; sandeha, *m.* 2. adhikāranirumbhana, *nt.*

Suspensory, *a.* olambamāna.

Suspicion, *n.* āsaṅkā; kaṅkhā; vimati, *f.* sandeha, *m.* °**cious,** *a.* 1. saṅkanīya; sāsaṅka; 2. saṅkākula; āsaṅkita.

Suspire, *v.i.* nissasati.

Sustain, *v.t.* 1. bharati; poseti; 2. pariharati; pavatteti; paṭipādeti; 3. sahati; vindati; dhāreti. *p.p.* bhata; posita; parihaṭa; °tita; °dita; sahita; °dita; dhārita. °**able,** *a.* bharitabba; vindanīya; dhāretabba. °**er,** *n.* dhārī; vinditu; bharitu, *m.* °**ment,** *n.* upatthambhana, *nt.*

Sustenance, *n.* 1. yāpana; jīvana, *nt.* jīvikā, *f.* 2. anna, *nt.* āhāra; jīvanādhāra, *m.*

Sustentation, *n.* jīvanavetana, *nt.*

Susurrus, *n.* nitthunana, *nt.* dubbalasadda, *m.* °**rant,** *a.* nitthunanta.

Suture, *n.* 1. sibbana; sambandhana, *nt.* 2. sibbanīmagga, *m.* 3. sīsasibbanī, *f.*

Suzerain, *n.* adhīsa, *m.*

Swab, *n.* pariyādāyakapuñchanī, *f. v.t.* (tāya) puñchati. *p.p.* °chita.

Swaddle, *v.t.* vatthehi paḷiveṭheti *or* oguṇṭheti. *p.p.* °ṭhita.

Swag, *v.i.* olambati. *p.p.* °bita. °**bellied,** *a.* lambodara, °**gy,** *a.* lambamāna.

Swagger, *v.i.* gabbitākārena carati; vikatthati. *p.p.* °carita; °thita.

Swain, *n.* 1. taruṇa-jānapadika; 2. vivāhatthī, *m.*

Swallow, *n.* 1. jalasakuṇa, *m.* 2. ajjhoharaṇa, *nt.* 3. galanāḷa, *m.* 4. āhārakabala, *nt. v.t.i.* gilati; ajjhoharati. *p.p.* gilita; ajjhohaṭa.

Swamp, *n.* anupa; palipa, *m. v.t.* osīdāpeti; nimuggāpeti. *p.p.* °pita. °**y,** *a.* palipayutta.

Swan, *n.* haŋsa, *m.* °**like,** *a.* haŋsasadisa. °**nery,** *n.* haŋsaposanaṭṭhāna, *nt.*

Sward, *n.* saddalabhūmi, *f.*

Swarm, *n.* ghaṭā, *f.* gumba; saṅkulasamūha, *m. v.i.* 1. gumbavasena sannipatati; 2. vāyamanto āruhati. *p.p.* °tita; °ārūḷha.

Swart, Swarthy, *a.* kāḷavaṇṇa.

Swash, *n.* udakakkhepasadda, *m.* *v.t.* vegena udakaŋ khipati.

Swathe, *n.* dussapaṭṭikā, *f.* *v.t.* paṭṭikāhi paḷiveṭheti. *p.p.* °ṭhita.

Sway, *n.* 1. pabhutta; ādhipacca; 2. dolāyana, *nt.* *v.i.* 1. dolāyati; 2. agatiŋ yāti. *v.t.* āṇaŋ pavatteti. *p.p.* °yita; °yāta; °titāṇa. — **backed,** *a.* onatapiṭṭhika.

Swear, *v.i.* sapati; sapathaŋ karoti. *v.t.* sapathaŋ kāreti. *p.p.* sapita; katasapatha; kāritasapatha. °**er,** *n.* sapathakārī, *m.* °**ing,** *n.* sapana, *nt.* sapatha, *m.*

Sweat, *n.* seda, *m.* *v.t.* sedaŋ moceti. *v.i.* sedo muccati. *p.p.* mocitaseda; muttaseda. °**er,** *n.* antarakañcuka, *m.* °**y,** *a.* sedatinta. °**iness,** *n.* sedakilinnatta, *nt.*

Sweep, *n.* 1. sammajjana, *nt.* 2. visayaṭṭhāna, *nt.* 3. sīghagamana, *nt.* 4. dhūmanettasodhaka, *m.* *v.t.* 1. sammajjati; 2. javenadhāvati. *p.p.* sammaṭṭha; °vita. °**er,** *n.* sammajjaka, *m.* °**ing,** *n.* sammajjana, *nt.* °**ings,** *n.* kacavara, *m.* saṅkārajāta, *nt.*

Sweet, *n.* madhurāhāra, *m.* khajjaka, *nt.* adj. 1. madhura; paṇīta; 2. cāru; manuñña. °**en,** *v.t.* madhurīkaroti. °**heart,** *n.* vallabha; piya; vivāhāpekkha, *m.* *f.* °**ly,** *adv.* madhurākārena. °**meat,** *n.* madhurakhajjaka, *nt.* °**ness,** *n.* madhuratta, *nt.* °**potato,** *n.* badālatā, *f.* °**scented,** *a.* sugandhī. °**voiced,** *a.* mañjubhāṇaka; madhurassara. °**tempered,** *a.* somma; pasannākāra.

Swell, *v.i.* uddhumāyati. *v.t.* vitthambheti. *p.p.* °yita; °bhita. °**ing,** *n.* uddhumāyana, *nt.* sopha *m.* 2. gaṇḍa, *m.*

Swelter, *n.* ghammādhikatta, *nt.* *v.i.* ghammena pīḷīyati *or* kilamati. *p.p.* °ḷita; °kilanta. °**try,** *a.* ghammābhitatta.

Swerve, *n.* uppathagamana; maggāpagamana, *nt.* *v.i.* supathā apayāti; ummagge yāti. *p.p.* °yāta. °**less,** *a.* apagamanarahita.

Swift, *a.* sīgha; turita; avilambita. °**ly,** *adv.* sīghaŋ; turitaŋ; āsu. °**ness,** *n.* sīghatta; turitatta, *nt.* java; vega, *m.*

Swill, *n.* 1. pakkhālana, 2. sagedha-pivana, *nt.* *v.t.i.* 1. pakkhāleti; 2. gedhena pivati. *p.p.* °lita; °pīta. °**er,** *n.* atimattapāyī, *m.*

Swim, *n.* udakaplavana; taraṇa, *nt.* *v.i.* udake plavati. *v.t.* udakaŋ tarati. *p.p.* °vita; tiṇṇodaka. °**mer,** *n.* plavaka; taritu, *m.* °**ming,** *n.* plavana; taraṇa, *nt.* °**mingly,** *adv.* anāyāsena; sukhena.

Swindle, *n.* vañcanā; palambhanā, *f.* *v.t.i.* see Cheat.

Swine, *n.* *pt.* 1. sūkaragaṇa; 2. nīcajana, *m.* °**herd,** *n.* sūkarapāla, *m.* °**ish,** *a.* sūkaropama.

Swing, *n.* 1. dolāyana, 2. dolāyitavatthu, *nt.* *v.i.* dolāyati; āviñjati. *v.t.* cāleti; pājeti; bhamāpeti. *p.p.* °yita; °jita; cālita; pājita; °pita. °**ing,** *a.* dolāyamāna. °**ing round,** āviñjanaka, *a.*

Swinge, *v.t.* daḷhaŋ potheti. *p.p.* °thita.

Swingle, *n.* sāṇadhovakadaṇḍa, *m. v.t.* sāṇaŋ sodheti. *p.p.* sodhitasāṇa.

Swipe, *v.t.* bāḷhaŋ paharati. *p.p.* °pahaṭa. °**er,** *n.* gāḷhappahāradāyī, *m.*

Swirl, *n.* salilāvaṭṭa, *m. v.i.* paribbhamati. *v.t.* bhame uppādeti. *p.p.* °bhanta ; °ditabhama.

Swish, *v.t.* vettādīni nabhe cāletvā saddam uppādeti.

Switch, *n.* 1. chinnapasākhā, *f.* 2. kittimakesapuñja, *m.* 3. vijjuppavāhaniyāmaka, *nt.* vijjubalakuncikā, *f. v.t.* 1. sākhāya tāḷeti; 2. vijjubalaŋ payojeti; 3. dhūmarathaŋ yathāmaggaŋ pāpeti. *p.p.* °ḷita ; °jitavijju° ; °pāpita. °**board,** *n.* vijjukuñcikāphalaka, *m. nt.*

Swollen, *a.* 1. uddhumāta ; sūna ; 2. saṅkhubhita.

Swoon, *n.* mucchā ; visaññitā, *f. v.i.* mucchati ; visaññīhoti. *p.p.* °chita ; °bhūta.

Swoop, *n.* opatana ; pakkhandana; ajjhottharaṇa, *nt. v.i.t.* sahasā ajjhottharati *or* pakkhandati. *p.p.* °thaṭa ; pakkhanta.

Swop, *n.* bhaṇḍavinimaya, *m. v.t.* bhaṇḍaŋ vinimeti. *p.p.* °mitabhaṇḍa.

Sword, *n.* khagga ; nettiŋsa, *m.* °**bearer,** °**sman,** *n.* khaggaddhara ; asiggāhaka, *m.* °**fish,** *n.* makaravisesa, *m.* — **and shield,** asi-camma, *nt.* **Blade of a —,** khaggatala ; asipatta, *nt.*

Sworn, *a.* abhisatta. °**foe,** *n.* balavaverī, *m.*

Swot, *n.* balavuggahaṇa, *nt. v.i.* atandito uggaṇhāti.

Sybarite, *n.* kāmabhogī, *m.*

Sycophant, *n.* çāṭukamya ; parūpajīvī, *m.*

Syllable, *n.* uccāriyakkhara ; vyañjanapada, *nt.*

Syllabus, *n.* niddesapaṇṇa, *nt.*

Syllogism, *n.* tidhābhūta-takka, *m.* °**gize,** *v.t.* takkaŋ dasseti.

Sylph, *n.* bhūtadevatā, *f.*

Sylvan, *a.* āraññaka.

Symbol, *n.* ciṇha ; visesalakkhaṇa, *nt.* °**ic,** °**ical,** *a.* ciṇhāyatta ; visesaviññāpaka. °**ism,** *n.* lakkhaṇapaddhati, *f.* lakkhaṇehi viññāpana, *nt.* °**ise,** °**ize,** *v.t.* lakkhaṇehi viññāpeti *or* nirūpeti. *v.i.* nidassanavasena pavattati. *p.p.* °pita ; °pavatta.

Symmetry, *n.* saṅgatāvayavatā ; anukūlatā; nigrodhaparimaṇḍalatā, *f.* °**ical,** *a.* yathāpamāṇayutta ; saṅgatāvayava. °**ically,** *adv.* saṅgatabhāvena. °**ize,** *v.t.* ubhayasamattaŋ pāpeti ; saṅgataŋ karoti. *p.p.* °pita ; °kata.

Sympathetic, *a.* anukampaka ; anumodaka.

Sympathy, *n.* anukampā ; samasukhadukkhatā, *f.* °**ize,** *v.i.* anukampati ; samanuñño hoti.

Symphony, *n.* samānassaratā, *f.* °**ic,** *a.* samasarayutta.

Symposium, *n.* 1. nānāmatasaṅgaha ; 2. madhupānussava, *m.* 3. dassanikasambhāsana, *nt.*

Symptom, *n.* pubbanimitta ; rogalakkhaṇa, *nt.* °**atic,** *a.* sūcaka; ñāpaka ; nimittabhūta. °**atology,** *n.* rogalakkhaṇa-vibhāga, *m.*

Synagogue, *n.* Yādava-devāyatana, *nt.*

Synchronize, *v.i.* samakāle vattati. *v.t.*samakālikaŋ karoti.*p.p.* °tita ; °kata. °**ism,** *n.* samakālikatta, *nt.* °**nous,** *a.* samakālika ; apubbācarima.

Syncopate, *v.t.* majjhavaṇṇaŋ lopeti. *p.p.* luttamaj°. °**ion,** *n.* majjhavaṇṇalopana, *nt.*

Syndicate, *n.* adhikārīmaṇḍala, *nt.* pālakasabhā, *f.*

Synod, *n.* dhammācariyasabhā.

Synonym, *n.* pariyāyavacana ; vevacana, *nt.* abhinnattha-sadda, *m.* °**ous,** *a.* tulyatthaka. °**ously,** *adv.* samānatthakavasena. °**ic,** pariyāyasaddappayojaka.

Synopsis, *n.* sārasaṅgaha, *m.* °**ptic,** *a.* sārasaṅgāhaka.

Synovial fluid, *n.* lasikā, *f.*

Syntactic, *a.* vākyaracanāpaṭibaddha.

Syntax, *n.* kārakayoga ; vākyaracanāvidhi, *m.*

Synthesis, *n.* saŋyoga, *m.* saŋhitā ; sandhi, *f.* °**thetic,** *a.* saŋyogāyatta ; saŋyutta.

Syphilis, *n.* upadaŋsaroga, *m.* °**lous,** *a.* upadaŋsātura.

Syringe, *n.* vatthi, *f.* siṅgaka, *nt.* *v.t.* vatthiŋ yojeti ; vatthiyā sodheti. *p.p.* vatthiyojita ; vatthisodhita.

Syrup, *n.* pānaka, *nt.*

Systaltic, *a.* phandamānaka ; saṅkoca-vitthambhanayutta.

System, *n.* paṭipāṭi, *f.* yojitakkama, *m.* 2. rīti ; paddhati ; 3. kappanā, *f.* °**atic,** *a.* kamānugata. °**atically,** *adv.* yathākkamaŋ ; yathānurūpaŋ. °**atize,** *v.t.* vavatthapeti ; niyameti. *p.p.* °pita ; °mita. °**atism,** *n.* vavatthāpana, *nt.*

Systemic, sakaladehāyatta.

Systole, *n.* hadayasaṅkocana, *nt.*

Syzygy, *n.* gahasaŋyoga, *m.* gahayuddha, *nt.*

T

Tabard, *n.* 1. sannāhoparikañcuka ; 2. dīnānaŋ uttarakañcuka, *m.*

Tabby, *n.* 1. jappakamahallikā, *f.* 2. dhūsarabilālī, *f.* 3. koseyyavisesa, *m.*

Tabefaction, *n.* sarīrahāni, *f.* dehapārijuñña, *nt.*

Tabernacle, *n.* dussakuṭikā, saŋhārimakuṭi, *f.* Yādavadevamandira, *nt.*

Tabes, *n.* khayaroga, *m.* **Tabetic,** *a. n.* khayarogātura, *m.*

Tablature, *n.* ālikhitacitta, *nt.*

Table, *n.* 1. phalakādhāra, *m.* 2. (for writing :) lekhanaphalaka, *m.* 3. (of contents :) mātikā, *f.* uddāna, *nt.* °**land,** *n.* sānu, *m.* *v.t.* 1. ādhārake ṭhapeti ; 2. lekhanādīni abhiharati. *p.p.* °ṭhapita ; abhihaṭalekhanādi.

Tablet, *n.* āvaṭṭikā, *f.* saṇṭhānaphalaka, *m. nt.*

Taboo, *n.* 1. paṭikkhepa, *m.* paccakkhāna, *nt.* 2. visuŋkatavatthu, *nt.* 3. visuŋkatapuggala, *m.* *v.t.* 1. puthakkaroti ; 2. paṭikkipati; paccakkhāti. *p.p.* °kata ; paṭikkhitta ; °khāta.

Tabor, *n.* mudiṅga, *m.*

Tabular, *a.* 1. phalakākāra ; 2. vaggavasena vibhatta ; kamānugata.

Tabulate, *v.t.* vaggavasena vibhajati; anukkamena likhati. *p.p.* °vibhatta ; °likhita. °**ion,** *n.* mātikāvasena ṭhapana, *nt.*

Tachometer, *n*. vegamāṇakayanta, *nt*.

Tacit, *a*. tuṇhībhāvena ñāpita *or* sūcita. °**urn**, *a*. appabhāsī. °**urnity**, *n*. appabhāsitā, *f*.

Tack, *n*. chattayuttāṇi. *f*. *v.t.* chattayuttāṇīhi ghaṭeti. *p.p.* °ṭita.

Tackle, *v.t.* 1. ubbāhati; 2. sīgham ussahati. *p.p.* °hita. *n*. 1. ubbāhakayanta, *nt*. 2. upakaraṇa, *nt*. 3. nivattāpaka, *m*.

Tact, *n*. cāturiya; kosalla; nepuñña, *nt*. °**ful**, *a*. catura; kusala; nipuṇa. °**fully**, *adv*. kosallena, nepuññena. °**less**, *a*. anipuṇa; adakkha.

Tactics, *n*. upāyakosalla; yuddhopāyakusalatta, *nt*.

Tactile, Tactual, *a*. phassapaṭibaddha, phusanīya.

Tadpole, *n*. bhekacchāpa, *m*.

Taffeta, *n*. vākapaṭṭavattha, *nt*.

Tag, *n*. 1. upadesavākya, *nt*. 2. pādukāpaṭṭikagga, *nt*. °**rag**, *n*. nīcajana, *m*.

Tail, *n*. puccha; naṅguṭṭha, *n*. vāladhi, *m*. *v.t.* vāladhiŋ yojeti. °**ed**, *a*. sapuccha. °**less**, *a*. apuccha.—**feather**, *n*. piccha; piñja, *nt*.

Tailor, *n*. tuṇṇavāya, *m*. °**ing**, *n*. tuṇṇakamma, *nt*.

Taint, *n*. kalaṅka; kalusa, *m*. dūsana, *nt*. *v.t.* kalaṅketi; dūseti; kalusayati. *p.p.* °kita; dūsita; °yita. °**less**, *a*. akalaṅka; viraja; nimmala.

Take, *v.t.* 1. gaṇhāti; ādāti; 2. harati; apaneti; 3. paṭiggaṇhāti. *p.p.* gahita; ādinna; haṭa; apanīta; paṭiggahita. — **away**, apaneti. — **a bath**, nahāyati. — **birth**, uppajjati. — **breath**, vissamati. — **care**, appamatto hoti.—**care of**, paṭijaggati.—**down**, oharati; oropeti. °**er**, *n*. gāhī; ādāyī, *m*. °**en up**, samādinna, *a*. — **flight**, palāyati. — **food**, bhuñjati.— **for granted**, tathā ti sampaṭicchati. — **heart**, dhitim uppādeti. — **hold of**, upādāti. — **in**, anto paveseti. °**ing**, *n*. gahaṇa, ādāna, *nt*. gāha, *m*. — **into account**, citte nidahati. — **notice**, sallakkheti. — **off**, (a garment, etc.) omuñcati.—**out**, nīharati. — **over**, adhikāraŋ gaṇhāti. — **place**, sijjhati. —**possession of**, āvisati; adhigaṇhāti. — **rebirth**, paccājāyati. — **a seat**, upavisati. — **to one's heels**, palāyati. — **up**, paggaṇhāti. — **upon oneself**, attani āropeti.

Taking, *a*. manohara. °**ly**, *adv*. manoharākārena.

Tale, *n*. 1. kiŋvadantī, *f*. ākhyāna; 2. pesuñña, *nt*. — **bearer**, pisuṇavādī, *m*. — **bearing**, pesuññaharaṇa, *nt*.

Talent, *n*. buddhippabhāva, *m*. nepuñña, *nt*. °**ed**, *a*. paññavantu. °**less**, *a*. nippañña; dummedha.

Talion, *n*. verasādhana, *nt*.

Talipot, *n*. tālarukkha, *m*.

Talisman, *n*. kavaca, *m*. parittāṇavatthu, *nt*. °**ic**, *a*. parittāṇabalayutta.

Talk, *v.i.t.* ālapati; sallapati; sambhāsati. *p.p.* °pita; °sita. *n*. ālāpa; sallāpa, *m*. sambhāsana; kathana, *nt*. °**ative**, *a*. mukhara; vācāla. °**ativeness**, *n.* bahubhāṇitā, *f.* °**er,** *n.* sallapaka; sambhāsaka, *m.* —**friendlily,** samullapati. — **nonsense,** palapati. — **over,** saññāpeti. — **round,** pariyāyena vadati.

Tall, *a.* 1. ucca; tuṅga; unnata; 2. vikatthaka. °**ness,** *n.* uccatā, *f.* unnatabhāva, *m.*

Tallow, *n.* vapā, *f.* — **faced,** *a.* paṇḍumukha.

Tally, *n.* 1. nāmaṅkita-salākā, *f.* 2. samānavatthu, *nt.* *v.i.* sameti. *p.p.* samita.

Talon, *n.* nakhapañjara, *m.*

Talus, *n.* gopphakaṭṭhi, *nt.*

Tamarind, *n.* ciñcā; tintiṇī, *f.*

Tamarisk, *n.* jhāvuka; picula, *m.*

Tambour, *n.* ekatalabheri, *f.* °**ine,** *n.* muraja, *m.*

Tame, *a.* danta; vinīta; gharavaḍḍhita. *v.t.* dameti; vineti sikkhāpeti. °**able,** *a.* damma; vineyya; damanāraha. °**er,** *n.* dametu; vinetu, *m.* °**ing,** damana; sikkhāpana, *nt.* °**ness,** *n.* dantatta, *nt.* **Difficult to —,** duddamīya; avidheya.

Tamil, *n.* 1. Damiḷabhāsā, *f.* 2. Damiḷajātika, *m.* °**ian,** *a.* Damiḷāyatta.

Tamper, *v.i.* 1. parakiccesu pavisati; 2. lekhanāni aññathā karoti; 3. lañcādīhi dūseti. *p.p.* °paviṭṭha; °katalekhana; °sita.

Tan, *n.* 1. kasaṭa-tacajāti, *f.* 2. tambavaṇṇa, *m.* *v.t.* 1. cammaŋ paṭisaṅkharoti; 2. tambavaṇṇaŋ karoti. *p.p.* °khata°; °ṇīkata. °**ner,** *n.* cammakāra, *m.* °**nery,** *n.* cammasodhanaṭṭhāna, *nt.* °**ning,** *n.* cammasaṅkharaṇa, *nt.*

Tandem, *adv.* ekassa pacchato; ekam anu.

Tang, *n.* ghaṇṭāsadisarāva, *m.* *v.t.* uccāsaddaŋ pavatteti. *p.p.* °titauccāsadda.

Tangent, *n.* phusanarekhā, *f.* °**gible,** *a.* phassavisayaka; phusanīya.

Tangle, *n.* jaṭā, *f.* *v.t.* jaṭeti; ākulīkaroti. *p.p.* jaṭita; °kata.

Tank, *n.* vāpi, *f.* jalāsaya, *m.* °**age,** *n.* 1. vāpigata-jalappamāṇa, *nt.* 2. āsaye ṭhapanāya vetana, *nt.* °**er,** *n.* telāsayayutta-nāvā, *f.*

Tantalize, *v.t.* icchābhaṅgaŋ karoti; iccham aparipūretvā pīḷeti. *p.p.* katicchābhaṅga; °pīḷita.

Tantamount, *a.* tulyaphala; samānatthaka.

Tantivy, *n.* pakkhandana, *nt.* adj. turita; sīgha.

Tantrum, *n.* kopāvesa, *m.*

Tap, *n.* 1. sanikākoṭana; 2. jalanāḷapidhāna, *nt.* *v.t.* 1. saṇikam ākoṭeti; lahuŋ abhihanati; 2. chiddaŋ karoti. *p.p.* °ṭita; °abhihata; katachidda.

Tape, *n.* dīghapaṭṭikā, *f.* *v.t.* dīghapaṭṭikāya ābandhati. *p.p.* °ābaddha.

Taper, *n.* sitthadīpikā, *f.* adj. anupubbatanuka. *v.i.* anupubbena sikharataŋ yāti. °**ing,** *a.* siṅgākāra; anupubbasikharībhūta.

Tapestry, *n.* citta-javanikā; *f.*

Tapia, *n.* varaṇarukkha, *m.*

Tapioca, *n.* guḷikā-piṭṭha, *nt.*

Tap-root, *n.* padhāna-mūla, *nt.*

Tapir, *n.* khuddhaka-khaggavisāṇa, *m.*

Tapster, *n.* majjabhājaka, *m.*

Tar, *n.* sajjurasa, *m. v.t.* sajjurasena lepeti. *p.p.* °pita.

Tarantula, *n.* visalūtikā, *f.*

Tardy, *a.* dandha ; dīghasuttika ; mandagatika. °**ily**, *adv.* mandaŋ ; sanikaŋ. °**iness**, *n.* dandhatta ; mantharatta, *nt.* °**igrade**, *a.* mandagatika.

Tare, *n.* 1. dhaññadūsaka, 2. vāhana-peḷādi-bhāra, *m.*

Target, *n.* lakkha ; vejjha, *nt.* °**eer**, *n.* phalakadhara, *m.*

Tariff, *n.* suṅkapaṇṇa, *nt.*

Tarnish, *n.* malinabhāva ; pabhānāsa, *m. v.t.* mandappabhaŋ *or* malinaŋ karoti. *v.i.* malinībhavati. *p.p.* malinīkata ; °bhūta.

Tarradiddle, *n.* musāvāda ; micchālāpa, *m.*

Tarry, *v.i.* vilambati ; cirāyati. *v.t.* vilambeti. *p.p.* °bita ; °yita. adj. sajjurasālitta.

Tart, *n.* phalamodaka, *m.* adj. 1. ambila ; kaṭuka ; 2. mammacchedaka.

Tartar, *n.* 1. dantamala ; 2. merayamala, *nt.* 3. Tārakadesavāsī, *m.*

Task, *n.* kicca ; kāriya, *nt.* kiccabhāra, *m. v.t.* kiccabhāre niyojeti. *p.p.* °jita. — **master**, *n.* kiccaniyojaka, *m.*

Tassel, *n.* suttagocchaka, *m.*

Taste, *n.* 1. rasa ; assāda, *m.* 2. ruci, *f. v.t.* assādeti ; sāyati. *p.p.* °dita ; sāyita. °**able**, *a.* assādanīya. °**er**, *n.* sāyaka, *m.* °**ful**, *a.* surasa ; rucikara. °**less**, *a.* virasa ; nirassāda. °**ing**, *n.* assādana, *nt.* °**y**, *a.* madhura ; sādurasa.

Tat, *n.* veḷukilañja, *m. v.t.* gantheti. *p.p.* °thita. °**ting**, *n.* ganthita-paṭṭikā, *f.*

Tatter, *n.* palaccara, *nt.* pilotikā, *f.* °**ed**, *a.* jiṇṇa ; palaccarabhūta.

Tattle, *n.* pajappana, *nt. v.i.* pajappati ; palapati. *p.p.* °pita. °**er**, *n.* pajappaka, *m.* °**ing**, *n.* palapana, *nt.*

Tattoo, *n.* 1. yāmabherināda ; yāmakāhala, *m.* 2. tace uṭṭhāpitarūpa, *nt. v.t.* 1. yāmabheriŋ vādeti ; 2. tace rūpāni samuṭṭhāpeti. *p.p.* vāditayā° ; °pitarūpa.

Taunt, *n.* garahā ; nindā, *f.* paribhava, *m. v.t.* nindati ; upārabhati ; garahati. *p.p.* °dita ; upāraddha ; °hita. °**ing**, *n.* nindana, *nt.* °**ingly**, *adv.* sopārambhaŋ ; sopahāsaŋ.

Taurine, *a.* usabhopama.

Taurus, *n.* usabharāsi, *m.*

Taut, *a.* asithila. °**ly**, *adv.* asithilākārena.

Tautology, *n.* pariyāyena punarutti, *f.* °**ist**, *n.* aññavacanehi tulyatthappakāsaka, *m.*

Tavern, *n.* pānāgāra, *nt.*

Tawdry, *a.* atimattālaṅkata ; niratthaka-sobhana. °**ily**, *adv.* bahisobhanākārena. °**iness**, *n.* asaṅgatasobhanatta, *nt.*

Tawny, *a.* piṅgala ; kapila.

Tax, *n.* kara ; bali ; suṅka, *m. v.t.* 1. karaŋ gaṇhāti *or* niyameti ; 2. accantaŋ pīḷeti. *p.p.* gahitakara ; °pīḷita. °**able**, *a.* karāraha ; karagāhiya. °**ation**, *n.* karaggāha, *m.* baliniyamana, *nt.* — **collector**, *n.* suṅkasaṅgāhaka, *m.*

Taxi, *n.* vetanika-sayaŋdhāvaka, *m.* — **meter**, gatadūramāṇaka, *nt.*

Taxidermy, *n.* anto pūretvā pasurūpasaṅkharaṇa, *nt.*

Taxis, *n.* vaggīkaraṇa, *nt.*

Taxology, *n.* vaggīkaraṇasattha, *nt.*

Tea, *n.* cāhāpaṇṇa, *nt.*

Teach, *v.t.* uggaṇhāpeti; sikkhāpeti. *p.p.* °pita. °**able**, *a.* sikkhanāraha. °**er**, *n.* ācariya; sikkhetu, *m.* °**er's fee**, *n.* gurudakkhiṇā, *f.* ācariyadhana, *nt.* °**er's teacher**, pācariya, *m.* °**ing**, *n.* ajjhāpana; sikkhāpana, *nt.*

Teak, *n.* phandanarukkha, *m.* (?)

Teal, *n.* jalakāka, *m.*

Team, *n.* 1. vāhakayuga, *nt.* 2. kīḷakagaṇa; 3. pūga, *m.* *v.t.* 1. yuge yojeti; 2. pūgena kammaŋ kāreti. *p.p.* °jita; °kāritakamma.

Tear, *n.* assu, *nt.* bappa, *m.* °**ful**, *a.* assumukha; assupuṇṇa. °**fully**, *adv.* assumukhena. °**less**, *a.* nirassuka.

Tear, *n.* chidda; vidāritaṭṭhāna, *nt.* *v.t.* vidāreti; padāleti. *p.p.* °rita; °lita. °**ing**, *n.* vidāraṇa; uppāṭana; uddālana, *nt.* — **off**, uppāṭeti. — **out**, ubbatteti. °**ing**, *a.* 1. vidāraka; 2. ghora; dāruṇa.

Tease, *n.* vihesaka, *m.* *v.t.* heṭheti; viheṭheti; hiŋsati; vihiŋsati. *p.p.* °ṭhita; °sita. °**ing**, *n.* vihesana, *nt.* °**er**, *n.*1. viheṭhaka, *m.* 2. dubbodhapañha, *m.*

Teat, *n.* cūcuka; thanagga, *nt.*

Technical, *a.* pāribhāsika; sippanissita. °**ly**, *adv.* sippāyattavasena. °**ity**, *n.* pāribhāsikasadda, *m.*

Technics, *n.* sippakalā, *f.*

Technique, *n.* kalākosalla, *nt.*

Technology, *n.* kalāviññāṇa, *nt.* sippavijjā, *f.*

Tectonic, *n.* nimmāṇasippa, *nt.* adj. (gharādi-) nimmāṇavisayaka.

Ted, *v.t.* (tiṇādiŋ) vikirati; viyūhati. *p.p.* vikiṇṇa; °hita.

Tedious, *a.* 1. āyāsakara; parissamāvaha; 2. mandapavattika. °**ly**, *adv.* āyāsakaratāya. °**ness**, *n.* āyāsakaratta, *nt.*

Teem, *a.* see **Abound**. °**less**, *a.* abahula; virala.

Teem, *v.t.* nikkhāmeti; nicchāreti; ossajati. *p.p.* °mita; °rita; ossaṭṭha.

Teens, *n.* *pl.* dvādasa-vīsati-antare vassagaṇanā, *f.*

Teethe, *v.i.* 1. dantā jāyanti; 2. dante chindati. *p.p.* jātadanta; chinnadanta. °**ing**, *n.* dantuggama, *m.*

Teetotal, *a.* majjanisedhanāyatta. °**er**, *n.* majjapaṭisedhī, *m.* °**ism**, *n.* majjapaṭisedhana, *nt.*

Teetotum, *n.* bhamarikā, *f.*

Tegument, *n.* āvaraka-camma, *nt.*

Telegram, *n.* vijjusandesa, *m.*

Telegraph, *n.* vijjusandesapesaka-yanta, *nt.* *v.t.* vijjusāsanaŋ peseti. °**ist**, *n.* vijjusāsanapesaka, *m.* °**ic**, *a.* vijjusāsanāyatta. °**y**, *n.* vijjusāsanavijjā, *f.*

Teleology, *n.* mūlahetuvijjā, *f.* paramatthavāda, *m.*

Telepathy, *n.* paracittajānana, *nt.*

Telephone, *n.* dūrabhāsana-(yanta), *nt.*

Telescope, *n.* dūradassaka, *nt.*

Television, *n.* dibbacakkhu, *nt.*

Tell, *v.t.i.* vadati ; bhāsati ; bhaṇati ; akkhāti ; ācikkhati. *p.p.* vutta ; °sita ; bhaṇita ; akkhāta ; °khita. °**er,** *n.* vattu ; akkhātu ; bhāsitu, *m.* °**ing,** *n.* kathana ; bhāsana, *nt.* °**tale,** *n.* pisuṇavādī, *m.*

Tellurian, *n.* paṭhavivāsī, *m.*

Tellurium, *n.* setalohavisesa, *m.*

Temenos, *n.* pujjaṭṭhāna, *nt.*

Temerarious, *a.* sāhasika ; nibbhaya.

Temerity, *n.* asamekkhakāritā, *f.*

Temper, *n.* 1. cittasabhāva, *m.* 2. dosapakati, *f.* 3. lohadaḷhatta, *nt.* 4. yojita-missana, *nt.* *v.t.* 1. siniddhaŋ *or* kammaññaŋ karoti ; 2. misseti ; saŋyojeti. *p.p.* siniddhakata ; °sita ; °jita. °**ance,** *n.* 1. parimitatta, *nt.* 2. niggaha ; saŋyama, *m.* °**ate,** *a.* 1. pamāṇayutta ; 2. saŋyata ; upasanta. °**ate in eating,** mitāhāra ; bhojane mattaññū, *a.* °**ately,** *adv.* mattaññutāya ; santākārena.

Temperament, *n.* puggalikasabhāva, *m.* °**al,** *a.* niccaparivattī.

Temperature, *n.* tejopamāṇa, *nt.*

Tempest, *n.* 1. vāyusaṅkhobha ; 2. mahākolāhala, *m.* °**uous,** *a.* saṅkhobhayutta. °**uously,** *adv.* khubhitākārena.

Temple, *n.* 1. devāyatana; devaṭṭhāna, *nt.* 2. lalāṭanta, *m.*

Temporal, *a.* 1. ihalokika ; 2. tāvakālika. °**ity,** *n.* 1. tāvakālikatta, *nt.* 2. saṅghika-dhana, *nt.* °**rary,** *a.* aciraṭṭhāyī ; sāmayika. °**rarily,** *adv.* kālikavasena.

Temporalty, *n.* upāsakagaṇa, *m.*

Temporize, *v.t.* tāvakālikaŋ karoti ; ayathā papañceti. *p.p.* °kata ; °cita.

Tempt, *v.t.* palobheti ; vimoheti. *p.p.* °bhita ; °hita. °**ation,** *n.* palobhana, *nt.* °**er,** *n.* palobhaka, *m.* °**ing,** *a.* palobhanaka ; cittākaḍḍhaka. °**ingly,** *adv.* palobhakākārena. °**ress,** *n.* palobhikā, *f.*

Ten, *a.* *n.* dasa, 3. °**fold,** *a.* dasavidha. — **thousand,** *n.* nahuta; dasa-sahassa, *nt.* — **times,** *adv.* dasakkhattuŋ. **In — ways,** dasadhā, *adv.*

Tenable, *a.* 1. rakkhanīya ; 2. takkena anapanetabba ; sādhakayutta. °**bility,** *n.* akhaṇḍiyatta, *nt.*

Tenacious, *a.* daḷhagāhī ; lagganasīla ; adātukāma. °**ly,** *adv.* daḷhagāhena. °**city,** *n.* daḷhagāha, *m.* saŋlaggana ; macchariya, *nt.*

Tenant, *n.* parasantaka-bhūmivāsī, *m.* °**ncy,** *n.* gharasuṅkadāna, *nt.* °**ry,** *n.* nivāsasuṅkadayījana, *m.* °**able,** *a.* suṅkagahaṇāraha.

Tend, *v.i.* poṇībhavati ; anuyāti. *v.t.* paṭijaggati ; poseti. *p.p.* poṇībhūta ; anuyāta ; °gita ; posita. °**ency,** *n.* poṇatta, *nt.* abhinivesa, *m.* °**er,** *n.* paṭijaggaka, *m.*

Tendentious, *a.* pakkhapāta-yutta ; agatigata.

Tender, *n.* 1. anuratha, *m.* upanāvā, *f.* 2. kammantāyācanapaṇṇa, *nt.* *v.t.* āyācanapaṇṇaŋ peseti. *p p.* pesitāyācana°.

Tender, *a.* mudu ; komala ; sukhumāla. *v.i.* upatiṭṭhati ; upakkhipati. *p.p.* upaṭṭhita ; upakkhitta. — **eyed,** *a.* dubbalakkhika. — **foot,** *n.* ādhunika, *m.* — **footed,** *a.* bhīrukajātika. — **hearted** *a.* muduhadaya. °**ly,** *adv.* sadayaŋ ; mudukaŋ. °**ness,** *n.* mudutta ; komalatta, *nt.*

Tendon, *n.* sandhibandhana, *nt.* mahāsirā, *f.*

Tendril, *n.* patāna, *nt.* latātantu, *m.*

Tenebrific, *a.* timisakara.

Tenebrous, *a.* tamāvuta.

Tenement, *n.* 1. thāvaradhana, *nt.* 2. āyattavatthu ; 3. vāsaṭṭhāna, *nt.*

Tenet, *n.* paṭiggahitamata, *nt.* siddhanta, *m.*

Tenon, *n.* āvuṇakaṅkusa, *m.*

Tenor, *n.* 1. adhippāya ; bhāvattha ; 2. pavattanākāra, *m.*

Tense, *a.* asithila ; daḷha. *n.* ākhyāta-kālabheda, *m.* °**ly,** *adv.* asithilākārena. °**ness,** °**ity,** *n.* asithilatta, *nt.* °**ion,** *n.* 1. dhārakasatti, *f.* 2. cittakkhobha, *m.*

Tensile, *a.* ākaḍḍhanakkhama.

Tensibility, *n.* ākaḍḍhanakkhamatā, *f.*

Tent, *n.* dussakuṭi, *f.* maṇḍapa, *m.* *v.t.* maṇḍapaŋ sampādeti. *v.i.* kuṭikāyaŋ vasati. *p.p.* sampāditama°; °vuttha.

Tentacle, *n.* phusanāvayava, *m.*

Tentative, *a.* paṭhamāvatthāgata ; parikkhaṇāya-kata.

Tenth, *a.* dasama.

Tenuity, *n.* tanutta, *nt.*

Tenuous, *a.* tanuka.

Tenure, *n.* adhikāravidhi, *m.*

Tepefy, *v.t.* manduṇhaŋ karoti. *v.i.* manduṇho bhavati. *p.p.* °kata ; °ṇhībhūta. °**faction,** *n.* manduṇhakaraṇa, *nt.*

Tepid, *a.* manduṇhayutta. °**ly,** *adv.* manduṇhākārena. °**ity,** °**ness,** *n.* manduṇhatta, *nt.*

Teraphim, *n.* gharadevapaṭimā, *f.*

Teratosis, *n.* vikaḷaṅgatā, *f.*

Tercentenary, *a.* *n.* tisatasaŋvaccharika.

Tercet, *n.* tika, *nt.*

Terebinth, *n.* sirivāsarukkha, *m.* °**ine,** *a.* saraladdavāyatta.

Terebrate, *v.t.* vinivijjhati. *p.p.* °viddha.

Teredo, *n.* kaṭṭhavedhī samuddapāṇī, *m.*

Tergiversate, *v.t.* 1. piṭṭhiŋ dasseti ; 2. pakkhantaraŋ saṅkamati. °**ion,** *n.* 1. pakkhantarasaṅkamaṇa ; 2. capalatta, *nt.*

Term, *n.* 1. adhivacana ; vevacana, *nt.* 2. kālaparicheda, *m.* 3. mariyādā, *f.* 4. *pl.* niyamāvali, *f.* *v.t.* abhidhāti ; ākhyāti. *p.p.* abhihita ; ākhyāta. °**less,** *a.* ananta ; apariyanta.

Terminate, *v.t.* osāpeti ; samāpeti ; *v.i.* osānaŋ pappoti ; nivattati. *p.p.* °pita ; °patta ; nivatta. °**nable,** *a.* pameyya ; osāpanīya. °**nal,** *n.* odhi ; anta, *m.*

adj. antima; antiya; osānabhūta. °**ion**, *n*. osāpana; pariyosāna, *nt*. (In gram:) vibhattipaccaya, *m*. °**ive**, *a*. osāpaka; antakara. °**tor**, *n*. osāpetu; antakārī, *m*.

Terminology, *n*. paribhāsā; vijjāyattasaddamālā, *f*. °**ical**, *a*. pāribhāsika. °**ically**, *adv*. pāribhāsikavasena.

Terminus, *n*. anta, *m*. osāna; pariyosāna, *nt*.

Termitè, *n*. upacikā, *f*.

Tern, *n*. tika, *nt*. °**ary**, *a*. tikayutta. °**ate**, *a*. tivaggayutta.

Terra, *n*. paṭhavī; medinī, *f*. °**cotta**, *n*. jhāma-mattikādimissitarūpa, *nt*. °**neous**, *a*. bhummaṭṭha; thalaja.

Terrace, *n*. vedikā, *f*. paghana; ālinda, *m*.

Terrapin, *n*. kumma, *m*.

Terraqueous, *a*. thala-jalāyatta.

Terrene, Terrestrial, *a*. bhumma; bhummaṭṭha; bhūminissita; ihalokika.

Terrible, *a*. ghora; dāruṇa; bhayānaka. °**ly**, *adv*. dāruṇākārena.

Terrify, *v.t*. uttāseti; bhāyāpeti. *p.p*. °sita; °pita. °**ic**, *a*. bhayaṅkara; bhayānaka. °**ically**, *adv*. bheravākārena.

Territory, *n*. janapada, *m*. vijita; raṭṭha, *nt*. °**ial**, *a*. janapadāyatta.

Terror, *n*. tāsa; uttāsa, *m*. bhaya, *nt*. bhīti, *f*. °**ism**, *n*. bhāyāpanena pālana, *nt*. °**ize**, *v.t*. bhāyāpeti; atisantāseti. °**struck**, *a*. bhayākula.

Terse, *a*. saṅkhitta; uttānattha. °**ness**, *n*. sugamatthatā, *f*. °**ly**, *adv*. samāsato.

Tertian, *n*. tīha-vārika-jara, *m*. adj. tīhika.

Tertiary, *n*. *a*. tatiyabhāvappatta.

Tessellate, *v.t*. caturassakehi vicitteti. *p.p*. °tita. °**ion**, *n*. caturassacittakaraṇa, *nt*.

Test, *n*. upaparikkhā; vīmaŋsā, *f*. *v.t*. upaparikkhati; vīmaŋsati. *p.p*. °khita; °sita.

Testacean, *n*. kosamaccha, *m*. °**ceology**, *n*. kosamacchavijjā, *f*. °**ceous**, *a*. kosamacchāyatta.

Testament, *n*. 1 accayadānapaṇṇa, *nt*. 2. Kiṭṭha-dhammagantha, *m*. °**ary**, *a*. accayadānanissita.

Testate, °**tor**, *n*. kata-accayadāna, *m*.

Tester, *n*. vitāna, *nt*.

Testicle, *n*. aṇḍakosa, *m*.

Testiculate, *a*. aṇḍasahita; aṇḍasadisa.

Testify, *v.i.t*. sapathena pakāseti; sakkhiŋ sādheti; samattheti. *p.p*. °sita; sādhitasakkhī; °thita.

Testimony, *n*. sakkhi; apadesa, *m*. sasapathapakāsana, *nt*. °**ial**, *n*. pamāṇapaṇṇa; sakkhipaṇṇa, *nt*.

Testy, *a*. dummana; anattamana. °**iness**, *n*. anattamanatā, *f*.

Tetanus, *n*. phandaka-roga, *m*.

Tetchy, *a*. kuppanasabhāva.

Tether, *n*. sandāna, *nt*. *v.t*. sandānena bandhati. *p.p*. sandānabaddha.

Tetrad, *n*. catukka, *nt*.

Tetragon, *n.* caturassavatthu, *nt.* °**al,** *a.* catukkaṇṇa.

Tetrapod, *a. n.* catuppada, *m.* °**y,** *n.* catuppadika (-gāthā), *f.*

Tetter, *n.* kuṭṭhavisesa, *m.* °**ous,** *a.* kuṭṭhātura.

Teucrian, *n.* Trojan-desavāsī, *m.*

Text, *n.* mūlagantha, *m.* °**book,** *n.* niyamita-potthaka, *m. nt.* °**ual,** *a.* mūlaganthāyatta.

Textile, *n.* vāyana, *nt.* adj. 1. vāyanapaṭibaddha ; 2. tantunimmita. 3. *pl.* vatthajāta, *nt.*

Texture, *n.* vāyitākāra ; nimmitākāra, *m.* °**less,** *a.* adissamānavāyima.

Thalamus, *n.* 1. itthāgāra, *nt.* 2. matthaluṅga-pacchābhāga, *m.*

Than, *conj.* Expressed by the abl. and suffix -*tara.* **More than that,** tato bahutaraŋ.

Thanatoid, *a.* maccusadisa ; matasadisa.

Thank, *n. v.t.* thometi ; pasaŋsati ; abhitthavati. *p.p.* °mita ; pasattha ; abhitthuta. °**ful,** *a.* kataññū ; thutipara. °**fully,** *adv.* kataññutāya. °**fulness,** *n.* kataññutā ; thutiparatā, *f.* °**less,** *a.* akatavedī. °**lessness,** *n.* akataveditā, *f.* °**worthy,** *a.* thometabba.

Thanks, *n. pl.* thuti ; thomanā, *f.* °**giving,** *n.* thutipūjā, *f.* °**giver,** *n.* anumodāpaka, *m.*

That, *a. pron.* ta. *conj.* iti. *adv.* tattakaŋ. — **man,** so. — **woman,** sā. — **thing,** taŋ. — **like,** *a.* tādisa. — **much,** *a.* tattaka. **After** —, tato pacchā, *ind.* **By** —, tena ; tadā, *adv.* **Like** —, tathā, *adv.* **With** —, tathā katvā.

Thatch, *n.* 1. chadana, *nt.* 2. chādaka-vatthu, *nt. v.t.* sañchādeti ; chādanaŋ niveseti. *p.p.* °dita ; nivesitachadana.

Thaumaturgy, *n.* iddhipāṭihāriya ; abbhutakamma, *nt.* °**ist,** *n.* pāṭihāriyadassaka ; iddhimantu, *m.*

Thaw, *n.* himavilīyana, *nt. v.i.* vilīyati. *p.p.* vilīna.

The, *a.* see **That.** *adv.* **The more the merrier,** yathādhikaŋ pīti vaḍḍhati.

Thearchy, *n.* devatāpālana, *nt.*

Theatre, *n.* 1. raṅgamaṇḍala, *nt.* naccasālā, *f.* 2. naccakalā, *f.* 3. vijjatthīsālā, *f.* 4. sallakattālaya, *m.* °**ical,** *a.* raṅgamaṇḍalocita ; raṅgāyatta. °**ically,** *adv.* raṅgocitākārena.

Theft, *n.* coriya ; theyya, *nt.*

Their, *pron.* tesaŋ ; tāsaŋ.

Theism, *n.* Issaranimmāṇavāda, *m.*

Theist, *n.* Issaravādī, *m.* °**ical,** *a.* Issaravādāyatta.

Theme, *n.* visaya ; visesapabandha, *m.*

Then, *adv.* 1. tadā ; 2. atha ; anantaraŋ. adj. taṅkālika. *conj.* tena hi ; tato. **By** —, tasmiŋ kāle. **Now and** —, kālantarena ; yadā kadāci. **Now** —, iṅgha passa.

Thence, *adv.* tato ; tasmā ; tena. °**forth,** tato pabhuti. °**forward,** tato paṭṭhāya *or* uttariŋ.

Theocracy, *n.* devapālitarajja, *nt.*

Theogony, *n.* devavaŋsavaṇṇanā, *f.*

Theology, *n.* devadhamma, *m.* °**ical,** *a.* devadhammāyatta. °**ically,** *adv.* devadhammānusārena. °**ion,** °**ist,** *n.* devadhammavidū, *m.*

Theomachy, *n.* devayuddha, *nt.*
Theomancy, *n.* anāgatakathana, *nt.*
Theomania, *n.* dhammummāda, *m.*
Theophany, *n.* devadassana, *nt.* devapātubhāva, *m.*
Theorem, *n.* pameyya ; sādhakehi sādhetabbakāraṇa, *nt.*
Theory, *n.* mata, *nt.* diṭṭhi, *f.* vāda, *m.* °**etic**, °**etical**, *a.* parikappanāyatta. °**ize**, *v.t.* parikappeti ; matavasena pakāseti.
Theosophy, *n.* 1. devañāṇa, *nt.* 2. yogavijjā, *f.* °**ist**, *n.* ñāṇayogavādī, *m.* °**ical**, *a.* devañāṇāyatta.
Therapeutic, *a.* *n.* ātaṅkahara ; roganivāraka.
There, *adv.* tattha ; tatra ; tahiŋ ; tahaŋ. °**abouts**, tattaka, *a.* °**after**, tato paraŋ, *adv.* °**at**, tasmiŋ ṭhāne. °**by**, ten' upāyena. °**fore**, *adv.* tasmā. °**from**, °**of**, tato, *adv.* °**in**, tasmiŋ. °**on**, °**upon**, tad upari ; tato paṭṭhāya. °**with**, °**withal**, *adv.* tena saddhiŋ ; api ca.
Theriac, *n.* visasamanosadha, *nt.*
Therm, *n.* uṇhamāṇa, *nt.* °**al**, *a.* ghammāyatta ; ghamma-māṇāyatta. °**antidote**, *n.* sītīkaraṇopakaraṇa, *nt.*
Thermometer, *n.* uṇhamāṇaka, *nt.*
Thermomotive, *a.* usumakampanāyatta.
Thermos, *n.* usumārakkhakabhājana, *nt.*
Theroid, *a.* tiracchānagatika.
Therology, *n.* khīrapāyīvijjā, *f.*
Thesaurus, *n.* nikhilakosa, *m.*
Thesis, *n.* 1. racanāvisaya ; 2. upādhidāyaka-nibandha, *m.*
Theurgy, *n.* uttarimanussadhamma, *m.*
Thews, *n.* *pl.* kāyikabala ; mānusikabala, *nt.*
Thick, *a.* 1. ghana ; bahala ; thūla ; 2. avirala. *adv.* aviralaŋ ; nirantaraŋ. °**head**, *n.* jala, *m.* °**ly**, *adv.* ghanatāya ; nirantaraŋ ; aviralaŋ. °**ness**, *n.* bahalatta, *nt.* °**set**, *a.* thūlasarīra. °**skinned**, *a.* sahanakkhama ; akampiya.
Thicken, *v.t.* bahalīkaroti. *v.i.* ghanībhavati. *p.p.* °kata ; °bhūta.
Thicket, *n.* vanagahana ; kuñja, *nt.*
Thief, *n.* cora ; thena ; takkara ; mosaka, *m.*
Thieve, *v.t.* coreti ; theneti. *p.p.* corita ; °nita. °**ry**, *n.* corikā, *f.* theyya ; corakamma, *nt.* °**ish**, *a.* corapakatika. °**ishness**, *n.* corapakati ; coretukāmatā, *f.*
Thigh, *n.* ūru ; satthi, *m.*
Thill, *n.* sakaṭadhura, *nt.*
Thimble, *n.* aṅgulitāṇaka ; sūcipaṭiggaha, *m.*
Thin, *a.* 1. tanu ; kisa ; 2. virala ; pelava. *v.t.* tanukaroti. *v.i.* tanuttaŋ yāti ; kisībhavati. *p.p.* tanukata ; °yāta ; °bhūta. °**ly**, *adv.* viralākārena ; tanutāya. °**ness**, *n.* tanutta ; viralatta, *nt.* °**skinned**, *a.* 1. tanuttaca ; 2. sukhobhiya.
Thing, *n.* 1. vatthu ; dabba, *nt.* 2. kāraṇa, *nt.* 3. siddhi, *f.*

Think, *v.t.i.* cinteti; vitakketi. °**able**, *a.* cintiya; cintanīya. — **about**, sallakkheti; anuvitakketi. °**er**, *n.* cintaka, *m.* °**ing**, *n.* cintana; vitakkana, *nt.* —**lightly**, (figurative:) tiṇāya maññati. — **over**, pakappeti; vicinteti. — **upon**, anuvicinteti. °**ingly**, *adv.* vicārapubbakaŋ.

Third, *a.* tatiya. °**ly**, *adv.* tatiyaŋ.

Thirst, *n.* 1. pipāsā; 2. āsā; taṇhā, *f.* *v.i.* pivāsati; abhilasti. *p.p.* °sita. °**less**, *a.* nittaṇha; nirāsa. °**y**, *a.* pipāsātura; sataṇha.

Thirteen, *n. a.* teḷasa; terasa, °**th**, *a.* terasama.

Thirty, *n. a.* tiŋsā; tiŋsati. *f.* — **five**, pañcatiŋsati, *f.* — **four**, catuttiŋsati, *f.* — **nine**, ekūnacattāḷīsati, *f.* — **seven**, sattatiŋsati, *f.* — **six**, chattiŋsati, *f.* — **three**, tettiŋsati, *f.* — **two**, battiŋsati; dvattiŋsati, *f.*

This, *a. pron.* ima. — **day**, ajjaṇha, *nt.* — **life**, itthatta, *nt.* diṭṭhadhamma, *m.* — **like**, *a.* evarūpa; īdisa. — **man**, ayaŋ, *m. Nom. sing.* — **woman** ayaŋ, *f. Nom. sing.* — **thing**, idaŋ, *nt. Nom. sing.* — **much**, ettaka, *a.*

Thistle, *n.* sakaṇṭakagacchavisesa, *m.*

Thither, see **There**. ° **wards**, taŋdisaŋ. *adv.*

Thong, *n.* varattā; naddhi, *f.* *v.t.* 1. naddhiŋ yojeti; 2. varattāya paharati. *p.p.* naddhiyojita; °pahaṭa.

Thor, *n.* Thanitadeva, *m.*

Thorax, *n.* uratthala, *nt.* khandhappadesa, *m.*

Thorn, *n.* kaṇṭaka, *m. nt.* — **apple**, *n.* ummattaphala, *nt.* °**less**, *a.* nikkaṇṭaka. °**y**, *a.* sakaṇṭaka. °**y hedge**, *n.* kaṇṭakādhāna, *nt.* kaṇṭakavati, *f.*

Thorough, *a.* thiratara; pariniṭṭhita. °**bred**, *a.* abhijāta; sammāvaḍḍhita. °**fare**, *n.* sādhāraṇamagga, *m.* °**going**, *a.* paripuṇṇa; anivattagāmī. °**ly**, *adv.* sammā; anūnaŋ; paripuṇṇākārena. °**ness**, *n.* thiratta; anūnatta, *nt.*

Thou, *pron.* tvaŋ; tuvaŋ. **Thee**, taŋ. **Thine**, tava; tuyhaŋ. **Thyself**, tvam eva.

Though, *conj.* kiñcāpi. **As** —, viya; iva. **Even** —, tathā pi.

Thought, *n.* cintā; cetanā, *f.* saṅkappa; parikappa, *m.* °**ful**, *a.* appamatta; samekkhakārī. °**fully**, *adv.* samekkha; vicintiya. °**fulness**, *n.* appamāda, *m.* parivīmaŋsana; vicārapubbaṅgamatta, *nt.* °**less**, *a.* pamatta; vicārahīna. °**lessly**, *adv.* sahasā; asamekkha. °**lessness**, *n.* avivekitā; vicārahīnatā, *f.*

Thousand, *n. a.* sahassa; dasasata, *nt.* — **eyed**, *a. n.* sahassakkha, *m.* — **spoked**, *a.* sahassāra. — **times**, sahassakkhattuŋ, *adv.* ° **fold**, *a.* sahassaguṇita.

Thrall, *n.* dāsa, *m.* °**dom**, *n.* dāsatta, *nt.*

Thrash, *v.t.* 1. atitāḷeti; 2. nitthusaŋ *or* nippalālaŋ karoti. *p.p.* °ḷita; nippalālīkata. °**ing**, *n.* 1. dhaññamaddana; 2. nippalālīkaraṇa, *nt.* °**ing floor**, khaḷamaṇḍala, *nt.*

Thread, *n.* sutta ; tanta, *nt.* tantu, *m.* *v.t.* 1. sūciyaŋ suttam yojeti ; 2. sutte āvuṇāti. *p.p.* °yojitasutta; °āvuta. °**bare,** *a.* khīṇatantuka ; jiṇṇasuttaka. °**worm,** *n.* tantupāṇaka, *m.* °**y,** *a.* tantusadisa ; suttamaya.

Threat, *n.* santajjana, *f.*

Threaten, *v.t.* santajjeti ; paribhāsati. *p.p.* °jita ; °sita. °**ing,** *a.* santajjaka ; pāripanthika. °**ingly,** *adv.* tajjanapubbakaŋ.

Three, *a.* *n.* ti. — **and a half,** aḍḍhuḍḍha, *m.* — **days,** tīha, *nt.* ° **fold,** *a.* tiguṇa; tivaṅgika. — **hundred,** *n.* tisata, *nt.* °**score,** *n.* *a.* saṭṭhi, *f.* tisso vīsatiyo, *f. pl.* — **storeyed,** *a.* tibhummaka. — **years old,** tivassika, *a.*

Threnode, °**ody,** *n.* sokagīta, *nt.* °**ial,** °**ic,** *a.* sokagītāyatta.

Thresh, *v.t.* maddati ; tāḷeti. *p.p.* °dita ; tāḷita. °**ing,** *n.* maddana, *nt.* — **floor,** *n.* khalamaṇḍala, *nt.*

Threshold, *n.* ummāra ; paḷigha, *m.* dehalī, *f.*

Thrice, *adv.* tikkhattuŋ.

Thrift, *n.* mitabbayatā, *f.* °**less,** *a.* amitabbaya ; vikiraka. °**lessly,** *adv.* asīmitavayena. °**lessness,** *n.* amitavayatta, *nt.* °**y,** *a.* mitabbayī.

Thrill, *n.* pharaṇā-pīti, *f.* *v.t.i.* pītiyā pharati ; udaggo hoti. *p.p.* °phuṭa ; udaggabhūta. °**ing,** *a.* lomahaŋsakara ; udaggakara.

Thrive, *v.i.* abhivaḍḍhati ; samijjhati. *p.p.* abhivuddha ; samiddha. °**ing,** *a.* abhivaḍḍhamāna. °**ingly,** *adv.* samiddhākārena.

Throat, *n.* kaṇṭha ; gala, *m.* galanāḷi, *f.* °**y,** *a.* 1. kaṇṭhuccārita ; kaṇṭhāyatta ; 2. mahākaṇṭha.

Throb, *n.* phandana ; vipphandana, *nt.* *v.i.* vipphandati. *p.p.* °dita. °**bing,** *a.* phandamāna.

Throe, *n.* balavavedanā ; pasūtivedanā, *f.*

Throne, *n.* 1. sīhāsana ; 2. rājatta, *nt.* *v.t.* rajje abhisiñcati. *p.p.* °abhisitta.

Throng, *n.* janasammadda, *m.* *v.t.* sambādheti *v.i.* sannipatati ; rāsībhavati. *p.p.* °dhita ; °tita ; °bhūta.

Throttle, *n.* galanāḷa, *m.* *v.t.* galaŋ nippīḷeti. *p.p.* °ḷitagala.

Through, *prep.* nissāya ; hetunā ; dvārena. *adv.* antarā ; antarena ; nirantaraŋ ; paripuṇṇaŋ. adj. abbocchinna. — **and through.** sukhumākārena ; sabbathā, *adv.* °**out,** *adv.* sabbattha ; nirantaraŋ. — **the favour,** vāhasā, *adv.* **Go** —, vindati.

Throw, *n.* khepa ; pāta, *m.* khipana, *nt.* *v.t.* khipati ; pāteti. *p.p.* khitta ; pātita. — **at,** upacchubhati. — **away,** chaḍḍeti ; apavijjhati. — **down,** avakkhipati ; nikkhipati. °**er,** *n.* chaḍḍetu ; khipaka, *m.* °**ing,** *n.* khipana, *nt.* — **into,** pakkhipati. — **off,** chaḍḍeti.

Thrush, *n.* 1. gāyaka-pakkhivisesa, *m.* 2. kaṇṭhapākaroga, *m.*

Thrust, *n.* nissāraṇa ; nikkaḍḍhana, *nt.* *v.t.* nissāreti ; nikkaḍḍhati. *p.p.* °rita ; °ḍhita.

Thud, *n.* patanasadda, *m.* *v.i.* sasaddaŋ patati.

Thug, *n.* ghātakacora, *m.*

Thumb, *n.* aṅguṭṭha, *m.*

Thump, *n.* pāṇippahāra; muṭṭhippahāra, *m.* *v.t.* muṭṭhinā paharati. *p.p.* °pahaṭa.

Thunder, *n.* thanita, *nt.* meghanāda, *m.* *v.i.* thanati. *v.t.* abhigajjati. *p.p.* °nita; °jita. **°bolt,** *n.* asani, *f.* kulisa, *nt.* **°clap,** *n.* meghagajjanā, *f.* **°er,** *n.* abhigajjitu, *m.* **°ing,** *a.* atimahanta; atithaddha. **°ous,** *a.* gajjanāsahita. **°storm,** *n.* meghanāditavuṭṭhi, *f.* **°struck,** *a.* 1. asanihata; 2. ativimhita.

Thurible, *n.* dhūpabhājana, *nt.*

Thurification, *n.* gandhadhūpana, *nt.*

Thursday, *n.* guruvāra, *m.*

Thus, *adv.* itthaŋ; evaŋ; iti. **— far,** ettāvatā, *ind.*

Thwart, *adv.* tiriyaŋ. *v.t.* paṭirodheti; moghīkaroti. *p.p.* °dhita; °kata.

Thy, *pron.* tava; tuyhaŋ. **°self,** tvam eva; tvam attanā va.

Tiara, *n.* makuṭa, *nt.* moḷi, *m.*

Tibia, *n.* jaṅghaṭṭhi, *nt.*

Tic, *n.* vadana-nahārusaṅkoca, *m.*

Tick, *n.* 1. ṭik-ṭik-sadda, *m.* 2. kīṭa-ūkā, *f.* *v.t.* ṭik-ṭik-saddaŋ pavatteti.

Ticket, *n.* pavesapatta; abhiññāṇapaṇṇa, *nt.*

Tickle, *n.* aṅgulipatodana, *nt.* *v.t.* aṅguliyā patudati. *p.p.* °dita. **°er,** *n.* 1. patudaka, *m.* 2. ubhatokoṭika-pañha, *m.*

Tide, *n.* 1. kālaparicheda; 2. kālika-jaluggama; uppāta, *m.* **°al,** *a.* jaluggamanāyatta.

Tidings, *n.* *pl.* pavatti; vutti, *f.* vuttanta, *m.*

Tidy, *a.* susaṇṭhapita; sobhana. **°ily,** *adv.* sobhanākārena. **°iness,** *n.* sobhanatta, *nt.*

Tie, *n.* 1. gaṇṭhi; saṅga, *m.* bandhana, *nt.* 2. gīveyyapaṭṭikā, *f.* *v.t.* bandhati; saṅghaṭeti. *p.p.* baddha or bandhita; °ghaṭita.

Tier, *n.* panti; seṇi, *f.* *v.t.* pantivasena yojeti. *p.p.* °jita.

Tiff, *n.* 1. manda-kalaha, *m.* 2. thokapibana, *nt.*

Tiffin, *n.* antarāhāra, *m.* *v.i.* antarāhāraŋ bhuñjati. *p.p.* bhuttantarāhāra.

Tiger, *n.* vyaggha; saddūla, *m.* **°ish,** *a.* vyagghasama.

Tight, *a.* gāḷha; daḷha; suvinaddha. *adv.* gāḷhaŋ; daḷhākārena. **°en,** *v.t.* daḷhīkaroti. *p.p.* °kata. **°ly,** *adv.* asithilaŋ; bāḷhaŋ. **°ness,** *n.* daḷhatta; asithilatta, *nt.*

Tigress, *n.* vyagghī, *f.*

Tike, *n.* narādhama, *m.*

Tile, *n.* chadaniṭṭhakā, *f.* *v.t.* iṭṭhakāhi chādeti. *p.p.* iṭṭhakāchanna. **°er,** *n.* 1. iṭṭhakāsampādaka; 2. chadanachādaka, *m.* **°ry,** *n.* iṭṭhakāvāpa, *m.*

Till, *prep.* *conj.* yāva. **— now,** yāvajjatanā, *ind.*

Till, *v.t.* kasati. *p.p.* kaṭṭha *or* kasita. **°er,** *n.* kassaka, *m.* **°able,** *a.* kasanāraha; kasikammayogga. **°age,** *n.* kasikamma, *nt.*

Tilt, *n.* 1. sattiyuddha, *nt.* 2. sakaṭāvaraṇa, *nt.* 3. passenonamana, *nt.* *v.t.* 1. poṇīkaroti; 2. kuntehi yujjhati. *p.p.* °kata; °jhita.

Timbal, *n.* maddala, *m.*

Timber, *n.* kaṭṭha, *nt.* dārusambhāra, *m.* — **yard**, *n.* kaṭṭhavikkayaṭṭhāna, *nt.*

Timbrel, *n.* ekatala-bherivisesa, *m.*

Time, *n.* 1. kāla; samaya, *m.* 2. velā, *f.* avasara, *m.* 3. vāra, *m.* *v.t.* kālaŋ niyameti *or* miṇāti. *p.p.* °mitakāla. °**keeper**, *n.* kālaniyāmaka, *m.* °**less**, ananta; anosāna. °**liness**, kālocitatā, *f.* °**ly**, *a.* yathākālika. — **of depression**, vipattikāla, *m.* — **of prosperity**, kālasampatti, *f.* °**piece**, *n.* saŋhārimaghaṭikāyanta, *nt.* — **table**, *n.* kālaniyamāvali, *f.* — **worn**, *a.* addhagata; paribhogajiṇṇa. **At all times**, sabbadā, *adv.* **At any** —, yadā kadāci, *ind.* **At the same** —, taṅkhaṇam eva; tad'eva. **For a long** —, cirāya, *ind.* **From** — **to** —, kālena kālaŋ. **In** —, yathāsamayaŋ *adv.*

Timid, *a.* dīna; kātara; bhīruka. °**ity**, *n.* bhīrukatta, *nt.* °**ly**, *adv.* dīnākārena.

Timocracy, *n.* dhanapati-pālana, *nt.*

Timorous, *a.* kātara; bhīruka. °**ly**, *adv.* dīnākārena. °**ness**, *n.* kātaratta, *nt.*

Tin, *n.* vaṅga-tipu, *nt.* *v.t.* 1. vaṅgatipunā lepeti; 2. vaṅgatipubhājane saŋrakkhati. *p.p.* °litta; °khita. °**smith**, *n.* vaṅgatipukāra, *m.*

Tinctorial, *a.* vaṇṇuppādaka.

Tincture, *n.* ābhāsa, *m.* *v.t.* thokaŋ misseti; appakaŋ vaṇṇaŋ uppādeti. *p.p.* °sita; °ditappavaṇṇa.

Tinder, *n.* aggitūla, *nt.*

Tinge, *n.* appakavaṇṇa, *m.* appakamissaṇa, *nt.* *v.t.* īsakaŋ rañjeti; appamattakaŋ vaṇṇaŋ deti. *p.p.* °jita; dinna°.

Tinker, *n.* tipukāra; lohabhaṇḍapaṭisaṅkhāraka, *m.* *v.t.* lohabhaṇḍāni saṅkharoti. *p.p.* saṅkhata°ḍa.

Tinkle, *n.* saṇana; jhanana, *nt.* *v.i.* saṇati; jhanati. *p.p.* saṇita; jhanita. °**ing**, *n.* kiṅkiṇināda, *m.*

Tinsel, *n.* jotamāna-tanuvaṅgapaṭṭa. *v.t.* jotamānapaṭṭehi alaṅkaroti. *p.p.* °kata.

Tint, *n.* vaṇṇa; raṅga, *m.* rajana, *nt.* *v.t.* rañjeti. *p.p.* rañjita.

Tiny, *a.* atikhuddaka.

Tip, *n.* 1. agga; sikhara, *nt.* koṭi, *f.* 2. pāritosika, *nt.* 3. mandākoṭana, *nt.* *v.t.* 1. mandam ākoṭeti; 2. poṇaŋ karoti; 3. pāritosikaŋ deti. *p.p.* °ṭita; poṇīkata; dinnapā°. °**ster**, *n.* assadhāvanapavattiñāpaka, *m.*

Tippet, *n.* uttarāsaṅgavisesa, *m.*

Tipple, *n.* tikhiṇamajja, *nt.* *v.i.t.* niccaŋ majjaŋ pivati. *p.p.* °pītamajja. °**er**, *n.* surādhutta, *m.*

Tipsy, *a.* surāmatta. °**ily**, *adv.* mattākārena. °**iness**, *n.* surāmattatā, *f.* surāmada, *m.*

Tiptoe, *n.* pādagga, *nt.* papada, *m.* *v.i.* pādaggena yāti.

Tiptop, *a.* visiṭṭhatama.

Tirade, *n.* dīghopārambhakathā, *f.*

Tire, *v.t.* āyāseti; kilameti. *v.i.* kilamati. *p.p.* °sita; °mita; kilanta. °**some**, *a.* āyāsakara. °**less**, *a.* akilanta.

Tire, *n.* 1. cakkanemi, *f.* 2. uṇhīsa; siroveṭhana, *nt.* *v.t.* nemiŋ yojeti. *p.p.* nemiyojita.

Tiro, Tyro, *n.* ādhunika, *m.*

Tissue, *n.* tanupaṭṭaka, *nt.*

Tit, *n.* 1. khuddakavatthu, *nt.* 2. paṭipahāra, *m.*

Titan, *n.* dānava; mahākāya; mahāthāma, *m.*

Titbit, *n.* madhura-khajjaka, *nt.*

Tithe, *n.* dasamabhāga, *m.* dasama bhāgika-bali, *m.* *v.t.* dasabhāgikabaliŋ gaṇhāti. *p.p.* gahitadasa°.

Titillate, *v.t.* patudati. *p.p.* °dita. °**ion**, *n.* aṅgulipatodana, *nt.*

Titivate, *v.t.i.* maṇḍeti; pasādheti. *p.p.* °ḍita; °dhita.

Title, *n.* 1. upādhi, *nt.* 2. adhikāra, *m.* 3. abhidhāna, *nt.* *v.t.* abhidhānaŋ ṭhapeti. *p.p.* ṭhapitābhidhāna. — **deed**, *n.* adhikāra-paṇṇa, *nt.* — **page**, *n.* pamukhapaṇṇa, *nt.*

Titter, *n.* mandahāsa, *m.* *v.i.* mandasaddena hasati. *p.p.* °hasita.

Tittle, *n.* appamattaka, *nt.* °**tattle**, *n.* samphappalāpa, *m.*

Titular, *a.* upādhimattaka.

To, *prep.* Expressed by Dat. *or* Suffix **tun** e.g. **To him**, tassa. **To go**, gantuŋ.—**wit**, yad' idaŋ. — **and fro**, ito c'ito.

Toad, *n.* maṇḍūka; bheka, *m.* °**eater**, *n.* cāṭukārī, *m.* °**stool**, ahicchattaka, *nt.*

Toady, *n.* parāyattavutti, *m.* *v.t.* ullapati; param ukkaŋseti. *p.p.* °pita; °sita. °**ism**, *n.* cāṭukamyatā, *f.*

Toast, *n.* 1. uttaribhaṅga, *m.* 2. thuticuṇṇikā, *f.* *v.t.* 1. bhajjati; 2. abhitthavati; subhāsaŋsanāya pivati; 3. avayave usumāpeti. *p.p.* bhaṭṭha; abhitthuta; °pīta; °pitāvayava. °**ing**, *n.* 1. bhajjana; 2. thomana, *nt.*

Tobacco, *n.* tamākhupaṇṇa, *nt.* °**nist**, *n.* tamākhuvāṇija, *m.*

Toboggan, *n.* himayānavisesa, *m.*

Tocsin, *n.* antarāya-ñāpakaghaṇṭā, *f.*

Today, *n. adv.* ajja.

Toddle, *n.* anipuṇagamana, *nt.* *v.i.* anipuṇākārena yāti.

Toddy, *n.* ambilasurā, *f.*

Toe, *n.* pādaṅguli, *f.* *v.t.* pādaṅgulīhi phusati *or* paharati. *p.p.* °phuṭṭha; °pahaṭa. **Great** —, pādaṅguṭṭha, *nt.*

Toff, *n.* 1. suvesī; 2. paññātapuggala, *m.*

Toffee, *n.* khajjakavisesa, *m.*

Together, *adv.* ekato; ekajjhaŋ.

Toil, *n.* parissama, *m.* kiccha, *nt.* āyāsa, *m.* *v.i.* yatati; vāyamati; āyāsena karoti. *p.p.* °kata. °**some**, *a.* āyāsakara.

Toilet, *n.* maṇḍana; pasādhana, *nt.* — **box**, *n.* gandhakaraṇḍa, *m.* — **powder**, *n.* vāsacuṇṇa, *nt.* — **stick**, *n.* añjanī, *f.*

Token, *n.* ciṇha; sārāṇīyavatthu, *nt.*

Tolerable, *a.* 1. sahanīya; 2. cirappavattaka. °**ness**, *n.* sahanakkhamatta, *nt.* °**ly**, *adv.* sayhākārena.

Tolerate, *v.t.* see **Endure**. °**rance**, °**ion**, *n.* adhivāsanā; khanti, *f.* khamana; sahana, *nt.* °**rant**, *a.* adhivāsaka; paramatasaha, *m.*

Toll, *n.* suṅka; kara, *m.* *v.t.* ghaṇṭaŋ vādeti. *v.i.* nadati. *p.p.*

vāditaghaṇṭa; °dita. °**able**, *a.* suṅkagāhiya. °**gate**, °**bar**, *n.* suṅkaṭṭhāna, *nt.* °**gatherer**, *n.* suṅkagāhaka, *m.* °**house**, suṅkaghara, *nt.*

Tom, *n.* pumpasu, *m.*

Tomato, *n.* takkālīphala, *nt.*

Tomb, *n.* susānathūpa, *m.* cetiya, *nt.* °**stone**, *n.* thūpasilā, *f.*

Tome, *n.* mahāpotthaka, *m. nt.*

Tomorrow, *adv.* sve; suve, *n.* dutiyadivasa; svātana, *m.*

Tom-tom, *n.* bheri, *f*, dundubhi, *m. v.i.* bheriŋ vādeti. — **beater**, *n.* bherivādaka, *m.*

Ton, *n.* bhāramāṇavisesa, *m.* (2,240 lb.).

Tone, *n.* 1. sara; nāda; dhani; 2. bhāva; āsaya, *m. v.t.* nādeti; vādeti. *p.p.* °dita.

Tongs, *n. pl.* saṇḍāsa, *m.*

Tongue, *n.* 1. jivhā; rasanā; 2. bhāsā; vāṇī, *f.* 3. ghaṇṭāpaharaṇī, *f. v.t.* jivhāya saddam uppādeti. °**less**, *a.* nijjivha. °**tied**, *a.* paṭisedhitakathana; kathāanipuṇa. **Hold one's —**, tuṇhī hoti. **Find one's —**, tuṇhī hutvā puna katheti.

Tonic, *n.* balavaḍḍhakosadha, *nt.* adj. balavaḍḍhaka. °**ity**, *n.* saṅkocana-pasāraṇakkhamatā, *f.*

To-night, *n.* ayaŋ ratti, *f. adv.* ajjarattiŋ.

Tonsil, *n.* galagaṇṭhi; galagaṇḍa, *m.* °**itic**, *a.* galagaṇḍayutta. °**litis**, *n.* kaṇṭhadāha, *m.*

Tonsorial, *a.* nahāpitāyatta; kesoropaṇāyatta.

Tonsure, *n.* matthakamuṇḍana; bhaṇḍukamma, *nt. v.t.* matthakaŋ muṇḍeti; kese voropeti. *p.p.* muṇḍitamatthaka; °pitakesa.

Too, *a.* adhika; accanta, *adv.* adhikaŋ; accantaŋ. *conj.* api; ca; c'eva. — **much**, atimattaŋ; ativiya, *adv.* — **soon**, atikhippaŋ, *adv.*

Tool, *n.* (kammakāra-) upakaraṇa, *nt. v.t.* pāsaṇe saṅkharoti. °**ing**, *n.* potthake mālākamma, *nt.*

Toot, *n.* kharasadda, *m. v.t.* kharasaddam uppādeti. *p.p.* °ditakhara°.

Tooth, *n.* danta; radana; rada; lapanaja; dasana, *m. v.t.* dante sampādeti *or* uppādeti. *p.p.* °ditadanta. °**ache**, *n.* dantasūla, *nt.* °**brush**, dantapoṇa, *m.* °**less**, *a.* dantarahita; galitadanta. °**pick**, *n.* dantasūci, *f.* °**relic**, *n.* dantadhātu; dāṭhādhātu, *f.* °**some**, *a.* surasa. °**somely**, *adv.* madhurākārena.

Tootle, *v.i.* nirantaraŋ nadati.

Top, *n.* 1. agga; sikhara, *nt.* matthaka, *m.* 2. bhamarikā, *f.* 3. pidhāna; 4. seṭṭhaṭṭhāna, *nt.* adj. aggeṭhita; sikharabhūta. *v.t.* 1. uggacchati; muddhani tiṭṭhati; 2. aggaŋ chindati; 3. pidhānaŋ yojeti; 4. sikharam āruhati. *p.p.* uggata; °ṭhita; chinnagga; yojitapidhāna; āruḷhasi°. °**hat**, *n.* unnatanāḷipaṭṭa, *m.* °**heavy**, *a.* uparigaruka. °**knot**, *n.* sikhā, *f.* °**most**, *a.* 1. uparitama; 2. atyucca.

Topaz, *n.* phussarāga (-maṇi), *m.*

Tope, *n.* thūpa, *m.* cetiya, *nt. v.i.* ativiya majjaŋ pivati. °**er**, *n.* atimajjapa, *m.*

Tophus, *n.* dehasandhisopha, *m.*

Topiary, *n.* gumbamaṇḍanasippa, *nt.*

Topic, *n.* visayakāraṇa, *nt.* mātikā, *f.* sīsapāṭha, *m.* °**al**, *a.* mātikāyatta. °**ally**, *adv.* visesakāraṇavasena.

Topography, *n.* 1. padesavitthāra-nirūpana; 2. dehakoṭṭhāsanirūpana, *nt.* °**pher**, *n.* ṭhānavitthāra-nirūpaka, *m.* °**phical**, *a.* padesavitthārāyatta.

Topper, *n.* matthakagāmī, *m.*

Topple, *v.i.* sikharato patati. *v.t.* sikharato pāteti. *p.p.* °tita.

Topsy-turvy, *adv.* viparivattaŋ; uddhapādaŋ.

Torch, *n.* ukkā; daṇḍadīpikā, *f.* — **of grass**, tiṇukkā, *f.* °**light**, *n.* ukkāloka, *m.*

Torment, *n.* abhipīḷana, *nt.* abhitāpa, *m.* kammakāraṇā, *f.* *v.t.* abhipīḷeti; abhitāpeti; vadheti. *p.p* °ḷita; °pita; vadhita. °**ing**, *a.* pīḷākara; hiŋsaka. °**or**, *n.* abhipīḷetu; vadhaka, *m.*

Tormina, *n.* udarasūla, *nt.*

Tornado, *n.* verambhavāta, *m.*

Torpedo, *n.* 1. amarāvisesa, *m.* 2. nāvānāsakayanta, *nt.*

Torpid, *a.* 1. apetasañña; visañña; 2. dandha. °**ity**, °**ness**, *n.* visaññitā, *f.*

Torpor, *n.* tandī, *f.* middha; līnatta, *nt.* °**ific**, *a.* anuttejanaka; līnattakara.

Torrefy, *v.t.* uṇhena sukkhāpeti; bhajjati. *p.p.* °pita; bhaṭṭha *or* bhajjita.

Torrent, *n.* 1. mahājalasota; 2. mahāmegha, *m.* 3. jaladhārā, *f.*

Torrid, *a.* gimhakalāpika; gimhādhika. °**ity**, *n.* gimhādhikatta, *nt.* — **zone**, *n.* gimhakalāpa; yugandharapabba, *m.*

Torsion, *n.* vyāvaṭṭana *nt.* °**sive**, *a.* vyāvaṭṭita.

Torso, *n.* kavandha-paṭimā, *f.*

Tort, *n.* aparādha, *m.* vajja, *nt.* °**ious**, *a.* sāparādha; hānikārī.

Tortile, *a.* vellita. °**ity**, *n.* vellitabhāva, *m.*

Tortoise, *n.* kumma; manthara; kacchapa, *m.* °**shell**, *n.* kacchapakapāla, *m.*

Tortuous, *a.* kuṭila; vaṅka; jimha. °**ly**, *adv.* jimhākārena.

Torture, *n.* kāraṇā; yātanā, *f.* vadha, *m.* *v.t.* 1. accantaŋ pīḷeti; kāraṇā kāreti; 2. vākyatthaŋ viparivatteti; 3. asammā yojeti. *p.p.* °ḷita; kāritakārana; °titavākya°; °jita. °**er**, *n.* kāraṇika; vadhaka, *m.* °**ous**, *a.* pīḷākara; hiŋsaka; vadhakara.

Tosh, *n.* kacavara, *m.* niratthakavatthu, *nt.* °**er**, *n.* anuyyogīsissa, *m.*

Toss, *n.* uddhaŋ-khipana; phandāpana, *nt.* *v.t.* uddhaŋ khipati; phandāpeti. *p.p.* °khitta; °pita. *v.i.* phandati; kampati. *p.p.* °dita; °pita. — **off**, ekavārena pivati. — **up**, upari khipati.

Tot, *n.* 1. khuddakavatthu, *nt.* 2. daharapuggala, *m.* 3. saṅkaletabba-gaṇanā, *f.* *v.t.* saṅkaleti; sampiṇḍeti. *p.p.* °lita; °ḍita.

Total, *n.* piṇḍitasaṅkhyā, *f.* adj. sakala; samagga; nissesa. *v.t.* sampiṇḍeti. *p.p.* °ḍita. °**ity**, *n.* sākalla, *nt.* paripuṇṇagaṇanā, *f.* °**ly**, *adv.* asesaŋ; nissesaŋ; sākallena.

Totter, *v.i.* pavedhati; jajjarāyati. *p.p.* °dhita; °yita. °**ing**, *a.* pavedhamana. °**ingly**, *adv.* sappavedhaŋ; sakampaŋ.

Touch, *n.* phusana, *nt.* phassa ; parāmāsa, *m. v.t.* phusati ; parāmasati. *p.p.* phuṭṭha ; parāmaṭṭha. °**able**, *a.* phusanīya ; āmasanīya. + **and go**, sāsaṅkāvatthā, *f.* °**ing**, *a.* hadayaṅgama. °**ing**, *prep.* uddissa ; adhikicca. °**ingly**, *adv.* hadayaṅgamākārena. °**stone**, *n.* sāṇa ; nikasa, *m.*

Touchy, *a.* sahasā kuppanasīla. °**iness**, *n.* sahasā kuppana, *nt.*

Tough, *a.* 1. kaṭhina ; dubbhejja ; thaddha ; 2. avidheya ; adamma ; 3. dukkara. °**en**, *v.t.* kaṭhinīkaroti. *p.p.* °kata. °**ish**, *a.* īsaŋkaṭhina. °**ly**, *adv.* thaddhākārena. °**ness**, *n.* thaddhatta, *nt.*

Tour, *n.* cārikā, *f.* desāṭana, *nt. v.i.* pariyaṭati ; desāṭanaŋ karoti. °**ist**, *n.* desāṭaka ; sañcārī, *m.*

Tournament, *n.* kīḷāyuddha, *nt.*

Tourney, *v.i.* kīḷāyuddhaŋ pavatteti. *p.p.* °titakīḷā°.

Tourniquet, *n.* dhamanitthambhaka-yanta, *nt.*

Touse, *v.t.* 1. parikaḍḍhati ; 2. asobhanaŋ karoti. *p.p.* °ḍhita ; °kata.

Tousy, *a.* ākulavyākula.

Tout, *n.* antaravāṇija, *m. v.i.* vāṇija-gāhakānam antare vattati. °**er**, *n.* vāṇija-gāhakamajjhavattī, *m.*

Tow, *v.t.* nāvaŋ rajjūhi ākaḍḍhati. °**line**, *n.* nāvākaḍḍhanarajju, *f.*

Toward, *a.* vidheya ; vineyya. °**ness**, *n.* vidheyyatta, *nt.*

Towards, *prep.* abhimukhaŋ.

Towel, *n.* udapunchanī, *f.*

Tower, *n.* aṭṭāla, *m. v.i.* uggantvā pavattati. °**ing**, *a.* unnata ; uggata.

Town, *n.* pura ; nagara, *nt.* nagarī ; purī, *f.* °**sman**, *n.* nagaravāsī, *m.* — **hall**, *n.* nagarasālā, *f.* santhāgāra, *nt.* °**let**, *n.* khuddakanagarī, *f.* °**ship**, *n.* nāgarikajanatā, *f.*

Toxic, *a.* visāyatta. °**ology**, *n.* visavijjā, *f.*

Toxin, *n.* rogahetuka-visa, *nt.*

Toxophilite, *n. a.* dhanusippābhilāsī, *m.*

Toy, *n.* kīḷābhaṇḍa, *nt. v.i.* kīḷati ; ramati. — **with**, upalālento tiṭṭhati. °**shop**, *n.* kīḷābhaṇḍāpaṇa, *m.*

Trace, *n.* 1. valañja ; padavalañja, *m.* 2. appaka-ciṇha ; aŋsumatta, *nt. v.t.* 1. valañjam anugacchati *or* anusarati ; gavesati ; 2. anusaṇṭhānaŋ sampādeti ; 3. thoka-thokaŋ vīmaŋsati. *p.p.* °anugata ; °saṭa ; °sita ; °ditānu° ; °sita. °**able**, *a.* gavesanakkhama.

Tracery, *n.* silāmaya-latākamma, *nt.*

Trachea, *n.* sāsanāḷa, *m.* °**al**, *a.* sāsanāḷāyatta. °**tomy**, *n.* sāsanāḷacchedana, *nt.*

Track, *n.* gatamagga, *m.* padavalañjāvali, *f. v.t.* anusarati ; padānupadikaŋ yāti. *p.p.* anusarita ; °yāta. °**less**, *a.* apada ; sañcārahīna.

Tract, *n.* 1. bhūmippadesa ; 2. laghu-gantha, *m.* °**able**, *a.* vidheya ; damma. °**ability**, *n.* vidheyatta, *nt.* °**ably**, *adv.* vidheyākārena.

Tractate, *n.* nibandha, *m.*

Traction, *n.* ākaḍḍhana, *nt.*

Trade, *n.* vaṇijjā, *f.* vāṇijja, *nt.* vohāra, *m.* *v.i.* vaṇijjaŋ *or* vohāraŋ karoti. °**er,** *n.* vāṇija, *m.* — **mark,** *n.* paṇyamuddā, *f.* °**sman,** *n.* āpaṇika, *m.* — **union,** *n.* kammanta-pūga; seṇī, *m.* °**wind,** *n.* nāvopakārīvāta, *m.*

Tradition, *n.* sampadāya; anussava; itihāsa, *m.* °**al,** *a.* pāramparika. °**ally,** *adv.* sampadāyavasena. °**al teaching,** vācanāmagga, *m.*

Traduce, *v.t.* abbhakkhāti. *p.p.* °khāta. °**er,** *n.* abbhācikkhaka; avaṇṇavādī, *m.*

Traffic, *n.* 1. gamanāgamana, *nt.* janasañcāra, *m.* 2. bhaṇḍavinimaya, *m.* *v.i.* see **Trade.** °**ker,** *n.* vāṇija; vohārūpajīvī, *m.*

Tragedy, *n.* 1. dāruṇasiddhi, *f.* 2. sokanta-nāṭaka, *nt.* °**ian,** *n.* sokantanāṭakayojaka, *m.*

Tragic, °**ical,** *a.* khedāvaha; dāruṇa. °**ally,** *adv.* dāruṇākārena.

Tragicomic, *a.* dukkhantasānanda. °**medy,** *n.* sokānandamissaka-nāṭaka, *nt.*

Trail, *n.* 1. anubaddhavatthu, *nt.* 2. anusaraṇapatha, *m.* *v.t.* 1. ābandhitvā ākaḍḍhati; bhūmiyam ākaḍḍhati; 2. gatamaggam anuyāti. *p.p.* °ḍhita; °anuyāta.

Train, *n.* 1. seṇī; mālā, *f.* 2. parivāra; 3. anukkama, *m.* 4. dhūmarathapanti, *f.* *v.t.* vineti; dameti; sikkhāpeti. *p.p.* vinīta; damita; °pita. °**er,** *n.* vinetu; dametu; sārathi, *m.* °**ing,** *n.* sikkhāpana; damana, *nt.* °**ing school,** ācariyasikkhāpanālaya, *m.*

Trait, *n.* visesa-guṇa, *m.*

Traitor, *n.* rājadubbhī; mittadohī; vissāsaghātī, *m.* °**ous,** *a.* dubbhaka; vissāsaghātaka. °**tress,** *n.* dubbhinī, *f.*

Tram (-car), *n.* vijjuratha, *m.*

Trammel, *n.* see **Fetter.**

Tramp, *n.* vaṇibbaka; vighāsāda, *m.*

Tramp, *v.i.* padasā carati. *v.t.* akkamati. *p.p.* °carita; akkanta. *noun* padasadda, *m.*

Trample, *v.t.* akkamati; maddati. *p.p.* akkanta; maddita. °**ing,** *n.* akkamana; maddana; mathana, *nt.*

Trance, *n.* 1. visaññitā; mucchā, *f.* 2. samādhi, *m.* *v.t.* moheti; vasīkaroti. *p.p.* mihota; °kata.

Tranquil, *a.* upasanta; aniñjana; nibbikāra. °**lity,** *n.* passaddhi; santi, *f.* upasama, *m.* santatta, *nt.* °**lize,** *v.t.* upasameti. *p.p.* °mita.

Trans-, *prep.* tiro; pāre.

Transact, *v.t.* sādheti; nipphādeti; anuṭṭhāti. *p.p.* sādhita; °dita; °ṭhita. °**ion,** *n.* 1. anuṭṭhāna; kicca, *nt.* 2. dānādāna, *nt.* °**ions,** *n. pl.* vijjādharasabhā-lekhana, *nt.* °**or,** *n.* kiccādhikārī, *m.*

Transcend, *v.t.* acceti; samatikkamati; samativattati. *p.p.* °kanta; °tita. °**ent,** *a.* atyuttama; atiseṭṭha. °**ental,** *a.* lokuttara; sabbātiga. °**entally,** *adv.* lokuttaravasena; sabbātigatāya.

Transcontinental, *a.* mahādīpantaragata.

Transcribe, *v.t.* paṭilikhati; puttikaŋ sampādeti. *p.p.* °khita; °ditaputtika. °**er,** *n.* puttikāsampādaka, *m.*

Transcript, *n.* paṭilipi; anulipi, *f.* °**ion,** *n.* paṭilikhana, *nt.* °**ional,** *a.* paṭilikhanāyatta.

Transfer, *n.* 1. ṭhānaparivattana, *nt.* 2. saṅkamanānuññā, *f. v.t.* aññaṭṭhānaŋ saṅkāmeti. *p.p.* °mita. °**able,** *a.* saṅkāmanīya. °**ence,** *n.* saṅkāmana, *nt.*

Transfigure *v.t.* vesaŋ parivatteti. *p.p.* °titavesa. °**ation,** *n.* vesaparivattana, *nt.*

Transfix, *v.t.* vinivijjhati. *p.p.* vinividdha.

Transform, *v.t.* rūpantaraŋ māpeti; ākāraŋ parivatteti. *p.p.* māpita°; °titākāra. °**ation,** *n.* rūpantaraparivattana, *nt.*

Transfuse, *v.t.* abbhantaraŋ paveseti. *p.p.* °sita. °**ion,** *n.* abbhantarappavesana, *nt.*

Transgress, *v.t.* aticarati; vītikkamati; vippaṭipajjati; ullaṇgheti. *p.p.* °rita; °mita; vippaṭipanna; °ghita. °**ion,** ullaṅghana; vītikkamana, *nt.* ajjhācāra, *m.* vippaṭipatti, *f.* °**or,** *n.* aticārī; ullaṅghaka, *m.*

Transient, *a.* anicca; aciraṭṭhitika; bhaṅgura. °**ly,** *adv.* aniccākārena; bhaṅguratāya. °**ence,** *n.* aniccatā; aciraṭṭhāyitā, *f.*

Transit, *n.* saṅkanti, *f.* saṅkama, *m.* aññattha-haraṇa, *nt. v.t.* tiriyaŋ yāti. °**ion,** *n.* saṅkamana; parivattana, *nt.* °**ional,** *a.* saṅkamanāyatta. °**ive,** *a.* saṅkamika: (In gram:) sakammaka.

Transitory, *a.* khaṇabhaṅgura. °**ily,** *adv.* addhuvatāya; aniccavasena. °**iness,** *n.* addhuvatta; athiratta, *nt.*

Translate, *v.t.* 1. anuvādeti; bhāsantaraŋ parivatteti; 2. viparivatteti. *p.p.* °dita; °tita. °**ion,** *n.* 1. anuvāda, *m.* bhāsāparivattana, *nt.* 2. aññathākaraṇa, *nt.* °**or,** *n.* anuvādī; bhāsantaraparivattaka, *m.*

Transliterate, *v.t.* aññakkharehi likhati. *p.p.* °khita. °**ion,** *n.* aññakkharehi likhana, *nt.*

Translucent, *a.* vinivijjha-dissamāna. °**nce,** *n.* pasannatta; vinivijjha-dissamānatta, *nt.*

Translucid, *a.* vimala; pasanna; pabhassara.

Transmarine, *a.* pārasāmuddika; samuddapāravattī.

Transmigrate, *v.i.* bhavantaraŋ yāti; saŋsāre saŋsarati. *p.p.* °yāta, °rita. °**ion,** *n.* bhavantaragamana, *nt.* saŋsāra, *m.* °**tory,** *a.* puna jāyamānaka; saŋsaranasīla.

Transmit, *v.t.* vyāpeti; gahetvā vissajjeti *or* peseti. *p.p.* °pita; °vissaṭṭha; °pesita. °**tal,** *n.* pesana; vyāpana, *nt.* °**ter,** *n.* vyāpaka; pesaka, *m.* °**mission,** *n.* vyāpana; pesana, *nt.* °**missive,** *a.* vyāpaka; pesanakara. °**missible,** *a.* vyāpanīya; pesanīya.

Transmogrify, *v.t.* iddhiyā vesaŋ parivatteti. °**ication,** sahasā-vesaparivattana, *nt.*

Transmute, *v.t.* dabbantaraŋ *or* vesantaraŋ parivatteti. *p.p.* °tita. °**ation,** *n.* vikatipāpana, *nt.*

Transparent, *a.* suppasanna; vinivijjha-passiya. °**ncy,** *n.* suppasannatta; vinivijjha-dissamānatta, *nt.* °**ly,** *adv.* atinimmalākārena; pabhassaratāya.

Transpierce, *v.t.* vinivijjha yāti; antopavisati. *p.p.* °yāta; °paviṭṭha.

Transpire, *v.t.* 1. lomakūpehi niggacchati; 2. pākaṭībhavati. *p.p.* °niggata; °bhūta.

Transplant, *v.t.* aññattha ropeti *or* patiṭṭhāpeti. *p.p.* °ropita; °pita. °**ation,** *n.* aññattharopaṇa; aññaṭṭhānapāpana, *nt.*

Transport, *n.* 1. aññaṭṭhānaharaṇa, *nt.* 2. accantapīti, *f.* 3. kopavega, *m.* *v.t.* 1. aññaṭṭhānaŋ harati; neti *or* pāpeti; 2. raṭṭhā nīharati *or* pabbājeti; 3. atipamodeti. *p.p.* °haṭa; °nīta; °pāpita °nīhaṭa; °jita; °dita. °**er,** *n.* bhaṇḍapesaka, *m.* bhaṇḍahārinī nāvā, *f.* °**able,** *a.* haraṇīya; aññattha nayanāraha.

Transpose, *v.t.* aññamañña-ṭhānavipallāsaŋ pāpeti. *p.p.* °pita. °**sal,** *n.* ṭhānavipallāsa; kamavipallāsa, *m.* °**ition,** *n.* vipallāsa, *m.* viparivattana, *nt.* °**itional,** *a.* vipallāsāyatta.

Transubstantiate, *v.* dabbaŋ vipallāseti *or* parivatteti. *p.p.* °sitadabba. °**ion,** *n.* dabbantaraparivattana, *nt.*

Transude, *v.i.* lomakūpehi niggacchati. *p.p.* °niggata. °**ation,** *n.* lomakūpehi niggamana, *nt.*

Transverse, *a.* *n.* tiriyaŋṭhita; tirobhūta. °**sal,** *a.* tiriyaŋ-patita. °**ly,** *adv.* tiriyaŋ.

Trap, *n.* adūhala; kūṭayanta, *nt.* *v.t.* adūhalena bandhati. *p.p.* adūhalabaddha. °**per,** *n.* adūhalika; vāgurika, *m.*

Trapan, see **Trepan.**

Trapes, *n.* dunnivasanā itthī, *f.*

Trappings, *n.* paricchada; kappana, *m.*

Trash, *n.* kacavara, *m.* *v.t.* pattādiŋ luñcati. *p.p.* °citapatta. °**y,** *a.* asāra; niratthaka.

Trauma, *n.* vaṇa, *m.* °**tic,** *a.* vaṇasahita.

Travail, *n.* pasavavedanā, *f.* *v.i.* pasūtivedanaŋ vindati.

Travel, *n.* pariyaṭana, *nt.* desacārikā, *f.* *v.i.* pariyaṭati; cārikaŋ carati. °**ler,** *n.* pathika; addhagū; desacārī, *m.* °**ling,** *n.* pariyaṭana; sañcaraṇa; addhānagamana, *nt.* cārikā, *f.*

Traverse, *a.* tiroṭhita. *v.t.* tiriyaŋ gacchati; tarati; atikkamati. *p.p.* °gata; tiṇṇa; atikkanta. (In law :) paṭikkhipati; paṭivirujjhati. *p.p.* °khitta; °viruddha. °**ly,** *adv.* tiriyaŋ; tiro.

Travesty, *n.* paralekhanānukaraṇa, *nt.* *v.t.* 1. paralekhanam anukaroti; 2. garukāraṇaŋ lahuttaŋ pāpeti. *p.p.* °kata; °pita.

Trawl, *n.* jāla; macchajāla, *nt.* *v.t.* jālena macche bandhati. *p.p.* °baddhamaccha. °**er,** *n.* 1. jālika, *m.* 2. macchagāhinī nāvā, *f.*

Tray, *n.* taṭṭikā, *f.*

Treachery, *n.* vissāsaghāta, *m.* dubbhana, *nt.* °**ous,** *a* dubbhaka. °**ously,** *adv.* dubbhanena. °**ousness,** *n.* vissāsaghātitā, *f.*

Treacle, *n.* ucchurasa, *m.* phāṇita, *nt.*

Tread (upon), *v.t.* akkamati; maddati; padaŋ nikkhipati. *p.p.* akkanta; °dita; nikkhittapada. *n.* padapāta, *m.* °**mill,** *n.* padapājita-yanta, *nt.*

Treason, *n.* rājadubbhana; kumantaṇa, *nt.* °**able,** *a.* rājadubbhanapariyāpanna.

Treasure, *n.* dhana; vitta, *nt.* vibhava, *m.* *v.t.* sañcināti; sambharati; nidahati. *p.p.* sañcita; sambhata; nihita *or* nidahita. °**er,** *n.* bhaṇḍāgārika; kosarakkhaka, *m.* — **pot,** *n.* nidhikumbhi, *f.* °**ry,** *n.* kosa, *m.* koṭṭhāgāra; dhanāgāra, *nt.* **Hidden —,** nidhi, *m.*

Treat, *n.* 1. sakkāra; saṅgaha, *m.* 2. parivesanā, *f.* 3. tikicchā, *f.* *v.t.* sakkaroti; saṅgaṇhāti. *v.i.* 1. ācarati; 2. paṭiññābandaŋ yāti; 3. tikicchati. *p.p.* sakkata; saṅgahita; °rita; °yāta; °chita. °**ment,** *n.* 1. sakkāra, *m.* 2. ācaraṇa, *nt.* 3. tikicchā, *f.* 4. nirūpanā, *f.* — **at length,** papañceti. — **kindly,** paṭisantharati. — **medically,** tikicchati. — **with,** samudācarati. — **with contempt,** avamāneti.

Treatise, *n.* nibandha; satthasaṅgaha, *m.* racanā, *f.*

Treaty, *n.* sandhānapaṇṇa, *nt.* saṅgara, *m.*

Treble, *a.* tiguṇa. *v.t.* tiguṇīkaroti. *p.p.* °kata.

Tree, *n.* rukkha; pādapa; viṭapī; duma; taru; sākhī; mahīruha, *m.* °**less,** *a.* apādapa; taruraahita. °**top,** *n.* dumagga, *nt.*

Trefoil, *a.* tiyaṅgulipattaka.

Trellis, *n.* gavakkhajāla, *nt.* *v.t.* gavakkhajālaŋ *or* dārujālaŋ yojeti. *p.p.* yojitadārujāla.

Tremble, *v.i.* pakampati; pavedhati; phandati. *p.p.* °pita; °dhita; °dita. °**ing,** *n.* kampana; phandana, *nt.* °**ing,** *a.* pavedhamāna. °**ingly,** *adv.* sakampaŋ.

Tremendous, *a.* atimahanta; atigaruka; bhayānaka. °**ly,** *adv.* atigarukatāya; bhayaṅkaratāya.

Tremor, *n.* santāsa; vepathu, *m.* kampana, *nt.* °**less,** *a.* akampa.

Tremulous, *a.* kampamāna; sacchambhī. °**ly,** *adv.* sappavedhaŋ; chambhitattena. °**ness,** *n.* chambhitatta, *nt.*

Trench, *n.* parikhā; digghikā, *f* *v.t.* 1. parikhaṇati; 2. parikhaŋ yojeti. *p.p.* parikhata; parikhāyojita. °**er,** *n.* 1. parikhāyojaka, *m.* 2. kaṭṭhabhājana, *nt.* °**er mate,** bhojanasahāyaka, *m.* — **upon,** akkamati.

Trenchant, *a.* tikhiṇa; mammacchedaka. °**ly,** *adv.* tikhiṇākārena.

Trend, *n.* poṇatta, *nt.* *v.i.* poṇībhavati. *p.p.* °bhūta.

Trepan, *n.* cakka-kakaca, *m.* *v.t.* 1. cakkakakacena chindati; 2. pamoheti; 3. pāsena bandhati. *p.p.* °chinna; °hita; pāsabaddha.

Trepidation, *n.* sampavedhana, *nt.* ubbega; saṅkhobha, *m.*

Trespass, *n.* nītyullaṅghana; yuttivītikkamana, *nt.* *v.t.* nītiŋ, yuttiŋ, *or* sikkhāpadaŋ ullaṅgheti *or* vītikkamati. *p.p.* °ghitanītika; vītikkantasikkhāpada.

°**er**, *n*. nītyullaṅghī ; aññāyappavesī, *m*.

Tress, *n*. alakā ; kesakuṇḍali ; kesarājī, *f*.

Triad, *n*. tika ; taya, *nt*.

Trial, *n*. anuvijjana ; abhiyuñjana ; upaparikkhana, *nt*. aṭṭavinicchaya, *m*.

Triangle, *n*. tikoṇaka, *nt*. °**gular**, *a*. tikoṇayutta. °**gulate**, *v.t.* tikoṇakaŋ karoti. *p.p*. °kata.

Tribe, *n*. gotta, *nt*. kulavisesa, *m*. gottaparamparā, *f*. °**al**, *a*. gottāyatta. °**alism**, *n*. gottāyattapālanavidhi, *m*.

Tribulation, *n*. 1. mahāvipatti, *f*. 2. balava-phandana, *nt*.

Tribunal, *n*. 1. vinicchayasabhā, *f*. 2. vinicchayāsana, *nt*.

Tribune, *n*. 1. mantikathikāsana, *nt*. 2. Roma-sacivasabhā, *f*.

Tribute, *n*. 1. suṅkapābhata, 2. thutipābhata, *nt*. °**ary**, *a*. 1. balidāyaka ; mahārajjavasavattī ; 2. upanadībhūta. *noun* : sākhānadī, *f*.

Trice, *n*. muhutta ; khaṇa, *m*.

Tricennial, *a*. tiŋsavassika.

Tricentinary, *n*. tisatavassa, *nt*.

Tricephalous, *a*. tisīsaka.

Trichiyasis, *n*. muttarogavisesa, *m*.

Trichogenous, *a*. kesavaḍḍhanaka ; aŋsuvaḍḍhanaka.

Trichord, *n*. titantika-vīṇā, *f*.

Trichotomy, *n*. (dehassa) tidhāvibhajana, *nt*.

Trick, *n*. kūṭopāya, *m*. nikati ; vañcanā, *f*. *v.t*. nikubbati ; vañceti. *p.p*. °bita ; °cita. °**ery**, *n*. sāṭheyya ; ketava, *nt*. °**ish**, *a*. vañcanasīla ; nekatika. °**ster**, *n*. kitava ; saṭha ; māyāvī, *m*. °**sy**, °**y**, *a*. kerāṭika ; nikatibahula ; kuṭilavuttī.

Tricolour, *n*. tivaṇṇadhaja, *m*. adj. tivaṇṇayutta.

Tricycle, *n*. ticakkaratha ; cakkattaya, *nt*.

Trident, *n*. tisūla, *nt*. °**ate**, *v.t.* tisūlayuttaŋ karoti. *p.p*. °kata.

Triennial, *a*. tivassika ; tivassavārika.

Trier, *n*. 1. ussahitu ; vāyamitu ; 2. anuvijjaka, *m*.

Trifid, *a*. tidhā-vibhatta.

Trifle, *n*. 1. parittakavatthu ; kiñcikkha, *nt*. 2. lahuka-kāraṇa ; asallakkhetabba, *nt*. *v.i.t*. lahukam ācarati ; na sallakkheti ; na gaṇeti. °**ing**, *a*. ittara ; oramattaka ; lahuka, agaṇetabba ; niratthaka. °**ingly**, *adv*. saparihāsaŋ ; lahuttāpādanena. °**er**, *n*. agarukārī, *m*. — **with**, avahasati ; avamaññati.

Trifoliate, *a*. tipattayutta.

Triform, *a*. tisaṇṭhānika.

Trifurcate, *a*. tisākhayutta.

Trig, *a*. suppasādhita. *v.t*. suṭṭhu pasādheti. *p.p*. °dhita.

Trigamy, *n*. 1. tibhariyatā ; 2. tipatikatā, *f*. °**mous**, *a*. 1. tipajāpatika ; 2. tibhattuka.

Trigonal, *a*. tikoṇaka.

Trigonometry, *n*. tikoṇamiti, *f*.

Trilateral, *a*. tibhuja ; tipassa.

Trilingual, *a*. tibhāsika.

Triliteral, *a*. tyakkharika.

Trillion, *n*. koṭippakoṭi, *f*.

Trim, *a*. suracita; paṭisaṅkhata ; susādhita. *v.t*. kappeti ; vibhūseti ; sobheti. *p.p*. °pita ; °sita ; °bhita. °**ly**, *adv*. sobhanākārena.

°**mer**, *n.* 1. pasādhaka ; kappaka ; 2. ubhayapakkhasevī, *m.* °**ming**, *n.* kappana, *nt.* °**mings**, *n. pl.* pasādhanūpakaraṇa, *nt.*

Trimonthly, *a.* temāsika.

Trine, *n.* tika, *nt.* *a.* tiguṇa ; tividha. °**al**, *a.* tividha.

Trinity, *n.* (pitu-putta-atta-) tika, *nt.* tividhākāra, *m.*

Trinket, *n.* appagghābharaṇa, *nt.*

Trinoctial, *a.* tirattika.

Trinominal, *a.* tināmika.

Trio, *n.* tivagga, *m.*

Trip, *n.* 1. cārikā, *f.* laghupariyaṭana, *nt.* 2. pakkhalana, *nt.* *v.i.t.* pakhalati ; khalitvā patati. *p.p.* °lita ; °tita. °**per**, *n.* pakkhalitu ; pamādabhāgī, *m.*

Tripartite, *a.* tibhāgayutta.

Triple, *a.* tividha ; tiguṇa. *v.t.* tiguṇīkaroti. *v.i.* tiguṇībhavati. *p.p.* °kata ; °bhūta.

Triplet, *n.* tivagga, *m.* tika, *nt.*

Triplicate, *a.* *n.* tiguṇa ; yāvatatiyaka. *v.t.* tiguṇīkaroti. °**ion**, *n.* tiguṇīkaraṇa, *nt.* °**city**, *n.* tiguṇībhāva, *m.* tivaggikatta, *nt.*

Tripod, *n.* tipāda-pīṭha, *nt.*

Tripudiate, *v.i.* pītiyā naccati ; jayapānaŋ pivati. *p.p.* °cita ; pītajayapāna.

Trisect, *v.t.* tidhā vibhajati. *p.p.* °vibhatta. °**ion**, *n.* tidhāvibhajana, *nt.*

Trisyllable, *n.* tyakkharapada, *nt.* °**bic**, *a.* tyakkharayutta.

Trite, *a.* niccopayutta ; abhiṇhappacārita ; atisāmañña. °**ly**, *adv.* nirasatāya. °**ness**, *n.* niccappayuttatā, *f.*

Triturate, *v.t.* sukhumaŋ cuṇṇeti. *p.p.* °ṇita. °**ion**, *n.* cuṇṇīkaraṇa ; piŋsana, *nt.*

Triumph, *n.* 1. jaya ; vijaya ; 2. vijayussava, *m.* *v.i.* jeti ; jināti. *p.p.* jita ; °**al**, *a.* vijayābaddha. °**ant**, *a.* jetu ; vijayī ; parājetu, *m.* °**antly**, *adv.* sajayaŋ ; vijayussavena.

Triumvirate, *n.* tiṇṇam ādhipacca, *nt.*

Trivial, *a.* see **Trifling**, °**ity**, appamattakatā ; agaṇetabbatā, *f.*

Trivium, *n.* tividha-sattha, *nt.* (i.e. vyākaraṇaŋ, takkasatthaŋ, alaṅkārasatthaŋ.)

Trodden, *p.p.* maddita ; akkanta.

Troglodyte, *n.* guhāvāsī, *m.*

Troll, *v.t.i.* 1. gāyati ; 2. balisena macche bādhati ; 3. cakkaŋ bhamāpeti. *p.p.* gīta ; °baddhamaccha ; °pitacakka.

Trolley, *n.* hatthavaṭṭaka-yāna, *nt.*

Trollop, *n.* gaṇikā, *f.*

Troop, *n.* 1. padāti ; patti, *f.* 2. yūtha ; gaṇa, *m.* 3. yuddhasenā, *f.* *v.i.* samosarati. *p.p.* samosaṭa. °**er**, *n.* assārohībhaṭa, *m.* —**ship**, *n.* senāhārakanāvā, *f.*

Trope, *n.* rūpakālaṅkāra, *m.*

Trophy, *n.* jayatthambha ; jayānussāraka, *m.*

Tropic, *n.* ayanāvaṭṭa, *m.* pl. yugandhara-pabba ; uṇhādhikadesa, *m.* °**al**, *a.* uṇhadesāyatta. —**of Cancer**, kakkaṭanivattana, *nt.* — **of Capricorn**, makaranivattana, *nt.*

Tropology, *n.* rūpakopamā, *f.*

Trot, *n.* sīghagamana, *nt.* *v.i.* mandaŋ dhāvati.

Troth, *n.* vissāsa, *m.* sacca, *nt.* **In** —, tathavasena.

Trouble, *n.* āyāsa, *m.* vyathā; pīḷā; duddasā, *f.* kasira; kiccha, *nt.* *v.t.* viheseti; upaddaveti; āyāseti. *p.p.* °sita; upadduta; °sita. °**ous**, *a.* duddasāpanna; kicchāpanna. °**some**, *a.* āyāsakara.

Trough, *n.* 1. ghāsadoṇī, *f.* 2. vīci-antara, *nt.*

Trounce, *v.t.* bāḷhaŋ tāḷeti. *p.p.* °ḷita.

Troupe, *n.* naṭagaṇa, *m.*

Trouser, *n.* nāḷīvasana, *nt.*

Trousseau, *n.* vadhukāvatthābharaṇa, *nt.*

Trow, *v.i.* maññati; saddahati. *p.p.* mata *or* maññita; °hita.

Trowel, *n.* sudhālepanī; pāṇikā; karaṇī, *f.*

Truant, *a.* *n.* kiccavimukha; palāyanasīla.

Truce, *n.* kālikasāma; yuddhavissāma, *m.*

Truck, *n.* 1. bhaṇḍavāhana, *nt.* 2. dabbavinimaya, *m.* *v.i.t.* 1. vinimeti; 2. kacchapuṭena vohāraŋ karoti. *p.p.* °mita; °katavohāra.

Truckle, *v.i.* dīnākārena vasībhavati. *p.p.* °bhūta.

Truculent, *a.* dāruṇasabhāva. °**nce**, *n.* dāruṇatta; caṇḍikka; niddayatta, *nt.*

Trudge, *n.* sāyāsa-gamana, *nt.* *v.i.* kicchena yāti.

True, *a.* sacca; tatha; yathābhūta; avitatha. — **friend**, kalyāṇamitta, *m.* °**ly**, *adv.* tacchato; yāthāvato; thetato. — **nature**, yāthāva, *nt.* °**ness**, *n.* avitathabhāva, *m.*

Truism, *n.* sammata-sacca, *nt.*

Truistic, *a.* saccasammata.

Trump, *n.* sappurisa; sujana; sādhujana, *m.* *v.t.* kūṭena jināti; vañceti. *p.p.* °jita; °cita.

Trumpery, *n.* niratthakavatthujāta, *nt.*

Trumpet, *n.* kāhala; dhamanavaŋsa, *m.* *v.t.* kāhalanādena viññāpeti. *p.p.* °pita. °**er**, *n.* kāhaladhamaka, *m.* — **flower**, pāṭalipuppha, *nt.* °**ting of an elephant**, kuñcanāda, *m.*

Truncal, *a.* khandhāyatta.

Truncate, *a.* aggacchinna. *v.t.* agge chindati. *p.p.* °chinna. °**tion**, *n.* aggacchindana, *nt.*

Truncheon, *n.* gadā, *f.* muggara; laguḷa, *m.*

Trundle, *n.* 1. āṇiyuttacakka, *nt.* 2. bhaṇḍavāhana, *nt.*

Trunk, *n.* 1. khandha, *m.* 2. ayopeḷā, *f.* 3. (— **of an elephant**:) soṇḍā, *f.* — **road**, mahāmagga, *m.*

Truss, *n.* palālaveṇī, *f.*

Trust, *n.* 1. saddahana, *nt.* vissāsa, *m.* 2. samappaṇa, *nt.* 3. pālakamaṇḍala, *nt.* *v.t.i.* 1. saddahati; vissasati; 2. samappeti. *p.p.* °hita; vissattha; °pita. —**deed**, samappaṇapaṇṇa, *nt.* °**ee**, *n.* āyuttaka; paradhanapālaka, *m.* °**eeship**, *n.* āyuttakadhura, *nt.* °**ful**, *a.* saddahanasīla. °**fully**, *adv.* vissāsena. °**less**, *a.* avissāsiya; asaddheyya. — **worthy**, *a.* saddheyya; paccayika; okappaniya. °**y**, *a.* saddheyya.

Truth, *n.* sacca; taccha; tatha, *nt.* °**ful**, *a.* saccavādī; saccasandha. °**fully**, *adv.* yathātathaŋ. °**fulness**, *n.* saccavāditā. °**less**, *a.* vitatha; asacca; musābhūta.

Try, *v.i.* 1. ussahati; vāyamati; parakkamati; yatati. *p.p.* °hita; °mita; parakkanta. *v.t.* 1. upaparikkhati; vīmaŋsati. 2. attaŋ vicāreti. *p.p.* °khita; °sita; vicāritaṭṭa. °**ing**, *a.* 1. parissamajanaka; 2. upaparikkhamāna. °**ingly**, *adv.* āyāsena.

Tryst, *n.* saṅketaṭṭhāna, *nt.* *v.t.* saṅketaŋ niyameti. *p.p.* °mitasaṅketa.

Tub, *n.* kaṭṭhabhājana, *nt.* *v.t.* kaṭṭhabhājane nahāpeti, °ropeti, °pakkhipati. *p.p.* °pita; °pakkhitta.

Tube, *n.* nāḷa, *m.* nāḷī; nāḷikā, *f.* °**ular**, *a.* nāḷākāra.

Tuber, *n.* kanda; āluva, *m.* °**ous**, *a.* sakandaka. °**cle**, *n.* kharapiḷakā, *f.*

Tuberculosis, *n.* kāsaroga, *m.* °**culous**, *a.* kāsarogātura.

Tuck, *n.* vali; vatthāvali, *f.* *v.t.* valīkaroti; valī yojeti. *p.p.* °kata; °jita.

Tuesday, *n.* kujavāra, *m.*

Tuft, *n.* gocchaka; thabaka, *m.* cūḷā; sikhā, *f.* °**y**, *a.* gocchakayutta.

Tug, *n.* ussāhenākaḍḍhana, *nt.* *v.t.* ussāhena ākaḍḍhati. *p.p.* °ḍhita. — **of-war**, rajjukaḍḍhana-kīḷā, *f.*

Tuition, *n.* sikkhāpana; ajjhāpana, *nt.* °**al**, *a.* ajjhāpanāyatta.

Tumble, *n.* 1. sahasā-patana; 2. uddhapādalaṅghana, *nt.* *v.i.* sahasā patati; pavaṭṭati. *v.t.* pavaṭṭeti; sahasā pāteti. *p.p.* °tita; °ṭita. °pātita. °**er**, *n.* pavaṭṭaka; laṅghaka, *m.* °**ing**, *n.* pavaṭṭana; pakkhalana, *nt.*

Tumefy, *v.i.* uddhumāyati. *v.t.* uddhumāyāpeti. *p.p.* °yita; °pita. °**facation**, *n.* uddhumāyana, *nt.*

Tumid, *a.* uddhumāta. °**ity**, *n.* uddhumātatta, *nt.* sopha, *m.*

Tumour, *n.* gaṇḍa; phoṭa.

Tumult, *n.* unnāda, *m.* ussāraṇā, *f.* °**uous**, *a.* unnādasahita; avupasanta; saṅkhubhita. °**uously**, *adv.* saṅkhubhitatāya.

Tune, *n.* laya; ninnāda, *m.* *v.t.* turiyabhaṇḍaŋ sajjeti; sussaraŋ karoti. *p.p.* °jitaturiya°; °kata. °**er**, *n.* turiyarāgasādhaka, *m.* °**ful**, *a.* madhurasarayutta. °**less**, *a.* amadhurassara.

Tunic, *n.* nivāsana-coḷa, *nt.*

Tunnel, *n.* ummagga; bhūmyantomagga, *m.*

Tup, *n.* meṇḍa; urabbha, *m.*

Turban, *n.* siroveṭhana; sīsaveṭhana, *nt.*

Turbid, *a.* āvila; lulita. °**ity**, *n.* āvilatta, *nt.* °**ly**, *adv.* āvilākārena.

Turbinate, *a.* bhamarikākāra.

Turbulent, *a.* saṅkhubhita; aticañcala; dāmarika. °**nce**, *n.* saṅkhobha, *m.* °**ly**, *adv.* saṅkhubhitākārena.

Turd, *n.* gomaya-piṇḍa, *m.*

Tureen, *n.* gambhīra-sūpathāli, *f.*

Turf, *n.* saddalabhūmi, *f.* *v.t.* saddalapiṇḍehi chādeti. *p.p.* °dita.

Turgid, *a.* uddhumāta. °**ity**, *n.* uddhumātatta, *nt.*

Turk, *n.* Turukkhadesīya, *m.* °**ey**, *n.* 1. Turukkhadesa, *m.* 2. mahākukkuṭavisesa, *m.* °**ish**, *a.* Turukkhajātyāyatta.

Turmeric, *n.* haḷiddā; haḷiddī, *f.*

Turmoil, *n.* saṅkhobha; sambhama, *m. v.t.* saṅkhobheti. *p.p.* °bhita.

Turn, *n.* 1 vāra; pariyāya, *m.* 2. āvaṭṭana, *nt.* 3. avatthā, *f.* 4. vaṅkaṭṭhāna, 5. aññathā parivattana, *nt. v.t.* 1. parivatteti; paribbhameti; 2. aññathā karoti; 3. cundakammaŋ karoti. *v.i.* 1. parivattati; paribbhamati; 2. aññathā hoti; 3. abhimukhī bhavati. *p.p.* °tita; °mita; °kata; katacundakamma; °tita; °bhūta; — **about,** viparivattati. — **against,** virujjhati. — **aside,** 1. apakkamati; 2. apaneti. — **away,** durīkaroti. — **back,** parāvattati; parāvatteti. — **down,** paṭikkhipati. — **into,** pāpeti. — **into money,** mūlaŋ nipphādeti. — **off,** 1. apasāreti; 2. pidahati. — **out,** nikkaḍḍhati. — **over,** āvajjeti; parivatteti. — **round,** anuparivattati. — **towards,** abhimukhī hoti. — **up,** *v.t.* ukkujjeti. *v.i.* pātubhavati; pākaṭībhavati. — **upon,** anapekkhito pahāraŋ deti. — **upside down,** paṭikujjeti. — **tail,** palāyati. — **turtle,** sabbathā adhomukhī hoti. — **a deaf ear,** nānukampati. — **one's back upon,** sevanaŋ cajati. **In** —, paṭipāṭiyā. **Out of** —, uppaṭipāṭiyā.

Turncoat, *n.* sapakkhacāgī, *m.*

Turner, *n.* 1. parivattetu; 2. cundakāra, *m.* °**y,** *n.* cundakārasālā, *f.*

Turnkey, *n.* kārāghara-kuñcikādhikārī, *m.*

Turnpike, *n.* maggasuṅkagāhaṭṭhāna, *nt.*

Turnstile, *n.* paribbhamanakadvāra, *nt.*

Turn-table, *n.* parivattiyavedikā, *f.*

Turpentine, *n.* sirivāsa; saraladdava, *m.*

Turpitude, *n.* 1. duṭṭhācāra *m.* 2. nīcatta, *nt.*

Turquoise, *n.* veḷuriya, *nt.*

Turret, *n.* niyyūha, *m.* °**ed,** *a.* niyyūhayutta.

Turtle, *n.* 1. kacchapa; 2. kapota, *m.*

Tusk, *n.* dāṭhā, *f.* °**er,** *n.* 1. dāṭhī; 2. sadāṭhahatthī, *m.*

Tussive, *a.* ukkāsanāyatta.

Tussle, *n.* kalaha, *m.* bāhuyuddha, *nt. v.i.* kalahaŋ karoti. *p.p.* katakalaha.

Tussock, *n.* 1. tiṇagumba; 2. kesakalāpa, *m.*

Tut, *intj.* dhī. *v.i.* dhikkaroti. *p.p.* dhikkata.

Tutelage, *n.* 1. bālārakkhā; 2. bālāvatthā, *f.*

Tutelary, *a.* ārakkhaka; pālakāyatta.

Tutenag, *n.* tuttha (-loha), *nt.*

Tutor, *n.* ajjhāpaka; ācariya, *m.* °**age,** *n.* ajjhāpana; sikkhāpana, *nt.* °**ess,** *n.* ācariyānī, *f.* °**ial,** *a.* ajjhāpanāyatta. °**ially,** *adv.* ajjhāpanavijjāvasena. °**ship,** *n.* ācariyapada, *nt.*

Twaddle, see **Prattle.**

Twain, *a.* yugalabhūta. *n.* yuga; yugala; dvika, *nt.*

Twang, *n.* ṭaṅkāra, *m. v.t.* jiyaŋ poṭheti; ṭaṅkāraŋ karoti. *p.p.* poṭhitajiya; kataṭaṅkāra.

Tweak, *n.* 1. vilikhana; 2. vegenākaḍḍhana, *nt. v.t.* 1. vilikhati; 2. vegena ākaddhati. *p.p.* °khita; °ḍhita.

Tweed, *n.* uṇṇāvatthavisesa, *m.*

Tweedledee, *n.* nāmamattakavisesa ; niratthakabheda, *m.*

Tweezer, *n.* saṇḍāsa, *m.* *v.t.* saṇḍāsena ākaḍḍhati. *p.p.* °ḍhita.

Twelfth, *a.* dvādasama.

Twelve, *a. n.* dvādasa.

Twenty, *n. a.* vīsati, *f.* °**five,** pañcavīsati, *f.* °**four,** catuvīsati, *f.* °**ieth,** *a.* vīsatima. °**nine,** ekūnatiŋsati, *f.* °**one,** ekavīsati, *f.* °**six,** chabbīsati, *f.* °**seven,** sattavīsati, *f.* °**three,** tevīsati, *f.* °**two,** bāvīsati ; dvevīsati ; dvāvīsati, *f.*

Twice, *adv.* dvikkhattuŋ ; dve vāre. °**born,** *a.* dija.

Twiddle, *v.i.* 1. mudhā kālaŋ khepeti ; 2. lahuŋ ākoṭeti. *p.p.* °pita ; °ṭita.

Twig, *n.* pasākhā, *f.* *v.t.* upaparikkhati; vijānāti. *p.p.* °khita; viññāta.

Twilight, *n.* padosa ; sañjhāloka, *m.*

Twin, *a.* yamaka ; yugalabhūta. *n.* yuga ; yugala, *nt.* *v.t.* yuganaddhaŋ karoti. *p.p.* °kata.

Twine, *n.* sutta ; tanta, *nt.* tantu, *m.* *v.t.* 1. veṭheti ; 2. suttaŋ santāneti. *p.p.* °ṭhita ; °nitasutta.

Twinge, *n.* tibbavedanā, *f.* *v.t.* tibbavedanaŋ uppādeti. *p.p.* °ditatibba°.

Twinkle, *n.* 1. taralajjuti, *f.* akkhinimesa, *m.* *v.i.* 1. taralaŋ dippati ; 2. ummesa-nimesaŋ karoti. °**ing,** *n.* 1. nimesa, *m.* 2. ujjalana. °**ing,** *a.* jotamāna.

Twirl, *n.* turitaparibbhamaṇa, *nt.* *v.i.* sīghaŋ paribbhamati. *v.t.* turitaŋ paribbhameti. *p.p.* °bhanta ; °mita.

Twist, *n.* veṭhana ; vyāvaṭṭana ; onahana ; vinandhana, *nt.* *v.t.* veṭheti ; vinandhati ; vyāvaṭṭeti ; onayhati. *p.p.* °ṭhita ; vinaddha ; °ṭita ; onaddha. — **over,** āveṭheti. °**er,** *n.* 1. veṭhaka, *m.* 2. vyāvaṭṭanayanta, *nt.*

Twit, *v.t.* paribhāsati ; upavadanto akkosati. *p.p.* °sita ; akkuṭṭha. °**tingly,** *adv.* sopārambhaŋ.

Twitch, *n.* sahasākaḍḍhana, *nt.* *v.t.* sahasā ākaḍḍhati. *p.p.* °ḍhita.

Twitter, *n.* cicciṭāyana, *nt.* *v.i.* cicciṭāyati. *v.t.* ciṭiciṭisaddaŋ pavatteti. *p.p.* °yita ; °tita-°sadda.

Two, *a. n.* dvi. — **and a half,** aḍḍhateyya, *nt.* — **days,** dvīha, *nt.* — **edged,** *a.* ubhatodhārāyutta. — **faced,** *a.* ubhatomukha. °**fold,** *a.* diguṇa ; duvidha. °**folded,** *a.* dupaṭṭa. °**foldness,** *n.* dvebhāva, *m.* — **inches,** dvaṅgula, *nt.* **In — ways,** dvidhā, *adv.*

Tyke, *n.* 1. sunakha ; 2. adhama, *m.*

Tylosis, *n.* pakhumadāha, *m.*

Tympanum, *n.* kaṇṇabheri, *f.*

Type, *n.* 1. ākāra, *m.* saṇṭhāna, *nt.* 2. muddākkhara, *nt.* *v.t.* lipiyantena muddāpeti. *p.p.* °pita. °**ify,** *v.t.* 1. paṭirūpena dasseti ; 2. nidassitabbaŋ karoti. °**foundry,** *n.* muddākkhara-sampādanaṭṭhāna, *nt.* °**ist,** *n.* lipiyantasāraka, *m.* °**writer,** *n.* lipiyanta, *nt.*

Typhoid, *n.* sannipātikajara, *m.*

Typhoon, *n.* sāhasikavāta, *m.*

Typhus, *n.* balava-sannipātajara, *m.*

Typical, *a.* nidassanabhūta. °**ly,** *adv.* pākatikavasena.

Typography, *n.* muddaṅkaṇa-sippa, *nt.*

Tyranny, *n.* pajāpīḷana; niṭṭhura-pālana, *nt.* °**ical,** *a.* niṭṭhura-pālanāyatta. °**ically,** *adv.* pajā-pīlakākārena. °**ize,** *v.t.* pasayha sāsati. °**icide,** *n.* pajāpiḷaka-ghātana, *nt.* °**nous,** *a.* pasayha-kārī; kurūrasāsana.

Tyrant, *n.* adhammikarāja; niṭ-ṭhurapālaka, *m.*

Tyriasis, *n.* sīpadaroga, *m.*

Tyre, *n.* cakkanemi, *f.*

Tyro, *n.* ādhunika, *m.*

U

Ubiquity, *n.* sabbavyāpitā, *f.* °**tous,** *a.* sabbatthavattī; sabba-vyāpī.

Udder, *n.* thanapuñja, *m.*

Udometer, *n.* meghamāṇaka-yanta, *nt.*

Ugly, *a.* 1. virūpa; duddasika; 2. kucchita. °**iness,** virūpatta; dubbaṇṇatta, *nt.*

Ulcer, *n.* vaṇa; aru, *m.* °**ate,** *v.t.* vaṇam uppādeti. *v.i.* vaṇīyati. *p.p.* °ditavaṇa; °yita. °**ation,** *n.* vaṇajanana, *nt.* °**ous,** *a.* vaṇapīlita.

Uliginose, *a.* sakaddamabhūmi-jāta.

Ulotrichous, *a.* uṇṇopamaloma-yutta.

Ulterior, *a.* 1. dūraṭṭha; 2. adis-samāna.

Ultimate, *a.* antima; carima. °**ly,** *adv.* ante; pariyosāne. °**imo,** *adv.* gatamāse. °**tum,** *n.* osā-nanivedana, *nt.*

Ultra, *prep.* ati; adhi. °**marine,** *a.* samuddapāraṭṭha, °**mun-dane,** *a.* lokuttara; lokātīta. °**violet,** *a.* adhikapāṭalavaṇṇa.

Ululate, *v.i.* ubbhukkati.

Umbel, *n.* chattākārapuppha-mañjarī, *f.*

Umbilical, *a.* nābhinissita.

Umblicus, *n.* nābhi, *f.*

Umbra, *n.* paṭhavīchāyā, *f.*

Umbrage, *n.* 1. asantuṭṭhi, 2. pattacchāyā, *f.* °**ous,** *a.* chāyā-sahita.

Umbrella, *n.* chatta; ātapatta, *nt.*

Umpire, *n.* pamāṇapurisa; niṇ-ṇetu; majjhaṭṭha. *v.i.* niṇṇeti. *p.p.* niṇṇita. °**ship,** *n.* niṇṇe-tubhāva, *m.*

Un, *prep.* Expressed by **a**- before consonants and **an**- before vo-wels; occasionally by **ni** or **vi,** e.g **aroga, anāmaya,** healthy. **Nitteja,** powerless. **Viraja,** passionless.

Unabated, *a.* anūna; aparihīna.

Unable, *a.* abhabba; asamattha; asakkonta. —**to bear,** asayha, *a.*

Unabridged, *a.* asaṅkhitta.

Unacceptable, *a.* asampaṭicchiya.

Unaccommodating, *a.* paṭisan-thāra-rahita.

Unaccountable, *a.* agaṇetabba; avitthāriya.

Unaccredited, *a.* abahumata.

Unaccustomed, *a.* aparicita; anipuṇa.

Unacquainted, *a.* asañjānanaka; asanthuta.

Unadorned, *a.* analaṅkata; am-aṇḍita.

Unaffected, *a*. 1. akampita ; 2. akittima ; adūsita ; pākatika.

Unagreeable, *a*. appiya ; amanāpa ; anabhimata.

Unaided, *a*. asahāya ; anupatthambha.

Unalienable, *a*. anaññasantakakaraṇīya.

Unalterable, *a*. anaññathākaraṇīya. °**ly**, *adv*. aviparivattiyatāya.

Unambiguous, *a*. advelhaka ; anāsaṅkiya ; visada.

Unambitious, *a*. anunnatikāma.

Unamiable, *a*. appiyasabhāva.

Unanimated, *a*. aviññāṇaka.

Unanimous, *a*. ekamatika ; avibhattamatika. °**ly**, *adv*. ekamatikatāya. °**mity**, *n*. ekamatikatā, *f*.

Unanswerable, *a*. niruttara ; avissajjiya ; appaṭivacanīya.

Unanticipated, *a*. anapekkhita.

Unappealable, *a*. uttarādhikaraṇaŋ anāharitabba ; apaṭikkosiya.

Unappeased, *a*. avupasamita.

Unapprised, *a*. puretaraŋ aviññāpita.

Unapproachable, *a*. anupasaṅkamiya ; durāsada.

Unappropriate, *a*. ananucchavika ; appatirūpa.

Unapproved, *a*. ananuññāta ; ananumata.

Unapt, *a*. asamattha ; anucita ; akammañña.

Unarm, *v.t*. nirāyudhaŋ karoti. *p.p*. °kata. °**ed**, *a*. asannaddha ; nirāyudha.

Unarrayed, *a*. asajjita ; paṭipāṭiyā ayojita.

Unascertained, *a*. anicchita ; avinicchita.

Unassailable, *a*. 1. duppasayha ; durāsada ; 2. ananuvajja.

Unassuming, *a*. avikatthaka ; anuddhata ; yathābhūta.

Unattached, *a*. nissaṅga ; anupādāna.

Unattainable, *a*. apattabba ; alabbhaneyya.

Unattempted, *a*. akatussāha.

Unauthentic, *a*. asaddheyya ; avissāsiya.

Unauthorized, *a*. anadhikata ; aladdhapaṭiñña.

Unavailing, *a*. niratthaka ; nipphala. °**ly**, *adv*. niratthakākārena.

Unavoidable, *a*. anivāriya ; ekantabhāvī.

Unaware, *a*. ajānanta ; anupaladdhika.

Unawares, *adv*. atakkitaŋ ; alakkhitaŋ.

Unawed, *a*. abhīta ; asantasita.

Unbaked, *a*. apakka ; arandhita.

Unbalanced, *a*. 1. ubhayasamattam apāpita ; asamabhārīkata ; 2. vikkhittacitta.

Unbar, Unbolt, *v.t*. vighāṭeti ; vivarati ; ghaṭikam apaneti. *p.p*. °ṭita ; vivaṭa ; apanītaghaṭika.

Unbearable, *a*. asayha ; akkhamanīya.

Unbeaten, *a*. aparājita.

Unbecoming, *a*. ananucchavika.

Unbefitting, *a*. ananurūpa ; anucita.

Unbefriended, *a*. asahāya ; sahāyarahita.

Unbegotten, *a*. sayañjāta.

Unbelief, *n*. asaddahana, *nt*.

Unbeliever, *n.* asaddahitu ; micchādiṭṭhika, *m.* °**ving,** *a.* asaddhahanaka ; assaddha.

Unbend, *v.i.* 1. parimuccati, 2. santhambhati. *v.t.* 1. parimoceti, 2. sithilīkaroti. *p.p.* parimutta ; °bhita ; °cita ; °kata. °**ing,** *a.* asithila ; anamya. °**ingly,** *adv.* avidheyyākārena.

Unbeseeming, *a.* ananucchavika; anucita.

Unbiassed, *a.* apakkhapāti ; agatirahita.

Unbind, *v.t.* bandhanaŋ moceti ; nibbeṭheti. *p.p.* °citaban° ; °ṭhita.

Unblamable, *a.* anavajja ; anupavajja ; agārayha.

Unblemished, *a.* akalaṅka ; niravajja.

Unblest, *a.* alakkhika ; aladdhāsiŋsana.

Unblown, *a.* apupphita ; mukulita.

Unblushing, *a.* ahirika ; nillajja.

Unborn, *a.* anuppanna.

Unbosom, *v.t.* savissāsaŋ pakāseti *or* pākaṭīkaroti. *p.p.* °sita ; °kata.

Unbound, *a.* abaddha ; mutta. °**ed,** *a.* asīmita ; aparicchinna ; ananta. °**edly,** *adv.* asīmitatāya; anantākārena.

Unbrace, *v.t.* ganṭhikaŋ moceti. *p.p.* mocitaga°.

Unbridled, *a.* uddāma ; adamma ; avidheya.

Unbroken, *a.* 1. abhinna ; akhaṇḍita ; 2. avicchinna.

Unbuilt, *a.* animmita ; akata.

Unburden, *v.t.* bhāram oropeti *or* nikkhipati. *p.p.* oropitabhāra ; nikkhitta°.

Uncalled, *a.* anāmantita. — **for,** *a.* anicchita ; anavassaka.

Uncanny, *a.* gūḷha ; rāhassaka.

Uncanonical, *a.* piṭakato bāhirabhūta.

Uncared, — **for,** asallakkhita ; arakkhita.

Uncase, *v.t.* kosato uddharati. *p.p.* °uddhaṭa.

Unceasing, *a.* nirantara ; abbocchinna ; sātatika. °**ly,** *adv.* nirantaraŋ ; avicchinnaŋ ; satataŋ.

Unceremonious, *a.* nirādara ; gāravarahita. °**ly,** *adv.* anādarena.

Uncertain, *a.* anicchita ; athira ; aniyata. °**ty,** *n.* vicikicchā, *f.* sandeha, *m.*

Unchain, *v.t.* bandhanā moceti. *p.p.* °cita.

Unchallenged, *a.* adassitavirodha.

Unchanging, *a.* nibbikāra.

Uncharitable, *a.* ananukampī ; adayāpanna. °**bly,** *adv.* niddayākārena.

Unchaste, *a.* kāmāsatta. °**ity,** *n.* kāmāsattatā ; abrahmacariyā, *f.*

Unciform, *a.* balisākāra.

Uncivil, *a.* asabbha ; avinīta.

Unclad, *a.* nagga ; anacchādita.

Unclaimed, *a.* 1. assāmika ; anāyatta ; 2. ayācita.

Uncle, (maternal :) mātula, *m.* (paternal:) 1. cūlapitu ; 2. mahāpitu, *m.*

Unclean, *a.* asuddha ; samala.

Unclose, see **Open.**

Unclouded, *a.* 1. vigatavalāhaka ; 2. vigatasaŋsaya.

Uncoil, *v.t.* bhoge nibbeṭheti. *p.p.* °ṭhitabhoga.

Uncomely, *a.* asobhana ; anucita.

Uncomfortable, *a.* aphāsujanaka.

Uncommon, *a.* asāmañña ; asādhāraṇa. °**ly,** *adv.* asāmaññatāya.

Uncommunicable, *a.* asambandhappavattika ; gamanāgamanarahita.

Uncomplaining, *a.* anujjhāyamāna.

Uncompleted, *a.* aniṭṭhita.

Uncomposed, *a.* asannihita.

Uncompounded, *a.* 1. amissita ; 2. asamāsita.

Unconcern, *n.* udāsīnatā ; upekkhā, *f.* °**ed,** *a.* upekkhaka ; asambandha.

Unconditional, *a.* apaṭiññābaddha. °**ly,** *adv.* paṭiññārahitatāya.

Unconfined, *a.* abādhita ; asambādha.

Unconfirmed, *a.* adaḷhīkata ; athirīkata.

Unconformity, *n.* ananuvattanatā, *f.*

Unconfused, *a.* avikkhitta ; samāhita.

Unconnected, *a.* visaŋsaṭṭha ; vippayutta.

Unconquerable, *a.* ajeyya ; ayojjha.

Unconscious, *a.* visañña ; mucchita. °**ly,** *adv* 1. visaññatāya ; 2. asañcicca. °**ness,** *n.* visaññitā ; mucchā, *f.*

Uncontested, *a.* vivādarahita ; appaṭipuggala.

Uncontrollable, *a.* adamma ; avasavattī. °**bly,** *adv.* adammākārena.

Uncontroverted, *a.* avivādita.

Unconventional, *a.* asammata ; apaññatta.

Unconverted, *a.* aparivattitabhattika.

Uncorrected, *a.* aparisodhita ; apaṭisaṅkhata.

Uncorrupted, *a.* adūsita.

Uncouple, *v.t.* viyojeti. *p.p.* °jita.

Uncouth, *a.* 1. apesala ; adakkha ; 2. duddasika ; asobhana.

Uncover, *v.t.* vivarati; avāpurati. *p.p.* vivaṭa ; °rita.

Uncreated, *a.* amāpita.

Uncritical, *a.* 1. avivecaka ; 2. vivecanaviruddha.

Uncrown, *v.t.* rajjā apaneti. *p.p.* °nīta.

Unction, *n.* vilepana ; abbhañjana, *nt.* °**tuous,** *a.* vilepana sadisa.

Uncultivated, *a.* akaṭṭha ; aropita ; akatakasikamma.

Uncurtailed, *a.* asaṅkhitta.

Undated, *a.* dinaniyamarahita.

Undaunted, *a.* abhīta ; anosakkita. °**ly,** *adv.* anosakkitākārena.

Undecayed, *a.* akhīṇa ; ajiṇṇa. °**ying,** *a.* akhīyamāna ; sassatika.

Undeceive, *v.t.* vibbhamam apaneti ; sammohato moceti. *p.p.* apanītavib° ; mocitasaṃ°.

Undecided, *a.* akatanicchaya.

Undefiled, *a.* adūsita ; akalaṅka ; nimmala.

Undefined, *a.* aparicchinna. °**nable,** *a.* aparicchedāraha. atīraṇīya.

Undemonstrative, *a.* gūḷhasabhāva ; asnehadassī.
Undeniable, *a.* apaṭikkhepanīya ; avivādiya ; nissandeha.
Under, *prep.* adho ; heṭṭhā ; oraŋ. adj. adhara ; adhoṭhita. °**bred,** *a.* asiṭṭha ; avinīta. °**buy,** *v.t.* ūnamūlena kiṇāti. °**current,** *n.* heṭṭhājalappavāha, *m.* °**estimate,** *v.t.* ūnamūlaŋ niyameti. °**fed,** *a.* asammāposita. °**garment,** *n.* antaravāsaka, *m.* °**growth,** adhovanagahana, *nt.* °**ground,** *a.* antobhummaṭṭha. °**hand,** *a.* gūḷha ; paṭicchanna. *adv.* raho. °**most,** *a.* atinīca ; adhotama. °**neath,** *adv.* adho; heṭṭhā. °**rate,** *v.t.* ūnagghaŋ niyameti.
Undergo, *v.t.* vindati ; anubhavati ; nigacchati ; paccanubhoti. *p.p.* °dita ; anubhūta ; °bhūta.
Undergraduate, *n.* upādhiapekkhī, *m.*
Underlay, *v.t.* adho ṭhapeti *or* nidahati. *p.p.* °ṭhapita ; °nihita.
Underlie, *v.i.* adho tiṭṭhati. *v.t.* adho patiṭṭhāpeti. *p.p.* °ṭhita ; °pita.
Underline, *v.t.* heṭṭhā rekhāya aṅketi. *p.p.* °aṅkita.
Underling, *n.* upajīvī ; anujīvī, *m.*
Undermine, *v.t.* 1. adho khaṇati ; 2. ummūleti. *p.p.* °khata; °lita.
Underplot, *n.* upakumantana, *nt.*
Under-secretary, *n.* upalekhaka, *m.*
Undersign, *v.t.* heṭṭhā hatthasaññaŋ yojeti.
Understand, *v.t.* bujjhati ; avagacchati ; vijānati. *p.p.* buddha; avagata ; viññāta. °**ing,** *n.* avabodha, *m.*
Undertake, *v.t.* ārabhati ; samādiyati ; sampaṭicchati. *p.p.* āraddha ; samādinna ; °chita. °**ing,** *n.* vyāpāra ; ārambha, *m.* kicca, *nt.* °**er,** *n.* anuṭṭhātu ; ārabhaka, *m.*
Undervalue, *v.t.* 1. agghaŋ hāpeti ; 2. lahumaññati ; avamāneti. *p.p.* hāpitaggha ; lahumata ; °nita.
Underwear, *n.* antovasana, *nt.*
Underwood, *n.* gumbagahana, *nt.*
Underworld, *n.* 1. adhobhuvana; pātāla, *nt.* 2. dhuttajana, *m.*
Undeserved, °**ving,** *a.* ananucchavika ; anucita.
Undesigned, *a.* atakkita ; appayojita.
Undesirable, *a.* appiya ; amanāpa.
Undetermined, *a.* anadhiṭṭhita ; aniyamita.
Undeterred, *a.* anolīna ; abhīta.
Undeveloped, *a.* abhāvita ; aparicita.
Undeviating, *a.* anuppathagāmī ; yathāmaggagāmī.
Undignified, *a.* asammānāraha ; bhaṭṭhayasa.
Undiminished, *a.* anūna ; paripuṇṇa.
Undiscernible, *a.* 1. avisada ; 2. adissamāna.
Undisciplined, *a.* avinīta ; asikkhita.
Undiscoverable, *a.* apātukaraṇīya ; ananvesanīya.
Undisguised, *a.* aparivattitavesa ; ujujātika ; pakatibhūta.
Undisturbed, *a.* nibbikāra ; asaṅkhubhita ; nirākula ; aniñjita.

Undivided, *a.* avibhatta.
Undo, *v.t.* 1. apacināti ; 2. ummoceti ; ugghāṭeti ; 3. parāvatteti. *p.p.* apacita ; °cita ; °ṭita ; °tita. °**ing,** *n.* apacinana ; ummocana ; parāvattana, *nt.*
Undoubted, *a.* asaṅkita ; nissaŋsaya. °**ly,** *adv.* jātu ; kāmaŋ ; have ; ekantena.
Undress, *v.t.* nivāsanāni apaneti *or* omuñcati. *p.p.* apanītani° ; omuttanivāsana.
Undue, *a.* ayogga ; anucita.
Undulate, *v.i.* taraṅgāyati ; unnatonatiŋ pāpuṇāti. *p.p.* °yita ; °patta. °**ing,** *a.* taraṅgāyamāna. °**ion,** *n.* taraṅgāyana, *nt.*
Unduly, *adv.* aññāyena.
Undutiful, *a.* anassava ; avidheya.
Undying, *a.* amara ; sassata; anassara ; ajarāmara.
Unearned, *a.* anajjita ; asambhata.
Unearth, *v.t.* ukkhaṇati ; uddharati ; bilato uṭṭhāpeti. *p.p.* ukkhata ; uddhaṭa ; °pita. °**ly,** *a.* alokika.
Uneasy, *a.* 1. aphāsuka ; 2. cintākula ; 3. anupasanta. °**ily,** *adv.* aphāsukatāya. °**ness,** *n.* 1. aphāsukatta, *nt.* 2. ubbega, *m.*
Uneducated, *a.* asikkhita ; anadhīta ; appassuta.
Unemployed, *a.* akiccappasuta ; nikkamma.
Unequal, *a.* asamāna ; visadisa. °**ity,** *n.* vesamma ; visamatta, *nt.* °**led,** *a.* atulya ; anupama. °**ly,** *adv.* asadisākārena.
Unequivocal, *a.* asandiddha ; sugamattha.
Unerring, *a.* akkhalanasīla ; avirajjhamāna ; pamādarahita.
Unessential, *a.* anavassaka; amukhya.
Uneven, *a.* asama ; visama. °**ness,** *n.* visamatta, *nt.*
Unexhortable, *a.* avacanīya ; anovadiya.
Unexpected, *a.* anapekkhita ; asambhāvita ; pāsaṅgika. °**ly,** *adv.* pāsaṅgikavasena ; sahasā.; anapekkhitaŋ.
Unexplored, *a.* avīmaŋsita ; anuparikkhita.
Unexposed, *a.* avivaṭa ; paṭicchanna.
Unfailing, *a.* avirajjhamāna ; ekanta ; dhuva.
Unfair, *a.* asobhana. °**ly,** *adv.* asobhanākārena. °**ness,** asobhanatta, *nt.*
Unfaithful, *a.* vissāsaghātaka ; asaddheyya.
Unfamiliar, *a.* aparicita ; asanthuta.
Unfasten, *v.t.* ugghāṭeti ; omuñcati. *p.p.* °ṭita ; omutta.
Unfathomable, *a.* appameyya ; ameyya ; agādha.
Unfavourable, *a.* ananukūla ; paṭipakkha ; viruddha.
Unfeeling, *a.* niṭṭhura ; niddaya. °**ly,** *adv.* niddayākārena.
Unfeigned, *a.* akittima ; avyāja, akuṭila.
Unfelt, *a.* avindita ; ananubhūta.
Unfetter, *v.t.* parimoceti ; saṅkhalikāhi moceti. *p.p.* °cita. °**ed,** *a.* asaṅga ; abandhana.
Unfinished, *a.* aniṭṭhita ; asamāpita.
Unfit, *a.* ayogga ; akkhama ; asamattha ; anucita. °**ly,** *adv.* ayoggākārena. °**ness,** *n.* anucitatta, *nt.*

Unfledged, *a.* 1. ajātapakkha ; 2. apariṇata.

Unfold, *v.t.* pasāreti ; pattharati ; vitthāreti. *p.p.* °rita ; patthaṭa ; °rita.

Unforeseen, *a.* avitakkita-pubba; sahasāpatta.

Unfortunate, *a.* 1. alakkhika ; dubbhaga ; 2. asubha ; amaṅgala. °**ly,** *adv.* mandabhāgyatāya ; abhāgyena.

Unfounded, *a.* amūlaka ; ahetuka ; appatiṭṭha.

Unfriendly, *a.* duṭṭhasabhāva ; mettirahita.

Unfruitful, *a.* aphala ; vañjha.

Unfulfilled, *a.* anipphanna ; aparipuṇṇa.

Unfurl, see **Unfold.**

Ungainly, *a.* asobhana. °**iness,** *n.* asobhanatta ; virūpatta, *nt.*

Ungenerous, *a.* adānasīla ; niranukampa.

Ungentle, *a.* kakkasa ; pharusa. °**manly,** *a.* anuttamapurisāraha.

Ungifted, *a.* avisiṭṭhapakatika.

Ungodly, *a.* adhammika.

Ungovernable, *a.* anassava ; avidheya ; dubbaca ; uddāma.

Ungracious, *a.* khala ; duṭṭha ; sagguṇahīna.

Ungrateful, *a.* akataññū ; akatavedī.

Ungrounded, *a.* appatiṭṭha; ahetuka ; amūlaka.

Ungrudging, *a.* anujjhāyamāna.

Unguarded, *a.* arakkhita ; anārakkha.

Unguent, *n.* gandhavilepana ; añjana, *nt.*

Ungula, *n.* 1. khura ; 2. nakha, *m.*

Unhallowed, *a.* 1. asuddha ; 2. apujja ; 3. dhammadessa.

Unhand, *v.t.* hatthato vissajjeti. *p.p.* °vissaṭṭha.

Unhandy, *a.* anipuṇa ; adakkha. °**ily,** *adv.* anipuṇākārena. °**iness,** *n.* anipuṇatta, *nt.*

Unhappy, *a.* 1. dukkhita ; dubbhaga ; 2. dummana. °**ily,** *adv.* dubbhagatāya ; dukkhitākārena. °**iness,** *n.* dubbhāgya, *nt.* alakkhī, *f.*

Unharmed, *a.* anupahata ; anupadduta.

Unhealthy, *a.* 1. rogāvaha ; asappāya ; 2. akallaka ; ābādhika.

Unheard, *a.* assutapubba.

Unheeded, *a.* asallakkhita.

Unhesitating, *a.* nirāsaṅka.

Unhindered, *a.* apaḷibuddha ; abādhita.

Unhinge, *v.t.* visandhīkaroti ; vikkhipati. *p.p.* °kata ; vikkhitta.

Unholy, *a.* apūta ; amahanīya ; pāpiṭṭha.

Unhoped, *a.* anapekkhita.

Unhorse, *v.t.* assapiṭṭhito pāteti. *p.p.* °tita.

Unhouse, *v.t.* gehato nikkaḍḍhati. *p.p.* °ḍhita.

Unhurt, *a.* anupahata ; akkhata. °**ful,** *a.* ahiŋsaka ; aheṭhaka.

Unhusk, *v.t.* tace apaneti. *p.p.* apanīta-taca.

Unicorn, *n.* khaggavisāṇa, *m.*

Uniform, *n.* samānacchādana, *nt.* adj. sarūpa ; ekākāra. °**ity,** *n.* ekākāratā ; avisesatā, *f.* °**ly,** *adv.* ekarūpena ; ekākārena.

Unify, *v.t.* ekīkaroti. *p.p.* °kata. °**ication,** *n.* ekattapāpana, *nt.*

Unimpeachable, *a.* anupavajja ; niddosa.

Unimpeded, *a.* 1. nirantara ; abbocchinna ; 2. bādhārahita.

Unimportant, *a.* agarubhūta ; amukhya ; agaṇetabba.

Uninclosed, *a.* aparikkhitta.

Unincorporated, *a.* saṅgame anosārita.

Uninflated, *a.* 1. anuddhumāta ; avātapūrita ; 2. anuddhata.

Uninhabited, *a.* vijana ; aniviṭṭha.

Uninstructed, *a.* ananusiṭṭha ; asikkhāpita.

Unintended, *a.* anadhippeta.

Unintentionally, *adv.* asatiyā ; asañcicca.

Uninviting, *a.* amanohara.

Union, *n.* 1. sāmaggi; 2. saṅgati, *f.* saṅgama, *m.* °**ist,** *n.* saṅgamika, *m.*

Unipersonal, *a.* ekapuggalika.

Unique, *a.* adutiya ; asama ; seṭṭhatama. °**ity,** *n.* asamatta ; atyuttamatta, *nt.*

Unit, *n.* ekaṅka, *nt.* °**y,** *n.* ekībhāva, *m.* °**arian,** *n.* advittavādī, *m.*

Unite, *v.t.* 1. saṅgameti ; sandhāneti ; 2. sampiṇḍeti ; saŋyojeti. *p.p.* °mita ; °nita ; °ḍita ; °jita. *v.i.* ekībhavati ; samosarati. *p.p.* ekībhūta ; samosaṭa. °**dly,** *adv.* ekībhāvena.

Universe, *n.* sakala-lokadhātu, *f.* °**al,** *a.* sabbalokika °**ally,** *adv.* sabbaso ; sabbathā ; sabbavyāpitāya. °**ality,** *n.* sabbabhummatta, *nt.*

University, *n.* nikhilavijjālaya, *m.* mahāvijjāyatana, *nt.*

Univocal, *a.* 1. ekatthaka ; 2. ekalaya.

Unjoin, *v.t.* viyojeti ; visileseti. *p.p.* °jita ; °sita.

Unjudiciously, *adv.* ayoniso.

Unjust, *a.* adhammika. °**ifiable,** *a.* yuttirahita ; sāvajja. °**ly,** *adv.* ayuttiyā ; aññāyena.

Unkempt, *a.* appasādhita.

Unkind, *a.* niddaya ; akāruṇika. °**ly,** *adv.* niddayaŋ. °**ness,** *n.* niddayatta, *nt.*

Unknown, *a.* aviññāta ; avidita ; apākaṭa. °**wable,** *a.* aviññeyya.

Unlamented, *a.* asocita.

Unlawful, *a.* nītiviruddha ; aññāyānugata.

Unlearned, *a.* anadhīta ; asikkhita ; asippa.

Unless, *conj.* no ce ; yadi na.

Unlettered, *a.* anuggahitakkharasamaya.

Unlicensed, *a.* aladdhānumatika ; adinnokāsa.

Unlike, *a.* asamāna ; visadisa. °**ly,** *a.* asambhaviya ; saṅkitasiddhika.

Unlimited, *a.* asīmita ; aparimita ; ananta.

Unload, *v.t.* bhāram oropeti ; otāreti *or* nikkhipati. *p.p.* orpitabhāra ; nikkhittabhāra.

Unlock, *v.t.* ugghāṭeti ; vivarati. *p.p.* °ṭita ; vivaṭa.

Unlucky, *a.* 1. dubbhaga ; 2. asubha ; avamaṅgala ; ariṭṭha. °**ily,** *adv.* dubbhāgyatāya. — **day,** duddina, *nt.* — **period,** duddasā, *f.*

Unmake, *v.t.* apacināti ; nāseti. *p.p.* °cita; nāsita. °**ing,** *n.* apacaya, *m.*

Unmanly, *a.* bhīruka; kātara; porisahīna.
Unmannerly, *a.* avinīta; gamma.
Unmask, *v.t.* 1. pakatiŋ *or* sakavesaŋ pāpeti; 2. pākaṭīkaroti. *p.p.* °pāpita; °kata.
Unmatched, *a.* appaṭipuggala.
Unmeaning, *a.* attharahita.
Unmeat, *a.* ananucchavika.
Unmendable, *a.* appaṭisaṅkhariya.
Unmerciful, *a.* akāruṇika; niddaya.
Unmerited, *a.* anaraha; laddhum-ayogga.
Unmindful, *a.* pamatta; sativippayutta.
Unmistakable, *a.* apakkhalanīya; atipākaṭa.
Unmitigated, *a.* 1. aladdhasahana; 2. anūnīkata.
Unmixed, *a.* amissita; asaṅkiṇṇa.
Unmolested, *a.* avihesita.
Unmotherly, *a.* amātāraha.
Unmoved, *a.* acala; thira; nibbikāra.
Unmurmuring, *a.* ananutthunanaka.
Unnatural, *a.* apākatika; sabhāvaviruddha.
Unnecessary, *a.* anavassaka; nippayojana.
Unnerve, *v.t.* dubbalīkaroti; viriyaŋ hāpeti. *p.p.* °kata; hāpitaviriya.
Unnoticed, *a.* asallakkhita; avidita.
Unnumbered, *a.* ayojitaṅka.
Unobjectionable, *a.* avirujjhanīya.
Unobstructed, *a.* abādhita; anorudha; (of mind:) vinīvaraṇa.
Unoccupied, *a.* apariggahita; anadhivuttha.
Unoffending, *a.* ahiŋsaka.
Unofficial, *a.* anadhikārāyatta.
Unopposed, *a.* virodharahita; abādhita.
Unostentatious, *a.* nirahaṅkāra.
Unpack, *v.t.* puṭaŋ bhindati; bhaṇḍikaŋ moceti. *p.p.* bhinnapuṭa; mocitabhṇḍika.
Unpalatable, *a.* virasa.
Unparalleled, *a.* anupameya; atulya.
Unpardonable, *a.* akkhamanīya; akkhamāraha.
Unpatriotic, *a.* vigatasadesālaya.
Unperceivable, *a.* aphusanīya; apariññeyya.
Unperformed, *a.* asādhita.
Unphilosophical, *a.* ñāyaviruddha.
Unpitied, *a.* ananukampita. °**tying**, *a.* niddaya.
Unpleasant, *a.* amanohara; appiya; aniṭṭha.
Unpolished, *a.* amaṭṭhakata.
Unpolite, *a.* dubbinīta; avinīta.
Unpoluted, *a.* apūtibhāta; adūsita.
Unpopular, *a.* mahājana-appiya.
Unpractical, *a.* asādhiya; appaṭipajjanakkhama. °**tised**, *a.* aparicita; abhāvita.
Unprecedented, *a.* abhūtapubba.
Unprejudiced, *a.* apakkhapātī; agatirahita.
Unprepared, *a.* assajjita; asaŋvihita.

Unpretending, Unpresuming, *a.* nirahaṅkāra ; avikatthaka.

Unprincipled, *a.* durācāra ; vicārahīna ; ayathāvidhika.

Unproductive, *a.* aphaladāyaka ; asāra.

Unproficient, *a.* avyatta ; anipuṇa.

Unprofitable, *a.* aphaladāyī ; niratthaka.

Unprogressive, *a.* anabhivuddhigāmī.

Unpromising, *a.* saṅkanīya ; āsaṅkiyaphala.

Unprompted, *a.* asamuttejita ; anussāhita.

Unpropitious, *a.* aniṭṭha ; amaṅgala ; asubha.

Unproved, *a.* asādhita; asiddhantagata ; anidassita.

Unpublished, *a.* appakāsita ; muddaṇena apākaṭīkata.

Unpunished, *a.* adaṇḍita.

Unqualified, *a.* 1. asammata; 2. anipuṇa ; 3. akammāraha.

Unquestionable, *a.* apaṭipucchiya ; asaṅkanīya.

Unravel, *v.t.* vijaṭeti; viniveṭheti; nibbeṭheti. *p.p.* °ṭita ; °ṭhita.

Unread, *a.* apaṭhita ; avācita.

Unready, *a.* asajjita ; aturita ; anucita.

Unreal, *a.* atatha ; ataccha ; asāra.

Unreason, *n.* mūḷhatta, *nt.* °able, *a.* abuddhigocara ; ayathābhūta ; aṭṭhānocita.

Unrecognizable, *a.* avijāniya ; dubbiññeyya.

Unrecommended, *a.* appasattha; asampaṭicchita.

Unrecorded, *a.* alikhita ; potthakānārūḷha.

Unredeemed, *a.* appaṭimocita.

Unrefined, *a.* 1. aparisodhita ; 2. avinītācāra.

Unregarded, *a.* agaṇita ; asallakkhita.

Unregenerate, *a.* appaṭisaṅkhata ; aparivattitasabhāva.

Unregretted, *a.* ananutāpī; apacchātāpī.

Unrejoicing, *a.* asammodamāna; anabhirata.

Unrelated, *a.* 1. aññātaka ; 2. asambandha.

Unrelenting, *a.* ananukampaka ; thaddhacitta ; niddaya.

Unreliable, *a.* asaddheyya.

Unremembered, *a.* vissarita ; pamuṭṭha.

Unremitting, *a.* avicchinna ; ahāyamāna ; nirantara.

Unremovable, *a.* acāliya ; thāvara.

Unrequited, *a.* aladdhaphala ; adinnahānika.

Unreserved, *a.* 1. asesita ; avisesita ; nissesa ; 2. pākaṭa.

Unresisted, *a.* adassitavirodha.

Unrest, *n.* anupasama ; āyāsa, *m.*

Unrestrained, *a.* asaŋyata ; adanta ; aniggahita.

Unrestricted, *a.* asīmita ; aparicchinna ; asambādha.

Unrighteous, *a.* adhammika; pāpiṭṭha.

Unripe, *a.* apakka; apariṇata; āmaka.

Unrivalled, *a.* atulya; appaṭipuggala ; appaṭisama.

Unrobe, *v.t.* cīvaram apaneti. *p.p.* apanītacīvara.

Unroll, *v.t.* pasāreti; nibbeṭheti. *p.p.* °rita ; °ṭhita.

Unroof, *v.t.* chadanam apaneti. *p.p.* apanītachadana.
Unroot, *v.t.* uddharati; ummūleti. *p.p.* uddhaṭa ; °lita.
Unruly, *a.* avidheya ; anassava ; dubbaca. °**iness**, *n.* avidheyatta ; dovacassa, *nt.*
Unsafe, *a.* saupaddava ; anārakkha ; sappaṭibhaya. °**ly**, *adv.* anārakkhaŋ ; sappaṭibhayaŋ.
Unsaintly, *a.* assamaṇāraha.
Unsaleable, *a.* avikkeyya.
Unsatisfactory, *a.* apariyattikara ; atuṭṭhijanaka. °**fied**, *a.* atitta ; appatīta.
Unsavoury, *a.* virasa ; asādurasa.
Unscrupulous, *a.* akukkuccaka ; asikkhāgaruka.
Unseal, *v.t.* lañchanam apaneti ; vivarati. *p.p.* apanītalañchana; vivaṭa.
Unsearchable, *a.* gavesitum asakya ; gūḷha.
Unseasonable, *a.* akālocita ; asāmayika.
Unseat, *v.t.* āsanā *or* ṭhānā uṭṭhāpeti *or* apaneti. *v.i.* ṭhānā cavati. *p.p.* °pita ; °apanīta ; °cuta.
Unseemly, *a.* ananucchavika ; asobhana.
Unseen, *a.* adiṭṭha ; adissamāna.
Unselfish, *a.* amāmaka ; paratthakāmī ; parahitakārī.
Unsentimental, *a.* akampiyasabhāva.
Unserviceable, *a.* akiccappayogāraha ; anupayogga.
Unsettle, *v.t.* khobheti ; ākulīkaroti. *p.p.* °bhita ; °kata.
Unsew, *v.t.* visibbeti ; sibbanam apaneti. *p.p.* °bita ; apanītasibbana.
Unshackle, *v.t.* saṅkhalikā moceti ; bandham apaneti. *p.p.* mocitasa° ; apanītabandhana.
Unshakable, *a.* akampiya ; avicāliya. °**ken**, *a.* akampita ; acala.
Unshapely, *a.* dussaṇṭhāna.
Unsheathe, *v.t.* ubbāhati ; kosato apaneti. *p.p.* °hita ; °nīta.
Unsheltered, *a.* aleṇa ; anārakkha ; agutta.
Unsightly, *a.* virūpa ; appiyadassana.
Unskilful, °**illed**, *a.* anipuṇa ; adakkha. °**ness**, *n.* anipuṇatta, *nt.*
Unsmeared, *a.* anupalitta.
Unsociable, *a.* na samājānucchavika. °**ness**, *n.* samājānucitatta, *nt.*
Unsoiled, *a.* amalina ; akalusita.
Unsolicited, *a.* anabhiyācita ; anārādhita.
Unsophisticated, *a.* avyāja ; akapaṭa ; adūsita.
Unsought, *a.* apariyesita.
Unsound, *a.* dubbala ; gilāna ; asāra.
Unsowed, *a.* avāpita ; aropita.
Unsparing, *a.* 1. amitavaya ; 2. akkhamanasīla.
Unspeakable, *a.* vācāvisayātīta ; vaṇṇanātikkanta.
Unspiritual, *a.* lokika; anajjhattika.
Unspoken, *a.* akathita.
Unspotted, *a.* 1. akalaṅka ; 2. asabala.
Unstable, *a.* athira ; addhuva.
Unstained, *a.* akalaṅka ; nimmala ; adūsita.
Unsteady, *a.* anavaṭṭhita ; capala ; cañcala ; lola.

Unstrained, *a.* 1. aparissāvita; 2. pākatika.

Unstudied, *a.* anuggahita; atakkita; anāciṇṇa.

Unsubstantial, *a.* nissāra; agayhūpaga; māyāmaya.

Unsuccessful, *a.* asamiddha; aphaladāyī; appattasiddhika. °**ly,** *adv.* nipphalākārena.

Unsuitable, *a.* anucita; ananucchavika; anupapanna. °**ly,** *adv.* asammā; ayathā.

Unsullied, *n.* niravajja; niddosa; akalaṅkita.

Unsupported, *a.* nirālamba; nirupatthambha.

Unsurpassed, *a.* niruttara; anabhibhūta. °**passable,** *a.* anatikkamiya; anabhibhavanīya.

Unsuspicious, *a.* nirāsaṅka; nibbematika.

Unswept, *a.* asammaṭṭha; asammajjita.

Unswerving, *a.* akampa; acala; thira.

Unsystematic, *a.* vidhiviruddha; akkamānuga.

Untainted, *a.* 1. adūsita; akalaṅka; 2. apūtibhūta.

Untamable, *a.* adamma; avineya.

Untamed, *a.* adanta; kūṭa.

Untaught, *a.* asikkhāpita.

Untenable, *a.* asamatthanīya; appaṭipādanīya; sādhanahīna.

Unthanked, *a.* anabhitthuta. °**kful,** *a.* athomanasīla; akataññū.

Unthinkable, *a.* acintiya.

Unthrifty, *a.* amitabbaya.

Unthoughtful, *a.* avīmaŋsaka; avicāraka.

Untidy, *a.* asobhana; malina.

Untie, *v.t.* ummoceti; ganṭhiŋ moceti. *p.p.* °cita.

Until, see **Till.**

Untimely, *a.* appattakāla; asāmayika; akālapayutta.

Untiring, *a.* akilāsu; anaṭṭhaviriya.

Unto, see **To.**

Untold, *a.* 1. avutta; 2. agaṇya; appameyya.

Untouched, *a.* anāmaṭṭha.

Untoward, °**ly,** *a.* 1. gabbita; dubbinīta; 2. asubha; abhaddaka; 3. anapekkhita.

Untrained, *a.* aparicita; akatupāsana; avinīta. — **horse,** assakhaluṅka, *m.*

Untried, *a.* anupaparikkhita; avicārita; avinicchita.

Untrue, *a.* asacca; atatha; vitatha. °**ly,** *adv.* micchā; vitathākārena.

Untrustworthy, *a.* apaccayika; asaddheyya.

Untruth, *n.* musā, *ind.* mosavajja; asacca; abhūta; alika. *nt.* °**ful,** *a.* musāvādī; asaccasandha.

Untwist, *v.t.* vijaṭeti; nibbeṭheti. *p.p.* °ṭita; °ṭhita.

Unusual, *a.* asātatika; asābhāvika.

Unutterable, *a.* akathanīya; anuccāriya.

Unvalued, *a.* aṭṭhapitaggha.

Unvaried, *a.* avisesita; sāmañña. °**rying,** *a.* avisesagāmī; nānattarahita.

Unveil, *v.t.* vivarati; pākaṭīkaroti. *p.p.* vivaṭa; °kata.

Unversed, *a.* anadhīta; appassuta; anipuṇa.

Unwarned, *a.* aniveditantarāya.

Unwarrantable, *a.* apaṭiññātabba. °**ted**, *a.* aladdhādhikāra; asampaṭicchita.

Unwary, *a.* pamatta; anārakkha. °**ily**, *adv.* pamattākārena; anārakkhatāya.

Unwashed, *a.* adhota.

Unwasted, *a.* akhīṇa; avināsita.

Unwavering, *a.* acala; thira.

Unwearied, *a.* akilanta; alīnaviriya.

Unwelcome, *a.* anabhimata; appiya; ananuññāta.

Unwell, *a.* gilāna; rogātura; akallaka.

Unwholesome, *a.* asappāya; ahita. °**ness**, *n.* asppāyatta, *nt.*

Unwieldy, *a.* 1. aparihāriya; 2. atithūla.

Unwilling, *a.* akāmaka; anicchamāna. °**ly**, *a.* akāmaŋ.

Unwind, *v.t.* nibbeṭheti. *p.p.* °ṭhita.

Unwinking, *a.* nimesarahita; sadājāgara; animisa.

Unwise, *a.* duppañña; buddhihīna. °**ly**, *adv.* mūḷhākārena; avidaddhatāya.

Unwitting, *a.* avicakkhaṇa. °**ly**, *adv.* asañcicca.

Unwonted, *a.* aparicita; asanthuta; asābhāvika.

Unworthy, *a.* anaraha; ananucchavika.

Unwounded, *a.* akkhata; aladdhappahāra.

Unwrap, *v.t.* veṭhanam apaneti. *p.p.* °nītaveṭhana.

Unwritten, *a.* alikhita.

Unwrought, *a.* 1. akatakamma; 2. asodhita.

Unyielding, *a.* avasagāmī.

Unyoke, *v.t.* viyojeti; yugā moceti. *p.p.* °jita; °cita.

Up, *prep. adv.* upari; uddhaŋ. — **and down**, uddham adho, *adv.* °**per**, *a.* upari ṭhita; uparima. °**permost**, *a.* uparitama.

Upbear, *v.t.* upatthambheti; unnāmeti. *p.p.* °bhita; °mita.

Upbraid, see **Reproach**.

Upbringing, *n.* posaṇa; vaḍḍhana; sikkhāpana, *nt.*

Upcast, *a.* uddhaŋkhitta.

Upheaval, *a.* unnāmana, *nt.* saṅkhobha, *m.*

Uphill, *a.* dukkara; duggama; durāroha.

Uphold, *v.t.* paggaṇhāti; upatthambheti; anumaññati. *p.p.* paggahita; °bhita; anumata. °**er**, *n.* upatthambhaka; paggahetu, *m.*

Upholster, *v.t.* kojavādayo sampādeti. °**er**, *n.* bhisikojavādisampādaka *m.* °**y**, *n.* gharūpakaraṇasampādana, *nt.*

Upkeep, *n.* paṭijaggana; pavattāpana, *nt.*

Upland, *n.* uccadesa, *m.*

Uplift, *v.t.* unnāmeti; uccāreti; ukkhipati. *p.p.* °mita; °rita; ukkhitta.

Upon, see **On**.

Upper, *a.* uparima. — **floor**, uparitala, *nt.* — **garment**, uttarisāṭaka, *nt.* — **part**, uparibhāga, *m.*

Uppish, *a.* uddhata; gabbita.

Upright, *a.* ujuka; avaṅka; akuṭila; uddhagata. °**ly**, *a.* avaṅkasabhāva. °**ness**, *n.* ajjava, *nt.*

Uprise, *v.i.* uddham uggacchati. *p.p.* °uggata. °**ing,** *n.* 1. uggamana. *nt.* 2. janasaṅkhobha, *m.*

Uproar, *n.* mahāsadda; kolāhala, *m.* °**ious,** *a.* mahāsaddappavattaka; saṅkhobhaka.

Uproot, *v.t.* ummūleti; uppāṭeti; samūhanati. *p.p.* °lita; °ṭita; samūhata. °**er,** *n.* ummūlaka; luñcaka, *m.*

Ups and downs, sukha-dukkha; patanuppatana, *nt.*

Upset, *v.t.* 1. viparivatteti; ākulīkaroti; 2. nikkujjeti. *p.p.* °tita; °kata; °jita. *n.* 1. vipallāsa; vikkhepa; 2. kalakala, *m.* 3. viparivattana, *nt.* adj. 1. viparivattita; ākulīkata; 2. vikkhittacitta; 3. akallaka.

Upshot, *n.* 1. paṭiphala, *nt.* 2. osānasiddhi, *f.*

Upside, *n.* uparipassa, *m.* °**down,** *adv.* adhomukhaŋ.

Upspring, *v.i.* uggacchati; ubbhavati. *p.p.* uggata; ubbhūta.

Upstairs, *adv.* uparitale.

Upstart, *n.* sahasā unnatippatta, *m.* *v.i.* sahasā uggacchati. *p.p.* °uggata.

Up-stream, *n.* paṭisota, *m.* *adv.* paṭisotaŋ.

Upturn, *v.t.* ukkujjeti; uparimukhaŋ karoti. *p.p.* °jita; °kata.

Upward, *a.* uddhaṅgama.

Upwards, *adv.* uddhābhimukhaŋ; uparimukhaŋ.

Uranium, *n.* seta-ghana-lohavisesa, *m.*

Urban, *a.* nāgarika; porī. — **council,** nagarasabhā, *f.*

Urbane, *a.* nagarajāta; vinīta; sādhusīla. °**ity,** *n.* nāgarikatta; sosīlya, *nt.* sabbhatā, *f.*

Urchin, *n.* 1. ceṭaka; avinītadāraka, *m.* 2. sallaka, *m.*

Ureter, Urethra, *n.* muttamagga; passāvamagga, *m.* °**itis,** *n.* muttamaggadāha, *m.*

Urge, *v.t.* ussāheti; uyyojeti. *p.p.* °hita; °jita.

Urgent, *a.* accāyika. °**ncy,** *n.* accāyikatta, *nt.* °**ly,** *adv.* atikhippaŋ; atituritaŋ.

Urine, *n.* mutta, *nt.* passāva, *m.* °**al,** *n.* 1. passāvakuṭi, *f.* 2. muttabhājana, *nt.* °**ary,** *a.* muttavisayaka. °**ate,** *v.i.* omutteti; passāvaŋ karoti. *p.p.* °tita; katapassāva. °**ation,** *n.* passāvakaraṇa, *nt.*

Urn, *n.* 1. bhasmakumbha; chavakumbha, *m.* 2. uṇhodakabhājana, *nt.*

Urticate, *v.t.* kapikacchūhi tāḷeti. *p.p.* °tāḷita.

Usable, *a.* upabhogāraha.

Usage, *n.* 1. upabhoga; 2. vohāra, *m.* 3. bhāsārīti, *f.*

Use, *n.* 1. payojana, *nt.* 2. upabhoga; paribhoga, *m.* 3. upasevanā, *f.* 4. cāritta, *nt.* *v.t.* 1. voharati; 2. upasevati; paribhuñjati; 3. ācarati. *p.p.* voharita; °vita; paribhutta; ācarita. *v.i.* paricayati. *p.p.* paricita. — **force,** pasahati. °**ful,** *a.* payojanāvaha; sopakāra. °**fully,** *adv.* sappayojanākārena. °**less,** *n.* nippayojana; niratthaka. °**lessly,** *adv.* nipphalākārena. °**lessness,** *n.* niratthakatta, *nt.*

Usher, *n.* pavesaka; paṭihārī, *m.* — **in,** paveseti.

Usual, *a.* sābhāvika ; pakatisiddha ; bāhulika ; avisiṭṭha. °**ly**, *adv.* sāmaññena ; pāyena ; bahuso.

Usurer, *n.* vaḍḍhigāhī, *m.*

Usurious, *a.* adhikavaḍḍhisahita. °**ly**, *adv.* sādhikavaḍḍhikaŋ.

Usurp, *v.t.* pasayha āyattīkaroti. *p.p.* °kata. °**ation**, *n.* balakkāra-gahaṇa, *nt.* °**er**, *n.* pasayha-gāhī, *m.*

Usury, *n.* vaḍḍhiyā iṇadāna, *nt.*

Utensil, *n.* upakaraṇa ; gehopakaraṇa, *nt.*

Uterine, *a.* ekakucchijāta.

Uterus, *n.* gabbhāsaya, *m.*

Utility, *n.* sappayojanatta, *nt.* °**arian**, *n.* atthasādhanatāpekkhī, *m.* °**arianism**, *n.* upayogitāvāda, *m.*

Utilize, *v.t.* upayojeti ; payojeti. *p.p.* °jita.

Utmost, *a.* parama ; accanta.

Utopian, *a.* manokappita.

Utter, *v.t.* udāneti ; udīreti ; vyāharati. *p.p.* °nita ; °rita ; vyāhaṭa. °**ance**, *n.* udīraṇa ; uggiraṇa, *nt.* samudāhāra, *m.* — **a cry**, vassati ; viravati.

Utter, *a.* accanta ; paripuṇṇa ; anūna. °**ly**, *adv.* sākallena ; accantaŋ ; paripuṇṇaŋ. °**most**, *a.* 1. parama ; uttama ; accadhika ; 2. dūratama.

Uvula, *n.* upajivhā, *f.*

Uxorious, *a.* bhariyāsatta. °**ness**, *n.* bhariyāvasitā, *f.*

V

Vacancy, *n.* 1. suññatā ; assāmikatā ; anadhivutthatā, *f.*

Vacant, *a.* ritta ; suñña ; assāmika ; anadhivuttha.

Vacate, *v.t.* cajati ; jahati ; vissajjeti. *p.p.* catta ; jahita ; vissaṭṭha. °**ion**, *n.* 1. cajana ; vissajjana, *nt.* 2. vissāmakāla, *m.*

Vaccinate, *v.t.* gopūyaŋ paveseti. *p.p.* °sitagopūya. °**ion**, *n.* masūrikānivāraka-patikāra, *m.*

Vacillate, *v.i.* dolāyati. *p.p.* °yita. °**ion**, *n.* dolāyana ; dveḷhakatta ; atthiratta, *nt.*

Vacuity, *n.* (vāta-) suññatta ; rittatta ; tucchatta, *nt.*

Vacuous, *a.* tuccha ; ritta.

Vacuum, *n.* rittaṭṭhāna, *m.* ākāsa, *m.* — **pump**, *n.* vātasuñña-udakākaḍḍhaka, *nt.*

Vagabond, *a. n.* niketanarahita ; vaṇibbaka, *m.* °**age**, *n.* vaṇibbakatta, *nt.*

Vagary, *n.* 1. sacchandacāra, *m.* 2. vipallattha-cintā, *f.*

Vagina, *n.* 1. kosākāravatthu, *nt.* 2. itthinimitta, *nt.*

Vagrant, *a. n.* aniyatavāsa ; pariyāhiṇḍaka ; akiccapasuta, *m.* °**ncy**, *n.* abaddhavāsatā ; akammasīlitā, *f.* °**ly**, *adv.* pariyāhiṇḍakatāya.

Vague, *a.* 1. avyatta ; avisada ; 2. avinicchita. °**ly**, *adv.* avisadākārena ; anicchayena. °**ness**, *n.* avisadatta ; apākaṭatta, *nt.*

Vail, *v.t.* gāravena sīsāvaraṇādiŋ apaneti ; garukaroti. *p.p.* garukata.

Vain, *a.* 1. niratthaka ; aphala ; mogha ; 2. uddhata ; dappita. °**glory**, *n.* vikatthana, *nt.* °**glorious**, *a.* 1. gabbita ; 2. vikatthanasīla. °**gloriously**, *adv.* gabbitākārena. °**ly**, *adv.* niratthakaŋ ; mudhā.

Vale, *n.* upaccakā, *f.*
Valediction, *n.* gamanāsiŋsanā, *f.* sotthivāda, *m.* °**tory,** *a.* subhāsiŋsanāyatta.
Valet, *n.* pādamūlika ; cullantevāsika ; paricāraka, *m.*
Valetudinary, *a.* akallaka ; gilāna.
Valiant, *a.* sūra ; vīra ; nibbhaya. °**ly,** *adv.* savikkamaŋ.
Valid, *a.* 1. sakāraṇa ; sasādhana; 2. pabala ; balappavattaka. °**ate,** *v.t.* pabalattaŋ pāpeti. *p.p.* °pāpita. °**ity,** *n.* 1. pabalatta ; thiratta ; 2. nītyanugatabala, *nt.* °**ly,** *adv.* pabalākārena ; akhaṇḍiyatāya.
Valise, *n.* hatthapasibbaka, *m.*
Valley, *n.* ninnabhūmi ; upaccakā, *f.*
Valour, *n.* parakkama ; vikkama, *m.* sūratta, *nt.* **Valorous,** *a.* dhitimantu ; savikkama. **Valorously,** *adv.* savikkamaŋ ; vīrākārena.
Value, *n.* 1. aggha, *m.* 2. payojana, *nt.* 3. mahatta, *nt.* *v.t.* 1. agghaŋ ṭhapeti *or* nirūpeti; 2. bahumaññati. *p.p.* ṭhapitaggha ; bahumata. °**able,** *a.* mahāraha ; mahaggha. *pl.* anagghavatthūni. °**ate,** *v.t.* agghaŋ nirūpeti. °**ation,** *n.* agghanirūpana, *nt.* °**ator,** *n.* agghanirūpaka ; agghāpaka, *m.* °**less,** *a.* aggharahita ; appaggha.
Valve, *n.* sayaŋvaṭṭaka-kavāṭa, *nt.* °**vular,** *a.* pidhānākāra.
Vamose, *v.i.* antaradhāyati ; apakkamati. *p.p.* antarahita ; apakkanta.
Vamp, *n.* mohinī ; mohetvā vilumpinī, *f.* *v.t.* palobheti ; sammoheti. *p.p.* °bhita ; °hita.
Vampire, *n.* 1. rudhirapāyīpisāca; 2. pasayhāvaharī, *m.* —**bat,** *n.* rudhirapāyinī jatukā. *f.*
Van, *n.* 1. bhaṇḍavāhīyāna, *nt.* 2. abhimukhasenā, *f.* *v.t.* yānena bhaṇḍāni harati. *p.p.* °haṭabhaṇḍa. °**guard,** *n.* senāmukha, *nt.* pamukhārakkhā, *f.*
Vandal, *n.* vijjākalāviddhaŋsī, *m.* °**ism,** *n.* sippīkammanāsana, *nt.*
Vane, *n.* ciṅgulaka, *nt.*
Vanish, *v.i.* antaradhāyati ; nirujjhati; atthaṅgacchati. *p.p.* antarahita; niruddha; °gata. °**ing,** *a.* antaradhāyamāna.
Vanity, *n.* 1. ahaṅkāra; tucchābhimāna, *m.* 2. tucchatta, *nt.*
Vanquish, *v.t.* parājeti ; abhibhavati. *p.p.* °jita ; °bhūta. °**er,** *n.* jetu ; abhibhū, *m.*
Vantage, *n.* lābha, *m.* payojana, *nt.*
Vapid, *a.* virasa ; nirasa. °**ity,** *n.* virasatā, *f.*
Vaporize, *v.t.* bappam uṭṭhāpeti. *p.p.* °pitabappa.
Vaporous, *a.* 1. sabappa ; bappayutta ; 2. asāra.
Vapour, *n.* 1. bappa, *m.* 2. matimatta, *nt.* *v.i.* 1. bappam uggacchati; 2. vikatthati. *p.p.* uggatabappa; °thita. °**er,** *n.* attasilāghī; vikatthī, *m.*
Vapulation, *n.* sākhāya tāḷana, *nt.*
Variable, *a.* viparivattanasabhāva; vipallāsāraha. °**bility,** vipariṇamana ; atthiratta, *nt.*

Variant, *a*. bhinna; nānāvidha. *n*. pāṭhabheda, *m*. °**nce**, *n*. 1. nānatta; visadisatta; 2. bhinnamatikatta, *nt*. °**ation**, *n*. 1. nānābhāva, *m*. vividhatta, *nt*. 2. visadisagamana, *nt*.

Varicoloured, *a*. nānāvaṇṇa.

Variegate, *v.t*. vicitteti; nānāvaṇṇaŋ karoti. *p.p*. °tita; °ṇīkata. °**ed**, *a*. kabara; kammāsa; sabala. °**ion**, *n*. sabalīkaraṇa, *nt*.

Variety, *n*. 1. pabheda, *m*. vividhatta; nānatta, *nt*. 2. visesajāti, *f*.

Variform, *a*. nānārūpa; vividhākāra.

Variola, *n*. masūrikā, *f*.

Various, *a*. anekavidha; vividha. °**ly**, *adv*. vividhākārena; anekadhā.

Varnish, *n*. majjanālepa, *m*. *v.t*. vaṇṇamaṭṭhaŋ karoti. *p.p*. °ṭhakata.

Vary, *v.i*. pabhijjati; nānābhavati. *v.t*. pabhedeti; rūpantaraŋ pāpeti. *p.p*. pabhinna; nānābhūta; °dita; °pita.

Vase, *n*. pupphādhāna, *nt*. bhaddakumbha, *m*.

Vassal, *n*. bhūmidāsa; parāyattabhūmivāsī, *m*. °**age**, *n*. bhūmidāsatta, *nt*.

Vast, *a*. atimahanta; ativitthiṇṇa. °**ly**, *adv*. ativisālavasena; yebhuyyena. °**ness**, *n*. ativitthiṇṇatta; atimahatta, *nt*.

Vaticinate, *v.t*. anāgataŋ pakāseti. *p.p*. °sitānāgata. °**ion**, *n*. anāgatāvīkaraṇa, *nt*.

Vault, *n*. 1. addhacandākārachadana-gabbha, *m*. 2. bhūmighara, *nt*.—**of heaven**, nabhomaṇḍala, *nt*.

Vaunt, *n*. attasilāghā, *f*. *v.i*. attānaŋ silāghati; vikatthati. *p.p*. °ghitatta; °thita. °**er**, *n*. attasilāghī, *m*.

Veal, *n*. vacchamaŋsa, *nt*.

Veer, *v.t*. maggaŋ parivatteti. *v.i*. matantaraŋ gaṇhāti. *p.p*. °titamagga; gahitama°.

Vegetable, *n*. haritaka, *nt*. sākasamūha; bhūtagāma, *m*.

Vegetarian, *n*. sākabhakkhī; nimmaŋsabhojī, *m*. °**ism**, *n*. ubbhidabhojitā, *f*.

Vegetate, *v.i*. ubbhijjati; virūhati. *p.p*. ubbhinna; virūḷha. °**ion**, *n*. ubbhidajāta, *nt*. bhūtagāma, *m*.

Vehement, *a*. aticaṇḍa; savega. °**nce**, *n*. caṇḍatta; savegatta, *nt*. °**ly**, *adv*. caṇḍākārena.

Vehicle, *n*. 1. vāhana; yāna; yogga, *nt*. ratha, *m*. 2. viññāpanupāya; 3. pavattanādhāra, *m*.

Veil, *n*. 1. āvaraṇa, *nt*. tirokaraṇī, *f*. 2. mukhajala, *nt*. 3. vyājopāya, *m*. *v.t*. paṭicchādeti; oguṇṭheti. *p.p*. °dita; °ṭhita.

Vein, *n*. dhamanī; sirā, *f*. °**y**, *a*. sirābahula; rekhāsahita.

Vellicate, *v.t*. sahasā ākaḍḍhati. *p.p*. °ḍhita.

Vellum, *n*. parimaddita-cammapaṭṭa, *nt*.

Velocipede, *n*. pādapājitayāna, *nt*.

Velocity, *n*. vega; java, *m*.

Velvet, *n*. siniddhaŋsuka-vatthavisesa, *m*.

Venal, *a*. lañcakhādaka. °**ity**, *n*. lañcavasikatā, *f*.

Vend, *v.t.* vikkiṇāti ; paṇeti. *p.p.* vikkīta ; paṇita. °**ee,** *n.* ketu ; kayika, *m.* °**er,** *n.* vikketu, *m.* °**ible,** *a.* vikkeyya.

Venerable, *a.* mahanīya ; garukātabba ; sambhāvanīya; gāravāraha. — **person,** āyasmantu; bhavanta, *m.*

Venerate, *v.t.* abhivādeti ; garukaroti ; māneti; vandati; pūjeti ; namassati. *p.p.* °dita ; °kata ; mānita ; °dita ; pūjita ; °sita. °**ion,** *n.* garukāra ; namakkāra, *m.* vandanā ; pūjanā ; abhivādanā, *f.* mānana, *nt.* °**or,** *n.* vandaka ; pūjaka, *m.*

Venereal, *a.* methuna-nissita.

Venery, *n.* 1. methuna, *nt.* 2. migava, *m.*

Vengeance, *n.* verasādhana; veranīyātana, *nt.*

Vengeful, *a.* veranīyātanasīla. °**ness,** *n.* verasādhakatta, *nt.*

Venial, *a.* satekiccha. °**ity,** *n.* satekicchatta, *nt.*

Venison, *n.* migamaŋsa, *nt.*

Venom, *n.* 1. visa ; garaḷa, *nt.* 2. usūyā ; anatthakāmatā, *f.* °**ed,** *a.* visadiddha. °**ous,** *a.* 1. savisa ; 2. issāyutta. °**ousness,** *n.* savisatta, *nt.*

Venous, *a.* dhamanīvisayaka.

Vent, *n.* vātacchidda ; niggamadvāra, *nt.* *v.t.* 1. nikkhāmeti ; 2. ajjhāsayaŋ pakāseti. *p.p.* °mita; °sitajjhāsaya. °**age,** *n.* 1. vātaniggama, *m.* 2. ajjhāsayappakāsana, *nt.* °**hole,** *n.* vātacchidda, *nt.* vāyunāḷa, *m.* °**less,** *a.* niggamadvāra-rahita.

Ventiduct, *n.* antobhummavātamagga, *m.*

Ventilate, *v.t.* 1. vātaŋ paveseti ; 2. ajjhāsayaŋ pakāseti. °**ion,** 1. vātappavesana; 2. ajjhāsayappakāsana, *nt.* °**tor,** *n.* vātamagga, *m.* kavāṭa, *nt.*

Ventral, *a.* udaranissita.

Ventricle, *n.* dehagatakuhara, *nt.* °**cose,** *a.* lambodara.

Venture, *n.* vīrakriyā, *f.* *v.i.* visahati. °**some,** °**ous,** *a.* vīrakriyāsatta ; nibbhaya. °**ously,** *adv.* vīrākārena.

Venue, *n.* 1. vinicchayaṭṭhāna ; 2. samāgamaṭṭhāna, *nt.*

Venus, *n.* Sukka ; Asuraguru, *m.*

Veracious, *a.* saccavādī ; saddheyyavacana. °**ly,** *adv.* saccavāditāya. °**city,** *n.* avithatatta, *nt.*

Veranda, °**dah,** *n.* ālinda, *m.* **Back** —, piṭṭhivaŋsa, *m.*

Verb, *n.* ākhyāta ; kriyāpada, *nt.* °**al,** *a.* 1. vācasika ; 2. kriyāyatta. °**al action,** vacīkamma, *nt.* °**alism,** *n.* saddamattavicāraṇā, *f.* °**alist,** *n.* saddamattavicāraka, *m.* °**ally,** *adv.* yathāsaddaŋ ; vacanavasena.

Verbatim, *adv.* padānupadaŋ ; padaso.

Verbiage, *n.* vacanabahulatta, *nt.*

Verbose, *a.* niratthakasaddappayogī ; atimattabhāṇī. °**ity,** *n.* saddabahulatā ; atibhāṇitā, *f.*

Verdant, *a.* 1. harita ; saddala ; 2. apariṇatabuddhī.

Verdict, *n.* adhikaraṇaniṇṇaya, *m.* adhikaraṇikatīraṇa, *nt.*

Verdure, *n.* 1. haritatta, *nt.* 2. rukkhalatāsamūha, *m.* °**ous,** *a.* 1. palāsavaṇṇa ; 2. rukkhalatāsañchanna.

Verge, *n*. 1. pariyanta, *m*. 2. adhikārayaṭṭhi, *m*. *f*. *v.i*. 1. passena onamati; 2. upatiṭṭhati; samīpaŋ yāti. *p.p*. °onata; °ṭhita; °yāta. °**er**, *n*. 1. adhikāradaṇḍadhārī; 2. devāyatane āsananiyāmaka, *m*.

Veridical, *a*. saccavādī; saddheyyavacana.

Verify, *v.t*. samattheti; pamāṇeti; tathataŋ sādheti. *p.p*. °thita; °ṇita; sādhitatathatta. °**ication**, *n*. samatthana; tathattasādhana, *nt*.

Verily, *adv*. nūnaŋ; khalu; ekaŋsena.

Verisimilitude, *n*. saccābhāsa. *m*. °**milar**, *a*. saccābhāsayutta.

Veritable, *a*. anvattha; yathābhūta. °**ity**, *n*. yāthāvatā; saccatā, *f*. °**bly**, *adv*. yathābhūtaŋ.

Verjuice, *n*. ambilayūsa, *nt*.

Vermicide, *n*. kīṭanāsakosadha, *nt*. °**dal**, *a*. kimināsaka.

Vermicular, *a*. kimisadisa.

Vermiculate, *a*. kimisaṅkiṇṇa. °**ion**, *n*. kimipuṇṇatta, *nt*.

Vermiform, *a*. kimisaṇṭhāna.

Vermilion, *n*. hiṅgulaka, *nt*.

Vermin, *n*. kimi; kīṭa, *m*. °**ous**, kīṭākiṇṇa. °**ate**, *v.i*. kimisaṅkiṇṇo hoti.

Vermiparous, *a*. kimijanaka.

Vermivorous, *a*. kimibhakkha.

Vernacular, *a*. sadesaja; nijadesika, *n*. sadesabhāsā; nijabhāsā, *f*. °**ism**, *n*. desabhāsāpayoga, *m*.

Vernal, *a*. vasantakālika.

Versatile, *a*. capala; lola. °**ity**, *n*. cāpalla, *nt*.

Verse, *n*. gāthā, *f*. pajja, *nt*. siloka, *m*. °**ed**, *a*. nipuṇa; vicakkhaṇa; vyatta; pavīṇa. °**ify**, *v.t.i*. pajjaŋ bandhati *or* racayati; pajjattaŋ parivatteti. *p.p*. baddhapajja; °tita. °**ification**, *n*. pajjaracanā, *f*. °**ifier**, *n*. pajjakāra, *m*.

Versicoloured, *a*. nānāvaṇṇa.

Version, *n*. anuvāda, *m*. bhāsantaraparivattana, *nt*.

Versus, *prep*. paṭi; virodhena.

Vertebra, *n*. piṭṭhikaṇṭaka, *nt*. °**te**, *a*. piṭṭhikaṇṭakayutta.

Vertex, *n*. sikhara; agga, *nt*. matthaka, *m*.

Vertical, *a*. uddhaŋṭhita. °**ly**, *adv*. uddhādhobhāvena; ujukamuddhaŋ.

Vertigo, *n*. sīsabhamaṇa, *nt*.

Verve, *n*. viriya, *nt*. dhiti, *f*. ussāha, *m*.

Very, *a*. 1. yathābhūta; yathātatha; 2. tadatthabhūta; 3. accanta; atimatta. *adv*. ati; accantaŋ; atimattaŋ. — **clear**, *a*. suvisada. — **difficult**, *a*. atidukkara. — **early**, *adv*. atippage'va. — **many**, *a*. subahu; atimatta. — **much**, *adv*. ativiya; atirekataraŋ. — **rich**, *a*. maddhanika.—**small**, *a*. ittara; atikhuddaka.

Vesica, *n*. muttāsaya, *m*.

Vesicate, *v.t*. phoṭake uppādeti. °**ion**, *n*. phoṭakuppādana, *nt*. °**ory**, *a*. phoṭakuppādaka.

Vesper, *n*. 1. sañjhopāsanā, *f*. 2. Sukkagaha, *m*. osadhītārakā, *f*. °**tine**, *a*. sāyaṇhika.

Vespiary, *n*. bhamarapaṭala, *nt*.

Vessel, *n*. 1. bhājana, *nt*. 2. pota, *m*. nāvā, *f*. 3. dhamanī, *f*.

Vest, *n.* 1. antarakañcuka; 2. nivāsana, *nt.* *v.t.* adhikāraŋ deti; adhikāradassakaŋ nivāseti. *v.i.* adhikāraŋ *or* upādhiŋ labhati. *p.p.* dinnādhikāra; nivāsita°; laddhādhikāra; laddhopādhika. °**ed**, *a.* patiṭṭhāpita; āyattīkata. °**ment**, *n.* adhikārāyatta-dīghakañcuka, *m.*

Vesta, *n.* 1. aggisalākā; 2. aggidevatā, *f.* °**al**, *a.* aggidevatāyatta. *n.* brahmacārinī, *f.*

Vestibule, *n.* 1. pavesasālā, *f.* abhimukhagabbha, *m.* 2. pavesamagga, *m.*

Vestige, *n.* lañchana; naṭṭhāvasiṭṭha, *nt.*

Vetch, *n.* māsajāti, *f.*

Veteran, *a.* *n.* 1. kataparicaya; 2. ñāṇavuddha; 3. topovuddha.

Veterinary, *n.* pasutikicchā, *f.* °**ian**, *n.* pasutikicchaka, *m.*

Veto, *n.* nisedhabala, *nt.* paṭisedhādhikāra, *m.* *v.t.* nisedheti; paṭisedheti. *p.p.* °dhita.

Vex, *v.t.* 1. kopeti; roseti; 2. bādheti; viheṭheti. *p.p.* kopita; rosita; bādhita; °ṭhita. °**ation**, *n.* 1. kopana; rosana; 2. viheṭhana, *nt.* 3. upatāpa; vighāta, *m.* °**atious**, *a.* 1. kopajanaka; ubbejaka; 2. viheṭhanaka. °**edly**, *adv.* saubbegaŋ; sakopaŋ.

Via, *n.* 1. magga, *m.* vīthi, *f.* 2. ākāsagaṅgā, *f.* *prep.* maggena; antarena; disāya.

Viable, *a.* jīvanakkhama. °**bility**, *n.* jīvanasamatthatā, *f.*

Viaduct, *n.* setusadisamagga, *m.*

Vial, *n.* kācatumba, *nt.*

Viand, *n.* āhāravatthu; bhojjavatthu, *nt.*

Viaticum, *n.* pātheyya; maggopakaraṇa, *nt.*

Vibrate, *v.i.* 1. vipphurati; 2. vipphandati; pakampati. *v.t.* vipphandeti; pakampeti. *p.p.* °rita; °dita; °pita; °dita. °**ion**, *n.* kampana; calana; phandana, *nt.* °**ive**, *a.* phandamāna; kampamāna.

Vicar, *n.* padesika-devapūjaka, *m.* °**age**, *n.* devapūjakanivāsa, *m.*

Vicarious, *a.* aññatthāya niyojita; parakiccapasuta.

Vice, *pref.* upa. *prep.* atthāya. °**chancellor**, *n.* nikhilavijjālaye upappadhāna, *m.* °**principal**, *n.* upapadhānācariya, *m.* °**roy**, *n.* rājapaṭinidhi; uparāja, *m.* — **royalty**, *n.* oparajja, *nt.*

Vice versa, *adv.* tappaṭipakkhena; paṭilomaŋ.

Vice, *n.* 1. duccarita, *nt.* aparādha; adhamma, *m.* 2. kaṭṭhapīḷaka, *m.* °**ious**, *a.* durācāra; kibbisakārī. °**iously**, *adv.* duṭṭhākārena; pāpacetasā.

Vicennial, *a.* vīsativassika.

Vicinage, *n.* āsannabhūmi, *f.* patiṭṭhita-padesa, *m.*

Vicinity, *n.* 1. samīpaṭṭhāna, *nt.* 2. ñātisambandha, *m.*

Vicissitude, *n.* vipariṇāma, *m.* avatthantara, *nt.* °**inary**, °**inous**, *a.* vipariṇāmadhamma.

Victim, *n.* 1. bhakkha; 2. gāhagata; antarāyappatta; 3. vañcanappatta, *m.* °**ize**, *v.t.* 1. upahārabaliŋ karoti; 2. antarāyaŋ pāpeti; 3. vañceti. *p.p.* °balikata; °pita; °cita.

Victor, *n*. jetu ; vijetu ; vijayī ; jayalābhī, *m*. °**ious**, *a*. vijitāvī ; jayaggāhī. °**ously**, *adv*. jayaggāhīlīlāya. °**y**, *n*. jaya ; vijaya; kaṭaggāha, *m*. jinana, *nt*.
Victress, *n*. vijitāvinī, *f*.
Victual, *v.t*. āhāropakaraṇāni sampādeti.
Victuals, *n*. āhāra, *m*. bhojana, *nt*.
Vide, *v.t*. passeyyāsi.
Vidimus, *n*. 1. saṅkhyāparikkhaṇa, *nt*. 2. saṅkhittalipi, *f*.
Vie, *v.i*. vijigiŋsati ; jetum icchati. *p.p*. °sita ; °chita.
View, *n*. 1. mata, *nt*. mati ; diṭṭhi, *f*. vāda, *m*. 2. dassana ; nirikkhaṇa ; parikkhaṇa, *nt*. 3. cakkhupatha ; dassanūpacāra, *m*. *v.t*. ikkhati ; passati ; oloketi ; upaparikkhati. *p.p*. ikkhita ; diṭṭha; °kita; °khita. — **holder**, *n*. matapakāsaka ; vādī, *m*. °**less**, *a*. adissamāna. — **point**, *n*. matabheda, *m*. **With a — to**, ajjhāsayena ; apekkhāya. **Field of** —, dassanapatha, *m*.
Vigil, *n*. jāgaraṇa, *nt*. appamāda, *m*. °**ance**, *n*. saŋrakkhaṇa ; jāgaraṇa, *nt*. appamāda, *m*. °**ant**, *a*. jāgara ; appamatta. °**antly**, *adv*. appamādena; sāvadhānaŋ ; jāgariyena.
Vigour, *n*. bala ; viriya, *nt*. thāma, *m*. satti, *f*.
Vigorous, *a*. 1. balavantu ; thāmavantu ; 2. daḷhatama. °**ly**, *adv*. atidaḷhaŋ ; mahussāhena.
Vile, *a*. nīca; hīna; nihīna; nikiṭṭha; kucchita. °**ly**, *adv*. nīcākārena ; adhamatāya. °**ness**, *n*. nīcatta ; adhamatta, *nt*.
Vilify, *v.t*. apavadati; upavadati; nindati. *p.p*. apavutta ; nindita. °**ication**, *n*. upavāda ; apavāda, *m*. nindana ; garahana, *nt*. °**ier**, *n*. upavādī ; garahī; nindaka, *m*.
Vilipend, *v.t*. avamaññati ; aguṇaŋ katheti. *p.p*. avamata; kathitāguṇa.
Villa, *n*. gāmika-mandira, *nt*.
Village, *n*. gāma ; saŋvasatha, *m*. °**er**, *n*. gāmika, *m*. — **folk**, *n*. gāmajana, *m*. — **headman**, *n*. gāmabhojaka, *m*. **Entrance to a** —, gāmadvāra, *nt*. **Inner** —, antogāma, *m*. **Neighbouring** —, dhuragāma, *m*.
Villain, *n*. khala ; dujjana ; dhutta ; pāpī ; narādhama, *m*. °**ous**, *a*. dujjanapakatika ; āgucārī ; duṭṭhasabhāva. °**ousness**, *n*. dujjanatta ; āgucāritta ; khalatta, *nt*. °**y**, *n*. dhuttabhāva; durācāra, *m*.
Vim, *n*. thāma, *m*. satti, *f*.
Vincible, *a*. jetabba, jeyya.
Vindicate, *v.t*. niravajjaŋ karoti ; dosaŋ sodheti. *p.p*. °kata ; sodhitadosa. °**ion**, *n*. dosamocana; niravajjakaraṇa, *nt*. °**tor**, *n*. dosasodhaka, *m*. °**ive**, *a*. vajjasamatthanaka.
Vindictive, *a*. verasādhanapara ; akkhamanasīla. °**ly**, *adv*. verasādhanavasena. °**ness**, *n*. verapaṭikaraṇa ; verasādhana, *nt*.
Vine, *n*. 1. latā ; 2. muddikā, *f*. °**clad**, *a*. muddikālatākiṇṇa. °**ry**, *n*. muddikāropaṇasālā, *f*. °**yard**, *n*. muddikāyatana, *nt*.
Vinegar, *n*. bilaṅga, *m*. sovīra, *nt*.
Vintage, *n*. muddikāphalasamaya, *m*. °**er**, *n*. muddikāocinaka, *m*.

Vintner, *n*. muddikāpānavikkayī, *m*.
Viol, *n*. cha-tantikavīṇā, *f*.
Viola, *n*. mahāvīṇā, *f*.
Violate, *v.t.* 1. ullaṅgheti; atikkamati; aticarati; 2. padhaŋseti. *p.p.* °ghita; atikkanta; °rita; °sita. °**ion**, *n*. 1. ullaṅghana; 2. padhaŋsana, *nt*. °**tor**, *n*. haṭhena dūsaka, *m*.
Violent, *a*. sāhasika; aticaṇḍa. °**ly**, *adv*. pasayha; balakkārena. °**nce**, *n*. sāhasa, *nt*. balakkāra, *m*.
Violet, *a*. pāṭala; nīlalohita. *n*. puppavisesa, *m*.
Violin, *n*. sāraṅgī, *f*. °**ist**, *n*. sāraṅgika, *m*.
Viper, *n*. gonasa (-sappa), *m*. °**ish**, *a*. gonasopama. °**ous**, *a*. pesuññavādī.
Virago, *n*. kalahappiyā; purisagatikā, *f*.
Virescence, *n*. haritatta, *nt*.
Virgate, *a*. kisa-ujubhūta.
Virgin, *n*. kaññā; kumārī; avivāhitā, *f*. °**ity**, *n*. kaññābhāva, *m*. °**al**, *a*. kaññānucchavika.
Virgo, *n*. kaññārāsi, *m*.
Viridescent, *a*. īsaŋharita. °**nce**, *n*. īsaŋharitatta, *nt*.
Virile, *a*. purisāyatta; thāmayutta. °**ity**, *n*. porisa, *nt*.
Virose, *a*. visayutta.
Virtu, *n*. lalitakalāpiyatā, *f*.
Virtue, *n*. sadācāra; guṇadhamma, *m*. sīla, *nt*. °**al**, *a*. vatthuto upalabbhamāna; yathātatha. °**ally**, *adv*. tattato; vatthuto; yathātthato. °**less**, *a*. dussīla; adhammika. °**ous**, *a*. susīla; sagguṇa; dhammika. °**ously**, *adv*. dhammikatāya. °**ousness**, *n*. dhammikatta; sosīlya, *nt*.
Virulent, *a*. visayutta; ugga; tibba; atipharusa. °**ly**, *adv*. tibbākārena. °**nce**, *n*. uggatta; atipharusatta, *nt*.
Virus, *n*. sannihitavisa, *nt*.
Visage, *n*. mukhasaṇṭhāna, *nt*. mukhavaṇṇa, *m*.
Vis-a-vis, *adv*. mukhāmukhaŋ; sammukhaŋ.
Viscera, *n*. *pl*. antādi-dehabbhantarika-koṭṭhāsā, *m*. °**te**, *v.t.* antādīni apaharati. *p.p.* apahaṭantādi.
Viscid, *a*. lagganapakatika. °**ity**, *n*. saŋlaggakatta, *nt*.
Viscin, *n*. niyyāsa-visesa, *m*.
Viscous, see **Glutinous**.
Visible, *a*. diṭṭhigocara; sandissamāna; sandiṭṭhika. °**bly**, *adv*. paccakkhato. — **thing**, rūpārammaṇa, *nt*. °**bility**, *n*. dissamānatta, *nt*.
Vision, *n*. 1. diṭṭhi, *f*. dassana, *nt*. 2. māyā, *f*. manonimmāṇa, *nt*. 3. ābhāsadassana, *nt*. °**ary**, *a*. manokappanāyatta; ābhāsamattāyatta.
Visit, *n*. abbhāgamana; upasaṅkamana, *nt*. *v.t.* upasaṅkamati; upagacchati. *p.p.* °saṅkanta; upagata. °**ant**, *n*. abbhāgāmī; āgantuka, *m*. °**ation**, *n*. 1. abbhāgamana; upaparikkhāya caraṇa, *nt*. 2. vipākadāna, *nt*. °**ing**, *a*. kālena kālaŋ upagacchamāna. °**ing card**, nāmādyaṅkitapaṇṇa, *nt*. °**or**, *n*. abbhāgāmī; atithi; āgantuka, *m*.
Visor, see **Mask**.
Vista, *n*. 1. antarena dassana *nt*. 2. tarupanti, *f*.

Visual, *a.* dassanāyatta ; diṭṭhigocara. — **cognition**, cakkhuviññāṇa, *nt.* — **organ**, *n.* cakkhāyatana, *nt.* °**ity**, *n.* dassanakkhamatta, *nt.* °**ize**, *v.t.* diṭṭhigocaraŋ karoti ; sacchikaroti. *p.p.* °kata.

Vital, *a.* 1. accāvassaka; 2. jīvāyatta ; jīvadhāraka. °**ity**, *n.* jīvadhārakatta; jīvitindriya, *nt.* °**ize**, *v.t.* sajīvaŋ karoti; balaŋ gāhāpeti. °**ization**, *n.* sajīvattapāpana ; sabalīkaraṇa, *nt.* °**ly**, *adv.* avassam eva. — **spot**, *n.* mammaṭṭhāna, *nt.*

Vitellus, *n.* aṇḍamiñjā, *f.*

Vitiate, *v.t.* dūseti ; misseti. *p.p.* dūsita ; missita. °**ion**, *n.* dūsana, *nt.*

Vitreous, *a.* kācūpama.

Vitrify, *v.t.* kācattaŋ pāpeti. *p.p.* °pāpita. °**ication**, *n.* kācattapāpana, *nt.*

Vituperate, *v.t.* akkosati ; garahati; nindati. *p.p.* °sita *or* akkuṭṭha ; °hita ; °dita. °**ion**, *n.* akkosana, *nt.* °**ive**, *a.* akkosaka ; paribhāsaka.

Viva, *n. intj.* ciraŋ jīvatu ! — **voce**, *n.* vācāhi upaparikkhaṇa, *nt. adv.* vacanamattena.

Vivacious, *a.* saussāha ; uttejita. °**ly**, *adv.* saussāhaŋ. °**city**, *n.* uttejitatta, *nt.*

Vivarium, *n.* pasuyyāna, *nt.* migadāya, *m.*

Vivid, *a.* 1. visada ; vibhūta ; atipākaṭa ; 2. dippamāna. °**ly**, *adv.* visadākārena. °**ness**, *n.* suvisadatta, *nt.*

Vivify, *v.t.* 1. sajīvaŋ karoti ; 2. uttejeti. *p.p.* sajīvakata ; °jita. °**ication**, *n.* ujjīvana ; uttejana, *nt.*

Viviparous, *a.* jalābuja ; gabbhaseyyaka.

Vivisect, *v.t.* sajīvapāṇino vicchindati. *p.p.* vicchinnasajīvapāṇī. °**ion**, *n.* sajīvapāṇivicchindana, *nt.*

Vixen, *n.* 1. sigālī ; 2. kalahakārinī, *f.*

Viz, *adv.* taŋ yathā ; seyyathīdaŋ.

Vizier, *n.* Mahammadikamahāmacca, *m.*

Vocable, *n.* vacana ; pada, *nt.*

Vocabulary, *n.* vacanamālā, *f.*

Vocal, *a.* saranissita ; vācasika. °**ist**, *n.* gāyaka ; sarabhāṇī, *m.* °**ize**, *v.t.* sarabhaññaŋ bhaṇati.

Vocation, *n.* 1. jīvanopāya ; vyāpāra, *m.* 2. avhāna, *nt.* °**al**, *a.* jīvanopāyāyatta.

Vocative, *n.* ālapanavibhatti, *f.* sambodhana, *nt.*

Vociferate, *v.t.* ukkosati ; mahāsaddena katheti. *p.p.* °sita; °thita. °**ion**, *n.* ukkosanā; ugghosanā, *f.* °**rance**, *n.* ugghosana, *nt.* mahāsadda, *m.*

Vociferous, *a.* mahāsaddayutta. °**ly**, *adv.* mahānādena. °**ness**, *n.* mahāghosatā, *f.*

Vogue, *n.* 1. vohāra ; pacāra, *m.* 2. pavattana, *nt.* 3. sammuti, *f.* **In** —, pacāragata, *a.*

Voice, *n.* sara ; sadda ; nāda, *m.* °**less**, *a.* nissadda. **Active** —, kattukāraka, *m.* **Passive** —, kammakāraka, *m.*

Void, *n.* suññaṭṭhāna, *nt.* ākāsa, *m.* adj. suñña ; ritta ; tuccha ; virahita. *v.t.* rittaŋ karoti. °**ance**, *n.* parivajjana; nicchāraṇa, *nt.* °**ly**, *adv.* suññākārena. °**ness**, *n.* suññatta, *nt.*

Volant, *a.* uḍḍīyanakkhama.

Volatile, *a.* 1. sīghena khīyamāna; 2. capala; cañcala. °**ize,** *v.t.* sīghaŋ khepeti *or* vipphāreti. *p.p.* °pita; °rita.

Volcano, *n.* aggibhūdhara; jālāmukhapabbata, *m.* °**nic,** *a.* 1. aggibhūdharāyatta; 2. aticaṇḍa.

Volitant, see **Volant.**

Volition, *n.* cetanābala, *nt.* adhimokkha, *m.* °**al,** *a.* cetanāyatta. °**ally,** *adv.* adhiṭṭhānabalena.

Volley, *n.* āyudhavuṭṭhi, *f.*

Volt, *n.* vijjubala-māṇa, *nt.* °**age,** *n.* vijjubalappamāṇa, *nt.*

Voluble, *a.* mukhara; vācāla. °**bility,** *n.* mukharatā, *f.* °**bly,** *adv.* mukhārākārena.

Volume, *n.* 1. saŋhati, *f.* saṅghāta, *m.* 2. (of a book:) gantha; potthaka, *m. nt.* °**inous,** *a.* 1. visāla; mahanta; 2. bahukaṇḍaka. °**inously,** *adv.* visālavasena.

Voluntary, *a.* secchāpubbaka; sacchandakārī. °**ily,** *adv.* sakaicchāya. °**teer,** *n.* secchāsevaka, *m.* *v.t.* sakaicchāya sevati *or* karoti.

Voluptuary, *a. n.* kāmāsatta.

Voluptuous, *a.* kāmabhogī. °**ly,** *adv.* kāmāsattatāya. °**ness,** *n.* kamabhogitā, *f.*

Vomit, *v.t.i.* vamati; uggāreti. *p.p.* vamita; °rita. *n.* chaddikā, *f.* vamathu, *m.* vamana, *nt.* °**ing,** *n.* vamana, *nt.* °**ory,** *n.* vamanakara. °**urition,** *n.* 1. abhiṇhavamana, *nt.* 2. vamanussāha, *m.*

Voracious, *a.* bahubhakkha; mahagghasa. °**ly,** *adv.* mahagghasatāya. °**ness,** *n.* odarikatta, *nt.*

Vortex, *n.* salilabbhama, *m.* āvaṭṭakavatthu; āvaṭṭana, *nt.*

Votary, *n.* vatasamādāyī; bhattimantu; sāvaka, *m.*

Vote, *n.* chandaka, *nt.* anumati, *f.* *v.t.* chandaŋ deti; anumatiŋ pakāseti. *p.p.* dinnachanda; °sitānumatī. °**er,** *n.* chandadāyī; anumatidāyī, *m.*

Votive, *a.* paṭiññāta.

Vouch, *v.t.* daḷhīkaroti; pamāṇayati. *p.p.* °kata; pamāṇita. °**er,** *n.* saccakārapaṇṇa, *nt.* °**safe,** *v.t.* anujānāti; anuggahaŋ paṭijānāti. *p.p.* anuññāta; paṭiññātānuggaha.

Vow, *n.* paṭiññā, *f.* vatasamādāna, *nt.* *v.t.* paṭijānāti; paṇidhiŋ ṭhapeti; sapathaŋ karoti. *p.p.* paṭiññāta; ṭhapitapaṇidhī; katasapatha.

Vowel, *n.* sara (-akkhara), *nt.*

Voyage, *n.* jalayātrā, *f.* samuddagamana, *nt.* *v.i.* nāvāya sañcarati. °**er,** *n.* nāvāya sañcārī, *m.*

Vraisemblance, *n.* saccābhāsa, *m.*

Vulgar, *a.* gamma; nikiṭṭha; adhama. °**ism,** *n.* asabbhavācāpayoga, *m.* °**ity,** *n.* gammatā; nīcatā, *f.* °**ize,** *v.t.* durācāraŋ sikkhāpeti. °**ly,** *adv.* asabbhākārena.

Vulnerable, *n.* bhejja; vejjha; suppadhaŋsiya. °**bility,** *n.* padhaŋsiyatā; bhejjatā, *f.*

Vulnerary, *a. n.* vaṇaropaka (-osadha), *nt.*

Vulpine, *a.* 1. sigālasadisa; 2. vañcaka; saṭha.

Vulture, *n.* gijjha, *m.* °**ine,** °**ish,** *a.* gijjhasadisa.

Vulva, *n.* itthinimitta, *nt.*

W

Waddle, *n.* haŋsagamana, *nt.* *v.i.* haŋsagatiyā gacchati. *p.p.* °gata. °**ingly,** *adv.* haŋsagatiyā.

Wade, *v.i.t.* kicchena yāti ; jale otaritvā gacchati. °**er,** *n.* 1. kicchena-yāyī ; 2. jalacarapakkhivisesa, *m.*

Wafer, *n.* madhupaṭalākārakhajjaka, *nt.*

Waft, *v.i.* udakena vuyhati ; vātena nīyati. *v.t.* (dhajādiŋ) kampeti. *p.p.* °vūḷha ; °nīta ; °pita. °**age,** *n.* vuyhana, *nt.*

Wag, *n.* 1. cālana, *nt.* 2. pahāsaka, *m.* *v.t.* cāleti ; kampeti ; vidhūpeti. *p.p.* cālita ; °pita. °**tail,** *n.* khañjarīṭa (-pakkhī), *m.*

Wage, *n.* vetana, *nt.* bhati, *f.* *v.t.* (war) yujjhati ; raṇam ārabhati, *p.p.* yujjhita; āraddharaṇa.

Wager, *n.* abbhuta ; paṇa, *m.* *v.t.* abbhutaŋ *or* paṇaŋ karoti. *p.p.* katabbhuta.

Waggish, *a.* keḷisīla ; pahāsaka.

Waggle, *v.t.i.* ito c'ito calati *or* cāleti. *p.p.* °calita ; °cālita.

Waggon, *n.* sakaṭa, *m.* °**er,** *n.* sākaṭika, *m.*

Waif, *n.* 1. assāmikavatthu, *nt.* 2. apariggahita-pāṇī, *m.* 3. anāthapurisa, *m.*

Wail, *n.* vilāpa ; parideva, *m.* akkandana, *nt.* *v.t.i.* vilapati ; paridevati ; kandati. *p.p.* °pita ; °vita ; °dita. °**ful,** *a.* vilapamāna ; sokapareta. °**ing,** *n.* rodana, *nt.*

Wainscot, *n.* bhittipadarāvaraṇa, *nt.* *v.t.* bhittiŋ padarehi āvarati. *p.p.* padarāvaṭabhittika.

Waist, *n.* kaṭi, *f.* majjha, *m.* °**band,** pāmaṅga ; kaṭisutta ; kāyabandhana, *nt.* °**cloth,** *n.* kacchabandhana, *nt.* °**deep,** *a.* kaṭippamāṇa.

Wait, *v.i.t.* 1. nivattati ; acchati ; 2. āgameti ; 3. upaṭṭhāti. *p.p.* °tita; °ṭhita. *n.* 1. āgamana ; 2. paccāsiŋsana, *nt.* °**er,** *n.* sevaka; paricāraka, *m.* — **for,** paccāsiŋsati; apekkhati. — **on,** upaṭṭhāti ; paricarati. °**ing,** *a.* acchamāna. °**ing room,** āgantukasālā ; pathikasālā, *f.* °**ress,** *n.* paricārikā ; parivesikā, *f.*

Waive, see **Abandon.**

Wake, *n.* jāgaraṇa, *nt.* appamāda, *m.* *v.i.* pabujjhati. *v.t.* pabodheti; sayanato uṭṭhāpeti. *p.p.* pabuddha ; °dhita ; °pita. °**ful,** *a.* appamatta ; jāgariyānuyutta. °**fully,** *adv.* appamādena ; jāgaratāya. °**fulness,** *n.* jāgariya ; avadhāna, *nt.* appamāda, *m.*

Waken, *v.t.* pabodheti ; uṭṭhāpeti. *v.i.* pabujjhati ; uṭṭhāti. *p.p.* °dhita ; °pita ; pabuddha ; uṭṭhita.

Wale, *n.* kasāhata-ciṇha, *nt.* *v.t.* kasāhananena ciṇhe uppādeti.

Walk, *n.* vicaraṇa; caṅkamaṇa, *nt.* sañcāra ; jaṅghāvihāra, *m.* *v.i.* sañcarati ; āhiṇḍati ; caṅkamati. °**er,** *n.* padika ; sañcaritu, *n.* °**ing,** *n.* sañcaraṇa, *nt.* °**ing stick,** kattarayaṭṭhi, *f.* **Prepared** —, caṅkama, *m.*

Wall, *n.* bhitti, *f.* kuḍḍa, *nt.* *v.t.* pākārena āvarati. *p.p.* °āvaṭa. °**plate,** saṅghāṭa, *m.*

Wallet, *n.* (hattha-) pasibbaka, *m.*

Wall-eye, *n.* nettakāca, *m.* °**ed,** *a.* nettakācayutta.

Wallop, *v.t.* adhikaŋ tāḷeti. *p.p.* °ḷita.

Wallow, *n.* paṅkāvāṭa, *m.* *v.i.* paṅke pavaṭṭati. *p.p.* °ṭita.

Walnut, *n.* vibhītakīvisesa, *m.*

Walrus, *n.* samuddahatthī, *m.*

Waltz, *n.* bhamananacca, *nt.* *v.i.* bhamananaccaŋ pavatteti.

Wan, *a.* vivaṇṇa ; uppaṇḍuka.

Wand, *n.* indajālika-yaṭṭhi, *f.*

Wander, *v.i.* āhiṇḍati; pariyaṭati; saŋsarati. *p.p.* saŋsarita. °**er,** *n.* pariyaṭaka ; paribbhamaka, *m.* °**ing,** *n.* saŋsaraṇa; sañcaraṇa, *nt.*

Wane, *v.i.* khīyati ; hāyati ; veti. *p.p.* khīṇa ; hīna. *n.* khaya ; vaya, *m.* hāni, *f.* °**ing,** *a.* khīyamāna.

Want, *n.* 1. apekkhā ; icchā, *f.* 2. abhāva, *m.* ūnatta, *nt.* 3. niddhanatta, *nt.* *v.i.* 1. apekkhati ; icchati ; 2. parihāyati. °**ing,** *a.* ūnaka; vikala. °**ing,** *prep.* vinā.

Wanton, *a.* 1. asaŋyata ; 2. kāmāsatta ; 3. yathākāmacārī ; 4. amattaññū. *n.* durācārinī, *f.* *v.i.* 1. dibbati ; 2. vilasati ; 3. kāmukatāya ācarati. °**ly,** *adv.* 1. savilāsaŋ ; 2. yathākāmaŋ. °**ness,** *n.* 1. vilāsitā ; 2. yathākāmcāritā, *f.* 3. abhimāna ; dappa, *m.*

War, *n.* yuddha; raṇa, *nt.* saṅgāma ; āhava, *m.* *v.i.* yujjhati ; saṅgāmeti. °**cry,** *n.* yuddhaghosa, *m.*—**chariot,** *n.* yuddharatha, *m.* °**fare,** *n.* yujjhana ; yuddhakaraṇa, *nt.* °**like,** *a.* raṇakāmī. — **office,** *n.* yuddhakiccālaya, *m.*

Warble, *n.* kūjana, *nt.* *v.i.* kūjati ; gāyati. *p.p.* kūjita ; gāyita. °**er,** *n.* 1. kūjaka, *m.* 2. pakkhivisesa, *m.*

Ward, *n.* 1. ārakkhā, *f.* 2. ārakkhaka, *m.* 3. anupadesa, *m.* *v.t.* 1. saŋrakkhati ; 2. nivāreti ; paṭibāhati. *p.p.* °khita ; °rita ; °hita. °**en,** *n.* saŋrakkhaka; pālaka, *m.* °**ing off,** paṭibāhana; nivāraṇa, *nt.* °**robe,** *n.* 1. vatthādhāna, *nt.* 2. nivāsana-pārupanāni, *nt. pl.* °**ship,** *n.* ārakkhakadhura, *nt.*

Ware, *n.* bhaṇḍajāta, *nt.* adj. see **Aware.** *v.t.* sāvadhāno *or* appamatto hoti. °**house,** *n.* bhaṇḍasālā, *f.*

Warm, *a.* 1. uṇha ; tatta ; 2. tikhiṇa ; uttejita. *v.t.* 1. tāpeti ; usumaŋ gaṇhāpeti ; 2. uttejeti. *p.p.* tatta ; gāhitausuma ; °jita. °**ly,** *adv.* sasnehaŋ ; saussāhaŋ. °**ness,** *n.* 1. tāpa ; uṇha, *m.* ghamma, *nt.* 2. tikhiṇatā ; 3. īhā, *f.* ussāha, *m.* °**blooded,** *a.* uṇhalohitayutta. °**hearted,** *a.* sadaya. °**th,** *n.* uṇhatta, *nt.*

Warn, *v.t.* pageva ñāpeti *or* nivedeti. *p.p.* °ñāpita ; °dita. °**ing,** *n.* āvedana ; nivedana ; puretarañāpana, *nt.*

Warp, *v.t.* parāvaṭṭeti ; saṅkoceti. *v.i.* āvaṭṭati ; sañkucati. *p.p.* °ṭita; °cita. *n.* āyata-tantavo, *m. pl.*

Warrant, *n.* adhikārapaṇṇa, *nt.* *v.t.* adhikāre niyojeti ; pamāṇayati. *p.p.* °jita ; °ṇita. °**able,** *a.* pamāṇīkātabba. °**ee,** *n.* laddhādhikārapaṇṇa, *m.*

Warrior, *n.* yodha ; yuddhabhaṭa, *m.* °**caste,** *n.* khattiyakula, *nt.*

Wart, *n.* cammakīla ; cammagaṇḍa, *m.* °**y,** *a.* cammakīlabahula.

Wary, *a.* appamatta ; sāvadhāna ; satimantu. °**ily,** *adv.* sāvadhānaŋ. °**iness,** *n.* sāvadhānatā ; appamāditā, *f.*

Was, *aor.* of **is,** āsi ; ahosi ; abhavi ; bhavi ; ahuvā.—**able,** asakkhi ; sakkuṇi.

Wash, *n.* dhovana ; pakkhālana, *nt.* *v.t.* dhovati ; vikkhāleti. *p.p.* °vita ; °lita. — **away,** pavāheti. — **basin,** *n.* dhovanapāti, *f.* °**er,** *n.* dhovaka, *m.* °**erman,** rajaka, *m.* °**erwoman,** *n.* rajakī, *f.* — **house,** *n.* dhovanasālā, *f.*

Washy, *a.* virasa ; niroja.

Wasp, *n.* bhamara, *m.* °**ish,** *a.* kodhana ; kujjhanasīla.

Wassail, *n.* surāchaṇa, *m.*

Waste, *n.* 1. kantāra, *m.* nijjanabhūmi, *f.* 2. khaya ; vaya, *m.* 3. nippayojanavatthujāta, *nt.* adj. 1. vijana ; 2. akatakasikamma ; 3. chaḍḍanīya. *v.t.* 1. hāpeti ; khepeti ; nāseti ; 2. vinipāteti. *v.i.* hāyati ; khīyati ; vinassati. *p.p.* hāpita ; khepita; nāsita ; °tita ; hīna ; khīṇa ; vinaṭṭha. °**ful,** *a.* vikiraṇasīla. °**fully,** *adv.* vikiraṇākārena. °**fulness,** *n.* asīmitavayatā, *f.* °**land,** *n.* jaṅgala, *nt.* aropitabhūmi, *f.* °**less,** *a.* akkhaya. °**pipe,** *n.* uccitṭhodakapaṇālī, *f.*

Wastrel, *n.* 1. dūsitavatthu ; dūsitabhaṇḍa, *nt.* 2. duppakatikadāraka, *m.*

Watch, *n.* 1. ārakkhā, *f.* 2. ārakkhaka, *m.* 3. yāma, *m.* 4. ghaṭikāyanta, *nt.* *v.t.* rakkhati ; pāleti. *v.i.* sāvadhāno hoti. *p.p.* °khita ; pālita ; sāvadhānabhūta. °**er,** *n.* rakkhī-purisa, *m.* °**ful,** *a.* appamatta ; sāvadhāna. °**fully,** *adv.* sāvadhānaŋ ; appamādena. °**fulness,** *n.* gutti, *f.* sāvadhānatta, *nt.* °**house,** *n.* rakkhāgāra, *nt.* °**maker,** *n.* ghaṭikāsaṅkhāraka, *m.* °**tower,** *n.* ghaṭikāaṭṭāla, *m.* *nt.* °**word,** *n.* saññāpaka-vacana ; āveṇikavacana, *nt.*

Water, *n.* jala ; udaka ; vāri ; ambu ; pānīya ; salila ; nīra ; toya, *nt.* *v.t.* jalena siñcati ; jalaŋ ākirati *or* vāheti. *p.p.* jalasitta ; ākiṇṇajala ; vāhita°. °**born,** *a.* vārija ; ambuja ; jalaja. °**carrier,** *n.* udahārī, *m.* °**clock,** *n.* jalahorāyanta, *nt.* °**course,** *n.* jalamātikā, *f.* °**fall,** *n.* nijjhara, *m.* °**jar,** *n.* bhiṅkāra, *m.* °**lily,** *n.* uppala, *nt.* °**less,** *a.* nirudaka. °**melon,** *n.* vallibha, *m.* °**nymph,** *n.* jaladevatā, *f.* °**pipe,** *n.* udakāyatikā, *f.* °**pool,** *n.* sobbha, *nt.* pokkharaṇī, *f.* — **pot,** *n.* ghaṭa ; udakumbha, *m.* °**shed,** opāna, *nt.* °**snake,** *n.* deḍḍubha, *m.* °**sprite,** dakarakkhasa, *m.* — **strainer,** *n.* parissāvana, *nt.* °**wheel,** *n.* ghaṭīyanta, *nt.* °**y,** *a.* jalabahula. **Free from —,** vodaka, *a.*

Wattle, *n.* 1. sākhābhaṅgavati, *f.* 2. kukkuṭagīvolambapesi, *f.*

Waul, *v.i.* biḷālaravaŋ pavatteti.

Wave, *n.* ūmi ; vīci, *f.* taraṅga, *m.* *v.t.* dhunāti ; kampeti. *v.i.* kampati ; calati. *p.p.* dhuta ; °pita ; calita. °**less,** *a.* ūmirahita. °**let,** *n.* khuddakavīci, *f.*

Waver, *v.i.* dolāyati ; kaṅkhati. *p.p.* °yita ; °khita. °**ing,** *a.* kaṅkhamāna ; dolāyamāna, °**ingly,** *adv.* sasaŋsayaŋ ; dveḷhakabhāvena.

Wavy, *a.* saūmika ; unnatonata.

Wax, *n.* 1. sittha, *nt.* 2. lākhā, *f.* jatu, *nt.* *v.t.* sitthena lepeti. *v.i.* vaḍḍhati. *p.p.* sitthalitta ; °ḍhita. °**en,** *a.* sitthamaya. °**modelling,** *n.* sitthakata-saṇṭhāna, *nt.* sitthākati, *f.* °**y,** *a.* sitthagatika.

Way, *n.* 1. magga ; patha ; pantha ; addhā, *m.* añjasa ; ayana ; vaṭuma, *nt.* 2. vidhi ; ākāra, *m.* 3. upāya, *m.* °**farer,** *n.* pathika ; addhika, *m.* °**faring,** *a.* addhānagāmī. °**lay,** maggaŋ āvaritvā gaṇhāti ; magge nilīyati. °**laying,** *n.* panthadūhana, *nt.* °**layer,** *n.* panthadūhaka, *m.* °**worn,** *a.* maggakilanta. **Give —,** apeti ; olīyati. **In another —,** aññathā, *adv.* **In this —,** itthaŋ ; evaŋ, *adv.* **In two —s,** dvidhā, *adv.* **In what —,** kathaŋ ; kenākārena, *adv.* **Make —,** apasarati. **On the —,** antarāmagge, *loc.* **Right —,** supatha, *m.* **This —,** ito, *adv.* **Wrong —,** kummagga ; uppatha, *m.*

Wayward, *a.* sericārī ; avasavattī. °**ly,** *adv.* sericāritāya. °**ness,** *n.* avasavattitā, *f.*

We, *pron. pl.* mayaŋ ; amhe.

Weak, *a.* dubbala ; khīṇabala ; hīnaviriya ; (in mind :) mandabuddhika. °**en,** *v.t.* dubbalīkaroti. *p.p.* °kata. °**ling,** *n.* dubbalapuggala, *m.* °**ly,** *a.* balahīna; mandaviriya. °**ness,** *n.* dubbalya ; asāmatthiya, *nt.* — **point,** *n.* randha ; dubbalaṭṭhāna, *nt.*

Weal, *n.* kalyāṇa ; subha, *nt.*

Wealth, *n.* dhana ; vitta ; sāpateyya, *nt.* vibhava, *m.* sampatti, *f.* °**iness,** *n.* sadhanatta, *nt.* °**y,** *a.* sadhana ; mahaddhana. **Greedy of —,** dhanalola, *a.* **Proud of —,** dhanamadamatta.

Wean, *n.* bālaka, *m.* *v.t.* thaññaŋ vajjetuŋ sikkhāpeti. °**ing,** *n.* thaññavajjana, *nt.*

Weapon, *n.* āyudha ; sattha ; paharaṇa, *nt.* °**less,** *a.* nirāyudha.

Wear, *n.* 1. khaya ; vaya, *m.* 2. paridahana ; nivāsana, *nt.* 3. vatthajāta, *nt.* *v.t.* 1. paridahati; nivāseti ; acchādeti ; 2. khepeti. *v.i.* khīyati. *p.p.* °hita ; °sita ; °dita ; °pita ; khīṇa. °**able,** *a.* acchādanāraha. °**er,** *n.* acchādetu, *m.* °**ing,** *n.* 1. acchādana ; 2. khīyana, *nt.* °**ing,** *a.* vihesakara.

Weary, *a.* 1. kilanta; parissanta; 2. nibbinna. *v.t.* viheseti ; kilameti ; āyāseti. *v.i.* kilamati. *p.p.* °sita; °mita ; kilanta. °**iness,** *n.* kilamatha, *m.* °**isome,** *a.* āyāsakara; vihesājanaka. °**isomeness,** *n.* āyāsakaratta, *nt.*

Weasand, *n.* kaṇṭhanāḷa ; sāsanāḷa, *m.*

Weasel, *n.* dīghaloma-nakulavisesa, *m.*

Weather, *n.* kālaguṇa ; utu, *m.* °**beaten,** *a.* 1. vātāhata ; vātavuṭṭhipīḷita ; 2. laddhaparicaya. °**gage,** °**gauge,** vātavāyanadisā, *f.* °**glass,** *n.* vāyumāṇaka, *m.* **Bad —,** duddina, *nt.* **Good —,** susamaya, *m.*

Weave, *n.* vāyana, *nt.* *v.t.* vināti. *p.p.* vīta. °**er,** *n.* tantavāya ; pesakāra, *m.* °**ing,** *n.* vāyana ; ganthana, *nt.*

Web, *n.* jāla, *nt.* °**footed,** *a.* jālapāda.

Wed, *v.t.* pāṇiggahaŋ *or* pariṇayaŋ karoti. *p.p.* katapariṇaya. °**ded,** *a.* gharabandhanabaddha. °**ding,** *n.* pāṇiggaha, *n.* gharabandhana, *nt.*

Wedge, *n.* kīla ; khīlaka, *m.* *v.t.* khīlaŋ yojeti. *p.p.* yojitakhīla.

Wednesday, *n.* Budhavāra, *m.*

Wee, *a.* atyappaka ; atikhuddaka.

Weed, *n.* tiṇajāti, *f.* *v.t.* niḍḍeti ; nipphalatiṇaŋ uddharati. *p.p.* °ḍita ; uddhaṭa° tiṇa.

Week, *n.* sattāha ; sattaratta, *nt.* °**ly,** *a.* sattāhika. *adv.* paṭisattāhaŋ.

Ween, *v.t.* maññati. *p.p.* maññita.

Weep, *v.i.t.* kandati ; paridevati ; vilapati. *p.p.* °dita ; °vita ; °pita. °**ing,** *n.* paridevana ; vilapana, *nt.* °**er,** *n.* paridevaka, *m.*

Weevil, *n.* dhaññanāsakakīṭa, *m.*

Weft, *n.* vāyane tirotanturāsi, *m.*

Weigh, *v.t.* 1. tuleti ; miṇāti ; 2. vīmaŋsati. *p.p.* tulita ; mita ; °sita. °**ing,** *n.* tulana, *nt.* °**er,** *n.* tuletu, *m.*

Weight, *n.* bhāra, *m.* garutta, *nt.* °**ily,** *adv.* bhāriyākārena. °**y,** *a.* bhāriya ; bhārayutta. °**iness,** *n.* bhāriyatta, *nt.* °**less,** *a.* appabhāra. **False —,** tulākūṭa, *nt.*

Weir, *n.* gaṅgārodhakāli, *f.*

Weird, *a.* amānusika ; gūḷha. *n.* bhāgya, *nt.* niyati, *f.*

Welcome, *n.* abhinandana, *nt.* svāgatavāda, *m.* adj. subha ; maṅgala ; iṭṭha. *intj.* svāgataŋ ! subhāgamanaŋ ! *v.t.* abhinandati ; sampaṭicchati ; sammāneti. *p.p.* °dita ; °chita ; °nita.

Weld, *v.t.* tāpetvā ghaṭeti *or* saŋyojeti. *p.p.* °ṭita ; °jita. °**er,** *n.* lohasandhānaka, *m.*

Welfare, *n.* attha, *m.* hita, *nt.* subhasiddhi, *f.* **— of others,** parahita, *nt.*

Welkin, *n.* ākāsa ; nabha, *m.*

Well, *n.* kūpa ; udapāna ; udakūpa, *m.* adj. anāmaya ; niroga. *adv.* suṭṭhu ; sammā ; sādhukaŋ. *intj.* sādhu ! sādhu ! °**born,** *a.* abhijāta. °**bred,** *a.* susikkhita. °**built,** *a.* sukata ; sumāpita. °**conducted,** *a.* suppaṭipanna. °**decked,** *a.* samalaṅkata. **— done,** *a.* sukata ; suniṭṭhita. **— doing,** *n.* hitakaraṇa, *nt.* **— doer,** *n.* hitakārī, *m.* **— disposed,** *a.* hitakāma ; hitesī. **— favoured,** *a.* cārudassana. **— fed,** *a.* suṭṭhuposita. **— founded,** *a.* suppatiṭṭhita. **— formed,** *a.* sughaṭita ; suracita. **—known,** *a.* pākaṭa ; abhiññāta ; vissuta. **— made,** *a.* susādhita ; susaṇṭhāna. **— meant,** *a.* suparikappita. **— nigh,** *adv.* kevalakappaŋ ; manaŋ. **— painted,** *a.* sucittita ; vaṇṇālitta. **— practised,** *a.* suparicita ; subhāvita. **— restrained,** *a.* susaññata. **— rid of,** sumutta, *a.* **— then,** handa, *ind.* **— to-do,** *a.* samiddha ; sukhita. **— touched,** *a.* suphassita. **— versed,** *a.* bahussuta. **— wisher,** *n.* subhāsaŋsī, *m.* **— wishing,** *a.* atthakāma ; hitakāma.

Welter, *n.* gottakalaha; pakkhantaravirodha, *m.* *v.i.* kalalādisu parivaṭṭati. *p.p.* °ṭita.

Wen, *n.* maŋsagaṇṭhi; vāyugaṇḍa, *m.*

Wench, *n.* 1. yuvatī; taruṇī; 2. gaṇikā, *f.*

Wend, see **Go.**

West, *n.* pacchimā; patīci, *f.* *adv.* pacchimena. °**ern**, °**erly**, *a.* pacchima; apācīna. °**erner**, *n.* pacchimadisāvāsī, *m.* °**ernmost**, *a.* atipacchimaka. °**wards**, *adv.* pacchimābhimukhaŋ.

Wet, *a.* alla; tinta; temita; kilinna. *n.* allatā, *f.* *v.t.* temeti; kiledeti. *p.p.* temita; °dita. °**ness**, *n.* tintatta, *nt.*

Whack, *n.* daḷhapothana, *nt.* *v.t.* daḷhaŋ potheti. *p.p.* °thita. °**er**, *n.* 1. mahattara-puggala, *m.* 2. mahattara-vatthu, *nt.* 3. mahattara-musā, *f.*

Whale, *n.* timiṅgala, *m.*

Wharf, *n.* nāvotaraṇaṭṭhāna, *nt.* nāvāsetu, *m.* *v.t.* 1. nāvaŋ setum upaneti; 2. nāvābhaṇḍaŋ setumhi nidahati. °**age**, *n.* bhaṇḍanidahanamūla, *nt.*

What, *pron.* 1. kiŋ, 2. ya, 3. kittaka, °**else**, kim aññaŋ ? °**ever**, yaŋ kiñci; yādi-saka, *a.* °**like**, kīdisa, *a.* — **sort of**, kathaŋvidha. *a.*

Wheat, *n.* godhuma, *m.*

Wheedle, *v.t.* cāṭukamyatāya upalāleti. *p.p.* °lita. °**er**, *n.* cāṭukāmī, *m.* °**lingly**, *adv.* cāṭukamyatāya.

Wheel, *n.* cakka, *nt.* *v.t.* āvaṭṭeti; paribbhameti. *v.i.* āvaṭṭati; paribbhamati. *p.p.* °ṭita; °mita; paribbhanta. °**barrow**, *n.* hatthasakaṭa, *m.* °**ed**, *a.* cakkayutta. °**er**, °**wright**, cakkakāra, *m.* °**y**, *a.* cakkasadisa.

Wheeze, *v.i.* sasaddaŋ passasati. *n.* sasanasadda, *m.*

Whelk, *n.* kapolapiḷakā, *f.*

Whelm, *v.t.* ajjhottharati; osīdāpeti. *p.p.* °thaṭa; °pita.

Whelp, *n.* pasupotaka, *m.*

When, *adv.* kadā ? °**ever**, yādā, *ind.*

Whence, *adv.* kuto ? yato.

Where, *adv.* kuhiŋ; kutra; kuttha; kattha; kahaŋ; kva, *conj.* yatra; yattha, yahiŋ. °**ever**, yattha; yattha katthaci. °**abouts**, *adv.* kasmiŋ ṭhāne. *n.* 1. patiṭṭhitaṭṭhāna; 2. vasanaṭṭhāna, *nt.* °**as**, *conj.* yasmā; yato; tathā pi. °**at**, tadā, *adv.* °**by**, *adv.* tena; tena hetunā; tasmā. °**for**, *adv.* kimatthaŋ ? °**fore**, *adv.* kissa hetu ? °**in**, *adv.* yatra. °**of**, kiŋ sandhāya. °**upon**, *adv.* tato; taṅkhaṇe; tena hetunā. °**withal**, *n.* āvassaka-dhanādi, *m.*

Whet, *n.* 1. nisāṇana; 2. uddīpana, *nt.* *v.t.* niseti; tejeti; tikhiṇayati. *p.p.* nisita; °jita; °yita. °**stone**, *n.* nikasa, sāṇa, *m.*

Whether, *adv.* kacci; kinti; uda vā; udāhu.

Whey, *n.* dadhimaṇḍa, *nt.*

Which, *pron.* (relative :) ya, 3. (Interrogative :) ka (=kiŋ), 3. — **of the two**, katara, *a.* — **of the many**, katama, *a.* °**ever**, yaŋ kiñci.

While, *n.* samaya ; kāla ; khaṇa, *m. conj. adv.* yāva . . . tāva ; tasmiŋ antare. *v.t.* (away :) khepeti; vītināmeti. **After a long —**, cirena ; dīghena addhunā. **For a —**, kiñci kālaŋ, *adv.* **Worth°**, sātthaka ; agghanaka. *a.*

Whilst, *conj.* tāva.

Whim, *n.* cāpalla ; matimatta, *nt.* sericāra, *m.* **°sical**, *a.* capala ; sericārī. **°sically**, *adv.* sericārena ; anavaṭṭhitatāya.

Whimper, *n.* aṭṭitarāva, *m. v.t.i.* aṭṭitassaraŋ pavatteti. *p.p.* °titaṭṭitassara.

Whine, *n.* anutthunana, *nt. v.i.* anutthunāti. *p.p.* °nita ; anutthuta.

Whinny, *n.* hesārava, *m. v.i.* hesāravaŋ pavatteti.

Whip, *n.* kasā, *f. v.t.* kasāya tāḷeti. *p.p.* °ḷita. **°per**, *n.* kasāhanaka, *m.* **°ping**, *n.* kasāhanana, *nt.* **— round**, sīghaŋ parivattati. **°snake**, *n.* nīlasappa, *m.* **°stock**, *n.* kasādaṇḍa, *m.*

Whirl, *n.* paribbhama ; āvaṭṭa, *m. v.t.* paribbhameti ; āvaṭṭeti. *v.i.* āvaṭṭati ; paribbhamati. *p.p.* °mita ; °ṭita ; paribbhanta. **°igig**, *n.* bhamanaka ; bhamaraka, *nt.* **°pool**, *n.* salilabbhama, *m.* **°wind**, *n.* vātamaṇḍalikā, *f.*

Whisht, **Whist**, *intj.* tuṇhī ; nissaddā hotha.

Whisk, *n.* cāmara, *m.* vījanī ; makkhikāvāraṇī, *f. v.t.* 1. vījeti; vidhūpeti ; 2. sīghaŋ puñchati. *p.p.* vījita ; °pita ; °chita.

Whisker, *n.* 1. kapolamassu, *nt.* 2. dāṭhikā, *f.*

Whisky, *n.* dhaññasurā, *f.*

Whisper, *n.* nikaṇṇikajappana, *nt. v.i.* upajappati. *p.p.* °pita. **°er**, *n.* kaṇṇajappaka, *m.* **°ing**, *n.* upajappana, *nt.* **°ingly**, *adv.* kaṇṇajappanavasena.

Whistle, *n.* 1. mukhakāhalanāda, *m.* 2. kāhala, *m. v.i.t.* mukhakāhalaŋ pavatteti.

Whit, *n.* bindumatta ; atyappaka, *nt.*

White, *a.* seta ; dhavala ; odāta ; sukka ; paṇḍara. *n.* 1. setavaṇṇa, *m.* 2. aṇḍassa setabhāga, *m.* 3. setanivāsana, *nt.* **°en**, *v.t.* dhavalīkaroti. *v.i.* dhavalībhavati. *p.p.* °kata ; °bhūta. **— ant**, *n.* upacikā, *f.* **— bear**, *n.* setaccha, *m.* **°bearded**, *a.* palitamassuka. **— elephant**, *n.* 1. sethahatthī, *m.* 2. niratthaka-vayakāraṇa, *nt.* **— lily**, *n.* setuppala ; kumuda, *nt.*—**livered**, *a.* bhīruka. **°ness**, *n.* dhavalatta, *nt.* **— paper**, *n.* rājāṇādīpaka-paṇṇa, *nt.* **°scab**, *n.* saṅkhakuṭṭha, *nt.* **°wash**, *v.t.* sudhāya lepeti. **°washer**, *n.* sudhālepaka, *m.*

Whither, see **Where**. **°soever**, yattha katthaci, *adv.*

Whitish, *a.* īsaŋpaṇḍara.

Whitlow, *n.* nakhagaṇḍa, *m.*

Whittle, *v.t.* 1. tikhiṇayati ; 2. anukkamena khepeti.

Who, *pron.* ko ? *m. sing.* **°ever**, yo koci, *m. sing.* **Whom**, kaŋ ? **Whose**, kassa ?

Whole, *a. n.* sakala ; nikhila ; kevala ; asesa ; nissesa ; sabba. **°hearted**, *a.* anaññavihita ; avikkhitta. **°ness**, *n.* sākalla, *nt.* **°ly**, *adv.* asesaŋ ; nissesaŋ ;

sabbaso. °**sale**, *n.* rāsivikkaya, *m.* °**some**, sappāyabhūta. °**someness**, *n.* sappāyatā, *f.*

Whoop, *n.* ukkuṭṭhi ; jayaghosa, *m.* *v.t.* ugghosena niggaṇhāti. *v.i.* ugghoseti. *p.p.* °niggahita ; °sita.

Whop, *v.t.* 1. tāḷeti ; 2. parājeti. *p.p.* tāḷita; °jita. *n.* sahasā patana, *nt.* °**ping**, *n.* atimahantavatthu, *nt.*

Whore, *n.* gaṇikā, *f.* *v.i.* kāmamicchācāraṃ ācarati. °**monger**, *n.* gaṇikāvallabha, *m.*

Why, *adv.* kasmā ? kena ? nanu. *n.* nimitta, *nt.* hetu, *m.* kāraṇa, *nt.*

Wick, *n.* dīpavaṭṭi, *f.*

Wicked, *a.* duṭṭha ; khala ; adhammika. °**ly**, *adv.* duṭṭhākārena. — **man**, *n.* narādhama ; asappurisa, *m.* °**ness**, *n.* duṭṭhatta ; kakkhaḷatta, *nt.*

Wicker, *a.* bidalamaya ; veḷupesikāmaya. °**work**, *n.* vilīvakamma, *nt.*

Wide, *a.* vitthata ; vitthiṇṇa ; puthula ; patthaṭa. °**en**, *v.t.* puthulīkaroti. °**ly**, *adv.* vitthiṇṇākārena. °**spread**, *a.* puthubhūta ; vitthārika.

Widow, *n.* vidhavā, *f.* °**ed**, *a.* matapatikā, *f.* °**er**, *n.* matabhariya, *m.* °**hood**, *n.* vidhavatta, *nt.*

Width, *n.* vitthāra, *m.*

Wield, *v.t.* 1. vase vatteti ; 2. pavatteti ; 3. vijambheti. *p.p.* °tita ; °bhita. — **the sceptre**, rajjaŋ kāreti. °**y**, *a.* suparihāriya.

Wife, *n.* bhariyā ; jāyā ; dutiyikā ; pajāpatī, *f.* kalatta, *nt.* dāra, *m.* — **and husband**, jāyāpatī ; jānipatī ; jayampatī, *m.* *pl.* °**hood**, *n.* jāyatta, *nt.* °**ly**, *a.* bhariyocita.

Wig, *n.* kittimakesakalāpa, *m.* *v.t.* daḷhaṃ akkosati. *p.p.* °akkuṭṭha. °**ging**, *n.* akkosana, *nt.*

Wild, *a.* 1. vanaja ; āraññaka ; 2. vāla ; caṇḍa ; adanta ; 3. vyākulacitta. °**boar**, *n.* vanavarāha, *m.* °**cat**, *n.* vanabiḷāra, *m.* °**goose chase**, niratthakavyāpāra, *m.* °**ly**, *adv.* adantākārena. °**ness**, *n.* 1. vanajatta ; 2. adantatta, *nt.* **Grow** —, vane jāyati.

Wilderness, *n.* 1. nijjanapadesa ; kantāra, *m.* 2. arañña, *nt.*

Wile, *n.* sāṭheyya ; ketava, *nt.* *v.t.* palobheti ; palambheti ; vañceti. *p.p.* °bhita ; °cita. °**y**, *a.* saṭha ; kūṭa.

Wilful, *a.* sacetanika ; secchāya kata ; yathākāmakata. °**ly**, *adv.* dovacassatāya ; seritāya. °**ness**, *n.* yathākāmacāritā, *f.*

Will, *n.* 1. chanda ; saṅkappa ; abhilāsa, *m.* icchā, *f.* 2. accayadānapaṇṇa, *nt.* *v.t.* and *aux.* icchati ; abhilasati ; ceteti. *p.p.* °chita ; °sita ; °tita. °**ing**, *a.* icchamāna ; kattukāma. °**ingly**, *adv.* sakecchāya. °**ingness**, *n.* kāmitā ; kattukāmatā, *f.* °**power**, *n.* cittabala ; adhiṭṭhānabala, *nt.* **At** —, yathākāmaŋ, *adv.* **With a** —, mahussāhena, *adv.*

Willy-nilly, *a.* akatanicchaya ; dveḷhakajāta. *adv.* icchante vā anicchante vā.

Wimble, *n.* ārāhattha, *m.* vedhanī, *f.*

Win, *n.* jaya ; vijaya ; kaṭaggāha, *m.* *v.t.i.* jināti ; parājeti ; abhibhavati. *p.p.* jita; °jita ; °bhūta. **— favour,** ārādheti. °**ner,** *n.* jetu ; kaṭaggāhī, *m.* °**ning,** *a.* jayaggāhī. °**some,** *a.* manohara.

Wince, *n.* aṭṭīyana ; vedanāya kampana, *nt.* *v.i.* vedanāya aṭṭīyati.

Wind, *n.* vāta ; vāyu ; anila ; māruta ; māluta ; pavana ; samīraṇa, *m.* vāya, *m.* *nt.* *v.t.* 1. (kāhalādiŋ) dhameti ; 2. vāyunā pūreti ; 3. vāyati. *p.p.* dhamita *or* dhanta; °rita; vāyita. °**bag,** *n.* jappanabahula; vācāla, *m.* °**fall,** *n.* 1. vātavāyana, *nt.* 2. anapekkhitalābha, *m.* °**gauge,** *n.* vāyuvegamāṇaka, *nt.* °**hover,** *n.* seṇa, *m.* °**lass,** *n.* bhārussāpakayanta, *nt.* °**less,** *a.* nivāta. °**mill,** *n.* vāyucālitayanta, *nt.* °**pipe,** *n.* kaṇṭhanāḷa, *m.* °**swept,** *a.* vātāhaṭa. °**ward,** *n.* vātavāyanadisā, *f.* adj. vātānugata. *adv.* vātābhimukhaŋ. °**y,** *a.* savāta ; vātabahula.

Wind, *n.* vellitavatthu ; veṭhana, *nt.* *v.t.* āvaṭṭeti ; āvelleti. *p.p.* °ṭita ; °lita. °**ing,** *a.* vaṅkabahula. °**ing,** *n.* āvellana, *nt.*

Window, *n.* vātapāna ; kavāṭa, *nt.* ālokasandhi, *m.* — **blind,** *n.* vātapānatirokaraṇī, *f.*

Wine, *n.* muddikāsava, *m.* °**bibber,** *n.* surādhutta, *m.*

Wing, *n.* 1. pakkha ; patta, *nt.* 2. (of an army :) senādala, *nt.* senāvibhāga, *m.* *v.t.* uḍḍeti ; pakkhe kampeti. *p.p.* uḍḍita ; kampitapakkha.

Wink, *v.i.* nimisati ; nimīleti. *p.p.* nimīlita. *n.* 1. nimesa, *m.* 2. nimesasaññā, *f.*

Winkle, *n.* sambukavisesa, *m.*

Winnow, *v.t.* opuṇāti ; vidhūpeti ; papphoṭeti. *p.p.* °ṇita ; °pita ; °ṭita. °**ing,** *n.* opuṇana, *nt.* °**ing basket,** suppa, *m.*

Winter, *n.* hemanta, *m.* sisira, *nt.* *v.i.t.* hemantaŋ khepeti; hemante (gavādiŋ) poseti. °**less,** *a.* hemantarahita. °**ly,** °**try,** *a.* hemantika ; sītavātabahula.

Wipe, *v.t.* puñchati ; parimajjati. *p.p.* °chita ; parimaṭṭha. °**er,** *n.* puñchanī, *f.* — **off,** — **out,** lopeti; vināseti; ummūleti. °**ing,** *n.* puñchana ,*nt.* lopa, *m.*

Wire, *n.* lohatantu, *m.* *v.t.* 1. lohatantavo yojeti ; 2. tantusāsanaŋ peseti. *p.p.* yojitalohatantū ; pesita°. °**less,** *a.* tanturahita ; vijjubalapesita. °**less message,** *n.* vijjuvegasāsana, *nt.* °**puller,** *n.* rahasipalobhaka, *m.*

Wiry, *a.* 1. lohatantusadisa ; 2. kisa-thāmavantu.

Wisdom, *n.* paññā; mati; buddhi ; medhā ; dhī, *f.* ñāṇa, *nt.* amoha, *m.*

Wise, *n.* ākāra ; vesa, *m.* adj. paññavantu ; dhīmantu ; matimantu ; medhāvī ; viññū ; vidū ; sappañña ; buddhimantu; °**acre,** *n.* paṇḍitamānī, *m.* °**ly,** *adv.* sampajaññena; yoniso. — **man,** *n.* paṇḍita ; vibudha ; vibhāvī ; dhīra, *m.* **In this —,** iminā ākārena.

Wish, *n.* icchā ; āsā ; ākaṅkhā ; āsaŋsā ; ruci, *f.* chanda ; manoratha ; abhilāsa, *m.* *v.t.i.* icchati ; abhilasati ; ākaṅkhati ; apekkhati ; patthеti. *p.p.* icchita ; °sita ; °khita ; °thita. °**ing**, *a.* ākaṅkhī ; apekkhī. °**er**, *n.* icchitu ; abhilasitu, *m.* °**fully**, *adv.* sābhilāsaŋ ; sākaṅkhaŋ. — **fulfilling tree**, kapparukkha, *m.* — **fulfilling gem**, cintāmaṇī, *m.*

Wistful, *a.* 1. accākaṅkhamāna; 2. cintāpara; alābhena ukkaṇṭhita. °**ly**, *adv.* accantāpekkhāya.

Wit, *n.* 1. paṭibhāṇa, *nt.* tikhiṇabuddhi, *f.* 2. parihāsasāmatthiya, *nt.* °**less**, *a.* appaṭibhāṇa.

Witch, *n.* māyākārī ; mohinī, *f.* *v.t.* pamoheti. *p.p.* °hita. °**craft**, *n.* māyā, *f.* indajāla, *nt.* °**ery**, *n.* indajālavijjā, *f.* °**ingly**, *adv.* mohanākārena.

With, *prep.* saha ; saddhiŋ. (Very often expressed by the Instrumental :) *purisena*, with the man. — **reference to**, uddissa ; upādāya ; sandhāya, *ind.*

Withal, *adv.* aparañ ca ; api ca.

Withdraw, *v.t.* 1. apakaḍḍhati ; paṭisaŋharati ; 2. paccosakkati. *p.p.* °ḍhita ; °haṭa, °kita. °**al**, *n.* 1. apakaḍḍhana; apanayana; 2. paccosakkana, *nt.* 3. uddhāra, *m.*

Wither, *v.i.* sussati ; milāyati. *p.p.* sukkha ; milāta. *v.t.* soseti ; milāyāpeti. *p.p.* sosita ; milāpita.

Withhold, *v.t.* orumbheti ; nirumbheti ; nivatteti. *p.p.* °bhita ; °tita.

Within, *adv. prep.* anto ; abbhantare. *n.* antobhāga, *m.* abbhantara, *nt.* — **the limits**, oraŋ ; orena. — **six months**, orena chammāsaŋ.

Without, *adv.* bahi ; bahiddhā ; *prep.* vinā ; aññatra. — **doubt**, nissaŋsayaŋ, *adv.* **Lying** —, bahiṭṭhita. *a.*

Withstand, *v.t.i.* paṭivirujjhati ; paccavaṭṭhāti. *p.p.* paṭiviruddha ; °ṭhita. °**er**, *n.* paṭivirodhī, *m.*

Witness, *n.* sakkhika ; apadisa, *m.* *v.t.* 1. paccakkhaŋ karoti ; 2. sakkhinā samatthayati. *v.i.* sakkhī bhavati. *p.p.* °kata ; °yita ; °bhūta. °**box**, *n.* sakkhipañjara, *m.* **Ear** —, sutasakkhī, *m.* **Eye** —, diṭṭhasakkhī, *m.*

Witty, *a.* nammālāpī; parihāsakusala. °**icism**, *n.* nammālāpakathana, *nt.* °**ily**, *adv.* parihāsacāturiyena. °**ingly**, *adv.* jānanto va.

Wive, *v.t.* dārapariggahaŋ karoti. *p.p.* katadāra°.

Wizard, *n.* māyākāra ; bhūtavejja, *m.* °**ry**, *n.* indajāla, *nt.*

Wizen, °**ed**, *a.* 1. valittaca; 2. kisadassana.

Woad, *n.* nīlī, *f.*

Wobble, *n.* dolāyana, *nt.* *v.i.* dolāyati ; pakampati. °**er**, *n.* dveḷhakajāta ; kampamānavāca, *m.*

Woe, *n.* dukkha ; dubbhāgya, *nt.* kheda, *m.* vipatti, *f.* °**ful**, *a.* sokāvaha ; dukkhakara. °**fully**, *adv.* khedakaratāya ; sadukkhaŋ.

Wold, *n.* akaṭṭhabhūmi, *f.*

Wolf, *n.* vaka ; koka, *m.* *v.t.* giddhatāya bhuñjati. °**ish**, *a.* 1. kokasadisa ; 2. vilumpaka ; 3. atigiddha. °**ishly**, *adv.* atigiddhatāya. °**ishness**, *n.* 1. dāruṇatta; 2. giddhatta, *nt.*

Woman, *n.* itthī ; nārī ; vanitā ; aṅganā ; thī ; mahilā ; abalā, *f.* mātugāma, *m.* °**hood**, *n.* itthibhāva, *m.* °**ish**, *a.* itthisadisa. °**kind**, *n.* itthigaṇa, *m.* °**ly**, *a.* vanitānucchavika ; itthiyogga.

Womb, *n.* gabbhāsaya, *m.*

Wonder, *n.* 1. vimhaya, *m.* 2. acchariya ; abbhuta, *nt.* *v.i.* vimhayam āpajjati. *p. p.* āpanna°. °**ful**, °**drous**, *a.* savimhaya ; abbhutajanaka. °**fully**, *adv.* abbhutākārena. °**ingly**, *adv.* savimhayaŋ.

Wont, *n.* paricaya ; satatavohāra, *m.* adj. paricayagata. *v. aux.* paricito hoti. °**ed**, *a.* paricita. °**ed nature**, pakati, *f.* paricitākāra, *m.*

Woo, *v.t.* vivāhāya abhilasati ; pemaŋ pakāseti. *p.p.* °sita ; °sitapema. °**er**, *n.* vivāhatthī, *m.*

Wood, *n.* 1. arañña ; vana, *nt.* aṭavi, *f.* 2. kaṭṭha ; dāru, *nt.* °**apple**, *n.* kapittha, *m.* °**cutter**, *n.* kaṭṭhacchedaka, *m.* °**en**, *a.* dārumaya. °**land**, *n.* rukkhagahaṇa-padesa, *m.* °**less**, *a.* vanarahita. °**nymph**, *n.* vanadevatā, *f.* °**pecker**, *n.* sārasa ; satapatta, *m.* °**reeve**, *n.* aṭavipālaka, *m.* °**sman**, vanavāsī, *m.* °**work**, *n.* dārukamma, *nt.* kaṭṭharacanā, *f.* °**y**, *a.* vanabahula ; araññagatika.

Woof, *n.* vāyane tirogatasuttajāta, *nt.*

Wool, *n.* uṇṇā, *f.* —**gathering**, *a.* anavaṭṭhitacitta. °**len**, *a.* uṇṇāmaya. *n.* uṇṇāvattha ; kambala, *nt.* — **draper**, *n.* kambalavāṇija, *m.* °**liness**, *n.* lomabahulatā, *f.* °**ly**, *a.* lomabahula.

Word, *n.* 1. vācā ; girā ; vāṇī, *f.* vacana ; bhāsita, *nt.* ālāpa, *m.* 2. pada, *nt.* *v.t.* padāni gantheti *or* racayati. °**iness**, *n.* padabāhulla, *nt.* °**ing**, *n.* racanāvilāsa, *m.* °**y**, *a.* padabahula ; vācābahula.

Work, *n.* 1. kamma ; kicca, *nt.* 2. vyāpāra ; kammanta, *m.* 3. nimmāṇa, *nt.* racanā, *f.* *v.t.* vidahati ; nimmiṇāti ; nipphādeti. *v.i.* kiccaŋ karoti ; vyāpāram āpajjati. *p.p.* vihita; °mita ; °dita ; katakicca ; °āpanna. °**able**, *a.* payojiya ; kammañña ; sukara, °**er**, *n.* kammakāra, *m.* °**er in bamboo**, vilīvakāra, *m.* °**ing**, *n.* 1. kammakaraṇa, *nt.* 2. katākāra, *m.* °**ing**, *a.* kiccappayutta ; kiccappayogāraha. °**ing class**, kammakārajanatā, *f.* °**manship**, *n.* kammakosalla, *nt.* — **on**, — **upon**, balaŋ pavatteti. — **out**, 1. gaṇanaŋ saṅkaleti ; 2. nibbeṭheti ; 3. avassakāraṇāni vijānāti. °**shop**, *n.* āvesana, *nt.* sippasālā, *f.*

World, *n.* loka, *m.* jagati, *f.* bhuvana, *nt.* — **beyond**, paraloka, *m.* — **circle**, *n.* cakkavāḷa, *m.* °**liness**, *n.* lokiyatta, *nt.* visayāsatti, *f.* °**ling**, *n.* visayāsatta ;

puthujjana, *m.* °**ly**, *a.* lokāyatta ; ihalokika. — **of desire**, kāmaloka, *m.* — **of the dead**, yamaloka, *m.*—**system**, *n.* lokadhātu, *f.* °**wide**, *a.* lokavitthata.

Worm, *n.* kimi ; kīṭa ; pulavaka, *m.* °**eaten**, *a.* kimikhādita. °**y**, *a.* kimibahula.

Worn, *a.* 1. khīṇa ; jiṇṇa ; 2. nivattha.

Worry, *n.* vihesā ; paritassanā, *f.* *v.t.* 1. āyāseti ; pīḷeti ; 2. (sunakho viya nantakaŋ) ḍasitvā vikirati. *v.i.* paritappati. *p.p.* °sita ; pīḷita ; °rita ; °pita. °**ing**, *a.* hiŋsaka ; vihesājanaka.

Worse, *a.* duṭṭhutara; atinikiṭṭha, *adv.* duṭṭhutaraŋ ; nikiṭṭhākārena.

Worship, *n.* paṇāma ; namakkāra, *m.* vandanā ; pūjanā, *f.* *v.t.* vandati ; namassati ; abhivādeti ; paṇamati ; mahati ; pūjeti. *p.p.* °dita ; °sita ; °mita ; mahita ; pūjita. °**ful**, *a.* vandanīya ; mahanīya. °**fully**, *adv.* atigāravena. °**per**, *n.* namassaka ; vandaka ; apacāyī ; pūjetu, *m.*

Worst, *n.* duṭṭhutamāvatthā, *f.* adj. asādhutama ; duṭṭhutama. *v.t.* parājeti ; abhibhavati. *p.p.* °jita ; °bhūta.

Worth, *n.* aggha ; mūlya, *nt.* adj. agghanaka. °**ily**, *adv.* yathārahaŋ ; yathocitaŋ. °**iness**, *n.* ocitya ; anucchavikatta, *nt.* °**less**, *a.* appaggha ; aggharahita. °**lessness**, *n.* niragghatta ; appagghatta, *nt.* °**y**, *a.* yogga ; araha ; ucita ; mānanīya. °**y for a monk**, sāmaṇaka, *a.* °**y of an offering**, dakkhiṇeyya, *a.* °**while**, *a.* āyāsagghanaka.

Wound, *n.* 1. vaṇa ; aru, *m.* khata, *nt.* 2. avaññā, *f.* *v.t.* 1. vaṇeti ; tudati ; 2. hiŋsati. *p.p.* vaṇita ; tunna ; °sita.

Wrangle, *n.* kalaha, *m.* bhaṇḍana, *nt.* *v.i.* bhaṇḍanaŋ karoti. *p.p.* katabhaṇḍana. °**er**, *n.* bhaṇḍanakārī, *m.*

Wrap, *n.* pāpuraṇa, *nt.* *v.t.* veṭheti ; oguṇṭheti ; onahati. *p.p.* °ṭhita. onaddha. — **in**, pārupati. °**per**, *n.* 1. bāhirāvaraṇa, *nt.* 2. paḷiveṭhaka. °**ping**, *n.* veṭhana; oguṇṭhana, pārupana, *nt.*

Wrath, *n.* baḷavakopa ; rosa ; appaccaya, *m.* °**ful**, *a.* kopāviṭṭha. °**fully**, *adv.* sakopaŋ ; kopāviṭṭhatāya.

Wreak, *v.t.* veraŋ paṭisādheti. *p.p.* °dhitavera.

Wreath, *n.* dāma ; hāra ; mālādāma, *m.* pupphāvali, *f.*

Wreathe, *v.t.* 1. gantheti ; 2. mālādāmaŋ pilandheti ; 3. āliṅgati. *p.p.* °thita ; °dhitamālā° ; °gita.

Wreck, *n.* 1. nāvābhaṅga, *m.* 2. vinaṭṭhabala ; vinaṭṭhayasa; 3. āsābhaṅga, *m.* *v.i.* bhijjati ; vinassati. *v.t.* bhañjati ; vināseti. *p.p.* bhinna ; vinaṭṭha ; bhaṭṭha ; °sita. °**age**, *n.* bhinnanāvāvasesa, *m.*

Wrench, *n.* 1. pasayhākaḍḍhana ; 2. viyogadukkha, *nt.* 3. āvaṭṭanīsaṇḍāsa, *m.* *v.t.* 1. āvaṭṭetvā ākaḍḍhati ; 2. ākaḍḍhitvā chindati ; 3. saṇḍāsena āvaṭṭeti. *p.p.* °ḍhita ; °chinna ; °ṭita.

Wrest, *v.t.* pasayha gaṇhāti *or* avaharati. *p.p.* °gahita ; °avahaṭa.

Wrestle, *n.* mallayuddha, *nt. v.i.t.* mallayuddhaŋ karoti. °**er,** *n.* muṭṭhimalla, *m.* °**ing,** *n.* mallayuddha, *nt.*

Wretch, *n.* alakkhika; dubbhaga; nissirīka, *m.* °**ed,** *a.* mandabhāgya; atidukkhita. °**ly,** *adv.* dīnākārena. °**ness,** *n.* dīnatta; dāḷiddiya; dobhagga, *nt.*

Wriggle, *n.* 1. saŋsappana; 2. vyāvaṭṭana, *nt. v.i.* 1. saŋsappati; 2. vyāvaṭṭati. *p.p.* °pita; °ṭita.

Wright, *n.* kārī; nimmāpaka; sampādetu, *m.*

Wring, *v.t.* gāḷhaŋ vyāvaṭṭeti *or* sampīḷeti. *v.i.* paripphandati. *p.p.* °ṭita; °ḷita. °dita. °**er,** *n.* sampīḷakayanta, *nt.*

Wrinkle, *n.* vali, *f.* bhaṅga, *m. v.i.* ākuñcati; valiŋ gaṇhāti. *v.t.* ākuñceti; valiŋ gāheti. *p.p.* °cita; valiggahita; valiggāhita.

Wrist, *n.* maṇibandha, *m.* °**let,** *n.* hatthavalaya, *nt.*

Writ, *n.* 1. porāṇalipi; 2. rājāṇā, *f.*

Write, *v.t.i.* likhati; racayati. *p.p.* likhita; racita. °**er,** *n.* 1. lipikāra; lekhaka; 2. ganthasampādaka, *m.* °**ing,** *n.* lekhana; likhana, *nt.* lipi, *f.*

Writhe, *n.* vipphandana, *nt. v.i.t.* vipphandati; visappati. *p.p.* °dita; °pita.

Wrong, *n.* 1. dosa, *m.* vajja, *nt.* aññāya; adhamma; apakāra; 2. pamāda; bhama, *m.* adj. 1. ayogga; sadosa; anucita; sāvajja; 2. asuddha; khalita; dūsita. *v.t.* apakaroti; aparajjhati. *p.p.* apakata; aparaddha. — **action,** *n.* duccarita; micchākammanta, *nt.* — **course,** *n.* agati, *f.* uppatha, *m.* — **doer,** *n.* apakārī; aparādhī, *m.* °**ful,** *a.* adhammika; sāvajja. °**fully,** *adv.* sāvajjākārena; adhammena. °**ly,** *adv.* ayathā; micchā; viparītena. — **means,** anupāya; adhamma, *m.* — **path,** kupatha; ummagga, *m.* — **view,** duddiṭṭhi; kumati, *f.* dummata, *nt.*

Wroth, *a.* atikuddha.

Wrought, *p.p.* from **Work,** kata; nimmita; sādhita; nipphādita.

Wry, *a.* āvaṭṭita. °**necked,** *a.* vaṅkagīva. °**ness,** *n.* vaṅkatta; jimhatta, *nt.*

X

Xanthic, *a.* pītavaṇṇa. īsaŋpītaka.

Xantippe, *n.* vadhakabhariyā, *f.*

Xenial, *a.* atithisakkārāyatta.

Xenodochy, *n.* āgantakasālā. *f.*

Xylography, *n.* dārukkiraṇasippa, *nt.*

Xylophagous, *a.* dārukhādaka.

Xyster, *n.* aṭṭhinimmajjakasattha, *m.*

Y

Yacht, *n.* kīḷānāvā, *f. v.i.* kīḷānāvāya ramati.

Yahoo, *n.* manussatiracchāna, *m.*

Yahveh, *n.* lokamāpaka, *m.*

Yak, *n.* camarī, *m.*

Yam, *n.* āluva; kanda, *m.*

Yank, *n.* sīghākaḍḍhana, *nt. v.t.* sīgham ākaḍḍhati. *p.p.* °ḍhita.

Yap, *n.* bhuṅkāra, *m. v.i.* bhuṅkaroti. *p.p.* °kata.

Yard, *n.* 1. aṅgaṇa; ājīra, *nt.* 2. dviratana, *nt. v.t.* gāvo aṅgaṇaŋ paveseti. — **of a mast,** kūpayaṭṭhi, *f.* °**stick,** māṇadaṇḍa, *m.*

Yarn, *n.* 1. vatthasutta, *nt.* 2. pariyaṭaka-vuttanta, *m. v.i.* vuttantaŋ katheti.

Yaw, *n.* nāvāya uppathagamana, *nt. v.i.* uppathaŋ yāti. *p.p.* °yāta.

Yawn, *n.* vijambhikā, *f.* jambhana, *nt. v.i.* vijambhati. *p.p.* °bhita.

Yea, *adv.* āma ; evaŋ. *noun :* sampaṭicchanā ; anumodanā, *f.*

Yean, *v.i.t.* potake vijāyati. *p.p.* vijātapotakā. °**ling,** *n.* mesapotaka ; ajapotaka, *m.*

Year, *n.* vassa ; saŋvacchara, *m. nt.* hāyana, *m.* — **after year,** anuvassaŋ, *adv.* °**ling,** *n.* ekavassika, *m.* °**ly,** *a.* anuvassika ; anusaŋvaccharika. *adv.* paṭivassaŋ. **Current** —, vattamānavassa, *nt.* **Last** —, gatavassa, *nt.* **Next** —, āgāmivassa, *nt.*

Yearn, *v.i.* icchati ; abhilasati ; īhati; kāmeti. *p.p.* icchita; °sita; īhita ; kāmita. °**ing,** *n.* abhilāsā, *f.*

Yeast, *n.* santānikā, *f.* kiṇṇa, *nt.*

Yell, *n.* ukkuṭṭhi, *f.* aṭṭarava, *m. v.i.t.* ukkosati ; aṭṭaravaŋ pavatteti. *p.p.* ukkuṭṭha ; pavattitaṭṭarava.

Yellow, *n.* pītavaṇṇa, *m.* adj. pīta ; haliddyābha. °**ish,** *a.* īsaŋpītaka. °**ish white,** *a.* paṇḍuvaṇṇa. °**myrobalan,** harītakī, *f.* — **robe,** kāsāyavattha ; samaṇacīvara, *nt.*

Yelp, *v.i.* sīghaŋ nadati *or* bhussati. *p.p.* °nadita ; °sita. °**ing,** *n.* sīghabhussana, *nt.*

Yeoman, *n.* 1. khettapāla ; 2. gahapati, *m.* °**ry,** *n.* 1. kassakagaṇa, *m.* 2. kassakabhaṭasenā, *f.*

Yes, *particle.* 1. āma ; evaŋ. 2. atha kiŋ ? 3. sādhu.

Yesterday, *adv.* hīyo ; hiyyo. *n.* gatadivasa, *m.*

Yesternight, *n.* gataratti, *f. adv.* hīyorattiyaŋ.

Yet, *adv.* tāva ; yāvedāni ; ajjāpi. *conj.* api ca ; tathā pi ; evaŋ sati pi.

Yield, *n.* uppāditavatthu ; uppanaphala, *nt.* udaya, *m.* samuṭṭhāna ; uṭṭhānakabhaṇḍa, *nt. v.t.* janeti ; uppādeti. *v.i.* vasaŋ yāti ; okāsaŋ deti. *p.p.* janita ; °dita ; °yāta ; dinnokāsa. °**ing,** *a.* 1. anukūla ; vasaga ; 2. samuṭṭhāpaka.

Yoke, *n.* 1. yuga ; dhura, *nt.* 2. kāja, *m.* 3. ghaṇṭādhārakadaṇḍa, *m.* 4. dāsatta ; bandhana; 5. sambandhana, *nt. v.t.* dhure yojeti ; yuge bandhati ; sambandheti. *p.p.* °jita ; yugabaddha, °dhita.

Yokel, *n.* jānapadika, *m.*

Yolk, *n.* aṇḍamiñjā, *f.*

Yon, Yonder, *a.* 1. asuka ; 2. pārima ; 3. nātidūra. *adv.* nātidūre ; amutra.

Yore, *n.* atītakāla, *m.* **Of** —, atīte ; pubbe ; purā.

You, *pron. pl.* tumhe.

Young, *a.* 1. taruṇa ; bāla ; 2. apariṇata. *n.* bālajana, *m.* — **animal,** *n.* potaka ; pillaka ; chāpa, *m.* °**er,** *a.* kaṇiṭṭha. °**er brother,** kaniṭṭhabhātu, *m.* °**er sister,** kaṇiṭṭhabhaginī, *f.* °**est,** *a.* sabbakaṇiṭṭha. — **girl,** *n.* daharā ; kumārī ; kaññā, *f.* — **leaf,** pallava, *m.* — **man,** yuva ; māṇava ; taruṇa, *m.* —

one, *n*. susu ; bālaka, *m*. — **plant**, gaccha, *m*. laṭṭhi, *f*. — **woman**, yuvatī ; taruṇī, *f*. °**ster**, *n*. māṇava ; kumāra, *m*.

Younker, *n*. kulaputta, *m*.

Your, *pron*. *a*. tavādhīna ; tumḥādhīna. °**self**, tvam attanāva. °**selves**, tumhe attanā va.

Youth, *n*. 1. yobbana ; yobbañña, *nt*. paṭhamavaya ; taruṇabhāva, *m*. 2. māṇava, *m*. 3. taruṇagaṇa, *m*. °**ful**, *a*. yobbanaṭṭha. °**fulness**, *n*. taruṇatta, *nt*.

Yowl, *n*. bhuṅkāra, *m*. *v.i*. bhuṅkaroti ; mahānādaŋ pavatteti. *p.p*. buṅkata ; °tita mahānāda.

Z

Zany, *n*. sevaka-vidūsaka, *m*. °**ism**, *n*. vidūsakakamma, *nt*.

Zeal, *n*. ussāha ; ātappa, *m*. viriya, *nt*. °**ous**, *a*. ussuka ; ātāpī ; saussāha. °**ously**, *adv*. saussāhaŋ ; sādhiṭṭhānaŋ ; uyyāmena.

Zebra, *n*. vanagadrabha, *m*.

Zenana, *n*. antepura ; itthāgāra, *nt*. orodha, *m*.

Zenith, *n*. 1. uddhabhāga ; 2. khamajjha, *m*. 3. uccatamaṭṭhāna, *nt*. paramakoṭi, *f*.

Zero, *n*. bindu ; suññalakkhaṇa, *nt*.

Zest, *n*. abhiruci, *f*. assāda, *m*.

Zetetic, *a*. vīmaŋsaka.

Zeus, *n*. devādhipati, *m*.

Zigzag, *n*. vaṅkamagga, *m*. vaṅkavatthu, *nt*. adj. kuṭilagatika. *v.i*. jimhaŋ yāti. *adv*. jimhākārena.

Zinc, *n*. tuttha, *nt*.

Zodiac, *n*. rāsicakka, *nt*. °**al**, *a*. rāsicakkāyatta.

Zoetrope, *n*. saŋsāracakka ; bhavacakka, *nt*.

Zoic, *a*. pāṇinissita.

Zone, *n*. pabba ; valaya ; maṇḍala, *nt*. **Temperate** —, īsadharapabba, *nt*. **Torrid** —, yugandharapabba, *nt*.

Zoo, *n*. pasuyyāna, *nt*. migadāya, *m*. °**graphy**, *n*. pasuvaṇṇanā, *f*. °**latry**, pasunamassanā, *f*. °**logy**, *n*. pasupakativijjā, *f*. °**logical**, *a*. pasuvijjāyatta. °**logist**, *n*. pasuvijjāvidū, *m*. °**tomy**, *n*. pasukāyaviccheda, *m*.

Zymotic, *a*. saṅkantika ; opasaggika (-rogāyatta).